The Challenge of the West

The Challenge of the West

Peoples and Cultures from the Stone Age to 1640

Volume I

Lynn Hunt
University of Pennsylvania

Thomas R. Martin
College of the Holy Cross

Barbara H. Rosenwein
Loyola University Chicago

R. Po-chia Hsia
New York University

Bonnie G. Smith
Rutgers University

D. C. Heath and Company
Lexington, Massachusetts   Toronto

Address editorial correspondence to:

D. C. Heath and Company
125 Spring Street
Lexington, MA 02173

Acquisitions Editor: James Miller
Developmental Editor: David Light
Production Editor: Janice Molloy
Designer: Henry Rachlin
Photo Researcher: Rose Corbett Gordon
Art Editor: Diane Grossman
Production Coordinator: Charles Dutton
Permissions Editor: Margaret Roll
Map Coordinator: Patricia Wakeley

Table of Contents Photograph Credits: p. xiii, Nimatallah/Art Resource, NY; p. xiv, Copyright British Museum; pp. xv and xvi, Scala/Art Resource, NY; p. xvii, Copyright British Museum; p. xviii, Scala/Art Resource, NY; p. xix, Giraudon/Art Resource, NY; p. xx, Art Resource, NY; p. xxi, By permission of the British Library; p. xxii, Hessische Landes- und Hochschul- Bibliothek, Darmstadt; p. xxiii, Staatsbibliothek Preussischer Kulturbesitz © Bildarchiv Preussischer Kulturbesitz, Berlin; p. xxiv, Erich Lessing/Art Resource, NY; p. xxv, Giraudon/Art Resource, NY; p. xxvi, Cameraphoto/Art Resource, NY; p. xxvii, The Metropolitan Museum of Art, Gift of Robert Lehman, 1955 (55.220.2); p. xxviii (top and bottom), Alinari/Art Resource

For permission to use copyrighted materials, grateful acknowledgment is made to the copyright holders listed on pages A-1 to A-3, which are hereby considered an extension of this copyright page.

Published simultaneously in Canada.

Printed in the United States of America.

International Standard Book Number: 0–669–12163–0

Library of Congress Catalog Number: 94–75072

10 9 8 7 6 5 4 3 2 1

ABOUT THE AUTHORS

Lynn Hunt, Annenberg Professor of History at the University of Pennsylvania, received her B.A. from Carleton College and her M.A. and Ph.D. from Stanford University. She is the author of *Revolution and Urban Politics in Provincial France* (1978), *Politics, Culture, and Class in the French Revolution* (1984), and *The Family Romance of the French Revolution* (1992); she is also the editor of *The New Cultural History* (1989) and the co-author of *Telling the Truth About History* (1994). She has been awarded fellowships by the Guggenheim Foundation and the National Endowment for the Humanities and is a Fellow of the American Academy of Arts and Sciences.

Thomas R. Martin, Jeremiah O'Connor Professor in Classics at the College of the Holy Cross, earned his B.A. at Princeton University and his A.M. and Ph.D. at Harvard University. He is the author of *Sovereignty and Coinage in Classical Greece* (1985) and collaborated on *Perseus 1.0: Interactive Sources and Studies on Ancient Greece* (1992), which was named the EDUCOM Best Software in Social Sciences (History) in 1992. He has received fellowships from the National Endowment for the Humanities and the American Council of Learned Societies and is councilor of the American Numismatic Society.

Barbara H. Rosenwein, professor of history at Loyola University Chicago, earned her B.A., M.A., and Ph.D. at the University of Chicago. She is the author of *Rhinoceros Bound: Cluny in the Tenth Century* (1982) and *To Be the Neighbor of Saint Peter* (1989), and co-author of *Saint Maïeul, Cluny et la Provence: Expansion d'une abbaye à l'aube du Moyen Age* (1994). She has received fellowships from the Guggenheim Foundation and the National Endowment for the Humanities.

R. Po-chia Hsia, professor of history at New York University, received his B.A. from Swarthmore College and his M.A. and Ph.D. from Yale University. He is the author of *Society and Religion in Munster, 1535-1618* (1984), *The Myth of Ritual Murder: Jews and Magic in Reformation Germany* (1988), *Social Discipline in the Reformation: Central Europe 1550-1750* (1989), and *Trent 1475: Stories of a Ritual Murder Trial* (1992). He has been awarded fellowships by the Woodrow Wilson International Center for Scholars, the National Endowment for the Humanities, the Guggenheim Foundation, and the Mellon Foundation.

Bonnie G. Smith, professor of history at Rutgers University, earned her B.A. at Smith College and her M.A. and Ph.D. at the University of Rochester. She is the author of *Ladies of the Leisure Class* (1981), *Confessions of a Concierge: Madame Lucie's History of Twentieth-Century France* (1985), and *Changing Lives: Women in European History Since 1700* (D. C. Heath, 1989). She has received fellowships from the Guggenheim Foundation, the Davis Center of Princeton University, and the American Council of Learned Societies.

PREFACE

Many American universities introduced Western civilization courses after World War I. Their intent was to explain what the United States had in common with its western European allies, that is, to justify American involvement in a European war. The emphasis on defending a shared tradition of Western values gained in urgency during World War II, but since the 1960s, and especially since the end of the Cold War, the wisdom of this approach has come into question. Even if everyone agreed on the purposes of teaching and learning about Western civilization, however, no one person or even team of authors could possibly master every field of scholarship and every national history that rightly enters into such an account. It is all the more important, therefore, to explain how we authors approached our task and what we hoped to accomplish.

The title of this book, *The Challenge of the West,* tells much about its general orientation. We focus on the contributions of a multitude of peoples and cultures to the making of Western values and traditions. But it is important to keep in mind that in the overall perspective of recorded human time, the very idea of the West is of recent vintage. It emerged as an idea in the fifteenth century, when the West began to dominate other areas of the globe through trade and colonization. The modern idea of the West as a trans-Atlantic entity—Europe and its colonial offshoots in North America—sharing common values and modes of social and political organization acquired distinctive meaning only at the end of the nineteenth century, when the United States joined the western European powers as a major industrial and colonizing force. Our task as authors has been to recount and analyze the evolution of these values and forms of organization, from the ancient ideas of community and individual responsibility to the modern forces of science and industry. We have consistently tried to place the West's emergence in a larger, world context, recognizing that it was not inevitable or predetermined but rather an unexpected, even surprising development.

As it secured technological and economic advantages, the West inevitably *challenged* other cultures, even dominated many of them for a time and destroyed some altogether. But in the late twentieth century, the West in turn faces challenges from other cultures and distinctively different modes of social and political organization in the rest of the world. To understand the West's ascent to dominance and the present-day challenges to that hegemony, it is imperative to set the history of the West's own internal unfolding into the context of its relations with the other cultures of the world. We consequently return again and again to the theme of Western relationships—economic, military, and cultural—with the wider world.

Peoples and cultures appear in the plural in our title because we want to emphasize the variety of groups, ethnicities, cultures, and nations that have played important roles in making the West. Cultures are whole ways of life, not always neatly confined within the state boundaries or standard chronologies of traditional history. Historians now pay increasing attention to the continuities and long-term trends in ordinary people's lives in the past. The age at which young people marry, the number of children they have, the houses they live in, the clothes they wear, and the ways they read and entertain themselves have all provided significant clues to the attitudes, values, and actions that shaped the West. They cannot replace the history of wars, changes of rulers, and shifts in political alignments, but they help to put those political events into a broader, more meaningful context.

The original, early-twentieth-century conception of Western civilization was much more narrow. Historians defined Anglo-American political institutions—representative, constitutional government and a free-market society—at the core of Western values. The Western civilization course effectively offered training in the history of diplomacy, warfare, and past politics for the next generation of leaders of the "free world." In 1919 one such course was described as creating "a citizen who shall be safe for democracy."

This view has a relatively long lineage, going back to eighteenth-century European writers who took for their model English religious tolerance (in fact limited to Protestants), freedom of the press, and constitutional monarchy (even when only a small proportion of adult men had the vote). The English agricultural expert and essayist Arthur Young, for example, offered a map of liberty in 1772:

> Asia is by the best accounts despotic throughout. . . . Africa comes next, and what misery involves that vast country! . . . In Europe itself, what disproportion between liberty and slavery! Russia, Poland, the chief of Germany, Hungary, Turkey, the greatest part of Italy, Spain, Portugal, France, Denmark and Norway. The following [free countries] bear no proportion to them, *viz* the British Isles, Sweden, Holland, Switzerland, and the Germanic and Italian states. And in America, Spain, Portugal and France, have planted despotism; only Britain liberty.

There is much in this picture that we would agree with still today. The English did indeed pioneer our modern Western conceptions of religious tolerance, freedom of the press, and constitutional government. Our sense of the geography of freedom, however, is both broader and more nuanced.

Historians today devote much more of their attention to the countries that did not follow the English model but developed their own distinctive routes, and to the groups—slaves, indigenous peoples, workers, women, immigrants—who labored in supposedly free societies without enjoying the guarantees of liberty until very recently. By pushing further and further back into the past, to the once derided "Dark Ages" of medieval times, to Greek and Roman precedents, back even to the very earliest settlements known in prehistoric times, historians of the West have revealed all the surprising turns, the routes not taken, and the alternatives once available and then lost as humans collectively made the decisions that have led us to where we are today. We go back in time so far not just to trace the emergence of the entity later known as the West but also to learn and to satisfy our curiosity about how peoples and cultures in the past organized themselves and experienced their worlds.

As democracy has expanded in meaning to include different religious groups, women as well as men, workers as well as employers, immigrants as well as natives, and peoples of all races and ethnicities, so, too, the history of what counts in the West has grown more capacious. We have tried to incorporate the history of once subordinate groups into our general narrative, showing how the struggles of daily life and ordinary people also helped to shape the Western past. We see these aspects not as colorful anecdotes or entertaining sideshows but rather as significant determinants of social and political relations. *Peoples* means *all* the people.

As Cold War barriers have broken down and the boundaries of the European Economic Community have expanded, the idea of Europe itself has changed. As a consequence, we make every effort to include Russia and eastern Europe in our story. It is hard to avoid the temptation of seeing eastern Europeans as "backward," "unfree," and certainly not Western like the rest of us, much as Arthur Young viewed them in the 1700s. But just as the West has begun to incorporate all its own peoples, so, too, it must confront its other geographical half—eastern Europe and Russia. Understanding the history of eastern Europe and its relationship to the West is one small step toward a meeting of cultures, perhaps even toward true integration that will render Young's version truly obsolete.

We have tried to present our account in a straightforward chronological manner. Each chapter covers all of the events, people, and themes of a particular slice of time; thus the reader will not be forced to learn about political events in one chapter and then backtrack to the social and cultural developments of the period in the next. We have followed this pattern from the very beginning, where we discuss the roots of Western civilization in prehistory and in the ancient Near East, to the very end, where we ponder the transforming effect of globalization on the idea of the West.

We believe that it is important, above all else, to see the interconnections—between politics and cultures; between wars and diplomacy, on the one hand, and everyday life, on the other; between so-called mainstream history and the newer varieties of social, cultural, and women's history. For this reason, we did not separate intellectual and cultural life or women's and social history into distinct chapters or sections. We have tried to integrate them chronologically throughout.

History will always be an interim report; every generation rewrites history as interests change and as new sources are discovered or known ones are reinterpreted. We have tried to convey the sense of excitement generated by new insights and the sense of controversy created by the clash of conflicting interpretations. For history is not just an inert thing, lying there in moldering records to be memorized by the next generation of hapless students. It is constantly alive, subject to pressure, and able to surprise us. If we have succeeded in conveying some of that vibrancy of the past, we will not be satisfied with what we have done—history does not sit still that long—but we will be encouraged to start rethinking and revising once again.

Special Pedagogical Features

A range of useful study aids has been built into *The Challenge of the West.* Each chapter begins with a vivid anecdote that draws readers into the atmosphere and issues of the times and raises the chapter's major themes; the chapters conclude with brief summaries that tie together the thematic strands and point readers onward. At the beginning of each chapter readers will find a list of important dates that introduces some of the key actors, events, and trends of the period. Timelines interspersed throughout the text give students a chronological overview of particular themes and processes. At the end of each chapter are carefully chosen bibliographies, first, of source materials ranging from political documents to novels, and second, of up-to-date interpretive studies that will aid those wishing to seek in-depth treatment of particular topics.

The text's full-color design features nearly 400 illustrations, including examples from material culture, the history of architecture, iconography, painting, cartoons, posters, and photography. The images come not only from Europe and the United States but also from Russia, Africa, and Asia. The illustrations combine well-known classics that are important for cultural literacy with fresh images that document, in particular, the lives of ordinary people and women. The text also contains more than 200 maps and graphs. Each chapter includes large maps that show major developments—wars, patterns of trade, political realignments, and so on—as well as smaller "spot" maps that immediately aid the student's geographical understanding of subjects ranging from the structure of Old Kingdom Egypt to the civil war in Yugoslavia.

Supplementary Program for the *Challenge of the West*

An extensive ancillary program accompanies *The Challenge of the West.* It is designed not only to assist instructors but to develop students' critical-thinking skills and to bolster their understanding of key topics and themes treated in the textbook. In the supplements as in the textbook, our goal has been to make teaching and learning enjoyable and challenging.

Students will find a valuable tool in *Studying Western Civilization: A Student's Guide to Reading Maps, Interpreting Documents, and Preparing for Exams,* by Richard M. Long of Hillsborough Community College. The guide includes helpful aids such as chapter outlines and summaries, vocabulary exercises, and a variety of self-tests on the chapter content. It also features primary-source excerpts (selected by the text authors) with interpretive questions, as well as map exercises to build geographical understanding of historical change. A two-volume set of documents provides students and instructors alike with hundreds of primary references, ranging from the classics of Western political, legal, and intellectual history to the freshest sources on social, cultural, and women's history.

The *Instructor's Guide,* prepared by Sara W. Tucker of Washburn University, includes annotated chapter outlines, lecture suggestions, and a wealth of teaching resources. The annotated chapter outlines are available on disk as the *Instructor's Toolkit.* D. C. Heath is also making available to adopters a Western civilization videodisc with 2,100 images that is barcoded, captioned, and indexed for classroom use.

Rounding out the supplementary resources are the *Computerized Testing Program,* which allows instructors to create customized problem sets for quizzes and examinations, and the accompanying printed *Test Item File.* More than 4,000 questions, prepared by Denis Paz of Clemson University and Jachin Warner Thacker of Western Kentucky University, are available in this testing program. Finally, we have produced a transparency set with some 100 full-color maps.

Acknowledgments

We first want to acknowledge the outstanding efforts and unstinting support of many people at D. C. Heath and Company in the development of this textbook. We thank History editor James Miller; developmental editors David Light, Debra Osnowitz, and Pat Wakeley; production editor Janice Molloy; designer Henry Rachlin; photo researchers Rose Corbett Gordon and Martha Shethar; production coordinator Charles Dutton; and permissions editor Margaret Roll.

Numerous colleagues around the country read and commented on the chapters, often at great length and with great insight. Here we thank those who contributed formal written reviews:

Dorothy Abrahamse, California State University, Long Beach; **Jeremy Adams,** Southern Methodist University; **Meredith Adams,** Southwest Missouri State University; **Thomas Adriance,** Virginia Polytechnic State University; **Kathleen Alaimo,** Xavier University; **James Alexander,** University of Georgia; **Kathryn Amdur,** Emory University; **Glenn J. Ames,** University of Toledo; **Susan Amussen,** Connecticut College; **Abraham Ascher,** City University of New York; **Achilles Avraamides,** Iowa State University; **James Banker,** North Carolina State University; **George Barany,** University of Denver; **John Barker,** University of Wisconsin, Madison; **Kenneth Barkin,** University of California, Riverside; **H. Arnold Barton,** Southern Illinois University; **Barrett Beer,** Kent State University; **Rodney Bell,** South Dakota State University; **Martin Berger,** Youngstown State University; **Patrice Berger,** University of Nebraska; **David Bien,** University of Michigan; **Rebecca Boehling,** University of Maryland, Baltimore County; **Donna Bohanan,** Auburn University; **Gordon Bond,** Auburn University; **Marilyn J. Boxer,** San Diego State University; **Jay Bregman,** University of Maine, Orono; **William Brennan,** University of the Pacific; **Renate Bridenthal,** City University of New York, Brooklyn College; **Jon Bridgman,** University of Washington; **E. Willis Brooks,** University of North Carolina; **Peter Brown,** Rhode Island College; **Paul Burns,** University of Nevada, Las Vegas; **Thomas Burns,** Emory University; **Stanley Burstein,** California State University, Los Angeles; **June K. Burton,** University of Akron; **Carter Carroll,** College of DuPage; **Jack Censer,** George Washington University; **Paul Chardoul,** Grand Rapids Junior College; **William Chase,** University of Pittsburgh; **Anna Cienciola,** University of Kansas; **Henry Clark,** Canisius College; **Catherine Cline,** Catholic University of America; **Marilyn Coetzee,** Denison University; **Gary Cohen,** University of Oklahoma; **William Cohen,** Hope College; **Susan Cole,** University of Illinois; **John J. Contreni,** Purdue University; **John Conway,** University of British Columbia; **Marc Cooper,** Southwest Missouri State University; **Ruth Schwartz Cowan,** State University of New York, Stony Brook; **Marvin Cox,** University of Connecticut; **Guy S. Cross,** Pennsylvania State University; **Paige Cubbison,** Miami-Dade Community College; **Robert V. Daniels,** University of Vermont; **Elinor M. Despalatovic,** Connecticut College; **Barbara Diefendorf,** Boston University; **Jeffrey Diefendorf,** University of New Hampshire; **John Patrick Donnelly, S.J.,** Marquette University; **Seymour Drescher,** University of Pittsburgh; **Katherine Fischer Drew,** Rice University; **Lawrence Duggan,** University of Delaware; **Chester Dunning,** Texas A&M University; **Evelyn Edson,** Piedmont Virginia Community College; **Geoffrey Eley,** University of Michigan; **Barbara Engel,** University of Colorado; **Amanda Eurich,** Western Washington University; **Barbara Evans Clements,** University of Akron; **John Evans,** University of Minnesota; **Theodore Evergates,** Western Maryland College; **Steven Fanning,** University of Illinois at Chicago; **Diane Farrell,** Moorhead State University; **Joanne Ferraro,** San Diego State University; **Arthur Ferrill,** University of Washington; **Elmar Fetscher,** University of Central Florida; **Monte Finkelstein,** Tallahassee Community College; **Robert Finlay,** University of Arkansas; **Nels W. Forde,** University of Nebraska; **John Freed,** Illinois State University; **Linda Frey,** University of Montana; **Ellen Friedman,** Boston College; **James Friguglietti,** Eastern Montana College; **Stephen Fritz,** East Tennessee State University; **James A. Funkhouser,** Edison State Community College; **Alison Futrell,** University of Arizona; **Alan Galpern,** University of Pittsburgh; **James Gentry,** College of Southern Idaho; **Bentley B. Gilbert,** University of Illinois at Chicago; **John Gillis,** Rutgers University; **Kees Gispen,** University of Mississippi; **R. Edward Glatfelter,** Utah

State University; **Abbott Gleason,** Brown University; **Penny Gold,** Knox College; **Richard Golden,** Clemson University; **Walter Gray,** Loyola University Chicago; **John Guilmartin,** Ohio State University; **James W. Hagy,** College of Charleston; **Charles Hamilton,** Simon Fraser University; **Barbara Hanawalt,** University of Minnesota; **Sarah Hanley,** University of Iowa; **Janine Hartman,** University of Cincinnati; **John Headley,** University of North Carolina; **David Hendon,** Baylor University; **Gerald Herman,** Northeastern University; **Holger Herwig,** University of Calgary; **Walter Hixson,** Michigan State University; **J. H. Hoffman,** Creighton University; **Daniel Hollis,** Jacksonville State University; **Blair Holmes,** Brigham Young University; **Rodney Holtzcamp,** College of DuPage; **David Hood,** California State University, Long Beach; **Jeff Horn,** Stetson University; **Donald Howard,** Florida State University; **David Hudson,** California State University, Fresno; **James W. Hurst,** Joliet Junior College; **John Hurt,** University of Delaware; **William Irvine,** Clendon College, York University; **Matthew Jaffe,** Antelope Valley Community College; **Barbara Jelavich,** Indiana University; **Carol Thomas Johnson,** University of Washington; **Yvonne Johnson,** Collin County Community College; **Richard Kaeuper,** University of Rochester; **Susan Karant-Nunn,** Portland State University; **Donald Kelley,** University of Rochester; **Joseph Kett,** University of Virginia; **William Keylor,** Boston University; **Joseph Kicklighter,** Auburn University; **Raymond Kierstead,** Reed College; **Carla Klausner,** University of Missouri, Kansas City; **Paul Knoll,** University of Southern California; **John Kohler,** Clayton State College; **Rudy Koshar,** University of Wisconsin, Madison; **Cynthia Kosso,** Northern Arizona University; **Z.J. Kostolnyik,** Texas A&M University; **Richard Kuisel,** State University of New York, Stony Brook; **P. David Lagomarsino,** Dartmouth College; **Ira M. Lapidus,** University of California; **David Large,** Montana State University; **Ann C. Lebar,** Eastern Washington University; **Helen Lemay,** State University of New York, Stony Brook; **Richard Levy,** University of Illinois at Chicago; **Richard Long,** Hillsborough Community College; **David Longfellow,** Baylor University; **Carolyn Lougee,** Stanford University; **William Lubenow,** Stockton State College; **J. Terrace Lyden,** St. Meinrad College; **Joseph Lynch,** Ohio State University; **Michael J. Lyons,** North Dakota State University; **Richard Mackey,** Ball State University; **Thomas Mackey,** University of Louisville; **Anne MacLennan,** Dawson College; **J.P. Madden,** Hardin Simmons University; **Sally Marks,** Rhode Island College; **Benjamin Martin,** Louisiana State University; **Ralph Mathisen,** University of South Carolina; **Margaret McCord,** University of Tampa; **Wade Meade,** Louisiana Technical University; **Meredith Medler,** St. Cloud State University; **Paul Michelson,** Huntington College; **James Mini,** Montgomery Community College; **Robert Moeller,** University of California; **Anthony Molho,** Brown University; **Michael Monheight,** University of South Alabama; **A. Lloyd Moote,** University of Southern California; **Marjorie Morgan,** Southern Illinois University; **Gordon Mork,** Purdue University; **Edward Muir,** Hagley Museum & Library; **John Kim Munholland,** University of Minnesota; **James Murray,** University of Cincinnati; **Philip Naylor,** Marquette University; **John Newell,** College of Charleston; **Gerald Newman,** Kent State University; **Martha Newman,** University of Texas, Austin; **Donald Niewyk,** Southern Methodist University; **Janet Nolan,** Loyola University Chicago; **Robert Nye,** Rutgers Center for Historical Analysis; **Dennis O'Brien,** West Virginia University; **Mary O'Neil,** University of Washington; **Robert Oden,** Dartmouth College; **Walter Odum,** Eastern Kentucky University; **Jeanne Ojala,** University of Utah; **William Olejniczak,** College of Charleston; **Richard Olson,** St. Olaf College; **Aristides Papadakis,** University of Maryland, Baltimore County; **Thomas Pesek,** Washington State University; **Dolores Peters,** St. Olaf College; **Michael Phayer,** Marquette University; **Ruth Pike,** Hunter College; **Linda Piper,** University of Georgia; **Jeremy Popkin,** University of Kentucky; **Johannes Postma,** Mankato State University; **Thomas Preisser,** Sinclair Community College; **Richard Price,** University of Maryland; **Anne Quartararo,** United States Naval Academy; **Hugh Ragsdale,** University of Alabama, Tuscaloosa; **Samuel Ramer,** Tulane University; **Orest Ranum,** Johns Hopkins University; **Marion Rappe,** San Francisco State University; **Norman Ravitch,** University of California, Riverside; **Charles Rearick,** University of Massachusetts, Amherst; **Virginia Reinberg,** Boston

College; **Kathryn Reyerson,** University of Minnesota; **Peter Riesenberg,** Washington University; **Harry Ritter,** Western Washington University; **John Roberts,** Lincolnland College; **Ronald Ross,** University of Wisconsin, Milwaukee; **Robin Rudoff,** East Texas State University; **Julius Ruff,** Marquette University; **Roland Sarti,** University of Massachusetts, Amherst; **Benjamin Sax,** University of Kansas; **Kenneth Schellhase,** Northern Michigan University; **Wolfgang Schlauch,** Eastern Illinois University; **R.A. Schneider,** Catholic University of America; **Robert Schnucker,** Northeast Missouri State University; **Sally Scully,** San Francisco State University; **Paul Seaver,** Stanford University; **David Sefton,** Eastern Kentucky University; **Kyle Sessions,** Illinois State University; **William Sewell,** University of Michigan; **Neil Shipley,** University of Massachusetts, Amherst; **Jane Slaughter,** University of New Mexico; **J. Harvey Smith,** Northern Illinois University; **Patrick Smith,** Broward Community College; **Ronald Smith,** Arizona State University; **Paul Spagnoli,** Boston College; **Elaine Spencer,** Northern Illinois University; **Jonathan Sperber,** University of Missouri, Columbia; **Zeph Stewart,** Center for Hellenic Studies; **Gale Stokes,** Rice University; **Gerald Strauss,** Indiana University; **Richard Sullivan,** Michigan State University; **Frederick Suppe,** Ball State University; **Francis Roy Swietek,** University of Dallas; **Edith Sylla,** North Carolina State University; **Emily Tabuteau,** Michigan State University; **William Tannenbaum,** Missouri Southern University; **Timothy Teeter,** Georgia Southern University; **David Tengwall,** Anne Arundel Community College; **Carol Thomas,** University of Washington; **Jason Thompson,** Western Kentucky University; **James Tracy,** University of Minnesota; **Sara Tucker,** Washburn University; **William Tucker,** University of Arkansas; **John Tuthill,** Georgia Southern University; **Gloria Tysl,** Illinois Benedictine College; **Ted Uldricks,** University of North Carolina, Asheville; **Johannes Ultee,** University of Alabama; **Raymond Van Dam,** University of Michigan; **Emily Vermuele,** Harvard University; **Robert Vignery,** University of Arizona; **Mack Walker,** Johns Hopkins University; **Sue Sheridan Walker,** Northeastern Illinois University; **Allan Ward,** University of Connecticut; **Bernard Wasserstein,** Brandeis University; **John Weakland,** Ball State University; **Robert Wegs,** University of Notre Dame; **Lee Shai Weissbach,** University of Louisville; **Eric Weitz,** St. Olaf College; **Robert Welborn,** Clayton State College; **Charlotte Wells,** University of Northern Iowa; **Peter Wells,** University of Minnesota; **Joseph Werne,** Southeast Missouri State University; **Victor Wexler,** University of Maryland; **Stephen D. White,** Wesleyan University; **Mary Wickwire,** University of Massachusetts, Amherst; **Ronald Witt,** Duke University; **Charles Wood,** Dartmouth College; **Neil York,** Brigham Young University; **Gordon Young,** Purdue University; **Reginald Zelnick,** University of California, Berkeley.

Professor Rosenwein especially wishes to thank Charles Brauner, Zouhair Ghazzal, Charles Radding, and Ian Wood for their assistance.

Professor Hunt extends special thanks to Caroline Bynum, Margaret Jacob, Sheryl Kroen, and Thomas Laqueur.

L.H.
T.R.M.
B.H.R.
R.P.H.
B.G.S.

CONTENTS

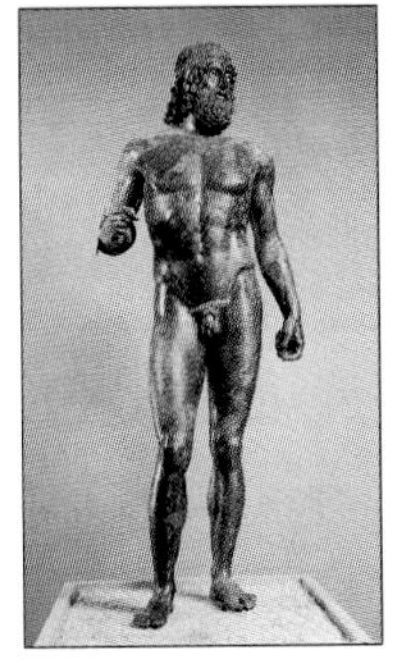

CHAPTER
8

The Heirs of the Roman Empire, 568–756 *269*

CHAPTER
9

CHAPTER

10

Vitality and Reform, 1054–1144 *341*

CHAPTER
11

An Age of Confidence, 1144–1215 377

CHAPTER
12

The Quest for Order and Control, 1215–1320 409

CHAPTER 15

PART
III

MAPS, CHARTS, AND GRAPHS

The B.C/A.D. System for Reckoning Dates

"When were you born?" "What year is it?" We customarily answer questions like this with a number, such as "1978" or "1995." Our replies are usually automatic, taking for granted the numerous assumptions Westerners make about dates. But to what do numbers such as 1978 or 1995 actually refer? In this book the numbers used to specify dates follow the system most commonly utilized in the Western secular world. This system reckons the dates of solar years by counting backward and forward from the putative date of the birth of Jesus Christ, nearly two thousand years ago.

Using this method, numbers followed by the abbreviation B.C., standing for "before Christ," indicate the number of years counting backward from the birth of Jesus. The larger the number after B.C. the earlier in history is the year to which it refers. The date 431 B.C., for example, refers to a year 431 years before the birth of Jesus and therefore comes earlier in time than the dates 430 B.C., 429 B.C., and so on. The same calculation applies to numbering other time intervals calculated on the decimal system: those of 10 years (a decade), of 100 years (a century), and of 1,000 years (a millennium). For example, the decade of the 440s B.C. (449 B.C. to 440 B.C.) is earlier than the decade of the 430s B.C. (439 to 430 B.C.). "Fifth century B.C." refers to the fifth period of 100 years reckoning backward from the birth of Jesus and covers the years 500 B.C. to 401 B.C. It is earlier in history than the fourth century B.C. (400 B.C. to 301 B.C.), which followed the fifth century B.C. Because this system has no year "zero," the first century B.C. covers the years 100 B.C. to 1 B.C. As for millennia, the second millennium B.C. refers to the years 2000 B.C. to 1001 B.C., the third millennium to the years 3000 B.C. to 2001 B.C., and so on.

Because B.C. indicates dates reckoned backward, adjectives such as "early" or "late" when applied to decades, centuries, or millennia B.C. refer to higher and lower numbers, respectively. For example, the two early decades of the fifth century B.C. are the 490s B.C. and the 480s B.C. The 420s B.C. is a late decade of the same century. The year 506 B.C. is a date in the late sixth century B.C. The date 2966 B.C. is in the early third millennium B.C. Similarly, the first quarter of the eighth century B.C. covers the twenty-five years from 800 B.C. to 776 B.C., whereas the second half of the same century consists of 750 B.C. to 701 B.C.

To indicate years counted forward from the birth of Jesus, numbers are preceded by the abbreviation A.D., standing for the Latin phrase *anno Domini* ("in the year of the Lord"). The date A.D. 1492, for example, translates as "in the year of the Lord 1492," meaning 1492 years after the birth of Jesus. Writing dates with A.D. following the number, as in 1492 A.D., makes no sense because it would amount to saying "1492 in the year of the Lord." It is, however, customary to indicate centuries by placing the abbreviation A.D. after the number. Therefore "first century A.D." refers to the period from A.D. 1 to A.D. 100. For numbers indicating dates after the birth of Jesus, of course, the smaller the number, the earlier the date in history. The fourth century A.D. (A.D. 301 to A.D. 400) comes before the fifth century A.D. (A.D. 401 to A.D. 500). The year A.D. 312 is a date in the early fourth century A.D., and A.D. 395 is a date late in the same century. When numbers are given without either B.C. or A.D., they are presumed to be dates after the birth of Jesus. For example, "eighteenth century" with no abbreviation accompanying it refers to the years A.D. 1701 to A.D. 1800.

No standard system of numbering years, such as the B.C./A.D. method, existed in antiquity. Different people in different parts of the world identified years with varying names and numbers. Consequently, it was difficult to match up the years in any particular local system with those in a different system. Each city of ancient Greece, for example, had its own method for keeping track of the years. The ancient Greek historian Thucydides therefore faced a problem in presenting a chronology for the war between Athens and Sparta, which began (by our reckoning) in 431 B.C. To try to explain to as many of his readers as possible the date the war had begun, he described its first year by three different local systems: "the year when Chrysis was in the forty-eighth year of her priesthood at Argos, and Aenesias was overseer at Sparta, and Pythodorus was magistrate at Athens."

A monk named Dionysius, who lived in Rome in the sixth century A.D., invented the system of reckoning dates forward from the birth of Jesus. Calling himself "Exiguus" (Latin for "the little," or "the small") as a mark of humility, he contributed to chronological reckoning by placing Jesus' birth 754 years after the foundation of ancient Rome. Others then and now believe his date for Jesus' birth was in fact several years too late. Many scholars today figure that Jesus was born in what would be 4 B.C. according to Dionysius's system, although a date a year or so earlier also seems possible.

Counting backward from the putative date of Jesus' birth to indicate dates earlier than that event represented a natural complement to reckoning forward for dates after it. The English historian and theologian Bede in the early eighth century was the first to use both forward and backward reckoning from the birth of Jesus in a historical work, and this system gradually gained wider and wider acceptance because it provided a basis for standardizing the many local calendars used in the western Christian world. Nevertheless, B.C. and A.D. were not used regularly until the end of the eighteenth century.

The system of numbering years from the birth of Jesus is not the only one still used. The Jewish calendar of years, for example, counts forward from the date given to the creation of the world, which would be calculated as 3761 B.C. under the B.C./A.D. system. Years are designated A.M. (an abbreviation of the Latin *anno mundi,* "in the year of the world") under this system. The Islamic calendar counts forward from the date of the prophet Muhammad's flight from Mecca, called the *Hijra,* in what would be the year A.D. 622 under the B.C./A.D. system. The abbreviation A.H. (standing for the Latin phrase *anno Hegirae,* "in the year of the Hegira," or "after the Hegira") indicates dates calculated by this system. Today the abbreviations B.C.E. ("before the common era") and C.E. ("of the common era") are often used, especially in Biblical studies, in place of B.C. and A.D., respectively, to allow the retention of numerical dates as reckoned by the B.C./A.D. system without the Christian reference implied by this system. Anthropology commonly reckons distant dates as "before the present" (abbreviated B.P.).

Finally, historians often label time by ages, eras, and other designations that people living in those periods would not have used. People living in the Stone Age, for example, did not refer to themselves as "Stone Age people." These historical labels can have various inspirations. The term *classical Greece,* for example, refers to the period from the Greek wars with Persia early in the fifth century B.C. to the death of Alexander the Great in 323 B.C. The label *classical* comes from art history and is meant to indicate a positive value judgment about the quality of the art of this time period. The term *Carolingian Age* refers to the period A.D. 751–987 and comes from the name of a prominent ruler, Carolus (Latin for "Charles"). The term *colonial America* in turn refers to the period in the seventeenth and eighteenth centuries before American independence, when British colonial government was in place. Terms such as *Stone Age, Bronze Age,* or *Iron Age* refer to the material used to make the most important tools in a given stretch of time.

These labels for periods of time are coined to make helpful generalizations about history, but we must remember that they are usually reflections of hindsight and potentially misleading if taken as indications of the ways people in the past may have viewed their own times. Today, for example, we routinely designated the year 323 B.C. as the end of what we call the Classical Age in Greek history and the beginning of the three centuries we refer to as the Hellenistic period—modern terms implying that the earlier period was better and finer than the later. But we cannot assume that Greeks alive in 323 B.C. would have agreed that it marked a watershed in their history or that the years before that year were necessarily better than after or should be called "classical." Likewise, today we might well ask whether we still live in the Iron Age or have moved into the Polymer Plastics Age.

Key to Symbols

✷	period of reign, term in office
✷	site of major battle

PROLOGUE

Before Civilization

The history of Western civilization is the story of what it has meant to live in the societies that first took shape in the ancient Near East, around the Mediterranean Sea, and in northern Europe. Eventually this story includes the New World of the Americas and the impact of Western civilization all over the globe. In telling this story, historians set themselves tasks that sound deceptively simple: to discover how people in these societies organized, supported, reproduced, and governed themselves; to understand what they thought about their world; and to search for reasons why the conditions of life and people's attitude toward life and death changed over time. To attempt these tasks requires the study not only of social, economic, and political history but also of religion, philosophy, literature, science, and art. Textbooks have often addressed these topics separately, yet they all *interact* to constitute the history of human culture, the complex sum of assumptions, traditions, and ideals that we rely on to guide our everyday lives. Because humans have the unique ability, through language, to pass their cultural heritage from generation to generation, the past inevitably influences the present. In this book we will look for the roots of that influence, paying special attention to the interplay between social and cultural changes and political power.

Our story of Western civilization's roots begins tens of thousands of years ago, in the Stone Age, so named because the people of the time had only stone, in addition to bone and wood, from which to fashion tools and weapons; they had not yet discovered the use of metals. Nor did these earliest humans know how to cultivate their own food. When the technology of agriculture was

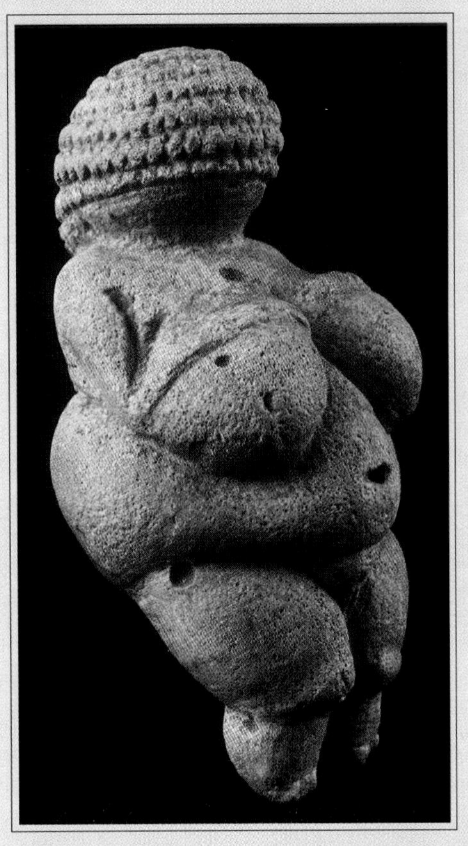

Venus of Willendorf
This Late Paleolithic statuette is characteristic of "Venus figurines" discovered at many European prehistoric sites. These figurines probably expressed a recognition of the importance and uncertainty of human fertility.

developed about ten thousand to twelve thousand years ago, humans experienced enormous changes and began to affect their environment in unprecedented ways. This transformation opened the way to the creation of cities and of political states (people living in a definite territory and organized under a government with leaders, officials, and judges). These new forms of human organization first appeared in the ancient Near East.* They evolved gradually and emerged at such distant places as India, China, and the Americas—whether through independent development or some process of mutual influence, we cannot say. The early cities and states of the ancient Near East, the Mediterranean island of Crete, and Greece exerted a profound impact on the course of Western civilization. The development of writing and metallurgy further transformed life. Despite regional differences in their circumstances, early peoples had in common the challenge of forging a sustainable and satisfying way of life under conditions strikingly different from those experienced by their predecessors, before the invention of agriculture.

*The meaning of the term *Near East,* like *Middle East,* has changed over time. Both terms originally reflected a European geographic point of view. During the nineteenth century, *Middle East* usually meant the area from Iran to Burma, especially the Indian subcontinent (then part of the British Empire); the *Near East* comprised the Balkan peninsula (today the territory of the formerly united Yugoslavia, Albania, Greece, Bulgaria, Romania, and the European portion of Turkey) and the eastern Mediterranean. The term *Far East* referred to the Asian lands that border the Pacific Ocean.

Today the term *Middle East* usually refers to the area encompassing the Arabic-speaking countries of the eastern Mediterranean region, Israel, Iran, Turkey, Cyprus, and much of North Africa. Ancient historians, by contrast, commonly used the term *ancient Near East* to designate Anatolia (often called Asia Minor, today occupied by the Asian portion of Turkey), Cyprus, the lands around the eastern end of the Mediterranean, the Arabian peninsula, Mesopotamia (the lands north of the Persian Gulf, today Iraq and Iran), and Egypt. Some historians exclude Egypt from this group on strict geographic grounds because it is in Africa, while the rest of the region lies in Asia. In this book we will observe the common usage of the term *Near East,* that is, to mean the lands of southwestern Asia and Egypt.

The Paleolithic Period

From fossil remains, anthropologists have identified a long period of development before the emergence of people with the same anatomical characteristics as humans of today. Many modern authorities date the most distant human ancestors several million years in the past and place their origin in sub-Saharan Africa, from where they moved out into the Near East, Europe, and Asia hundreds of thousands of years ago. The human type called *homo sapiens,* the immediate ancestor of the modern type (called *homo sapiens sapiens,* an anthropological term that means "wise, wise human being") first appeared several hundred thousand years ago in Africa in the Paleolithic (Greek for "Old Stone") period. The Stone Age can be divided roughly into an older period, the Paleolithic, whose beginnings extend at least four hundred thousand years into the past (some estimates say seven hundred thousand), and a more recent period, the Neolithic ("New Stone") period, which began about ten thousand to twelve thousand years ago.

The Spread and Organization of Paleolithic Peoples

Humans in the Paleolithic period lived a radically different life from the settled existence most of us now take for granted: they roamed all their lives, moving around because they had to find their food in the wild. Although they knew a great deal about their environment, they had not yet learned to produce their own food by growing crops and raising animals. Instead they hunted wild game for meat, fished in lakes and rivers, collected shellfish if they could, and gathered wild plants, fruits, and nuts. Because they had to survive by hunting and gathering their food, we refer to these early humans as *hunter-gatherers. Homo sapiens sapiens* was the last of a long line of populations to live by hunting and gathering, the way of life that characterized human experience for by far the greatest span during which humans have inhabited the earth.

Some of the African *homo sapiens* population migrated into the rest of the world at least one hundred thousand years ago, such as the type known as *homo sapiens Neanderthalensis,* so named because archaeologists have found their remains in Germany's Neanderthal valley. *Homo sapiens sapiens* apparently began to leave Africa about forty-five thousand to forty thousand years ago, during the last part of the Paleolithic period. They first moved into Asia and Europe and later into the Americas and Australia, transversing then–existent land bridges. When *homo sapiens sapiens* first appeared in Asia and Europe, they encountered *homo sapiens* populations that had migrated much earlier. How *homo sapiens sapiens* came to replace completely these earlier peoples such as the Neanderthals remains unknown. Although humans by this time had developed spoken language, the invention of writing still lay tens of thousands of years in the future. These early hunter-gatherers therefore left no documents to tell us about their lives, and archaeologists and anthropologists who study prehistory, the period before written records, must rely on other sources of information.

We cannot say for certain why some hunter-gatherers left Africa in the Paleolithic period yet others stayed. Periodic, extended fluctuations in climate that made the plains of Africa more arid may have influenced migration. Persistently drier conditions would have driven some local game animals north in search of moisture, and some of the mobile human populations who hunted them would have followed. No evidence exists, however, to explain how people at the time would have decided whether to migrate.

Archaeological discovery of objects left at early human campsites has revealed much about the lives of hunter-gatherers of different anthropological types. Anthropologists have even been able to speculate about the lives of ancient hunter-gatherers from comparative studies of certain modern populations because a few small groups of people, such as the !Kung San who inhabit the Kalahari Desert in southern Africa, still live by hunting and gathering. Thus, archeology and anthropology allow us to reconstruct some outlines of the life of Paleolithic hunter-gatherers. They probably banded together in groups of about twenty-five individuals who hunted and foraged for food that they shared with each other. Because women of childbearing age had to nurse their young, they would have found it difficult to roam far from their camp. They and the smaller children gathered food closer to home by foraging for edible plants and catching small animals. The plant food they gathered constituted the bulk of the diet of hunter-gatherer populations. Men probably did most of the hunting of large and sometimes dangerous animals, which often took place far from camp. Prehistoric groups thus tended to divide their main labor—finding food—between men and women.

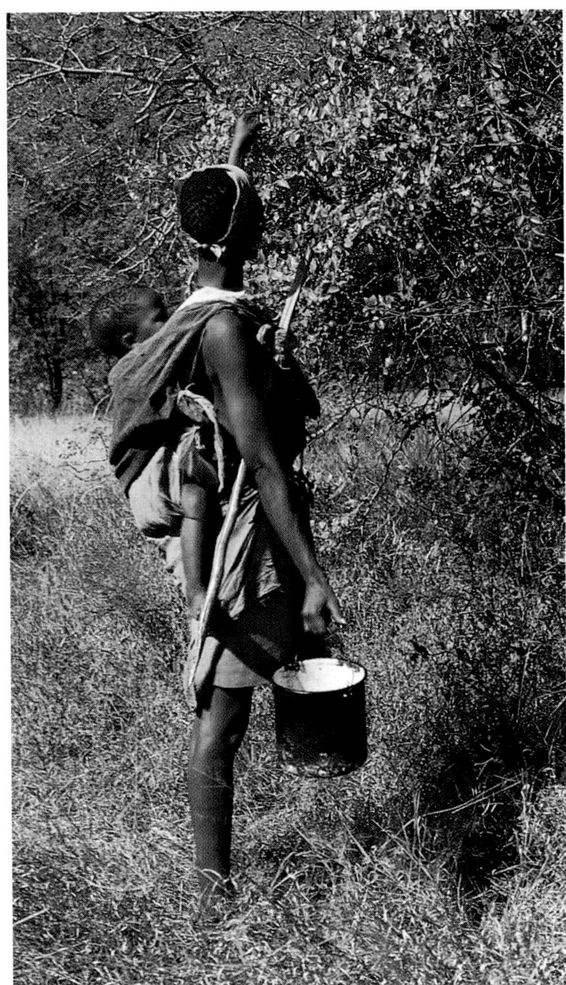

A Modern Hunter-Gatherer
This woman gathering food from wild plants in Africa exemplifies the only way human beings could support themselves before the invention of agriculture. Women's responsibilities for small children meant that they could not roam as far from home as men did on their hunts.

Because both men and women made an essential contribution to the group's support, these prehistoric bands perhaps did not divide power and status according to gender. In fact, early hunter-gatherer society (the organization of their communal relationships with one another) may have been largely egalitarian; that is, all adults, regardless of gender, may have shared decision making about the group's organization and actions. Furthermore, hunter-gatherers lacked laws, judges, and political institutions in the modern sense. Nevertheless, differences in prestige probably existed among some ancient hunter-gatherers. Modern hunter-gatherer groups, for example, sometimes observe prestige differences according to gender, such as assigning greater value to the meat hunted by men than to the plant food gathered by women, despite the latter's greater contribution to the continuing sustenance of the group. Older people likely enjoyed higher social status in ancient hunter-gatherer populations because of their greater knowledge. Their age also set them apart in an era when most people died of disease or accidents before they were thirty.

Recent archaeological discoveries of Paleolithic graves containing weapons, tools, animal figurines, ivory beads, and bracelets show not only that humans in the Old Stone Age attached special, perhaps religious, significance to death but also suggest that they recognized social differences among individuals based on other grounds. We can surmise that persons buried with such elaborate care and expenditure enjoyed superior wealth, power, or status. These rich burials may indicate that some Paleolithic groups organized themselves into *hierarchies,* social systems that ranked certain people as more important than others. One important component of the story of early Western history is the evidence for *social differentiation,* the marking of certain people as wealthier, more respected, or more powerful than others in their group.

The Knowledge and Beliefs of Hunter-Gatherers

Paleolithic hunter-gatherers did not roam randomly in their search for food. Each group tended to stay within its own territory. If they behaved anything like modern hunter-gatherers, they ranged over an area that averaged roughly sixty miles across in any one direction. Because no one had yet domesticated oxen or horses or built wheeled vehicles for transport, hunter-gatherers had to walk everywhere and to carry their belongings with them, under their own power. Although this constant exercise kept them in robust condition, they counted on their knowledge as well as their strength. For example, they planned ahead for cooperative hunts at favorite spots, such as river crossings, where they were likely to find large game animals. They also established their camps in regular locations that past experience had shown to be particularly good spots for gathering wild plants. They sought shelter from the weather in caves or rough dwellings made from branches and animal skins. Occasionally they built more elaborate shelters, such as the domelike hut found in western Russia that was constructed from the bones of mammoths. Nevertheless, although hunter-gatherers might return year after year to the same places where they had found food in the past, their temporary dwellings could never become permanent homes. They had to move in order to survive.

Their mobility and skill at hunting constituted only part of the store of knowledge that Paleolithic people assembled. Over time they developed considerable skill at shaping tools such as hammers and blades from stone, wood, and bone. Almost everything these people possessed they either found or made in the area covered by their wanderings. When they encountered other bands, however, hunter-gatherers could exchange goods. Whenever possible they bartered with each other for attractive objects. The objects exchanged in this way could travel great distances from their point of origin: for example, seashells used as jewelry made their way inland through repeated swaps from one group to another. Such exchanges, known from at least the late Paleolithic period, foreshadowed the development of international trade that would later forge far-reaching connections among distant parts of the world.

Prehistoric humans had many skills that their ancestors had passed down to them. Their forebears taught them how to make tools and how to fashion ornaments to wear on the clothing they created from animal skins. Their knowledge of making fire proved essential for survival during the extended winters of periodic ice ages, when the

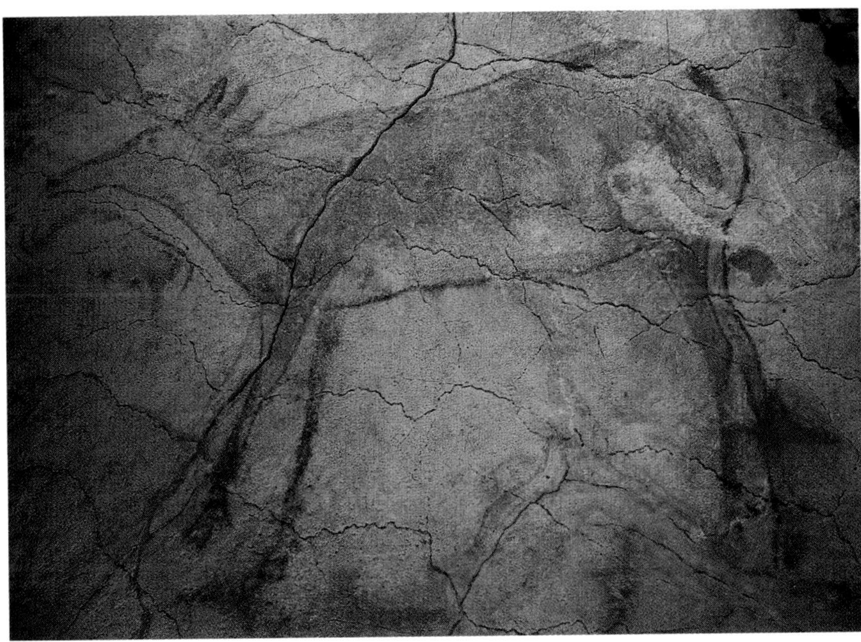

Paleolithic Painting
This deer was one of an entire herd painted on the ceiling of a cave in Altamira, Spain, about fifteen thousand years ago. Prehistoric people often painted the animals they hunted.

northern European glaciers moved much farther south than usual. The coldest part of the most recent Ice Age, for example, started about twenty thousand years ago and created a harsh climate in much of Europe for nearly ten thousand years. Their control of fire also helped hunter-gatherers survive by cooking foods. Cooking was an important technological innovation because it made edible and nutritious food out of some plants, such as wild grain, that were indigestible when raw.

But the skills of these hardy people went beyond mere survival. They sculpted statuettes of human figures, presumably for religious purposes. For example, tiny female statuettes (called Venus figurines by modern archaeologists after the Roman goddess of sexual love), sculpted with extra-large breasts, abdomens, buttocks, and thighs, have turned up in excavations of Paleolithic sites all over Europe. The exaggerated features of these female figurines suggest that the people to whom they belonged had a special set of beliefs and probably community rituals about fertility and birth. The care with which they buried their dead—the corpses decorated with red paint, flowers, and seashells—conveys a concern with the mystery of death and perhaps some belief about an afterlife. The late Paleolithic cave paintings found in Spain and France show the artistic ability of the hunter-gatherer populations of early Europe and also hint at their religious beliefs. Using strong, dark lines and earthy colors, artists of this period painted on the walls of caves that were apparently set aside as special places and not used as day-to-day shelters. The paintings, which depict primarily large animals, suggest that these powerful beasts and the dangerous hunts for them played a significant role in the life and religion of these prehistoric people. We still do not understand the significance of many of their beliefs, such as the meaning of the signs (dots, rectangles, and hands) that they often drew beside their paintings of animals.

Despite their varied knowledge and technological skills, prehistoric hunter-gatherers lived precarious lives dominated by the relentless search for something to eat. Survival was a risky business at best. Groups survived only if they learned to cooperate effectively in securing food and shelter, to profit from technological innovations like the use of fire and tool making, and to teach their children the knowledge, beliefs, and social traditions that had helped make their society viable. Paleolithic history matters in the story of Western civilization because successful hunter-gatherers passed on to later societies these traits that comprised their strategy for survival in a harsh world.

The Neolithic Period

Compared with the enormous length of time humans lived exclusively as hunter-gatherers, the origins of our modern way of life are relatively recent. Daily life as we know it depends on agriculture and the domestication of animals, developments that began about ten thousand to twelve thousand years ago. These radical innovations in the way humans acquired food caused fundamental changes in the ways they lived.

Neolithic Origins of a Modern Way of Life

Precisely how people learned to sow and to harvest crops and to raise animals for food remains a mystery. Recent archaeological research indicates that it took several thousand years to gain this knowledge. The process began in southwestern Asia when the climate there became milder and wetter than it had been in the preceding period. This favorable change in the weather promoted the growth of fields of wild grains in the Fertile Crescent, an arc of relatively well-watered territory bounded by desert and mountains, which stretched from modern Israel northward across Syria, and then southeast down to the plain of the lower stretches of the Tigris and Euphrates rivers in what is now southern Iraq. The hunter-gatherer populations who then inhabited the Fertile Crescent began to gather more and more of their food from these now easily available and increasingly abundant stands of wild cereal grains. The ample food supply in turn promoted fertility, which led to population growth, a process that might have already begun as a result of a milder climate. The more people that were born, the greater the corresponding need to exploit the food supply efficiently to feed these new, hungry mouths. Perhaps thousands of years of repeated trial and error were necessary before humans in the Fertile Crescent learned to plant part of the seeds from one crop to produce another crop. Because Neolithic women, as foragers for plant food, had the greatest knowledge of plant life, they probably played the major role in the invention of agriculture and the tools needed to practice it, such as digging sticks and grinding stones. For a long time, they did most of the agricultural labor, while men continued to hunt.

During this same period, people also learned to breed and herd animals for food. The sheep was the first animal domesticated as a source of meat, beginning about 8500 B.C. (The dog had been domesticated much earlier but was not principally used as a meat source.) The domestication of animals had become common throughout the Near East by about 7000 B.C. In this early period of domestication some people continued to move around to find grazing land for their animals, living as what we call *pastoralists.* They may have also cultivated small, temporary plots from time to time when they found a suitable area. Others, relying increasingly on growing crops, kept small herds close to their settlements. Thus men, women, and children alike could tend the animals. The earliest domesticated herds seem to have been used only as a source of meat, not for so-called secondary products such as milk and wool.

Once Neolithic hunter-gatherers in the Fertile Crescent learned how to grow crops and raise animals, tremendous changes in human life ensued. Called the Neolithic, or somewhat loosely, agricultural, revolution, these changes laid the foundation for the way of life we today regard as normal. For example, to raise permanent crops, people had to cease roaming and settle in one location. Farming communities thus began to dot the landscape of the Fertile Crescent as early as 10,000 B.C.; they shared the region with more mobile pastoralists. Moreover, parents needed to have more children to practice agriculture effectively. Much larger than the fleeting settlements of Paleolithic hunter-gatherers, villages of farming families boasted permanent houses built from mud-bricks. The earliest houses were apparently circular huts, such as those known from Jericho in Palestine (the region at the southeastern corner of the Mediterranean, where modern Israel is located). Perhaps two thousand people lived at Jericho around 8000 B.C. Their huts formed a haphazardly arranged settlement without formal streets, and it stretched over about twelve acres. The village's most striking feature was the massive fortification wall around its perimeter. Three meters thick, the wall was crowned with a stone tower ten meters in diameter, which even included an internal flight of stairs.

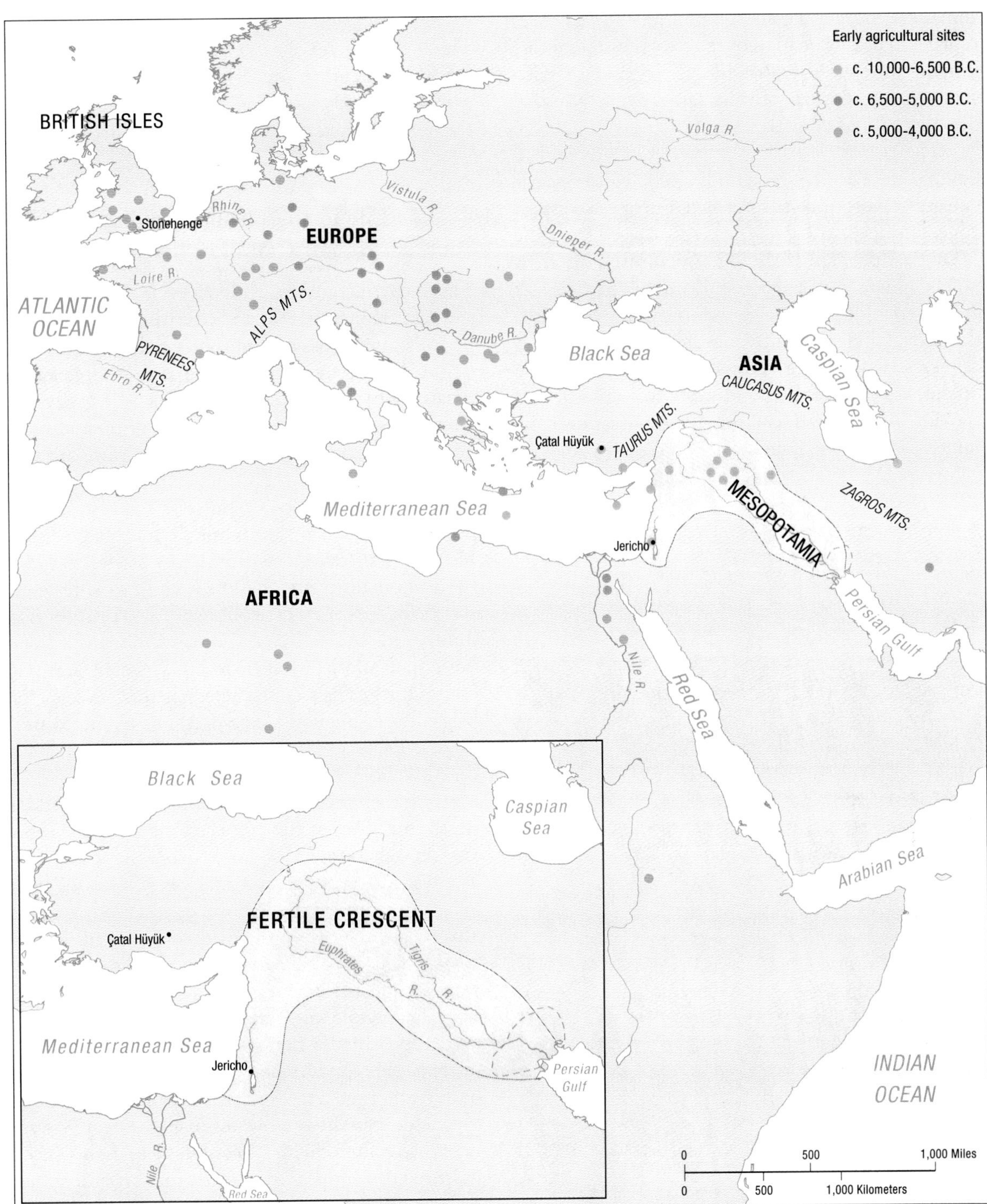

The Development of Agriculture

This walled, permanent community of farmers represented a dramatic contrast to the Paleolithic hunter-gatherers' way of life. This kind of constructed environment with its large, densely settled population was something entirely new.

The knowledge of agriculture gradually spread beyond the Fertile Crescent. By 4000 B.C. the agricultural revolution had reached Europe's western edge. Farmers slowly migrating westward from the Near East probably brought agriculture into areas where it was not previously known, although it also seems likely that people in other regions of the world independently developed farming and domesticated animals. However Neolithic people outside the Fertile Crescent came to know of this startling new way to live, their lives were never the same after they became farmers instead of hunter-gatherers. Above all, fundamental changes occurred in the way people responded to population flux. The Neolithic revolution clearly shows the importance of demography—the study of the size, growth, density, distribution, and vital statistics of the human population—in understanding historical change.

Tower in the wall of Neolithic Jericho
Built around 8000 B.C., the stone wall around Jericho in Palestine is one of the earliest such defenses known.

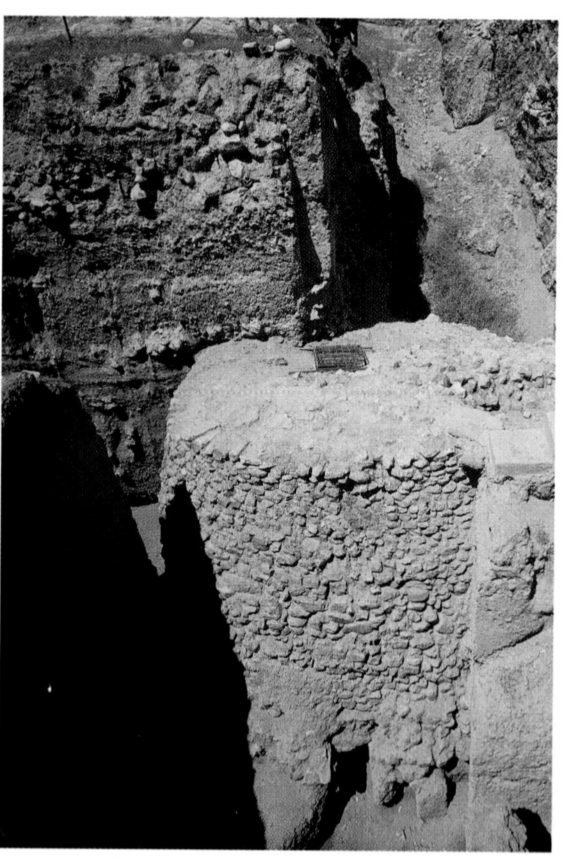

Life in the Neolithic Village of Çatal Hüyük

The most intriguing evidence yet discovered for the vast changes in human life during the Neolithic period comes from an archaeological site northwest of the Fertile Crescent, in the region later called Anatolia by the Greeks and Asia Minor by the Romans (now Turkey). There, on an upland plain near a river, a massive mound rises from the surrounding open countryside. Known to us only by its modern Turkish name, Çatal Hüyük (pronounced "Chatal Hooyook," meaning "Fork Mound"), this site was home to a settled agricultural population. By 6500 B.C., and probably considerably earlier, the people at Çatal Hüyük had built mud-brick houses nestled chock-a-block with one another to form a permanent farming community. They constructed their houses in the basically rectangular shape used in current domestic architecture, but with one striking difference: they had no doors in their outer walls. Instead they entered their homes by climbing down a ladder through a hole in the flat roof. Because this hole also served as a vent for smoke from the family fire, getting into a house at Çatal Hüyük could be a grimy business. But the absence of exterior doors also meant that the walls of the community's outermost houses could serve as a general fortification wall for the settlement.

The people of Çatal Hüyük produced their own food. In the fields stretching out below the mound, the villagers planted and harvested wheat, barley, and vegetables such as field peas. To increase the yield, they diverted water from the nearby river to irrigate their fields. Beyond these fields, they pastured the domesticated cattle that provided their main supply of meat and, by this time, hides and milk. (Sheep and goats were the norm elsewhere in the Near East as the principal domesticated animals.) They still hunted, too, as we can tell from the paintings of hunting scenes, reminiscent of the cave paintings of much earlier times, they drew on the walls of some of their buildings. Unlike hunter-gatherers, however, these villagers no longer depended on the hit-or-miss luck of the hunt or risked being killed by wild animals to acquire meat and leather. At its height, the population supported in this way probably numbered as many as six thousand.

The diversity of occupations practiced at Çatal Hüyük marked another significant change from the past and hinted at the economic complexity of later societies. Because the community could produce enough food to support the village without everyone having to work in the fields or herd cattle, some people could develop crafts as full-time occupations. Craft specialists continued to fashion tools, containers, and ornaments using traditional materials—wood, bone, hide, and stone—but they now also worked with the material of the future: metal. So far, archaeologists are certain only that metalworkers at Çatal Hüyük knew how to fashion lead into pendants and to hammer naturally occurring lumps of copper into beads and tubes for jewelry. Because traces of slag have been found on the site, however, the workers may also have begun to develop the technique of smelting metal from ore. This tricky process—the basis of true metallurgy and the foundation of much modern technology—required temperatures of 700 degrees centigrade. Other workers at Çatal Hüyük specialized in weaving textiles; the scraps of cloth discovered there are the oldest examples of this craft ever found. Like other early technological innovations, metallurgy and the production of cloth apparently also developed independently in other places.

Trade also figured in the economy of this early village. Through trade, the people of Çatal Hüyük acquired goods, such as shells from the Mediterranean Sea to wear as ornaments and a special flint from far to the east to shape into ceremonial daggers. The villagers could trade for these prized materials by offering obsidian, a local volcanic glass whose glossy luster and capacity to hold a sharp edge made it valuable. The trading contacts the villagers negotiated with other settlements meant that their world was not made up merely of isolated communities. On the contrary, they already seem to have started down the path of economic interconnection among far-flung communities—a pattern familiar in our world today.

The nearby volcano that rendered obsidian proved in the end to be as dangerous as it had been profitable. Çatal Hüyük never recovered from a volcanic eruption that destroyed it, probably about a thousand years after its foundation. A remarkable wall painting suggests that the people of Çatal Hüyük regarded the volcano as an angry god whom they needed to propitiate, and shrines found by excavators show how much their religious beliefs meant to the villagers. They outfitted these special rooms with representations of bulls' heads and female breasts, perhaps as symbols of male and female elements in their religion. Like the hunter-gatherers before them, they sculpted figurines depicting amply endowed women who perhaps represented goddesses of birth. This evidence of their fascination with the secrets of life and fertility finds its mirror image in the evidence of their deep interest in the mystery of death: skulls displayed in the shrines and wall paintings of vultures devouring headless corpses. We cannot tell whether the village had priests or priestesses with special authority for religious matters, just as we cannot know precisely what sort of political organization the villagers had. We can feel confident, however, that the people of Çatal Hüyük had some sort of social and political hierarchy. The need to plan and regulate irrigation, trade, and the exchange of food and goods between farmers and crafts producers presumably created a need for leaders with more authority than was required to maintain order in hunter-gatherer bands. Furthermore, households that were successful in farming, herding, crafts production, and trade generated wealth surpluses that distinguished them from others whose efforts proved less fortunate. In short, the villagers did not live in an undifferentiated, egalitarian, or leaderless society.

The equality between men and women that may have existed in hunter-gatherer society had also disappeared by the late Neolithic period. The reasons for this shift remain unclear, but they perhaps involved gradual changes in agriculture and herding over many centuries. Farmers began to use plows pulled by animals sometime after about 4000 B.C. to cultivate land that was more difficult to sow than the areas cultivated in the earliest period of agriculture. Men apparently operated the plows, perhaps because plowing required more physical strength than digging with sticks and hoes. Men also predominated in tending the larger herds that had become more common now that grazing animals such as cattle were kept as sources of milk and sheep were raised for wool. The herding of a community's animals tended to take place at a distance from the home settlement because new grazing land had to be found continually. As with hunting in hunter-gatherer populations, men, free from having to nurse children, took on this task. Women probably became more tied to the central settlement because they had to bear and raise more children to support agriculture. The responsibility for new labor-intensive tasks also fell to women. For example, they now turned milk into cheese and yogurt and made cloth by spinning and weaving wool. However the transition occurred, the predominance of men in agriculture in the late Neolithic period and the accompanying changes in the lives of women apparently led to women's loss of equality with men.

Permanent homes, large families, relatively reliable food supplies from agriculture and animal husbandry, specialized occupations, and hierarchical societies in which men have held the most power have characterized Western history from the Neolithic period forward. For this reason the broad outlines of the life of Neolithic villagers might seem so familiar to us as to be unremarkable. But their way of life probably would have astounded the hunter-gatherers of the earlier Paleolithic period. The Neolithic revolution marked a turning point in human history. Now that farmers and herders could produce a surplus of food to support other people, specialists in art, architecture, crafts, religion, and politics could multiply as never before. Hand in hand with these developments came an increasing social differentiation and a division of labor by gender that saw men begin to take over agriculture and women take up new tasks at home. These developments reflected the apportionment of power in the society. The surpluses created by the Neolithic revolution opened the way to the development of Western civilization as we know it.

The Challenge of the West

Cloth Merchants, Roman Relief

PART I

The Emergence of the West, from Earliest Times to A.D. 567

What do we mean by *Western civilization?* Historians use *Western* in this context to refer mainly to the history of Europe. The term *Europe* comes from the ancient Greeks, who gave that name to the Greek mainland; it means "[the place of] the setting of the sun." The Greeks referred to regions east of them as "the place where the sun rises," and they judged themselves very different from the inhabitants of those areas. Thus the notion of a distinctive Western civilization arose from the interaction of peoples in the ancient Near East and Greece. But what exactly is *civilization?* Historians define the concept not by making value judgments but by examining the level of complexity of human activity. Thus they see the embryo of civilization in the momentous changes of twelve to fourteen thousand years ago, when the development of agriculture produced the first farming communities. The material needs of such communities—for irrigation, tools, and defense—led to an increasing division of labor and an accelerating tendency to value some people more than others.

By around 3000 B.C., the ranking of people to construct a social hierarchy had grown more complex as farming settlements in the Near East swelled into large cities. We can certainly say that civilization had begun by this time. In politics, the growth of hierarchy culminated in the development of monarchical government. The idea of a supreme ruler seemed natural—a reflection of the superiority of gods to humans. The need to ensure divine favor by proper performance of religious rituals on behalf of the ruler and the whole community created another source of complexity. Furthermore, the invention of writing and the development of metallurgical technology led to more specialized jobs.

Deeply influenced by their Near Eastern and Egyptian neighbors, the first European civilizations emerged in the eastern Mediterranean, especially on the island of Crete and the Greek islands and mainland. About three thousand years ago, a period of crisis profoundly disrupted these civilizations and their older counterparts to the east. The Near East recovered faster from these disasters than Greece, and the Assyrians soon built a great empire from Mesopotamia to Syria in the tradition of their forerunners.

Having regained their prosperity by about 750 B.C., the Greeks created a new form of political and social organization that would prove enormously significant for Western civilization: the democratic city-state, or *polis.* Although ancient Greek democracy coexisted with slavery and excluded women from politics, it introduced the radically new principle of including the poor as citizen-participants alongside the rich. The Greeks, however, never created political unity: it was left to Rome to become the political master of the Mediterranean. The Romans had no real technological advantage over those whom they came to dominate. But unlike the Greeks, who only rarely admitted outsiders to full membership in the city-state, the Romans assimilated others into their society. This characteristic allowed the Romans to organize a political domain greater than any the Western world had seen.

Roman rule's vast expansion took place during the Republic, a state that in theory was governed by the people but in practice was dominated by a few upper-class families. The leaders of these families brought down the Republic by engaging in civil wars; what emerged was a monarchy disguised as an improved republic, which we call the Roman Empire. For the first two centuries of this new system, the Roman emperors presided over relative peace. Cities prospered and grew, and the needs of huge urban populations significantly expanded interactions across the Mediterranean world. Civil wars, combined with epidemics and other natural disasters, dramatically weakened the empire in the third century. A century later the emperor Constantine instituted the most striking change in the period—and the most enduring legacy for later Western civilization—when he made Christianity the official state religion.

By the end of the fourth century A.D., the Roman Empire struggled to accommodate large numbers of Germanic peoples from northern Europe seeking safety and prosperity inside Roman territory. Peoples in and outside the empire had long interacted along its frontier zones, but now conflict between the old-time inhabitants of the empire and the newcomers periodically erupted into violence. These intense changes overwhelmed Roman governmental institutions in the western half of the empire in the fifth century and led to the creation of kingdoms that were ruled by newcomers but populated by old and new inhabitants. These new states, constructed from Germanic and Roman traditions, would be the connection between antiquity and medieval Europe. The eastern half of the empire, by contrast, maintained its traditional identity, which combined Greek and Near Eastern populations, and it endured politically for another thousand years as what we call the Byzantine Empire. The legacies of ancient times to later Western civilization were thus transmitted through two distinct channels, stemming from the western and the eastern halves of the former Roman Empire.

CHAPTER

I

The First Civilizations in the West

Around 2600 B.C. a king named Gilgamesh ruled the city of Uruk (today Warka, Iraq). Gilgamesh became a legendary figure in ancient Mesopotamia ("the land between the rivers"), the great plain of the Tigris and Euphrates rivers where Western civilization first emerged and settlers built the earliest cities. The *Epic of Gilgamesh* spun a tale of heroic adventures that took Gilgamesh to the ends of the earth. The ultimate goal of his quest was immortality. By diving to the bottom of the sea and seizing the magic plant of rejuvenation, Gilgamesh gained the secret of eternal life. But as he and his boatman traveled home with their treasure, misfortune struck:

> *. . . they stopped for the night. Gilgamesh saw a pool whose water was cool, and went down into the water and washed. A snake smelt the fragrance of the plant. It came up silently and carried off the plant. As it took it away, it shed its scaly skin. Thereupon Gilgamesh sat down and wept. . . . He spoke to Ur-shanabi the boatman: "For what purpose, Ur-shanabi, have my arms grown weary? For what purpose was the blood inside me so red? I did not gain an advantage for myself. . . . I shall give up, and I have left the boat on the shore." . . . They reached Uruk the sheepfold. Gilgamesh spoke to . . . the boatman: "Go up on to the wall of Uruk, Ur-shanabi, and walk around, inspect the foundation platform and scrutinize the brickwork! Testify that its bricks are baked bricks, and that the Seven Wise Ones must have laid its foundations! One square mile is city, one square mile is orchards, one square mile is claypits, as well as the open ground of [the goddess] Ishtar's temple. Three square miles and the open ground comprise Uruk."*

Cuneiform Tablet
Mesopotamian scribes wrote using pointed sticks to make wedge-shaped marks (cuneiform) on soft clay tablets, which were preserved by baking. This earliest form of writing developed as Western civilization became more urbanized and more economically and socially complex.

When Gilgamesh concedes defeat in his quest for immortality, he consoles himself with thoughts of Uruk, which he describes with pride. His finely built city gives meaning to his life in the end.

To Gilgamesh, Uruk represented the pinnacle of his life's achievement. To people today, cities can also be a source of pride, a measure of human accomplishment—a symbol of civilization even. In fact, modern notions of what "civilization" means usually include the development of cities as an integral characteristic. Other attributes usually deemed essential for a society to be called "civilized" include the ability to write and keep written records, the use of a formal set of laws enforced and regulated by a hierarchical political organization, a developed system of agriculture, and the capability to build large structures. Using these criteria, we find evidence of the first civilizations in southwestern Asia and Egypt as early as the fourth and third millennia B.C. These earliest civilizations developed in the Bronze Age, which followed the Neolithic Age in the late fourth millennium. During that era, crafts producers first learned to combine copper with tin to make the metal alloy bronze, a material that revolutionized the production of luxury goods, tools, and most of all weapons. This technological innovation made people eager to acquire supplies of metal, by force if necessary. Through trade, contacts made in travel, and perhaps migration, these early civilizations of the ancient Near East significantly influenced the development of the civilizations that later emerged on the Mediterranean island of Crete and in Greece.

Important Dates

c. 3500 B.C.* First cities established and writing developed in Sumer

c. 3100–3000 B.C. King Menes unites Upper and Lower Egypt

c. 3000 B.C. Stone temples constructed on Malta

c. 2600 B.C. King Gilgamesh rules the city of Uruk in Sumer

c. 2575 B.C. Great Pyramid of Cheops constructed at Giza in Egypt

c. 2350 B.C. Sargon establishes the Akkadian empire

c. 2200 B.C. Earliest Cretan palaces constructed

c. 1792–1750 B.C. Reign of Hammurabi, king of Babylon

Early fifteenth century B.C. Reign of Queen Hatshepsut of Egypt

c. 1400 B.C. Earliest Mycenaean palaces constructed in Greece

c. 1285 Battle of Egyptian King Ramesses II with the Hittites at Kadesh in Syria

Early or mid-thirteenth century B.C. Exodus of the Hebrews from Egypt

c. 1200 B.C. Disturbances across the eastern Mediterranean region

The First Civilizations in the Near East

More than any other single factor, living in cities has traditionally been associated with the concept of civilization. Historians usually reserve the term *city* for densely populated settlements with special features such as fortified walls, major buildings used for religious and political purposes, and a complex political administration. Because some and occasionally all of these elements appeared in embryonic form in early Neolithic villages, such as Jericho and Çatal Hüyük, the growth of cities proper seems to have been an evolutionary rather than a revolutionary process. The first cities truly worthy of the name were built in Mesopotamia.

The Earliest Cities: Sumer

Urban settlements large enough to be called cities had emerged in southwestern Asia by about 3500 B.C.† Most of these early cities clustered in Mesopotamia. Cities first emerged there in the alluvial land at the southern end of the plain, where the hot weather and fertile soil made for good farming conditions when river water was diverted to the

*The abbreviation c., standing for the Latin *circa,* means "approximately" and is used to indicate dates about which some uncertainty exists.

†Most dates in ancient Near Eastern history must be regarded as tentative because our evidence simply does not allow precision.

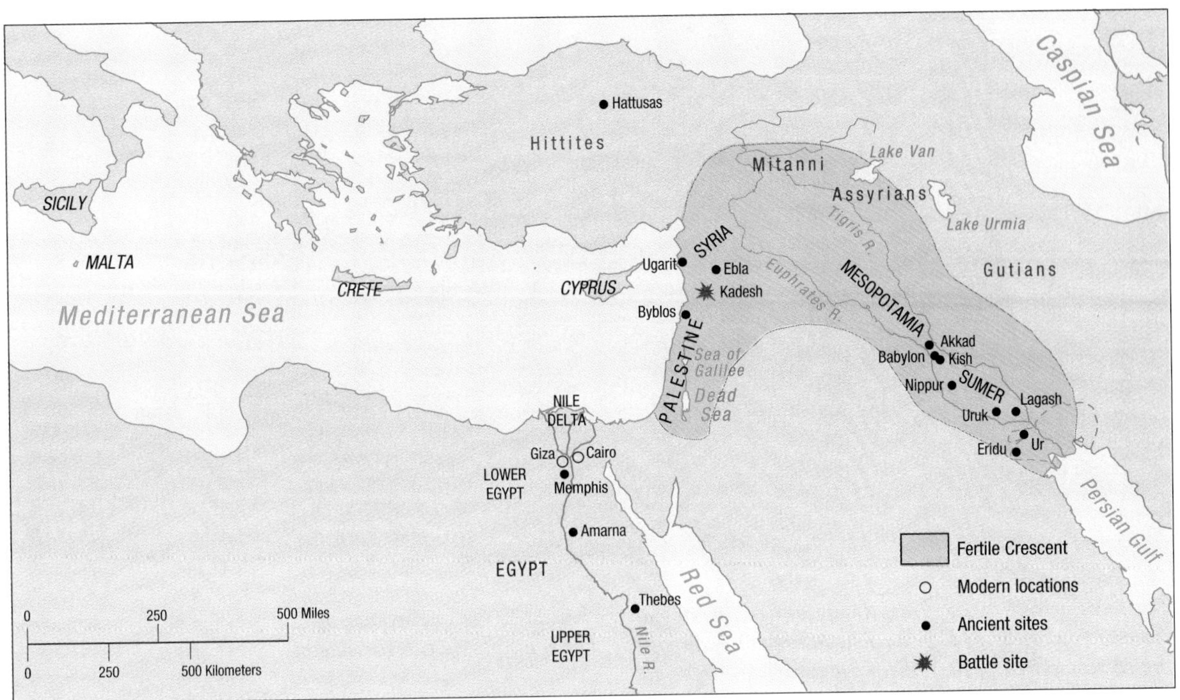

The Early Civilizations of the Near East and Egypt

fields via a complex system of irrigation canals that made up for the scarcity of rainfall. By 3000 B.C. the Sumerians, the people from the southern Mesopotamian territory called Sumer, dominated this part of the Fertile Crescent. They established sizable cities there, such as Uruk (the Erech of the Bible), Eridu, and Ur, which grew up around great temples built of mud-brick and whose control extended to the agricultural land outside the cities. This geographical arrangement—an urban center exercising political and economic control over the countryside around it—is often called a *city-state.* In later Greek history the city-state is associated with self-governance by an assembly of male citizens. Assemblies of male citizens probably decided major issues under the leadership of a council of elders in the earliest Mesopotamian cities, too, but this feature waned as strong monarchies developed. Although we do not know the precise organization of early Sumerian city-states, we do know that they saw themselves as separate political entities and regularly squabbled with one another.

The Sumerians' prosperity stemmed from the surpluses yielded by their farms and their development of trade routes to exchange these surpluses for materials not available in their locale. Through hard work and ingenuity, they grew plants and raised animals on the rich soil of their river plains, where summer temperatures often reached 120 degrees and canals diverted water for irrigation. The strongly flowing rivers required careful attention because they tended to change course unpredictably, causing devastating floods—an ironic danger in the desert. The Sumerians traded their surpluses of grain, vegetable oil, woolens, and leather for products such as metals, timber, and precious stones. Sumerian sea trade regularly reached as far east as India. Technological innovation also strengthened the early Mesopotamian economy: around 3000 B.C. the wheel was invented in a form sturdy enough to be used on carts. The ability to transport loads on wheeled vehicles greatly aided the Sumerians in agriculture and commerce.

By about 2500 B.C. most Sumerians inhabited walled cities populated with twenty thousand or more residents, some many more. Their mud-brick houses consisted of rooms grouped around an open court. Most people lived in only one or two rooms, but the wealthy constructed two-story dwellings that had a dozen or more rooms. But rich and poor

The Ziggurat of Ur
The massive size of ziggurats (temples) like this one at Ur indicated the importance of the worship of the gods in ancient Mesopotamian culture. For the scale, notice the size of the car compared to that of the ziggurat.

alike suffered the ill effects of a domestic water supply often contaminated by sewage. No system of waste disposal existed beyond the pigs and dogs who scavenged in the streets and open spaces where garbage was unceremoniously dumped.

Inside the cities' walls, the great temple-towers (ziggurats) soared as high as ten stories, emphasizing the centrality of religion to the Sumerians. They viewed the gods as their absolute masters to whom they owed total devotion. The Sumerians demonstrated their religious devotion most visibly by giving their gods tremendous material support. The revenues from numerous fields and the toil of gangs of semifree laborers supported the ziggurats and their religious activities, which were supervised by powerful priests and priestesses. These priests and priestesses also administered the gods' considerable property. The priest or priestess of the city's chief divinity, which differed from place to place, enjoyed extremely high status.

Although the temples and their support systems predominated in the economy of Sumerian cities, some private households also held significant power. Like the temples, wealthy households derived income from the agricultural land they controlled. Also like the temples, private individuals could own slaves. Slavery existed in many forms in the ancient Near East, and no single description of the social and legal position of slaves can cover all the permutations. People became slaves by being captured in war, by being born to slaves, by voluntarily selling themselves or their children because they were too impoverished to survive on their own, or by being sold under duress to satisfy debts they could not otherwise pay. Foreigners enslaved as captives in war or in raids dispatched to acquire slaves had an inferior position compared to citizens who fell into slavery to pay off debts. Children whose parents dedicated them as servants to the gods, although counted as slaves, could rise to prominent positions in the temple administrations. In general, however, slavery was a state of near-total dependency on other people and legal exclusion from most normal social relations; most slaves worked without compensation and lacked almost any legal rights.

Although slaves sometimes formed relationships with free persons and frequently married each other and had families, they had no guarantee that their family members would not be sold. Slaves in the most inferior position could be bought, sold, beaten, or even killed by their masters—they counted as commodities, not as people. Slaves worked in domestic service, craft production, and

Royal Finery from Ur
Women from the royal court of Ur in Sumer wore elaborate jewelry of gold and lapis lazuli. This headdress was found in a royal tomb containing the bodies of sixty-eight women similarly outfitted.

farming, but their economic significance compared to that of free workers in early Mesopotamia is still disputed. Free persons appear to have performed the majority of state labor as a kind of corvée service (paying a tax with labor rather than money). Under certain conditions slaves could be manumitted (set free), for example, by the provisions of their masters' wills or by purchasing their freedom from the earnings they could sometimes accumulate. Manumission, however, remained only a faint possibility for most slaves.

The complex, hierarchical political organization—what we would call the state—of Sumerian cities directly affected their economy. In theory the gods ruled Sumerian cities, a notion that made the state a theocracy (government by gods) and gave the priests and priestesses a say in secular affairs. By about 2700 B.C., however, the state as it existed in Sumerian cities had a supreme temporal, or worldly, ruler—a king—with a council of older men as his advisers. Diverse factors contributed to the emergence of this highly structured political organization: the similarity to the rule of the divine world by a chief god, the increasing need for supervision of the cities' complex economic systems, and above all the necessity of having a military commander to lead the defense of the community against raiders and rivals eager to seize its riches, its land, and its water supply.

As befitted his status, a Sumerian king and his family lived in an elaborate palace that rivaled the scale of the great temples. It served as the secular administrative center for the city and its surrounding territory. Another major function of the king's palace was to store the enormous wealth the royal family accumulated. The Sumerian state demanded that a significant portion of its economic surplus be dedicated to displaying the superior status of its royal leaders. Archaeological excavation of the immense royal cemetery in Ur, for example, has revealed the dazzling extent of these riches. The rulers of Ur took with them to their graves spectacular possessions crafted in gold, silver, and precious stones. These graves also yielded grislier evidence of the exalted status of the king and queen: the bodies of the servants and retainers who were sacrificed to serve their royal masters after death.

The spectacle of wealth and power that evidently characterized Sumerian kingship suggests just how great the gap between the upper and lower ranks of Sumerian society had become. The days of relative equality between men and women were also long gone. Patriarchy—domination by men in political, social, and economic life—was already established in these first cities. Although a Sumerian queen was respected because she was the wife of the king and the mother of the royal children, the king ruled. The high priestess of the city's patron god owed most of her elevated status to her relationship with the king, with whom she celebrated the annual religious ritual of the sacred wedding during the New Year holiday. This reenactment of a mythological story of the marriage of the goddess Inanna and the god Dumuzi supposedly ensured successful reproduction in the city's population that year.

The Sumerians were the first people to develop a system of writing based on nonpictorial symbols. Some scholars think people used small tokens to represent quantities of items before the invention

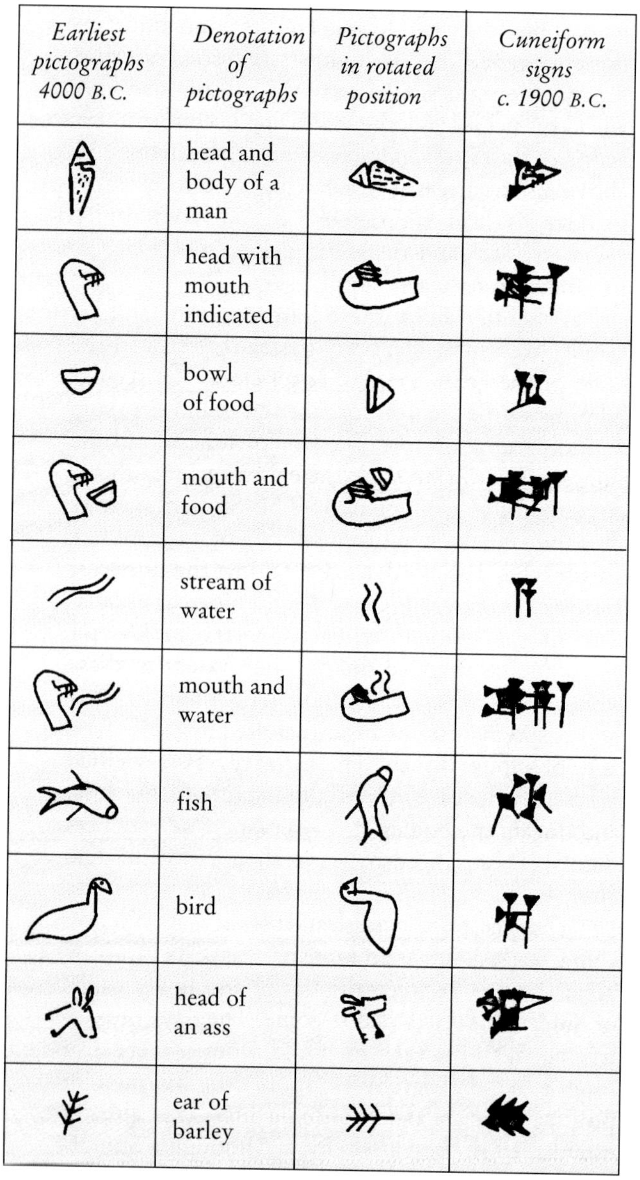

Earliest pictographs 4000 B.C.	*Denotation of pictographs*	*Pictographs in rotated position*	*Cuneiform signs c. 1900 B.C.*
	head and body of a man		
	head with mouth indicated		
	bowl of food		
	mouth and food		
	stream of water		
	mouth and water		
	fish		
	bird		
	head of an ass		
	ear of barley		

Sample of Sumerian Cuneiform

of writing. Food producers, for example, might need to verify the amount of grain, the number of animals, or the quantity of some other commodity they were having someone else deliver. They would therefore seal the appropriate number of tokens in a clay ball to prevent tampering. Unfortunately, this method of accounting had a critical flaw: the receiving agent had to shatter the ball to check the number of items delivered against the number of tokens, which obviously prevented these balls from becoming permanent records. People eventually avoided this particular problem by representing the number of tokens inside the ball with an equivalent number of marks scratched on the outside. These marks symbolically represented the number of objects. A natural next step in the process of using symbols to express meaning was drawing small pictures on clay tablets to represent objects. At first these pictographs symbolized concrete objects only, such as a cow. Eventually the pictographs and signs came to represent the sounds of spoken language. Sumerian writing was not an alphabet, in which a symbol represents the sound of a single letter, but a mixed system of phonetic symbols and pictographs that represented the sounds of entire syllables and often stood for entire words.

The Sumerians' fully developed script is now called *cuneiform* (from *cuneus,* Latin for "wedge") because of the wedge-shaped marks impressed into clay tablets to record spoken language. Other peoples in this region subsequently adopted cuneiform to write their own languages. For a time, writing was largely a professional skill mastered by only a few men and women, known as scribes, and was used mostly in accounting. Eventually, writing was used for other purposes, above all to record the culture's stories, previously preserved only in memory and speech. Thus written literature began. The world's oldest poetry by a known author was composed by Enheduanna in the twenty-third century B.C. She was a priestess, prophetess, and princess, the daughter of King Sargon of Akkad. Her poetry, written in Sumerian, praised the life-giving goddess of love, Inanna (or Ishtar). Some later princesses, who wrote dirges, love songs, lullabies, and prayers, continued the Mesopotamian tradition of royal women as authors. The number of literate women and men in the general population was probably quite small. By 2000 B.C., Mesopotamians in various places had begun to record their myths, such as the epic of Gilgamesh. Stories about Gilgamesh had circulated orally for centuries, but now they were permanently recorded in cuneiform.

The evolution of writing had a tremendous impact on the organization of society as well as on the forms of literature. Powerful men such as kings, priests, and wealthy landowners could control their workers even more strictly because they could keep precise track of who had paid, who still owed, and the amounts of debt. A scribal administrative class developed and began to keep documents. Most significantly, writing provided a powerful new tool for passing on a culture to later generations.

Bronze Age Metallurgy

About the same time cities emerged in Mesopotamia, crafts producers there and in other areas of the Mediterranean world developed advanced techniques for working with bronze, lead, silver, and gold. Devising innovative ways to alloy metals at high temperatures, smiths fashioned new luxury goods and better tools for agriculture, construction, and warfare. Most revolutionized by this new technology was the field of weaponry. Pure copper weapons, which had been available for some time, had offered few advantages over stone weapons because they easily lost their shape and edge. Bronze, with its strength and ability to hold a razor edge, enabled smiths to produce durable and deadly metal daggers, swords, and spearheads. Weapons of bronze soon became standard equipment for every prosperous man in the Bronze Age. Cities without metal ore had to develop trade contacts or conquer territories with mines.

Bronze Age smiths could also create daggers and swords that were far more than utilitarian implements for hunting and war. The sometimes lavish decorations added to these weapons displayed the owners' wealth and status. Such weapons also underscored the division between men and women in society, because they signified the masculine roles of hunter and warrior that had emerged long ago in the division of labor of hunter-gatherers. The development of metallurgy had other social consequences as well. People's desire to accumulate wealth and to possess status symbols stimulated demand for metals and for the skilled workers who could create these coveted articles: lavishly adorned weapons for men; exquisitely crafted jewelry made from exotic materials, such as imported ivory, for both women and men. Growing numbers of craftspeople swelled the size of Bronze Age settlements. Greater availability of such items made even more people want them. People began to question whether they were paid appropriately for their labor. They now expected to acquire wealth in metal, not just in foodstuffs, animals, or land.

The Akkadian Empire

Weaponry played such a large role in Mesopotamia's history because the cities there constantly battled one another for control. Historical documents reveal that the city of Kish achieved political supremacy in the so-called Early Dynastic Period during the middle of the third millennium B.C. In about 2350 B.C., however, a new power emerged when Sargon, the ruler of Akkad, north of Sumer, declared himself supreme and eventually dominated the region militarily. Sargon was Akkadian, not Sumerian. The Akkadians were one of the peoples we call Semitic based on the characteristics of their language. The Sumerians were a non-Semitic people; their language seems to have been unique to them. But aside from using different languages, the Akkadian and Sumerian cultures appear to have been identical. From Sargon's records of his career as a commander and ruler, we learn that he launched campaigns of conquest far to the north and south of his homeland, building by force the first empire (a political unit that includes a number of territories or peoples ruled by a single sovereign leader) recorded in history. A poet of about

The Akkadian Empire

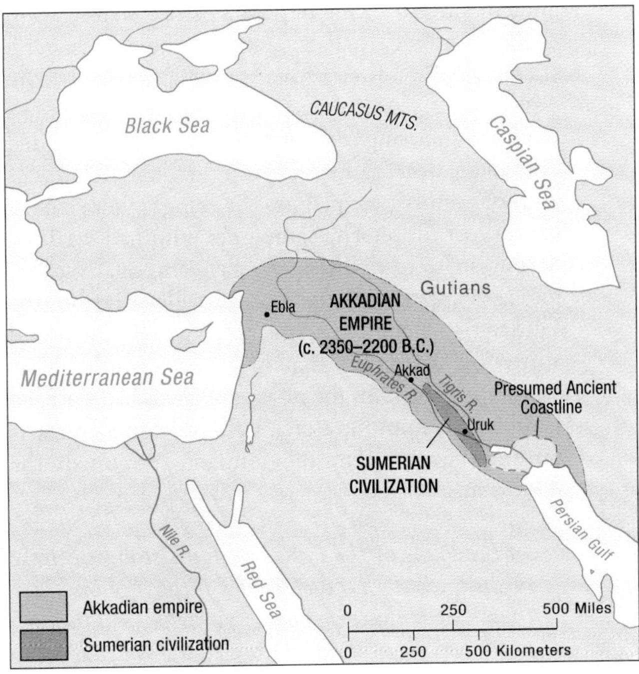

2000 B.C. attributed Sargon's success to the favor of the god Enlil: "to Sargon the king of Akkad, from below to above, Enlil had given him lordship and kingship."

Sargon's energetic grandson, Naram-Sin, continued the family tradition of military expeditions to conquer distant lands. By 2250 B.C. he had severely damaged Ebla, a large city whose site has only recently been discovered in what is now Syria, over five hundred miles from Naram-Sin's home base in Mesopotamia. Archaeologists have unearthed many cuneiform tablets at Ebla, some of them in more than one language. These discoveries may mean that Ebla had thrived as an early center of learning.

Although Sargon and Naram-Sin warred so aggressively partly because success in battle proved their worthiness to rule, they also harbored other motives for their imperialism. The Akkadian conquerors wanted a reliable supply of metal. Effective weapons required bronze, which necessitated acquiring copper and tin. We still do not know where the Mesopotamians obtained the tin they needed to make bronze. Tin is not found in the Near East today; the closest source appears to be in what is now Afghanistan, far to the northeast. The Mesopotamians may have imported tin from there by caravan. Because of the increasing dependency on metals from the Bronze Age on, ancient states lacking deposits of raw materials in their territories had to acquire them either by trade or by conquering lands that contained them.

This early Akkadian empire did not last. Attacks from neighboring hill peoples, the Gutians, ended Akkadian dominance in Sumer around 2200 B.C. and continued to plague the kings there for a century or more. The same poet who had credited Sargon's rise to divine favor gave an equally theological explanation for the vast devastation the Gutians—a people, he sneered, "whose form and stuttering words are that of a dog"—inflicted on Sumer. Naram-Sin, the poet explained, had enraged Enlil by his impious attack on a holy site. In retribution the god sent the Gutians to punish the Akkadians:

> *In the gates of the land the doors stood deep in dust, all the lands raised a bitter cry on their city walls. . . . The large fields and acres produced no grain, the flooded acres produced no fish, the watered gardens produced no honey and wine. . . . The people droop helplessly because of their hunger.*

Mesopotamian Mythology and Early Laws

This description of the plight of Sumer near the end of the third millennium B.C. reveals how precarious human life remained despite the development of complex, urban, and literate societies. The myths preserved in Mesopotamian literature reveal a belief in the gods' awesome power over humans and in the limits of human control over the circumstances of life. The themes of Mesopotamian mythology not only lived on in their own poetry and songs but also powerfully influenced the mythology of distant peoples, most notably the Greeks in later times.

A long narrative poem, the *Epic of Creation*, tells the Mesopotamian version of how all things came into being. A violent struggle among the gods supposedly created the universe. The poem depicts these primeval deities as unruly and violent. The first two gods, the female Tiamat and the male Apsu, have a blazing argument when Apsu threatens to get rid of their four generations of descendants because their incessant noise keeps him from sleeping. Eventually the fearsome male god Marduk—"four were his eyes, four were his ears; when his lips moved, fire blazed forth"—becomes the supreme deity by destroying Tiamat, her army of snaky monsters, and the gods allied with her in a gory battle. Marduk then fashions human beings out of the blood of Tiamat's chief monster. He creates people not to honor or love them but to demand that they serve and entertain their divine masters.

The *Epic of Gilgamesh* relates the adventures of Gilgamesh (whom we met on his quest for immortality at the beginning of the chapter). This popular poem has numerous versions (none complete, unfortunately) in different Near Eastern languages. In the Mesopotamian story, Gilgamesh is a tyrant who enthusiastically beds all the young women of Uruk and orders the young men to construct a temple and walls for the city. When the city's distressed inhabitants implore the mother of the gods to give them a rival to Gilgamesh, she creates the man of nature, Enkidu. After a wrestling match that ends in a draw, Enkidu and Gilgamesh become friends instead of enemies and set out to conquer Humbaba (or Huwawa), the ugly giant of the Pine Forest. The two comrades also defeat the Bull of Heaven after Gilgamesh offends the goddess Ishtar, but the gods doom Enkidu to die not long after this moment of triumph. In despair over human frailty, Gilgamesh sets out, as we saw, to find the secret of immortality, only to have his quest foiled by a thieving snake. He subsequently realizes that immortality can come only from great achievements and the memory they perpetuate.

The late Sumerian version of the Gilgamesh Epic includes a description of a cataclysmic flood that covers the earth. The gods send the flood to Mesopotamia, but one man is warned of the impending disaster and told to build a boat. He then loads his vessel with his relatives, other humans skilled in crafts, his possessions, domesticated and wild animals, and "the seed of all living things, all of them." After a week of torrential rains he and his passengers disembark to repopulate and rebuild the earth. This story is a striking predecessor to the later Biblical account of the flood and the story of Noah's ark.

The early civilizations of Mesopotamia tenaciously faced the constant challenges posed by social and political existence. They created the earliest recorded sets of public regulations and laws aimed at improving society, at least as defined by the rulers. Uruinimgina,* for example, a ruler of the city of Lagash in the twenty-fourth century B.C., promulgated the earliest known directives for reforming society and government. He sought to strengthen his own position as the central authority by weakening the powers of rich landowners and winning popular support by protecting the poor against unjust seizure of their property. His reforms subsequently influenced the famous set of written laws of Ur-Nammu, king of Ur in the late twenty-second century. Ur-Nammu expressed a commitment to, in his words, "the principles of truth and equity," under which "the orphan was not delivered up to the rich man; the widow was not delivered up to the mighty man; the man of one shekel [a small unit of value] was not delivered up to the man of one mina [a much larger unit of value]." This official concern with protecting the less powerful from exploitation introduces a moral dimension to law that recurs in later codes, such as that of Hammurabi of Babylon.

*His name was formerly read on cuneiform tablets as "Urukagina."

But even the comfortable inhabitants of walled cities had only limited protection from disaster, sickness, and starvation. According to the cuneiform poem that records his death, Ur-Nammu himself died fighting the Gutians, "abandoned on the battlefield like a crushed vessel."

The Old Kingdom of Egypt

Africa was home to the other great Near Eastern civilization of the third millennium B.C.: Egypt, a fertile region that snaked along the banks of the Nile River. The region's population included a diversity of people, whose skin color ranged from light to very dark. A significant proportion of ancient Egyptians, especially in Upper Egypt, would perhaps be regarded as black by the standards of modern racial classifications, which ancient people did not observe. Except in the delta of the Nile near the Mediterranean Sea, where the great river fanned out into several channels and swamps, the habitable territory of Egypt encompassed only the lush fields extending several miles away from the river on either side for about seven hundred miles from north to south. This narrow strip was fertile because late every summer the Nile, swollen by melting snow from the mountains far to the south, overflowed its banks for several weeks to months. This annual inundation enriched the soil with nutrients from the river's silt and prevented the accumulation of harmful deposits of mineral salts. Because of the dark color of this ribbon of fields, the Egyptians called their country the "Black Land." Immediately beyond this fertile strip stretched vast, nearly impassable deserts (the "Red Land"). So abrupt is the transition between these two areas that even today a person can stand with one foot in the Black Land and one in the Red Land. The deserts protected the Egyptians from attack except through the Nile delta and from the Nile valley on the southern frontier with Nubia. The surpluses that a multitude of hard-working farmers produced in the lush Nile valley made Egypt prosperous. Date palms, vegetables, grasses for pasturing animals, and grain grew in abundance. From their ample supplies

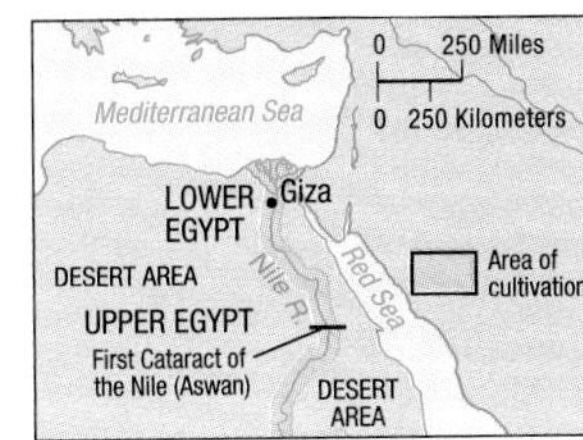

Old Kingdom Egypt

The Harvest in Egypt
This Egyptian painting depicts agriculture along the fertile banks of the Nile River. Techniques of harvesting and winnowing grain (separating the edible core from the inedible chaff) have changed little in many parts of contemporary Egypt.

Preparing Grain in the Traditional Way
Some people today still use the method of winnowing grain that ancient Egyptians used: throwing it into the air by hand so the breeze can blow the light chaff away from the heavier core.

of grain the Egyptians made bread and beer, their favorite beverage. Like the Sumerians, who brewed eleven different types, the Egyptians relished beer.

Despite the relative geographic isolation their surrounding mantle of desert gave the Egyptians, they had contacts with southwest Asia and felt the influence of Sumerian civilization. The Egyptians may have learned about writing from the Sumerians, but they wrote in their own scripts rather than cuneiform. For the most formal texts they used an ornate pictographic script known as *hieroglyphs* (Greek for "sacred carving or writing"). Both Sumerian and Egyptian life centered around religion. The Egyptians worshipped a great variety of gods, who were often represented in art and literature as creatures with both human and animal features. The priests who administered the temples, sacrifices, and festivals of the various Egyptian gods gained a preeminent place in the social and political life of Egypt, second only to the kings and queens who ruled Egypt after its unification.

Twenty-five hundred years of Egyptian royal dynasties began when King Menes (sometimes identified as Narmer) united the previously separate territories of Upper (southern) Egypt and Lower (northern) Egypt around 3100–3000 B.C. Menes' reign culminated a long process of the centralization of power. Egyptian political history thereafter revolves around the waxing and waning of a strong central authority. At times, for example, the priests or the governors of different regions promoted their own interests at the expense of the king's, causing a decentralization of authority that led to instability. The Egyptians regarded the king as a god in human form, such as the son of the sun god. Because the Egyptians recognized the

The Goddess Sakhmet
Egyptian legend taught that this lioness-headed deity had exacted vengeance on the human race when the gods were angry. She was also regarded as the creator of the people of Syria, Palestine, and the Libyan desert.

Hieroglyphic sign	*Meaning*	*Sound value*
	vulture	glottal stop
	flowering reed	consonantal I
	forearm and hand	ayin
	quail chick	W
	foot	B
	stool	P
	horned viper	F
	owl	M
	water	N
	mouth	R
	reed shelter	H
	twisted flax	slightly guttural
	placenta (?)	H as in "loch"
	animal's belly	slightly softer than h
	door bolt	S
	folded cloth	S
	pool	SH
	hill	Q
	basket with handle	K
	jar stand	G
	loaf	T

Sample of Egyptian Hieroglyphs

mortality of the reigning king, they probably differentiated the human existence of the individual king and the divine institution of the monarchy. In the Egyptian view the monarchy incorporated the divine force creating harmony and stability, called *ma'at.* Often translated as "truth," or "justice," or "righteousness," *ma'at* expressed the ideal of the beneficent and honorable administration the king as a divine being was supposed to provide his people. Their special religious status distinguished the Egyptian kings from the Sumerian kings, who ruled only as temporal lords in a state devoted to the gods.

Egypt also differed politically from the quarreling city-states of Sumer in its early tradition of unification under one monarch. This central political system gave enormous power to the kings of the so-called Old Kingdom, which lasted from 2686 to 2181 B.C., one of the three major chronological divisions of ancient Egyptian history.* (The Middle Kingdom extended from 2050 to 1786 B.C., the New Kingdom from 1567 to 1085 B.C.) The kings (known by the time of the New Kingdom as *pharaoh,* which means "the Great House," that is, the royal palace and estate) exhibited their authority and resources in their building programs. They built a few cities; their capital, Memphis (south of modern Cairo), grew into a metropolis packed with mammoth structures. But it was outside Memphis that the Old Kingdom kings erected the most stunning manifestations of their might: the pyramids, which served as royal tombs and as the centerpieces of elaborate groups of buildings for royal ceremonies. Although we now know that the pyramids were not the first megalithic (Greek for "of large stones") monuments in the world, they still rank as the grandest. The Old Kingdom monarchs marshaled their resources and population to construct these huge complexes. Imhotep, chief architect of King Djoser around 2650 B.C., became famous for overseeing the construction of the first large pyramid, the Step Pyramid at Saqqara, Egypt's earliest monument built entirely of stone. King Sneferu subsequently had a much larger pyramid built at Dahshur. But king Cheops, around 2575 B.C., commissioned the biggest of them all—the Great Pyramid at Giza outside Cairo. At around four hundred eighty feet high, it stands taller than a forty-story skyscraper. Covering over thirteen acres, its dimensions of roughly seven hundred sixty feet per side required more than two million blocks of limestone weighing on the average two and a half tons, with some as heavy as fifteen tons.

The pyramids and the funerary buildings linked to them were outfitted elaborately to provide the kings with material delights for their existence in the world of the dead. Gilded furniture; sparkling jewelry; exquisite objects of all kinds, from the domestic to the exotic—the dead kings took it all with them. Archaeologists have even uncovered two full-sized cedar ships buried next to the Great Pyramid; they evidently conveyed King Cheops on his journey into eternity. A hieroglyphic text from around 2300 B.C., addressed to the god Atum, expresses the hope that an Old Kingdom ruler entombed in his pyramid has a secure afterlife: "O Atum, put your arms around King Nefer-ka-Re, around this construction work, around this pyramid. . . . May you guard lest anything happen to him evilly throughout the course of eternity." The kings of Egypt—and presumably their subjects as well—coped with the idea of death as best they could; their lavish preparations for death clearly indicate their strong belief in an afterlife.

Almost all the extant art from ancient Egypt comes from tombs or temples, further testimony to the kings' consuming interest in the afterworld and proper relations with the gods. Egyptian artists of the Old Kingdom excelled in stonework, from carved ornamental jars to massive portrait statues of the kings. These statues invariably represent the subject either standing stiffly with his left leg advanced or sitting on a chair or throne. Artists sculpted the parts of the bodies according to a predetermined set of proportions, and molded the faces into an idealized style that befitted the special religious status of the monarchs. The formalism of this sculpture illustrates how much Egypt's rulers valued order and predictability. The concern for a certain decorum appears in the Old Kingdom literature the Egyptians called *Instructions*, known today as *wisdom literature*. These texts convey precepts for appropriate behavior for high officials. In the *Instruction of Ptahhotep,* for example, the king advises his minister Ptahhotep to tell his son, who will succeed him in office, not to be arrogant or overconfident just because he is well educated and to seek advice from the ignorant as well as the wise.

Even by today's standards the massive pyramid complexes are marvels of engineering and human labor. The effort required to supply workers and materials for such enormous projects, intentionally or not, furthered the organization of a centralized state. Old Kingdom rulers had to develop a stronger government administration just to oversee their great construction projects. Egyptian

*The uncertainty that characterizes the chronology of ancient Mesopotamia also pertains to the dates for ancient Egypt, despite the apparent precision implied by the custom of giving specific dates for the reigns of kings, and so on.

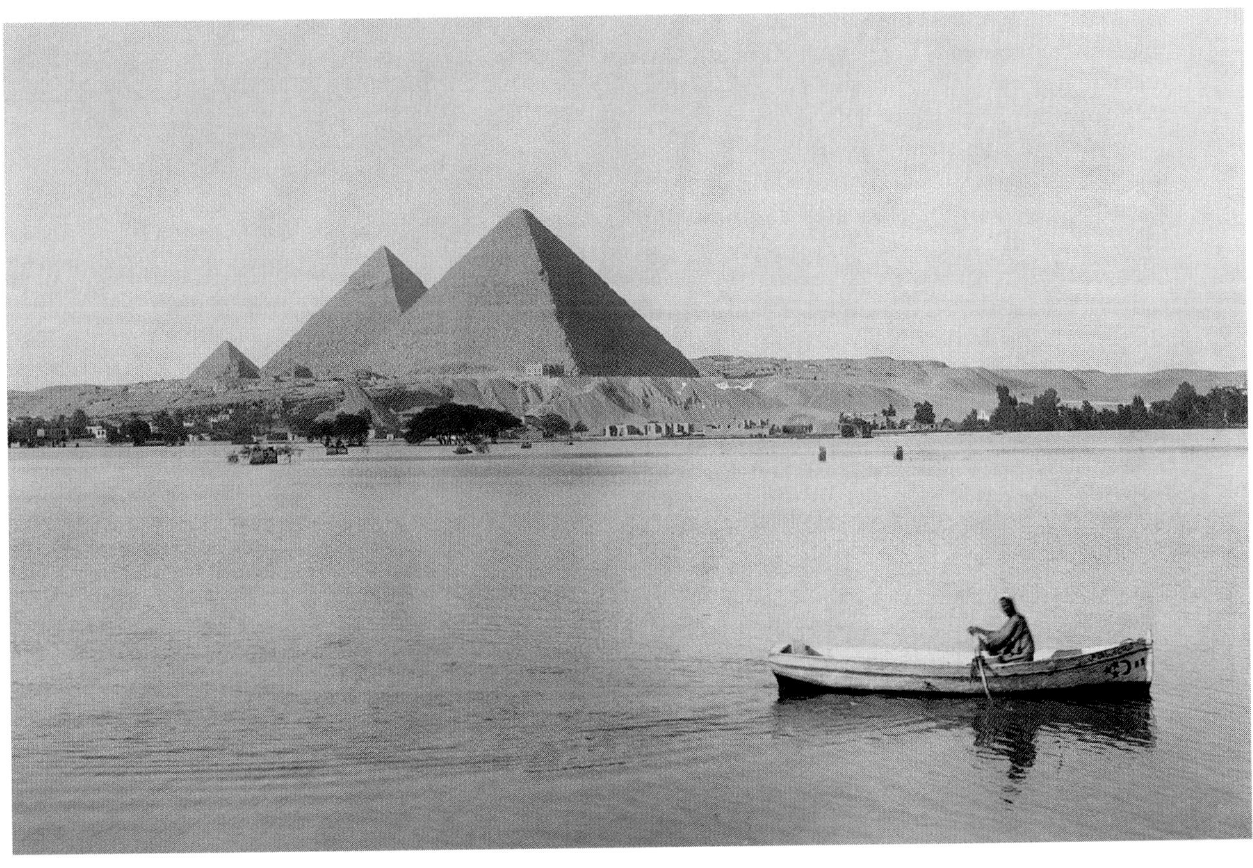

The Great Pyramids
The largest of the Egyptian pyramids, built during the Old Kingdom, loomed over the Nile River at Giza. This picture shows the Nile spreading over its banks in one of its annual inundations before the modern Aswan Dam ended them.

society consequently evolved into a more structured hierarchy. The king and queen, whose job included producing children to continue the ruling dynasty, topped the social pyramid. Brothers and sisters in the royal family could marry, perhaps because such matches were believed necessary to preserve the status of the royal line or to imitate the marriages of the gods. The priests and the royal administrators, including the commanders of the army, ranked next in the hierarchy, but their standing was far below the king and queen. The common people, who did all the manual labor, comprised the massive base of this figurative pyramid of free people in Egypt. Free workers built most of the pyramids for wages or as corvée service to the state. Slaves captured in foreign wars served the royal family and the temples in the Old Kingdom. Privately owned slaves in domestic service did not become common until the Middle Kingdom.

Women in ancient Egypt generally had the same legal rights as men. They could pursue lawsuits, testify in cases, and initiate divorces. Old Kingdom portrait statues vividly express the equal status of wife and husband: each figure is the same size and sits on the same kind of chair. (In New Kingdom art, however, wives appear smaller than their husbands and more relegated to the background.) In general, Egyptian women devoted themselves to private life, managing their households and property, whereas men functioned more in public life. When their husbands went to war or were killed in battle, women often took on the responsibilities their husbands had shouldered, especially concerning the public management of the family's holdings. Some women held government posts, served as priestesses, and practiced medicine.

Producing heirs and preparing for death were not an Egyptian king's only responsibilities. His special status as a religious figure required him to ensure the welfare of his country by following certain rituals. Protocol strictly regulated his every activity, setting a specific time for him to bathe, take a walk, or even make love to his wife. Above all, the king was obliged to marshal the numinous power necessary to make sure the Nile flooded every year. When climate changes beginning around 2350 B.C. caused the annual inundations to shrink and therefore eventually led to famines, the apparent loss of the king's ability to ensure prosperity undermined his political authority and contributed to the breakup of the Old Kingdom. This failure of the kings' efficacy exposed a serious weakness in Egyptian kings' justification of their power: they could not always keep Egypt well fed. Regional governors probably increased their power considerably when these continuing crop failures proved the king could not guarantee the safety of the harvest. These local administrators, who had assisted the kings over the centuries, already had significant power and independence from central authority. When King Peyi II lingered on the throne for over ninety years, the relaxation of royal authority led to the dissolution of the Old Kingdom. The economic chaos and political anarchy that characterized the First Intermediate Period (2181–2050 B.C.) resembled the disruption of society the Gutians had caused in Sumer at about the same time.

The first civilizations of Mesopotamia and Egypt fell for different reasons—the former ravaged by savage neighbors, the latter splintered by rebellious insiders. Archaeological evidence reveals that many settlements in Europe suffered grave damage during this same general period, around 2000 B.C. Although Europe had no cities during this time, the prehistoric societies of Europe had been transformed by a Neolithic revolution. We need to go back in time to trace the history of this metamorphosis and to examine its connection with the evolutionary process that had previously changed the face of the ancient Near East.

Technological and Social Change in Late Prehistoric Europe

At the time the villagers of Çatal Hüyük were already raising their own food, in the seventh millennium B.C., most European peoples still lived as hunter-gatherers. But over the next two to three thousand years, the way of life of many who dwelled in Europe underwent sweeping changes. Some of the same social and technological innovations that marked the Near East's transition to civilization also occurred in Europe. Recent research has caused us to rethink the nature of some of these changes in late prehistoric Europe.

Diffusion and Independent Innovation

Agricultural techniques gradually became known across Europe after their beginnings in the Fertile Crescent. The Neolithic farmers of Europe transformed the landscape of their continent, clearing vast tracts of dense forest. Considering the tools they had available (ax blades fashioned from bone or chipped rocks, wood or bone hoes), their clearing of so much land stands as one of the most remarkable modifications of the natural environment humans have ever accomplished. People began farming all across Europe: in balmier locales near the Mediterranean Sea, such as on the peninsulas formed by Greece and Italy; in upland plateaus nestled against the great east-west chain of mountains that divides southern Europe from the much colder north; in the huge plain of northern Europe that extends east into Russia north of the mountains; and eventually, around 4000 B.C., even on the windswept islands we know as the British Isles. Because the climates of these areas varied as much as their physical features, the kinds of farming undertaken and the crops grown in each region also differed.

What sparked the innovations that transformed Europe in the Neolithic and Bronze Ages? How did European peoples learn to farm and domesticate animals and later to build monumental stone constructions and to use the techniques of copper metallurgy? How much of this knowledge came from Mesopotamia and Egypt, and what, if anything, did the Europeans invent? Until recently most historians believed diffusion of technology answered these questions; they theorized that farmers, herders, architects, and metalworkers migrated to Europe from the Near East, either as settlers or as invaders. With them came the technologies of agriculture, stone construction, and copper metallurgy; that is, these emigrants diffused technological knowledge from the Near East over all of Europe.

New scientific techniques, refined only in the late 1960s, forced historians to reevaluate this diffusion theory. The most important technique, radiocarbon dating, allows scientists to determine the age of prehistoric organic materials found in excavations. By examining the amount of radioactive carbon-14 in ancient bones, seeds, hides, wood, and other materials, laboratory analysts can establish the length of time since the death of the material being tested. Dates obtained in this way have a certain margin of error, but scientists have refined the accuracy of radiocarbon dating by comparing their results with the chronological evidence obtained from counting the internal rings of long-lived trees. These new methods for dating archaeological material have led to a complete reworking of the chronology of Europe in the Neolithic and Bronze Ages. We now know, for example, that farming communities had already appeared in Greece and the mountains immediately to the north (the Balkans) in the early seventh millennium B.C. In this case the idea of migration as a source of cultural change may still hold, because the domesticated grains these communities grew had come from the Near East, probably brought in by migrating farmers. But the domestication of cattle that took place in this region at least as early as in the Near East suggests that the indigenous population of Europe also fostered innovation independently.

Megaliths and Metallurgy

The new dating techniques also reveal that local innovation accounts for the use of megaliths to build monumental structures in Neolithic Europe. Before radiocarbon dating, the pyramids of Egypt were thought to be the earliest megalithic stone constructions. The diffusion hypothesis postulated that migrating Egyptian architects supervised the construction of the large, stone chamber-tombs that are built into the ground along the far western edge of Europe. But radiocarbon dating of materials from these tombs has shown that the earliest of them were built before 4000 B.C., more than a thousand years before the pyramids. It is therefore impossible that the Neolithic inhabitants of western Europe learned to construct megalithic structures from Egyptians. The inhabitants of the Mediterranean island of Malta (south of Sicily) also erected substantial temples of stone before 3000 B.C., obviously without Egyptian advice. These Maltese temple complexes are the earliest freestanding stone monuments in the world. The new dating techniques have also shown that the local population, not visitors from the East, built Stonehenge in what is now southern England. This precisely aligned assemblage of mammoth stones was erected between 2100 and 1900 B.C., possibly to track the movements of the sun and the moon. Although Europeans in the Neolithic Age, or even in the subsequent Bronze Age, had no cities like those of the Near East, they had developed sophisticated megalithic building techniques.

Radiocarbon dates also indicate that Europeans probably did not learn copper metallurgy from Mesopotamian metalsmiths. If Near Eastern smiths had taught Europeans how to smelt copper, we would expect to find evidence that metallurgy began much earlier in the Near East than in Europe. But copper metallurgy developed in various European locations around the same time it did in the Near East. By the fourth millennium B.C., for example, Balkan smiths could cast copper ax heads with the hole for the ax handle in the correct position. Moreover, these smiths of southeastern Europe learned to make bronze in the same period their Near Eastern counterparts did. The Bronze Age therefore started in Europe at roughly the same time as in the Near East. This simultaneous development of metallurgy in such widely separated places can be explained only by independent local innovation.

Our new knowledge of chronology makes explaining the changes in prehistoric Europe even more complicated. Outsiders obviously did not introduce megalithic architecture and metallurgy to Europe. Even though we can still speculate that

Stonehenge
People in southern England erected these megaliths between 2100 and 1900 B.C. most likely to track the different positions of the sun and the moon.

migrating farmers from the Near East were responsible for spreading agriculture throughout Europe, we must also credit Europe's native populations with the capacity to make technological and social innovations independent of outside influence.

The Puzzle of the Indo-Europeans

One of the ongoing debates concerning European prehistory after the Neolithic revolution involves the question of whether peoples collectively labeled as Indo-Europeans migrated to Europe over the course of many centuries and radically changed the nature of its established societies. Some historians hypothesize that the final wave of Indo-European migration became a violent invasion that resulted in the devastation that archaeology reveals occurred in Europe around 2000 B.C. Some believe the Indo-Europeans prompted major changes in European languages, religion, and political organization. And some say these Indo-European newcomers imposed patriarchy on the societies of Neolithic Europe. Deciding whether the scattered evidence for the Indo-Europeans truly means they were responsible for such changes presents an intriguing puzzle of historical interpretation.

The evidence of language reveals that there is a mystery to be solved. Linguists long ago recognized that one ancient language was the ancestor of most of the major ancient and modern languages of western Europe (including English), of the Slavic languages, of the Persian language of Iran, and of some languages spoken in India. Those who had once spoken the original language (it eventually disappeared, splitting into its many branches) are called Indo-Europeans. Because all who spoke the original Indo-European language died long before the invention of writing, the only traces of that language survive in features of the languages descended from Indo-European. We can tell, for example, that Indo-European had only one word for *night,* which survives in English "night," Spanish "noche," French "nuit," German "Nacht," Russian "noch," Vedic (the type of Sanskrit used in the ancient epic poetry of India) "nakt-," and so on.

Scholars still do not know how the various tongues descended from the original Indo-European language emerged in locations scattered from India to Europe. Perhaps Indo-Europeans migrated to these different regions from their homeland (whose location is unknown). Over time these now separate groups could have developed their own versions of the ancestral language. The words that descended from the original Indo-European vocabulary offer a few hints about the nature of the early Indo-European society. For example, the name of their chief divinity, a male god, survives in the similar sounds of "Zeus pater" and "Jupiter," the names given to the chief god in Greek and Latin, respectively. So we surmise that Indo-European society was patriarchal: the father was not merely a parent but the adult male in charge of the household as well as the public world. Other words indicate that Indo-European society was also patrilocal (the bride joined the groom's family) and patrilineal (the line of descent was traced through the father). Indo-Europeans also had the notion of king, a detail suggesting they had a ranked, socially differentiated society. Scholars usually assume the original Indo-Europeans were also warlike and competitive.

A frequently cited interpretation of the significance of the Indo-Europeans argues that these newcomers transformed what had been an egalitarian, peaceful, and matrifocal (centered on women as mothers) society into a hierarchical, warlike, and patriarchal one. The principal gods of the original Europeans were female, the argument further postulates, but they were now displaced by the male deities of the Indo-Europeans. The major point of this theory is that modern Western culture can find its patriarchal beginnings in this Indo-European onslaught.

This theoretical reconstruction of the way European society became patriarchal remains speculative and controversial. Opponents of the theory argue that we should not even assume the Indo-Europeans moved into the European continent as distinct groups powerful enough to overturn local traditions. Perhaps, even, Indo-European society never differed much from the kind of society that had evolved in late prehistoric Europe. In other words, European patriarchy might have originated in Europe itself, much earlier.

One competing theory suggests that male hunter-gatherers had already started human society on the road toward patriarchy in the Paleolithic Age by stealing women from each other's bands. They may have sought these women to produce children and thereby increase their band's population and strength. In this way men could have dominated women long before the Indo-European invasions supposedly began. The indigenous society of Europe would thus have been patriarchal.

Alternatively, the loss of equality between men and women may have resulted from the changes accompanying the development of plow agriculture and large-scale herding in late Neolithic Europe. Those who minimize the significance of the Indo-Europeans as a source of cultural change argue further that the Indo-Europeans should not be blamed for the widespread destruction of European sites near the end of the third millennium. Instead, they suggest, exhaustion of the soil, leading to intense competition for land, and internal political turmoil probably caused the devastation.

The significance of the Indo-Europeans in Neolithic Europe remains an unsolved mystery. We know for certain that most members of historical European civilization spoke Indo-European languages, worshipped a male chief god, paid homage to female divinities, and lived in patriarchal societies. But we still cannot be sure how and when these fundamental characteristics of ancient Western society originated.

Venus Figurine
Archaeologists have discovered small female figures, like this one from Romania, in many Neolithic sites in Europe. Their shape suggests they may have been symbols of human fertility.

The First Civilizations in Europe

The first civilizations of Europe arose in the aftermath of the destruction that swept Europe around 2000 B.C. They were created by the early Bronze Age populations of the islands and on the coast of the Aegean Sea, a section of the eastern Mediterranean Sea between Greece and Anatolia (Asia Minor; today the western part of Asian Turkey). These people had advanced technologies, elaborate architecture, striking art, and a marked taste for luxury. They also inhabited a dangerous world whose perils ultimately overwhelmed all their civilized sophistication.

The Palace Society of Minoan Crete

The earliest civilization of the Aegean region emerged on the large island of Crete around 2200 B.C. People had inhabited this large fertile island for several thousand years; the first settlers probably came from nearby Anatolia about 6000 B.C. Like their contemporaries elsewhere in Europe, these pioneers established small settlements near agricultural land. In the third millennium B.C., however, new technological capabilities began to affect Cretan society.

As elsewhere, advances in metallurgy influenced the people of Crete. But the emergence of what is called Mediterranean polyculture—the cultivation of olives and grapes as well as grain in one agricultural system—changed Crete more profoundly. This system, which still dominates Mediterranean agriculture, had two important consequences: the food supply increased, stimulating population growth; and agriculture became diversified and specialized, producing valuable new products such as olive oil and wine. Because old methods were inadequate for storing and transporting these commodities, artisans invented and began manufacturing huge storage jars that could accommodate these products, in the process adding another specialized skill to their craft. Craftspeople and agricultural workers, producing their wares using sophisticated but time-consuming techniques, no longer had time to grow their own food or make the goods, such as clothes and lamps, they needed for everyday life. They now bartered the products they made for food and other goods.

The Early Civilizations of Greece and the Aegean Sea

Society became increasingly interdependent, both economically and socially, in the palace society of Crete. In the smaller villages of early Neolithic Europe, reciprocity had governed exchanges among the population of self-sufficient farmers. Reciprocal exchange promoted social relationships rather than economic gain: I give you some of what I produce, and you in return give me some of what you produce. We exchange, not because either of us necessarily needs what the other produces, but to reaffirm our social alliances in a small group. Bronze Age society in the Aegean region reached a level of economic interdependence based on redistribution that was far more complex than even the larger Neolithic villages like Çatal Hüyük.

The palace society, named for its sprawling, many-chambered buildings, began to appear on Crete around 2200 B.C. Today this palace society is called *Minoan,* after King Minos, the legendary Cretan ruler known only from Greek myths. The palaces housed the rulers and their menials and served as central storage facilities. The general population clustered around the palaces in houses adjacent to one another. Some other settlements dotted outlying areas. Earthquakes leveled the first Minoan palaces about 1700 B.C., but the Cretans rebuilt on an even grander scale in the succeeding centuries. Accounting records preserved on clay tablets reveal that these new palaces were the hub of the island's economy.

Probably influenced by Egyptian hieroglyphs, the first written records of Crete used a pictographic script to symbolize objects. This system evolved into a more linear form of writing that expressed phonetic sounds. Unlike cuneiform or hieroglyphs, this system was a true syllabary—a character represented the sound of each syllable of a word. The Cretan version of this script, which originated sometime after 2000 B.C., is today called Linear A.

The records kept in Cretan script were lists: accounts of goods received and goods paid out, inventories of stored goods, livestock, landholdings, and personnel. The Minoans kept records of everything from chariots to perfumes. The receipts record payments owed, with any deficits in the amount actually paid in carefully noted. The records of disbursements from the palace storerooms cover ritual offerings to the gods, rations to personnel, and raw materials for crafts production, such as metal issued to bronzesmiths. None of the tablets records any exchange rate between different categories of goods, such as a ratio stating how much grain was equivalent to a sheep. Nor do the tables reveal any use of bullion as money. (The invention of coinage lay a thousand years in the future.)

The economic system of Minoan Crete appears to have been controlled by the palaces: the king or his representatives decided how much each producer had to contribute and what each would receive for subsistence. Similar redistributive economic systems based on official monopolies, not a market economy, had existed in Mesopotamia for some time. Like them, the logistics of operating the Cretan arrangement were complicated. For example, the palaces' vast storage areas were filled with hundreds of gigantic jars containing olive oil and wine; nearby storerooms were crammed with bowls, cups, and dippers. Scribes meticulously recorded what came in and what went out. This process of economic redistribution applied to craft specialists as well as to food producers, and the palaces' administrative officials set quotas for craftspeople. Although not everyone is likely to have participated in the redistribution system, it apparently dominated the Cretan economy, minimizing the exchange of goods through markets. People in the countryside may have sold goods to one another occasionally. But these small markets never rivaled the palace system. The palaces probably oversaw overseas trade as well.

From all indications this system worked smoothly and peacefully for centuries. Although contemporary settlements elsewhere around the Aegean Sea and in Anatolia had elaborate defensive walls, Minoan Crete had none. The palaces, towns, and even isolated country houses apparently saw no need to fortify themselves against each other. The remains of the newer palaces, such as the one at Knossos—with its hundreds of rooms in five stories, storage jars capable of holding 240,000 gallons, a form of indoor plumbing, and colorful scenes painted on the walls—have led many to conclude that Minoans, at least those who lived in the palace society, were prosperous, peaceful, and contented. The prominence of women in palace frescoes and the numerous figurines of buxom goddesses found on Cretan sites have prompted speculation that Minoan society was a female-dominated culture.

Minoan Contact with Mycenaean Greece

The upper class of Minoan Crete maintained extensive overseas contacts, using another innovation of the third millennium: the longship. Their sea travel in search of trade goods took them not only to Egypt and the other civilizations of the Near East but also to the islands of the Aegean and southern Greece, where another society, the Mycenaean, flourished. Archaeologists have uncovered the Bronze Age site of Mycenae in the Peloponnese (the large peninsula that is southern Greece). Although neither Mycenae nor any other settlement ever ruled Bronze Age Greece as a united state, Mycenaean has become the general term for the Bronze Age civilization of mainland Greece in the second millennium B.C.

Nineteenth-century archaeologists discovered treasure-filled Mycenaean graves. Constructed as stone-lined shafts, these graves contained entombed dead and their golden jewelry, including heavy necklaces festooned with pendants; gold and silver vessels; bronze weapons decorated with scenes of wild animals inlaid in precious metals; and delicately painted pottery that were buried with them. The first excavator of Mycenae thought he had found the grave of King Agamemnon, who commanded the Greeks at Troy in Homer's poem *The Iliad*, but we now know the shaft graves date to the sixteenth century B.C., long before the Trojan War. The artifacts point to a warrior culture organized in independent settlements ruled by powerful commanders who enriched themselves by raiding near and far as well as dominating local farmers.

Another kind of burial chamber, called *tholos* tombs—spectacular underground domed chambers built in beehive shapes from closely fitted stones—marks the next period in Mycenaean society, which began in the fifteenth century B.C. The architectural details of the *tholos* tombs and the style of the burial goods found in them testify to the far-flung contacts Mycenaean rulers maintained throughout the eastern Mediterranean, but particularly with Minoan Crete.

The evidence of contact between the Minoans and the Mycenaeans raises a thorny problem. The art and goods of the Mycenaeans in the middle of the second millennium B.C. display many motifs clearly reminiscent of Cretan design. The archaeologist who excavated Knossos therefore argued that the Minoans had inspired Mycenaean civilization by sending colonists to the mainland, as they undeniably had to various Aegean islands, such as Thera. This "demotion" of Mycenaean civilization offended the excavators of Mycenae, and a debate ensued over the relationship between the two cultures. They were certainly not identical. The Mycenaeans made burnt offerings to the gods; the Minoans did not. The Minoans scattered sanctuaries across the landscape in caves, on mountaintops, and in country villas; the mainlanders did none of this. When the Mycenaeans started building palaces in the fourteenth century B.C., unlike the Minoans they designed them around megarons—rooms with huge ceremonial hearths and thrones for the rulers. Some palaces had more than one megaron, which could soar two stories high with columns to support a roof above the second-floor balconies.

The mystery surrounding the relationship between the Minoans and the Mycenaeans deepened with the startling revelation of documents found in the palace at Knossos, in which a Cretan script had been adapted to Greek—these documents are the famous Linear B tablets, whose pictographic script was based on Linear A. Because these tablets dated from before the final destruction of the palace in about 1370 B.C., they meant that the palace administration had been keeping its records in a foreign language for some time. Presumably this change means that Mycenaeans had come to dominate Cretans, but whether by violent invasion or some kind of peaceful accommodation remains unknown. The Linear B tablets imply that Mycenae had not long, if ever, remained a secondary power to Minoan Crete.

The Zenith of Mycenaean Society

A glimpse of Mycenaean society in its maturity demonstrates the nature of its power. War was clearly the principle concern of those Mycenaean men who could afford its expensive paraphernalia. Contents of Bronze Age tombs in Greece reveal that no wealthy Mycenaean male went to his grave without his fighting equipment. The complete suit of Mycenaean bronze armor found in a fourteenth-century B.C. tomb in the northeastern Peloponnese shows how extensive a warrior's equipment could be. This warrior was buried in a complete bronze cuirass (chest guard) of two pieces (front and back), an adjustable skirt of bronze plates, bronze greaves (shin guards), shoulder plates, and a collar. On his head had rested a boar's-tusk helmet with metal cheekpieces. Next to his body lay his leather shield, bronze and clay vessels, and a bronze comb with gold teeth. Originally his bronze swords had lain beside him, but tomb robbers had stolen them. The expense of these grave goods implies that armor and weapons were so central to a Mycenaean man's identity that he could not do without them, even in death.

Mycenaean warriors could ride into battle in the latest in military hardware—the lightweight, two-wheeled chariot pulled by horses. These revolutionary vehicles, sometimes assumed to have been introduced by Indo-Europeans migrating from Central Asia, first appeared not long after 2000 B.C. in various Mediterranean and Near Eastern societies. The first Aegean representation of such a chariot occurs on a Mycenaean grave marker from about 1500 B.C. Wealthy people evidently desired this new form of transportation not only for war but also as proof of their social status.

The Mycenaeans seem to have spent more on war than on religion. In any case, they did not construct any large religious buildings like the giant temples of the Near East. Although the nature of Bronze Age mainland religion remains largely obscure, many scholars assume the Mycenaeans primarily worshiped the male-dominated pantheon traditionally associated with the martial culture of the Indo-Europeans. The names of numerous deities known from later Greek religion occur in the Linear B tablets.

Bronze Age Mycenaean traders and warriors both journeyed far from home, mainly by sea travel. Mycenaeans established colonies at various locations along the coast of the Mediterranean. Seaborne Mycenaean warriors also dominated and probably usurped the palace society of Minoan Crete in the fifteenth and fourteenth centuries B.C., presumably in wars over commercial rivalry in the Mediterranean. By the middle of the fourteenth century B.C., the Mycenaeans had displaced the Minoans as the preeminent civilization of the Aegean.

The Near East and Greece to the End of the Second Millennium B.C.

The Bronze Age development of extensive sea travel for trading and raiding put the cultures of the Aegean and the Near East in closer contact than ever before. The ease and speed of transportation by water, compared to the difficulty of travel by land in a world largely without roads, encouraged interaction between the older civilizations at the eastern end of the Mediterranean and the younger ones to the west. Minoan and Mycenaean voyagers alike particularly favored visiting Egypt, because they valued exchanging goods and ideas with such a prosperous and complex civilization. The civilizations of Mesopotamia and Anatolia after 2000 B.C. overshadowed those of Crete and Greece: their cities were much larger, and their written legal codes were much more highly developed and extensive. By around 1200 B.C., however, turmoil caused by internal strife and the movements of many peoples throughout the eastern Mediterranean and the Near East seriously damaged the political stability, economic prosperity, and international contacts of the societies of most of these lands.

The Kingdoms of Mesopotamia and Anatolia

The Gutians who had overwhelmed the Akkadian empire near the end of the third millennium B.C. did not set up a lasting political structure. The Third Dynasty of Ur, founded by the Sumerian lawgiver King Ur-Nammu (✱2112–2095 B.C.*), reestablished some stability in Sumer by about 2050 B.C. Frequent warfare with rivals for territory, however, fatally weakened the Third Dynasty after about a century. Until after 1000 B.C., Mesopotamia underwent complex and often turbulent changes. Economic difficulties caused by soil pollution may have disrupted political stability in Mesopotamia in the second millennium B.C. The intensive irrigation necessary there had increased the salinity of the fields, hindering production of the agricultural surpluses that could make a state rich. And in Anatolia, to the northwest, the Hittite kingdom arose as a formidable rival to Mesopotamia. No single Mesopotamian state dominated the region in this long period; only after 1000 B.C. did the Assyrians revive their power. Despite its troubles during the early second millennium B.C., Mesopotamia nevertheless experienced the growth of two characteristic features of civilization: private, large-scale commercial enterprise and extensive collections of written laws.

The Assyrians, descended from the Akkadians, lived in the northeastern portion of Mesopotamia. These Semitic people of seminomadic origins freed themselves from Sumerian rule of the Ur III dynasty in the twentieth century B.C. and gained prosperity as an independent kingdom by taking advantage of their geographical location next to Anatolia and establishing trading ties. The various city-states of Anatolia had become the principal source of raw materials such as wood, copper, and silver for the rest of the ancient Near East in the early second millennium B.C. Adapting to their country's lack of natural resources, the Assyrians concentrated on producing woolen textiles to export in return for the raw materials of Anatolia.

Although Mesopotamian societies had traditionally operated mainly under state monopolies in redistributive economic systems, by 1900 B.C. the Assyrian kings allowed private individuals to transact large international commercial deals on their own initiative. Assyrian investors staked traders for a cargo of cloth and travel expenses. The traders then formed donkey caravans to travel the hundreds of miles to Anatolia, where they could make huge profits. After repaying investors' origi-

*The ✱ indicates date of reign or term in office.

nal investment, the traders split the profits with them. Hired hands received their pay from any profits. This system motivated the participants to maximize profits, and the enormous profits these entrepreneurs could earn reflected the equally large risks of the business. Regulations existed to deal with fraud by the trader as well as losses in transit. The Assyrian domestic economy still centered on a redistributive system similar to those of the Aegean, but this emergent profit-driven international trade foreshadowed the shape of many economies of the later Greco-Roman world.

Attacks by the aggressive kingdom of the Mitanni in Anatolia cost Assyria its prosperity and independence, but strong Assyrian kings fought to recover them by the thirteenth century B.C. King Tiglath-Pileser I (*c. 1114–1076 B.C.) successfully protected Assyria in its frequent wars with the Babylonian kingdom in Mesopotamia, the Phrygians of Anatolia, and the Aramaeans from Syria. But by about 1000 B.C. incessant Aramaean attacks had ground down the power of Assyria, leaving no single state able to dominate the area.

In hierarchical societies such as those of the ancient Near East, social life required official rules. This need for laws became more pressing as the expansion of private trade and property ownership further complicated life in a centralized monarchy. Although we know Sumerian kings promulgated laws as early as about 2400 B.C., King Hammurabi (*c. 1792–1750 B.C.) of Babylon instituted the most famous Mesopotamian laws. His Amorite ancestors, another seminomadic Semitic people, began migrating into Mesopotamia and Syria from 2200 to 2000 B.C. Eventually the Amorites established a powerful kingdom centered in Babylon. After long struggles in the early eighteenth century B.C., Hammurabi became the dominant power in southern Mesopotamia (though he never assembled an extensive empire).

Hammurabi's laws legally divided society into three categories: free men and women, commoners, and slaves. The criteria for differentiating the first two levels of free people remain uncertain, but the terms did express a social hierarchy. An attacker who caused a pregnant woman of the free class to miscarry, for example, paid twice the fine levied for the same offense against a woman of the class of commoners. Among social equals, the principle of "an eye for an eye" (in Latin *lex talionis,* "law of retaliation") prevailed in cases of physical injury. But a member of the free class who killed a commoner was not executed, only required to pay monetary compensation. Most of the laws concerned the king's interests as a property owner who leased innumerable tracts of land to tenants in return for rent or services. The laws imposed severe penalties for offenses against property, including mutilation or a gruesome death for crimes as varied as theft, wrongful sales, and careless construction. Women had some legal rights in this patriarchal society, although their rights were more limited than men's. They could make business contracts and appear in court. A wife could divorce her husband for cruelty; but a husband could divorce his wife for any reason. The inequality of the divorce laws was tempered in practice, however, because a woman could recover the property she had brought to her marriage, a fact that represented a considerable disincentive for a man to end his marriage.

Although written laws helped prevent the kinds of arbitrary decisions unwritten laws could allow, the major omissions in Hammurabi's laws show that he was not attempting to codify, or systematize, the law comprehensively. For example, criminal law receives less attention than a full codification would require. Furthermore, the documents of the period show almost no evidence that Hammurabi's laws were applied; in practice, penalties were often less severe than the law specified. Common, or unwritten, law presumably governed most of everyday life. Hammurabi's laws publicized a royal ideal; they did not necessarily reflect reality. Why did Hammurabi have his laws written down? He announces his reasons in the prologue and epilogue to his collection: to give all his subjects a chance to have certain knowledge of the rules governing them and to demonstrate his status as a just king before his god and his people. Above all, Hammurabi had his laws inscribed on a polished stone slab in a temple because he wanted to show Shamash, the sun god and god of justice, that he had fulfilled the social responsibility imposed on him as a divinely installed monarch—to ensure justice and the moral and material welfare of his people. That responsibility corresponded to the strictly hierarchical vision of society that characterized all Mesopotamian societies.

The situations and conflicts covered by Hammurabi's laws illuminate many aspects of the lives of city-dwellers in ancient Mesopotamia. Crimes of burglary and assault apparently plagued urban residents. Marriages were arranged by the groom and the bride's father, who sealed the agreement with a legal contract. The husband dominated the household, although the state retained the right to decide cases of disinheritance. The detailed laws on surgery make clear that doctors practiced in the cities.

Information gleaned from archaeological excavations and surviving literature and other documents supplement what we know about the lives of early Mesopotamians. Their cities had many taverns and wine shops, often run by women proprietors, possibly attesting to the city-dwellers' enjoyment of spirits and a convivial atmosphere. Because disease was believed to have supernatural origins, Mesopotamian medicine included magic as well as treatment with potions and diet. A doctor might prescribe an incantation as part of his therapy. Magicians or exorcists offered medical treatment that depended primarily on spells and on interpreting signs such as the patient's dreams or hallucinations. Contaminated drinking water caused many illnesses because sewage disposal was rudimentary (as in most cities until the twentieth century). Relief from the odors and crowding of the streets could be found in the open spaces set aside for city parks. The oldest known map in the world, an inscribed clay tablet showing the outlines of the Babylonian city of Nippur about 1500 B.C., shows a substantial area designated for this purpose.

Mesopotamian achievements in mathematics and astronomy had a profound effect that endures to this day. Mathematical specialists knew how to employ algebraic processes to solve complex problems, and they could derive the roots of numbers. They discovered the system of place-value notation, in which the quantity indicated by a numeral is affected by its place in a sequence. We have also inherited from Mesopotamia the system of reckoning based on powers of sixty that we use in the division of hours and minutes and degrees of a circle. The Mesopotamians used both this sexagesimal system and a decimal system of numeration. Their expertise in recording the paths of the stars and planets across the night sky probably arose from their desire to make predictions about the future based on the astrological belief that the movement of celestial bodies directly affected human life. Astrology never lost its popularity in Mesopotamia. But the charts and tables compiled by Mesopotamian stargazers laid a basis for scientific astronomy.

The centralized Babylonian administration forged by Hammurabi failed not long after his death, and a decentralized political system characterized Babylonia until about 1460 B.C. At that time the Kassites once again unified it. Some Kassites had first come to Babylon as agricultural workers, but others invaded. The centralized political system the Kassites created endured for 250 years, longer than any other Babylonian dynasty. The Kassites assimilated much of the Mesopotamian culture. Perhaps their willingness to adopt Mesopotamian customs helped prevent revolts by making their rule seem less onerous.

To the northwest of Mesopotamia other important kingdoms thrived in Syria and Anatolia in the middle centuries of the second millennium B.C. Our scanty sources reveal little about the powerful kingdom of Mitanni or the Hurrian people who constituted the majority of its population. From about 1550 to 1350 B.C., Mitanni dominated the region around the northern reaches of the Euphrates River. Then the Hittite king Suppiluliumas I forced it to become a subservient ally of his kingdom in Anatolia. The Hittites, who spoke an Indo-European language but took their method of writing from the Mesopotamians, probably came from the Caucasus area between the Black and Caspian Seas into the highland plateau of central Anatolia and wrested control from the indigenous population by about 1750 B.C. Their capital, Hattusas, grew into an expansive city with straight streets, huge palaces, massive defensive walls and towers of stone, and many sculptures of animals, warriors, and the royal rulers. The Hittite monarchy maintained its rule by forging personal alliances—cemented by marriages and oaths of loyalty—with the noble families of the kingdom. Judging from their appearance in documents, royal letters, and foreign treaties, Hittite queens apparently played a prominent role in public life. Hittite public religion combined worship of deities inherited from the original Anatolian population with those of Indo-European extraction. The king served as high priest, and his ritual purity was paramount. His drinking water had to be strained, for example; once when a hair was found in his water jug, the water carrier was executed.

In the periods during which ties with the nobility remained strong and the kingdom therefore preserved its unity, the Hittite kings aggressively campaigned to extend their power. A Hittite army raided as far as Babylon in 1595 B.C., weakening the Amorite kingdom and contributing to its eventual replacement by the Kassites. Hittites eventually dominated Anatolia and Syria, and in the battle of Kadesh about 1285 B.C. the Hittite king Muwatallis prevented the Egyptian king Ramesses II from recovering Egypt's Syrian possessions. The economic strength of the Hittite kingdom depended on its effective defense of the international trade routes by which it secured essential raw materials, especially metals. Scholars no longer accept the once popular idea that the Hittites owed their imperialistic success to a special knowledge of making weapons from iron, although Hittite craftsmen did smelt iron from which they made ceremonial implements. (Not until after 1200 B.C.—at the end of the Hittite kingdom—did iron objects become common in the Mediterranean world.) The Hittite army did excel in the use of chariots and perhaps this skill gave them the edge in their evident military success. Nevertheless, the unified Hittite kingdom fell in the twelfth century B.C. in the catastrophes that struck eastern Mediterranean societies at that time.

The New Kingdom in Egypt

In Egypt the social order continued to depend on the flooding Nile to bring prosperity and the ability of the royal family to build political unity. The famine and civil unrest of the First Intermediate Period (2181–2050 B.C.) thwarted attempts by the princes of Thebes in Upper Egypt to reestablish political unity. King Mentuhotep II finally reunited Egypt in the Middle Kingdom (2050–1786 B.C.). Gradually the monarchs of the Middle Kingdom restored the divine authority their Old Kingdom predecessors had lost. They pushed the boundaries of Egypt farther to the south and expanded contacts to the northeast in ancient Palestine and Syria and to the northwest in Crete. In the midst of all this activity, the Egyptians retained a warm pride in their homeland, as the vigorous literature of this period demonstrates. The main character of the Middle Kingdom tale *The Story of Sinuhe*, for example, reported that he lived a luxurious life while in Syria: "It was a good land. . . . Figs were in it, and grapes. . . . Bread was made for me as daily fare, wine as daily provision, cooked meat and roast fowl." But the point of the tale was his eagerness to come home to Egypt.

By the Second Intermediate Period (1786–1567 B.C.), nature had again undermined the kings' hold on a unified Egypt: famines caused by irregular Nile floods weakened the population. A people, whose real name is unknown but whom the Egyptians called Hyksos (meaning "Rulers of Foreign Lands"), took advantage of this debilitation and invaded Egypt. These Semites from the Syria-Palestine region had taken over Lower Egypt by around 1670 B.C. Recent archaeological discoveries have emphasized the role of the Hyksos settlers in transplanting elements of their culture to Egypt. These interlopers introduced such innovations as new musical instruments, the olive, and the war chariot and increased Egypt's contact with other states in the Near East.

Eventually, the leaders of Thebes fought once again to reunite their land. Amosis finally won their war of liberation from the Hyksos around 1567 B.C., initiating the New Kingdom (1567–1085 B.C.). The New Kingdom kings, known as pharaohs, no longer brooked local political rivals, such as the provincial governors, although they were prudent enough to acknowledge other powerful monarchs in the world. In fact, the New Kingdom pharaohs regularly exchanged letters on matters of state with their "brother kings," as they called them, elsewhere in the Near East. They also fought campaigns abroad. Wars to the south in Nubia and the Sudan won them access to gold and other precious materials, while the raids into Palestine and Syria by Thutmosis I (died c. 1512 B.C.) gave notice of the Egyptian interest in conquering the coastal lands of the eastern Mediterranean. These fighting pharaohs of Egypt presented themselves as the incarnations of a warrior god, but they also practiced the wiles of diplomacy. Thutmosis III, for example, forged defensive alliances with both the Babylonians and the Hittites in the fifteenth century B.C.

Massive riches supported the power of the New Kingdom pharaohs. Egyptian traders exchanged fine goods such as ivory for foreign luxury goods, such as Mycenaean painted pottery.

The Egyptian kings displayed their wealth most conspicuously in the enormous sums they spent to build temples of stone. Nothing the people of Europe and the Aegean constructed in this period remotely compared to these structures. Queen Hatshepsut of the fifteenth century B.C. renewed this tradition with the great complex at Deir el Bahri near Thebes, which includes a temple dedicated to the god Amon and to her own funerary cult. After the death of her husband, Thutmosis II, Hatshepsut proclaimed herself "female king" as co-regent with her young stepson Thutmosis III. By doing so she shrewdly sidestepped Egyptian ideology, which made no provision for a queen to reign in her own right. The relief sculpture she commissioned to portray the expedition she dispatched to gather myrrh in Punt (probably Somalia, southeast of Egypt) faithfully records the characteristics of the people, flora, and fauna of this land renowned for its spices. This work of art is the first recorded anthropological report of a foreign culture.

As fellow divine beings, the pharaohs had a deep personal interest in the standing of Egypt's legions of traditional gods. The various gods of the Egyptian pantheon oversaw all aspects of life and death, with particular emphasis on the afterlife. The cults of the main gods, who were honored with glorious temples, were integral in the religious life of both the general population and the leaders. The principal festivals of the gods, for example, offered occasions for public celebration. A calendar based on the moon governed the dates of religious ceremonies. (The Egyptians also developed a calendar for administrative and fiscal purposes that had 365 days, divided into 12 months of 30 days each, with the extra 5 days added before the start of the next year. Our modern calendar is based on this civil calendar.)

The New Kingdom pharaohs promoted the state god Amen-Re of Thebes until he overshadowed the other gods. This Theban cult incorporated and subordinated the other gods without denying either their existence or the continued importance of their priests. But the pharaoh Amenhophis IV, known as Akhenaten, went a step further during his reign in the fourteenth century B.C. when he began to tout the cult of Aten, who represented the shining disk of the sun. This new cult excluded the other deities and their supporters, although it perhaps should not be called pure monotheism

Queen Hatshepsut of Egypt
This statue shows Hatshepsut dressed in the distinctive garb of a pharaoh to demonstrate her claim to rule. She had the statue placed in a temple she built outside Thebes.

The Contents of King Tut's Tomb
Egyptian royalty packed their tombs with everything they would need in the afterlife. Over the years thieves broke into most Egyptian tombs, but Tutankhamun's escaped detection until an achaeologist opened it in 1922.

(the worship of only one god) because Akhenaten seems not to have denied the divine associations of the king, and the population presumably went on venerating the ruler as before. Chiseling the names of the other, now disgraced deities out of inscriptions and building a new capital for his god at modern Amarna, Akhenaten neglected practical affairs as he obsessively tried to force his new version of official religion on recalcitrant priests and other followers of the traditional cults. He also attempted to imbue royal Egyptian art with more realistic portraiture, even allowing court artists to reveal his own angular face and dumpy physique. Ultimately, his failure to attend to government business left financial distress and a weakened defense as legacies to his successors, such as the boy king Tutankhamun. Akhenaten's religion did not survive his reign.

The pharaohs following Tutankhamun in the thirteenth and twelfth centuries B.C. had their hands full protecting their territories outside Egypt. They faced heavy competition for control of Palestine and Syria from the Hittites. Pharaoh Ramesses II finally settled the issue by making a sophisticated treaty with the Hittite king around 1269 B.C. and then marrying the king's daughter. Remarkably, both Egyptian and Hittite copies of this landmark in diplomatic history survive. In it the Egyptians and Hittites pledged to be "at peace and brothers forever." Ramesses II continued the pharaonic building tradition with a passion. Fully half the temples remaining in Egypt today come from his reign. The architecture of Egypt's rectangular buildings of stone studded with columns served as a model for the style of the later temples of Greece.

Archaeology does not clearly reveal whether the prosperity of the New Kingdom rulers trickled down to the general free population. The rhythm of the lives of most ordinary people still revolved around the relation between their labor and the annual inundations of the Nile. During the months when the river stayed between its banks they worked their fields along the water's course, rising very early in the morning to avoid the searing heat. Their obligation to work on royal building projects came due when the flooding halted agricultural tasks and freed them to move to workers' quarters erected next to the building sites. Although slaves became more common as household workers in the New Kingdom, mostly free workers doing corvée service labored on the mammoth royal construction projects of this period. Surviving texts reveal that they lightened the burden of their labors by singing songs and telling adventure stories.

Ordinary people devoted much attention to deities outside the royal cults, to gods they hoped would protect them in their daily lives. They venerated Bes, for instance, a dwarf with the features of a lion, as a protector of the household and carved his image on amulets, beds, headrests, and the handles of mirrors. People also continued to spend much time and effort on preparing for the next life. Those who could afford it arranged to have their bodies mummified and their tombs outfitted with all the paraphernalia needed for the journey to their new existence. An essential piece of equipment for a corpse was a copy of the *Book of the Dead,* a collection of magic spells to ward off dangers and ensure a successful verdict in the divine judgment that people believed every soul had to pass to avoid a second death. In the underworld, the dead underwent a mystical union with the god Osiris.

Magic played a large role in their lives, too, as they sought spells and charms from professional magicians to seek relief from disease and injury, ward off demons, smooth the often rocky course of love, and exact revenge on enemies. As with the homage they paid minor deities, these personal dealings with the supernatural probably meant more to their everyday lives than the cults of the major divinities.

Later pharaohs of the New Kingdom had less opportunity for building projects because they had to spend much of their time fighting foreign invaders from all directions. During the twelfth century B.C. this pressure from outside eventually overwhelmed even the heroics of commanders such as the warrior pharaoh Ramesses III. Once again the centralization of authority that gave Egypt its political and military strength dissipated.

Hebrew Origins

The religious rather than the political history of this Semitic people profoundly affected the roots of Western civilization. The enduring influence of the Hebrews (or Israelites, the descendants of Jacob, who was also called Israel) has stemmed above all from the impact of the book that eventually became the Hebrews' sacred scripture—the Hebrew Bible, known to Christians as the Old Testament—on Judaism, Christianity, and Islam. Unfortunately, neither the opening books of the Hebrew Bible nor archaeological research provides a clear picture of the origins of the Hebrews. A reconstruction of the earliest period of Hebrew history depends on limited and controversial evidence.

The Hebrew Bible reports that the patriarch Abraham and his followers left the Mesopotamian city of Ur to migrate to "the land of Canaan" (ancient Palestine). Because other Semitic peoples, such as the Amorites and the Aramaeans, are known to have moved throughout the Fertile Crescent in the early second millennium, the story of Abraham's journey perhaps reflects this era and can be dated about 1800 B.C. When the Hebrews finally reached Palestine (at the southeast corner of the Mediterranean Sea), they continued their traditional existence as seminomads, tending flocks of animals and living in temporary tent settlements. They occasionally planted barley or wheat for a season or two, but they would then move to new pasturage; they never settled down or formed a political state in this period. Political and military power in Canaan resided in the local city-states, kingdoms, and tribes already established there.

Abraham's son Isaac led his people to live in various locations in keeping with the demands of a pastoral way of life and also to avoid further disputes with local Canaanites over grazing rights. Isaac's son Jacob, the story continues, moved to Egypt late in life; Jacob's son, Joseph, brought his father and other relatives there to escape famine in Canaan. Joseph had used his intelligence and charisma to rise to an important position in the Egyptian administration. The Biblical story of the movement of some Hebrews to Egypt represents a crucial event in the early history of the Hebrews; it may reflect a time when drought forced some of the Hebrews, se[illegible] save their flocks, to migrate grad[illegible] hwest Asia into the Nile delta of E[illegible] ably migrated during

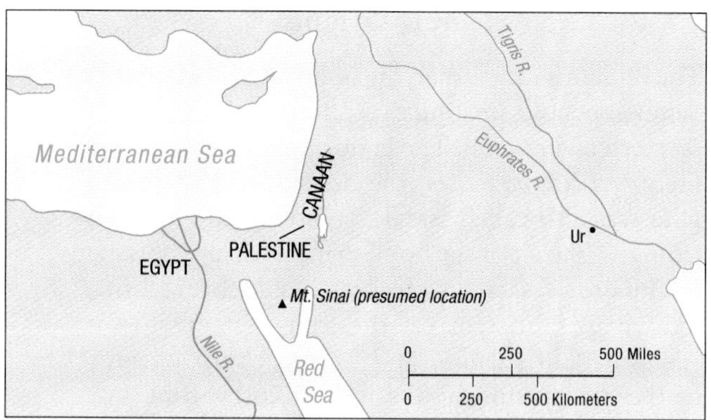

Locations in Early Hebrew History

the seventeenth or sixteenth century B.C. But unlike the Hyksos, who invaded Egypt, these Hebrew immigrants lacked military might. Although they apparently lived peacefully in Egypt for a long time, by the thirteenth century B.C. the pharaohs had conscripted male Hebrews into slave labor gangs for farming and for construction work on the large building projects.

Toward the end of the Bronze Age, groups of Hebrews left Egypt, part of widespread social foment in the Near East that also included displaced people from the cities of Canaan. The Hebrew Bible tells this story in the Biblical book Exodus. The Hebrew deity Yahweh (incorrectly called Jehovah in Christian tradition) instructed Moses to lead the Hebrews out of bondage in Egypt. Yahweh then sent ten plagues to compel the pharaoh to free the Hebrews. When the pharaoh, who may have been Ramesses II in the second half of the thirteenth century B.C., tried to recapture the fleeing Hebrews, Yahweh miraculously parted the Red Sea to allow the Hebrews to escape. When the pharaoh's army tried to follow, the water swirled back together, drowning the Egyptians.

The Biblical narrative of the Exodus then moves to a seminal moment in ancient Hebrew history: the formalizing of a covenant between the Hebrews and their deity, who reveals himself to Moses on Mt. Sinai in the desert northeast of Egypt. The covenant consisted of an agreement between the Hebrews and their deity that, in return for the Hebrew's promise to worship him as their only divinity and to live by his laws, he would make them his chosen people and lead them into a promised land of safety and prosperity. This binding agreement between the Hebrew people and their deity built on the earlier pledges of the patriarchs Abraham, Isaac, and Jacob, all of which demanded human obedience to divine law and promised punishment for unrighteousness. The Hebrew Bible sets forth the religious and moral code the Hebrews had to follow both in the Ten Commandments (found in 20 Exodus and 5 Deuteronomy), which required the worship of Yahweh; the honoring of parents; and abstention from murder, adultery, theft, lying, and covetousness; and in the other laws described in the Pentateuch, or Torah (the first five books of the Hebrew Bible).

Aside from the Ten Commandments, most of the Pentateuchal laws shared the traditional form of Mesopotamian laws: if someone does a certain thing to another person, then the following punishment is imposed on the perpetrator. They also dealt with similar issues, such as property rights, and even had much content in common with Mesopotamian laws, such as those of Hammurabi. For example, both Hammurabi's laws and Hebrew law considered negligence in the case of the owner of an ox whose animal had gored another person. The owner was penalized only if he had been warned about his beast's tendency to gore yet done nothing to restrain it. Also like Hammurabi's laws, Hebrew law expressed an interest in the welfare of the poor as well as the rich; but in addition it secured protection for the lower classes and people without power, such as strangers, widows, and orphans. The same law applied to all without regard to their position in the social hierarchy, and the severity of punishments did not depend on a person's social class. Hebrew law furthermore did not allow vicarious punishment—a Mesopotamian tradition specifying, for example, that a rapist's wife be raped or that the son of a builder whose faulty work caused the death of another's son be killed. Women and children had certain legal protection, although their rights were less extensive than men's. For example, wives had less freedom to divorce their husbands than husbands had to divorce their wives, much as in the laws of Hammurabi. Crimes against property never carried the death penalty, as they frequently did in other Near Eastern societies. Hebrew law also protected slaves against flagrant mistreatment by their masters. Slaves who lost an eye or even a tooth from a beating were to be freed.

Like free people, slaves enjoyed the right to rest on the Sabbath, the holy day of the seven-day Hebrew week.

Because the earliest parts of the Hebrew Bible were composed in about 950 B.C., long after the Exodus, their account of the creation of the covenant and the Hebrew laws deals with a distant, undocumented time. Many uncertainties persist in our understanding of the process by which the Hebrews acquired their distinctive religion and way of life, but it seems clear that both took much longer to evolve than the Biblical account describes. The early Hebrews probably worshipped a variety of gods, including spirits believed to reside in natural objects such as trees and stones. Yahweh may have originally been the deity of the tribe of Midian, to which Moses' father-in-law belonged. The form of the covenant with Yahweh conformed to the ancient Near Eastern tradition of treaties between a superior and subordinates, but its content differed from other ancient Near Eastern religions because it made him the exclusive deity of his people. In the time of Moses, Yahweh religion was not yet the pure monotheism it would later become because it did not deny the existence of other gods. Rather, it was monolatry (worshiping one god only). Because in the ensuing centuries some Hebrews worshiped other gods as well, such as Baal of Canaan, it seems that the covenant with Yahweh and fully formed Hebrew monotheism did not emerge until well after 1000 B.C.

The Hebrews who fled from Egypt with Moses made their way back to Canaan, but they were still liable to attack from the Egyptian army. The first documentary reference to their presence in Palestine comes from an inscribed monument erected by the pharaoh Merneptah in the late thirteenth century B.C. to commemorate his victory in a military expedition there. The returning Hebrew tribes joined the Hebrews who had remained in Canaan and had somehow carved out territory for themselves there. The twelve Hebrew tribes remained ethnically, politically, and even religiously diverse from 1200 to 1000 B.C. and lacked a strong central authority. In the twelfth century B.C., they began to suffer depredations from the attacks of raiders from outside Canaan. The presence of these raiders testified to the violent disruptions that had begun to afflict a wide area of the ancient Mediterranean and Near East.

Regional Disruptions

A state of political equilibrium, in which kings corresponded with one another and traders traveled all over the area, characterized the Mediterranean and Near Eastern world of the early thirteenth century B.C. By about 1200 B.C., however, hard times had begun to hit not only small, loosely organized groups like the Hebrews in Canaan, but also major political states. The New Kingdom in Egypt had fragmented; foreign invaders had destroyed the powerful Hittite kingdom in Anatolia; Mesopotamia underwent a period of political turmoil; and the palace societies of the Aegean had disintegrated. Explaining all the catastrophes that occurred in the Mediterranean region from about 1200 to 1000 B.C. remains one of the most difficult puzzles in ancient history.

Egyptian and Hittite records document foreign invasions in this period, some of them from the sea. According to his own account, the pharaoh Ramesses III around 1182 B.C. defeated a fearsome coalition of seaborne invaders from the north, who had fought their way to the edge of Egypt:

> *All at once the peoples were on the move, dispersed in war. . . . No land could stand before their arms. . . . They laid their hands upon the lands as far as the circuit of the earth, their hearts confident and trusting: "Our plans will succeed!" . . . Those who reached my frontier, their seed is not, their heart and their soul are finished forever and ever. . . . They were dragged in, enclosed, and prostrated on the beach, killed, and made into heaps from head to tail.*

These sea peoples, as they are called, comprised many different groups. Some had been mercenary soldiers in the armies of the rulers they then turned against. Some came from far away to raid. And some were Mycenaean warriors who had been displaced by the economic troubles of their homeland, probably looking for more prosperous places to settle. What evidence we have for the history of the sea peoples indicates that no one, unified group pillaged the eastern Mediterranean in a single tidal wave of violence but rather that many disparate bands wracked the region. A chain reaction of attacks and flights in a recurring and expanding cycle put even more bands on the move. In the end all this turbulence revised the demographic map of the Mediterranean. The reasons for all this commotion remain mysterious, but its dire consequences for Near Eastern and Greek civilization are clear.

The once mighty Hittite kingdom fell about 1200 B.C. when raiders finally cut its supply lines of raw materials and invaders penetrated its borders. The capital city, Hattusas, was razed and never reinhabited, although smaller Neo-Hittite principalities survived for another five hundred years before succumbing to the armies of the Neo-Assyrian kingdom.

Egypt's New Kingdom repelled the sea peoples only through great military effort; the danger at sea created by these raiders left the Egyptian international trade network throughout the Mediterranean in shambles. Power struggles between the pharaoh and the priests also undercut the centralized authority of the monarchy. By the middle of the eleventh century B.C., Egypt had shrunk to its old territorial core along the banks of the Nile. Egypt's credit was ruined along with its international stature. When an eleventh-century B.C. Theban temple official traveled to Phoenicia to buy cedar for a ceremonial boat, the city's ruler demanded cash in advance. Although the Egyptian monarchy continued for centuries after the New Kingdom, continued power struggles between pharaohs and priests combined with frequent attacks from abroad prevented the reestablishment of centralized authority. No Egyptian dynasty was ever again an active and aggressive international power.

The calamities of this time also affected the copper-rich island of Cyprus and the flourishing cities along the eastern coast of the Mediterranean Sea. The Greeks later called these coastal peoples the Phoenicians (from the Greek *phoenix* meaning "shellfish"). The inhabitants of cities like Ugarit on the coast of Syria thrived on international maritime commerce and enjoyed a lively polyglot cultural milieu. Although a catastrophic attack by the sea peoples overwhelmed Ugarit and other areas of this region, one of its most brilliant accomplishments survived. In this crossroads of cultures the first alphabet had been developed from about 1700 to 1500 B.C.; its later form eventually became the base of the ancient Greek and Roman alphabets and hence of modern Western alphabets. Using the letters of an alphabet was simpler and more flexible than working with the other writing systems of the ancient Near East. An alphabetic system with pictures that stood for only one sound had also begun to develop in Egypt around 1600 to 1550 B.C. to write foreign words and names.

Raiders from the north, called Philistines, settled in Palestine and attacked the Canaanites and the Hebrews repeatedly in the eleventh century B.C. (The term *Palestine* was perhaps later derived from the word *Philistine*.) The Hebrew tribes appointed military leaders and legal authorities called judges in an attempt to unify their loose confederation during this period of near anarchy. One of these judges, Deborah, led an Israelite coalition force to victory over a Canaanite army.

The turmoil of this period reached far to the east and to the west of the eastern end of the Mediterranean. A scarcity of sources obscures the course of events in Mesopotamia, but we do know the Kassite kingdom in Babylonia collapsed, and the Assyrians were confined to their homeland. Invasions by the Semitic peoples known as Aramaeans and Chaldeans seem to have devastated western Asia and Syria. The Aramaeans established several small independent states in Syria, foreshadowing their future importance in that area and the later popularity of their language as an international tongue in the Near East.

The Mycenaeans had reached their pinnacle after 1400 B.C. The enormous domed tomb at Mycenae, called the Treasury of Atreus, belongs to this period. Its elaborately decorated facade and soaring roof testify to the confidence the Mycenaean warrior princes had in their power. The last phase of the extensive palace at Pylos on the west coast of the Peloponnese also dates to this time. It boasted glorious wall paintings, storerooms bursting with food, and a royal bathroom with a built-in tub and intricate plumbing. But these prosperous Mycenaeans inhabited a violent world. Ominous signs of danger first appeared during this period of affluence. Linear B tablets from Pylos record the disposition of troops to guard this unwalled site around 1200 B.C. The palace inhabitants of eastern Greece, such as those at Mycenae and nearby Tiryns, now constructed such massive stone walls that the later Greeks thought giants had built them. These fortifications could have protected these coastal palaces against attackers from the sea, who could have been either outsiders or other seafaring Greeks. But the wall around the in-

THE FOUNDATIONS OF CIVILIZATION IN THE WEST

Mesopotamia and Anatolia	Old and New Kingdom Egypt	Europe and the Aegean
c. 3500 B.C. First cities established; writing developed in Sumer; copper metallurgy already known	**c. 3100–3000 B.C.** King Menes unites Upper and Lower Egypt	**c. 5000 B.C.** Substantial houses built in many locations
c. 3000 B.C. Sumerians dominate; the wheel invented for vehicles	**2686–2181 B.C.** Old Kingdom	**c. 4000–3000 B.C.** Copper metallurgy under way in eastern Europe
c. 3000–2500 B.C. Bronze metallurgy under way	**c. 2650 B.C.** Imhotep builds the first pyramid for King Djoser	**c. 3000 B.C.** Stone temples constructed on Malta
c. 2600 B.C. King Gilgamesh rules the city of Uruk	**c. 2575 B.C.** Great Pyramid of Cheops constructed at Giza	**c. 3000–2000 B.C.** Mediterranean polyculture developed
c. 2350 B.C. Sargon establishes the Akkadian empire	**c.1670–1567 B.C.** The Hyksos dominate Lower Egypt	**c. 2200 B.C.** Earliest Cretan palaces constructed
2112–2095 B.C. King Ur-Nammu founds the Third Dynasty of Ur and promulgates set of written laws	**1567–1085 B.C.** New Kingdom	**c. 2100–1900 B.C.** Final phase of construction of Stonehenge
c. 1900 B.C. Private enterprise under way in Assyria	**Early fifteenth century B.C.** Reign of Queen Hatshepsut	**c. 1500–1450 B.C.** Earliest Mycenaean *tholos* tombs built
c. 1800 B.C. Abraham and his family migrate from Ur to Palestine	**Early fourteenth century B.C.** Reign of Akhenaten	**c. 1370 B.C.** Palace of Knossos destroyed
c. 1792–1750 B.C. Reign of Hammurabi, king of Babylon	**c. 1285 B.C.** Battle of Ramesses II with the Hittites at Kadesh in Syria	**c. 1300–1200 B.C.** High point of Mycenaean palace culture
c. 1750 B.C. Hittites begin to establish a kingdom in Anatolia	**c. 1269 B.C.** Treaty of Ramesses II with the Hittites	**c. 1200 B.C.** Disturbances across the Aegean region
c. 1200 B.C. Fall of the Hittite kingdom	**Early or mid-thirteenth century B.C.** Exodus of the Hebrews from Egypt	**c. 1000 B.C.** Destruction of Mycenaean palace culture completed
	c. 1182 B.C. Ramesses III turns back the sea peoples	

land palace at Gla in central Greece, where no foreign pirates could reach, confirms that above all the Mycenaeans had to defend themselves against other Mycenaeans. Never united in one state, the Mycenaeans by the late thirteenth century B.C. fought each other at least as much as they did foreigners.

Internal turmoil and the cataclysmic effects of major earthquakes offer the most plausible explanation of the destruction of the palaces of mainland Greece in the period after 1200 B.C. Jealous rulers regularly battled each other for status and gain. Near constant warfare burdened the elaborate economic balance of the redistributive economies of the palaces and hindered recovery from the damage apparently caused by earthquakes. The eventual failure of the palace economies devastated many Mycenaeans, who depended on this redistributive system for their subsistence. The later Greeks remembered an invasion of Dorians (Greek speakers from the north) as the reason for the disaster, but the Dorians who did move to the south most likely came in groups too small to cause such damage by themselves. Indeed, small-scale movements of people characterized this era. Bands of warriors with no prospects at home swarmed the eastern Mediterranean around 1200 B.C.

The damage done to Greek society by the dissolution of the redistributive economies of Mycenae took centuries to repair. Only Athens seems to have escaped wholesale disaster. In fact, Athenians of the fifth century B.C., prided themselves on their unique status among the peoples of classical Greece: "sprung from the soil" of their homeland, they had not been forced to emigrate in the turmoil that engulfed the rest of Greece in the twelfth and eleventh centuries B.C. Other Greeks were less fortunate. Uprooted from their homes, they wandered abroad in search of new territory to settle. The Ionian Greeks, who later inhabited the central coast of western Anatolia, emigrated from the mainland during this period. To an outside observer, Greek society at the end of the Bronze Age might have seemed destined for irreversible economic and social decline, even oblivion. The next chapter shows how wrong this prediction would have been.

Conclusion

The basis of our modern way of life arose from the technological and social changes associated with the Neolithic revolution, which began over ten thousand years ago. Over the course of many centuries, hunter-gatherer society transformed into a more settled style of life. People in the Near East learned to farm and domesticate animals for food; such an agricultural system could sustain a growing population and support even more people to work the land. As the knowledge of agricultural technology slowly spread from the Fertile Crescent to the western lands of Europe around 4000 B.C., human society developed well-defined social hierarchies. Marked social differentiation corresponding to differences in wealth and power had now become a standard in Western society, as had a patriarchal social system, in which men dominated political and economic life and exerted power over women in most realms of society.

Beginning about 3500 B.C. the first cities began to develop, in Mesopotamia. Although local conditions inhibited the emergence of cities in some areas, such as Europe, in this early period, societies structured more centrally grew up outside southwestern Asia, especially in Egypt along the fertile banks of the Nile River. These changes started a general trend toward economic specialization and political centralization. The knowledge of writing, which first emerged in the Near [illegible] e developments. Written law codes testify to the complex political and legal organization of Mesopotamian society. Mesopotamian and Egyptian accomplishments in art, architecture, astronomy, calculations of calendars, mathematics, and medicine influenced later developments, just as the mythology and the religion of the Hebrews inspired later peoples.

Prehistoric societies in Europe may have been influenced by an influx of Indo-European peoples. The peoples of prehistoric Europe developed technologies, such as megalithic architecture and metallurgy, independently of similar developments in Egypt and the other lands of the Near East. The need to secure raw materials for metallurgy and other commodities not available locally led to the establishment of trade connections throughout the European and Mediterranean worlds. Competition for resources and the desire to appropriate the prosperity of others led to warfare and political takeovers, especially in Mesopotamia and the Aegean. In this latter region, violent strife of this kind probably led to the domination of Minoan civilization by the Mycenaeans. The Mycenaeans lost their civilization because of war and damage from earthquakes. After 1200 B.C. the peace, prosperity, and international trade of the Near East and Greece were shattered during a mysterious period of history characterized by the violent wanderings of raiders like the sea peoples.

Suggestions for Further Reading

Source Materials

Dalley, Stephanie. *Myths from Mesopotamia: Creation, the Flood, Gilgamesh, and Others.* 1989. New, authoritative translations of Mesopotamian myths.

Grayson, A. K., and D. B. Redford, eds. *Papyrus and Tablet.* 1973. A topically arranged selection of translated texts from ancient Egypt and Mesopotamia.

Pritchard, James B. *The Ancient Near East in Pictures Relating to the Old Testament.* 2d ed. 1969. An invaluable anthology that contains many fascinating pictures depicting ancient Near Eastern culture. Comes with a supplement.

———. *Ancient Near Eastern Texts Relating to the Old Testament.* 3d ed. 1969. An indispensable anthology of the literary and documentary evidence for ancient Near Eastern culture. A useful supplement also included.

Interpretive Studies

Aldred, Cyril. *The Egyptians*, Rev. ed. 1984. An illustrated introduction to ancient Egyptian history and culture. (Generally, Aldred's dates for events in Egyptian history have been used in this chapter.)

Baines, J., and J. Malek. *Atlas of Ancient Egypt.* 1980. A superbly illustrated introduction to ancient Egyptian history and culture.

Chadwick, John. *The Mycenaean World.* 1976. A clear introduction to Bronze Age Greece by an authority on Linear B.

Champion, Timothy, Clive Gamble, Stephen Shennan, and Alasdair Whittle. *Prehistoric Europe.* 1984. A demanding presentation of archaeological evidence.

Childe, V. Gordon. *The Dawn of European Civilization.* 6th ed. 1958. A classic work by the most famous "diffusionist." For an excellent discussion of the significance of Childe's work, see Ruth Tringham, "V. Gordon Childe 25 Years After: His Relevance for the Archaeology of the Eighties," *Journal of Field Archaeology* 10 (1983): 85–100.

Ehrenberg, Margaret. *Women in Prehistory.* 1989. A study of women's important contributions to the development of agriculture and of their social status in Europe from the Paleolithic Age to the Iron Age.

Frankfort, Henri, H. A. Frankfort, John A. Wilson, Thorkild Jacobsen, and William A. Irwin. *The Intellectual Adventure of Ancient Man: An Essay on Speculative Thought in the Ancient Near East.* 1946. Reissued with updated bibliography, 1977. Lectures on the myth and thought of the ancient Egyptians, Mesopotamians, and Hebrews.

Gimbutas, Marija. *The Goddesses and Gods of Old Europe, 6500–3500 B.C.: Myths and Cult Images.* New ed. 1984. An updated presentation of the author's views on the matrifocal nature of Neolithic European culture.

James, T. G. H. *An Introduction to Ancient Egypt.* 1979. An excellent guide to the diverse history of ancient Egypt.

Knapp, A. Bernard. *The History and Culture of Ancient Western Asia and Egypt.* 1988. A concise, comprehensive introduction covering prehistoric times to the fourth century B.C.

Kramer, Samuel Noah. *The Sumerians: Their History, Culture, and Character.* 1963. Provides extensive coverage of Sumerian culture.

Lerner, Gerda. *The Creation of Patriarchy.* 1986. A provocative survey of patriarchal ancient civilizations by a feminist historian.

Lesko, Barbara, ed. *Women's Earliest Records from Ancient Egypt and Western Asia.* 1989. A collection of wide-ranging articles and responses on the history of women in ancient Egypt, Mesopotamia, and Israel.

Macqueen, J. G. *The Hittites.* Rev. and enl. ed. 1986. A fast-moving survey of this complex kingdom.

Miller, J. Maxwell, and John H. Hayes. *A History of Ancient Israel and Judah.* 1986. A survey from the end of the second millennium B.C. until the sixth century B.C., with valuable discussions of the difficulties in understanding the earliest history of the Hebrews.

Oates, Joan. *Babylon.* Rev. ed. 1986. Introduces the history and archaeology of Babylonia from the time of Sargon until after Alexander the Great.

Oppenheim, A. Leo. *Ancient Mesopotamia: Portrait of a Dead Civilization.* Rev. ed. completed by Erica Reiner. 1977. A standard work with a helpful appendix on chronology.

Piggott, Stuart. *The Earliest Wheeled Transport from the Atlantic Coast to the Caspian Sea.* 1983. A full treatment of the "technological explosion" that brought to Europe the invention of the wheel and its use in transport, and the domestication of the horse.

Redford, Donald B. *Akhenaten: The Heretic King.* 1984. A revised look at this maverick pharaoh and his monotheistic religion.

Renfrew, Colin. *Before Civilization: The Radiocarbon Revolution and Prehistoric Europe.* 1979. An introduction to the new dating techniques, arguing strongly against the diffusionist explanation of change in prehistoric Europe.

Roux, Georges. *Ancient Iraq.* 2d ed. 1980. Surveys Mesopotamian history from Paleolithic times to the Greco-Roman period.

Sanders, N. K. *The Sea Peoples: Warriors of the Ancient*

Mediterranean, 1250–1150 B.C. Rev. ed. 1985. Reviews the different areas affected by these disparate groups of raiders.

Sarna, Nahum M. *Exploring Exodus: The Heritage of Biblical Israel.* 1986. An interpretative discussion of the period of the Covenant in Hebrew history.

Tigay, Jeffrey H. *The Evolution of the Gilgamesh Epic.* 1982. A comprehensive history of the versions of the Mesopotamian epic poem about Gilgamesh.

Tringham, Ruth. *Hunters, Fishers, and Farmers of Eastern Europe, 6000–3000* B.C. 1971. Investigates the causes of cultural change, considering both diffusion and indigenous invention.

Vermeule, Emily. *Greece in the Bronze Age.* 1972. A stimulating treatment of this complex subject.

Willetts, R. F. *The Civilization of Ancient Crete.* 1977. Cretan history from earliest times until the eve of the classical period.

CHAPTER 2

New Paths for Western Civilization, c. 1000–500 B.C.

According to a story told by the Greek writer Plutarch, around 594 B.C. a foreign king touring Greece visited Solon, the most renowned lawmaker of ancient Athens. At the time, Solon was drawing up a new set of laws at the request of his fellow Athenians, who hoped a revised law code would end the social and political turmoil their self-governing community of free citizens was then experiencing. When the king discovered what Solon was doing, he burst into laughter, saying to the lawmaker, "Do you actually believe your fellow citizens' injustice and greed can be kept in check this way? Written laws are more like spiders' webs than anything else: they tie up the weak and the small fry who get stuck in them, but the rich and the powerful tear them to shreds." Solon replied, "People abide by their agreements when neither side has anything to gain by breaking them. I am writing laws for the Athenians in such a way that they will clearly see it is to everyone's advantage to obey the laws rather than to break them."

This story, like many anecdotes about conversations from the past, may not be historically accurate. But whether or not this particular conversation ever took place is not important. Solon certainly existed and indeed revised the laws of Athens. The point of the story is that it reflects the Greeks' attempts to create systems of law that applied equally to all the free men of the community. In Solon's time the question of whether written laws would promote justice and peace in Athenian society remained unanswered. The earlier political systems of the Near East, though sometimes allowing certain prominent male citizens outside the royal family to participate, had relied on the strong, centralized authority of monarchs.

A Spartan Dancer
This bronze statuette shows the graceful style of Spartan art before it faded away as Sparta developed its regimented way of life, one of the many significant changes in Greek society that took place in the Archaic period.

Solon's Athens exemplified a different type of community that had begun to emerge in Greece around 750 B.C.: self-governing city-states.

Greek city-states contrasted significantly with earlier political and social institutions. They had no traditional monarchy, which still prevailed, for example, in Assyria and other contemporary societies of the Near East; they extended the rights of ordinary citizens, guaranteeing the community's free males, poor as well as rich, a role in state policy making as well as new legal and political rights, and granting women valuable status and additional legal rights; and in some cases they created democratic governments.

To understand the forces behind the advent of Greek city-states in the eighth century B.C. and the momentous consequences for later Western history, we must first trace the political, economic, and social changes that occurred following the great disruptions that characterized the years 1200 to 1000 B.C. The Near East after 1000 B.C. reinstituted the traditional political and social systems of its past: those of monarchy. Although the Hebrews lost their independence in this period, Judaism's transformation into a true monotheistic religion represented a significant development. The enduring power of the Hebrews' religious ideas, which greatly influenced Christianity and Islam, thus joins the novel patterns of life and thought that appeared in the early Greek city-states as the foremost legacies of this period (c. 1000–500 B.C.) to later Western civilization.

Important Dates

Late eleventh century B.C. Saul becomes ancient Israel's first king

c. 1000–900 B.C. Greece experiences severe depopulation and poor economic conditions

c. 900 B.C. Neo-Assyrians create an empire

c. 800 B.C. Phoenicians begin colonization in western Mediterranean

776 B.C. First Olympic Games held in Greece

c. 750 B.C. Greeks begin to create city-states

c. 750–550 B.C. Greek colonies founded all around the Mediterranean

604–562 B.C. Nebuchadnezzar II reigns in Babylon, conquers Judah, destroys the central Hebrew temple in Jerusalem, and exiles most Hebrews to Babylon

594 B.C. Athenians appoint Solon to recodify laws to try to end social unrest

560–530 B.C. Cyrus founds Persian kingdom

510 B.C. Athenian aristocrats and Spartans free Athens from tyranny

508 B.C. Cleisthenes begins to reform Athenian democracy

The Early Greek Dark Age and Revival in the Near East

The turmoil during 1200–1000 B.C. weakened or obliterated many city-states and kingdoms in Greece and the Near East. Many of the people who survived suffered grinding poverty. We know little about this period of devastation or the recovery that followed because few literary or documentary sources exist to supplement the incomplete information provided by archaeology. Both because conditions were so gloomy for so many people and because our view of what happened in these years is dim, historians often refer to the era beginning in the twelfth and eleventh centuries B.C. as a Dark Age. The Greeks did not fully regain their strength until about 750 B.C. In contrast, the Near East recovered much sooner, ending its Dark Age around 900 B.C.

The Poverty of the Early Greek Dark Age

The depressed economic conditions in Greece after the fall of Mycenaean civilization typify the desperately reduced circumstances so many people in the Mediterranean and the Near East had to endure during the worst years of the Dark Age. One of the most startling indications of the severity of life in the early Dark Age is that the Greeks apparently lost their knowledge of writing when Mycenaean civilization fell. The Linear B script the Mycenaeans used was difficult to master and probably known only by a few specialists, the scribes who maintained palace records. They wrote only to track the flow of goods in and out of the palaces. When the

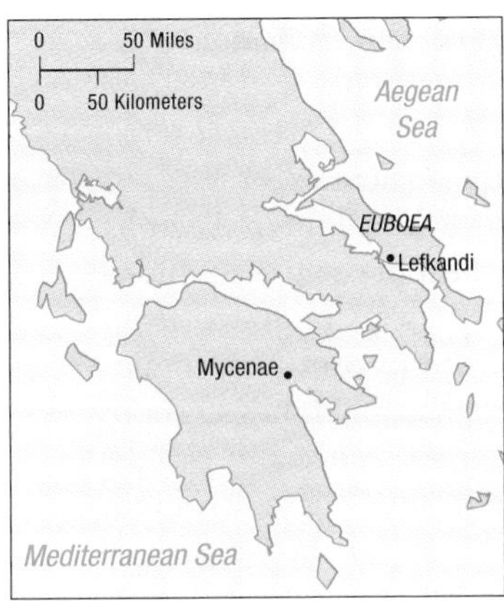

Dark Age Greece

redistributive economy of Mycenaean Greece collapsed, the Greeks no longer needed scribes or writing. Oral transmission kept Greek cultural traditions alive.

Later Greeks believed that, following the downfall of the Mycenaeans, a Greek-speaking group from the north—the Dorians—began to invade central and southern Greece. But archaeologists have not discovered any distinctive remains attesting Dorian incursions, and many scholars do not believe these invasions occurred.

Archaeological excavations have shown that the Greeks cultivated much less land and had many fewer settlements in the early Dark Age than at the height of Mycenaean prosperity. No longer did powerful rulers ensconced in stone fortresses preside over several towns and faraway but tightly organized territories, with the redistributive economies they controlled providing a tolerable standard of living for farmers, herders, and a wide array of craft workers. The many ships filled with adventurers, raiders, and traders that had plied the Mediterranean during the Bronze Age had dwindled to a paltry few. Developed political states no longer existed in Greece, and the people eked out their existence as herders, shepherds, and subsistence farmers bunched in tiny settlements—about twenty people in many cases. The Greek population decreased in the early Dark Age. As the population shrank, less land was cultivated, leading to a decline in food production. The diminished food supply in turn prompted a further drop in the population. These two processes reinforced one another in a vicious circle, multiplying the negative effects of both.

The Greek agricultural economy remained complex despite the withering away of many traditional forms of agriculture. More Greeks than ever before made their living by herding animals. This increasingly pastoral way of life meant that people became more mobile: they needed to move their herds to new pastures once the animals had overgrazed their current location. If the herders were lucky, they might find a new spot where they could grow a crop of grain if they stayed long enough. As a result of this less settled style of life, people built only simple huts and got along with few possessions. Unlike their Bronze Age forebears, Greeks in the Dark Age had no monumental architecture, and they ceased depicting people and animals in their principal art form, the designs on ceramics.

We might assume that the general level of poverty throughout the Greek population in the Dark Age would have resulted in more egalitarian communities. However, archaeologists have recently analyzed contents of graves that suggest that Greek society, perhaps as early as 1050 B.C., had reinstituted a system of social hierarchy. Evidence for this hierarchy shows up clearly in the tenth century B.C. site now known as Lefkandi on the island of Euboea, off the eastern coast of the Greek mainland. There

A Rich Woman's Burial in Dark Age Greece
This burial from the tenth century B.C. dramatically reveals the wealth of some Greeks in the late Dark Age. This woman was buried with her gold jewelry, including an unusual chest ornament.

archaeologists have discovered the richly furnished graves of a man and a woman, who died about 950 B.C. The dead woman wore elaborate gold ornaments that testify to her exceptional wealth. The couple were buried under a building more than one hundred fifty feet long with wooden columns on the exterior. The striking architecture and riches in their graves imply that they enjoyed high social status during their lives and perhaps received a form of ancestor worship after their death. Probably few such wealthy and therefore powerful people lived during this time, but the graves at Lefkandi prove that marked social differentiation had again emerged in the Greek world. Strains in this hierarchical organization later set the stage for the birth of Greece's self-governing city-states.

Resurgent Kingdoms in the Near East

Although the Near East recovered from the devastation of its Dark Age more rapidly than Greece did, no political change comparable to the creation of the Greek city-state occurred. Instead the tradition of centralized authority was renewed. From Anatolia to Egypt to Mesopotamia, kingdoms large and small constituted the most prominent and powerful states, just as in the past. Some of these states were weaker than they had been before the Dark Age—especially Egypt, which had lost its status as an international power. The new Assyrian kingdom, however, put together the greatest territorial empire yet seen in the ancient Near East.

The Near East

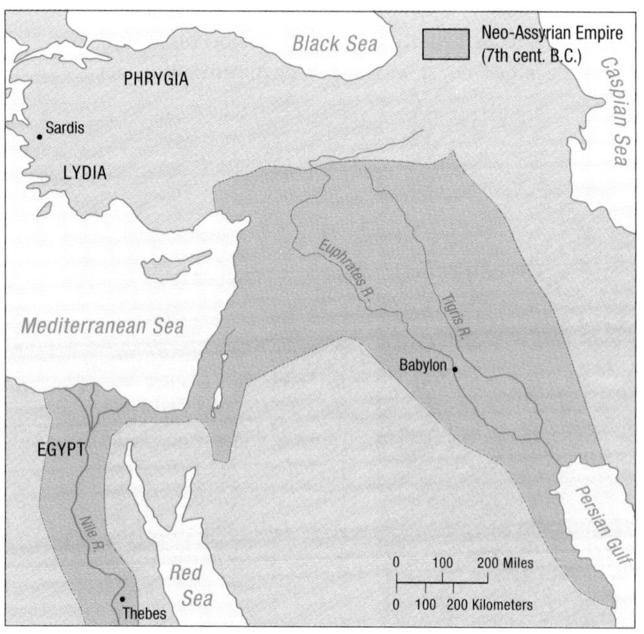

The collapse of the Hittite kingdom in Anatolia had opened the way for the Phrygians, an Indo-European people who had perhaps migrated from Thrace, the spur of the European continent immediately to the west. The Phrygian kingdom's strength derived from the raw materials, especially metals, found in Anatolia. So wealthy did these resources make Phrygia that at the height of the kingdom's prosperity in the eighth century B.C., its ruler, known to the Greeks as Midas, became a legendary figure noted for his hoards of gold. About 695 B.C., however, a northern people called the Cimmerians invaded and destroyed the Phrygian kingdom. Eventually the kingdom of Lydia, in southwestern Anatolia, expanded to control the former territory of the Phrygians. Lydia also became famous for its material wealth, as symbolized by the phrase "as rich as Croesus," which recalls the Lydian king Croesus (*c. 560–546 B.C.), who bestowed fabulous gifts on religious sanctuaries in Anatolia and Greece. But as before the Dark Age, wealth proved no insurance against disaster. In 546 B.C. the first Persian king, Cyrus, conquered Lydia after Croesus tried to push eastward into Persian territory.

The greatest international power in the Near East during this period was Assyria. Beginning around 900 B.C., the armies of the Neo-Assyrian ("New Assyrian") kingdom drove westward against the Aramaean states in Syria until they finally punched through to the Mediterranean coast. The desire to acquire metals and to secure access to seaborne trade routes to transport these metals probably fueled this enterprise. Eventually the Assyrian kings forced many of the people they conquered to move to Assyria to work on huge building projects in the kingdom's principal cities. So many Aramaeans were transplanted that their language had practically replaced Assyrian as the everyday language of Assyria by the eighth century B.C. Many Aramaeans also rose to prominent positions in the Assyrian army and in government administration. Assyrian imperial government was distinguished by its elaborate and well-organized record keeping, which relied on expert scribes.

Military imperialism pervaded Neo-Assyrian society, which seems to have been dominated by male warriors. Infantrymen provided the backbone of the Assyrian army; trained warriors excelled in the use of technology such as siege towers, battering rams, and swift chariots for carrying archers. Campaigns against foreign lands brought in revenues to supplement the domestic economy, which was based on agriculture, stock raising, and international trade. Conquered peoples who escaped deportation to Assyria had to pay annual tribute, and all citizens were expected to contribute to Assyrian prosperity. When the Phoenicians (who lived on the coast of Syria) eventually came under Assyrian control, they specialized in supplying raw materials and luxury goods such as incense, wine, dyed linens, glasswork, and ivory. So economically valuable did this commerce become to the Neo-Assyrian kingdom that it left the Phoenician cities largely autonomous. The Phoenicians conducted business and settled colonies throughout the Mediterranean, as far west as today's Spain. In 814 B.C. they founded the colony of Carthage in western North Africa, a settlement that grew into a great city. Within a century of its foundation sometime before 750 B.C., the Phoenician settlement on the site of modern Cadiz in Spain had become a city thriving on economic and cultural interaction with the indigenous Iberian population. A Phoenician expedition commissioned by an Egyptian pharaoh completed the first recorded circumnavigation of Africa around 600 B.C.

When not making war, Assyrian men spent much time hunting wild animals, the more dangerous the quarry the better. The king, for example, hunted lions as proof of his vigor and power. Royal lion hunts provided a favorite subject for Assyrian sculptors, who mastered the artistic technique of carving long relief sculptures that narrated a connected story. Although the Assyrian imperial administration devoted much time and energy to preserving documents in its archives, literacy apparently mattered far less to Assyrian males than war and hunting. Only one king is known to have learned to read and write in his youth. Neo-Assyrian public religion, which included deities imported from Babylon, reflected the prominence of war in Assyrian culture. Several cults, including that of Ishtar, the goddess of love, fertility, and war, glorified warfare. The Assyrians' passion for monumental architecture manifested itself in huge temples erected to the gods. The temples' staffs of priests and slaves grew so numerous that the revenues from temple lands could no longer support them, and the kings had to supply extra funds.

The Neo-Assyrian monarchs pursued an aggressive policy of foreign expansion. Tiglath-pileser III (*744–727 B.C.) extended Assyrian control over portions of Syria-Palestine and conquered Babylon, while Esarhaddon (*680–669 B.C.) added Egypt to the Neo-Assyrian empire, dramatic proof of the weakness that had characterized Egypt since the fall of the New Kingdom. Their vast empire fell, however, when the Neo-Assyrian nobility stopped cooperating with the kings and Assyria's many enemies combined forces to invade. By 612 B.C. these temporary allies, spearheaded by the newly independent Chaldean dynasty of Babylon, had destroyed the Assyrian capital at Ninevah.

This new Babylonian kingdom took over much of the Neo-Assyrian empire. Like the Aramaeans, who had earlier settled in Babylonia in such great numbers that Aramaean had replaced Babylonian as the common tongue, the Chaldeans of the Neo-Babylonian kingdom were a Semitic people who had originally been seminomads. They absorbed traditional Babylonian culture and preserved much ancient literature like the Gilgamesh Epic and other Mesopotamian myths; they also created many new works of prose and poetry. Educated people read this literature and recited it publicly for the enjoyment of the illiterate. Particularly popular were wisdom literature and texts that prophesied the future. Babylonian advances in astronomy became so influential that the word *Chaldean* came to mean *astronomer* in Greek. As in the past, the primary motivation for observing the stars was the belief that the gods communicated with humans by signs, through such natural phenomena as celestial movements and eclipses, abnormal births, the way smoke curled upward from a fire, and the trails of ants. The interpretation of these phenomena as messages from the gods exemplified the mixture of science and religion characteristic of ancient Near Eastern thought.

The Neo-Babylonian kingdom reached its zenith under Nebuchadnezzar II (*604–562 B.C.). He adorned Babylon with massive buildings, such as the rebuilt temple of the chief god, Marduk; the famous Hanging Gardens (whose original design, perhaps a ziggurat, remains uncertain); and the beautiful city gate dedicated to the goddess Ishtar.

Blue-glazed bricks and lions molded in yellow, red, and white decorated the portal's walls, which were thirty-six feet high. (This gate, reconstructed from the ruins found at Babylon, today stands in a Berlin museum.) Internal strife fatally weakened the kingdom, however, in the reign of Nabonidus (*c. 555–539 B.C.). He caused a revolt among the priests who championed Marduk by promoting the cult of Sin, the moon god of the Mesopotamian city of Harran, and then retired for ten years to an oasis in the Arabian desert, leaving his son in Babylon to deal with the unrest. Nabonidus finally returned to Babylon, but in a failed attempt to stem an invasion led by the Persian Cyrus, who presented himself as the restorer of traditional Babylonian religion.

The Character of Persian Rule

The kingdom of Persia had taken shape when Cyrus (*560–530 B.C.) established himself as its first king by overthrowing the monarchy of the Medes. The Median kingdom, centered in what is today northern Iran, had emerged in the late eighth century B.C., and it had joined Babylonia in destroying the Neo-Assyrian kingdom in 612 B.C. Median power then extended as far as the border of Lydia in central Anatolia. The languages of the Medes and the Persians descended from Indo-European; the language of today's Iran derives from ancient Persian. By taking over Lydia in 546 B.C., Cyrus also acquired dominion over the Greek city-states of Ionia (the western coast of Anatolia) that the Lydian king Croesus had previously subdued. Cyrus's son Cambyses conquered Egypt in 525 B.C. The expansion of Persian power under Cyrus and Cambyses set the stage for the great conflict between Persia and Greece in the early fifth century B.C.

When King Darius I (*522–486 B.C.) ascended to the throne the Persian kingdom, whose ancestral heart lay in southern Iran east of Mesopotamia, covered a vast territory stretching east-west from Afghanistan to Turkey and north-south from inside the southern border of the former Soviet Union to Egypt and the Indian Ocean. Its heterogeneous population numbered in the millions. Darius created a smoothly functioning administrative structure for

The Great King of Persia
This relief sculpture from the palace at Persepolis depicts the proper way to show respect to the Persian king. The larger size of the king and his son behind him symbolizes their greater status.

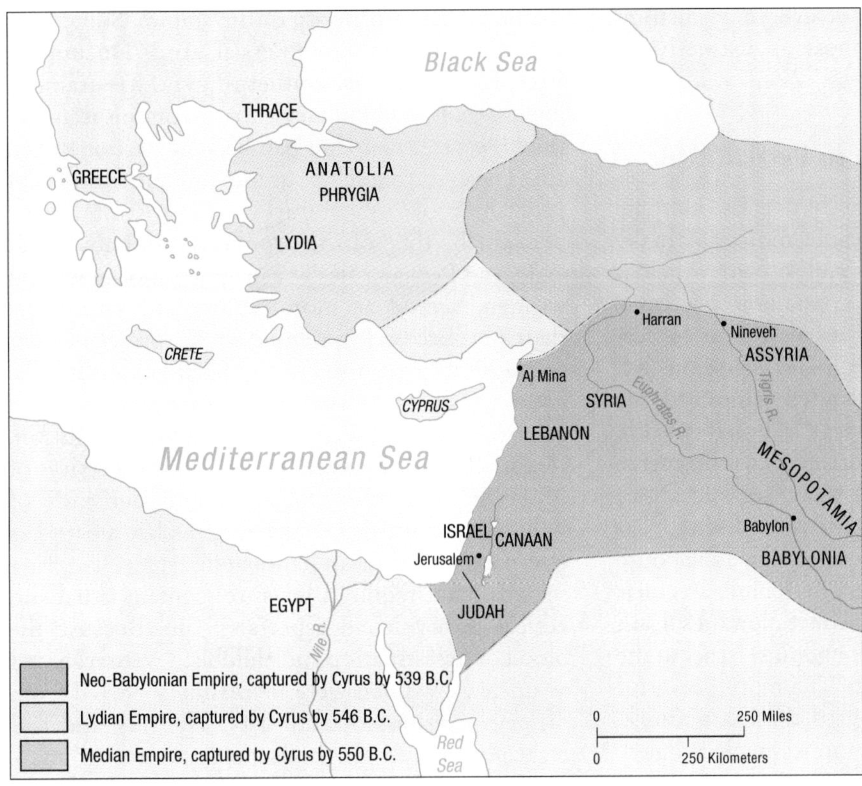

Expansion of the Persian Empire by Cyrus

the empire based on Assyrian precedents. Provincial governors (satraps) ruled enormous territories with little, if any, direct interference from the king. Their duties included keeping order, enrolling troops when needed, and sending revenues to the royal treasury. The Persian kings taxed the many different subject peoples of the kingdom in food, precious metals, and other valuable commodities and demanded from them levies of soldiers to staff the royal army. A system of roads and a courier system for royal mail facilitated communications among the far-flung administrative centers of the imperial provinces.

The revenues of its realm made the Persian monarchy wealthy beyond imagination. Everything about the king emphasized his grandeur and his superiority to ordinary mortals. His purple robes were more splendid than anyone's; the red carpets spread for him to walk upon could not be trod by anyone else; his servants held their hands before their mouths in his presence to muffle their breath so that he would not have to breathe the same air as they; in the sculpture adorning his palace, he appeared larger than any other human. To display his concern for his loyal subjects, as well as the gargantuan scale of his resources, the king provided meals for some fifteen thousand nobles, courtiers, and other followers every day, although he himself ate hidden from the view of his guests. The Greeks, in awe of the Persian monarch's power and his lavish style of life, referred to him as "The Great King."

As absolute autocrats, the Persian kings believed they were superior to all humans. They did not, however, regard themselves as gods, but rather as the agents of the supreme god of Persian religion, Ahura Mazda. Persian religion, based on the teachings of the prophet Zoroaster, was dualistic, perceiving the world as the arena for the ongoing battle between good and evil. Unlike other ancient Near Eastern peoples, such as the Hebrews, the Persians did not sacrifice animals. Fire, kindled on special altars, played an important part in their religious rituals. Despite their autocratic rule, the ancient Persian kings usually did not interfere with the religious practices or everyday customs of their subjects, not even those as distinctive as the Hebrews'.

Israel from Monarchy to Persian Rule

The Hebrews achieved their first truly national organization with the creation of a monarchy in the late eleventh century B.C. Saul became ancient Israel's first king by fighting to limit Philistine power over the Hebrews in Canaan, and his successors David (*c. 1010–970 B.C.) and Solomon (*c. 961–922 B.C.) brought the united nation to the height of its prosperity. Israel's national wealth, largely derived from import-export commerce conducted through its cities, was displayed above all in the great temple richly decorated with gold leaf that Solomon built in Jerusalem to be the house of the Hebrews' god, Yahweh. This temple was their premier religious monument. After Solomon's death the monarchy split into two kingdoms: Israel in the north and Judah in the south. The more powerful Mesopotamians later subjugated these kingdoms. Tiglath-pileser III of Assyria forced much of Palestine to become a tribute-paying, subject territory, destroying Israel in 722 B.C. and deporting its population to Assyria. In 597 B.C. the Babylonian king Nebuchadnezzar II conquered Judah and captured its capital, Jerusalem. Ten years later he destroyed its temple to Yahweh and banished the Hebrew leaders and much of the population to Babylon. The Hebrews ever after remembered the sorrow of this exile. Their history from then on was that of a people subject to the political domination of others, save for a period of independence during the second and first centuries B.C.

When the Persian king Cyrus overthrew the Babylonians in 539 B.C., he permitted the Hebrews to return to Palestine, which was called Yehud from the name of the southern Hebrew kingdom Judah. From this geographical term came the name *Jews,* the customary designation for the Hebrews after their Babylonian exile. Cyrus allowed the Jews to rebuild their main temple in Jerusalem and to practice their religion. The priests of the Jerusalem temple, the literal and figurative center of Judaism, became the leaders of the Jewish community. Like other Persian subjects, the Jews were allowed to live as they pleased as long as they did not disrupt the peace and prosperity of the empire. Some Jews apparently served in the Persian army. Documents from Elephantine in southern Egypt, for example, mention a Jewish military garrison on this island in the Nile, after that land had become part of Persia.

The enduring religious ideas and institutions of Judaism took shape during the postmonarchic period (the time of the prophets), the Babylonian exile, and Persian rule. The prophets, both men and women, served as moral critics and preachers; their purpose was to remind the Hebrews of their responsibility to observe the Sinai covenant. The great prophets of the eighth through the sixth centuries B.C., such as Amos, Hosea, Isaiah, Huldah, Jeremiah, and Ezekiel, taught the necessity of observing the religious and moral demands of Yahweh and warned that failing to live up to the covenant would mean national disaster. Observing the covenant required Jews to maintain ritual and ethical purity in all aspects of life. Because the blood of menstruation and childbirth were regarded as unclean, women were increasingly barred from official positions of authority. The husband had legal power over the household, subject to intervention by the male elders of the community, and only he could initiate divorce proceedings. Marrying non-Jews was forbidden, as was any work on the Sabbath (the holy day of the week). Ethics applied not only to ordinary crimes but also to financial dealings. Taxes and offerings had to be paid to support and honor the sanctuary of Yahweh, and debts had to be forgiven every seventh year.

The prophets assailed their people for falling short of the standards of behavior imposed by the covenant. They interpreted the conquests of the Hebrew kingdoms by the Neo-Assyrians and Neo-Babylonians as divine punishments for worshiping gods other than Yahweh and oppressing the poor. After the destruction of the temple at Jerusalem, the prophets' message turned from doom to hope, with the promise of national regeneration if the people returned to the covenant. An anonymous prophet whose words are recorded in the second half of the book of Isaiah hailed the Persian king Cyrus as an agent of Yahweh who had liberated the people from their exile in Babylon. Some prophets also preached about the coming end of the present world following a great crisis, a judgment by Yahweh, and salvation leading to a new world order. This apocalypticism ("uncovering" of the future), reminiscent of Babylonian prophecy texts, greatly influenced early Christianity later on.

By the Persian period, Judaism had become a monotheistic religion based on the recognition of certain books as authoritative scripture. The identification of sacred texts as the center of Jewish religion proved the most crucial development for the later history not only of Judaism, but of Christianity and Islam as well. These scriptures were assembled by editing earlier Hebrew traditions to form the Torah, the first five books of the Hebrew Bible, which under the Jewish leader Ezra in the fifth century B.C. was recognized as the sacred literature of the Jewish community. The books of the prophets found in the Hebrew Bible were probably also edited at this time and began to be accepted as authoritative.

Although the early Hebrews were never politically, economically, or militarily preeminent in the Near East, their religious ideas greatly influenced the later course of Western history. Through the continuing vitality of Judaism and its impact on the doctrines of Christianity and Islam, the early Jews bequeathed ideas whose effects have endured to this day: the belief in monotheism and the idea, based on the notion of covenant, that nations can have a divinely ordained destiny if they obey the divine will. These religious concepts constitute one of the most significant legacies to Western civilization from the Near East of the first half of the first millennium B.C.

Remaking Greek Civilization

In Greece the Dark Age of depopulation and poverty persisted longer than in the Near East. Although Greek economic improvement is evident as early as about 900 B.C., not until around 750 B.C. did political states, now of a new kind, develop again and the Dark Age end. The history of Greece in these centuries, though often obscure, laid the foundation for the pronounced social, political, and intellectual changes associated with the creation of the Greek city-state. The impact of these changes on Western history has been profound.

The Greek Dark Age

c. 1000 B.C. Almost all important Mycenaean sites except Athens destroyed by now

c. 1000–900 B.C. Greatest depopulation and economic loss

900–800 B.C. Early revival of population and agriculture; iron now beginning to be used for tools and weapons

c. 800 B.C. Greek trading contacts initiated with Al Mina in Syria

776 B.C. First Olympic Games held

c. 775 B.C. Euboeans found trading post on Ischia in the Bay of Naples

c. 750–700 B.C. Homeric poetry recorded in writing after Greeks learn to write again; Hesiod composes his poetry; Oracle of Apollo at Delphi already famous

The Start of Economic Revival

Evidence from burials shows that Greeks in more and more locations had become conspicuously wealthy by about 900 B.C. The hierarchical arrangement of society was evidently spreading throughout Greece, and the few men and women at the pinnacle of society could afford to have expensive material goods placed in their tombs with them. Earlier in the Dark Age the best grave offerings a dead person could expect were a few clay pots. The exceptional contents of rich graves point to significant metallurgical and economic changes already under way by the ninth century B.C.

Two burials from Athens illustrate the changes that occurred in metallurgical technology for war and agriculture, advances that eventually helped end Greece's Dark Age. The earliest grave, from about 900 B.C., consisted of a pit into which a clay pot to hold the dead man's cremated remains was placed. Metal weapons, including a long sword, spearheads, and knives, surrounded the pot. Placing weapons in a male's grave was a burial tradition continued from the Bronze Age; but these arms were forged from iron, not bronze. This difference reflects a significant shift in metallurgy that took place throughout the Mediterranean region during

Model Granary
Found in a ninth-century woman's tomb in Athens, this model imitates the shape of grain storage facilities. Its decoration reflects the geometric style of Greek art.

the early centuries of the first millennium B.C.: iron displaced bronze as the principal metal used to make weapons and tools. For this reason historians also refer to the Dark Age in Greece as the Early Iron Age.

The Greeks, like others in the Near East, turned to iron because they could no longer obtain the tin needed to mix with copper to make bronze. The international trading routes once used to bring tin to Greece and the Near East from distant sources had been disrupted in the upheaval associated with the sea peoples and the widespread turmoil that began around 1200 B.C. Iron ore was available locally in Greece and elsewhere throughout the Near East. The Greeks probably learned to smelt iron through contact with people from the island of Cyprus, who in turn had learned it from people in southern Anatolia. Iron eventually replaced bronze in many uses, above all for agricultural tools, swords, and spear points. Bronze was still used for shields and armor, however, perhaps because it was easier to shape into thinner, curved pieces. The lower cost of iron tools and weapons meant that more people could afford them; and because iron is harder than bronze, implements kept their sharp edges longer. Better and more plentiful farming implements of iron eventually helped increase food production, a development reflected by evidence from the second burial.

The second grave, from about 850 B.C., held the remains of a woman and her treasures, including gold rings and earrings, a necklace of glass beads, and an unusual storage chest of baked clay. The necklace was imported from Egypt or Syria, and the style of the gold jewelry was also that of the Near East. These objects reflected Greek trade with the more prosperous civilizations of that region, a relationship whose influence on Greece increased as the Dark Age faded in the next century. The most intriguing object from the burial is the terra-cotta chest, which was painted with intricate, precise, and regular designs. (This style, which modern art historians call Geometric, is characteristic of the late Dark Age.) On its top were sculpted five beehivelike urns that are miniatures of granaries (structures for storing grain). If these models were important enough to be buried as objects of special value, we can deduce that actual granaries and the grain they held were precious commodities. This deduction in turn means that by 850 B.C. agriculture had already begun to recover from the devastation of the early Dark Age. Whether the woman owned grain fields we cannot know, but from her sculpted chest we can glimpse the significance of farming for her and her contemporaries. Increased agriculture production in this period accompanied a resurgence in population. Historians cannot determine whether a rise in population led to the raising of more grain, or whether improve-

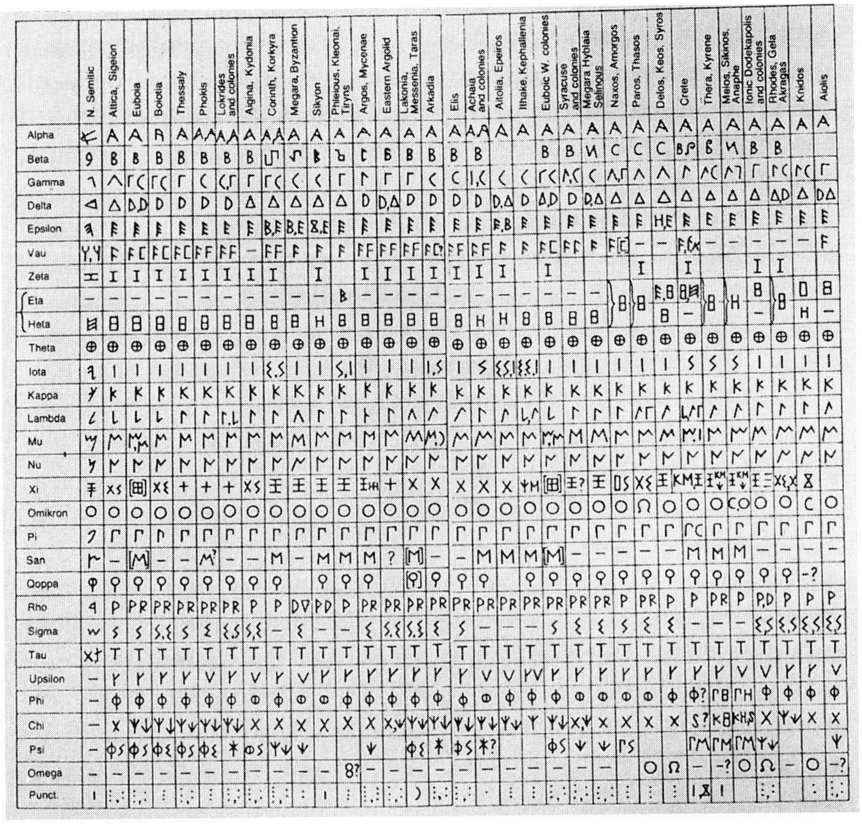

Phoenician and Greek Alphabets
This chart shows how the Greeks imitated the Phoenician alphabet. The Semitic alphabet appears in the first column of letters, followed by sets of letters used by various groups in Greece.

ments in agricultural technology and the cultivation of more fields spurred population growth by increasing the number of people the land could support. These two developments reinforced one another: as the Greeks produced more food, the better-fed population reproduced faster; and as the population grew, more people could produce more food. The repopulation of Greece in the late Dark Age established the demographic conditions under which the new political forms of Greece were to emerge.

The Social Values of Aristocratic Greek Society

People like the couple from Lefkandi and the woman buried with the granary model at Athens constituted the aristocracy that emerged during the later part of the Greek Dark Age. The term *aristocracy* comes from Greek and means "rule of the best"—"the best" in this case referred to the people with the highest social status and the most wealth and political influence. Although aristocrats in this period seem to have controlled a disproportionate share of their communities' wealth and power, their acceptance into the aristocracy was not based on their resources alone. The key to being a proper aristocrat was to be born into a family that the rest of society considered aristocratic. We can only speculate about the various ways in which families might have originally gained this designation and thus became entitled to pass on their status. Some aristocratic families in the Dark Age might have inherited their status as descendants of the most prominent families of the Bronze Age; some might have made themselves aristocrats during the Dark Age by amassing wealth and befriending less fortunate people who were willing to acknowledge their benefactors' superior status in return for material help; and some might have acquired aristocratic status by monopolizing control of essential religious rituals.

Like the agricultural revival and population growth of the late Dark Age, the aristocrats' code of social values became a fundamental component of Greece's emerging political forms. This code underlies the stories told in the *Iliad* and the *Odyssey,* two book-length poems that first began to be written down about the middle of the eighth century B.C., at the very end of the Dark Age. The Greeks had relearned writing as a result of contact with the literate civilizations of the Near East. Sometime between about 950 and 750 B.C. the Greeks modified a Phoenician alphabet to represent the sounds of their own language; the English alphabet used today is based on this Greek version. The Greeks believed that Homer, a blind poet from the Greek region called Ionia (today the western coast of Turkey), composed the *Iliad* and the *Odyssey.* Although Homer may have been the first to put these poems into the form in which we have them today, countless Greek poets, influenced by Near Eastern epic tales, had sung of these stories for centuries, orally transmitting cultural values from one generation to the next. The behavioral code portrayed in these poems reflects Greek aristocratic values before the rise of political systems based on citizenship.

The primary characters in Homer's poems are aristocrats. The men are warriors, such as Achilles, a hero of the *Iliad.* This poem tells part of the legendary story of a Greek army attack on the city of Troy, a stronghold located in northwestern Anatolia. (Although historians have long believed the Trojans were not Greeks, the poems offer no certain clues to their ethnic identity.) In the *Iliad's* representation of the Trojan War, which the Greeks believed occurred four hundred years before Homer's time, Achilles is "the best of the Greeks" because he is an incomparable "doer of deeds and speaker of words." Achilles' overriding concern both in word and in action is with the eternal glory and recognition he can win with his "excellence" (the best translation for *arete,* a word with a range of meanings). Like all aristocrats, Achilles feared the disgrace of failing to live up to the code of excellence. Under the aristocratic code, failure and wrongdoing produced public shame more than private feelings of guilt.

This quest for excellence was a distinctive feature of the aristocratic code of values presented in Homer's poems, and it was pursued by women as well as men. For an aristocratic woman such as Penelope, the wife of Odysseus, the hero of the *Odyssey,* excellence meant preserving her household and property using her intelligence, beauty, social status, and intense fidelity to her husband. This curatorship required great stamina and ingenuity in resisting the demands of her husband's rivals at home while he was away for twenty years, fighting the Trojan War and then sailing home in a journey fraught with danger. In real life the role of aristocratic women was to develop the excellence that Penelope embodied to set themselves apart from ordinary people. A life not spent trying to attain excellence and the fame that accompanied it was considered contemptible.

Excellence as a competitive value for male Greek aristocrats showed up clearly in the Olympic Games, a religious festival in honor of Zeus, king of the Greek gods. The games were held at Zeus's sanctuary at Olympia, in the northwestern Peloponnese (the large peninsula that forms southern Greece), every four years beginning in 776 B.C. During these great celebrations aristocratic men competed in running events and wrestling as individuals, not on national teams as in the modern

Warriors in Training
Young men in Greece trained for war with sports such as javelin and discus throwing.

Olympic Games. The emphasis on physical prowess and fitness, competition, and public recognition by other men corresponded to the ideal of Greek masculine identity as it developed in this period. In a rare departure from the ancient Mediterranean tradition against public nakedness, Greek athletes competed without clothing. Competitions such as horse and chariot racing were added to the Olympic Games later, but the principal event remained a sprint of about two hundred yards, called the *stadion.* Winners originally received no financial prizes, only a garland made from wild olive leaves and the prestige of victory. In later Greek athletic competitions valuable prizes were often awarded. Admission was free to men; women were barred, on pain of death, but they had their own separate festival at Olympia on a different date in honor of Zeus's wife, Hera. Although we know less about the women's games, literary sources report that virgins competed on the Olympic track in a foot race five-sixths as long as the men's *stadion.* In later times professional athletes dominated international games, including the Olympics. They made good livings from appearance fees and prizes won at various games held throughout Greece. The most famous athlete was Milo, from southern Italy. Winner of the Olympic wrestling crown six times beginning in 536 B.C., he was renowned for showy stunts such as holding his breath until his blood expanded his veins so much that he could snap a cord tied around his head.

The Olympic Games originally centered on showcasing the aristocrats' innate superiority to ordinary people, as the fifth-century B.C. poet Pindar made clear in praising a family of victors: "Hiding the nature you are born with is impossible. The seasons rich in their flowers have many times bestowed on you, sons of Aletes [of Corinth], the brightness that victory brings, when you achieved the heights of excellence in the sacred games." The organization of the festival as an event for all Greek aristocrats—the Olympics were pan-Hellenic, that is, open to all Greeks—nevertheless indicates the trend toward communal activity that was under way in Greek society and politics by the mid-eighth century B.C. The sanctuary at Olympia provided a setting for public gatherings, with surrounding space for crowds to assemble. An international truce of several weeks was declared so that competitors and spectators from all Greek communities could travel to and from Olympia in security; wars in progress were put on hold for the duration of the games.

The arrangements for the Olympic games demonstrate that in the eighth century B.C., Greek aristocratic values of individual activity and the pursuit of excellence were beginning to be channeled into a new context appropriate for a changing society. This new regard for communal interests was another important precondition for the creation of Greece's new political forms.

Religion in Greek Myth as the Voice of the Community

Throughout the history of ancient Greece, religion provided the context for almost all communal activity. Sports events, such as the Olympic Games, took place at religious festivals honoring specific deities. War proceeded according to the signs of divine will that civil and military leaders identified in animal sacrifices and in omens derived from such natural occurrences as unusual weather. Sacrifices, the central event of Greek religious rituals, were performed before crowds in the open air on public occasions that involved communal feasting afterward on the sacrificed meat. Greek religion was based on *myths* (Greek for "stories" or "tales") about the gods and goddesses and their relationships to humans. In the eighth century B.C. the Greeks began to write down their myths. The poetry of Hesiod preserved from this period reveals how religious myths, as well as the economic changes and social values of the time, contributed to the feeling of community that underlay the creation of new political structures in Greece.

Hesiod employed myth to reveal the divine origin of justice. His long poem the *Theogony* ("Genealogy of the Gods") details the birth of the race of gods from primeval Chaos ("void" or "vacuum") and Earth, the mother of Sky and numerous other offspring. Hesiod explained that when Sky began to imprison his siblings, Earth persuaded her fiercest son, Kronos, to overthrow him violently because "Sky first contrived to do shameful things." When Kronos later began to swallow up all his own children, Kronos's wife Rhea (who was also his sister) had their son Zeus depose his father by force in retribution for his evil deeds. These vivid stories, which had their origins in Near Eastern myths like those of the

Woman at Altar
Greek women played a role in public and private religious ceremonies. Here a woman in rich clothing pours a libation onto a flaming altar while carrying a religious symbol in her left arm.

Mesopotamian Epic of Creation, carried the message that existence, even for deities, entailed struggle, sorrow, and violence. Even more significant, however, they showed that a concern for justice had been a component of the divine order of the universe from the beginning.

In his poem *Works and Days,* Hesiod identified Zeus as the fount of justice in human affairs, a marked contrast to Homer's portrayal of Zeus as concerned mainly with the fates of his favorite aristocratic warriors. Hesiod presents justice as a divine quality that will assert itself to punish evildoers: "For Zeus ordained that fishes and wild beasts and birds should eat each other, for they have no justice; but to human beings he has given justice, which is far the best." Aristocratic men dominated the distribution of justice in Hesiod's day. They controlled their family members and household servants. Others outside their immediate households became their followers by acknowledging their status as leaders. Because these followers were roughly equal in wealth and status among themselves, they needed a figure of stronger authority to settle their disputes and organize defense against raids or other military threats. In anthropological terms aristocrats operated as chiefs of bands. An aristocratic chief was empowered to settle arguments over property and duties, to oversee the distribution of rewards and punishments, and usually to head the religious rituals deemed essential to the group's security. A chief's power to coerce unwilling members of his band was limited, however. When decisions affecting the entire group had to be made, his leadership depended on his ability to forge a consensus. Hesiod describes how an effective chief exercised leadership: "When his people in their assembly get on the wrong track, he gently sets matters right, persuading them with soft words." In short, a chief could lead his followers only where they were willing to go.

Hesiod reveals that a state of heightened tension had developed between aristocratic chiefs and the peasants (the free proprietors of small farms, who might own a slave or two, oxen to work their fields, and other movable property of value). Their property made peasants the most influential group among the men, ranging from poor to moderately well-off, who made up the bands of followers of aristocratic chiefs in late Dark Age Greece. Assuming the perspective of a peasant farming a small holding, Hesiod insisted that the divine origin of justice should be a warning to "bribe-devouring chiefs," who settled disputes among their followers and neighbors "with crooked judgments." This feeling of outrage commoners evidently felt at not receiving equal treatment served as yet another stimulus for the gradual movement toward new forms of political organization in Greece.

The Creation of the Greek City-State

During the Archaic Age (c. 750–500 B.C.) the Greeks developed the most widespread and influential of their new political forms, the city-state, or polis. *Polis,* from which we derive our word *politics,* is usually translated as *city-state* to emphasize its difference from what we today think of as a city. As in many earlier states in the ancient Near East,

Archaic Greece

the polis included not just an urban center but also countryside for some miles around that various small settlements occupied. Members of the polis lived both in the central town and also in the surrounding villages. Together these people made up a community of citizens constituting a political state, and it was this partnership among citizens that represented the distinctive political characteristic of the polis. Only men had the right to participate in politics, but women still counted as members of the community legally, socially, and religiously. A particular god or goddess, as, for example, Athena at Athens, presided over each polis as protector and patron. Different communities could choose the same deity as their protector; Sparta, Athens's chief rival in later times, also chose Athena as its patron. The members of a polis constituted a religious association obliged to honor the state's patron deity as well as the community's other gods. The community paid homage and respect to the deities through cults, which were regular sets of public religious activities overseen by priests and priestesses and funded by polis members. Animal sacrifices, the central ritual of a city-state's cults, demonstrated the polis members' respect and piety for their patron.

A polis was independent of neighboring *poleis* (plural form of *polis*), and its citizens were politically unified. Never before had a state been organized on the concept of citizenship for all its free inhabitants, even if, as some scholars think, the Greeks were influenced in the organization of the polis by their contact in the eighth century with the states of Phoenicia. Citizenship was a distinctive organizing concept because it assumed (in theory) certain basic levels of legal equality, essentially the expectation of equal treatment under the law—except for women, whose sexual behavior and control of property were governed by different regulations. But the general legal equality the polis provided did not depend on a citizen's wealth. Because a distinguishing social hierarchy characterized the history of the ancient Near East and Greece in the Bronze Age and had once again become common in Greece by the late Dark Age, it is remarkable that a notion of legal equality, no matter how incomplete it may have been in practice, became the basis for the reorganization of Greek society in the Archaic Age. The polis remained the preeminent form of political and social organization in Greece until the beginning of the Roman Empire, eight centuries later. The other most common new form of political organization in Greece was the *ethnos* ("league" or "federation"), a flexible form of association over a broad territory that was itself sometimes composed of city-states.

The most famous ancient analyst of Greek politics and society, the philosopher Aristotle (384–322 B.C.), later insisted the emergence of the polis had been the inevitable result of the forces of nature. "Humans," he said, "are beings who by nature live in a polis." Anyone who existed outside the community of a polis, Aristotle only half-jokingly maintained, must be either a beast or a deity. By "nature," Aristotle meant the combined effect of social and economic forces. But the natural world of Greece, especially its geography, also influenced the creation of this radical new way of organizing human communities.

The Physical Environment of the City-State

The ancient Greeks never constituted a nation in the modern political sense because their independent city-states lacked a unifying organization. They identified with each other culturally, however, because they spoke the same language and worshiped the same deities, although with local variations. Their homeland lay in and around the Aegean Sea, a part of the Mediterranean Sea dotted with numerous islands, both large and small, and flanked on the west by the Balkan peninsula and on the east by the coast of Anatolia.

Regardless of where they lived, most Greeks never traveled very far from home; what few long-distance travelers there were went by sea. Overland transport was slow and expensive because rudimentary dirt paths served as the only roads in the predominantly mountainous terrain where most Greeks lived. Greece's rivers were practically useless as avenues for trade and communication because most of them slowed to a trickle during the many months each year of little or no rainfall. The most plentiful natural resource of the mountains of mainland Greece was timber for building houses and ships. Some deposits of metal ore were also scattered throughout Greek territory, as were clays suitable for pottery and sculpture. Various quarries of fine stone such as marble provided material for special buildings and works of art. The uneven distribution of these resources meant that some areas were considerably richer than others.

Although none of the mountains wrinkling the Greek landscape rose higher than ten thousand feet, their steep slopes separated the city-states. Only 20 to 30 percent of the total land area was arable. The scarcity of level terrain in most areas ruled out the large-scale raising of cattle and horses; pigs, sheep, and goats were the common livestock. The domestic chicken had also been introduced from the Near East by the seventh century B.C. The "Mediterranean" climate (intermittent heavy rain during a few months and hot, dry summers) also limited a farmer's options. Because the amount of annual precipitation varied so much, farming was a precarious business of boom and bust. Farmers mostly grew barley, the cereal staple of the Greek diet. Wine grapes and olives were the other most important crops. Wine diluted with water was the Greeks' preferred beverage; olive oil was the main source of fat in their diet and was also used, for example, as a cleaning agent and a base for perfumes.

So jagged was the coastline of mainland Greece that almost all its communities lay within forty miles of the sea. Their proximity to the Mediterranean Sea allowed Greek entrepreneurs convenient access to one another and to potentially lucrative international trade, especially with Egypt and the Near East. But sea travel meant dangers from pirates and storms. Prevailing winds and fierce gales almost ruled out sailing in winter. Even in calm conditions sailors hugged the coast as much as possible and preferred to put in to shore at night for safety. As Hesiod commented, merchants needing to make a living took to the sea "because an income means life to poor mortals, but it is a terrible fate to die among the waves."

By isolating the city-states and making communication difficult, the mountainous geography of Greece contributed to the tradition of independence, indeed of noncooperation, among the city-states. A single island could be home to multiple city-states; Lesbos, for example, had five. Because few city-states controlled enough arable land to support a large population, communities of only several hundred to several thousand people were the rule even after the rise in the Greek population at the end of the Dark Age. By the fifth century B.C., Athens' population of male citizens numbered in the tens of thousands, but this was a rare exception. Such a large population could be sustained only by the constant importation of food paid for through trade and other revenues.

Economic Revival and Colonization

Some Greeks had emigrated to Ionia as early as the ninth century B.C. Starting around 750 B.C., however, Greeks began to settle much farther from the Greek mainland. Within two hundred years, Greek colonies existed in present-day southern France, Spain, Sicily and southern Italy, North Africa, and along the coast of the Black Sea. Eventually the Greek world encompassed nearly fifteen hundred city-states. (The Greeks established their new form of government wherever they settled.) The revival of international trade in the Mediterranean in this era may have provided the original stimulus for Greeks to venture from their homeland, where the economy was still depressed. Some Greeks with commercial interests, especially in acquiring natural resources such as metal to export back to their lands of origin, moved to foreign settlements, such as those founded in Spain by Phoenicians from Palestine.

Greeks also established trading posts abroad. By 800 B.C. traders from Euboea had already set up commercial contacts with a community on the Syrian coast at a site now called Al Mina. Men wealthy enough to finance risky expeditions by sea ranged far from home in search of metals. The basic strategy of this entrepreneurial commodity trading is described in the *Odyssey,* where the goddess Athena once appears disguised as a metal trader: "I am here . . . with my ship and crew on our way across the wine-dark sea to foreign lands in search of copper; I am carrying iron now." By about 775 B.C., Euboeans, who seem to have been particularly active explorers, had also founded a trading settlement on the island of Ischia, in the Bay of Naples off southern Italy. There they processed iron ore

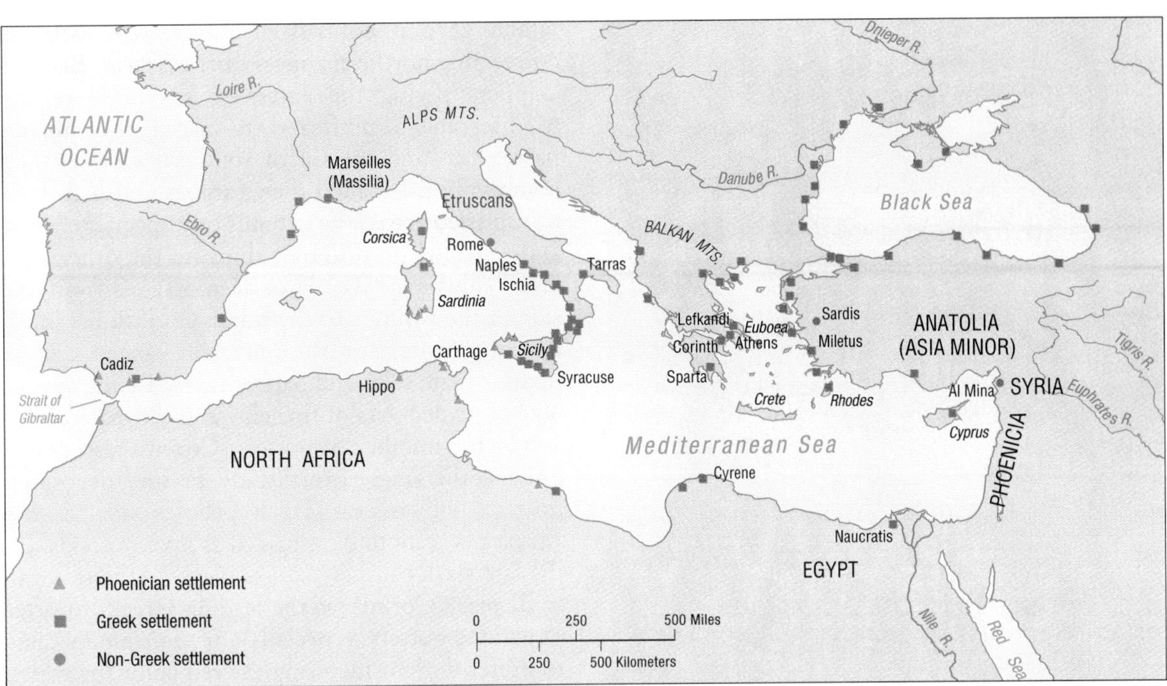

Phoenician and Greek Settlements, c. 800–500 B.C.

imported from the Etruscans, who lived in central Italy. Archaeologists have documented the expanding overseas network of the eighth century B.C. by finding Greek pottery at more than eighty sites outside Greece; for the tenth century, by contrast, only two pots that were carried abroad have been found.

Although commercial interests may have first motivated Greeks to emigrate, the population explosion that had begun in the late Dark Age had by around 750 B.C. caused a severe scarcity of arable land, a condition that induced many more of them to move abroad permanently in the mid-eighth century B.C. Good farming land was the most desirable form of wealth for Greek men, so the shortage caused tension in the male population. Emigration alleviated some of the strain, because landless men often went abroad to acquire their own fields in the new city-states. Sometimes the local inhabitants welcomed the colonists, especially if they settled on previously unoccupied land; sometimes the native peoples greeted them hostilely, and they had to fight for land. Because only males apparently went on these colonizing expeditions, they had to find wives among the locals, either through peaceful negotiation or by kidnapping.

The Greeks' participation in international trade and colonization increased their contact with the peoples of Anatolia and the Near East. They admired and envied these older civilizations for their wealth, such as the gold of the Phrygian kingdom of Midas, and their cultural accomplishments, such as the lively pictures of animals on Near Eastern ceramics, the magnificent temples of Egypt, and the alphabets of the Phoenician cities (which, as we saw, the Greeks adapted for their own use). During the early Dark Age, Greek artists had stopped portraying people or other living creatures, but the pictures they saw on pottery imported from the Near East in the late Dark Age and early Archaic Age inspired them to once again draw figures in their paintings. The style of Near Eastern reliefs and freestanding sculptures also influenced Greek art of the period. Greeks sculpted figures that stood stiffly, staring straight ahead, in imitation of Egyptian statuary. When the improving economy of the later Archaic Age allowed Greeks to revive monumental architecture in stone, many temples for the worship of the gods and goddesses emulated Egyptian architectural designs. In the sixth century B.C. the Greeks began to mint coins,

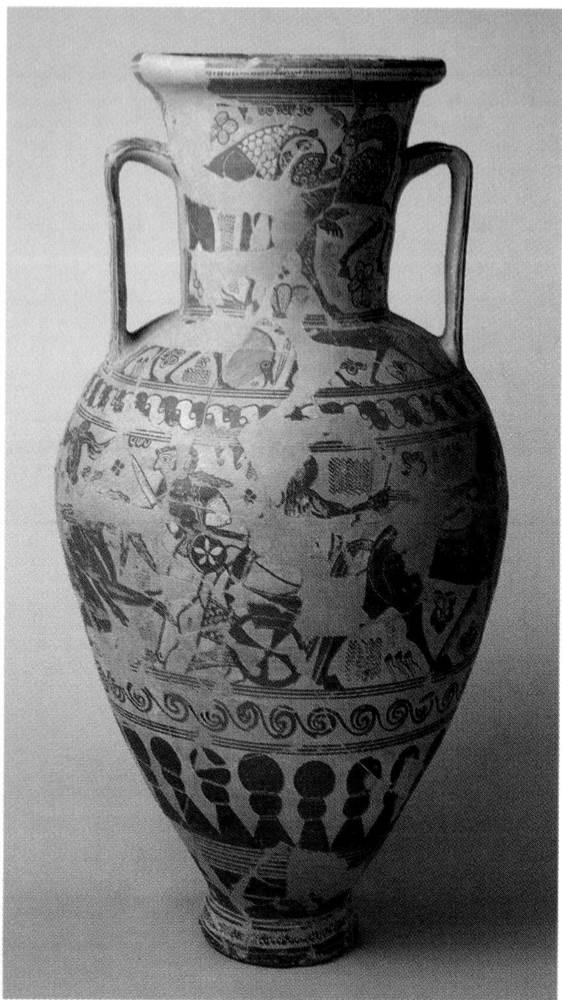

The Reappearance of Figures in Greek Art
Trading voyages brought Greeks of the Archaic Age into contact with the art of the civilizations of the Near East and led them to reintroduce human and animal figures into their own art. This painted vase from the seventh century B.C. shows the hero Heracles heading off to battle a monster.

a technology they learned from the Lydians, who invented coinage in the seventh century B.C. Long after this innovation, however, most economic exchanges involved barter, especially in the Near East. Highly monetized economies took centuries to develop.

Success in competing for international markets affected the fortunes of Greek city-states during this period. Corinth, for example, grew prosperous from ship building and its geographical location, which gave it control of the narrow isthmus connecting northern and southern Greece. Because shippers plying the east-west sea lanes of the Mediterranean preferred to avoid the stormy passage around the tip of southern Greece, they commonly off-loaded their cargoes and had them transported across the isthmus on a special roadbed and reloaded on different ships on the other side. Small ships may even have been dragged from one side of the isthmus to the other. Corinth became a bustling center for shipping and earned a large income from sales and harbor taxes. Taking advantage of its deposits of fine clay and the expertise of a growing number of potters, Corinth also developed a thriving export trade in fine decorated pottery, which non-Greek peoples such as the Etruscans seem to have prized as luxury goods. By the late sixth century B.C., however, Athens began to displace Corinth as the leading Greek exporter of painted pottery, especially after consumers came to prefer designs featuring the red color for which its clay was better suited than Corinth's.

Greeks always solicited approval from their deities before setting out from home, whether for commercial voyages or colonization. The god most frequently consulted about sending out men to colonize was Apollo in his sanctuary at Delphi, a hauntingly beautiful spot in the mountains of central Greece. The Delphic sanctuary began to win international renown in the eighth century B.C. because it housed an oracular shrine in which a prophetess, the Pythia, spoke the will of Apollo in response to visitors' questions. The Delphic oracle functioned for only a few days over nine months of the year, and demand for its services was so high that the sanctuary operators rewarded generous contributors with the privilege of jumping to the head of the line. Most visitors to Delphi consulted the oracle about personal matters such as marriage and having children. The oracle at Delphi continued as a force in Greek international affairs in the centuries to come.

Aristocrats and Common People in the Rise of the City-State

One insurmountable difficulty in ascertaining the reasons city-states began to emerge in Greece around 750 B.C. is that most of the surviving evidence pertains only to Athens, which because of its large population and extensive territory was not a

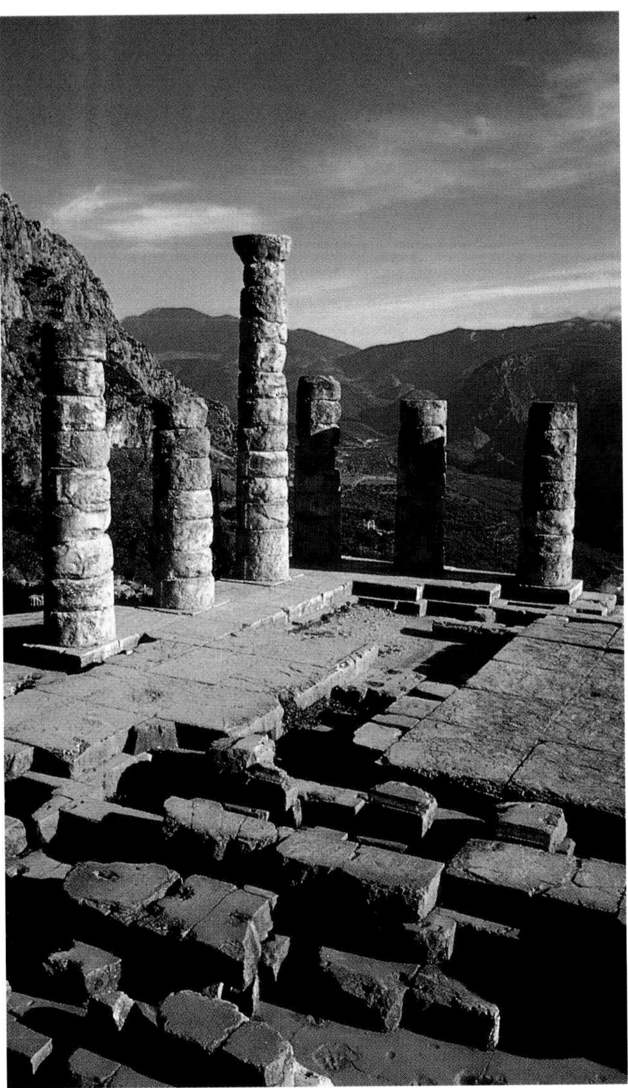

Apollo's Temple at Delphi
The sanctuary of Apollo at Delphi, situated high above a dramatic valley, became an internationally famous oracle. Greeks and others sought advice from the oracle on a wide variety of questions affecting their lives.

typical city-state. But by using the information from Athens and various literary sources and other documents, we can draw some general conclusions about how and why the Greeks broke with the traditional form of political organization that depended on a centralized authority and instead gradually instituted the citizen-based city-states.

The economic revival of the Archaic Age and the population growth in Greece evident by the eighth century B.C. certainly gave momentum to the process. Men who acquired substantial property from success in commerce or agriculture could now demand a greater say in political affairs from the hereditary aristocrats. Theognis of Megara, a sixth-century B.C. poet, gave voice to the aristocrats' distress at the opening of new avenues to social and political influence: ". . . men today prize possessions, and noble men marry into 'bad' [that is, nonaristocratic] families and 'bad' men into noble families. Riches have mixed up lines of breeding . . . and the good breeding of the citizens is becoming obscured." The population increase in this era probably came mostly in the ranks of the poor. Such families raised more children to help farm more land, which had been vacant after the depopulation of the early Dark Age. The growing number of poorer folk apparently resented and reacted against the inequitable treatment they received from aristocratic leaders, who sometimes acted as petty kings in their local territory and dispensed lopsided justice to those with less wealth and power.

For the city-state to function as a political institution in which all free men had a share, nonaristocratic men had to insist on equitable treatment, even if aristocrats were to remain in leadership positions and carry out the policies agreed on by the group. The concept of citizenship responded to that demand. Citizenship above all carried certain legal rights, such as access to courts to resolve disputes, protection against enslavement by kidnapping, and participation in the religious and cultural life of the city-state. It also implied involvement in politics, although the degree to which poor men shared political power varied among the city-states. The right to hold public office, for example, could be limited in some cases to owners of a certain amount of property or wealth. Most notably, citizen status distinguished free men and women from slaves and *metics,* foreigners who had limited legal rights and permission to reside in a city-state that was not their homeland. Thus even the poor had a distinction that set them apart from others. Yet despite the legal guarantees of citizenship, social and economic inequality among male citizens persisted in the city-states.

Women's citizenship was crucial because it identified them as a specific group and gave them social status and legal rights denied slaves and metics. Certain religious cults were reserved for citizen women only. Citizen women were legally protected against being kidnapped and sold into slavery. They also had recourse to the courts in disputes over property, but they could not represent themselves—men spoke for them, a requirement that reveals their subordinate legal status. The traditional paternalism of Greek society, with men acting as "fathers" to regulate the lives of women and safeguard their interests as defined by men, demanded that all women have male guardians to protect them physically and legally. Women received no rights to participate in politics. They were not permitted to attend political assemblies, nor could they vote. They could serve as priestesses, however, and they had access to the initiation rights of the popular cult of Demeter at Eleusis, near Athens. This internationally renowned cult may have served as a sort of safety valve for the pressures created by life in Greek city-states, because it promised protection from evil and a better fate in the afterworld for everyone, regardless of class or gender.

The Poor as Citizens

Despite the limited equality of the Greek city-state, especially in practice, this new form of political organization nevertheless represented a significant break with the past. One of the most striking developments in the polis was the extension of at least some political rights to the poor. We cannot be certain why poor men were allowed a say in political matters. For a long time, historians attributed the general widening of political rights in the city-state to a so-called hoplite revolution, but recent research has undermined the plausibility of this theory. *Hoplites* were infantrymen who wore metal body armor, and they constituted the main strike force of the militias that defended each city-state in this period. The hoplites marched into combat shoulder to shoulder in a rectangular formation called a *phalanx*. Staying in line and working as part of the group were the secrets to successful phalanx tactics. In the words of the seventh-century B.C. poet Archilochus, a good hoplite was "a short man firmly placed upon his legs, with a courageous heart, not to be uprooted from the spot where he plants his feet." Greeks had fought in phalanxes for a long time, but until the eighth century B.C. only aristocrats and a few of their nonaristocratic followers could afford the equipment to serve as hoplites. In the eighth century B.C., however, a growing number of men had become prosperous enough to buy metal weapons, especially because the use of iron had made them more readily available. Presumably these new hoplites, because they bought their own equipment and trained hard to learn phalanx tactics to defend their community, felt they should also enjoy political rights. According to the theory of a hoplite revolution, these new hoplites forced the aristocrats to share political power by threatening to refuse to fight, which would cripple the community's military defense.

The theory correctly assumes that new hoplites had the power to demand and receive a voice in politics. But the hoplites were not poor. How, then, did poor men win political rights? If contributing to the city-state's defense as a hoplite was the only grounds for meriting the political rights of citizenship, the aristocrats and the hoplites had no obvious reason to grant poor men anything. Yet poor men did become politically empowered in many city-states, with some variations. All male citizens, regardless of their wealth, eventually were entitled to attend, speak in, and vote in the communal assemblies that made policy decisions for the city-states. The hoplite revolution fails to explain completely the development of the city-state mostly because it cannot account for the extension of rights to poor men. Furthermore, not many men were wealthy enough to afford hoplite armor until the middle of the seventh century B.C., well after the initial formation of the city-state.

No satisfactory alternative or extension to the theory of hoplite revolution as the reason for the rise of city-states yet exists. The laboring free poor—the workers in agriculture, trade, and crafts—contributed to the city-state's economic strength, but it is hard to see how their value as laborers could have been translated into political rights. The better-off elements in society certainly did not extend the rights of citizenship to the poor out of any romanticized vision of poverty as spiritually noble. As one contemporary put it, "Money is the man; no poor man ever counts as good or honorable." Perhaps tyrants (sole rulers who seized power unconstitutionally in some city-states) boosted the status of poor men. Tyrants could have granted greater political rights to poor or disfranchised men as a means of marshaling popular support. Another, more speculative possibility is that the aristocrats and hoplites had simply become less cohesive as a political group, thereby weakening opposition to the growing idea of poor men that it was unjust to be excluded from political participation. According to this view, when the poor agitated for power the aristocrats and hoplites had no united front to oppose them, making compromise necessary to prevent destructive civil unrest.

In any case the hallmark of politics in developed Greek city-states was the practice of citizen men making decisions communally—as a whole in democratic states and to a lesser extent in oligarchies (the Greek word *oligarchy* means "rule by the few"). Aristocrats continued to influence, sometimes dominate, Greek politics even after the emergence of city-states. But the unprecedented political power nonaristocratic men came to wield in city-states constituted the most remarkable feature of the political organization of Greek society in the Archaic Age.

The Emergence of Slavery in Greece

The only evidence of slavery in the Dark Age, which appears in the poetry of Homer and Hesiod, reveals complex relationships among free and unfree people. Some people captured in war evidently became chattel slaves, completely dominated by their masters. Other dependent people described in the poems seem more like inferior members of their owners' households. They lived under virtually the same conditions as their superiors and had families of their own. Slavery apparently had its own dismal hierarchy during this time.

Chattel slavery became widespread in Greece only after about 600 B.C. Eventually slaves became cheap enough that people of even moderate means could afford one or two. But even wealthy Greek landowners never acquired gangs of hundreds of slaves such as those who kept up Rome's water system under the Roman Empire. Maintaining a large number of slaves year-round in ancient Greece would have been uneconomical because the crops cultivated required short periods of intense labor punctuated by long stretches of inactivity. Slaveowners did not want to feed and house slaves who had no work.

By the fifth century B.C. slaves accounted for up to one-third of the total population in some city-states. Even so, most labor was still performed by small landowners and their families themselves, sometimes hiring free workers. (The special system of slavery in Sparta was a rare exception to this situation.) Chattel slaves did all kinds of labor. Household slaves, often women, had the least dangerous existence. They cleaned, cooked, fetched water from public fountains, helped the wife with the weaving, watched the children, accompanied the husband as he did the marketing, and performed other domestic chores. Yet they could not refuse if their masters demanded sexual favors. Slaves who worked in small manufacturing businesses, such as those of potters or metalworkers, and slaves who worked on farms often labored alongside their owners. Rich landowners, however, might appoint a slave supervisor to oversee the work of their field slaves while they remained in town. Slaves who worked in the narrow, landslide-prone tunnels of Greece's few silver and gold mines had the worst lot. Many died doing this dangerous, dark, and backbreaking job.

Many slaves were war captives; others were non-Greeks pirates or raiders had seized from the rough regions to the north and east of Greek territory. The fierce bands in these areas would also capture and sell each other to slave dealers. Greeks also enslaved fellow Greeks, especially those defeated in war (who were not members of the same city-state as their owners). Rich families prized Greek slaves with some education because they could be used as tutors for children—no schools existed in this period, and few people learned how to read and write.

Some slaves worked as public slaves; they were owned by the city-state rather than an individual. They had a measure of independence, living on their own and performing specialized tasks. In Athens, for example, public slaves eventually certified the authenticity of the city-state's coinage. Temple slaves "belonged" to the deity of the sanctuary, for which they worked as servants. Some female temple slaves served as sacred prostitutes, and their earnings helped support the sanctuary.

Slaveowners could punish, even kill, their slaves with impunity. But beating working slaves severely enough to cripple them or executing able-bodied slaves made no economic sense—in essence the master would be destroying part of his property. For this reason such treatment was probably limited. Under the best conditions, household slaves with humane masters might live lives free of violent punishment. They might even be allowed to join their owners' families on excursions and attend religious rituals. However, without the right to a family of their own, without property, and without legal or political rights, they remained alienated from regular society. In the words of an ancient commentator, chattel slaves lived lives of "work, punishment, and food." Although their labor helped maintain the economy of Greek society, it rarely benefited them. Yet despite the misery of their condition, Greek slaves—outside Sparta—almost never revolted on a large scale, perhaps because they were of too many different origins and nationalities and too scattered to organize. Sometimes owners manumitted their slaves, and some promised freedom at a future date to encourage their slaves to work hard. Freed slaves did not become citizens in Greek city-states but instead mixed into the population of metics. They were still expected to help out their former masters when called upon.

The creation of citizenship as a category to define membership in the exclusive group of people constituting a polis inevitably highlighted the contrast between those included in the category of citizens and those outside it, especially slaves. Freedom from control by others was a necessary precondition to become a citizen with political rights, which in the city-states meant being a free-born adult male. The strongest contrast citizenship produced, therefore, was that between free and unfree. In this way, the development of a clear idea of personal freedom in the formation of the city-state as a new political form may ironically have encouraged the complementary development of chattel slavery in the Archaic Age. The rise in economic activity in this period probably also encouraged the importation of slaves by increasing the demand for labor. In any case, slavery as it developed in the Archaic Age reduced unfree persons to a state of absolute dependence; they were the property of their owners. As Aristotle later put it, slaves were "living tools."

Archaic Elegance in Sculpture
This damaged statue from the late Archaic period shows the elegant and colorful clothing, elaborate hairstyle, and slight smile that distinguished sculptural portraiture of women in this era. The statue would have been dedicated to a divinity.

Family Life in the City-State

The emergence of widespread slavery in the city-state made households bigger and added new responsibilities for women, especially rich women, whose lives were devoted to maintaining their households. While their husbands farmed, participated in politics, and met with their male friends, wives managed the household (*oikonomia*, Greek for "economics"). They were expected to raise the children, supervise the preservation and preparation of food, keep the family's financial accounts, weave cloth for clothing, direct the work of the household slaves, and see to them when they were ill. Women's work ensured the family's economic

An Ancient Greek Wedding Procession
This painted vase depicts the procession that brought the bride to the groom's house, the central event in an ancient Greek wedding.

self-sufficiency and allowed the male citizens the time to participate in public life.

Poor women worked outside the home, often as small-scale merchants in the public market that occupied the center of every settlement. Only in Sparta did women have the freedom to participate in athletic training along with men. In all other city-states women engaged in public life solely at funerals, state festivals, and religious rituals. Women could perform public duties in various official cults; for example, women officiated as priestesses in more than forty cults in Athens by the fifth century B.C. Women holding these posts often had considerable prestige, practical benefits such as a salary paid by the state, and greater freedom of movement in public.

When women married they became legal wards of their husbands, as they previously had been of their fathers. Marriages were arranged by men. A woman's guardian—her father, or if he were dead, her uncle or her brother—would commonly betroth her to another man's son while she was still a child, perhaps as young as five. The betrothal was an important public event conducted in the presence of witnesses. The guardian on this occasion repeated the phrase that expressed the primary aim of marriage: "I give you this woman for the plowing [procreation] of legitimate children." The marriage itself customarily took place when the girl was in her early teens and the groom ten to fifteen years older. Hesiod advised a man to marry a virgin in the fifth year after her menarche, when he himself was "not much younger than thirty and not much older." A legal marriage consisted of the bride moving to her husband's house; the procession to his house served as the ceremony. The woman brought to the marriage a dowry of property (perhaps land yielding an income, if she were wealthy) and personal possessions that formed part of the new household's assets and could be inherited by her children. Her husband was legally obliged to preserve the dowry and to return it in case of a divorce. Divorce procedures had more to do with power than with law: a husband could expel his wife from his home; a wife, in theory, could leave her husband on her own initiative to return to the guardianship of her male relatives. However, her husband could force her to stay. Except in certain cases in Sparta, monogamy was the rule in ancient Greece, as was a nuclear family (that is, husband, wife, and children living together without other relatives in the same house). Citizen men could have sexual relations without penalty with slaves, foreign concubines, female prostitutes, or willing preadult citizen males. Citizen women had no such sexual freedom, and adultery carried harsh penalties for both parties, except at Sparta.

Greek citizen men placed Greek citizen women under their guardianship both to regulate marriage and procreation and to maintain family property. This paternalistic attitude allowed Greek men to control human reproduction and consequently the distribution of property, an urgent concern in the reduced economic circumstances of the Dark Age. According to Greek mythology, women were a necessary evil. Zeus supposedly created the first woman, Pandora, as a punishment for men in his vendetta against the demigod Prometheus for giving fire to humans. Pandora subsequently loosed "evils and diseases" into the previously trouble-free world by removing the lid from the box the gods had filled for her. Many

Greek men probably shared Hesiod's opinions about women: he saw the female sex as "big trouble" but thought any man who refused to marry to escape the "troublesome deeds of women" would come to "destructive old age" all alone, with no heirs. In other words, a man needed a wife so he could sire children who would care for him during his waning years and so his descendants would preserve his holdings after his death. Although Greek citizen women were subordinate to men by custom and by law, their lives incorporated social and religious duties essential to the welfare of their own families and of their city-state.

Oligarchy, Tyranny, and Democracy in the City-States

Although the Greek city-states differed in size and natural resources, they shared certain fundamental political institutions and social traditions: citizenship, slavery, the legal disadvantages and political exclusion of women, and the continuing influence of aristocrats in society and politics. During the Archaic Age, however, these common traits mutated in strikingly different ways in the various city-states. In some oligarchic city-states, such as Sparta, only a few men exercised meaningful political power. Tyrants dominated sporadically in other city-states. Tyranny, passed down from father to son, existed at various times throughout the Greek world, from city-states on the island of Sicily in the west to Samos off the coast of Ionia in the east. Still other city-states instituted early forms of democracy ("rule by the people"), allowing all male citizens to participate in governing. Although some assemblies of men had influenced kings in certain early states in the ancient Near East, never had any group of people been invested with the amount of political power the Greek democracies gave their male citizens. The Athenians established Greece's most renowned democracy, in which male citizens enjoyed individual freedom unprecedented in the ancient world. These varied paths of political and social development illustrate the great challenge Greeks faced as they struggled to construct new ways of life during the Archaic Age. In the course of this endeavor they also began to formulate different ways of understanding the physical world, their relations to it, and their relationships with each other.

The Political Evolution of Sparta

Sparta was an oligarchy in which military readiness overrode all other concerns. During the Archaic Age, this city-state developed the mightiest infantry force in Greece. Spartans were renowned for their self-discipline—a cultural value that manifested their militaristic bent. Sparta's easily defended location—nestled on a narrow north-south plain between rugged mountain ranges in the southeastern Peloponnese, in a region called Laconia—gave it a secure base. Sparta had access to the sea through a harbor situated some twenty-five miles south of its urban center, but this harbor opened onto a dangerous stretch of the Mediterranean whipped by treacherous winds and currents. Thus enemies could not threaten the Spartans by sea; this relative isolation from the sea kept the Spartans from becoming adept sailors. Their interests and their strength lay on the land.

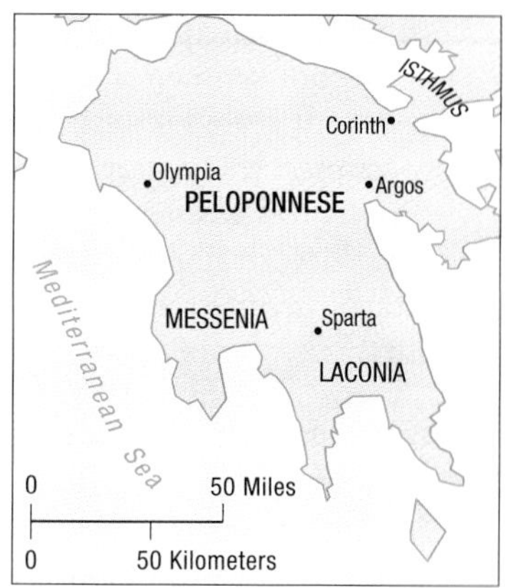

The Peloponnese

The Greeks believed the Spartans emigrated from central Greece and conquered the indigenous inhabitants of Laconia and settled in at least four small villages, two of which apparently dominated the others. These early settlements later joined and formed the core of what eventually became the city-state of Sparta. The Greeks called this process of political unification, in which most people continued to live in their original villages even after one village began to serve as the center of the new city-state, *synoecism* ("union of households"). One apparent result of the compromises required to forge Spartan unity was the retention of two hereditary military leaders of high prestige, the kings. These kings, perhaps originally the leaders of the two dominant villages, served as the religious heads of Sparta and commanders of its army. Their power to make decisions and set policy was not absolute, however, because they operated not as pure monarchs but as leaders of the oligarchic institutions that governed the Spartan city-state. Rivalry between the two royal families periodically led to fierce disputes. Because having two supreme military commanders paralyzed the Spartan army when the kings disagreed on strategy in the middle of a military campaign, the Spartans eventually decided that the army would be commanded by only one king at a time.

The "few" who made policy in Sparta were a group of twenty-eight men over sixty years old, joined by the two kings. This group of thirty, called the *gerousia* ("council of old men"), formulated proposals that were submitted to an assembly of free adult males. This assembly had only limited power to amend the proposals put before it; mostly it was expected to approve the council's plans. Rejections were rare because the council retained the right to withdraw a proposal when the reaction to it in the assembly foreshadowed a negative vote. "If the people speak crookedly," according to Spartan tradition, "the elders and the leaders of the people shall be withdrawers [of the proposal]." The council could then resubmit the proposal later, after marshaling support for its passage.

A board of five annually elected *ephors* ("overseers") counterbalanced the influence of the kings and the *gerousia.* Chosen from the adult male citizens at large, the ephors convened the *gerousia* and the assembly, and they exercised considerable judicial powers of judgment and punishment. They could even bring charges against a king and imprison him until his trial. The creation of the board of ephors diluted the political power of the oligarchical *gerousia* and the kings; the ephors' job was to ensure the supremacy of law. The Athenian Xenophon later reported:

> *All men rise from their seats in the presence of the king, except for the ephors. The ephors on behalf of the polis and the king on his own behalf swear an oath to each other every month: the king swears that he will exercise his office according to the established laws of the polis, and the polis swears that it will preserve his kingship undisturbed if he abides by his oath.*

The Spartans demanded obedience to the law; laws were their guide for proper behavior in all matters. When the ephors entered office, for example, they issued an official proclamation to the men of Sparta: "Shave your moustache and obey the laws." The Spartan law-based political system evolved from about 800 to 600 B.C. A Spartan leader named Lycurgus is credited with reforming early Spartan laws, but the dates and nature of his changes remain unknown. The Spartans believed he had consulted the oracle of Apollo at Delphi to receive the laws from the gods. They called the gods' response the Rhetra ("spoken laws"). Unlike other Greeks, the Spartans never wrote down their laws. Instead they preserved their system from generation to generation with a unique, highly structured way of life based on a particular economic foundation.

The Economic Foundation of Spartan Militarism

The distinctiveness of the Spartans' way of life was fundamentally a reaction to their living in the midst of people whom they had conquered in war and enslaved, but who greatly outnumbered them. To maintain their superiority, Spartan men turned themselves into a society of vigilant soldiers. They accomplished this transformation by radically restructuring traditional family life and enforcing strict adherence to all the laws. Through constant, daily reinforcement of their strict code of values, the Spartans ensured their survival against the enemies they had created by subjugating their neighbors. The seventh-century B.C. poet Tyrtaeus, whose verses exemplify the high quality of the poetry produced before Sparta's military culture began to devalue and exclude such achievements, expressed that code:

> *I would never remember or mention in my work any man for his speed afoot or wrestling skill, not if he was huge and strong as a Cyclops or could run faster than the North Wind, nor more handsome than Tithonus or richer than Midas or Cinyras, nor more kingly than Pelops, or had speech more honeyed than Adrastus, not even if he possessed every glory—not unless he had the strength of a warrior in full rush.*

The supreme male value was martial courage.

Some of the conquered inhabitants of Laconia continued to live in self-governing communities.

These so-called *perioikoi* ("those who live round about") were required to serve in the Spartan army and pay taxes, but they lacked citizen rights. Perhaps because they retained their personal freedom and property, the *perioikoi* never rebelled against Spartan control. Far different was the fate of the conquered people who ended up as *helots* (derived from the Greek word for "capture"). Later commentators described the helots as "between slave and free" because they were not owned by individual Spartans but rather belonged to the whole community, which alone could free them. Helots had a semblance of family life because they were expected to produce children to maintain their population. They labored as farmers and household slaves so Spartan citizens would not have to do such "demeaning" work. Spartan men in fact wore their hair very long to show they were "gentlemen" rather than laborers, for whom long hair was inconvenient.

When the arable land of Laconia, which was held predominantly by aristocrats, proved too limited to support the citizen population of Sparta, the Spartans attacked their Greek neighbors to the west, the Messenians. In the First (c. 730–710 B.C.) and Second (c. 640–630 B.C.) Messenian Wars, the Spartan army captured the territory of Messenia, which amounted to 40 percent of the Peloponnese, and reduced the Messenians to helots. With the addition of the tens of thousands of people in Messenia, the total helot population now more than outnumbered that of Sparta, whose male citizens at this time probably numbered between eight thousand and ten thousand. The Messenians' despair is reflected in their legend of King Aristodemus, who sacrificed his beloved daughter to the gods of the underworld in an attempt to enlist their aid against the invading Spartans. When his campaign of resistance at last failed, in grief he slew himself on her grave. Deprived of their freedom and their city-state, the Messenian helots were ever after on the lookout for a chance to revolt against their Spartan overlords.

In their private lives, helots could keep some personal possessions and practice their religion, as could slaves generally in Greece. Publicly, however, helots lived under the constant threat of officially sanctioned violence. Every year the ephors formally declared war between Sparta and the helots, allowing any Spartan to kill a helot without any civil penalty or fear of offending the gods by unsanctioned murder. By beating the helots frequently, forcing them to get drunk in public as an object lesson to young Spartans, making them wear dogskin caps, and generally humiliating them, the Spartans consistently emphasized the "otherness" of the helots. In this way Spartans erected a moral barrier between themselves and the helots to justify their harsh abuse of fellow Greeks.

Their labor made helots valuable to the Spartans. In addition to farming the plots of land the state allotted to individual Spartan households for their sustenance and working as household servants, by the fifth century B.C., Laconian and Messenian helots alike also accompanied Spartan hoplite warriors on the march, carrying their heavy gear and armor. In the words of Tyrtaeus, helots worked "like donkeys exhausted under heavy loads; they lived under the painful necessity of having to give their masters half the food their ploughed land bore." This compulsory rent of 50 percent of everything produced by the helots working on each family's assigned plot was supposed to amount to seventy measures of barley each year to the male master of the household and twelve to his wife, along with an equivalent amount of fruit and other produce. In all, this food was enough to support six or seven people. Because Spartan men did not have to work their own land, they devoted themselves to full-time training for war. Contrasting the freedom of Spartan citizens from ordinary work with the lot of the helots, the later Athenian Critias commented, "Laconia is the home of the freest of the Greeks, and of the most enslaved."

The Structured Life of Spartans

From childhood on, life in Sparta revolved around military preparedness. Boys lived at home only until their seventh year, when they were sent to live in communal barracks with other males until they were thirty. They spent most of their time exercising, hunting, training with weapons, and being acculturated to Spartan values by listening to tales of bravery and heroism at the common meals presided over by older men. Discipline was strict, to prepare young males for the hard life of a soldier on campaign. For example, the boys were not allowed to speak at will. They were also underfed purposely so they would learn stealth by stealing food. (If they were caught, punishment and disgrace followed immediately.) One famous Spartan tale taught how seriously boys were supposed to fear such failure: having successfully stolen a fox, which he was hiding under his clothing, a Spartan youth died because he let the panicked animal rip out his insides rather than be detected in the theft. By the Classical Age, older boys were dispatched to live in the wilds for a period as members of the "secret band" whose job it was to murder any helots who seemed likely to foment rebellion. Spartan men who could not survive the tough conditions of their childhood training fell into social disgrace and were not certified as Equals, the official name for adult males entitled to full citizen rights of participation in politics and to the respect of the community. Only the sons of the royal family were exempted from this training, perhaps to avoid a potential social crisis if a king's son failed to stay the course.

Each Equal had to gain entry to a group that dined together at common meals, in a so-called common mess, each of which had about fifteen members. The new member was admitted on the condition that he contribute a regular amount of barley, cheese, figs, condiments, and wine to the mess from the produce provided by the helots working on his family plot. Some meat was apparently contributed too, because Spartan cuisine was infamous for a black, bloody broth of pork condemned as practically inedible by other Greeks. Perhaps it was concocted from the wild boars Spartan men loved to hunt, an activity for which messmates were formally excused from the compulsory communal meals. If any member failed to keep up his contributions, he was expelled from the mess and lost his full citizenship rights. The experience of spending so much time in these common messes schooled Sparta's young men in the values of their society. There they learned to call all older men "father" to emphasize that their primary loyalty was to the group and not to their genetic families. There they were chosen to be the special favorites of males older than themselves to build bonds of affection, including physical love, for others at whose side they would have to march into deadly battle. There they learned to take the rough joking of army life for which Sparta was well known. In short, the common mess took the place of a boy's family and school when he was growing up and remained his main social environment once he reached adulthood. Its function was to mold and maintain his values consistent with the demands of the one honorable occupation for Spartan men: an obedient soldier. Tyrtaeus enshrined the Spartan male ideal in his poetry: "Know that it is good for the polis and the whole people when a man takes his place in the front row of warriors and stands his ground without flinching."

Spartan women were known throughout the Greek world for their relative freedom. Some Greeks thought it scandalous that Spartan girls exercised with boys while wearing scanty outfits. Spartan women were supposed to use the freedom from labor provided by the helot system to keep themselves physically fit to bear healthy children and to raise them as strict upholders of Spartan values. The male ideal for Spartan women appears in the late seventh century B.C. in the work of Alcman, a poet who wrote songs female and male choruses performed at Spartan civic and religious occasions. The dazzling leader of a women's chorus, he wrote, "stands out as if among a herd of cows someone placed a firmly-built horse with ringing hooves, a prizewinner from winged dreams."

Although Sparta deliberately banned money to discourage the accumulation of material goods, women, like men, could own land privately. More and more land came into the hands of women in later Spartan history because the male population declined through losses in war, especially during the Classical Age. Spartan women with property enjoyed special status, because Spartan law forbade dividing the land originally allotted to a family. This law meant that in a family with more than one son, all the land went to the eldest son. Fathers with multiple sons therefore needed to find their younger sons brides who had inherited land and property from their family because they had no brother surviving. Otherwise, younger sons might fall into dire poverty.

With their husbands so rarely at home, women directed the households, which included servants, daughters, and sons until they left for their communal training. As a result, Spartan women exercised more power in the household than did women elsewhere in Greece. Until he was thirty a Spartan husband was not allowed to live with his family, and even newlywed men were expected to pay only short visits to their wives by sneaking into their own houses at night. This Spartan custom was not the only one other Greeks found bizarre. Spartans also had no prohibition against adultery, and, if all parties agreed, a woman could have children by a man other than her husband.

Spartan women were free from some of the restrictions imposed on women in other Greek city-states so they could more easily fulfill their basic function: to produce manpower for the Spartan army. By the Classical Age the ongoing problem of producing enough children to keep the Spartan citizen population from shrinking had grown acute. Men were legally required to get married, with bachelors subjected to fines and public ridicule. Women who died in childbirth were the only Spartans allowed to have their names placed on their tombstones, a mark of honor for their sacrifice to the state.

All Spartan citizens were expected to put service to their city-state before personal concerns because Sparta's survival was continually threatened by its own economic foundation, the great mass of helots. Because Sparta's well-being depended on the systematic exploitation of these enslaved Greeks, its entire political and social system required a staunch militarism and conservative values. Change meant danger. Although the Spartans institutionalized equality in the form of the common mess, they denied social and political equality to ordinary male citizens, an inevitable inequality in an oligarchy. Whatever other Greeks may have thought of the particulars of the Spartan system, they admired the Spartans' unswerving respect for their laws as a guide to life in hostile surroundings, albeit of their own making.

Tyranny in the City-States

Opposition to aristocratic and oligarchic domination brought the first Greek tyrants to power (although never in Sparta). The most famous early tyrant arose at Corinth around 657 B.C. in protest to the rule of the aristocratic family called the Bacchiads. Under Bacchiad rule in the eighth and early seventh centuries B.C., Corinth had blossomed into the most economically advanced city in archaic Greece. The Corinthians had progressed so far in naval engineering, for example, that other Greeks contracted with them to have ships built. Corinth's strong fleet helped the Bacchiads in founding overseas colonies at Corcyra in northwest Greece and Syracuse on Sicily, city-states that would themselves become major naval powers.

The Bacchiads fell into disfavor despite the city's prosperity, because they ruled violently. Cypselus, an aristocrat whose mother was a Bacchiad, readied himself to take power by becoming popular with the masses: "he became one of the most admired of Corinth's citizens because he was courageous, prudent, and helpful to the people, unlike the oligarchs in power, who were insolent and violent," according to a later historian. Cypselus engineered the overthrow of Bacchiad rule with popular support and a favorable oracle from Delphi. He then ruthlessly suppressed rival aristocrats, but his popularity remained so high that he could govern without the protection of a bodyguard. Corinth added to its economic strength during Cypselus's rule by exporting large quantities of fine pottery, especially to markets in Italy and Sicily. Cypselus founded additional colonies along the sailing route to the western Mediterranean to promote Corinthian trade in that direction.

When Cypselus died in 625 B.C. his son Periander succeeded him. Periander aggressively continued Corinth's economic expansion by founding colonies on the coasts both northwest and northeast of Greek territory to increase trade with the interior regions there, which were rich in timber and precious metals. He also pursued commercial contacts with Egypt, an interest commemorated in the Egyptian name Psammetichus he gave to one of his sons. The city's prosperity encouraged crafts, art, and architecture to flourish. The foundations of the great stone temple to Apollo begun in this period can still be seen. Unlike his father, however, Periander lost popular support by ruling harshly. He kept his power until his death in 585 B.C., but the hostility that persisted against him led to the overthrow of his son and successor, Psammetichus, within a short time. The opponents of tyranny thereupon installed a government based on a board of eight magistrates and a council of eighty men.

Greek tyranny represented a distinctive type of rule for several reasons. Although tyrants were by definition rulers who usurped power by force rather than inheriting it like legitimate kings, they

The Archaic Temple of Apollo at Corinth
This Doric-style building dating to the sixth century B.C. *is one of the earliest surviving stone temples. The rocky acropolis of Corinth looms in the background.*

too established family dynasties to maintain their tyranny. Also, the tyrants were usually aristocrats, or at least near-aristocrats, who rallied support for their coups among nonaristocrats. In city-states where landless men may have lacked full citizenship or felt substantially disfranchised in political life, tyrants may have garnered backing by extending citizenship and other privileges to these groups. Moreover, tyrants usually preserved the existing laws and political institutions of their city-states.

As at Corinth, most tyrannies needed to cultivate support among the masses of their city-states to remain in power because their armies were composed primarily of commoners. The dynasty of tyrants on the island of Samos in the eastern Aegean Sea, who came to power about 540 B.C., built enormous public works to benefit their city-state and provide employment. They began constructing a temple to Hera meant to be the largest in the Greek world, and they dramatically improved the urban water supply by excavating a great tunnel connected to a distant spring. This marvel of engineering, with a channel eight feet high, ran for nearly a mile through a 900-foot-high mountain. Later tyrannies in city-states on Sicily similarly graced their cities with beautiful temples and public buildings.

By working in the interests of their peoples, some tyrannies, like that founded by Cypselus, maintained their popularity for decades. Other tyrants experienced bitter opposition from aristocrats jealous of the tyrant's power or provoked civil war by ruling brutally and inequitably. The poet Alcaeus of the city-state of Mytilene on the island of Lesbos in the northeastern Aegean, himself a rebellious aristocrat, described such strife around 600 B.C.: "Let's forget our anger; let's quit our heart-devouring strife and civil war, which some god has stirred up among us, ruining the people but bestowing the glory on our tyrant for which he prays." Although today the English word *tyrant* labels a brutal or unwanted leader, tyrants in archaic Greece did not always fit that description. Greeks evaluated tyrants based on their behavior, opposing the ruthless and violent ones but welcoming the fair and helpful ones.

The Early Struggle for Democracy at Athens

Greeks explained significant historical changes, such as the founding of communities or the codification of law, as the work of an individual "inventor" from the distant past. The Athenians traced back the origins of their city-state to a single man. Athenian legends credited Theseus with founding the polis of Athens by the synoecism of villages in Attica, the name given to the peninsula that formed the territory of the Athenian city-state. Because Attica had several ports along its coast, the Athenians were much more oriented to seafaring than were the landlocked Spartans. Theseus made an appropriate mythical founder for Athens: he was described as a traveling adventurer, sailing, for example, to Crete to defeat the Minotaur, a cannibalistic monster, half human and half bull. Theseus embodied the characteristics Athenians valued: courage, adventurousness, and fairness.

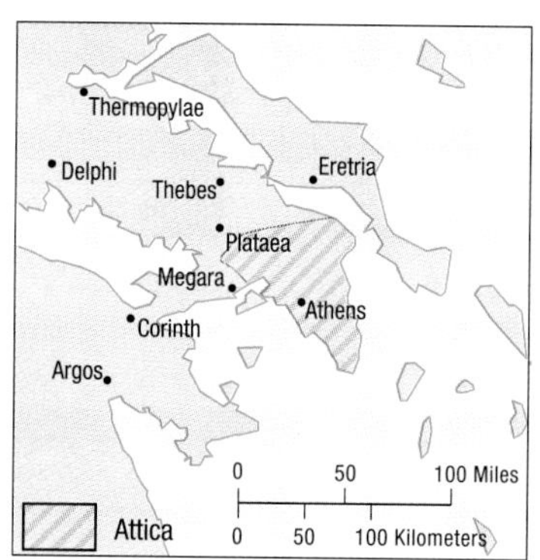

Attica and Central Greece

Unlike most other important sites inhabited in the Mycenaean period, Athens had not suffered catastrophic destruction at the end of the Bronze Age. Nevertheless, its population shrank in the Early Dark Age, which depressed its economy. By around 850 B.C., however, archaeological evidence shows that the Athenian agricultural economy was reviving. As economic conditions improved in the early Archaic Age, the population of Attica apparently expanded at a phenomenal rate from about 800 to 700 B.C., the free peasants constituting the fastest growing segment of the population. The free peasants evidently began to insist on having a say in making Athenian policies because they felt justice demanded at least limited political equality. Some of these small landowners became wealthy enough to afford hoplite armor, and these men probably pressed the aristocrats who had previously ruled Athens as a relatively broad oligarchy for concessions. Because rivalries among the aristocrats prevented them from uniting to oppose these demands, they had to respond to these pressures to ensure the allegiance of the hoplites, on whom Athenian military strength depended.

By the late seventh century B.C., Athens's male citizens—rich, middle class, and poor—had established the beginnings of a limited form of democratic government. Determining why they moved strongly toward democracy instead of, for example, a narrow oligarchy like Sparta's remains difficult. Two factors perhaps encouraged the incipient democracy at Athens: rapid population growth, and a rough sense of egalitarianism among male citizens that survived the frontierlike conditions of the early Dark Age, when most people had shared the same meager existence. But these conditions affected all of Greece in the Archaic Age. Why then did not all the other city-states evolve into democracies? Perhaps the rapidness of population growth among Athenian peasants gave them greater clout than elsewhere. Their power and political cohesiveness were evident as early as 632 B.C., when they rallied "from the fields in a body," according to a later historian, to foil the attempted coup of an Athenian nobleman named Cylon, who with some other aristocrats had planned to install a tyranny. Influential aristocrats like Solon and Cleisthenes, who later worked to strengthen Athenian democracy for differing reasons, also made democracy more viable at Athens.

The scanty evidence seems to indicate that by the seventh century B.C. all freeborn adult male citizens of Athens could attend open meetings, in a body called the assembly, which elected nine magistrates called *archons* (rulers) annually. The archons, still all aristocrats, headed the government and rendered verdicts in disputes and criminal accusations. As before, aristocrats still dominated Athenian political life—they used their influence to make sure they were elected archons, perhaps by marshaling their traditional bands of followers and by making alliances with other aristocrats. The right of middle-class and poor men to serve in the assembly had only limited value at this time because little business besides electing archons was conducted when the assembly gathered. It probably convened rarely in this period, and then only when the current archons decided it should.

Aristocratic political alliances often proved temporary, however, and rivalries among jealous aristocrats continued under early Athenian democracy. In the aftermath of Cylon's attempted tyranny, an Athenian named Draco was appointed in 621 B.C., perhaps after pressure by the hoplites, to establish a code of laws promoting stability and equity. Unfortunately, Draco's laws further destabilized the political situation; the Athenians later remembered them as having been as harsh as the meaning of his name—"dragon, serpent." (Our word *draconian,* meaning excessively severe, reflects this view.) The well-being of Athens's free peasants deteriorated as well; their circumstances had been eroding slowly for a long time. This condition also undermined social peace. Later Athenians did not know the cause of this economic crisis—only that it pitted the rich against the middle class and the poor.

Many poor Athenians had apparently lost their land to wealthier proprietors by the late seventh century B.C. Athenian farms often operated at subsistence level, and a bad year could mean starvation. Even if crops were abundant in a given year, farmers had no easy way to convert the surplus into imperishable capital they could store to offset future lean years. (Coinage was invented only in the late seventh century B.C., and it did not come into common use for a long time.) To survive, farmers often had to borrow food and seed. When they could borrow no more, they had to leave their land and find a job to support their families, most likely a job working for other, more successful farmers. The more successful farmers, who perhaps employed more effective methods or maybe were simply more fortunate than farmers who failed, could use and eventually buy the land of failed farmers. This process meant that fewer and fewer people gradually controlled or accumulated most of the arable land. The crisis became so acute that impoverished peasants were even being sold into slavery to pay off debts. Finally, twenty-five years after Draco's legislation, civil war threatened to break out. In desperation the Athenians in 594 B.C. gave Solon special authority to revise their laws to deal with the emergency.

As he explains in his autobiographical poetry, Solon tried to steer a middle course between the demands of the rich to preserve their financial advantages and the pleas of the poor to redistribute the land held by wealthy landowners. His famous "shaking off of obligations"—some sort of reduction or cancellation of debts—somehow freed those farms whose ownership had become formally encumbered without, however, actually redistributing any land. He also forbade selling Athenians into slavery for economic reasons and liberated citizens who had become slaves in this way, commemorating his success in verses he wrote: "To Athens, their home established by the gods, I brought back many who had been sold into slavery, some justly, some not. . . ."

Attempting to balance political power between rich and poor, Solon ranked male citizens into four classes according to their income: "five-hundred-measure men" (those with an annual income equivalent to that much agricultural produce), "horsemen" (income of three hundred measures), "yoked men" (two hundred measures), and "laborers" (less than two hundred measures). The higher a man's class, the higher the government office for which he was eligible; laborers were barred from all posts. Solon did, however, reaffirm the right of the laborer class to participate in the assembly. He probably created a council of four hundred men to prepare an agenda for the assembly, although some scholars believe this innovation occurred later than Solon's time. Aristocrats could not dominate the council's deliberations because its members were chosen by lot, probably only from the top three classes. Solon may also have initiated a schedule of regular meetings for the assembly. These reforms added impetus to the assembly's legislative role and thus indirectly laid a foundation for the political influence the laborer class would gradually acquire over the next century and a half.

Solon's classification scheme was another step toward democracy because it allowed for upward social mobility: if a man increased his income, he could move up the scale of eligibility for office. Because income was not directly taxed, ambitious entrepreneurs could make more profit and benefit from what they earned. Solon's reforms gave Athenian male citizens a political and social system far more open to individual initiative and change than that of Sparta.

Equally important to restoring stability in a time of crisis was Solon's ruling that any male citizen could bring charges on a wide variety of offenses against wrongdoers on behalf of any victim of a crime. Furthermore, people who believed a magistrate had rendered unfair judgments against them now had the right to appeal their case to the assembly. With these two measures, Solon involved ordinary citizens, not just the predominantly aristocratic magistrates, in the administration of justice. He balanced these judicial reforms acknowledging the common people, however, by granting broader powers to the "Council which meets on the Hill of the god of war Ares," which we call the Areopagus (meaning "Ares' hill"). Archons became members of the Areopagus after their year in office. This body of ex-archons could, if the members chose to, wield great power, because it judged the most serious cases—in particular, any accusations against archons themselves. Solon probably expected the Areopagus to use its power to protect his reforms as well.

For its place and time, Athens's emerging democracy was remarkable, even at this early stage in its evolution, because it granted all male citizens the possibility of participating meaningfully in making laws and administering justice. But not everyone admired Solon's system. The same king who had scoffed at Solon's lawmaking reportedly also found Athenian democracy ludicrous. Observing the procedure in the Athenian assembly, he expressed his amazement that leading aristocratic politicians could only recommend policy in their speeches, while the male citizens as a whole voted on what to do: "I find it astonishing," he remarked, "that here wise men speak on public affairs, while fools decide them." Some Athenians agreed with the king, and did their best to undermine Solon's reforms. Such oligarchic sympathizers continued to challenge Athenian democracy periodically throughout its history.

Contentiousness among aristocrats, combined with the continued discontent of the poorest Athenians, lay behind the strife in the mid-sixth century B.C. that led to Athens's first tyranny. At this time an Athenian aristocrat named Pisistratus, helped by his upper-class friends and the poor, whose interests he championed, launched an effort to make himself sole ruler by force. He finally established himself securely as tyrant at Athens in 546 B.C. Pisistratus made funds available to help peasants acquire needed farm equipment. He provided employment for poorer men while benefiting Athens, hiring them to build roads and work on such major public works as a great temple to Zeus and fountains to increase the supply of drinking water. His tax on agricultural production, one of the rare instances of direct taxation in Athenian history, financed the loans to farmers and the building projects. He also arranged for judicial officials to go on circuits through the outlying villages of Attica to hear cases, thus saving farmers the trouble of having to leave their fields to seek justice in Athens. Like the earlier tyrants of Corinth, he promoted the economic, cultural, and architectural development of Athens. Athenian pottery, for example, now began to crowd out Corinthian in the export trade.

Hippias, the eldest son of Pisistratus, continued the tyranny after his father's death in 527 B.C. He governed by making certain that his relatives and friends occupied magistracies. But for a time he also allowed his aristocratic rivals to hold office, thereby defusing some of the tension created by their jealousy of his superior status. Eventually, however, the aristocratic family of the Alcmaeonids arranged to have the Spartans send an army to expel Hippias. In the ensuing vacuum of power, the leading Alcmaeonid, Cleisthenes, sought support among the masses by promising democratic reforms when his bitterest aristocratic rival became an archon in 508 B.C. When the rival tried to block Cleisthenes' reforms by calling in the Spartans again, the Athenian people united to force him and his foreign allies out. The conflict between Athens and Sparta ended quickly but sowed the seeds of mutual distrust between the two city-states.

His popular support gave Cleisthenes the authority to begin to install the democratic system for which Athens has become famous, and the importance of his reforms led later Athenians to think of him as a principal founder of their democracy. First he made the villages of the countryside and the neighborhoods of the city of Athens the constituent units of Athenian political organization. Organized in these units, called *demes,* the male citizens participated directly in the running of their government: in deme registers they kept track of which males were citizens and therefore eligible at eighteen to attend the assembly and vote on laws and public policies. The demes in turn were grouped into ten so-called tribes for other political functions, such as choosing fifty representatives by lot from each tribe to serve for one year on the council of five hundred, which replaced Solon's council of four hundred. The number of representatives from each deme was proportional to its population. Most important, the ten men who served each year as "generals," the officials with the highest civil and military authority, were elected one from each tribe. Cleisthenes' reorganization was complex; its general aim seems to have been to undermine existing political alliances among aristocrats in the interests of greater democracy.

By about 500 B.C., Cleisthenes had devised an Athenian democracy based on direct participation by as many adult male citizens as possible. That he could institute such a system successfully in a time of turmoil and that it could endure, as it did, means that Cleisthenes must have been building on preexisting conditions favorable to democracy. As an aristocrat looking for popular support, Cleisthenes certainly had reason to establish the kind of system he thought ordinary people wanted. That he based his system on the demes, most of which were country villages, suggests that some democratic notions may have stemmed from the traditions of village life. Possibly the idea of widespread participation in government gained support from the villagers' customary way of dealing with each other on relatively egalitarian terms: each man was entitled to his say in running local affairs and had to persuade others of the wisdom of his recommendations. Because many aristocrats seem to have preferred to reside in the city, their ability to dominate discussion in the demes was reduced. In any case the idea that persuasion, rather than force or status, should constitute the mechanism for political decision making in the emerging Athenian democracy fit well with the spirit of intellectual changes rippling through Greece in the late Archaic Age.

New Ways of Thought

Poetry was the only form of Greek literature until the late Archaic Age. The earliest Greek poetry, that of Homer and Hesiod, had been confined to a single rhythm. A much greater rhythmic diversity characterized the new form of poetry, called lyric, that emerged during the Archaic Age. Lyric poems were much shorter than the narrative poetry of Homer or the didactic poetry of Hesiod, and they encompassed many forms and subjects, but they were always performed with the accompaniment of the lyre (a kind of harp that gives its name to the poetry). Choral poets like Alcman of Sparta wrote songs for groups to perform on public occasions to honor the deities, to celebrate famous events in a city-state's history, for wedding processions, and to praise victors in athletic contests. Lyric poets writing songs for solo performance at social occasions stressed a personal level of expression on a variety of topics. Solon and Alcaeus, for example, wrote poems focused on contemporary politics. Others deliberately adopted a critical attitude toward traditional values such as strength in war. For example, Sappho, a lyric poet from Lesbos born about 630 B.C. and famous for her poems on love, wrote, "Some would say the most beautiful thing on our dark earth is an army of cavalry, others of infantry, others of ships, but I say it's whatever a person loves." In this poem Sappho was expressing her longing for a woman she loved, who was now far away. Archilochus of Paros, who probably lived in the early seventh century B.C., became famous for poems on themes as diverse as friends lost at sea, mockery of martial valor, and love gone astray. The bitter power of his poetic invective reportedly caused a father and his two daughters to commit suicide when Archilochus angrily ridiculed them after the father had ended Archilochus's affair with his daughter Neobule. Some modern literary critics think the poems about Neobule and her family are fictional, not autobiographical, and were meant to display Archilochus's dazzling talent for "blame poetry," the mirror image of lyric poetry as the poetry of praise. Mimnermus of Colophon, another seventh-century B.C. lyric poet, rhapsodized about the glory of youth and lamented its brevity: "no longer than the time the sun shines on the plain." Lyric poets' focus on the individual's feelings represented a new stage in Greek literary sensibilities, one that continues to inspire much poetry today.

Greece's earliest prose literature was written in the late Archaic Age. Thinkers we now usually call philosophers, but who could also be described as theoretical scientists studying the physical world, created Greek prose to express their new ways of thought. These thinkers, who came from the city-states of Ionia, developed radically new explanations of the human world and its relation

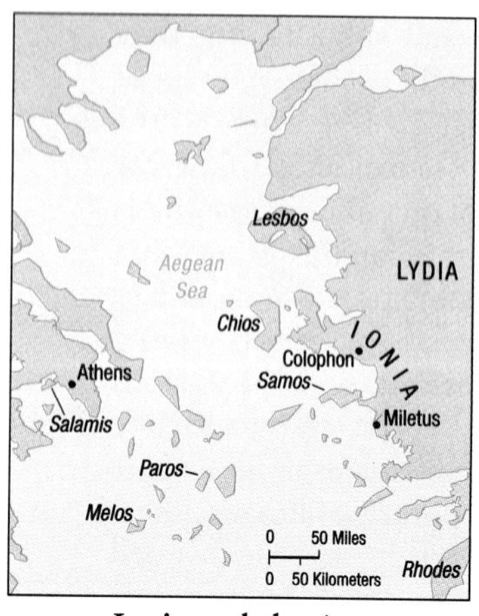

Ionia and the Aegean

to the gods and goddesses. Thus began the study of philosophy in Greece. Ionia's geographical location next to the non-Greek civilizations of Anatolia, which had contact with the older civilizations of Egypt and the Near East, permitted Ionian thinkers to acquire knowledge and intellectual inspiration from their neighbors in the eastern Mediterranean area. Because Greece in this period had no formal schools at any level, thinkers like those from Ionia made their ideas known by teaching pupils privately and giving public lectures. Some Ionian thinkers composed poetry to explain their theories and gave public recitations. People who studied with these thinkers or heard their presentations then helped spread the new ideas.

Knowledge from the ancient Near East inspired Ionian thinkers, just as it influenced Archaic Age Greek artists. Greek vase painters and specialists in decorating metal vessels imitated Near Eastern designs depicting animals and luxuriant plants; Greek sculptors produced narrative reliefs such as those of Assyria and statues modeled on the Egyptian style. Egypt also inspired Greek architects to use stone for columns, ornamental details, and eventually entire buildings.

Information about the regular movements of the stars and planets developed by astronomers in Babylonia proved especially key in helping Ionian thinkers reach their conclusions about the nature of the physical world. The first of the Ionian theorists, Thales (c. 625–545 B.C.), who came from the city-state of Miletus, was said to have predicted a solar eclipse in 585 B.C., an accomplishment implying he had been influenced by Babylonian learning. Modern astronomers doubt Thales actually predicted the eclipse, but the story shows how eastern scientific and mathematical knowledge influenced Ionian thinkers. Working from such knowledge as the observed fact that celestial bodies moved in a regular pattern, thinkers like Thales and Anaximander (c. 610–540 B.C.), also from Miletus, drew the revolutionary conclusion that the physical world was regulated by a set of laws of nature rather than by the arbitrary intervention of divine beings. Pythagoras, who emigrated from Samos to southern Italy about 530 B.C., taught that patterns and relationships of numbers explained the entire world. His doctrines inspired systematic study of mathematics and the numerical aspects of musical harmony.

The Ionian thinkers insisted the workings of the universe could be revealed because natural phenomena were neither random nor arbitrary. The universe, the totality of things, they named *cosmos* because this word meant an orderly arrangement that is beautiful. The order of the cosmos encompassed not only the motions of heavenly bodies but also the weather, the growth of plants and animals, human health and well-being, and so on. Because the universe was ordered, it was intelligible; because it was intelligible, events could be explained by thought and research. The thinkers who deduced this view believed they needed to give reasons for their conclusions and to persuade others by arguments based on evidence. They believed, in other words, in logic (derived from the Greek term *logos,* meaning, among other things, "a reasoned explanation"). This mode of thought represented a crucial first step toward science and philosophy as these disciplines endure today. The rule-based view of the causes of events and physical phenomena developed by these thinkers contrasted sharply with the traditional mythological view of causation. Naturally, many people had difficulty accepting such a startling change in their understanding of the world, and the older tradition explaining events as the work of deities lived on alongside the new approach.

The ideas of the Ionian thinkers probably spread slowly because no means of mass communication existed, and few men could afford to spend the time to become their followers and then return home to explain these new ways of thought to others. Magic remained an important preoccupation in the lives of the majority of ordinary people, who retained their notions that deities and demons frequently and directly affected their fortunes and health, as well as the events of nature. Even though their ideas probably had only a limited effect on the ancient world, the Ionian thinkers had initiated a tremendous development in intellectual history: the separation of scientific thinking from myth and religion. Some modern scholars call this development the birth of rationalism. But it would be unfair to label the myths and religious ways of ancient people irrational if that word is taken to mean "unthinking" or "silly." They realized their lives were subject to forces beyond their control and understanding, and it was not unreasonable to attribute supernatural origins to the powers of nature or the ravages of disease. The new scientific ways of thought insisted, however, that observable evidence had to be sought and theories of explanation had to be logical. Just being old or popular no longer bestowed truth on a story purporting to explain natural phenomena. In this way, the Ionian thinkers parted company with the traditional ways of thinking of the ancient Near East as found in its rich mythology and repeated in the myths of early Greece.

Developing the idea that people must give reasons to explain their beliefs, rather than just make assertions others must believe without evidence, was the most important achievement of the early Ionian thinkers. This insistence on rationality, coupled with the belief that the world could be understood as something other than the plaything of divine whims, gave humans hope that they could improve their lives through their own efforts. As Xenophanes from Colophon (c. 580–480 B.C.) put it, "The gods have not revealed all things from the beginning to mortals, but, by seeking, human beings find out, in time, what is better." Xenophanes, like other Ionian thinkers, believed in the existence of gods, but he nevertheless assigned the opportunity and the responsibility for improving human life to humans themselves.

Conclusion

At the start of the Dark Age the future looked bleak in Greece and the ancient Near East. The Near East recovered its political and economic strength more quickly than did Greece, and the Neo-Assyrian kingdom used its military force to build the most extensive empire the region had yet seen—even Egypt, which had never revived as an international power, became part of this empire. The Neo-Babylonian kingdom of the Chaldeans succeeded Assyria as the greatest power in the Near East, but it then fell to the new kingdom of Persia. By 500 B.C., Persia far exceeded even the greatest extent of the earlier Assyrian empire. These kingdoms essentially continued or revived the political and social institutions of their predecessors in the Near East—rule by a strong, centralized authority. The most significant innovations in Near Eastern history in this period occurred in religious history: the consolidation of the Hebrew religion as a true monotheism, whose tenets required Jews to observe strict rules of ethical and ritual purity to maintain their covenant with Yahweh, and the editing of the Hebrew Bible to produce sacred scriptures as the basic texts of Judaism.

The Dark Age truly devastated Greece. The tightly organized redistributive economy and the splendid palaces of the Mycenaean period had been destroyed. Along with them had gone the traditional social and political organization. Much farmland lay vacant or out of cultivation. The population had shrunk to a fraction of its former size. No one, it seems, any longer knew how to write. By around 750 B.C., however, the conditions of life in Greece were strikingly different. The population had grown so rapidly that a shortage of arable land had forced colonists to found new settlements abroad, which were also founded for trade. A developing sense of Greek identity and communal spirit had promoted the creation of pan-Hellenic centers, such as Olympia with its games and Delphi with its oracle of Apollo. Roused by a desire for the justice that poets taught had the support of the deities, the free peasants of Greece somehow wrested a share of political power from aristocrats and hoplites in Greece's emerging new political form, the independent city-state. The creation of citizenship as the conceptual and organizational basis of the Greek city-state represented a major innovation. The concept of citizenship, though restricted in its political rights to male citizens, emphasized the notion of personal freedom. Chattel slavery contrasted sharply with the ideas of its citizenship. Trade with the Near East once again brought Greeks into contact with the ideas of its civilizations, reintroduced literacy to Greece, and influenced Greek art and mythology.

Geography and the varying courses of local history led to different political and social developments in different city-states in the Archaic Age. Tyrants promoted prosperity in city-states like Corinth. Sparta evolved into an oligarchy and adopted a distinctive way of life designed to exploit a subject population, thereby obligating Spartans to devote all their energies to maintaining their state's military strength. The communal organization of Sparta largely separated men's and women's lives, requiring men to train for war and women to manage both households and farms. Throughout Greece, women were legal wards of their fathers, husbands, or male relatives, with only limited rights of their own. While maintaining their paternalism toward women, Athenian men gradually developed a democracy based on certain egalitarian principles for rich and poor men alike, a revolutionary development for the ancient world.

Equally revolutionary was the change in ways of thought inspired by Ionian thinkers in the Archaic Age. By arguing that the universe was based on laws of nature, which humans could explain through reason and research, they established the conceptual basis for science and philosophy. By their example as well as their theories, they encouraged humans to believe that individual initiative could help "find out what is best." Thus they valued an intellectual freedom that corresponded to the value of political freedom—unequally distributed though it may have been by the exclusion of women and slaves—in the city-state.

It was during the Archaic Age of Greece that the values that have so profoundly affected Western civilization first began to emerge. But the Greek world and its new values would soon face a grave threat from the awesome kingdom of Persia.

Suggestions for Further Reading

Source Materials

Barnes, Jonathan. *Early Greek Philosophy.* 1987. An excellent, brief introduction to the Ionian thinkers followed by excerpts in context from them and other early Greek philosophers.

Crawford, Michael, and David Whitehead. *Archaic and Classical Greece: A Selection of Ancient Sources in Translation.* 1983. A collection of excerpts from literature and historical documents with useful introductions and annotations.

Hesiod, *Theogony; Works and Days.* Available in various translations such as one by Apostolos N. Athanassakis, 1983, as well as in the bilingual edition published in the Loeb Classical Library series.

Homer, *Iliad; Odyssey.* Available in various translations such as one by Robert Fitzgerald, 1974, 1961, respectively, as well as in the bilingual edition published in the Loeb Classical Library series.

Rhodes, P. J. *The Greek City States: A Source Book.* 1986. A collection of sources arranged in sections of explanatory narrative.

Sappho. Her poems, many of which survive only in fragmentary form, are available, along with the poems of Alcaeus, in *Greek Lyric I,* 1982, a bilingual edition published in the Loeb Classical Library series. Jeffrey M. Duban, *Ancient and Modern Images of Sappho: Translations and Studies in Archaic Greek Love Lyric,* 1983, includes translations of Sappho, Alcman, Anacreon, Archilochus, and Ibycus.

Interpretive Studies

Boardman, John. *The Greeks Overseas: Their Early Colonies and Trade.* New ed. 1980. A survey of Greek colonization and overseas commerce.

Boardman, John, et al. *The Oxford History of the Classical World.* 1986. Articles on central historical topics as well as Homer, myth and Hesiod, lyric poetry, and philosophy.

The Cambridge Ancient History. 2d ed. Vol. III, Part 3, *The Expansion of the Greek World, Eighth to Sixth Centuries B.C.* 1982. An authoritative survey of Greek history in the Archaic Age.

Cartledge, Paul. *Sparta and Lakonia: A Regional History, 1300–362 B.C.* 1979. A survey beginning in the late Bronze Age with emphasis on geography and the material conditions affecting Spartan history.

Coldstream, J. N. *Geometric Greece.* 1977. Detailed treatment of Greece in the ninth and eighth centuries B.C. with much discussion of artifacts.

Donlan, Walter. *The Aristocratic Ideal in Ancient Greece: Attitudes of Superiority from Homer to the End of the Fifth Century B.C.* 1980. An interpretation of the functioning of concepts such as honor, excellence, and justice in Greek society.

Emlyn-Jones, C. J. *The Ionians and Hellenism: A Study of the Cultural Achievements of Early Greek Inhabitants of Asia Minor.* 1980. An assessment of the art, literature, and philosophy of the Ionians from the eighth to the sixth century B.C.

Finley, M. I. *Ancient Slavery and Modern Ideology.* 1980. A discussion of the nature of ancient slavery as compared to more modern systems of slavery.

———. *Early Greece. The Bronze and Archaic Ages.* Rev. ed. 1981. A brief, readable introduction to Greek history to the dawn of the Classical Age with emphasis on the difficulties of clear interpretation.

———. *The World of Odysseus.* 2d ed. 1965. A standard work on the question of how much history can be found in Homeric poetry.

Finley, M. I., and H. W. Pleket. *The Olympic Games: The First Thousand Years.* 1976. A survey of the history of the games throughout antiquity.

Fitzhardinge, L. F. *The Spartans.* 1980. A well-illustrated survey of Spartan history and society.

Forrest, W. G. *The Emergence of Greek Democracy, 800–400 B.C.* 1966. A provocative classic in the field arguing that developments at Sparta set the stage for the rise of democracy.

Garlan, Yvon. *Slavery in Ancient Greece.* Rev. ed. Translated by Janet Lloyd. 1988. A comprehensive discussion of the varying categories of Greek slavery.

Guthrie, W. K. C. *A History of Greek Philosophy.* Vol. 1, *The Earlier Presocratics and the Pythagoreans.* 1962. The standard, detailed introduction to the Ionian thinkers and other early Greek philosophers.

Hurwitt, Jeffrey M. *The Art and Culture of Early Greece, 1100–480 B.C.*. 1985. A detailed treatment of the cultural significance of Greek art before the Classical Age.

Jeffrey, L. H. *Archaic Greece: The City-States, c. 700–500 B.C.* 1976. Political history of the Greek world in the Archaic Age presented geographically.

Morris, Ian. *Burial and Ancient Society: The Rise of the Greek City-State.* 1987. Stimulating, high-level discussion of the archaeological evidence for the social conflicts that provided the context for the rise of the city-state.

Murray, Oswyn. *Early Greece.* 1980. An accessible survey that places archaic Greece in the context of Mediterranean civilization of the time, especially the Near East.

Snodgrass, Anthony. *Archaic Greece: The Age of Experiment.* 1980. An exceptionally stimulating presentation of the Archaic Age as a period of great innovation and change.

———. *The Dark Age of Greece.* 1971. An extensive treatment making the most of the limited evidence available for this period.

Starr, Chester G. *The Economic and Social Growth of Early Greece, 800–500 b.c.* 1977. A brief and readable account of the interdependency of economic and social changes in the Archaic Age.

———. *Individual and Community: The Rise of the Polis, 800–500 B.C.* 1986. A compact survey of the balancing of communal interests and the emerging concept of individual freedom in the Archaic Age.

Swaddling, Judith. *The Ancient Olympic Games.* 1980. A brief, illustrated survey of the history of the games.

Wilbur, J. B., and H. J. Allen. *The Worlds of the Early Greek Philosophers.* 1979. A discussion of the philosophers of early Greece in their historical contexts.

CHAPTER

3

The Greek Golden Age, c. 500–403 B.C.

The greatest military danger ever to threaten ancient Greece began with a diplomatic misunderstanding. Fearing the Spartans would again try to intervene at Athens in support of the city's aristocratic faction opposed to democracy, the Athenians in 507 B.C. sent ambassadors to ask for a protective alliance with the king of Persia, Darius I (*522–486 B.C.). The Persian Empire was now the largest, richest, and militarily strongest power in the ancient world. The Athenian emissaries met with a representative of Darius at Sardis, the Persian headquarters in western Anatolia (modern Turkey). When the royal intermediary had heard their plea for help, he replied, "But who in the world are you and where do you live?"

The dynamics of this incident reveal the forces motivating the conflicts that would dominate the military and political history of mainland Greece during the fifth century B.C. First, the two major powers in mainland Greece—Sparta and Athens—remained wary of each other. When the Spartan army had backed Cleisthenes' rival in a power struggle over who would become the leader of Athens, they had been expelled by Athenian soldiers in a humiliating defeat. Spartans began to view Athenians as foes, a feeling reciprocated at Athens after the abortive Spartan interference, during which the Spartan troops had forced some seven hundred Athenian households into temporary exile. Second, the kingdom of Persia had expanded far enough west that the Greeks were becoming aware of its awesome might. Yet neither the Persians nor the mainland Greeks knew much about each other. Their mutual ignorance opened the door to explosive wars.

New Directions in the Classical Age
The pose of this bronze figure exemplifies the implied motion of the new style developed by Greek artists during the Classical Age. Political and intellectual life also moved in new directions.

Even though one bloody conflict after another raged through Greece in the fifth century B.C., beginning with war against Persia, Athens's international power, economic prosperity, and artistic, literary, and intellectual endeavors flourished during this turmoil-filled century. Athenian accomplishments of the fifth century B.C. have had such an enduring impact that historians call this period a Golden Age. This Golden Age coincided with the beginning of the Classical Age of Greek history, a modern designation that covers the period from about 500 B.C. to the death of Alexander the Great in 323 B.C. During its Golden Age, Athens was the preeminent society in ancient Greece and indeed throughout the Mediterranean basin. (Because we know much more about Athens than about any other place or society in the ancient world during the fifth century B.C., we necessarily focus there.) Unfortunately for the Athenians, their Golden Age ended in the closing decades of the fifth century B.C., as a result of a protracted war with Sparta that ultimately engulfed most of the Greek world. Ironically, a period of such cultural blossoming both ended and began with destructive wars.

Important Dates

490 B.C. King Darius sends Persian force against Athens; battle of Marathon

480 B.C. King Xerxes leads Persian invasion of Greece; battles of Thermopylae and Salamis

477 B.C. Athens assumes leadership of the Greek alliance (Delian League)

461 B.C. Ephialtes passes political and judicial reforms to strengthen Athenian democracy

446 B.C. Athens and Sparta sign a peace treaty meant to last thirty years

431 B.C. The Peloponnesian War begins between Athens and Sparta

421 B.C. Nicias induces Athens and Sparta to sign a peace treaty

415–413 B.C. Athenian expedition against Syracuse in Sicily renews the war

404 B.C. Athens surrenders to Sparta

404–403 B.C. The Thirty Tyrants suspend democracy at Athens and conduct a reign of terror

403 B.C. Athenians overthrow the Thirty Tyrants and restore democracy

Clash Between Persia and Greece

The Athenian ambassadors who had gone to Sardis accepted the customary Persian terms for an alliance by giving tokens of earth and water to the king's representative, thereby indicating Athens's recognition of the superiority of Darius, who acknowledged no one as his equal. The Athenian assembly, although outraged at their envoys' symbolic submission to a foreign power, never overtly repudiated the alliance and therefore unwittingly set in motion a sequence of events that culminated in invasions of mainland Greece by the enormous army and navy of Persia. The Persian kingdom outstripped mainland Greece in every category of material resources, from precious metals to soldiers. The wars between Persia and Greece pitted the equivalent of an elephant against a small swarm of mosquitoes. In such a conflict a Greek victory seemed improbable, to say the least. Equally improbable—given the propensity toward disunity and even mutual hostility of the independent Greek city-states—was that a coalition of these city-states would unite to repel the common enemy.

The Beginning of the Persian Wars

The most famous series of wars in ancient Greek history—the so-called Persian Wars, which were fought in the 490s B.C. and in 480–479 B.C.—broke out with a revolt in Ionia (the western coast of Anatolia), where the Greek city-states had come under Persian control. The Ionian Greeks had first lost their independence not to the Persians but to the Lydians, who had overpowered them during Croesus's reign (*c. 560–546 B.C.). Buoyed by this success and his legendary riches, Croesus had next tried to conquer territory in Anatolia that had previously been in the Median kingdom, but Cyrus, the Persian king, defeated him and captured his territory.

By 499 B.C., Ionia had rebelled against the tyrannies the Persian kings had installed there, in keeping with their policy of supporting local tyrants who were supposed to keep their city-states loyal to Persia. The Athenian assembly voted to join the city-state of Eretria on the neighboring island of Euboea in sending military aid to the Ionian rebels. Their combined force proceeded as far as Sardis, Croesus's old capital and now a Persian headquarters. After razing much of Sardis, however, the Athenians and Eretrians fled home when a Persian counterattack repelled them, causing them to retreat in disarray. Subsequent campaigns by Persian commanders crushed the Ionian rebels by 494 B.C. King Darius then sent a general, Mardonius, to reorganize the city-states of Ionia into democratic regimes, which Persia now permitted because Darius had seen the problems unpopular tyrannies could cause.

King Darius was furious when he learned that the Athenians had aided the Ionian revolt: not only had they dared attack his kingdom, but they had done so after indicating their submission to him through their alliance. The Greeks later claimed that to keep him from forgetting his vow to punish their disloyalty, Darius ordered one of his slaves to say to him three times at every meal, "Sire, remember the Athenians." In 490 B.C., Darius dispatched a flotilla of ships carrying soldiers that burned Eretria and landed on the northeastern coast of Attica near a village called Marathon. The Persians brought with them the elderly Hippias, exiled son of Pisistratus, expecting to reinstall him as their puppet tyrant of Athens. Because the Persian troops outnumbered the citizen militia of Athenian

The Persian Wars

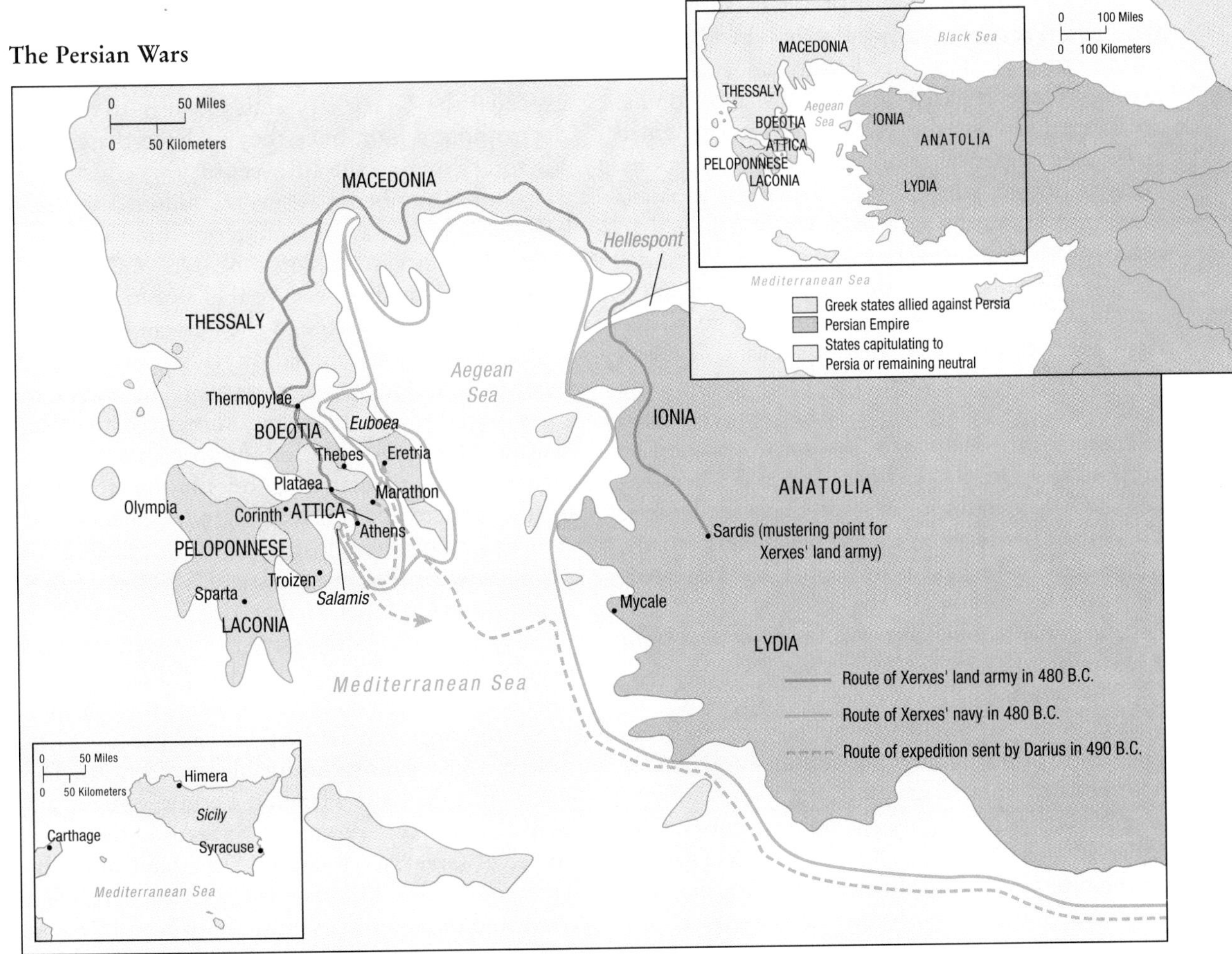

hoplites, the Athenians asked Sparta and other Greek city-states for military help. The Athenian courier dispatched to Sparta became famous because he ran the hundred and forty miles from Athens to Sparta in less than two days. But by the time the battle of Marathon erupted, the only additional troops to arrive were a contingent from the small city-state of Plataea in Boeotia, the region just north of Athenian territory.

Everyone expected the Persians to win. The Athenian and Plataean soldiers, who had never before seen Persians, grew anxious just at the sight of the Persians' outlandish (to Greek eyes) outfits. Nevertheless, the Athenian generals—the board of ten men elected each year as the civil and military leaders—never let their men lose heart or back down. Carefully planning their tactics to minimize the time their soldiers would be exposed to the deadly arrows of Persian archers, the generals, led by the aristocrat Miltiades (c. 550–489 B.C.), sent their hoplites straight toward the Persian line at a dead run. The Greeks dashed across the Marathon plain in their clanking metal armor under a hail of arrows. Once engaged in hand-to-hand combat with the Persians, the Greek hoplites benefited from their superior armor and longer weapons. After a furious struggle they drove the Persians back into a swamp; any invaders who failed to escape to their ships were killed.

The Athenian army then hurried the twenty-six miles from Marathon to Athens to guard the city against a Persian naval attack. (Today's marathon races commemorate the exploit of a runner who, so the story goes, had been sent ahead to announce the victory to the city, whereupon he dropped dead from the effort.) When the Persians saw the Athenian troops in place, they sailed home. The Athenians rejoiced in disbelief. The Persians, whom they had feared as invincible, had retreated. For decades afterward the greatest honor an Athenian man could claim was to say he had been a "Marathon fighter."

The symbolic importance of the battle of Marathon far outweighed its military significance. The defeat of his punitive expedition enraged Darius because it injured his pride, not because it represented any threat to his kingdom's security. The Athenian men who constituted the city-state's army, on the other hand, had dramatically demonstrated their commitment to preserving their freedom. The unexpected victory at Marathon boosted Athenian self-confidence, and the city-state's soldiers and leaders thereafter boasted that they had withstood the feared Persians on their own, without Sparta's help.

The Great Invasion of 480–479 B.C.

This newly won confidence helped steel the Athenians against the gigantic Persian invasion of Greece in 480 B.C. Darius had vowed to avenge the defeat at Marathon, but it took so long to marshal forces from all over the far-flung Persian kingdom that he died before an attack could be launched. His son, Xerxes I (*486–465 B.C.), therefore led the massive force of infantry and ships that invaded the Greek mainland. So immense was Xerxes' army, the Greeks later claimed, that it required seven days and seven nights of continuous marching to cross the Hellespont strait, the narrow passage of sea between Anatolia and mainland Greece, on a temporary bridge lashed together from boats and pontoons. Xerxes expected the Greek city-states simply to surrender without a fight once they realized the size of his forces, which the fifth-century B.C. historian Herodotus numbered as several million but modern scholars estimate at around one hundred thousand. The city-states in northern and central Greece did just that because their location placed them directly in the line of the Persian forces and their small size precluded any hope of effective defense. The Boeotian city-state of Thebes, about forty miles north of Athens, supported the Persian invasion, probably hoping to gain an advantage over its Athenian neighbors in the aftermath of the anticipated Persian victory. Thebes and Athens had become hostile to one another about 519 B.C., when Plataea successfully sought Athenian protection from Theban dominance.

Thirty-one Greek states, however, located mainly in central Greece and the Peloponnese, formed a coalition to fight the Persians, and they chose the Spartans as their leaders because they fielded Greece's most formidable hoplite army. The coalition, called the Hellenic League, sought aid from Gelon, the tyrant of Syracuse, the most powerful Greek city-state on the island of Sicily. The appeal failed, however, when Gelon demanded command of either the Greek sea or land forces in return for his assistance, a price the Spartan and Athenian leaders were unwilling to meet. In this same period, Gelon was battling Carthage over territory in Sicily, and in 480 B.C. his forces defeated a massive Carthaginian expedition at Himera, on the island's northern coast. Some historians have suggested that the Carthaginian incursion into Sicily and the Persian invasion of mainland Greece were purposely coordinated to embroil the Greek world in a two-front war in the west and the east simultaneously.

The Spartans showed their courage when three hundred of their men led by King Leonidas, along with allies, held off Xerxes' huge army for several days at the narrow pass called Thermopylae ("warm gates") in central Greece. The Spartan troops refused to be intimidated. A Spartan hoplite summed up their attitude by his reputed response to the remark that the Persian archers were so numerous that their arrows darkened the sky in battle. "That's good news," said the Spartan warrior. "We will get to fight in the shade." The pass was so narrow that the Persians could not use their superior numbers to overwhelm the Greek defenders, who were better one-on-one warriors. Only when a local Greek, hoping for a reward from Xerxes, revealed a secret route around the pass was the Persian army able to massacre the Greek defenders, attacking them from the front and the rear simultaneously.

The Athenians soon proved their mettle. Rather than surrender when Xerxes arrived in Attica with his army, they abandoned their city. Women, children, and noncombatants packed their belongings as best they could and evacuated to the northeast coast of the Peloponnese. The Athenian commander Themistocles (c. 528–462 B.C.), purposely spreading misinformation in his characteristically shrewd manner, maneuvered the other, less aggressive Greek leaders into facing the larger Persian navy in a sea battle in the narrow channel between the island of Salamis and the west coast of Attica. Athens was able to supply the largest contingent to the Greek navy at Salamis because the assembly had been financing warship construction ever since a rich strike of silver had been made in Attica in 483 B.C. The proceeds from the silver mines went to the state, and at the urging of Themistocles the assembly had voted to use the financial windfall to build a navy for defense rather than to disburse the money to individual citizens. As at Thermopylae, the Greeks at the battle of Salamis in 480 B.C. used their country's topography to their advantage. The narrowness of the channel prevented the Persians from using all their ships at once and minimized the advantage of their ships' greater maneuverability. In the close quarters of the Salamis channel, the heavier Greek ships could use their underwater rams to sink the less sturdy Persian craft. When Xerxes observed that the most energetic of his naval commanders appeared to be the one woman among them, Artemisia, ruler of Caria (the southwest corner of Anatolia), he remarked, "My men have become women, and my women, men."

The Greek victory at Salamis sent Xerxes back to Persia, but he left behind an enormous infantry force under his best general and an offer for the Athenians: if they would capitulate, they would remain unharmed and become his overlords of the other Greeks. The assembly refused, the population evacuated again, and Xerxes' general sacked Athens for the second time in two years. In 479 B.C. the Greek infantry headed by the Spartans under the command of a royal son named Pausanias (c. 520–470 B.C.) outfought the Persian infantry at Plataea in Boeotia, and a Greek fleet routed the Persian navy at Mycale in Ionia. The coalition of Greek city-states had thus done the incredible: protected their homeland and their independence from the strongest power in the world.

The Greeks' superior armor and weapons and resourceful use of their topography to counterbalance the Persians' greater numbers help explain their victories on the military level. But what is truly remarkable about the Persian Wars is the decision of the warriors of the thirty-one Greek city-states of the Hellenic League to fight in the first place. They could easily have surrendered and agreed to become Persian subjects to save themselves. Instead, encouraged to resist by the citizens of their communities, they eventually triumphed together against seemingly overwhelming odds. Because the Greek forces included not only aristocrats and hoplites but also thousands of poorer men who rowed the warships, the effort against the Persians cut across social and economic divisions. The Hellenic League's decision to fight the Persian Wars demonstrated courage inspired by a deep commitment to the ideal of political freedom that had emerged in the Archaic Age.

Athenian Confidence in the Golden Age

The struggle against the Persians occasioned a rare instance of city-state cooperation in ancient Greek history. The two most powerful city-states, Athens and Sparta, had put aside their mutual hostility to share the leadership of the united Greek military forces. Their attempt to continue this alliance after the Persian Wars, however, ended in failure, despite the lobbying of pro-Spartan Athenians who believed the two city-states should be partners rather than rivals. Out of this failure arose the so-called Athenian empire, a modern label that accurately describes Athens' new vision of itself after the defeat of the Persians. No longer were Athenians satisfied being co-members of the association of Greek city-states: they fancied a much grander role for themselves.

The Establishment of the Athenian Empire

The victorious Greeks decided in 478 B.C. to continue a naval alliance to attack the Persian outposts that still existed in far northern Greece and western Anatolia, especially Ionia. The Spartan Pausanias, commander of the victorious Greek infantry forces at the battle of Plataea, led the first expedition. But his arrogant and violent behavior toward both his Greek troops and local Greek citizens in Anatolia, especially women, quickly led to disaffection with Spartan leadership among the Greek allies. (This kind of outlaw conduct became common for Spartan men in powerful positions when away from home; their regimented training apparently left them ill prepared to operate humanely and effectively once they had escaped the constraints imposed by their way of life in Sparta.)

By 477 B.C. the Athenian aristocrat Aristides (c. 525–465 B.C.) had persuaded the other Greeks to request Athenian leadership of the alliance against the Persians. Under Athenian direction the alliance took on a permanent organizational structure. Member states swore a solemn oath never to desert the coalition. The members were located predominantly in northern Greece, on the islands of the Aegean Sea, and along the western coast of Anatolia—the areas most exposed to Persian attack. Most of the independent city-states of the Peloponnese, however, remained in the alliance with the Spartans that they had established long before the Persian Wars. Now Athens and Sparta each dominated a coalition of allies. Sparta and its allies, which modern historians refer to as the Peloponnesian League, had an assembly to set policy, but no action could be taken unless the Spartan leaders agreed to it. The alliance headed by Athens, referred to today as the Delian League because its treasury was originally located on the Aegean island of Delos, also had an assembly of representatives to make policy. Members of the alliance were supposed to share equally in making decisions, but in practice Athens was in charge.

The Athenian representatives came to dominate this "democracy" as a result of the special arrangements made to finance the alliance's naval operations. Aristides based the different levels of "dues" the various member city-states were to pay each year on their size and prosperity. Larger member states were to supply entire triremes (warships) complete with crews and their pay; smaller states could share the cost of a ship and crew or simply contribute cash, which would be added to others' payments.

Over time, more and more Delian League members paid their dues in cash rather than by furnishing warships. It was beyond their capacities to build ships as specialized as triremes (narrow vessels built for speed—they held three banks of oarsmen on each side and had a battering ram attached to the bow) and to train crews in the intricate teamwork required to work the oars (one hundred seventy rowers were needed). Athens, far larger than most of the allies, had the shipyards and skilled workers to build triremes as well as an abundance of men eager to earn pay as rowers. Therefore Athens built and manned most of the alliance's triremes, supplementing the allies' dues with its own contribution. The oarsmen came from the poorest class in society, and their essential contribution to the navy earned them not only money but also additional political influence in Athenian democracy as naval strength became the city-state's principal source of military power.

Because most allies eventually lacked warships of their own, members of the Delian League had no effective recourse if they disagreed with decisions made for the league as a whole by Athens. The

Athenian assembly dispatched the superior Athenian fleet to compel discontented allies to adhere to league policy and to continue paying their annual dues (which because they were compulsory were really "tribute"), thereby becoming the dominant power in the league. As Thucydides observed, rebellious allies "lost their independence," making the Athenians as the league's leaders "no longer as popular as they used to be."

Within twenty years after the battle of Salamis the Delian League had expelled almost all the Persian garrisons that had continued to hold out in some city-states along the northeastern Aegean coast and had driven the Persian fleet from the Aegean Sea, ending the Persian threat to Greece for the next fifty years. Athens meanwhile grew stronger from its share of the spoils captured from Persian outposts and the tribute paid by Delian League members. By the middle of the fifth century B.C., league members' tribute totaled an amount equivalent to perhaps $200 million in contemporary terms (assuming $80 as the average daily pay of an ordinary worker today). For a state the size of Athens (around thirty thousand to forty thousand adult male citizens at the time), this annual income meant prosperity.

The Athenian assembly decided how to spend the city-state's income. Rich and poor alike had a self-interested stake in keeping the fleet active and the allies paying for it. Well-heeled aristocrats like Cimon (c. 510–450 B.C.), the son of Miltiades, the victor of Marathon, enhanced their social status by commanding successful league campaigns and then spending their portion of the spoils on benefactions to Athens. Such financial contributions to the common good were expected of wealthy and prominent men. Political parties did not exist in ancient Athens, and political leaders formed informal circles of friends and followers to support their agendas. Disputes among these aristocratic leaders often stemmed more from competition for public offices and influence in the assembly than from disagreements over policy matters. Arguments about policy tended to revolve around how Athens should exercise its growing power internationally, not whether it should refrain from interfering with the affairs of the other Delian League members to further Athenian interests. The numerous Athenian men of lesser means who rowed the Delian League's ships came to depend on the income they

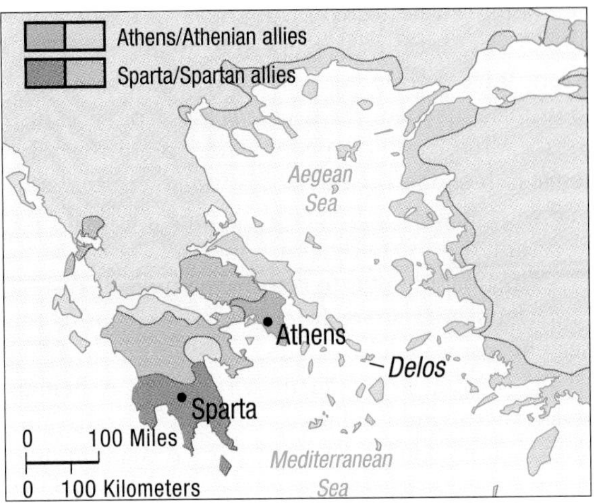

The Delian and Peloponnesian Leagues

earned on league expeditions. Thus alliance was transformed into empire, despite Athenian support of democratic governments in some allied city-states previously ruled by oligarchies. The Athenians believed their conversion from partner to leader was justified because it kept the Delian League strong enough to protect Greece from the Persians.

The Democratic Reform of the Athenian System of Justice

In the decades following the Persian Wars, both the military and political importance of the poorer men who powered the Athenian fleet grew. As these citizens came to recognize that they provided the foundation of Athenian security and prosperity, they apparently felt the time had come to make the administration of justice at Athens just as democratic as the process of making policy and passing laws in the assembly, which was open to all male citizens over eighteen years old. Although at this time the assembly could serve as a court of appeals, the nine archons (annual magistrates of the city-state) and the Areopagus council of ex-archons rendered most judicial verdicts. The nine archons had been chosen by lot rather than by election since 487 B.C., thus making access to those offices a matter of chance and not liable to domination by wealthy aristocrats who could afford expensive electoral campaigns. Filling public offices by lot was considered democratic because it gave all eligible contestants an equal chance. But even democratically selected magistrates were susceptible to corruption, as were the members of the Areopagus. A different judicial system was needed to insulate the men who decided cases from pressure by socially prominent people and from bribery by those rich enough to buy a favorable verdict. Laws that were enacted democratically meant little if they were not applied fairly and honestly.

The final impetus to reform the judicial system came from a crisis in foreign affairs. Cimon, the hero of many Delian League campaigns, marshaled all his prestige to persuade a reluctant Athenian assembly to send hoplites to help the Spartans suppress a serious helot revolt in 462 B.C. Cimon, like many Athenian aristocrats, had always admired the Spartans, and he was known for registering his opposition to assembly proposals by saying, "But that is not what the Spartans would do." His Spartan friends soon changed their minds about Athenian assistance, however, and sent Cimon and his army home. Spartan leaders feared the democratically inclined Athenian soldiers might decide to help the helots throw off Spartan domination.

This humiliating rejection of their help outraged the Athenian assembly and provoked renewed hostility between the two city-states. The disgrace it brought Cimon carried over to his fellow aristocrats, thereby establishing a political climate ripe for further democratic reforms. A man named Ephialtes seized the moment in 461 B.C. and convinced the assembly to pass measures limiting the power of the Areopagus and, more important, to set up a judicial system of courts run by male citizens over thirty years old chosen by lot for each case. The reforms made it virtually impossible to influence or bribe the citizen jurors because the jurors for each court were selected only on the day of the trial, all trials were concluded in one day, and juries were large (from several hundred to several thousand). The only official present kept fights from breaking out. Jurors made up their minds after hearing speeches by the persons involved. The accuser and the accused were required to speak for themselves, although they might pay someone else to compose the speech they would deliver and ask others to speak in support of their arguments. A majority vote of the jurors ruled, and no appeals were allowed.

The structure of the new court system reflected the underlying principles of what scholars today

Ostraka
These two ostraka *(inscribed potsherds that were used as ballots in the process of ostracism) were broken from the same pot. The upper piece bore the name of Cimon, the lower one the name of Themistocles.*

call the "radical" democracy of Athens in the mid-fifth century B.C. This system involved widespread participation by a cross section of male citizens, random selection of most public officeholders, elaborate precautions to prevent corruption, equal protection under the law for citizens regardless of wealth, some legal restrictions on citizen women, and the majority's authority over any minority or individual. A striking example of majority rule was a procedure called *ostracism* (from *ostracon,* meaning a "piece of broken pottery," the material used for ballots). Once a year, at a meeting just for this purpose, all male citizens were eligible to cast a ballot on which they had scratched the name of one man they thought should be exiled. If at least 6,000 ballots were cast, the man whose name appeared on the greatest number was compelled to live outside the borders of Attica for ten years. He suffered no other penalty, and his family and property could remain behind undisturbed. Ostracism was emphatically not a criminal penalty, and men returning from their exile had undiminished rights as citizens. Probably no more than several dozen men were actually ostracized after the first recorded instance in 488 B.C.; the practice fell into disuse after about 416 B.C.

Ostracism served as a mechanism for blaming an individual for a failed policy the assembly had originally approved. Cimon, for example, was ostracized after the disastrous attempt to cooperate with Sparta during the helot revolt. An ostracism could also stem from a man's personal eminence, if he became so prominent that he could dominate the political scene and thus seem a threat to democracy. An anecdote about Aristides, who set the original level of dues for the Delian League members, illustrates this situation. Aristides was nicknamed "The Just" because he was reputedly so fairminded. On the day of the balloting for an ostracism, an illiterate man from the countryside handed Aristides a potsherd and asked him to scratch the name of the man's choice for ostracism on it:

> *"Certainly," said Aristides. "Which name shall I write?"*
> *"Aristides," replied the countryman.*
> *"Very well," remarked Aristides as he proceeded to inscribe his own name. "But tell me, why do you want to ostracize Aristides? What has he done to you?"*
> *"Oh, nothing; I don't even know him," sputtered the man. "I'm just sick and tired of hearing everybody refer to him as 'The Just.' "*

Although Aristides was indeed ostracized in 482 B.C. (though he was recalled in 480 B.C. to fight the Persians), this anecdote may well be apocryphal. Nevertheless, it makes a valid point: the Athenians assumed that the right way to protect democracy was always to trust the majority vote of freeborn, adult male citizens, without any restrictions on a man's ability to say what he thought was best for democracy. This conviction required making allowances for irresponsible types like the illiterate countryman who complained about Aristides. It rested on the belief that the cumulative political wisdom of the majority of voters would outweigh the eccentricity and ignorance of the few.

The Policies of Pericles

This idea that democracy was best served by involving a cross section of the male citizenry received further support in the 450s B.C. when Pericles (c. 495–429 B.C.), whose mother was the niece of the democratic reformer Cleisthenes, successfully proposed that state revenues be used to pay a daily stipend to men who served on juries, in the council of the five hundred, and in other public offices filled by lot. Without this stipend poorer men would have found it difficult to leave their regular work to serve in these time-consuming positions. By contrast, the most influential public officials—the annual board of ten generals, who oversaw both military and civil affairs, especially public finances—were elected and received no stipend. The assembly elected these generals because their posts required expertise and experience—conditions that random selection could not guarantee. They were not paid mainly because rich men, who had access to the education and resources required to handle this job, were expected to win election as generals. Generals were compensated by the prestige their office carried. The stipend received by other officials and jurors was not lavish, certainly no more than an ordinary worker could earn in a day, but it enabled poorer Athenians to serve in government. Like Cleisthenes before him, Pericles became the most influential Athenian leader of his era by devising innovations to strengthen the egalitarian tendencies of Athenian democracy.

In 451 B.C., Pericles sponsored a law stating that henceforth citizenship would be conferred only on children whose mother and father were both Athenians. Previously, the offspring of Athenian men who married non-Athenian women had been granted citizenship. Aristocratic men in particular had tended to marry rich foreign women, as Pericles' own maternal grandfather had done. The new law enhanced the status of Athenian mothers and made Athenian citizenship more exclusive. The citizens of Athens began to see themselves as part of an elite group.

Pericles initially pursued an aggressive foreign policy against Spartan interests in Greece and against Persian domination of Egypt and the eastern Mediterranean. The disastrous results of the campaigns of the 450s B.C. against Persian territory and the accelerating acrimony with the Spartans convinced the assembly to cease any further expeditions in the eastern Mediterranean after 450 B.C. When operations against Sparta and other members of the Peloponnesian League also failed, Pericles in the winter of 446–445 B.C. engineered a peace treaty with Sparta designed to freeze the balance of power in Greece for thirty years and thus preserve Athenian dominance in the Delian League. Although he remained the most powerful man in Athens during this period, winning election as general fifteen consecutive years beginning in 443 B.C., Pericles had to withstand severe criticism for his policies, both domestic and foreign. His championing of a building program of large temples raised fierce objections over expenses, and his judgment came under attack for a war in 441–439 B.C. with the people of the island of Samos, a valuable Delian League ally. But Pericles soon faced an even greater challenge when relations with Sparta worsened in the mid-430s B.C. over Athenian backing of some rebellious Spartan allies. Corinth, a crucial Spartan ally, threatened to defect to the Delian League unless Sparta acted to prevent Athenian interference with Corinth's own allies. The Spartans finally demanded the Athenians withdraw their embargo of Megara, a Spartan ally, or face war, but Pericles prevailed upon the assembly to refuse all compromises. His critics claimed he was sticking to his hard line against Sparta and trying to provoke a war in order to revive his fading popularity. Pericles retorted that no accommodation to Spartan demands was possible because Athenian freedom of action was at stake. By 431 B.C. the thirty-year peace made in 445 B.C. had been shattered beyond repair. The protracted Peloponnesian War (as modern historians call it) began in that year and ultimately ended the Athenian Golden Age.

The Urban Landscape of Athens

Private homes, both in the city and the countryside, retained their traditional modest size even during Athens' great prosperity in the fifth century B.C. Farmhouses were usually clustered in villages, while homes in the urban center were wedged higgledy-piggledy against one another along narrow, winding streets. The residences of rich people followed the same basic design as other urban homes, which grouped bedrooms, storerooms, and dining rooms around small, open-air courtyards, only on a grander scale. Wall paintings or works of art were not yet common as decorations for private homes. Sparse furnishings and simple furniture were the rule. Sanitary facilities usually consisted of a pit dug just outside the front door, which was emptied by collectors paid to dump the contents outside the city at a distance set by law. Poorer people rented houses or small apartments.

Private patronage funded some public improvements, such as the landscaping with shade trees and running tracks that Cimon paid to have installed in open areas. On the edge of the central market square and gathering spot at the heart of the city, called the *agora,* was the renowned Painted Stoa. *Stoas* were narrow buildings open along one side whose purpose was to provide shelter from sun or rain. The crowds of men who came to the agora daily to chat about politics and local affairs would cluster inside the Painted Stoa, whose walls were decorated with paintings of great moments in Greek history commissioned from the most famous painters of the time, Polygnotus and Mikon. That one of the stoa's paintings portrayed the battle of Marathon, in which Cimon's father, Miltiades, had won glory, was only appropriate because the building had been paid for and donated to the city by the husband of Cimon's sister, probably with financial assistance from Cimon. The social values of Athenian democracy called for aristocratic men like Cimon and his brother-in-law to provide such gifts for public use to show their goodwill toward the city-state and thereby earn increased social eminence. Wealthy citizens were also expected to fulfill costly liturgies, or public services, such as fully equipping a warship or providing theatrical entertainment at city festivals. To a certain extent this liturgical system for wealthy men compensated for the lack of any regular income or property taxes in ancient Athens.

Athens received substantial revenues from harbor fees, sales taxes, and the "dues" of its Delian League allies. Buildings paid for by public funds constituted the most conspicuous architecture in classical Athens. The scale of these public buildings was usually no greater than the size required to fulfill their function, such as the complex of buildings on the agora's western edge in which the council of five hundred held its meetings and the public archives were kept. Because the assembly convened in the open air on a hillside above the agora, it required no building, just a speaker's platform. In 447 B.C., however, Pericles instigated a great project atop the acropolis, the mesalike promontory at the center of the city, which towered over the agora. Most conspicuous were a mammoth gate building with columns straddling the broad entrance to the acropolis at its western end and a new temple of Athena to house a huge image of the goddess. These buildings easily cost more than the modern equivalent of a billion dollars, a phenomenal sum for an ancient Greek city-state. Pericles' political enemies railed at him for squandering public funds. The program may have been financed partly from Delian League

The Civic Center of Athens
This model shows the public buildings of the west side of the agora of Athens, the city's physical and governmental center. The two large buildings in the foreground were not built until Roman times.

tributes. Substantial funds certainly came from sales taxes and harbor taxes and from the financial reserves of Athena's sanctuaries, which like those of the other gods throughout Greece received both private donations and public support.

The new temple built for Athena became known as the *Parthenon,* meaning "the house of the virgin goddess." As the patron goddess of Athens, Athena had long had another sanctuary on the acropolis. Its focus was an olive tree regarded as the sacred symbol of Athena, who ensured the economic health of the Athenians. The Parthenon honored Athena in a different capacity: as a warrior serving as the divine champion of Athenian military power. Inside the Parthenon a gold and ivory statue well over thirty feet high portrayed the goddess in battle armor and holding in her outstretched hand a six-foot statue of the figure of Victory (*Nike* in Greek). Like all Greek temples, the Parthenon was meant as a house for its divinity, not as a gathering place for worshipers. In its general design the Parthenon was representative of the standard architecture of Greek temples: a rectangular box on a raised platform, a plan the Greeks probably derived from the stone temples of Egypt. The box, which had only one small door at the front, was fenced in by columns all around. The columns were carved in the simple style called Doric, in contrast to the more elaborate Ionic and Corinthian styles that have often been imitated in modern buildings (for example, in the Corinthian-style facade of the Supreme Court Building in Washington, D.C.).

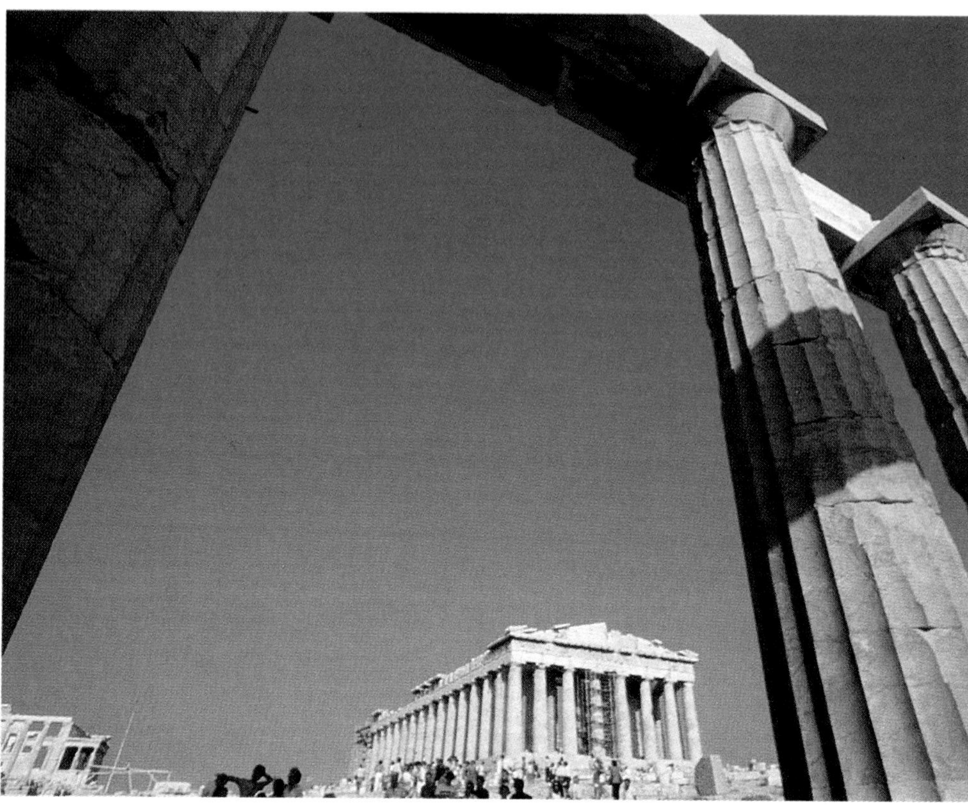

Architectural Grandeur *This photograph gives an idea of the size of the majestic gateway to the Athenian acropolis and the dramatic framing effect it produced for visitors as they passed through toward the Parthenon temple in the distance.*

Only priests and priestesses could enter the temple, but public religious ceremonies took place outside.

The Parthenon was remarkable for its great size and elaborate decoration. Constructed from twenty thousand tons of Attic marble, it stretched nearly two hundred thirty feet in length and a hundred feet wide, with eight columns across the ends instead of the six normally found in Doric style, and seventeen instead of thirteen along the sides. Its massive look conveyed an impression of power. Because perfectly rectilinear architecture appears curved to the human eye, subtle curves and inclines were built into the Parthenon to produce an illusion of completely straight lines: the columns were given a slight bulge in their middles, the corner columns were installed at a slight incline and closer together, and the platform was made slightly convex. By overcoming the distortions of nature, the Parthenon's sophisticated architecture and technical refinements made a confident statement about human ability to construct order that was both apparent and real.

Fifth-Century Athens

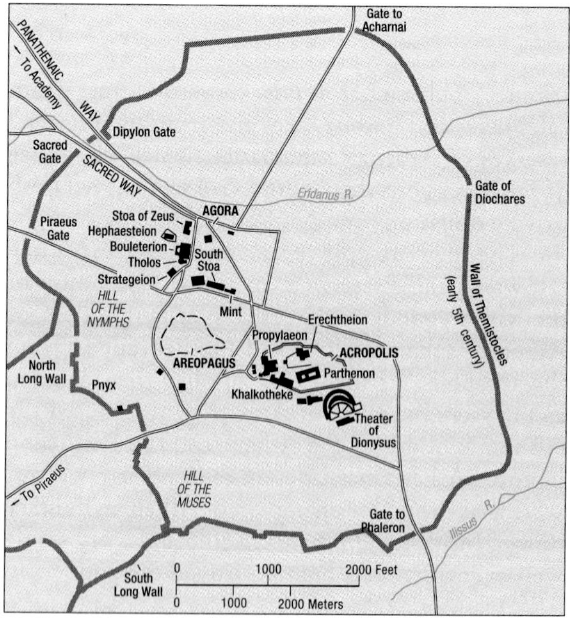

The sculptural decoration of the Parthenon also proclaimed Athenian confidence about their city-state's relationship with the gods. Sculptured panels ran along its exterior above the columns, and tableaux of sculptures appeared in the triangular spaces (pediments) underneath the roof line at either end of the building. Although these decorations were a regular part of the Doric style, the Parthenon also incorporated a unique sculptural feature for a Doric building. A continuous band of figures was carved in relief around the top of the walls inside the porch formed by the columns along the edges of the building's platform. This sort of frieze usually appeared only on Ionic-style buildings. Adding a frieze in Ionic style to a Doric-style temple was a striking departure meant to attract attention. The Parthenon's frieze depicted the Athenian religious ritual in which a procession of citizens paraded to the acropolis to present Athena in her olive-tree sanctuary a new robe woven by specially selected Athenian girls. Depicting the procession in motion, like a filmstrip in stone, the frieze showed men riding spirited horses, women walking along carrying sacred implements, and the gods gathering together at the head of the parade to observe their human worshipers. As usual in the sculptured decoration on Greek temples, the frieze sparkled with shiny metal attachments serving, for example, as the horsemen's reins and with brightly colored paint enlivening the figures and the background.

The Acropolis of Athens
This rocky promontory, with its three marble temples to the goddess Athena, was the city's religious center.

No other city-state had ever gone beyond the traditional function of temples—glorifying and paying homage to the community's special deities—by adorning a temple with representations of its citizens. The Parthenon frieze made a unique statement about how Athenians perceived their relationship to the gods. Even if the deities carved in the frieze were understood to be separated from and perhaps invisible to the humans in the procession, a temple adorned with pictures of citizens, albeit idealized citizens of perfect physique and beauty, amounted to a claim of special intimacy between the city-state and the gods. Presumably this assertion reflected the Athenian interpretation of their success in helping turn back the Persians, in achieving leadership of a powerful naval alliance, and in amassing wealth that made Athens richer than all its neighbors in mainland Greece. The Parthenon, like the rest of Pericles' building program, honored the deities with whom the city-state identified and expressed Athenian confidence that the gods looked favorably on their empire. Their success, the Athenians would have said, proved that the gods were on their side.

The Message of Sculpture

Like the design of the sculpture on the outside of the Parthenon, the enormous size and expense of the freestanding figure of Athena inside the temple expressed the innovative and confident spirit of Athens in its Golden Age. The statue's creator, the Athenian Phidias, gained such fame that he became a close friend of Pericles and was invited by other Greek city-states to sculpt great statues for their temples. (Phidias's social stature was exceptional,

The Parthenon Frieze *These blocks from the Ionic frieze around the Parthenon at Athens show the gods seated as observers of a procession. The complex folds of their clothing characterized the classical style of Greek sculpture.*

however. Aristocrats considered most sculptors and artists low status because they labored with their hands. Only the few fortunate talented enough to become famous were welcomed in high society.)

Other Greek artists as well as sculptors experimented with new techniques and artistic approaches in this period, but freestanding sculpture most clearly demonstrates the new and various ways in which the human form was rendered in the fifth century B.C. Such sculptures could be either public (that is, paid for with city-state funds, as were the Parthenon's) or private (paid for by individuals). But Greeks who ordered pieces of private art did not yet use them to decorate the interiors of their homes. Instead they displayed them publicly, for a variety of purposes. Privately commissioned statues of gods could be placed in a sanctuary as a proof of devotion. In the tradition of offering lovely crafted objects to divinities as commemorations of important personal experiences such as economic successes or victories in athletic contests, people also donated sculptures of physically beautiful humans to the sanctuaries of the gods as gifts of honor. Wealthy families would commission statues of their deceased members, especially if they had died young, to be placed above their graves as memorials of their virtue. In every case private statues were meant to be seen by other people. In this sense private sculpture in the Golden Age served a public function: it broadcast a message to an audience.

Archaic statues had been characterized by a stiff posture imitating the style of freestanding Egyptian figures. Egyptian sculptors used this style, unchanged, for centuries. Greek artists, however, had begun changing their style by the time of the Persian Wars, and in the fifth century B.C. new poses became more prevalent in freestanding sculpture, continuing the trend toward movement visible in the sculpture attached to temples. Human males were still generally portrayed nude as athletes or warriors, and females were still clothed in fine robes. But their postures and their physiques were becoming more naturalistic. In the Archaic Age, male statues had been rendered in a uniform pose: striding forward with their left legs, arms held rigidly at their side. Classical Age male statues might have the body's weight on either leg and bent arms. Their musculature was now anatomically correct rather than sketchy and almost impressionistic, as had been the style in the sixth century B.C. Female statues, too, had more relaxed poses and natural clothing, which hung in a way that hinted at the shape of the body underneath instead of disguising it. The faces of classical sculptures reflected an impassive calm rather than the smiles that had characterized archaic figures.

The sculptors who devised these daring new styles preferred to work in bronze, though marble was also popular. Creating bronze statues, which were cast in molds made from clay models, required a particularly well-equipped workshop with furnaces, tools, and foundry workers skilled in metallurgy. Properly prepared bronze had the tensile strength to allow outstretched poses of arms and legs, which could not be done in marble without supports. (Hence the intrusive tree trunks and other such supports introduced in the marble copies made in Roman times of Greek statues in bronze. These Roman copies are often the only surviving examples of the originals.) The strength and malleability of bronze allowed innovative sculptors like the Athenian Myron and Polyclitus of Argos to develop the freestanding statue to its physical limits. Myron, for example, sculpted a discus thrower crouched at the top of his backswing. The figure not only assumes an asymmetrical pose but also seems to burst with the tension of the athlete's effort. Polyclitus's renowned statue of a walking man carrying a spear gives a different impression from every angle of viewing. The feeling of motion it conveys is palpable. The same is true of the famous statue by an unknown sculptor of a female (perhaps the goddess of love Aphrodite) adjusting her diaphanous robe with one upraised arm. The message these statues conveyed to their ancient audience was one of energy, motion, and asymmetry in delicate balance. Archaic statues impressed viewers with their appearance of stability; not even a hard shove seemed likely to budge them. Statues of the Classical Age, by contrast, showed greater range of motion and a variety of poses and impressions. The spirited movement of some of these statues suggests the energy of the times but also reflects the possibility of change and instability.

Continuity and Change in the Golden Age of Athens

Even though the cultural and social life of Athens in the fifth century B.C. underwent unprecedented changes, many central aspects of Athenian society remained unchanged. The result was a mix of innovation and tradition. Tragic drama developed as a publicly supported art form. A new and upsetting (to traditionalists) form of education for wealthy young men with ambitions in public life emerged. Public life remained confined and limited for upper-class women. Women of the poorer classes, however, had more opportunity for contact with the public, male world because they had to work to help support their families. The interplay of continuity and change created a tension that was tolerable until the pressure of war with Sparta strained Athenian society to the breaking point. All these events took place against the background of traditional Greek religion, which permeated public and private life.

Greek Religion in the Classical Period

The Athenians' attitude toward their deities in the mid-fifth century B.C. corresponded to the basic tenet of Greek religion: humans both as individuals and as groups honored the gods to thank them for blessings received and to receive blessings in return. Those honors consisted of sacrifices, gifts to the gods' sanctuaries, and festivals of songs, dances, prayers, and processions. A seventh-century B.C. bronze statuette, which a man named Mantiklos gave to a (now unknown) sanctuary of Apollo to honor the god, makes clear why individuals gave such gifts. On its legs Mantiklos inscribed his understanding of the transaction: "Mantiklos gave this from his share to the Far Darter of the Silver Bow [Apollo]; now you, Apollo, do something for me in return." This idea of reciprocity underlay the Greek understanding of the divine. Deities did not love humans, though in some mythological stories they took earthly lovers and produced half-divine children. Rather they supported humans who paid them honor and did not offend them. Gods whom humans offended retaliated by sending such calamities as famine, earthquake, epidemic disease, or defeat in war.

The greatest difficulty for humans lay in anticipating what might offend a deity. Fortunately, some of the gods' expectations were codified in a moral order with rules for human behavior. For example, the Greeks believed that the gods demanded hospitality for strangers and proper burial for family members and that they punished human arrogance and murderous violence. Oracles, dreams, divination, and the prophecies of seers were all regarded as clues to what humans might have done to anger the gods. Offenses could be acts such as forgetting a sacrifice, violating the sanctity of a temple area, or breaking an oath or sworn agreement made to another person. People believed the deities were especially concerned with certain transgressions, such as violating oaths, but generally uninterested in common crimes, which humans had to police themselves. Homicide was such a serious offense, however, that the gods were thought to punish it by casting a *miasma* (state of pollution) upon murderers and upon all those around them. Unless the members of the affected group purified themselves by punishing the murderer, they could all expect to suffer divine punishment such as bad harvests or disease.

The Greeks believed their gods occasionally experienced sorrow in their dealings with one another, but essentially were immune to tragedy because they were immortal. The twelve most important gods, headed by Zeus, were envisioned assembling for banquets atop Mt. Olympus, the highest peak in mainland Greece. Like the human aristocrats of Homer's stories, the gods resented any slights to their honor. "I am well aware that the gods are competitively envious and disruptive towards humans" is Solon's summary of their nature in one famous (and probably fictitious) anecdote that tells of him giving advice to Croesus before the Lydian king lost his kingdom to the Persians.

To interact with a god, people prayed, sang hymns of praise, offered sacrifices, and presented gifts at the deity's sanctuary. In these sanctuaries a person could honor and thank the deities for blessings and propitiate them when misfortune, taken as a sign of divine anger at human behavior, had struck the petitioner. Private individuals offered sacrifices at home with the household gathered around, and sometimes the family's slaves were allowed to join. Priests and priestesses, who in most cases were chosen from the citizen body as a whole, conducted the sacrifices of public cults. The priests and priestesses of Greek cults were usually attached to a particular sanctuary or shrine and did not seek to influence political or social matters. Their special knowledge consisted in knowing how to perform traditional religious rites. They were not guardians of theological orthodoxy, as are some clergy today, because Greek religion had no systematic theology or canonical dogma, nor did it have any institutions to oversee doctrine.

The ritual of sacrifice provided the primary occasion of contact between the gods and their worshipers. Most sacrifices were regularly scheduled events on the community's civic calendar. Athenians demonstrated their piety toward the deities of the city-state's official cults on the first eight days of every month. For example, they celebrated Athena's birthday on the third day of each month and Artemis's, the goddess of wild animals who was also the special patroness of the Athenian council of five hundred, on the sixth. Artemis's brother, Apollo, was honored on the seventh day. Athens boasted of having the most religious festivals in all of Greece, with nearly half the days of the year featuring one, some large and some small. Not everyone attended all the festivals; hired laborers' contracts specified how many days off they received to attend religious ceremonies. Major occasions such as the Panathenaia festival, whose procession was portrayed on the Parthenon frieze, attracted large crowds of both women and men. The Panathenaia festival honored Athena not only with sacrifices and parades but also with contests in music, dancing, poetry, and athletics. Valuable prizes were awarded to the winners. Some festivals were for women only: one was the three-day festival for married women in honor of Demeter, goddess of agriculture and fertility.

Different cults had differing rituals, but sacrifice served as their focus. Sacrifices ranged from the bloodless offering of fruits, vegetables, and small cakes to the slaughter of large animals. Looking back on fifth-century B.C. Athens, the orator Lysias explained the necessity for public sacrifice: "Our ancestors handed down to us the most powerful and prosperous community in Greece by performing the prescribed sacrifices. It is therefore proper for us to offer the same sacrifices as they, if only for the sake of the success which has resulted from those rites." The sacrifice of a large animal provided an occasion for the community to assemble and reaffirm its ties to the divine world and, by sharing the roasted meat of the sacrificed beast, for the worshipers to benefit personally from a good relationship with the gods. The feasting that followed a blood sacrifice was especially significant because meat was comparatively rare in the Greek diet. The actual killing of the animal followed strict rules meant to ensure the purity of the occasion. The elaborate procedures required for a blood sacrifice show how seriously and solemnly the Greeks regarded the sacrificial killing of animals. The victim had to be an unblemished do-

Animal Sacrifice
The sacrifice of large animals was an important Greek religious ceremony. Here, women place garlands on the animals before they are killed to show that they are specially chosen.

mestic animal, specially decorated with garlands and induced to approach the altar as if of its own volition. The assembled crowd maintained strict silence to avoid possibly impure remarks. The sacrificer sprinkled water on the victim's head so it would, in shaking its head in response to the sprinkle, appear to consent to its death. After washing his hands, the sacrificer scattered barley grains on the altar fire and the animal's head and then cut a lock of the animal's hair and threw it on the fire. Following a prayer, he swiftly cut the animal's throat while musicians played flutelike pipes and female worshipers screamed, presumably to express the group's ritual sorrow at the victim's death. The carcass was then butchered, with some portions thrown on the altar fire so their aromatic smoke could waft its way upward to the god of the cult. The rest of the meat was then distributed among the worshipers.

Greek religion also encompassed many activities besides those of the cults of the twelve Olympian deities. Families marked significant moments such as birth, marriage, and death with prayers, rituals, and sacrifices. Greeks honored their ancestors with offerings made at their tombs, consulted seers about the meanings of dreams and omens, and sought out magicians for spells to improve their love lives or curses to harm their enemies. Particularly important both to the community and to individuals were hero cults, rituals performed at the tomb of a man or woman, usually famous for performing extraordinary feats in the distant past, whose remains were thought to retain special power. This power was local, whether for revealing the future through oracles, for healing injuries and disease, or for providing assistance in war. The only hero to whom cults were established all over the Greek world was the strongman Heracles (or Hercules, as his name was later spelled by the Romans). His superhuman feats gave him an appeal as a protector in many city-states.

The cult of Demeter and her daughter Kore (or Persephone), headquartered at Eleusis, a settlement on the west coast of Attica, attracted followers from all parts of the world. The central rite of this cult was called the Mysteries, a series of initiation ceremonies into the secret knowledge of the cult. If they were free of pollution (for example, if they had not been convicted for murder, committed sacrilege, or had contact with a birth or death), all free speakers of Greek from anywhere in the world—women and men, adults and children—were eligible for initiation, as were some slaves who worked in the sanctuary. Initiation proceeded in several stages. The main stage took place during an annual festival lasting almost two weeks. So important were the Eleusinian Mysteries that the Greek states observed an international truce of fifty-five days to allow travel to and from the festival even from distant corners of the Greek world. Prospective initiates participated in a complicated set of ceremonies that culminated in the revelation of Demeter's central secret after a day of fasting. The secret was revealed in an initiation hall constructed solely for this purpose. Under a roof fifty-five yards square supported on a forest of interior columns, the hall held three thousand people standing around its sides on tiered steps. The most eloquent proof of the sanctity attached to the Mysteries of Demeter and Kore is that throughout the thousand years during which the rites were celebrated, we know of no one who ever revealed the secret. To this day all we know is that it involved something done, something said, and something shown. It is certain, however, that initiates were promised a better life and a better fate after death. "Richly blessed is the mortal who has seen these rites; but whoever is not an initiate and has no share in them, that one never has an equal portion after death, down in the gloomy darkness" are the words describing the benefits of initiation in the sixth-century B.C. poem *The Hymn to Demeter.*

The Eleusinian Mysteries were not the only mystery cult of the Greek world, nor were they unique in their concern with what lay beyond death. Most mystery cults also emphasized protection for initiates in their daily lives, whether against ghosts, illness, poverty, shipwrecks, or the countless other dangers of ancient Greek life. Divine protection was accorded, however, as a reward for appropriate conduct, not by any abstract belief in the gods. For the ancient Greeks, gods expected honors and rites, and Greek religion required action from its worshipers. Greeks had to pray and sing hymns honoring the gods, perform sacrifices, and undergo purifications. These rites represented an active response to the precarious conditions of human life in a world in which early death from disease, accident, or war was commonplace. Furthermore, the Greeks believed the gods sent both good and bad into the world. As a result the Greeks did not expect to reach paradise at some future time when evil forces would finally be vanquished forever. Their assessment of existence made no allowance for change in the relationship between the human and the divine. That relationship encompassed sorrow as well as joy, punishment in the here and now, and perhaps the uncertain hope for favored treatment both in this life and in an afterlife for initiates of the Eleusinian Mysteries and other similar cults.

The Development of Athenian Tragedy

The complex relationship between gods and humans formed the basis of classical Athens's most enduring cultural innovation: the tragic dramas performed over three days at the major annual festival of the god Dionysus held in the late spring. These plays, still read and produced on stage, were presented in ancient Athens as part of a drama contest, in keeping with the competitive spirit characteristic of many events held in the gods' honor. Tragedy reached its peak as a dramatic form in the fifth century B.C.

Every year, one of Athens's magistrates chose three playwrights to present four plays each at the festival. Three were tragedies and one a satyr play in which actors portrayed the half-human, half-animal (horse or goat) satyrs featured in this more lighthearted form of theater. The term *tragedy*—derived, for reasons now lost, from the Greek words for "goat" and "song"—referred to plays with plots that involved fierce conflict and characters that represented powerful forces. Tragedies were written in verse and used solemn language; they were often based on stories about the violent consequences of the interaction between gods and humans. The story often ended with a resolution to the trouble—but only after considerable suffering.

The performance of Athenian tragedies bore little resemblance to conventional modern theater productions. They took place during the daytime in an outdoor theater sacred to Dionysus, built into the slope of the southern hillside of Athens's acropolis. This theater held around fourteen thousand spectators overlooking an open, circular area in front of a slightly raised stage platform. To ensure fairness in the competition, all tragedies had to have the same number of cast members, all of whom were men: three actors to play the speaking roles (all male and female characters) and fifteen chorus members. Although the chorus leader sometimes engaged in dialogue with the actors, the chorus primarily performed songs and dances in the circular area in front of the stage, called the orchestra. Because all the actors' lines were in verse with special rhythms, the musical function of the chorus was simply to enhance the overall poetic nature of Athenian tragedy.

Even though scenery on the stage was sparse, a good tragedy presented a vivid spectacle. The chorus wore elaborate, decorative costumes and performed intricate dance routines. The actors, who wore masks, used broad gestures and booming voices to reach the upper tier of seats. A powerful voice and prodigious vocal skills were crucial to a tragic actor because words represented the heart of a tragedy, in which dialogue and long speeches were far more common than physical action. Special effects were, however, part of the spectacle. For example, a crane allowed actors playing the roles of gods to fly suddenly onto the stage, like superheroes in a modern movie. The actors playing the lead roles, called the protagonists ("first competitors"), competed against each other for the designation of best actor. So important was a first-rate protagonist to a successful tragedy that actors were

The Theater of Dionysus at Athens
This theater, cut into the south slope of the Acropolis, held some fifteen thousand spectators for performances in honor of the god Dionysus. The stone seats, wall, and stage date to the Roman period.

assigned by lot to the competing playwrights of the year to give all three an equal chance to have the finest cast. Great protagonists became enormously popular, although unlike many playwrights, they were not usually aristocrats and did not move in upper-class social circles.

The author of a slate of tragedies in the festival of Dionysus also served as director, producer, musical composer, choreographer, and sometimes even actor. Only men of some wealth could afford the amounts of time such work demanded because the prizes in the tragedy competition were probably modest. As citizens, playwrights also fulfilled the normal military and political obligations of Athenian men. The best known Athenian tragedians—Aeschylus (525–456 B.C.), Sophocles (c. 496–406 B.C.), and Euripides (c. 485–406 B.C.)—all served in the army, held public office at some point in their careers, or did both. Aeschylus fought at Marathon and Salamis; the epitaph on his tombstone, which says nothing of his great success as a playwright, reveals how highly he valued his contribution to his city-state as a citizen-soldier: "Under this stone lies Aeschylus the Athenian, son of Euphorion . . . the grove at Marathon and the Persians who landed there were witnesses to his courage."

Aeschylus's pride in his military service illustrates a fundamental characteristic of Athenian tragedy: it was at its base a public art form, an expression of the polis that explored the ethical quandaries of humans in conflict with the gods and with one another in a polis-like community. Even though most tragedies were based on stories that harkened back to a time before the polis, such as tales of the Trojan War, the moral issues the plays illuminated always pertained to the society and obligations of citizens in a city-state. In *Antigone* (441 B.C.), for example, Sophocles presented a drama of harsh conflict between the family's moral obligation to bury its dead in obedience to divine command and the male-dominated city-state's need to preserve its order and defend its values. Antigone, the daughter of Oedipus, the now-deceased former king of Thebes, clashes with her uncle, the new ruler, when he forbids the burial of one of Antigone's two brothers on the grounds that he had been a traitor. This brother had attacked Thebes after the other brother had broken an agreement to share the kingship. Both brothers died in the ensuing battle, but Antigone's uncle had allowed the burial only of the brother who had remained in power. When Antigone defies her uncle by symbolically burying the allegedly traitorous brother by sprinkling dust on his body, her uncle condemns her to die. He realizes his error only when he receives bad omens from the gods. His decision to punish Antigone ends in utter disaster: Antigone hangs herself before Creon can free her, and his son and then his wife kill themselves in despair. In this horrifying story of anger and death, Sophocles deliberately exposes the right and wrong on each side of the conflict. Although Antigone's uncle eventually acknowledges a leader's responsibility to listen to his people, the play offers no easy resolution of the competing interests of divinely sanctioned moral tradition expressed by a woman and the political rules of the state enforced by a man.

A striking aspect of Greek tragedies is that these plays written and performed by men frequently feature women as central, active figures. At one level the depiction of women in tragedy allowed men accustomed to spending most of their time with other men to peer into what they imagined the world of women was like. But the heroines portrayed in fifth-century B.C. Athenian tragedies also served as vehicles to explore the tensions inherent in the moral code of contemporary society by strongly reacting to men's violations of that code, especially as it pertained to the family. The heroines exhibit what Greeks regarded as masculine qualities. Sophocles' Antigone, for example, confronts the male ruler of her city because he deprived her family of its prerogative to bury its dead. Antigone is remarkable in fearlessly criticizing a powerful man in a public debate about right and wrong. Sophocles shows a woman who can speak like an Athenian man.

Sophocles' plays concerned difficult ethical problems in the context of the polis and thus suggest the social and political function of Athenian tragedy. His plays were overwhelmingly popular. In a sixty-year career as a playwright he competed in the drama festival about thirty times, winning at least twenty times and never finishing less than second. Because winning plays were selected by a panel of ordinary male citizens who were influenced by the audience's reaction, Sophocles' record clearly means his works appealed to the many men who attended the drama competition of the festival of Dionysus. (The evidence concerning women's attendance is unclear, but it suggests they could be present.) Their precise understanding of his messages and those of others' tragedies we cannot know, but they must have been aware that the central characters of the plays were figures who fell into disaster from positions of power and prestige. Their reversals of fortune come about not because they are absolute villains but because, as humans, they are susceptible to a lethal mixture of error, ignorance, and *hubris* (violent arrogance). The Athenian empire was at its height when audiences at Athens attended the plays of Sophocles. The presentation of the plays at the festival of Dionysus was preceded by a procession in the theater to display the money Athens received from the tribute of its allies that year. Thoughtful spectators may have reflected on the possibility that Athens's current power and prestige, managed as it was by humans, remained hostage to the same forces that controlled the fates of the heroes and heroines of tragedy. Tragedies certainly appealed to audiences because they were entertaining, but they also had an educational function: to remind male citizens, those who in the assembly made policy for the city-state, that success engendered complex moral problems too formidable to be fathomed casually or arrogantly.

Property, Social Freedom, and Athenian Women

Athenian women exercised power and earned status in both private and public life through their roles in the family and in religion, respectively. Their exclusion from politics, however, meant that their contributions to the city-state might well be overlooked by men. One heroine in a tragedy by Euripides, Melanippe, vigorously expresses this judgment in a speech denouncing men who denigrate women:

> *Empty is the slanderous blame men place on women; it is no more than the twanging of a bowstring without an arrow; women are better than men, and I will prove it: women make agreements without having to have witnesses to guarantee their honesty. . . . Women manage the household and preserve its valuable*

property. Without a wife, no household is clean or happily prosperous. And in matters pertaining to the gods—this is our most important contribution—we have the greatest share. In the oracle at Delphi we propound the will of Apollo, and at the oracle of Zeus at Dodona we reveal the will of Zeus to any Greek who wishes to know it.

Euripides' heroine Medea insists that women who bear children are due respect at least commensurate with that granted men who fight as hoplites:

People say that we women lead a safe life at home, while men have to go to war. What fools they are! I would much rather fight in the phalanx three times than give birth to a child even once.

Greek drama sometimes emphasized the areas in which Athenian women contributed to the polis: publicly by acting as priestesses and privately by bearing and raising legitimate children, the future citizens of the city-state, and by managing the household's property. Women had certain property rights in classical Athens, although these rights were granted more to benefit men than to acknowledge women's legal rights. Women could control property, even land—the most valued possession in Greek society—through inheritance and dowry, although they faced more legal restrictions than men did when they wanted to sell their property or give it away as gifts. Like men, women were supposed to preserve their property to hand down to their children. Daughters did not inherit any of their father's property on his death if he had any living sons, but perhaps one household in five had only daughters, to whom the father's property then fell. Women could also inherit from other male relatives who had no male offspring. A daughter's share in her father's estate came to her in her dowry at marriage. A son whose father was still alive when the son married might also receive a share of his inheritance at that time, to allow him to set up a household. A husband legally controlled the property in his wife's dowry, and their respective holdings frequently became commingled. In this sense husband and wife co-owned the household's common property, which was apportioned to its separate owners only if the marriage were dissolved. The husband was legally responsible for preserving the dowry and using it for the support and comfort of his wife and any children she bore him. A man often had to put up valuable land of his own as collateral to guarantee the safety of his wife's dowry if, for example, she brought to the marriage money or farm animals that he was to manage. Upon her death her children inherited the dowry. The expectation that a woman would have a dowry encouraged marriage within groups of similar wealth and status. As with the rules governing women's rights to inheritances, customary dowry arrangements supported the society's goal of enabling males to establish and maintain households, because daughters' dowries were usually less valuable than their brothers' inheritances and therefore kept the bulk of a father's property attached to his sons.

The same goal shows up clearly in Athenian laws concerning heiresses. If a father died leaving only a daughter, his property devolved upon her as his heiress, but she did not own it in the sense that she could dispose of it as she pleased. Instead (in the simplest case) her father's closest male relative—her official guardian after her father's death—was required to marry her, with the aim of producing a son. The inherited property then belonged to that son when he reached adulthood. This rule theoretically applied regardless of whether the heiress was already married (without any sons) or whether the male relative already had a wife. The heiress and the male relative were both supposed to divorce their present spouses and marry each other, although in practice the rule could be circumvented by legal subterfuge. This rule preserved the father's line and kept the property in his family. The practice also prevented rich men from getting richer by engineering deals with wealthy heiresses' guardians to marry and therefore merge estates. Above all it prevented property from piling up in the hands of unmarried women. At Sparta, Aristotle reported, precisely this agglomeration of wealth took place as women inherited land or received it in their dowries without—to Aristotle's way of thinking—adequate regulations promoting remarriage. He claimed that women had come to own 40 percent of Spartan territory. Athenian men regulated women's access to property and therefore to power more successfully.

Medea's comment that women were said to lead a safe life at home reflected the expectation that

Athenian women from the propertied class would avoid frequent or close contact with men who were not family members or in the family's circle of friends. Women of this socioeconomic level were supposed to spend much of their time in their own homes or the homes of women friends. Women dressed and slept in rooms set aside for them, but these rooms usually opened onto a walled courtyard where the women could walk in the open air, talk, supervise the domestic chores of the family's slaves, and interact with other members of the household, male and female. Here in her "territory" a woman would spin wool for clothing while chatting with women friends who had come to visit, play with her children, and give her opinions on various matters to the men of the house as they came and went. Poor women had little time for such activities because they, like their husbands, sons, and brothers, had to leave their homes, often only a crowded rental apartment, to work. They often set up small stalls to sell bread, vegetables, simple clothing, or trinkets.

A woman with servants who answered the door herself would be reproached as careless of her reputation. And a proper woman left her home only for an appropriate reason. Fortunately, Athenian life offered many occasions for women to get out: religious festivals, funerals, childbirths at the houses of relatives and friends, and trips to workshops to buy shoes or other domestic articles. Sometimes her husband escorted her, but more often she was accompanied only by a servant and had more opportunity to act independently. Social protocol demanded men to refrain from speaking the names of respectable women in public conversations and speeches in court unless practical necessity demanded it.

A Greek Woman at the Shoemaker
This Athenian vase shows a woman being fitted for a pair of custom-made shoes by a craftsman and his young assistant. Following Greek custom, the woman did not shop alone but was accompanied by her husband.

Because they stayed inside or in the shade so much, rich women maintained very pale complexions. This pallor was much admired as a sign of an enviable life of leisure and wealth. Women regularly used powdered white lead to give themselves a suitably pallid look. Presumably, many upper-class women viewed their limited contact with men outside the household as a badge of their superior social status. In a gender-segregated society such as that of upper-class Athens, a woman's primary personal relationships were probably with her children and the other women with whom she spent most of her time.

Men restricted women's freedom of movement partly to avoid uncertainty about the paternity of their children (by limiting their wives' opportunities for adultery) and to protect the virginity of their daughters. Given that citizenship defined the political structure of the city-state and a man's personal freedom, Athenians felt it crucial to ensure a boy truly was his father's son and not the offspring of some other man, who could conceivably be a foreigner or a slave. Furthermore, the preference for keeping property in the father's line meant that the sons who inherited a father's property needed to be his legitimate sons. Women who bore legitimate children immediately earned higher status and greater freedom in the family, as explained, for example, by an Athenian man in this excerpt from his remarks before a court in a case in which he had killed an adulterer whom he had caught with his wife:

> *After my marriage, I initially refrained from bothering my wife very much, but neither did I allow her too much independence. I kept an eye on her. . . .But after she had a baby, I started to trust her more and put her in charge of all my things, believing we now had the closest of relationships.*

Bearing male children brought special honor to a woman because sons meant security for parents.

The Pleasures of a Symposium *Wealthy Greek men frequently joined friends for a* symposium, *a drinking party usually with hired female entertainers. The man at the right is about to fling the dregs from his wine cup, a messy game called* kottabos.

Sons could appear in court in support of their parents in lawsuits and protect them in the streets of Athens, which for most of its history had no regular police force. By law, sons were required to support their parents in their old age. So intense was the pressure to produce sons that stories of women who smuggled in male babies born to slaves and passed them off as their own were common. Such tales, whose truth is hard to gauge, were credible only because husbands customarily stayed away at childbirth.

Men, unlike women, were not penalized for sexual activity outside marriage. "Certainly you don't think men beget children out of sexual desire?" wrote the upper-class author Xenophon. "The streets and the brothels are swarming with ways to take care of that." Men could have sex with female slaves, who could not refuse their masters, or patronize various classes of prostitutes, depending on how much money they wanted to spend. A man could not keep a prostitute in the same house as his wife without offending his wife and her family, but otherwise he incurred no censure or disgrace by paying for sex. The Greeks called the most expensive female prostitutes "companions." Usually from another city-state than the one in which they worked, companions were physically attractive and could usually sing and play musical instruments, which they did at men's dinner parties (to which wives were not invited). Many companions lived precarious lives subject to exploitation and even violence at the hands of their male customers. The most accomplished companions, however, could attract lovers from the highest levels of society and become sufficiently rich to live in luxury on their own. This independent existence strongly distinguished them from citizen women, as did the freedom to control their own sexuality. Equally distinctive was their cultivated ability to converse with men in public. Companions entertained men with their witty, bantering conversation. Their characteristic skill at clever taunts and verbal snubs allowed companions a freedom of speech denied to "proper" women. Only very rich citizen women of advanced years, such as Elpinike, the sister of Cimon, could occasionally indulge in a similar freedom of expression. She once publicly rebuked Pericles for having boasted about the Athenian conquest of Samos after its rebellion. When other Athenian women praised Pericles for his success, Elpinike sarcastically remarked. "This really is wonderful, Pericles, . . . that you have caused the loss of many good citizens, not in battle against Phoenicians or Persians, like my brother Cimon, but in suppressing an allied city of fellow Greeks."

Education, the Sophists, and New Intellectual Developments

Athenians learned the norms of respectable behavior not in school but in the family and in the course of everyday life. Public schools as we know them did not yet exist. Only well-to-do families could afford private teachers, to whom they sent their sons to learn to read, write, perhaps sing or play a musical instrument, and train for athletics and military service. Physical fitness was considered so vital for men, who could be called up for military service from the age of eighteen until sixty, that the city-state provided open-air exercise facilities for daily workouts. Men also discussed politics and exchanged news at these gymnasia. The daughters of wealthy families often learned to read, write, and do simple arithmetic, presumably from instruction at home; a woman with these skills would be better prepared to manage a household and help her future husband run their estate.

Poorer girls and boys learned a trade and perhaps some rudiments of literacy by assisting their parents in their daily work, or if they were fortunate, by being apprenticed to skilled crafts producers. Outside the ranks of the prosperous the level of literacy in Athenian society was low: only a few poor people could do much more than perhaps sign their names. The inability to read did not impede most people, who could find someone to read aloud to them any written texts they needed to understand. The predominance of oral rather than written communication meant that people were accustomed to absorbing information by ear (those who could read usually read out loud), and Greeks were very fond of songs, speeches, narrated stories, and lively conversation.

Young men from prosperous families traditionally acquired the advanced skills to participate successfully in the public life of Athenian democracy by observing their fathers, uncles, and other older men as they debated in the assembly, served as councilors or magistrates, and spoke in court cases. In many cases an older man would choose an adolescent boy as his special favorite to educate. The boy would learn about public life by spending his time in the company of the older man and his adult friends. During the day the boy would observe his mentor talking politics in the agora, help him perform his duties in public office, and work out with him in a gymnasium. Their evenings would be spent at a symposium (a drinking party for men and companions), which would encompass a range of behavior from serious political and philosophical discussion to riotous partying. Such a mentor-protégé relationship commonly included homosexual love as an expression of the bond between the boy and the older male, who would normally be married. Although neither male homosexuality outside a mentor-protégé relationship nor female homosexuality in general were socially acceptable, the homosexual behavior between older mentors and younger protégés was generally considered appropriate, as long as the older man did not exploit his younger companion physically or neglect his education in public affairs. Athenian society encompassed a wide range of bonds among men, from political and military activity, to training of mind and body, to sexual practices.

In the second half of the fifth century B.C. young men who sought to polish their political skills had access to a new kind of teacher. These teachers were called *sophists* ("wise men"), a label that acquired a pejorative connotation (preserved in the English word *sophistry*) because they were so clever at public speaking and philosophic debates. The earliest sophists practiced in parts of the Greek world outside Athens, but from about 450 B.C. on they began to travel to Athens, which was then at the height of its material prosperity, to search for pupils who could pay the hefty prices the sophists charged for their instruction. Wealthy young men flocked to the dazzling demonstrations these itinerant teachers put on to showcase their eloquence, an ability they claimed they could impart to students. The sophists offered what every ambitious young man wanted to learn: the skill to persuade his fellow citizens in the debates of the assembly and the council or in lawsuits before large juries. For those unwilling or unable to master the new rhetorical skills, the sophists (for stiff fees) would write speeches the purchasers delivered as their own compositions.

The most famous sophist was Protagoras, a contemporary of Pericles, from Abdera in northern Greece. Protagoras emigrated to Athens around 450 B.C., when he was about forty, and spent most of his career there. His oratorical skills and upright character so impressed the men of Athens that they chose him to devise a code of laws for a new colony to be founded in Thurii in southern Italy in 444 B.C. Some of Protagoras's beliefs eventually aroused considerable controversy; one was his agnosticism: "Whether the gods exist I cannot discover, nor what their form is like, for there are many impediments to knowledge, [such as] the obscurity of the subject and the brevity of human life."

Equally controversial was Protagoras's denial of an absolute standard of truth, his assertion that every issue has two, irreconcilable sides. For example, if one person feeling a breeze thinks it warm, whereas another person thinks it cool, neither judgment can be absolutely correct because the wind simply is warm to one and cool to another.

Protagoras summed up his subjectivism (the belief that there is no absolute reality behind and independent of appearances) in the much-quoted opening of his work *Truth* (most of which is now lost): "Man is the measure of all things, of the things that are that they are, and of the things that are not that they are not." "Man" in this passage (*anthropos* in Greek, hence our word "anthropology") seems to refer to the individual human, whether male or female, whom Protagoras makes the sole judge of his or her own impressions.

The sophists alarmed many traditionally minded men, who thought the sophists' facility with words might be used (by them or by their pupils) to destabilize social and political traditions. In a culture like that of ancient Greece, where laws, codes of proper behavior and morals, and religious ideals were expressed and transmitted from generation to generation orally, a persuasive and charismatic speaker could potentially wield as much power as an army of warriors. Many feared people would be swayed by the style of silver-tongued sophists and accept the substance of what they said, which often contradicted the truths commonly held.

Tension Between Intellectual and Political Forces in the 430s B.C.

The teachings of sophists like Protagoras made many Athenians nervous, especially because leading figures like Pericles flocked to hear them. Two related views sophists taught aroused special concern: the idea that human institutions and values were only matters of convention, custom, or law *(nomos)* and not products of nature *(physis)*, and the idea that because truth was relative, speakers should be able to argue either side of a question with equal persuasiveness. The first view implied that traditional human institutions were arbitrary rather than grounded in immutable nature, and the second rendered rhetoric an amoral skill. The combination of the two ideas seemed exceptionally dangerous because it threatened the shared public values of the polis with unpredictable changes. Protagoras insisted his doctrines were not hostile to democracy, especially because he argued that every person had an innate capability for "excellence" and that human survival depended on the rule of law based on a sense of justice. Members of the community, he argued, should be persuaded to obey the laws not because they are based on absolute truth, which does not exist, but because it is expedient for people to live by them. A thief, for example, who might claim he thought a law against stealing was not appropriate, would have to be persuaded that the law forbidding theft was to his advantage because it protected his own property and the community in which he, like all humans, had to live in order to survive.

Protagoras's views were not the only source of disquietude for many Athenian men disturbed by intellectual developments. Philosophers such as Anaxagoras of Clazomenae in Ionia and Leucippus of Miletus propounded unsettling new theories about the nature of the cosmos in response to the provocative physics of the Ionian thinkers of the sixth century B.C. Most people probably thought Anaxagoras's general theory postulating an abstract force he called "mind" as the organizing principle of the universe was too obscure to worry about. But the details of his theory offended those who held to the assumptions of traditional religion. For example, he argued that the sun was in truth nothing more than a lump of flaming rock, not a divine entity. Leucippus, whose doctrines were made famous by his pupil Democritus of Abdera, invented an atomic theory of matter to explain how change was possible and indeed constant. Everything, he argued, consisted of tiny, invisible particles in eternal motion. Their random collisions caused them to combine and recombine in an infinite variety of forms. This physical explanation of the source of change, like Anaxagoras's analysis of the nature of the sun, seemed to deny the validity of the entire superstructure of traditional religion, which explained events as the outcome of divine forces.

Many people feared the teachings of the sophists and philosophers would offend the gods and therefore erode the divine favor they believed Athens enjoyed. Just like a murderer, a teacher spouting sacrilegious doctrines could bring miasma and therefore divine punishment on the whole community. So deeply felt was this anxiety that Pericles' friendship with Protagoras, Anaxagoras, and other controversial intellectuals gave his rivals a weapon to use against him when political tensions came to a head in the 430s B.C. as a result of the threat of war with Sparta. Pericles' opponents criticized him as sympathetic to dangerous new ideas as well as autocratic in his leadership.

Other new ideas also emerged in the mid-fifth century B.C. In historical writing, for example, Hecataeus of Miletus, born in the later sixth century B.C., had earlier opened the way to a broader and more critical vision of the past. He wrote both an extensive guidebook to illustrate his map of the world as he knew it and a treatise criticizing mythological traditions. The Greek historians writing immediately after him concentrated on the histories of their local areas and wrote in a spare, chronicle-like style that made history into little more than a list of events and geographical facts. Herodotus of Halicarnassus (c. 485–425 B.C.), however, built on the foundations laid by Hecataeus in writing his *Histories,* a groundbreaking work in its wide geographical scope, its critical approach to historical evidence, and its lively narrative. To describe and explain the clash between East and West represented by the wars between Persians and Greeks in the early fifth century B.C., Herodotus searched for the origins of the conflict both by delving deep into the past and by examining the cultural traditions of all the peoples involved. He recognized the relevance and the delight of studying other cultures as a component of historical investigation.

New developments in Greek medicine in this period are associated with Hippocrates of Cos, a younger contemporary of Herodotus. Details about the life and thought of this most famous of all Greek doctors are sketchy, but he certainly made great strides in putting medical diagnosis and treatment on a scientific basis. Earlier medical practices had depended on magic and ritual. Hippocrates apparently viewed the human body as an organism whose parts must be understood as part of the whole. Greek doctors characteristically searched for a system of first principles to serve as a foundation for their treatments, but no consensus emerged. Even in antiquity medical writers disagreed about the theoretical foundation of Hippocrates' medicine. Some attributed to him the view, popular in later times, that four elements, called humors (fluids), make up the human body: blood, phlegm, black bile, and yellow bile. This intellectual system corresponded to the division of the inanimate world into four parts as well: the elements earth, air, fire, and water.

Most important, Hippocrates taught that the physician should base his knowledge on careful observation of patients and their response to remedies. Empirically grounded clinical experience, he insisted, was the best guide to treatments that would not do the sick more harm than good. Hippocratic medical doctrine apparently made little or no mention of a divine role in sickness and its cures, although various cults in Greek religion, most famously that of the god Asclepius, offered healing to petitioners. Hippocrates' contribution to medicine is remembered today in the oath bearing his name that doctors swear at the beginning of their professional careers.

The impact of the developments in history and medicine on ordinary people is hard to assess, but their misgivings about the new trends in education and philosophy definitely heightened the political tension in Athens in the 430s B.C. These intellectual developments had a wide-ranging effect because the political, intellectual, and religious dimensions of life in ancient Athens were so intertwined. A person could discuss the city-state's domestic and foreign policies on one occasion, novel theories of the nature of the universe on another, and whether the gods were angry or pleased with the community every day. By the late 430s B.C. the Athenians had new reasons to worry about each of these topics.

The End of the Golden Age

Tension between Athens and Sparta had peaked by the time a team of Spartan representatives arrived in Athens for diplomatic negotiations in 432 B.C. The Spartan representatives issued an ultimatum stating that war could be averted only if the Athenians revoked their economic sanctions against Megara, a city-state allied to Sparta. Such legalistic wranglings hid the larger issue of power that fueled the hostility between Athens and Sparta. The Spartan leaders feared the Athenians would use their superior long-distance offensive weaponry—the naval forces of the Delian League—to destroy Spartan control over the members of the Peloponnesian League. The majority in the Athenian assembly resented Spartan interference in their freedom of action.

When the negotiations collapsed, the result was the devastating Peloponnesian War, which dragged on from 431 to 404 B.C. and engulfed almost the entire Greek world. The history of the conflict reveals the general unpredictability of war and the consequences of the repeated reluctance of the Athenian assembly to negotiate peace terms instead of simply dictating them. Athens's losses of population and property had a disastrous, although temporary, effect on its international power, revenues, and social cohesiveness.

The Strategy of the Peloponnesian War

The Spartans took an intransigent stance with the Athenians to placate their allies—notably the Megarians and, more important, the Corinthians. The latter had threatened to withdraw from the Peloponnesian League and form a different international alliance if the Spartans delayed any longer in backing them in their dispute with the Athenians over a rebellious Corinthian ally. In this way the actions of lesser powers nudged the two great powers, Athens and Sparta, over the brink into war.

Most of our knowledge of this decisive war comes from the history written by the Athenian Thucydides (c. 460–400 B.C.), himself a commander in the early years of the war (until the assembly banished him for losing an outpost to the enemy).

Alliances of the Peloponnesian War

During his exile, Thucydides interviewed witnesses from both sides of the conflict. His perceptive account of the causes and events of the war made his book a pioneering work of history presented as the narrative of great contemporary events and power politics. For example, he revealed that Pericles convinced his fellow citizens to reject the Spartan demands with these arguments:

> *If we do go to war, harbor no thought that you went to war over a trivial affair. For you this trifling matter is the assurance and the proof of your determination. If you yield to their demands, they will immediately confront you with some larger demand, since they will think that you only gave way on the first point out of fear. But if you stand firm, you will show them that they have to deal with you as equals. . . . When our equals, without agreeing to arbitration of the matter under dispute, make claims on us as neighbors and state those claims as commands, it would be no better than slavery to give in to them, no matter how large or how small the claim may be.*

Athens's fleet and fortifications made its urban center impregnable to direct attack. Already by the 450s B.C. the Athenians had encircled the city center with a massive stone wall and fortified a broad corridor with a wall on both sides leading all the way to the main harbor at Piraeus five miles to the west. Military siege machines of this period were unable to broach such walls. Consequently, no matter how agricultural production of Attica was damaged in the course of the war, the Athenians could feed themselves by importing food by ship through their fortified port. They could pay for the food with the huge financial reserves they had accumulated from the dues of the Delian League and the income from their silver mines. The Athenians could also retreat safely behind their walls if the superior Spartan infantry attacked. From this seemingly invincible position they could launch surprise attacks against Spartan territory by sending their warships behind enemy lines and landing troops before the Spartans could prepare to defend themselves.

This two-pronged strategy, which Pericles devised, was simple: avoid set battles with the Spartan infantry even if Athenian territory was ravaged, and attack Sparta from the sea. In the end, he predicted, the superior resources of Athens would enable it to win a war of attrition. The difficulty in carrying out Pericles' plan was that many Athenians who resided outside the urban center had to abandon their homes and fields to the depredations of the Spartan army when it invaded Attica. As Thucydides reports, people hated coming in from the countryside where "most Athenians were born and bred; they grumbled at having to move their entire households [into Athens] . . . , abandoning their normal way of life and leaving behind what they regarded as their true city." When in 431 B.C. the Spartans invaded Attica for the first time and began to destroy the countryside, the country-dwellers of Attica became enraged as, standing in safety on Athens's walls, they watched the smoke rise from their property as the Spartans torched it. Pericles only barely managed to stop the citizen militia from rushing out despite the odds to take on the Spartan hoplites. The Spartan army returned home after about a month in Attica because it lacked the structure for resupply over a longer period and could not risk being away from Sparta too long for fear of helot revolt. For these reasons the annual Spartan invasions of Attica in the early years of the war never lasted longer than forty days each.

The Unpredictability of War

The innate unpredictability of war undermined Pericles' strategy, especially as an epidemic disease ravaged Athens's population for several years beginning in 430 B.C. The disease struck while the Athenians were jammed together in unsanitary conditions behind their walls to escape Spartan attack. The symptoms were gruesome: vomiting, convulsions, painful sores, uncontrollable diarrhea, and fever and thirst so extreme that sufferers threw themselves into cisterns vainly hoping to find relief in the cold water. The rate of mortality was so high it crippled Athenian ability to man the naval expeditions Pericles' wartime strategy demanded. Pericles himself died of the disease in 429 B.C. He apparently had not anticipated the damage to Athens that the loss of his firm leadership could mean. The epidemic also seriously hampered the war effort by destroying Athenian confidence in their relationship with the gods. "As far as the gods were concerned, it seemed not to matter whether one worshiped them or not because the good and the bad were dying indiscriminately," was Thucydides' description of the population's attitude at the height of the epidemic.

The epidemic hurt the Athenians materially by devastating their population, politically by removing their foremost leader, and psychologically by damaging their self-confidence. Nevertheless, they fought on. In 425 B.C., in fact, their general Cleon won an unprecedented victory by capturing some one hundred twenty Spartan Equals and about one hundred seventy allied troops in a battle at Pylos in the western Peloponnese. No Spartan soldiers had ever before surrendered under any circumstances. They had always taken as their martial creed the sentiment expressed by the legendary advice of a Spartan mother as she handed her son his shield as he went off to war: "Come home either with this or on it," meaning he should return either as a victor carrying his shield or as a corpse carried upon it. By this date, however, the population of Spartan Equals had been so reduced that even the loss of a small group was devastating. The Spartan leaders therefore offered the Athenians favorable peace terms in return for the captives. At Cleon's urging the Athenian assembly refused to make peace.

The lack of wisdom in this decision became clear with the next unexpected development of the war: a sudden reversal in the Spartan policy against waging military expeditions far from home. In 424 B.C. the Spartan general Brasidas led an army on a daring campaign against Athenian strongholds in far northern Greece, hundreds of miles from Sparta. He adroitly meshed diplomacy with brilliant military tactics employing speed and surprise to bring Athens's allies in this crucial region over to Sparta's side. Brasidas's success robbed Athens of access to gold mines and a major source of timber for building warships. (The loss of Amphipolis, an Athenian colony controlling a main route into the interior and its rich resources, was what led the assembly to exile Thucydides—he was the commander in this area.) Cleon then commanded a counterattacking expedition with the aim of recovering Athens's valuable northern possessions. But both Cleon and Brasidas were killed in battle before Amphipolis in 422 B.C., thus depriving each side of its most energetic military leader and opening the way to negotiations. Peace came in 421 B.C. when both sides agreed to resurrect the balance of forces just as it had been in 431 B.C.

Still, factions in both city-states clamored for war, and fighting resumed when the brash young Athenian commander Alcibiades (c. 450–404 B.C.) formed a temporary coalition between Athens and Argos, a bitter rival of Sparta for power in the Peloponnese. The coalition disintegrated after being defeated by Sparta's forces at the battle of Mantinea in 418 B.C. The "peacetime war" continued in 416 B.C. when the Athenians besieged the tiny island of Melos, a community sympathetic to Sparta that had taken no active part in the war, and killed the men and sold the women and children into slavery just to demonstrate their strength. In 415 B.C. the war recommenced on a large scale when Alcibiades convinced the Athenian assembly to launch a massive naval campaign against Sicily to seek its great riches and prevent any Sicilian cities from aiding the Spartans. His aggressive dreams of martial glory appealed especially to young men who had not yet experienced the realities of war. The arrogant flamboyance of Alcibiades' private life and his evident political ambitions had made him many enemies in Athens, and they managed to get him recalled from the expedition's command by accusing him of having participated in a sacrilegious mockery of the Eleusinian Mysteries and being mixed up in the vandalizing of statues called Herms just before his expedition sailed. Herms, stone posts with sculpted sets of erect male organs and a bust of the god Hermes, stood throughout the city as protectors

Mainland Greece and Sicily

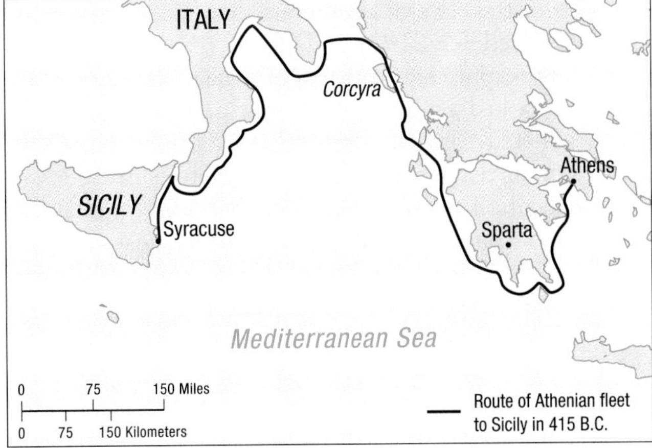

against infertility and bad luck. The vandals outraged the public by knocking off the statues' phalluses. Alcibiades' reaction to the charges was a shock: he deserted to Sparta. The remaining Athenian generals so mismanaged the Sicilian expedition that it ended in total defeat at Syracuse in 413 B.C.

Alcibiades' defection caused Athens enormous trouble because he used his knowledge of the Athenian situation to aid Sparta. On his advice the Spartans established a permanent base of operations in the Attic countryside in 413 B.C. Spartan forces could now raid the Athenian countryside year-round. Twenty thousand slaves working in Athens's silver mines sought refuge in the Spartan camp. An oligarchic coup briefly overturned Athenian democracy in 411 B.C., but Athens soon regained its traditional form of government and fought on, despite the support Sparta now began to receive from Persia. By backing a rebel against the Persian king some five to ten years earlier, Athens had lost any chance for help from King Darius II, who was ready to provide money in return for acknowledgment of his right to control the Greek city-states of Anatolia. Sparta made this concession and received Persian funding. Aggressive Spartan action at sea, with a fleet financed largely by this aid, forced Athens to surrender in 404 B.C. After twenty-seven years of near continuous war, the Athenians were at the mercy of their enemies.

The Spartans resisted the Corinthians' demand for the utter destruction of Athens because they feared Corinth and Thebes might grow too strong if Athens no longer existed to serve as a counterweight. Instead they installed a regime of antidemocratic Athenian aristocrats, who became known as the Thirty Tyrants. These men came from the class of aristocrats that had traditionally despised democracy and embraced oligarchy. Brutally suppressing their opposition, these oligarchs embarked on an eight-month period of terror in 404–403 B.C. The orator Lysias, for example, reported that their henchmen seized his brother for execution as a way of stealing the family's valuables, even ripping the gold earrings from the ears of his brother's wife. An Athenian democratic resistance movement soon arose, and it seized power from the Thirty Tyrants in Athens after a series of bloody street battles in 403 B.C. Fortunately for the democrats, a split in the Spartan leadership fueled by the competing ambitions of its two most prominent men had prevented effective Spartan military support for the tyrants. To end the internal strife that threatened to tear Athens apart, the newly restored democracy proclaimed an amnesty, the first known in Western history, under which all further charges and official recriminations concerning the period of terror in 404–403 B.C. were forbidden. Athens's government was once again a functioning democracy; its financial and military strength, however, were shattered, and its society harbored the memory of a bitter divisiveness that no amnesty could dispel.

Response to War in Athens

The Peloponnesian War took its toll on Athens's domestic life as well as its political harmony and international power. It ruined the lives of the many people who lived in the countryside, because the Spartan invaders had wrecked their homes. The crowded conditions in the city led to friction between city-dwellers and the refugees from the rural areas. The economy suffered from the interruptions to agriculture and the loss of income from the silver mines after 413 B.C. Some public building projects were kept going, like the Erectheum temple to Athena on the acropolis, to demonstrate the Athenian will to carry on and also to infuse some money into the crippled economy. But the war had depleted the funds available for many nonmilitary activities. The scale of the great dramatic festivals, for example, had to be cut back. The financial situation had become so desperate by the end of the war that Athenians were required to turn in their silver coins and exchange them for an emergency currency of bronze thinly plated with silver. The regular silver coins, along with gold coins that were minted from golden objects borrowed from Athens's temples, were then used to pay war expenses.

The war caused many men and women to make drastic changes in the way they earned a living. Wealthy families that had money and valuable goods stored up could weather the crisis by using their savings, but most people had no financial cushion. When enemies destroyed their harvests, farmers used to toiling in their own fields had to scrounge for work as day laborers in the city. Men who rowed the ships of the Athenian fleet could earn regular wages, but they had to spend long periods away from their families and faced death in every battle. Craftspeople and small merchants in the city still had their livelihoods, but their business suffered because consumers had less money to spend. Especially hard hit were many previously moderately well-off women whose husbands and brothers died during the conflict. Such women had traditionally done weaving at home for their own families and supervised the work of household slaves, but the men had earned the family's income by farming or practicing a trade. With no one to provide for them and their children, they were forced to work outside the home to support their families. The only jobs open to them were low-paying occupations traditional for women, such as baby nurse or weaver or some occupations as laborers in such areas as vineyard work, for which not enough men were available to meet the need. Although these circumstances brought more women into public view, they were still not included in Athenian political life.

The Chorus of a Greek Comedy
The Greek comedies of the fifth century B.C. sometimes sported choruses of actors dressed as animals, such as these horses carrying riders. A musician playing pipes for their dance stands at the left.

The stresses of everyday life during trying times were reflected in Athenian comedies produced during the war. Besides tragedies and satyr plays, comic plays were the other main form of dramatic art in ancient Athens. Like tragedies, comedies were composed in verse and had been presented annually since early in the fifth century B.C. They formed a separate competition in the Athenian civic festivals in honor of Dionysus in the same outdoor theater used for tragedies. Women could probably attend, although the evidence for this is ambiguous. Comedies' all-male casts consisted of a twenty-four-member chorus in addition to regular actors. The beauty of the soaring poetry of the choral songs of comedy was matched by the ingeniously imaginative fantasy of its plots, which almost always ended with a festive resolution of the problems with which they had begun. In the *Birds,* by Aristophanes, for example, produced in 414 B.C., two men try to escape the hassles of everyday life at Athens. They run away to seek a new life in a world called Cloudcuckooland that is inhabited by talking birds, portrayed by the chorus in colorful bird costumes.

The immediate purpose of a comic playwright was to create beautiful poetry and raise laughs in the hope of winning the award for the festival's best comedy. Much of the humor of Athenian comedy had to do with sex and bodily fuctions, and much of its ribaldry was delivered in a stream of imaginative profanity. The plots dealt primarily with current issues and personalities. Insulting attacks on prominent men such as Pericles or Cleon, the victor of Pylos, were a staple. Pericles apparently instituted a ban on such attacks in response to fierce treatment in comedies after the revolt of Samos in 441–439 B.C., but the measure was soon rescinded. Cleon was so outraged by the way he was portrayed on the comic stage by Aristophanes (c. 455–385 B.C.), the only comic playwright of the fifth century B.C. from whose works entire plays have survived, that he sued the playwright. When Cleon lost the case, Aristophanes responded by pitilessly parodying him as a reprobate foreign slave in *The Knights* of 424 B.C. Other well-known men who were not portrayed as characters could come in for insults as sexually effeminate and cowards. Women characters portrayed as figures of fun and ridicule in comedy seem to have been fictional.

Although slashing satire directed against the mass of ordinary citizens seems to have been unacceptable, Athenian comedies often criticized government policies that had been approved by the assembly by blaming political leaders for them. The strongly critical nature of comedy was never more evident than during the war years. Several of

Comedies of Aristophanes Produced During the Peloponnesian War (431–404 B.C.)

427 B.C. *Banqueters*
Not preserved; apparently involved an argument between a spendthrift son and his father

426 B.C. *Babylonians*
Not preserved; apparently attacked politicians, leading Cleon to prosecute Aristophanes

425 B.C. *Acharnians*
Comic hero makes peace with Sparta for his family

424 B.C. *Knights*
Attack on Cleon as a deceitful demagogue

423 B.C. *Clouds*
Controversial portrayal of Socrates as an arrogant sophist

422 B.C. *Wasps*
Parody of old men's passion for serving as jurors in Athens

421 B.C. *Peace*
Comic hero flies to the gods on a giant dung beetle to retrieve the goddess Peace

414 B.C. *Birds*
Comic heroes seek quiet life but end up establishing an empire among the birds in Cloudcuckooland

411 B.C. *Lysistrata*
Athenian and Spartan women ally in a sex strike to compel men to make peace

411 B.C. *Women at the Festival of Demeter*
Women take revenge on the dramatist Euripides for unflattering portrayal of women in his tragedies

405 B.C. *Frogs*
The god Dionysus goes to Hades to bring back the tragedian Aeschylus to teach the Athenians old-fashioned virtue once again

Aristophanes' popular comedies had plots in which characters arranged peace with Sparta, even though the comedies were produced while the war was still being fiercely contested. In *The Acharnians* of 425 B.C., for example, the protagonist arranges a separate peace treaty with the Spartans for himself and his family while humiliating a character who portrays one of Athens's prominent military commanders of the time. The play won first prize in the comedy competition that year.

The most remarkable of Aristophanes' comedies are those in which the main characters are powerful women who compel the men of Athens to overthrow basic policies of the city-state. Most famous is *Lysistrata* of 411 B.C., named after the female lead character of the play. In it the women of Athens join with the women of Sparta to force their husbands to end the Peloponnesian War. To make the men agree to a peace treaty, the women first seize the acropolis, where Athens's financial reserves are kept, and prevent the men from squandering them further on the war. They then beat back an attack on their position by the old men who have remained in Athens while the younger men are out on campaign. When their husbands return from battle, the women refuse to have sex with them. This strike, which is portrayed in a series of risqué episodes, finally coerces the men of Athens and Sparta to agree to a peace treaty.

Lysistrata presents women acting bravely and aggressively against men who seem bent on destroying their family life by staying away from home for long stretches while on military campaign and on ruining the city-state by prolonging a pointless war. In other words, the play's strong women take on what were usually masculine roles in the ancient Greek city-state and assert their collective power to preserve the community's traditional way of life. Lysistrata emphasizes this point in the speech in which she insists that women have the intelligence and judgment to make political decisions: "I am a woman, and, yes, I have brains. And I'm not badly off for judgment. Nor has my education been bad, coming as it has from my listening often to the conversations of my father and the elders among the men." She came by her knowledge in the traditional way, by learning from older men. Her old-fashioned training and good sense allowed her to see what needed to be done to protect the community. Like the heroines of tragedy, Lysistrata is a reactionary; she wants to put things back the way they were. To do that, however, she has to act like a revolutionary. Perhaps Aristophanes was telling Athenian men that all Athenians should find a new vision to preserve old ways, lest they be lost.

Conclusion

The Athenians had much to lose in their war with Sparta because the Golden Age of Athens in the fifth century B.C. had been a time of prosperity, political stability, international power, and artistic and cultural accomplishment. Athenians, both men who fought on land and sea and women who kept their households together during the evacuation of 480–479 B.C., had won great glory in the unexpected victory of the Greek alliance against the Persians. This stunning triumph could have occurred, the Athenians believed, only because the gods smiled upon them with special favor and because the Athenians displayed their superior courage, intelligence, and virtue.

Athens's high-handed application of its military prominence soon led to problems, however, as allied city-states unhappy with the new imbalance of power rebelled. Important allies in the Delian League, such as the Samians, were unwilling to take orders in what was supposed to have been a democratically governed alliance. By the time the Spartans threatened war in the late 430s B.C., Athens no longer commanded an alliance of loyal partners on whom it could depend for support.

The dues of the Delian League, in combination with the income from Attica's silver mines, brought Athens previously unimaginable wealth in the Golden Age. The new revenue allowed the Athenians to embark on a spectacular building program and to offer regular employment to thousands of poorer men as trireme rowers. The problematic aspect of this change in the financial fortunes of the Athenians was that it depended on their maintaining hegemony over allies who chafed at their control. Athenians' prosperity led them to act as an imperial power in relation to their fellow Greeks, a policy their opponents called the equivalent of enslavement, the very issue for which Athens had once stood shoulder to shoulder with these same allies against the Persians.

While the Athenians extended their control in the Aegean region, they developed new democratic procedures, which provided greater political participation for rich and poor men alike. Poor men benefited from reforms in the court system that allowed all Athenian men to be involved in dispensing justice. Under the leadership of Pericles, poorer men also gained greater access to political life after stipends became available for jurors and many officeholders. New opportunities to play a role in political life were not extended to women, however. Upper-class women remained restricted to their households, their friends, and their participation in public religious cults. Poorer women helped support themselves and their families, often as small-scale merchants and crafts producers. Legally, Athenian women's control of their own property and their ability to act on their own behalf in matters of law were still restricted. The tension between continuity and change was evident in many of the tragedies written and performed in the fifth century B.C., in which characters engage in intense conflicts concerning their relationship with the gods and with other people.

Further changes helped undermine the new democratic relationship among Athenian men. The additional opportunities for the advanced education of wealthy young men introduced by the sophists certainly made their pupils more skillful participants in Athenian democracy. The techniques of persuasion taught by Protagoras and his fellow teachers of oratory enabled a man to advance his opinions on policy with great effect or defend himself staunchly in court. Because only wealthy men could afford instruction from a sophist, however, this new education worked against the egalitarian principles of Athenian participatory democracy by giving an advantage to the rich. In addition, the relativism of Protagoras and the physical explanation of the universe expounded by philosophers like Anaxagoras struck traditionally minded Athenians as dangerous to the values of the city-state.

The Athenian Golden Age was framed by war. The successful outcome of the Persian Wars had boosted the Athenians to power in Greece and prosperity at home. The Peloponnesian War had quite a different impact on Greece's premier city-state and its jealous competitors and unwilling allies. The pressures of war upset the traditional pattern of life for many people, especially women who were forced to work outside the home for the first time. Among the consequences of the Peloponnesian War was a restructuring of political power in the ancient Greek world.

Suggestions for Further Reading

Source Materials

Aristophanes. *Lysistrata; The Acharnians; The Clouds.* Translated by A. H. Sommerstein. 1973. A lively rendering of three famous comedies from fifth-century B.C. Athens.

Fornara, Charles W. *Translated Documents of Greece and Rome.* Vol. 1, *Archaic Times to the End of the Peloponnesian War.* 2d ed. 1983. A briefly annotated collection of inscriptions, documents, and historical sources.

Grene, David, and Richmond Lattimore, eds. *The Complete Greek Tragedies.* 9 vols. 1953–1991. Translations of all surviving Athenian tragedies of the fifth century B.C.

Herodotus. *The Histories.* Available in various translations such as that of Aubrey de Sélincourt, 1972, as well as in a bilingual edition published in the Loeb Classical Library series. The principal ancient source for the history of the Persian Wars and a compendium of intriguing stories about the interactions of Greeks and other peoples.

Lefkowitz, Mary R., and Maureen B. Fant. *Women's Life in Greece and Rome: A Source Book in Translation.* 1982. Selections from documents and literature on many aspects of women's lives.

Plutarch. *Life of Themistocles; Aristides; Cimon; Pericles.* Available in various translations such as that of Ian Scott-Kilvert, *Plutarch: The Rise and Fall of Athens,* 1960, as well as in a bilingual edition published in the Loeb Classical Library series. Lively biographies of the great men of classical Athens.

Thucydides. *The Peloponnesian War.* Available in various translations such as that of Rex Warner, 1972, as well as in a bilingual edition published in the Loeb Classical Library series. The only surviving fifth-century B.C. account of the development of the Athenian empire (Book 1, sections 89–117) and the principal ancient source for the Peloponnesian War.

Interpretive Studies

Boardman, J., N. G. L. Hammond, D. M. Lewis, and M. Ostwald, eds. *The Cambridge Ancient History.* Vol. IV, *Persia, Greece, and the Western Mediterranean, c. 525 B.C. to 479 B.C.* 2d ed. 1988. An authoritative survey covering the Persian Empire, the Ionian revolt, and the Persian Wars.

Brommer, Frank. *The Sculptures of the Parthenon.* 1979. A magnificent photographic record of the sculptural decoration of the Parthenon, with descriptions.

Burkert, Walter. *Greek Religion.* Translated by John Raffan. 1985. A vast, scholarly catalog of Greek religious practices.

Camp, John M. *The Athenian Agora: Excavations in the Heart of Classical Athens.* 1986. A splendidly illustrated survey of the buildings and monuments of Athens' civic center and their functions.

Cook, J. M. *The Persian Empire.* 1983. A colorful, readable complement to Olmstead's work.

Davies, J. K. *Democracy and Classical Greece.* 1978. A survey of classical Greek history with frequent discussion on the evidence of documents.

De Romilly, Jacqueline. *A Short History of Greek Literature.* 1985. A comprehensive survey including discussions of poetry, philosophy, history, rhetoric, and medical writings.

Dodds, E. R. *The Greeks and the Irrational.* 1951. A stimulating and enormously influential treatment of Greek religion and thought that remains a classic despite some outdated views.

Dover, K. J. *Aristophanic Comedy.* 1972. An introduction to Athenian Old Comedy in general and to the eleven surviving plays of Aristophanes in particular.

Easterling, P. E., and J. V. Muir, eds. *Greek Religion and Society.* 1985. Readable essays on topics including views of life after death, temples, festivals, oracles, and divination.

Ehrenberg, Victor. *From Solon to Socrates.* 2d ed. 1973. A wide-ranging survey of Greek history and civilization in the sixth and fifth centuries B.C.

Finley, M. I. *Democracy Ancient and Modern.* Rev. ed. 1973. A provocative series of lectures that advocate applying the principles of Athenian participatory democracy to modern democracies.

Goldhill, Simon. *Reading Greek Tragedy.* 1986. Introduces the many different approaches modern critics take in interpreting Greek tragedy.

Guthrie, W. K. C. *A History of Greek Philosophy,* Vol.

2, *The Presocratic Tradition from Parmenides to Democritus.* 1965. The standard introduction to Greek philosophy in the fifth century B.C.

———. *A History of Greek Philosophy,* Vol. 4, pt. 1, *The Sophists.* 1971. A thorough discussion of the evidence for the sophists' views.

Joint Association of Classical Teachers. *The World of Athens: An Introduction to Classical Athenian Culture.* 1984. A clearly written handbook arranged topically (originally produced to accompany the Joint Association of Classical Teachers' Greek course).

Kerferd, G. B. *The Sophistic Movement.* 1981. A readable introduction to the thought and the impact of the fifth-century B.C. sophists.

Lacey, W. K. *The Family in Classical Greece.* Rev. ed. 1980. The standard survey of the subject, for a general audience.

McGregor, Malcom F. *The Athenians and Their Empire.* 1987. A detailed introduction to the military and administrative history of the Athenian empire.

Mikalson, Jon D. *Athenian Popular Religion.* 1983. Investigates the religious beliefs and practices of the Athenian people.

Olmstead, A. T. *History of the Persian Empire.* 1948. Still the most comprehensive survey of the subject for the general reader.

Parke, H. W. *Festivals of the Athenians.* 1977. Describes the chief ceremonial occasions of Athens according to their order in the calendar year.

Parker, Robert. *Miasma: Pollution and Purification in Early Greek Religion.* 1983. An extensive treatment of these central themes in Greek life, attributing their importance to a desire for order.

Pollitt, J. J. *Art and Experience in Classical Greece.* 1972. A lively interpretation of the messages conveyed by classical Greek art.

Powell, Anton. *Athens and Sparta: Constructing Greek Political and Social History from 478 B.C.* 1988. A stimulating treatment of the main topics of classical Greek history, including an extensive section on Athenian citizen women.

Robertson, D. S. *Greek and Roman Architecture.* 2d ed. 1971. A detailed survey of the techniques of Greek architecture.

Schaps, David M. *Economic Rights of Women in Ancient Greece.* 1979. Explores the rights and disadvantages of women with regard to property, inheritance, dowry, and commerce.

Sealey, Raphael. *Women and Law in Classical Greece.* 1990. Analyzes women's rights in marriage, property ownership, and questions of inheritance.

Woodford, Susan. *Cambridge Introduction to the History of Art: Greece and Rome.* 1982. A concise introduction to the development of Greek art, especially sculpture, with excellent illustrations and suggestions for further reading.

Wycherly, R. E. *How the Greeks Built Cities.* 2d ed. 1976. Examines the relationship of architecture and town planning to ancient Greek life.

CHAPTER

4

Remaking the Mediterranean World, 403–30 B.C.

The School of Plato
This mosaic from Roman times presents an idealized view of Plato's school of philosophy, the Academy, in Athens. Platonism was one of the great legacies of Greece's Golden Age.

Before going to fight in the Peloponnesian War, an Athenian man named Diodotus had appointed his brother guardian of his three children and left behind a large amount of money and property for their care. The brother happened to be the children's grandfather—their mother was his daughter. After Diodotus was killed in battle, his brother misappropriated much of the funds and eventually claimed he could no longer support the two boys, who would thereafter have to fend for themselves. Their sister was already married, with a dowry from her father's money.

We learn from testimony in a lawsuit brought on the boys' behalf about 400 B.C. by their sister's husband that their mother had done her utmost to dissuade her father from abandoning the boys. She insisted that her father and his friends be brought together so she could address them, saying that her boys' misfortune was so grievous that she must speak out even though she was unaccustomed to speaking in the presence of men. She then asked her father in front of his friends how he could mistreat her children so heartlessly:

> *Even if you did not feel ashamed before any person, you should have feared the gods . . . you thought it right to expel these children of your daughter from their own house in worn-out clothes, shoeless, without a servant, without bedding, without cloaks, without the furniture that their father left them, without the money he entrusted to you . . . you are throwing them out to become dishonored and beggars instead of people of means, and yet you feel no fear of the gods nor shame before me, who knows the facts, nor do you remember your brother, but you think money is more important than anything.*

This incident, whose outcome is not recorded, illustrates both the continuing importance of family as the center of Greek society and the special pressures war could bring. Families always tried to solve their difficulties among themselves before resorting to legal action, and women played an influential part in this process. But the Peloponnesian War had recently ended and conditions in Athens remained precarious. Children turned out of their homes during such times probably had little chance of surviving, much less prospering. So an ordinary mother took an extraordinary step out of her traditional role to confront her father in front of other males in an effort to save her sons.

Similarly complex interplays of continuity and change characterized Greek history on many levels after the Peloponnesian War. Greek society remained relatively stable at the household level, but a succession of wars among Greece's leading city-states in the wake of the Peloponnesian War weakened their ability to withstand the expansion of the kingdom of Macedonia, the region north of Greece. The success of their monarchy led Macedonians to establish new kingdoms in Egypt and the Near East. The new governments also affected the course of literature, art, and science. Religion and philosophy headed down new paths, too, though many traditional cults and ideas remained popular.

Important Dates

399 B.C. Socrates is tried and executed at Athens

359 B.C. Philip II becomes Macedonian king

348 B.C. The philosopher Plato dies

338 B.C. Philip defeats a Greek alliance at the battle of Chaeronea to become the leading power in Greece

336 B.C. Philip is murdered; Alexander takes over as king

334 B.C. Alexander leads an army of Greeks and Macedonians against Persia

326 B.C. Alexander's army mutinies in India

323 B.C. Alexander dies

322 B.C. The philosopher Aristotle dies

306–304 B.C. The Successors of Alexander declare themselves to be kings

The Aftermath of the Peloponnesian War

Strife among prominent city-states vying for power continued to plague Greece in the years following the Peloponnesian War. The losses of population, the ravages of epidemic disease, and the financial hardship brought on by war caused severe difficulties for Athens. Those who had been banished by the Thirty Tyrants fought back and reclaimed Athens as a democracy in 403 B.C. In an attempt to quell social and political animosities wrought by the humiliations and deprivations endured during the brief but vicious rule of the tyrants, both sides agreed to an amnesty forbidding prosecutions for crimes committed during that time. But this measure did not truly restore the harmony that defeat in war and the dispossession of democratic privileges had shattered. The most prominent casualty of the divisive bitterness of the time was the famous philosopher Socrates, whose trial for impiety in 399 B.C. resulted in a death sentence. The Athenian household—family members and their personal slaves—somehow managed to hold together and survived as the fundamental unit of the city-state's society and economy.

Rebuilding Athenian Society

Many Athenian households lost fathers, sons, or brothers in the Peloponnesian War. Resourceful families found ways to compensate for the economic strain such personal tragedies could create. The writer Xenophon (c. 428–354 B.C.) told of an Athenian named Aristarchus, whose income had severely diminished because of the war and whose household had grown because of the sisters, nieces, and female cousins who had moved in with him. He found himself unable to support a household of fourteen, not counting the slaves. Aristarchus's friend Socrates reminded him that his female relatives knew how to make men's and women's cloaks, shirts, capes, and smocks, "the work considered the best and most fitting for women." Although the women had previously made clothing only for the family, Socrates suggested they now begin to sell it for profit. Others sewed clothing or baked bread for sale, and Aristarchus could tell the women in his house to do the same. The plan succeeded financially, but the women complained that Aristarchus was now the only member of the household who ate without working. Socrates advised his friend to reply that the women should think of him as sheep did a guard dog—he earned his share of the food by keeping the wolves away from the sheep.

Many Athenian households produced manufactured goods, as did small shops and a few larger enterprises. Among the larger concerns were metal foundries, pottery workshops, and the shield-making company that employed 120 slaves owned by the family of Lysias (c. 459–380 B.C.); businesses bigger than this did not exist during this period.

Working Women
This vase shows a woman spinning wool for clothing, which was made at home whenever possible.

Lysias, an educated metic (resident alien) from Syracuse whose father had been recruited by Pericles to live in Athens, began to earn his living by writing speeches for others after the Thirty Tyrants seized his property in 404 B.C. He wrote the speech the brother-in-law of Diodotus's sons delivered in court. Metics could not own land in Athenian territory without special permission, but they had legal rights in Athenian courts that foreigners without metic status lacked. In return they paid taxes and served in the army when called upon. Lysias lived near Piraeus, the harbor of Athens, as did many metics, who played a central role in the international trade of such goods as grain, wine, pottery, and silver from Athens's mines, commodities that passed through Piraeus. The long walls that connected the city with the port, destroyed at the end of the war, were rebuilt by 393 B.C. at the urging of the great naval commander Conan as part of the Athenian navy's revival. These walls again ensured the safety of traders going in and out of Athens, a signal that trade could resume to prewar levels. Another sign of Athens's recovering economic health was the renewed minting of its famous silver coins to replace the emergency bronze ones created during the last years of the war.

Grain imported through Piraeus was crucial for fourth-century B.C. Athens. Even before the war, Athenian farmers had been unable to produce enough of this dietary staple to feed the population. The Spartan invasions had damaged farm buildings and equipment, making the situation even worse. Sparta had established a year-round base at Decelea near Athens from 413 to 404 B.C., giving their forces ample opportunity to demolish Athenian resources, which they could not do on the short campaigns customary in Greek warfare. The invaders probably even cut down Athenian olive trees, the source of valuable olive oil. These trees took a generation to replace because they grew so slowly. After the war, Athenian property owners worked hard to restore their land and businesses not only to benefit themselves but also to provide for their heirs. Athenian men and women felt strongly that their property, whether land, money, or belongings, should be preserved for their descendants. For this reason, Athenian law allowed men who squandered their inheritance or an inheritance entrusted to them, as did Diodotus's brother, to be prosecuted. The same spirit underlay the requirement that parents ensure

Greek Women at a Fountain
Wearing the standard long robes and hair coverings of their time, women in a Greek city collect water from a large and decorative municipal fountain.

their children's livelihood, either by leaving them income-producing property or training them in a skill.

Most working people probably earned just enough to feed and clothe their families. Athenians usually had only two meals a day, a light lunch in midmorning and a heavier meal in the evening. Bread baked from barley or, for richer people, wheat constituted the main part of their diet. A family bought its bread from small bakery stands, often run by women, or made it at home, with the wife directing and helping the household slaves grind the grain, shape the dough, and bake it in a pottery oven heated by charcoal. Those few households wealthy enough to afford meat from time to time often grilled it over coals on a pottery brazier. Most people ate vegetables, olives, fruit, and cheese as the bulk of their diet; they had meat only at animal sacrifices paid for by the state. The wine everyone drank, usually much diluted with water, came mainly from local vineyards. Water was fetched from public fountains and brought to the house in jugs, a task the women of the household performed or made sure the household slaves did. Many state-owned slaves had escaped from the mines in the countryside during the war, but few privately owned domestic slaves tried to run away. All but the poorest families continued to have at least one or two slaves to do household chores and look after the children. If a mother did not have a slave to serve as a wet nurse to suckle her infants, she would hire a poor free woman for the job if her family could afford the expense.

Socratic Knowledge

The conviction and execution of Socrates (469–399 B.C.), the most famous philosopher of the late fifth century B.C., was the most infamous event in the history of Athens after the Peloponnesian War. Socrates' life had been devoted to combating the idea that justice should be equated with the power to work one's will. His death, coming as it did during a time of social and political turmoil, indicated the tenuousness of Athenian justice in practice. His mission to find valid guidelines for leading a just life and to prove that justice is better than injustice under all circumstances gave Greek philosophy a new direction: an emphasis on ethics. Although thinkers before him, especially poets and dramatists, had wrestled with moral issues, Socrates was the first philosopher to make ethics and morality his primary concern.

Compared to most sophists, Socrates lived in poverty, for he disdained material possessions. Still he served as a hoplite in the army and supported his wife and several children. He may have inherited some money, and he also received gifts from wealthy admirers. He paid so little attention to his physical appearance and clothes that many Athenians regarded him as eccentric. Sporting, in his words, a stomach "somewhat too large to be convenient," he wore the same nondescript cloak summer and winter and scorned shoes no matter how cold the weather. His physical stamina was legendary, both from his tirelessness as a soldier and from his ability to outdrink anyone at a symposium.

Whether participating at a symposium, strolling in the agora, or watching young men exercise in a gymnasium, Socrates spent his time in conversation. He and his fellow Athenians valued and took great pleasure in speaking with each other at length. He wrote nothing; our knowledge of his ideas comes from others' writings, especially those of his pupil Plato. Plato's dialogues, so called because they present Socrates and others in extended conversation about philosophy, portray Socrates as a relentless questioner of his fellow citizens, foreign friends, and various sophists. Socrates' questions aimed at unsettling his interlocutors (his partners in the conversation), forcing them to examine the basic assumptions of their way of life. Employing what has come to be called the Socratic method, Socrates never directly instructed his conversational partners; instead he led them to answers to his probing questions that refuted their presumptions.

This indirect method of searching for the truth often left Socrates' interlocutors puzzled because they found themselves forced to conclude that they were ignorant: ideas they had believed inviolate had been proven false. Socrates insisted that he too was ignorant of the best definition of virtue but that his wisdom consisted of knowing that he did not know. He was trying to improve rather than undermine his interlocutors' beliefs, even though, as one put it, a conversation with Socrates made a man feel as numb as if he had just been stung by a stingray (a sea creature whose venom paralyzes its victims). Through reasoning, Socrates wanted to discover universal standards for morality. He especially attacked the sophists' view that conventional morality served as the "fetters that bind nature." They proclaimed that only the weak and foolish believed in accepted standards of right and wrong; for such sophists, it was natural and fitting for the strong to take whatever they could. This declaration, Socrates asserted, equated human happiness with power and "getting more."

Socrates believed passionately that justice was better for humans than injustice and that morality was justified because it created happiness. He argued that just behavior, or virtue, was identical to self-knowledge and that true knowledge of justice would inevitably lead people to choose good over evil and therefore to have truly happy lives, regardless of their material wealth, because they would then be true to their nature. Because Socrates believed self-knowledge alone was sufficient for happiness, he claimed that no one knowingly behaved unjustly and that behaving justly was always in the individual's self-interest. It might seem, he maintained, that individuals could promote their interests by cheating or using force on those weaker than themselves, but this appearance was deceptive. It was in fact ignorance to believe that the best life was the life of unlimited power to pursue whatever one desired. Instead the most desirable human life was concerned with virtue and guided by rational reflection. Moral knowledge was all one needed for the good life, as Socrates defined it.

The Condemnation of Socrates

Unlike the sophists, Socrates offered no courses and took no fees. But his effect on many people was as unsettling as the relativistic doctrines of the sophists had been. Indeed Socrates' rebuttal of his fellow conversationalists' most cherished certainties, though expressed indirectly through his method of questioning, made some of his interlocutors decidedly uncomfortable. Unhappiest of all were fathers whose sons, after listening to Socrates reduce someone to utter bewilderment, tried the same technique at home on their parents. Men who experienced this reversal of the traditional hierarchy of education between parent and child—the father was supposed to educate the son—felt that Socrates, however unintentionally, was undermining the stability of society by questioning Athenian traditions. We do not know what Athenian women thought of Socrates. The realities of Athenian society meant that Socrates circulated primarily among men and addressed his ideas to them and their situations. Reportedly he had numerous conversations with Aspasia, the courtesan who lived with Pericles for many years. Plato, in one of his dialogues, depicts Socrates attributing his ideas on love to a woman, the otherwise unknown priestess Diotima of Mantinea.

The public perception that Socrates could be a danger to conventional society gave Aristophanes the inspiration for his comedy *Clouds* of 423 B.C. In the play, Socrates is presented as a cynical sophist who, for a fee, offers instruction in the Protagorean technique of making the weaker argument the stronger. When Socrates' instruction transforms the protagonist's son into a rhetorician able to argue that a son has the right to beat his parents, the protagonist ends the comedy by burning down Socrates' Thinking Shop, as it is called in the play.

Athenians who felt that Socrates posed a danger to conventional society had their fears confirmed in the careers of Alcibiades and, especially, Critias, one of the Thirty Tyrants. Socrates' critics blamed him for Alcibiades' contempt for social conventions because Alcibiades had been one of Socrates' most devoted supporters. Critias,

Socrates *This statuette depicts the homely face and awkward figure that the philosopher Socrates joked about in describing himself.*

another prominent follower, played a leading role in the murder and plunder perpetrated by the Thirty Tyrants in 404–403 B.C. In blaming Socrates for the crimes of Critias, Socrates' detractors chose to overlook his defiance of the Thirty Tyrants when they had tried to involve him in their violent schemes and his utter rejection of the immorality Critias had displayed.

The hostility some Athenians felt toward Socrates after the horrors of the Thirty Tyrants encouraged the distinguished Athenian Anytus, who had suffered personally under this regime, to join with two other, less notable men in prosecuting Socrates in 399 B.C. Because the amnesty precluded bringing any charges directly related to the period of tyranny, they accused Socrates of impiety. Athenian law did not specify precisely what offenses constituted impiety, so the accusers had to convince the jurors that Socrates had committed a crime. As usual in Athenian trials, no judge presided to rule on what evidence was admissible or how the law should be applied. Speaking for themselves as the prosecutors, as also required by Athenian law, the accusers argued their case against Socrates before a jury of 501 that had been assembled by lot from that year's pool of eligible jurors (male citizens over thirty years old). The prosecutors' case featured both a religious and a moral component. They accused Socrates of not believing in the gods of the city-state and of introducing new divinities, actions they labeled as impiety. They also charged that he had lured the young men of Athens away from Athenian moral conventions and ideals. After the prosecutors concluded their remarks, Socrates spoke in his own defense, per Athenian law. Plato writes that Socrates used this occasion not to rebut all the charges or beg for sympathy, as jurors expected in serious cases, but to reiterate his unyielding dedication to goading his fellow citizens into examining their preconceptions. This irritating process of constant questioning, he maintained, would help them learn to live virtuous lives. Furthermore, they should care not about their material possessions but about making their true selves—their souls—as good as possible. He vowed to remain their stinging gadfly no matter what the consequences.

After the jury narrowly voted to convict, standard Athenian legal procedure required the jurors to decide between alternative penalties proposed by the prosecutors and the defendant. Anytus and his associates proposed death. In such instances the defendant was then expected to offer exile as an alternative, which the jury usually accepted. Socrates, however, replied that he deserved a reward rather than a punishment, until his friends at the trial prevailed upon him to propose a fine as his penalty. The jury chose death. Socrates accepted his sentence with equanimity because, as he put it in a famous paradox, "no evil can befall a good man either in life or in death." In other words, nothing can take away the knowledge that is virtue, and only the loss of that wisdom could ever count as a true evil. He was executed in the customary way, by being given a poisonous drink concocted from powdered hemlock. The silencing of Socrates did nothing to restore Athenian confidence or the feelings of invincibility that had characterized their Golden Age. Ancient sources report that the Athenians soon came to regret the condemnation and execution of Socrates as a tragic mistake that left a blot on their reputation.

The International Struggle for Power

In the fifty years after the Peloponnesian War, Sparta, Thebes, and Athens struggled for international power in the Greek world. Athens never regained the economic and military strength it had wielded in the fifth century B.C., perhaps because its silver mines no longer produced at the same level. Nevertheless, after the reestablishment of democracy in 403 B.C., Athens again became a major force in international politics. Sparta's widespread attempts to extend its power after the Peloponnesian War gave Athens and the other Greek city-states ample opportunity for diplomatic and military action. In 401 B.C. the Persian satrap (provincial governor) Cyrus, son of a previous king, hired a mercenary army to try to unseat Artaxerxes II, who had ascended to the Persian throne in 404 B.C. Xenophon, who joined Cyrus's army, wrote *Anabasis,* which included a stirring account of the expedition's disastrous defeat at Cunaxa near Babylon and the arduous journey home made by the terrified Greek mercenaries from Cyrus's routed army. Sparta had supported Cyrus's rebellion, thereby arousing the hostility of Artaxerxes. The Spartan general Lysander, the victor over Athens in the last years of the Peloponnesian War, pursued an aggressive policy in Anatolia and northern Greece in the 390s B.C., and other Spartan commanders meddled in Sicily. Thebes, Athens, Corinth, and Argos thereupon formed an anti-Spartan coalition because they felt this Spartan activity threatened their interests at home and abroad.

In a reversal of the alliances at the end of the Peloponnesian War, the Persian king initially supported Athens and the other Greek city-states against Sparta in the so-called Corinthian War, which lasted from 395 to 386 B.C. This alliance ultimately failed because both the king and the Greek allies pursued their own self-interests rather than peaceful accommodation. The war ended with Sparta once again cutting a deal with Persia. In a blatant renunciation of its claim to defend Greek freedom, Sparta acknowledged the Persian king's right to control the Greek city-states of Anatolia in return for permission to secure Spartan interests in Greece without Persian interference. Their agreement, called the King's Peace, of 386 B.C., effectively returned the Greeks of Anatolia to their dependent status of a century past, before the Greek victory in the Persian Wars of 490–479 B.C.

Spartan forces attacked city-states all over Greece in the years after the peace. In Athens the rebuilt walls restored its invulnerability to invasion. A new kind of foot-soldier, called a peltast (armed now with a light leather shield, instead of a heavier bronze one, javelins, and sword) made Athenian ground forces more mobile and fleet, a development attributed to the Athenian general Iphicrates. Athens's reconstructed navy built up its offensive strength. By 377 B.C., Athens had again become the leader of a naval alliance of Greek city-states, called the Second Athenian League. But this time the league members insisted their rights be specified in writing to prevent a recurrence of high-handed Athenian behavior. Sparta's hopes for lasting power were dashed in 371 B.C. when a resurgent Thebes defeated the Spartan army at Leuctra in Boeotia and then invaded the Spartan homeland in the Peloponnese. At this point the Thebans seemed likely to challenge Jason, tyrant of Pherae in Thessaly, for the position of the dominant military power in Greece.

The alliances of the various city-states shifted often in the many conflicts during the early decades of the fourth century B.C. The threat from Thessaly faded with Jason's murder in 370 B.C., and the former enemies Sparta and Athens temporarily allied against the Thebans in the battle of Mantinea in the Peloponnese in 362 B.C. Thebes won the battle but lost the war when its great leader Epaminondas was killed at Mantinea and no credible replacement for him could be found. The Theban quest for dominance in Greece had failed. Xenophon succinctly summed up the situation after 362 B.C. with these closing remarks from the history he wrote of the Greeks in his time: "Everyone had supposed that the winners of this battle would be Greece's rulers and its losers their subjects; but there was only more confusion and disturbance in Greece after it than before." The truth of his analysis was confirmed when the Second Athenian League fell apart in a war between Athens and its allies over the close ties some allies were developing with Persia and Macedonia.

All the efforts of the various major Greek city-states to extend their hegemony over mainland Greece in this period failed. By the mid 350s B.C. no Greek city-state had the power to rule more than itself. The struggle for supremacy in Greece that had begun eighty years earlier with the outbreak of the Peloponnesian War had finally ended in a stalemate of exhaustion that opened the way for a new power—the kingdom of Macedonia.

New Directions in Philosophy and Education

One reason the sophists who flocked to Athens in the fifth century B.C. stirred up controversy was that many people felt their teachings undermined time-honored moral traditions. Their relativistic doctrines implied that justice in reality meant, to paraphrase Thucydides describing Athenian wartime behavior, the strong seizing all that their power permits and the weak enduring what they are forced to accept. The fourth-century B.C. philosopher Plato attacked this doctrine in the course of his many intellectual pursuits. Plato's famous pupil, Aristotle, combined his teacher's passion for theoretical philosophy with a scientific curiosity about the phenomena of the natural world. Their work helped create a new foundation for ethical and scientific inquiry. But many believed the ideas of Plato and Aristotle were too theoretical, too far removed from the realities of everyday life to have much relevance to the concrete concerns of a public career. Men like the orator Isocrates insisted that a proper education centered on rhetoric and practical wisdom.

The Writings of Plato

Socrates' fate profoundly affected his most brilliant follower, Plato (c. 428–348 B.C.), who even though an aristocrat nevertheless withdrew from political life after 399 B.C. The condemnation of Socrates apparently convinced him that citizens in a democracy were incapable of rising above narrow self-interest to knowledge of any universal truth. In his works dealing with the organization of society, Plato bitterly rejected democracy as a justifiable system of government. Instead he sketched what he saw as the philosophical basis for ideal political and social structures among humans. His utopian vision had virtually no effect on the actual politics of his time, and his attempts to advise Dionysius II (✱367–344 B.C.), tyrant of Syracuse in Sicily, on how to rule as a true philosopher ended in utter failure. But political philosophy was only one of Plato's interests, which ranged from astronomy and mathematics to metaphysics (theoretical explanations for phenomena that cannot be understood through direct experience or scientific experiment). After Plato's death his ideas attracted relatively little attention among philosophers for the next two centuries; but they were revived and debated vigorously in the Roman era. The sheer intellectual power of Plato's thought and the controversy his ideas have engendered throughout the years have established him as one of the great philosophers.

Plato intended his dialogues to provoke readers into thoughtful reflection rather than to spoon-feed them a predetermined set of beliefs. His views apparently changed over time—nowhere did he present one cohesive set of doctrines. He seems to have disagreed with Socrates' insistence that fundamental knowledge meant moral knowledge based on inner reflection. Plato concluded that knowledge meant truths that are independent of the observer and can be taught to others. He acted on this latter belief by founding the Academy, a shady gathering spot just outside the walls of Athens, which he named after a local hero whose shrine was nearby. The Academy was not a school or college in the modern sense but rather an informal association of people who studied philosophy, mathematics, and theoretical astronomy under Plato's guidance. Intellectuals gathered at the Academy for nine hundred years after Plato died; in some periods distinguished philosophers directed it, but at other times mediocre thinkers held court there.

Plato taught that we cannot define and understand absolute virtues such as goodness, justice, beauty, or equality by the concrete evidence of these qualities in our lives. Any earthly examples will in some other context display the opposite quality. For example, always returning what one has borrowed might seem just. But what if a person who has borrowed a friend's weapon is confronted by that friend, who wants the weapon back to commit murder? In this case returning the borrowed item would be unjust. Examples of equality are also only relative. The equality of a stick two feet long, for example, is evident when it is compared with another two-foot stick. Paired with a three-foot stick, however, it is unequal. In sum, in the world that humans experience with their senses, every virtue and every quality is relative to some extent.

Plato refused to accept the relativity of virtues as reality. He developed the theory that virtues cannot be discovered through experience; rather they are absolutes that can be comprehended only by thought and that somehow exist independently of human existence. In some of his works, Plato referred to the separate realities of the pure virtues as Forms; among the Forms were Goodness, Justice, Beauty, and Equality. He argued that the Forms were invisible, invariable, and eternal entities located in a higher realm beyond the empirical world of humans. According to Plato, the Forms are the only true reality; what humans experience through their senses are the impure shadows of this reality. Plato's views on the nature and significance of Forms altered throughout his career, and his later works seem quite divorced from this theory. Nevertheless, Forms exemplify both the complexity and the wide range of Plato's thought. His theory of Forms elevated metaphysics, the consideration of the ultimate nature of reality beyond the reach of the human senses, to a central and enduring issue for philosophers.

Plato's idea that humans possessed immortal souls distinct from their bodies established the concept of *dualism,* a separation between spiritual and physical being. This notion influenced much of later philosophical and religious thought. In a dialogue Plato wrote late in his life, he said the preexisting knowledge possessed by the immortal human soul is in truth the knowledge known to the supreme deity. Plato called this god the Demiurge ("craftsman") because the deity used knowledge of the Forms to craft the world of living beings from raw matter. According to Plato, because a knowing, rational god created the world, the world has order. Furthermore, the world's beings have goals, as evidenced by animals adapting to their environments in order to thrive. The Demiurge wanted to reproduce the perfect order of the Forms in the material world, but the world turned out imperfect because matter is imperfect. Plato believed the proper goal for humans is to seek perfect order and purity in their own souls by making rational thoughts control their irrational desires, which are harmful. The desire to drink wine to excess, for example, is irrational because the drinker fails to consider the hangover to come the next day. Those who give in to irrational desires fail to consider the future of both their body and soul. Finally, because the soul is immortal and the body is not, our present, impure existence is only one passing phase in our cosmic existence.

One version of Plato's utopian vision is found in his most famous dialogue, the *Republic.* This work, whose title would be more accurate as *System of Government,* primarily concerns the nature of justice and the reasons people should be just instead of unjust. Like a just soul, a just society would have its parts in proper hierarchy. Plato presents these parts as three classes of people, distinguished by their ability to grasp the truth of Forms. The highest class constitutes the rulers, or "guardians," as Plato calls them, who are educated in mathematics, astronomy, and metaphysics. Next come the "auxiliaries," whose function is to defend the polis. The lowest class comprises the "producers," who grow the food and make the objects the whole population requires. Each part contributes to society by fulfilling its proper function.

According to Plato's *Republic,* women as well as men can be guardians because they possess the same virtues and abilities as men, except for a disparity in physical strength between the average woman and the average man. The axiom justifying the inclusion of women—namely, that virtue is the same in women as in men—is a notion Plato may have derived from Socrates. The inclusion of women in the ruling class of Plato's utopian city-state represented a startling departure from the actual practice of his times. Indeed never before in Western history had anyone proposed that work be allocated in human society without regard to gender. Moreover, to minimize distraction, guardians are to have neither private property nor nuclear families. Male and female guardians are to live in houses shared in common, to eat in the same mess halls, and to exercise in the same gymnasiums. They are to have sexual relations with various partners so that the best women can mate with the best men to produce the best children. The children are to be raised together in a common environment by special caretakers. Although this scheme would supposedly free women guardians from child-care responsibilities and enable them to rule equally with men, Plato fails to mention that women guardians would in reality have a much tougher life than men because they would be pregnant frequently and undergo the strain and danger of giving birth. But he evidently does not disqualify women from ruling on this account. The guardians who achieve the highest level of knowledge in Plato's ideal society would qualify to rule over the ideally just state as philosopher-kings.

The severe regulation of life Plato proposed for his ideally just state in the *Republic* was an outgrowth of his tight focus on the question of a rational person's true interest. Furthermore, he insisted that objective truths can be found in the fields of politics and ethics by using reason. Despite his harsh criticism of existing governments, such as Athenian democracy, Plato recognized the practical difficulties in implementing radical changes in the way people actually lived. Indeed his late dialogue *The Laws* shows him wrestling with the question of improving the real world in a less radical, though still authoritarian, way than in the *Republic.* Plato hoped that instead of ordinary politicians, whether democrats or oligarchs, the people who know truth and can promote the common good would rule because their rule would be in everyone's real interest. For this reason above all, he passionately believed the study of philosophy mattered to human life.

Aristotle, Scientist and Philosopher

Plato's most brilliant follower was Aristotle (384–322 B.C.). Aristotle's great reputation as a thinker in science and philosophy rests on his influence in promoting scientific investigation of the natural world and in developing rigorous systems of logical argument. The enormous influence of Aristotle's works on later scholars, especially those of the Middle Ages, has made him a monumental figure in the history of Western science and philosophy.

The son of a wealthy doctor from Stagira in northern Greece, Aristotle came to Athens at the age of seventeen to study in Plato's Academy. In 335 B.C., Aristotle founded his own informal philosophical school in Athens, named the Lyceum, later called the Peripatetic School after the covered walkway *(peripatos)* in which its students carried on conversations while strolling out of the glare of the Mediterranean sun. Aristotle lectured with dazzling intelligence and energy on nearly every branch of learning: biology, medicine, anatomy, psychology, meteorology, physics, chemistry, mathematics, music, metaphysics, rhetoric, political science, ethics, and literary criticism. He also worked out a sophisticated system of logic for precise argumentation. Creating a careful system to identify the forms of valid arguments, Aristotle established grounds for distinguishing a logically sound case from a merely persuasive one. He first named contrasts such as "premise versus conclusion" and "the universal versus the particular," concepts featured in thought and speech ever since. He also studied the process of explanation itself, formulating the influential *doctrine of four causes.* According to Aristotle, four different categories of explanation exist that are not reducible to a single, unified whole: form (defining characteristics), matter (constituent elements), origin of movement (similar to what we commonly mean by "cause"), and *telos* (aim or goal). This doctrine exemplifies Aristotle's care never to oversimplify the complexity of reality.

Apparently an inspiring teacher, Aristotle encouraged his followers to conduct research in numerous fields of specialized knowledge. For example, he had student researchers compile reports on the systems of government of 158 Greek city-states. Much of Aristotle's philosophical thought reflected the influence of Plato, but he also refined and even rejected ideas his teacher had advocated. He denied the validity of Plato's theory of Forms, for example, on the grounds that the separate existence Plato postulated for them did not make sense. This position typified Aristotle's general preference for explanations based on common sense rather than metaphysics. By modern standards his scientific thought relied little on mathematical models of explanation and quantitative reasoning; but mathematics in his time had not yet become sophisticated enough for such work. His method also differed from that of modern scientists because it did not include controlled experiments. Aristotle believed that investigators had a better chance of understanding objects and beings by observing them in their natural setting than under the artificial conditions of a laboratory. His coupling of detailed investigation with perceptive reasoning worked especially well in such physical sciences as biology, botany, and zoology. For example, as the first scientist to try to collect and classify all the available information on the animal species, Aristotle recorded the facts about more than five hundred different kinds of animals, including insects. Many of his findings represented significant advances in learning. His recognition that whales and dolphins were mammals, for example, which later writers on animals overlooked, was not rediscovered for another two thousand years.

Some of Aristotle's most influential discussions concentrated on understanding qualitative concepts that humans tend to take for granted, such as time, space, motion, and change. Through careful argumentation he probed the philosophical difficulties that lie beneath the surface of these familiar notions, and his views on the nature of such things powerfully affected later thinkers. Aristotle was conventional for his times in regarding slavery as natural based on the argument that some people were by nature bound to be slaves because their souls lacked the rational part that should rule in a human. Individuals propounding the contrary view were rare, although one fourth-century B.C. orator, Alcidamas, asserted that "God has set all men free; nature has made no one a slave." Also in tune with his times was Aristotle's conclusion that women were by nature inferior to men. His view of women's inferiority was based on faulty notions of biology. He wrongly believed, for example, that in procreation the male's semen actively gave the fetus its form, whereas the female passively provided its matter. He justified his assertion that females were less courageous than males by dubious evidence about animals, such as the report that a male squid would stay by as if to help when its mate was speared but that a female squid would swim away when the male was impaled. Although erroneous information led Aristotle to evaluate females as incomplete males, he believed human communities could be successful and happy only if both women and men contributed. Aristotle argued that marriage was meant to provide mutual help and comfort but that the husband should rule.

Aristotle departed sharply from the Socratic idea that knowledge of justice and goodness was all a person needed to behave justly. He argued that people's souls often possess knowledge of what is right but that their irrational desires overrule this knowledge and lead them to do wrong. People who know the misery of gluttony still stuff themselves, for example. Recognizing a conflict of desires in the human soul, Aristotle advocated achieving self-control by training the mind to win out over instincts and passions. Self-control did not mean denying human desires and appetites; rather it meant striking a balance between suppressing and heedlessly indulging physical yearnings, of finding "the mean." Aristotle claimed that the mind should rule in finding this balance because the intellect is the finest human quality and the mind is the true self, indeed the godlike part of a person.

Aristotle regarded science and philosophy not as abstract subjects isolated from the concerns of ordinary existence but as the disciplined search for knowledge in every aspect of life. That search epitomized the kind of rational human activity that alone could bring the good life and genuine happiness. Some modern critics have pointed out that Aristotle's work lacks a clear moral code. Even so, he did the study of ethics a great service by insisting that standards of right and wrong have merit only if they are grounded in character and aligned with the good in human nature and do not simply consist of lists of abstract reasons for behaving in one way rather than another; that is, an ethical system must be relevant to the actual moral situations humans experience. In ethics, as in all his scholarship, Aristotle distinguished himself by insisting that the life of the mind and experience of the real world are inseparable components in the quest to define a worthwhile existence for humans.

Practical Education and Rhetoric

Despite his interest in subjects such as the history of the constitutions of states and the theory and practice of rhetoric, Aristotle remained a theoretician in the mold of Plato. This characteristic set him apart from the major educational trend of the fourth century B.C., which emphasized practical wisdom and training that applied directly to the public lives of upper-class male citizens in a swiftly changing world. The most important component of this education was rhetoric, the skill of persuasive public speaking, which itself depended not only on oratorical techniques but also on the knowledge of the world and of human psychology that speakers required to be effective. The ideas about education and rhetoric that emerged in this period had a tremendous impact on later Greeks and Romans and on others long after.

Even many who had admired Socrates, who had dismissed such matters, believed in the general value of practical knowledge and rhetoric. Xenophon, for example, knew Socrates well enough to write extensive memoirs re-creating many conversations with the great philosopher. But he also wrote a wide range of works in history, biography, estate management, horsemanship, and the public revenues of Athens. The subjects of these treatises reveal the manifold topics Xenophon considered essential to the proper education of men.

The ideas of the famous Athenian orator Isocrates (436–338 B.C.) exemplified the dedication to rhetoric as a practical skill that Plato rejected as utterly wrong. Isocrates was born to a rich family and studied with sophists and thinkers, including Socrates. Because he lacked the voice to address large gatherings, Isocrates composed speeches for other men to deliver and endeavored to influence public opinion and political leaders at Athens and abroad by publishing his own speeches. He regarded education as the preparation for a useful life doing good in matters of public importance. He sought to develop an educational middle ground between the theoretical study of abstract ideas and purely crass training in rhetorical techniques for influencing others to one's personal advantage. In this way he stood between the ideals of Plato and the promises of unscrupulous sophists.

Isocrates believed that rhetoric was the skill men who aspired to public office must master. Becoming a good rhetorician, he insisted, required natural talent and practical experience in worldly affairs, which trained orators to understand public issues and the psychology of the people whom they had to persuade for the common good. Isocrates saw rhetoric not as a device for cynical self-aggrandizement but as a powerful tool for human betterment, if wielded by properly gifted and trained men with developed consciences. (Women could not become orators because they were excluded from politics.) Isocrates' emphasis on rhetoric and its application in real-world politics won many more adherents among men in Greek and, later, Roman culture than did Plato's vision of the philosophical life, and it came to exert great influence when revived in Renaissance Europe, two thousand years later.

Throughout his life, Isocrates tried to put his doctrines to use by addressing works to powerful leaders whose policies he wanted to influence. In his later years he believed Greece had become so unstable that he promoted the cause of pan-Hellenism—political harmony among all the Greek city-states—by urging Philip II, king of Macedonia, to unite the Greeks under his leadership in a crusade against Persia. This radical recommendation was Isocrates' practical solution to the persistent conflicts among Greek city-states and to the social unrest created by friction between the richer communities and the many poor areas in Greece. Isocrates believed that if the fractious city-states accepted Philip as their leader in a common alliance, they could avoid wars among themselves and relieve the impoverished population among them by establishing Greek colonies on land to be carved out of Persian-held territory in Anatolia. That a prominent Athenian would openly appeal for a Macedonian king to save the Greeks from themselves reflected the startling new political and military reality that had emerged in the Greek world by the mid-fourth century B.C.

The Restructuring of Power in Greece and the Near East

The kingdom of Macedonia soon filled the power vacuum that had been created by the futile wars the Greek city-states waged against one another in the early fourth century B.C. Macedonia was a rough land of mountains and lowland valleys just north of Greece. Life there was harder than in Greece because the climate was colder and more dangerous and because the Macedonians' western and northern neighbors periodically launched devastating raids into Macedonian territory. The Macedonians were especially vulnerable to these raids because

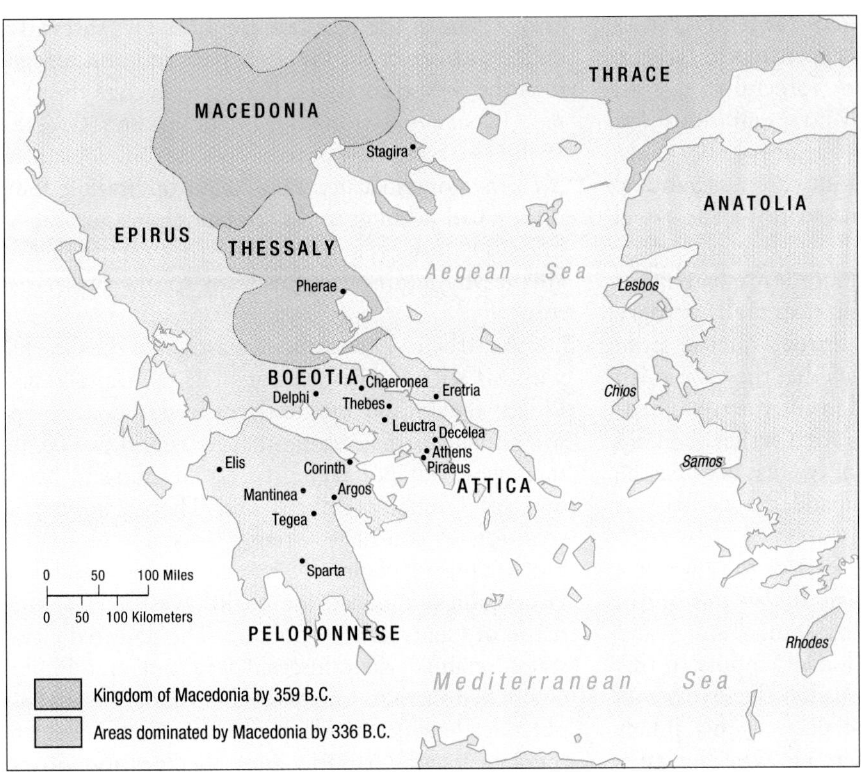

The Expansion of Macedonia

they generally lived in small villages and towns without protective walls. That this formerly minor kingdom became the greatest power in Greece and conquered the Persian Empire ranks as one of the major surprises in ancient military and political history.

The Creation of Macedonian Power

Macedonian tradition dictated that the king listen to his people, who were used to addressing their monarch with considerable freedom of speech. This custom constrained the king's power; he could govern effectively only as long as he maintained the support of the most powerful aristocrats, who counted as the king's social equals and controlled large bands of followers. Fighting, hunting, and heavy drinking were the favorite pastimes of these men. The king was expected to demonstrate his prowess in these activities to show he was a Macedonian "man's man" capable of heading the state. Macedonian queens and royal mothers received respect in this male-dominated society because they came from powerful families in the Macedonian nobility or the ruling houses of lands bordering Macedonia. In the king's absence these royal women often vied with the king's designated representative for power at court.

Macedonians had their own language, related to Greek but not comprehensible to Greeks. The aristocrats who dominated Macedonian society routinely learned to speak Greek because they thought of themselves and indeed all Macedonians as Greek by blood. At the same time, Macedonians looked down on the Greeks to the south as a soft lot unequal to the adversities of life in Macedonia. The Greeks reciprocated this scorn. The famed Athenian orator Demosthenes (384–322 B.C.) lambasted the Macedonian king Philip II (*359–336 B.C.) as "not only not a Greek nor related to the Greeks, but not even a barbarian from a land worth mentioning; no, he's a pestilence from Macedonia, a region where you can't even buy a slave worth his salt." Barbed verbal attacks like this characterized Demosthenes' speeches on foreign and domestic policy to the Athenian assembly, where he consistently tried to convince his fellow Athenians to oppose Macedonian expansion in Greece.

Demosthenes spoke so forcefully against Philip because he recognized how ambitious and potentially dangerous he was—against heavy odds, Philip had forged Macedonia into an international power. Before Philip's reign, strife in the royal family and disputes among the leading aristocrats had been so common that Macedonia had never united sufficiently to mobilize its full military strength. Macedonian kings feared violence from their own countrymen so much that they stationed bodyguards both outside and inside the royal bedroom. Macedonian princes married earlier than did most men, soon after the age of twenty, because the instability of the kingship demanded male heirs as soon as possible.

The situation was grave in 359 B.C., when a force of Illyrians, hostile neighbors to the north, slaughtered the current Macedonian king and around four thousand Macedonian troops. In this moment of crisis, Philip persuaded the aristocrats to recognize him as king in place of his infant nephew, for whom he was serving as regent after the king's death in battle. Philip then rallied the army by teaching the infantrymen an unstoppable new tactic. Macedonian troops carried thrusting spears fourteen to sixteen feet long, which they had to hold with two hands. Philip drilled his men in handling these heavy weapons in a phalanx formation, whose front line bristled with outstretched spears like a lethal porcupine. With the cavalry of aristocrats deployed as a strike force to soften up the enemy and protect the infantry's flanks, Philip's reorganized army promptly routed Macedonia's attackers and defeated his local rivals to the kingship.

Philip then embarked on a whirlwind of diplomacy, bribery, and military action to force the Greek city-states to acknowledge his superiority. He financed his ambition by prodigiously spending the gold and silver coins he had minted from the ore of Macedonia mines and those captured in Thrace. A Greek contemporary, the historian Theopompus of Chios, labeled Philip "insatiable and extravagant; he did everything in a hurry . . . he never spared the time to reckon up his income and expenditure." By the late 340s B.C., Philip had cajoled or coerced most of northern Greece to follow his lead in foreign policy. His goal then became to lead a united Macedonian and Greek army against the Persian Empire. He shrewdly culled a thorn from Greece's past and announced it as the reason to attack Persia: to avenge the 480 B.C. Persian invasion of Macedonia and Greece. Philip also feared the potentially destabilizing effect his reinvigorated army would have on his kingdom if they had nothing to do. To launch his grandiose invasion, however, he needed to strengthen his alliance by adding the forces of southern Greece to it.

At Athens, Demosthenes castigated the Greeks with his stirring rhetoric for their failure to resist Philip: they stood by, he thundered, "as if Philip were a hailstorm, praying that he would not come their way, but not trying to do anything to head him off." Finally, Athens and Thebes headed a coalition of southern Greek city-states to try to block Philip's plans. In 338 B.C., Philip and his Greek allies trounced the coalition's forces at the battle of Chaeronea in Boeotia. The defeated city-states retained their internal freedom, but Philip compelled them to join an alliance under his undisputed leadership. (Modern scholars call this alliance the League of Corinth, after the location of its headquarters.) The course of later history proved the battle of Chaeronea a decisive turning point in Greek history: never again would the city-states of Greece make foreign policy for themselves without considering, and usually following, the wishes of outside powers. This change marked the end of the Greek city-states as independent actors in international politics, though they did remain the basic economic and social units of Greece. Macedonia's King Philip and his son Alexander now stepped onto center stage. The people of the Greek city-states became subjects or allies of the new kingdoms these two rulers and their successors carved out. The Hellenistic kingdoms, as these new monarchies are called, like the Roman provinces that eventually replaced them as political masters of the Greeks, depended on the local leaders of the Greek city-states to collect taxes for the imperial treasuries and to ensure the loyalty and order of the citizens.

Alexander's Conquest of Persia

A Macedonian assassinated Philip in 336 B.C. Unconfirmed rumors speculated that the murder had been instigated by one of his several wives, Olympias, a princess from Epirus to the west

Alexander Winning the Battle of Issus
This wall-sized, Roman-era mosaic shows Alexander attacking the Persian king at Issus in 333 B.C. Based on a famous painting, it shows dramatic foreshortening—a technique that added a three-dimensional feeling to the work—as in the horse's hindquarters.

of Macedonia. Philip's son by her, Alexander (356–323 B.C.), promptly murdered potential rivals for the throne and won recognition as king. In several lightning-fast campaigns, he subdued Macedonia's traditional enemies to the west and north. Next he forced the southern Greeks, who had defected from the Macedonian-led League of Corinth at the news of Philip's death, to rejoin the alliance. To demonstrate the price of disloyalty, Alexander destroyed Thebes in 335 B.C. as punishment.

With Greece begrudgingly quiescent, Alexander in 334 B.C. led a Macedonian and Greek army into Anatolia to fulfill his father's plan to avenge Greece by attacking Persia. Alexander's astounding success in conquering the entire Persian Empire while in his twenties earned him the sobriquet "the Great" in later ages. In his own time his greatness consisted of his ability to motivate his men, however reluctantly, to follow him into hostile, unknown regions. Alexander inspired his troops with his reckless disregard for his own safety. He often plunged into the enemy's front line at the head of his men, sharing the danger of the common soldier. No one could miss him in his plumed helmet, vividly colored cloak, and armor polished to reflect the sun. So intent on conquering distant lands was Alexander that he rejected advice to delay his departure from Macedonia until he had married and fathered an heir, to forestall instability in case of his death. He further alarmed his principal adviser by giving away virtually all his land and property in order to strengthen the army, thereby creating new landowners who would furnish troops. "What," he was asked, "do you have left for yourself?" "My hopes," he replied. Those hopes centered on constructing a heroic image of himself as a warrior as splendid as the incomparable Achilles of Homer's *Iliad.* Alexander always kept a copy of the *Iliad* under his pillow, along with a dagger. Alexander's aspirations and his behavior represented the ultimate expression of the Homeric vision of the glorious conquering warrior, still the prevailing ideal of male Greek culture.

Alexander cast a spear into the earth of Anatolia when he crossed the Hellespont strait from Europe to Asia, thereby claiming the Asian continent for himself in Homeric fashion as "territory won by the spear." The first battle of the campaign, in 334 B.C. at the River Granicus in western Anatolia, proved the worth of Alexander's Macedonian and Greek cavalry, which charged across the river and up the bank to rout the opposing Persians and their Greek mercenaries. Alexander visited Midas's old capital of Gordion in Phrygia, where an oracle had promised the lordship of Asia to whoever could loose a seemingly impenetrable knot of rope tying the yoke of an ancient chariot preserved in the city. The young Macedonian, so the story goes, cut the Gordian knot with his sword. In 333 B.C. the Persian king, Darius, finally faced Alexander in battle at Issus, near the southeastern corner of Anatolia. Alexander's army defeated its more numerous opponents with a characteristically bold strike of cavalry through the left side of the Persian lines followed by a flanking maneuver against the king's position in the center. Darius had to flee from the field to avoid capture, abandoning his wives and daughters, who had accompanied his campaign in keeping with royal Persian tradition. Alexander's scrupulously chivalrous treatment of the Persian royal women after their capture at Issus reportedly boosted his reputation among the peoples of the Persian Empire.

When Tyre, a heavily fortified city on the coast of what is now Lebanon, refused to surrender to him in 332 B.C., Alexander employed the artillery towers, armored battering rams, and catapults flinging boulders developed by his father to breach its walls. The capture of Tyre rang the death knell of supposedly impregnable walled city-states. Although effective attacks on cities with defensive walls remained rare even after Alexander because well-constructed city walls still presented formidable barriers, Alexander's success at Tyre increased the terror of a siege for a city's general population. No longer could a city-state's citizens confidently assume their defensive system could withstand the technology of their enemy's offensive weapons indefinitely. The now present fear that armed warriors might actually penetrate into the city made it much harder psychologically for city-states to remain united in the face of threats from aggressive enemies.

Alexander next conquered Egypt, which had fallen to Persian conquest in 525 B.C., regained its independence later for a time, and then once again been taken over by the Persian Empire. Hieroglyphic inscriptions show that he probably presented himself as the successor to the Persian king as the land's ruler rather than as an Egyptian pharaoh. On the coast, to the west of the Nile River, he founded a new city in 331 B.C. and named it Alexandria after himself. Alexandria was the first of many cities he founded, as far east as Afghanistan. During his time in Egypt, Alexander also paid a mysterious visit to the oracle of the god Ammon, whom the Greeks regarded as identical to Zeus, at the oasis of Siwah far out in the western Egyptian desert. Alexander told no one the details of his consultation with the oracle, but the news leaked that he had been informed he was the son of Ammon and that he joyfully accepted the designation as true.

In 331 B.C., Alexander crushed the Persian king's main army at the battle of Gaugamela in northern Mesopotamia (near the border of modern Iraq and Iran). He subsequently proclaimed himself king of Asia in place of the Persian king. For the heterogeneous populations of the Persian Empire, the succession of a Macedonian to the Persian throne changed their lives very little. They continued to send the same taxes to a remote master, whom they rarely if ever saw. As in Egypt, Alexander left the local administrative system in place, even retaining some Persian governors. His long-term aim seems to have been to forge an administrative corps composed of Macedonians, Greeks, and Persians working together to rule the territory he and his army conquered.

The Expedition to India

So fierce was Alexander's love of conquest and adventure that he next led his army farther east into territory hardly known to the Greeks. He pared his force to reduce the need for supplies, which were hard to acquire in the arid country through which they were marching. Each hoplite in Greek armies customarily brought a personal servant to carry his armor and pack. Alexander, imitating Philip, trained his men to carry their own equipment, thereby creating a leaner force by cutting the number of army servants significantly. As with all

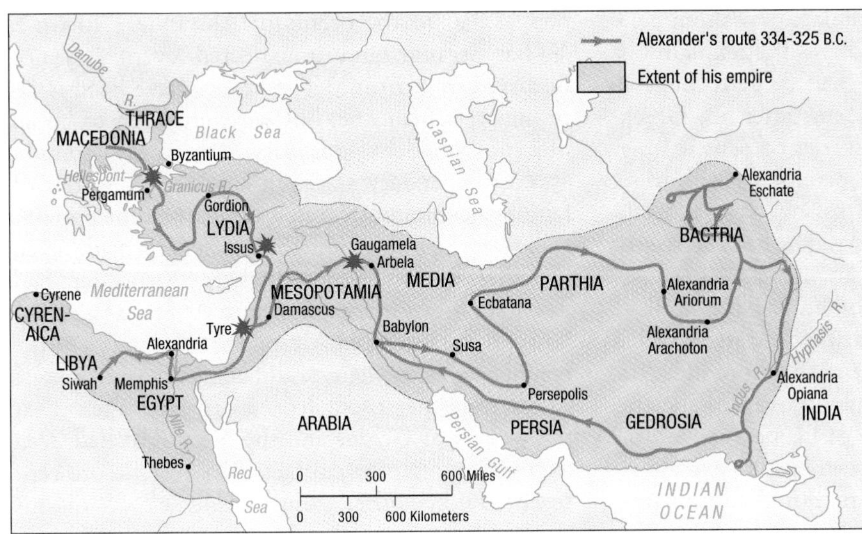

Alexander's Route to India and Back

ancient armies, however, many noncombatants trailed after the fighting force: merchants who set up little markets at every stop, prostitutes, women whom soldiers had taken as mates along the way, and their children. Although supplying these hangers-on was not Alexander's problem, their foraging for themselves made it harder for Alexander's quartermasters to find what they needed to supply the army proper.

From the heartland of Persia, Alexander in 329 B.C. marched northeast into the trackless steppes of Bactria (modern Afghanistan). When he proved unable to subdue completely the highly mobile locals, who avoided pitched battles in favor of the guerrilla tactics of attack and retreat, Alexander settled for an alliance that he sealed by marrying the Bactrian princess Roxanne in 327 B.C. From Bactria, Alexander headed east into India. He probably intended to push all the way through to China in search of the edge of the farthest land on the earth, which Aristotle, who had once tutored the young Alexander, had taught was a sphere. Seventy days of marching through monsoon rains, however, shattered the nerves of the soldiers. In the spring of 326 B.C. they mutinied on the banks of the Hyphasis River (the modern Beas) in western India. Alexander was forced to agree to lead them in the direction of home. Their return cost many casualties as they proceeded first southward along the Indus River and then westward, with some troops sailing along the coast, some taking a northern route, and Alexander leading a contingent through the harsh Gedrosian desert. They finally reached safety in the heartland of Persia in 324 B.C. Alexander promptly began planning an invasion of the Arabian peninsula and, after that, of all North Africa west of Egypt.

By the time Alexander had returned to Persia he had dropped all pretense of ruling over the Greeks as anything other than an absolute monarch. Despite his earlier promise to respect the internal freedom of the Greek city-states, he impinged on their autonomy by issuing a peremptory decree ordering them to restore citizenship to the many exiles who had been created over the previous decades of war in Greece and whose status as wandering, stateless persons was creating unrest. Even more striking was his announcement that he wished to receive the honors due a god. Initially dumbfounded by this request, the leaders of most Greek city-states soon complied by sending honorary delegations to him as if he were a god. The Spartan Damis pithily expressed the only prudent position on Alexander's deification open to the cowed Greeks: "If Alexander wishes to be a god, we agree that he be called a god." Scholars continue to debate Alexander's motive for wanting the Greeks to acknowledge him as a god, but few now accept a formerly popular theory that he sought divinity because he believed the city-states would then have to obey his orders as originating from a divinity, whose authority would supersede that of all earthly regimes. Scholars now think personal rather than political motives best explain his request. He almost certainly had come to believe he was actually the son of Zeus; after all, Greek mythology contained many stories of Zeus mating with a human female and producing children. Most of those legendary offspring were mortal, but Alexander's conquests proved he had surpassed them. His feats must be superhuman because they exceeded the bounds of human possibility. Alexander's accomplishments demonstrated that he had achieved godlike power and therefore must be a god himself. Alexander's divinity was, in ancient terms, a natural consequence of his power.

Alexander's overall aims can best be explained as interlinked goals: the conquest and administration of the known world and the exploration and possible colonization of new territory beyond. Conquest through military action was a time-honored pursuit for Macedonian aristocrats like Alexander. He included non-Macedonians in his administration and army because he needed their expertise, not because he wished to promote an abstract notion of what has been called "the brotherhood of man." Alexander's explorations benefited numerous scientific fields from geography to botany because he took along scientifically minded writers to collect and catalog the new knowledge they acquired. The far-flung cities that he founded served as loyal outposts for keeping the peace in conquered territory and providing warnings to headquarters in case of local uprisings. They also created new opportunities for trade in valuable goods such as spices that were not produced in the Mediterranean region.

Alexander's plans to conquer Arabia and North Africa were extinguished by his premature death from a fever and heavy drinking on June 10, 323 B.C. He had been suffering for months from depression brought on by the death of his best friend, Hephaistion. Close since their boyhoods, Alexander and Hephaistion were probably lovers. Like Pericles, Alexander had made no plans about what should happen if he died unexpectedly. His Bactrian wife, Roxanne, gave birth to their first child a few months after Alexander's death. When at Alexander's deathbed his commanders asked him to whom he bequeathed his kingdom, he replied, "To the most powerful."

The Athenian orator Aeschines (c. 397–322 B.C.) well expressed the bewildered reaction many people had to the events of Alexander's lifetime: "What strange and unexpected event has not occurred in our time? The life we have lived is no ordinary human one, but we were born to be an object of wonder to posterity." Alexander certainly attained legendary status in later times. Stories of fabulous exploits attributed to him became popular folk tales throughout the ancient world, even reaching distant regions where Alexander had never set foot, such as deep into Africa. The popularity of the legend of Alexander as a symbol of the heights a warrior-hero could achieve served as one of his most persistent legacies to later ages. That the worlds of Greece and the Near East had been brought into closer contact than ever before represented the other long-lasting effect of his astonishing career.

The Development of a Hellenistic Culture

The word *Hellenistic* was coined in the nineteenth century to designate the period of Greek and Near Eastern history from the death of Alexander the Great in 323 B.C. to the death of Cleopatra VII, the last Macedonian queen of Egypt, in 30 B.C. (By 30 B.C. the Romans had become the dominant power in the eastern Mediterranean.) The term *Hellenistic* conveys the idea that a mixed, cosmopolitan form of social and cultural life combining Hellenic (that is, Greek) traditions with indigenous traditions emerged in the eastern Mediterranean region in the aftermath of Alexander's career. Greek ideas and practices had their greatest impact on the urban populations of Egypt and southwestern Asia. The many people who farmed in the Near Eastern countryside and rarely visited the cities had much less contact with Greek ways of life.

Significant social and cultural changes of the Hellenistic period occurred against the backdrop of a new form of kingship, compounded of Macedonian and Near Eastern traditions, which became the predominant political structure in the eastern Mediterranean after Alexander's premature death. The kings who founded the Hellenistic kingdoms were self-proclaimed monarchs with neither a blood relationship to any traditional royal family line nor any special claim to a particular territory. (For this reason historians often describe such a kingdom as a "personal monarchy.") They transformed themselves into kings using their military might, their prestige, and their ambition.

The Creation of Successor Kingdoms

After Alexander's death his mother, Olympias, tried for several years to establish her infant grandson, Alexander's son by Roxanne, as the Macedonian king under her protection. Her plan foundered because Alexander's former army commanders wanted to rule instead, and within twenty years, three of his most powerful generals had established new kingdoms in place of the old. Antigonus (c. 382–301 B.C.) took over in Anatolia, the Near East, Macedonia, and Greece; Seleucus (c. 358–281 B.C.) in Babylonia and the East as far as India; and Ptolemy (c. 367–282 B.C.) in Egypt. Because these men became the de facto heirs to the largest parts of Alexander's conquests, they were referred to as the "successor kings."

Antigonus tried to conquer the other kingdoms to reunite Alexander's domain, but the other successor kings temporarily banded together and defeated his forces and killed him at the battle of Ipsus in Anatolia in 301 B.C. Seleucus then added Syria to his kingdom. Antigonus's son, Demetrius (c. 336–283 B.C.), regained the Macedonian throne from about 294 to 288 B.C., but further defeats forced him to spend his last years in benign captivity as a helpless guest under the thumb of Seleucus. Demetrius's son, Antigonus Gonatas (c. 320–239 B.C.), reestablished his family's kingdom in Macedonia around 276 B.C., but the city-states of southern Greece remained nominally independent. The Seleucid kingdom had to cede its easternmost territory early in its history to the Indian king Chandragupta (∗323–299 B.C.), founder of the Mauryan dynasty, and later lost most of Persia to the Parthians, a north Iranian people. The Ptolemaic kingdom retained its control of the rich land of Egypt. By the middle of the third century B.C., the three kingdoms had reached a balance of power that precluded their expanding much beyond their core territories. Even so, the Hellenistic monarchs remained competitive, especially in conflicts over contested border areas. The armies of the Ptolemaic and Seleucid kingdoms, for

Principal Hellenistic Kingdoms and Locations

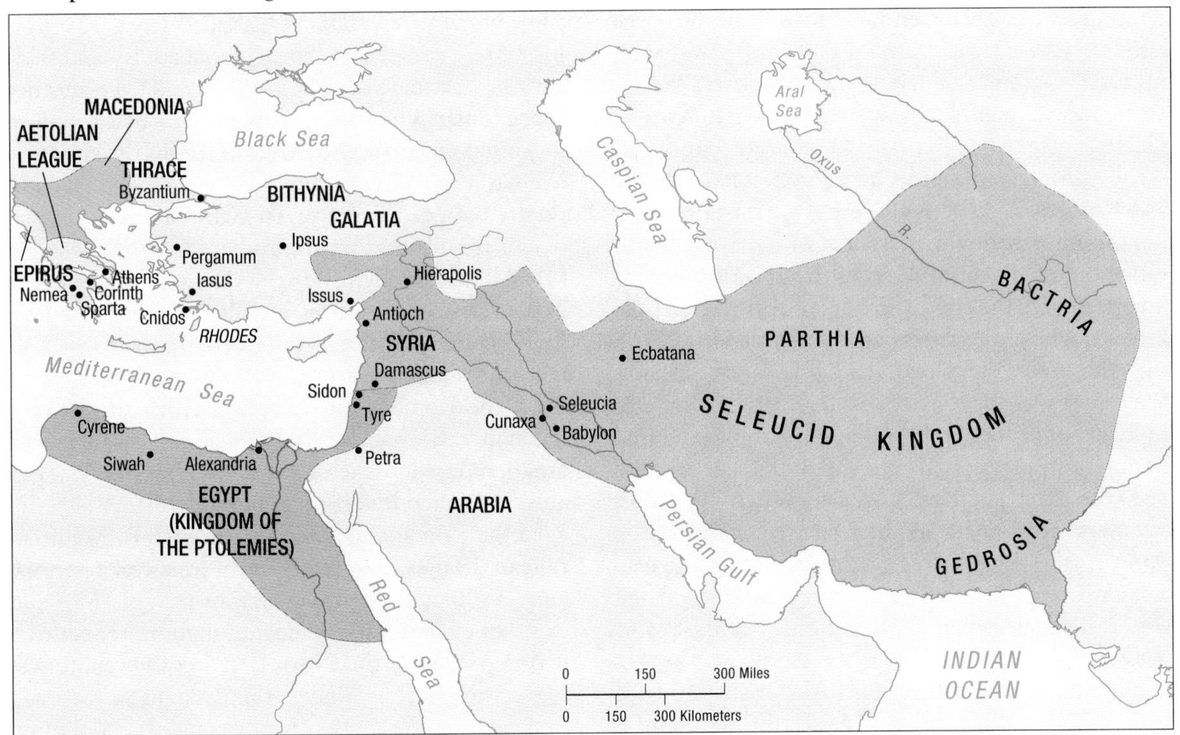

Theater at Hellenistic Pergamum *Prosperous cities like Pergamum in western Anatolia (Asia Minor) built steeply pitched theaters that seated thousands of spectators for dramas and festivals.*

example, periodically engaged in a violent tug-of-war over Palestine and Syria.

Some smaller, regional kingdoms also developed in the Hellenistic period. Most famous was the kingdom of the Attalids in Anatolia, with the wealthy city of Pergamum as its capital. The Attalids were strong enough to defeat the large band of Celtic people, called Celts or Gauls, who invaded Anatolia from northern Europe in 278 B.C., and confine them to an area thereafter known as Galatia, after their name. (A separate band had invaded Macedonia and Greece in 279 B.C.) As far away as central Asia, in modern Afghanistan, a new kingdom formed when Diodotus I led a successful rebellion of Bactrian Greeks from the Seleucid kingdom in the mid-third century B.C. These Greeks, whose ancestors had been settled in Bactria by Alexander the Great, had flourished because their land was the crossroads for overland trade in luxury goods between India and China and the Mediterranean world. By the end of the first century B.C. the Bactrian kingdom had fallen to Asian invaders from north of the Oxus River (now the Amu Daria), but the region continued to serve as a cauldron for the interaction of the artistic, philosophical, and religious traditions of East and West.

The successor kings adopted different strategies to meet the goal shared by all new political regimes: to establish a tradition of legitimacy for their rule. Legitimacy was essential if they were to found a royal line that had a chance of enduring beyond their deaths. As a result, Hellenistic queens enjoyed a high social status as the representatives of distinguished families, who then became the mothers of a line of royal descendants. The successors' positions ultimately rested on their personal ability and their power. Lysimachus (c. 360–281 B.C.), another Macedonian who temporarily carved out a kingdom in Thrace and Asia Minor, summed up the situation in a letter to a Greek city: "My rule depends mostly on my own excellence *(arete)*, and on the good will of my friends and on my forces."

All the Hellenistic kingdoms in the eastern Mediterranean region eventually fell to the Romans. Diplomatic and military blunders by the Macedonian kings beginning in the third century B.C. first drew the Romans into Greece, which they dominated by the middle of the second century B.C. Smaller powers, such as the city-state of Rhodes and the Attalid kings in Pergamum, further encouraged the Romans to intervene in eastern Mediterranean affairs. Despite its early losses of territory and later troubles from both internal uprisings and external enemies, the Seleucid kingdom remained a major power in the Near East for two centuries. Nevertheless, it too fell to the Romans in the mid-first century B.C. As for Egypt, even though

Ptolemy II (*282–246 B.C.) created difficulties for his successors by imposing disastrous financial measures to pay for a war in Syria, the Ptolemaic kingdom survived the longest. Eventually, however, its growing weakness forced the Egyptian kings to summon intermittent Roman support. When Queen Cleopatra chose the losing side in the Roman civil war of the late first century B.C., a Roman invasion in 30 B.C. ended her reign and the long succession of Ptolemaic rulers.

The Organization of Hellenistic Kingdoms

The armies and navies of Hellenistic kingdoms provided security against internal unrest as well as external enemies. Unlike the citizen militias of the classical period's city-states, professional soldiers made up Hellenistic royal forces. The Greek city-states of the Hellenistic period also hired mercenaries increasingly, as had the Persian kings, instead of mustering citizens. To develop their military might, the Seleucid and Ptolemaic kings vigorously promoted immigration by Greeks and Macedonians, who received land grants in return for military service. When this source later dwindled, the kings had to rely more on the local populations, often employing indigenous troops. Military expenditures rose because the kings faced ongoing pressure to pay their mercenaries regularly and because technology had developed more expensive artillery, such as catapults capable of flinging a projectile weighing one hundred seventy pounds a distance of nearly two hundred yards. Hellenistic navies were expensive because warships were larger, with some dreadnoughts requiring hundreds of men as crews. War elephants, popular in Hellenistic arsenals for their shock effect on enemy troops, were also extremely costly to maintain.

Hellenistic kings initially depended mostly on Greek and Macedonian immigrants to administer their kingdoms. The title "king's friends" identified the inner circle of advisers and courtiers. Like Alexander before them, however, the Seleucids and the Ptolemies also employed indigenous men in the middle and lower levels of their administrations. Even if local men had successful careers in government, however, only rarely were they admitted to the highest ranks of royal society, such as the king's friends. Greeks and non-Greeks tended to live in separate communities. Greeks and Macedonians generally saw themselves as too superior to mix with locals.

Local men who aspired to a government career bettered their chances of succeeding if they learned to read and write Greek in addition to their native languages. This bilingualism qualified them to fill positions communicating the orders of the highest ranking officials, all Greeks and Macedonians, to the local farmers, builders, and crafts producers. The Greek these administrators learned was *koine* ("common Greek"), a standardized form of Greek based on the Athenian dialect. For centuries koine was the common language of commerce and culture from Sicily to the border of India. The New Testament was written in koine during the early Roman Empire, and it was the parent language of Byzantine and modern Greek.

Administrators' principal jobs were to maintain order and to direct the kingdom's tax systems. In many ways the goals and structures of Hellenistic royal administrations recalled those of the earlier Assyrian, Babylonian, and Persian empires. They kept order among the kingdom's subjects by mediating between disputing parties whenever possible, but they could call on troops serving as police if necessary. Overseeing tax collection could be complicated. For example, in Ptolemaic Egypt, the most tightly organized Hellenistic kingdom, royal officials collected customs duties of 50 percent, $33\frac{1}{3}$ percent, 25 percent, or 20 percent depending on the type of goods imported. The renowned Ptolemaic organization was based on methods of central planning and control inherited from much earlier periods of Egyptian history. Officials continued to administer royal monopolies, such as that on vegetable oil, to maximize the king's revenue. Ptolemaic administrators, in a system much like modern schemes of centralized agriculture, decided how much land farmers should sow in oil-bearing plants, supervised production and distribution of the oil, and set all prices for every stage of the oil business. The king, through his officials, also often entered into part-

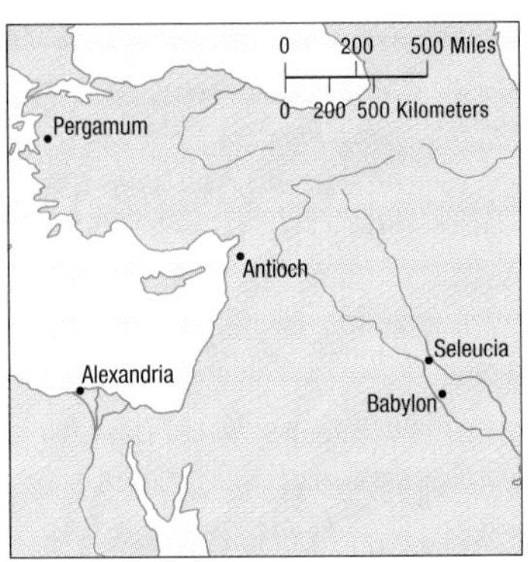

Principal Hellenistic Cities of the Eastern Mediterranean

Model of Priene
This model of the city of Priene in Anatolia shows the rectilinear layout of buildings and streets, with an agora at the center, that characterized Greek cities in the classical and Hellenistic periods.

nerships with private investors to produce more revenue.

Cities were the economic and social hubs of the Hellenistic kingdoms. In Greece some cities outside the Macedonian kingdom tried to increase their strength (to counterbalance that of the monarchies) by banding together into new federal alliances, such as the Achaean League in the Peloponnese and the Aetolian League in northwestern Greece. Making decisions for the league in a common assembly, these cities agreed to use, for example, the same coinage and weights and measures, and to offer equal legal protection for their citizens. Many Greeks and Macedonians now lived in new cities founded by Alexander and the successor kings in the Near East. Hellenistic kings also reestablished existing cities to bring honor to themselves and to introduce new immigrants and social patterns supportive of their policies. The new settlements had the traditional features of classical Greek city-states, such as gymnasiums and theaters. Although these cities often also possessed such traditional political institutions of the city-state as councils and assemblies for citizen men, the limits of their independence depended strictly on the king's will. When writing to the city's council, the king might express himself in the form of a polite request, but he expected his wishes to be fulfilled as if they were commands. These cities often had to pay taxes directly to the king.

The kings needed the goodwill of the wealthiest and most influential city-dwellers—the Greek and Macedonian urban elites—to keep order in the cities and ensure a steady flow of tax revenues. These wealthy people had the crucial responsibility of collecting taxes from the surrounding countryside as well as from their cities and sending them on to the royal treasury. The kings honored and flattered these members of the cities' upper class to secure their favor and cooperation. Accommodating cities would receive benefactions from the king to pay for expensive public works like theaters and temples or restorations after such natural disasters as earthquakes. The wealthy men and women of the urban upper classes in turn helped keep the general population tractable by providing donations and loans that secured a reliable supply of grain to feed the city's residents, subsidize teachers and doctors, and construct public works. The Greek tradition of the wealthy and the aristocrats of a city-state making contributions for the common good was therefore continued in a new way, through the social interaction of the kings and the urban upper classes.

The kings also needed to court the good graces of well-to-do members of the local populations. Because indigenous cities had long been powerful in Syria and Palestine, for example, the kings had to develop cordial relations with their leading citizens. Non-Greeks and non-Macedonians from eastern regions also moved westward to Hellenistic Greek cities in increasing numbers. Jews in particular moved from Palestine to Asia Minor, Greece, and Egypt. The Jewish community eventually became an influential minority in Alexandria, the most important Hellenistic city. In Egypt the king also had to come to terms with the priests who controlled the temples of the traditional Egyptian gods, because the temples owned large tracts of arable land worked by tenant farmers. The linchpin in the organization of the Hellenistic kingdoms was the system of mutual rewards by which the kings and their leading subjects—Greeks, Macedonians, and indigenous elites—became partners in government and public finance.

The successor kingdoms nevertheless amounted to foreign rule over local populations by kings and queens of Macedonian descent. Although monarchs had to maintain harmony with the urban elites and the favored immigrants in their kingdoms, royal power pervaded the lives of the kingdoms' subjects, above all in meting out justice. Seleucus, for one, claimed this right as a universal truth: "It is not the customs of the Persians and other peoples that I impose upon you, but the law which is common to everyone, that what is decreed by the king is always just." Even Antigonus's successors, who claimed to lead the Greeks in a voluntary alliance that allegedly reestablished Philip's League of Corinth, frequently interfered in the internal affairs of the Greek city-states. Like the other kings, they regularly installed their own governors and garrisons in cities where loyalty was suspect.

The Layers of Hellenistic Society

Hellenistic society in the eastern Mediterranean world was clearly divided into separate layers. The royal family and the king's friends topped the hierarchy. The Greek and Macedonian elites of the major cities ranked next. Just under them came the wealthy and aristocratic upper classes of the indigenous cities, the leaders of large minority urban populations, and the traditional lords and princes of local groups maintaining their ancestral domains in more rural regions. Lowest of the free population were the masses of small merchants, crafts producers, and laborers. Slaves remained where they had always been, outside the bounds of society, although those who worked at court could live physically comfortable lives.

Poor people performed the overwhelming bulk of the labor required to support the economies of the Hellenistic kingdoms. Agriculture remained the economic base, and conditions for farmers and field workers changed little over time. Many worked on the royal family's huge agricultural estates, but in city-states that retained their countrysides free peasants still worked small plots as well as on the larger farms of wealthy landowners. Rural people rose with the sun and began working before the heat became unbearable, raising the same kinds of crops and animals as their ancestors had with the same simple hand tools and beasts of burden. Perhaps as many as 80 percent of all adult men and women, free as well as slave, had to work the land to produce enough food to sustain the population. Along certain international routes, however, trade by sea thrived. More than eighty thousand amphoras (large ceramic jars used to transport commodities such as olive oil and wine) made on the Greek island of Rhodes, for example, have been found in Ptolemaic Egypt. Consortiums of foreign merchants turned the Aegean island of Delos into a busy transportation hub for the cross-shipping of goods, such as the ten thousand slaves a day the port could handle. In the cities, poor women and men could work as small merchants, peddlers, and artisans, producing and selling goods such as tools, pottery, clothing, and furniture. Men could sign on as deck hands on the merchant ships that sailed the Mediterranean and Indian oceans.

In the Seleucid and Ptolemaic kingdoms a large portion of the rural population existed in a state of dependency somewhere between free and slave. The "peoples," as they were called, farmed the estates belonging to the king, who owned the most land in the kingdom. Theoretically, the king owned all his kingdom's land because Alexander had claimed it as "won by the spear." In practice, however, the king ceded much territory to cities and favored individuals. The peoples were not landowners but compulsory tenants. Although they could not be sold like chattel slaves, they were not allowed to move away or abandon their tenancies. They owed a certain quota of produce per area of land to the king as if rent to a landlord. The rent was sufficiently heavy that the peoples had virtually no chance of improving their economic lot in life.

The social and political status of women in the Hellenistic world depended on the social layer to which they belonged. Hellenistic queens, like their Macedonian predecessors, commanded enormous riches and received honors commensurate with their elevated status. They usually exercised power only to the extent that they could influence their husbands' decisions, but in some cases they ruled on their own when no male heir existed. Because the Ptolemaic royal family observed the pharaonic tradition of brother-sister marriage, royal daughters as well as sons could rule. Arsinoë II (c. 316–270 B.C.), the daughter of Ptolemy I, first married the Macedonian successor King Lysimachus, who gave her four towns as her personal domain. After Lysimachus's death she married her brother, Ptolemy II of Egypt, and exerted at least as much influence on policy as he did. The virtues publicly praised in a queen reflected traditional Greek values for women. When the city of Hierapolis around 165 B.C. passed a decree in honor of Queen Apollonis of Pergamum, for example, it praised her piety toward the gods, her reverence toward her parents, her distinguished conduct toward her husband, and her harmonious relations with her "beautiful children born in wedlock."

Some queens evidently paid special attention to the condition of women. About 195 B.C., for example, the Seleucid queen Laodice gave a ten-year endowment to the city of Iasus in southwestern Asia Minor to provide dowries for needy girls. Her endowment reflected the wealthy's increasing concern for the welfare of the less fortunate during the Hellenistic period. The royal families led the way in this tendency toward philanthropy as part of their cultivation of an image of generosity befitting kings and queens, in the best tradition of Greek aristocratic benefaction. That Laodice funded dowries shows that she recognized the importance to women of owning property, the surest guarantee of a certain respect and a measure of power in their households.

Most women still remained under the control of men. "Who can judge better than a father what is to his daughter's interest?" remained the dominant creed of fathers with daughters. Once a woman married, "husband" and "wife's" replaced "father" and "daughter's" in the creed. Upper-class women continued to live separated, most of the time, from men not members of their families; poor women still worked in public. Greeks continued to abandon infants they could not or would not raise—girls were abandoned more often than boys. Other peoples, such as the Egyptians and the Jews, did not practice abandonment, or exposure, as it is often called. Exposure differed from infanticide because the parents expected someone else to find the child and rear it, albeit usually as a slave. The third-century B.C. comic poet Posidippus overstated the case by saying, "A son, one always raises even if one is poor; a daughter, one exposes, even if one is rich." Daughters of wealthy parents were not usually abandoned, but up to 10 percent of other infant girls were. In some limited ways, however, women achieved greater control over their own lives in the Hellenistic period. The rare woman of exceptional wealth could enter public life, for example, by making donations or loans to her city and being rewarded with an official post in her community's government. Of course, such posts were less prestigious and important than in the days of the independent city-states, because the king and his top adminstrators now controlled the real power. In Egypt, women acquired greater say in the conditions of marriage because contracts, a standard procedure, gradually evolved from an agreement between the groom and the bride's parents to one made by the bride and groom themselves.

Even with power based in the cities, most of the population continued to live where people always had—in small villages in the countryside. There different groups of people lived side by side but nevertheless separately. In one region of Anatolia, for example, twenty-two different languages were spoken. Life in the new and refounded Hellenistic cities developed independently of indigenous rural society. Urban life acquired special vitality because the Greek and Macedonian residents of these cities, surrounded by the non-Greek countryside, tended to stay in them more than had their predecessors in the classical city-states, who had usually gone back and forth frequently between city and countryside to attend to their rural property, participate in local festivals, and worship in local shrines. Now the city-dwellers' activities centered more and more on the city. Urban existence also offered new advantages over country life because of the endowments the wealthy bestowed on their cities. On the island of Samos, for example, wealthy contributors endowed a foundation to finance the distribution of free grain to all the citizens every month so that food shortages would no longer trouble their city. State-sponsored schools for educating children, often funded by wealthy donors, also sprang up in various Hellenistic cities. In some places girls as well as boys could attend school. Many cities also began ensuring the availability of doctors by sponsoring their practices. Patients still had to pay for medical attention, but at least they could count on finding a doctor when they needed one. The wealthy whose donations and loans made many of the cities' new services possible were paid back by the respect and honor they earned from their fellow citizens. Philanthropy even touched international relations occasionally. When an earthquake devastated Rhodes, many cities joined kings and queens in sending donations to help the Rhodians recover. In return, the Rhodians showered honors on their benefactors by appointing them to prestigious municipal office and erecting highly visible inscriptions expressing the city's gratitude.

Wealthy non-Greeks adopted Greek habits more and more in the process of adapting to the new social hierarchy. Diotimus of Sidon (in Lebanon), for example, although not Greek by birth, had a Greek name and pursued the premier Greek sport, chariot racing. He traveled to Nemea in the Peloponnese to enter his chariot in the race at the prestigious festival of Zeus there. When he won he put up an inscription in Greek to announce that he was the first Sidonian to do so. He announced his victory in Greek because koine Greek had become the international language of the eastern Mediterranean coastal lands. The explosion in the use of Greek by non-Greeks certainly indicates the emergence of an international culture based on Greek models, which rulers and their courts, the urban upper classes, and intellectuals all adopted during the Hellenistic period. The most striking evidence of the spread of Greeks and Greek throughout the Hellenistic world comes from Afghanistan. There, Asoka (✱c. 268–232 B.C.), third king of the

Woman with a Fan *Inexpensive terra-cotta figurines like this one imitated the poses and elaborate drapery of bronze and marble sculpture.*

Mauryan dynasty and a convert to Buddhism, used Greek as one of the languages in his public inscriptions that announced his efforts to introduce his subjects to Buddhist traditions of self-control such as abstinence from eating meat. Even in far-off Afghanistan, non-Greeks communicated with the Greeks they encountered in Greek.

Literature and Art Under New Conditions

As the use of the Greek language spread throughout the Hellenistic world, Greek literature began to reflect the new conditions of life. The burlesquing of contemporary people and politics characteristic of comedy in fifth-century B.C. Athens, for example, disappeared along with the city-state's autonomy. Comic dramatists like Menander (c. 342–289 B.C.) and Philemon (c. 360–263 B.C.) now presented plays with timeless plots concerning the trials and tribulations of fictional lovers, in works not unlike modern soap operas. These comedies of manners, as the genre is called, proved so popular that later Roman comedy writers imitated their style.

Poets such as Theocritus (c. 300–260 B.C.) from Syracuse in Sicily and Callimachus (c. 305–240 B.C.) from Cyrene in North Africa, both of whom came to Alexandria under the patronage of the Ptolemies, made individual emotions a central theme in their work. Their poetry broke new ground in demanding great intellectual effort as well as emotional engagement from the audience. Only the erudite could fully appreciate the allusions and complex references to mythology that these poets employed in their elegant poems, which were mostly much shorter than Homeric epics. Theocritus was the first Greek poet to express the splitting between the town and the countryside, a poetic stance corresponding to a growing reality. His pastoral poems, the *Idylls,* emphasized the discontinuity between the environment of the city and the bucolic life of the country-dweller, although the rural people depicted in Theocritus's poetry appeared in idealized landscapes rather than the actual Egyptian fields. Nevertheless, his *Idylls* reflected the fundamental social division of the Ptolemaic kingdom between the food consumers of the town and the food producers of the countryside.

The themes of Callimachus's prolific output underscored the division between the intellectual elite and the uneducated masses in contemporary society. "I hate the crowd" describes Callimachus's authorial stance toward poetry and its audience. A comparison between Callimachus's work and that of his literary rival, Apollonius of Rhodes, emphasizes the Hellenistic preference for intellectually demanding poetry. Even though Apollonius wrote long epics (including one about Jason and the Argonauts) instead of short poems, Apollonius's verses also displayed an erudition only readers with a literary education could understand. Like the earlier lyric poets, who in the sixth and fifth centuries B.C. often wrote to please rich patrons, these Hellenistic authors necessarily had to consider the tastes of royal patrons, who were paying the bills. In one poem expressly praising his patron, Ptolemy II, Theocritus spelled out the quid pro quo of Hellenistic literary patronage: "the spokesmen of the Muses [that is, poets] celebrate Ptolemy in return for his benefactions."

The Hellenistic kings promoted intellectual life principally by offering to support scholars financially if they relocated to the royal capitals, proving royal magnanimity and grandeur. The Ptolemies won this particular competition by making Alexandria the leading intellectual center of the Hellenistic world. There they established the world's first scholarly research institute. Its massive library had the impossible goal of trying to collect all the books (that is, manuscripts) in the world; it grew to hold a half million scrolls, an enormous number for the time. Linked to it was a building in which the hired scholars dined together and produced encyclopedias of knowledge such as *The Wonders of the World* and *On the Rivers of Europe* by Callimachus (he was a learned prose writer as well as a poet). The name of this building, the Museum (meaning "place of the Muses," the Greek goddesses of learning and the arts), is still used to designate institutions that preserve and promote knowledge. The output of the Alexandrian scholars was prodigious. Their champion was Didymus (c. 80–10 B.C.), nicknamed "Brass Guts" for his indefatigable writing of nearly four thousand books.

None of the women poets known from the Hellenistic period seem to have enjoyed royal

The Masks of Comedy *This sculpted panel shows the kinds of masks with exaggerated expressions worn by comic actors on stage.*

patronage. But women excelled in writing epigrams, a style of short poems originally used for funeral epitaphs (for which Callimachus was famed). In this era the epigram expressed a wide variety of personal feelings, love above all. Elegantly worded epigrams written by women from diverse regions of the Hellenistic world—Anyte of Tegea in the Peloponnese, Nossis of Locri in southern Italy, Moero of Byzantium—still survive. Women, from courtesans to respectable matrons, figured as frequent subjects in their poems. No Hellenistic literature better conveyed the depth of human emotion that their epigrams, such as Nossis' poem on the power of Eros (Love, regarded as a divinity): "Nothing is sweeter than Eros. All other delights are second to it—from my mouth I spit out even honey. And this Nossis says: whoever Aphrodite has not kissed knows not what sort of flowers are her roses."

Like their literary contemporaries, Hellenistic sculptors and painters featured human emotions prominently in their works. Classical artists had consistently imbued their subjects' faces with a serenity that represented an ideal rather than reality. Numerous examples, usually surviving only in later copies, show that Hellenistic artists tried to depict emotions more naturally in a variety of genres. In portrait sculpture, Lysippus's famous bust of Alexander the Great captured the young commander's passionate dreaminess. A sculpture from Pergamum by an unknown artist commemorates the third-century B.C. Attalid victory over the plundering Gauls by showing a defeated Gallic warrior stabbing himself after having killed his wife to prevent her enslavement by the victors. A large-scale painting of Alexander battling with the Persian king Darius portrayed Alexander's intense concentration and Darius's horrified expression (page 125). The artist, who was probably either Philoxenus of Eretria or a Greek woman from Egypt named Helena (one of the first female artists known), used foreshortening and strong contrasts between shadows and highlights to accentuate the emotional impact of the picture.

To appreciate fully the appeal of Hellenistic sculpture, we must remember that, like earlier Greek sculpture, it was painted in bright colors. The fourth-century B.C. sculptor Praxiteles reportedly remarked that his best statues were "the ones colored by Nicias" (a leading painter of the time). But Hellenistic art differed from classical art in its social context. Works of classical art had been commissioned by the city-states for public display or by wealthy individuals to donate to their city-state as a work of public art. Now sculptors and painters created their works more and more as commissions

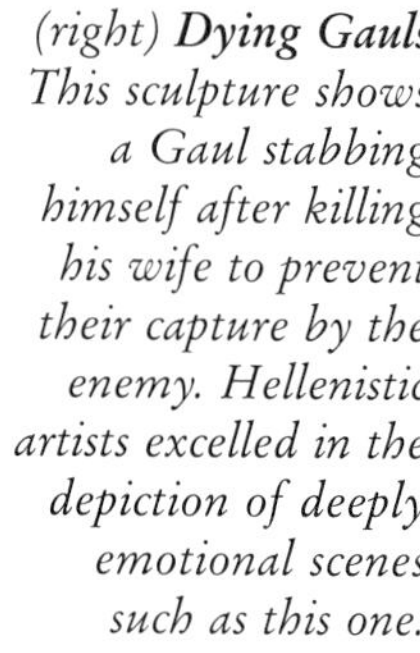

(right) ***Dying Gauls*** *This sculpture shows a Gaul stabbing himself after killing his wife to prevent their capture by the enemy. Hellenistic artists excelled in the depiction of deeply emotional scenes such as this one.*

(far right) ***Realism in Hellenistic Sculpture*** *Sculptors during the Hellenistic period often depicted subjects that reflected the harsh reality of everyday life, such as this woman bowed by age and the burden she carries.*

from royalty and from the urban elites who wanted to show they had artistic taste like their social superiors in the royal family. To be successful, artists had to please their rich patrons, and so the increasing diversity of subjects that emerged in Hellenistic art presumably represented a trend approved by kings, queens, and the elites. Sculpture best reveals this new preference for depictions of humans in a wide variety of poses, many from private life (again in contrast with classical art). Hellenistic sculptors portrayed subjects never before shown: foreigners (such as the dying Gaul), drunkards, battered athletes, wrinkled old people. The female nude became a particular favorite, presumably for male owners. A naked Aphrodite, which Praxiteles sculpted for the city of Cnidos, became so renowned that Nicomedes, king of Bithynia in Asia Minor, later offered to pay off Cnidos's entire public debt if he could have the statue. The Cnidians refused.

A lasting innovation of Hellenistic art was the depiction of abstract ideas as sculptural types. Such statues were made to represent ideas as diverse as Peace and Insanity. Modern statues such as the Statue of Liberty belong in this artistic tradition. Modern neoclassical architecture also imitates the imaginative public architecture of the Hellenistic period, whose architects often boldly combined the Doric and Ionic style of architectural decoration on the same building and energized the Corinthian order with florid decoration.

Innovation in Philosophy, Science, and Medicine

Greek philosophy in the Hellenistic period reached a wider audience than ever before. Although the masses of working poor as usual had neither the leisure nor the resources to attend philosophers' lectures, the more affluent members of society studied philosophy in growing numbers. Theophrastus (c. 370–285 B.C.), Aristotle's most brilliant pupil, lectured to crowds of up to two thousand in Athens. Most philosophy students continued to be men, but women could now join the groups attached to certain philosophers. Kings competed to attract famous thinkers to their courts, and Greek settlers took their interest in philosophy with them, even to the most remote Hellenistic cities. Archaeological excavation of a city located thousands of miles from Greece on the Oxus River in Afghanistan, for example, turned up a Greek philosophical text as well as inscriptions of moral advice imputed to Apollo's oracle at Delphi.

Fewer Hellenistic thinkers concentrated on metaphysics. Instead they focused on philosophical materialism, a doctrine asserting that only things made of matter truly existed. It therefore denied the concept of soul Plato described and ignored any suggestion that such nonmaterial phenomena could exist. The goal of much philosophical inquiry now centered on securing human independence from the effects of chance or worldly events by withdrawing from as much of the business of daily life as possible and cultivating calmness in the face of all troubles. Scientific investigation of the physical world became a specialty separate from philosophy. Hellenistic philosophy was regularly divided into three related areas: logic (the process for discovering truth), physics (the fundamental truth about the nature of existence), and ethics (the way humans should achieve happiness and well-being as a consequence of logic and physics). The most significant new philosophical schools of thought were Epicureanism and Stoicism. (Epicurean and Stoic doctrines became exceptionally popular among upper-class Romans.) The various philosophies of the Hellenistic period in many ways asked the same question: what is the best way for humans to live? Different philosophies recommended different paths to the same answer: individual humans must attain personal tranquility to achieve freedom from the turbulence of outside forces. For Greeks the changes in political and social life accompanying the rise to dominance of the Macedonian and later Hellenistic kings make this focus understandable. Outside forces in the persons of aggressive kings had robbed the city-states of their freedom of action internationally, and the fates of city-states as well as individuals now rested in the hands of distant, often fickle monarchs. More than ever before, human life and opportunities for free choice seemed poised to careen out of the control of individuals. It therefore made sense, at least for those wealthy enough to spend time philosophizing, to look for personal, private solutions to the unsettling new conditions of life in the Hellenistic era.

Epicureanism took its name from its founder, Epicurus (341–271 B.C.), who settled his followers in Athens in a house amidst a verdant garden (hence The Garden as the name of his informal school). Under Epicurus the study of philosophy assumed a social form that broke with tradition, because he admitted women and slaves as regular members of his group. His lover, Leontion, became notorious for her treatise criticizing the views of Theophrastus. Epicurus believed humans should pursue pleasure, but his notion of pleasure had a unique definition. He insisted that true pleasure consisted of an "absence of disturbance" from pain and the everyday turbulence, passions, and desires of ordinary human existence. A sober life lived in the society of friends apart from the cares of the common world could best provide this essential peace of mind. This teaching represented a serious challenge to the ideal of Greek citizenship, which required men of means to participate in city-state politics and for citizen women to engage in public religious cults.

Humans should above all be free of worry about death, Epicurus taught. Because all matter consisted of microscopic atoms in random movement, as Democritus and Leucippus had earlier theorized, death was nothing more than the painless disassociation of the body's atoms. Moreover, all human knowledge must be empirical, that is, derived from experience and perception. Phenomena that most people perceive as the work of the gods, such as thunder, do not result from divine intervention in the world. The gods live far away in perfect tranquility, paying no attention to human affairs. Humans therefore have nothing to fear from the gods, in life or in death.

The Stoics recommended a different, less isolationist path for individuals. Their name derived from the Painted Stoa in Athens, where they discussed their doctrines. Zeno (c. 333–262 B.C.) from Citium on Cyprus founded Stoicism, but Chrysippus (c. 280–206 B.C.) from Cilicia in Asia Minor did the most to make it a comprehensive guide to life. Stoics believed humans should make the pursuit of

The Stoa of Attalus in the Athenian Agora
This long building with columns, a gift to Athenians from King Attalus II of Pergamum in the second century B.C., offered a shady place for conversation and meetings. The stone building in the foreground is a church from a later period.

virtue their goal. Virtue, they said, consisted of putting oneself in harmony with universal Nature, the rational force of divine providence that directed all existence under the guise of Fate. Reason as well as experience should be used to discover the way to that harmony, which required the "perfect" virtues of good sense, justice, courage, and temperance. According to the Stoics the doctrines of Zeno and Chrysippus applied to women as well as men. In fact, the Stoics advocated equal citizenship for women and doing away with the conventions of marriage and families as the Greeks knew them. Zeno even proposed unisex clothing as a way to obliterate unnecessary distinctions between women and men.

The Stoic belief that everything that happened was fated created for them the question of whether humans truly have free will. Employing some of the subtlest reasoning ever applied to this fundamental issue, Stoic philosophers concluded that purposeful human actions did have significance. A Stoic should therefore take action against evil, for example, by participating in politics. Nature, itself good, did not prevent vice from occurring, because virtue would otherwise have no meaning. What mattered in life was the striving for good, not the result. To be a Stoic also meant to shun desire and anger while enduring pain and sorrow calmly, an attitude that informs the current meaning of the word *stoic.* Through endurance and self-control, a Stoic attained tranquility. Stoics did not fear death because they believed people lived over and over again infinitely in identical fashion to their present lives. This repetition would occur as the world would be destroyed by fire periodically and then reformed after the conflagration.

Other schools of thought carried on the work of earlier philosophical leaders such as Plato and Pythagoras. Still others, like the Sceptics and the Cynics, struck out in idiosyncratic directions. Sceptics aimed at the same state of personal imperturbability as did Epicureans, but from a completely different premise. Following the doctrines of Pyrrho (c. 360–270 B.C.) from Elis in the Peloponnese, they believed that secure knowledge about anything was impossible because the human senses yield contradictory information about the world. All people can do, they insisted, is to depend on appearances of things while suspending judgment about their reality. Pyrrho's thought had been influenced by the Indian ascetic wise men (the magi) he met while a member of Alexander the Great's entourage. The basic premise of scepticism inevitably precluded any unity of doctrine.

Cynics ostentatiously rejected every convention of ordinary life, especially wealth and material comfort. They believed humans should aim for complete self-sufficiency. Whatever was natural was good and could be done without shame before anyone; according to this idea, even public defecation and fornication were acceptable. Women and men alike should be free to follow their sexual inclinations. Above all, Cynics should disdain the comforts and luxuries of a comfortable life. The name *Cynic,* which meant "like a dog," reflected the common evaluation of this ascetic and unconventional way of life. The most famous early Cynic, Diogenes (died 323 B.C.) from Sinope on the Black

Sea, was reputed to wear borrowed clothing and sleep in a big storage jar. Almost as notorious was Hipparchia, a female Cynic of the late fourth century B.C. She once bested an obnoxious philosophical opponent named Theodorus the Atheist with the following argument, which recalled the climactic episode between father and son in Aristophanes' *Clouds:* "That which would not be considered wrong if done by Theodorus would also not be considered wrong if done by Hipparchia. Now if Theodorus strikes himself, he does no wrong. Therefore, if Hipparchia strikes Theodorus, she does no wrong."

Science benefited from its widening divorce from philosophy during the Hellenistic period. Historians have called this era the Golden Age of ancient science. Various factors contributed to this flourishing of thought and discovery: the expeditions of Alexander had encouraged curiosity and increased knowledge about the extent and differing features of the world; royal patronage supported scientists financially; and the concentration of scientists in Alexandria promoted a fertile exchange of ideas that could not otherwise take place because of the difficulty of travel and communication. The greatest advances came in geometry and mathematics. Euclid, who taught at Alexandria around 300 B.C., made revolutionary progress in the analysis of two- and three-dimensional space. The utility of Euclidean geometry still endures. Archimedes of Syracuse (287–212 B.C.) was an arithmetical polymath who calculated the approximate value of pi and devised a way to manipulate very large numbers. He also invented hydrostatics (the science of the equilibrium of a fluid system) and mechanical devices such as a screw for lifting water to a higher elevation. Archimedes' shout of delight, "I have found it" (*heureka* in Greek), when he solved a problem while soaking in his bathtub has been immortalized in the modern expression "Eureka!"

The sophistication of Hellenistic mathematics affected other fields that also required complex computations. Aristarchus of Samos early in the third century B.C. first proposed the correct model of the solar system by theorizing that the earth revolved around the sun, which he also identified as being far larger and far more distant than it appeared. Later astronomers rejected Aristarchus's heliocentric model in favor of the traditional geocentric one because calculations based on the orbit he postulated for the earth failed to correspond to the observed positions of celestial objects. Aristarchus had made a simple mistake: he had postulated a circular orbit instead of an elliptical one. (It would be another eighteen hundred years before the heliocentric system would be recognized by the Polish astronomer Copernicus [A.D. 1473–1543] as the correct one.) Eratosthenes of Cyrene (c. 275–194 B.C.) pioneered mathematical geography. He calculated the circumference of the earth with astonishing accuracy by simultaneously measuring the length of the shadows of widely separated but identically tall structures. Ancient scientists in later periods, especially the astronomer and geographer Ptolemy, who worked in Alexandria in the second century A.D., would improve and refine the image of the natural world elaborated by Hellenistic researchers. But the basic ideas of these Hellenistic scientists dominated Western scientific thought until the advent of modern science.

Greek science was as quantitative as it could be given the limitations of ancient technology. Precise scientific experimentation was not possible because no technology existed for the precise measurement of very short intervals of time. Measuring tiny quantities of matter was also next to impossible. But the spirit of invention prevailed in spite of these difficulties. Ctesibius of Alexandria (born c. 310 B.C.), a contemporary of Aristarchus, devised machines operated by air pressure. In addition to this

Intellectuals in Third-Century Alexandria

Euclid from Alexandria(?) (born c. 340 B.C.)
mathematician

Ctesibius of Alexandria (born c. 310 B.C.)
mechanical engineer

Callimachus from Cyrene (c. 305–240 B.C.)
poet, encyclopedist

Theocritus from Syracuse (c. 300–260 B.C.)
poet

Herophilus of Chalcedon (born c. 300 B.C.)
physician and anatomist

Eratosthenes of Cyrene (c. 275–194 B.C.)
polymath

Aristophanes from Byzantium (c. 257–180 B.C.)
literary scholar

invention of pneumatics, he built a working water pump, an organ powered by water, and the first accurate water clock. His fellow Alexandrian of the first century A.D., Hero, continued the Hellenistic tradition of mechanical ingenuity by building a rotating sphere powered by steam. This invention did not lead to viable steam engines, perhaps because the metallurgical technology to produce metal pipes, fittings, and screws was not yet developed. As in the modern world, much of the engineering prowess of the Hellenistic period was applied to military technology. The kings hired engineers to design powerful catapults and wheeled siege towers many stories high, which were capable of battering down the defenses of walled cities. The most famous large-scale application of technology for nonmilitary purposes was the construction of a lighthouse three hundred feet tall (the Pharos) for the harbor at Alexandria. Using polished metal mirrors to reflect the light from a large fire fueled by wood, it shone many miles out over the sea. Awestruck sailors regarded it as one of the wonders of the world.

Medicine also shared the progressive mood exemplified by Hellenistic science. The increased contact between Greeks and people of the Near East in this period made the medical knowledge of the ancient civilizations of Mesopotamia and Egypt better known in the West and gave an impetus to the study of human health and illness. Around 325 B.C., Praxagoras of Cos discovered the value of measuring the human pulse in diagnosing illness. A bit later, Herophilus of Chalcedon (born c. 300 B.C.), working in Alexandria, became the first scientist in the West to study anatomy by dissecting human cadavers. Anatomical terms Herophilus coined are still used (such as *duodenum,* a section of the small intestine). Other Hellenistic advances in understanding anatomy included the discovery of the nerves and nervous system. Anatomical knowledge, however, outstripped knowledge of human physiology. The earlier idea that human health depended on the balance of four humors remained the dominant theory in physiology. A person was healthy—in "good humor"—so long as the correct proportions of the four humors were maintained. Because illness was thought to result from an imbalance of the humors, doctors prescribed various regimens of drugs, diet, and exercise to restore balance. Doctors also believed that drawing blood from patients could help rebalance the humors. (This practice of "bleeding" was used into the 1800s.) Doctors thought many illnesses in women were caused by displacements of the womb, which they wrongly believed could move around in the body.

Transformation in Hellenistic Religion

The expansion and diversification of knowledge that characterized Hellenistic intellectual life was matched by the growing diversity of religious practice. The traditional cults of Greek religion remained very popular, but new cults, such as those that deified ruling kings, responded to changing political and social conditions. Preexisting cults that previously had only local significance, such as that of the Greek healing deity Asclepius or the mystery cult of the Egyptian goddess Isis, grew prominent all over the Hellenistic world. In many cases, Greek cults and indigenous cults from the eastern Mediterranean meshed and shared practices, each influencing the other. Their traditions blended well because their cults were found to share many assumptions about how to remedy the troubles of human life. In other instances, local cults and Greek cults existed side by side, with some overlap. The inhabitants of villages in the Fayum district of Egypt, for example, continued worshiping their traditional crocodile god and mummifying their dead according to the old ways but also paid homage to Greek deities. In the tradition of polytheistic religion, people could worship in both old and new cults.

New Hellenistic cults picked up a prominent theme of Hellenistic philosophy: a concern for the relationship between the individual and what seemed the controlling, unpredictable power of the divinities Luck and Chance. Greek religion had always addressed randomness at some level, but the chaotic course of Greek history since the Peloponnesian War had made human existence appear more unpredictable than ever. Yet advances in astronomy revealed the mathematical precision of the celestial sphere of the universe. Religious experience now had to address the apparent disconnection between that heavenly uniformity and the shapeless chaos of life on earth. One increasingly popular approach to bridging that gap was to rely on astrology for advice deduced from the movement of the stars and planets, thought of as divinities.

In another approach offering devotees protection from the capricious tricks of Chance or Luck, the gods of popular Hellenistic cults promised salvation of various kinds. One form of salvation could come from powerful rulers, who enjoyed divine status in what are known as ruler cults. These cults were established in recognition of great benefactions. The Athenians, for example, deified the Macedonians Antigonus and his son Demetrius as savior gods in 307 B.C., when they bestowed magnificent gifts on the city and restored democracy (which had been abolished in 321 B.C. by another Macedonian). Like most ruler cults, this one expressed both spontaneous gratitude and a desire to flatter the rulers in the hope of obtaining additional favors. As a rule, the Antigonid kings had no divine cult in their honor in Macedonia, but many cities in the Ptolemic and Seleucid kingdoms instituted ruler cults for their kings and queens. An inscription put up by Egyptian priests in 238 B.C. concretely described the qualities appropriate for a divine king and queen:

> *King Ptolemy III and Queen Berenice, his sister and wife, the Benefactor Gods, . . . have provided good government . . . and [after a drought] sacrificed a large amount of their revenues for the salvation of the population, and by importing grain . . . they saved the inhabitants of Egypt.*

Healing divinities offered another form of protection to anxious individuals. Scientific Greek medicine had rejected the notion of supernatural causes and cures for disease ever since Hippocrates had established his medical school on the Aegean island of Cos in the late fifth century B.C. Nevertheless, the cult of Asclepius, son of Apollo, who offered cures for illness and injury at his many shrines, grew popular during the Hellenistic period. Suppliants seeking Asclepius's help would sleep in special dormitories at his shrines to await dreams in which he prescribed healing treatments. These prescriptions emphasized diet and exercise, but numerous inscriptions set up by grateful patients also testified to miraculous cures and surgery performed while the sufferer slept. The following example is typical:

> *Ambrosia of Athens was blind in one eye. . . . She . . . ridiculed some of the cures [described in inscriptions in the sanctuary] as being incredible and impossible. . . . But when she went to sleep, she saw a vision; she thought the god was standing next to her . . . he split open the diseased eye and poured in a medicine. When day came she left cured.*

Other cults proffered secret knowledge as a key to worldly and physical salvation. They believed protection from physical danger was more urgent than the care of the soul or the afterlife. The Mysteries of Demeter at Eleusis, however, continued to address a person's soul and the afterlife. The mystery cults of the Greek god Dionysus and, in particular, the Egyptian goddess Isis gained followers in this period. The popularity of Isis, whose powers extended over every area of human life, received a boost from King Ptolemy I, who established an official seat for her cult in Alexandria. He also refashioned the Egyptian deity Osiris in a Greek mold as the new god Sarapis, whose job was to serve as Isis' consort. Sarapis reportedly performed miracles of rescue from shipwreck and illness. The cult of Isis, who became the most popular female divinity in the Mediterranean, involved extensive rituals and festivals incorporating features of Egyptian religion mixed with Greek elements. Disciples of Isis apparently hoped to achieve personal purification as well as the aid of the goddess in overcoming the sometimes demonic influence of Chance and Luck on human life.

That an Egyptian deity like Isis could achieve enormous popularity among Greeks (and Romans in later times) alongside the traditional gods of Greek religion, who also remained popular, is the best evidence of the cultural cross-fertilization of the Hellenistic world. Equally striking on this score was that many Jews, especially those living in the large Jewish communities that had grown up in Hellenistic cities outside Palestine, such as Alexandria, adopted the Greek language and many aspects of Greek culture. The Hebrew Bible was even translated into Greek in Alexandria in the early third century B.C., reportedly at the request of King Ptolemy II. Hellenized Jews largely retained the ritual practices and habits of life that defined traditional Judaism, and they refused to worship Greek gods. Hellenistic politics and culture also affected the Jewish community in Palestine. The region, caught between the great kingdoms of the Ptolemies in Egypt and the Seleucids in Syria, was controlled militarily and politically by the

Ptolemies in the third century B.C. and by the Seleucids in the second century B.C. Both the Ptolemies and the Seleucids allowed the Jews to live according to their ancestral tradition under the political leadership of a high priest in Jerusalem. Internal dissension among Jews erupted in second-century B.C. Palestine over the amount of Greek influence that was compatible with traditional Judaism. The Seleucid king Antiochus IV (*175–163 B.C.) intervened in the conflict in support of an extreme Hellenizing faction of Jews in Jerusalem, who had taken over the high priesthood. In 167 B.C., Antiochus converted the main Jewish sanctuary there into a Greek temple and outlawed the practice of Jewish religious rites such as observing the Sabbath and circumcision. A revolt led by Judah the Maccabee eventually won Jewish independence from the Seleucids after twenty-five years of war. The most famous episode of the Maccabean Revolt was the retaking of the temple in Jerusalem and its rededication to the worship of the Jewish god, Yahweh, a triumphant moment commemorated by Jews ever since on the holiday of Hanukkah. That Greek culture attracted Jews, whose strong traditions reached far into antiquity, provides a striking example of the transformations that affected many—though far from all—people of the Hellenistic world.

Conclusion

After Athens recovered its prosperity following the Peloponnesian War, the city-state was again strong enough to participate in the struggles among Sparta, Corinth, and Thebes over political and military dominance in Greece in the first half of the fourth century B.C. When the wars and shifting alliances of the city-states in this period led to weakness and instability after the battle of Mantinea in 362 B.C., a power vacuum resulted, which the kingdom of Macedonia promptly filled through the actions of its aggressive king, Philip II. The conquests of Philip and his son, Alexander the Great, eventually led to the restructuring of the political landscape of the eastern Mediterranean world. The philosophers Socrates, Plato, and Aristotle, whose careers together spanned the period from before the Peloponnesian War through the life of Alexander the Great, gave new directions to Greek thought in ethics, metaphysics, logic, and scientific investigation of the natural world.

The personal monarchies of the Hellenistic kings both exploited the long-term structures of government already established in their conquered territories and built up an administrative system staffed by Greeks and Macedonians. Indigenous elites as well as Greeks and Macedonians cooperated with the Hellenistic monarchs in governing their society, which was divided along hierarchical ethnic lines. To enhance their image of magnificence, the kings and queens of the Hellenistic world supported writers, artists, scholars, philosophers, and scientists, thereby encouraging the distinctive energy of Hellenistic intellectual life. The traditional city-states continued to exist in Hellenistic Greece, but their external freedom was constrained by the need to stay on good terms with powerful monarchs. With the ultimate control of political power removed from their hands, citizen men tended less and less to constitute militias to defend the city-state, a task increasingly performed by hired mercenaries.

The diversity of the Hellenistic world encompassed much that was new. Its queens commanded greater wealth and status than any women since the queens of the New Kingdom of Egypt. Its philosophers, such as Epicurean and Stoic scholars, defined different paths humans could take to achieve personal tranquility in a tumultuous world. Its scientists and doctors expanded the range of human knowledge enormously. Its new cults expressed a yearning for protection from the perils of life shared by worshipers from varied backgrounds. At the same time, its most fundamental elements remained unchanged—the labor, the poverty, and the necessarily limited horizons of the mass of ordinary people working in its fields, vineyards, and pastures.

Suggestions for Further Reading

Source Materials

Aristotle. *The Complete Works.* 2 vols. Edited by Jonathan Barnes. 1984. Translations of the writings of Aristotle, including the *Constitution of Athens.*

Arrian. *The Campaigns of Alexander.* Translated by Aubrey de Sélincourt. 1971. The best ancient account of Alexander's exploits, by a historian of the early Roman Empire. Also available in the Loeb Classical Library series.

Austin, M.M. *The Hellenistic World from Alexander to the Roman Conquest: A Selection of Ancient Sources in Translation.* 1981. Excerpts of sources from political, social, and economic history, with useful introductions to each selection.

Plato. *The Collected Dialogues.* Edited by Edith Hamilton and Huntington Cairns. 1961. Contains the translated writings of Plato.

Plutarch. *The Age of Alexander: Nine Greek Lives.* Translated by Ian Scott-Kilvert. 1973. A selection of biographies of famous Greek men of the fourth and third centuries B.C., including Alexander, Demosthenes, and Demetrius. All Plutarch's biographies are available in the Loeb Classical Library series.

Xenophon. *A History of My Times.* Translated by Rex Warner. 1979. A translation of the *Hellenica,* which continues *The Peloponnesian War* by Thucydides and covers events in Greek history until 362 B.C. The Loeb Classical Library series publishes all of Xenophon's works in seven volumes, including *The Oeconomicus,* on household management.

Interpretive Studies

Adcock, F.E. *The Greek and Macedonian Art of War.* 1957. The classic introduction to the strategy and technology of the subject.

Barnes, Jonathan. *Aristotle.* 1982. A succinct yet comprehensive introduction to the thought of Aristotle.

Bowman, Alan K. *Egypt After the Pharaohs, 332 B.C.–A.D. 642.* 1986. A topically arranged and well-illustrated survey.

The Cambridge Ancient History. Vol. VII, pt. 1, *The Hellenistic World.* 2d ed. 1984. Surveys Hellenistic history from the death of Alexander to 217 B.C., with an emphasis on political history but including sections on culture, economy, science, agriculture, and building and town planning.

Gosling, J.C.B. *Plato.* 1973. A critical discussion of some of the central ideas of Plato.

Grant, Michael. *From Alexander to Cleopatra: The Hellenistic World.* 1982. A readable survey of political and intellectual history.

Green, Peter. *Alexander to Actium: The Historical Evolution of the Hellenistic Age.* 1990. A massive, vividly written volume with many provocative interpretations.

Hamilton, J.R. *Alexander the Great.* 1973. A reliable introduction to the Macedonian background and career of Alexander.

Hornblower, Simon. *The Greek World, 479–323 B.C.* 1983. An interpretative survey of Greek history in the Golden Age and the fourth century B.C.

Lewis, Naphtali. *Greeks in Ptolemaic Egypt.* 1986. Case studies in the social history of Greek immigrants to Egypt.

Long, A.A. *Hellenistic Philosophy: Stoics, Epicureans, Sceptics.* 2d ed. 1986. A scholarly yet readable introduction to the main developments in Greek philosophy during the Hellenistic period.

Martin, Luther. *Hellenistic Religions: An Introduction.* 1987. An intriguing analysis of the social and intellectual changes in Greek religion after the Classical Age.

Phillips, E.D. *Greek Medicine.* 1973. An introduction to the subject, presented chronologically.

Pollitt, J.J. *Art in the Hellenistic Age.* 1986. A comprehensive treatment of the various genres of Hellenistic art.

Pomeroy, Sarah B. *Women in Hellenistic Egypt: From Alexander to Cleopatra.* 1984. Includes histories of women from slaves to queens.

Richter, G.M.A. *Portraits of the Greeks.* Rev. ed. 1984. Includes illustrations of Aristophanes, Socrates, Plato, Aristotle, Alexander, Hellenistic kings and queens, and many others.

Snyder, Jane M. *The Woman and the Lyre: Women Writers in Classical Greece and Rome.* 1989. Includes women poets and philosophers of the Hellenistic period.

Tarn, W.W. *Hellenistic Civilization.* 3d ed. Revised by G.T. Griffith. 1961. A still valuable survey with a broad range.

Tcherikover, Victor. *Hellenistic Civilization and the Jews.* Translated by S. Applebaum. A classic study of the contacts between Jews and Greeks in the Hellenistic period.

White, K.D. *Greek and Roman Technology.* 1984. A splendidly illustrated survey including Hellenistic inventions.

Witt, R.E. *Isis in the Greco-Roman World.* 1971. Surveys the cult of Isis from its Egyptian roots to the worlds of Greece and Rome.

CHAPTER

5

The Rise and Fall of the Roman Republic,

c. 800–44 B.C.

Romulus, the legendary first king of Rome, reputedly vanished forever during a windstorm. The legend goes on to say that his people felt distressed about the mysterious loss of their king and suspected his aristocratic advisers had murdered him. To calm the crowd, Julius Proculus, a prominent citizen, explained the king's disappearance:

> *Romulus, the father of our city, descended from the sky at dawn this morning and appeared to me. In awe and reverence I stood before him, praying that it would be right to look upon his face. "Go," Romulus said to me, "and tell the Romans that by the will of the gods my Rome shall be capital of the world. Let them learn to be soldiers. Let them know, and teach their children, that no power on earth can stand against Roman arms." Having spoken these words, he returned to the sky.*

According to legend, this speech placated the people of early Rome by assuring them of their king's immortality.

This story about Romulus's mandate to Rome, though certainly fictional, summed up the way the Romans eventually came to view their destiny: the gods willed that Rome should rule the world by military might. But simultaneously the legend highlights the tensions between Roman aristocrats and the mass of Roman citizens. This tale shows a member of the upper class manipulating the ordinary people of Rome by deceiving them. Most significant, the story implies that the aristocrats hated the monarchy whereas the common people were content to be ruled by a king. This part of the legend foreshadowed a fundamental discord that periodically plagued the Roman state as it developed over the centuries from a monarchy to a republic to an empire: all

Julius Caesar the Dictator
When Julius Caesar placed his portrait and the inscription "Caesar, perpetual dictator" on coins, he flaunted his breaking of the prohibition against a dictator serving indefinitely. This sort of self-aggrandizing led to civil war and the destruction of the Roman Republic.

Romans gradually came to believe it their fate to rule others by conquest, but at crucial moments in Roman history the upper and lower classes clashed over the way power should be shared.

According to tradition, seven kings ruled Rome in succession after its legendary foundation by Romulus and his brother Remus in 753 B.C., in the same period the city-states emerged in Greece. (Like all dates for events in early Roman history, we cannot be certain this one is absolutely accurate.) The Roman Republic was created around 509 B.C. when some disgruntled aristocrats expelled the last recorded king of Rome. The word *republic,* which the Romans used to describe the new political system these aristocrats established, comes from the Latin phrase *res publica* ("public property" or "commonwealth") and distinguishes this period (509–27 B.C.) from the era of the seven kings (753–509 B.C.).

Roman history is the story of the expansion of Rome's power far beyond its origins as a tiny settlement in central Italy. Starting as villagers with only a patch of territory to their name, the Romans eventually dominated Europe, North Africa, and the ancient Near East. From the sixth century B.C., Roman republican government distributed social, economic, and political power among the Roman people. By the late second century B.C., however, internal strife had weakened the republic, which began to disintegrate early in the first century B.C. as political violence escalated. During the middle of the first century B.C., ferocious conflicts brought anarchy to the streets of Rome and nearly paralyzed its government. The assassination of Julius Caesar in 44 B.C. ushered in a decade and a half of climactic political conflict and civil war that finally destroyed the republic. Augustus (63 B.C.–A.D. 14) eventually quelled the violence and by 27 B.C. had transformed Rome's republican government into what we call the Roman Empire.

Important Dates

753 B.C. Rome founded under a monarchy

509 B.C. Roman Republic established

451–449 B.C. Formulation of the Twelve Tables, Rome's first written law code

264–241 B.C. First Punic War between Rome and Carthage

Late third century B.C. Appearance of Roman literature

218–201 B.C. Second Punic War between Rome and Carthage

149–146 B.C. Third Punic War between Rome and Carthage

91–87 B.C. Social War between Rome and its Italian allies

60 B.C. First Triumvirate of Julius Caesar, Pompey the Great, and Marcus Crassus

49–45 B.C. Civil war, with Caesar emerging the victor

44 B.C. Caesar appointed as dictator for life, assassinated in same year

The Development of Early Rome

Trying to understand the history, chronology of events, and politics of early Rome is especially challenging because no contemporary written sources for this period exist. The Roman Livy (59 B.C.–A.D. 17) and his Greek contemporary, Dionysius of Halicarnassus, who lived in Rome for many years beginning in 30 B.C., wrote the most extensive accounts of early Roman history. But these authors compiled their histories of Rome more than seven hundred years after Rome was founded. Inevitably, their interpretations of events that happened so long ago were colored by the concerns of their own time, the period during which the Romans were transforming their republic into an empire. Archaeological evidence adds only a limited amount of information to the conclusions of Livy and Dionysius. For these reasons, any reconstruction of early Roman and Italian history necessarily contains some unexplainable gaps, uncertainties, and educated guesses. Exactly how this tiny settlement grew into the greatest power in the Mediterranean region remains one of history's mysteries.

The Geography of Early Rome

Geography certainly played a part in Rome's rise to greatness. Rome's location in central Italy gave the settlement access to fertile farmland and a nearby harbor on the Mediterranean Sea. The terrain of Italy is a jumble of plains, river valleys, hills, and mountains crowded into a narrow, boot-shaped

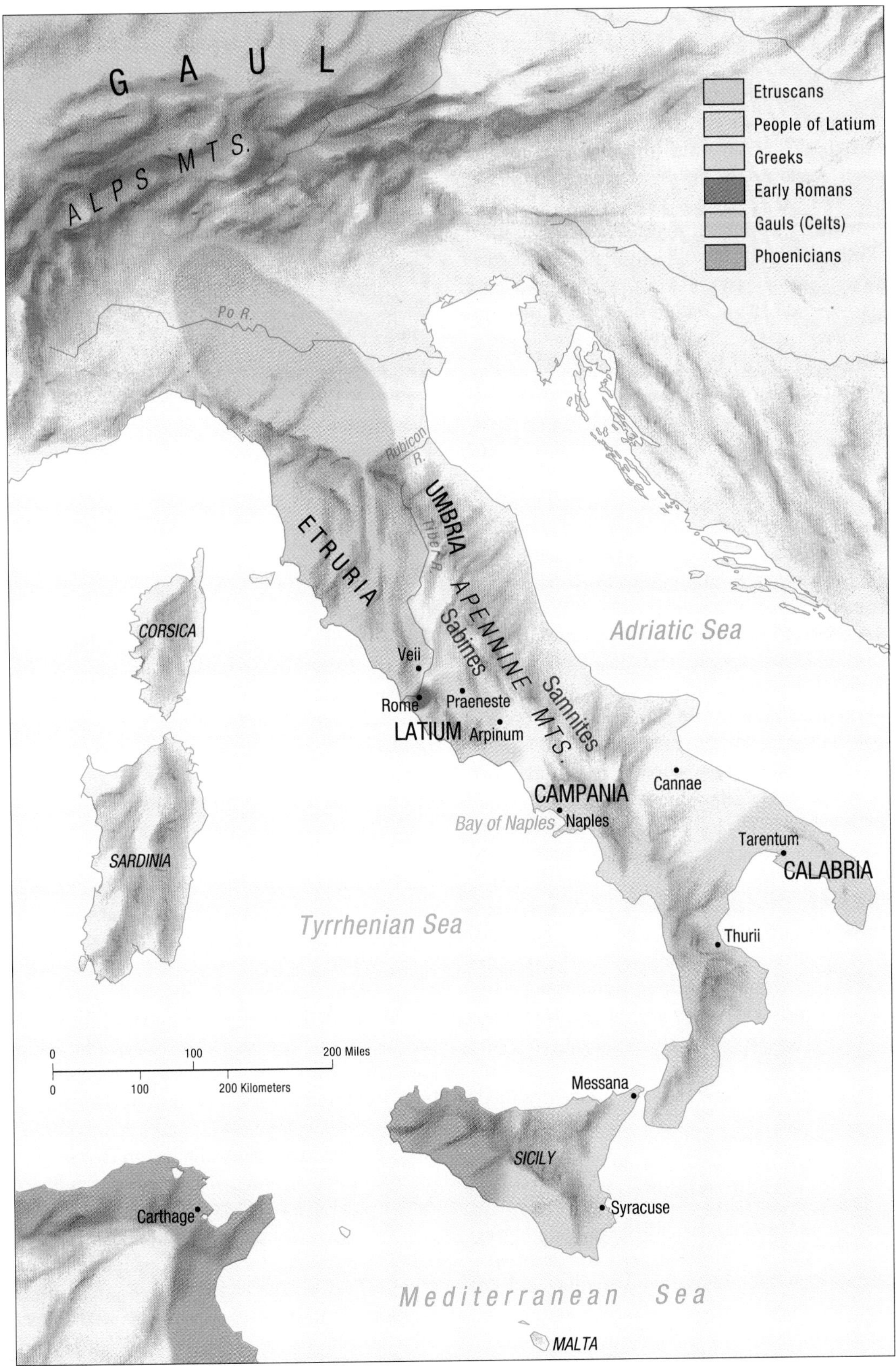
GAUL
ALPS MTS.
Etruscans
People of Latium
Greeks
Early Romans
Gauls (Celts)
Phoenicians
Po R.
Rubicon R.
UMBRIA
Tiber R.
ETRURIA
APENNINE MTS.
Sabines
Samnites
CORSICA
Adriatic Sea
Veii
Rome
Praeneste
LATIUM
Arpinum
CAMPANIA
Cannae
Bay of Naples
Naples
Tarentum
CALABRIA
SARDINIA
Tyrrhenian Sea
Thurii
0
100
200 Miles
0
100
200 Kilometers
Messana
SICILY
Carthage
Syracuse
Mediterranean Sea
MALTA

Ancient Italy

peninsula. A large, rich plain lies at its upper end, north of the Po River. Mountains farther north, the towering Alps, divide this plain from continental Europe and provide Italy a natural barrier that makes invasion from the north difficult. To the south of the Alps, another mountain range, the Apennines, separates the northern plain from central and southern Italy. The Apennines then snake southeastward through the peninsula like a knobby spine. Hills and small coastal plains flank this central mountain chain on east and west, with the western plains larger and blessed with more rainfall than the eastern ones. An especially fertile area, the Campanian plain, surrounds the Bay of Naples on Italy's southwestern coast. Compared to the relentlessly mountainous terrain of Greece, Italy's expansive plains were much more conducive to agriculture and animal husbandry. The more open geography of Italy also made political unification easier, at least on the physical level.

Rome originally occupied some hilltops above one of the western lowland plains. Fortunately for the farmers who inhabited early Rome, their land was fertile and their weather mild. Most important for its future, Rome was situated ideally for contact with the outside world. The settlement controlled a useful crossing spot on the Tiber River, astride a natural route for northwest-southeast land communication along the western side of the peninsula as well as northward along the river's valley. The Mediterranean Sea, offering numerous opportunities for trade and exploration, lay only fifteen miles west of Rome, at the mouth of the Tiber. Furthermore, Italy stuck so far out into the Mediterranean that east-west ship traffic could not help but find its way there. Geography put Rome at the natural center of both Italy and the Mediterranean world. Livy summed up Rome's geographical advantages this way: "With reason did gods and men choose this site for our city—all its advantages make it of all places in the world the best for a city destined to grow great."

The Etruscans

The early Romans had many different neighbors in ancient Italy. The people of the area surrounding Rome, called Latium, were poor villagers like the Romans. These people spoke the same language as the Romans, an early form of Latin. To the south, Greeks had established colonies on the Campanian plain as early as the eighth century B.C. But the Etruscans, who lived north of Rome in a region of central Italy called Etruria, most influenced the early Romans. Because the Etruscan language has not yet been fully deciphered, our understanding of Etruscan origins and culture is limited. We do not know what language group Etruscan belongs to, but it seems not to be Indo-European. The fifth-century B.C. Greek historian Herodotus believed the Etruscans had immigrated to Italy from Lydia in Anatolia, but Dionysius of Halicarnassus reported they had always inhabited Italy. Whatever their origins, the Etruscans were a prosperous people who dwelled in independent towns nestled on central Italian hilltops. They produced fine art work, jewelry, and sculpture, and they imported luxurious objects, such as large painted vases, from Greece and other Mediterranean lands. Magnificently colored wall paintings, which still survive in some of their tombs, portray funeral banquets and games, evidence of their society's sophistication.

The refined Etruscans influenced their more rustic neighbors, the early Romans, in numerous ways. The Romans based many essential features of their official religion on Etruscan practices, among them the tradition of erecting temples divided

An Etruscan Couple
This terra-cotta sarcophagus portrays an Etruscan married couple reclining together at a meal, symbolizing the harmony of their union in life.

Etruscan-style Banqueting *This painting in an Etruscan tomb depicts couples reclining as they drink wine and converse. Pictures of musicians playing for the party decorated the adjoining wall.*

into three sections for worshiping a triad of main gods: for the Romans, they were Jupiter, the king of the gods; Juno, the queen of the gods; and Minerva, the goddess of wisdom. The Romans also learned from the Etruscans the practice of divining the gods' will by looking for clues in the shapes of slaughtered animals' entrails (a process called haruspicy). Official divinations regularly preceded significant Roman public actions to ensure that the gods did not oppose the intended plan. Roman society even derived its fundamental social hierarchy—the patron-client system—from the Etruscan tradition by which people were obligated to each other as patrons (social superiors) and clients (social inferiors). The Roman convention of allowing women to join men for social gatherings probably also originated in Etruscan society. Tomb paintings confirm what Aristotle reported: respectable Etruscan women participated in banquets, apparently in an equal position with the men who attended, not in some subservient role. (In Greek society the only women who ever attended dinner parties with men were courtesans, hired musicians, and slaves.)

Rome's first political system, a monarchy, was also rooted in Etruscan precedents; Etruscan kings even ruled Rome for a time. And the Romans modeled their army, a citizen militia of heavily armed hoplites who fought in formation, on the Etruscan military. When Rome began to emerge from its early poverty and obscurity, many developments that fed its growth were grounded in Etruscan culture: the Greek alphabet (which the Romans learned from the Etruscans and used to write their own language); trade with other areas of the Mediterranean, which promoted economic growth; and sound civil engineering, which helped transform early Rome from a village to a complex, urban society.

The Political Background of the Republic

The distant ancestors of the Romans were Indo-European-speaking peoples who had migrated to Italy from the interior of Europe at an unknown date, certainly many centuries before Rome was founded. By the eighth century B.C., Romans lived in a small village of huts on Palatine Hill, one of the seven hills that eventually formed the heart of the city of Rome. The culture of the neighboring people of Latium so resembled that of Rome's early inhabitants that some Latin people had merged with the Romans in a loose political alliance. This first stage of Rome's growth foreshadowed the basic principle of its later expansion: incorporate certain outsiders into the Roman state by giving them political rights and in some cases by making them Roman citizens. This process of integration contrasted with the exclusionist policies of the Greek city-states and resulted in some ethnic diversity in early Rome.

Slaves in Rome had an opportunity for upward social mobility, a condition unusual in the ancient world. Although Roman slaves were chattel slaves, like those in Greece, slaves freed by Roman citizens received Roman citizenship if they could acquire enough money to buy their freedom or if they were manumitted in their owner's will. Freed slaves still owed special obligations to their former owners, and they were barred from holding Roman elective office or serving in Rome's legions. Otherwise these freedmen and freedwomen, as they were officially designated, had full civic rights, such as legal marriage. Children born to freedmen and freedwomen were granted citizenship without any limitations.

Rome's practice of expanding its territory by appropriation sometimes led to violence. The legend of the kidnapping of the Sabine women during the rule of Rome's first king illustrates that those who would not join Rome peaceably were often forced. As Livy tells the tale, when Romulus feared Rome would wither because it lacked enough women to marry the village's men and bear children to increase the population, he sent envoys to all the surrounding peoples to ask for the right of intermarriage. The ambassadors were instructed to say that although Rome was only a tiny hamlet, the gods had granted it a brilliant future and Rome's more prosperous neighbors should not disdain an alliance with this people of destiny. Everyone refused the Roman request. Romulus therefore invited Rome's neighbors to a religious festival, to which the Sabine men and their wives and children came from their villages just northeast of Rome. By prearrangement, Rome's men kidnapped the unmarried Sabine women and fought off attacks launched to rescue them. Romulus told the women they would be cherished as beloved wives, and the men of Rome married the captives, who became citizens. A massive Sabine counterattack on Rome resulted in a bloody battle that halted only when the Sabine women rushed between the warring men. They implored their new husbands, the Romans, and their parents and brothers, the Sabines, either to cease the slaughter or kill them on the spot to end the war. The men thereupon made peace and agreed to merge their populations under Roman rule. Besides showing the potential for violence inherent in Rome's policy of expansion through assimilation, this legendary story exemplifies Rome's self-image as a military power destined to rule.

Tensions could arise even when immigrants joined the Roman state peacefully. Another legend of early Rome recounts that the fifth king of Rome, named Tarquin the Elder, was an Etruscan whose wife, Tanaquil, prodded him to emigrate from Etruria to make their fortune in the new city. There he became an adviser to the king and then his successor, reaching the throne peacefully. But Tarquin was murdered in a political power struggle. Tanaquil acted boldly, however, and secured the crown for her son-in-law. This story symbolized the opportunities for immigrants to early Rome and perhaps prompted many to move there. Where else in the ancient world could a foreigner resettle and become king of his new community? Tarquin's unfortunate demise, however, suggested that some Romans strongly disapproved of having an Etruscan rule them.

In the period of the kings (753–509 B.C.), Rome became a large settlement for its time, but hardly glorious. People lived in thatched-roof huts on the hills of Rome surrounding an open area at the foot of the hills called the forum. Using Etruscan engineering techniques, the Romans in the sixth century B.C. drained this formerly marshy section so the land could be used as the public center of their emerging city. Coincidentally, the Romans created the forum at about the same time the Athenians fashioned the agora, the open, public center of their growing city. By this time the Romans controlled some three hundred square miles of Latium, enough agricultural land to support a population of thirty thousand to forty thousand people.

The later kings of Rome clashed with the city's upper class. These rich aristocratic families resented the monarchy's power and authority. The kings, in turn, feared that a powerful aristocrat might try to overthrow them. The aristocrats were especially disturbed by the monarchy's general popularity. To secure allies against their upper-class rivals, the kings had cultivated support from citizens possessing enough wealth to furnish their own weapons

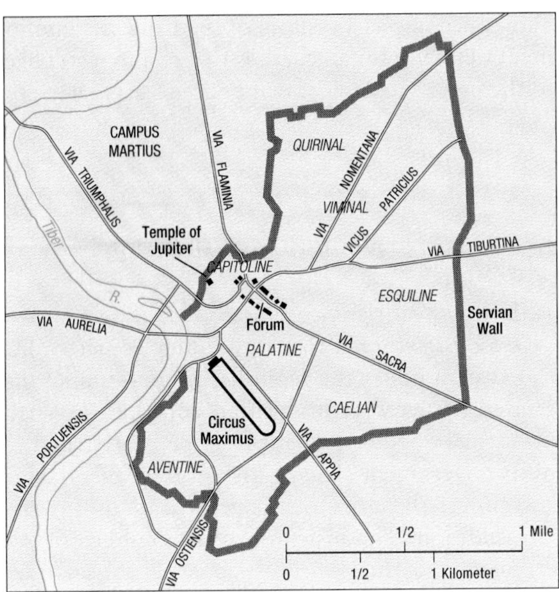

Early Rome

but not enough money or social standing to count as members of the upper class. However, public support did not save King Tarquin the Proud, the seventh and last king of Rome. In 509 B.C. aristocrats deposed him, ostensibly for a vicious crime his son committed: the rape at knifepoint of Lucretia, a virtuous Roman woman. Despite pleas from her husband and father not to blame herself, Lucretia committed suicide after denouncing her attacker. Lucretia subsequently became a kind of martyr, an example of the ideal Roman woman: chaste, courageous, and honorable, preferring death to any possible sullying of her moral reputation. This story also illustrates the double standard Roman men held regarding women: foreign women, such as the Sabines, could be kidnapped and coerced into forced marriages, but the rape of a woman of their own class was cause for moral outrage.

Labeling themselves liberators, the aristocrats who ousted Tarquin the Proud abolished the monarchy on the grounds that crimes such as the rape of Lucretia sprang from rule by one man, which they equated with tyranny. The distrust of monarchy became a central feature of the aristocratic republic and was enshrined in the famous legend of the Roman warrior Horatius, who single-handedly held off an Etruscan bid to reimpose a king on the Romans after Tarquin the Proud had been deposed. As Livy told the story, Horatius, while blocking the enemy's access to Rome over the bridge crossing the Tiber River, berated the Etruscans as slaves who had lost their freedom because they were ruled by haughty kings. For upper-class Romans, a compelling reason to install a new system of government—the republic—was to make one-man rule impossible.

The Struggle of the Orders

The republic as a system of government evolved slowly. After expelling Tarquin the Proud, the Romans took more than two hundred years to work out a stable arrangement for society and politics. Turmoil between the elite (called the patricians) and the rest of Rome's citizen population (the plebeians), the republic's two "orders" in Roman parlance, marked these centuries. Historians refer to this period as "the struggle of the orders."

A clear picture of this conflict eludes us, as it did the Roman historians we depend on for our information about early Rome. We do know that patricians were privileged citizens and that the only way to become a patrician was to be born to the right family: certain families were patrician, and no others could achieve this status. Patricians constituted only a tiny percentage of the population but nearly monopolized the secular and religious offices of early republican government; they were usually extremely wealthy as well. Patrician men were early Rome's social and political leaders, and they often controlled large bands of followers. A recently discovered inscription to the war god Mars, for example, says that "the comrades of Publius Valerius" erected the monument. These men designated themselves followers of the patrician Valerius rather than Roman citizens, even in a dedication to a national deity. Another patrician family, the Fabians, was able to raise a private army from among its many followers to fight against the neighboring town of Veii in 479 B.C. when no general militia force could be assembled. Patricians proudly advertised their status. In the early republic they wore red shoes to set themselves apart. Later they changed to the black shoes worn by all senators but adorned them with a small metal crescent to mark their special station.

Economic and social issues fueled the struggle between the patricians and the plebeians. Most plebeians wanted more land for farming and relief from the crushing debts that the poor among them incurred just to survive. The patricians, on the other hand, tried to protect their privileges by walling themselves off socially from the plebeians. No matter how rich a plebeian family was (and some were), it could not rival a patrician family in prestige. The patricians even banned intermarriage between the orders as a tactic for sustaining their social exclusion.

To force change in such matters as intermarriage, the plebeians periodically resorted to drastic measures. More than once, disputes became so bitter that they physically withdrew from the city to a temporary settlement on a neighboring hill, and the men refused to serve in the army. This tactic of secession worked because it depleted the city's military strength. The patricians, numbering only some one hundred thirty families in the early republic, could not defend Rome by themselves and were obliged to compromise with the plebeians. Over time the two orders hammered out a series of written laws to guarantee the plebeians more political clout and upward social mobility. The earliest code of Roman law, called the Twelve Tables, was enacted between 451 and 449 B.C. in response to a plebeian secession. The Twelve Tables encapsulated the prevailing legal customs of early Rome's agricultural society in simply worded provisions such as, "If plaintiff calls defendant to court, he shall go," and "If a wind causes a tree from a neighbor's farm to be bent and lean over your farm, action may be taken to have that tree removed." Although these laws did not make plebeians the social equals of patricians, they marked a turning point in the plebeians' struggle to obtain legal recognition and equality. In Livy's words, these laws prevented the patrician public officials who judged most legal cases from "arbitrarily giving the force of law to their own preferences." Emphasizing matters such as disputes over property, the Twelve Tables demonstrated the Romans' overriding interest in civil law. Roman criminal law never became extensive, so courts never had a full set of rules to guide their verdicts in all cases. Magistrates decided most cases without juries. Trials before juries became common only in the late republic of the second and first centuries B.C. So important did the Twelve Tables become as a symbol of the Roman commitment to justice for all citizens that children still had to memorize its laws four hundred years later.

The Roman Constitution

Although historians commonly use the term *Roman Constitution* in referring to the Roman political system under the republic, Rome—unlike the United States with its written constitution—had no formal document that prescribed the structure of its government. The history of the Roman constitution is the story of the growth of an unwritten tradition. The institutions of republican government and their various powers evolved over time through trial and error, and in some cases duties and responsibilities overlapped among institutions or were divvied up piecemeal among them. Different assemblies having a variety of structures elected magistrates and made policy decisions according to their own rules, contributing to the complex messiness of Roman republican government. One feature was clearcut, however: as in Greece, the Roman tradition of public life excluded women from formal participation. Only men could vote or hold political office.

The Consuls and the Senate

From the beginning of the republic, two elected magistrates, later called consuls, shared the highest state office. Consuls held office for only a year and were not supposed to serve consecutive terms. Having two magistrates serve annual terms prevented what Roman aristocrats detested in monarchies: the continued concentration of political authority in the hands of one person. The kings of Rome, in truth, had not customarily made important decisions by themselves but had acted only after consulting with a body of advisers. The tradition that government officials should seek advice continued under the republic. The highest magistrates consulted a body called the Senate, which had 300 members during most of the republic. (The general and politician Sulla increased the membership to 600 as part of his reforms in 81 B.C., Julius Caesar raised it to 900 in the mid-40s B.C., and

Augustus brought it back to 600 by 13 B.C.) Originally, the kings had chosen senators from among Rome's most distinguished men. Under the republic, the highest magistrates at first selected senators from the pool of patricians and plebeians who had previously served as lesser magistrates. Two magistrates of high prestige, called censors, later chose senators from the same group. The censors could also expel men from the senate for alleged immoral conduct; all they needed to do to remove a senator was to place a black dot opposite his name on the roll. In time the Senate exerted tremendous influence over republican domestic and foreign policy, state finance, official religion, and all types of legislation. Senators were especially involved in decisions about declaring and conducting wars. Because republican Rome fought wars almost continually, this Senate function was critical.

The Senate's influence stemmed not from any constitutional right to legislate, but solely from its members' social status. The senators could not enact laws, only advise the republic's magistrates, signaling either their consent to or disapproval of various courses of action. No official power compelled the magistrates to heed the senators' wishes. But the unwritten yet understood code that governed the relationship between the senators and the magistrates, which also reflected the essence of Roman politics and society, demanded that the magistrates comply with the senators' recommendations. The senators' high social status gave their opinions the force—even if not the form—of law. Any magistrate who refused the Senate's "advice" found his political career in severe jeopardy. And since magistrates aspired to become members of the Senate, they could ill afford to offend that body. Senators were not shy about advertising their social status: their black, high-top shoes and tunics embroidered with a broad, purple stripe made them highly visible.

The Senate decided what advice to offer in an ostensibly democratic procedure—majority vote of the members. Even in senatorial democracy, however, status counted. Before a vote the most distinguished senator had the right to express his opinion first. The other senators then followed in descending order of prestige. The opinions of the most eminent, usually older senators carried great weight. Only a junior senator who did not aspire to being a senior senator would dare give an opinion that differed from theirs.

The Course of Offices

Republican Rome had a roster of annually elective offices. These offices were ranked according to their prestige in what is called the *cursus honorum* ("course of offices"). After 337 B.C. all offices were open equally to patricians and wealthy plebeians. Various assemblies elected men to these posts. An ambitious and successful Roman man would climb this ladder by winning election to one post after another, each more important than the preceding one. After up to ten years of service on military campaigns as a young man, he would begin by seeking the lowest of the chief annual offices, that of *quaestor.* This post in financial administration was usually filled by a man in his late twenties or early thirties; his duties involved overseeing revenues and payments for the treasury in the capital, for commanders on campaign, and in the overseas provinces Rome established beginning in the third century B.C. Eventually, laws set minimum age requirements for the various offices. After Sulla in 81 B.C. prescribed strict regulations for progress through the *cursus honorum,* a man who had been a quaestor was automatically eligible to be chosen as a senator when a place opened up in the Senate.

A Roman man aspiring to higher office would often seek election as an *aedile* after serving as a quaestor. Aediles had the irksome duty of looking after Rome's streets, sewers, temples, markets, and the like. After either his quaestorship or his aedileship, if he served one, a man sought election as a *praetor,* a prestigious magistracy whose responsibilities included the administration of justice. With fewer praetorships than quaestorships (the number of both changed over time), competition for them was fierce, and only men of wealth and high social status could proceed directly from quaestor to praetor. The praetorship's distinction came mainly from the praetors' role as commanders of military forces when needed. Military success, like high birth and wealth, won a man status in Roman society. Only those who achieved the highest status could hope to become a *consul,* the epitome of social and political success under the republic. Consuls were older men; according to Sulla's regulations they were supposed to be at least forty-two years old. The two consuls had a voice in every important matter of state and served as the supreme commanders of Roman armies in the field. Like praetors, their military power could extend beyond their one-year term of office if they were needed to command abroad. Ex-magistrates on these tours of duty were called *propraetors* and *proconsuls.* Their special grant of power ended when they returned to Rome.

During their term of office, consuls and praetors were endowed with a power called *imperium* (from which comes our word *empire*). It was imperium that gave them the right to demand Roman citizens to obey their orders and to command an army on military expeditions. It also bestowed the official right to perform the rites of divination called *auspicia* (auspices), another Etruscan legacy to Rome. Roman tradition required consuls and praetors to use the auspices to discern the gods' will concerning significant public events such as elections, inaugurations, a magistrate's entrance into a province, and military operations.

Finally, the Roman government included two special, nonannual magistrates, *censors* and *dictators.* Every five years, two censors were elected to serve for eighteen months. Censors were ex-consuls, elder statesmen with the exceptional prestige and wisdom necessary to carry out their crucial duties. They conducted a census of all male Roman citizens and the amount of their property so male citizens could be classified for conscription and taxes levied. The censors decided who would fill openings in the Senate, and they would strike from its rolls any man they believed to have behaved immorally. They also supervised state contracts and oversaw the renewal of official prayers to ensure the gods' goodwill toward the Roman people.

The office of dictator was the sole instance of one-man rule sanctioned by Roman tradition. Chosen by the Senate on rare occasions to lead the republic at times of extreme crisis, such as a military emergency, a dictator had absolute power to make decisions. His term of office, however, was six months at the most. The most famous dictator was Cincinnatus. His conduct as dictator in 458 B.C. epitomized the Roman ideal of selfless public service: in only sixteen days he defeated an enemy threat-

Roman Expansion, 500–44 B.C.

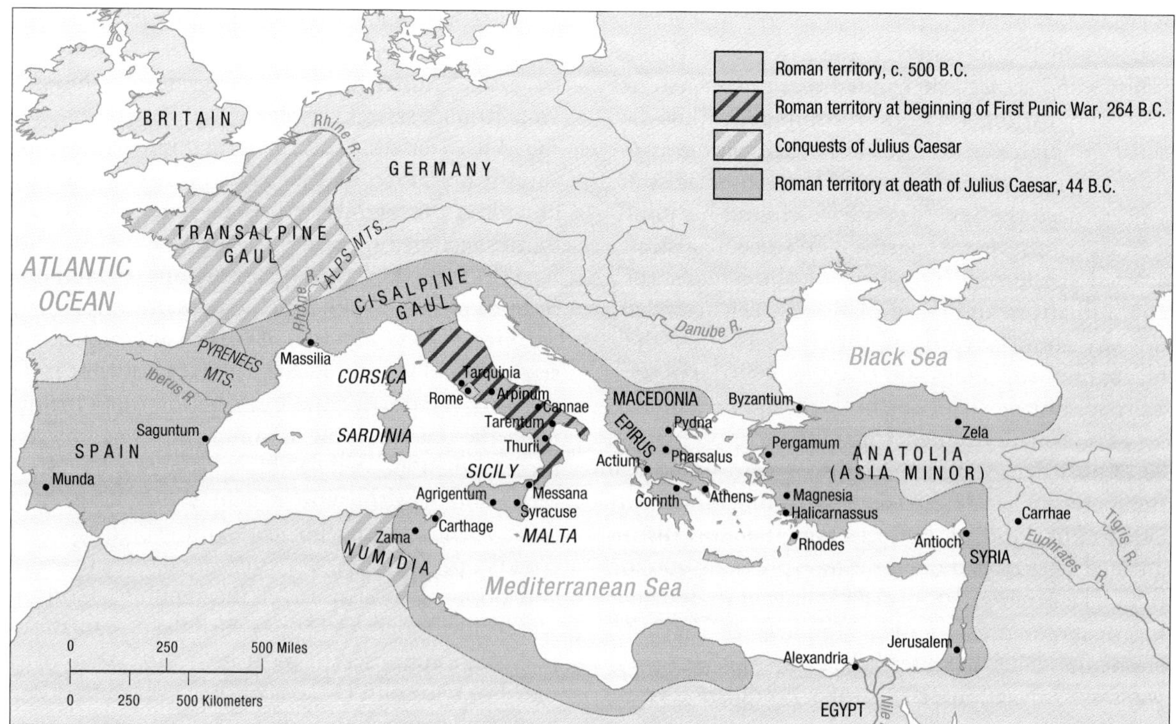

ening Rome and then immediately laid down his supreme power to return to his former existence as a farmer working a modest plot with his own hands.

In republican Rome, as in ancient Greece, the only honorable and desirable career for a man of high social standing was holding public office, or as we might label it, a career in government. Public office added to a successful man's social status. Following Etruscan tradition, Roman men displayed their status obviously. For example, twelve attendants preceded a consul wherever he went. Each attendant, called a *lictor,* carried the *fasces,* the symbol of the consul's imperium. Inside the city limits the fasces consisted of a bundle of sticks to symbolize the consul's right to beat citizens who disobeyed his orders; outside the city an ax was added to the sticks to signify his right to execute disobedient soldiers in the field. Lictors also accompanied praetors, who also had imperium; but praetors had only six lictors instead of twelve, indicating that they had less status than the consuls.

The value of a public career had nothing to do with earning money, at least not in the early republic. In fact, Roman officials earned no salaries. On the contrary, they were expected to spend their own money, supplemented by that of family and friends, on their careers. Roman political expenses could be crushing. Candidates spent large sums, their own or borrowed, to win popular support by entertaining the electorate, for example, with lavish shows that featured gladiators (trained fighters) and wild beasts, such as lions and tigers imported from Africa. Financing such exhibitions could put a candidate deeply in debt. Once in office a magistrate had to pay for public works such as roads, aqueducts, and temples that benefited the whole populace, fulfilling the expectation that a public officeholder would serve the common good. Their rewards were originally only the status their positions carried and the esteem they could win by meritorious service to the republic. But as the Romans gradually came to control more and more overseas territory through warfare, the opportunity to make money became an increasingly important component of a public career. Magistrates could enrich themselves legitimately with booty gained while commanding in successful foreign wars. While administering the Roman provinces created from conquered territory, less scrupulous magistrates extorted money and other valuables from the local people and financed their political careers with these profits of war.

The Assemblies

The free, adult male citizens of Rome met in outdoor gatherings called assemblies to pass laws, hold certain trials, and elect magistrates. Roman tradition required assemblies to be summoned by a magistrate, held only on days proper under religious law, and sanctioned by favorable auspices. Assembly members voted only on matters presented by the magistrates, whose proposals could not be amended. Women were barred from the assemblies, where voting took place, but like noncitizens they could attend (but not speak at) the public discussion meeting, called a *contio,* that preceded assemblies. All official policy debates were supposed to occur at the *contio.* The presiding magistrate decided which assembly members could speak at a *contio* and thus could guide the course of the debate. Nevertheless, the *contio* provided an opportunity for those excluded from voting to express their approval or disapproval of issues by their reactions to the speakers' remarks.

The organizational complexity of the major republican assemblies almost defies description. The most significant point about the assemblies is that the members voted in groups; that is, the men in the various assemblies were divided into groups according to criteria particular to each assembly and voted within these groups. The members of a group cast their individual votes to determine their group's single vote. Each group's single vote, regardless of the number of members in the group, counted the same in determining the assembly's decision by simple majority vote. In other words, the one-man, one-vote principle applied only within groups.

Group voting severely limited the democracy of the assemblies. The Centuriate Assembly offers the clearest example of the effects of this procedure. This important assembly elected censors, consuls, and praetors; enacted laws; declared war and peace; and could inflict the death penalty. The groups in this assembly, called *centuries* (hence the assembly's name), were meant to correspond to the divisions of the male citizens when they were drawn up as an army. As in the city-states of archaic and classical Greece, early Rome relied not on a standing army financed by taxes but on a citizen militia, in which every male citizen armed himself at his own expense as best he could. This principle of national defense through individual contributions meant that the richer citizens had more and better weapons than did the poorer, more numerous citizens. Consequently, the rich were seen as deserving more power in the assembly, to reflect their greater military expenses. In line with this principle, cavalrymen, who incurred the highest military costs, made up the first 18 groups of the assembly. The following 170 groups consisted of foot soldiers ranked in property classes from highest to lowest according to the amount of their expenditure. The next 5 groups comprised noncombatants. Some of these were military engineers of higher status, but the last group, the proletarians, was composed of those too poor to afford military arms and thus barred from serving as soldiers. All they contributed to the state were their offspring (their *proles,* hence the word *proletarian*).

In essence, the groups of the Centuriate Assembly corresponded to the distribution of wealth in Roman society. Far more men belonged to the groups at the bottom of the social hierarchy than to those at the top. The proletarians, for example, formed the largest group. But their group still had only one vote. The groups voted in order from richest to poorest, and the polling ended as soon as a majority had been reached. The voting procedure in the Centuriate Assembly allowed the rich to vote as a block and thus muster a majority of group votes well before the voting reached the groups of the poor. When the elite voted together, the Centuriate Assembly could make a decision without the wishes of the lower classes ever being heard.

The Tribal Assembly also voted by groups. Roman men were divided into groups, called tribes, according to where they lived. The structuring of the tribes gave wealthy rural landowners disproportionate influence. In its original form the Tribal Assembly excluded patricians. Meeting as the Tribal Assembly of the Plebeians, the assembly conducted nearly every form of public business, including holding trials. In 287 B.C. its resolutions, called *plebiscites,* were officially recognized as laws, making it a principal source of Roman legislation. The recognition of these "resolutions of the plebs" as legally binding ended the struggle of the orders because it formalized the power of the people in helping set policy and define Roman justice. Later, the Tribal Assembly could also meet in a second form that included patricians as well as plebeians. When convened in this form it was called the Tribal Assembly of the People and elected the quaestors, the two curule aediles (the aedileships of the highest prestige, originally open only to patricians), and the six senior officers of each army legion (called military tribunes). The Tribal Assembly of the People also enacted laws and held minor trials.

The Tribal Assembly of the Plebeians elected the plebeian aediles and, most important, the ten *tribunes,* special and powerful magistrates devoted to protecting the plebeians' interests. As plebeians themselves, tribunes derived their power not from official statutes but from the sworn oath of the plebeians to protect them against all attacks. This inviolability of the tribunes, called sacrosanctity, allowed them the right to *veto* (a Latin word meaning "forbid") other tribunes and to intercede in other government bodies and with other officials on behalf of the plebeians. Tribunes could use their power to block the actions of magistrates, prevent the passage of laws, suspend elections, and counter the advice of the Senate. Their clout, derived from the threat of a plebeian secession, gave tribunes an extraordinary potential to influence Roman government. Tribunes who tried to exercise their full powers could become the catalysts for bitter political disputes, and the office itself became controversial because tribunes sometimes seemed to operate with scant regard for the Senate's wishes.

The republic's political system, with its jumbled network of offices and assemblies, lacked an overall structure to consolidate it. Many different political bodies enacted laws, or in the Senate's case, opinions that amounted to laws. Yet Rome had no judicial body, such as the U.S. Supreme Court, that could resolve disputes about the validity of conflicting laws. The republic's political well-being and stability did not depend on clearly defined institutions of government but rather on a reverence for tradition, the "way of the elders [or ancestors]." This reliance on tradition ensured that the most socially prominent and the richest Romans dominated government—because the "way of the elders" was their way.

Roman Social Institutions

Social institutions that reflected the Roman tradition of deriving power from social status supported Rome's developing political system. A complex social hierarchy that subordinated clients to patrons but also obligated the patron to the client bolstered political relationships. Roman family life was legally based on the father's overwhelming authority, but in practice his power was limited by the expectation that he would consult others before making important decisions. Education was intended primarily for males and designed to make them good citizens. Similarly, the public cults of Roman religion supported the goals of the republic.

The Client-Patron System

The client-patron system institutionalized the differences in status so key in Roman society. A patron was a man of superior status who could provide *kindnesses,* as they were officially called, to those people of lower status who paid him special attention. These were his clients, who in return for his kindnesses owed him *duties.* Patrons could also be the clients of still more distinguished men, just as clients could be the patrons of those below them in the social hierarchy. Under this pervasive system, Roman society developed an interlocking network of personal relationships that obligated people to each other. These obligations were binding. The Twelve Tables, for example, declared any patron who defrauded his client an outlaw. The Romans regarded the client-patron relationship as one of friendship with clearly defined roles for each party. A sensitive patron would greet a client as "my friend," not as "my client." A client, on the other hand, would honor his patron by addressing him as "my patron."

The client's duties included supporting his patron financially and politically. In early Rome tradition dictated that a client had to help fund dowries for his patron's daughters. A client could also be called upon to lend money to his patron when the latter was a magistrate and incurred large expenses in providing the public works expected of him in office. In political life a client was expected to aid in the election campaign when his patron or one of his patron's friends sought a magistracy. Clients could be especially helpful in swinging votes to their patrons' side in the elections that took place in the two forms of the Tribal Assembly. Furthermore, because it was a mark of great status for a patron to have numerous clients surrounding him like a swarm of bees, the patron expected his clients to gather at his house early in the morning and accompany him to the forum. A Roman aristocrat needed a large, fine house to hold his throng of clients and to entertain his social equals, and a crowded house signified social success.

Patrons' kindnesses to their clients took various forms. By the time of the empire, the patron was supposed to provide a picnic basket of food for the breakfast of his clients who clustered on his doorstep at daybreak. Under the republic, a patron might help a client get started in a political career by supporting his candidacy or might provide financial support from time to time. A patron's most important kindness was the obligation to support a client and his family if they got into legal difficulties, such as in lawsuits involving property, which were common. People of lower social status had a distinct disadvantage in the Roman judicial system if they lacked influential friends to help protect their interests. The aid of a patron well versed in public speaking was particularly needed, because in court both accusers and accused either had to speak for themselves or have friends speak for them. Rome had no state-sponsored prosecutors or defenders, nor any lawyers to hire. Priests monopolized knowledge of the law and customary procedures until the third century B.C. By that time, however, prominent men known to be experts on law, called jurists, had begun to play a central role in the Roman judicial system. Although jurists frequently developed their expertise by serving in Roman elective office, they operated as private citizens, not officials, in their role of giving legal advice to other citizens and magistrates. The reliance on jurists, a distinctive feature of Roman republican justice, endured under the empire.

The mutual obligations that constituted a client-patron relationship were supposed to be stable and long lasting. In many cases client-patron ties would endure over generations. Ex-slaves, who automatically became the clients for life of the masters who had manumitted them, often passed on to their children their relationship with the patron's family. Romans with contacts abroad could acquire clients among foreigners; particularly distinguished and wealthy Romans sometimes had entire foreign communities as their clients. With its emphasis on duty and permanence, the client-patron system epitomized the Roman view that social stability and well-being were achieved by faithfully maintaining the ties that linked people to one another. This view reflected a central concept in Roman morality, that of *fides* (from which our word *fidelity* derives), the trustworthy honoring of the web of various obligations among people that defined so much of Roman public and private life.

Power in Roman Families

Republican Rome was a patriarchal society, and under Roman law the father of the family possessed the *patria potestas* ("power of a father") over his children, no matter how old, and his slaves. *Patria potestas* made the father the sole owner of all the property acquired by anyone in the household. As long as their father was alive, no son or daughter could own anything, accumulate money, or possess any independent legal standing—in theory at least. In practice, however, adult children could acquire personal property and money, much as favored slaves might build up some savings. By law the father also held power of life and death over these members of the household. However, fathers rarely exercised this power on anyone except infants. Exposing unwanted babies, so that they would die, be adopted, or be raised as slaves by strangers, was an accepted practice to control the size of families and dispose of physically imperfect infants. Statistics on exposure of infants are lacking, but baby girls suffered this fate more often than boys—a family enhanced its power more by investing its resources in its sons.

Few fathers contemplating the drastic decision to execute an adult member of their household would have made the decision completely on their own. As in government, where senators advised the magistrates, or in legal matters, where jurists shared their expertise, Romans in private life regularly conferred with others on important family issues to seek a consensus. Each Roman man had his own circle of friends and relatives, his "council," whom he consulted before making significant decisions. In this way decision making in the Roman family resembled the process in the Roman republic. A father's council of friends would certainly have advised him to think again if he proposed killing his adult son except for an extremely compelling reason. For example, one outraged father had his son put to death in 63 B.C. because his son had committed treason by joining a conspiracy to overthrow the government. Such violent exercises of a father's power happened rarely.

A wife also lived under her husband's power unless her marriage agreement specifically prohibited it. By the late republic "free" marriages were by far the most common. In free marriages the wife remained in her father's power as long as he lived. But probably few aged fathers actually controlled the lives of their mature, married daughters: because so many people died young in the ancient world, few fathers survived long enough to oversee the lives of their adult daughters. By the time most Roman women married, in their late teens, half of them had already lost their fathers. Because males generally did not marry until their late twenties, by the time they married and formed their own household, only one man in five still had a living father. Like a son whose father had died, an adult woman without a living father was relatively independent. Legally she needed a male guardian to conduct business for her, but the guardianship of adult women was primarily an empty formality by the first century B.C. A later jurist commented on women's freedom of action even under a guardian: "the common belief, that because of their instability of judgment women are often deceived and that it is only fair to have them controlled by the authority of guardians, seems more specious than true. For women of full age manage their affairs themselves."

Women grew up fast in Roman society. Tullia (c. 79–45 B.C.), the daughter of the famous politician and orator Cicero (106–43 B.C.), was engaged at twelve, married at sixteen, and widowed by twenty-two. Women of wealth often led busy lives. They oversaw the household slaves, monitored the nurturing of their young children by wet nurses, accompanied their husbands to dinner parties, and often kept account books to track the property they personally owned. Wealthy men spent much of their time outside the house visiting friends or pursuing public careers, but they used their homes extensively to meet with and entertain their circle of clients and friends.

Children played at home or in the streets, and their education, if their family could afford formal schooling, was provided by tutors at home or in the quarters of private teachers. A mother's power in shaping the moral outlook of her children was especially valued in Roman society and constituted a major component of female virtue. Women like Cornelia, an aristocrat of the second century B.C. and mother of two famous tribunes, the Gracchus brothers, won enormous respect for their accomplishments both in raising outstanding citizens and managing property. When her distinguished husband died, Cornelia refused an offer of marriage from the Ptolemaic king of Egypt so she could oversee the family estate and educate her daughter and two sons. Her other nine children had died. The number of children she bore exemplifies the fertility and stamina required of a Roman wife to ensure the survival of her husband's family line. Cornelia was renowned for entertaining important people and for her stylish letters, which were still being read a century later. Her sons, Tiberius and Gaius Gracchus, grew up to be among the most influential—and controversial—politicians of the late republic.

Recent archaeological discoveries suggest that by the end of the republic some women owned large businesses, such as brick-making companies. Because both women and men could control property, prenuptial agreements to outline the rights of both partners in the marriage were common. Legally, divorce was a simple matter, with fathers

A Mother's Gift
This bronze urn for holding toilet articles dates from the end of the fourth century B.C. and bears two inscriptions: "Dindia Malconia gave this to her daughter" and "Novios Plautios made me in Rome." Its engraving shows scenes from the story of the Argonauts.

A Roman Food Store
This sculpture shows a woman selling food in a store. Roman women could own property, and this woman may have been the shop's owner.

usually keeping the children after the dissolution of a marriage. Most poor women, like poor men, had to toil for a living, but few occupations allowed women. Usually they had to settle for jobs selling things in small shops or from stands. Even if their families produced crafts, the predominant form of producing goods in the Roman economy, women normally sold rather than made the goods the family manufactured. The men in these families usually worked the raw materials and finished the goods. Those women with the worst luck or from the poorest families often ended up as prostitutes. Prostitution was legal, but prostitutes were regarded with contempt. Roman law forbade female prostitutes to wear a *stola,* the long robe reserved for married women, to signal their lack of chastity: they therefore wore the outer garment of men, the toga.

Women in the mainstream of Roman society could wield political influence. Nevertheless, the impact even wealthy Roman women had on politics was almost exclusively indirect, through their influence on their husbands and male children and relatives outside the household. Women seem to have participated in very few public demonstrations in the course of republican history, and they apparently were well-off women protesting limits imposed on their riches and display of status. For example, in 215 B.C., at the height of a wartime financial crisis, the tribune Oppius had a law passed forbidding women from possessing more than a half ounce of gold, wearing multicolored clothing in public, or riding in horse-drawn carriages within a mile of Rome or other Roman towns except for public religious events. His measure presumably was intended to quiet public discontent over resources controlled by wealthy women at a time when the republic faced an acute need for funds, even though the Senate had required women to contribute to the war's expenses two years earlier. In 195 B.C., after the war, the women affected by Oppius's law successfully rallied to have the restrictions lifted. They forced the political men of Rome to rescind the law by pouring out into the streets of Rome to express their demands to the magistrates and besiege the houses of the two tribunes who had been using their veto power to block repeal. Even this dramatic exception to the ordinary public behavior of Roman women shows that they could exercise political power only through their effect on the male citizens who controlled politics. Cato (234–149 B.C.), a famous senator and author who had bitterly opposed the repeal of Oppius's law, hinted at the limited reality of women's power in public life with a biting comment directed at his fellow politicians: "All mankind rule their wives, we rule all mankind, and our wives rule us."

The Goals of Roman Education for Public Life

As in Greece, only well-to-do families could afford formal education for their children. If parents in the many crafts-producing families knew how to read, write, and do simple calculations, then they could pass that knowledge on to their children, who labored alongside them. Roman children of wealthier families customarily received their basic education at home. In the early republic, parents did the educating, at least until the children reached the age of seven, when they might be sent to classes offered by independent schoolmasters in their lodgings. Fathers carefully instructed their sons in the rudiments of masculine virtue, especially physical training, fighting with weapons, and courage. If the slaves purchased to tend children were literate, they helped educate them (a practice derived from Greece). Girls usually received less training than boys, but in upper-class households both girls and boys learned to read. Repetition was the usual teaching technique, with corporal punishment frequently used to keep pupils attentive. Aristocratic girls would be taught literature, perhaps some music, and the basics of making conversation (for dinner parties). A principal aim of the education of women was to prepare them for the important role Roman mothers were expected to play in instilling respect for Roman social and moral traditions in their children.

Rhetoric—the skill of persuasive public speaking—dominated an upper-class Roman boy's curriculum because it was crucial to a successful public career. To win elections, a man had to persuade men to vote for him; to win legal cases, he had to speak effectively in the courts, where lawsuits were the vehicle for building political coalitions and fighting personal feuds. A boy would hear rhetorical techniques in action by accompanying his father, a male relative, or a family friend to public meetings, assemblies, and court sessions. By listening to the speeches he would learn to imitate winning techniques. Wealthy parents would also hire special teachers to instruct their sons in the skills and general knowledge an effective speaker requires. Roman rhetoric owed much to Greek rhetorical techniques, and many Roman orators studied with Greek teachers of rhetoric. When Roman textbooks on rhetoric began to be written in the second century B.C., they reflected material derived from Greek works.

Cicero was the republic's finest example of how far rhetorical skill could carry a man. His father paid for Cicero to leave home and study rhetoric in both Rome and Greece. There he developed the brilliant style of public speaking that allowed him to overcome his lack of prestige (his family came from a small Italian town rather than Rome). Cicero began his rhetorical career by defending men accused of crimes, a relatively safe debut for an unknown orator because defendants were grateful for such help and prosecutors usually did not retaliate against the defendants' supporters. Prosecution was far riskier because a man who lodged an accusation against a powerful public figure could expect his target to seek revenge by bringing a countercharge. Cicero therefore electrified the Roman political community in 70 B.C. when his speech accusing Gaius Verres of flagrant corruption in office drove the ex-provincial governor into exile. In 63 B.C., Cicero achieved the pinnacle of success by being elected consul, the first man in decades from a family without consuls in its history to reach that office. Throughout his career, Cicero used his rhetorical skills to attempt to reconcile warring factions of aristocrats, and he became the speaker feared by more politicians than any other. Later orators studied his speeches, many of which he published after he had delivered them, to absorb the techniques of their carefully structured arguments, clarity of expression, and powerful imagery. Cicero also wrote influential treatises in which he explained his rhetorical doctrines and his belief that to be a good speaker a man had to develop moral excellence. Cicero heeded the advice he once received on the importance of rhetoric: "excel in public speaking. It is the tool for controlling men at Rome, winning them over to your side, and keeping them from harming you. You fully realize your own power when you are a man who can cause your rivals the greatest fears of meeting you in a trial."

Marcus Tullius Cicero
This bust of the famous orator Cicero portrays him as concerned but resolute.

Religion in the Interests of the State and Family

In the early republic the patricians who dominated political offices also controlled the public cults of Roman religion. But by 300 B.C. aristocratic plebeians began to serve as religious officials. Men and women from the top of the social hierarchy filled the priesthoods that directed official worship of the many Roman gods. The people who acted as priests and priestesses were not usually professionals who devoted their lives solely to religious activity; rather, they were fulfilling one aspect of a successful Roman's public life. As in Greek public religion, the duty of these directors of religion was to ensure the gods' goodwill toward the state, a crucial relationship the Romans called the *pax deorum* ("peace of/with the gods"). To maintain the gods' favor toward Rome, priests and priestesses conducted frequent festivals, sacrifices, and other rituals that conformed strictly with ancestral tradition. Because Rome came to house hundreds of shrines and temples, these sacred activities required much time, energy, and expense. The most important board of priests, which had fifteen members for most of the republic's history, advised magistrates on their religious responsibilities as agents of the Roman state. The leader of this group, the *pontifex maximus* ("highest priest"), served as the head of state religion and the ultimate authority on religious matters affecting government. The political power of the *pontifex maximus* motivated Rome's most prominent men to seek the post, which by the third century B.C. was filled by a special election in the Tribal Assembly. Roman government and Roman public religion were inextricably intertwined. No official occasion could proceed without a preparatory religious ritual; the agenda of every Senate meeting began with any religious business; and commanders with imperium regularly sought to discern the will of the gods through various forms of divination.

Many religious festivals reflected the concerns of an agricultural community with an unstable future, the circumstances of early Rome. Roman religion traditionally sought to protect farming, the basis of the community's life. Prayers therefore commonly requested the gods' aid in ensuring good crops, warding off disease, and promoting healthy reproduction among domestic animals and people. In urgent times the Romans even sought foreign gods to protect them, such as when the government imported the cult of the healing god Asclepius from Greece in 293 B.C. hoping he would save Rome from a plague. Private individuals worshiped other foreign gods, such as the Greek god Dionysus, called Bacchus by the Romans. The worship of Bacchus stirred controversy because the cult's secret meetings aroused fears of potential political conspiracies. As long as foreign or new religious cults did not appear to threaten the stability of the state, however, they were permitted to exist and the government took no interest in their doctrines.

Official Roman religious rituals did not vary significantly over time because Romans felt that changing the customary honors paid to the gods was potentially offensive to them and thus hazardous to the community. The religion of the late republic preserved many ancient rituals, such as the Lupercalia festival. During its celebration, naked young men streaked around Palatine Hill, lashing any women they met with strips of goatskin. Women who had not yet borne children would run out to be struck, believing this would help them become fertile. At the Saturnalia festival at the winter solstice, a time Christians much later in the Roman Empire adopted for Christmas, the social order temporarily turned topsy-turvy. As the playwright and scholar Accius (c. 170–80 B.C.) described the Saturnalia, "people joyfully hold feasts all through the country and the towns, each owner acting as a waiter to his slaves." The social inversion of masters and servants both released tensions caused by the inequalities of ordinary life and reinforced the slaves' ties to their owners by symbolizing kindness from the latter, which the former had to repay with faithful service.

Romans viewed their chief deity, Jupiter, who corresponded to the Greek god Zeus, as a powerful, stern father. Juno, queen of the gods, and Minerva, goddess of wisdom, joined Jupiter to form the central triad of the state cults, in imitation of Etruscan practice. These three deities shared Rome's most revered temple on Capitoline Hill. Worshipers offered them regular sacrifices as the protectors of the city—guarding Rome's physical safety and prosperity was their major function in Roman religion. These and the numerous other major gods of Roman public religion had only limited connections with human morality, with certain exceptions, such as Jupiter's responsibility to punish those who broke oaths. Roman tradition did not acknowledge the anthropomorphic gods as the primary originators of the society's moral code, in contrast, for example, to the Hebrew belief that Yahweh handed down the Ten Commandments and other laws governing human life. In the first century B.C., Cicero explained the general nature of Rome's official religion with this description of Jupiter's official titles: "We call Jupiter the Best (*Optimus*) and Greatest (*Maximus*) not because he makes us just or sober or wise but, rather, healthy and rich and prosperous."

Romans nevertheless incorporated a strict morality in their religious consciousness by regarding abstract moral qualities such as *fides* as special divine beings or forces. Also regarded as divine was *pietas* (a Latin word that provides the root of the English word *piety*). *Pietas* connoted a sense of devotion and duty—to family, to friends, to the republic, to keeping one's word. A temple to *pietas* dedicated in Rome in 181 B.C. housed a statue of this moral quality represented as a female divinity in anthropomorphic form. This personification of abstract moral qualities provided a focus for the rituals associated with their cults. Another revered quality was *virtus* (derived from the Latin word for *man—vir*; the root of the English word *virtue*), a primarily masculine value stressing courage, strength, and loyalty. But *virtus* also included wisdom and moral purity, qualities that aristocrats were expected to display in their public and private lives. In this broader sense *virtus* applied to women as well as men. The religious aura surrounding moral qualities emphasized that they were ideals to which every Roman should aspire.

The republic also supported the worship of many other special deities. The shrine of Vesta, the goddess of the hearth and therefore a protector of the family, housed the official eternal flame of Rome. The Vestal Virgins, six unmarried women sworn to chastity for terms of thirty years, tended Vesta's shrine. Their most important duty was to protect the flame, because as the historian Dionysius of Halicarnassus reported, "the Romans dread the extinction of the fire above all misfortunes, looking upon it as an omen which portends the destruction of the city." If a Vestal Virgin was convicted of a minor offense, the *pontifex maximus* publicly flogged her. Should the flame happen to go out, the Romans assumed one of the Vestal Virgins had broken her vow of chastity; a Vestal Virgin convicted of breaking that vow was carried on a funeral bier, as if a living corpse, to be entombed in an underground chamber, where she was walled up to die. Female chastity symbolized the safety and protection of the Roman family structure and thus the preservation of the republic itself.

A Roman Household Shrine
This wooden cabinet, carved to resemble a temple, held statuettes of the gods worshiped in a Roman home, the Lares and Penates. Its lower section held glassware and ornaments.

Reverence for the cult of Vesta was only one way in which Roman religion was associated with the family as well as the state. As part of private religion, each Roman family maintained a sacred space in its home for small shrines housing its Penates (spirits of the pantry) and Lares (spirits of the ancestors), who were connected with keeping the family well and its moral traditions alive. The statuettes representing these family spirits signified the family's respect for its heritage, a commitment made explicit by the habit of hanging death masks of distinguished ancestors on the walls of the home's main room as reminders of the virtuous ideals of the family and the responsibility of the current generation to live up to ancestral standards. The strong sense of family tradition instilled by these practices and by instruction from parents (especially mothers) represented the principal source of Roman morality. The shame of losing public esteem by tarnishing this tradition, not the fear of divine punishment, was the strongest deterrent to immoral behavior.

Many other divine spirits were believed to participate in crucial moments in life, such as birth, marriage, and death. So pervasive was religious activity in Roman existence that special rituals accompanied activities as diverse and commonplace as breast-feeding babies and spreading manure to fertilize crops. People performed these rituals in search of protection from harm in a world fraught with dangers and uncertainties.

The Foreign Wars of the Republic

War and expansion propelled republican domestic and foreign policy and made conquest and military service central to the lives of Romans. During the fifth and fourth centuries B.C. the Romans fought war after war in Italy until Rome became the most powerful state on the peninsula. In the third and second centuries B.C. they fought wars far from home in the West, the North, and the East, but above all they battled Carthage, a powerful state in Africa (modern Tunisia). Their success in these campaigns made Rome the premier power in the Mediterranean.

Expansion in Italy

The Romans believed they were militarily successful because they respected the will of the gods. Reflecting on the earlier history of the republic, Cicero claimed, "we have overcome all the nations of the world, because we have realized that the world is directed and governed by the gods." Believing that the gods supported defensive wars as just, the Romans always insisted they fought only in self-defense. The most debated question about Roman expansion under the republic is the extent to which this claim was valid.

Rome and Central Italy

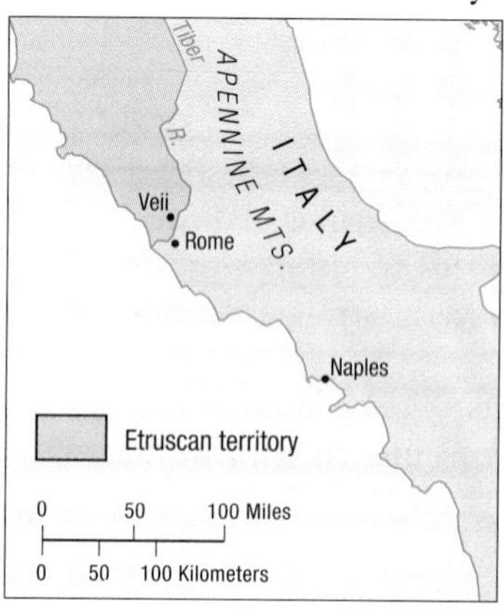

After a victory over their Latin neighbors in 499 B.C., the Romans spent the next hundred years warring with the Etruscan town of Veii, a few miles north of the Tiber River. Their eventual victory in 396 B.C. doubled Roman territory. By the fourth century B.C. the Roman infantry legion had surpassed the Greek and Macedonian phalanx as an effective fighting force. Its internal division into squads gave it greater mobility on the battlefield, and the open space left between soldiers gave them enough room to throw their spears and hack with their cut-and-thrust swords, specially designed for this formation. Even a devastating sack of Rome in 387 B.C. by marauding Gauls (Celts) from the distant north proved only a temporary check. By around 220 B.C. Rome controlled all of Italy south of the Po River.

The conduct of the wars of conquest in Italy was brutal. When the Romans won, they sometimes enslaved many of the defeated or forced them to give up large parcels of their land. Yet the Romans also regularly struck generous peace terms with former enemies. Some defeated Italians immediately became Roman citizens; others gained limited citizenship without the right to vote; still other communities received treaties of alliance. No conquered Italian peoples had to pay taxes to Rome. All, however, had to render military aid to the Romans in future wars. These new allies then received a share of the booty, chiefly slaves and land, that Rome and its allied armies seized on victorious campaigns against a new crop of enemies. In this way the Romans adroitly co-opted their former opponents by making them partners in the spoils of conquest, an arrangement that in turn enhanced Rome's wealth and authority.

To ensure the security of Italy, the Romans planted colonies of citizens throughout the country and constructed a network of roads up and down the peninsula. These roads connected the diverse peoples of Italy, hastening the creation of a more unified culture dominated by Rome. Latin, for example, came to be the common language. But Rome too was influenced by the new contacts. In southern Italy the Romans found sophisticated cities like Naples, which had been founded hundreds of years before by Greek colonists. Greek communities like Naples, too weak to resist Roman armies, were overpowered. But though Rome dominated them militarily, they never surrendered their artistic traditions. In fact the Greek traditions in art, music, and literature provided models for Roman developments in the arts. When in the late third century B.C., Roman authors began to record history for the first time, they imitated Greek forms and aimed at Greek readers, even to the point of writing in Greek.

Rome's urban population grew tremendously during this period. By around 300 B.C. perhaps one hundred fifty thousand people lived within its walls. Newly built aqueducts funneled fresh water to this burgeoning population, and the plunder from successful wars financed a massive building program inside the city. Outside the city about seven hundred fifty thousand free Roman citizens inhabited various parts of Italy on land taken from the local peoples. Much conquered territory was declared public land, supposedly open to any Roman to use for grazing flocks. Many rich landowners, however, ended up controlling huge parcels of this land for their private benefit. This illegal monopolization of public land later created enormous strife between rich and poor.

The ranks of the rich included both patricians and plebeians, an alliance of the wealthy and politically successful that amounted to a new kind of upper class, a new kind of "order," exploiting the expanding Roman territories. They derived their wealth mainly from agricultural land and booty gained as officers in military expeditions. Rome levied no regular income or inheritance taxes, so financially prudent families could pass down this wealth from generation to generation. Families in the top social stratum in this new upper class consisted of those who at some point had a consul in the family. They called themselves "the nobles" in honor of this illustrious achievement. (Some historians think a praetor in the family also earned this status.) Rich Roman men with no consul on their family tree tried fervently to win election as consul to bestow nobility on themselves and their descendants.

The First and Second Punic Wars

The nobles, the elite of Roman society, dominated republican politics during the third and second centuries B.C. War preoccupied Roman government in this period. From 280 to 275 B.C. the Romans battled the forces of Pyrrhus (319–272 B.C.), the king of Epirus in northwest Greece, who had brought an army to southern Italy to aid the Greek city of Tarentum against Rome. Rome's alliance with another Greek city in southern Italy, Thurii, had drawn Roman forces into conflict with Tarentum, which feared the growing Roman involvement in its region. But the enemy Rome soon focused on was Carthage, a prosperous and sophisticated state located across the Mediterranean Sea in North Africa. Phoenicians had colonized Carthage (near modern Tunis) in the late ninth century B.C. The Romans therefore called the Carthaginians the *Punici,* their word for Phoenicians (hence the adjective *Punic*). Punic riches stemmed from large, well-managed agricultural estates and a thriving maritime commerce. Long experience at sea meant that the Carthaginians completely outstripped the Romans in naval capability. Rome and Carthage were both oligarchic republics, and for centuries they had maintained peaceful relations because their economic interests and political domains had not yet overlapped. But by the mid-third century B.C. the Romans, who had expanded their power to the southern tip of Italy's boot, came face to face with the power of Carthage, which had settlements on the islands of Sicily and Sardinia.

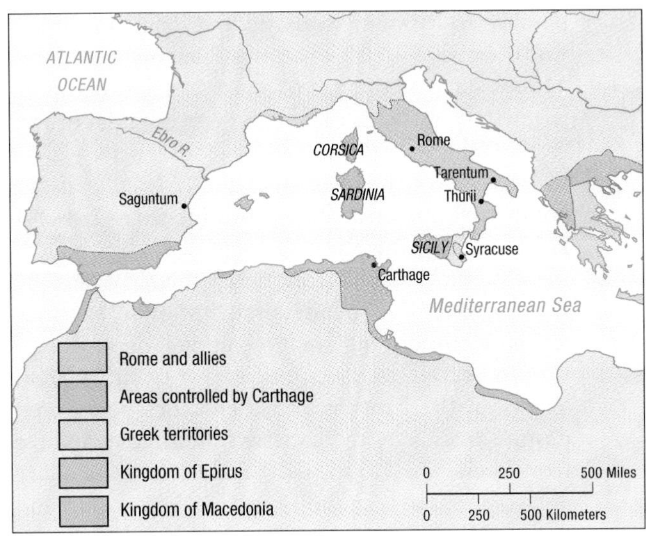

First Punic War

Hostilities between Rome and Carthage erupted in 264 B.C. over a petty local affair in the region where their respective spheres of power met. A beleaguered band of mercenaries in Messana at Sicily's northeastern tip appealed to both cities for help in settling a violent dispute there. The Roman senators disagreed about what to do, but a patrician consul, Appius Claudius, persuaded the people to demand a Sicilian expedition by raising hopes of lucrative conquest. The troops dispatched to Messana were the first Roman military foray outside Italy. That the Romans could see Messana across the narrow strait separating Sicily from Italy made the leap into foreign adventures easier. When Carthage simultaneously sent a force to Messana, a fierce war exploded between the competing powers. The First Punic War (264–241 B.C.) lasted a generation and revealed why the Romans so consistently conquered their rivals: they were prepared to spend as much money, sacrifice as many troops, and stick it out as long as necessary to prevail. In the course of this twenty-three-year war, the Romans and their allies persevered despite losing more than five hundred warships from their newly built navy and perhaps as many as two hundred fifty thousand men from their land and sea forces. The Greek historian Polybius, writing a century later, regarded the First Punic War as "the greatest war in history in its duration, intensity, and scale of operations."

At the end of the First Punic War the Romans were the masters of Sicily, a large island made prosperous by its fertile soil. Their domination of Sicily proved so profitable that in 238 B.C. the Romans seized the nearby islands of Sardinia and Corsica from the Carthaginians. In 227 B.C. the Romans turned Sicily into one overseas province and Sardinia and Corsica into another. Thus began the Roman provincial system. New praetors were created to serve as governors; their job was to keep the provinces peaceful and out of enemy hands. Roman provincial governors used local administrative arrangements. For example, in Sicily they collected the same taxes that the earlier Greek kingdom there had levied. The province's indigenous people did not become Roman citizens. Eventually, taxes the noncitizens of the provinces paid provided great wealth to the Roman state, as well as opportunities for personal enrichment to the upper-class Romans who served in high offices in the republic's provincial administrations.

The Romans also made alliances in Spain, where the Carthaginians had long had important interests. When Saguntum, a city located in the Carthaginian-dominated part of Spain, appealed to Rome for help against Carthage, the Senate responded favorably despite an apparent pledge in 226 B.C. not to interfere in Spain south of the Ebro River. When Saguntum fell to a Carthaginian siege, Roman fear of a revived and powerful Carthage led to the Second Punic War (218–201 B.C.).

The Second Punic War became a vicious life-and-death struggle for both sides. First, the Carthaginian general Hannibal (247–182 B.C.) shocked the Romans by marching troops and war elephants over the Alps into Italy. With their treacherous, snowy passes, these high mountains had seemed a secure barrier against human invasion, to say nothing of warm-climate behemoths like elephants. Then, after Hannibal had followed up some early victories by killing more than thirty thousand Romans at the battle of Cannae in 216 B.C., he hoped to provoke widespread revolts among the numerous Italian cities allied to Rome. But disastrously for him, most Italians remained loyal to Rome. His alliance with King Philip V of Macedonia (238–179 B.C.) in 215 B.C. forced the Romans to fight in Greece as well, but they refused to crack. Hannibal made Romans' lives miserable by marching up and down Italy, ravaging Roman territory for fifteen years. The best the Romans could do militarily was to engage in stalling tactics, made famous by Fabius, called "the Delayer."

War Elephant
The Carthaginian commander Hannibal astonished the Romans in the Second Punic War by marching over the Alps into Italy with elephants. The huge animals were trained to charge the enemy on the battlefield.

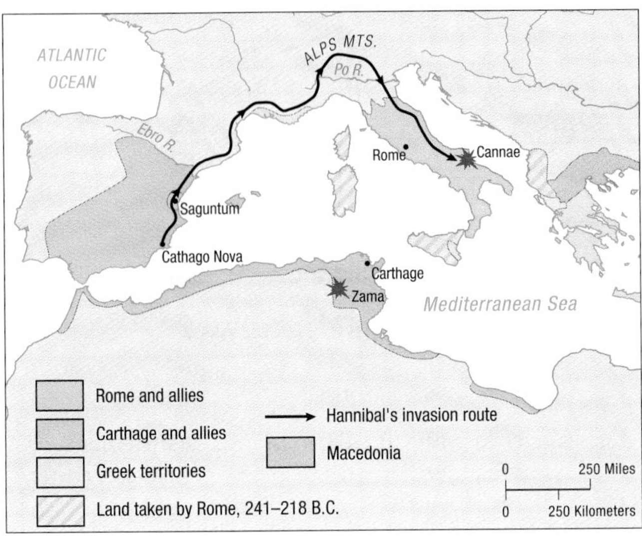

Second Punic War

Eventually Hannibal had to abandon his rampages in Italy to rush his army back to North Africa in 203 B.C., when the Romans, led by their general Scipio, daringly attacked Carthage itself. After battling in the field in Spain and Italy for thirty-four years, Hannibal was defeated in his home territory in North Africa at the battle of Zama in 202 B.C. by Scipio, who was dubbed "Africanus" to commemorate his triumph. The victorious Romans imposed a punishing peace settlement on the Carthaginians in 201 B.C., forcing them to scuttle their navy, pay huge war indemnities scheduled to last for fifty years, and relinquish their territories in Spain. The Romans subsequently had to fight a long series of wars with the indigenous Spanish peoples for control of the area, but the enormous profits reaped from Spain's mineral resources made the effort worthwhile. The revenues from Spain's silver mines, for example, financed expensive building projects in Rome.

The end of the Second Punic War allowed the Romans to resume their efforts to subjugate the Gauls (Celts) in northern Italy, who inhabited the rich plain of the Po River. By about 220 B.C., Rome controlled the Po valley. The Romans felt no qualms about their aggressive and bloody campaigns against these northern peoples, whom they lumped together as barbarians along with the Carthaginians and others to the west and north of Italy. Because the Romans respected the military prowess of the Gauls and, remembering their sack of Rome in 387 B.C., feared invasion from them, Romans considered their attacks on these peoples defensive and just, on the theory that the best defense is a good offense. Most important for their self-justification was that the Romans regarded themselves morally superior to all "barbarians." For example, they condemned the Carthaginians for their practice of occasionally sacrificing children to try to secure divine favor in times of great trouble for Carthage.

New Consequences of War

Before the First Punic War, Roman warfare had followed the normal Mediterranean pattern of short campaigns timed not to interfere with the fluctuating labor needs of agriculture. This seasonal warfare allowed men to remain home during the times of the year they needed to sow and harvest their crops and oversee the mating and culling of their flocks of animals. The campaigns of the First Punic War, prolonged year after year, disrupted this pattern. The women in farming families, like those in urban families, normally worked in and around the house, not in the fields. A farmer absent on military campaigns therefore had two choices: rely on a hired hand or slave to manage his crops and animals, or have his wife try to take on what was traditionally man's work in addition to her usual tasks of bringing water, weaving cloth, storing and preparing food, caring for the family's children, and managing the slaves.

The story of the consul Regulus, who led a Roman army to victory in Africa in 256 B.C., reveals the severe problems a man's absence could cause. When the man who managed Regulus's four-and-one-third acre farm died while the consul was away fighting Carthage, a hired hand absconded with all the farm's tools and livestock. Regulus implored the Senate to send a general to replace him so he could return home to prevent his wife and children from starving on his derelict farm. The senators took measures to save Regulus's family and property from ruin because they wanted to keep Regulus as a commander in the field, but ordinary soldiers could expect no such special aid. Women and children in the same plight as Regulus's family faced disaster because they had no marketable skills even if they moved to a city in search of work. Even unskilled jobs were scarce, because slaves

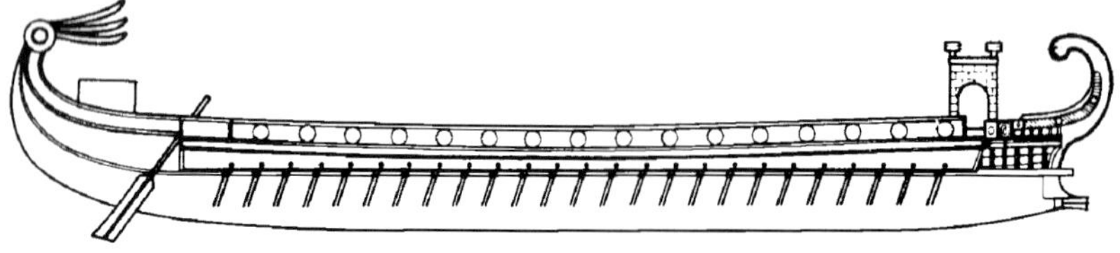

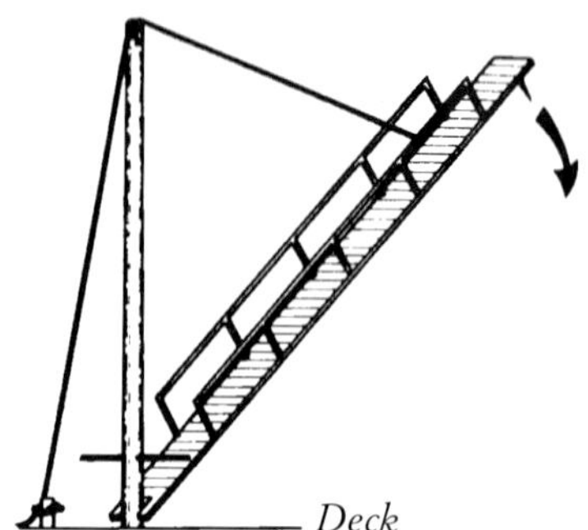

Roman Warship and "Raven"
The Romans mounted spiked boarding ramps ("ravens"), like the one depicted here, on the bows of warships. Roman soldiers could then cross onto enemy ships and turn sea battles into land battles, at which they excelled.

worked in domestic service and family members labored in small-scale manufacturing businesses run by families. Many rural women, reduced to destitution by their husbands' absence or death in war, could survive only by becoming urban prostitutes. The new style of warfare thus had the unintended consequence of disrupting the traditional forms of life in the Roman countryside, the base of Rome's agricultural economy. At the same time, women in the propertied classes amassed even more wealth through dowry and inheritance as the men in their families, who filled the elite positions in the army, brought home the greater share of booty to which their high rank entitled them under the Roman system of distributing the spoils of war.

The need to fight at sea in the Punic Wars forced Rome to develop new military technology, but these innovations applied only to weaponry. Agricultural and manufacturing technology did not benefit from the inventions that supplemented Rome's military power. Most remarkably, the Romans built a navy from scratch during the First Punic War and then overcame their inferiority to the Carthaginians in naval warfare with an ingenious technical innovation, a beam fitted with a long spike at its outer end positioned on the prows of their warships. In battle they snared enemy ships by dropping these spiked beams, called ravens because of their resemblance to the sharp-beaked bird, onto the enemy ship's deck. Roman troops then boarded the captive ship to fight hand to hand, their specialty. So successfully did the Romans learn and apply naval technology that they lost very few major sea battles in the First Punic War. One famous loss in 249 B.C. they characteristically explained as divine punishment for the consul Claudius Pulcher's sacrilege before the battle. In accordance with the religious requirement that a commander take the auspices, he had sacred chickens on board ship. Before battle could be engaged, a commander had to observe the birds feeding energetically as a sign of good fortune. When his chickens, no doubt seasick, refused to eat, Claudius hurled them overboard in a rage, sputtering, "Well, then, let them drink!" He thereupon lost 93 of his 123 ships in a spectacular naval defeat. As a result, Claudius had to stand trial at Rome and was condemned to pay a very heavy fine.

The Roman Problem in Greece

The Romans felt less confident when confronting the Greeks, as they did on a large scale in the second century B.C., than when coercing people they regarded as barbarians. They found it harder to claim the preeminence of their own customs—a typical ethnocentric chauvinism—when faced with the illustrious culture of the cities and kingdoms of Greece and Asia Minor. In 200 B.C. the Senate again sent Roman forces abroad eastward to fight Philip V of Macedonia (who had been allied with Hannibal from 215 B.C. until he made peace with Rome on favorable terms in 205 B.C.). In 200 B.C. the senators were responding to a plea from Pergamum and Rhodes to prevent an alliance between the Macedonian and Seleucid kingdoms, which these smaller powers feared would overcome them. After thrashing Philip in the Second Macedonian War (200–197 B.C.), the Roman commander Flamininus in 196 B.C. proclaimed the "freedom of the Greeks." The cities and federal leagues of Greece naturally thought the proclamation meant they could behave as they liked. They misunderstood.

The Romans rationalized that they had become the Greeks' patron through the kindness of proclaiming their freedom. The idea that this act of friendship (as the Romans defined friendship) created strong ties of obligation between the superior Roman patron and the inferior (yet liberated) Greek clients understandably eluded the Greeks. The Greek system of personal and political obligations differed vastly from the Roman client-patron system; Greeks based their foreign allegiances on the idea of contracts between independent and equal partners. As so often in history, trouble developed because two parties failed to realize that common and familiar words like *freedom* and *friendship* could carry very different implications in different societies. The Greeks, taking the Roman proclamation of freedom literally, resisted Roman efforts to intervene in the local disputes that continued to disrupt Greece and Macedonia after 196 B.C. The Romans regarded Greek intransigence as a betrayal of the client's duty to acquiesce to the patron's wishes. They were especially upset by the military support that certain Greeks solicited from King Antiochus III (c. 242–187 B.C.), the Seleucid monarch who invaded Greece after the Romans had withdrawn in 194 B.C. The Romans therefore crushed Antiochus and his allies in what is called the Syrian War (192–188 B.C.), parceled out his territories to friendlier states in the region, and again withdrew to Italy. When the energetic policy of the Macedonian king Perseus (*179–168 B.C.) led King Eumenes of Pergamum to ask Rome to return to Greece, a Roman army fought Perseus's forces in the Third Macedonian War (171–168 B.C.) and won a decisive victory at the battle of Pydna. It took yet another twenty years before Rome decisively restored peace for the benefit of its friends and supporters in Greece and Macedonia. Rome formally incorporated Macedonia and Greece into the Roman provincial system after the so-called Fourth Macedonian War (148–146 B.C.). In 146 B.C. the Roman commander Mummius destroyed the famous and wealthy city of Corinth as a calculated act of terror to show what continued resistance to Roman domination would mean.

The year 146 B.C. also saw the annihilation of Carthage at the end of the Third Punic War (149–146 B.C.). The war had begun when the Carthaginians, who had once again revived economically after paying the indemnities imposed by Rome after the Second Punic War, retaliated against their neighbor, the Numidian king Masinissa, a Roman ally who had been aggressively provoking them for some time. Carthage finally fell before the blockade of Scipio Aemilianus (185–129 B.C.), the adopted grandson of Scipio Africanus. Romans razed Carthage and converted Carthaginian territory into a Roman province. This disaster did not obliterate Punic social and cultural ways, however, and under the Roman Empire this part of North Africa became distinguished for its economic and intellectual vitality, which emerged from a synthesis of Roman and Punic traditions.

The Reasons for Roman Imperialism

The destruction of Carthage as an independent state was a response, posthumously as it happened, to the oft-expressed wish of the crusty and influential Roman senator Cato. For several years before 146 B.C., Cato had taken every opportunity in senatorial debate to intone, "Carthage must be destroyed!" Cato presumably had two reasons for his insistence. One was fear that a resurgent Carthage would again threaten Rome. Another was a desire to eliminate Carthage as a rival for the riches and glory Roman aristocrats could accumulate through expansion in the Mediterranean area. Historians seem to agree with Cato's reasoning at least, advancing two main reasons to explain Roman imperialism under the republic: fear for Roman security that induced the Senate to advise preemptive strikes against those perceived as enemies, and Roman aristocrats' eagerness for the fabulous wealth that could be gained by capturing booty as commanders in foreign military campaigns. Along with wealth came the especially valued prestige and glory of having been a successful military leader and the chance to serve as a provincial governor.

In the third and second centuries B.C., the process of Roman imperial conquest and administration beyond the shores of Italy was neither simple nor uniform. No single principle determined its course. The Romans used various methods depending on the subject peoples and their locations. In the western Mediterranean the Romans followed their conquests by immediately imposing direct rule and maintaining a permanent military presence. In Greece and Macedonia they preferred to rule indirectly, through compliant local governments. Roman aristocrats befriended their Greek counterparts to promote their common interests in keeping the peace. By 146 B.C., Rome's power extended across two-thirds the length of the Mediterranean, from Spain to Greece. In 133 B.C. the king of Pergamum, Attalus III, increased Roman power with an astonishing bequest: he left his kingdom to Rome in his will. The Romans could not have achieved so much had they not been both tenacious in fighting and adaptable in governing what they conquered.

The Consequences of Roman Expansion

Although Romans greatly expanded their power, territory, and wealth and came into contact with new peoples and cultures during their conquests, these gains came at a price. The city of Rome was no longer a close-knit and insular community. Centuries of war had also widened the gap between the social classes. Military victory brought an influx of riches to some, mostly the nobles and others at the top of the social hierarchy, enhancing their already prominent economic and social status; but the demands of military expeditions created hardships for many more men, whose service to their republic brought them increased burdens rather than rewards. The exposure to foreign peoples and their different traditions during campaigns waged far from home influenced Rome's society and culture, effecting some changes that were largely unanticipated and often controversial.

The Beginnings of Literature in Latin

Roman activity in the East greatly intensified their contact with the Greeks, which had begun when Rome expanded its power into southern Italy and Sicily. The first Roman history was written about 200 B.C.—in Greek. The earliest literature in Latin, which was exclusively poetry, also owed a debt to Greek models. By the time Romans came into frequent contact with Greek literature in the third century B.C., it had already been shaped by the Hellenistic trend toward exotic erudition. The great classics of Greek literature nevertheless still retained their appeal, such as Homer's *Iliad,* with its concentration on the pain of war, and *Odyssey,* with its tales of fabulous adventure and travel. The first work of literary Latin, in fact, was an adaptation of the *Odyssey* written sometime after the First Punic War (264–241 B.C.). Remarkably, the author was not a Roman but a Greek from Tarentum in southern Italy, Livius Andronicus. A former prisoner of war, he lived in Rome after being freed, taking his master's name. Many of the most famous early Latin authors were not native Romans. They came from all over: the poet Naevius (died 201 B.C.) from Campania, south of Rome; the poet Ennius (died 169 B.C.) from even farther south, in Calabria; the comic playwright Plautus (died c. 184 B.C.) from north of Rome, in Umbria; his fellow comedy writer Terence (c. 190–159 B.C.) from North Africa. These writers gave Latin literature an eclectic pedigree and testified to the intermingling of cultures in the Roman world—a process well under way by this time.

Literature shows clearly that Rome found strength and vitality by combining the foreign and the familiar. Plautus and Terence, for example, wrote their famous comedies in Latin for Roman audiences, but they adapted their plots from Greek comedies. They displayed their genius by keeping the settings of their comedies Greek while creating sprightly characters who were unmistakenly Roman in outlook and behavior. The comic figure of Plautus's *The Braggart Warrior,* for one, mocked the pretensions of Romans who claimed elevated social status on the basis of the number of enemies they had slaughtered.

Not all Romans applauded Greek influence. Cato, although he studied Greek himself, repeatedly thundered against the deleterious effect the "effete" Greeks had on the "sturdy" Romans. He established Latin as an appropriate language for prose with the publication of his history of Rome, *The Origins* (written between 168 and 149 B.C.), and of his treatise on running a large farm, *On Agriculture* (published about 160 B.C.). He glumly predicted that if the Romans ever became infected with Greek literature, they would lose their dominions. In fact, despite its debt to Greek literature, early Latin literature reflected traditional Roman values. Ennius, for example, was inspired by Greek epic poetry to compose his path-breaking Latin epic, *Annals,* a

Greek Style in Rome
Built in the late second century B.C., *this building is the earliest surviving marble temple in Rome. Its purely Greek style reveals how heavily Greece had influenced Rome by this date.*

poetic version of Roman history. But its contents were anything but subversive of ancestral tradition, as a famous line demonstrates: "On the ways and the men of old rests the Roman commonwealth." As it turned out, the unanticipated social and economic changes brought on by Roman imperialism were far more troubling than Greek influence on Roman culture.

The Rewards of Conquest

Rome's aristocrats reaped rich political and material rewards from Roman imperialism in the third and second centuries B.C. The increased need for commanders to lead military campaigns abroad meant more opportunities for successful men to enrich themselves from booty. By using their gains to finance public buildings, they could enhance their reputations while benefiting the general population. Building new temples, for example, was thought to increase everyone's security because the Romans believed it pleased their gods to have more shrines in their honor. In 146 B.C. a victorious general, Caecilius Metellus, paid for the first Roman temple built of marble. This temple to Jupiter started a trend toward magnificence in the architecture of Roman public buildings.

Eventually, territorial expansion created a need for military and political leadership that the usual number of magistrates could no longer handle. More and more magistrates therefore had their powers prolonged to command armies and administer the provinces. Because a provincial governor ruled by martial law, no one in the province could curb a greedy governor's appetite for graft, extortion, and plunder. Not all Roman magistrates were corrupt, of course, but some did use their unsupervised power to squeeze all they could from the provincials. Normally such offenders faced no punishment because their colleagues in the Senate preferred to excuse each other's depredations; the notorious Verres prosecuted by Cicero in 70 B.C. was a rare exception. Ostentatious, large country villas became a favorite symbol of wealth. The new taste for luxurious living became a matter of controversy because it contradicted Roman aristocratic ideals, which emphasized private moderation and frugality. Cato, for example, made his ideal Roman the military hero Manius Curius (died 270 B.C.), legendary for his meals of turnips boiled in his humble hut. The new opportunities for extravagance financed by the fruits of expansion abroad strained this tradition of austerity.

The Plight of Small Farmers in Italy

The economic basis of the republic was agriculture. For centuries, farmers working little plots had been the backbone of Roman agricultural production. These small property owners also constituted the principal source of soldiers for the Roman army (men were required to own a certain amount of property before they could enlist). The republic faced grave economic, social, and military difficulties when the successful wars of the third and second centuries B.C. ironically turned out to be disastrous for many small farmers and their families throughout Italy.

The farmers' troubles started with Hannibal's years of ravaging Italy at the end of the third century B.C., during the Second Punic War. The presence of a Carthaginian army had made it hard for farmers to keep up a regular schedule of planting and harvesting in the regions Hannibal terrorized, and Fabius's defensive tactics of delay and attrition had exacerbated their losses. Their problems multiplied in the second century B.C., when many farmers had to spend years away from their fields fighting in Rome's nearly constant military expeditions abroad. More than 50 percent of Roman adult males spent at least seven years in military service during this period, leaving their wives and children to cope as best they could. Because women were not trained to do agricultural labor, their family farms often failed unless their slaves and hired laborers (assuming they could afford such help) were diligent, honest, and lucky enough to keep production going. Many farmers and their families fell into debt and were forced to sell their land. Rich landowners then bought many small plots and created large estates. Landowners further increased their holdings by illegally occupying the public land Rome had confiscated from defeated peoples in Italy. The rich gained vast estates, called *latifundia,* worked by slaves as well as free laborers. They had a ready supply of slaves because of the many captives taken in the same wars that displaced Italy's small farmers. In the words of one modern scholar, "Roman peasant soldiers were fighting for their own displacement."

Not all regions of Italy suffered as severely as others, and some impoverished farmers and their families in the badly affected areas managed to remain in the countryside by working as day laborers for others. Many displaced people, however, emigrated to Rome, where the men looked for work as menial laborers and women might hope for some piecework making cloth—but often were forced into prostitution. This influx of desperate people swelled the poverty-level population in the city, and the difficulty these landless, urban poor had supporting themselves made them a potentially explosive element in Roman politics. They were willing to support any politician who promised to address their needs. They also represented a problem for Rome because they had to be fed to avert food riots. Like Athens in the fifth century B.C., Rome by the late second century B.C. needed to import grain to feed its huge urban population. The Senate supervised the market in grain to prevent speculation and to ensure wide distribution in times of shortage. Supplying low-priced (and eventually free) grain to Rome's poor at the state's expense became one of the most contentious issues in late republican politics.

The Splintering of Aristocratic Politics

The plight of those who had lost their land attracted the attention of the brothers Tiberius Gracchus (died 133 B.C.) and Gaius Gracchus (died 121 B.C.), aristocrats of distinguished lineage. (Their mother Cornelia was the daughter of Scipio Africanus.) Their actions in favor of dispossessed farmers were probably not altogether altruistic—they had scores to settle with their political rivals and could gain popular support by championing these farmers. But we would be overly cynical to deny their apparent sympathy with the displaced families. Tiberius, the older brother, eloquently dramatized the tragic dimensions of the situation.

> *The wild beasts that roam over Italy have their dens. . . . But the men who fight and die for Italy enjoy nothing but the air and light; without house or home they wander about with their wives and children. . . . They fight and die to protect the wealth and luxury of others; they are styled masters of the world, and have not a clod of earth they can call their own.*

As tribune in 133 B.C., Tiberius outraged the Senate by having the Tribal Assembly of the Plebeians adopt reform laws designed to redistribute public land to landless Romans without the senators' approval, a formally legal but extremely nontraditional maneuver. Also unprecedented was his convincing the assembly to depose a fellow tribune, who had been vetoing Tiberius's legislation. Tiberius further broke with tradition by circumventing the will of the Senate on the question of financing this agrarian reform. Before the Senate could render an opinion on whether to accept the bequest of all his property the recently deceased king of Pergamum, Attalus III, made to Rome, Tiberius moved that the gift be used to equip the new farms that were to be established on the redistributed land.

When Tiberius announced his intention to stand for reelection as tribune for the following year, he violated the republican constitution. Even some of his supporters abandoned him, because the "way of the elders" forbade serving consecutive terms. What happened next signaled the beginning of the end of the republic's political health. An ex-consul, Scipio Nasica, instigated a surprise attack on his cousin, Tiberius, by a group of senators and their clients. This aristocratic mob clubbed Tiberius and some of his adherents to death on Capitoline Hill in late 133 B.C.. Thus began the sorry history of murder as a political tactic in the republic.

Gaius Gracchus, tribune in 123 B.C. and again in 122 B.C., despite tradition, also initiated reforms that threatened the Roman elite, including keeping alive the agrarian reforms initiated by his brother. He also introduced laws to assure grain to Rome's citizens at subsidized prices, to mandate public works projects throughout Italy to provide employment for the poor, and to found colonies abroad. Most revolutionary of all were his proposals to give Roman citizenship to some Italians and to establish jury trials for senators accused of corruption as provincial governors. The citizenship proposal failed. The creation of a system to prosecute corrupt senators became an intensely controversial issue because it threatened the power of the ruling oligarchy in the Senate to protect its own members and their families. The new juries were to be manned not by senators but by members of the social class called *equites* (meaning "equestrians" or "knights"). These were wealthy men without public careers, who came mostly from the local landed aristocracy with family origins outside Rome proper. In the earliest republic the equestrians had been what the word suggests—men rich enough to own horses for cavalry service. But by this time equestrians had become a kind of second-class aristocrats, whose political ambitions were often thwarted by the dominant aristocrats in the Senate. Senators drew a distinction between themselves and equestrians by maintaining that it was unseemly for a senator to soil his hands in commerce, an activity some equestrians embraced rather than pursue their limited opportunities for a public career. A law passed by the tribune Claudius in 218 B.C. made it illegal for senators and their sons to own large-capacity cargo ships, but senators nevertheless sometimes did have commercial interests. They masked their income from this source by clandestinely employing intermediaries or favored slaves to do the work and then return the profits to their senatorial backers. The legislation authorizing equestrians to compose juries to try senators accused of malfeasance in the provinces marked the emergence of the equestrians as a political force in Roman politics, to the dismay of the Senate.

Gaius acquired a bodyguard to try to protect himself against violence from senatorial enemies bent on blocking his program. The senators in 121 B.C. used the violence they had themselves initiated as an excuse to issue the "ultimate decree" for the first time, a vote of the Senate advising the consuls to take whatever measures were necessary to defend the republic. The consul Opimius was therefore granted implicit permission to use military force inside the city of Rome, where magistrates ordinarily had no such power. To escape arrest, Gaius had one of his slaves cut his throat. The deaths of Tiberius and Gaius Gracchus prompted the disintegration of the cohesive oligarchy that had dominated Roman government. Both the reforming brothers and their murderers came from the upper class, which could no longer govern through a consensus that protected its interests. From now on, Roman aristocrats increasingly saw themselves either as supporters of the *populares,* who sought power by promoting the interests of the common people (*populus*), or as members of the *optimates,* who supported the "best people" (the *optimi,* meaning the nobles) and relied on aristocratic political sentiment. Some identified with one faction or the other out of genuine allegiance to its policies. Others picked a group to support based simply on political expediency; depending on which side promoted their own political advancement, they would pretend to be sincere proponents of either the people or the upper class. In any case this division of the Roman upper class into political factions persisted as a source of friction and violence until Augustus finally imposed peace and the unity of one-man rule at the end of the first century B.C.

The Rise of the "New Man"

Even as Rome's traditional ruling elite was losing its cohesiveness, the republic continued to need effective military leaders. Seventy thousand slaves from the *latifundia* in Sicily revolted from 134 to 131 B.C. A war with an ungrateful client king in North Africa, Jugurtha, began in 112 B.C. Not long after, formidable bands of Celtic tribesmen began to menace the northern border of Italy. In response to the disarray of the upper class and these threats, a new force arose in Roman politics—the man not born into the charmed circle of the highest nobility at Rome but nevertheless able to force his way to fame, fortune, influence, and the consulship by sheer ability as a military leader. This "new man" challenged the traditional political dominance of the Roman aristocracy.

The Origin of Client Armies

The man who set this new political force in motion, Gaius Marius (c. 157–86 B.C.) came not from Rome but from the wealthy aristocracy of Arpinum, a town in central Italy. Ordinarily, an equestrian like Marius had little chance of cracking the ranks of Rome's ruling oligarchy of noble families, who virtually monopolized the office of consul. The best an equestrian could usually hope for in a public career was to advance to the junior ranks of the Senate as the dutiful client of a powerful noble. Fortunately for Marius, however, Rome at the end of the second century B.C. had a pressing need for men who could lead an army to victory. Marius made his reputation by running for office in the interests of noble patrons, marrying above his social rank into a famous patrician family (from whose line Julius Caesar would be born in 100 B.C.), and serving with distinction in the North African war. Capitalizing on his military record and popular dissatisfaction with the nobles' conduct of the war against Jugurtha, Marius won election as one of the consuls for 107 B.C. In Roman terms this election made him a "new man"—that is, the first man in the history of his family to become consul. "New men" were rare in the republic. Marius had gained distinction because of his military prowess. His success, first as a general in the African war and then against the invasions of Italy by the "barbarian" Teutones and Cimbri, led to his election as consul for an unprecedented six terms by 100 B.C., including consecutive terms, a practice previously illegal.

So celebrated was Marius that the Senate voted him a triumph, Rome's ultimate military honor. On the day of a triumph the general who had earned this award rode through the streets of Rome in a military chariot. His face was painted red for reasons the Romans could no longer remember. Huge crowds cheered him. His army traditionally lambasted him with off-color jokes, perhaps to ward off the evil eye at this moment of supreme glory. For a similar reason a slave rode behind him in the chariot and kept whispering in his ear, "Look behind you, and remember that you are a mortal." For a former equestrian like Marius to be granted a triumph was a mammoth social coup.

Despite his triumph, the "best people" never fully accepted Marius. They saw him as an upstart and a threat to their preeminence. Marius's mainstay of support came from the common people and wealthy equestrians, who favored his attempt to break into the nobility or were concerned that the incompetence of senatorial leaders would ruin their economic interests abroad. His dramatic reform of entrance requirements for the army made him particularly popular with poor men. Previously, only men with property could enroll as soldiers. Marius opened the ranks even to proletarians. For these men who had virtually nothing, serving in the army meant an opportunity to better their lot by acquiring booty under a successful general. They willingly traded the risk of getting killed in combat for a chance to seize some property for themselves while on military campaigns. The republic at this time made no provisions for regular rewards to ex-soldiers; their fortunes depended on the success and generosity of their general, who could keep the lion's share of booty for himself and his high-ranking officers. Proletarian troops naturally felt grateful to a commander who led them to victory and then generously divided the spoils with them. Troop loyalty became more and more directed at their commander, not to the republic, and poor Roman soldiers began to behave as an army of clients following their patron, the general. Marius, who created this potential source of power, was only the first to use it to promote his own career. He lost his political importance soon after 100 B.C., when he no longer commanded armies and had alienated his own supporters. His enemies among the *optimates* succeeded in keeping him from power. When others who came after Marius proved even more successful in employing client armies as tools in political struggles, the fall of the republic could no longer be avoided.

Uprisings and the War with the Allies

Rome's Italian allies shared in the bounty of military victory, but because most of them lacked Roman citizenship, they had no voice in decisions concerning Roman domestic or foreign policy, even when their interests were directly involved. This political disability made them increasingly unhappy as wealth from conquest piled up in Italy in the late republic. The allies wanted a share in the growing prosperity of the upper class. Gaius Gracchus had seen the wisdom of including the allies and tried to extend Roman citizenship to the loyal allies of Rome in Italy, who would have increased his own power by becoming his clients. His enemies, however, had convinced the Roman people that they would lessen their own political and economic power by granting these people citizenship.

The allies' discontent finally erupted in the Social War of 91–87 B.C. (so called because the Latin word for "ally" is *socius*). The Italians formed a confederacy to fight Rome, minted their own coins to finance their operations, and died valiantly in the field. One ancient source claims the war took three hundred thousand casualties. In the end the Roman army proved victorious in battle, but the allies won the political war. The Romans granted the Italians the citizenship for which they had begun their rebellion. From this time on the freeborn peoples of Italy south of the Po River enjoyed the privileges of Roman citizenship. Most important, if their men made their way to Rome, they could vote in the assemblies. The bloodshed of the Social War was the unfortunate price paid to reestablish Rome's early principle of seeking strength through including people in the political process through citizenship.

Farther from Rome, the conquered peoples of Asia Minor chafed under Roman rule. King Mithridates VI of Pontus (120–63 B.C.) won the support of these populations for a rebellion because they so bitterly resented the notorious Roman tax collectors. Groups of Romans from the class of the *equites* formed private companies that bid for provincial tax contracts. Such a group would agree to deliver a set amount of revenue to the Roman republic in return for the right to collect taxes in a certain province. These "tax farmers," as they are called, could keep as profit any additional amount their collectors, called publicans, managed to obtain, an arrangement that gave them great incentive to exploit the provincials. It is no wonder that Mithridates found a sympathetic ear in Asia Minor for his charge that the Romans were "the common enemies of all mankind." He reportedly capitalized on these hostile feelings to engineer the slaughter of thousands of Roman residents in Asia Minor and create a crisis for Roman authority there in the First Mithridatic War (88–85 B.C.).

The Demise of Roman Republic Tradition

The Social War and the threat from Mithridates brought a ruthless Roman noble named Lucius Cornelius Sulla (c. 138–78 B.C.) to power. He came from a patrician family that had lost much of its status. Anxious to restore his line's prestige, Sulla had first schemed to advance his career while serving under Marius against Jugurtha. His subsequent military success against the allies in the Social War propelled him to the prominence he coveted: he won election as consul for 88 B.C. The Senate promptly rewarded him with the mission of fighting Mithridates.

Marius, now the jealous enemy of his former subordinate Sulla, connived to have the command against Mithridates transferred to himself just as Sulla was marshaling an army. Sulla's reaction to this setback showed that he understood the source of power that Marius had gained by creating a client army. Instead of accepting the loss of the command, Sulla led his Roman army against Rome itself. All his officers except one deserted him in horror at

The Kingdom of Mithridates VI of Pontus

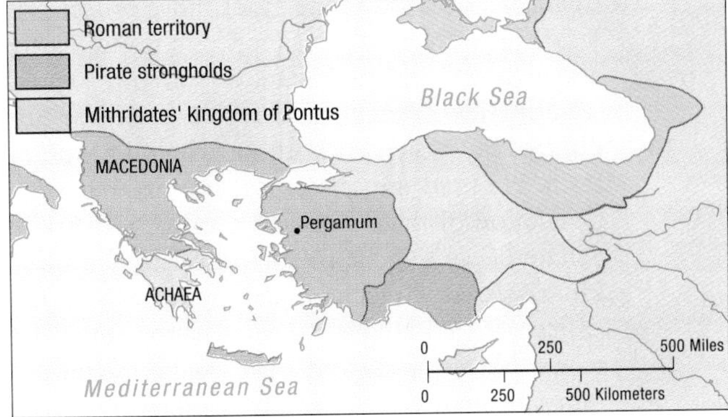

this unthinkable outrage. His common soldiers, by contrast, followed him to a man. Neither they nor their commander shrank from starting a bloody civil war. When Sulla took Rome, he killed or exiled his opponents. His men went on a rampage in the capital city. He then led them off to campaign in Asia Minor despite a summons to stand trial.

When Sulla marched against Mithridates, Marius and his friends regained power in Rome and embarked on their own reign of terror. Murderous violence had become frighteningly routine in Roman politics. Marius soon died of natural causes, but his friends held undisputed power until 83 B.C., when Sulla returned to Italy after forcing Mithridates to make peace and provide funds for Sulla's army. Another civil war ensued. Sulla's enemies joined some of the Italians, especially the Samnites from central and southern Italy, to hold him off for nearly two years. The climactic battle of the war took place in late 82 B.C. at the Colline Gate of Rome. The Samnite general whipped his troops into a frenzy against Sulla by shouting, "The last day is at hand for the Romans! These wolves that have made such ravages upon Italian liberty will never vanish until we have cut down the forest that harbors them."

Unfortunately for the Samnites, they lost the battle and the war. Sulla proceeded to exterminate them and distribute their territory to his supporters. He also brutally massacred his opponents at Rome by means of proscription. This practice, which became a frequent weapon in Roman civil war, meant posting a list of those supposedly guilty of treasonable crimes so that anyone could hunt them down and execute them. Because the property of those proscribed was confiscated, Sulla's supporters fraudulently added to the list the name of anyone whose wealth they desired. The Senate in terror appointed Sulla dictator without any limitation of term. He used the office to legitimize his reorganization of the government, under which the Senate became the supreme power in the state. He reversed Gracchan jury reforms so that equestrians no longer judged senators. He tried to disable the tribunate by forbidding the tribunes from offering legislation without the prior approval of the Senate and barring any man who became a tribune from holding any other magistracy thereafter. Minimum age limits were imposed for holding the various posts in the sequence of the course of offices. In short, Sulla's vision was that of a state completely dominated by the "best people"—a repudiation of the idea of the "new man."

Convinced by an old prophecy that he had only a short time to live, Sulla retired to private life in 79 B.C. and indeed died the next year. His remarkable career had starkly revealed the strengths and the weaknesses of the social and political traditions of the later republic. First, success in war had come to mean profits for common soldiers and commanders alike, primarily from selling prisoners of war into slavery and seizing booty. This incentive to war made it all the harder to resolve problems peaceably. Many Romans were so poor that they preferred war to a life without prospects. Sulla's troops in 88 B.C., for example, did not want to disband because they had their eyes on the riches they hoped to win in a war against Mithridates. Second, the pervasiveness of the client-patron system meant that poor soldiers felt stronger ties of obligation to their general, who acted as their patron, than to their republic. Sulla's men obeyed his order to attack Rome because they owed obedience to him as their patron and could expect benefits in return. Sulla obliged them by permitting the plundering of Rome and of the vast riches of Asia Minor.

Finally, the concern of aristocrats with public status worked both for and against the republic's stability. When the desire for status motivated important men to seek office to promote the welfare of the population as a whole—the traditional ideal of an aristocratic public career—it was a powerful force for social peace and general prosperity. But pushed to its extreme, as in the case of Sulla, the concern for personal standing based on personal prestige and individual wealth could overshadow all considerations of public service. Sulla in 88 B.C. simply could not bear to lose the glory and status that a victory over Mithridates would bring. He preferred to initiate a civil war rather than to see his cherished status diminished.

The republic was doomed once its leaders and its followers forsook the "way of the elders" that valued respect for the peace and prosperity of the republic and its constitution above personal gain. Sulla's career helps to reveal how the social and political structure of the republic contained the seeds of its own destruction.

The End of the Republic

The great generals whose names dominate the history of the republic after Sulla all took him as their model: while professing allegiance to the state, they relentlessly pursued their own advancement. The motivation—that a Roman aristocrat could never have too much glory or too much wealth—was a corruption of the finest ideals of the republic. In their fevered pursuit of self-aggrandizement they ignored the honored tradition of public service to the commonwealth. Pompey and Caesar gained glory and prodigious amounts of money for themselves, but the brutal civil war they eventually fought against each other's armies ruined the republic and opened the way for the return of monarchy to Rome after an absence of nearly five hundred years.

The Irregular Career of Pompey

Gnaeus Pompey (106–48 B.C.) had forced his way onto the scene in 83 B.C. when Sulla first returned to Italy after defeating Mithridates. Only twenty-three years old at the time, he gathered a private army from his father's clients in Italy and joined Sulla, for whom he won victories in Italy and, soon thereafter, in Sicily and North Africa, where Sulla's rivals had fled. These successes meant that Sulla could not refuse Pompey's bold demand for a triumph. A triumph honoring such a young man, who had never held a formal magistracy, shattered another ancient tradition of the republic. Pompey did not have to wait his turn for acclaim or earn his accolades only after years of service. Because he was so powerful, he could demand his stamp of glory from Sulla on the spot. As Pompey said to Sulla, "People worship the rising, not the setting, sun." Pompey's "triumph" betrayed the hollowness of Sulla's vision of the Roman republic. Sulla had proclaimed a return to the rule of the "best people" and, according to him, Rome's finest political traditions. Instead he fashioned a regime controlled by violence and power politics. His government reforms disintegrated in the decade after his death. A modern historian offers a blunt assessment: "The Sullan oligarchy had a fatal flaw: it governed with a guilty conscience."

The course of Pompey's subsequent career shows how the traditional checks and balances of republican government failed to operate in the late republic. After helping suppress a rebellion in Spain and a massive slave revolt in Italy led by the escaped gladiator Spartacus, Pompey demanded and won election to the consulship in 70 B.C., well before he had reached the legal age of forty-two or even held any elective office. Three years later he received a command with unprecedented powers to exterminate the pirates currently infesting the Mediterranean. He smashed them in a matter of months. This success in 67 B.C. made him wildly popular with the urban poor at Rome, who depended on a steady flow of imported grain subsidized by the state; with the wealthy commercial and shipping interests, which depended on safe sea lanes; and with coastal communities everywhere, which had suffered from the pirates' raids. The next year the command against Mithridates, who was still stirring up trouble in Asia Minor, was taken away from the general Lucullus so it could be given to Pompey. Lucullus had made himself unpopular with his troops by curbing their looting of the province and with the publicans by regulating their extortion of the defenseless provincials. Pompey conquered Asia Minor and the ancient Near East in a series of bold campaigns. He marched as far south as Jerusalem, which he captured in 63 B.C. When he then annexed Syria as a province, he initiated Rome's formal presence in that part of the world and created a client kingdom.

Pompey's success in the East was spectacular. People compared him to Alexander the Great and referred to him as *Magnus* ("Great"). Not one for self-effacement, he boasted that he had increased Rome's provincial revenues by 70 percent. He distributed money equal to twelve and a half years' pay each to his soldiers. Moreover, during his time in the East he operated largely on his own initiative. He never consulted the Senate when he set up new political arrangements for the territories he conquered. For all practical purposes he behaved more like an independent king than a Roman magistrate. He had pithily expressed his attitude early in his career when replying to some foreigners after they had objected to his treatment as unjust. "Stop quoting the laws to us," he told them. "We carry swords."

Pompey's enemies at Rome feared him and tried to strengthen their own positions while he was abroad. His principal foes among them were two unscrupulous aristocrats, the fabulously wealthy Marcus Licinius Crassus (died 53 B.C.), who had defeated Spartacus, and the young Julius Caesar (100–44 B.C.). They promoted themselves as *populares,* concerned with the plight of the common people. And there was much cause for concern. The population of Rome had soared to perhaps a million people. Hundreds of thousands of them lived crowded together in shabby apartment buildings no better than slums. Work was hard to find. Many people subsisted on the dole of grain the government distributed at a subsidized low price. The streets of Rome were dangerous because the city had no police force. To make matters worse, Rome was grappling with special economic problems in the 60s B.C., perhaps a result of the falling value of land that Sulla's confiscations had created by flooding the market with properties for sale. Credit seems to have been in short supply at the very time those in financial difficulties were trying to borrow their way back to respectability.

The conspiracy of Lucius Sergius Catilina in 63 B.C. reveals to what lengths debt and poverty could drive people. Catiline, as he is known in English, was a debt-ridden aristocrat who rallied a band of fellow upper-class debtors and victims of Sulla's confiscations to his cause. Frustrated in his attempts to win the consulship, he planned to use violence to seize tyrannical power, with the aim of redistributing wealth and property to his supporters after their victory. The consul Cicero, however, discovered the plot before the conspirators could murder him and the other consul and forced them to flee to northern Italy, where a Roman army killed them in battle. Even if their misguided plot had brought them power, Catiline and his co-conspirators never had a realistic chance of redressing their grievances. They would have had to kill all the currently successful property owners! Nevertheless, their futile effort demonstrates the desperation of many people at Rome, even aristocrats, during this period.

When Pompey returned from the East in 62 B.C., the "best people" shortsightedly refused to support his settlement of the ancient Near East or the reward of land to the veterans of his army. This setback forced Pompey to negotiate with Caesar and Crassus. In 60 B.C. these three formed an informal troika, commonly called the First Triumvirate (that is, "coalition of three men"), to advance their own interests. They succeeded. Pompey got laws to confirm his eastern arrangements and give land to his veterans; Caesar got the consulship for 59 B.C. along with a special command in Gaul for five years; Crassus got financial breaks for the Roman tax collectors in Asia Minor, whose support helped make him powerful and in whose business he had a stake. This astounding coalition of former political enemies provided each triumvir (member of the triumvirate) a means for achieving his personal ambitions: Pompey wanted status as patron to his troops and to the territories he had conquered; Caesar wanted the consulship and the chance to win glory and booty from fighting "barbarians"; and Crassus wanted increased financial profits for himself and his clients so he could remain politically competitive with Pompey and Caesar, whose military and political reputations far exceeded his. The First Triumvirate was an association formed only for the advantage of the moment. Because its three members shared no common philosophy of governing, their cooperation lasted only as long as they continued to profit from it personally.

The first triumvirs recognized the potentially transitory nature of their coalition, and they used a popular form of political alliance to try to give their arrangement some permanence: they contracted marriages among one another. Women were the pawns traded back and forth in these alliances. In 59 B.C., for example, Caesar married his daughter Julia to Pompey. She had been engaged to another man, but this political marriage now took precedence to create a bond between Caesar and Pompey. Pompey simultaneously soothed Julia's jilted fiance by having him marry Pompey's daughter, who had been engaged to yet somebody else. Through these marital machinations, the two powerful antagonists now had a common interest: the fate of Julia, Caesar's only daughter and Pompey's new wife. (He had divorced his second wife after Caesar

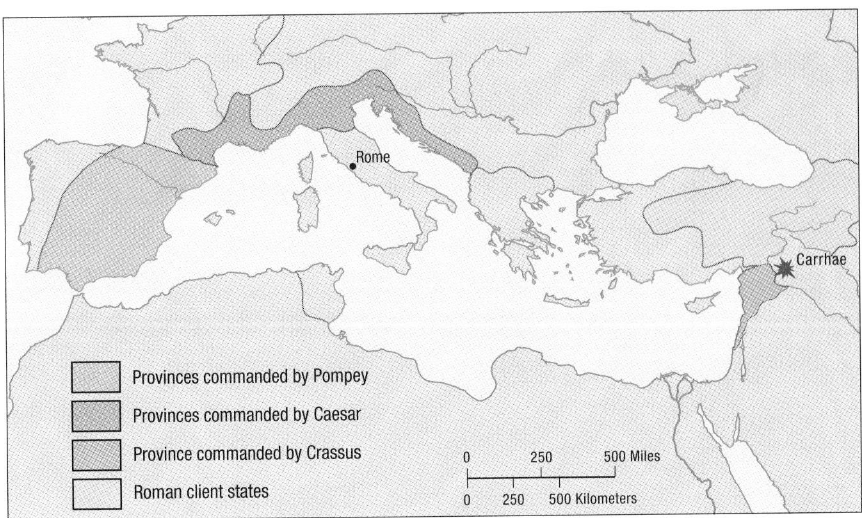

Provincial Commands of the "First Triumvirate"

allegedly had seduced her.) Pompey and Julia apparently fell deeply in love in their arranged marriage. As long as Julia lived, Pompey's affection for her helped restrain him from an outright break with her father, Caesar. But when she died in childbirth in 54 B.C., the bond linking Pompey and Caesar was severed.

The Victory of Caesar

Caesar had left Rome to take up a command in Gaul (modern France) in 58 B.C. For the next nine years he attacked one "barbarian" people after another throughout what is now France, the western part of Germany, and even the southern end of Britain. The slaves and booty his army seized not only paid off the enormous debts he had incurred in his political career but also enriched him and his soldiers. For this reason above all, his troops loved him. His political enemies at Rome dreaded him even more as his military successes mounted; his supporters meanwhile tried to prepare the ground for his eventual return to Rome. The two sides' rivalry soon exploded into violence. By the mid-50s B.C., political gangs of young men regularly roamed the streets of Rome in search of opponents to beat up or murder. Street fighting reached such a pitch in 53 B.C. that it was impossible to hold elections, and no consuls were chosen that year. The triumvirate completely dissolved that same year with the death of Crassus in battle at Carrhae in northern Mesopotamia; in an attempt to win the military glory his career so conspicuously lacked, he had led a Roman army across the Euphrates River to fight the Parthians, an Iranian people whose military aristocracy headed by a king ruled a vast territory stretching from the Euphrates to the Indus River. In 52 B.C. the most extreme *optimates*—Caesar's most determined enemies—took the extraordinary step of having Pompey appointed as sole consul for the year. The traditions of republic government had plainly fallen into the dust. When Caesar prepared to return to Rome in 49 B.C., he too wanted a special arrangement to protect himself. He demanded the consulship for 48 B.C.

When the Senate responded by ordering him to surrender his command, Caesar, like Sulla before him, led his army against Rome. As he crossed the Rubicon River in northern Italy in early 49 B.C., he uttered the famous words signaling the start of a bitter civil war: "The die is cast." His troops followed him without hesitation, and the people of the towns and countryside of Italy cheered him on enthusiastically. He had many backers in Rome, too, among the many to whom he had lent money or political support. Some of those glad to hear of his coming were ruined aristocrats, who hoped to recoup their once-great fortunes by backing Caesar against the rich. These were in fact the people whom Caesar had always refused to help politically or financially, saying to them, "What you need is a civil war."

The enthusiastic response of the masses to Caesar's advance induced Pompey and Caesar's enemies in the Senate to transport their forces to

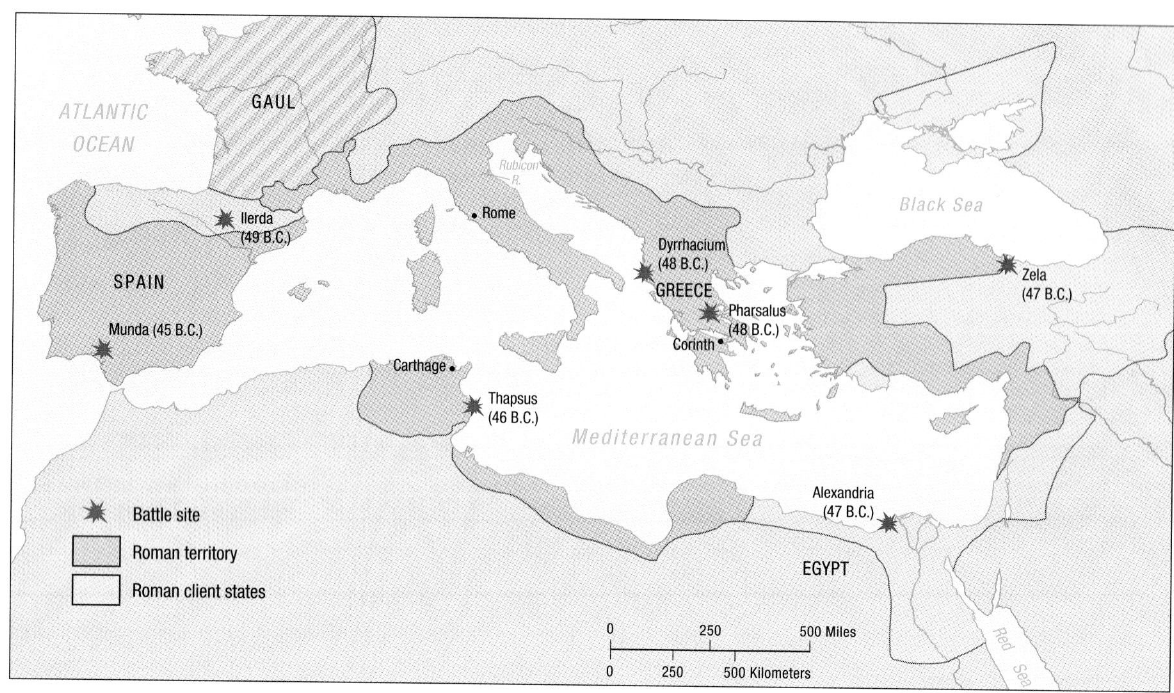

Julius Caesar's Battles During the Civil War (49–45 B.C.)

Greece for training before facing Caesar's experienced troops. Caesar entered Rome peacefully, soon departed to defeat the army his enemies had raised in Spain, and then followed Pompey to Greece in 48 B.C. There he nearly lost the war when Pompey cut off his supplies with a blockade. But his loyal soldiers stuck with him even when they were reduced to eating bread made from roots. When Pompey saw what Caesar's troops were willing to subsist on he lamented, "I am fighting wild beasts." The high morale of Caesar's army and Pompey's weak generalship eventually combined to bring Caesar a stunning victory at the battle of Pharsalus in 48 B.C. Pompey fled to Egypt, where he was treacherously murdered by the ministers of the boy-king Ptolemy XIII (63–47 B.C.), who had earlier exiled his sister and co-ruler, Queen Cleopatra VII (69–30 B.C.), and supported Pompey in the war. Caesar followed Pompey to Egypt and won a difficult campaign against Ptolemy's army that ended with the drowning of the pharaoh in the Nile and the return to the Egyptian throne of Cleopatra, who had begun a love affair with Caesar. He next had to spend three years battling his remaining Roman enemies in North Africa and Spain. But by 45 B.C. he had won the civil war. Now he faced the intractable problem of ruling Rome.

Caesar's predicament had deep roots. Experience had shown that only a sole ruler could end the chaotic violence of factional politics in the first century B.C., but the oldest tradition of the republic was its abhorrence of monarchy. Cato had best expressed the Roman aristocrats' feelings about monarchy: "A king," he quipped, "is an animal that feeds on human flesh." Caesar's solution was to rule as king in everything but name. He first had himself appointed dictator in 48 B.C., with his term in this traditionally temporary office eventually extended to a lifetime tenure around 44 B.C. "I am not a king," he insisted. But the distinction was meaningless. As dictator he controlled the government despite the appearance of normal procedures. Elections for offices continued, for example, but Caesar manipulated the results by recommending candidates to the assemblies, which his supporters dominated. Naturally his recommendations were followed. His policies as Rome's ruler were ambitious and broad. He reduced debt moderately; limited the number of people eligible for subsidized grain; initiated a large program of public works, including the construction of public libraries; established colonies for his veterans in Italy and abroad; reestablished Corinth and Carthage as commercial centers; proclaimed standard constitutions for Italian towns; and extended citizenship to such non-Romans as the Cisalpine Gauls (those on the Italian side of the Alps). He also admitted non-Italians to the Senate when he expanded its membership from 600 to 900. Unlike Sulla, he did not proscribe his enemies. Instead he prided himself on his clemency, whose recipients were, by Roman custom, bound to be his grateful clients. In return, he received unprecedented honors, such as a special golden seat in the Senate house and the renaming of the seventh month of the year after him (*Julius*, hence our *July*). He also regularized the Roman calendar by initiating a year of 365 days, which was based on an ancient Egyptian calendar and roughly forms the basis for our modern calendar.*

His office and his honors pleased most Romans but outraged the narrow circle of the "best people." These men resented their exclusion from power and their domination by one of their own, a "traitor" who had deserted to the other side in the perpetual conflict between the republic's rich and poor. A band of senators consequently stabbed Julius Caesar to death on March 15 (the Ides of March), 44 B.C. in the Senate house at the foot of a statue of Pompey. The liberators, as they called themselves, had no concrete plans for governing Rome. They apparently believed the traditional political system of the republic would somehow reconstitute itself without any action on their part and without further violence; in their profound naiveté they ignored the bloody reality of the previous forty years, starting with Sulla. In fact, rioting broke out at Caesar's funeral as the common people vented their anger against the upper class that had robbed them of their hero. Far from presenting a united front, the aristocrats resumed their squabbles with one another to secure political power. By 44 B.C. the republic was damaged beyond repair.

*This so-called Julian calendar introduced an extra day every four years (the idea of a "leap year"), but this modification still left a discrepancy between the calendar and the solar year. In 1582 the Roman Catholic church under Pope Gregory XIII introduced the modern (Gregorian) calendar, which eliminated leap years in century years not evenly divisible by 400, such as 1800 and 1900. Protestant European countries adopted the Gregorian calendar only much later—Great Britain, for example, in 1752. In Russia the Julian calendar remained in effect until 1918, after the Bolshevik Revolution.

Commemorating the Murder of Caesar *Julius Caesar's assassins minted this coin in 43 B.C. The inscription says, "Ides of March," the date of the murder. The cap between the daggers symbolized liberty; the conspirator Brutus had his own portrait stamped on the other side of the coin.*

Realism in Late Republican Literature and Portraiture

Because the sources of creativity are so diverse, historians necessarily must be cautious about postulating overly specific relationships between authors' and artists' works and the events of their times. The events of the late republic, however, were directly reflected in some of the contemporary literature. In the work of other authors, as in sculptural portraiture, we can suspect, although not prove, a connection to the conditions of the times.

Contemporary references to Roman affairs provided directly relevant material for some of the poems of Catullus (c. 84–54 B.C.). He moved to Rome from the province of Cisalpine Gaul in northern Italy, where his family had been sufficiently prominent to entertain Julius Caesar when he had been governor of that area. That connection did not prevent Catullus from including Caesar among the politicians of the era whose sexual behavior he savaged with his witty and explicit poetry. Catullus also wrote poems on more timeless themes, love above all. He employed a literary style popular among a circle of poets who modeled their Latin poems on the elegant Greek poetry of Hellenistic authors such as Callimachus. Catullus's most famous series of love poems concerned his passion for a married woman named Lesbia, whom he entreated to think only of the pleasures of the present: "Let us live, my Lesbia, and love, and value at one penny all the talk of stern old men. Suns can set and rise again: we, when once our brief light has set, must sleep one never-ending night. Give me a thousand kisses, then a hundred, then a thousand more. . . . "

Sculpture for a Roman Couple's Grave
Wealthy Romans frequently commissioned sculptures of themselves for their tombs, such as this one showing a couple standing together to signify their marriage bond.

Catullus's call to live for the moment, heedless of convention, well suited a time when the turmoil of Rome could make the concerns of tradition seem irrelevant.

The many prose works of Cicero, the master of rhetoric, also directly concerned events of his time. Fifty-eight of his speeches survive in the revised versions he published, and their eloquence and clarity established the style that later European prose authors tried to match when writing polished Latin—the common language of government, theology, literature, and science throughout Europe for the next fifteen hundred years and more. Cicero also wrote many letters to his family and friends in which he commented frankly on political infighting and his motives in pursuing his own self-interest. The over 900 surviving letters offer a vivid portrait of Cicero's joys, sorrow, worries, pride, and love for his daughter. For no other figure from the ancient world do we have such copious and revealing personal material.

During periods when he temporarily withdrew from public affairs because his political opponents held the upper hand, Cicero wrote numerous works on political science, philosophy, ethics, and theology. He was not an original thinker in philosophy and ethics, taking his inspiration mainly from Greek philosophers, but he adapted their ideas to Roman life and infused his writings on these topics with a deep understanding of the need to appreciate the uniqueness of each human personality. His doctrine of *humanitas* ("humanness, the quality of humanity") combined various strands of Greek philosophy, especially Stoicism, to express an ideal for human life based on generous and honest treatment of others and an abiding commitment to morality derived from natural law (the right that exists for all people by nature, independent of the differing laws and customs of different societies). This ideal would exercise a powerful and enduring influence on later Western ethical philosophy. Cicero's legacy comes from his philosophical works and the style of his Latin prose, not from his distinguished political career. What he passed on to later ages was perhaps the most attractive ideal to come from ancient Greece and Rome: the spirit of *humanitas*.

The poet Lucretius (c. 94–55 B.C.) indirectly reflected the uncertainty and violence of his times. By explaining the nature of matter as composed of tiny, invisible particles called atoms, his long poem called *On the Nature of Things* sought to dispel the fear of death, which in his words, served only to feed "the running sores of life." Dying, his poem taught, simply meant the dissolution of the union of atoms, which had come together temporarily to make up a person's body. There could be no eternal punishment or pain after death, indeed no existence at all, because a person's soul, itself made up of atoms, perished along with the body. Lucretius took this "atomic theory" of the nature of existence from the work of the Greek philosopher Epicurus (341–270 B.C.), whose views on the atomic character of matter were in turn derived from the work of the fifth-century B.C. thinkers Leucippus and Democritus. Although we do not know when he began to compose his poem, Lucretius was still working on it at Rome during the 50s B.C. when politically motivated violence added a powerful new danger to life in Rome. Romans in Lucretius's time had ample reasons to need reassurance that death had no sting.

We might also surmise that the starkly realistic style of Roman portraiture of men in the first century B.C. reflected a recognition of life's harshness in this turbulent period, even for those wealthy enough to have likenesses of themselves sculpted in marble. The Roman upper-class tradition of making death masks of ancestors and displaying them in their homes presumably contributed to the artistic style of realistic portraiture. Another influence on this veristic, or "truthful," style may have been the taste in Hellenistic Greek sculpture for unflattering representations of human stereotypes, such as drunkards or elderly people. In any case the many portraits of specific individuals that survive from this era did not try to hide unflattering features. Long noses, receding chins, deep wrinkles, bald heads, careworn looks—all these were sculpted. Portraits of women from the period, by contrast, were generally more idealized, and children were not portrayed until the early empire. Because either the men depicted by the portraits or their families paid for the busts, they presumably wanted the subject's experience of life to show. Perhaps this insistence on realism mirrored the toll exacted on men who participated in the brutal arena of late republican politics.

Conclusion

The greatest challenge in studying the Roman Republic is to understand how such a powerful and militarily successful state lost its political stability. From its beginnings the republic flourished because the small farmers of Italy produced agricultural surpluses. These surpluses supported a growth in population that supplied the soldiers for a strong army of citizens and allies. The Roman willingness to endure great losses of life and property helped make this army invincible in prolonged conflicts. Rome might lose battles, but never wars. Because Rome's wars initially brought profits, peace seemed a wasted opportunity. Aristocratic commanders especially liked war because they could win glory and riches to enhance their status in Rome's social hierarchy.

But the continued wars of the republic had unexpected consequences that spelled disaster. Many of the small landowners on whom Italy's prosperity depended were ruined. When the dispossessed flocked to Rome, which had a temporarily booming economy because of the influx of booty from overseas, they created a new, unstable political force: the urban mob subject to the violent swings of the urban economy. The upper class escalated their competition with each other for the increased career opportunities constant war presented. These rivalries became unmanageable when successful generals began to extort advantages for themselves instead of the republic by acting as patrons to their client armies of poor troops. In this dog-eat-dog atmosphere, violence and murder became the preferred means for settling political disputes. But violent actions provoked violent responses. The powerful ideas of Cicero's ethical philosophy, which greatly influenced later thinkers, went ignored in the murderous conflicts of the civil wars that wracked Rome. No reasonable Roman could have been optimistic about the chances for an enduring peace in the aftermath of Caesar's assassination. That Augustus would forge such a peace less than fifteen years later would have seemed an impossible dream in 44 B.C. But history is full of surprises.

Suggestions For Further Reading

Source Materials

Lefkowitz, Mary R., and Maureen B. Fant. *Women's Life in Greece and Rome.* 1982. A collection of primary sources arranged by topics.

Lewis, Naphtali, and Meyer Reinhold. *Roman Civilization: Sourcebook I: The Republic.* 1990. An indispensable collection of annotated primary sources on a wide variety of subjects.

Livy. *The Early History of Rome; Rome and Italy; The War with Hannibal; Rome and the Mediterranean.* 1971, 1982, 1965, and 1976, respectively. Detailed narratives full of lively stories, written at the time of Augustus.

Plutarch. *Makers of Rome; Fall of the Roman Republic.* 1965 and 1972 (rev. ed.), respectively. Sprightly biographies of prominent figures from the republic, written by this prolific Greek author about A.D. 100.

Polybius. *The Rise of the Roman Empire.* 1979. A history of how Rome came to dominate the Mediterranean world written by a Greek of the second century B.C.

Interpretive Studies

Astin, Alan E. *Cato the Censor.* 1978. A scholarly account of the political and literary career of Cato.

Badian, E. *Publicans and Sinners: Private Enterprise in the Service of the Roman Republic.* 1972. A study of the economic and political role of Rome's primary big-business interests, its tax farmers.

———. *Roman Imperialism in the Late Republic.* 2d ed. 1968. Explains Roman expansion as a response to a perceived need for military defense.

Beard, Mary, and Michael Crawford. *Rome in the Late Republic.* 1985. A provocative interpretation of later republican history, especially on the relationship between religion and politics.

Boardman, John, Jasper Griffin, and Oswyn Murray, eds. *The Oxford History of the Classical World.* 1986. Brief, interpretive chapters covering the political, economic, social, and literary history of the republic.

Boëthius, Axel. *Etruscan and Early Roman Architecture.* 2d ed. 1978. Copiously illustrated discussion of republican architecture.

Bonfante, Larissa, ed. *Etruscan Life and Afterlife: A Handbook of Etruscan Studies.* 1986. Articles on the main aspects of Etruscan civilization in the light of recent research.

Brunt, P. A. *Social Conflicts in the Roman Republic.* 1971. A brief, authoritative account of the struggle of the orders and the social problems of the later republic.

Christ, Karl. *The Romans.* 1984. A topically arranged introduction to Roman civilization.

Cornell, Tim, and John Matthews. *Atlas of the Roman World.* 1982. A concise historical summary linked to excellent and colorful maps.

Crawford, Michael. *The Roman Republic.* 1978. A survey that emphasizes primary sources in its narrative.

Earl, Donald. *The Moral and Political Tradition of Rome.* 1967. A standard work on the ethical conceptions of the Roman aristocracy.

Errington, R. M. *The Dawn of Empire: Rome's Rise to World Power.* 1972. A detailed textbook on Roman wars and expansion in the third and second centuries B.C.

Gardner, Jane. *Women in Roman Law and Society.* 1986. Especially thorough treatment of the legal status of women in Roman history.

Gelzer, Matthias. *Caesar: Politician and Statesman.* 6th ed. Translated by Peter Needham. 1968. A classic work by a great German scholar of the earlier twentieth century.

Harris, William V. *War and Imperialism in Republican Rome, 327–70 B.C.* Corrected ed. 1985. A detailed discussion arguing that the desire for profits and social prestige motivated Roman expansion.

Henig, Martin, ed. *A Handbook of Roman Art.* 1983. An illustrated survey.

Hopkins, Keith. *Conquerors and Slaves: Sociological Studies in Roman History.* Vol. I. 1978. A controversial treatment of the effect increasing wealth had on Roman institutions, especially slavery.

Keaveney, Arthur. *Sulla: The Last Republican.* 1982. A biography that takes a sympathetic approach to Sulla's career.

Leach, John. *Pompey the Great.* 1978. A biography that emphasizes political history.

Nicolet, Claude. *The World of the Citizen in Republican Rome.* Translated by P. S. Falla. 1980. A scholarly treatment of a citizen's responsibilities and privileges under the republic.

Ogilvie, R. M. *Early Rome and the Etruscans.* 1976. A readable analysis of the murky history of early Rome.

———. *Roman Literature and Society.* 1980. A discussion of the history of Roman literature in its social context.

Potter, T. W. *Roman Italy.* 1987. An innovative survey of the history of the Italian countryside in Roman antiquity.

Rawson, Beryl, ed. *The Family in Ancient Rome.* 1986. A collection of essays by different authors.

Scullard, H. H. *From the Gracchi to Nero: A History of Rome, 133 B.C. to A.D. 68.* 5th ed. 1982. The classic introduction to this period.

Warmington, B. H. *Carthage.* 1964. A comprehensive but concise survey of Carthaginian history.

CHAPTER

6

The Roman Empire, 44 B.C.–A.D. 284

Building the Roman Empire
This concrete and stone bridge, financed by eleven local communities in Roman Spain in A.D. 106, soared one-hundred fifty feet over a river below. Construction on this massive scale testified to the early Roman Empire's prosperity and shared culture.

In A.D. 69 a general named Vespasian (A.D. 9–79,✱69–79) became the ninth Roman emperor. One day his son, Titus, complained about the fee the imperial government charged for entering public latrines. Most people in Rome had to use these facilities because they had no bathroom where they lived. But Vespasian's son protested that it was unworthy of the emperor of the Roman world to derive revenue from such an undignified source. The emperor thereupon pulled out a small coin and held it to his son's nose, asking, "Does it stink?" With this demonstration, Vespasian made the point that the government could not afford to be too particular about the sources of its income.

Because the Roman Empire, like the republic before it, had few direct taxes, finding enough money to pay government expenses posed problems. Although certain taxes were collected, no personal income tax was levied. The empire's tax system was just one of the economic, social, and political traditions handed down from republican times that affected the imperial government's freedom of action. In fact, Roman attachment to "the ways of the elders" created a dangerous situation after Caesar's murder in 44 B.C. The old style of politics—competition among aristocratic men for status and power—had failed to bring peace and social stability, because personal success had become more important than the tradition of service to the commonwealth. The republic's collapse meant that Roman government needed a major overhaul to function effectively again. But abandoning the republican model of governing was too great a departure from ancestral tradition for the Romans. In response to this predicament, Augustus (63 B.C.–A.D.14, ✱27 B.C.–14 A.D.), the man who eventually succeeded Caesar as the most powerful Roman leader, consciously erected a new political system upon what had come before. He appealed to Roman reverence for tradition by keeping old institutions—the Senate, the magistrates, the client-patron system, for example—while fundamentally reshaping the distribution of power by creating a sole ruler. Augustus's justification for this new system, which we call the Roman Empire, was that it reestablished the old system the way it should have been. He deftly masked the reality of sweeping change, however, by propaganda in which innovation was called restoration, and the powerful new emperor was called merely the "first man" of the state. In this way tradition appeared to have been preserved when in fact it had been reinvented. The system Augustus created restored peace to the Roman world and endured until a prolonged political and economic crisis fatally weakened it in the third century A.D. By then, Christianity had emerged as a growing new religion, setting the stage for the religious and cultural transformation of the Roman Empire in the following centuries.

Important Dates

43 B.C. Octavian, Antony, and Lepidus form the Second Triumvirate

31 B.C. Octavian defeats Antony and Cleopatra at Actium in western Greece

27 B.C. Octavian announces the restoration of the republic and takes the title Augustus, thus beginning the principate

c. A.D. 5 Election of magistrates begins to be removed from the assemblies and placed under the control of the Senate and the emperor (process completed under Tiberius)

A.D. 41 Senate fails to restore the republic after Emperor Gaius's murder

A.D. 68–69 Civil war during the Year of the Four Emperors

A.D. 98 Last recorded instance of the passage of a law by a Roman assembly

A.D. 193 Praetorian guards auction off the rule of Rome after Emperor Commodus's murder

A.D. 212 Emperor Caracalla confers Roman citizenship on almost all free inhabitants of the empire (*Constitutio Antoniniana*)

A.D. 251–253 Serious epidemic spreads across the Roman world

A.D. 258–275 Prices rise by almost 1000 percent in many regions in an economic crisis

The Pax Romana: *Unity After Civil War*

The process of developing a new Roman political system headed by a sole ruler was accomplished neither quickly nor peacefully. In the long run, however, the new arrangement brought an extended period of peace for most people who lived inside the boundaries of Rome's empire. This tranquil time, sometimes called the *pax Romana* ("Roman peace"), was particularly welcome after the horrors of the civil wars between Caesar and his opponents and among the potential heirs to Caesar's power after his assassination. The story of the transformation of the republic into the empire begins with this gruesome struggle of Roman against Roman after the death of the dictator Caesar.

Caesar's Heir

When Julius Caesar was murdered, his grandnephew Gaius Octavius, as Augustus was then named, was eighteen years old. The reading of Caesar's will revealed that he had adopted Octavius as his son and made him heir to a considerable fortune. (Roman families without sons often adopted an adult man, who then took over a son's responsibilities: continuing the family name and keeping the property in the male line.) Octavius, as Caesar's adopted son, took the name Gaius Julius Caesar Octavianus (known today as Octavian). He immediately thrust himself into the middle of the hornet's nest of Roman politics. The political infighting at Rome was ferocious, as politicians competed to fill the vacuum of power created by Caesar's sudden death. The most prominent competitor was Mark Antony (83–30 B.C.), who had served as a military commander under Caesar and had been his colleague as consul at the time of the murder. Antony patched together a temporary peace in Rome by convincing the Senate that it must carry out Caesar's various reforms to placate Caesar's veterans and secure the goodwill of the ordinary people of Rome, who had loved Caesar. Caesar's assassins were sent to posts in the provinces so their

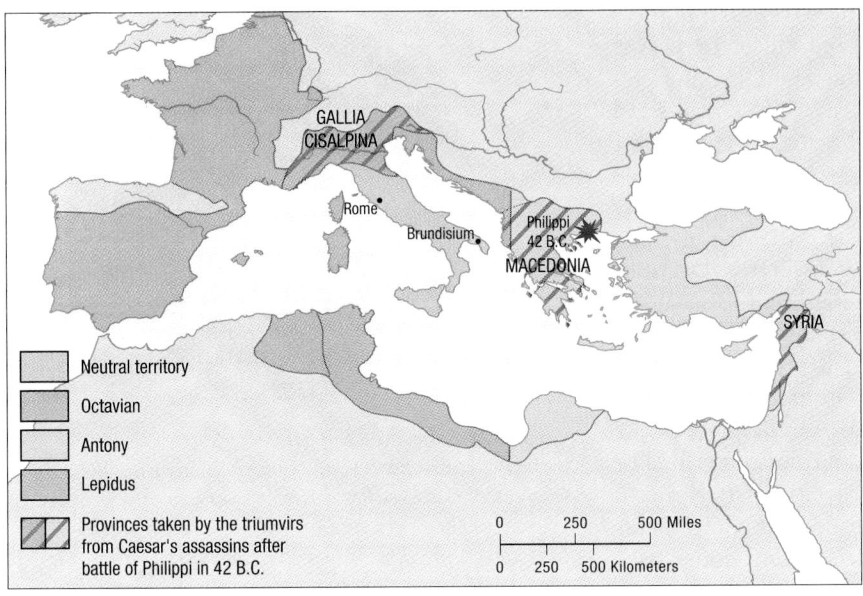

Territorial Division of the Second Triumvirate by 40 B.C.

presence in Rome would not further provoke the people. Antony gained the support of Lepidus, who commanded Caesar's veterans, by promising him the post of *pontifex maximus* (which Caesar had held). Antony's ascent to dominant leadership seemed a sure thing until Octavian's new status as Caesar's adopted son was revealed and his evident ambitions made him an unwelcome obstacle to Antony's dream.

Because the veterans of Caesar's army now supported Octavian out of loyalty to their murdered commander, the Roman senators tried to use him as a political counterweight to Antony, even after Octavian demonstrated his disdain for regular procedure by illegally assembling an army on his own. Many senators thought they could control the inexperienced young man more easily than they could Antony, who they feared was aiming for dictatorial power. Cicero baldly asserted, "We will praise and honor the youngster and then get rid of him." The Senate directed the consuls of 43 B.C. to help Octavian against Antony, who was besieging Decimus Brutus, one of Caesar's assassins and now a provincial governor in Cisalpine Gaul (northern Italy). Octavian's troops headed north and forced Antony to retreat across the Alps. Meanwhile, the two consuls of 43 B.C. apparently died of battle wounds, although rumor said that Octavian had poisoned one of them. Octavian proved that discarding him was not going to be an easy task: he marched his army back to Rome and demanded that he and an obscure relative be appointed consuls for the rest of 43 B.C. The Senators yielded and gave Octavian and his relative the consulships for the remainder of the year, once again disregarding the tradition that required a man to progress gradually through the course of offices to reach the pinnacle of power. This acquiescence to the demands of powerful military men, as in Pompey's irregular career, seemed more and more to be standard practice rather than a rare exception to tradition.

From Second Triumvirate to Civil War

Because the Roman armies, led by Octavian, Antony, and Lepidus (now a provincial governor in Narbonese Gaul, today southern France), balked at fighting each other, their commanders decided to reconcile and join forces to compel the Senate to recognize their supremacy. The three leaders met in the presence of their armies in November 43 B.C. to form the so-called Second Triumvirate. Unlike the First Triumvirate (60 B.C.), this alliance received official sanction when the triumvirs compelled the Senate to pass a law bestowing on them responsibility for reconstituting the state. Their power was now unrivaled, and the republic was in truth, if not in law, defunct. Octavian and Antony, who overshadowed the more lethargic Lepidus, ruthlessly proscribed the real and imagined enemies of Caesar, thereby declaring them outlaws to be hunted down and killed. In 42 B.C. the Senate recognized Caesar as a god, making Octavian the son of a divinity. Meanwhile, Cassius and Marcus Brutus, leaders in the conspiracy against Caesar, had been extorting money from the provinces of the eastern Mediterranean in an attempt to mount resistance to the triumvirate. (Antony had executed the conspirator Decimus Brutus, whose army had deserted him.) But at the battles of Philippi in Macedonia, in October 42 B.C., Antony defeated Cassius and Brutus while illness kept Octavian in his tent. The two conspirators committed suicide, and the uneasy partners in the triumvirate agreed to divide the Roman world. The pact made at Brundisium in southern Italy in 40 B.C. gave Italy and the western provinces to Octavian, the eastern provinces to Antony, and Africa to Lepidus.

Octavian secured Italy as his power base by settling veterans from his army on land confiscated from Italians who had supported Cassius and Brutus, causing great hardship and discontent for many. Those who lost their land had few options besides emigrating to Rome to join the poor masses there. From 39 to 36 B.C. Octavian fought a bitter war against the republican general Sextus Pompey in the western Mediterranean, who threatened to cut off grain shipments to Rome from that region and thus foment unrest among the urban poor, the recipients of subsidized grain. The brilliant naval operations of Octavian's general Agrippa finally vanquished Sextus. When Lepidus challenged Octavian's right to control Sicily after Sextus's defeat, Octavian trounced Lepidus's army and forced him out of the triumvirate into private life. The stage was now set for a confrontation between Octavian and Antony, men whose individual ambitions were too great to share Rome's rule. While Octavian had been fighting Sextus, Antony had been conducting military campaigns to increase his power in the ancient Near East. In the course of diplomatic negotiations over the reorganization of Roman-controlled territory in the eastern Mediterranean, he met and fell in love with Cleopatra VII (69–30 B.C.), the remarkable queen who had earlier entranced Caesar. Through her wit and intelligence, Cleopatra had made Caesar and then Antony her political supporters and her lovers.

Cleopatra, Queen of Egypt
This silver coin, inscribed "Queen Cleopatra, Younger Goddess," portrays her wearing a crown and swathed in pearls. The other side bore a portrait of Mark Antony to commemorate their partnership in ruling the Eastern Mediterranean.

Because Cleopatra commanded a sizable fleet and a rich country, her alliance with Antony strengthened his position in his rivalry with Octavian. Playing on the Roman fear of foreigners, Antony's enemies in Rome launched a propaganda campaign claiming that he planned to take over the Roman world and share it with Cleopatra. Octavian promptly moved to crush the pair. He shrewdly required the residents of Italy and the western provinces to swear a personal oath of allegiance to him, effectively making them all his clients in the traditional Roman system of patronage. The civil war ended in Antony's ignominious defeat in 31 B.C., at the naval battle of Actium in northwest Greece. Cleopatra fled with her ships to Egypt, and Antony followed. There she committed suicide in 30 B.C. as Octavian's armies advanced. To rob Octavian of the chance to parade her as a captive in his triumph in Rome, Cleopatra ended her life by allowing a poisonous snake, a symbol of royal authority, to bite her.

The capture of Egypt in 30 B.C. left Octavian without a viable military rival in the Roman world. It also made him fabulously rich because Egypt essentially became his private property, to be inherited by future Roman emperors. Egypt also exported much grain to Rome, providing a third of the city's annual needs. Rome's emperors needed Egyptian grain to feed the urban poor, who might riot if

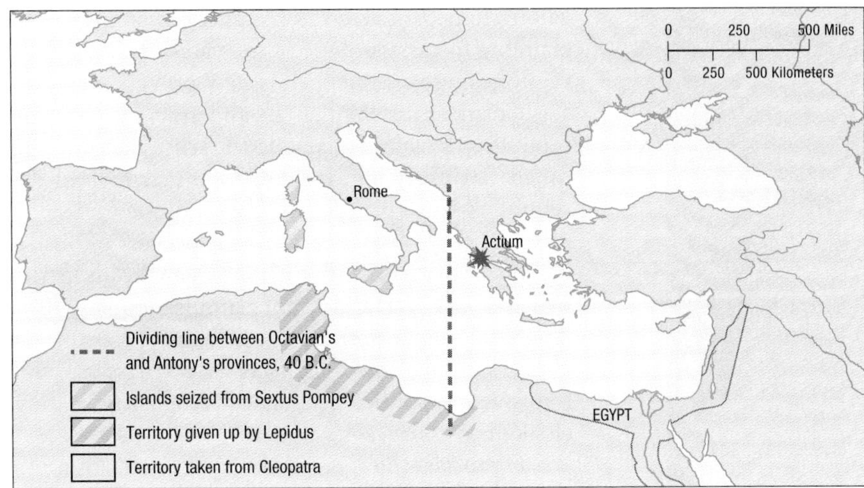

Territories Gained by Octavian, 40–30 B.C.

shortages occurred. Preserving the revenues and exports from Egypt always remained a priority for Rome's emperors. About ten years later, for example, Rome went to great lengths to head off a threat to the region's security by making concessions to Candace, the queen of Nubia, whose army had fought the Roman defenders of southern Egypt to a standstill.

The Creation of the Principate

After again distributing land to veterans of his army to create more settlements loyal to him, Octavian formally announced in 27 B.C. that he was restoring the republic. It was up to the Senate and the Roman people, he proclaimed, to decide how to preserve it thereafter. Recognizing that Octavian possessed real power in this unprecedented situation, the Senate promptly asked him to safeguard the restored republic and gave him the honorary name "Augustus." Octavian had wanted to change his name to Romulus, after Rome's legendary first king, but as an ancient observer reports, "when he realized the people thought this preference meant he longed to be their king, he accepted the title of Augustus instead, as if he were more than human; for everything that is most treasured and sacred is called *augustus.*"

The system of government Augustus created to replace the republican system is called the *principate,* from the Latin word *princeps* (meaning "first man," the root of the English word *prince*). Augustus used this term to describe his position as ruler, but modern historians usually refer to the *princeps* as the emperor, from the title *imperator.* This was a republican honorary designation meaning "military commander" that troops bestowed on their general after a great victory, and it became customary to give this title to every *princeps* to signify his control over the army.

In the years after 27 B.C. the annual election of consuls and other officials, the continuation of the Senate, and the passing of legislation in the assemblies of the people maintained the facade of republican normality. In truth, Augustus exercised power because he controlled the army. To preserve appearances, however, Augustus made sure the Senate periodically renewed its formal approval of his powers. An arrangement decreed in 23 B.C. promoted stability after Augustus had nearly died from two severe illnesses—with no successor ready—and opposition had arisen from disgruntled aristocrats. Augustus resigned his consulship and ceased to hold it in later years, making room for other upper-class men to gain this coveted post. The Senate in turn granted Augustus the power of a consul without him needing to hold the office, declaring that his imperium was greater than that of any actual consul. He also received a lifetime grant of the power of a tribune, giving him the authority to halt the action of all magistrates, the assemblies, and the Senate. Finally, he controlled the state treasury. The

Roman Family Pride
This Roman senator holds busts of his ancestors. Prominent Romans kept such items in their homes to display their lineage.

senators granted supreme power—the power of a king—to Augustus but camouflaged it in these republican trappings so they and he could claim they had restored the republic and its traditions.

Augustus's choice of *princeps* as his title instead of "king" or "dictator" was a cleverly calculated move. In the republic, *princeps* had designated the most prestigious man in the Roman Senate, the leader other senators looked to for guidance. By calling himself a *princeps,* Augustus was implicitly claiming to carry on one of the valued traditions of republican government. His new powers were described in terms familiar to and respected by the republic's citizens, conveying the sense that nothing much was changing. In fact, Augustus revised the republic's basic power structure: no one under the republic could have exercised the powers of both a consul and a tribune without even holding the offices, and certainly not simultaneously. But Augustus did just that: the principate became in effect a monarchy disguised as a corrected and improved republic, headed by Augustus, a king cloaked as a *princeps.*

Historians disagree about Augustus's motives in establishing the principate: some argue that he was a cynical despot bent on suppressing the traditional freedoms of the republic; others insist that he had little choice but to impose an autocratic system to stabilize a world jolted by the violence of aristocratic rivals for power. To evaluate the principate, we must recognize the demands on Augustus to balance his society's need for peace, Rome's traditional commitment to its citizens' freedom of action, and his own political ambitions.

Augustus's constitutional position has been aptly described by the wonderfully paradoxical phrase "first among equals." In his own account of his career, the *Res gestae* ("Things Accomplished"), he wrote that he ruled not by power but through his moral authority (*auctoritas*)—that is, people would regard his advice as the equivalent of commands. In this way the traditional Roman paternalism in social relations, represented by the client-patron system, was officially transferred to politics. It was not a hollow gesture when Augustus was named "father of his country" in 2 B.C., in Roman eyes the greatest honor he could receive. With the emergence of the principate, Rome had a sole ruler who presided over the people like a Roman father: stern but caring, expecting obedience and loyalty from his children, and obligated to nurture them in return. The goal of such an arrangement was stability and order, not political freedom.

Augustus's loyal troops backed up his moral authority. Like the generals of the late republic, he had given his veterans land to sustain their loyalty in the years of civil war, and he continued to pay attention to their needs. He institutionalized the strategy of using military strength to secure political rule by constituting the army as a permanent,

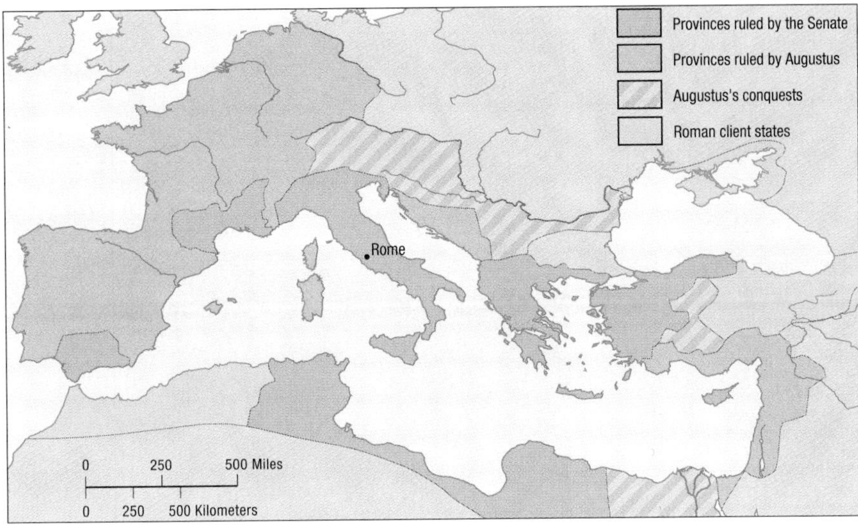

The Roman Empire Under Augustus

standing force with defined responsibilities and benefits. As *princeps* he established regular terms of service and for the first time guaranteed soldiers that they would receive substantial benefits after their retirement. To pay the costs of maintaining this permanent army, Augustus imposed an inheritance tax; this direct tax mainly affected the rich and thus was unpopular with the upper classes. The soldiers, in return for the *princeps'* patronage, obeyed and protected him. For the first time in Roman history, troops, called praetorians, were stationed in Rome itself. These soldiers were Augustus's bodyguards, a visible reminder that the superiority of the Roman emperor, as we will call him for convenience, was in reality guaranteed by the threat of force as well as the weight of his moral authority.

The Precariousness of City Life in Augustan Rome

Augustus remained Roman emperor until his death in A.D. 14. The greatest benefit of his rule was peace within the empire after the nearly constant civil war that had plagued Roman Italy for more than fifty years. At last the government could attend to economic and social problems, a response that the Roman tradition of paternalism demanded. The most pressing problems were in Rome itself, a teeming city of more than a million inhabitants, many of whom had too little to eat and not enough jobs. A variety of archaeological and literary sources allow us to sketch a composite picture of life in Augustan Rome. Although some of the sources refer to times after Augustus and to cities other than Rome, they nevertheless help us understand this period; economic and social conditions were essentially the same in all Roman cities throughout the early centuries of the empire.

Rome's inhabitants, except for the rich, had hard lives. The population of Augustan Rome was vast for the ancient world; no European city would have nearly this many people again until London in the 1700s. Such a huge population meant overcrowding. The streets were packed: "One man jabs me with his elbow, another whacks me with a pole; my legs are smeared with mud, and from all sides big feet step on me" is one resident's description of walking in Rome. To ease congestion in the narrow streets, the city banned carts and wagons in the daytime. This regulation made Rome's nights noisy with the creaking of axles and the shouting of drivers caught in traffic jams.

Most people lived in small apartments in multistoried buildings called *insulae* ("islands"). These dwellings outnumbered private houses by twenty-six to one. The first floor of the building usually housed shops, bars, and simple restaurants. Graffiti of all kinds—political endorsements for municipal elections, the posting of rewards for the return of stolen property, personal insults, and what we would call advertising—frequently decorated the exterior walls. Well-off tenants occupied the lower stories. The higher the floor in the building, the

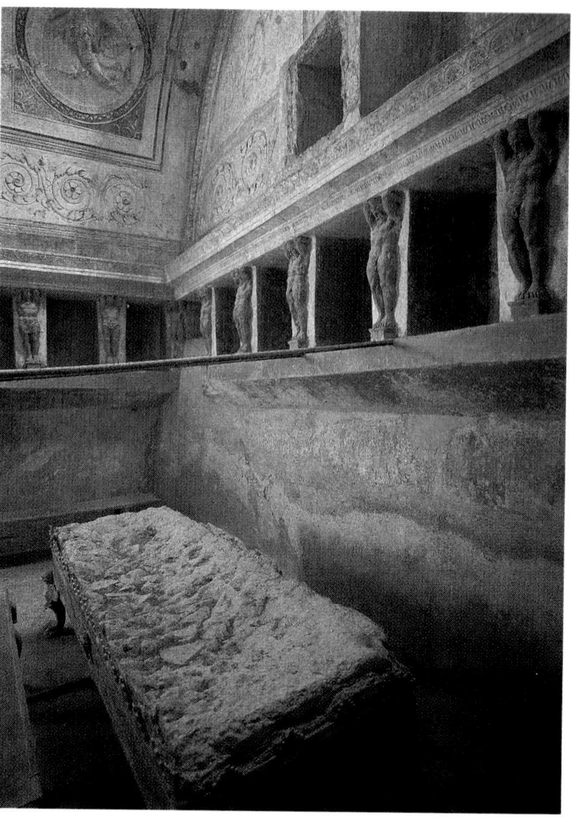

(above) ***Roman Snack Bar***
This establishment on the first floor of an apartment building at Ostia, the port of Rome, was typical of the small restaurants of Roman cities. Customers could take out food and drink or sit for a more leisurely meal.
(right) ***Roman Public Bath***
This "warm room" (tepidarium) *from a luxuriously decorated Roman bath included couches on which clients could rest.*

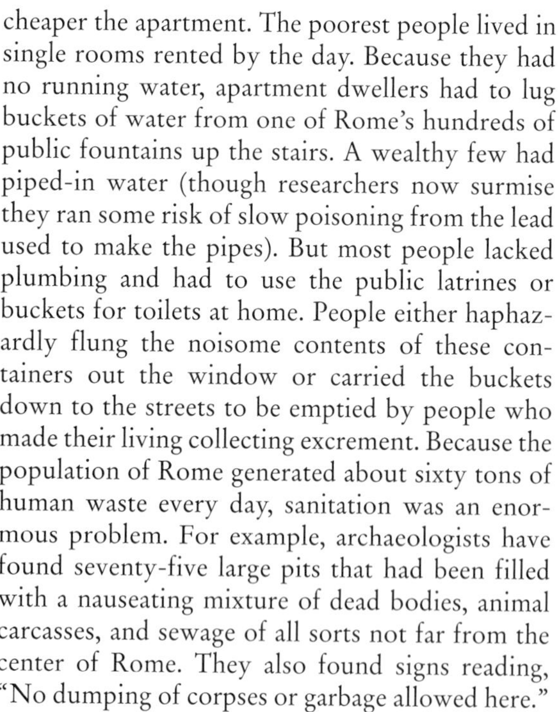

cheaper the apartment. The poorest people lived in single rooms rented by the day. Because they had no running water, apartment dwellers had to lug buckets of water from one of Rome's hundreds of public fountains up the stairs. A wealthy few had piped-in water (though researchers now surmise they ran some risk of slow poisoning from the lead used to make the pipes). But most people lacked plumbing and had to use the public latrines or buckets for toilets at home. People either haphazardly flung the noisome contents of these containers out the window or carried the buckets down to the streets to be emptied by people who made their living collecting excrement. Because the population of Rome generated about sixty tons of human waste every day, sanitation was an enormous problem. For example, archaeologists have found seventy-five large pits that had been filled with a nauseating mixture of dead bodies, animal carcasses, and sewage of all sorts not far from the center of Rome. They also found signs reading, "No dumping of corpses or garbage allowed here."

To keep clean, people used public baths. Because admission fees were low, almost everyone could afford to go to the baths daily. Imperial Rome had scores of these establishments, which like modern health clubs served as centers for exercising and socializing as well as washing. Bath patrons progressed through a series of increasingly warm, humid areas until they reached a saunalike room. Bathers swam naked in their choice of hot or cold pools. The sexes bathed apart, either in separate rooms or at different times of the day, and women had full access to the public baths.

In Rome, as in all ancient cities, unsanitary conditions prevailed despite the many baths, fountains with running water, and the ongoing efforts of officials (the aediles) to keep the streets clean. Bathing was thought to be particularly valuable for sick people, for example, and the baths contributed to the spread of communicable diseases. Furthermore, although the Roman government in its concern for public sanitation built a sewer system, its contents emptied untreated into the city's Tiber

River. The technology for sanitary disposal of waste simply did not exist. People regularly left human and animal corpses in the streets, to be gnawed by vultures and dogs. The poor were not the only people affected by such conditions: a stray mutt once brought a human hand to Vespasian's table while he was eating lunch. Flies buzzing everywhere and a lack of mechanical refrigeration contributed to frequent gastrointestinal ailments; the most popular amulet of the time was supposed to ward off stomach trouble. Although the wealthy could not eliminate such discomforts, they made their lives more pleasant with amenities such as having snow brought from the mountains to ice their drinks and having their slaves clean their airy houses, which were built around courtyards and gardens.

City residents faced other hazards besides infectious disease. Broken crockery and other debris were routinely hurled out of the upper stories of apartment buildings and rained down like missiles on unwary pedestrians below. "If you are walking to a dinner party in Rome," one poet remarked, "you would be foolish not to make out your will first. For every open window is a source of potential disaster." The *insulae* could be dangerous to their inhabitants as well as to passersby because they were in constant danger of collapsing. Roman engineers, despite their expertise in using concrete, brick, and stone as durable building materials, lacked the technology to calculate precisely how much stress their constructions could stand. Builders trying to cut costs paid little attention to engineering safeguards in any case, which led Augustus to impose a height limit of seventy feet on new apartment buildings, a regulation that unscrupulous operators largely ignored. Often built in valleys because the sunny hilltops were occupied by the homes of the rich, these apartment buildings were also susceptible to floods. Fire presented an even greater risk; one of Augustus's many services to the urban masses was to provide Rome with the first public fire department in Western history. He also established Rome's first police force, despite his reported fondness for stopping to watch the frequent brawls that the crowding in Rome's streets encouraged. The squalid conditions and commonplace violence that characterized Augustan Rome were in fact a normal part of city life in antiquity.

Roman Street in Herculaneum
Multi-storied houses abutting directly onto streets paved with flat stones characterized prosperous Roman towns. This street in Herculaneum was preserved by the volcanic eruption of Mt. Vesuvius in A.D. *79.*

Augustus also tried to improve the condition of the urban masses by assuring an adequate food supply for Rome's poor, many of whom could find only sporadic employment. He viewed this as part of his responsibility as the patron of all the people, and he freely drew upon his own vast fortune to help pay for imported grain. Distributing free grain to Rome's poor had been a tradition for decades, but the scale of Augustus's dole system was immense: two hundred fifty thousand recipients were entitled to the distributions. Because many of these poor people had families, this statistic suggests that perhaps seven hundred thousand people in Rome depended on the government for their grain, the basic food staple of most Romans. Poor people usually made this grain, a form of wheat not well suited for baking bread, into a watery porridge, which they washed down with cheap wine. If they were lucky, they might have some beans, leeks, or sheep lips on the side. The rich, as we learn from a surviving Roman cookbook, ate more delectable dishes, such as spiced roast pork or lobster, often flavored with a sweet-and-sour sauce concocted from honey and vinegar.

Slaves and Spectacles

To produce the agricultural products Rome's consumers required, both free laborers and slaves toiled on farms throughout Italy. The conditions of slavery under the empire remained much as they had been under the late republic, when Rome's foreign wars resulted in a great influx of foreign slaves to Italy. Slaves working in agriculture or manufacturing that required a lot of physical strength often endured grueling existences. Most such slaves were men, although slave women might be assistants to the foremen who managed gangs of rural slave laborers. An ancient author offers this grim description of slave men at work in a flourmill in the eastern part of the empire: "Through the holes in their ragged clothes you could see all over their bodies the scars from whippings. Some had on only loincloths. Letters had been branded on their foreheads and irons manacled their ankles." Worse than the mills were the mines, where the foremen constantly flogged the slave miners to keep them working in such a dangerous environment.

Slaves who worked as household servants had an easier physical existence. Although Roman households employed more male than female slaves, many domestic slaves were women, who worked as nurses, maids, kitchen help, and clothesmakers. Some male slaves ran businesses for their masters, and they were often allowed to keep part of the profits as an incentive. Female household slaves had less opportunity to earn money. Masters sometimes granted tips for sexual favors. Female prostitutes, who were mostly slaves owned by men, had more chances to make money for themselves. Slaves who somehow acquired funds would sometimes buy slaves themselves, thereby creating a kind of slave hierarchy. A male slave, for example, might buy a female slave for a mate. Slaves could thus sometimes have a semblance of a family life, though a formal, legal marriage was impossible because the man and woman remained their master's property, as did their children. If truly fortunate, slaves could save enough to buy themselves from their masters or could be manumitted by their masters' wills. They then became free Roman citizens. Some tomb epitaphs testify to affectionate feelings certain masters had for their slaves, but even household slaves could suffer miserable lives if their masters were cruel. Slaves had no recourse; if they retaliated against their owners because of inhumane treatment, their punishment was death.

The most visible slaves were the men and women who fought as gladiators for public entertainment. Women, perhaps daughters trained by their gladiator fathers, first appeared in the arena during the republic and continued to fight in public until the emperor Septimius Severus (*A.D. 193–211) banned their appearance. Not all gladiators were slaves; prisoners of war and condemned criminals could also be forced to fight. Gladiatorial combat was often to the death, but the crowd could shout for a defeated fighter to be spared if he or she had shown special courage. Free men and women also voluntarily enrolled themselves as gladiators in return for a fee. Early in the first century A.D., the Senate apparently became alarmed at the number of citizens entering this disreputable occupation. It forbade men and women of senatorial or equestrian rank and all freeborn women under the age of twenty from fighting as gladiators or appearing on stage as entertainers, another unsavory profession by upper-class standards.

Under the republic, private individuals had financed gladiatorial combats as part of a distinguished man's funeral. Gladiatorial shows became the rage under the empire in cities across the Roman world. Augustus himself paid for more than five thousand pairs of gladiators to fight it out in spectacular festivals staged at Rome. Gladiatorial shows and chariot races were staged as the main attractions at celebrations of great occasions, such as a victory in war. These shows provided a main source of a city's public entertainment. Theatrical productions also flourished. Mimes were the most popular form of theater; these dramas of everyday life and explicit sexual farces were unique in employing female actresses to play female roles.

Enormous crowds of men and women attended shows in Rome and in cities across the empire to watch chariot races, bouts between gladiators, mock naval battles on artificial lakes, fights between humans and savage beasts, and displays of exotic African animals that sometimes mangled condemned criminals as a form of capital punishment. Tens of thousands of spectators would crowd into amphitheaters to see the gladiatorial combats, with women segregated in the uppermost tiers of seats. To make the fights more unpredictable, Romans matched gladiators with different kinds of weapons. One favorite kind of bout pitted a lightly armored fighter, called a "net-man" because he used a net and a trident, against a more heavily armored "fish-man," so named from the design of his helmet crest. Chariot racing held in the Circus Maximus stadium at Rome drew gigantic crowds of perhaps two hundred thousand people. Women could sit next to men at chariot races, at which betting was a great attraction. Crowds at these events could be rowdy. One contemporary source described his fellow Roman sports fans: "Look at the mob coming to the show—already they're out of their minds! Aggressive, heedless, already in an uproar about their bets! They all share the same suspense, the same madness, the same voice." As the Roman Empire gradually became more autocratic, mass gatherings such as sports events or theater productions became a medium for ordinary people to communicate with the emperors, who were expected to attend. On more than one occasion, for example, the poor rioted in the amphitheaters or the Circus Maximus to confront the emperor and express their concern about a shortfall in the free grain supply.

Communicating the Emperor's Image

The emperor sent messages to the populace through media both small and large. In the ancient world, coins were the only mass-produced source of official messages and therefore could function something like modern political advertising. Coins produced in the imperial mints carried propaganda messages such as Augustus's title "father of his country" to remind people of their emperor's moral authority over them, or "the roads have been rebuilt" to emphasize the emperor's personal generosity in paying for highway construction. Augustus had to do something about Italy's roads and bridges because Rome's wealthy men had failed to fulfill their traditional duty of funding such public works projects. The rich now preferred to show their public-spirited munificence by paying for elegant buildings such as temples or halls for law courts instead of low-visibility projects such as fixing the roads, which did not garner them as much publicity and prestige.

Augustus outmaneuvered the aristocracy by turning the construction of public buildings into a virtual monopoly of the emperor. Dipping into his overwhelmingly vast fortune, he paid to erect grand buildings in Rome, winning glory for his generosity. These projects served utilitarian purposes but also communicated a particular image of the emperor to the Roman people. The vast imperial forum (public square) Augustus built illustrates how his image was conveyed. To commemorate the victory over Caesar's assassins at Philippi in 42 B.C., Augustus had vowed to build a temple to Mars, the Roman god of war, and Venus, the Roman goddess of love, whom Julius Caesar had claimed as his divine ancestor and thus made Augustus's relative, too. In 2 B.C. the massive temple, constructed on a lofty podium, was completed. Out from the temple, the forum's centerpiece, stretched two-story colonnades and curved statue galleries displaying famous heroes from Roman history. The forum served various practical purposes, such as providing space for religious services and the formal ceremonies marking the passage into adulthood of upper-class Roman boys. It also communicated an image of the emperor who had paid for it: the imposing size and the elevation of the temple communicated the benefactor's grandeur; the statues indicated his respect for the lessons of history about the proper goals for a Roman man; and the fulfillment of the promise to build the forum testified to his loyalty to the gods, the valued quality of *pietas.* These messages constituted Augustus's ideology of empire, which he wished his subjects to accept. As with his patronage of the urban poor through the distribution of free food, he was trying to promote political and social stability while at the same time win glory and status for himself in traditional Roman fashion. With his many prestigious achievements, Augustus overshadowed his rich and aristocratic contemporaries. His successors in ruling Rome imitated his methods of reinforcing the emperor's image as the Roman world's preeminent figure.

Under the empire the upper class of Rome never regained the political dominance it had enjoyed during the republic. Even the wealthiest of the elite could not compete with the emperor because of the power he derived from his command of a standing army and from his control of the treasury. Moreover, as patron of upper-class Romans, the emperor was often bequeathed wealth in the wills of his clients and became even richer. Finally, the upper class failed to reproduce itself sufficiently, perhaps because its members felt that the expense and trouble of raising children threatened their high standard of living. Children became so rare among this class that Augustus passed a law designed to encourage more births by granting special legal privileges to the parents of three or more children. In the same spirit he also promulgated new laws intended to strengthen marriage ties and made adultery a criminal offense. Ironically, he had to exile his own daughter—his only child—and a granddaughter after adultery scandals. He also banished Ovid (43 B.C.–A.D. 17), ostensibly for writing poems like *The Art of Love* and *Love Affairs,* in which the poet as part of his complex reflection on Roman society playfully described how to flirt at the races or deceive a spouse. Augustus's legislation had little effect, however, and the prestigious old families withered away under the empire, aided by banishment and execution if they ran seriously afoul of the emperors. Recent demographic research suggests that three-quarters of the families of senatorial status died out in every generation. New people from below the senatorial class who won the emperors' favor continuously took their places in the social hierarchy.

Despite often poor health, Augustus ruled as emperor until his death at age seventy-five in A.D. 14. The length of his reign (forty-one years) helped institutionalize the changes in Roman government he brought about with the principate. As the Roman historian Tacitus later remarked, by the time Augustus died, "almost no one was still alive who had seen the republic." The gradual dying out of the important families of the republic over the following decades eliminated a major source of potential opposition to the new system. And Augustus could destroy those who got in his way. Rome's urban masses favored the empire because their rich patron, the emperor, looked out for their needs. Through his longevity, his rapport with the army, and his crafty manipulation of the traditional vocabulary of Roman politics to disguise his power, Augustus ensured the transformation of the republic into the empire. His position as a sole ruler also effectively redefined the Roman constitution, which under the republic had been incompatible with monarchy.

New and Old Education in Imperial Rome

Although some traditional educational practices remained unchanged in the transformation of the republic into an empire, Roman education's primary subject, rhetoric, underwent important changes. Since the republic, mastering rhetoric had been a major goal in the education of young Roman men because persuasive speaking skills had traditionally been the key to success for men in politics and the courts. The ability to make stirring speeches had been such a powerful weapon in the late republic that it had catapulted a man like Cicero, who lacked distinction as a military leader, to the political forefront. Cicero's stinging attacks on Antony, in fact, so enraged him that he ordered Cicero murdered during the proscriptions of 43 B.C. In a grisly display of his hatred of Cicero's words, Antony had the orator's severed head and hands nailed up for display at Rome's center, where Cicero had so often spoken.

Under the empire the study of rhetoric changed. The supremacy of the emperor ruled out the kind of freewheeling political debate and decision making in which rhetoric had been so important in the late republic. The subject matter of rhetorical training now, one orator complained, "is far removed from reality." Instead of matters concerning government, he went on, students debated topics such as "a rape victim's alternatives,"or "cures for the plague" in stilted, grandiloquent style. Despite this shying away from current politics, rhetorical studies continued to dominate Roman education under the empire. Ambitious men now needed rhetorical skills to praise the current emperor on the numerous public occasions that promoted his image as a competent and compassionate ruler as well as for legal matters and the trials of government officials. The power of rhetoric was thus redirected from its republican aim of influencing votes to a new imperial goal: legitimizing and strengthening the new Roman system of government.

Rome had no free public schools, so the poor were lucky to pick up even rudimentary knowledge from their harried parents; even wealthier people rarely pursued their education further than acquiring practical skills. A character in the *Satyricon,* a satirical literary work of the first century A.D., expressed this utilitarian attitude toward education succinctly: "I didn't study geometry and literary criticism and worthless junk like that. I just learned how to read the letters on signs and how to work out percentages, and I learned weights, measures, and the values of the different kinds of coins."

As the historian Tacitus described, the Roman ideal called for mothers to teach their children right and wrong:

> *Once upon a time children were reared not by a hired nurse in her den but at their mother's breast and on her lap. For her the highest merit was to keep house and raise the children. An older female relative of high character was chosen to look after the family's children, and in her presence nobody dared to say anything rude or do anything wrong. She governed not only the children's lessons and tasks but also recreation and play.*

Under the empire servants or hired teachers usually looked after the children of families with some means. They would send their sons and daughters to private elementary schools from the ages of seven to eleven to learn reading, writing, and basic arithmetic. Teachers used rote methods in the classroom, with frequent corporal punishment for mistakes. Some children went on to the next three years of school, in which they were introduced to literature, history, and grammar. Only a few boys thereafter advanced to the study of rhetoric.

For the Romans, advanced study principally concerned literature, history, ethical philosophy, law, and dialectic (determining the truth by identifying contradictions in arguments). Mathematics and science were little studied for themselves, but Roman engineers and architects necessarily became extremely proficient at calculation. Rich men and women would pursue their interest in books by having slaves read aloud to them. Reading required manual dexterity as well as literacy because books, instead of being bound page by page, consisted of continuous scrolls made from the papyrus reed or animal skin. A reader had to unroll the scroll with one hand and simultaneously roll it up with the other.

Celebrated Ideals in Literature and Portraiture

New literature blossomed in the time of Augustus. Modern critics call the period from about 100 B.C. through Augustus's reign the Golden Age of Latin literature. Although writers like the historian Livy (54 B.C.–A.D. 17) and the encyclopedist Varro (116 B.C.–27 B.C.) produced volume after volume in prose, the most glamorous literature of Augustus's age was poetry. Augustus himself tried to write poetry, and he served as the patron of a circle of writers and artists. The emperor did not approve of an irreverent wit like Ovid. His favorites, Horace (65–8 B.C.) and Virgil (70–19 B.C.), were more amenable to the establishment. Horace, for example, celebrated Augustus's victory over Antony and Cleopatra at Actium in a poem opening with the line, "Now is the time for a toast." Virgil's most famous work was *The Aeneid,* an epic poem inspired by Homeric poetry, which told the legend of the Trojan Aeneas, the most distant ancestor of the Romans and therefore a predecessor of Romulus, Rome's first king. In this poem, Virgil tempered his praise of the Roman state and Aeneas's great virtues, especially *pietas,* with a dramatic recognition of the price he paid for success. According to Virgil, Aeneas's flight from the ruins of Troy displayed his piety in obeying the gods' command to found a new city in Italy as the base for future Roman expansion and glory. In the course of doing his duty, however, Aeneas paid a heavy personal price. He had to desert the woman he loved, Dido, queen of Carthage, thereby establishing the background for the hostility between Romans and Carthaginians, which erupted into the bloody Punic Wars. To found a new state in Italy, Aeneas also had to fight fierce wars against indigenous peoples. In *The Aeneid,* Virgil explored with deep emotion the paradoxical pairing of human success and human suffering. On another level, *The Aeneid* also underscored the complex mix of gain and loss that followed the Augustan transformation of Roman politics and society. In the poem the gods teach the pious (in the Roman sense) Aeneas the moral code of ruling: be merciful to the conquered but lay low the haughty. Augustus followed this same code.

When Augustus was growing up, the complexity of human experience had characterized the style of sculptural portraits: busts sculpted in the late republic were starkly realistic. The sculptures Augustus ordered after he became emperor displayed a more idealized style, reminiscent of classical Greek sculpture and the portraits of Alexander the Great by Lysippus. In renowned works of art such as the First Gate statue of himself or the sculpted frieze on his Altar of Peace, Augustus was portrayed as serene and dignified, not careworn and sick, as he often was. As with his monumental architecture, Augustus used sculpture to project a calm and competent image of himself as, to use the vocabulary of his propaganda, the "restorer of the world."

Much of the poetry and portraiture of the new empire reflected Augustus's chosen vision of himself: the great father selflessly restoring peace to his war-torn people. This image lulled Romans into accepting a new way of life without realizing the hidden costs. Augustus was a generous patron to Rome's poor, and he did force reluctant aristocrats to contribute to maintaining the state's infrastructure and supporting the standing army. But underneath his benevolence lay a vein of ruthlessness. Many people were murdered under the proscriptions of 43 B.C. Many lost their homes in the confiscations that provided land for his army veterans. And perhaps most telling, the ironic guarantee of the *pax Romana* was the threat of Augustus's force as commander of the army. The free discussion and agreement among citizens that had been the most cherished ideal of the Roman Republic had been lost—they were the price of social and political order in the monarchy of the early Roman Empire.

The Political and Social Amalgam of the Early Empire

When Augustus died in A.D. 14, no procedure existed for selecting a new emperor because open concern with imperial succession would have been incompatible with Augustus's insistence that the republic had been restored. During his lifetime, Augustus had tried to ensure that a son would indeed succeed him. But he had no natural son, and the men he adopted as his heirs died prematurely. Finally he had settled on Tiberius (42 B.C.–A.D. 37, ✱A.D. 14–37), a distinguished military commander who was the son of his wife Livia by a previous marriage. Tiberius paid a steep personal price for the emperor's favor: Augustus forced him to divorce his beloved wife, Vipsania, to marry Augustus's daughter, Julia, a marriage that proved disastrously unhappy. After Augustus's funeral and some awkward debate, the Senate formally asked Tiberius to take over the state. He accepted with apparently genuine reluctance. In this hesitant fashion, then, the imperial government set a precedent for the succession of a new emperor after the death of the preceding ruler. Nevertheless, the Roman Empire was not yet fully rooted as a political institution.

The Consolidation of Monarchy Through Politics and Religion

At first Tiberius tried to govern in cooperation with the Senate. He did, however, end the pretense that the republic still lived on by completing the transfer of the election of magistrates from the assemblies of the people to the Senate, a process Augustus had begun. Giving this power to the Senate provided the emperor with greater control over elections because he could direct the appointment of senators, and it pleased the senators because they no longer had to try to win public favor by campaigning. Furthermore, for some offices, Tiberius indicated his favorite candidates and thus ensured their election. The people, one Roman historian reported, "did not complain about the loss, except for some trivial grumbling." Another commentator applauded the change by asserting that the emperor's selection of winning candidates meant "genuine merit has replaced clever campaigning." Eventually, Tiberius decreased the importance of the Senate in Roman government, a trend that following emperors continued until the emperor's control over the election of magistrates and the passing of legislation became absolute.

Events after Tiberius's death demonstrated that most of the Roman upper class had no deep-seated desire for a genuine restoration of the republic. Tiberius had designated as the next emperor his young grandnephew Gaius (A.D. 12–41, ✱37–41), who was also the great grandson of Augustus's sister. Gaius has since become known as Caligula ("Baby Boots"), the nickname soldiers gave him as a child because he wore little leather shoes imitating theirs. He ruled through cruelty and violence, and his lack of any serious training in the skills of governing and his prodigal spending made his administration worse. He developed a hatred for the Senate and pushed the principate closer to open autocracy in the style of Hellenistic monarchy. He frequently outraged Roman social conventions by appearing on stage as a singer and actor, fighting mock gladiatorial combats, and appearing in public in women's clothing or costumes imitating statues of the gods. His demand for honors normally reserved for the gods earned him a reputation as a megalomaniac. His plan to have a statue of himself placed in the main Jewish temple in Jerusalem caused severe unrest among the Jews there. When two officers of the praetorian guard murdered Caligula in A.D. 41 to avenge personal insults, some senators debated the idea of truly restoring the republic by refusing to choose a new emperor. They soon capitulated, however, when Claudius (10 B.C.–A.D. 54, *A.D. 41–54), Augustus's grandnephew and Caligula's uncle, obtained the backing of the praetorian guard with promises of money. The praetorians forced the Senate to acknowledge Claudius as the new emperor; as he pointed out to the senators, without troops they had no other choice. The succession of Claudius under the threat of the use of force against the Senate made it abundantly clear that soldiers would always insist on having an emperor, a patron to look after their interests. It also revealed that any senatorial yearnings for the return of a republic would never be fulfilled.

From the reign of Claudius on, the emperors and the senatorial class developed a patron-client relationship; no longer could senators dream of reestablishing their former primacy in government, although they retained great status and expected the emperor to listen to their concerns respectfully. As patron the emperor chose the Senate members and then fostered their careers in public office. Claudius expanded the pool of imperial clients by enrolling men from a Roman province (Transalpine Gaul) in the Senate for the first time, an important change foreshadowing the crucial roles provincials would eventually play in the society and politics of the Roman Empire. As the emperor's clients, senators were supposed to remain loyal to him and support his programs. Tensions of course persisted. Many senators remained hostile toward Claudius because they resented the power play he had used to become emperor and because he kept pushing them to be dutiful. They also objected to the broad administrative powers Claudius gave to some freedmen on his personal staff, a key step in developing an imperial administration. Finally, senators accused Claudius of being too influenced by his first wife, Messalina, and after her execution following a sexual scandal, his next wife, Agrippina.

At the age of sixteen, Nero (A.D. 37–68, *54–68) succeeded Claudius as emperor. Nero was Claudius's grandnephew and adopted son, whose mother, Agrippina, had married Claudius (her uncle) to ensure Nero's succession to the throne. The rumor that she hastened the event by feeding Claudius poisoned mushrooms cannot be confirmed. Nero's passion for singing and acting in public earned him the contempt of the upper class, who despised actors. The spectacular public festivals he put on and the cash he distributed to the masses in Rome kept him generally popular with the poorer people throughout his reign, although a giant fire in Rome in A.D. 64 aroused suspicions that he might have ordered the conflagration to clear the way for new building projects. As Nero grew older, he increasingly oppressed the upper class, and his strong preference for Greek culture offended traditional Romans. He even toured Greece in 67 and 68 A.D. to compete as a singer in the pan-Hellenic games; naturally, he won all the events he entered. While there, he announced "the freedom of Greece" in imitation of Flamininus's famous proclamation in 196 B.C. But for the Greeks this declaration rang as hollow as the previous one; Greece still remained part of the Roman Empire. To raise money for his profligate spending, Nero would trump up charges against wealthy men and women in order to seize their property. The revolts of three powerful provincial governors drove him to commit suicide in A.D. 68, when the praetorian guard was bribed to switch its loyalty to one of the governors. Assisted by one of his freedmen, Nero cut his own throat with the parting words, "To die! And such a great artist!"

Vespasian (A.D. 9–79, *69–79) became emperor after a year of civil war in which three others tried and failed to hold the throne (the Year of the Four Emperors, as it is called today). All the emperors from Augustus to Nero had come from one group of aristocratic families known as the Julio-Claudians.

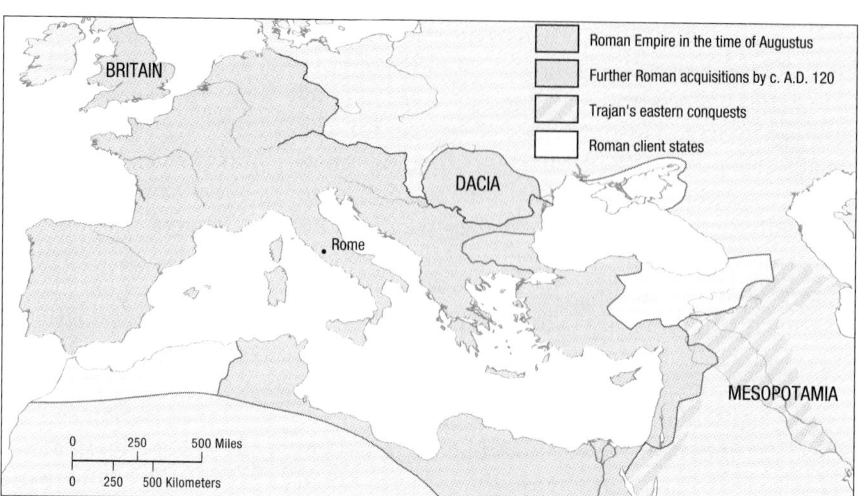

The Expansion of the Roman Empire

Vespasian, who was succeeded by his sons Titus (A.D. 39–81, ✶79–81) and Domitian (A.D. 51–96, ✶81–96), belonged to a different family, the Flavians. Their rule demonstrated that the Roman monarchy was not necessarily the inherited property of a single family group but rather a prize that could be won in competition and transferred to a new family dynasty. To legitimize his position, Vespasian had the Senate issue a law proclaiming his right to the powers exercised by previous emperors, probably in keeping with similar decrees passed for earlier emperors. Because respect for tradition was such a powerful force among the Romans, such proclamations in effect institutionalized the Roman Empire as a political system by acknowledging the precedents for the emperor's rule.

Vespasian also sought to secure his position by encouraging the spread of the imperial cult (worship of the emperor as a living god) in the provinces outside Italy, where most of the empire's population resided. With Julius Caesar as precedent, Augustus and Claudius had been declared gods after their deaths as a mark of great honor, and temples had been built for regular sacrifices to them. In the eastern provinces of the empire, however, people had spontaneously begun to worship the ruling emperor as a living god as early as the reign of Augustus. They had earlier expressed their respect for top officials and generals of the Roman Republic in this way. The deification of the current ruler seemed normal to them because they had honored their kings as divinities for centuries, even before the Romans had conquered them. The imperial cult broadcast the same image of the emperor to the people of the provinces as the city's architecture and sculpture did to the people of Rome: he was larger than life, worthy of loyal respect, and a source of potential benefactions. Because emperor worship was already well established in Greece and the ancient Near East, Vespasian concentrated on spreading it in the provinces of Spain, southern France, and North Africa. Italy, however, had no temples to the living emperor. Traditional Romans scorned the imperial cult as a provincial aberration. Vespasian, known for his wit, revealed his personal attitude toward deification when, as he lay dying, he muttered, "Oh me! I'm afraid I'm becoming a god."

Although the emperor Trajan (✶A.D. 98–117) fought extensive campaigns to try to expand the Roman Empire northward across the Danube River into Dacia (today Romania) and eastward into Mesopotamia, most emperors of the second century A.D. followed a less aggressive set of goals: to maintain law and order inside the vast empire's boundaries; to keep the army strong enough to defend the border regions; to provide free food and entertainment for the poor in Rome; to initiate public building projects both in the capital and the provinces; to furnish occasional relief to provincial communities after natural disasters, such as the devastating earthquakes common in the eastern empire; and, most important, to collect enough taxes to pay for all this. The imperial government was quite small compared to the size of the empire being administered. As under the republic, governors with small staffs were sent to the provinces, which eventually numbered about forty. In Rome the emperor employed a substantial palace staff, and several officials called *prefects,* who came from the equestrian ranks, oversaw the city itself. The Roman Empire had no swollen bureaucracy during this time: no more than several hundred top Roman officials governed a population of around 50 million.

The Roman Empire could operate with so few high officials because it fostered the traditional republican ideal of public service in the upper classes in the provinces outside Italy. A tax on provincial agricultural land (Italy was exempt) provided the principal source of the empire's revenue. The local officials of the provincial cities, which were self-governing, collected this tax. In this decentralized system the wealthy and public-spirited people who ran these cities were personally responsible for seeing that the appropriate amount of tax money was forwarded to the central Roman administration. The level of taxation varied from province to province, but taxes everywhere seem to have been particularly difficult for the poor to pay, perhaps more because they were so destitute than because taxes were especially high. Most emperors under the early empire attempted to keep taxes low. As Tiberius put it once when refusing a request from provincial governors for tax increases, "I want you to shear my sheep, not skin them alive."

Because rich and powerful men and women in the provincial cities had to make up from their own pockets any shortfall in tax revenues from their community, their responsibility could be expensive. The prestige of their position, however, made the risk worthwhile. The emperor rewarded some faithful public servants with priesthoods in the imperial cult, a local honor open to both men and women. Or they could petition the emperor for special help for their area after an earthquake or a flood. In other words, the members of the local social elite were the patrons of their communities and the clients of the emperor. The decentralized Roman tax system certainly made possible financial corruption and exploitation of the lower classes, but the more enlightened emperors tried to minimize such depredations. As long as there were enough rich people in the provinces satisfied with the characteristically Roman value system of financial obligations and nonmaterial rewards, the empire could function effectively. It ran so smoothly by the second century A.D. that modern historians have labeled this period a Golden Age.

Social Distinctions in the Empire's Golden Age

In the second century A.D. more people in the Roman Empire experienced peace and relative prosperity than ever before. As always, the upper classes constituted a tiny portion of the population. Only about one in every fifty thousand had enough money to qualify for the highest-ranking class, the senatorial order (so named because men of this class could be appointed to the Senate). Men in the senatorial class sported a broad purple stripe on their tunics, an emblem of their status. Men of the second highest order, called equestrians even though they no longer had anything to do with horses, had to have a substantial amount of wealth and to come from a family that had been freeborn for two generations. About one in a thousand belonged to the equestrian class. Equestrians could display their status by wearing a gold ring and a narrow purple stripe on their outer garment. The third highest order consisted of the propertied and influential people who served as local council members in provincial towns. Members of this class were called *curiales* because their ownership of a legal minimum of property made them eligible to serve as magistrates (*decurions*) on their municipal city council (*curia*). To retain their special status, they also had to pay for festivals, sacrifices, and public works. Rich women as well as men could become *curiales.*

The requirement that equestrians come from freeborn families signifies a remarkable aspect of the demography of the Roman Empire: much of the population in many areas had slaves as ancestors. Moreover, many men and women in the empire had themselves once been slaves but had either bought their freedom or been manumitted in their masters' wills. These freedmen and freedwomen often worked as craftspeople or merchants in the cities and on farms in the countryside. During the first century A.D. some of them became prominent members of the emperor's personal staff and thus of the empire's central administration. Although ordinary freedmen and freedwomen formed the economic backbone of the empire, the rich scorned

A Roman Couple
This painting from a house in Pompeii probably portrays the wealthy baker P. Paquius Proclus and his wife. He holds a scroll and she holds a wax-covered writing tablet and stylus to proclaim their literacy.

them. Cicero had long before expressed a typical upper-class republican attitude that persisted under the empire: "The occupations of all workers, merchants, craftsmen, dancers, and actors are vulgar and unsuitable for gentlemen."

Those who were not members of the social elite faced even greater disadvantages than social snobbery. Even in a so-called Golden Age people at the bottom of the economic heap continued to endure a desperate existence. The republican distinction between the "better people" (*honestiores*) and "humbler people" (*humiliores*) became more pronounced throughout the principate, and by the third century A.D. it pervaded Roman legal affairs. No detailed description of the criteria for dividing people into "better" and "humbler" survives, but we do know the "better people" included senators, equestrians, *curiales,* and retired army veterans. Everybody else (except for slaves, who counted as property, not people) made up the vastly larger group of "humbler people." These people faced their gravest disadvantage if they were brought to trial: the law imposed harsher penalties on *humiliores* than on *honestiores,* even for the same crimes. A person was probably classified as "better" or "humbler" at his or her trial. Humbler people convicted of capital crimes were regularly executed by being crucified or torn apart by wild animals before a crowd of spectators. Better people rarely suffered the death penalty, but if they were condemned, they received a quicker and more dignified execution by the sword. When being questioned in criminal investigations, humbler people could also be tortured, even if they were Roman citizens. Romans regarded this inequality under the law fair on the grounds that a person's higher status reflected a higher level of genuine merit. As one provincial governor expressed it, "nothing is more unequal than equality itself."

In Roman society one important function of law was to make discriminations among people. Romans prided themselves on their ability to order their society through law. As Virgil said, the Roman mission was "to establish law and order within a framework of peace." Perhaps the most distinctive characteristic of Roman law was its recognition of the principle of equity. Equity meant using law to bring about what was "good and fair" even if the letter of the law had to be ignored to do so. A concern for equity led Roman legal thinkers to insist, for example, that the intent of parties in a deal outweighed the words of their contract and that the burden of proof lay with the accuser rather than the accused. The emperor Trajan ruled that no one should be convicted on the grounds of suspicion alone because it was better for a guilty person to go unpunished than for an innocent person to be condemned. These principles of Roman law influenced most legal systems in modern Europe.

A concern for fairness and compassion also extended to other aspects of Roman life under the empire. Both public and private sources assisted the poor, especially if the aid might promote agriculture. The emperors initiated welfare assistance for needy children, although their aim was to encourage Romans to have more children. Wealthy people sometimes adopted children in their communities. One North African man gave enough money to support 300 boys and 300 girls each year until they grew up. The relative value of male and female children in Roman society is evident in these efforts: boys often received more aid than did girls under these assistance programs.

Marriage and Medicine

The status of some Roman women improved under the empire. Beginning in the late republic, Roman women had started to gain more power over property and divorce. Rich Roman women could operate almost as free agents by the time of the empire because marriage no longer gave the husband legal authority over whatever property the wife had received from her parents. A wife could instigate and obtain a divorce and still retain control over the property she had owned as a single woman, just as widows did. Most women continued to work at low-paying jobs, such as dressmakers or fish sellers, and had little property to control. For them an improved legal status had little or no effect on their economic status. As before, the poorest women often had to resort to prostitution to earn money.

Just as under the republic, girls in the Roman Empire often married in their early teens or even younger. Although marriages were usually arranged between spouses who hardly knew each other, husbands and wives could grow to admire and love each other. A butcher in Rome put up this memorial to his dead wife, who had the virtues Roman husbands deemed appropriate for a married woman: "She was my one and only wife, chaste in body and displaying a loving spirit. She remained faithful to her faithful husband. Always cheerful, even when times were tough, she never neglected her duties."

Complications during childbirth and after delivery could easily lead to the mother's death. Roman women often began bearing children in their early teens, when complications are more common, and Roman medicine could do little to cure any resulting illness or infection. Midwives and folk practitioners provided some information about sex and childbirth, but knowledge about such matters probably came mostly from family members. Young women who were not told about sex and pregnancy sometimes suffered dismal consequences. The upper-class government official Pliny, for example, once sent the following report to the grandfather of his third wife, Calpurnia: "You will be very sad to learn that your granddaughter has suffered a miscarriage. She is a young girl and did not realize she was pregnant. As a result she was more active than she should have been and paid a high price for her lack of knowledge by falling seriously ill." Male specialists were also ill informed about the process of reproduction; gynecologists erroneously recommended the days just before and after menstruation as the best time to become pregnant.

Concern about reproduction permeated marriage. Because so many children died young, families had to produce numerous children to keep from disappearing. The tombstone of Veturia, a soldier's wife married at eleven, tells a typical story: "Here I lie, having lived for twenty-seven years. I was married to the same man for sixteen years and bore six children, five of whom died before I did." Not all people wanted children, and some ways to prevent pregnancy were known and freely practiced. Women's contraceptive methods included using a tuft of wool as a diaphragm or drinking a potion prepared from the sap of the silphium plant, a now extinct species of giant fennel that grew near Cyrene in North Africa. Recent medical research seems to confirm that a drug made from silphium would have been an effective contraceptive or abortifacient and helps explain why the plant was worth more than its weight in silver as an export. Some women resorted to less expensive aids believed to deter conceiving, such as wearing a spider's head on a necklace as a magical charm. The available methods of abortion, which was a controversial practice, were extremely dangerous. The Roman emphasis on child bearing in marriage brought its own hazards to women, but to remain single represented social failure for a Roman girl.

Once children were born, they were cared for by both their mothers and any household help in all but the more affluent families. Women who could afford child care routinely had their babies attended to and breast-fed by wet nurses. Scholars disagree on whether this practice weakened the ties of affection between Roman mothers and their children. Inevitably, some babies were not wanted by their parents. The practice of exposure continued during the empire, more so for baby girls than baby boys.

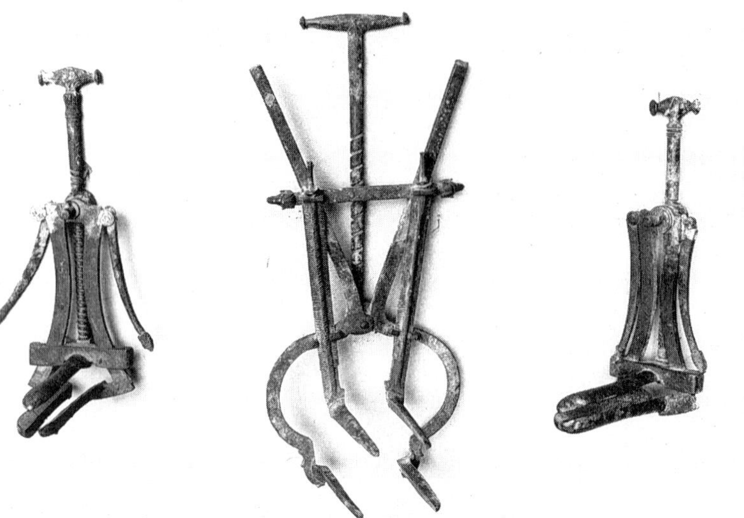

Roman Medical Instruments *Ancient medical practitioners used a variety of metal tools for surgery and other treatments. The most elaborate tools were obstetrical.*

Most therapies of everyday Roman general medicine were comparable to those used in Hellenistic Greece. Treatments were mainly limited to potions, such as the drink of wild boar's manure boiled in vinegar customarily given to chariot drivers who had been injured in crashes. Roman technology did, however, provide carefully crafted instruments for surgery and for physical examinations of female and male patients. Many doctors were freedmen from Greece and other provinces, and they usually had only informal training. The public considered their occupation low status, unless the doctor served the emperor or other members of the upper class. The most famous court physician of the Roman Empire was Galen (c. A.D. 129–199), who began his career ministering to gladiators but eventually became the doctor of the emperor Marcus Aurelius (*A.D. 161–180). Galen accepted the traditional theory of the four bodily humors, but he also increased medical knowledge. In anatomy, for example, he demonstrated by careful dissection that the blood circulates through the arteries as well as the veins. He also studied neurology, physiology, pharmacology, and diet, and the many books he wrote to explain his doctrines affected later medical thought tremendously. Particularly influential were his ideas that doctors should constitute an elite profession and that medical science required systematic, comprehensive knowledge of health and illness rather than the compartmentalized specialization frequent in his times.

The Merging of Cultures in the Roman Provinces

By the second century A.D. the provinces of the Roman Empire covered a vast territory stretching from Spain to Mesopotamia in one direction and from the British Isles to North Africa in the other. These provinces contained a wide diversity of peoples speaking different languages, observing different customs, dressing in distinctive styles, and worshiping various divinities. In the rural areas of the empire, Roman contact had virtually no effect on local customs. Where new towns were built, however, Roman influence was evident. Many towns in the western empire originated with the settlements peopled by army veterans the emperors had spread around the provinces, and others grew up around Roman forts. Some regions sprouted cities much earlier than others. Prominent men from Roman towns in Spain, for example, had successful public careers at Rome by the first century A.D. Eventually even emperors came from Roman families in the provinces; Trajan, whose family had settled in Spain, was the first.

The growth of Roman towns in regions the Romans had considered barbarian was most conspicuous in what is today Europe west of the Rhine River. Prominent modern cities such as Trier and Cologne near Germany's western border started as Roman towns. Even in this part of the empire, however, the countryside remained much less influenced

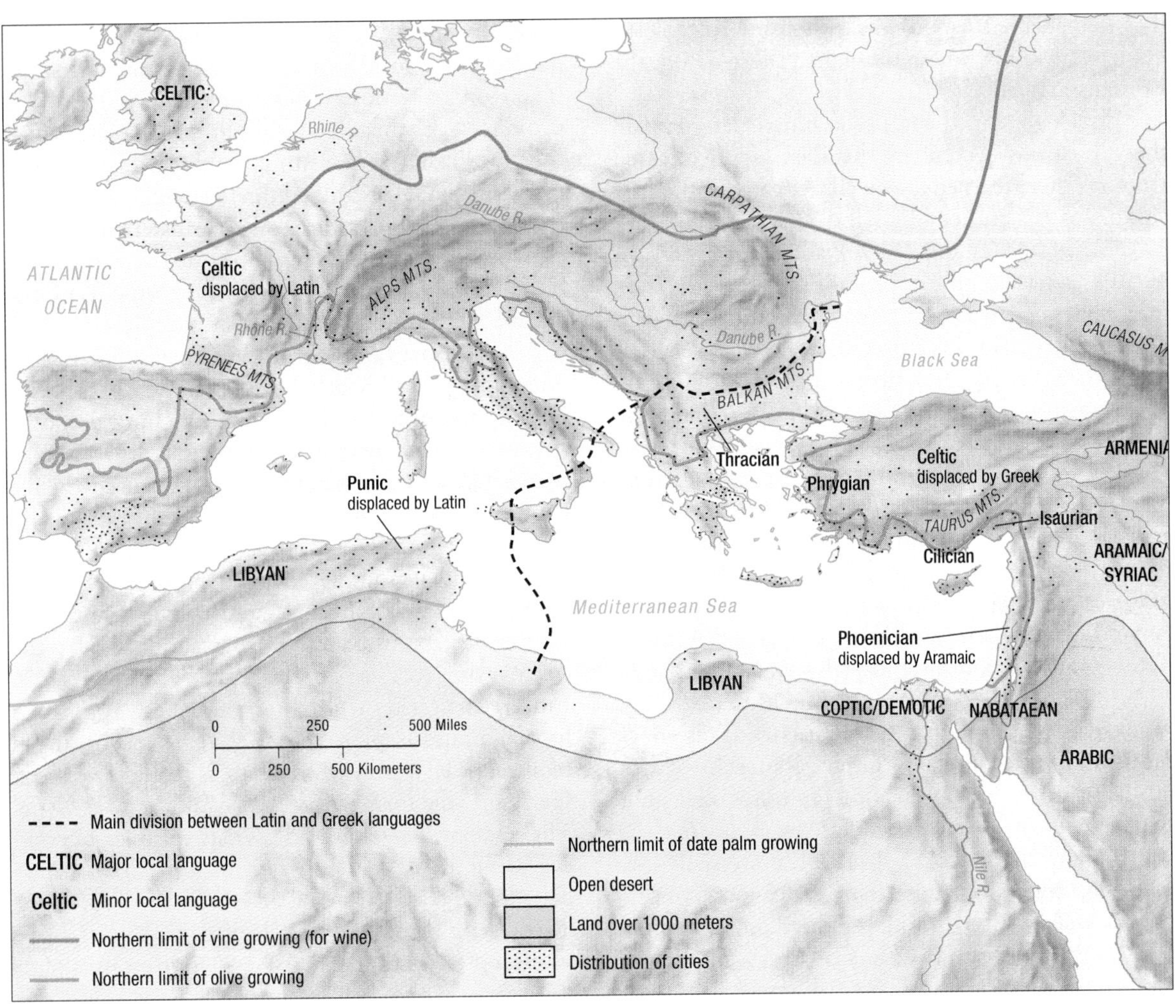

Natural Features and Languages of the Roman World

by the Roman presence. Moreover, the Romans and "Romanized" provincials in the towns were themselves affected by local traditions. In such provinces as Gaul, Britain, and North Africa, the interaction of Romans and provincials produced new, mixed cultural traditions. *Romanization* of the western provinces meant a gradual merging of Roman and local culture, not the unilateral imposition of Roman ways of life on provincials. Romanization also raised the standard of living for many people in the provinces as roads and bridges improved, trade increased, and agriculture flourished under the peaceful conditions secured by the Roman army. Where Roman troops were stationed in the provinces, their need for supplies meant new business for farmers and merchants. Non-Romans who lived more prosperously under Roman rule than ever before found Romanization easy to take.

The Eastern provinces of the Roman world retained their Greek and Near Eastern character under the empire. Such great cities as Alexandria in Egypt and Antioch in Syria had been thriving for centuries. Compared to Rome, they had more individual houses for the well-to-do, fewer blocks of high-rise tenements, and equally magnificent temples. The local elites of the eastern cities easily fit into the Roman system of patronage as the clients of the emperor and the patrons of their communities. They had long ago become accustomed to the comparable paternalistic social relationships that had formed part of the system of rule of the Hellenistic kings, who had reigned there before the Romans arrived.

Greek remained the predominant language in these bustling centers in the East, and educated Romans there learned it as well. Already in the first century A.D., authors like the poets Lucan (A.D. 39–65), Statius (c. A.D. 45–96), and Martial (c. A.D. 40–104) and the philosophical essayist and tragedian Seneca (c. 4 B.C.–A.D. 65) had contributed to a revival in Latin literature, what literary scholars called its Silver Age. Its most famous authors, such as the historian Tacitus (c. A.D. 56–120) and the satiric poet Juvenal (c. A.D. 65–130), wrote with acid wit and verve. By the middle of the second century A.D., however, Greek literature experienced a renaissance that relegated Latin literature to second rank. New trends, often inspired by the work of Hellenistic authors, blossomed in Greek literature. Second-century authors like Chariton and Achilles Tatius penned romantic novels. Lucian (c. A.D. 117–180) composed satirical dialogues that fiercely mocked both people and gods. As part of his enormous and varied literary output, Plutarch (c. A.D. 50–120) wrote biographies of famous Greek and Roman men as character studies.

In much of the eastern Roman Empire, daily life, including education and artistic endeavors, continued to follow Greek models. The Roman emperors lacked any notion of themselves as missionaries who had to impose Roman civilization on foreigners. Rather, they saw themselves primarily as peacekeepers and preservers of law and social order. They allowed the traditional Greek forms of civic life and government to continue largely unchanged. The willing cooperation of the upper classes of the provinces in the task of governing the empire was crucial in making it possible for the emperors to provide these benefits.

The Army and the Limits of the Roman Empire

The strength of the Roman imperial army was also crucial in ensuring the empire's stability. Because Roman rule maintained the privileged position of local elites, stable and peaceful provinces had no need for garrisons of troops. Roman soldiers were a rare sight in many places. Even Gaul, which had originally resisted its Roman conquerors with an almost suicidal frenzy, was, according to a contemporary witness, "kept in order by 1,200 troops—hardly more soldiers than it has towns." Most of the Roman troops were concentrated in the provinces on the northern and eastern fringes of the empire. There the Romans feared that the local residents, less Romanized than provincials closer to the center of the empire, might cause trouble, and that hostile neighbors living just beyond the boundaries of imperial territory would raid the empire's outlying towns and farms.

The Roman army in the late republic and the Augustan period had been an engine of prosperity because its success in war brought in huge amounts of capital that more than compensated for its cost to the treasury. Prisoners of war, captured by the thousands, were sold as slaves. The victorious army also seized movable property of all kinds as war booty. And it conquered great expanses of land, providing new tax revenues. (Augustus's capture of Egypt was the most spectacular addition.) By the end of Augustus's reign, the territory of the Roman Empire encircled the Mediterranean Sea. Augustus's most ambitious plan was to extend the northern frontier eastward into what is today western Germany, the former Czechoslovakia, and Austria. The part of his scheme designed to push beyond the Rhine River failed disastrously in A.D. 9, when his general Varus was wiped out in the Teutoburg Forest with three legions (a legion was a unit of five thousand to six thousand troops). For months after this catastrophe, Augustus stormed around the palace with his hair and beard untrimmed, pounding his head on a door while shouting, "Varus, give me back my legions!" The Rhine River subsequently marked the easternmost extent of Roman territory in Europe.

The loss of Varus's troops left the Roman army with twenty-five legions, which nominally contained six thousand men each at full strength, but retirements and losses usually kept each legion at least several hundred men below full enrollment. Soldiers enlisted for terms of twenty to twenty-five years. The famous discipline and maneuverability in battle of the Roman legions stemmed from their organization into smaller units under a precise system of command. Each legion consisted of ten cohorts, each cohort of three maniples, and each maniple of two centuries. A century, named for its theoretical strength of 100 men, was commanded by a centurion. Drawn from the nonaristocratic ranks of society, centurions maintained

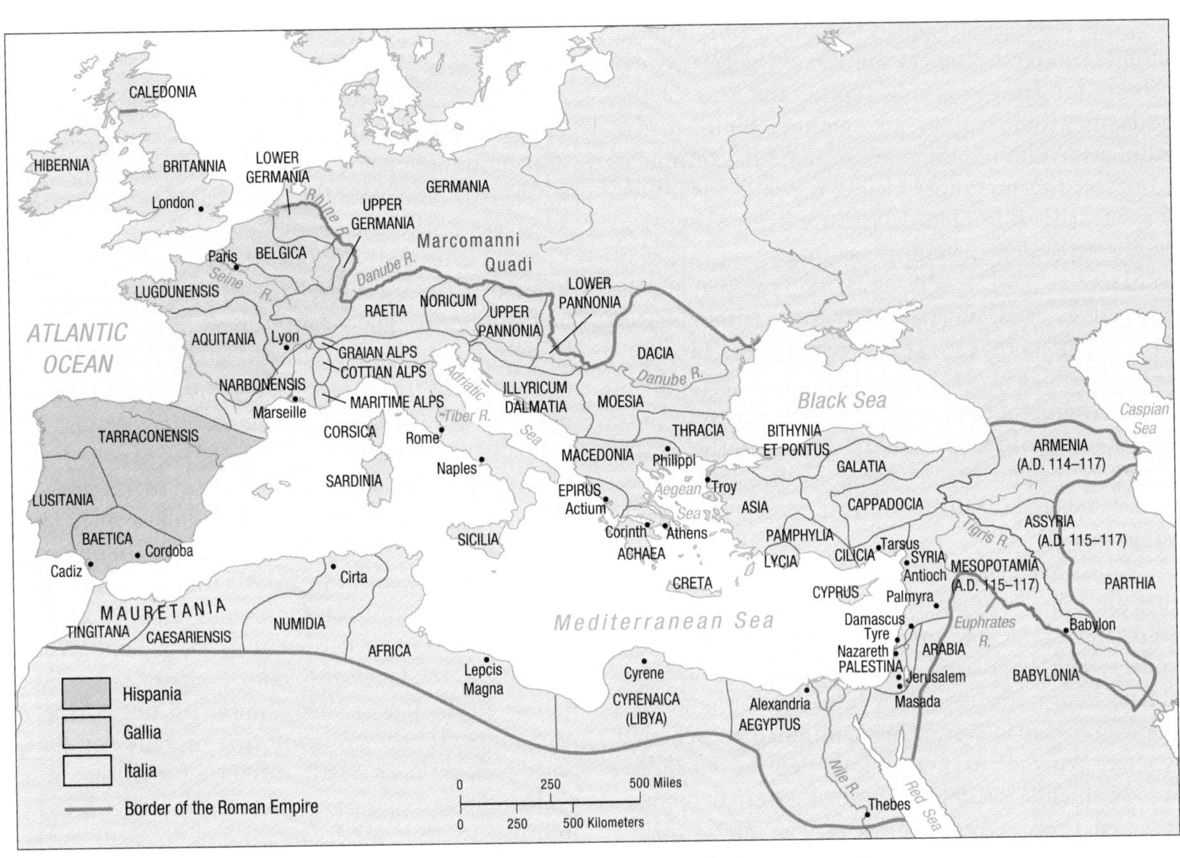

The Provinces of the Roman Empire at its Largest Extent (Second Century A.D.)

discipline and provided invaluable advice to the aristocratic officers, who normally lacked long experience in military service. The best centurions could reach the rank of *primus pilus* ("chief unit commander"), the leader of a legion's first century. These successful military men earned the social rank of equestrians and a retirement benefit of 600,000 sesterces (a basic unit in Roman coinage).* An ordinary legionary soldier earned 900 sesterces a year in the first century A.D., from which expenses were deducted, and received 12,000 sesterces on retirement. Members of the emperor's praetorian guard earned far greater sums. Soldiers' regular pay was supplemented by the substantial bonuses (donatives) that emperors paid on their accession and other special occasions. The material rewards made an army career very desirable for many men, and enlistment counted as a privilege restricted to free male Roman citizens. The Roman army also included auxiliary units manned by noncitizens, often specialized troops such as cavalry, archers, and slingers. The auxiliaries, whose numbers probably approached that of the regular legionary soldiers, learned some Latin and were introduced to Roman customs by serving under Roman commanders. Little is recorded about the terms of their service, but upon discharge from the army they received Roman citizenship for themselves and their descendants. In this way the Roman army served as an indirect instrument in spreading the Roman way of life.

*Meaningful calculations of the value of ancient money are difficult because prices changed over time and varied from region to region. Some items, especially cloth, were proportionally more expensive in antiquity than today because the lack of mass production kept prices high. In the first century A.D., table wine in the taverns of Pompeii in southern Italy cost from one-quarter to one sesterce per pint, and a loaf of bread in the same period cost about three-quarters of a sesterce. The notoriously frugal Cato in the second century B.C. paid 400 sesterces for one outfit of clothing (toga, tunic, and shoes). The cost of a blanket in A.D. 202 is recorded as 100 sesterces.

The theoretical Roman military goal remained infinite conquest. Virgil in *The Aeneid* had expressed this notion by portraying Jupiter, the king of the gods, as promising "empire without limit" to the Romans. Although imperial propaganda continued to reflect this grandiose vision, the military reality was usually different. Emperors after Augustus rarely expanded the empire significantly; one was Trajan (A.D. 53–117, *98–117), who campaigned as far east as Mesopotamia after succeeding Nerva (A.D. 30–98 *96–98). Trajan's successor, Hadrian (A.D. 76–138, *117–138), however, had to relinquish these conquests. Most emperors concentrated on maintaining order within the empire rather than trying to extend it; but some acquired additions that lasted, and the dream of further conquest never vanished.

Controversial recent scholarship has suggested that the emperors paid less attention to formulating a coherent policy of defense against potential invaders than historians often assume, because no matter how unrealistic their hopes of foreign conquest sometimes were they continued to see the Roman army primarily as an offensive weapon. Arrangements for defense against external threats received a relatively low priority. The safety of the empire probably owed more to geography than to a preconceived defensive strategy. The great deserts stretching along its frontiers in North Africa and the ancient Near East provided natural obstacles to invasion. The troops positioned near the empire's frontiers did serve a defensive purpose besides squelching local disturbances. They alerted Rome if attacked and could mobilize to repel any invaders, such as the Germanic bands that often crossed the Danube and Rhine rivers (easier to cross than the great deserts) to raid Roman territory. But the defense of the empire against threats from outside was often more a matter of responding to attacks after the fact than of planning ahead to prevent them.

The army's mobility depended on a vast network of roads and bridges stretching across the empire all the way to its frontier zones. The Romans made these roads primarily for infantry on the march rather than for wheeled vehicles, and their surfaces could be bumpy and their grades steep: Roman engineers punched these rough, straight roads through otherwise nearly impassable terrain, such as marshes and dense forests. Civilians used the roads for travel, but land transportation was generally too expensive for trade goods, which therefore went by sea.

The most significant threats to the empire's safety occurred on its northern and eastern frontiers. During the reigns of Antoninus Pius (A.D. 86–161, *138–161) and Marcus Aurelius (A.D. 121–180, *161–180), the Germanic peoples north of the Danube constantly menaced Roman settlements. Roman prosperity lured their bands of warriors bent on booty. These bands lived in family groups loosely united by shared beliefs and customs. The men in these tribes usually fought in ragtag bands of raiders, but the Marcomannic wars against the Romans (A.D. 166–172, 177–180) provoked the Germanic tribes into reorganizing themselves as more regular armies. The Germanic armies that emerged from this process caused the empire enormous difficulties from this time forward. The Romans also employed Germanic warriors as auxiliary soldiers in their own army because they had recognized the Germans' valor ever since the fierce battles Julius Caesar had fought on his northern campaigns. It is a sad irony that Marcus Aurelius, who would have vastly preferred the life of a philosopher to that of a soldier, had to spend years fighting in the northern wilderness against the Germanic peoples the Quadi and the Marcomanni.

Roman Roads
Stone-paved roads like the Via Appia, which led south out of Rome, connected the empire's capital to other cities. These routes facilitated swift marches by Rome's armies.

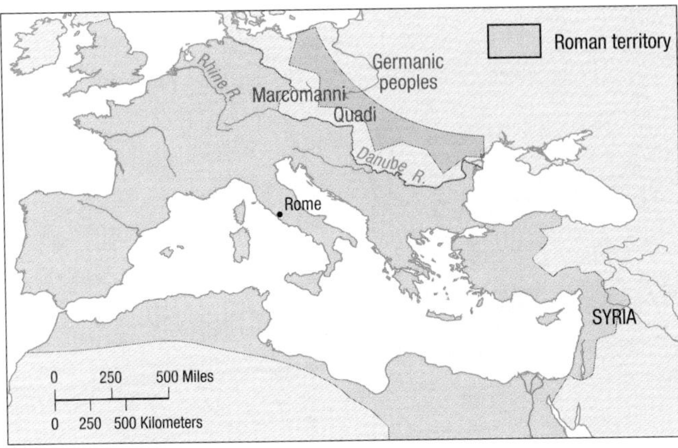

Pressures on the Northern Frontier, Second Century A.D.

Remarkably, despite the rigors of war, he persisted in writing down his musings on life, in Greek. The resulting book, *The Meditations,* offers often gloomy but touching reflections on the human condition, such as his belief that people exist for each other. "Either make them better, or just put up with them," he advised.

The revolt of a Roman general in Syria who hoped to become emperor himself forced Aurelius to abandon any plan of establishing unchallenged Roman control in the eastern Danube region. The best he could do was to settle bands of rough-hewn, non-Roman locals south of the river and hope they would serve as a buffer against the hostile groups to the north. Aurelius therefore established a precedent for settling Germanic peoples, barbarians to the Romans, in Roman territory to try to secure peace. This policy, born of desperation, was an early hint that in the long run the only way to preserve the Roman Empire was to find ways to accommodate all those who wished to live within its territory.

The Economic Origins of the Crisis of the Third Century A.D.

The emperors from Nerva through Marcus Aurelius are known as "the five good emperors" because their relations with the Roman upper class were generally less hostile than those of infamous past tyrants like Caligula or Nero or those future rulers like Commodus (A.D. 161–192, *180–192). Commodus was Aurelius's son, whom he designated as his successor at the age of nineteen despite Commodus's obvious cruelty. Aurelius's choice of Commodus ended the custom followed by each of the previous four emperors, who designated the best available man as his successor by adopting him as his son. Commodus embarked on a reign marred by murdering his closest associates and scandalously appearing in the arena as a gladiator, dispatching wild beasts by the score and battling other fighters who did not try to lose just to make the emperor look good. When Commodus's advisers bribed an athlete to strangle him in a wrestling match, no one regretted the end of his reign, especially not the neglected military. The political chaos that ensued, however, could hardly have been worse. The praetorians murdered the first successor to Commodus and then demanded huge bribes to support further candidates for the throne. It had long been the custom for a new emperor to pay a donative to the troops in Rome, but this time the praetorians auctioned off the throne of the Roman Empire to the highest bidder. The winner lasted only a couple of months. A soldier, Septimius Severus (A.D. 145–211, *193–211), then took over.

Severus was a soldier's emperor who came from the great North African city of Lepcis Magna in what is today Libya. He vigorously pursued the imperial dream of foreign conquest with campaigns beyond the ends of the empire in Mesopotamia and Scotland. By his time the Roman army had expanded by a hundred thousand more troops than under Augustus, enrolling perhaps as many as three hundred fifty thousand to four hundred thousand regular and auxiliary troops (some historians believe the number to be substantially smaller). Army life was harsh because the troops trained constantly. Soldiers had to be fit enough to carry their forty-three pound packs up to twenty miles in five hours, swimming any rivers in their way. Because a Roman legion on the march built a fortified camp every night, the troops essentially carried all the makings of a wooden-walled city with them everywhere they went. As one ancient commentator noted, "Roman infantrymen were little different from loaded pack mules." Huge quantities of supplies were required to support the army. At one temporary fort in a frontier area, for example, archaeologists found a supply of a million iron nails—ten tons' worth. The same encampment required seventeen miles of timber for its barracks walls. To outfit a single Roman legion with tents took fifty-four thousand calf hides.

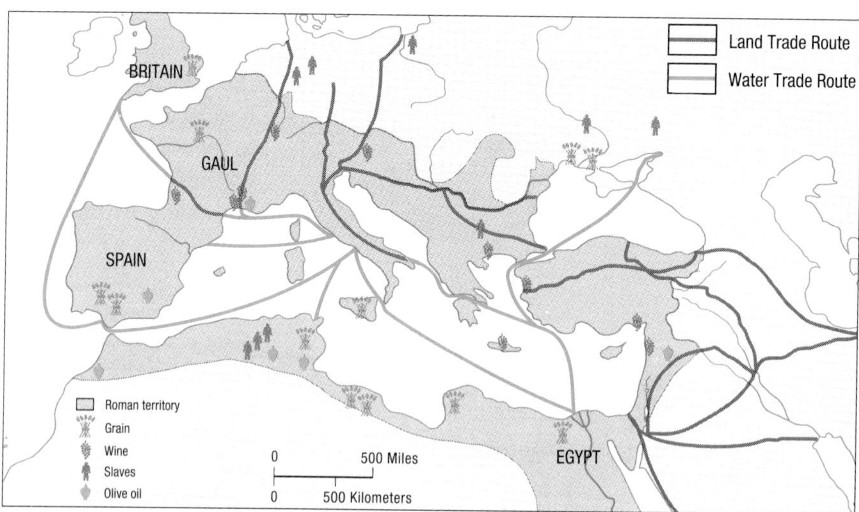

Trade Routes in the Roman Empire

Successful conquests had dwindled under the empire, and the army had become a source of negative instead of positive cash flow to the Roman treasury. The economy had not expanded sufficiently to compensate for the difference. Economic changes of the early empire had reestablished the traditional Mediterranean pattern of mainly intraregional commerce for bulk commodities. During the late republic and Augustan period, a nontraditional pattern had developed when central Italian producers established a flourishing export trade to the western provinces. For example, immense quantities of wine and olive oil were shipped to the markets of Gaul and Spain. Gangs of slaves working on Italian plantations produced these cash crops specifically for export. In the first centuries of the empire, however, the western regions developed their own local production by tenant farmers whose prices undercut those of the imports from Italy.

With the loss of these export markets, Italian producers in the second century A.D. increasingly rid themselves of their slave gangs and changed over to a more diverse mix of agriculture and stock raising by tenants, who were mostly free men and women. Their products met the increased demand from imperial Rome and other Italian markets, which the peaceful conditions of the early empire had encouraged. Even olive oil was now imported to Italy from Spain, to be replaced by A.D. 200 by oil from North Africa. These African imports took over because they could piggyback at little cost on the constant traffic of ships bringing African grain to Italy. These shipments constituted taxes levied on the province of Africa and supplied the state-sponsored giveaway of grain to the urban masses in Rome. In other words, only the existence of this state-organized and financed transportation system allowed African producers to sell their products abroad at a profit. Otherwise, the high cost of transporting goods in antiquity made such trade often impractical. Transportation over land was so slow and difficult that the costs of shipments often doubled and tripled after even short trips. Shipments by sea moved slowly, too. A superfast ship could sail from Egypt to Rome's port in a week, but an ordinary voyage lasted fifty days. Under these conditions the only consistent long-range trade was in luxury items such as spices, ivory, or silk. Roman merchant ships in search of such exotic treasures for import at exorbitant prices regularly sailed as far east as India and Ceylon (today Sri Lanka).

The Roman government's need for revenue had grown faster than the empire's tax base. The state needed more income because the army had grown by a third and inflation had driven up prices. A principal cause of inflation under the early empire may have been, ironically, the long period of peace that promoted increased demand for the empire's relatively static production of goods and services. Over time, some emperors responded to inflated prices by debasing imperial coinage in a vain attempt to cut government costs for purchasing goods and services. By putting less silver in each coin without changing its face value, emperors hoped to create more cash with the same amount of precious metal. But merchants simply raised prices to make up

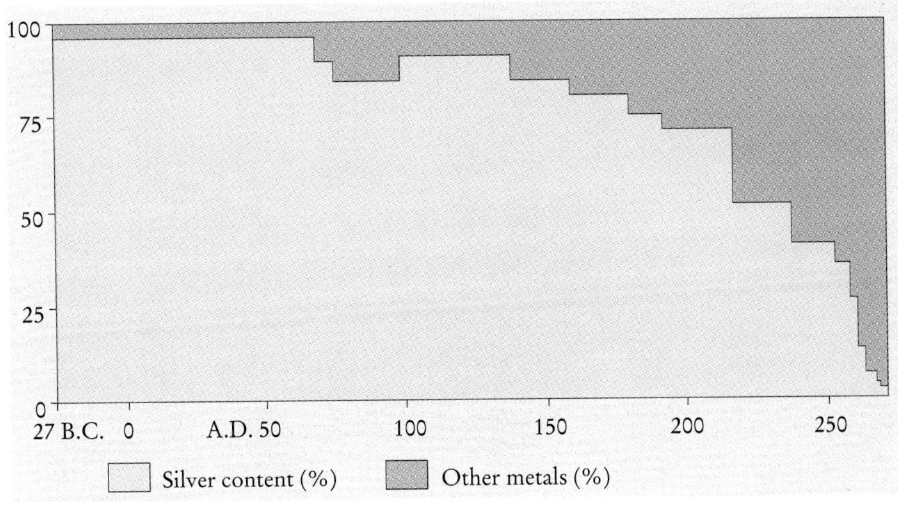

Roman Imperial Silver Coinage, 27 B.C.–A.D. 272

for the loss in value from the debased currency, increasing the momentum of the inflationary spiral.

The Political Catastrophe After Severus

By the time Severus became emperor in A.D. 193, inflation had diminished the value of the soldiers' wages to virtually nothing after the cost of basic supplies and clothing had been deducted from their pay. They routinely expected the emperors as their patrons to favor them with gifts of money, especially when a new emperor was first chosen. Severus set out to improve conditions for the soldiers more fundamentally. He ended the prohibition against troops' marrying while in service and raised their pay by a third. This pay raise for an army a third larger than in Augustus's time further strained the imperial budget and increased inflationary pressures. For Severus the financial consequences of his military policy were of no concern. His deathbed advice to his sons was to "stay on good terms with each other, be generous to the soldiers, and pay no attention to anyone else."

Severus's sons followed their father's advice only on the last two points. Caracalla (A.D. 188–217, *211–217) seized the throne by murdering his brother Geta. Caracalla's profligate reign signaled the end of the relative peace and prosperity of the early Roman Empire. He increased the soldiers' pay by another 40 percent to 50 percent and spent gigantic sums on building projects such as the largest public baths Rome had ever seen. Caracalla's extravagant spending put added pressure on the people responsible for collecting taxes and on those who had to pay them. Caracalla's most famous enactment, the granting in A.D. 212 of Roman citizenship to almost every man and woman in the empire except slaves (Constitutio Antoniniana), had a financial goal. Because only citizens paid inheritance taxes and fees for freeing slaves, an increase in citizens meant an increase in revenues, much of which was earmarked for the army. Despite this tactic, Caracalla wrecked the imperial budget and paved the way for the ruinous inflation to come in the third century A.D. He summed up his disastrous policy once when his mother upbraided him for his excess. "Never mind, mother," he said, drawing his sword, "we shall not run out of money as long as I have this."

Political instability accompanied the financial weakening of the empire. After Macrinus, the commander of the praetorians, murdered Caracalla to make himself emperor, Caracalla's female relatives convinced the army to overthrow Macrinus in favor of a young male relative. The restored dynasty did not last long, however, and by A.D. 235 the secret was out: bribing the soldiers was the way to become emperor. The following forty-nine years included numerous rebellions by pretenders to the throne and the reigns of over twenty separate emperors, sometimes more than one claiming rule at the same time. (The total number of emperors varies depending on how many men claiming rule in this tumultuous period are counted as genuine emperors.) Many of these emperors were members of local elites in the Balkan region of the empire

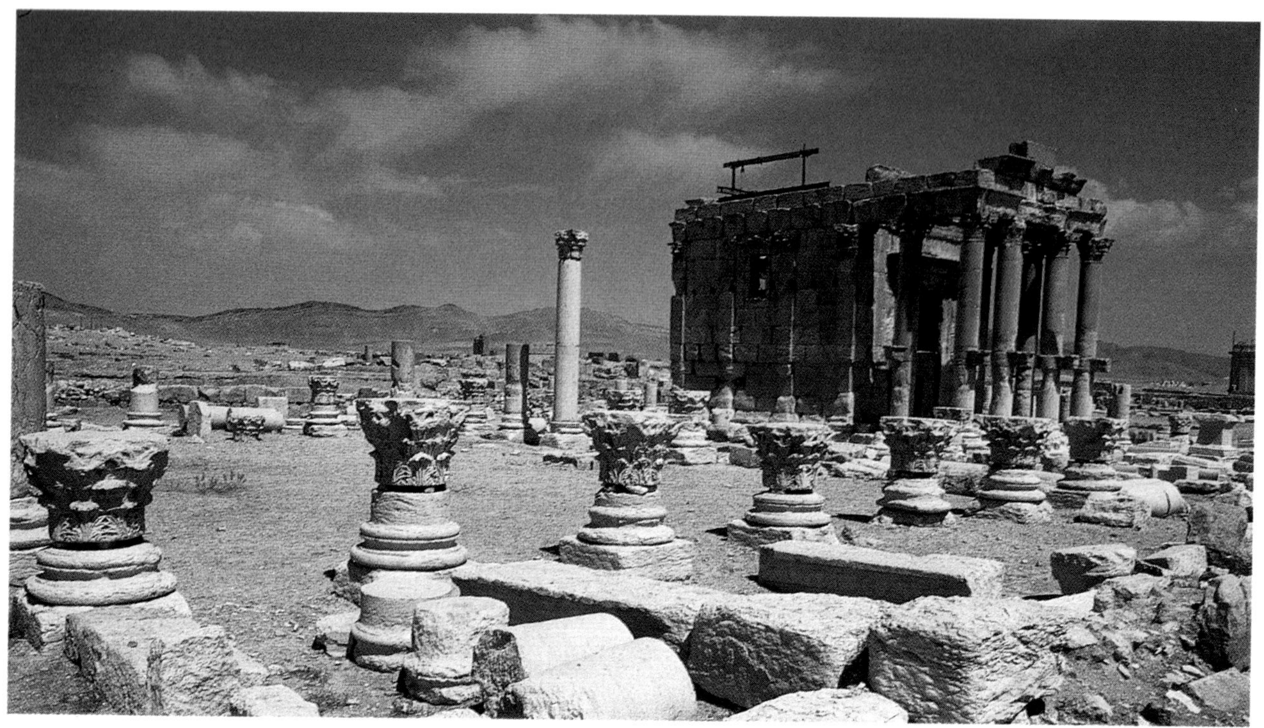

Palmyra in Syria
Located at an oasis on a caravan trade route between Syria and Mesopotamia, Palmyra, the city of Queen Zenobia, flourished under the Roman Empire. Its architecture combined Greek, Roman, and Near Eastern styles.

and had risen through the ranks because of their military prowess. Their skill was needed because the foreign enemies of Rome took advantage of this period of crisis to attack, especially along the eastern frontier. Roman fortunes hit bottom when Shapur I, king of the Sassanid Empire of Persia, rolled over a Roman army and captured the emperor Valerian (✱A.D. 253–260) during a Persian invasion of Syria in A.D. 260. Even the tough Aurelian (✱A.D. 270–275) could manage only defensive operations, such as recovering Egypt and Asia Minor from Zenobia, the warrior queen of Palmyra in Syria. He also had to encircle Rome with a massive wall to ward off surprise attacks from northern tribes who were already smashing their way into Italy.

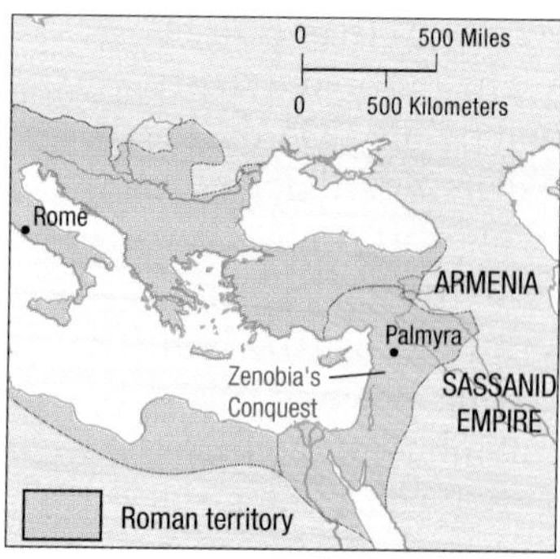

Territory of Zenobia, Queen of Palmyra, A.D. 269–272

This period of political anarchy, hyperinflation, and military disaster in the middle of the third century A.D. had dire repercussions for people of every status in the empire. Natural disasters compounded the social crisis when devastating earthquakes and a virulent plague struck the Mediterranean region in the middle of the third century A.D. The population declined significantly as food supplies became less dependable, civil war killed soldiers and civilians alike, and epidemic diseases ravaged large regions of the empire. The loss of population meant fewer soldiers for the army, whose efficiency as a defense and police force deteriorated severely in any case under the pressures of political and financial chaos. More regions of the empire therefore became vulnerable to raids, and the attacks of invaders and the roving bands of robbers who became more and more common as economic conditions worsened scourged the countryside and its residents. Agricultural producers, the main support of the Roman economy, found it increasingly difficult to pay the higher

Fates of Roman Emperors to A.D. 235

Died of natural causes	*Assassinated, executed, or forced to commit suicide*
Augustus (✱27 B.C.–A.D. 14)	*Gaius, also known as Caligula (✱A.D. 37–41)*
Tiberius (✱A.D. 14–37)	*Claudius (✱A.D. 41–54)*
Vespasian (✱A.D. 69–79)	*Nero (✱A.D. 54–68)*
Titus (✱A.D. 79–81)	*Galba (✱A.D. 68–69)*
Nerva (✱A.D. 96–98)	*Otho (✱A.D. 69)*
Trajan (✱A.D. 98–117)	*Vitellius (✱A.D. 69)*
Hadrian (✱A.D. 117–138)	*Domitian (✱A.D. 81–96)*
Antoninus Pius (✱A.D. 138–161)	*Commodus (✱A.D. 180–192)*
Marcus Aurelius (✱A.D. 161–180)	*Pertinax (✱A.D. 193)*
Lucius Verus (✱A.D. 161–169, co-emperor)	*Didius Julianus (✱A.D. 193)*
Septimius Severus (✱A.D. 193–211)	*Caracalla (✱A.D. 211–217)*
	Geta (✱A.D. 211–212, co-emperor)
	Macrinus (✱A.D. 217–218)
	Elagabalus (✱A.D. 218–222)
	Severus Alexander (✱A.D.. 222–235)

taxes the government demanded. Tenant farmers, called *coloni,* were legally compelled to stay on the land they rented until they paid their taxes, a restriction that applied to their children if any bills were left unpaid. Because revenues from the countryside could not meet the emperors' demands for money, the *curiales,* who were responsible for collecting a set amount of taxes, were often driven to bankruptcy as a result of making up the difference from their own pockets. Consequently, it became extremely difficult to find people willing to serve as local officials. The old way of public service, in which rich and prominent members of society financed public works and acted as patrons to those lower on the social hierarchy, increasingly broke down. Some of the wealthy elite who were supposed to serve as local council members even moved away from their own towns to escape the demands of government service. Others joined the army or petitioned the emperor for a special exemption from public service and its financial obligations. In short, during this period the political and social structure on which the empire had depended for more than two hundred years was gutted, and the separation between rich and poor in Roman society became more marked than ever before.

The economic and political crisis of the Roman Empire was resolved at the end of the 200s, when new patterns of life and government began to emerge. The most significant changes in the later Roman Empire revolved around the importance of Christianity.

The Emergence of Early Christianity

Christianity began as a kind of splinter group within Judaism. The Jewish and Roman worlds did not readily embrace the new Christian movement, however, and virtually every book of the New Testament refers to the resistance the adherents of this new faith faced. As long as believers in Jesus remained members of Jewish synagogues, they found opponents in their fellow Jews. But the main opposition to the new movement came from the non-Jewish Roman world. The appeal and strength of Christianity flowed from its message of salvation, its early believers' sense of mission, and the strong bonds of community it inspired. The new religion's inclusion of women and slaves allowed it to draw members from the entire population. To understand early Christianity we must appreciate developments within Judaism in the Greek and Roman periods.

The Jews Under Greek and Roman Rule

After Alexander conquered the ancient Near East in the late fourth century B.C., the territory called Judaea, where many Jews lived, was controlled at different times by the Ptolemies, whose kingdom centered in Egypt, and by the Seleucids, who ruled Syria. These Hellenistic dynasties fought over Judaea because it occupied the land route between Egypt and Syria. Both the Ptolemaic and the Seleucid kings customarily allowed the Jews in Judaea to govern themselves according to Jewish law. After winning independence from the Seleucid kingdom in the Maccabean revolt that ended in 142 B.C., Judaea was ruled as an independent kingdom by the Hasmoneans, descendants of the Maccabees, until Pompey placed it under Roman control in 63 B.C.

The Romans allowed the Jews a certain measure of independence under local rulers, the most famous of whom was Herod the Great (✱37–4 B.C.). Herod's taste for a Greek style of life, which broke Jewish law, made him unpopular with his Jewish subjects despite his magnificent rebuilding of the temple in Jerusalem. In A.D. 6, after a decade of unrest following Herod's death, Augustus began the tradition of sending governors to Judaea directly from Rome. These officials, first known as prefects, then as procurators, imposed high taxes, but the Jews retained the right to practice their religion. The Roman policy of ruling primarily with an eye to increasing their own wealth and power provoked a Jewish uprising, which the Romans harshly repressed. A full-scale war broke out in A.D. 66 and did not end until 70, when the emperor Domitian's son, Titus, conquered Jerusalem. He ordered his troops to destroy the great temple and sell much of the city's population into slavery. Only a small band of guerrillas, known as "knife-men" from the short sword they used to kill their opponents, held out on the mountain fortress of Masada that Herod had built. After a long siege the Romans finally broke through the walls, only to find that the rebels, including almost all their families, had committed mass suicide the preceding night rather than allow themselves to be captured. The remnants of Jewish resistance to Roman rule flared up again sixty years later. Under the leadership of Simon Bar Kokhba, in the time of the Emperor Hadrian, the Jews fought a bloody war (A.D. 132–135) against the Romans, which once again ended in a crushing defeat. Jerusalem thereafter became a pagan city named Aelia Capitolina, which Jews were forbidden to enter.

Their harsh experiences of economic and political repression raised for many Jews the question of divine justice: How could a just God allow the wicked to prosper and the righteous to suffer? At the time of the persecution under the Seleucid king Antiochus IV, which resulted in the Maccabean revolt, a complex of emerging ideas began to answer this question, not only for the Jews of that time but for many Jews, Christians, and Muslims in later ages. According to this worldview, evil powers, divine and human, controlled the present world. This regime would soon end, however, when God and his agents would conquer the forces of evil. A final judgment would follow, after which the wicked would receive eternal punishment and the righteous eternal reward. Apocalypticism, as this worldview is usually designated today (from the Greek word for "uncovering" or "revelation"), proved immensely popular, especially among the Jews living in Judaea under Roman rule. Often associated with apocalypticism was the ancient belief that a divine agent, sometimes designated the "anointed one" (Hebrew, "Meshiah" or "Messiah"; Greek, "Christ") would initiate the final battle against the forces of evil. Several figures in the early Roman period claimed this title, including Simon Bar Kokhba, the leader of the second Judaean revolt against the Romans. The most important figure for world history, however, was Jesus of Nazareth.

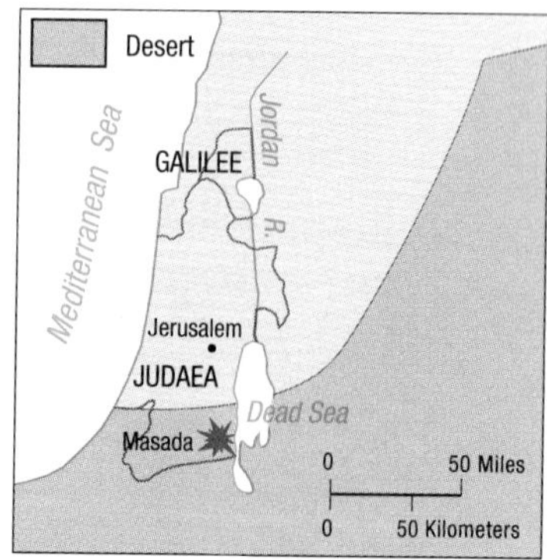

Judea in the First Centuries B.C. and A.D.

Jesus of Nazareth and the Spread of His Teachings

Jesus of Nazareth (c. 4 B.C.–A.D. 30)* began his career as a teacher and healer in his native Galilee, the northern region of Palestine. The New Testament Gospels, written between about A.D. 70 and 90, offer the earliest accounts of Jesus' life. They begin the story of his public ministry with his baptism by John the Baptist, who preached a message of the need for repentance for sins in the face of the

*An explanation of the apparent anomaly of dating the birth of Jesus to 4 B.C. is in the section on dates before the Prologue.

coming final judgment. John was executed by Herod Antipas (✱4 B.C.–A.D. 39), a son of Herod the Great, whom the Romans supported as ruler of Galilee; Herod feared John's apocalyptic preaching might provoke riots. After John's death, Jesus in some respects continued his mission by proclaiming the imminence of God's kingdom. He stressed that this kingdom was open to everyone, regardless of their social status or apparent sinfulness in the eyes of the world. The Gospels interpret Jesus' healings and exorcisms as signs of his conquering the power of Satan, whom those who believed the apocalyptic worldview regarded as the ruler of this world. The Roman prefect Pontius Pilate (✱A.D. 26–36), who no doubt viewed Jesus' popularity with the crowds as a threat to public order in politically volatile Judaea, ordered Jesus' execution in Jerusalem in A.D. 30.

In contrast to the fate of many other charismatic leaders the Romans executed, Jesus' influence did not end with his death. His followers reported that he had been raised from the dead, and they set about convincing other Jews that he was the promised anointed one, the Messiah, who would soon return to judge the world and usher in God's kingdom. At this point those who believed that Jesus was the Messiah had no thought of starting a new religion. They considered themselves good Jews and continued to follow the commandments of the Sinai covenant.

Painting of the "Good Shepherd"
This third century A.D. fresco shows the Good Shepherd carrying the bowl of milk that Christians received on their baptism to symbolize their entry into the Promised Land.

A radical change took place with the conversion of Paul of Tarsus, a pious Jew with Roman citizenship who had formerly persecuted those who accepted Jesus as the Messiah. After a religious experience that he interpreted as a direct revelation from Jesus, Paul became a follower of Jesus, or a Christian (follower of Christ), as members of the new movement came to be known. Paul taught that accepting Jesus' death as the ultimate sacrifice for the sins of humanity was the only way of becoming regarded as righteous in the eyes of God. Those who accepted Jesus as divine and followed his teachings could expect to attain salvation in the world to come.

Although Paul stressed the necessity of ethical behavior, especially the rejection of sexual immorality and worship of pagan gods, he taught that there was no need to keep all the provisions of the Jewish law. His main mission was to the non-Jews of Syria, Asia Minor, and Greece, and he did not require the males who entered the movement to undergo the Jewish initiation rite of circumcision. This tenet and his teachings that his congregations did not have to keep the Jewish dietary laws or celebrate the Jewish festivals led to tensions with the followers of Jesus who lived in Jerusalem, who believed Christians had to follow Jewish law. Roman authorities executed Paul around A.D. 64, labeling him a criminal troublemaker.

After the destruction of Jerusalem in A.D. 70, Paul's position on the proper relationship between Christians and Jewish law won out. His impact on the new movement can be gauged by his thirteen letters that appear in the New Testament, a collection of twenty-seven early Christian writings. Christians came to regard the New Testament as having equal authority with the Jewish Bible, which they now called the Old Testament. Christianity, whose adherents were now predominantly non-Jewish, became a separate religion. Its early congregations were composed mainly of what we might call urban middle-class men and women, with some richer and some poorer members. Women as well as men could hold offices in these congregations, and the first head of a congregation we hear of in the New Testament was a woman. Most early Christians were city-dwellers because teachers like Paul preached primarily in the cities, where contact with crowds of people was easier than in the smaller communities of the countryside.

Persecution and Martyrdom

Unlike Jews, Christians espoused a novel faith, not a traditional religion handed down from their ancestors, and so deserved no special treatment as far as Rome was concerned. Rome furthermore viewed Christians as potential political and social subversives because they proclaimed as king a man the Roman government had crucified as a criminal. Christian ritual also led to accusations of cannibalism in a setting of sexual promiscuity because Christians symbolically ate the body and drank the blood of Jesus during their central rite, which they called the Love Feast. In short, Romans saw Christians as a dangerous new threat to ordinary society.

The Roman historian Tacitus vividly describes the persecution of Christians in Rome in A.D. 64. In that year an inferno of fire destroyed block after block of the *insulae* of apartments in Rome. The urban masses blamed the emperor Nero for the destruction of their homes, believing the fire was his way of clearing the slums to make room for his own pet building program. To divert the mob's rage, Nero accused the Christians of Rome of being the arsonists. He chose them as scapegoats because he knew non-Christians would believe Christians committed criminal acts. As Tacitus reports, Nero had Christians "covered with the skins of wild animals and mauled to death by dogs, or fastened to crosses and set on fire to provide light at night." The harshness of their punishment ironically earned the Christians some sympathy from the general population of Rome.

After the persecution under Nero, the Roman government acted against Christians only intermittently. No law under the early empire specifically forbade Christianity, but Christians were easy prey for Roman officials, who could punish them or order their deaths in the name of maintaining public order. The action of Pliny as a provincial governor in Asia Minor illustrates the Christians' predicament. In about A.D. 112 he had to decide the fate of some Christians local people had brought to his notice. He asked those accused of practicing this new religion if they were indeed Christians, urging those who admitted it to reconsider. Those who denied they had ever been Christians, as well as those who stated they were former Christians who no longer believed, Pliny freed after they sacrificed to the spirit of the emperor and cursed Christ to prove the truth of their statements. He executed those who persisted in declaring themselves Christians.

Fortunately for historians, Pliny reported this incident in a letter to the emperor Trajan, which has survived, along with Trajan's reply. The Christians Pliny executed were killed not because he found them guilty of any crimes but because they refused to surrender their religion and therefore to pay the usual honor to recognized divinities and to the emperor. From the official Roman point of view, Christians had no right to retain their religion if it created disturbances. Trajan's letter to Pliny shows, however, that the government had no policy of tracking down Christians. They concerned the government only when their presence was so disruptive that non-Christians complained to the authorities or the authorities noticed their refusal to participate in official sacrifices. At those times, Roman officials were prepared to execute Christians who would not renounce their religion—just for being Christians—on the grounds that they would suppress anyone whose existence unsettled the peace and order of society.

Perhaps the Romans felt hostile toward Christians mostly because they feared that tolerating them would offend the gods of traditional Roman religion—that is, Romans believed their safety and welfare depended on preserving the *pax deorum* ("peace of/with the gods"). This "contract" between the state and the divine called for humans to pay due respect to the gods of the official cults. Otherwise the gods would retaliate by sending disasters into the world. The Christians' refusal to participate in the imperial cult particularly troubled Romans. Because the Christians denied the existence of the Roman gods and the divine associations of the emperor, they naturally seemed likely to provoke the anger of the gods and therefore deserved blame for natural catastrophes. Tertullian (c. A.D. 160–225), a North African Christian teacher trained in Latin rhetoric, summed up pagan feeling about the danger Christians represented to their safety: "If the Tiber River overflows, or if the Nile fails to flood; if a drought or an earthquake or a famine or a plague hits, then everyone immediately shouts, 'To the lions with the Christians.'"

In response to persecution, Christian intellectuals like Tertullian and Justin (c. A.D. 100–165), a Palestinian Christian who became a prominent Christian teacher in Rome, defended their cause by arguing that the Romans had nothing to fear from the Christians. Far from teaching immorality and subversion, these writers insisted, Christianity taught an elevated moral code and respect for authority. Christianity was not a foreign superstition but the true philosophy that combined the best features of Judaism and Greek philosophy and was thus a fitting religion for the Roman world. Tertullian pointed out that Christians actually prayed for the safety of the empire: "We invoke the true god for the safety of the emperors. We pray for a fortunate life for them, a secure rule, safety for their families, a courageous army, a loyal Senate, a virtuous people, a world of peace."

Persecution did not destroy Christianity, and there is much truth in Tertullian's assertion that "the blood of the martyrs is the seed of the Church." The Christians regarded public trials and executions as an opportunity to become witnesses ("martyrs" in Greek) to their faith. Their willingness to die for their religion, recorded by Christians in stirring accounts, must have impressed many nonbelievers and drawn them to the new faith. Christian martyrs' firm conviction that their deaths would lead directly to heavenly bliss allowed them to face excruciating tortures with courage. Some courted martyrdom. Ignatius (c. A.D. 35–107), the bishop of Antioch, begged the Roman church not to intervene on his behalf after his arrest: "Let me be food for the wild animals (in the arena) through whom I can reach God," he pleaded. "I am God's wheat, to be ground up by the teeth of beasts so that I may be found pure bread of Christ." Similarly, the martyr Perpetua, in writing about her experiences leading up to her execution in about A.D. 203, revealed the depth of emotion prospective martyrdom could elicit for martyrs and their families. She poignantly described her father's bitter grief at her determination to die for her religion. A mother nursing a young infant, she gave up her child and went willingly to a painful death rather than save herself by denying her faith. Stories recounting the courage of martyrs like Perpetua inspired Christians facing hostility from non-Christians and helped shape the identity of this new religion as a faith that gave its adherents the spiritual power to endure great suffering.

The Development of Christian Institutions

The earliest Christians had expected Jesus to return to pass final judgment on the world during their lifetimes. When these expectations about the timing of the physical coming of the kingdom of God were not met, Christians transformed their religion from an apocalyptic Jewish sect into one that would survive over the long term. Over time they developed religious organizations and institutions that supported the survival of their religion. Paul's early congregations had no clear-cut hierarchy because the members thought none was needed, given that they believed the ordinary world would soon end. Each Christian was also seen as possessing different spiritual gifts, with none superior to the other. By the end of the first century A.D., however, Christian congregations began to organize themselves hierarchically. In the congregations of the cities and towns around the Roman Empire, officials called *bishops* gained the authority to define doctrine and conduct, with authority that superseded the *elders*, or leaders, of local churches. The development of the *episcopate* (leadership by bishops, from the Greek word *episkopos*, meaning "overseer, bishop") combatted the splintering effect of the differing interpretations of Christianity that emerged in the early church. Bishops had the power to define what was true doctrine (orthodoxy) and what was not (heresy), and they used their authority over congregations to try to maintain as much uniformity in belief as possible. Most important, bishops decided who could participate in Christian worship, especially the Eucharist, or Lord's Supper, which many regarded as necessary for achieving eternal life. Exclusion meant the loss of salvation. For all practical purposes the meetings of the bishops of different cities constituted the Christian church as a whole, though the church was by no means a unified organization in this early period.

Only men could be bishops, a rule reflecting the spirit of Paul's view that Christian women should be subordinate to Christian men, just as slaves should be subordinate to their masters. In the congregations of Paul's time, women had held positions of leadership unusual in the Jewish and Roman world, and their active participation in the early movement probably contributed to Roman suspicions of Christianity. By the time bishops began to be recognized, however, women were usually relegated to inferior positions in many churches. In the second and third centuries women still had positions of authority in some Christian groups. The late second-century prophetesses Prisca and Maximilla, for example, proclaimed the apocalyptic message of Montanus that the Heavenly Jerusalem would soon descend in Asia Minor. Second-century Christians could also find proof that women could preach and baptize in fictional literature such as *The Acts of Paul and Thecla.* In this story, Thecla calls off her engagement to a prominent noble in order to follow Paul and help him spread the Christian message and found churches. Her mother's words reflect her family's horror at her decision: "My daughter, like a spider bound at the window by that man's words, is controlled by a new desire and a terrible passion." Like the invented literary character Thecla, many Christian women chose a life of celibacy and service to their church. Their commitment to chastity as proof of their devotion to Christianity gave these women the power to control their own bodies by removing their sexuality from the control of men. It also bestowed social status upon them among other Christians, as women with a special closeness to God. By rejecting the traditional roles of wife and mother and by becoming leaders, at least among similarly minded women, celibate Christian women achieved a measure of independence and authority generally denied them in the non-Christian world.

Gnostics

Unlike Judaism and the traditional religions of Greece and Rome, Christianity placed belief ahead of practice as the primary criterion of who was a good and genuine member of the religion. Defining "right" belief, Christian orthodoxy, thus became a critical issue. From the first century A.D. to the present, disagreements about doctrine and accusations of heresy have separated one Christian group from another, sometimes with violent consequences.

One of the great battles over Christian doctrine in the second and third centuries A.D. was the struggle between Gnostics and other Christians. The Gnostics believed an inferior or evil god, in disobedience to the high god, from whom all spirit derives, created the material world. This creator god was the God of the Old Testament, who kept humans in ignorance by claiming he was the only god and by imposing laws on them to keep them enslaved. Salvation could be achieved only by rejecting the material world and recognizing that the soul's true origin and destiny were with the high god. He periodically sent various redeemers into the world to reveal the truth to humanity. According to some Gnostics, the first of these redeemers was the snake in the Garden of Eden, who tried to impart true knowledge to Adam and Eve. The final redeemer was Jesus, who handed down his secret spiritual message to his apostles after his resurrection. It was this saving knowledge (Greek *gnosis*) the Gnostics said they offered the world.

Christian opponents of Gnosticism fought what they saw as its heretical doctrines not only through sophisticated theological treatises refuting its tenets but also through accounts attacking Gnosticism's leaders and demonstrating the power of the orthodox faith. The *Acts of Peter,* for example, told how the apostle Peter fought a duel in Rome with Simon the Magician, the reputed founder of Gnosticism. When Simon demonstrated his power by flying around Rome, Peter used his own magic to cause Simon to crash. The Roman emperor, the story continued, later put Peter to death after the emperor's mistresses converted to Christianity and refused to have sex with him anymore.

Judging from the spirited attacks on it by Church authorities, we can surmise that Gnosticism presented a formidable challenge to what was to become orthodox Christianity. The Gnostic message of redemption through esoteric revelation and rejection of the material world, rather than through belief in the death and physical resurrection of Jesus, as well as its rejection of the Old Testament and its God, represented a radically different form of Christianity from the orthodoxy represented in the New Testament. Ultimately, Gnosticism faded out because most Christians, especially those in positions of power and prosperity, were not ready to turn away from this world and cut all ties to Judaism's Bible. Much of Christianity's appeal resided in Jesus' identity as a man who had been raised from the dead in the recent past; he was not a figure of ancient mythology or a spirit from an alien world. Early Christianity gave its believers the feeling that their God was close to them, loved them, and bound them together to love each other with tenderness and compassion, rich and poor alike, in a community in this world and the next.

Parallel Religious Experience in Paganism

The diverse nature of early Christianity was matched by the diversity of pagan religion under the early empire. In A.D. 200 the overwhelming majority of people in the Roman world were still polytheists. Their deities ranged from the stalwarts of the state cults, such as Jupiter and Minerva, to spirits traditionally thought to inhabit local groves and springs. Several popular new cults also emerged. The Iranian god Mithras developed a large following among merchants and soldiers as the god of the morning light, a superhuman hero requiring ethical conduct and truthful dealings from his followers. But tradition excluded women from Mithraism, and this restriction put the cult at a disadvantage in expanding its membership. In the third century A.D., the emperors enthusiastically introduced worship of the sun as the supreme deity of the empire as part of the official religion. The cult of the goddess Isis, however, best shows how paganism as well as Christianity could provide believers with a religious experience arousing strong personal emotions and demanding a moral way of life.

Isis was a deity of ancient Egyptian religion, and her cult had already attracted Romans by the time of Augustus. He tried to suppress it because it was Cleopatra's religion, but Isis' stature as a loving, compassionate goddess who cared for the suffering of each of her followers made her cult too popular to crush. The Egyptians said it was her tears for famished humans that caused the Nile to flood every year and bring them good harvests. Her image was that of a loving mother, and in art she was often shown nursing her son. A central doctrine of her cult concerned the death and resurrection of her husband, Osiris. Isis promised her followers hope for life after death for themselves, too. Her

Mithras and the Bull
The all-male cult of the god Mithras originated in Persia and became especially popular among soldiers. Here Mithras's role in creation is symbolized by his slaying a bull, from whose blood springs life and vegetation.

cult was open to both men and women, and a preserved wall painting shows people of both dark- and light-skinned races officiating at her rituals.

Like Christianity, the cult of Isis expected its adherents to behave morally. In inscriptions put up for all to read, Isis was portrayed as expressing her expectations for her followers by referring to her own civilizing accomplishments: "I broke down the rule of tyrants; I put an end to murders; I caused what is right to be mightier than gold and silver." A similar concern for upright conduct by Isis' devotees was described in the novel *The Golden Ass* by Apuleius (born A.D. 123), a wealthy and well-educated Roman from North Africa. The hero of his story, Lucius, had trouble obeying Isis' laws of chastity and obedience. At the end of the book, however, Isis' power purified Lucius in a miraculous transformation and prepared him for a new life. Lucius's prayer to her expressed his intense joy after having been spiritually reborn: "O

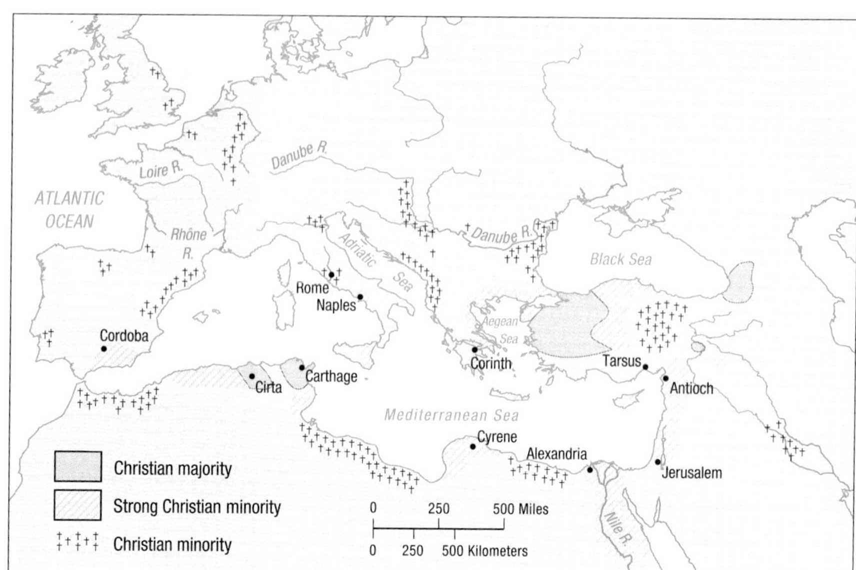

Christian Populations, c. A.D. 300

holy and eternal guardian of the human race, who always cherishes mortals and blesses them, you care for the troubles of miserable humans with a sweet mother's love. Neither day nor night, nor any moment of time, ever passes by without your blessings."

Other pagan cults also required their adherents to lead morally upright lives. Numerous inscriptions from remote villages in Asia Minor, for example, record the confessions of pagan peasants to sins such as sexual transgressions for which their local god had imposed harsh penance on them. Mithraism required its followers to adhere to a strict moral code. For many upper-class Romans in the early empire, the tenets of Stoic philosophy, derived from the teachings of the Greek Zeno (335–263 B.C.), directed their personal lives. Stoics believed in self-discipline above all, and their code of personal ethics left no room for riotous conduct. As the Roman Stoic Seneca (died A.D. 65) put it, "It is easier to prevent harmful emotions from entering the soul than it is to control them once they have entered." For the Stoics the universe was guided by a single creative force that incorporated reason, nature, and divinity. Humans shared in the essence of this universal force and found happiness by living in accordance with it.

Other philosophical challenges caused Christian intellectuals to defend the new faith. Origen (c. A.D. 185–255), for example, argued that Christianity was both true and superior to pagan philosophy as a guide to correct living. At about the same time, however, pagan belief achieved its most philosophical formulation in the works of Plotinus (c. A.D. 205–270). Plotinus's spiritual philosophy, called Neoplatonism (meaning "New Platonism") because it developed new doctrines based on Plato's philosophy, influenced many educated Christians as well as pagans. Plotinus's religious doctrines focused on a human longing to return to the universal Good from which human existence was derived. By turning away from the life of the body through the intellectual pursuit of philosophy, individual souls could ascend to the level of the universal soul, becoming the whole of which, as individuals, they formed a potential part. This mystical union with what the Christians would call God could be achieved only through strenuous self-discipline in personal morality as well as intellectual life. Neoplatonism's stress on spiritual purity gave it a powerful appeal to Christian intellectuals.

Pagan systems of belief, like those of the cult of Isis or the philosophy of the Stoics and Neoplatonists, paralleled those of Christianity in their ability to provide guidance, comfort, and hope to people through good times or bad. The bad times of the economic and political crisis of the third century A.D. gave particular relevance and appeal to the spiritual relief these creeds could offer. It was in this period of crisis that Christianity came under the most violent attack yet. The emperor Decius

(*A.D. 249–251) instituted a systematic persecution of Christians, styling himself "Restorer of the Cults" while proclaiming, "I would rather see a rival to my throne than another bishop of Rome." He ordered all inhabitants of the emperor to prove their loyalty to the welfare of the state by participating in a sacrifice to its gods. Christians who refused were killed.

Conclusion

The Roman Empire began when Augustus created the principate, a new political system of disguised monarchy. The principate endured because it restored peace and stability while maintaining the political vocabulary of the republic and many of its offices. As the patron of all Romans, the emperor exercised paternalistic authority over them in the tradition of the client-patron system. Ultimately, however, his power rested on his control of the army. The succession of Claudius with the backing of the praetorian guard blatantly revealed that force made emperors and set a precedent that would be followed on later occasions when the succession was disputed.

Perhaps the most significant economic trend under the early empire was the shift in the impact of the Roman army. During the republic and the reign of Augustus, the army had been a successful offensive force whose conquests strengthened the empire's economy. Thereafter, only rarely did emperors use it to conquer territory and bring in capital in the form of booty and slaves. When the army spent most of its time maintaining internal security or repelling invaders, as it did for long stretches under the early empire, it severely drained the empire's resources, especially because it had grown by perhaps a third since Augustus's time.

The loss of conquest as a source of income helped precipitate a breakdown in the traditional Roman system of patronage, which had always provided a foundation for the financial and social health of the cities and towns of the empire. Later emperors who lacked the full treasury Augustus enjoyed could no longer function as patrons of the population of the empire in the same generous way as he. The decline in imperial revenues increased the financial pressure on the wealthy elites of the provinces to support public services. When they could no longer meet the government's demand for revenue without ruining their fortunes, these people began to look for ways to escape their traditional duties as patrons.

Roman traditions faced further challenge with the emergence of Christianity. The separation of Christianity from its Jewish origins created a new religion that appealed to men and women across the empire, although its members were still a minority by A.D. 200. The emperor Decius's persecution of them shows the depth of the Roman Empire's troubles in the third century A.D. Authorities sought out Christians to punish because, as so often in history, it was more convenient to blame difficult problems on outsiders rather than those in the government's inner circle. The crisis of the third century A.D. in reality occurred as the culmination of long-term trends complicated by the coincidence of the natural disasters that devastated the Mediterranean world at this time. This combination of events had pushed the Roman Empire to the brink of near anarchy and economic collapse by the 280s A.D. The remarkable history of the changes that brought about a recovery and the equally remarkable transformation of the Roman Empire into a Christian Empire form the next part of the story.

Suggestions for Further Reading

Source Materials

Juvenal. *The Sixteen Satires.* 1967. Stinging satires on Roman urban life under the early empire. Also available in a bilingual Latin/English edition in the Loeb Classical Library series.

Kraemer, Ross E., ed. *Maenads, Martyrs, Matrons, Monastics: A Sourcebook on Women's Religions in the Greco-Roman World.* 1988. A topically arranged selection of sources on the religious experiences of women in Greco-Roman paganism, Judaism, and Christianity.

Lefkowitz, Mary R., and Maureen B. Fant. *Women's Life in Greece and Rome: A Source Book in Translation.* 1982. Contains selected sources on the occupations, daily life, and political and religious experiences of women.

Lewis, Naphtali, and Meyer Reinhold, eds. *Roman Civilization: Sourcebook II: The Empire.* 1990. Offers a wide selection of sources arranged chronologically and topically, with useful introductions to each excerpt; includes political and administrative history.

Suetonius. *The Twelve Caesars.* 1979. Biographies of the rulers of Rome from Caesar to Domitian by an insider with access to the imperial archives. Also available in a bilingual Latin/English edition in the Loeb Classical Library series.

Tacitus. *The Annals; The Histories.* 1978; 1975. A caustic narrative of the imperial reigns from A.D. 14 to 70 by a premier historical stylist. Also available in a bilingual Latin/English edition in the Loeb Classical Library series.

Interpretive Studies

Balsdon, J. P. V. D. *Romans and Aliens.* 1979. A fascinating account of Roman attitudes toward non-Romans in the empire, and vice versa.

Birley, Anthony. *Marcus Aurelius: A Biography.* Rev. ed. 1987. An engaging biography of the most philosophical Roman emperor, which uses Aurelius's own book, *The Meditations.*

Chadwick, Henry, and G. R. Evans. *Atlas of the Christian Church.* 1987. Includes a brief, masterful survey of the history of the early church, with an emphasis on theological and doctrinal history.

Christ, Karl. *The Romans.* 1984. A topically arranged introduction to Roman civilization.

Cornell, Tim, and John Matthews. *Atlas of the Roman World.* 1982. A concise historical survey linked to excellent and colorful maps.

Earl, Donald. *The Age of Augustus.* 1968. An accessible discussion of all aspects of the Augustan age, with many illustrations.

Frend, W. H. C. *The Rise of Christianity.* 1984. An exhaustive study including Jewish background and doctrinal history.

Garnsey, Peter, and Richard Saller. *The Roman Empire: Economy, Society, and Culture.* 1987. A detailed thematic treatment of the political, social, economic, religious, and cultural life of the principate (27 B.C.–A.D. 235).

Grant, Michael. *Cleopatra.* 1972. A readable biography of the last member of the royal line of the Ptolemies.

———. *The Roman Emperors: A Biographical Guide to the Rulers of Imperial Rome, 31 B.C.–A.D. 476.* 1985. Contains short biographies of the Roman emperors from Augustus to Romulus Augustulus.

Greene, Kevin. *The Archaeology of the Roman Economy.* 1986. Presents recent archaeological evidence for trade, transport, finances, and agriculture in the Roman Empire.

Henig, Martin, ed. *A Handbook of Roman Art: A Comprehensive Survey of All the Arts of the Roman World.* 1983. Features broad coverage, including architecture, with many illustrations.

Isaac, Benjamin. *The Limits of Empire: The Roman Army in the East.* 1989. A reassessment of the Roman army's role as more directed toward conquest and internal security than defense against foreign invasion.

Jackson, Ralph. *Doctors and Diseases in the Roman Empire.* 1988. A stimulating study of illness, medical treatment, and the interaction of doctors and healing divinities in the Roman imperial world.

MacMullen, Ramsay. *Paganism in the Roman Empire.* 1981. A comprehensive survey of the great variety of pagan religious beliefs and practices in the Roman Empire.

Meeks, Wayne A. *The First Urban Christians: The Social World of the Apostle Paul.* 1983. A study of what it was like to be an ordinary Christian in Paul's time.

Scarborough, John. *Roman Medicine.* 1969. A wide-ranging introduction for a nonspecialist audience.

Schürer, Emil. *The History of the Jewish People in the Age of Jesus Christ (175 B.C.–A.D. 135).* Rev. ed. 4 vols. 1973, 1979, 1986. An authoritative scholarly work on the history of the Jews in the late republic and early empire.

Sitwell, N. H. H. *Roman Roads of Europe.* 1981. Discusses the Roman road system province by province, and includes many color illustrations.

Stambaugh, John E. *The Ancient Roman City.* 1988. A synthesis of Roman social history in the context of urban architecture and the physical space of the city.

Stambaugh, John E., and David L. Balch. *The New Testament in Its Social Environment.* 1986. A clearly presented introduction to the social world of early Christianity, in the valuable series *The Library of Early Christianity.*

Thompson, Lloyd A. *Romans and Blacks.* 1989. A study of Roman attitudes toward blacks, arguing that skin color was an aesthetic rather than a social issue.

Webster, Graham. *The Roman Imperial Army of the First and Second Centuries A.D.* 3d ed. 1985. Discusses all aspects of the Roman military in this period.

Witt, R. E. *Isis in the Greco-Roman World.* 1971. An account for a general audience of the cult of Isis in ancient Egypt, Greece, and Rome.x

CHAPTER 7

The Fragmentation and Transformation of the Late Roman Empire, 284–568

The Soaring Architecture of Santa Sophia
Golden mosaics originally shone from the high walls and domes of Santa Sophia ("Holy Wisdom"), Emperor Justinian's great church in Constantinople. Its magnificence reflected the scope of Justinian's dream to reunite the eastern and western parts of the Roman Empire.

The dry sands of Egypt have preserved many ancient documents written on paper made from the reeds of the papyrus plant. One typical example from the third century, a personal letter from an Egyptian woman named Isis to her mother, was found among the remains of a village near the Nile River. The letter offers us a tantalizing glimpse of some of the unsettling changes that affected the lives of many people in the Roman Empire of the time.

> *I make supplication for you every day before the lord Sarapis and his fellow gods. I want you to know that I have arrived in Alexandria safely after four days. I send fond greetings to my sister and the children and Elouath and his wife and Dioscorous and her husband and children and Tamalis and her husband and son and Heron and Ammonarion and . . . Sanpat and her children. And if Aion wants to be in the army, let him come. For everybody is in the army.*

Unfortunately, we do not know the relations between Isis and each person she mentioned, with their mixture of Greek and Semitic names. Nor can we tell whether Isis knew how to write or, as was common, had hired a scribe.

Why did Isis go to Alexandria? Why did Aion want to become a soldier? Why was "everybody" in the army? The answers suggest the many dimensions of the third-century crisis in the Roman Empire. Perhaps economic troubles forced Isis to leave her home to look for work in the largest city in her area. Perhaps Aion wanted to join the army to better his condition. Perhaps it seemed that everybody was in the army because the political crisis of the empire frequently led to military conflicts. These possibilities seem plausible in the context of the primary challenge facing the Roman Empire by the second half of the third century: to restore the state's traditional function as the guarantor of peace and order through military force, government administration, and enough economic prosperity to prevent turmoil.

Rome's rulers also faced growing religious tensions between Christians and pagans like Isis (named after the Egyptian goddess). By the end of the fourth century this conflict had been formally resolved in favor of Christianity, which became the empire's official religion. Yet the social and cultural effects of this transformation took much longer to settle because pre-Christian Roman traditions persisted. Eventually, the western and eastern sections of the empire split into two systems. In the western portion, Germanic peoples organized their tribes into kingdoms whose authority eventually replaced centralized Roman rule. They and the inhabitants of the former Roman provinces there lived side by side, each keeping some customs of their heritage intact but merging other parts of their disparate cultures and developing a new sense of ethnic identity. These new kingdoms and the general decentralization of authority set the pattern for the later political divisions of medieval western Europe. Provinces in the eastern Roman Empire stayed under Roman rule for another thousand years, even though hostile neighbors frequently wrenched away some of the empire's territory in wars. This eastern part of the empire became the Byzantine Empire, a power that endured until the mid-1400s. Starting in the third century, the Roman world began to evolve into two distinct entities—the West and the East—whose fates would unfold along separate paths.

Important Dates

c. 285 Anthony withdraws to the Egyptian desert to become the first known Christian monk

301 Emperor Diocletian issues the Edict on Maximum Prices

312 Constantine defeats Maxentius and converts to Christianity

313 Co-emperors Constantine and Licinius abolish official hindrances to Christianity and proclaim a policy of religious tolerance

361–363 Emperor Julian the Apostate tries to restore paganism as Rome's official religion, but fails

378 The Visigoths defeat the eastern emperor Valens at the battle of Adrianople

391 Emperor Theodosius bans pagan sacrifice and closes the temples

410 The army of Alaric, king of the Visigoths, sacks Rome

476 The German commander Odoacer deposes the final western emperor, Romulus Augustulus

529 The Byzantine emperor Justinian orders the closing of the Academy originally founded by Plato in Athens

538 Justinian dedicates the Church of the Holy Wisdom in Constantinople

c. 540 Benedict of Nursia draws up his regulations for monastic life (The Rule of St. Benedict)

The Reorganization of the Roman Empire

The Roman Empire reemerged from the economic and political crisis in the mid-third century as a unified state ruled by a strong central authority. The penetration of the empire's borders by different invaders over several decades, however, had imposed a pressing need to reorganize its defenses and its system of collecting revenue. In the religious arena the pagan emperors confronted the thorny issue of a growing Christian church, whose presence was now felt throughout the Roman world. The definitive responses to these challenges came during the reign of the emperors Diocletian (∗284–305) and Constantine (∗306–337).

Administrative and Military Reforms

Diocletian was an uneducated military man from Dalmatia (a region in what used to be Yugoslavia). His courage and intelligence propelled his rise through the ranks to commander of the emperor

Numerian's personal bodyguard. When Numerian (*283–284) was assassinated soon after taking the throne, the army made Diocletian emperor to avenge the crime. Diocletian swiftly executed the commander of the praetorian guard, Numerian's father-in-law, as the murderer and defeated other rivals for the throne. As emperor, Diocletian used his exceptional talent for administration and control to reorganize the structure of the Roman Empire, reasserting its tradition of centralized authority. The imperial administration needed revamping so the provinces could be governed more effectively; this meant restoring tax revenues and setting new limits on the provincial administrators' power, making it possible for Rome to keep them from rebelling. The third-century invasions had clearly demonstrated that military reforms were necessary; the empire had to have better defensive strategies. The imperial Roman army had two traditional purposes: fighting wars of conquest to satisfy the emperors' desires for glory, booty, and territory, and suppressing unrest in the outlying provinces. Defense, which had previously been considered secondary to offense, became crucial when a double threat arose along the empire's frontiers. The Sassanids, who had created a new Persian Empire, menaced Roman territory in the east, while bands of Germanic warriors raided the empire along its nearly three-thousand-mile-long northern frontier along the Rhine and Danube rivers.

Diocletian's administrative reforms divided the empire into four districts, each with its own ruler, capital city, and military forces. No longer did a single emperor rule the Roman Empire. Under the *tetrarchy* ("rule by four rulers"), as the new system was called, two of the rulers were the senior members (*augusti;* singular, *augustus*) and two the junior (caesars). The *augusti* adopted the caesars as their sons and made them heirs to their thrones to try to prevent the civil wars that had regularly erupted in the third century when a new emperor had to be chosen. When an *augustus* retired or died, his caesar took over as *augustus* and then selected and adopted a new caesar for the junior position. Diocletian himself became the *augustus* of the eastern half of the empire and lived there in Nicomedia, near the Bosphorus Strait in western Asia Minor; and he dominated the *augustus* in the western empire, Maximian. Under Diocletian's arrangement the city of Rome lost its special position as the capital; Diocletian did not even visit Rome until 303, nearly twenty years after becoming emperor. The generals who now determined the empire's fate came from rough lands in the provinces, and the Senate of Rome had lost all power to control them. The northern city of Milan was better located to defend Italy and this became one of Diocletian's new capitals; the others were Nicomedia, Sirmium, near the Danube River border, and Trier, near the Rhine River border. Italy was henceforth just another section of the empire, on an equal footing with the other imperial provinces and subject to the same taxation system (except for the district of Rome itself).

To increase administrative efficiency and prevent provincial governors from becoming too powerful, Diocletian reduced the size of the old provinces, thereby creating new ones and doubling the total number of provinces. The now more than one hundred provinces were divided into twelve groups, called *dioceses,* each headed by a vicar who reported to one of the four praetorian prefects. At this time each emperor had as his principal assistant a prefect who traveled with him wherever he went. Later in the fourth century the prefects were permanently assigned to head the four territorial districts of the empire, which became known as prefectures. Naturally, the increased number of subdivisions required a larger imperial staff. Diocletian chose the administrators almost exclusively from the equestrian class, men who had risen through the military ranks from relatively humble beginnings; the traditional senatorial domination of the top offices in Roman provincial administration thus ceased. Diocletian also departed from tradition by beginning to separate military from civil authority, a development concluded by his successor, Constantine. Governing the provinces and commanding troops now became separate functions overseen by different men, reducing the possibilities of individual officials rebelling against the central government.

Diocletian revised Roman military strategy both by greatly increasing the size of the Roman army and by devising a new defense against invaders. He stationed troops on the frontiers (the *frontiersmen*) under regional commanders. The frontiersmen settled on the land with their families to farm the area they guarded. But they were not just a peasant militia called out only in times of trouble. They served as sentries, warning the empire of any threats along its borders, and as fighting troops, buffering the interior in case of attack. Constantine,

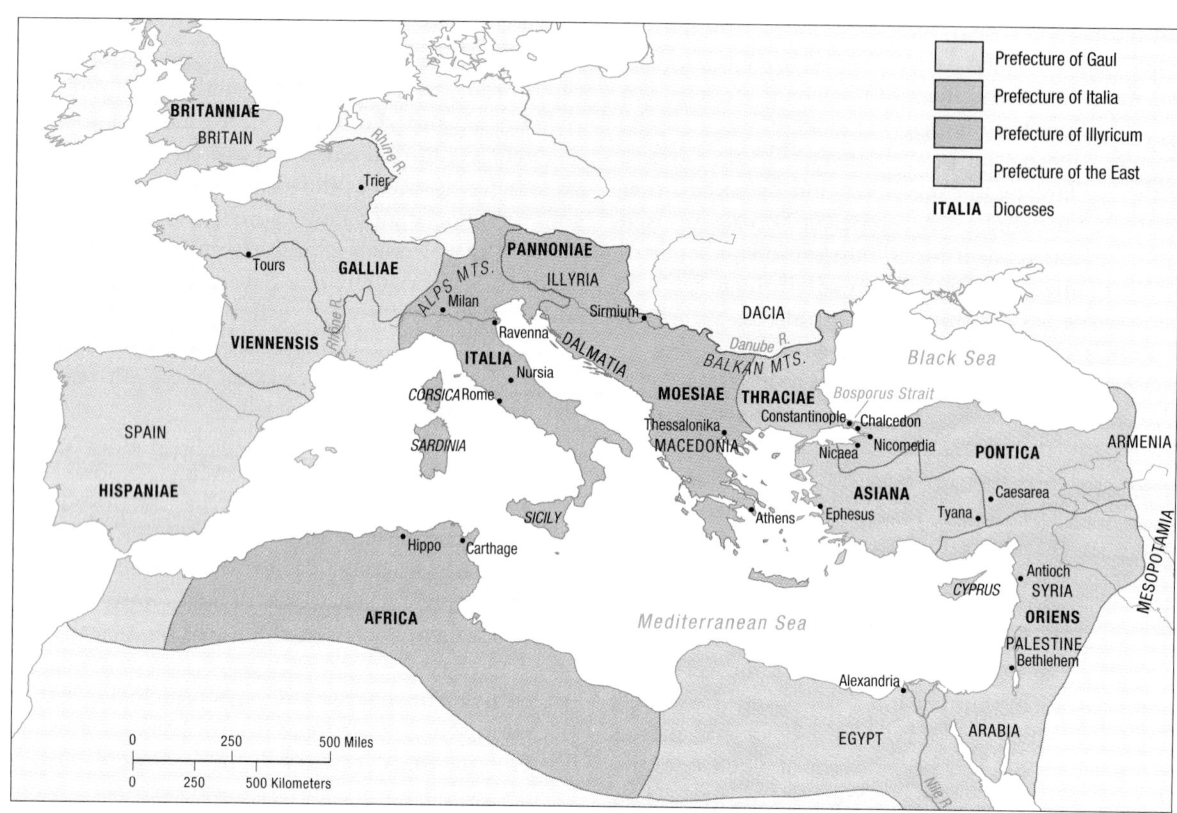

Dioceses of Diocletian, c. 300, and the Later Geographical Prefectures

who became sole emperor in 324 after nearly two decades of civil wars, dramatically modified Diocletian's strategy by reducing the emphasis on stationary defense in the frontier regions. He created a number of centrally located, mobile contingents (the *convoyers*) based in a zone of forts well to the rear, who would be dispatched by an area commander to meet any enemy force that had broken through the frontiersmen.

The military reforms of Diocletian and Constantine succeeded in temporarily ending the danger of invasions. Later emperors again tried to employ the army for conquest, especially against Persia, and thought little about defense. But any territory they acquired never stayed in the empire for long, and Rome's history as a relentless and seemingly invincible conqueror of foreign land ended.

The reforms Diocletian initiated made the empire more stable and therefore helped it emerge by about 300 from the worst crisis in its history. But this reorganization was no cure-all. The tetrarchy introduced a significant weakness by increasing the number of rulers and thus the opportunities for conflict among them. Constantine sought to correct this flaw by eliminating joint rule, but in the long run it proved impossible for one emperor to govern the entire empire.

Tax Reform

The most urgent consequence of Diocletian's reforms was the need to raise more revenue to pay the increased costs of administration and defense, especially because the civil wars and unrest of the mid-third century had ruined the government financially. Simply paying the troops, for example, was considerably more expensive than before because the army had been expanded. Some scholars estimate Diocletian's army to have been as large as five hundred thousand men—an increase of more than one hundred thousand over the size of the third-century armies. By modern standards the Roman army was not extraordinarily big relative to the size of the empire's population, which totaled at least several tens of millions. Nevertheless, the cost of the army severely burdened the structurally weak imperial financial system. The system had been stressed almost to the breaking point by the devaluation of Roman currency in the third century and the accompanying hyperinflation. Prices soared to unheard-of levels. High prices caused people to hoard whatever they could buy, driving up prices even higher. "Hurry and spend all my money you have; buy me any kinds of goods at whatever prices they are available," wrote one official to his servant on hearing of another impending devaluation. In 301, Diocletian tried to curb inflation with an elaborate system of wage and price controls. His Edict on Maximum Prices, which blamed high prices on profiteers of "unlimited and frenzied avarice," forbade hoarding and set ceilings on the amounts that could legally be charged or paid for about a thousand goods and services. The edict, promulgated only in the eastern part of the empire, soon became ineffective because merchants refused to cooperate, and government officials proved unable to enforce it, despite the threat of death or exile as the penalty for violations.

Devaluation and inflation had destroyed the old revenue system, under which people paid taxes in money that the government then used to buy goods and services. Diocletian and Constantine revised the empire's revenue system so it relied mainly on taxation in kind: most citizens now had to pay tax assessments largely in goods and services rather than in coinage. Taxation in kind remained the empire's principal source of revenue until the end of the fourth century, when payments were more and more commuted into gold and silver. In earlier times the Roman government had occasionally requisitioned supplies for the army, sometimes even paying for them. But now the state regularly demanded goods in lieu of monetary taxes. These "taxes"—barley, wheat, meat, salt, wine, vegetable oil, horses, camels, mules, and so on—provided food and transport animals for the army.

The government used a complex formula to determine tax assessments. The major components of the system, which varied in different regions of the empire, were a tax on land, assessed according to its productivity, and a head tax on individuals. In some areas, both men and women from the age of about twelve to sixty-five paid the full tax, but in others women paid only one-half the tax assessment or none at all. It is unclear how the head tax applied to people living in cities; they may have been liable only for a tax on their property, if they had any, and for periodic unpaid labor, especially on public works projects. By Constantine's reign every kind of urban business people, from shopkeepers to prostitutes, owed monetary taxes, and members of the senatorial class, who were exempt from the general tax system, were subject to various levies. The compulsory public services levied on the mutual support organizations (*collegia*) in which urban crafts producers and shopkeepers were traditionally organized also constituted an important, often burdensome, form of taxation. These services ranged from cleaning the municipal drains to repairing dilapidated buildings. The *collegia* either had to do the work themselves or pay for others to do it. In another effort to guarantee essential materials at the lowest cost, the government established state factories to manufacture armaments and to weave and dye cloth to provide fine garments for imperial officials and uniforms for soldiers.

The new tax system could work only if agricultural production remained stable and the government could control the people liable for the head tax. Hence Diocletian further restricted the movement of the *coloni,* or tenant farmers, the empire's economic base. Tenant farmers had traditionally been free to move to different farms under different landlords as long as their debts were paid. Now, male tenant farmers, as well as their wives in those areas in which women were assessed for taxes, were increasingly tied to a particular plot. Their children also had to stay on and farm their allotted land throughout their lives, thereby making agriculture a hereditary occupation. Binding the rural population to the land simultaneously stabilized agricultural production and made it easier to assess and collect the head tax. Each year the government calculated its budget solely on the amount of revenue its plans required and then gathered that amount by dividing it by the number of assessments on people and land in the empire. Over time, more and more taxes were imposed without much regard for how much people could pay. The tax on land eventually reached one-third of its gross yield, and the increasing tax burden on the rural population led to revolts in some areas, especially fifth-century Spain.

The government also deemed some occupations outside agriculture essential and prohibited such workers from taking other jobs. Crucial in preventing riots, for example, was assuring a supply of free grain for Rome's poor, following a tradition begun in the Roman Republic. About one hundred twenty thousand people in Rome were now entitled to receive free bread produced in state bakeries. The state bakers could not leave their jobs, and anyone who acquired a baker's property had to assume that occupation. A man marrying the daughter of a baker in Rome had to take up his father-in-law's trade and keep it even in the event of a divorce. Shippers in the state-regulated system of seaborne transport, who brought grain to Rome, were also legally bound to their occupation. From Constantine's reign on, the sons of military veterans had to serve in the army, which was a lifetime career. Army recruits, like workers in the imperial armament factories, were branded on the arm so that runaways could be identified.

It had always been common in the ancient world for a son to take up his father's trade, but this custom increasingly became a legal obligation in the late Roman Empire, at least in the West. As the economy in the West deteriorated in later years, the western emperors prohibited a greater variety of crafts producers and shopkeepers from leaving their jobs. The government's goal was to keep up civic services by maintaining a supply of workers in essential occupations and regularly requiring them to donate labor. The more prosperous eastern empire never imposed a similar degree of regulation.

The Curial Class and Autocracy

In the long term the empire's increasing demand for revenue and compulsory services from citizens had a tremendous impact on the propertied class in the cities and towns, the *curiales.* In this period almost all men in the curial class were obliged sooner or later to serve as unsalaried council members, who had to use their own funds if necessary to provide costly municipal services. This arrangement stemmed from the Roman tradition that the wealthy should use their riches for the public benefit in return for honor and prestige. The *curiales* were responsible for services such as repairing aqueducts, supplying animals for the imperial postal and land-transport system (an expensive service that carried official mail and valuables such as gold and silver), and feeding and lodging troops. For the central government the *curiales'* most important obligation was to collect taxes in their region. Although this responsibility provided them an opportunity to profit by raking off more taxes than were legally due, it also committed them to making up any shortfalls, which had become increasingly common because of the third-century economic crisis, from their own pockets.

Curiales varied in wealth, and in smaller towns the property qualification for this status could be relatively low. Many poorer *curiales* owned nothing more than a small farm, and the burden of having to make up tax deficits often crushed them. The regulations governing *curiales* usually referred to men, but women and orphans with property also had the same obligations to make up tax shortfalls and pay for public services. The financial responsibility of the curial class increased during the reigns of Constantine and his immediate successors. By then the imperial government demanded even the income that cities had traditionally received from their indirect taxes, such as sales taxes, customs fees, and rent on publicly owned lands. Now that the cities had lost their private tax revenues, the *curiales* struggled harder than ever to fulfill their official obligations to help pay for their city's waterworks and other communal needs.

Curiales essentially inherited their status, because property that passed from generation to generation in even a moderately wealthy family automatically made its possessors members of the curial class. For centuries, having civic-minded and propertied citizens in curial positions in the cities and towns had been critical to the empire's financial welfare. This system was now clearly breaking down, as more and more *curiales* could no longer afford their financial responsibilities. A telling indication of the dire change in the curial system was that compulsory service on a municipal council became one of the punishments for a minor crime. Eventually, to prevent *curiales* from escaping their obligations, imperial policy forbade them to move away from the town where they had been born. They even had to ask official permission to travel. *Curiales* had only two avenues of escape. They could obtain an exemption from service by using their connections to petition the emperor, by bribing the appropriate officials, or by taking up one of the occupations (such as service in the army, imperial administration, or the church) that relieved people of the financial burdens of the curial class. Or they could flee, abandoning home and property. Because the obligations of exempt or fugitive *curiales* were simply passed on to those unfortunates still around, the scramble to gain exemptions increased exponentially.

The tax reform of the later third century, however, improved Roman imperial finances compared to the disastrous conditions of mid-century, and this relative financial stability helped restore peace to the provinces in Diocletian's time. Still, the failure of the Edict on Maximum Prices foreshadowed the problems this rigid centralization of economic activity would cause later on, as the government's increased demand for revenue severely outpaced the population's ability to pay. Official attempts to direct the economy reflected the autocratic nature of imperial rule. Collaboration between emperor and Senate in ruling the empire, the hallmark of the principate and a tradition that rulers such as Marcus Aurelius had genuinely respected, became a thing of the past. Culminating a century-long trend, Diocletian was now formally recognized not as *princeps,* or "leader," but rather as *dominus,* or "Lord."

From the Latin word *dominus* comes the term historians use to designate Roman imperial rule from Diocletian onward—the *dominate.* The autocracy and theology of the dominate reflected traditions of rule in the ancient Near East and the Hellenistic kingdoms. To mark their supreme status as autocrats ruling without any peers other than each other, emperors as "Lords" dressed themselves in jeweled robes and surrounded themselves with courtiers and ceremony. A series of veils separated the palace's waiting rooms from the inner space where the emperor held audiences. Officials marked their rank in the strictly hierarchical imperial administration with grandiose titles such as "most perfect" and wore special shoes and belts with their costly clothing. In their style and propaganda the imperial courts of the late Roman Empire more closely resembled that of the Great King of Persia a thousand years earlier than that of the first Roman emperors. Continuing a trend already visible in the time of earlier emperors like Caracalla (*211–217), the architecture of the dominate reflected the image of its rulers as all-powerful autocrats. When Diocletian built a public bath in Rome, its size rivaled that of the baths Rome's most extravagant earlier emperors constructed. The soaring vaults and domes of the Baths of Diocletian covered a space over three thousand feet long on each side.

As in the past, religious language was used to mark the emperor's special status above mere humans. The title *et deus* ("and God") could be added to *dominus,* for example, as a mark of supreme honor. Diocletian also adopted the title *Jovius,* claiming himself descended from Jupiter (Jove), the chief Roman god. In so designating himself, Diocletian was following the lead of emperors from at least as early as the mid-third century. His fellow *augustus,* Maximian, boasted of his own descent from Hercules (the son of Jupiter, and thus subordinate to Diocletian). The emperors did not take these titles to present themselves as gods like the traditional deities of Roman religion. Rather their titles expressed the sense of complete respect and awe they expected from their subjects and also demonstrated that government on earth replicated divine organizations. Just as the deified hero Hercules had been his father's helper, so Maximian was Diocletian's loyal supporter, his "son." This theological framework for legitimating imperial rule had roots in Hellenistic kingship, and its linking of father and son as rulers and benefactors of humans found a parallel in Christian theology. After his conversion to Christianity, Constantine (like the Christian emperors following him) continued this tradition, by believing God had appointed him ruler.

The Christianizing of the Empire

By the end of the fourth century, imperial support for paganism, like that Diocletian provided, was abolished, and Christianity became the official religion of the Roman state. Many people remained pagans, but most of the empire's population had adopted the new faith. The sense of community Christianity brought to its believers, its openness to men and women of all classes, and the advantages of belonging to the sanctioned state religion gave it a social appeal to complement its theological promise of personal salvation. The startling transformation of the Roman Empire into a Christian state proved the most influential legacy from

Greco-Roman antiquity to the later history of the Western world.

Confrontation Between Pagans and Christians

Diocletian firmly believed in the traditional pagan divinities and the established religion of the Roman state. He made clear his attitude toward new religions in a letter to a provincial governor: "Through the providence of the immortal gods, eminent, wise, and upright men have in their wisdom established good and true principles. It is wrong to oppose these principles or to abandon the ancient religion for some new one. . . . " Diocletian obviously feared that any weakening of Roman polytheism would have dire consequences for the state.

Having survived periods of persecution and developed an institutional organization that extended all over the Roman world, Christianity had become prominent in the empire by Diocletian's time. Indeed a Christian church had been built in sight of Diocletian's imperial headquarters in Nicomedia. Every city of any size had a church. Large cities had a central church, presided over by a bishop, as well as smaller churches. Bishops appointed the priests, deacons, and deaconesses who ministered to their city's Christian congregations. Bishops also controlled the congregations' finances and admitted or expelled their members. This hierarchical system set Christianity apart from paganism, whose priests and priestesses had never presided over organizations like those bishops controlled. Some bishops commanded great wealth through their congregations, which increasingly received donations from rich Christians. Many donors were widows, who controlled the property of their households after the death of their husbands and could therefore decide on its disposal. Their generosity accorded them status and prominence in their congregations.

The bishops in the very largest cities, such as Rome, Alexandria, Antioch, and Carthage, became the most influential Christian leaders. The main bishop of Carthage, for example, oversaw at least one hundred local bishops in the surrounding area. Regional councils of bishops exercised supreme authority in appointing new bishops and deciding the doctrinal disputes that frequently polarized bishops and congregations. Christianity was still a religion of small, diverse, and separate groups spread throughout the empire, and they frequently clashed over theology and practice. The bishop of Rome later emerged as the supreme leader of the western church, but in the fourth century, when Christianity had no single center, he did not yet dominate. The preeminence the bishop of Rome eventually gained is recognized in his designation as *pope* (from *pappas*, a Greek word for "father"), the title still used for the head of the Roman Catholic church. Many bishops other than the bishop of Rome were called popes, however, especially in the western empire, and the title did not specifically denote the bishop of Rome for several hundred years. Although the bishop of Rome's rise to dominance in the western Christian church depended principally on the wealth and power he commanded, later popes found a scriptural basis for their position in the New Testament (Matt. 16:18–19). There Jesus speaks to the apostle Peter: "You are Peter, and upon this rock I will build my church. . . . I will entrust to you the keys of the kingdom of heaven. Whatever you bind on earth shall be bound in heaven. Whatever you loose on earth shall be loosed in heaven." Because Peter's name in Greek and Aramaic means "rock" and because Peter was believed to have been the first bishop of Rome, later bishops of Rome claimed that this passage recognized their superior position.

Christianity started as an urban religion and spread to the countryside only gradually. The continuing strength of traditional polytheism in the thousands of tiny villages of the empire is symbolized by the word *pagan*, which derives from a Latin word meaning "country person." Pagans still constituted most of the population around 300 in both city and country. At this time, Christians may have numbered as few as 5 percent of the empire's people, and certainly no more than 20 percent. By now, however, the government and the pagan majority no longer feared the Christians were political subversives bent on destroying public order and overthrowing Roman rule in a violent revolution. The empire had no official policy of toleration, but neither did it sponsor further violence against Christians after vicious but relatively short-lived persecutions under the emperors Decius and Valerian in the mid-third century—at least not until the so-called Great Persecution, which Diocletian launched in 303. He sought first to purge his administration of Christians and then issued edicts to destroy churches, seize Christians' property, and execute Christians who refused to participate in Roman religious rituals. He feared the Christians' refusal to worship the traditional gods would anger the state's deities and lead them to punish him and his empire. In the western part of the empire the violent persecution stopped after about a year; in the eastern portion it continued until early 313 in some areas. As a result, a number of Christians became martyrs, and their gruesome public executions aroused the sympathy of some of their pagan neighbors.

Christians and pagans debated passionately about whether there was one God or many and about what kind of interest the divinity (or divinities) took in the world of humans. But Christian and pagan beliefs sometimes resembled each other as well. The imperial theology of rule on earth by father and son paralleled the Christian doctrine of God the Father and Jesus the Son as rulers in heaven. The tendency of the emperors to choose a particular god as their protector faintly echoed Christian monotheism. Both pagans and Christians also assigned a potent role to spirits and demons as ever-present influences on human life. The two beliefs occasionally converged. For example, a silver spoon used in the worship of the pagan forest spirit Faunus has been found engraved with a fish, the common symbol whose Greek letters (ΙΧΘΥΣ) stood for "Jesus Christ the Son of God, the Savior."

The differences between pagans and Christians, however, far outweighed their similarities. Pagans from the emperor to the common people still participated in frequent festivals and sacrifices to many different gods. Why, pagans asked, did the many festivals and joyous occasions of polytheistic worship not satisfy the Christians' yearning for contact with divinity? Pagans also found it incomprehensible that Christians could believe in a savior who had not only failed to overthrow Roman rule but had even been executed as a common criminal. The Romans' gods, by contrast, had bestowed a world empire on their worshipers. Moreover, pagans pointed out, cults such as that of the goddess Isis and philosophies such as Stoicism insisted that only the pure of heart and mind could be admitted to their fellowship. Christians, on the other hand, sought out the impure. Why, asked perplexed pagans, would Christians want to associate with sinners?

An African Dedication to Saturn
This inscribed sculpture from North Africa depicts the solar god Saturn, who had been the chief god of Carthage under the name of Baal Hammon. The sculpture was dedicated in 323 and reflects the persistence of local pagan religion in the Roman Empire in the time of Constantine, the first Christian emperor.

By the fourth century, Christian intellectuals had been defending their faith against such accusations for more than one hundred years, with their pagan counterparts refuting these defenses as quickly as they appeared. For example, whereas some Neoplatonists tried to find points of correspondence between their doctrines and Christian theology, others mounted withering attacks, such as *Against the Christians* by Porphyry (c. 234–305), a Greek scholar who ironically was devoted to the doctrines of the Neoplatonist Plotinus that also appealed to some Christians. Porphyry presented a detailed critique of both the Old Testament and the New Testament and denigrated the prominence that women could achieve in Christian congregations. He also asserted that Jesus' contemporary, the magician Apollonius of Tyana, had been a greater wonder worker because he could criticize the authorities and then vanish after they arrested him. In short, argued Porphyry, Christians were unjustified in claiming they possessed the sole version of religious truth, for no doctrine that provided "a universal path to the liberation of the soul" had ever been devised.

Porphyry's most powerful accusation motivated Diocletian and another fiercely anti-Christian tetrarch named Galerius to launch the Great Persecution in 303. Porphyry charged that the Christians by their innovative worship of Jesus and their refusal to participate in acts of worship in the imperial cult were corroding the ability of the ancestral religion of the Roman state to maintain the goodwill of the gods toward the Roman people. The empire's recovery from the worst effects of the third-century crisis proved to its autocratic rulers that they had regained divine favor, and they were anxious not to lose it again. Therefore they ordered Christians to turn over their scriptures and sacred treasures to Roman officials and to participate in state-sponsored sacrifices; those who refused were tortured until they complied or executed if they remained obstinate. By escalating pagan fears about Christianity's effect on Rome's fate into the violence of persecution, however, Diocletian and Galerius only undermined the peace and order of society that their other reforms had been intended to restore.

Constantine's Conversion

Official persecution of Christians remained possible as long as the emperor adhered to the traditional Roman religion. Fortunately for Christians, Diocletian's successor, Constantine, converted to Christianity and soon ended further persecution. He also set in motion the process that eventually made Christianity the late Roman Empire's official religion. Constantine's conversion occurred when he was a Roman general, one of several commanders who claimed to be the *augusti* and were vying with each other over who would rule the empire.

Protracted civil war had followed Diocletian's retirement because of ill health in 305. Constantine and another caesar, Maxentius, eventually faced off at Rome in 312, culminating their military struggle for control of the western empire. Constantine had previously received unfavorable omens from pagan gods during his campaign, but just before the crucial confrontation at Rome he experienced a dream-vision promising him the support of the Christian God. His Christian biographer, Eusebius (c. 260–340), later reported that Constantine had also seen a vision of Jesus' cross in the sky surrounded by the words, "In this sign you shall be the victor." Constantine ordered his soldiers to emblazon their shields with the Christogram or *labarum,* a monogram composed of the first two Greek letters of the word *Christ* (chi, X, and rho, P) superimposed on one another. These entwined letters later became the official symbol of the Christian emperors. When Constantine's army defeated and killed Maxentius at the Battle of the Milvian Bridge in 312, the emperor attested that the miraculous power of Christianity's God needed no further demonstration; he was now a Christian believer—and the new *augustus* of the western empire. Constantine renounced the pagan gods he had worshiped until this momentous turning point—in particular his chosen protecting divinity, the Unconquered Sun—and declared the Christian God his divine guardian.

Although Constantine's conversion did not immediately make the Roman Empire a Christian state, it did officially end the persecutions soon thereafter and led to a policy of religious toleration. One version of this new policy promulgated by Constantine and the eastern *augustus,* Licinius (who did not become a Christian), survives in the so-called Edict of Milan. This edict, which Licinius announced in 313, proclaimed free choice of religion for everyone and referred to the "highest divinity"—an imprecise term designed to satisfy both pagans and Christians. Despite this official policy for toleration of all religions, the edict clearly favored the Christians (proof of Constantine's patronage), repeatedly emphasizing that all official impediments to the practice of their religion were to be removed. Constantine matched his moral support of Christianity with practical backing. He returned all property seized from Christians during the Great Persecution to its previous owners, requiring the imperial treasury to compensate those who had bought the confiscated property at auction (to avoid resentment among non-Christians). Constantine also gave the Lateran basilica (meaning a long rectangular hall, derived from the Greek word for "belonging to the king") to the bishop of Rome for his headquarters.

Over time, Constantine provided Christianity with many advantages, such as exempting its clergy from taxation and from service as *curiales.* He gave bishops the authority to decide legal cases on appeal from the civil judiciary system. When bitter doctrinal disputes broke out among Christians, however, he personally presided over councils of bishops to try to settle them. In 321 the Lord's Day (Sunday) was made a holy day on which no official business or manufacturing work could be performed. It was a mark of Constantine's shrewdness in handling religious matters that he called this new Christian holiday Sunday. The name was suitably ambiguous; pagans could argue that the name equally honored an important ancient deity: the sun.

Constantine's declaration of Sunday as a holiday led to the gradual imposition of a calendar of seven-day weeks, replacing the old Roman system of nine-day cycles marked by market days. Christians had adopted the seven-day week from the Hebrews, who in turn had maintained an ancient Babylonian tradition. The popularity of astrology in the Mediterranean world had already given some momentum to the idea of reckoning time in units of seven days. Many Christians and pagans subscribed to astrological beliefs, such as that each day was guided by a particular celestial power: Sun, Moon, Mars, Mercury, Jupiter, Venus, and Saturn, respectively. This tradition is commemorated in the names for various days of the week in most modern Western languages.

Constantine increased imperial support for Christianity cautiously, recognizing that he had to move slowly in an empire still permeated by polytheism and populated by a majority of non-Christians. Christian symbols gradually appeared on the imperial coinage, but they were placed alongside the images of pagan gods. Moreover, Constantine maintained official ties with the ancient pagan imperial cults. For example, he respected tradition by continuing to hold the office of *pontifex maximus* ("chief priest"), which Roman emperors had filled ever since Augustus. Constantine's conversion did not cost him the support of the empire's pagan majority. After all, imperial tradition allowed him to choose a special deity as his protector, and his success in battle showed the wisdom of his choice. When the Senate of Rome voted Constantine a triumphal arch to commemorate his great victory in 312, its members officially recognized the divine favor demonstrated by his success. In the inscription on the arch, which still stands, the senators discreetly sidestepped the question of precisely which god had helped Constantine, referring only to "divinity."

Colossal Statue of Constantine
This gigantic head came from a statue of Emperor Constantine. The thirty-foot-high statue sat at the end of a towering basilica.

Constantine chose the ancient city of Byzantium, near the mouth of the Black Sea, to serve as his capital—the "new Rome." Refounded as Constantinople ("the city of Constantine," today Istan-

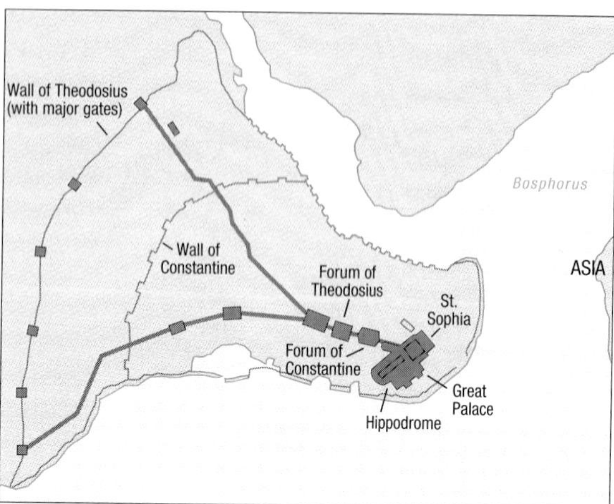

Constantinople

bul, in Turkey) in 324 and formally inaugurated six years later, the capital was centrally and strategically located on an easily fortified peninsula astride the principal land routes from the western to eastern Mediterranean region. To recall the glory of pagan Rome and thus claim for himself the political legitimacy carried by the memory of the old capital of the empire, Constantine graced his new capital with a forum, an imperial palace, a hippodrome for chariot races, and numerous statues of the traditional gods. But to mark his new religious allegiance, he started construction on the great Church of the Holy Wisdom (St. Sophia), which in its later form became one of the architectural marvels of late antiquity. Like the pagan Roman emperors before him, Constantine realized the value of mortar and stone for building his own immortal reputation.

Autocracy and the Growing Strength of Christianity

Because Constantine presented his support of Christianity as a continuation of the Roman tradition of securing divine goodwill for the empire, he was able to minimize opposition from pagans. In 324 he consolidated his power by ousting his pagan colleague Licinius in a bloody struggle more concerned with political domination than religion. Constantine thereafter ruled as sole emperor over a united empire, strongly reasserting the ancient tradition of centralized authority familiar from ancient Near Eastern history and Hellenistic kingship. He increased the blatantly autocratic image and reality of rule under the dominate that Diocletian had initiated. Ceremony to reinforce the emperor's status became even more elaborate as petitioners at the imperial court were expected to prostrate themselves and kiss the hem of his purple and gold robe adorned with precious stones. Upon his head rested a diadem (a headband of precious metal studded with jewels). His image was erected in every law court and church in which a bishop presided. Even though they ruled a more fragmented empire, the emperors who succeeded Constantine perpetuated this autocratic style, which they, too, justified as a manifestation of their especially close relationship with the supreme deity.

The structure of the new state-supported Christian church that emerged under Constantine paralleled the imperial autocracy. Early Christianity's relatively loose, democratic form had by now been replaced by a rigid hierarchy based on the authority of bishops. Since the second century, bishops had claimed they had special authority. Now, deriving from the New Testament the power that Jesus had bestowed on the apostles, bishops ruled their congregations almost as monarchs.

Beginning with Constantine, all power was openly vested in the Roman emperors. They commanded the army, issued laws, and exercised supreme judicial authority. The old aristocracy based on birth and inherited wealth, which had always participated in governing the empire, gradually gave way to a new aristocracy of salaried imperial administrators chosen and rewarded by the emperors. Constantine completed the separation of civil and military functions, begun by Diocletian, to prevent the same official from exercising both forms of power. Old symbols of prestige, such as membership in the Senate or the consulship, remained intact; but though these high-ranking officials retained significant financial and legal privileges, they no longer had any real political power. Both pagans and Christians could aspire to such status. Still, despite their desire to conciliate pagans, Constantine and his immediate successors used their autocratic rule to promote Christianity and gradually limit pagan worship. At some point before he died, Constantine may even have issued an edict forbidding pagans to sacrifice. His son Constans, ruling in the west, certainly forbade pagan sacrifice in 341, but the ban seems to have proved largely ineffectual. Throughout the empire, official support for Christianity increased the number of conversions. Soldiers, for example, now found it comfortable to be Christian and still serve in the army. Earlier, Christian soldiers had sometimes created disciplinary problems by renouncing their military oath. As one senior infantryman had said at his court martial in 298 for refusing to continue his duties, "A Christian serving the Lord Christ should not serve the affairs of this world." Once the emperors had become Christians, soldiers could justify military duty as serving the affairs of Christ.

Christianity's openness to women, who were barred from some pagan cults such as Mithraism, promoted the growth of the new religion—it could draw its strength and increase its membership from the entire population. Many men who wanted public careers were still reluctant to embrace Christianity fully, fearing that a public Christian affiliation would inhibit their participation in the oaths, sacrifices, and festivals that remained enormously important in the official ceremony of Roman life. Women's exclusion from public careers correspondingly freed them from this constraint. Augustine (354–430), the famous Christian theologian, eloquently recognized women's contribution to the strengthening of Christianity in a letter he wrote to the unbaptized husband of a baptized woman: "O you men, who fear all the burdens imposed by baptism. You are easily bested by your women. Chaste and devoted to the faith, it is their presence in large numbers that causes the Church to grow." Although women no longer held high offices in the church hierarchy as they had in the beginning of Christianity, they could earn renown and status not only by giving their property to their congregation but also by renouncing earthly marriage to dedicate themselves to Christ. Consecrated virgins and widows who chose not to remarry thus joined large donors as especially respected women.

Christianity grew because it offered believers a strong sense of community in this world as well as the promise of salvation in the next. Wherever Christians traveled or migrated, they could find a warm welcome in a new congregation. Christian congregations became even more popular by emphasizing such charitable works as caring for the poor, widows, and orphans. By the mid-third century, for example, the church in Rome was supporting 1,500 widows and other poor persons. The practice of hospitality, fellowship, and philanthropy, which pagans had always valued as well, was enormously important in the ancient world because people had to depend mostly on their relatives and friends for practical help and advice; state-sponsored social services were rare and limited.

Only one concerted attempt to restore the empire's pagan traditions was made. In 361, Julian (*361–363) became emperor and tried to restore polytheism as the official religion. A relative of Constantine and a successful military commander, Julian gained the throne in a civil war against his Christian cousin, Constantius, the reigning emperor. Julian had been baptized, but he later rejected Christianity—hence he was known as Julian the Apostate—in favor of a strict Neoplatonism. Constantius's politically motivated murders of Julian's father in 337 and brother in 354 might have influenced Julian's rejection of Christianity. But he was in any case a well-read and deeply religious man who expressed his belief in a supreme deity corresponding to Greek philosophical traditions: "This divine and completely beautiful universe, from heaven's highest arch to earth's lowest limit, is tied together by the continuous providence of god, has existed ungenerated eternally, and is imperishable forever." Julian's attempt to suppress Christianity failed, however, perhaps in part because his religious vision seemed too abstract and his image too effete. When he lectured to a large audience in Antioch, for example, the crowd made fun of his philosopher's beard instead of listening to his message. Julian's early death in battle against the Sassanids in 363 ended this last-ditch effort to reinstate polytheism as the Roman state religion.

The emperors who followed Julian chipped away at paganism by slowly removing its official privileges, completing the process Constantine had initiated. During the overlapping reigns of Gratian (*367–383), Valentinian II (*375–392), and Theodosius I (*379–395), all the cults of pagan polytheism were officially suppressed. In 382 came the highly symbolic gesture of removing the altar and statue of Victory, which had stood in the Senate house in Rome for centuries, along with a ban on government support for pagan cults. Symmachus (c. 340– 402), a pagan senator who held the prestigious post of prefect of Rome, objected to what he saw as an outrage to the Roman religious tradition of diversity. Symmachus spoke eloquently in this last protest of the old pagan aristocracy against the new religious order: "We all have our own way of life and our own way of worship. . . . So vast a mystery cannot be approached by only one path." But the emperors held firm at the direction of Ambrose (c. 339–397), the bishop of Milan. Ambrose insisted that in moral matters the emperors had to submit to the church. So unassailable was Ambrose's influence in the newly Christian empire that in 390 he compelled the emperor Theodosius to perform a humiliating public penance as atonement for a bloody massacre at Thessalonica. The emperor had ordered the killings after a crowd there had murdered a general, who had earlier arrested their favorite charioteer on a charge of pederasty. Ambrose cowed the emperor by refusing him Communion until Theodosius laid aside his crown and purple robe and tearfully stood among the ordinary members of Ambrose's congregation in Milan to beseech the bishop for absolution from his sin. Ambrose's assertion of spiritual authority over even an emperor foreshadowed the disputes between ecclesiastical and secular leaders over the boundaries of their respective authority that flared up repeatedly in later European history.

Official paganism in the Roman Empire ended in 391 when Theodosius again prohibited pagan sacrifices, which had evidently continued despite earlier bans. Cutting off public funding for sacrifices severed any connection between pagan religion and the Roman state. Following Gratian's lead, Theodosius rejected the title of *pontifex maximus.* Furthermore, Theodosius made divination by the inspection of entrails punishable as high treason and closed all the pagan temples, confiscating their sites. Many temples, among them the Parthenon in Athens, became Christian churches. Worship of Jesus or homage to a Christian saint, for example, replaced the cult of Asclepius in many of that god's healing sanctuaries. The ban on public support for pagan cults did not require individual pagans to convert to Christianity, nor did it forbid non-Christian schools. The Platonic Academy in Athens, for example, continued for another 140 years. Nor did capable non-Christians such as Symmachus find themselves denied successful careers in the imperial administration under the Christian emperors of the late fourth century and even later. But pagans were now the outsiders in a Roman Empire that had officially been transformed into a monarchy devoted to the Christian God. The church thus became the focus for state-supported Christianity.

Unlike pagan religion, Judaism was not disestablished in the Christian Roman Empire, but the religion of the Jews faced increasing legal restrictions. For example, imperial decrees eventually banned Jews from holding government posts. But Jews frequently had to assume the financial burdens of *curiales* without receiving the honor of curial status. By the late sixth century, Jews were barred from making wills, receiving inheritances, or testifying in court. Although these developments began the long process that made Jews into second-class citizens in later European history, they did not disable Judaism. Magnificent synagogues existed in late Roman Palestine, where some Jews still lived, although most had been dispersed throughout the cities of the empire and the lands to the east. The study of Jewish law and lore flourished in this period, during which the massive compilations known as the Palestinian and the Babylonian Talmuds and the scriptural commentaries of the Midrash were produced. These works of religious scholarship laid the foundation for later Jewish life and practice.

Christian Disputes over Religious Truth

Serious controversies among Christians over what they should believe became more visible as Christianity was becoming official and no longer had to contend with pagan cults for recognition. Bitter disputes frequently arose over what views constituted orthodoxy (the official doctrines of the church as enforced by church councils) as opposed to heresy (from the Greek word meaning a "private choice"). Church authorities had always been concerned with defining orthodoxy. Now, with official support for Christianity, the state inevitably joined in these disputes. The emperor became ultimately responsible for enforcing orthodox creed (a summary of beliefs), although that creed could vary from emperor to emperor and from one council of bishops to another.

Theological questions about the nature of the Trinity of Father, Son, and Holy Spirit caused the deepest divisions. A severe argument ensued, for example, when a priest named Arius (c. 260–336) from Alexandria maintained that Jesus, as the son of God the Father, had not existed eternally; rather, God had created his son from nothing and bestowed on him his special status. Thus, Jesus was not coeternal with God and not divine by nature. This doctrine, known as Arianism, found widespread support among ordinary people, perhaps because it relieved the difficulty of understanding how a son could be as old as his father and because its subordination of son to father corresponded to the norms of family life. Arius used popular songs to make his views known, and people everywhere became engrossed in the controversy. "When you ask for your change from a shopkeeper," one observer remarked in describing Constantinople, "he harangues you about the Begotten and the Unbegotten. If you inquire how much bread costs, the reply is that 'the Father is superior and the Son inferior'; if in a public bath you ask 'Is the water ready for my bath?' the attendant answers that 'the Son is of nothing.'"

Many Christians became so incensed over Arianism's apparent denigration of Jesus that Emperor Constantine intervened to try to restore ecclesiastical peace and to find the answers to Arius's troubling questions. Despite his lack of any official position in the church hierarchy, Constantine convened the Council of Nicea in 325 with 220 bishops, who tried to settle the dispute over Arius's teachings. The bishops voted to banish Arius to Illyria, a rough region in the Balkan mountains, and issued a creed declaring that the Father and the Son were indeed "of one substance" and coeternal. Constantine's changing reactions to Arius reflected how perplexing he found Arius's issues: he recalled Arius from exile some years after the council, only to reproach him again not long after. Many of the Germanic peoples who later came to live in the empire were converted to Arian Christianity, and the dispute between Arian and non-Arian Christians raged for centuries.

Other persistent disputes about the nature of the incarnate Christ also set Christians at odds with one another, especially in the eastern empire. Nestorius, a Syrian who became bishop of Constantinople in 428, argued that Christ incarnated two separate persons, one divine and one human. (The orthodox position held that Christ was one person with a double nature, simultaneously God and man.) Nestorianism enraged orthodox Christians by rejecting the designation *theotokos* (Greek for "bearer of God") as an appellation of Mary, the mother of Jesus. Orthodox Christians used the word as a theological expression of their growing devotion to the Virgin as the mother of God. The bishops of Alexandria and Rome had Nestorius deposed and his doctrines officially rejected at councils held in 430 and 431; they condemned his writings in 435. Nestorian bishops in the eastern empire refused to accept these decisions, however, and they formed a separate church centered in Persia. Nestorian Christians continued to flourish there for centuries, generally enjoying the support of Persia's non-Christian rulers. Eventually, Persia's Nestorian church established Christian communities that still endure in Arabia, India, and China.

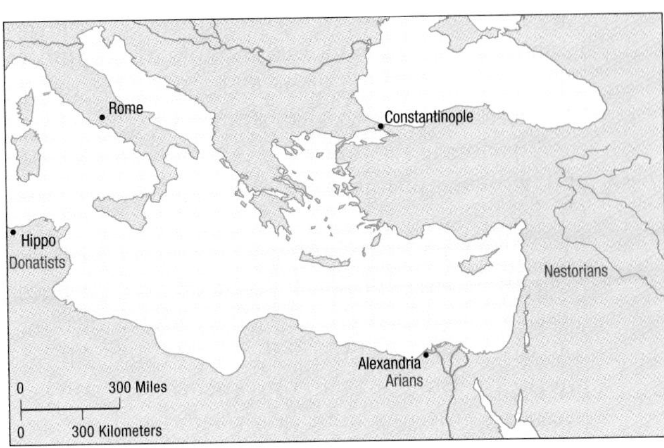

Original Areas of Christian Religious Disputes

Monophysites rivaled Nestorians in the fierceness of their convictions about the nature of Christ, but disagreed with them as ardently as they did with orthodox Christians. Monophysitism (from the Greek words meaning "of a single nature") maintained that Christ had a single—divine—nature. The emperor Marcian (*450–457) convened five hundred to six hundred bishops in 451 at the Council of Chalcedon to deal with the Monophysitical views of the prominent monk Eutyches of Constantinople, a vehement opponent of Nestorianism. The council issued the Chalcedonian Definition to repudiate the theological views of both Eutyches and Nestorius. Adherents of Monophysitism thereupon organized themselves in a persistent opposition movement to the orthodox church, although internal disputes created many varying forms of Monophysite doctrine. The bitter rift between the orthodox church and Monophysite Christians over the fundamental issue of the nature of Christ was never healed, despite repeated negotiations during the following centuries. Intolerance and violence characterized both sides. Rejecting Chalcedonian orthodoxy, Monophysites in Egypt (the Coptic church), Ethiopia, Syria, and Armenia formally separated from the orthodox ecclesiastical hierarchy in the sixth century. Deep-seated theological divisions such as Nestorianism and Monophysitism had political consequences later, when heretical Christians in the east found that they often had greater freedom of worship and protection from violence under non-Christian rulers in Persia and Arabia.

Economic and social differences among Christians sometimes fueled the fire of theological disputes, as the clash between orthodoxy and Donatism in North Africa shows. A dispute arose there in the fourth century over whether to readmit to their old congregations those Christians who had escaped martyrdom during the Great Persecution by cooperating with imperial authorities. Some North African Christians felt these lapsed members should be forgiven, but the Donatists (followers of the North African priest Donatus) insisted that the church should not be polluted with such "traitors." Most important, Donatists insisted, unfaithful priests and bishops could not administer the sacraments. So bitter was the clash that it even sundered Christian families. A son threatened his mother thus: "I will pass over to the party of Donatus, and I will drink your blood." Augmenting the theological issues of the controversy were the economic differences between many Donatists, who tended to be poorer country people, and their opponents, largely Christian landowners and urban residents. Violence leading to bloodshed erupted between government forces and roving bands of Donatist rebels, whom the authorities called encirclers (*circumcelliones*) from their technique for attacking the buildings of country estates. The Donatist controversy persisted despite repeated efforts to settle it. Finally, a conference of more than five hundred bishops and an imperial representative met in Carthage in 411 to resolve the conflict, but their decision against the Donatists and the subsequent persecution of Donatists by the authorities only embittered the rebels. Donatist doctrines endured in North Africa for at least another century.

Augustine's Impact on Christianity

No one person had a stronger impact on the formation of what eventually came to be the orthodox doctrines of later Western Christianity than Augustine. Born to a Christian mother and pagan father in the hill country of North Africa west of Carthage, Augustine (354–430) was exceptionally well read in the Latin classics, although he knew little Greek. His reading of Cicero's now-lost work *Hortensius,* he later said, "converted him to philosophy." He absorbed the ideas of Plato through his study of Neoplatonism. Augustine began his career by teaching rhetoric at Carthage. He had a son by a mistress there and was befriended by the famous pagan aristocrat, Symmachus, after moving to Italy. In 386, however, he converted to Christianity under the influence of his mother and Ambrose, bishop of Milan. From 395 until his death, Augustine served as the bishop of Hippo, a small seaport in North Africa, where he had to balance his interest in study and writing with a bishop's busy schedule.

Augustine's reputation rests on his writings, not on his work as a bishop. For the next thousand years his works would be the most influential texts in Western Christianity, save for the Bible. He wrote so prolifically in Latin about religion and philosophy that a later scholar was moved to declare: "The man lies who says he has read all your works." Augustine deeply affected later thinkers with his views on the role of authority in human life. His most influential exposition of the proper role of secular authority came in his *City of God,* a "large and arduous work," as he called it. The book's immediate purpose was to refute those who expected that Christianity, like the pagan cults it had replaced, would automatically guarantee Christians earthly success and to counter those who rejected any place for the state in a Christian world. For example, some pagans asserted that the sack of Rome by Germanic marauders in 410 was divine retribution for the official abandonment of the pagan gods; Augustine sought to reassure Christians troubled by this calamity that their faith had not caused Rome's defeat. His larger aim, however, was to redefine the ideal state as a society of

Christians. Not even Plato's doctrines offered a true path to purification, Augustine asserted, because the real opposition for humans was not between emotion and reason. Emotion, especially love, was natural and desirable, but only when directed toward God. Humans were misguided to look for value in life on earth. Earthly life was transitory. Only life in God's heavenly city had meaning.

Nevertheless, Augustine said, secular law and government were required because humans are inherently imperfect. God's original creation in the Garden of Eden was full of goodness, but humans lost their initial perfection by inheriting a permanently flawed nature after Adam and Eve had disobeyed God. Their disobedience caused humans to fall from God's grace and permanently destroyed the harmony between the human will and human desires that had existed in the paradise of Eden. The doctrine of original sin—a subject of theological debate since at least the second century—purported that humans suffered from a hereditary moral disease that turned the human will into a disruptive force. Augustine insisted that only God's grace could bring salvation from this evil. The corruption of the human will meant that governments had to use coercion to try to suppress vice, even if they had little power to inculcate virtue. Although desperately inferior to the ideal that would exist if humans were not flawed, civil government was based on a moral order and should endeavor to imitate divine justice. In this way its actions could serve as an extension of divine providence, imposing order on the chaos of human life after the Fall from grace in the Garden of Eden. The state had a right to compel people to remain united to the church, by force if necessary.

Order in society, Augustine asserted, could turn to comparatively good purposes such inherently evil practices as slavery. Augustine detested slavery, but he acknowledged that well-treated slaves in rich homes were materially better off than destitute free laborers. Social institutions like slavery were lesser evils than the violent troubles that would follow if anarchy were to prevail. Christians therefore had a duty to obey the emperor and participate in political life. Soldiers, too, had to follow their orders. Torture and capital punishment as judicial procedures, on the other hand, had no place in a morally upright government. The purpose of secular authority was to maintain a social order based on a moral order. Augustine was certainly no advocate of separation of church and state, but neither did he mean that bishops should rule over emperors, as some later thinkers interpreted his views.

In *City of God,* Augustine sought to show a divine purpose, not always evident to humans, in the events of history. He presented the destiny of the earthly city as hell and of the divine city as heaven but spelled out no specific theory of history and did not predict the future. All that Christians could know with certainty was that history progressed toward an ultimate goal. But only God could know the meaning of each day's events. What could not be doubted was God's guiding power.

> *To be truthful, I myself fail to understand why God created mice and frogs, flies and worms. Nevertheless, I recognize that each of these creatures is beautiful in its own way. For when I contemplate the body and limbs of any living creature, where do I not find proportion, number, and order exhibiting the unity of concord? Where one discovers proportion, number, and order, one should look for the craftsman.*

The repeated "I" in this example exemplified the intense personal engagement Augustine brought to matters of faith and doctrine. Many other Christians shared this intensity, a trait that energized their disagreements over orthodoxy and heresy.

New Patterns of Life

Striking changes in social and intellectual life occurred in the late Roman Empire and in the following centuries, when the Roman world was increasingly separating into eastern and western halves. Christian thinkers, principally Augustine, viewed human sexual desire as much more of a problem than pagan Roman tradition had considered it. Many devout Christians, unsatisfied with their lives in the ordinary world and no longer being martyred by a hostile state, looked for new ways to express their piety and emulate the suffering of Jesus. In increasing numbers, especially in the eastern empire, people disengaged from secular society and became monks, living lives of self-denial.

Christian Reevaluation of Sexual Desire

A fundamental issue Christians disagreed on was the proper attitude toward sexual desire. Augustine's views eventually became the orthodox position. Throughout his life Augustine had pondered how to define the proper relationship between the soul and the body in a life of virtue. Both Christian and pagan thinkers had struggled with this issue for centuries. Augustine's knowledge of Stoicism inclined him as a young man to reject all self-indulgence, but (he wrote) his sensual desires continued unabated. His ten-year adherence to the doctrines of Mani (c. 216–276) exacerbated this conflict. Mani, a sage from Mesopotamia, had created a new religion that emphasized self-denial. Contrary to mainstream Christian doctrine, Mani had taught that the crucifixion of Jesus should be understood as a symbol of humanity's suffering, not as a historical event: no redeemer sprung from God could have been physically born or killed. Furthermore, the universe was split between good and evil, represented by the forces of light and dark, respectively. This dualism, Mani argued, better accounted for the origin of evil in the world than the Christian notion of a god who had permitted evil despite his omnipotence. Mani's code of extreme asceticism (the practice of strict self-denial; from the Greek *askesis,* meaning "training") not only forbade indulgence in food and drink, but also demanded celibacy from its most advanced devotees, a rank Augustine never achieved. Augustine later immersed himself in Neoplatonism, a philosophy that also denigrated the physical side of human existence. Augustine's autobiographical *Confessions,* written shortly before 400, revealed his deep conflict between his sexual desire and the philosophies he had studied. Only after a long period of reflection and doubt could he pledge his future chastity as part of his conversion to Christianity.

Christian Art
Christians adapted Roman artistic style to portray Biblical scenes, like this one of Adam and Eve, which decorated the sarcophagus of a fourth-century Roman official.

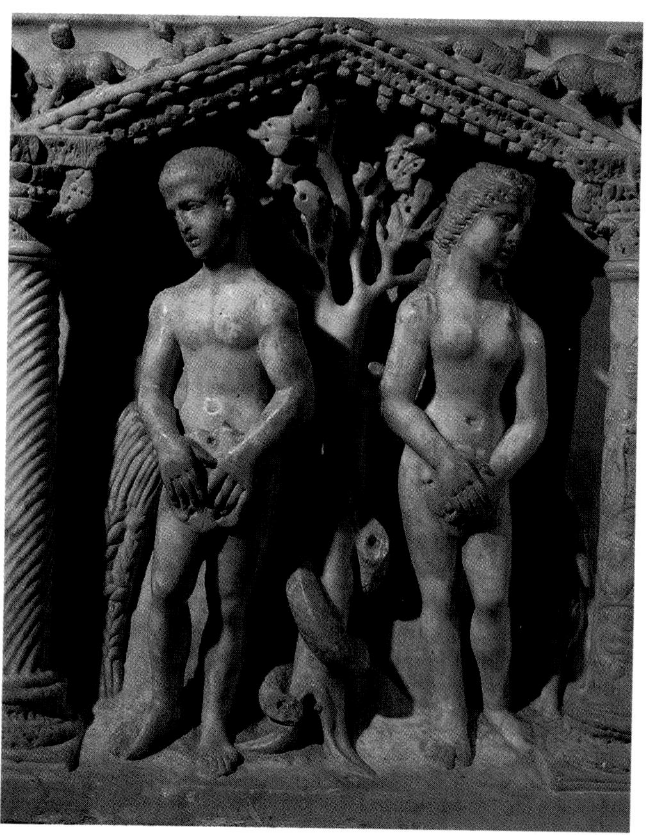

Augustine chose sexual abstinence because he believed Adam and Eve's disobedience in the Garden of Eden had forever ruined the original, perfect harmony God created between the human will and human passions. According to Augustine, God punished his disobedient children by imposing an eternal conflict on humans: sexual desire would forever become a disruptive force in human life because humans could never completely control it through their will. Not even conversion and the purifying effect of baptism could wash away this legacy of Original Sin. Augustine reaffirmed the value of marriage in God's plan, but sexual intercourse even between loving spouses carried the melancholy reminder of humanity's fall from grace. A married couple should "descend with a certain sadness" to the task of procreation, the only unblameworthy reason for sex. Sexual pleasure could not be a human good. The only completely virtuous course was to renounce sex, through the power of God's grace. But Augustine recognized that most Christians could not do this. Only God could put an end to this struggle through his mysterious grace of salvation: "You have made us for Yourself, and our hearts are restless till they find rest in You."

Augustine formed his doctrines on sexual desire against a long background of Christian thought. The apostle Paul in the first century had recommended sexual renunciation for Christians who could bear it. Christians of Paul's day expected the imminent end of the world and the coming of the kingdom of God on earth; thus, they were not concerned that celibacy for all would mean the end of society because no more children would be born. The theologian Origen (c. 185–254) had written that to maintain virginity was to assert one's freedom from the demands of ordinary society, which expected citizens to marry and bear children to perpetuate the state. So fervently did he reject sexuality that at about the age of twenty he had himself castrated. This operation, when performed on adult men, renders them infertile without removing sexual desire or ability and was far from unknown in the third and fourth centuries. By being castrated men sought not necessarily to end their sexual activity (although Origen certainly did) but to free themselves from obligations to head a household, raise children, and provide for a family.

Jerome (c. 348–420), one of Augustine's contemporaries, ennobled virginity and sexual renunciation as the highest Christian virtues, greater even than martyrdom. He greatly influenced Christian thought by his strong personality and energetic scholarship. The bishop of Rome entrusted Jerome with the crucial task of accurately translating the Bible into Latin. Jerome's translation, known as the Vulgate ("popular") edition, became the most widely used version of the Bible in the western church. Both Augustine and Jerome rejected one of the traditional assumptions underlying Roman family life: that sex between loving spouses was desirable as a personal pleasure and a civic responsibility to produce children. They would have approved of the sentiment expressed in the inscription on the tombstone of Simplicia, a Christian woman who rejected marriage: "she paid no heed to producing children, treading beneath her feet the snares of the body."

Like pagan and Jewish ascetics before them, Christian ascetics rejected the traditional idea that reproduction was a fundamental human responsibility. The powerfully argued theology of ascetics had an impact on Christianity despite their relatively few adherents. Virgin women, widows who did not remarry, and spouses who gave up conjugal sex had special status in the church. Their congregations honored these people because their renunciation of sex testified powerfully to their dedication to God. Their devoutness reflected the purity of angels and the sacrifice of earlier Christian martyrs. In Jerome's words, virginity was a "daily martyrdom." Because Constantine had earlier revoked Augustus's laws on marriage, people no longer felt any legal pressure to marry or bear children. Celibate men and women had equal legal standing to married people. Women could even refuse to marry, so better to worship God. The religious dedication of celibate women improved their educational opportunities because it justified their insistence that they be taught Greek and Hebrew to read the Bible. Rape, intended to force the victim to marry her assailant, apparently became more common as men feared a shortage of women would prevent them from forming households and continuing their lineages. By the end of the fourth century, pressure was growing to choose priests and bishops who had never had sexual relations rather than widowers or men who did not have sex with their spouses. This call for male virgins in ecclesiastical service represented a dramatic change in tradition, which had previously propounded virginity as a virtue exclusively for women.

Despite early Christianity's respect for those who forswore sex, Augustine's conception of Original Sin and his insistence that sexual desire was inescapably tainted with sin aroused vehement opposition from scholarly critics such as Pelagius, a monk from Britain (died after 419), and his follower Julian (c. 386–454), an Italian bishop. These critics of Augustine, called Pelagians, argued that humans can take the initial steps toward salvation by their own choice, independent of God's grace, and that the human will was not irretrievably deformed. They insisted that humans are free to choose good and shed their bad inclinations. As Pelagius put it, "If I ought, I can." The doctrine of Original Sin, Pelagians objected, deprived people of their choice to sin or not to sin by making sin inevitable. Moreover, as Julian asserted, sex was God's merciful gift to humanity as a defense against time and death, a guarantee of immortality through the bearing of children. In response to views like those of Ambrose that "a legal husband must not allow himself to be tempted, through love of sensuous delight, to play the adulterer to his own wife," Julian insisted that sexual pleasure was the "chosen instrument of any self-respecting marriage . . . acceptable in and of itself and blameworthy only in its excesses." These pointed objections to Augustine's interpretation of Original Sin, combined with the support Pelagians found among some bishops, led Augustine and Jerome to counterattack energetically and denounce the Pelagians as heretics. When most of the empire's bishops joined the bishop of Rome in condemning the Pelagian view in 418, the Augustinian view linking sexual desire and Original Sin was on its way to becoming the orthodox position of the western Christian church, a victory that profoundly influenced the subsequent development of official Christian attitudes toward human sexuality.

The First Christian Monks

The appearance of monks, both male and female, represented a new pattern of Christian life.* The word *monk* (from the Greek *monos,* meaning "single, solitary") described the essential experience of monasticism: these people withdrew from everyday society to live an ascetic life as a demonstration of their devotion to God. They wore the roughest clothes, ate barely enough food to survive, and renounced sex. This disengagement from the world corresponded to the notion of separateness and apartness that was theoretically fundamental to the Christian identity. Christians saw themselves as spiritually set apart from ordinary society by their bonds to Christ, which were supposed to take precedence over their ties to the community and even their own families. Monks gave Christian separateness a literal dimension by physically removing themselves not only from secular life but also from regular Christian congregations.

When Christian monasticism emerged in the latter half of the third century, choosing to live an ascetic life was not a revolutionary phenomenon. Self-styled followers of the sixth-century B.C. Greek philosopher Pythagoras and also Cynic philosophers had practiced certain forms of abstinence. Jewish monastic communities already existed. The missionaries spreading the doctrines of Mani in third-century Mesopotamia also practiced asceticism. Non-Christian philosophers had long taught that humans should exercise sexual restraint because physical passion interfered with reason's rule in the human soul.

Christian monasticism was distinctive not in its practice of asceticism, but rather in the large number of people who over the following centuries abandoned their normal existence to become monks. The first Christian monks emerged in Egypt. These monks lived as solitary hermits in extremely ascetic conditions to seek a relationship with God unsullied by the demands of the body and material comforts. Although earlier Christian ascetics had certainly existed, the first known Christian monk was a prosperous Egyptian farmer named Anthony (c. 251–356). One day, Anthony abruptly abandoned all his property after hearing a sermon based on Jesus' admonition to a rich young man to sell his possessions and give the proceeds to the poor (Matt. 19:21). Placing his sister in a home for unmarried women, Anthony lived as an ascetic on the outskirts of his village at the edge of the desert for some fifteen years, rejecting family life and marriage. In about 285 he withdrew from even limited contact with the secular world by moving into an isolated region. He wanted to be a hero for God. About 305 he reemerged to inspire disciples and then, after 313, withdrew to the desolation of a barren mountain to live out his life in surroundings whose quiet emptiness echoed his spiritual serenity.

Christians chose to emulate Anthony's disengagement from society for a variety of reasons, social and economic as well as theological. Prosperous Christian villagers in Egypt (like Anthony), for example, from whose ranks many early monks came, lived under constant social tension because they had to negotiate continually with each other in managing the flooding of the Nile to control agriculture. Their obligation to be cooperative, combined with their religious beliefs, made anger socially unacceptable. This pressure to conform to social norms was accompanied by worry about the heavy taxes that successful producers always owed. Like the fourth-century *curiales* who deserted their posts and their possessions, these villagers often found ordinary life unbearable. Some early Egyptian monks also came from very poor backgrounds. For them, monastic asceticism seemed little different from everyday life, with its famine-level diet and malnutrition that suppressed sexual desire. Still

*Because monastic women were not called nuns until a later period, *monk* here will refer to women as well as men.

others believed that Christians should literally suffer for their sins, just as Jesus had suffered on the cross. By becoming monks, Christians hoped to achieve the inner peace promised by detachment from worldly concerns. But the reality of monastic life was constant struggle, not least against the dreams and visions of earthly pleasures (of food more than sex) that haunted those who had renounced their previous lives.

Christian monasticism spread from Egypt across the late Roman world. As in so many areas of ancient life, regional differences characterized its practice. In Syria, for example, "holy women" and "holy men" attracted great attention for their deeds of piety, such as Symeon's (390–459) living atop a tall pillar for thirty years; people gathered at the foot of his perch to hear him preach. With the emergence of this kind of highly visible public holiness, Christianity developed a new group of living heroes. Christians in Egypt came to believe that the piety of the land's male and female monks ensured the annual flooding of the Nile, the duty once associated with the magical power of the ancient pharaohs.

Because the empire was increasingly Christian, martyrdom was virtually impossible. Monasticism allowed people another way to follow Jesus' model. Their aura of holiness seemed to endow monastic people with special wisdom. They were often asked to arbitrate disputes in the villages of fourth- and fifth-century Syria, where the undoing of many large estates and their powerful landlords through economic crisis had left a vacuum of authority. Monks with reputations for exceptional holiness exercised even greater influence after death. The relics—body parts or clothing—of these saints (people venerated after their deaths for their special holiness) became treasured sources of protection and healing. Christian relics thus took over a function previously fulfilled by relics of heroes in pagan religion, like the bones of Theseus that the fifth-century B.C. general Cimon had returned to classical Athens to the delight of the people there.

The Development of Monastic Communities

The earliest monks usually lived alone. Organized communities of monks living together appeared around 320 in the Nile valley. Military-style discipline was the paramount vow, subjecting the monks to God's will and the monastery's rules. People in monasteries separated themselves from worldly concerns and possessions, but not from fellow ascetics. Men and women founded such coenobitic ("life in common") monasteries all over the Roman world. Male and female monastic communities were sometimes located side by side, although an individual monastery had only men or women. Coenobitic monks grew their own food, made their own clothes, and crafted what few tools and goods their sparse life required. Some monasteries strove for self-sufficiency to minimize transactions with the outside world. Basil ("the Great") of Caesarea (c. 330–379), however, put together different monastic requirements and created a model that became important in the eastern empire. For example, he required monks to perform charitable service outside the monastic community, such as ministering to the sick, which led to the foundation of the first hospitals, attached to monasteries.

Members of social elites joined monasteries for a variety of motives, but one common reason was the long-standing Roman tradition that sexual desire, although natural and not evil, had to be strictly controlled. Monasticism provided a way to achieve that control with the support of like-minded people. Because monks as individuals kept a vow of poverty, rich people entering monasteries donated their land, buildings, and wealth to the monastic community. Rich Christian women were prominent donors to and founders of monasteries. For example, Paula (347–404), a widow of distinguished Roman ancestry, donated her fortune to establish monasteries in Palestine. Christian women of means could attain a certain independence by traveling the world on their own to visit holy places and using their fortunes to set up monastic communities for women. These female communities, however, sometimes existed under the protection and moral supervision of the local bishop or of the male abbot (head of a monastery) from a neighboring monastery. (Physical protection was necessary because even in a monastery a woman from a propertied family might be kidnapped, raped, and thus forced to marry, allowing her husband to gain control of her inheritance.) Monasteries also acquired resources from those who were healed of illness or injury after praying to a saint whose relics had been housed in the monastery. Those who recovered from their afflictions, believing they had experienced a miracle through direct contact with God,

Monastery of St. Catherine in the Sinai
In 527 the Byzantine emperor Justinian built this stronghold in the desert of the Sinai peninsula as proof of his piety and as protection for the monks who were to live there.

often expressed gratitude by donating money or property. Some were so inspired that they devoted their lives to serving that monastic community.

The nature of the monasteries' relations with their secular neighbors and the degree of austerity imposed on the monks varied by region. The most isolationist and ascetic monasticism was practiced in the eastern empire. Some western monasteries, such as those established by the followers of Martin of Tours (c. 316–397), an ex-soldier famed for his pious deeds, and those filled by aristocrats in Gaul, were also known for their austerity. Benedict from Nursia in central Italy (c. 480–553) devised what became the most influential monastic code in the West, and its tenets established a western monasticism that was generally milder than the East's strict asceticism. His Rule, as such organizational codes came to be known, prescribed the monks' daily routine of prayer, Scriptural readings, and manual labor. Benedict's Rule divided the day into seven parts, each with a compulsory service of prayers and lessons, but no Mass. The required worship for each part of the day was called the liturgy and became part of monastic practice. Unlike the harsh regulations of Egyptian and Syrian monasticism, Benedict's code did not isolate the monks from the outside world or deprive them of sleep, adequate food, or warm clothing. Benedict's monks lived very simply, however, all wearing standard garb and eating the same plain food. Although the abbot had full authority over the institution, Benedict's Rule instructed him to listen to what every member of the community, even the youngest monk, had to say before deciding important matters. The abbot disciplined the monks, but not so severely as to "sadden" or "overdrive" them. He was not allowed to beat them for lapses in discipline, as sometimes happened under other, stricter systems. The Benedictine Rule eventually became the standard for western monasteries.

Thousands of Christians became monks in the fourth century and thereafter. Some had been given as babies to a monastery by parents who could not raise them or were fulfilling pious vows. The practice of turning over children to monasteries, called oblation, helped replenish the monastic population. Jerome, himself a monk in a monastery for men that was located next to one for women, once gave this advice to a mother who decided to send her young daughter to a monastery:

> *Let her be brought up in a monastery, let her live among virgins, let her learn to avoid swearing, let her regard lying as an offense against God, let her be ignorant of the world, let her live the angelic life, while in the flesh let her be without the flesh, and let her suppose that all human beings are like herself.*

When she reaches adulthood as a virgin, he added, she should avoid the baths so she would not be seen naked or give her body pleasure by dipping in the warm pools. Jerome promised that in recompense for the dedication of her daughter, the child's mother would bear sons. Evidently even in Christian society, boys were more valued than girls.

By the early fifth century many adults were joining monasteries as a reaction against the worldliness and secularity of ordinary Christians. Some men fled from the army to enter monastic communities. For women, monasticism offered a rare opportunity to achieve status and recognition comparable to that of men; as Jerome explained: "We evaluate people's virtue not by their gender but by their character, and deem those to be worthy of the greatest glory who have renounced both status and riches." Monasticism endured because it attracted a steady stream of adherents who sought a way to serve God and be saved in the next world. Many also found the austerity of a community of like-minded members of the same sex more desirable than a civilian life of family, property, and secular responsibilities. Speaking of Italy, Jerome joyfully related that "monastic establishments for virgin women became numerous, and there were countless numbers of hermits. So numerous were God's servants that monasticism, which had previously been a term of reproach, became one of honor."

As Jerome implied, not all Christians approved of the shift in morals and manners of life that monasticism represented. The theologian Origen had argued against monastic withdrawal: renunciation of the world, he said, was not achieved by physically removing oneself to the desert. Bishops had little reason to rejoice when devoted members of their congregations became monks and thus ceased to serve as supporters or financial contributors benefiting their local churches. Monasticism also represented a possible threat to the bishops' authority, despite the fact that monasteries in the Benedictine Rule generally granted bishops the right to oversee them, and that bishops had to perform essential rituals such as consecrating abbots and altars. Both anchorite ("solitary") and coenobitic monks were less closely controlled and guided by the episcopal ("headed by bishops") hierarchy of the Christian church than were the members of ordinary congregations: monks earned their authority by their own action; that is, they acquired their special status of holiness not by having it bestowed by the church but by their own act of renunciation and their obedience to their monastery's rule. One of the few ways by which bishops could control charismatic monks who were attracting large followings was to reintegrate them into the church's hierarchy by compelling them to take positions ministering to congregations. Bishops and monks did share a spiritual goal—salvation and service to God. The distinctiveness of monasticism was that its members pursued this goal not by seeking to unite the physical, human side of their nature with the spiritual, divine side—the kind of union exemplified in Christian doctrine by Jesus as the incarnation of God—but rather by separating the two.

Transformations in a Divided Empire

In its new role as the official religion of the Roman Empire, Christianity was the primary unifying force in an otherwise divided state. The essentially independent emperors who ruled the East and the West cooperated in theory only. Constantine had abolished the tetrarchy but had designated his three surviving sons as heirs to his throne, hoping they would share power peaceably. Yet they fought one another after their father's death, so that divided responsibility among eastern and western emperors became the general practice. This division continued ever after because the empire had become too large for one ruler to govern efficiently and defend effectively against major military threats.

The eastern emperor continued Constantine's tradition of making Constantinople his capital. In 404 the emperor Honorius (*395–423) selected Ravenna, on Italy's northeastern coast, as the western imperial headquarters because its walls and marshes protected it from attack by land, while its excellent port kept it from being starved out in a siege. The geographical division between the two realms of the empire roughly followed a northwest–southeast line between Italy and Greece. The eastern half was largely populated by Greeks and the indigenous peoples of the eastern Mediterranean. It was richer than the West, had more large cities, and was easier to defend. The western half encompassed the diverse peoples of Roman North Africa and western Europe. The western empire's northern border had little natural protection from the Germanic peoples across the Rhine and the Danube, who for centuries had traded with Romans and served as mercenaries in their army. These northern provinces found it difficult to defeat Germanic bands raiding for booty.

The empire's two halves eventually experienced markedly different fates. For example, the three-tiered administrative structure (prefectures/diocese/province) inaugurated by Diocletian lasted only until 476 in the West but until the seventh century in the East. The most important change, however, was in the demography of the western empire, where in the late fourth century, Germanic peoples started moving into its northern regions in unprecedented numbers. Their growing presence eventually transformed the military, political, and social structures of Roman Europe.

Germanic Society

The various peoples whom we call ancient Germans and whom the Romans regarded as barbarians had never been part of a unified nation or single political entity. Moreover, they probably had little sense of a common identity before they settled in Roman territory in large groups. The word *German* in this context therefore refers only to some common linguistic origins of these peoples, not to an ancient and strongly shared ethnicity.

In their original homelands in northern Europe, these Germanic peoples lived in small settlements whose economies depended on farming, herding, and iron working. One common form of German house was constructed of interwoven branches and reeds on a timber frame, built large enough to house the family's people and cattle; the animals' body heat helped warm the house during the region's cold winters. Cattle were also valued highly for food and as measures of prestige. German society consisted of a welter of diverse groups loosely led by men averse to strong central authority. Even groups with clearly defined leaders were constituted as chiefdoms, whose members could be only persuaded, not compelled, to follow the chief. The chiefs maintained their status by giving gifts to their followers and by leading warriors on frequent raids against their neighbors to seize cattle and slaves. German society was patriarchal: men headed German households and exercised authority over their women, children, and slaves. German women

Marks of Identity
This skull sports the kind of topknot in the hair that some Germanic peoples used to identity themselves as members of a particular group.

were valued above all for their ability to bear children, and rich men could have more than one wife and perhaps concubines as well. A clear division of labor made women responsible for agriculture, pottery making, and the production of textiles, while men worked iron and herded cattle. Men acquired prestige through their prowess as warriors and their possessions. Warfare and its accompaniments preoccupied German men, as their ritual sacrifices of weapons preserved in northern European bogs have shown. Women had certain rights of inheritance and could control property, and married women received a dowry of one-third of their husbands' property.

Households were organized into clans on kinship lines based on maternal as well as paternal descent. The members of a clan were supposed to keep peace among themselves, and violence against a fellow clan member was the worst possible offense. Clans in turn grouped themselves into very loose and fluctuating coalitions called tribes. People belonged to tribes by claiming a common, though distant, kinship or by being allowed to join the group regardless of their ethnic origin if they observed tribal tradition. Tribes and their armies seem to have been polyethnic, including even non-German people. Members of a particular tribe identified themselves primarily by their clothing, hair styles, jewelry, weapons, religious cults, and oral stories. These distinctions seem to have formed a stronger sense of tribal identity and rivalry than did the different, though related, languages the different tribes spoke. An assembly of the tribe's free male warriors provided the only form of tribal political organization. Some tribes had leaders, whom historians have called kings, but their functions were restricted mostly to religious and military matters. Tribes could be very unstable and prone to internal conflict. Clans frequently feuded, with bloody consequences, and tribal law tried to set boundaries to the violence acceptable in seeking revenge. Tribal stability was also threatened by bands of young warriors who collected around leaders known for their ability to organize raids and seize plunder. These warrior bands operated outside the political and social control of the larger tribal group, somewhat like modern urban gangs.

Germanic peoples along the frontiers of the Roman Empire came into frequent contact with Romans during the early empire, and they developed a taste for Roman goods as marks of prestige. This desire for the material fruits of Roman civilization led more and more Germans to enter Roman territory, where they could also hope to escape the frequent attacks from other groups. At the same time, German men regularly found employment as soldiers recruited by the Roman emperors. Both Germans and Romans, then, used and needed one another from early imperial times. Germanic families in small groups had begun to settle in the outer fringe of the northern frontier zones by the second century; others had raided in Roman territory. Among these families were a group, related to the peoples later known as Goths, who roamed and marauded in the eastern provinces for thirty years, beginning in 238, before they were finally defeated. After epidemic disease and civil war had decimated the empire's population during the third-century crisis, the emperors encouraged many more Germans to settle in Roman territory because they were eager to recruit German warriors. By Constantine's time, German settlers provided a significant proportion of the military forces of the western empire. The men in these groups usually farmed less than in their homelands and depended on Roman pay for their incomes; the government ensured their cooperation and obedience by paying their military wages. By the late fourth century many Roman provincials and Germans had lived side by side for a long time.

From the Visigoths to the Franks

The settled provincial life of Roman northern Europe was suddenly disturbed in the late fourth century when thousands of Germanic people started moving from central Europe into the northern Roman frontier areas. Although the experiences of these groups varied, many were fleeing in panic from the Huns, nomads from the steppes of central Asia, who had invaded German territory north of the Danube River in 376. The appearance alone of the Hunnic warriors terrified the Germans—the Huns' skulls were elongated from having been bound between boards in infancy and their arms were covered with fantastic tattoos. The Hunnic cavalry was particularly frightening because its horsemen could wield their powerful composite bows of wood and bone while riding full tilt.

The Germanic peoples who came to be known as Visigoths ("West Goths") composed the first groups in this period to escape from the Huns into Roman territory. Like other Germans, in their homelands the Visigoths seem to have been broadly polyethnic, with no overwhelming sense of a particular ethnic or political identity (although the extent to which they might have conceived of themselves as a particular ethnic group is debatable). Intense pressure from the Huns compelled them to request permission in 376 to move into the Balkans. The emperor granted the appeal on the condition that their warriors enlist in the Roman army to battle the Huns.

The movement of the Visigoths into the Roman Empire was not an invasion or a carefully planned migration but rather a flight to safety of people who had been forced out of their traditional homes and who were now a horde of squatters. Greedy and incompetent Roman officers charged with helping these refugees failed miserably to provide for even their basic needs. As the Visigoths approached starvation, Roman officials forced them to sell some of their own people into slavery in return for dogs to eat. In desperation, the Visigoths rebelled. In 378 they defeated and killed the eastern emperor Valens (*364–378) at Adrianople in Thrace. His successor, Theodosius I (*379–395), then had to allow them to settle permanently in Roman territory and pay them a large annual subsidy, which enabled them to survive. In contrast to earlier policy on Germanic settlements inside the empire, the Visigoths were subject to their own laws and government instead of Roman institutions, but they were designated as "federates" (allies) of the empire, obliged to support its safety and prosperity. After Theodosius's reign the Visigoths began to move westward when their subsidies were cut off and their future in the eastern empire seemed threatened. In 410, under their commander Alaric, who resented his failure to obtain an important command in the empire, they stunned the Roman world by briefly occupying and sacking Rome itself. For the first time since the Gauls eight hundred years before, a foreign force held the ancient capital. The Visigoths destroyed many areas around Rome and terrorized its people, as expressed in Alaric's comment to the Romans after he had demanded all their gold, silver, movable property, and foreign slaves: "What will be left to us?" they asked him. "Your lives," he replied. The Roman government finally agreed to settle the Visigoths in southwestern Gaul (present-day France) in 418, once again as federates of the empire. Within a century they had expanded into Spain. Visigothic control of much of Spain would last until the Arab conquest in 711.

In their new territories the Visigoths gradually replaced the chiefdom structure of earlier Germanic society in favor of a kingdom with a strong central ruler. Their religion was Arian Christianity. New problems created by living close to Romans, especially disputes over property, led the Visigothic kings to develop the first-known written laws from Germanic society. Written in Latin and heavily influenced by Roman legal traditions, these laws used fines and compensation as the primary method for resolving disputes. Visgothic law applied to Visigoths, and perhaps also to Romans living in Visigothic territory. Official arrangements for subsidizing Visigothic settlement are also obscure; some large Roman landowners may have had to divide their estates with Visigothic nobles. Romans often retained full possession of their property, however, and paid the German leaders the taxes they had previously paid the Roman government, and many Romans worked as Visigothic advisers, lawyers, and tax collectors. As federates of the western empire, the Visigoths in 451 even helped the western emperor successfully defend Gaul against the onslaught of the Hunnic king Attila (*434–453), whose conquests extended from the Alps to the Caspian Sea.

Clovis (*485–511), the son of a federate of the Roman Empire and the king of another Germanic tribe called the Salian Franks, eventually overthrew Visigothic control of Gaul. Frankish men had regularly served in the Roman army ever since the imperial government had settled the tribe in a rough northern border area (now in the Netherlands) in the early fourth century and had allowed it gradually to move south into more civilized Roman territory. Clovis then extended his kingdom at the expense of surrounding Germanic groups in Gaul. His wife, Clotilda, was a Christian, and the bishop and historian Gregory of Tours (538–594) reports the famous story of her urging her husband to convert from the traditional paganism of the Germanic tribes. According to this tale, around 500, Clovis became an orthodox Christian (not an Arian like so many German converts to Christianity) to fulfill a vow he had made: when a battle had been going against him, he had sworn to be baptized if Clotilda's Christian God would grant him a victory. His army followed suit in adopting the new religion. Clovis's support of orthodoxy then won him the favor of orthodox Christians, who looked to him as a defender against such Arian Christian Germans as the Visigoths. Recent research, however, suggests that Clovis may have been an Arian all along. In any case, Clovis defeated the Visigothic king in 507 with support from the eastern Roman emperor. When that emperor named him an honorary consul, Clovis celebrated his new status by having himself crowned with a diadem.

Clovis's kingdom, called Merovingian after the legendary Frankish ancestor Merovech, foreshadowed the kingdom that would emerge much later as the forerunner of modern France. Clovis's ruthlessness—he murdered almost all his relatives to acquire their wealth and followers—contributed to the durability of his monarchy, as recognized by Gregory, who later praised Clovis's violent toughness in the history he wrote of the Franks. Clovis's ability to organize his society in the best Roman tradition also helped him provide stability. He insisted on written laws, for example—a Roman rather than a Germanic tradition. Preserved as the Code of Salic Law, his collection of laws promulgated in Latin had as a principal goal the promotion of social order through uniform sanctions for specific crimes. Clovis formalized a system of fines intended to regulate the divisive feuds and vendettas between individuals and clans that often broke out in Germanic society. The most prominent component of this system was *Wergild,* the payment a murderer had to make as compensation for his crime. Most of the *Wergild* was paid to the victim's kin, but the king received perhaps one-third of the amount. The differing amounts of *Wergild* imposed offer a glimpse of the relative values of different categories of people in Frankish society. The compensation for murdering a freeborn man, young girl, and a woman past childbearing age (specified as sixty years old) was 200 gold coins. This fine was large, sufficient to buy 200 cattle. The *Wergilds* for women of childbearing age, boys under twelve, and men in the king's retinue were 600 gold coins. The fine was tripled if the murder had occurred in the victim's home or at the hands of conspirators. The *Wergild* for ordinary slaves was 35 coins.

Above all, Clovis's kingdom derived its strength from his cultivation of good relations with his kingdom's Roman nobles, including the bishops of the towns. The bishops' support was key both because these men frequently came from the upper classes, at least in cities, and because they could be appointed to their post by popular acclaim, as happened with Martin (died 397), bishop of Tours. Bishops therefore represented a point of contact between the upper classes and the population at large. His support from ecclesiastical leaders and large landowners helped Clovis control the population of Gaul now that the Roman provincial administration in the western empire had largely disappeared, undermined by the diversion of taxes to German hands. Although the Merovingian dynasty was weakened when in 511 Clovis divided it among his four sons (recalling the Roman tetrarchy), it endured for another two hundred years, far longer than several other Germanic kingdoms in the West. The Merovingians survived because they had achieved a workable symbiosis between Germanic military prowess and Roman aristocratic social power.

Vandals, Anglo-Saxons, and Ostrogoths

Another major movement of Germanic peoples occurred when an enormous number of men, women, and children crossed the Rhine River into Roman territory in 406, perhaps also driven by the Huns. Known as the Vandals, these Germans had traditionally lived by agriculture and fought as infantry. They cut a swath of destruction through Gaul on their way to Spain (the modern word *vandal,* meaning "destroyer of property," perpetuates the memory of their destructiveness). In 429, eighty thousand Vandals ferried across the Mediterranean Sea to Roman North Africa. There they initially became federates of the western empire, but soon threw off their allegiance to Roman government. They took the region by force and ended its traditional tax shipments of grain and vegetable oil to Rome. The Vandals caused tremendous hardship for local inhabitants by systematically confiscating Roman property in the countryside rather than (like the Visigoths) allowing property owners to make periodic payments to "ransom" their land. In 455 they attacked and plundered Rome. Vandal naval expeditions in the Mediterranean further disrupted commerce and the transportation of food from North Africa to both the western and the eastern empires. The eastern empire nearly bankrupted itself to finance military expeditions to oust the Vandals from North Africa and to restore the transport of supplies. These efforts failed until 534, when the forces of the eastern emperor Justinian (*527–565) finally overthrew the Vandal kingdom.

Another movement of Germanic peoples, although involving fewer people than the others, occurred at the northwestern edge of the empire and affected Britain, from where Roman legions had been recalled by about 407 to defend Italy against the Visigoths. From the 440s onward, Angles from the area that is now Denmark and Saxons from the northwestern region of modern Germany invaded Britain. There they carved out a territory for themselves by wresting land from the native Celtic peoples, especially the Picts and Scots, as well as Britain's remaining Roman inhabitants. Gradually the eastern regions of Britain were transformed by the Germanic culture of the now-dominant Anglo-Saxons. The Celtic peoples of Britain lost most of their language and other cultural traditions, including those introduced by the Romans, and they lost contact with Christianity, which survived only in Wales and Ireland.

Elsewhere in the West, Roman customs had slowly merged with those of the Germanic peoples. Germans held administrative posts in the remnants of western imperial government and commonly served in the army, often as high officers. The German Ricimer, serving as commander in chief of the western empire's armed forces composed of various groups of non-Roman troops, was so powerful that he determined which Romans would serve as emperors in the West for nearly twenty years until his death in 472. Similarly, the commander Orestes made his young son, Romulus Augustulus, emperor in Ravenna in 475. But Odoacer, a non-Roman general from the Danube region, killed the father and overthrew the son in 476 after the troops turned against Orestes: he had unwisely refused their demands for more money. Odoacer, who like Orestes had earlier served the Hunnic king Attila, then proceeded to reign as an independent king, not as Romulus's successor.

Historians have traditionally fixed 476 as the date of the "fall" of the Roman Empire and the beginning of the European Middle Ages. But in fact the empire continued after that because Odoacer, in ruling Italy, acknowledged his subordinate status to the eastern emperor. Odoacer was himself deposed in 493 at the behest of the eastern emperor. Theodoric the Great, who overthrew Odoacer, was king of the Ostrogoths ("East Goths"), another mixed population group that included some Romans as well as Germans and had originally been allowed into Roman territory in the mid-fifth century. Until his death in 526, Theodoric administered his Ostrogothic kingdom from the traditional western imperial capital at Ravenna. Although the rank and file of Ostrogothic society often remained hostile to those Romans not in the tribe, Theodoric nevertheless saw an advantage in accommodating Roman aristocrats. He especially needed their support to maintain the novel arrangement under which a king ruled the fractious Ostrogoths, who as members of a Germanic tribe were accustomed to very loose authority. Moreover, Theodoric and his Ostrogothic nobles wanted to enjoy the luxurious life of the empire's aristocracy, not destroy it. As a young man, Theodoric had received a Roman upbringing in Constantinople while living there as a hostage (a kind of diplomatic exchange common to the times), and he appreciated Roman customs and institutions. He therefore allowed the Senate and the consulships to continue, while Goths dominated the leadership of the army. Himself an Arian Christian like the other Ostrogoths, he nevertheless announced a policy of religious toleration: "No one can be forced to believe against his will." In practice, he did sometimes take harsh measures against orthodox Christians, especially if their loyalty was suspect. The army of the eastern emperor Justinian destroyed Theodoric's Ostrogothic kingdom in Italy in the mid-sixth century. The eastern empire then ruled the former Ostrogothic territory in northern Italy until another Germanic people, the Lombards, settled there in 568 and established their own kingdom.

From Cities to Countryside in the West

While movements of Germanic peoples were transforming political and cultural life in the late Roman world, its landscape was also changing. Some cities, particularly those where the emperors made their capitals, rose to new prominence and prosperity; urban communities in other areas shriveled. Ravenna, the western imperial capital, with its glorious cathedral and churches embellished with colorful mosaics, prospered and grew at Rome's expense, as did Constantinople. The violence of some of the Germanic immigrations severely damaged many towns in the northern regions of the western empire; there the emphasis increasingly shifted to the countryside. Wealthy aristocrats built sprawling villas as their headquarters on extensive estates located at a distance from the dangerous frontier regions. Staffed by *coloni,* these estates became independent economic units capable of self-defense and self-sufficiency. Their owners consequently shunned participation in municipal administration, the traditional lifeblood of the empire. The nobles' riches and power further allowed them to avoid their obligations to the Roman government, taxes above all. One Roman aristocrat in Gaul described his life on a country estate as "close to the sources of delight and distant from ambition."

The contrasts between urban and rural life could be striking. Synesius (c. 370–413), a bishop in eastern North Africa, remarked that the emperor was such a remote figure to local people in his area that few knew his name; some people thought the legendary Greek king Agamemnon was still ruling, he joked. In Augustine's home region farther to the west, some peasants still spoke Punic, the ancient Carthaginian language, six hundred years after the Roman conquest. Carthage, on the other hand, was a vibrant Roman city with architecture rivaling the capitals' great buildings and all the refinements of Roman urban life, from baths to theaters. It became the Vandal capital after its capture in 439.

The eastern empire largely retained its economic vitality. Its many cities teemed with merchants from far and wide, and its wealthiest inhabitants spent freely on luxury goods imported from the east: silk, precious stones, and prized spices such as pepper. Rich and poor alike, urban people enjoyed the spirited religious festivals and spectacular games that frequently filled the public gathering places. Chariot racing was a special passion of the masses in cities big enough to support a racetrack. The situation in many parts of the western empire grew grimmer, however, as its economic infrastructure deteriorated. Roads and bridges fell into disrepair as the cities and the provincial administrations ceased to maintain them. Self-sufficient Roman nobles on their estates had no interest in a restored central authority with the power to collect taxes. By avoiding taxes, the rich alienated the poor, financially strangled Roman provincial administration, and effectively privatized most services, even justice and law and order. Nobles in the West could

Late Roman Country Estate
This mosaic depicts the kind of large country house and grounds that wealthy Romans made into self-sufficient, even fortified, retreats in the later empire.

be astonishingly rich compared to the anemic finances of the western empire. The pagan aristocrat Symmachus, for example, owned three houses in Rome and fifteen villas scattered throughout Italy. The very wealthiest senators (the social and financial rank surviving from republican times) could have an annual income rivaling that of even an entire province. The Germanic kingdoms propped up the tottering structures of Roman provincial government only to support their local regimes, not to revitalize the empire.

Decreased population as a result of the third-century crisis meant a smaller-scale economy in many regions despite the great wealth of a few. Furthermore, inflation again mounted in the fourth century because Constantine had put an enormous quantity of gold confiscated from pagan temples into circulation. The most vivid demonstration of depopulation and economic failure in the late empire was the abandonment of farmlands. A veritable flight from the land ensued: first the *coloni* ran away; then their landlords followed because they remained responsible for the tax due from the land even though its workers were now gone. As much as 20 percent of arable Roman territory became deserted in the most seriously affected areas. The abandonment of taxable land increased the demands for revenues from those who remained and encouraged the authorities to bring in still more German settlers. The desertion of the land further weakened the economy; the economic downturn then severely restricted the government's ability to finance imperial defense, especially in the West. The difficulty of the late Roman world in defending itself, which resulted from economic failure and depopulation, was its greatest administrative weakness.

Coloni had few incentives to endure the increasingly harsh conditions of their lives because their status had become virtually indistinguishable from that of slaves. They still retained more legal rights than slaves—for example, they could bring charges in court for criminal offenses committed against them—but the difference in power between landlords and tenants was so great that it resembled the relationship between masters and slaves. For example, *coloni* could not bring civil suits against their landlords except on a charge of exacting excessive rent. In justifying this restriction, the law indeed spoke of tenants who were tied to the land as the virtual equivalent of slaves: "They seem almost bound in a kind of servitude to those to whom they are subject by their annual payments of rent and by the obligation of their status. It is all the less to be tolerated that they should dare to bring (civil) charges against those by whom, as by owners, they can without doubt be sold together with their possessions." *Coloni,* like poor peasants who owned only tiny plots and like peddlers in the towns, always lived on the edge of disaster; bad harvests could leave them with no recourse except to flee to a large city to beg. The famous rhetoric teacher Libanius (c. 314–493) described such a scene in his hometown of Antioch in 384: "Famine had filled our city with beggars, some of whom had abandoned their fields because they lacked even grass to eat, since it was winter, and some had abandoned their native cities." Such destitution contrasted starkly with the enduring affluence of the wealthy urban classes of the empire and the general prosperity enjoyed by the proprietors of productive farms in areas that escaped raids by invaders and natural disasters. As always, the economic health of the empire varied from region to region over time.

The tying of tenants to the land and making selected occupations into hereditary obligations increased the categories of unfree people in the late Roman Empire. Slaves, of course, still constituted the least-free category. Few slaves now worked in agriculture, but they were common as household servants, assistants in the emperors' entourages, and workers in certain imperial enterprises such as the mint. Christians continued to buy and sell slaves, although Christian influence on law did lead to slaves being allowed to marry. Children born to married slaves, however, remained slaves. Gregory (c. 330–395), bishop of Nyssa, was the first Christian of stature to denounce slavery as an institution. More common was the view of Augustine, who sadly reported that he saw no way of abolishing slavery. He concluded it was an outcome of the fall of humans from God's grace.

Mixing of Roman and German Ways in the West

The western Roman Empire of the fifth and sixth centuries experienced a mixing of Roman and German customs that brought the styles of people's lives closer together in significant ways, although differences still persisted. In practice it mattered little to most people that a Roman emperor no longer ruled the western empire, and in many areas German settlement did not mean catastrophic disruption. Some land cultivated by previous inhabitants was confiscated and given to the new settlers, but sometimes the land the Germans farmed was uninhabited land that had fallen out of cultivation during the loss of population in the third century. Moreover, Germans often became in effect absentee landlords by being granted as rent the taxes due from lands on which the previous owners were allowed to remain, retaining their homes and property. Roman authorities had to forgo the tax revenue the old inhabitants of these lands now paid the Germans, but agricultural production continued, and as soldiers the Germans contributed to the region's defense.

Augustine had said that the city of God had as much room for Goths as for Romans. So did the western Roman Empire. As it developed inside Roman territory, German society transformed from its traditional tribal structure into monarchies, built upon landowning aristocracies, and developed new notions of ethnic identity. Moreover, the successful German kings cooperated with the Roman provincial nobility, despite their differences in Christian faith (many Germans were Arian Christians, while most ethnic Romans were orthodox). As their traditions came into contact with Roman traditions, the Germans were "Romanized." The other side of the historical coin, of course, was that the western Roman Empire was simultaneously changed by the effects of the move-

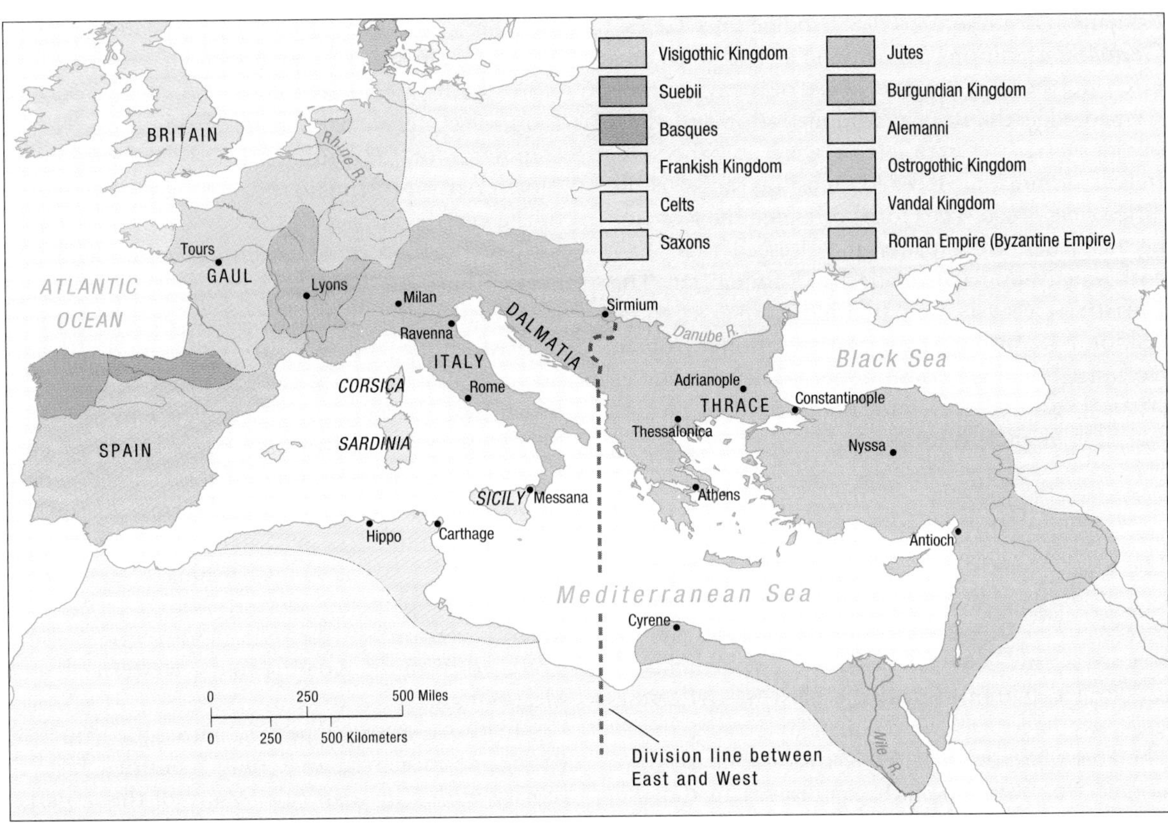

Peoples and Kingdoms of the Roman World, c. 526

ments of many Germanic peoples into Roman territory. This "barbarization," as it is sometimes called, has often been blamed for the West's weakening. But the German influence was more an effect than a cause. The western empire's weakness had its origins in the civil wars and epidemics of the third century, which decimated its population, precipitated its economic decline, and shattered its peace and order. The Germanic peoples' migrations to the West and the demographic and cultural transformations their presence brought had been made possible by these earlier blows to Roman military, political, and social well-being.

As the two societies began to co-exist, they found they shared assumptions about the fundamental relationship between men and women. The traditional patriarchy of the Germanic tribes continued in the new Gothic kingdoms established in Roman territory and corresponded to Roman customs. Both Romans and Germans also practiced some of the new Christian customs that affected traditionally devalued members of the community—women and the poor. For example, Christians allowed poor women and men to be buried near the graves of saints, on equal terms with aristocrats; and rich women could become prominent in their congregations if they donated generously to Christian causes. Yet women in general remained largely under male control.

Shifts in political power also altered the ways in which Roman and German men interacted. Because Romans and Germans served together in the army, military service exposed ordinary men from both societies to one another. Roman noblemen in Gaul had to be clever in dealing with the now-dominant Gothic kings. Sidonius Apollinaris, a well-connected noble from Lyons (c. 430–479), for example, once purposely lost a backgammon game to the Visigothic king as a way of getting the king to approve a request for a favor. Sidonius's skill in delivering flattering orations allowed him to succeed under a series of rulers; he was appointed bishop of a region in south-central Gaul and tried to prevent the Goths from exploiting

Romans. An undercurrent of indigenous Celtic-Germanic traditions persisted in the western empire's northern provinces. These old ways simply reemerged as the Roman administration and elites of the western empire left or were absorbed. As Italian dominance receded, tensions and visible differences arose. The Goths offended the Romans because they wore pants and dressed their hair with smelly pomades made from animal fat. The Christian clergy perpetuated old Roman sartorial fashion by continuing to wear traditional Roman clothing. For this reason modern Christian ecclesiastical vestments resemble the clothing of the upper class of ancient Rome.

The Byzantine Empire

The eastern empire (called the Byzantine Empire by modern historians after the old name—Byzantium—of its capital, Constantinople) largely escaped massive German population movements of the kind that transformed the West by deflecting the newcomers westward, often by paying them. The East therefore suffered less economic dislocation in the fifth and sixth centuries than did the West. The inhabitants of the eastern empire regarded themselves as the heirs of ancient Roman culture: they referred to themselves as Romans. Although Latin remained the language of government and of command in the army until the seventh century, many people in the eastern empire spoke Greek as their native language (westerners referred generically to easterners as Greek). The eastern empire's population was quite heterogeneous, however, and a traveler in its provinces would have heard many different languages and seen many styles of dress.

Fearing that contact with Germans and other northern peoples would "barbarize" their empire just as it had the West, the eastern emperors did everything they could to preserve the "Romanness" of their world. As early as the end of the fourth century, for example, they had forbidden residents of Constantinople to dress in Germanic style—in pants, boots, and clothing made from animal furs—instead of traditional Roman garb. Unfortunately for such dreams of maintaining pure Roman cultural traditions, military needs compelled the Byzantine army to hire many Germans and Huns.

Ironically, the eastern emperors needed these "barbarian" mercenaries because through the reign of Justinian (527–565) they repeatedly tried to overthrow the Germanic kingdoms in the West. They launched these expeditions attempting to restore the former unity of the Roman Empire, to acquire western tax revenues, and to revive the shipments of foodstuffs formerly received from North Africa. Justinian, the most famous emperor in the early centuries of the eastern empire's long history, pursued these campaigns with characteristic enthusiasm. Born to a Latin-speaking family in a small Balkan town, Justinian acquired a Roman education and was promoted rapidly in imperial service thanks to the patronage of his uncle, Justin, who became eastern emperor in 518. Justinian succeeded Justin nine years later, and like Augustus, surrounded himself with skilled generals, especially the brilliant Belisarius. Justinian's military commanders eventually recaptured Italy, the Dalmatian coast, Sicily, Sardinia, Corsica, part of southern Spain, and western North Africa. Justinian's version of the old empire for a time stretched from the Atlantic to the western edge of Mesopotamia.

Justinian strengthened the autocratic nature of Byzantine monarchy and fully identified his authority with Christian rule. Many of the imperial political traditions and ceremonies had originated in the early and therefore pagan Roman Empire. Justinian managed to sustain the ancient tradition of the Roman emperor's visible supremacy while recasting the symbols of rule in a Christian context. A gleaming mosaic in his church at San Vitale in Ravenna, for example, displayed his vision of the emperor's role: Justinian stood at the center of the cosmos shoulder to shoulder with both the ancient Hebrew patriarch Abraham and Christ. No wonder Justinian proclaimed the emperor the "living law," an old idea made explicit for the first time. His autocracy also reduced the autonomy of the eastern empire's cities. City councils ceased to govern as more and more imperial officials were installed throughout the eastern provinces. *Curiales* were still responsible for assuring payment of the full amount of taxes from their area due the central government, but they no longer enjoyed the compensating reward of deciding local matters. Now the imperial government dominated all aspects of decision making and status. Men of property from the provinces who aspired to power and prestige knew they could best satisfy their ambitions by entering the imperial administration, whether in the capital or the provinces. They also

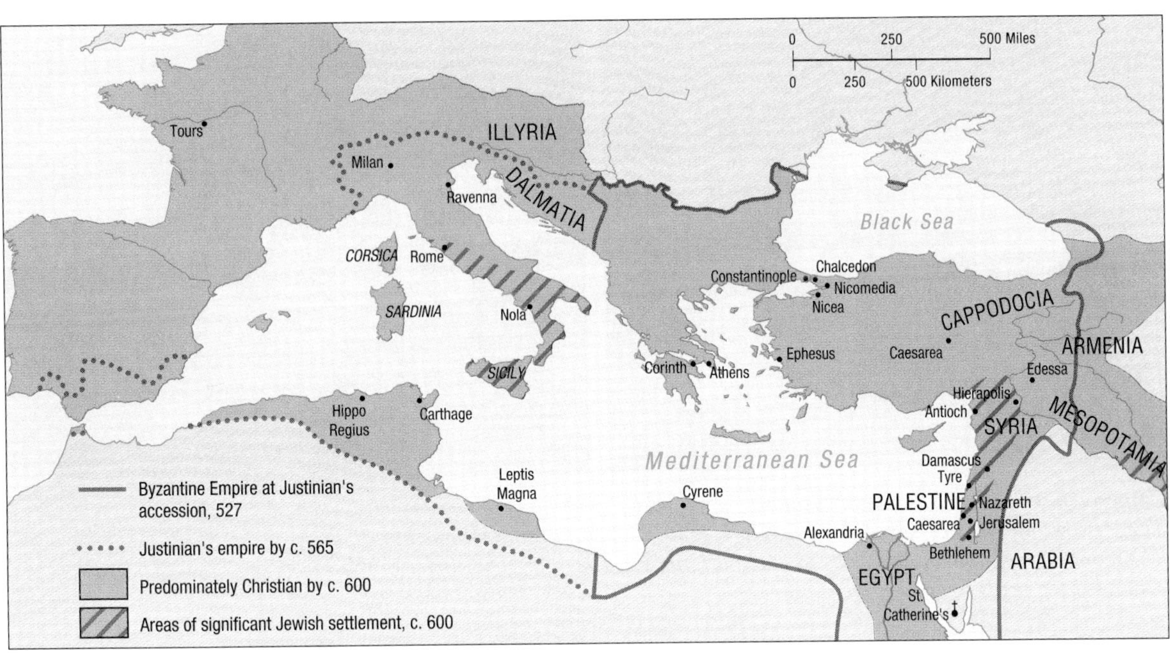

Justinian's Empire and the Spread of Christianity up to 600

realized the great financial advantage of an imperial post: it freed them from the financial burdens of the *curiales.*

Justinian's attempt to reunite the Roman Empire by crushing the German kingdoms came at enormous cost to the economic infrastructure of the West and the finances of the East. His extended military campaigns against the Goths in Italy caused death and destruction on a massive scale. To finance the expeditions, the emperor squeezed even more taxes out of his already overburdened population. Worsening his financial straits was the need to pay large amounts of money every year to hostile neighbors to keep them from attacking the eastern empire while he directed his attention westward. This protection money went to various peoples in the north and, most of all, to the Sassanids in Mesopotamia. Banditry increased in many areas as the economic situation deteriorated, and crowds poured into the capital from rural areas, seeking relief from poverty. In the 540s a horrific epidemic killed perhaps a third of the people in the eastern empire; a quarter of a million succumbed in Constantinople alone, half the capital's population. The loss of so many people meant vacant agricultural land, reduced tax revenues, and a shortage of army recruits. The epidemic devastated the cities and towns of the East, and their continuing weakness made them ill-equipped to respond to the crises that would come in the seventh century, when the Byzantine Empire faced aggressive challenges from Persians and Arabs.

Justinian also strained imperial finances with his urban building program, which drained the West of many builders and craft specialists. Some of his projects were public works, like the huge cistern built in Constantinople, whose roof supported by a forest of columns still stands. Also surviving, although modified through the centuries, is his magnificent reconstruction of Constantine's Church of the Holy Wisdom (St. Sophia, in Istanbul). Facing the palace, the location of St. Sophia corresponded to Justinian's interlacing of imperial and Christian authority. Abandoning the conventional basilica-style architecture of Christian churches, Justinian's architects erected a huge building on a square plan capped by a dome 107 feet across and soaring 160 feet above the floor below. Its interior walls glowed like the sun from the light reflecting off their four acres of gold mosaics. Imported marble of every color added to the sparkling effect. When he first entered his just-completed masterpiece, dedicated in 538, Justinian exclaimed, "Solomon, I have outdone you." (He was referring to the Biblical story of the glorious temple King Solomon built for the ancient

Emperor Justinian and Empress Theodora
These sparkling mosaics from Ravenna, Italy, show Emperor Justinian and Empress Theodora leading court processions to make offerings at the altar. The circles (nimbi) *around their heads signify holiness.*

Hebrews.) Justinian's costly building projects did provide employment, but like his wars to reunite the Roman Empire, they were ultimately justified by the traditional ethos of Roman rulers: the pursuit of glory and a magnificent imperial image were the proper goals of an emperor.

Further reflecting his zeal for reform, Justinian had the laws of the empire codified to try to bring greater consistency and uniformity to the often confusing welter of rules that different emperors had revised and enacted over the centuries. A team of scholars condensed millions of words of regulations to produce the *Digest.* This collection of laws, which superseded the Theodosian Code of 438, influenced legal scholars for centuries. Justinian's experts also compiled a textbook for law students, the *Institutes,* which continued to appear in law-school reading lists until modern times.

The emperor's costly projects left his successors a legacy of bankruptcy and imposed a terrible burden on the general population. So heavy and so unpopular were his taxes and so notorious was his tax collector, the ruthless John of Cappadocia, that they provoked a major riot in 532. This so-called Nika Riot almost ended the emperor's reign. It epitomized the tumultuous life in the eastern capital. The residents of Constantinople had long divided themselves into factions called the Blues and the Greens, names derived from the racing colors of the teams of charioteers around whom the groups had originally formed as ardent fans. By Justinian's time, the Blues and Greens had come to detest each other more out of religious hatred than sports rivalry. The Blues favored orthodox Christian doctrines, whereas the Greens supported Monophysitism. When the Blues and Greens met in Constantinople's hippodrome to watch races, for example, they often came to blows over their theological differences. In 532, however, they unexpectedly united against the emperor, shouting "Nika! Nika!" ("Win! Win!") as their battle cry. After nine days of violence in which much of Constantinople was burned, Justinian was ready to abandon his throne and flee in panic, but his wife, Theodora, sternly rebuked him: "Once born, no one can escape dying, but for one who has held imperial power it would be unbearable to be a fugitive. May I never take off my imperial robes of purple, nor live to see the day when those who meet me will not greet me as their sovereign." Justinian then sent in troops, who quelled the disturbance by slaughtering thirty thousand rioters trapped in the hippodrome.

Empress Theodora dramatically showed the influence women could achieve in the eastern imperial family. Uninhibited by her humble origins (she was the daughter of a bear trainer and had been an actress with a scandalous reputation), Theodora had married into royalty and, like those born into it, could rival anyone in influence and wealth. John

Lydus, a contemporary government official, judged her "superior in intelligence to any man." Some ancient reports suggest that she had a hand in every aspect of Justinian's rule until her death in 548. But Theodora was exceptional. The luxurious and powerful position of royal women bore no resemblance to the lives of most women in this part of the Roman world. For them the pattern of life reflected ancient tradition. For example, both Christian and non-Christian women were expected to minimize their contact with men outside their families. They could not fulfill various public functions, such as witnessing wills. Women and children were subject to the authority of their husbands and fathers, and women veiled their heads (though not their faces). Pagan and Christian sexual mores overlapped significantly, but Christian theologians generally went beyond Roman tradition in frowning on remarriage and supporting increased legal penalties for sexual offenses. Nevertheless, female prostitutes, often poor women desperate for income, continued to abound in the streets and inns of eastern cities, just as in earlier days.

Following the tradition of Roman imperial rule, Justinian considered it his sacred duty to ensure the well-being of the empire and its subjects. Their welfare, he believed, depended especially on the religious purity of the empire, which could not flourish if God became angered by the presence of those who offended him. As emperor, Justinian decided who the offenders were. He zealously enforced long-standing laws against pagans and heretics. For example, he compelled pagans, both in cities and the countryside, to be baptized or forfeit their lands and official positions. Three times he purged heretical Christians whom he could not reconcile to his version of orthodoxy. And his laws made male homosexual relations illegal for the first time in Roman history. Homosexual marriage, apparently not uncommon earlier, had been officially prohibited in 342, but civil sanctions had never before been imposed on men engaging in homosexual activity. All the previous emperors, for example, had taxed male prostitutes. The legal status of homosexual activity between women is less clear; it probably counted as adultery when married women were involved and was thus a crime. For Justinian the use of the force and sanctions of the law against pagans, heretics, and people convicted of homosexual relations expressed his devotion to God and his concern for his own reputation as a pious and successful ruler. In this sense, Justinian's compulsion to purify the empire was part of the same imperial program that promoted the building of magnificent Christian basilicas.

Transformation and Divisiveness

The social, cultural, and political changes in the late Roman Empire took place gradually in a process of transformation. The widespread idea that maintains the empire started on a decline in the third century and then in the fifth century fell, meaning disappeared, stems perhaps more than anything else from the great renown of the title of the English historian Edward Gibbon's multivolume work *The Decline and Fall of the Roman Empire* (published 1776–1788). Gibbon recognized that the Roman Empire did not disappear in 476 with the deposition of the western emperor Romulus Augustulus, because he continued his mammoth history until the Turks captured Constantinople in 1453, the final end of the eastern empire. Its so-called decline and fall therefore lasted more than a thousand years. Gibbon entitled his history when he published its first volume in 1776, twelve years before he finished the final volume that reached the events of 1453. (He might well have chosen a different title had he completed writing the long story of the eastern Roman Empire before he named his work, and the erroneous idea that the Roman Empire fell once and for all in 476 might not have gained such currency.) The end of the short reign of Romulus Augustulus in 476 undeniably marked a change, because he was the last Roman emperor in the West. No longer did one central authority head Roman government there; a welter of local administrations and Germanic kingdoms now governed. In this narrow sense the western empire did fall; but that distinction has little, if any, historical significance. The reality of political power in the West remained the same after 476 as it had been for generations before: German commanders and troops dominated the Roman army and therefore controlled the western empire's political fate.

The most remarkable aspect of the transformation of the late Roman Empire was the divergence of its western and eastern portions. For centuries to come, the East largely retained its centralized authority, complex financial administration, and sense of being the continuation of the ancient Roman Empire. The western empire changed far more profoundly, and the decentralization of authority there plus the impact of the influx of Germanic peoples turned it into something markedly different. The traditional practices of Roman administration faded away in the western provinces as the German kingdoms became more independent. By Romulus's reign in the late fifth century, the annual revenues at the western emperor's disposal had shrunk to a small fraction of the eastern emperor's. Tax revenues that previously would have supported the central government now enriched German potentates and Roman nobles. The violence that had sometimes accompanied the appearance of large groups of Germanic peoples in the West had also weakened the economy in some regions. The western empire found these losses especially difficult to overcome because its population had probably never recovered its former size after the disasters of the third century.

Both halves of the Roman world probably did share at least one experience in this period: an increasing lack of social cohesiveness and a sense of belonging among their populations. A tremendous gulf had always separated rich and poor Romans, and theological disputes had divided Christians from the earliest years of their new religion. Nevertheless, as these tendencies became more pronounced in the later Roman Empire, people grew more alienated from one another and thus less able to find cooperative solutions to their society's problems.

People of limited means and status found it increasingly difficult to get government officials to issue permits, redress grievances, and deal with the many other affairs of daily life requiring official intervention. Romans of all social ranks had always relied on personal connections when dealing with the government, sometimes seeking preferential treatment, sometimes simply trying to ensure that officials did what they were supposed to do. The administration of late Roman imperial government imposed special burdens on citizens, however, not only because its officials continued to expect generous tips routinely, but also because there were now considerably more officials to tip. Because interest rates were high, people could incur onerous debt trying to raise the cash to pay high officials to act on important matters. Many officials depended on this system to augment their generally paltry salaries. John Lydus, for example, who worked in Justinian's administration, earned thirty times his annual salary in payments from petitioners during his first year in office. The emperors approved petitioners' payments to their officials as a way to keep salary costs down, and they published an official list of the maximum bribes officials could exact. The idea was to keep officials from crippling the administration by pricing their services too highly. The increased importance of paying extra in return for service obviously made it harder and harder for people without much money to obtain help from government officials.

Another source of divisiveness in the late Roman Empire was the increasing autocracy of the emperors and the severity of the legal penalties they imposed as lawmakers. Already in the second century the legal scholar Gaius had argued that the emperor's decrees had the full force of law without any need for Senate approval. In the late Roman world the emperors employed many legal scholars to tell them that their word alone was law. Indeed the emperors came to be above the law because they were not bound even by the decrees of their predecessors, and they thus had less interest than ever in consulting the aristocracy, ruling by consensus, and observing tradition. The emperors depended on their personal staff for advice and grew farther apart from the aristocrats. The emperors also used their greater legal powers to increase the severity of judicial penalties for crimes, continuing a trend already evident during the Great Persecution. For example, the law mandated that if, after due warnings, officials did not keep their "greedy hands" off bribes (presumably exorbitant ones), "they shall be cut off by the sword." Constantine revived the ancient punishment of tying certain malefactors in a leather sack with snakes and drowning them in a river. The guardians of a young girl who allowed a lover to seduce her were punished by having molten lead poured into their mouths. Fewer condemned criminals, however, were dispatched to the amphitheater to die as gladiators or by fighting animals. Nevertheless, punishments grew especially harsh for the large segment of the population legally designated as *humiliores* ("humbler people"). The upper ranks of the population (*honestiores*) could generally escape harsh treatment for crimes. Although the lack of direct evidence for what common people felt makes generalization uncertain, the increased severity with which the government punished the masses could hardly have strengthened their sense of attachment to the Roman state, whose privileges were more than ever before limited to the wealthy and socially well-connected.

The late Roman world was also split spiritually by frequent, bitter controversies over Christian doctrine and by the disengagement from everyday society epitomized by monasticism. These divisions in Christianity disrupted society much more than had the formation of new pagan cults in earlier times. Whereas paganism had incorporated new divinities and new practices without rejecting time-honored traditions, Christianity required its adherents to serve only one divinity in a prescribed fashion. But Christian orthodoxy required political enforcement, and not even the growing secular power of church officials sufficed either to persuade or to compel unwilling believers to accept orthodox views. In some cases, oppressed Christians fled the empire, as when the Nestorians moved to Persia. Emperors like Justinian tried to convince heretical Christians to return to orthodox theology and the hierarchy of the church, but they did not shrink from using force when persuasion failed. Rulers took these extreme measures believing that they were helping to save lost souls. But the persecution of Christian subjects by Christian emperors symbolized the dire consequences of divisiveness for the late Roman world.

The Survival of Roman Language and Education

Language and literature in the later Roman Empire represented a continuation of tradition because they clearly reflected their earlier Roman heritage; but they were also transformed through the demographic changes and conflicts among the inhabitants of the Roman world and the ever-increasing influence of Christianity. As Roman and Germanic traditions mingled, creating new ways of life in the western empire, "Romanness" there became something that one acquired more by education rather than by birth or ethnic origin. Upper-class Roman and German men of the late empire came to share a taste for education in traditional Roman subjects, rhetoric above all. German leaders who gained this learning became the intellectual peers of educated Roman men, while remaining their political superiors in the new kingdoms. The German tribes originally had no written language, but a script for writing the Goths' spoken tongue was invented in the late fourth century so the Bible could be translated into Gothic. The Germans who forged successful careers in the western empire before the formation of the Germanic kingdoms, especially those who served in the Roman army, learned to write and speak Latin. (For more than a thousand years, in fact, Latin would remain the principal language of official communication in Europe.) Familiarity with classical texts, although limited, remained the distinguishing mark of an educated person. Augustine had a friend who knew Virgil so well that if someone quoted him a line of the poet's work, he could recite the preceding line.

Some Roman scholars and intellectuals viewed German influence as a threat because they feared Roman literary and cultural traditions would gradually be obliterated in the new Germanic kingdoms. Latin literature had experienced a renaissance at the end of the fourth century and the beginning of the fifth century with great prose works like those of Augustine and Jerome. Poetry had again flourished in Latin, too, as in the evocative poem by Ausonius of Bordeaux (c. 310–395) that describes the natural wonders of the Moselle River (which flows from what is now France into Germany). Christian poets, such as Paulinus of Nola (353–431) also began writing in Latin. Several generations later, Boethius and Cassiodorus, both of whom worked for Ostrogothic kings of Italy, became famous for their scholarly efforts to preserve the traditions of Roman literature and philosophy. Boethius (c. 480–524) rose to the consulship under Theodoric, but he was subsequently imprisoned on suspicion of treason and later executed. Boethius's scholarship was motivated by his "fear that many things which are now known soon will not be." This worry that classical learning might be forgotten led him to want to translate Plato and Aristotle into Latin and provide commentaries to explain the texts. He was killed, however, before he had progressed very far with this work. His *Consolation of Philosophy*, written in prison when he had no recourse to a library, nevertheless abounded in references to classical texts and was filled with Neoplatonic doctrines. Cassiodorus (c. 490–585) spent time in Constantinople but returned to Italy to live in a monastery he had founded. There he developed a new monastic goal,

Christ as the Sun God *This mosaic from a second-century Roman catacomb portrays Christ as the radiant Sun God driving his chariot, illustrating how Christian art made use of pagan traditions.*

the copying of manuscripts to keep their contents alive as old ones disintegrated, which became a function for the monks in monasteries he founded. Cassiodorus wrote his book *Institutions* to prescribe the works a person of superior education should read. His ideal curriculum included secular texts as well as Scripture and Christian literature, encapsulating the cultural diversity of the late Roman Empire.

Pagan literature in Latin continued to be widely read because no other suitable texts existed for basic education. Educated Christians therefore received at least a rudimentary knowledge of some pre-Christian classics. And such an education was necessary for a distinguished career in government service. In the words of an imperial decree of 360, "No person shall obtain a post of the first rank unless it shall be shown that he excels in long practice of liberal studies, and that he is so polished in literary matters that words flow from his pen faultlessly." Christian literature, which flourished in the late empire, followed distinguished pagan models. Classical eloquence, for example, was used to disseminate Christian theology and guidance. When Ambrose composed the first systematic description of Christian ethics for young priests, he consciously imitated the great Roman writer Cicero. Writers employed the dialogue form pioneered by Plato to refute heretical Christian doctrines, and traditions of laudatory biography survived in hagiography, or saints' lives. These works demonstrated how Christianity could use literature to promote religion. Moreover, Christians often communicated their beliefs and emotions in paintings, mosaics, and carved reliefs that combined pagan and Christian traditions of representation. A famous mosaic of Christ with a sunburst surrounding his head, for example, recalled pagan depictions of the radiant Sun as a god.

The development of specifically Christian literature was accompanied by a significant technological evolution in the production of manuscripts (books). Pagan literature had always been written mainly on sheets made of thin animal skin or paper made from the papyrus plant. This material was then attached to a rod at either end to make a scroll, which the reader unrolled to read. For ease of use, Christians preferred their literature in the form of the *codex*—a book with bound pages. During the fourth century the codex became the standard form of book production in the Roman world. Because it was less susceptible to damage and could contain text more efficiently than scrolls, which were cumbersome for long works, the codex aided the preservation of literature. This technological innovation helped keep the memory of ancient Greco-Roman culture as embodied in its literature from disappearing as it evolved into new forms during and after the late Roman Empire.

New literary developments also helped perpetuate the memory of classical learning. Around 470, for example, the pagan Martianus Capella in Vandal Carthage composed an allegory in Latin prose and verse to tell the story of Philology, the goddess of learning, accompanied by her handmaidens, the seven Liberal Arts (grammar, rhetoric, logic, arithmetic, geometry, astronomy, and music), ascending to the heavens where Philology was to marry the god of eloquence, Mercury. Such elaborate allegories later became a very popular literary form.

But despite such continuing importance of classical Greek and Latin literature, preserving pagan literature became increasingly problematic. By the fifth century, knowledge of Greek in the West had faded so drastically that very few could read Homer's *Iliad* and *Odyssey*—the traditional foundations of a pagan literary education—in the original. Classical Latin fared better, and well-read Christians like Augustine and Jerome knew ancient Latin literature extremely well. But they also saw

(far left) ***The Old Form of the Book*** *This sculpture from a Roman sarcophagus shows a man reading a book in the form of a scroll, which had to be unrolled and then rolled up again as its reader proceeded through the text.*

(left) ***The New Form of the Book*** *This mosaic from the church of S. Vitale in Ravenna (completed in 546) shows the evangelist Mark holding a codex, a kind of book featuring bound pages that Christians favored for their scriptures over traditional scrolls.*

the Latin classics as potentially too seductive for a pious Christian. Jerome in fact once had a nightmare of being condemned on Judgment Day because he had been a Ciceronian instead of a Christian. Like Greek, Latin survived in a form increasingly different from the classical language of an earlier time. The Latin of literature became simpler in the late empire. For example, Benedict's Rule used colloquial, nonclassical words to make the code intelligible to simply educated monks. Educated people, however, frequently preferred an ornate style recalling Greek Hellenistic poetry and the Latin prose of the second century. This preference reflected the educational gap between the masses and the few who could appreciate traditional literature.

In the eastern empire the region's original Greek culture reemerged as the dominant influence. Men of affairs, such as the emperor Julian and his fourth-century contemporary Libanius, the influential pagan rhetorician from Antioch, produced copious works in Greek that dealt with religion, politics, and intellectual issues. Novels with plots of romance and adventure captured the imagination of a wide public. Schoolboys memorized passages from Homer, as they had in classical Greece. The most famous Byzantine historian, Procopius, a high official under Justinian, wrote both his conventional *History of the Wars of Justinian* and his provocative *Secret History,* a scurrilous attack on the policies and personal habits of Justinian and Theodora, in a classical Greek style. Educated members of the upper class tried to speak in the Greek forms of ancient times. This tendency sprang from the traditionally narrow notion of education in Roman society: training in elite knowledge whose purpose was to separate its holders from the masses. Ordinary Greek speakers used koine ("common" Greek) that kept evolving away from classical models. Already in the fourth century, for example, some people were ceasing to use the classical Greek word *hydor* for "water" and instead using *nero*—the word used in modern Greek.

The administration of the eastern empire was bilingual, with Latin remaining the language of law and the army throughout this period. For example, Justinian's code of laws, the *Digest,* was written in Latin. But in court cases people routinely spoke Greek, and Greek translations of the codified laws soon became available. Latin scholarship in the eastern empire received a boost when Justinian's wars in Italy impelled Latin-speaking scholars to flee for safety to Constantinople. Their labors there helped to conserve many works of Latin literature that might otherwise have disappeared, because conditions in the West were hardly conducive to safekeeping ancient learning, except in such rare instances as the monasteries founded by Cassiodorus.

The handing down of knowledge from classical antiquity suffered a great symbolic blow when Justinian in 529 closed the Academy in Athens, originally founded by Plato. The emperor shut down this famous pagan school after nine hundred years of operation because he was outraged by its virulently anti-Christian head, Damascius. But fortunately for the future of classical texts, Justinian did not attack non-Christian learning at large. The Neoplatonist school at Alexandria, for example, he simply ignored, perhaps because its leader, John Philoponus (c. 490–570), was a Christian. In addition to Christian theology, Philoponus wrote commentaries on the works of Aristotle; some of his ideas anticipated those of Galileo. Philoponus symbolizes the synthesis of old and new that was one of the fruitful outcomes of the transformation of the late Roman world—that is, he was a Christian in sixth-century Egypt, heading a school founded long before by pagans, studying the works of an ancient Greek philosopher as the inspiration for his forward-looking scholarship.

Conclusion

The most significant and enduring development in the history of the late Roman Empire was that masses of people converted to Christianity. Pagans continued their traditions long after Christianity had become the empire's official religion in the late fourth century, and Judaism maintained its vitality, but Christian doctrines and patterns of life were now assured a central role in Western civilization. The autocratic rule of the late Roman emperors and the development of a hierarchy of monarchical bishops helped secure Christianity's success.

Demographic changes also helped set the stage for the future, especially in the western region of the now-divided empire. The movements of polyethnic tribes—Visigoths, Vandals, Anglo-Saxons, Ostrogoths, and Lombards—into the western empire created a new culture that meshed Roman and German traditions and led to the formation of Germanic kingdoms in place of Roman provincial administration. The damage many European and North African cities and towns suffered in this period, combined with a loss of population in many places, weakened the economic and political infrastructure of the region for a long time to come, making the area difficult to defend. In the eastern empire, largely unchanged by the movements of Germanic peoples (except in the Balkans), urban life remained vital until the increasing autocracy of the Byzantine Empire and the ravages of the epidemic of the 540s severely weakened its cities. The administrative efficiency and financial health of the East deteriorated because, in the words of a recent scholar, the government and the cities directly competed for the same human and financial resources. The government attracted more and more of the urban elites into imperial administration, where their offices automatically entitled them to exemption from the financial responsibilities imposed on municipal *curiales.* The dwindling supply of *curiales* meant that the cities and towns experienced chronic difficulties in fulfilling their traditional role as the collectors of revenues for the imperial government.

Taxation became ever heavier as the emperors tried to raise money to pay the army, to bribe foreign enemies not to attack, and to erect glorious buildings to demonstrate their grandeur. People in cities benefited from the emperors' public works projects, but the urban poor, along with their compatriots in the countryside, found little comfort in a government that pinched them for taxes and served them only if they could pay its officials or otherwise obtain favors.

Monasticism represented the most visible manifestation of many people's longing for a dramatic change in their lives. Becoming a monk was a way to escape everyday cares and, through the continual worship of God, to attain a level of personal contentment many people felt secular life could not match. The problem presented by withdrawal from ordinary life was that it might satisfy an individual's needs but offered no resolution to the difficulties facing a society in crisis.

Suggestions for Further Reading

Source Materials

Augustine. *City of God.* Translated by Henry Bettenson. 1984. The major theological work of one of Christianity's most influential thinkers.

———. *Confessions.* Translated by Henry Chadwick. 1991. Augustine's spiritual autobiography.

Geanakoplos, D. J. *Byzantium: Church, Society, and Civilization Seen Through Contemporary Eyes.* 1984. A collection of excerpts from primary sources on many aspects of Byzantine life.

Hillgarth, J. L., ed. *Christianity and Paganism, 350–750: The Conversion of Western Europe.* Rev. ed. 1986. A selection of documents and literary texts concerning the spread of Christianity in western Europe.

Kraemer, Ross S., ed. *Maenads, Martyrs, Matrons, Monastics: A Sourcebook on Women's Religions in the Greco-Roman World.* 1988. Includes sources through the late Roman world, with extensive coverage of asceticism and monasticism.

Procopius. *History of the Wars; Secret History; Buildings.* Edited by Averil Cameron. 1967. An abridged edition of the diverse works of this sixth-century Byzantine official, including his scathingly gossipy *Secret History.*

Interpretive Studies

Bowersock, G. W. *Julian the Apostate.* 1978. An elegantly written study of the last pagan emperor of Rome.

Brown, Peter. *Augustine of Hippo.* 1967. The standard biography of this seminal figure in early Christianity.

———. *The Body and Society: Men, Women, and Sexual Renunciation in Early Christianity.* 1988. A masterful and provocative treatment of a fundamental episode in the shaping of Western attitudes toward sexuality.

———. *The World of Late Antiquity, A.D. 150–750.* 1971. The most intriguing brief introduction to the transformation of the Roman world into the early medieval world.

Cochrane, Charles N. *Christianity and Classical Culture.* Rev. ed. 1944. An enduring analysis of the impact of Christianity on thought and action in the Roman world from the first to the fourth century.

Dodds, E. R. *Pagan and Christian in an Age of Anxiety.* 1965. A classic introduction to religious experience in the Roman world from the late second century to the time of Constantine.

Geary, Patrick J. *Before France and Germany: The Creation and Transformation of the Merovingian World.* 1988. A sprightly analysis of the diverse forces and traditions involved in the formation of the Germanic kingdoms in Roman Europe.

Gibbon, Edward. *The Decline and Fall of the Roman Empire.* Edited by J. B. Bury. 1946. An annotated edition of this still stimulating classic work, whose first volume was originally published in 1776.

Heather, P. J. *Goths and Romans, 322–448.* 1991. A study of the interaction of Goths with the Roman Empire, arguing that these Germans originally had a stronger sense of ethnic identity than is usually acknowledged.

Isaac, Benjamin. *The Limits of Empire: The Roman Army in the East.* 1989. A refreshingly revisionist argument that Roman military planning was often haphazard and not very geared toward defense.

James, Edward. *The Franks.* 1988. A readable treatment of the history and customs of this Germanic people.

Jones, A. H. M. *The Decline of the Ancient World.* 1966. An abbreviated version of his multivolume work combining chronological narrative and topical analysis.

———. *The Later Roman Empire.* 2 vols. 1964. Still the most complete account by an expert with profound knowledge of this vast subject.

MacMullen, Ramsay. *Christianizing the Roman Empire, A.D. 100–400.* 1984. An interpretive survey of the process through which Christianity became the dominant religion in the Roman Empire.

———. *Constantine.* 1969. A clearly written introduction to the career of the first Christian emperor.

———. *Corruption and the Decline of Rome.* 1988. A controversial indictment of the role of official corruption in the weakening of the late Roman Empire.

Mango, Cyril. *Byzantium: The Empire of New Rome.* 1980. A wide-ranging study of Byzantine social, cultural, and intellectual history.

Murray, Alexander C. *Germanic Kinship Structure.* 1983. A tightly argued study of bilateral kinship relationships in the Germanic tribes.

Ostrogorsky, George. *History of the Byzantine State.* Rev. ed. 1969. The standard scholarly treatment of the subject, primarily concerned with political, diplomatic, and military history.

Pagels, Elaine. *Adam, Eve, and the Serpent.* 1988. A thought-provoking interpretation of the effect of Augustine's concept of the doctrine of original sin.

Rousselle, Aline. *Porneia: On Desire and the Body in Antiquity.* Translated by Felicia Pheasant. 1988. A compendium of fascinating evidence on attitudes toward the human body and sexuality.

Wolfram, Herwig. *History of the Goths.* Rev. ed. Translated by Thomas J. Dunlap. 1988. A comprehensive study of the ethnogenesis of the Goths and what it meant to be German in a Roman world.

Masons and Sculptors, Stained Glass in Chartes Cathedral, France

PART

II

The Quickening of the West, 568–1560

With the end of imperial rule in the West, northern and central Europe became an important historical stage as new political, economic, and cultural communities competed and cooperated with one another as well as with the older communities of the Mediterranean and the Near East. New peoples, speaking new languages, came on the scene: joining those who spoke Latin, Greek, and Germanic and Celtic tongues were Slavic peoples and immigrants from the steppes of western Asia. Once Europe's dense forests were cut back and its thick grasslands tamed, the way was opened for population growth, the emergence of cities, and the development of centralized states.

Although these changes were under way, no one in the sixth century proclaimed the end of the ancient world or the beginning of the Middle Ages. Only much later, when some people self-consciously imitated the art and literature of classical antiquity, did the idea of a "middle age in between" the classical and modern period emerge. Thus the intellectual movement known as the Renaissance (meaning "rebirth") created the Middle Ages. Nevertheless, the Renaissance itself represented a period of retrenchment of medieval institutions and attitudes.

The Middle Ages called on the legacy of antiquity. Byzantine emperors, Muslim caliphs, and German kings followed Roman administrative and legal traditions; scholars revived interest in Greek and Roman philosophy and literature; and churchmen built on the theology and commentary of the great spokesmen for the early church. The very idea that the Roman Empire had ended seemed absurd, for emperors continued to rule in the East until 1453; and new-style Western emperors, the first of whom was crowned in the year 800, governed into the nineteenth century.

The Middle Ages also replaced some ancient practices with its own enduring traditions. In place of slavery, peasants settled on the land in households; wage labor began; and the use of water mills, heavy plows, and massive looms marked the beginning of industry. For the first time, cities were more hubs of commercial activity than centers of politics and religious ritual. Latin ceased to be spoken, while the ancestors of modern languages such as French, German, English, and Spanish became literary as well as oral languages. Medieval scholars created unique syntheses of divine revelation and human knowledge. Twelfth-century troubadour poets and religious mystics created a new literature of love, and a few centuries later Renaissance humanists spoke to the experiences and concerns of lay men and women in courts and cities.

National states ruled by kings overturned the ancient Roman model of empire. The contours of these states foreshadowed the current political map of Europe. Ever on the move, Western medieval kings, warriors, and churchmen pushed eastward along the Baltic coast, southward into the Holy Land, and westward to Ireland. So although the Mediterranean was still the focus of Western culture at the beginning of the Middle Ages, by the end of the period a New World had been "discovered" and Westerners were transplanting their brand of civilization across the Atlantic.

The Middle Ages saw the rise and fall of a united Christendom. The hierarchical church, led by a pope and his bishops, asserted its authority and power in the twelfth and thirteenth centuries, when it clashed with the Western emperor. But even in the twelfth century, for many people this hierarchical conception of the church was partly overshadowed by other potent manifestations of divine power, from miracles at the shrines of saints to the monastic devotions of monks. The papal view conflicted as well with the growing power of monarchs and princes, with the rising prestige of pious lay groups, and with new visions of the world set out by scholars. In the sixteenth century, leaders of the religious movement known as the Reformation rebelled against the medieval papacy and forever split Christian Europe into rival sects.

In everyday parlance today, the term *Middle Ages* has two meanings. Sometimes it connotes the so-called Dark Ages, a period of ignorance, intolerance, and violence. At other times it suggests an age of chivalry and romance, of knights in shining armor and damsels in distress. Although each image contains a bit of truth, the whole truth is far more complex and specific. Seventh-century illiteracy must not obscure the twelfth century's surge of scholarship or the creation of a new institution, the university. Cruel intolerance of Jews and other groups in the twelfth century does not negate the acceptance of Jews in tenth-century society. Medieval life was marred by violence but also soothed and steadied by peace movements and other attempts to channel and control warfare. Knighthood and the romantic literature that portrayed it were products of the eleventh and twelfth centuries, a response to specific conditions of the era. As these conditions passed away, they brought in their wake a new world, constrained in its turn to build upon and change the legacy of the Middle Ages.

CHAPTER

8

The Heirs of the Roman Empire, 568–756

According to a writer who was not very sympathetic to the Byzantines, Emperor Heraclius (✱610–641) had a dream: "Verily [he was told] there shall come against thee a circumcised nation, and they shall vanquish thee and take possession of the land." Heraclius thought the vision betokened a rising of the Jews, and he ordered mass baptisms in all his provinces. "But," continued the story,

> *after a few days there appeared a man of the Arabs, from the southern districts, that is to say, from Mecca or its neighborhood, whose name was Muhammad; and he brought back the worshipers of idols to the knowledge of the One God. . . . And he took possession of Damascus and Syria, and crossed the Jordan and dammed it up. And the Lord abandoned the army of the Romans before him.*

This tale, however fanciful, alerts us to the most astonishing development of the seventh century: the Arabs conquered much of the Roman Empire and became one of its heirs. The western and eastern parts of the empire, both diminished, were now joined by yet a third—Arab and Muslim—power. The resulting triad has endured in various guises to the present day: the western third of the old Roman Empire became western Europe; the eastern third, occupying what is now Turkey, Greece, and part of the Balkans, became part of eastern Europe and helped to create Russia; and North Africa, together with the area of the ancient Near East (now called the Middle East), remains the Arab world.

As diverse as these cultures are today, they share some of the same roots and

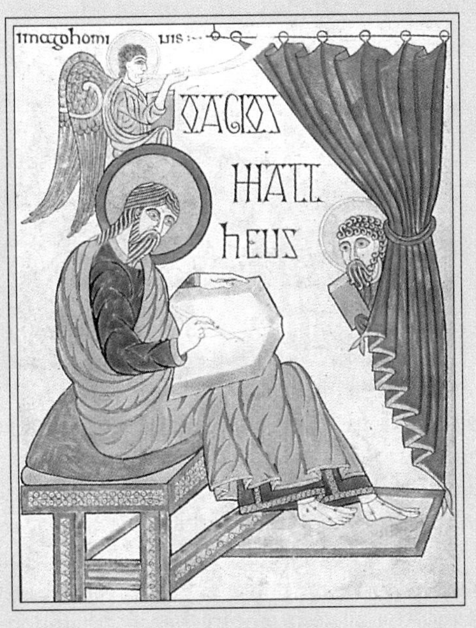

Lindisfarne Gospels Evangelist Page
Far both in time and spirit from the classical Mediterranean world, the seventh-century English monks who drew this picture of St. Matthew transformed classical human and architectural representations into bold and decorative designs.

assumptions. All were heirs of Hellenistic and Roman traditions; most important, each believed in monotheism. The western and eastern halves of the empire had Christianity in common, although they differed at times in interpreting it. The Arab world's religion, Islam, accepted the same one God as Christianity but considered Jesus one of God's prophets rather than his son.

The history of the seventh and eighth centuries is a story of adaptation: in different ways, all three heirs combined elements of their Roman heritage with new values, interests, and conditions. The divergences among them resulted inevitably from disparities in geographical and climatic conditions, material and human resources, skills, and various local traditions. But these differences should not blind us to the fact that the Byzantine, Muslim, and western European worlds were sibling cultures.

Important Dates

c. 570–632 Life of Muhammad, prophet of Islam

590–604 Papacy of Gregory the Great

622 *Hijra* to Medina and beginning of Islamic calendar

657 Queen Balthild, wife of Clovis II, king of the Franks, becomes regent during her son's minority

664 Synod of Whitby; English king opts for Roman Christianity

687 Battle of Tertry; Pippin II becomes mayor of two Frankish kingdoms

726–843 Period of iconoclasm at Byzantium

751–768 Pippin III rules as king of the Franks

Byzantium: A Christian Empire Under Siege

The Byzantine emperor Justinian had tried to recreate the old Roman Empire. On the surface he succeeded. The map of his empire once again included Italy, North Africa, and the Balkans. Vestiges of old Roman society persisted: an educated elite maintained its prestige, town governments continued to function, and old myths and legends were retold in poetry and depicted on silver plates and chests. By the beginning of the seventh century, however, the eastern empire began to undergo a transformation as striking as the one that had earlier remade the western half. From the last third of the sixth century, Byzantium was almost constantly at war, and its territory shrank drastically. Cultural and political change came as well. Cities—except for a few such as Constantinople—decayed, and the countryside became the focus of government and military administration. In the wake of these shifts the old elite largely disappeared, and classical learning gave way to new forms of education, mainly religious in content. The traditional styles of urban life, dependent on public gathering places and community spirit, faded away.

Byzantium at War

The state of nearly constant warfare against invaders of the Byzantine Empire persisted from the last third of the sixth century to the middle of the eighth century. To the west Byzantium faced the Lombards, a Germanic people from Pannonia (modern Hungary), some of whom had been used by Justinian's generals in their destructive war against the Ostrogoths in Italy. In 568, pursued by a Turkic people known as the Avars, the Lombards had invaded Italy and pushed back the Byzantines. Byzantium's western foothold shrank severely, although it retained nominal control over a swath of land through the middle of Italy called the Exarchate of Ravenna, of which Rome was a part. Byzantium also kept control of the toe and heel of the Italian boot, the island of Sicily, and Venice. But most of Italy was now out of the eastern emperor's grasp, and he would soon lose more land and power elsewhere.

To the north the Byzantines had to ward off tribal groups attacking from just beyond the Danube. First were the Slavs, who, much like the Germans of earlier centuries, combined sedentary agriculture with raiding expeditions. Lightly armed and fleet, Slavic raiding parties could not breach the Byzantine walled cities of the Balkans, but they easily devastated the countryside, looting and taking prisoners, then riding their swift horses to safety across the Danube River.

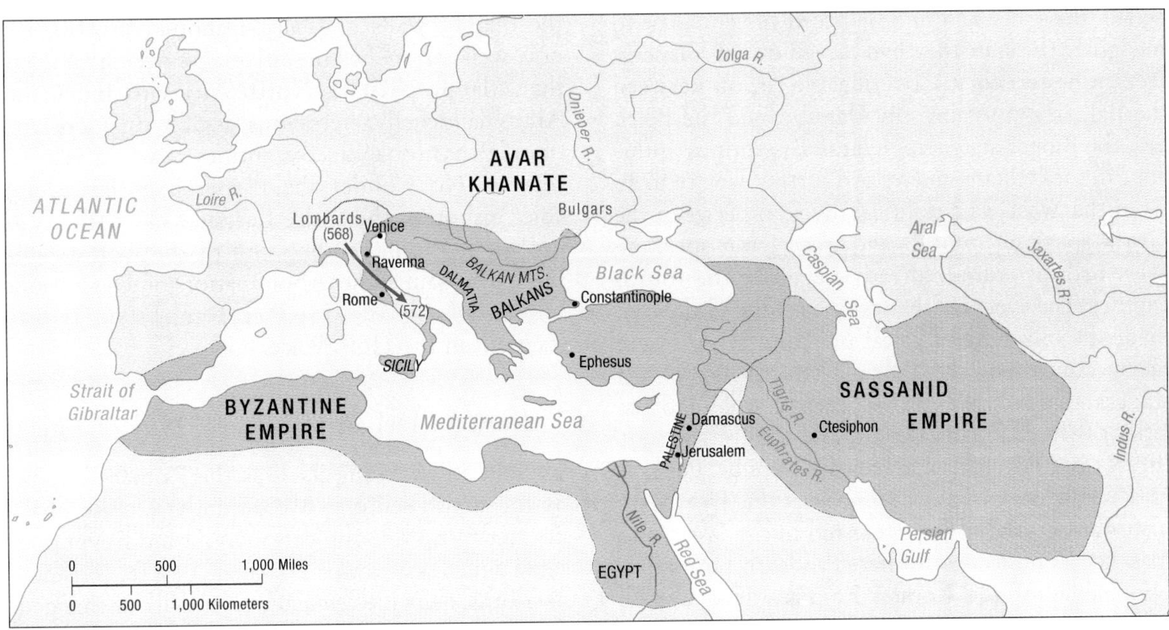

Byzantine and Sassanid Empires, c. 600

Soon, however, the Slavs were joined by the Avars. These nomadic pastoralists and warriors were driven into Europe from the east by rival tribes at their backs, as well as lured by visions of conquest and plunder. Under their ruler, called a *khagan,* the Avars forged a formidable military force. By the 560s they had settled in Pannonia, organizing a state with fixed borders and subjecting local Slavic and Hunnic tribes. From this base, Avar armies, bolstered by their more numerous (if less well organized) tribal allies, besieged the cities in the Balkans. Throughout the last third of the sixth century and into the seventh, they fought the Byzantine forces. They raided mostly on the Dalmatian coast, but sometimes struck down into Greece or marched (and sailed, in small boats) as far as the Bosphorus. In 626, for example, they attacked Constantinople. But here the Avars found a veritable fortress, surrounded by nearly impregnable walls and further defended by the formidable Byzantine fleet. The attack of 626, at least, was foiled.

Meanwhile, Slavs and Avars were penetrating more peacefully—through simple settlement—into the Balkans. Sometimes displacing, more often intermingling with the indigenous population, they absorbed local agricultural techniques and burial practices while imposing their language and religious cults. By 626 the Avars were waning as a fighting force, and their client tribes rebelled against them. Now a new people, the Croats, established themselves in the western Balkans, and another, related group called the Serbs moved a little to the south of what is now Serbia. Both new groups were successful conquerors because they boasted a well-disciplined cavalry, just as the Avars had. However, again like the Avars, they were not very numerous and depended on allied support. The population of the entire Balkan region by the end of the seventh century was mostly Slavic peasantry. The Croats and Serbs soon assimilated with these Slavs, adopting much of their language and culture. By the beginning of the eighth century, the ethnic mix that would eventually form the population of the present-day Balkans had largely been established.

From the Byzantines' point of view the arrival of the Croats and the Serbs and the weakening of Avar power hardly mattered, for Byzantium was attacked in turn by the Bulgars. These originally Turkic people came from the Black Sea region, where after forging a multiethnic federation led by a chief, they had been pushed out (in a familiar pattern) by yet another group. Entering what is now Bulgaria in the 670s, they defeated the

Byzantine army and in 681 forced the emperor to recognize the state they had carved out of formerly Byzantine territory. Covering the region between the Balkan mountains, the Danube, and the Black Sea, the Bulgar state crippled the Byzantines' influence in the Balkans and helped further isolate them from the West. The political division between the Greek-speaking world and the Latin-speaking West had, of course, already begun in the fourth century. The events of the seventh century, however, made the split both physical and cultural. Avar and Slavic control of the Balkans effectively cut off trade and travel between Constantinople and the cities of the Dalmatian coast, and the Bulgar state threw a political barrier across the Danube. Perhaps as a result of this physical separation, Byzantine historians ceased to be interested in the West, and its scholars no longer bothered to learn Latin. The two halves of the Roman Empire, once united, communicated very little in the seventh century.

Byzantium was unsuccessful in the Balkans mostly because it simultaneously had to fight the Persians on its eastern border. The Sassanid Empire was a superpower of the early seventh century (it included the regions known today as Iran and Iraq), and it fought with Byzantium off and on during the late sixth century. War broke out once again in 604, and from then until 620, Persian armies won resounding victories against Byzantines, taking, for example, Damascus in 613, Jerusalem the following year, and Egypt in 619. But Emperor Heraclius reorganized his army and inspired his troops to avenge the sack of Jerusalem, thus turning the tide and regaining all lost territory by 627.

The significance of this period of war lay not in the taking and retaking of territory but in the sapping of both Persian and Byzantine military strength. Exhausted, these empires were now vulnerable to attack by the Arabs, whose military prowess was to create a new empire and spread a new religion, Islam. In the 630s, Arab armies overran Palestine and Jerusalem. In 637 they defeated the Persians at the very gates of their capital, Ctesiphon. During the 640s they invaded North Africa, and by 651 all of Persia was in Muslim hands. Now the two superpowers that faced one another were Byzantine and Arab. For more than two hundred years, from the 640s to the 860s, they remained at war, not always locked in battle but nevertheless continually threatening one another. Each year between 673 and 678, Arab forces attacked the mighty walls of Constantinople. In 718–719, now well entrenched in settlements stretching from the Atlantic coast of North Africa to India, the Arabs launched a ferocious assault on Constantinople that took the Byzantines nearly a year to repulse. No wonder the Patriarch of Jerusalem, chief bishop of the entire Levant, saw in the Arab onslaught the impending end of the world: "Behold," he said, "the Abomination of Desolation, spoken of by the Prophet Daniel [9:27], that standeth in the Holy Place."

From an Urban to a Rural Way of Life

Though still viewing itself as the Roman Empire, by the eighth century, Byzantium was quite small. Former Byzantine subjects in Syria and Egypt now came under Arab sway. For them, despite their new overlords, daily life remained essentially unchanged. Non-Muslims paid a special tax to their conquerors, but they could practice their own religions. In the countryside they were permitted to keep and farm their lands, and their cities remained centers of government, scholarship, and business.

Ironically, the most radical transformations for seventh- and eighth-century Byzantines occurred not in the territories lost but in the shrunken empire itself. Under the ceaseless barrage of war, many towns, formerly bustling nodes of trade and centers of the imperial bureaucratic network, vanished or became unrecognizable in their changed way of life. The public activity of marketplaces, theaters, and town squares gave way to the family table and hearth. City baths, once places where people gossiped, made deals, and talked politics and philosophy, disappeared in most Byzantine towns—with the significant exception of Constantinople. Warfare reduced some cities to rubble, and when they were rebuilt, the limited resources available went to construct thick walls and solid churches instead of marketplaces and baths. Marketplaces moved to overcrowded streets that looked much like the souks of the modern Middle East. People under siege sought protection rather than community pastimes. In the Byzantine city of Ephesus, for example, the citizens who built the new walls in the seventh century did not enclose the old public edifices but rather their homes and churches.

Along with the decline of the cities came a further deterioration in the class of local town

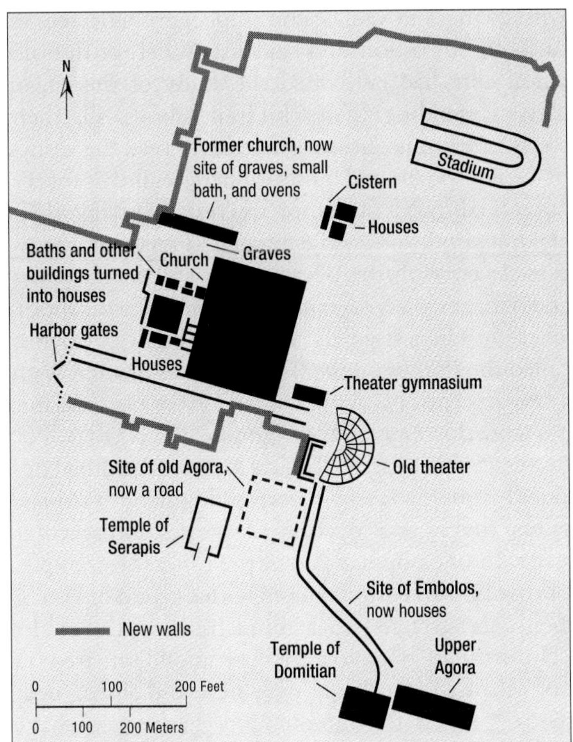

City of Ephesus
The center of classical Ephesus had been the Agora and the Embolos (a wide street, paved with marble and rimmed by shops and monuments). After the seventh century, the city was partially destroyed, its population declined, and the rebuilt city—without Agora or Embolos—was located to the north and protected by walls.

A New Rural Ideal
While incessant wars led to the depopulation of the Byzantine Empire and the decline of its cities, rural life gained importance both in reality and as a pastoral ideal. This mosaic on the floor of the imperial palace at Constantinople, probably made in the seventh century, shows an idyllic view of the farm.

councilors (the *curiales*), the elite that for centuries had mediated between the emperor and the people.* The pressures of war against the Arabs brought a change in Byzantine society parallel to the West a few centuries before, spelling the end of the curial class. But an upper class nevertheless remained: as in the West, bishops and their clergy continued to form a rich and powerful upper stratum even within declining cities.

Indeed, Constantinople and a few other urban centers retained much of their old vitality. Some industry and trade continued, particularly the manufacture of fine silk textiles. These were the prestige items of the time, coveted by enemies as well as friends, and their production and distribution was monitored by the government. In the mid-sixth century, silkworms from China had been introduced into the empire, relieving Byzantium's dependence on imports of raw silk. State-controlled factories produced the very finest fabrics, which legally could be worn only by the emperor, his court, and his friends. In private factories, merchants, spinners, and weavers turned raw silk into slightly less luxurious cloth for both internal consumption and foreign trade. Even though Byzantium's economic life became rural and barter-based in the seventh and eighth centuries, the skills, knowledge, and institutions of urban workers made long-distance trade and the domestic manufacture of luxury goods possible. The full use of these resources, however, had to await the end of centuries of debilitating wars.

As urban life declined, agriculture, always the basis of the Byzantine economy, became the center of its social life as well. But unlike the West, where an extremely rich and powerful elite dominated the agricultural economy, the Byzantine Empire of the seventh century was predominantly a realm of free and semifree peasant farmers. On their small plots of land they grew food, herded cattle, and tended vineyards. In the shadow of decaying urban cen-

*See Chapter 7.

ters, the social world of the farmer was narrow. "If two farmers agree one with the other before two or three witnesses to exchange land," says the legal compilation called the Farmers' Law, "let their determination and their exchange remain firm and secure and unassailable." Two or three neighbors were enough to ratify a land transfer. Farmers interacted mostly with their families or with monasteries. The buffer once provided by the curial class was gone; these families now felt the impact of imperial rule directly. In turn, the emperors of the seventh and eighth centuries tried to give ordinary family life new institutional importance. Imperial legislation narrowed the grounds for divorce and set new punishments for marital infidelity. Husbands who committed adultery were whipped and fined, and their noses were slit. Female adulterers suffered a similar penalty. Abortion was prohibited, and new protections were set in place against incest with children. Mothers were given equal power with fathers over their offspring and, if widowed, became the legal guardians of their minor children and controlled the household property.

New Military and Cultural Forms

The transformations of the countryside went hand in hand with political, military, and cultural reforms. Determined to win wars on many fronts, the imperial government exercised greater autocratic control, abetting the decline of the curial class, wresting power from other elite families, and encouraging the formation of a middle class of farmer-soldiers. In the seventh century an emperor, possibly Heraclius, divided the empire into military districts called *themes* and put all civil matters there into the hands of generals, *strategoi* (singular, *strategos*). Landless men were lured to join the army with the promise of land and low taxes; they fought side by side with indigenous farmers, who provided their own weapons and horses. The *strategoi*, who received no land but rather a handsome salary and the promise of a hefty share of any booty, not only led the local troops into battle but also served as the emperor's regional tax collectors. The *strategoi* soon became the vanguard of a new elite and began to dominate the rural scene. Nevertheless, between about 650 and 800 the reorganization of the countryside worked to the peasants' advantage.

The military and social changes brought about by the new network of *themes* went hand in hand with changes in values; and these were reflected, in turn, in education and culture. Whereas the old curial elite had cultivated the study of the pagan classics, sending their children (above all, their sons) to schools or tutors to learn to read the works of Greek poets and philosophers, eighth-century parents showed far more interest in giving their children, both sons and daughters, a religious education. Even with the decay of urban centers, cities and villages often retained an elementary school. There teachers used the *Psalter* (a book of poems, called the *Psalms*, in the Bible) as their primer. With a few exceptions, which would later become important, this new culture ignored the classics. For two centuries, secular, classical learning remained decidedly out of favor, whereas dogmatic writings, saints' lives, and devotional works took center stage. In one popular tale of the time, for example, a prostitute arriving at an inn with a group of young men was attracted to a monk reading the Bible. "Unfortunate one, you are very impudent; are you not ashamed of coming over here and sitting next to us?" asked the monk. "No, Father . . . I have hope in the Son of the living God that after today I shall not remain in sin," replied the penitent woman. Thereupon she followed the monk and entered a monastery for women.

Religion and Politics: The Clergy and Iconoclasm

The importance placed on religious learning and piety complemented both the autocratic imperial ideal and the powers of the bishops in the seventh century. While the bishops consolidated their positions as the elite of the cities, Byzantine emperors ruled as religious as well as political figures. In theory, imperial and church power were separate but interdependent. In fact, the emperor functioned as the head of the church hierarchy, appointing the chief prelate, the patriarch of Constantinople; formulating Christian doctrine; calling church councils to determine dogma; and setting out the criteria for bishops to be ordained. Beginning with Heraclius, the emperors considered it one of their duties to baptize Jews forcibly, persecuting those who would not convert. In the view of the imperial court, this was part of the ruler's role in upholding orthodoxy.

Bishops functioned as state administrators, not in spite of being churchmen but rather because the spiritual and secular realms were understood to be inseparable. Bishops acted as judges and tax collectors. They distributed food in times of famine or siege, provisioned troops, and set up military fortifications. As part of their charitable work, they cared for the sick and the needy. Byzantine bishops were part of a three-tier system: they were appointed by "metropolitans," bishops who headed up an entire province; and these metropolitans, in turn, were appointed by the patriarchs, bishops with authority over whole regions. Theoretically, monasteries were under limited control by the local bishop, but in fact they were enormously powerful institutions that often defied episcopal and even imperial authority. Because monks commanded immense prestige as the holiest of God's faithful, they could influence the many issues of church doctrine that wracked the Byzantine church.

The most important of these issues revolved around icons. Icons were images of holy people—Christ, the Virgin, saints—that were far more than mere representations to Byzantine Christians. Icons were believed to be infused with holy power that directly affected people's daily life as well as their chances for salvation.

Many seventh-century Byzantines made icons the focus of their religious devotion. To them, icons were like the incarnation of Christ; they turned spirit into material substance. Thus, the icon manifested in physical form the holy person whom it depicted. Some Byzantines actually worshiped icons; others, particularly monks, considered icons a necessary part of Christian piety. As the monk St. John of Damascus put it in a vigorous defense of holy images, "I do not worship matter, I worship the God of matter, who became matter for my sake, and deigned to inhabit matter, who worked out my salvation through matter."

But other Byzantines abhorred icons. Most numerous of these were the soldiers on the frontiers, who were shocked by Arab triumphs. They found the cause of their misfortunes in the Biblical injunction against graven images. When they compared their defeats to Muslim successes, they could not help but notice that Islam prohibited all representations of the divine. To these soldiers and others who shared their view, icons revived pagan idolatry and desecrated Christian divinity. As iconoclastic (anti-icon or, literally, icon-breaking) feeling grew, some churchmen became vociferous in their opposition to icons. As one church council of 754 put the issue, "What avails, then, the folly of the painter who from sinful love of gain depicts that which should not be depicted—that is, with his polluted hands he tries to fashion that which should only be believed in the heart and confessed with the mouth."

Byzantine emperors shared these religious objections, but they also had important political reasons for distrusting icons. First, they were anxious to support their troops in every way. Second, icons diffused loyalties, setting up intermediaries between worshipers and God that undermined the emperor's exclusive place in the divine and temporal order. Third, the emphasis on icons in monastic communities made the monks potential threats to imperial power; the emperors hoped to use this issue to break the power of the monasteries. Fourth, some churchmen had begun to question the emperor's right to interfere in religious affairs. Thus the issue of icons became a test case of imperial authority.

The controversy climaxed in 726, after Emperor Leo III the Isaurian (*717–741) had defeated the Arabs besieging Constantinople in 717 and 718 and turned his attention to consolidating his political position. In the wake of the victory, officers of the imperial court tore down the great golden icon of Christ at the gateway of the palace and replaced it with a cross. In protest, a crowd of iconodule (literally, icon-worshipping) women went on a furious rampage. This event marked the beginning of the period of iconoclasm (icon-smashing); soon afterward, Leo ordered all icons destroyed, a ban that remained in effect, despite much opposition, until 787. A modified ban would be revived in 815 and last until 843.

Iconoclasm had an enormous impact on daily life. At home, where people had their own portable icons, it forced changes in private worship: the devout had to destroy their icons or worship them in secret. Iconoclasm meant ferocious attacks on the monasteries: splendid collections of holy images were destroyed; vast properties were confiscated; and monks were ordered to marry. In this way iconoclasm destroyed communities that might otherwise have served as centers of resistance to imperial power.

Wracked by wars, its cities devastated, its frontiers shrunk, its dominance over the Christian church challenged, Byzantium experienced hard times in the seventh and eighth centuries. But it proved resilient. Building on its inheritance of administrative skills, land resources, and control over religious symbols and the hierarchy of the Christian church, the Byzantine state adapted to changing circumstances. The new *theme* organization in the countryside effectively countered frontier attacks. The Byzantine cavalry, clad in heavy iron—the "boiler boys" (*cataphracts*)—were the human equivalent of modern tanks and could easily mow down less well-armed enemy soldiers. And "Greek fire," invented in the seventh century, proved an ingenious and deadly weapon. It was a combustible oil, shot through tubes or sprayed from a pump, that burst into flames upon hitting its target. Greek fire was especially effective against ships, since the burning oil floated on water. Its creation was part of the general reorganization and reorientation of Byzantine institutions that allowed the state to survive against the Arab onslaught under the banner of Islam.

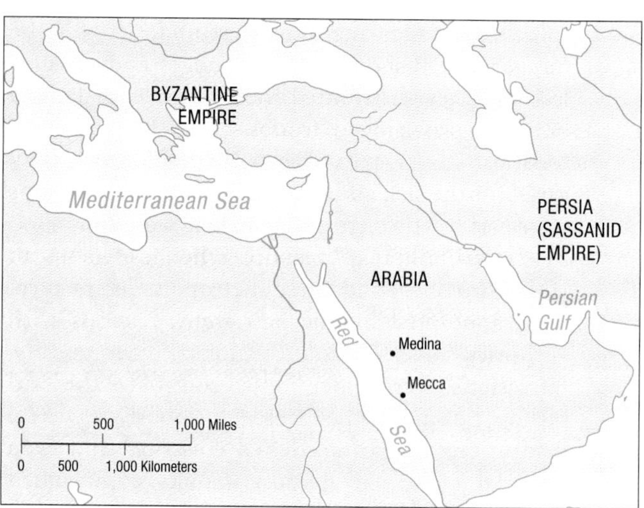

Arabia in Muhammad's Lifetime

Islam: A New Religion and a New Empire

Islam, meaning "submission" to the will of God, is the religion of people who call themselves Muslims. Its roots are in the same soil as Christianity and Judaism: the Fertile Crescent and the Iranian hinterland. Indeed the Muslims' God is the God of Abraham, Moses, and Jesus. Emerging in seventh-century western Arabia (today Saudi Arabia), in the shadow of Persian and Byzantine culture, Islam thrived initially among nomadic herding peoples. Their world contained few cities and placed little emphasis on the political and cultural institutions of a polis-centered life. Whereas Greco-Roman civilization rimmed the Mediterranean Sea, Arabian life was based inland, in the desert, where water was the very source of life: "The heavens and the earth were an integrated mass, then We split them and made every living thing from water," says God in the Qur'an,* the Holy Recitation that serves Muslims much as the Bible does Christians and Jews.

Yet much of the Greco-Roman heritage would become grafted irrevocably onto Islamic culture. First, and perhaps most important, was that the Muslim conquerors allowed older monotheistic religions to persist in their new empire. This was particularly important to groups espousing forms of Christianity not considered orthodox by Byzantine emperors. For example, Monophysite Christians, who believed Christ's nature wholly divine—not both divine and human—constituted a large part of the population of Syria, Egypt, and northern Iraq. Under Byzantine rule they had suffered forced conversions and savage persecutions. People such as these welcomed Muslim overlords. Second, the Arabs soon became used to a settled existence, initially in garrison towns separate from the cities of the ancient world but then gradually in urban centers resembling those that had flourished before their conquest. Finally, Muslims absorbed into their ranks members of the native population who converted to Islam, and at the same time they adopted many of the traditions of the ancient world, above all its literary, philosophical, and scientific heritage.

Bedouin Tribal Society

Pre-Islamic Arabia became aware of wider currents through contact with the Persians and Byzantines,

*Older books use *Koran*, but the new standardized transliteration of Arabic worked out by Islamicists dictates a different spelling.

who in their wars against one another employed Arab tribesmen as mercenaries and encouraged border tribes to organize buffer states. Elsewhere in Arabia, Romanized Jews and Monophysites, refugees from Byzantine persecution, settled in town-oases alongside native populations. But most Arabs did not have sustained, regular contact with these refugees. Most were Bedouins who lived in tribes—loose confederations of clans, or kin-groups—that herded flocks for meat and milk and traded (or raided) for grain, dates, and slaves. Poor Bedouin tribes herded sheep, whereas richer ones kept camels—extremely hardy animals, splendid beasts of burden, and good producers of milk and meat. (The word *Arab* was the name camel nomads called themselves.)

Tribal, nomadic existence produced its own culture, including a common language of extraordinary delicacy, precision, and beauty. In the absence of written language, the Bedouins used poetry and story-telling to transmit their traditions, simultaneously entertaining, reaffirming values, and teaching new generations.

Modern Bedouins
There are still Bedouins in the modern Middle East, as in Muhammad's time. They live as nomads, in small groups, with their belongings carried by camels.

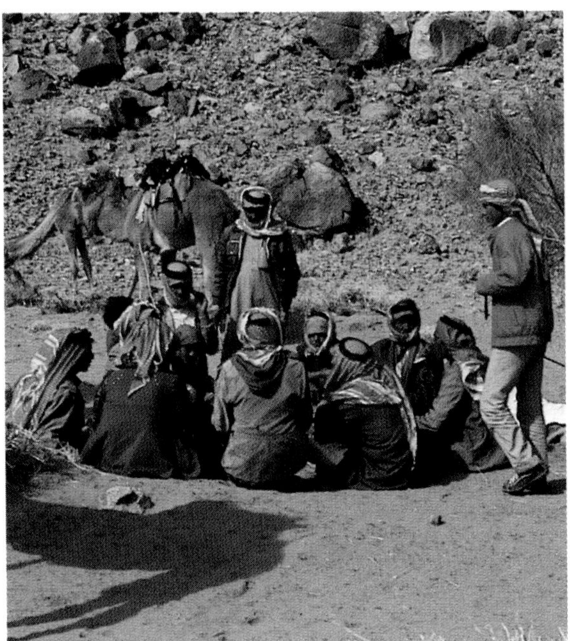

Even in town-oases, where permanent settlements arose, the clan was the key social institution and focus of loyalties. Clans grouped together in tribes, their makeup shifting as kin-groups joined or left. These associations, however changing, nevertheless saw outsiders as rivals, and tribes constantly fought with one another. Yet clan rivalry was itself an outgrowth of the values the various tribes shared. Bedouin men prized "manliness," which meant far more than sexual prowess. They wanted to be brave in battle and feared being shamed. Manliness also entailed an obligation to be generous, to give away the booty that was the goal of intertribal warfare. Women were often part of this booty; a counterpart to Bedouin manliness was therefore the practice of polygyny (having more than one wife at the same time). Bedouin wars rarely involved much bloodshed; their main purpose was to capture and take belongings. It was not much of a step from this booty-gathering to trading and from there to the establishment of commercial centers.

Although historians once thought Mecca, the birthplace of Muhammad and therefore of Islam, served as a commercial center for the eastern luxury trade with the Byzantine Empire, recent reviews of the evidence cast doubt on this view. Nevertheless, Mecca did play a commercial role. Meccan caravans, for example, were organized to sell Bedouin products—mainly leather goods and raisins—to more urbanized areas in the north, at the border between Arabia and Syria. More important, Mecca had for centuries been one of the foci of Bedouin life because it contained a shrine, the Ka'ba. Long before Muhammad was born, the Ka'ba, hedged about with 360 idols, served as a sacred place within which war and violence were prohibited. The tribe that dominated Mecca, the Quraysh, controlled access to the shrine and was able to tax the pilgrims who flocked there as well as sell them food and drink. In turn, plunder was transformed into trade as the visitors bartered with one another on the sacred grounds, assured of their security.

The Prophet Muhammad and Islamic Society

Thus Muhammad was born (c. 570) in a center with two important achievements—one religious, the other commercial. His early years were inauspicious: orphaned by the age of six, he spent two years with his grandfather and then came under the care of his uncle, a leader of the Quraysh tribe. Eventually, Muhammad became a trader. At the age of twenty-five, he married Khadija, a rich widow much older than he. They had at least four daughters and lived (to all appearances) happily and comfortably. Yet Muhammad would sometimes leave home and spend a few days in a nearby cave in prayer and contemplation, reflecting a model of piety that had also inspired early Christians.

Then beginning in 610 and continuing until he died in 632, Muhammad heard a voice speaking what he came to identify as the words of God (Allah means "the God" in Arabic). "Recite!" began the voice, and to Muhammad it entrusted a special mission: to speak God's words, to live by them, eventually to preach them, and to convert others to follow them. The holy book of Islam, the Qur'an, means "recitation"; each of the verses, or *suras*, are understood to be God's revelation as told to Muhammad, then recited in turn by Muhammad to a scribe who wrote them down word for word. The first revelations emphasized the greatness, mercy, and goodness of God; the obligations of the rich to the poor; and the certainty of Judgment Day. In time they covered the gamut of human experience and the life to come; for the Muslim the Qur'an contained the sum total of history, prophecy, and the legal and moral code by which men and women should live: "Do not set up another god with God, . . . Do not worship anyone but Him, and be good to your parents. . . . Give to your relatives what is their due, and to those who are needy, and the wayfarers."

The Qur'an emphasized the nuclear family—a man, his wife, and children—as the basic unit of Muslim society. It cut the tribespeople adrift from the protection and particularism of the tribe but gave them in return an identity as part of the *ummah*, the community of believers, who shared both a belief in one God and a set of religious practices. Islam depended entirely on individual belief and adherence to the Qur'an. Muslims had no priests, no mass, no intermediaries between the divine and the individual. Instead, Islam stressed the relationship between the individual and God, a relationship characterized by gratitude to and worship of God, by the promise of reward or punishment on Judgment Day "when the sky is cleft asunder"; and by exhortations to human kindness: "Do not oppress the orphan,/And do not drive the beggar away." The Ka'ba, with its many idols, had gathered together tribes from the surrounding vicinity. Muhammad, with his one God, forged an even more ecumenical religion.

The Image of Mecca
In this sixteenth-century depiction of Mecca, the Ka'ba is in the center. The lines, like spokes in a wheel, connect to the names of the Islamic countries.

The first to convert was Muhammad's wife and then a few friends and members of his immediate family. Discontented young men, often eluded by commercial success, joined his converts, as did some wealthy merchants. Soon, however, the new faith polarized Meccan society. Muhammad's insistence that all other cults be abandoned brought him into conflict with leading clan members of the Quraysh tribe, who found their own positions of leadership and livelihood threatened. Lacking political means to expel him, they insulted Muhammad and harassed his adherents.

Disillusioned with his own tribe and with Mecca, where he had failed to make much of an impact, Muhammad tried to find a place and a population receptive to his message. Most important, he expected support from Jews, whose monotheism (he thought) prepared them for his own faith. When a few of Muhammad's converts

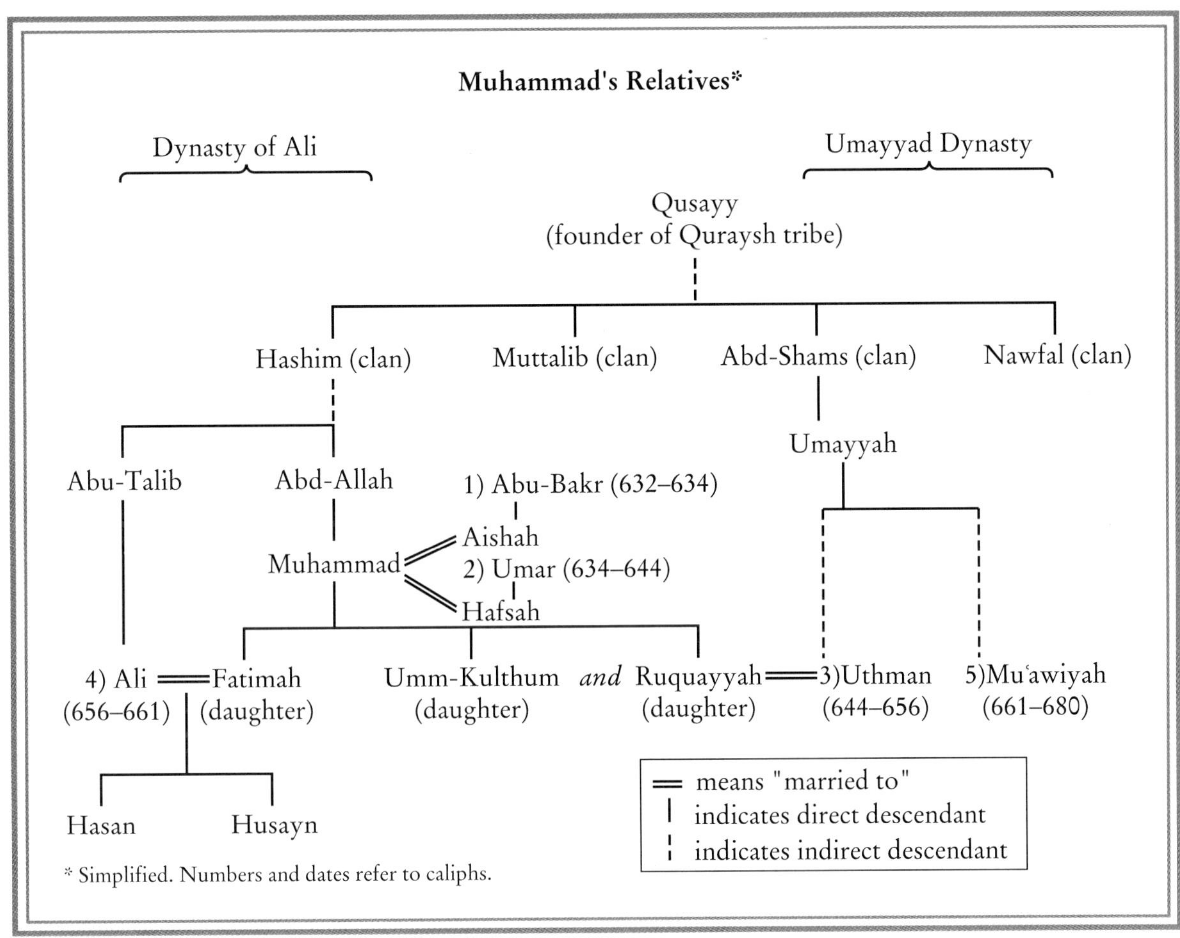

* Simplified. Numbers and dates refer to caliphs.

from Medina promised to protect him if he would join them, he eagerly accepted the invitation, largely because Medina had a significant Jewish population. In 622 Muhammad made the *Hijra*, or emigration, to Medina, an oasis about two hundred miles northeast of Mecca. This journey proved a crucial event for the fledgling movement. At Medina, Muhammad found followers ready not only to listen to his religious message but also to regard him as the leader of their community. They expected him, for example, to act as a neutral and impartial judge in their interclan disputes. Muhammad's political position in the community set the pattern by which Islamic society would be governed afterward; rather than add a church to political and cultural life, as the Romans had done with Christianity, the Muslims made their political and religious institutions inseparable. After Muhammad's death the *Hijra* was named the first year of the Islamic calendar; it marked the beginning of the new Islamic era.†

At Medina, Muhammad established the *ummah*, a single community distinct from other people. But the Muslims were not content to confine themselves to a minor outpost at Medina. Above all, it was essential for the success of the new religion to control Mecca, still a potent holy place. Muhammad's following was not large enough to launch a direct siege on the city, so he first attacked Meccan caravans that were going to and from Syria. The Muslims no longer felt bound by the etiquette

†Thus 1 A.H. (1 *Anno Hegirae*) on the Muslim calendar is equivalent to A.D. 622 (*Anno Domini* 622) on the Christian calendar.

that had previously regulated warfare and had emphasized raiding over killing. In 624 Muhammad led a small contingent to ambush a huge caravan brimming with goods; at the battle of Badr, aided by their position near an oasis, he and his followers killed forty-nine of the Meccan enemy, took numerous prisoners, and confiscated rich booty. The Qur'an commentary on the battle was, "It was not you who killed them, but God did so. You did not throw what you threw (sand into the eyes of the enemy at Badr), but God, to bring out the best in the faithful by doing them a favor of His own." Thus traditional Bedouin plundering was grafted on to the Muslim duty of *jihad* (literally "striving," but often translated as "holy war").

The battle of Badr was a great triumph for Muhammad, who was now able to consolidate his position at Medina, gaining new adherents and silencing all doubters. The Jews at Medina, whom Muhammad had at first seen as allies, had not converted to Islam as he had expected. Organized by clans, like their Arab neighbors, the Jews controlled important date groves and dominated the city's trades and crafts. Right after the battle of Badr, seizing on a minor dispute as a pretext, Muhammad attacked the Jewish Qaynuqa clan, expelling them from Medina. In the following year he drove out most of the rest, dividing their lands among himself and his converts. The remaining Jewish men were eventually executed, and the women and children sold into slavery.

At the same time Muhammad broke with the Jews, he distanced himself from Judaism and instituted new practices to define Islam as a unique religion. Among these were the *zakat*, a tax on possessions to be used for alms; the fast of Ramadan, which took place during the month in which the battle at Badr had been fought; the *hajj*, a yearly pilgrimage to Mecca; and the *salat*, formal worship at least three times a day (later increased to five), which could include the *shahadah*, or profession of faith: "there is no divinity but God, and Muhammad is the messenger of God." Emphasizing his repudiation of Jewish traditions, Muhammad now had the Muslims turn their prayers away from Jerusalem, home of the Jews, toward Mecca and the Ka'ba. Detailed regulations for these practices, sometimes called the "five pillars of Islam," were worked out in the eighth and early ninth centuries.

Meanwhile, the fierce rivalry between Mecca's clans and Medina's Muslims began to spill over into the rest of the Arabian peninsula as both sides strove to win converts. Muhammad sent troops to subdue Arabs north and south. In 630 he entered Mecca with 10,000 men and took over the city, assuring the Quraysh of leniency and offering alliances with its leaders. By this time the prestige of Islam was enough to convince clans elsewhere to convert. Through a combination of force, conversion, and negotiation, Muhammad was able to unite many, though by no means all, Arabic-speaking tribes under his leadership by the time of his death in 632.

In so doing, Muhammad brought about important social transformations. As they "submitted" to Islam, Muhammad's converts formed not a clan or tribe but rather a brotherhood bound together by the worship of God. It was also something of a sisterhood, for women were accepted into the Muslim community and their status enhanced. Islam prohibited all infanticide, for example, a practice that had long been used largely against female infants; and at first, Muslim women joined men during the prayer periods that punctuated the day. Men were allowed to have up to four wives at one time, but they were obliged to treat them equally; their wives received dowries and had certain inheritance rights. But beginning in the eighth century, women began to pray apart from the men. Adopting a symbol of upper-class superiority—the veil worn by noble Byzantine women to separate them symbolically from humbler folk—Muslim women veiled themselves as a symbol of their separation from the public, male world. Like Judaism and Christianity, Islam retained the practices of a patriarchal society in which women's participation in community life was circumscribed.

Even though Islamic society was a new sort of community, in many ways it functioned as a tribe or rather a "supertribe," obligated to fight common enemies, share plunder, and resolve peacefully any internal disputes. Muslims participated in group rituals, such as the *salat* and public recitation. The Qur'an was soon publicly sung by professional reciters, much as the old tribal poetry had been. Most significantly for the eventual spread of Islam, Muslim men continued to be warriors. They took up where Meccan traders had been forced to leave off; along the routes once taken by caravans to Syria, their armies reaped profits at the point of a sword. But this differed from intertribal fighting; it was the "striving" of people carrying out the injunction of God against unbelievers. "Strive, O Prophet," says the Qur'an, "against the unbelievers and the hypocrites, and deal with them firmly. Their final abode is Hell: And what a wretched destination!"

Muhammad's successors commanded a force to reckon with: fully armed, on horseback, and employing camels as convoys, they stormed the Near East, already weakened by war. In the 630s and 640s alone, they invaded the areas that today comprise Iran and Iraq (both part of the Sassanid Empire) and Syria and Egypt (held by the Byzantines). Where they conquered, the Muslims built garrison cities from which soldiers requisitioned taxes and goods. Sometimes whole Arab tribes, including women and children, were imported to settle conquered territory, as happened in parts of Syria. In other regions, such as Egypt, a small Muslim settlement at Fustat sufficed to gather the spoils of conquest.

Muhammad's Successors

In founding a new political community in Arabia, Muhammad reorganized traditional Arab society as he cut across clan allegiances and welcomed converts from every tribe. His political power in this community of believers was far greater than that of any former tribal chief, for Muslims believed Muhammad to be the chosen prophet of God, the source of law. Around him formed a new elite, based not so much on ties of kinship or the traditional virtues of manliness, but rather on closeness to Muhammad and participation in his movement's crucial events, above all the *Hijra*. His was a personal government, and it did not outlive him. His successors needed other models to rule the vast territories they conquered, and so they adapted the machinery of government of the Byzantines and, later, the Persians. In so doing, the Muslims further sank their roots into the soil of the Roman Empire and became one of its heirs.

The death of Muhammad marked a crisis in the government of the new state. The *caliphs* (literally "successors") who followed Muhammad did not assume authority without dispute. The first four caliphs came from the new elite, the Muslims in the prophet's inner circle, but each of them had to face opposition from other would-be leaders and their supporters. Abu-Bakr (∗632–634), the first caliph, was Muhammad's father-in-law, as was Umar (∗634–644), who was largely responsible for the policies that encouraged Islamic expansion and its new administrative and political order.

The third caliph, Uthman (∗644–656), was a member of the Umayyad family and son-in-law (by marriage with two daughters) of Muhammad; but his position aroused jealousy among other clan members of the "inner circle." Growing discontent—in part based on enmities dating back to the days at Mecca, partly on the new circumstances of conquest, and partly on different religious sensibilities—exploded in bloodshed and rioting. Uthman championed Meccan tradesmen; but Muslim soldiers were unhappy with his distribution of high offices and revenues, accusing him of favoritism and injustice. They looked to Ali—a member of the Hashim clan (to which Muhammad had belonged) and also (like Uthman) Muhammad's son-in-law—to put things right.

In 656 Uthman was murdered by a group of these discontented soldiers, and civil war broke out between the followers of Ali and the supporters of Muʿawiyah, leader of the Umayyad family. For a short time Ali was recognized as caliph in nearly all regions; but on the brink of defeat by Muʿawiyah, he was assassinated by one of his erstwhile supporters. Although some of Ali's followers elevated his son Hasan to the caliphate, Hasan negotiated with Muʿawiyah a graceful retirement for himself. The caliphate was now (661) in Umayyad hands.

Nevertheless, the *Shiʿat Ali*, the followers of Ali, did not fade away. Ali's memory lived on among groups of Muslims (the *Shiʿites*) who saw in him a symbol of justice and righteousness. For them Ali's death was the martyrdom of the only true successor to Muhammad. They remained faithful to his dynasty, shunning the "mainstream" caliphs of the other Muslims (*Sunni* Muslims, as they were later called). The Shiʿites awaited the arrival of the true leader—the *imam*—who in their view could come only from the house of Ali and his wife (daughter of Muhammad) Fatimah. The enmity between Shi'ite and Sunni Muslims, based on this dispute over the legitimacy of Muhammad's successors, continues even today.

Under the Umayyads the Muslim world became a state with its capital at Damascus, today the capital of Syria. Borrowing from the institutions well known to the civilizations they had just conquered, the Arabs issued coins and hired former Byzantine and Persian officials. They made Arabic a tool of centralization, imposing it as the language of government on regions not previously united linguistically. Taxes poured into Damascus, and military expeditions continued. Muslim armies, still predominantly Arab, took all of North Africa between 643 and 711, and troops then crossed the Strait of Gibraltar northward into Spain, conquering most of the Visigothic Kingdom by 718. At the same time, other armies marched east, taking the Indus valley (today Pakistan) between 710 and 713. Their thrust eastward was stopped only in 751, in a defeat by Chinese forces, just beyond the Jaxartes River (today the Syr Darya River) southeast of the Aral Sea; in the west their farthest reach brought them almost to the banks of the Loire in France. Constantinople, almost alone among the cities under attack, held fast against its Arab besiegers. For Byzantium this period was one of unparalleled military crisis, the prelude to iconoclasm. For the Muslim world, now a multiethnic society of Muslim Arabs, Syrians, Egyptians, Iraqis, and so on, it was a period of settlement, new urbanism, and literary and artistic flowering.

Yet the question of Islamic government was not settled. In 750 a civil war brought a new dynasty—the Abbasids—to the caliphate. The Abbasids found support in an uneasy coalition of Shi'ites and non-Arabs who had been excluded from Umayyad government and now demanded a place in political life. The new regime signaled a revolution. The center of the Islamic state shifted

Arab Coin
The Arabs learned coinage and minting from those whom they conquered. This silver dirham *from the seventh century is based on a Byzantine model; the word* dirham *is derived from the Greek* drachma.

Expansion of Islam to 750

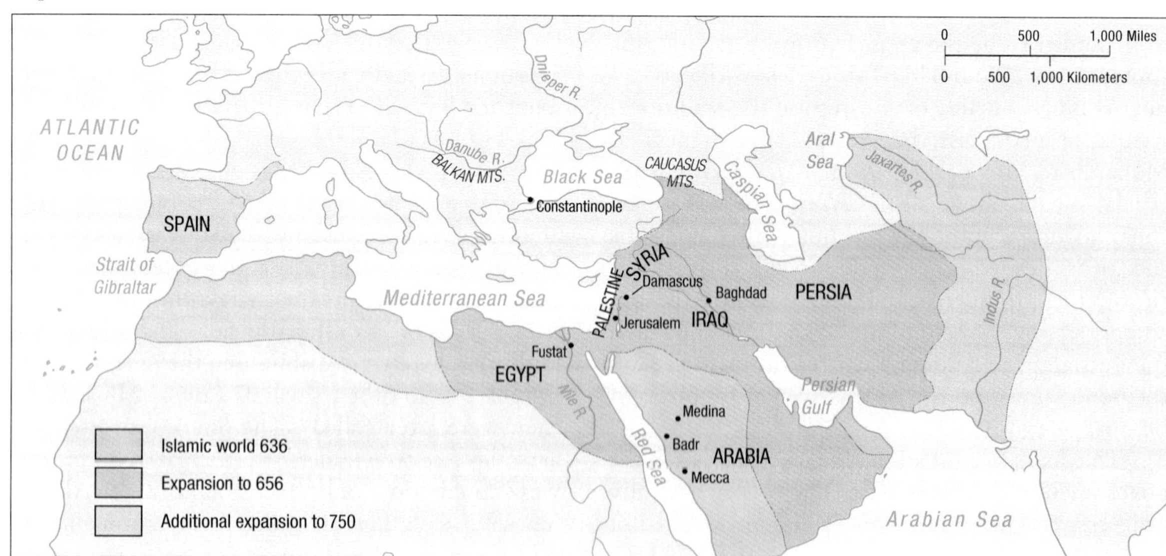

Umayyad Mosque
The mosaics in this mosque, built at Damascus in the eighth century, adopted classical motifs.

from Damascus, with its roots in the Roman tradition, to Baghdad, a new capital city built by the Abbasids in the heart of Persian culture. Here the Abbasid caliphs imitated the Persian King of Kings and adopted the court ceremony of oriental potentates. Administration grew increasingly centralized: the caliph controlled the appointment of regional governors; his staff grew, and their jobs became more complex. Although some Shiʿites were reconciled to this new regime, others, a minority, continued to tend the flame of Ali's memory—and the justice and purity it stood for.

Peace and Prosperity in Islamic Lands

Ironically, the Arab conquerors brought peace. While the conquerors stayed within their fortified cities or built magnificent hunting lodges in the deserts of Syria, the conquered went back to work, to study, to play, or (in the case of Christians and Jews, who were considered "protected subjects," *dhimmis*) to worship as they pleased. At Damascus, local artists and craftspeople worked on the lavish decorations for a mosque in a neoclassic style at the very moment Muslim armies were storming the walls of Constantinople. Here too, St. John of Damascus inherited from his Christian father the job of financial officer for the new Arab government. Leaving the Byzantine institutions in place, the Muslim conquerors allowed Christians and Jews to retain their posts and even protected dissidents. In the 730s, for example, safe under Muslim rulers, John wrote treatises against the Byzantine imperial iconoclastic decrees. No one at Constantinople could have acted with such impunity. John later retired to a monastery near Jerusalem to live the quiet life of an ascetic and write poetry and prose.

During the seventh and eight centuries, Muslim scholars wrote down the hitherto largely oral Arabic literature. They determined the definitive form for the Qurʾan and compiled pious "reports" about the Prophet (*hadith* literature). Scribes composed these works in exquisite handwriting; Arab calligraphy became an art form. A new literate class, composed mainly of the old Persian and Syrian elite now converted to Islam and schooled in Arabic, created new forms of prose writing, from official documents to essays on topics ranging from hunting to ruling. Umayyad poetry explored new worlds of thought and feeling. Patronized by the caliphs, who found in poetry an important source of propaganda and a buttress for their power, the poets also found a wider audience that delighted in their clever use of words, their satire, and their invocations of courage, piety, and sometimes erotic love:

I spent the night as her bed-companion,
each enamoured of the other,
And I made her laugh and cry, and stripped
her of her clothes.
I played with her and she vanquished me; I
made her happy and I angered her.
That was a night we spent, in my sleep,
playing and joyful,
But the caller to prayer woke me up. . . .

Such poetry scandalized conservative Muslims, brought up on the ascetic world-denying tenets of the Qur'an. But this love poetry was a product of the new urban civilization of the Umayyad period, where wealth, cultural mix, and the confidence born of conquest inspired diverse and experimental literary forms.

The Arabs, who at best had lived in the shadow of Roman civilization, exploded into Western civilization in the seventh century under the impetus of their inspired religious and military leader, Muhammad. Their armies conquered peoples and states from the Jaxartes River in the east to the Pyrenees in Spain. Although the Arabs were originally nomadic Bedouins, they quickly assimilated many aspects of the cultures they conquered. By the end of the Umayyad period, Islamic civilization was multiethnic, urban, and sophisticated, a true heir of Roman and Persian traditions.

The Western Kingdoms

With the demise of Roman imperial government in the West, the primary institutions providing power and stability in Europe were kinship networks, church patronage, royal courts, and wealth derived from land and plunder. In contrast to Byzantium, where an emperor still ruled as the successor to Augustus and Constantine, drawing upon an unbroken chain of Roman legal and administrative traditions, political power in the West was more diffuse. Churchmen and rich magnates, sometimes one and the same men, held sway. Power derived as well from membership in royal dynasties, such as that of the Merovingian kings, who traced their ancestry back to a sea monster whose magic ensured the fertility and good fortune of the Franks. Finally, people believed power lodged in the tombs and relics of saints, who represented and wielded the divine forces of God. Although the patterns of daily life and the procedures of government in the West remained recognizably Roman, they were also in the process of change, borrowing from and adapting local traditions. In its merging of cultures, Europe resembled the Islamic world.

Frankish Kingdoms with Roman Roots

The Franks had established themselves as dominant in Gaul during the sixth century, and by the seventh century the limits of their Merovingian kingdoms roughly approximated the eastern borders of present-day France, Belgium, the Netherlands, and Luxembourg. Moreover, the Merovingian kings had subjugated many of the peoples beyond the Rhine, foreshadowing the contours of modern Germany. Although the little-Romanized northern and eastern regions were important to the Frankish kingdoms, the core of these kingdoms was Roman Gaul; and their inhabitants lived with the vestiges of Rome at their very door.

Travelers making a trip to Paris in the seventh century, perhaps on a pilgrimage to the tomb of St. Denis, for example, would probably rely on river travel, even though some Roman roads would still be in fair repair. (They would prefer water routes because land travel was very slow and because even large groups of travelers on the roads were vulnerable to attacks by robbers.) Like the roads, other structures in the landscape would seem familiarly Roman. Coming up the Rhône from the south, voyagers would pass Roman amphitheaters and farmlands neatly and squarely laid out as they had been by Roman land surveyors. The great stone palaces of villas would still dot the countryside.

What would be missing, if the travelers were very observant, would be thriving cities. Hulks of cities remained, of course, and they served as the centers of church administration; but gradually during the late Roman period, many urban centers had lost their commercial and cultural vitality. Depopulated, many survived as mere skeletons,

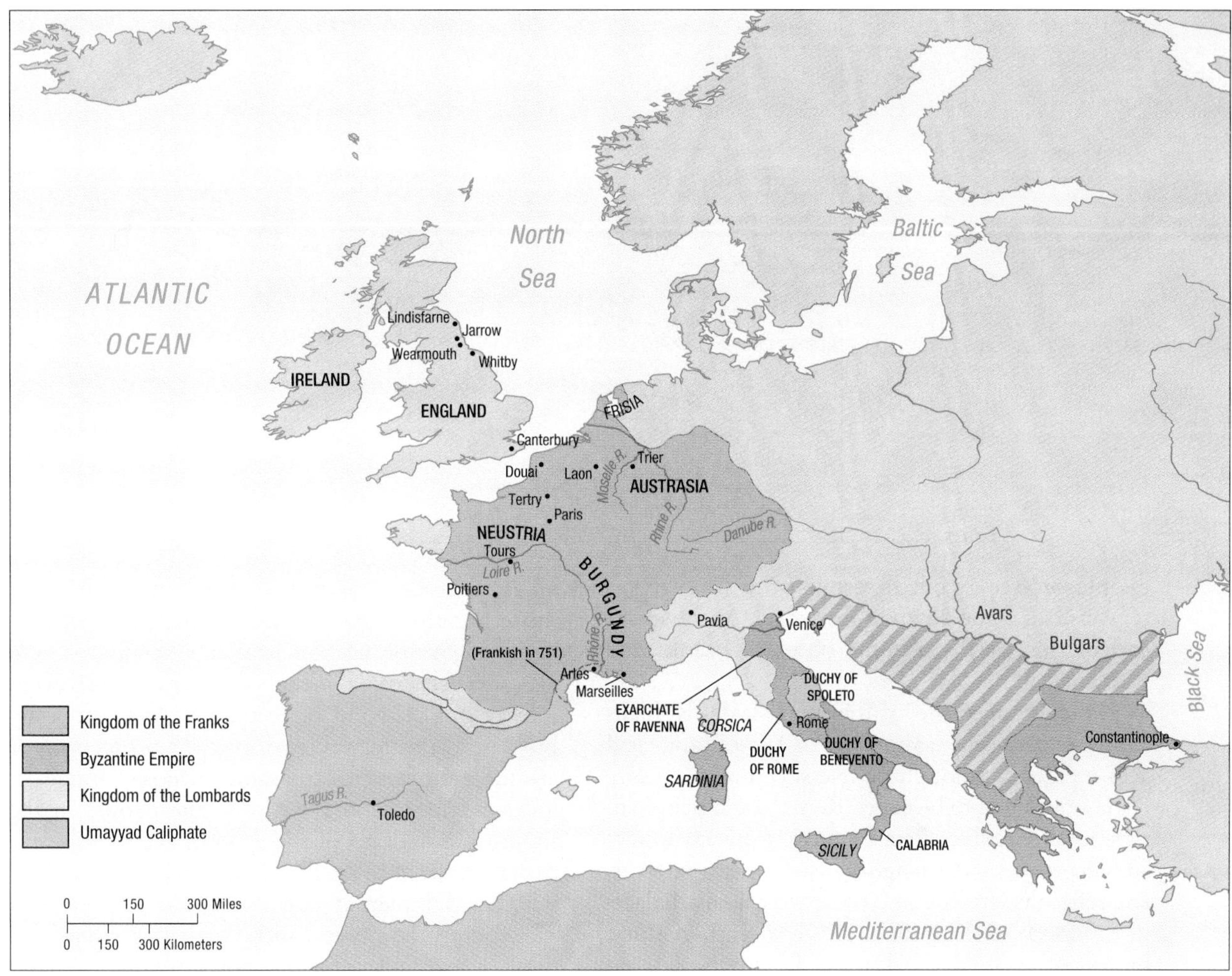

Europe in the Eighth Century

with the exception of such thriving commercial centers as Arles and Marseilles. Moreover, if the travelers were to approach Paris from the northeast, they would pass through dense, nearly untouched forests as well as land more often used as pasture for animals than for cereal cultivation. These areas would not have been much influenced by Romans, and they would represent far more the farming and village settlement patterns of the Franks. Yet even on the northern and eastern fringes of the Merovingian kingdoms some structures of the Roman Empire remained. Fortresses were still standing at Trier (near Bonn, Germany, today), and great stone villas, such as the one excavated by archaeologists near Douai (today in France, near the Belgian border), loomed over the more humble wooden dwellings of the countryside.

In the south, gangs of slaves still might occasionally be found cultivating the extensive lands of wealthy estate owners, as they had done since late Republican times. Scattered here and there, independent peasants worked their own small plots as they, too, had done for centuries. But for the most part, seventh-century travelers would find semifree peasant families settled on little holdings, their *manses*—including a house, a garden, and cultivable land—for which they paid dues and owed labor services to a landowner. Some of these peasants were descendants of the *coloni* (tenant farmers) of the late Roman Empire; others were the sons and daughters of slaves, now provided with a small plot of land; and a few were

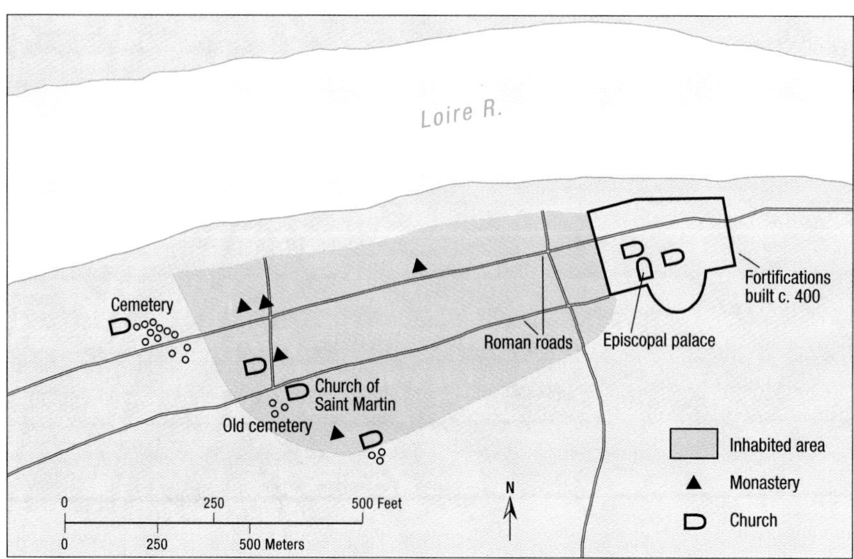

Tours, c. 600

people of free Frankish origin who for various reasons had come down in the world. At the lower end of the social scale, the status of Franks and Romans had become identical.

At the upper end of the social scale, Romans (or more precisely, Gallo-Romans) and Franks had also merged. Although people south of the Loire River continued to be called Romans and people to the north Franks, their cultures were strikingly similar: they shared language, settlement patterns, and religious sensibilities. There were many dialects in the Frankish kingdoms in the seventh century, but most were derived from Latin, though no longer the Latin of Cicero. "Though my speech is rude," Gregory, bishop of Tours (*c. 573–c. 594), wrote at the end of the sixth century,

> *I have been unable to be silent as to the struggles between the wicked and the upright; and I have been especially encouraged because, to my surprise, it has often been said by men of our day, that few understand the learned words of the rhetorician but many the rude language of the common people.*

Thus Gregory began his *Histories,* a precious source for the Merovingian period. He was trying to evoke the sympathies of his readers, a traditional Roman rhetorical device; but he also expected that his "rude" Latin—the plain Latin of everyday speech—would be understood and welcomed by the general public.

Whereas the Gallo-Roman aristocrat of the fourth and fifth centuries had lived with his *familia*—his wife, children, slaves, and servants—in isolated villas, aristocrats of the seventh century lived in more populous settlements: in small villages surrounded by the huts of peasants, shepherds, and artisans. The early medieval village, constructed mostly out of wood or baked clay, was generally built near a waterway or forest for protection, or around churches (for the same purpose). Intensely local in interests and outlook, the people in the Frankish kingdoms of the seventh and eighth centuries clustered in small groups next to protectors, whether rich men or saints.

Tours—the city in which Gregory, the historian of plain speech, was bishop—exemplified this new-style settlement. Once a Roman city, Tours's main focus was now outside the city walls, where a church had been built. The population of the surrounding countryside was pulled to this church as if to a magnet, for it housed the remains of the most important and venerated person in the locale: St. Martin. This saint, a fourth-century soldier-turned-monk, was long dead, but his relics—his bones, teeth, hair, and clothes—remained at Tours, where he had served as bishop. There, in the succeeding centuries, he remained a supernatural force: a protector, healer, and avenger through whom God manifested divine power. In Gregory of Tours's view, for example, Martin's relics (or rather God *through* Martin's relics) had prevented armies from plundering local peasants. Nor was Martin the only human to have great supernatural power; all of God's saints were miracle workers.

At the tomb of St. Illidius in Clermont (now Clermont-Ferrand), for example, it was reported that "the blind are given light, demons are chased away, the deaf receive hearing and the lame the use of their limbs." In the early Middle Ages the church had no formal procedures for proclaiming saints; rather, holiness was "recognized" by influential local people and the local bishop. Even a few women were so esteemed: "[Our Savior] gave us as models [of sanctity] not only men, who fight [against sinfulness] as they should, but also women, who exert themselves in the struggle with success," wrote Gregory as a preface to his story of the nun Monegundis, who lived with a few other ascetic women and whose miracles included curing tumors and prompting paralyzed limbs to work again. No one at Tours doubted that Martin had been a saint, and to tap into the power of his relics his church was constructed in the cemetery directly over his tomb. For a man like Gregory of Tours, the church was above all a home for the relics of the saints. Whereas in the classical world the dead had been banished from the presence of the living, in the medieval world the holy dead held the place of highest esteem.

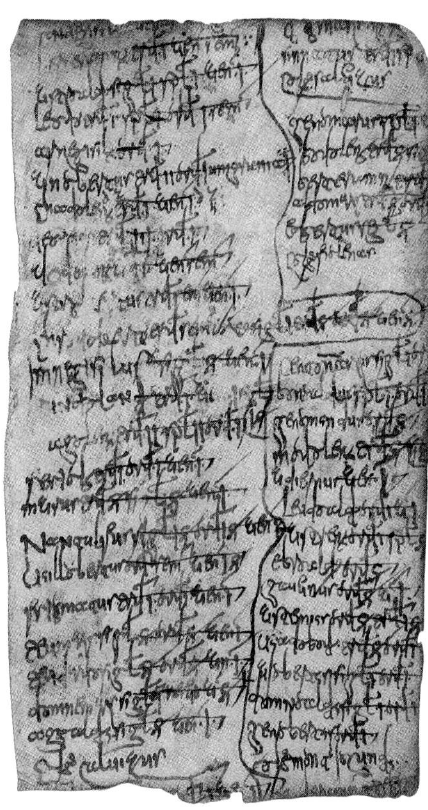

Peasant Dues
This seventh-century ledger sheet from the church of St. Martin of Tours lists the dues owed by tenants on St. Martin's estates.

Economic Hardship in a Peasant Society

Relics were important protectors for people who lived on the very edge of survival, as seventh- and eighth-century Europeans did. Studies of Alpine peat bogs show that from the fifth to the mid-eighth centuries glaciers advanced and the mean temperature in Europe dropped. This climatic change spelled shortages in crops, exacerbating the problems of primitive farming. The dry, light soil of the Mediterranean region had been easy to till, and wooden implements were no liability there. But the northern soils of most of the Merovingian world were heavy, wet, and difficult to turn and aerate. The primary fertilizer was animal dung. We know from chronicles, histories, and saints' lives that crop shortages, famines, and diseases were a normal part of life. For the year 591 alone, Gregory of Tours reported that

> *a terrible epidemic killed off the people in Tours and in Nantes. Each person who caught the disease was first troubled with a slight headache and then died. . . . In the town of Limoges a number of people were consumed by fire from heaven for having profaned the Lord's day by transacting business. . . . There was a terrible drought which destroyed all the green pasture. As a result there were great losses of flocks and herds. . . . [Elsewhere] the hay was destroyed by incessant rain and by the rivers which overflowed, there was a poor grain harvest, but the vines yielded abundantly.*

The meager population of the Merovingian world was too large for its productive capacities. Technological limitations meant a limited food supply; and agricultural work was not equitably or efficiently allocated and managed. A leisure class of landowning warriors and churchmen lived off the work of peasant men, who tilled the fields, and peasant women, who gardened, brewed, baked, and wove cloth. Surpluses did occasionally develop, whether from peaceful agriculture or plunder in warfare, and these were traded, although not in an impersonal, commercial manner. Most economic transactions of the seventh and eighth centuries were part of a gift economy, a system of give and take: booty was taken, tribute demanded, harvests hoarded, and coins struck, all to be redistributed to friends, followers, and dependents. Those benefiting from this largess included religious people and institutions: monks, nuns, bishops; monasteries and churches. We still have a partial gift economy today. At holidays, for example, goods change hands for social purposes: to consecrate a holy event, to express love and friendship, to "show off" wealth and status. In the Merovingian world, the gift economy was the dynamic behind many other moments when goods and money changed hands. Kings and other rich and powerful men and women amassed gold, silver, ornaments, and jewelry in their treasuries and grain in their storehouses to mark their power, add to their prestige, and prove their generosity.

Some economic activity in the seventh century was purely commercial. Impersonal transactions took place especially in long-distance trade, in which the West supplied human and raw materials like slaves, furs, and honey and in return received luxuries and manufactured goods such as silks and papyrus from the East. Trade was a way in which the three descendants of the Roman Empire kept in tenuous contact with one another. Seventh- and eighth-century sources speak of Byzantines, Syrians, and Jews as the chief intermediaries. Some continued to live in the still thriving port cities of the Mediterranean. Gregory of Tours especially associated Jews with commerce, complaining that they sold things "at a higher price than they were worth."

Despite the hostility toward Jews that Gregory's words reveal, Jews in seventh- and eighth-century Europe were not usually persecuted. (The exception was Visigothic Spain, where both church and monarchy legislated with great thoroughness against the Jews.) In many regions—in Burgundy and along the Rhône River valley, for example—Jews were almost entirely integrated into every aspect of secular life. They used Hebrew in worship, but otherwise they spoke the same languages as Christians and used Latin in their legal documents. Their children were often given the same names as Christians (and, in turn, Christians often took Biblical names, such as Solomon); they dressed as everyone else dressed; and they engaged in the same occupations. Many Jews planted and tended vineyards, in part because of the importance of wine in synagogue services, in part because the surplus could easily be sold. Some Jews were rich landowners, with slaves and dependent peasants working for them; others were independent peasants of modest means. Whereas some Jews lived in towns with a small Jewish quarter where their homes and synagogues were located, most Jews, like their Christian neighbors, lived on the land. Only much later, in the tenth century, would their status change, setting them markedly apart from Christians.

Silver, Gold, and Garnet Brooch
Precious ornaments such as this, which comes from a seventh-century aristocrat's tomb, were used to display status and might become part of a gift exchange.

Nor were women as noticeably set apart from men in the Merovingian period as they had been in Roman times. As in the Islamic world, Western women received dowries and could inherit property. In the West they could be entrepreneurs as well: we know of at least one enterprising peasant

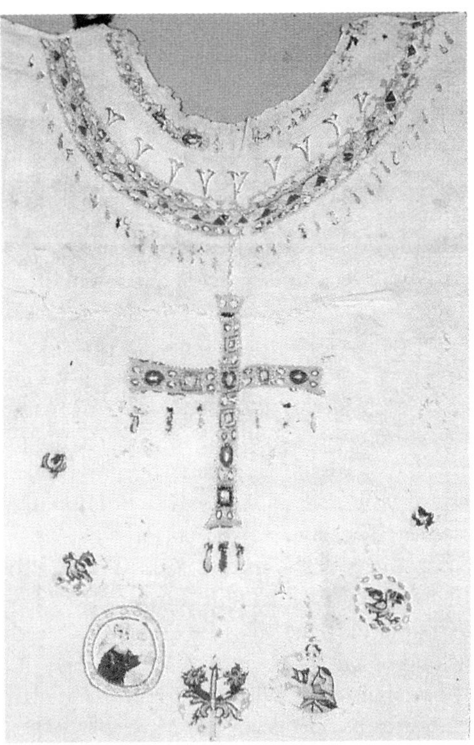

Symbolic Jewels
The embroidery on this blouse depicts the jewels worn by Merovingian aristocratic women. Tradition has it that this particular blouse belonged to Queen Balthild: rather than wear real jewels, she distributed them to the poor and contented herself with their memento in embroidery.

woman who sold wine at Tours to earn extra money. Along with their economic power, peasant women enjoyed a good deal of social independence; for example, they—rather than their parents or their lords—chose husbands from the men in the villages. This was a function of demographics—the fact that rich Merovingian men had several wives and mistresses meant that eligible women were in short supply for other men. A woman's legal status determined the social rank of her children: if a free-woman married a male slave, the children of the union were recognized as free. Such marriages contributed to the upward mobility of ambitious peasants; although, of course, the children of slave women would have the status of slaves, even if their father were free. Some women catapulted to even higher positions. Balthild (who died c. 680), a slave in the king's household but "beautiful, clever and of strong character," as her biographer described her, attracted the attention of King Clovis II (*639–657). Their marriage produced three sons, all of whom became kings; and after Clovis's death in 657, during the minority of her oldest son, Queen Balthild served as regent for her son until he came of age. She staunchly opposed slavery and infanticide and lent equally strong support to monasteries and pious clerics. Male slaves could never rise to royal power; but some became royal favorites and achieved wealth and status that way. Andarchius, for example, born a slave, became a scholar and an ambassador for a Merovingian king.

The Powerful in Merovingian Society

Aristocratic men, who lived mostly in rural areas, controlled the activities of women more closely than did men of the lower classes. Merovingian aristocrats did not form a separate legal group, but they held hereditary wealth, status, and political influence. Noble parents determined whom their daughter was to marry, for such unions bound together whole kindreds rather than simply husbands and wives. As was true for brides of the lower classes, aristocratic wives received a dowry (usually land) over which they had some control; if they were widowed without children, they were allowed to sell, give away, exchange, or rent out those estates as they wished. Moreover, men could give women property outright in written testaments. Fathers so often wanted to share their property with their daughters that an enterprising compiler drew up a formula for scribes to follow when drawing up such wills. It began:

> *For a long time an ungodly custom has been observed among us that forbids sisters to share with their brothers the paternal land. I reject this impious law: God gave all of you to me as my children and I have loved you all equally, therefore you will all equally rejoice in my goods after my death. . . . I make you, my beloved daughter, an equal and legitimate heir in all my patrimony.*

Because of such bequests, dowries, and other gifts, many aristocratic women were very rich. Childless widows frequently gave grand and generous gifts to the church from their vast possessions. But a woman need not have been a widow to control enormous wealth: in 632, for example, the nun Burgundofara, who had never married, drew up a will giving her monastery the land, slaves, vineyards, pastures, and forests she had received from her two brothers and her father. In the same will she gave other property near Paris to her brothers and sister. Aristocratic women maintained close ties with their relatives. They did what they could to find powerful husbands for their sisters and prestigious careers for their brothers; in turn, they relied on their relatives for personal support.

Though legally under the authority of her husband, a Merovingian woman often found ways to take control of her life and of her husband's life as well. Queens like Fredegund, wife of Chilperic, plotted against her husband's brothers, bribed bishops to speak against her enemies, and poisoned her stepson. Tetradia, wife of Count Eulalius, left her husband, taking all his gold and silver, because

> *he was in the habit of sleeping with the women-servants in his household. As a result he neglected his wife. He used to knock her about when he came from these midnight exercises. As a result of his excesses, he ran into serious debt, and to meet this he stole his wife's jewellery and money.*

At a court of law Tetradia was sentenced to repay Eulalius four times the amount she had taken from him, but she was allowed to keep and live on her own property. Other women were able to exercise behind-the-scenes control through their sons. Artemia, for example, used the prophecy that her son, Nicetius, would become a bishop to prevent her husband from taking the bishopric himself. Although the prophecy eventually came to pass, well into his thirties, Nicetius remained at home with his mother, working alongside the servants and teaching the younger children of the household to read the Psalms.

Some women exercised direct power. As mentioned, Balthild, the mother of a king, acted as her son's regent before he came to power. Rich widows with fortunes to bestow wielded enormous influence. Some Merovingian women were abbesses, rulers in their own right over female monasteries and sometimes over "double monasteries," with separate facilities for men and women. These could be very substantial centers of population: the female monastery at Laon, for example, had 300 nuns in the seventh century.

Housed in populous convents or monopolized by rich men able to support several wives and mistresses at one time, women were scarce in society at large and therefore valuable. Marriage, especially the most formal kind, was expensive for an upper-class man. He had to pay a dowry to his bride; and after the marriage was consummated, he gave her a morning gift. A less formal marriage, and less expensive, was the *Friedelehe*, in which a man "abducted" his wife in a kind of elopement. These were not clandestine marriages, however, and they too involved payment of the morning gift. Churchmen had many ideas about the value of marriages, but in practice they had little to do with the matter. No one got married in a church. The purpose of marriage, as it was understood in the seventh and eighth centuries, was procreation. The marriage bed, not the altar, was its focus. For aristocrats marriage existed to maintain the family.

Aristocrats lived lives of leisurely abundance. At the end of the sixth century, for example, Bishop Nicetius inhabited a palace that commanded a view of his estates overlooking the Moselle River:

> *From the top you can see boats gliding by on the surface of the river in summertime; it has three stories and when you reach the top, the edifice seems to overshadow the fields lying at its feet. . . . On these slopes, formerly sterile, Nicetius has planted juicy vines, and green vineshoots clothe the high rock that used to bear nothing but scrub. Orchards with fruit-trees growing here and there fill the air with the perfume of their flowers.*

Sixth-century aristocrats with wealth and schooling like Nicetius still patterned their lives on those of Romans, teaching their children Latin poetry and writing to one another in phrases borrowed from Virgil.

Less than a century later, however, aristocrats no longer adhered to the traditions of the classical past. Most important, they spoke a language far removed from literary Latin. New-style aristocrats paid little attention to Latin poetry. Some still learned Latin, but they cultivated it mainly to read the Psalms. A religious culture emphasizing Christian piety over the classics was developing in the West at the same time as in Byzantium.

The new religious sensibility was given powerful impetus by the arrival (c. 591) on the Continent of the Irish monk St. Columbanus (c. 543–615).

The Merovingian aristocracy was much taken by Columbanus's brand of monasticism, which stressed exile, devotion, and discipline. The monasteries St. Columbanus established in both Gaul and Italy attracted local recruits, some of them grown men and women, from the aristocracy, but many were young children given to a monastery by their parents. This practice (called *oblation*) was not only accepted but also often considered essential for the spiritual well-being of both the children and their families. Irish monasticism introduced aristocrats on the Continent to a deepened religious devotion. Those aristocrats who did not actively join or patronize a monastery still often read (or listened to others read) books about penitence, and they chanted the Psalms.

Along with their religious activities, male aristocrats of the mid-seventh century spent their time honing their skills as warriors. To be a great warrior in Merovingian society, just as in the otherwise different world of the Bedouin, meant more than just fighting: it meant perfecting the virtues necessary for leading armed men. Aristocrats affirmed their skills and comradeship in the hunt; they proved their worth in the regular taking of booty; and they rewarded their followers afterward at generous banquets. At these feasts, following the dictates of the gift economy, fellowship was combined with the redistribution of wealth, as lords gave abundantly to the retainers who surrounded them.

Bishops were generally also aristocrats and ranked among the most powerful men in Merovingian society. Gregory of Tours, for example, considered himself the protector of "his citizens" at Tours. When representatives of the king came to collect taxes there, Gregory stopped them in their tracks, warning them that St. Martin would punish anyone who tried to tax his people. "That very day," Gregory reported, "the man who had produced the tax rolls caught a fever and died." Gregory then obtained a letter from the king, "confirming the immunity from taxation of the people of Tours, out of respect for Saint Martin."

Like other aristocrats, many bishops were married even though church councils demanded celibacy. For example, Bishop Priscus of Lyon had a wife, Susannah, and a son. As the overseers of priests, however, bishops were expected to be their moral superiors and refrain from sexual relations with their wives. Since bishops were ordinarily appointed late in life, long after they had raised a family, this did not threaten the ideal of a procreative marriage.

Atop the aristocracy were the Merovingian kings, rulers of the Frankish kingdoms from about 486 to 751. The dynasty owed its longevity to good political sense: it had allied itself with local lay aristocrats and ecclesiastical authorities. The kings relied on these men to bolster their power derived from other sources: their tribal war leadership and access to the lion's share of plunder; their quasi-magical power over crops and fertility; and their appropriation of the taxation system, the fisc (public lands), and the legal framework of Roman administration. The kings' courts functioned as schools for the sons of the aristocracy, tightening the bonds between royal and aristocratic families and loyalties. When kings sent officials—counts and dukes—to rule in their name in various regions of their kingdoms, these regional governors worked with and married into the aristocratic families that had long controlled local affairs, so that the kings' officials themselves merged with local aristocrats.

The king acted as arbitrator and intermediary for the competing interests of these aristocrats while taking advantage of local opportunities to appoint favorites and garner prestige by giving out land and privileges to supporters and religious institutions. Both kings and aristocrats, therefore, had good reason to want a powerful royal authority. Gregory of Tours's history of the sixth century is filled with stories of bitter battles between Merovingian kings, as royal brothers fought over territories, wives, and revenues in seemingly endless vendettas. Yet what seemed like royal weakness and violent chaos to the bishop was in fact one way in which the kings focused local aristocratic enmities, preventing them from spinning out of royal control. By the beginning of the seventh century, three relatively stable Frankish kingdoms had emerged: Austrasia to the northeast; Neustria, with its capital city at Paris; and Burgundy, incorporating the southeast. These divisions were so useful to local aristocrats and the Merovingian dynasty alike that even when royal

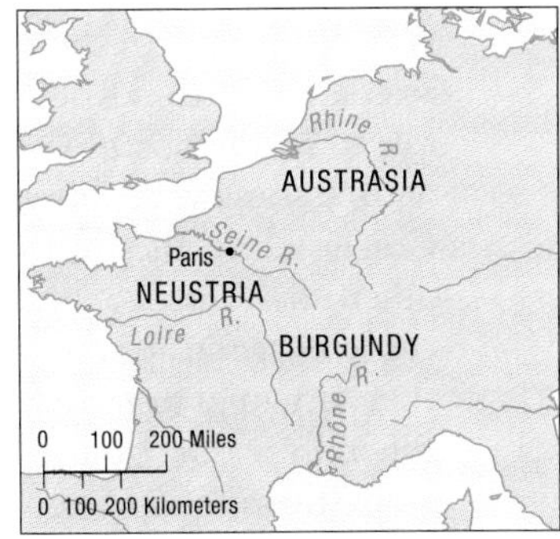

The Frankish Kingdoms

power was united in the hands of one king, Clothar II (✷613–623), he made his son the independent king of Austrasia.

The very power of the kings in the seventh century, however, gave greater might to their chief court official, the mayor of the palace. In the following century, allied with the Austrasian aristocracy, one mayoral family would displace the Merovingian dynasty and establish a new royal line, the Carolingians.

Christianity and Classical Culture in England and Ireland

The Merovingian kingdoms exemplify some of the ways in which Roman and non-Roman traditions combined. Anglo-Saxon England shows still another in its formation of a learned monastic culture. The impetus for this culture came not from native traditions but from Rome and Ireland. After the Anglo-Saxon conquest, England gradually emerged politically as a mosaic of about a dozen kingdoms ruled by separate kings, all of whom traced their ancestry to the god Woden. Like Clovis, the English kings carved out their territories and made good their authority by battling rival leaders and tribes; but unlike Clovis, the Anglo-Saxon kings did not find a strong Christian aristocracy with which to ally. No proud and dignified bishops met them at their cities' gates, for by the time of the Anglo-Saxon invasions the cities were mere shells and the Romans who built them had fled. The British Christians who remained were either absorbed into the pagan culture of the invaders or pushed west into Wales or north into Scotland, where Christianity survived.

Christianity was reintroduced in England from two directions. In the south of England, missionaries arrived from Rome, sent by Pope Gregory the Great. In the north of England, Irish monks came with a somewhat different brand of Christianity. Converted in the fifth century by St. Patrick and other missionaries, the Irish had rapidly evolved a church organization that corresponded to its rural clan organization. Abbots and abbesses, who generally came from powerful dynasties, headed monastic *familiae*, communities composed of blood relatives, servants, slaves, and, of course, monks or nuns. Bishops were often under the authority of abbots, and the monasteries rather than cities were the centers of population settlement in Ireland.

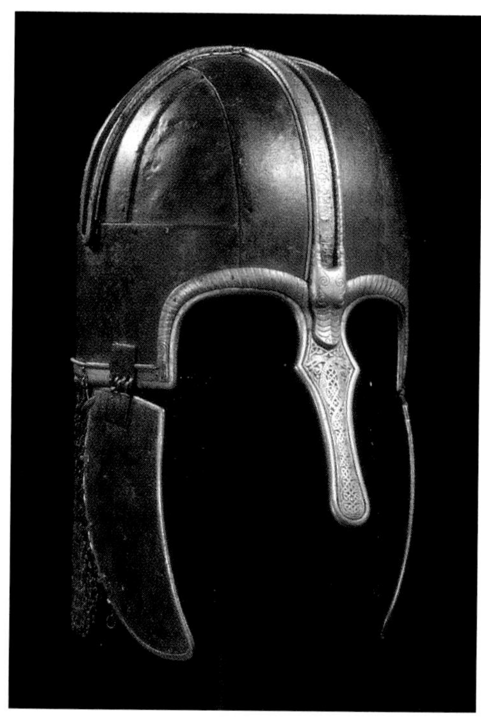

Warrior Helmet
The English aristocracy of the seventh and eighth centuries was largely a class of warriors. Finely wrought helmets like this one were made of iron and copper alloy and were worn only by the very richest warriors; the others had to be content with leather.

Because their families and communities were so important, pious Irishmen considered self-imposed exile to be one of the greatest sacrifices they could make for God. St. Columbanus, according to his seventh-century biographer,

> *longed to go into strange lands, in obedience to the command which the Lord gave Abraham: "Get thee out of thy country, and from thy kindred, and from thy father's house, into a land that I will show thee."*

In 635 another monk, Aidan, left Ireland to found a monastery, Lindisfarne, on the coast of northern England.

Thus Christianity had already arrived in England from one direction when, in 596, Pope Gregory the Great sent churchmen to Kent, England's southernmost kingdom. The missionaries, under the leadership of Augustine (not the same Augustine as the bishop of Hippo), intended to convert the king and through him his people. Arriving in 597, Augustine and his party brought with them Roman practices at odds with those of Irish Christianity, stressing ties to the pope and the organization of the church under bishops rather than abbots. Using the Roman model, they divided England into territorial units (*dioceses*) headed by an archbishop and bishops. Augustine, for example, became archbishop of Canterbury. A major bone of contention between the Roman and Irish churches was the calculation of the date of Easter. Both sides thought that Christians could not be saved unless they observed the day of the Resurrection properly and on the right date, but they argued on behalf of entirely different dates.

Aidan had close ties with the king of Northumbria (in the north of England), and he and his disciples were given royal support to preach Christianity and the Irish position on Easter. In the south of England the Roman view prevailed, and it eventually triumphed in the north as well when the Northumbrian king, Oswy, organized a synod at Whitby (664). There Wilfred, a churchman raised in the north but zealous on behalf of the Roman position, convinced Oswy that Rome spoke with the voice of St. Peter, the heavenly doorkeeper. Oswy opted for the Roman calculation of Easter and embraced the Roman church as a whole.

The path to the Roman triumph had been well prepared. To many English monks, Rome had great prestige; for them, it was a treasure trove of knowledge, piety, and holy objects. Benedict Biscop (c. 630–690), the founder of two important English monasteries, Wearmouth and Jarrow, made many arduous trips to Rome, bringing back relics, liturgical vestments, and even a cantor to teach his monks the proper melodies in a time before written musical notation. Above all, he went to Rome to get books. At his monasteries in the north of England, he built up a grand library. In Anglo-Saxon England as in Ireland, both of which lacked a strong classical tradition from Roman times, a book was considered a precious object, to be decorated as finely as a garnet-studded brooch.

The Anglo-Saxons and Irish Celts had a thriving oral culture but extremely limited uses for writing. Books became valuable only when these societies converted to Christianity. Just as Islamic reliance on the Qur'an made possible a literary culture under the Umayyads, so Christian dependence on the Bible, written liturgy, and patristic thought helped make England and Ireland centers of literature and learning in the seventh and eighth centuries. Under Archbishop Theodore (*669–690), who had studied at Constantinople and was one of the most learned men of his day, a school at Canterbury was established where students mined Latin and even some Greek manuscripts to comment on Biblical texts. Men like Benedict Biscop soon sponsored other centers of learning, and here again the texts from the classical past were used. Although women did not found famous schools, many abbesses ruled over monasteries that stressed Christian learning. Here as elsewhere, Latin writings, even pagan texts, were studied diligently, in part because Latin was so foreign a language that mastering it required systematic and formal study. One of the Benedict Biscop's pupils was Bede (673–735), a monk and historian of extraordinary

Lindisfarne Gospels Text Page
To the monks who copied the Gospels in the north of England, the book was a precious object, to be decorated much as a brooch might be enhanced. Here the letters that begin a chapter are treated as part of a design.

breadth. Bede in turn taught a new generation of monks who became a kind of brain trust for late eighth-century rulers.

The vigorous pagan Anglo-Saxon oral tradition was only partially suppressed; much of it was adapted to the new Christian culture. Bede told the story of Caedmon, a layman who had not wanted to sing and make up poems, as he was expected to do at the convivial feasts of warriors. One night, slipping out of the dinner hall to sleep with the animals in the barn, Caedmon had a dream: he was commanded by an unknown man to sing about Creation. In his sleep Caedmon dreamed an Anglo-Saxon poem that praised God as author of all things. He became a kind of celebrity, joined a monastery, and spent the rest of his days turning "whatever passages of Scripture were explained to him into delightful and moving poetry in his own English [that is, Anglo-Saxon] tongue." Although Bede himself translated Caedmon's poem into Latin when he wrote down the tale, he encouraged and supported the use of Anglo-Saxon, urging Christian priests, for example, to use it when they instructed their flocks. Sometimes Bede himself wrote in Anglo-Saxon: he was translating the Gospel of St. John into the vernacular at the time of his death. In contrast to other European regions, where the vernacular was rarely written, Anglo-Saxon came to be a written language used in every aspect of English life, from government to entertainment.

After the Synod of Whitby, the English church was tied by doctrine, friendship, and conviction to the church of Rome. An influential Anglo-Saxon monk and bishop, Wynfrith even changed his name to the Latin Boniface to symbolize his loyalty to the Roman church. Preaching on the Continent, Boniface (680–754) worked to set up churches in Germany and Gaul that, like the ones in England, looked to Rome for leadership and guidance. His zeal would give the papacy new importance in the West.

Visigothic Unity and Lombard Division

In contrast to England, southern Gaul, Spain, and Italy had long been part of the Roman Empire and preserved many of its traditions. Nevertheless, as they were settled and fought over by new peoples, their histories came to diverge dramatically. When Clovis defeated the Visigoths in 507, their vast kingdom, which had sprawled across southern Gaul into Spain, was dismembered, and the Franks and Ostrogoths vied for its control. By mid-century, however, the Ostrogoths were too busy struggling against Justinian's forces to be concerned with matters outside Italy, and the Franks came into possession of most of the Visigothic kingdom in southern Gaul, while in Spain the Visigothic king survived only to meet with fierce revolts by rebellious nobles and townsmen.

The Visigothic king Leovigild (✶569–586) at last established territorial control over most of Spain by military might. But no ruler could hope to maintain his position there without the support of the Hispano-Roman population, which included the great landowners and leading bishops; and their backing was unattainable while the Visigoths remained Arian.* Leovigild's son, Reccared (✶586–601), took the necessary step in 587. Two years later, at the Third Council of Toledo, most of the Arian bishops followed their king by announcing their conversion to Catholicism, and the assembled churchmen enacted decrees for a united church in Spain.

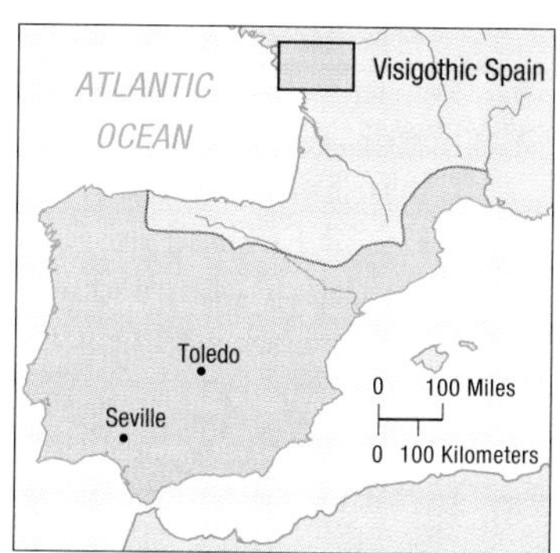

Visigothic Spain, c. 600

Thereafter the bishops and kings of Spain cooperated to a degree unprecedented in other regions. While the king gave the churchmen free reign to set up their own hierarchy (with the bishop of Toledo at the top) and to meet regularly at synods to regulate and reform the church, the bishops in turn supported their Visigothic ruler. A leading writer of the period, Bishop Isidore of Seville (✶c. 600–636), argued that the king ruled as a minister of the Christian people. Rebellion against him was tantamount to rebellion against Christ. The Spanish bishops reinforced this idea by anointing the king, daubing him with holy oil in a ritual that paralleled the ordination of priests and demonstrated divine favor. Toledo became the city not only where the highest bishop presided but also where the kings were "made" through anointment.

*See Chapter 7.

While the bishops in this way made the king's cause their own, their lay counterparts, the great landowners, helped supply the king with troops, allowing him to maintain internal order and repel his external enemies.

Ironically, it was precisely the centralization and unification of the Visigothic kingdom that proved its undoing. When the Arabs arrived in 711, they needed only to kill the king, defeat his army, and capture Toledo to deal it a crushing blow.

By contrast, the Lombard king faced at all times a hostile papacy in the center of Italy and virtually independent dukes in the south of Italy who, although theoretically royal officers, in fact ruled Benevento and Spoleto on their own behalf. Although many Lombards were Catholics, others, including important kings and dukes, were Arian. The "official" religion varied with the ruler in power. Rather than signal a major political event, then, the conversion of the Lombards to Catholic Christianity occurred gradually, ending only around the mid-seventh century. Partly as a result of this slow development, the Lombard kings, unlike the Visigoths, Franks, or even the Anglo-Saxons, never enlisted the wholehearted support of any particular group of churchmen.

Lacking strong and united ecclesiastical favor, Lombard royal power still had strong bulwarks. Chief among these were the traditions of leadership associated with the royal dynasty, the kings' control over large estates in northern Italy and their military ability, and the Roman institutions that survived in Italy. Although the Italian peninsula had been devastated by the wars between the Ostrogoths and the Byzantine Empire, the Lombard kings took advantage of the still-urban organization of Italian society and economy, assigning dukes to city bases and setting up a royal capital at Pavia. Recalling emperors like Constantine and Justinian, the kings built churches, monasteries, and other places of worship in the royal capital, maintained the walls, and minted coins. Revenues from tolls, sales taxes, port duties and court fines filled their coffers, although (and this was a major weakness) they could not revive the Roman land tax. Like other Germanic kings, the Lombards issued law codes that revealed a great debt to Roman legal collections such as those commissioned by Justinian. Although individual provisions of the law code promulgated by King Rothari (*636–652), for example, reflected Lombard traditions, the code also suggested the Roman idea that the law should apply to all under his rule, not just Lombards: "We desire," Rothari wrote,

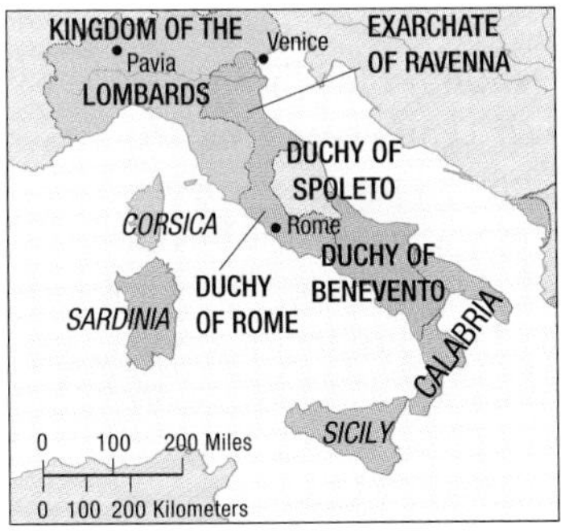

> *that these laws be brought together in one volume so that everyone may lead a secure life in accordance with the law and justice, and in confidence thereof will willingly set himself against his enemies and defend himself and his homeland.*

Unfortunately for the Lombard kings, the "homeland" they hoped to rule was not united under them. As soon as they began to make serious headway into southern Italy against the duchies of Spoleto and Benevento, the pope feared for his own position in the middle and called on the Franks for help.

Lombard Italy

Political Tensions and Reorganization at Rome

By the end of the sixth century the position of the pope was anomalous. On the one hand, believing himself the successor of St. Peter and head of the church, he buttressed this claim with real secular power. Pope Gregory the Great (*590–604) in many ways laid the foundations for the papacy's later spiritual and temporal ascendancy during his tenure. He made the pope the greatest landowner in Italy; he organized the defense of Rome and paid for its army; he heard court cases, made treaties, and provided welfare services. The missionary expedition he sent to England was only a small part of his involvement in the rest of Europe. For example, Gregory maintained close ties with the churchmen in Spain who were working to convert the Visigoths from Arianism to Catholicism; and he wrote letters to the Merovingian queen Brunhilda, assuring her that faith in God would help solidify her rule. A prolific author of spiritual works and Biblical exegeses, Gregory digested and simplified the ideas of church fathers like St. Augustine, making them accessible to a wider audience. His prac-

Byzantium and Rome
*This mosaic, commissioned by Pope Theodore (*642–649), shows the strong influence of Byzantine styles on early seventh-century Roman art, attesting to the political, cultural, and theological links between Rome and Constantinople.*

tical handbook for the clergy, *Pastoral Rule*, was matched by practical reforms within the Church: he tried to impose in Italy regular episcopal elections and to enforce clerical celibacy.

But the pope was not independent: he was only one of many bishops in the Roman Empire, which was now ruled from Constantinople; and he was therefore juridically tied to the emperor and Byzantium. For a long time the emperor's view on dogma, discipline, and church administration prevailed at Rome. This authority began to unravel in the seventh century. In 691 Emperor Justinian II convened a council that determined 102 rules for the church, and he sent the rules to Rome for papal endorsement. Most of the rules were unobjectionable, but Pope Sergius I was unwilling to agree to the whole because it permitted priestly marriages (which the Roman church did not want to allow), and it prohibited fasting on Saturdays in Lent (which the Roman church required). Outraged by Sergius's refusal, Justinian tried to arrest the pope, but Italian armies (theoretically under the emperor) came to the pontiff's aid, while Justinian's arresting officer cowered under the pope's bed. The incident reveals that some local forces were already willing to rally to the side of the pope against the emperor. By now Constantinople's influence and authority over Rome was tenuous at best. Sheer distance, as well as diminishing imperial power in Italy, meant the popes were in effect the leaders of the parts of Italy not controlled by the Lombards.

The gap between Byzantium and the papacy widened in the early eighth century as Emperor Leo III tried to increase the taxes on papal property to pay for his all-consuming war against the Arab invaders. The pope responded by leading a general tax revolt. Meanwhile, Leo's fierce policy of iconoclasm collided with the pope's tolerance of images. In the West, Christian piety focused not so much on icons as on relics, but the papacy was not about to allow sacred images to be destroyed. The pope argued that holy images could and should be venerated—but not worshiped. His support of images reflected popular opinion as well. A later commentator wrote that iconoclasm so infuriated the inhabitants of Ravenna and Venice that "if the pope had not prohibited the people, they would have attempted to set up a [different] emperor over themselves."

These difficulties with the emperor were matched by increasing friction between the pope and the Lombards. The Lombard kings had gradually managed to bring the duchies of Spoleto and Benevento under their control, as well as part of the Exarchate of Ravenna. By the mid-eighth century, the popes feared that Rome would fall to the Lombards, and Pope Zachary (*741–752) looked northward for friends. He created an ally by sanctioning the deposition of the last Merovingian king and his replacement by the first Carolingian king, Pippin III the Short (*751–768). In 753 a subsequent pope, Stephen II (*752–757), called on Pippin to march to Italy with an army to fight the Lombards. Thus events at Rome had a major impact on the history of not only Italy but the Frankish kingdom as well.

The Rise of the Carolingians

The popes were not dealing with naive upstarts; the Carolingians,* part of an aristocratic kin network accustomed to power and buttressed by vast estates in Austrasia, had long prepared to take over. The Carolingians were among many aristocratic families on the rise during the Merovingian period, a time of great competition and alliances among kindred groups. Consolidating power through marriages, royal grants, and probably also episcopal offices, the Carolingians also served as the mayor of the palace (chief minister) for the Merovingian kings in Austrasia. In 687 one Carolingian mayor, Pippin II (d. 714), made a bold move: at the battle of Tertry he defeated the mayor of the palace of Neustria. More important than this victory for his dynasty's success, Pippin allied himself with the aristocrats of Neustria through marriages and patronage. For example, he married his son Drogo to Anstrud, daughter of the most important Neustrian family. Because of these alliances, Pippin was able to assume the mayor's office in Neustria as well as in Austrasia.

*The name *Carolingian* derives from Carolus, the Latin name of several of the dynasty's most famous members, including Charles Martel and Charlemagne (or Charles the Great).

The son of Pippin II, Charles Martel (mayor, *714–741), was also a warrior and politician. Although he spent most of his time fighting vigorously against opposing aristocratic groups, later generations would recall with nostalgia his defeat of a contingent of Muslims between Poitiers and Tours in about 732. In contending against regional aristocrats who were carving out independent lordships for themselves, Charles and his family turned aristocratic factions against one another, rewarded supporters, crushed enemies, and dominated whole regions by controlling monasteries that served as focal points for both religious piety and land donations. Allying themselves with these influential religious and political institutions, the Carolingians took advantage of a fatal biological problem of the last Merovingian kings: few of them survived to adulthood. The exalted place of the aristocracy in Merovingian society made it likely that a number of powerful groups would emerge as autonomous rulers. The Carolingians' astonishing feat was to counteract this disintegration.

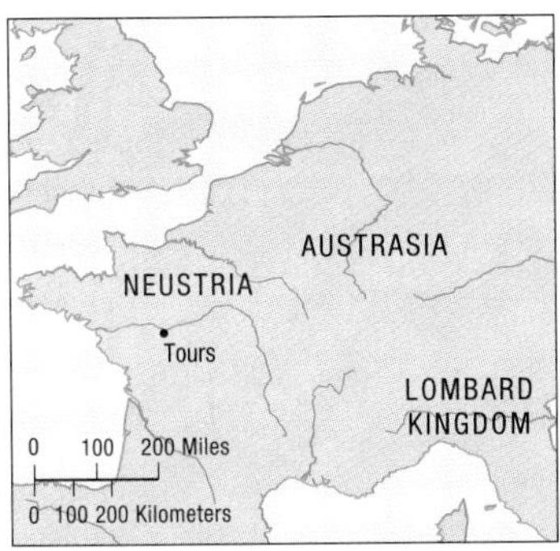

Rise of the Carolingians

The Carolingians chose their allies well. Anglo-Saxon missionaries like Boniface, who went to Frisia (today, the Netherlands) and Germany, helped them expand their control, converting the population as a prelude to conquest. Many of the areas Boniface reached had long been Christian, but the churches there had followed local or Irish models rather than Roman. Boniface, who came to Germany from England as the pope's ambassador, set up a hierarchical church organization and founded monasteries dedicated to the Rule of St. Benedict rather than to the Columbanian or other traditions. His newly appointed bishops were loyal to Rome and the Carolingians, not to regional aristocracies. They knew that their power came from papal and royal fiat rather than from local power centers. The Carolingians enhanced their own position by enforcing Boniface's reforms and allying themselves with the new episcopacy and with the pope at Rome.

Although at first men like Boniface worked indirectly to bring about the Carolingian alliance

Heirs of the Roman Empire

Byzantium

604–627 Persians and Byzantines at war

610–641 Reign of Emperor Heraclius

626 Avars defeated at the walls of Constantinople

717–741 Reign of Emperor Leo III the Isaurian

718–719 Major Arab attack on Constantinople repulsed

726–843 Period of iconoclasm

Islam

c. 570 Muhammad born at Mecca

610 Muhammad first hears the word of God

622 *Hijra*, the emigration to Medina and the beginning of the Islamic calendar

624 Battle of Badr, Islamic victory against the Meccans; expulsion of Jewish Qaynuqa clan from Medina

632 Arabs largely united under Muhammad; death of Muhammad

661–750 Umayyad caliphate

711–718 Muslim troops take North Africa and Spain

713 Muslim armies take the Indus valley

The West

590–604 Gregory the Great is pope at Rome

c. 591 Columbanus, an Irish monk, arrives on the Continent

596–597 Augustine of Canterbury sent to England by Pope Gregory the Great to convert the Anglo-Saxons

664 Synod of Whitby; Northumbrian King Oswy opts for Roman Christianity

680–754 Life of Boniface, an Anglo-Saxon missionary with strong ties to Rome

687 Battle of Tertry; Pippin II becomes mayor of both Austrasia and Neustria

714–741 Charles Martel is mayor of Neustria and Austrasia

751–768 Reign of Pippin III, king of the Franks (first of the Carolingian dynasty)

756 So-called Donation of Pippin

with the papacy, Pippin III and his supporters cemented the partnership when they decided that the time was ripe to depose the Merovingian king. Having petitioned Pope Zachary to legitimize their actions, the Carolingians readily returned the favor a few years later when the pope asked for their help in defense against hostile Lombards. The request signaled a major shift. Hitherto the papacy had been part of the Byzantine Empire; but in 754 it turned to the West. In that year the papacy and the Franks formed a close, tight alliance based, as their agreement put it, on *amicitia, pax et caritas* (mutual friendship, close relations, and Christian love). In 756 Pippin launched a successful campaign against the Lombard king that ended with the so-called Donation of Pippin, a peace accord between the Lombards and the pope. The treaty gave back to the pope cities that had been wrested from the Exarchate of Ravenna by the Lombard king. The new arrangement recognized what the papacy had long ago created: a territorial "republic of St. Peter" ruled by the pope, not by the Byzantine emperor. Henceforth the fate of Italy would be tied largely to the policies of the pope and the Frankish kings to the north, not to the emperors of the East.

The Carolingian partnership with Roman-style churchmen gave the dynasty a new kind of Christian aura, expressed in symbolic form by anointment. Carolingian kings, as Visigothic kings had been, were rubbed with holy oil on their foreheads and on their shoulders in a ceremony that reminded contemporaries of the Old Testament kings, such as David, who had been anointed by God. The son of Pippin III, Charles the Great, would be known to history as Charlemagne; but his nickname, David—the Hebrews' heroic king tells us better the image he cultivated of himself.

Conclusion

The three heirs of the Roman Empire—Byzantines, Muslims, and the peoples of the West—built upon three distinct legacies. Byzantium directly inherited the central political institutions of Rome; its people called themselves Romans; its emperor was the Roman emperor; and its capital, Constantinople, was the new Rome. Sixth-century Byzantium also inherited the cities, laws, and religion of Rome. Despite many changes in the seventh and eighth centuries—contraction of territory, urban decline, disappearance of the old elite, a ban on sacred images—the Byzantine Empire never entirely lost its Roman character. Byzantium itself remained an important and thriving city, with trade and manufacturing continuing even in the darkest hours of war and with administrative and fiscal institutions allowing the emperor to reorganize and adapt government to new demands. Education maintained vestiges of classical traditions even as it was reoriented to Christian texts. By 750, however, Byzantium was less Roman than it was a new resilient political and cultural entity, a Christian polity on the borders of the new Muslim empire.

The Muslims were the stepchildren of the Roman world, with Islam built on Jewish monotheism and only indirectly on Roman Christianity. Under the guidance of the Prophet Muhammad, Islam became both a coherent theology and a tightly structured way of life with customs defined in the Qur'an and based on Arabian tribal life. Once the Muslim Arabs embarked on military conquests, however, they too became heirs of Rome, preserving its cities, hiring its civil servants, and adopting its artistic styles. Drawing upon Roman traditions, the Muslims created a powerful Islamic state, with a capital city in Syria, regional urban centers elsewhere, and a culture that tolerated a wide variety of economic, religious, and social institutions so long as the conquered paid taxes to their Muslim overlords.

The West also inherited Roman institutions and transformed them with great diversity. In Italy and at Rome itself, the traditions of the classical past remained living parts of the fabric of life. The roads remained, the cities of Italy survived (although depopulated), and both the popes and the Lombard kings ruled in the traditions of Roman government; otherwise they would not have written out peace treaties. In Spain the Visigothic kings allied themselves with a Hispano-Roman elite that maintained elements of the organization and vigorous intellectual traditions of the late empire. In England, however, once the far-flung northern summit of the Roman Empire, the Roman legacy had to be reimported in the seventh century, as pagan Anglo-Saxon kings accepted Christianity from Roman missionaries and monks learned Latin as a new, exotic language. Frankish Gaul built on Roman traditions that had long been transformed by provincial and Germanic custom. There, for example, Roman-style coins became precious gifts, and such Roman government tasks as tax collecting were adopted to the interests of Frankish aristocratic factions.

All three heirs to Rome suffered the ravages of war. In all three societies the social hierarchy became simpler, with the loss of "middle" groups like the *curiales* at Byzantium and the near-suppression of tribal affiliations among those who professed Islam. As each of the three heirs shaped Roman institutions to its own uses and advantages, each also strove to create a religious polity. In Byzantium the emperor was a religious force, presiding over the destruction of images. In the Islamic world the caliph was the successor to Muhammad, a religious and political leader. In the West the Carolingians were anointed rulers of the Franks. Despite their many differences, all these leaders had a common understanding of their place in a divine scheme; they were God's agents on earth, ruling over God's people.

Suggestions for Further Reading

Source Materials

Bede, *A History of the English Church and People*. Translated by Leo Sherley-Price. 1991. The most important source for the history of the conversion of the English, written by an extraordinary eighth-century monk.

Geanakoplos, Deno John, ed. and trans. *Byzantium: Church, Society, and Civilization Seen Through Contemporary Eyes*. 1986. Contains translations of key primary source documents.

Gregory of Tours. *The History of the Franks*. Translated by Lewis Thorpe. 1976. Our major source for the history and the mentality of the Merovingian world. Gregory called this work his *Histories*, but Thorpe's translation refers to it by its later name.

Lewis, Bernard, ed. and trans. *Islam: From the Prophet Muhammad to the Capture of Constantinople*. 2 vols. 1987. A useful collection of documents concerned with the politics, war, religion, and economy of the Islamic world.

Interpretive Studies

Beeston, A. F. L. et al., eds. *Arabic Literature to the End of the Umayyad Period*. 1983. A collection of essays by specialists on every aspect of Umayyad literature.

Brown, Peter R. L. *The World of Late Antiquity, a.d. 150–750*. 1971. An exceptionally masterful but brief survey of the transition from the ancient to the medieval world, beautifully illustrated.

Browning, Robert. *The Byzantine Empire*. 1980. A thoughtful survey of change in Byzantium.

Chapelot, Jean, and Robert Fossier. *The Village and House in the Middle Ages*. Translated by Henry Cleere. 1985. Written jointly by a historian and an archaeologist. This text is a detailed study of the material remains of medieval settlements.

Collins, Roger. *Early Medieval Spain: Unity in Diversity, 400–1000*. 1983. Studies the Visigothic Kingdom and its transformation under the Muslims.

Crone, Patricia. *Meccan Trade and the Rise of Islam*. 1987. A controversial work that questions Mecca's place as a center of trade.

Donner, Fred McGraw. *The Early Islamic Conquests*. 1981. Concentrates on the tribal and religious forces behind the early Arab-Muslim expansion.

Dvornik, Francis. *Byzantium and the Roman Primacy*. Translated by Edwin A. Quain. 1966. A masterful study of the growth and development of the notion of papal primacy in the context of Byzantine political history.

Fine, John V. A., Jr. *The Early Medieval Balkans: A Critical Survey from the Sixth to the Late Twelfth Century*. 1991. A unique study that looks at the Balkans from the point of view of the people who settled there rather than from the Byzantines' perspective.

Geary, Patrick J. *Before France and Germany. The Creation and Transformation of the Merovingian World*. 1988. An insightful synthesis of the newest research on the period.

Goffart, Walter. *The Narrators of Barbarian History (a.d. 550–800): Jordanes, Gregory of Tours, Bede, and Paul the Deacon*. 1988. Examines early medieval histories as literary texts and as implicit statements about the task of the historian.

Grierson, Philip. "Commerce in the Dark Ages: A Critique of the Evidence." *Transactions of the Royal Historical Society* 5th ser. 9 (1959): 123–139. A path-breaking study in which the notion of the gift economy is used to explain problematic aspects of the early medieval economy.

Haldon, J. F. *Byzantium in the Seventh Century: The Transformation of a Culture*. 1990. An important and comprehensive survey of continuity and change in Byzantine society, culture, and institutions.

Hallenbeck, Jan T. *Pavia and Rome: The Lombard Monarchy and the Papacy in the Eighth Century*. 1982. A clear and detailed account of the relationship between the Lombard kings and the popes in the eighth century.

Herlihy, David. *Medieval Households*. 1985. An important synthesis of historical knowledge about the varieties of and changes in medieval family units, written by an authority in the field.

Hodges, Richard, and David Whitehouse. *Mohammed, Charlemagne and the Origins of Europe. Archaeology and the Pirenne Thesis*. 1983. Two archaeologists discuss the evidence concerning trade and economic vitality in the early Middle Ages.

Hodgson, Marshall G. S. *The Venture of Islam: Conscience and History in a World Civilization*. Vol. 1, *The Classical Age of Islam*. 1974. An authoritative account of the early period of Islamic history.

Hussey, Joan M. *The Orthodox Church in the Byzantine Empire*. 1986. Covers the organization of the Greek Orthodox church and the controversies that beset it until the fall of Byzantium in 1453.

James, Edward. *The Origins of France. From Clovis to the Capetians, 500–1000*. 1982. A survey of the transformations that turned Gaul into France.

———. *The Franks*. 1988. Brings together written and archaeological materials in a careful and insightful appraisal of Frankish culture through the seventh century.

Kennedy, Hugh. *The Prophet and the Age of the Caliphates: The Islamic Near East from the Sixth to the Eleventh Century*. 1986. A detailed political history of early Islam.

Kitzinger, Ernst. *Early Medieval Art*. rev. ed. 1983. Treats art as a window onto changes in attitudes and ideas about this world and the hereafter.

Lapidus, Ira. *A History of Islamic Societies*. 1988. A panoramic overview of the history of Islamic civilization from its beginnings to the twentieth century.

Latouche, Robert. *The Birth of Western Economy: Economic Aspects of the Dark Ages*. Translated by E. M. Wilkinson. 1961. A careful look at trade, farming, and urban life in the early Middle Ages.

Lewis, Bernard. *Islam and the Arab World: Faith, People, Culture*. 1976. Various topics treated in short and richly illustrated articles by different experts.

Noble, Thomas F. X. *The Republic of St. Peter: The Birth of the Papal State, 680–825*. 1984. Discusses the papacy during a major period of transition.

Norwich, John Julius. *Byzantium: The Early Centuries*. 1989. A well-written introduction that concentrates on political figures.

Ostrogorsky, George. *History of the Byzantine State*. rev. ed. Translated by J. M. Hussey. 1969. The standard and essential one-volume account of Byzantine history.

Peters. F. E. "The Commerce of Mecca Before Islam." In *A Way Prepared: Essays on Islamic Culture in Honor of Richard Bayly Winder*, edited by Farhad Kazemi and R. D. McChesney. 1988. Presents a nuanced view of the economic role of Mecca in the period before Muhammad.

Riché, Pierre. *Education and Culture in the Barbarian West: Sixth Through Eighth Centuries*. Translated by John J. Contreni. 1975. A monumental study of the shift from lay classical culture to religious culture in early medieval Europe.

Ruthven, Malise. *Islam in the World*. 1984. An excellent introduction to the history of Islam and its importance in the modern world.

Van Dam, Raymond. *Leadership and Community in Late Antique Gaul*. 1985. Gaul before and during the time of Gregory of Tours.

Waddy, Charis. *Women in Muslim History*. 1980. Focuses on the part played by women at decisive moments in Islam's history.

Watt, William Montgomery. *Muhammad: Prophet and Statesman*. 1961. A scholarly and sympathetic biography of the Prophet.

Weitzmann, Kurt. *The Icon: Holy Images, Sixth to Fourteenth Century*. 1978. A beautifully illustrated guide to the topic by the dean of Byzantine art-historical studies.

Wemple, Suzanne Fonay. *Women in Frankish Society. Marriage and the Cloister, 500–900*. 1981. A pioneering study of women in the Merovingian and Carolingian periods.

Wickham, Chris. *Early Medieval Italy: Central Power and Local Society, 400–1000*. 1981. An important survey of complex transformations, based on primary sources and anthropological insights.

Wood, Ian. *The Merovingian Kingdoms, 450–751*. 1994. A comprehensive and penetrating study.

CHAPTER

9

The Remaking of Three Societies, 756–1054

In 841 a fifteen-year-old boy named William went to serve at the court of King Charles the Bald. William's father was Bernard, an extremely powerful noble. His mother was Dhuoda, a well-educated, pious, and able woman; she administered the family's estates in the south of France while her husband occupied himself in court politics and royal administration. In 841, however, politics had become a dangerous business. King Charles, named after his grandfather Charlemagne, was fighting with his brothers over his portion of the Carolingian Empire, and Bernard (who had been a supporter of Charles's father, Louis the Pious) held only a precarious position at the young king's court. In fact, William was sent to Charles's court as a kind of hostage, to ensure Bernard's loyalty. Anxious about her son, Dhuoda wanted to educate and counsel him, so she wrote a *Handbook* of advice for William, outlining what he ought to believe about God, about politics and society, about his obligations to his family, and above all, about his duties to his father, which she emphasized even over loyalty to the king:

> *In the human understanding of things, royal and imperial appearance and power seem preeminent in the world, and the custom of men is to account those men's actions and their names ahead of all others. . . . But despite all this . . . I caution you to render first to him whose son you are special, faithful, steadfast loyalty as long as you shall live.*

William heeded his mother's words, with tragic results: when Bernard ran afoul of Charles and was executed, William died in a failed attempt to avenge his father.

Learned Women
In the eighth through the eleventh century many noblewomen were well educated and important patrons of the arts. This illustration is from a book of the Gospels commissioned by a German noblewoman, Abbess Hitda, who is depicted offering the manuscript to St. Walburgis.

Dhuoda's *Handbook* reveals the volatile political atmosphere of the mid-ninth century, and her advice to her son points to one of its causes: a crisis of loyalty. Loyalty to emperors and kings competed with allegiances to local authorities; and those, in turn, vied with family ties. Between 756 and 1054, European political structures changed in fundamental ways, reflecting the pressures of these competing loyalties. At the beginning of this period, centralized rulers controlled huge realms; by its end, these realms had fragmented into smaller, more local units. Eventually in the West, as these units sometimes broke apart further, sometimes joined together, the modern map of western Europe began to take shape. The Islamic world also separated into regional states. Of the three heirs of the Roman Empire—Byzantium, the Islamic world, and western Europe—only Byzantium remained relatively unchanged politically, retaining its imperial monarchy. However, under its influence new political entities in the Balkans and Russia emerged.

Important Dates

768–814 Charlemagne rules as king of the Franks

786–809 Caliphate of Harun al-Rashid

843 End of iconoclasm at Byzantium; Treaty of Verdun: Frankish kingdom divided

c. 870–c. 1025 Macedonian renaissance at Byzantium

871–899 Reign of King Alfred the Great in England

969–1171 Fatimid Dynasty in Egypt

976–1025 Reign of Byzantine Emperor Basil II Bulgaroctonos

1054 Schism between Roman Catholic and Greek Orthodox churches

Byzantium: Renewed Strength and Influence

By the middle of the ninth century, Byzantium was recovering well, both economically and militarily, from its debilitating wars. Beginning in the mid-ninth century and lasting until 1025, Byzantine forces advanced on all fronts, recapturing Crete (960) and Antioch (969) from the Muslims and consolidating control over southern Italy. In 1014 Emperor Basil II Bulgaroctonos (*976–1025)—his epithet meant "Slayer of the Bulgars"—ended two centuries of indecisive battles by destroying the fledgling Bulgar state and incorporating its territories into Byzantium. Victories such as these gave new prestige to the army and to the imperial court, contributing to important social and economic changes.

Most significant, a vital new elite emerged from the military reorganization of the seventh and eighth centuries. The heirs of some of the peasant-soldiers settled on virtually tax-free land, adding to their holdings and forming a new class of large

Basil II Bulgaroctonos
Despite the Bulgars' conversion to Byzantine Christianity, they were continually at war with the Byzantine state until 1014, when Emperor Basil II defeated them decisively. In this illustration, made just after his victory, Basil is shown in triumph, with the Bulgarians prostrate at his feet.

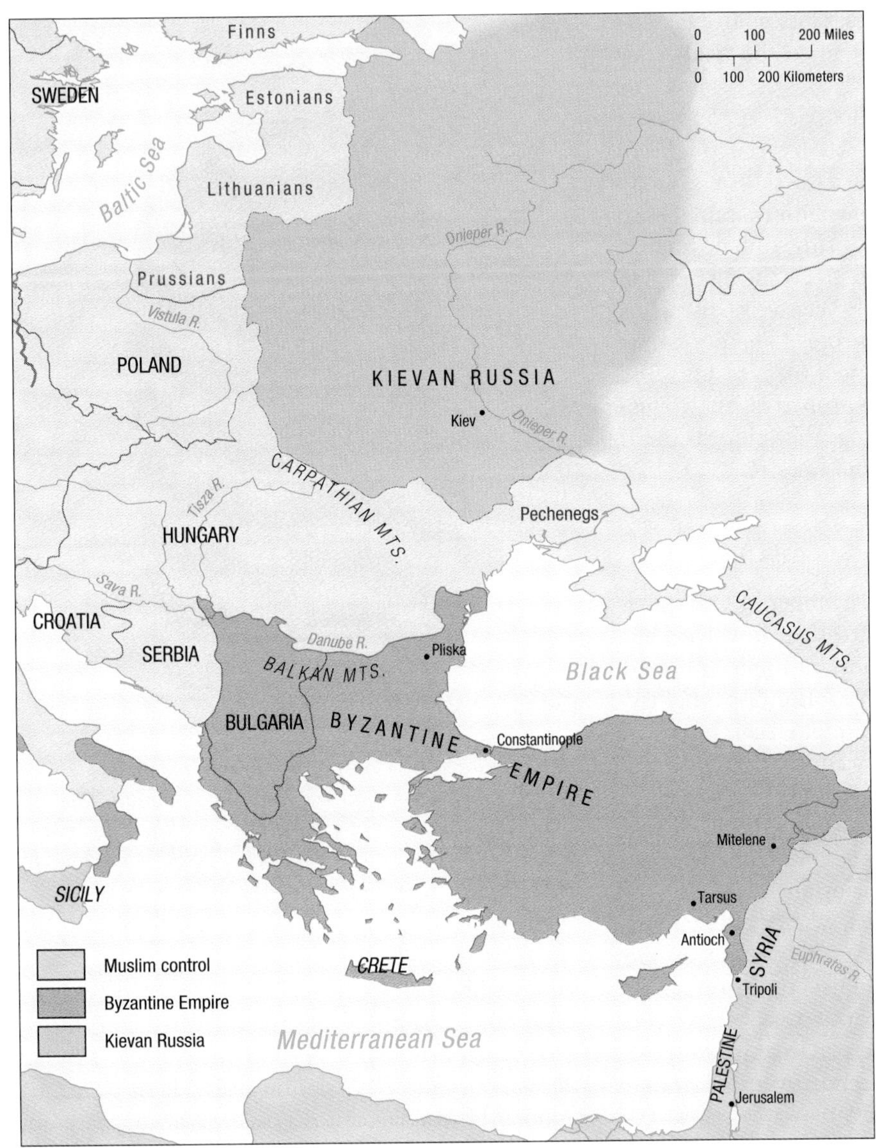

Kievan Russia and Byzantium, c. 1000

landowners. Many smaller peasants, unable or unwilling to pay their taxes,were compelled to give up their small freeholds to become dependents of these great landlords. They still tilled the soil, but they no longer owned it.

The most powerful of the large landowners were the generals, the *strategoi*, who had been set up as imperial appointees to rule the new districts, the *themes*, and who now found their prestige enhanced by victory. The *strategoi* took orders from the emperor or empress (during the period 756–1054 three powerful women ruled, generally as regents for their young sons), who told them when to prepare for campaigns and summon troops. But the *strategos* also exercised considerable power on his own. One *strategos*, Michael Lachanodracon, disbanded the monasteries in his *theme* and sold off their property on his own initiative, sending the proceeds to the imperial treasury as a gesture of comradery with his war companion, Emperor Constantine V. Although individual *strategoi* could be demoted or dismissed by irate emperors, most *strategoi* formed a powerful hereditary class of landowners. In these ways, the social hierarchy of Byzantium began to resemble that of western Europe, where grand estates owned by aristocrats were farmed by peasants whose tax and service obligations bound them to the fields they cultivated.

Some Byzantine emperors tried to counteract this new development. Moved by the plight of peasants who had been forced to sell or give up their properties to powerful men, for example, Basil II guaranteed their right to bring suit no matter how much time had elapsed since their land had been appropriated. "We have been very disturbed on behalf of the poor," he wrote. "The poor man ought in no case to be prevented from seeking and gaining the return of his own property." Such legislation slowed, but did not stop, the subjugation of the peasantry in the Byzantine Empire.

Art Sponsored by Constantine Porphyrogenitos
In this relief, carved during the rule of Constantine Porphyrogenitos out of a piece of jasper, the artist rendered Christ in a gesture of blessing with body-clinging drapery that reflected pagan classical Greek styles.

The Macedonian Renaissance

The most vocal and visible members of the new elite resided not in the countryside, however, but in the imperial court at Constantinople. Flushed with victory, reminded of Byzantium's past glory, they now revived classical intellectual pursuits. Basil I (*867–886) from Macedonia founded the imperial dynasty that presided over the so-called Macedonian renaissance (c. 870–c. 1025). Those now in power in Byzantium came from families that had bided their time during the dark days of the seventh and eighth centuries, when the Byzantine Empire had been under siege and the Byzantine emperors had suppressed the use and production of icons. Even in those anxious times, however, some of the educated elite had persisted in studying the classics in spite of the trend toward a simple religious education.

Now, with the empire slowly regaining its military eminence and with icons permanently restored in 843 by Empress Theodora, this scholarly elite thrived again. Byzantine artists produced new works of art, and emperors and other members of the new court society, liberated from sober taboos, sponsored sumptuous artistic productions. Emperor Constantine VII Porphyrogenitos (*913–959) wrote books of geography and history and financed the work of other scholars and artists. He even supervised the details of his craftspeople's products, insisting on exacting standards: "Who could enumerate how many artisans the Porphyrogenitos corrected? He corrected the stonemasons, the carpenters, the goldsmiths, the silversmiths, and the blacksmiths," wrote a historian supported by the same emperor's patronage. When a westerner, Liutprand, bishop of Cremona, visited Porphyrogenitos's court, he marveled at its luxury and called the emperor himself "a skillful artist." Unfortunately, none of Porphyrogenitos's own work survives; but some art produced under his patronage shows extraordinary mastery of classical techniques in the modeling of figures and suggestion of three-dimensional space and atmosphere.

Other members of the imperial court also supported writers, philosophers, and historians. Scholars wrote summaries of classical literature, encyclopedias of ancient knowledge, and commentaries on classical authors. Others copied manuscripts of religious and theological commentaries, such as the Homilies of St. Gregory Nazianzen, liturgical texts, Bibles, and Psalters. They hoped to revive the intellectual and artistic achievements of the heyday of imperial Roman rule. But the Macedonian renaissance could not possibly succeed in this endeavor: too much had changed since the time of

The Macedonian Renaissance
The figures in this Psalter illustration appear to live and move in a landscape and to have a relationship with one another, as in classical art. The figures, too, are modeled on classical prototypes: for example, King David, the supposed author of the Psalms, is patterned on Orpheus, the famous musician of pagan mythology.

Justinian. Nevertheless, the renaissance permanently integrated classical forms into Byzantine political and religious life. A jasper carving of Christ in a gesture of blessing illustrates this point: the theme is religious, but the figure of Christ, with his lively movement and naturally falling drapery, recalls classical models.

The merging of classical and Christian traditions is clearest in manuscript illuminations (painted illustrations). Both at Byzantium and in the West, artists chose their subjects by considering the texts they were to illustrate and the ways in which previous artists had handled particular themes. They drew upon traditional models to convey long-hallowed information. Artists thus worked within certain constraints in order to make their subjects identifiable. In much the same way that a modern illustrator of Santa Claus relies on a tradition dictating a plump man with a bushy white beard, medieval artists depended on particular visual cues. These characteristics constituted the iconography of their subject. For example, the artist of one illuminated Psalter who wanted to illustrate King David, the supposed poet of the Psalms, turned to a model of Orpheus, the enchanting musician of Greek mythology. The style of this artist's painting—an atmospheric setting in which solid, weighty figures appear to act—was also based on classical models.

The Wealth and Power of Byzantium

New wealth matched Byzantium's revived power. The emperors drew revenues from vast and growing imperial estates. For example, when the usurper Emperor Romanos I Lacapenos (*920–944) reconquered Mitelene on his eastern front, he incorporated it directly into imperial property. Emperors could levy revenues and services on the general population at will—requiring them to build bridges and roads, to offer lodging to the imperial retinue, and to pay taxes in cash. These taxes increased over time, partly because of fiscal reforms and partly because of population increases. The approximately 7 million people who lived in the empire in 780 had swelled to about 8 million less than a century later.

The emperor's or empress's power extended over both civil administration and military command. The only check on his or her authority was the possibility of an uprising, either at court or in the army. This is one reason that emperors surrounded themselves with eunuchs: castrated men were believed unfit for imperial office, and they could not have ambitions for their sons. Eunuchs were employed in the civil service; they held high positions in the army; and they were important palace officials. Eunuchs had a privileged place in Byzantine administrations because they were less liable than others to have an independent power base. Emperors, supported by their wealth and power, negotiated from a position of strength with other rulers. Embassies were exchanged, and the Byzantine court received and entertained diplomats with elaborate ceremonies. One such diplomat, Liutprand of Cremona, reported on his audience with Constantine Porphyrogenitos:

> *Leaning upon the shoulders of two eunuchs I was brought into the emperor's presence. At my approach [mechanical] lions began to roar and birds to cry out, each according to its kind. . . . After I had three times made obeisance to the emperor with my face upon the ground, I*

Muslim and Byzantine Interaction
This silk, which shows lions that symbolize the emperor's greatness, was produced at Constantinople between 976 and 1025. The style reflects silks produced in the Islamic world at about the same time and attests to the close relations between the two cultures.

> *lifted my head, and behold! the man whom just before I had seen sitting on a moderately elevated seat had now changed his raiment and was sitting on the level of the ceiling. How it was done I could not imagine, unless perhaps he was lifted up by some such sort of device as we use for raising the timbers of a wine press.*

Although this elaborate court ceremonial clearly amused Liutprand, its real function was to express the serious, sacred, concentrated power of imperial majesty. Liutprand missed the point, because he was a westerner unaccustomed to such displays.

The emperor's wealth relied on the prosperity of an agricultural economy organized for trade. State control and entrepreneurial enterprise were delicately balanced in Byzantine commerce. Although the emperor controlled craft and commercial guilds (such as those in the silk industry) to ensure imperial revenues and a stable supply of valuable and useful commodities, entrepreneurs organized most of the fairs held throughout the empire. Foreign merchants traded within the empire, either at Constantinople or in certain border cities. Because this international trade intertwined with foreign policy, the Byzantine government considered it a political as well as an economic matter. Emperors issued privileges to certain "nations" (as, for example, the Venetians, Russians, and Jews were called), regulating the fees they were obliged to pay and the services they had to render. At the end of the tenth century, for example, the Venetians bargained to reduce their customs' dues per ship from thirty *solidi* (coins) to two; in return they promised to transport Byzantine soldiers to Italy whenever the emperor wished. Merchants from each nation were lodged at state expense in certain areas of the city for about three months in order to transact their business. The Syrians, although Muslims, received special privileges: their merchants were allowed to stay at Constantinople for six months. In return, Byzantine traders were guaranteed protection in Syria, and the two governments split the income from the taxes on the sales Byzantine merchants made there. Thus Byzantine trade flourished in the Levant (the region bordering the southeastern part of the Mediterranean Sea) and, thanks to Venetian intermediaries, with the Latin West.

Equally significant was trade to the north. Byzantines may have mocked the "barbarians," dressed in animal skins, who lived beyond the Black Sea. Nevertheless, many Byzantines wore furs from Russia. Byzantines also imported Russian slaves, wax, and honey. Some Russians even served as mercenaries in the Byzantine army. The relationship between the two peoples became even closer at the end of the tenth century.

The Creation of Slavic States in the Balkans and Russia

The shape of modern Eastern Europe grew out of the Slavic kingdoms created during the period from the mid-eighth to the mid-tenth century. Byzantine influence predominated in some of these societies, notably Russia, Bulgaria, and Serbia.* Other new realms—the ancestors of the modern Polish, Czech, Slovak, and Croat states—eventually fell into the orbit of the Latin West.

By 800, Slavic settlements dotted the area from the Danube River down to Greece and from the Black Sea to Croatia. The Bulgar khagan ruled over the largest realm, populated mostly by Slavic peoples and situated northwest of Constantinople. Under Khagan Krum (*c. 803–814) and his son, Slavic rule stretched west all the way to the Tisza River in modern Hungary. At about the same time as Krum's triumphant expansion, however, the Byzantine Empire began its own campaigns to conquer, convert, and control these Slavic regions.

The Byzantine offensive began under Emperor Nicephorus I (*802–811), who waged war against the Slavs of Greece in the Peloponnesus, set up a new Christian diocese there, organized it as a new military *theme*, and forcibly resettled Christians in the area to counteract Slavic paganism. The Byzantines followed this pattern of conquest as they pushed northward. By the end of the ninth century Byzantium ruled all of Greece. Still under Nicephorus, the Byzantines launched a massive attack against the Bulgarians, took the chief city (Pliska), plundered it, burned it to the ground, and then marched against Krum's encampment in the Balkan Mountains. Krum took advantage of his position, however, attacked the imperial troops, killed Nicephorus, and brought home the emperor's skull in triumph. Cleaned out and lined with silver, the skull served as the victorious Krum's drinking goblet. In 816 peace was drawn up between the two sides that lasted for thirty years. But hostility remained latent, and wars between the Bulgarians and Byzantines broke out with increasing intensity. Skirmishes in 846, 852, and 863 gave way to longer wars in 894–897 and throughout the tenth century. The Byzantines slowly advanced, at first taking Bulgaria's eastern territory, and then, in a slow and methodical conquest (1001–1018) led by Emperor Basil II, aptly called the "Bulgar-Slayer," subjecting the entire region to Byzantine rule.

Meanwhile, the Byzantines also embarked on a religious offensive. In 863 they sent two brothers, Cyril and Methodius, as missionaries to Old (or Great) Moravia, a Slavic domain probably centered along the Sava River. Cyril and Methodius, well-educated Greeks, spoke one dialect of Slavic fluently. They devised an alphabet for Slavic based on Greek forms (the ancestor of the modern Cyrillic alphabet used in Russia, Bulgaria, and Serbia, for example). They also created a written language, later called Old Church Slavonic, based on their dialect of Slavic mixed (when they found it necessary, especially for theological ideas) with Greek words. Armed with translations of the Gospel and other church writings, they began preaching in Moravia.

At about the same time, the Byzantines attacked Bulgaria and forced the khagan, Boris, to accept Christianity. Boris had already decided to convert to Christianity, but under Frankish rather than Byzantine auspices. He capitulated reluctantly and was forced to give up his Frankish alliance and accept Byzantine missionaries and churchmen, who used the methods and writings of Cyril and Methodius.

With the arrival around 899 of a new group of invaders, the Magyars, into the Danubian basin, the Slavic world was effectively divided. Those Slavs bordering on the Frankish kingdom, such as the Czechs and Poles, came under influences that tied them to the church at Rome rather than to the Byzantine church. But Bulgaria became a Byzantine province. The Serbs, encouraged by Byzantium to oppose the Bulgarians, began to form the state that would become Serbia, in the shadow of Byzantine interests and religion. Other small Slavic principalities, such as the future Montenegro, tried to maintain their independence by playing papal and Byzantine interests off against one another.

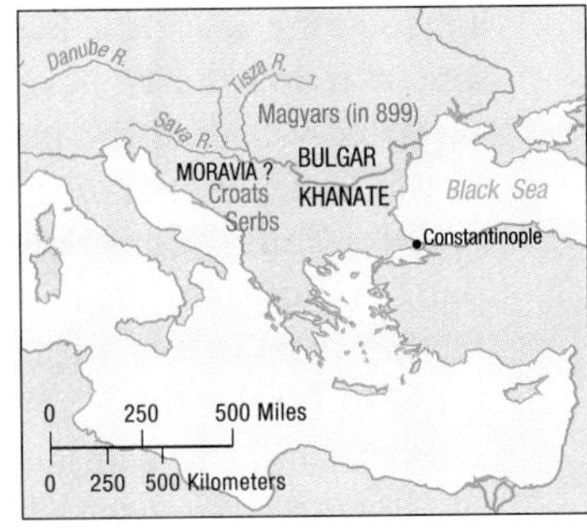

The Balkans, c. 800–900

*Terms like these, which imply boundaries and national identities, are modern. Throughout the period discussed here, boundaries were vague, and although people had a sense of ethnic identity, the nature of this identity and even the name of the ethnic group was very fluid and changeable. Perhaps most important, such identity was not connected with a particular place. Thus a term like *Croatia* refers here to the region in which the Croats were settled rather than to a nation-state in the modern sense.

Ninth- and tenth-century Russia lay outside the sphere of direct Byzantine rule, but like Serbia and Bulgaria, it came under increasingly strong Byzantine cultural and religious influence. Vikings—Scandinavian adventurers who ranged over vast stretches of ninth-century Europe seeking trade, booty, and land—had penetrated Russia from the north and imposed their rule over the Slavs inhabiting the broad river valleys connecting the Baltic Sea with the Black Sea and thence with Constantinople. Like the Bulgars in Bulgaria, the Scandinavian Vikings gradually blended into the larger Slavic population. At the end of the ninth century, one Dnieper valley chief, Oleg, established control over most of the tribes in southwestern Russia and forced peoples farther away to pay tribute. The tribal association he created formed the nucleus of Kievan Russia, named for the city that had become the commercial center of the region and is today the capital of Ukraine.

Kievan Russia and Byzantium began their relationship with war, developed it through trade agreements, and finally sustained it by religion. Around 905, Oleg launched a military expedition to Constantinople, forcing the Byzantines to pay a large indemnity and open their doors to Russian traders in exchange for peace. Although a few Christians already lived in Russia—along with Jews and probably some Muslims—the Russians' conversion to Christianity was spearheaded by a Russian ruler later in the century. The grand prince of Kiev and all Russia, Vladimir (✱c. 980–1015), and the Byzantine emperor, Basil II, agreed that Vladimir should adopt the Byzantine form of Christianity. He took the new name Basil in honor of the emperor and married the emperor's sister, Anne; then he reportedly had all the people of his state baptized in the Dnieper River.

Vladimir's conversion represented a wider pattern, not only of the Christianization of Slavic realms such as Old Moravia, Serbia, and Bulgaria but also (under the auspices of the Roman church rather than the Byzantine) of the rulers and peoples of Poland, Hungary, Denmark, and Norway. Russia's conversion to Christianity was especially significant, because Russia was geographically as close to the Islamic world as to the Christian and might conceivably have become an Islamic land. By converting to Christianity, Russians made themselves heirs to Byzantium, assuming its church, customs, art, and political ideology, although with modifications. For example, their language of worship was not Greek but Old Church Slavonic, which they readily understood. Similarly, Russian builders modeled their new churches on Byzantine forms but adapted them to indigenous needs, such as pitching roofs steeply to prevent snow from accumulating during the harsh Russian winters. Russia's adoption of Christianity linked it to the Christian world. But choosing the Byzantine rather than the Roman form of Christianity later served to isolate Russia from western Europe, because in time the Greek and Roman churches became increasingly estranged over beliefs, practices, and administration.

Russian rulers at times sought to cement relations with central and western Europe, which in turn were tied to Rome. Prince Iaroslav the Wise (✱1019–1054) forged such links through his own marriage and those of his sons and daughters to rulers and princely families in France, Hungary, Sweden, and Norway. Iaroslav encouraged intellectual and artistic developments that would connect Russian culture to the classical past. According to an account written about a half century after his death, Iaroslav

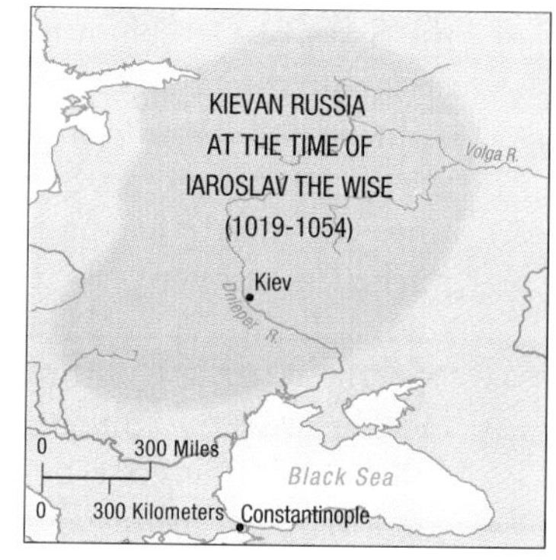

Rise of Kievan Russia at the Time of Iaroslav

> *applied himself to books and read them continually day and night. He assembled many scribes to translate from the Greek into Slavic. He caused many books to be written and collected, through which true believers are instructed and enjoy religious education.*

At his own church of St. Sophia, at Kiev, which copied the one at Constantinople, Iaroslav created a major library.

When he died, Iaroslav divided his kingdom among his sons. Civil wars broke out between the brothers and eventually between cousins, shredding what unity Russia had known. Massive invasions by outsiders, particularly from the region of the steppes (grassy plains), further weakened Kievan rulers, who were eventually displaced by princes from northern Russia. At the crossroads of East and West, Russia could meet and adopt a great variety of traditions; but its situation also opened it to unremitting military pressures.

The Rise of Independent Islamic States

The Abbasids' overthrow of the Umayyads in 750 marked the end of exclusively Arab and Syrian control over the Islamic state. From their new capital in Baghdad (still the capital of present-day Iraq), the Abbasids built an empire based largely on Persia's political traditions and Iraq's prosperous commercial and agricultural economy. With a military force to bolster their claim to represent Islam as Muhammad's successors, the Abbasids dominated the Islamic world in the eight and ninth centuries, until regional and religious discontents and loyalties eventually undermined their hegemony and led to the formation of separate states.

Fragmentation and Diversity

The Abbasid caliph Harun al-Rashid (*786–809) presided over a flourishing empire from Baghdad. (He and his court are immortalized in *Thousand and One Nights*, a classic of world literature, which is a series of anonymous stories about Scheherezade's efforts to keep her husband from killing her by telling him a story each night for 1,001 nights.) Charlemagne, Harun's contemporary, was very impressed with the elephant Harun sent him as a gift, along with monkeys, spices, and medicines. But these items were mainstays of everyday commerce in Harun's Iraq. For example, a mid-ninth-century list of imports inventoried "tigers, panthers, elephants, panther skins, rubies, white sandal, ebony, and coconuts" from India; "silk, chinaware, paper, ink, peacocks, racing horses, saddles, felts, [and] cinnamon" from China.

The Abbasid dynasty began to decline after Harun's death, mostly because of economic problems. Obliged to support a huge army and increasingly complex civil service, the Abbasids found their tax base inadequate. They needed to collect revenues from their provinces, such as Syria and Egypt, but the most powerful people within those regions often refused to send the receipts. After Harun's caliphate, ex-soldiers, seeking better salaries, recognized different caliphs and fought for power in savage civil wars. The caliphs tried to bypass the regular army, made up largely of free Muslim foot soldiers, by turning to slaves, bought and armed to serve as mounted cavalry. This expedient failed, however, and in the tenth century the caliphs became increasingly powerless; independent rulers established themselves in the various regions of the Islamic world. To support themselves militarily, many of these new rulers themselves turned to independent military commanders who led armies of Mamluks—Turkish slaves or freedmen trained as professional mounted soldiers. Mamluks were well paid to maintain their mounts and arms, and many gained renown and high positions at the courts of regional rulers. Anushtakin al-Disbari, for example, a Turk from Transoxania who was captured and sold as a slave as a youth, proved himself an able soldier and administrator and garnered an appointment as governor of Palestine and Syria, a position he held until his death in 1041.

Thus in the Islamic world, as in the Byzantine Empire, a new military elite arose. But the Muslim and Byzantine elites differed in key ways. Whereas the Byzantine *strategoi* were rooted to particular regions, the Mamluks were highly mobile. They were organized into tightly knit companies bound together by devotion to a particular general and by a strong esprit de corps. They also easily changed employers, moving from ruler to ruler for pay.

Religion also contributed to political fragmentation. In the tenth century one group of Shi'ites, calling themselves the Fatimids (after Fatimah, Muhammad's daughter and wife of Ali), began a successful political movement. Allying with the Berbers in North Africa, the Fatimids established themselves in 909 as rulers in the region now called Tunisia. The Fatimid Ubayd Allah claimed to be not only the true *imam*,* descendant of Ali, but also the *mahdi*, the "divinely guided" messiah, come to bring justice on earth. In 969 the Fatimids declared

*By this time some Shi'ite groups believed that each *imam* after Ali had designated his successor, so that at any given time a single true *imam*, even if he had no political role, held power. This "line" of *imams* was called the *imamate*; Ubayd Allah claimed to belong to it.

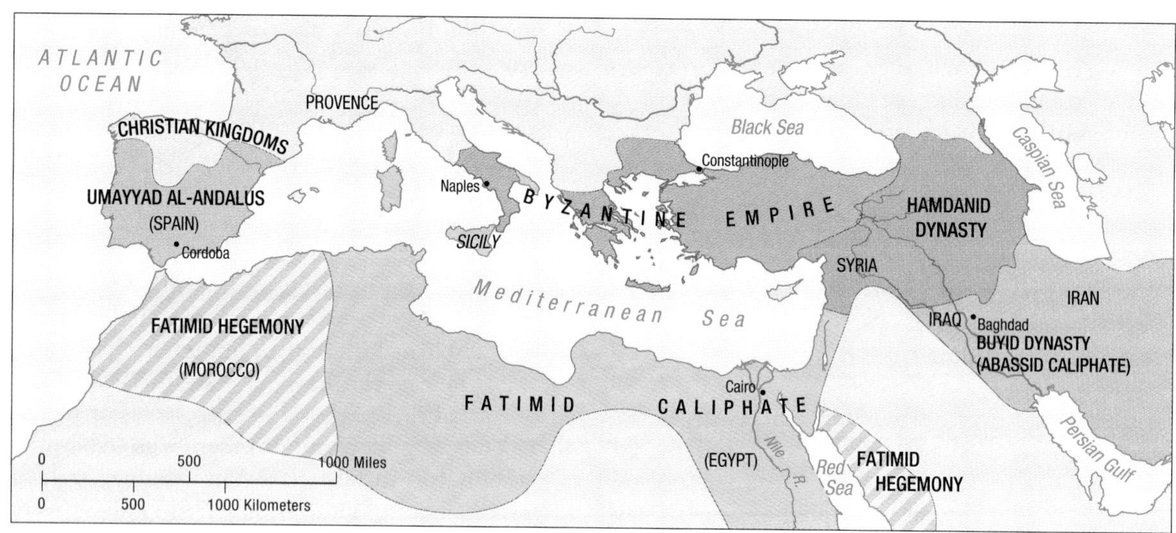

Islamic States, c. 1000

themselves rulers of Egypt. Their dynasty lasted for about two hundred years. Fatimid leaders also controlled North Africa, Arabia, and even Syria for a time. Under the Fatimids, Muslims followed Shi'ite customs and festivals, such as celebrating the day on which Muhammad was supposed to have recognized Ali as his successor. Shi'ism became predominant in much of the Islamic world until the arrival of the Sunni Seljuk Turks in the mid-eleventh century.

With the fragmentation of political and religious unity, each of the tenth- and early eleventh-century Islamic states built upon regional traditions under local rulers. Although western Europeans called all Muslims Saracens without distinction, Muslims in fact came from different regions, races, and traditions. Whereas the Shi'ites dominated Egypt, for example, Sunni Muslims ruled al-Andalus (Spain).

Unlike the other independent Islamic states, which were forged during the ninth and tenth centuries, the Spanish emirate of Cordoba (so called because its ruler took the secular title *emir*, commander, and fixed his capital at Cordoba) was created at the very start of the Abbasid caliphate. Abd al-Rahman, a member of the Umayyad family, founded the emirate. During the Abbasid revolution, he fled to Morocco, gathered an army, invaded Spain, and in 756, after only one battle, was declared emir. He and his successors ruled a broad range of peoples, including many Jews and Christians. After the initial Arab conquest of Spain, the Christians had adopted so much of the new language and so many of the customs that they were called "Mozarabs," that is, "like Arabs." The Arabs allowed them freedom of worship and let them live according to their own laws. Some Mozarabs were content with their status; others converted to Islam; still others intermarried (most commonly, Christian women married Muslim men and raised their children as Muslims). A vocal and determined minority of Christians chafed under Muslim rule. At Cordoba in about 850, some of these malcontents openly declared Muhammad "the damned and filthy prophet," courting martyrdom. About fifty Christians were executed for blasphemy before the episode ended. Strict new measures against Christians resulted.

In the tenth century, however, tensions in al-Andalus eased enormously. Under Abd al-Rahman III (912–961) who took the title caliph in 929 (three caliphates now existed: Fatimid, Abbasid, and Umayyad), members of all religious groups were given absolute freedom of worship and equal opportunity to rise in the civil service. Concurrently, Abd al-Rahman initiated important diplomatic contracts with Byzantine and European rulers. He felt strong enough not to worry much about the weak and tiny Christian kingdoms squeezed into northern Spain, between the Duero River and the Atlantic Ocean. At about the same time as the

Macedonian renaissance at Byzantium, al-Rahman and his son, al-Hakam II (*961–976), presided over a brilliant court culture, patronizing scholars, poets, and artists. The library at Cordoba contained the largest collection in Europe, and the traditions of philosophy and scholarship established there would survive many political changes and even the breakup of the Caliphate of Cordoba into *taifas* in 1031.

Commercial Unity

Although the regions of the Islamic world were diverse, they maintained a measure of unity. Their principal bond was the Arabic language. At once poetic and sacred (for it was the language of the Qur'an), Arabic was also the language of commerce and government from Baghdad to Cordoba. Moreover, despite political differences, borders were open: a craftsman could move from one place to another; a landowner in Morocco might very well own property in al-Andalus; a young man from North Africa would think nothing of going to Baghdad to find a wife; a young girl purchased as a slave in Mecca might become part of a prince's harem in Baghdad. With no national barriers to trade and few regulations (though every city and town had its own customs' dues), traders regularly dealt in far-flung, various, and often exotic goods.

Although we might expect that Islam itself was the primary reason for this internationalism, open borders extended to non-Muslims as well. For example, historians know a great deal about the Jewish community at a city near present-day Cairo, Egypt. The Jews who lived there left all their writings, including many notes and shopping lists, in a depository (*geniza*) of their synagogue. The *geniza* preserved these documents for burial. Originally only writings that contained the name of God were buried, but soon anything written in Hebrew was placed in the *geniza*. By chance, the materials in the Cairo *geniza* were preserved, and they show us the world of the Mediterranean between the tenth and the thirteenth centuries more vividly than any other single set of documents. Above all, they reveal a cosmopolitan middle-class society, occupied with trade, schooling, marriages, divorces, poetry, litigation—the issues and activities of everyday life. For example, some of these documents show us that middle-class Jewish women disposed of their own property and that widows often reared and educated their children on their own.

The Tustari brothers, Jewish merchants from southern Iran whose lives are illuminated by the *geniza* documents, typified the commercial activity in the Arabic-speaking world. By 1026 they had established a flourishing business in Egypt. Although the Tustaris did not have "branch offices," informal contacts allowed them many of the same advantages and much flexibility: friends and family in Iran shipped them fine textiles to sell in Egypt, and the Tustaris exported Egyptian fabrics to sell in Iran. Dealing in fabric could yield fabulous wealth, for

Jews Under Muslim Rule
This letter, written c. 1000 in Hebrew, ended up among the geniza *documents near Cairo. It illustrates the far-flung connections of Jewish merchants: the writer, who lived in Tunisia, writes to an acquaintance in Egypt about business matters in Spain.*

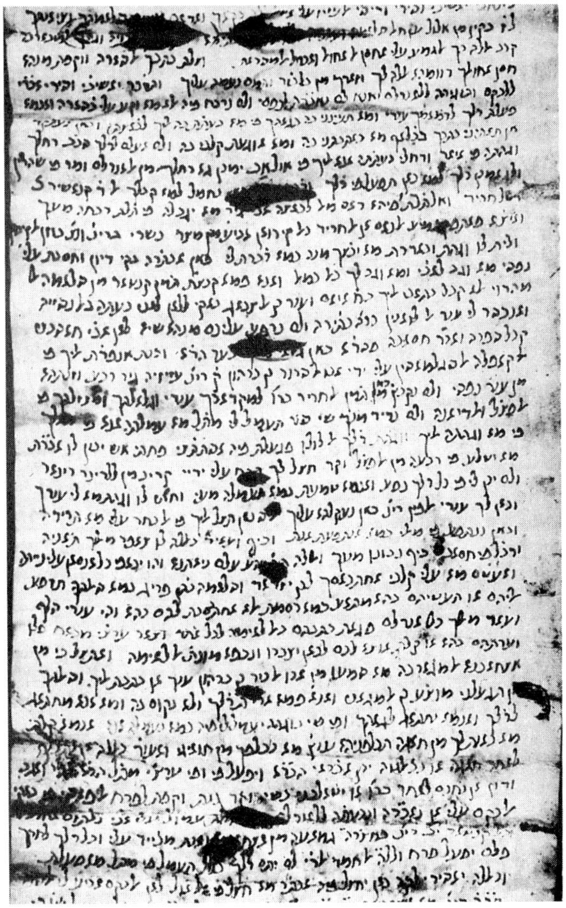

cloth was essential not only for clothing but also for home decoration: textiles covered walls; curtains separated rooms. The Tustari brothers held the very highest rank in Jewish society and had contacts with Muslim rulers. The son of one of the brothers converted to Islam and became *vizier* (chief minister) to the Fatimids in Egypt. But the sophisticated Islamic society of the tenth and eleventh centuries supported networks even more vast than those represented by the Tustari family. Muslim merchants brought tin from England; salt and gold from Timbuktu; amber, gold, and copper from Russia; and slaves from every region.

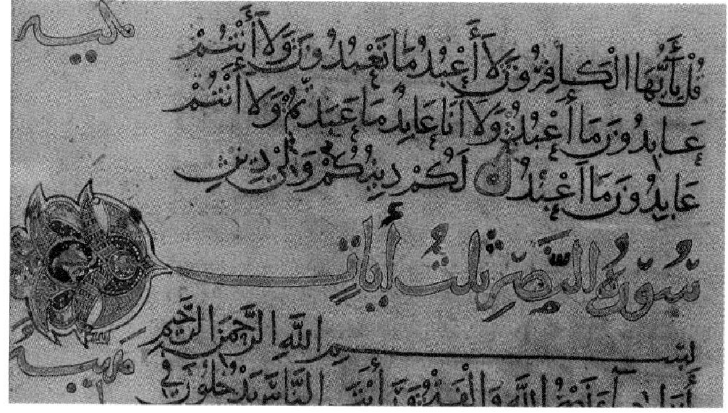

Arabic Calligraphy
This page from the Qur'an was copied by Ibn al-Bawwab, who helped develop a new form of Arabic cursive called naskhi *script around 1000.*

The Islamic Renaissance

Just as cosmopolitan as the merchants were the many scholars, both Jewish and Muslim, who traveled from Baghdad to Cordoba in search of learning or in hopes of teaching or other employment. Unlike the Macedonian renaissance of Byzantium, which was concentrated in Constantinople, a "Renaissance of Islam" occurred throughout the Islamic world. It was particularly dazzling in such urban court centers as Cordoba. Rather than hindering cultural activity, the dissolution of the caliphate into separate political entities multiplied the centers of learning and intellectual productivity.

Already in the eighth century, the Abbasid caliphs endowed research libraries and set up centers for translation where scholars culled the writings of the ancients, including the classics of Persia, India, and Greece. Scholars read, translated, and commented on the works of neo-Platonists and Aristotle. They imported texts from India, in which (around the mid-ninth century) an Arabic intellectual discovered Hindu numerical notation. Arab mathematicians realized the remarkable potential of these numbers: they added the zero and contributed significantly to algebraic theory (from the Arabic *al-jabr,* meaning "reunification"). Al-Khwarizmi wrote his famous book on equation theory in about 825. Other scholars, such as Alhazen (c. 1000), wrote further studies on cubic and quadratic equations. No wonder the numbers 1, 2, 3, and so on were known as "Arabic numerals" when they were introduced into western Europe in the twelfth century.

The newly independent Islamic rulers supported science as well as mathematics. Unusual because she was a woman was al-Asturlabi, who followed her father's profession as a maker of astrolabes (which measured the altitude of the sun and stars in order to calculate time and latitude) for the court at Syria. More typical were men like Ibn Sina (980–1037), known in the West as Avicenna, who wrote books on logic, the natural sciences, and physics. His *Canon of Medicine* systematized earlier treatises and reconciled them with his own experience as a physician. Active in the centers of power, he served as vizier to various rulers. In his autobiography he spoke with pleasure and pride about his intellectual development:

> *One day I asked permission [of the ruler] to go into [his doctors'] library, look at their books, and read the medical ones. He gave me permission, and I went into a palace of many rooms, each with trunks full of books, back-to-back. In one room there were books on Arabic and poetry, in another books on jurisprudence, and similarly in each room books on a single subject. I read the catalogue of books of the ancients and asked for those I needed. . . . When I reached the age of eighteen, I had completed the study of all these sciences.*

Ibn Sina's words reveal the importance of Arabic literature and Islamic law, even for a physician. Islamic governments put special emphasis on patronizing religious writings. *Hadith* or "tradition" literature, which recorded the sayings or actions of Muhammad as transmitted by a chain of informants, achieved its authoritative form in the ninth and tenth centuries.

In contrast to Byzantine scholars, whose work focused primarily on enhancing the prestige of the ruling classes, Islamic scholars had more pragmatic goals—to be physicians to the rich, teachers to the young, and contributors to passionate religious debates. They generally wrote "working manuscripts" rather than elegantly illuminated texts, and they used paper—relatively cheap sheets made of wood pulp and imported from China—rather than the expensive parchment that kept manuscripts in Byzantium and Europe out of the hands of all but the very rich.* Arabic manuscripts were made beautiful, however, by the further development of calligraphy in the so-called *naskhi* script.

*Parchment is made from animal skin.

The Creation and Division of a New Western Empire

Byzantium, the Islamic world, and Europe in the eighth and early ninth centuries all had monarchical governments, but this characteristic was one of the few they shared. In what is today western Europe, the Carolingians elaborated an exalted ideal of anointed kingship, but they exerted their power at the local level unevenly. They depended largely on the personal loyalties of their bishops, governors, and military men (counts, margraves, and—a title given out sparingly—dukes). These governors and other powerful men eventually began to go their own way, building castles, collecting public dues, hearing court cases without royal supervision; in effect, they carved out independent principalities. Like the king, these new rulers relied on personal loyalties, forming bonds of fealty (fidelity, trust, and service) with their vassals, who served them as armed and mounted warriors. The resulting system of decentralized loyalties is often called feudalism.

Public Power and Private Relationships

The Carolingian rulers maintained their political power in part through kin networks and personal alliances. Their sons served as semiautonomous rulers of subkingdoms, their daughters married powerful nobles in the kingdom. Personal alliances were forged with vassals and *fideles* (literally, "faithful men"), with whom they had a relationship of mutual trust and interdependency. Their counts were *fideles* to whom the kings entrusted the public functions—holding courts, collecting dues, calling local freemen to arms—in the various regions of their realm. In addition to a share in the revenues of the county, the counts received benefices, later also called fiefs (pronounced "feefs"), which were temporary grants of land given in return for service. These short-term arrangements often became permanent, however, once a count's son inherited the job and the fiefs of his father. By the end of the ninth century, fiefs were often property that could be passed on to heirs.

From the middle Latin word for fief comes the word *feudal*, and historians often call the social and economic system created by the relationship between vassals, lords, and fiefs *feudalism*.* Medieval feudalism included the institutions created by the personal bonds between lords and vassals; the military style of life and values they shared; the small, local regions they dominated; and the economic system based on manors and dependent serfs that buttressed them. In the course of the ninth and tenth centuries, more and more members of the upper classes became part of feudalism, as vassals pledged themselves to a lord and lords tied themselves to vassals. By the eleventh century many members of the upper military classes considered these relationships ideal, and they were celebrated in poetry, defined in learned treatises, and described by observant chroniclers.

The chroniclers made clear that becoming the vassal of a lord often involved both ritual gestures and verbal promises. Witnessed by others, the vassal-to-be knelt and, placing his hands between

*The term *feudalism* has had (and continues to have) many different meanings. In France in the eighteenth century, it meant the system of privilege nobles enjoyed and the condition of unfree dependency serfs (peasants) suffered on the great estates they farmed for the nobility. In the nineteenth century, Karl Marx used *feudalism* to refer to a system dominated by a military ruling class of property owners. Many historians in England continue to use this definition. More recently, however, some historians have tried to differentiate between *manorialism*, involving serfs and landlords, and *feudalism*, involving only members of the upper classes. Still other historians find the term *feudalism* useless, precisely because it has so many different meanings.

the hands of his lord, said, "I promise to be your man." This act, known as homage, was followed by the promise of fealty, which the vassal swore with his hand on relics or a Bible. Then the vassal and the lord kissed. In an age in which many people could not read, a public ceremony like this represented a visual and verbal contract. Vassalage bound the lord and vassal to one another with reciprocal obligations: they would help, not harm, one another. The lord would provide food, clothing, and perhaps a fief for the vassal. The vassal would fight for his lord and counsel him.

Carolingian Warfare and Imperial Power, 750–850

This sort of feudalism was only just beginning in the time of the early Carolingian kings. The power of these kings rested on the prestige of their office, their inheritance of Merovingian administrative traditions, their alliance with the papacy and other churchmen, their ability to expand their kin networks through marriage, and their success at war, from which they gained land and plunder to distribute to their followers, whether vassals or not.

The most famous Carolingian king was Charles (*768–814). He was called "the Great" ("le Magne" in Old French) by his contemporaries, and epic poems portrayed Charlemagne as a just, brave, wise, and warlike king. In a biography written by Einhard, his friend and younger contemporary, and patterned closely upon Suetonius's *Lives of the Caesars*, Charlemagne was the very model of a Roman emperor. Other scholars at his court described him as another David, the anointed Old Testament king. Modern historians are less dazzled than his contemporaries were, knowing that even before Charlemagne's death Carolingian power had begun to wane. Nevertheless, Charlemagne's vision—an empire that would unite the martial and learned traditions of the Roman and Germanic worlds with the legacy of Christianity—remained a European goal long after Charlemagne and his dynasty had turned to dust. His vision lay at the core of his own political activity, his building programs, and his active support of scholarship and education.

Becoming sole ruler of the Franks after the death of his brother, Carloman, in 771, Charlemagne spent the early years of his reign conquering lands in all directions and subjugating the conquered peoples. In 773 he moved south and invaded Italy, seizing the crown of the Lombard kings and claiming northern Italy. Affirming the popes' rights to rule the region around Rome, Charlemagne nevertheless retained the title given to his father: *patrician* (a nebulous term at the time, meaning something like "protector") of the Romans. He then moved northward and began a long and difficult war against the Germanic Saxons, concluded only after over thirty years of fighting, during which he forcibly annexed Saxon territory and converted the Saxon people to Christianity. To the southeast Charlemagne waged a campaign against the Avars, the people who had fought the Byzantines almost two centuries before. His biographer Einhard exulted, "all the money and treasure that had been years amassing was seized, and no war in which the Franks have ever engaged within the memory of man brought them such riches and such booty." To the southwest Charlemagne led an expedition to Spain. Although suffering a notable but local defeat at Roncesvalles in 778, he did set up a *march*, or military buffer region, between al-Andalus and his own realm.

By the 790s Charlemagne's kingdom stretched eastward to the Saale River (today in eastern Germany), southeast to what is today Austria, and south to Spain and Italy. Such hegemony in the West was unheard of since the time of the Roman Empire. Flushed with success, Charlemagne began to act according to the old Roman model by sponsoring building programs to symbolize his authority, standardizing weights and measures, and acting as a patron of intellectual and artistic efforts. He built a capital city at Aachen, complete with a church patterned on one built by Justinian at Ravenna. He even dismantled the columns, mosaics, and marble from the church at Ravenna and carted them northward to use in constructing his new church. He initiated a revival of Christian and classical learning. To discourage corruption, Charlemagne appointed special officials, called *missi dominici* (meaning "those sent out by the lord king"), to oversee the counts on the king's behalf. These men, chosen from the same aristocratic class as bishops and counts, traveled in pairs to make a circuit of regions of the kingdom. As one of Charlemagne's capitularies (summaries of royal

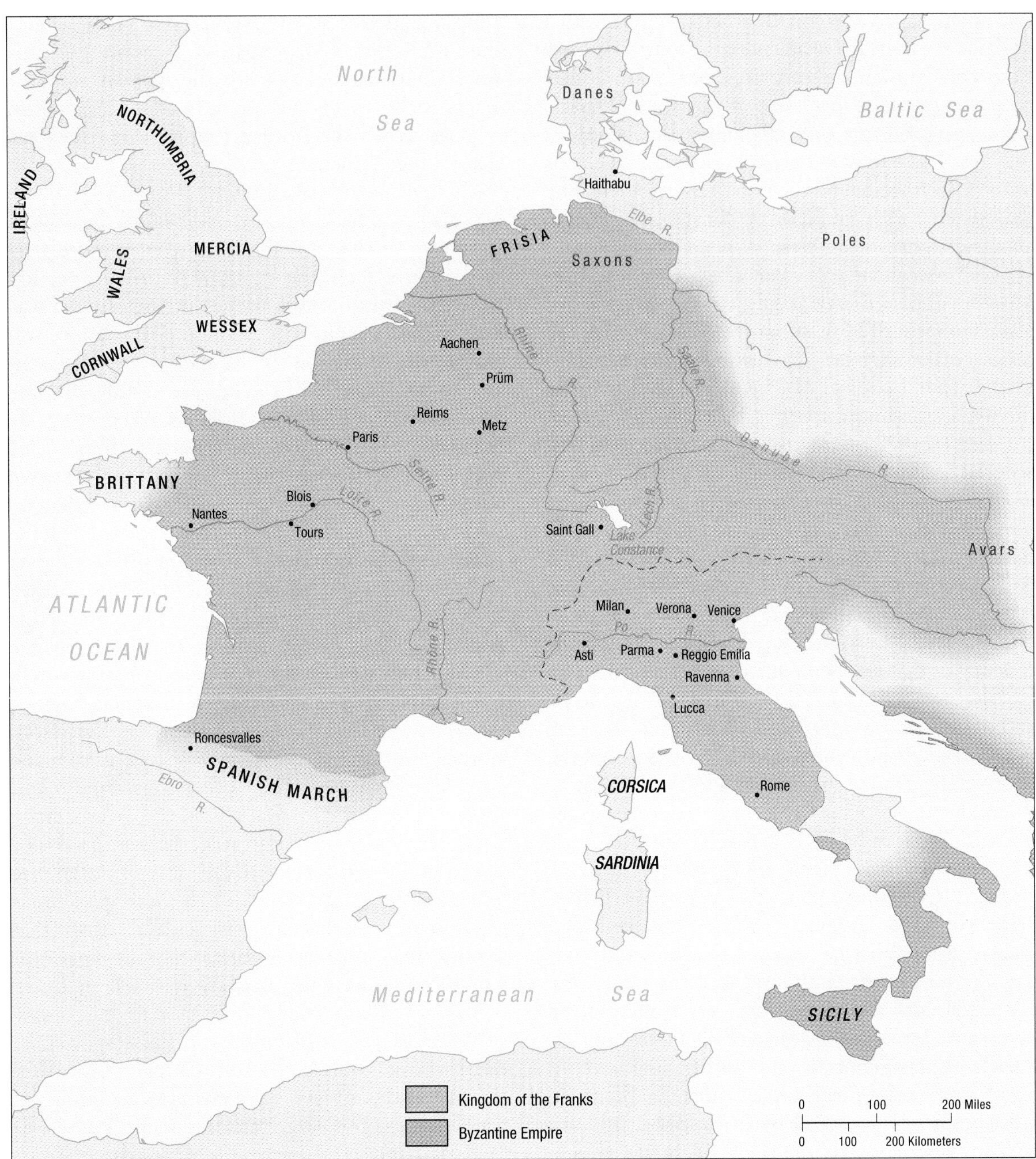

Charlemagne's Empire

decisions) put it, the *missi* "are to make diligent inquiry wherever people claim that someone has done them an injustice, so that the *missi* fully carry out the law and do justice for everyone everywhere, whether in the holy churches of God or among the poor, orphans, or widows."

While Charlemagne was busy imitating Roman emperors through his conquests, his building programs, his legislation, and his efforts at church reform, the papacy was beginning to claim imperial power for itself. At some point, perhaps in the mid-750s, members of the papal chancery forged a document, called the Donation of Constantine, that declared the pope the recipient of the fourth-century Emperor Constantine's crown, cloak, and military rank along with "all provinces, palaces, and districts of the city of Rome and Italy and of the regions of the West." The tension between the imperial claims of the Carolingians and the pope was heightened by the existence of an emperor at Constantinople who also had rights in the West. A pope like Hadrian I (*772–795) maintained a balance between these three powers, urging Charlemagne to recognize papal claims to most of Italy, supporting Charlemagne in turn in other affairs, and assenting to the decisions of the second council of Nicea, presided over by the Byzantine empress Irene. But Hadrian's successor, Leo III (*795–816), tipped the balance. In 799, accused of adultery and perjury by a faction of the Roman aristocracy, Leo narrowly escaped being blinded and having his tongue cut out. He fled northward to Charlemagne, who had him escorted back to Rome under royal protection and who arrived there himself in late November 800 to an imperial welcome orchestrated by Leo. On Christmas day of that year, Leo put an imperial crown on Charlemagne's head and the "Romans"—the clergy and nobles who were present—acclaimed the king Augustus. The pope hoped in this way to exalt the king of the Franks, to downgrade the Byzantine ruler, and to enjoy the role of "emperor maker" himself.

About twenty years later, when Einhard wrote about this coronation, he said that the titles of "emperor" and "Augustus" at first so displeased Charlemagne "that he declared that he would not have set foot in the church the day that they were conferred, although it was a great feastday, if he could have foreseen the design of the Pope." In fact, Charlemagne did not use any title but king for over a year afterward. But it is unlikely that Charlemagne was completely surprised by the imperial title; his advisors certainly had been thinking about claiming it. He might have hesitated because he feared the reaction of the Byzantine empress, as Einhard went on to suggest, or he might well have objected to the papal role in his crowning rather than to the crown itself. When he finally did call himself emperor, after establishing a peace with Empress Irene, he used a long and revealing title: "Charles, the most serene Augustus, crowned by God, great and peaceful Emperor who governs the Roman Empire and who is, by the mercy of God, king of the Franks and the Lombards." According to this title, Charlemagne was not the Roman emperor crowned by the pope but rather God's emperor, who governed the Roman Empire along with his many other duties.

Charlemagne's son, Louis the Pious (*814–840), was also crowned emperor, and he took his role as guarantor of the Christian empire even more seriously. He brought the monastic reformer Benedict of Aniane to court and, harnessing his authority as king, issued a capitulary in 817 imposing a uniform way of life (based on the Rule of St. Benedict) on all the monasteries of the empire. Although some monasteries opposed this legislation, and in the years that followed the king was unable to impose his will directly, this moment marked the effective adoption of the Benedictine rule as the monastic standard in the West. Louis also standardized the practices of his notaries, who issued his documents and privileges, and he continued to use *missi* to see that justice was done in the various parts of his realm.

In a new development of the coronation ritual, Louis's first wife, Ermengard, was crowned Augusta by the pope in 816. In 817 their firstborn son, Lothar, was given the title emperor and made co-ruler with Louis. Their other sons, Pippin and Louis (later called "the German"), were made subkings under imperial rule. Louis the Pious hoped in this way to ensure the unity of the empire while satisfying the claims of all his sons. Should any son die, only his firstborn could accede to that throne, thus preventing further splintering. But Louis's hopes were thwarted by events. Ermengard died, and Louis married Judith, the daughter of one of the most powerful families in the kingdom. In 823 she and Louis had a son, Charles. Thereafter the provisions of 817 were changed a number of times to accommodate Charles (later known as "Charles the Bald," the king to whose court Dhuoda's son William was sent). The sons of Ermengard, bitterly discontented, rebelled against their father and fought one another. A chronicle written during the period suggests that nearly every year was filled with family tragedies:

> *[For 830] Pippin, who had with him a large proportion of the people, with Lothar's consent took away from the Emperor [Louis] his royal*

Ancestry and Progeny of Louis the Pious

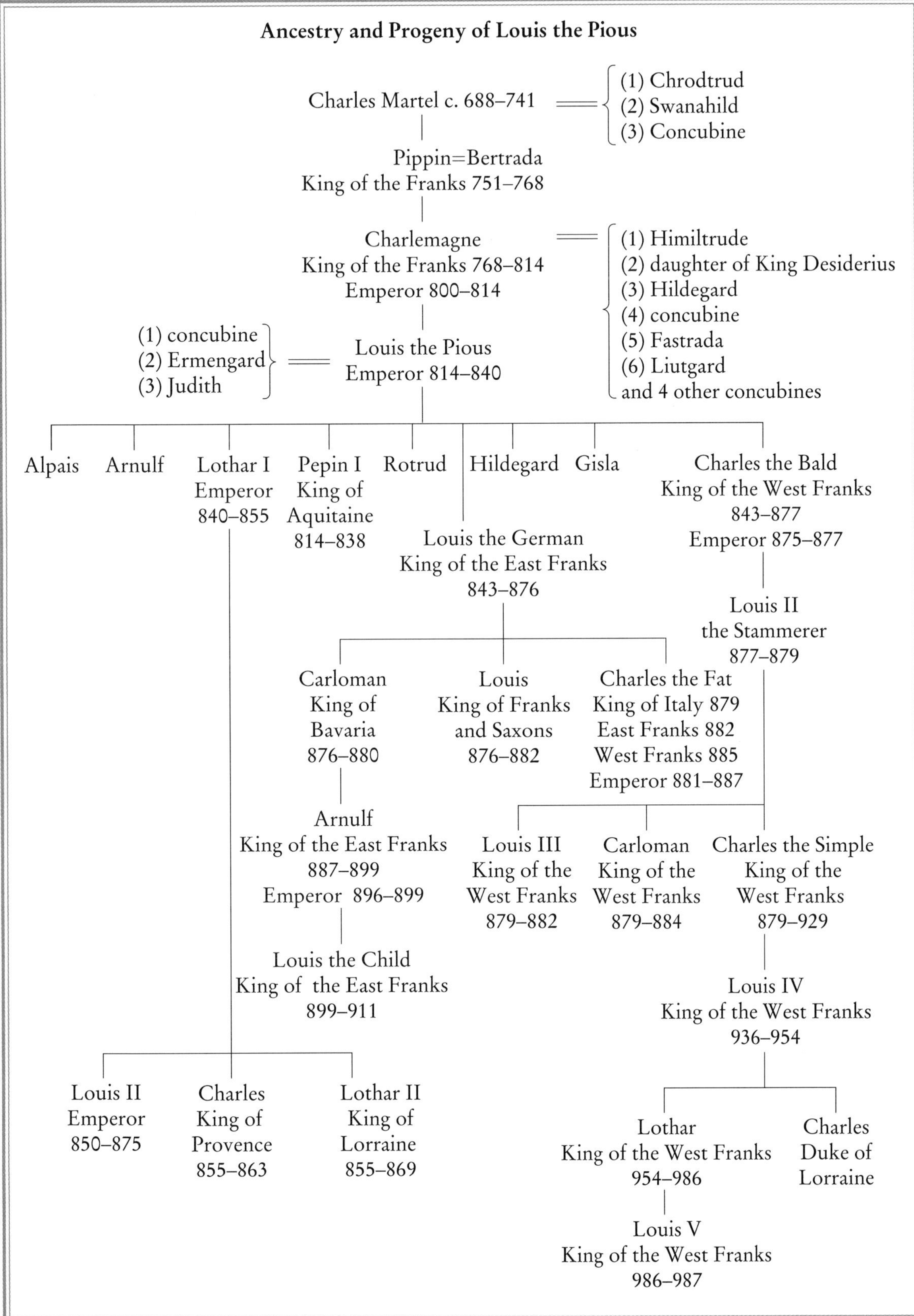
Charles Martel c. 688–741
(1) Chrodtrud
(2) Swanahild
(3) Concubine
Pippin=Bertrada
King of the Franks 751–768
Charlemagne
King of the Franks 768–814
Emperor 800–814
(1) Himiltrude
(2) daughter of King Desiderius
(3) Hildegard
(4) concubine
(5) Fastrada
(6) Liutgard
and 4 other concubines
(1) concubine
(2) Ermengard
(3) Judith
Louis the Pious
Emperor 814–840
Alpais
Arnulf
Lothar I
Emperor
840–855
Pepin I
King of
Aquitaine
814–838
Rotrud
Hildegard
Gisla
Charles the Bald
King of the West Franks
843–877
Emperor 875–877
Louis the German
King of the East Franks
843–876
Louis II
the Stammerer
877–879
Carloman
King of
Bavaria
876–880
Louis
King of Franks
and Saxons
876–882
Charles the Fat
King of Italy 879
East Franks 882
West Franks 885
Emperor 881–887
Arnulf
King of the East Franks
887–899
Emperor 896–899
Louis III
King of the
West Franks
879–882
Carloman
King of the
West Franks
879–884
Charles the Simple
King of the
West Franks
879–929
Louis the Child
King of the East Franks
899–911
Louis IV
King of the West Franks
936–954
Louis II
Emperor
850–875
Charles
King of
Provence
855–863
Lothar II
King of
Lorraine
855–869
Lothar
King of the West Franks
954–986
Charles
Duke of
Lorraine
Louis V
King of the West Franks
986–987

power, and also his wife [Judith] whom they veiled and sent to the convent of St-Radegund at Poitiers. [Louis regained control of the situation, however.] [For 833] [Louis] had not been staying [at Aachen] for many days when news arrived that his sons had again got together in an alliance to revolt against him and were aiming to attack with a large force of his enemies. . . . Lothar came from Italy bringing Pope Gregory with him, Pippin from Aquitaine, and Louis from Bavaria with a very large number of men. [This time Louis was imprisoned. He was released by his sons Louis the German and Pippin, who now joined against their brother Lothar.]

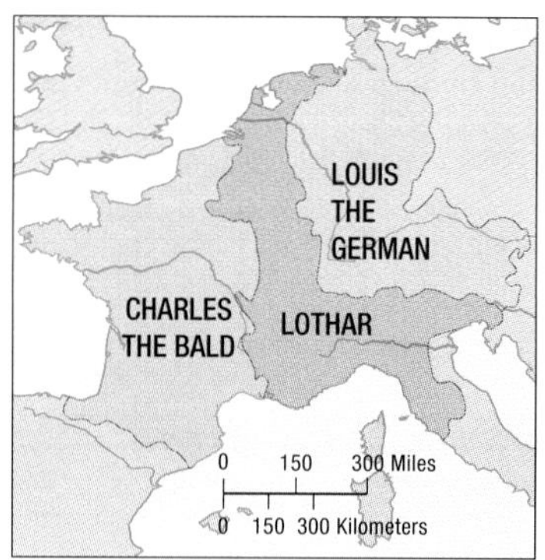

Treaty of Verdun

Family battles such as these continued, both during Louis's lifetime and, with great vigor, after his death. In 843, with the Treaty of Verdun, the three remaining brothers (Pippin had died in 838) finally arrived at an arrangement that would roughly describe the future political contours of western Europe. The western third, bequeathed to Charles the Bald (✶843–877), would eventually become France; the eastern third, handed to Louis the German (✶843–876), would become Germany. The "Middle Kingdom," which was given to Lothar (✶840–855) along with the imperial title, had a different fate: parts of it were absorbed by France and Germany, and the rest eventually formed the modern states of the Netherlands, Belgium, Luxembourg, Switzerland, and Italy.

In 843 the European-wide empire of Charlemagne had dissolved. Forged by conquest, it had been supported by a small privileged aristocracy with lands and offices stretching across the whole of it. Their loyalty, based on shared values, real friendship, expectations of gain, and sometimes ties of vassalage and fealty, was crucial to the success of the Carolingians. The empire had also been supported by an ideal, shared by educated laymen and churchmen alike, of imperialism and Christian belief working together to bring good order to the earthly state. But powerful forces worked against the Carolingian empire. Once its borders were fixed and it could no longer expand, the aristocrats lost their expectation for new lands and offices. They put down roots in particular regions and began to gather local followings of *fideles* and vassals. Powerful local traditions such as different languages also undermined imperial unity. Finally, as Dhuoda revealed, some people disagreed with the imperial ideal. Asking her son to put his father before the emperor, she demonstrated her belief in the primacy of the family and the intimate and personal ties that bound it together. Dhuoda's ideal did not eliminate the emperor (European emperors would continue to reign until World War I), but it represented a new sensibility that saw real value in the breaking apart of Charlemagne's empire into smaller, more intimate, more local units.

Land and Power

The Carolingian economy contributed to both the rise and the dissolution of the Carolingian empire. At the onset its wealth came from land and plunder. After the booty from war ceased to pour in, the Carolingians still had access to money and goods. To the north, in Viking trading stations like Haithabu (today Hedeby, in northern Germany), archaeologists have found Carolingian glass and pots alongside Islamic coins and cloths, which tells us that the Carolingian economy meshed with that of the Abbasid caliphate. Silver from the Islamic world probably came north up the Volga River through Russia to the Baltic Sea. There the coins were melted down, the silver traded to the Carolingians in return for wine, jugs, glasses, and other manufactured goods. The Carolingians turned the silver into coins of their own, to be used throughout the empire for small-scale local trade.

Despite such far-flung networks of trade, land provided the most important source of Carolingian wealth and power. Like the landholders of the late Roman Empire and the Merovingian period, Carolingian aristocrats held many estates, scattered throughout the Frankish empire. But in the Carolingian period these estates were reorganized and their productivity carefully calculated. Modern historians often call these estates *manors*.

Typical was the manor called Villeneuve St. Georges, which belonged to the monastery of St.-Germain-des-Prés (today in Paris) in the ninth century. Villeneuve consisted of arable fields, vineyards, meadows where animals could roam, and woodland, all scattered about the countryside rather than connected in a compact unit. The land was not tilled by slave gangs, as had been the custom on great estates of the Roman Empire, but by peasant families, each one settled on its own manse, which consisted of a house, a garden, and small pieces of the arable land. They farmed the land that belonged to them and also worked the *demesne*, the very large manse of the lord (in this case the abbey of St.-Germain). These peasant farms marked a major social and economic development: the peasant household of the Carolingian period was the precursor of the modern nuclear family.

Peasants at Villeneuve practiced the most progressive sort of plowing, known as the three-field system, in which they farmed two-thirds of the arable land at one time. They planted one-third with winter wheat and one-third with summer crops, and left one-third fallow (to restore its fertility). The crops sown and the field of fallow land then rotated, so that land use was repeated only every three years. This method of organizing the land produced larger yields (because two-thirds of the land was cultivated each year) than the still prevalent two-field system, where only half of the arable land was cultivated one year, the other half the next.

All the peasants at Villeneuve were dependents of the monastery. Unlike slaves, they could not be separated from their families nor displaced from their manse; but they owed dues and services to St.-Germain. Their obligations varied enormously, depending on the status of the peasants and the manse they held. One family, for example, owed four silver coins, wine, wood, three hens, and fifteen eggs every year, and the men had to plow the fields of the demesne land. Another family owed the intensive labor of working the vineyards. One woman was required to weave cloth and feed the chickens. Peasant women spent much time at the lord's house in the *gynecaeum*—the women's workshop, where they made and dyed cloth and sewed garments—or in the kitchen, as cooks. Peasant men spent most of their time in the fields.

The Carolingian Renaissance

With the wealth coming in from trade and the profits of their estates, the Carolingians supported a revival of learning that began in the 790s and continued for about a century. Parallel in some ways to the renaissances of the Byzantine and Islamic worlds, the Carolingian renaissance revived the learning of the past. Scholars studied Roman imperial writers like Suetonius and Virgil; they read and

Adam and Eve as Carolingian Peasants
This full-page illumination from the Grandval Bible, dating from 834–843, depicts the story of Genesis. In the bottom tier, illustrating the expulsion from the Garden, Eve suckles her baby while Adam tills the soil. Like Adam, Carolingian peasants had primitive tools with which they eked out a precarious existence from the soil.

Freedom and Expressiveness in Carolingian Art
The Utrecht Psalter was made at Reims during the reign of Louis the Pious. Drawn in a sketchy, quick, lively style, each illustration corresponds to the verses of the psalms. For the thought in Vulgate Psalm 43 (in other editions 44) verse 7 depicted here, "For I will not trust in my bow; neither shall my sword save me," the artist drew a quiver filled with arrows and a sword discarded on the ground near the Psalmist, who leads a group of soldiers.

commented on the works of the church fathers; and they worked to establish complete and accurate texts. Their accomplishments helped to enhance royal glory, educate officials, reform the liturgy, and purify the faith.

The English scholar Alcuin (c. 732–804), a famous member of the circle of scholars whom Charlemagne recruited to form a center of study, brought with him the traditions of Anglo-Saxon scholarship that had been developed by men like Benedict Biscop and Bede. Invited to Aachen, Alcuin became Charlemagne's chief advisor, writing letters on the king's behalf, counseling him on royal policy, and tutoring the king's household, including the women. Charlemagne's sister and daughter, for example, often asked Alcuin to explain passages from the Gospel to them. Charlemagne entrusted Alcuin with the task of preparing an improved edition of the Vulgate (the Latin Bible).

Scholarship complemented the alliance between the church and the king symbolized by Charlemagne's anointment. In the Carolingian age, distinctions between politics and religion were meaningless: kings considered themselves appointed by the grace of God, often based their capitularies on Biblical passages, involved themselves in church reform, appointed churchmen on their own initiative, and believed their personal piety a source of power.

Just as in the Byzantine renaissance, artists often illuminated Carolingian texts using classical or patristic models. To these models Carolingian artists added exuberant decoration and design, often rendering architectural elements as bands of color and portraying human figures with great liveliness and verve. Greek pictorial models came from Byzantium, and perhaps some Carolingian artists themselves came originally from Greece, refugees from Byzantium during its iconoclastic period. Other pictorial models, from Italy, provided the kings' artists with examples of the sturdy style of the late Roman Empire. In turn, Carolingian art became a model for later illuminators. The Utrecht Psalter, for example, made at Reims in about 820, was copied by artists in eleventh-century England.

The Carolingian program was ambitious and lasting, even after the Carolingian dynasty had faded to a memory. The work of locating, understanding, and transmitting models of the past continued in a number of monastic schools. In the materials they studied, the questions they asked, and the answers they suggested, the Carolingians offered a mode of inquiry fruitful for subsequent generations. In the twelfth century, scholars would build upon the foundations laid by the Carolingian renaissance. The very print of this textbook depends upon one achievement of the Carolingian period: modern letter fonts are based on the new letter forms, called Caroline minuscule, invented in the ninth century to standardize manuscript writing and make it more readable.

Muslim, Viking, and Magyar Invasions

Like the Roman emperors they emulated, Carolingian kings and magnates confronted new groups along their borders. The new peoples—Muslims to the south, Vikings to the north, and Magyars to the east—were feared and hated; but like the Germanic tribes that had entered the Roman Empire, they also served as military allies. As royal sons fought one another and as magnates sought to carve out their own principalities, their alliances with the newcomers helped integrate the outsiders swiftly into European politics. The impact of these foreign groups hastened, but did not cause, the dissolution of the empire.

Although Muslim armies had entered western Europe in the eighth century, the ninth-century Muslims were a different breed: they were freebooters, working independently of any caliph or other ruler. Taking advantage of Byzantium's initial weakness, in 827 they began the slow conquest of Sicily, which took nearly one hundred years. During the same century, Muslim pirates set up bases on Mediterranean islands and strongholds in Provence (today in southern France) and near Naples (today in southern Italy). Liutprand of Cremona reported on the activities of one such group:

> *[Muslim pirates from al-Andalus], disembarking under cover of night, entered the manor house unobserved and murdered—O grievous tale!—the Christian inhabitants. They then took the place as their own . . . [fortified it and] started stealthy raids on all the neighboring country. . . . Meanwhile the people of Provence close by, swayed by envy and mutual jealousy, began to cut one another's throats. . . . But inasmuch as one faction by itself was not able to satisfy upon the other the demands of jealous indignation, they called in the help of the aforesaid Saracens.*

The Muslims at this base, set up in 891, robbed, took prisoners, and collected ransoms. But they were so useful to their feuding Christian neighbors that they were not ousted until 972, when they caused a scandal by capturing the holiest man of his era, Abbot Maieul of Cluny. Only then did the count of Provence launch a successful attack against their lair.

The Vikings came from the north, from Scandinavian lands that would eventually become Denmark, Norway, and Sweden. They shared the same language, and to their victims they were all one: the Franks called them Northmen; the English called them Danes. They were, in fact, much less united than their southern contemporaries thought. When they began voyages at the end of the eighth century, they did so in independent bands. Merchants and pirates at the same time, Vikings followed a chief, seeking profit, prestige, and land. Many traveled as families: husbands, wives, children, and slaves.

The Vikings perfected the art of navigation. In their longships they crossed the Atlantic, settling Iceland and Greenland and (about A.D. 1000) landing on the coast of North America. Eastward, they voyaged through watercourses and portaged to the Volga River or the Dnieper, eventually seizing Kiev and creating the first Russian state. Other Viking bands navigated the rivers of Europe. The Vikings were pagans, and to them monasteries and churches—with their reliquaries, chalices, and crosses—were storehouses of booty. "Never before," wrote Alcuin, who experienced one attack, "has such terror appeared in Britain as we have now suffered from a pagan race. . . . Behold the church of St. Cuthbert spattered with the blood of the priests of God, despoiled of all its ornaments."

England confronted sporadic attacks by the Vikings in the 830s and 840s. By mid-century, Viking adventurers regularly spent winters there. The Vikings did not just destroy. In 876 they settled in the northeast of England, plowing the land and preparing to live on it. The region where they settled and imposed their own laws was later called the *Danelaw*.

In Wessex, the southernmost kingdom of England, King Alfred the Great (*871–899) bought

Viking Ship
Ships were the major technological reason for Viking success. A replica of the Gokstad Ship, pictured here, crossed the Atlantic in 1893 in less than a month.

Muslim, Viking, and Magyar Invasions

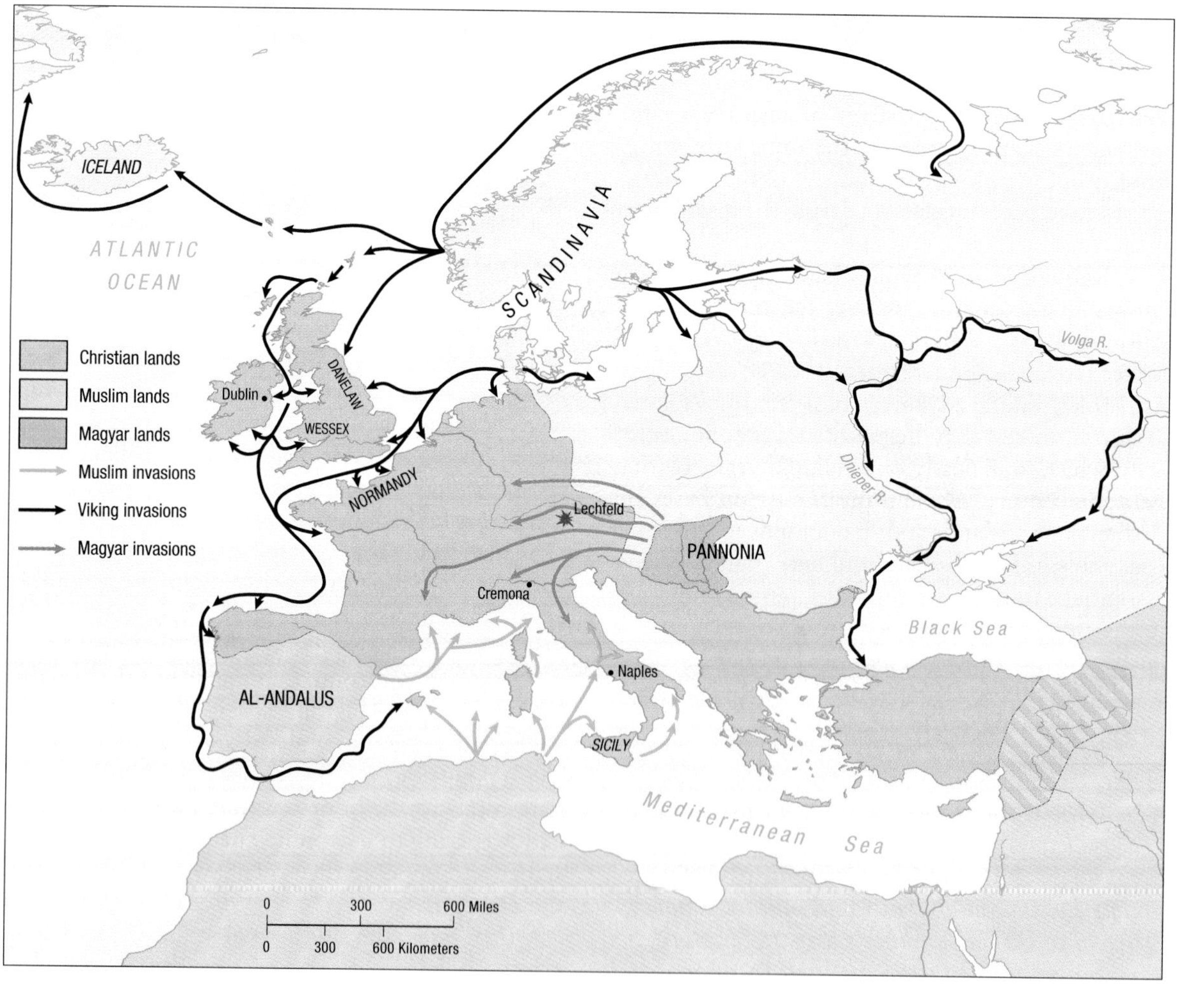

Christian lands
Muslim lands
Magyar lands
Muslim invasions
Viking invasions
Magyar invasions

ICELAND
ATLANTIC OCEAN
SCANDINAVIA
Dublin
DANELAW
WESSEX
NORMANDY
Lechfeld
PANNONIA
Cremona
Volga R.
Dnieper R.
Black Sea
AL-ANDALUS
Naples
SICILY
Mediterranean Sea
0 300 600 Miles
0 300 600 Kilometers

time and peace by paying tribute and giving hostages. Such tribute, later called *Danegeld*, was collected as a tax that eventually became the basis of a relatively lucrative taxation system in England. Then in 878, Alfred led an army that, as his biographer put it, "gained the victory through God's will. He destroyed the Vikings with great slaughter and pursued those who fled . . . hacking them down." Thereafter the pressures of invasion eased as Alfred reorganized his army, set up strongholds, and deployed new warships.

Vikings also attacked Ireland, setting up fortified bases along the coast from which they attacked and plundered churches and monasteries. But they also established Dublin as a commercial center and, in the tenth century, began to intermarry with the Irish and convert to Christianity.

On the Continent, too, the invaders set up trading emporia and settled where originally they had raided. Beginning about 850, their attacks became well-organized expeditions for regional control. At the end of the ninth century, one contingent settled in the region of France that soon took their name: Normandy, the land of the Northmen. The new inhabitants converted to Christianity during the tenth century. Rollo, the Viking leader in Normandy, accepted Christianity in 911, at the same time Normandy was formally ceded to him by the Frankish king Charles the Simple (or Straightforward).

Although most Vikings adopted the sedentary ways of much of the rest of Europe, some of their descendants continued their voyages and raids. In southern Italy the popes first fought against and then made peace with the Normans, who in the early eleventh century traveled southward from Normandy to hire themselves out as warriors. They fought for the Byzantines or the Muslims, siding with whoever paid them best.

The Magyars (or Hungarians) were latecomers to the West. Originally a nomadic people from the Asian steppes, they were pushed westward by the pressures of other steppes people. Moving into the middle Danubian plains, they helped the Franks destroy Old Moravia (c. 899) and from their bases in present-day Hungary raided far to the west. They attacked Germany, Italy, and even northern Gaul frequently between 899 and 955. Then in the summer of 955, one marauding party of Magyars was met at the Lech River by the German king Otto I, whose army decimated them. Otto's victory, his subsequent military reorganization of his eastern frontiers, and the cessation of Magyar raids around this time made Otto a great hero to his contemporaries. However, historians today think the containment of the Magyars had more to do with their internal transformation from nomads to farmers than with their military defeat.

The Emergence of Local Rule

The invasions shocked the inhabitants of western Europe, and they demonstrated the structural weaknesses of the Carolingian empire. Charlemagne's conquests had removed buffer groups, such as the Saxons and the Avars, bringing the Franks face to face with peoples used to living in mobile communities, quick to seize the opportunity to raid. As the Carolingian empire ceased to expand, the counts and other magnates stopped looking to the king for new lands and offices and began to develop and exploit what they already had. They built castles, set up markets, collected revenues, kept the peace, and began to see themselves as independent regional rulers.

The myth of the Carolingian kingdom—that it was united by one man crowned by God—never quite died. Yet by the end of the tenth century, Charlemagne's empire lay in fragments. In the region that would become France, local magnates exercised most powers of government and commerce. In Italy, bishops in the cities took over most government functions. They built fortifications around their churches and sometimes extended their power to the surrounding countryside, as happened at Asti, Parma, and Reggio Emilia by the 960s. In Germany and England, kings continued to wield power, but there, too, local lords challenged royal authority. The new rulers increased their wealth and power through improved agricultural productivity and direct control of the land and its inhabitants.

Agricultural Growth in the Post-Carolingian Age

New methods of cultivation and a growing population helped transform the rural landscape. With a growing number of men and women to work the land, the lower classes now had more mouths to feed and faced the hardship of food shortage. Landlords began reorganizing their estates to run more profitably. In the tenth century the three-field system became more prevalent; heavy plows came into wider use; and horses (more efficient than oxen) were harnessed to pull the plows. The result was surplus food and a better standard of living for nearly everyone.

In search of greater profits, some lords lightened the dues and services of peasants temporarily to allow them to open up new lands by draining marshes and cutting down forests. Some landlords converted dues and labor services into money payments, a boon for both lords and peasants. Lords gained liquidity: they now had money to spend on what they wanted rather than hens and eggs they might not need or want. Peasants benefited because their tax was fixed despite inflation. Thus, as the prices of their hens and eggs went up, they could sell them on the market, reaping a profit in spite of the dues they owed their lords.

By the tenth century many peasants lived in populous rural settlements, true villages. In the midst of a sea of arable land, meadow, wood, and wasteland, these villages developed a sense of community. Boundaries—sometimes real fortifications, sometimes simple markers—told nonresidents to keep out and to find shelter in huts located outside the village limits. The church often formed the focal point of local activity: there people met, received the sacraments, drew up contracts, buried their parents and children. Religious feasts and festivals joined the rituals of farming to mark the seasons. The church dominated the village in another way: men and women owed it a tax called a *tithe* (equivalent to a tenth of their crops or income, whether paid in money or in kind), which was first instituted on a regular basis by the Carolingians. Village peasants developed a sense of common purpose based on their practical interdependence, as they shared oxen or horses for the teams that pulled the plow or turned to village craftsmen to fix their wheels or shoe their horses. A sense of solidarity sometimes fostered banding together to ask for privileges as a group. Near Verona, Italy, for example, twenty-five men living around the castle of Nogara in 920 joined together to ask their lord, the monastery of Nonantola, to allow them to lease plots of land, houses, and pasturage there in return for a small yearly rent and the promise to defend the castle. The abbot of Nonantola granted their request.

Village solidarity could be compromised, however, by varied and conflicting loyalties and obligations. A peasant in one village might very well have one piece of land connected with a certain manor and another bit of arable field on a different estate; and he or she might owe several lords different kinds of dues. Even peasants of one village working for one lord might owe him varied services and taxes. At a manor belonging to Autun Cathedral in France, for example, Rictred and Gautier held one manse and owed two shillings in March and twelve pennies (equal to one shilling) in May, or else a pig worth the same amount; they also owed labor, which they could redeem for twelve more pennies. On the same manor, however, a church endowed with three manses owed ten shillings but no labor services; presumably the priest living there paid the dues.

Various obligations such as these were even more striking across the regions of Europe. The principal distinction was between free peasants, such as small landowners in Saxony and other parts of Germany, and unfree peasants, who were especially common in France and England. In Italy peasants ranged from small independent landowners to leaseholders (like the tenants at Nogara); most were both, owning a parcel in one place and leasing another nearby.

Post-Carolingian Territorial Lordships

As the power of kings weakened, the system of peasant obligations became part of a larger system of local rule. When landlords consolidated their power over their manors, they collected not only dues and services but also fees for the use of their flourmills, bakehouses, and breweries. Some built castles, fortified strongholds, and imposed the even wider powers of the *ban*: the rights of public power to collect taxes, hear cases, levy fines, and muster men for defense.

In France, for example, as the king's power waned, political control fell into the hands of counts and other princes. By 1000, castles had become the key to their power. In the south of France, power was so fragmented that each man who controlled a castle—a castellan—was a virtual ruler, although often with a very limited reach. In northwestern France territorial princes, basing their rule on the control of *many* castles, controlled much broader regions. For example, Fulk Nerra, Count of Anjou (987–1040), built more than thirteen castles and captured others from rival counts. By the end of his life, he controlled a region extending from Blois to Nantes along the Loire valley.

Castellans extended their authority by subjecting everyone near their castle to their ban. Peasants, whether or not they worked on a castellan's estates, had to pay him a variety of dues. Castellans also established links with the more well-off landholders in the region, tempting or coercing them to become vassals. Lay castellans often supported local monasteries and controlled the appointment of local priests. But churchmen themselves sometimes held the position of territorial lords, as, for example, the archbishop of Milan in the eleventh century.

The development of virtually independent local political units, dominated by a castle and controlled by a military elite, marks an important turning point in western Europe. Although this development did not occur everywhere simultaneously (and in some places it hardly occurred at all), the social, political, and cultural life of the West was now dominated by landowners who saw themselves as both military men and regional leaders. This phenomenon paralleled certain changes in the Byzantine and Islamic worlds; at just about the same time, the Byzantine *strategoi* were becoming a landowning elite and Muslim provincial rulers were employing Mamluk warriors. But crucial differences existed. The *strategoi* were still largely under the emperor's command, whereas Muslim dynasties were dependent on mercenaries. In contrast, castellans acted as quasi-kings; they were the lords of their vassals, whom they had kissed in token of their sworn bond of mutual service.

Warfare and a New Warrior Class

The castellans were part of a social transformation in post-Carolingian France (and elsewhere to a lesser extent) in which two classes emerged: an unfree laboring class of peasants and a free class of fighters. Naturally, many gradations existed within the warrior group. Kings still had great prestige and in some places, such as Germany, considerable power; counts and castellans had local influence, though their authority varied from place to place. Other nobles included local magnates, who might be both vassals of more powerful lords and lords of less powerful vassals. Knights were considered members of the nobility in some regions and warriors of lower status in others.

Warfare was the occupation of most noblemen and knights, who fought one another for honor, power, land, and the profits of control. But battles affected more than the elite fighting forces, as Raoul Glaber, an eleventh-century monk, observed in his account of the battle of Nouy (1044). The battle pitted the son of Fulk of Anjou, Geoffrey Martel, against the sons of Count Odo II of Blois over control of the city of Tours, which had been part of Odo's territory:

> *[Geoffrey] had gathered a great army and had been besieging the city for more than a year when the two sons of Odo came against him in force, meaning to fight in order to aid the beleaguered and starving city. When Geoffrey realized this, he prayed for the aid of St. Martin, promising to restore to this holy martyr, and indeed all other saints, any property of theirs which he had stolen. Then he took his standard, attached it to his lance, and marched out against his enemies with a great force of cavalry and infantry. When the two armies came close fear so struck the troops of the two brothers that they were all unable to fight. There is no doubt at all that victory over his enemies went to the man who had piously invoked the aid of St. Martin. . . . It is true that the sons of Odo had robbed the poor of St. Martin in order to supplement the pay of their troops.*

At Nouy the elite fighters, armed and mounted on horses, composed the cavalry. Subordinate to them were the foot soldiers, neither nobles nor knights but rather men compelled to go to war under Geoffrey's ban. The unhappy citizens of Tours were harassed by both sides, subjected to Geoffrey's siege and Odo's sons' robbery. Still another group suffered from these warriors: the peasants and clergy concerned with the "property of St. Martin" and other saints, which Geoffrey had plundered.

Most knights lived in the households of their lord, unmarried, hoping eventually to earn a fief

Patrilineal "Family Portrait"
In the twelfth century, Siboto, count of Falkenstein (in southern Germany), drew up a "family portrait" reflecting the new patrilineal mode: his daughters were literally "not in the picture." But Siboto's wife was included, and their first-born son was named after Siboto's maternal grandfather. Thus the transition to the patrilineal model did not deny a place to women altogether.

from their lord, then find a wife, father a family, and become lords themselves. No matter how old they might be, these unmarried men were called "youths" by their contemporaries. Such perpetual bachelors were something new, the result of a profound transformation in the organization of families and inheritance. Before about 1000, noble families had recognized all their children as heirs and had divided their estates accordingly. In the mid-ninth century, Count Everard and his wife, for example, willed their large estates, scattered from Belgium to Italy, to their four sons and three daughters (although they gave the boys far more than the girls, and the oldest boy far more than the others). By the end of the tenth century, however, adapting to diminished opportunities for land and office and wary of fragmenting the estates they had, French nobles changed both their conception of their family and the way its property passed to the next generation. Recognizing the overriding claims of one son, often the eldest, they handed down their entire inheritance to him. The heir, in turn, traced his lineage only through the male line, backward through his father and forward through his own eldest son. Such patrilineal families (tracing their bloodline only through the father and one of his sons) left many younger sons without an inheritance and therefore without the prospect of marrying and founding a family; instead they lived at the courts of the great as "youths," or they join the church as clerics or monks. The development of territorial rule and patrilineal families went hand in hand, as fathers passed down to one son undiminished not only manors but titles, castles, and the authority of the ban.

Patrilineal inheritance tended to bypass daughters and so worked against aristocratic women, who lost the power that came with inherited wealth. In families without sons, however, widows and daughters did inherit property; but land given out as a fief, normally for military service, was not usually given to a woman. Thus a major source of control over land, people, and revenues was denied to them. Yet women played an important role in this warrior society. A woman who survived childbirth and the death of her husband could marry again and again, becoming a peace broker as she forged alliances between great families and powerful "lords" on behalf of her younger sons. In the early eleventh century, for example, Agnes, the daughter of a count, first married the duke of Aquitaine, and after his death married Geoffrey Martel, count of Anjou. When her first husband died, her sons were still young, and she wielded ducal powers in Aquitaine and disposed of property there in her own name. In some areas women could carry out military service by using a male proxy. And wives often acted as lords of estates when their husbands were at war.

The Containment of Violence

Constant warfare benefited territorial rulers in the short term, but in the long run their revenues suffered as armies plundered the countryside and sacked the walled cities. Bishops, who were themselves from the class of lords and warriors, worried about the dangers to church property. Peasants cried out against wars that destroyed their crops or forced them to join regional infantries. Monks and religious thinkers were appalled at violence that was not in the service of an anointed king. By the end of the tenth century, all classes clamored for peace.

Beginning in the south of France, sentiment against local violence was harnessed in a movement called the Peace of God. At meetings of bishops, counts, and lords, and often crowds of lower-class men and women, proclamations setting forth the provisions of this Peace were issued: "No man in the counties or bishoprics shall seize a horse, colt, ox, cow, ass, or the burdens which it carries. . . . No one shall seize a peasant, man or woman," ran the decree of one council held in 990. Anyone who violated this peace was to be excommunicated: cut off from the community of the faithful, denied the services of the church and the hope of salvation.

The peace proclaimed at local councils like this limited some violence but did not address the problem of conflict between armed men. A second set of agreements, the Truce of God, soon supplemented the Peace of God. The truce prohibited fighting between warriors at certain times: on Sunday because it was the Lord's day; on Saturday because it was a reminder of Holy Saturday; on Friday because it symbolized Good Friday; and, finally, on Thursday because it stood for Holy Thursday. Enforcement of the truce fell to the local knights and nobles, who swore over saints' relics to uphold it and to fight anyone who broke it.

The Peace of God and Truce of God were only two of the mechanisms by which violent confrontations were contained or defused in the tenth and eleventh centuries. At times, lords and their vassals mediated wars and feuds in assemblies sometimes called feudal courts. In other instances, monks or laymen tried to find solutions to disputes that would leave the honor of both parties intact. Rather than try to establish guilt or innocence, winners or losers, these methods of adjudication often resulted in compromises on both sides. When a woman named Eve and the monastery of Cluny contested the ownership of a piece of property, both sides won: Cluny got the property; but Eve received money, a special place in the monks' prayers, and a burial plot in Cluny's cemetery.

Life in the early Middle Ages did not become less contentious because of these expedients, but the attempts to contain violence did affect society. Some aggressiveness was channeled into the church-sanctioned militias mandated by the Truce of God. At other times, disputes prodded neighbors to readjust their relationships and become friends. Churchmen made the rituals of swearing to uphold the peace part of church ceremony, the oaths backed by the power of the saints. In this way any bloodshed involved in apprehending those who violated the peace was made holy. Geoffrey Martel sought to sanctify his own violence by placating St. Martin when he battled for Tours; Raoul Glaber, who reported the incident, thought Geoffrey had succeeded and his victory was the manifestation of St. Martin's power.

The Cities of Italy: An Urban Localism

Northern Italy had also been part of the Carolingian empire, and local rule was as much a feature there as in post-Carolingian France. But in Italy, power was exercised from the cities. The urban centers of the Roman Empire had never quite disappeared, and in the tenth century many great landlords who in France would have built their castles in the countryside instead constructed their family seats within the walls of cities like Milan and Lucca. Churches, as many as fifty or sixty, were built within the city walls, the proud work of rich laymen and women or of bishops. From their perch within the cities, the great landholders, both lay and clerical, denominated the countryside.

Italian cities also functioned as important marketplaces. Peasants sold their surplus goods there; artisans and merchants lived within the walls; foreign traders offered their wares. These members of the lower classes were supported by the noble rich, who depended, even more than elsewhere, on cash to satisfy their desires. In the course of the ninth and tenth centuries, both servile and free tenants became renters who paid in currency.

The social and political life in Italy was conducive to a familial organization somewhat different from the patrilineal families of France. To stave off the partitioning of their properties among heirs, families organized themselves by formal contract into *consorteria*, in which all male members shared the profits of the family's inheritance and all women were excluded. The consorterial family became a kind of blood-related corporation, a social unit upon which early Italian businesses and banks would later be modeled.

In some ways Rome in the tenth century closely resembled other central Italian cities. Large and powerful families who built their castles within its walls and controlled the churches and monasteries in the vicinity dominated and fought over it.

The urban area of Rome had shrunk dramatically in the early Middle Ages, and it no longer commanded an international market: the population depended on local producers for their food, and merchants brought their wares to sell under its walls. Yet the mystique of Rome remained. Although it was no longer the hub of a great empire, it was still the *see*, the center of church authority, of the bishop of Rome. The pope (his special name since the ninth century) claimed the highest position in the church on the basis of "Petrine theory": citing a passage in Matthew's Gospel, the pope argued that he was the successor of St. Peter, the "rock" upon whom Christ had founded his church, the superior of all bishops, the holder of the keys of the kingdom of heaven.

Although this Petrine theory had relatively little practical impact during the ninth and tenth centuries, the papacy did command great prestige. Rome was the goal of pilgrims; and the papacy was the prize of powerful families, like that of Alberic, prince of Rome, whose son became John XII (*955–963). In the second half of the tenth century the king of Germany, Otto I (*936–973), considered Rome so essential to his imperial ambitions that he invaded it, put his own appointee on the papal throne, and had himself crowned emperor there. Rome's myth made it an international jewel.

Regional Kingship in the West

As a consequence of the splintering of the Carolingian empire, the western king of the Franks—who would only later receive the territorial title of king of France—was a relatively weak figure in the tenth and eleventh centuries. The German and English kings had more power, controlling much land and wealth and appointing their followers to both secular and ecclesiastical offices.

In France* during most of the tenth century, Carolingian kings alternated on the throne with kings from a family that would later be called the Capetian. As the Carolingian dynasty waned, the most powerful men of the kingdom—dukes, counts, and important bishops—prevented serious civil war by electing Hugh Capet (*987–996). This event marked the end of Carolingian rule and the beginning of the new dynasty that would last, handing down the royal title from father to son, until the fourteenth century. In the eleventh century the reach of the Capetian kings was limited by territorial lordships in the vicinity. The king's scattered but substantial estates lay in the north of France, in the region around Paris—the Ile-de-France (literally "the island of France"). His castles and his vassals were there. Independent castellans, however, controlled areas nearby, such as Montmorency, less than ten miles from Paris. In the sense that he was a neighbor of castellans and not much more powerful militarily than they, the king of France was just another local magnate. Yet the Capetian kings had considerable prestige. They were anointed with holy oil, and they represented the idea of unity inherited from Charlemagne. Most of the counts, at least in the north of France, became their vassals, swearing fealty and paying homage to the kings as feudal lords. As vassals they did not promise to obey the king, but they did vow not to try to kill or depose him.

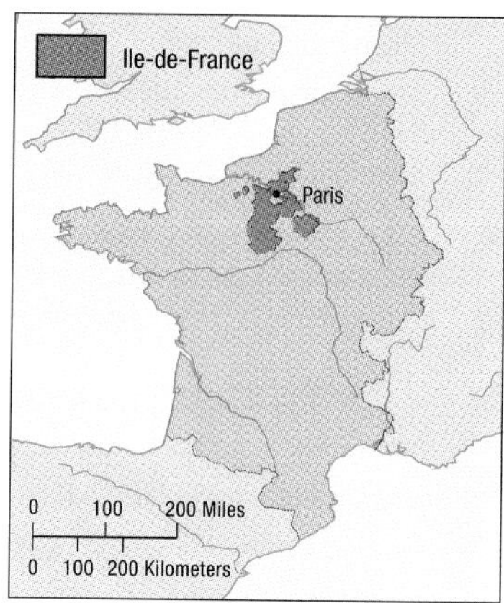

The Kingdom of the Franks Under Hugh Capet

In contrast with the development of territorial lordships in France, Germany's fragmentation hardly began before it was reversed. Five duchies (regions dominated by dukes) emerged in Germany in the late Carolingian period, each much larger than the counties and castellanies of France. With the death of the last Carolingian king in Germany, Louis the Child, in 911, the dukes elected one of themselves king. Then, as the Magyar invasions increased, the dukes gave the royal title to the duke of Saxony, Henry I (*919–936), who proceeded to set up fortifications and reorganize his army, crowning his efforts with a major defeat of a Magyar army in 933.

Otto I, the son of Henry I, was an even greater military hero. In 951 he marched into Italy and

*Terms such as "France," "Germany," and "Italy" are used here for the sake of convenience; they do not imply that these regions had the characteristics of modern nation-states.

The Empire of Otto I

took the Lombard crown. At the battle at the Lech River (the Battle of Lechfeld) in 955 he and his troops beat back the Magyars decisively. Against the Slavs, with whom the Germans shared a border, Otto set up marches from which he could make expeditions and stave off counterraids. After the pope crowned him emperor in 962, he claimed the Middle Kingdom carved out by the Treaty of Verdun and cast himself as the agent of Roman imperial renewal.

Otto's victories brought tribute and plunder, ensuring a following but also raising the German nobles' expectations for enrichment. He and his successors, Otto II (*973–983), Otto III (*983–1002)—not surprisingly, the dynasty is called the Ottonian—and Henry II (*1002-1024), were not always able or willing to provide the gifts and inheritances their family members and followers expected. To maintain centralized rule, for example, the Ottonians did not divide their kingdom among their sons: like castellans in France, they created a patrilineal pattern of inheritance. But the consequence was that younger sons and other potential heirs felt cheated out of their inheritance, and disgruntled royal kin led revolt after revolt against the Ottonian kings. The rebels found followers among the aristocracy, where the trend toward the patrilineal family prompted similar feuds and thwarted expectations.

Relations between the Ottonians and the German clergy were less rancorous. With a ribbon of new bishoprics along his eastern border, Otto I appointed bishops, gave them extensive lands, and subjected the local peasantry to their overlordship. Like Charlemagne, Otto believed that the well-being of the church in his kingdom depended on him. The Ottonians placed the churches and many monasteries of Germany under their special protection. Bishops were given the powers of the ban, allowing them to collect revenues and call men to arms. Answering to the king and furnishing him with troops, they became royal officials, while also carrying out their pastoral and religious duties. German kings claimed the right to select bishops, even the pope at Rome, and to "invest" them by participating in the ceremony that installed the bishop in his office. The higher clergy joined royal court society; most first came to the court to be schooled; then, in turn, they taught the kings, princes, and noblewomen there.

Like all the strong rulers of the day, whether in the West or in the Byzantine and Islamic worlds, the Ottonians presided over a renaissance of learning. For example, the tutor of Otto III was Gerbert (c. 945–1003), the best-educated man of his time. Placed on the papal throne as Sylvester II, Gerbert knew how to use the abacus and to calculate with Arabic numerals. He "used large sums of money to pay copyists and to acquire copies of authors," as he put it. He studied the classics as models of rhetoric and argument, and he loved logic and debate. Not only did churchmen and kings support Ottonian scholarship, but to an unprecedented extent noblewomen in Germany also

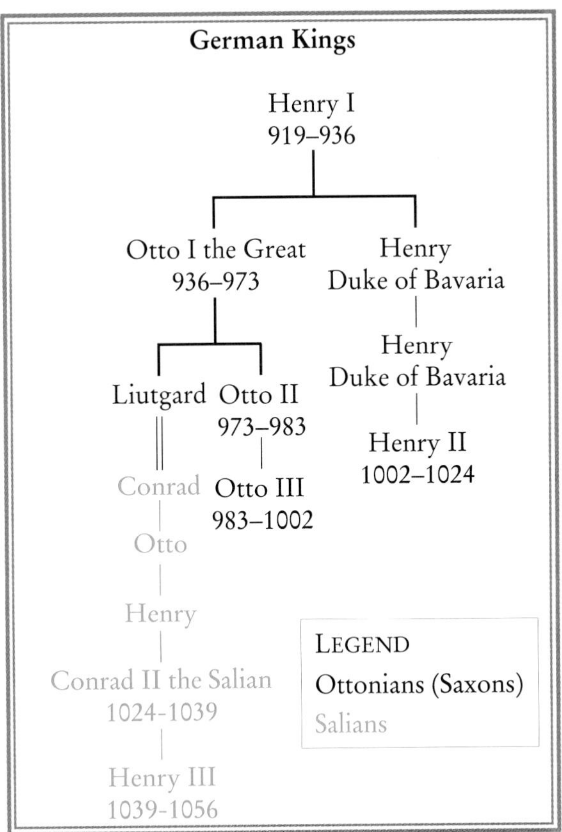

Sacral Kingship
The Ottonian kings were sacral, that is, anointed by God. This illumination from 1002-1014 shows Christ placing a crown on the heads of King Henry II and his wife, Queen Kunigunde, flanked by Saints Peter and Paul. Below are the symbols of empire. The artistic style reflects Byzantine influence, but the exaggerated gesture and simplicity of the background is unique to Ottonian art.

acquired an education and participated in the intellectual revival. Aristocratic women spent much of their wealth on learning. Living at home with their kinsfolk and servants or in convents that provided them with comfortable private apartments, noblewomen wrote books and occasionally even Roman-style plays. They also supported other artists and scholars.

Despite their military and political strength, the kings of Germany faced resistance from dukes and other powerful princes, who hoped to become petty rulers themselves. The Salians, who succeeded the Ottonians, tried to balance the power among the German dukes but could not meld them into a corps of vassals the way the Capetian kings tamed their counts. In Germany vassalage was considered beneath the dignity of free men. Instead of relying on vassals, the Salian kings and their episcopal supporters used ministerials, men who were legally serfs, to collect taxes, administer justice, and fight on horseback. Ministerials retained their servile status even though they often accumulated wealth and rose to high position. Under the Salian kings, ministerials became the mainstay of the royal army and administration.

In late ninth-century England, King Alfred also developed new mechanisms of royal government, instituting reforms that his successors continued. He fortified settlements throughout Wessex and divided the army into two parts, one with the duty of defending these fortifications (or *burhs*), the other with the job of operating as a mobile unit. Alfred also started a navy. These military innovations cost money, and the assessments fell on peasants' holdings.

Burhs might afford regional protection, but in Alfred's view they would be effective only if religion were strengthened as well. In the ninth century, people interpreted invasions as God's punishment for a sinful people; sin, then, was the real culprit. Hence Alfred began a program of religious reform by bringing scholars to his court to write and to educate others. Above all, Alfred wanted to translate key religious works from Latin into Anglo-Saxon (or Old English). He was determined to "turn into the language that we can all understand certain books which are the most necessary for all men to know." Alfred and scholars under his guidance translated works by Gregory the Great, Boethius, and St. Augustine. Even the Psalms were rendered into Anglo-Saxon. Whereas in the rest of ninth- and tenth-century Europe Latin remained the language of scholarship and writing, separate from the language people spoke, in England the vernacular was a literary language. With Alfred's work giving it greater legitimacy, Anglo-Saxon came to be used alongside Latin for both literature and administration. It was the language of royal *writs*, which began as terse directives from the king or queen to their officials.

Alfred's reforms strengthened not only military defense, education, and religion but also royal power. He consolidated his control over Wessex and fought the Danish kings, who by the mid-870s had taken Northumbria, northeastern Mercia, and East Anglia. Eventually, as he harried the Danes who were pushing south and westward, he was recognized as king of all the English not under Danish rule. He issued a law code, the first by an English king for a century. Unlike earlier codes, drawn up for each separate kingdom of England, Alfred drew his laws from all of the English kingdoms. In this way Alfred became the first king of all the English.

Alfred's successors rolled back the Danish hegemony in England. "Then the Norsemen departed in their nailed ships, bloodstained survivors of spears," wrote one poet about a battle the Vikings lost in 937. But many Vikings remained. Converted to Christianity, their great men joined Anglo-Saxons in attending the English king at court. As peace returned, new administrative subdivisions were established throughout England: shires and hundreds, districts used for judicial and taxation purposes. The powerful men of the kingdom swore fealty to the king, promising to be enemies of his enemies, friends of his friends. England was united and organized to support a strong ruler.

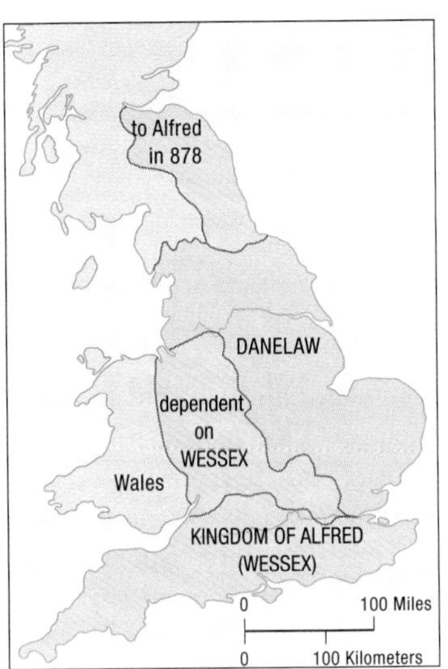

England in the Era of Alfred the Great

An English king like Edgar (*957–975), Alfred's grandson, commanded all the possibilities early medieval kingship offered. He was the sworn lord of all the great men of the kingdom. He controlled appointments to the English church and sponsored monastic reform. In 973, following the continental fashion, he was anointed. The fortifications of the kingdom were in his hands, as was the army, and he took responsibility for keeping the peace by proclaiming certain crimes—arson and theft—to be under his special jurisdiction and mobilizing the machinery of the shire and hundred to find and punish thieves.

Despite its apparent centralization, England was not a unified state in the modern sense, and the king's control over it was often tenuous. Many royal officials were great landowners who (as on the Continent) worked for the king because it was in their best interest. When it was not, they allied with different claimants to the throne. The kingdom built by Alfred and his successors could fragment easily, and it was easily conquered. At the beginning of the eleventh century the Danes invaded England, and Cnut (Canute), who would soon be king of Denmark, became king of England (*1017–1035); in 1030 he became ruler of Norway as well. Yet under Cnut, English kingship did not change much. By the mid-tenth century the kings of Denmark and their people had become Christian, and Cnut's conquest of England, bitterly opposed though it was, kept intact much of the administrative, ecclesiastical, and military apparatus already established. In any event, by Cnut's time Scandinavian traditions had largely merged with those of the rest of Europe, and the Vikings were no longer an alien culture.

King Alfred's Jewel
This jewel bears an Anglo-Saxon inscription that says, "Alfred ordered me to be made." It may have been used as a "pointer" (to point to a passage in a manuscript) or as a book mark. It demonstrates the relationship between fine craftsmanship and manuscript production, both of which flourished in the age of King Alfred.

The Emergence of Central Europe

Cnut's expansion was nearly matched by that of the German kings, for whom the region from the Elbe to Russia formed a vast frontier both tempting and threatening. The Slavs who lived in present-day eastern Germany and Poland offered opportunities for plunder, and the Germans waged wars against them with zeal. Otto I indicated his plans to expand by establishing the archbishopric of Magdeburg without any eastern boundary so that it could increase as far as future conquests and conversions to Christianity would allow.

Whereas Byzantine influence predominated in Russia and the Balkans, German military pressure and papal interests fostered the emergence of Christian monarchies in what are today Croatia, Hungary, the Czech and Slovak Republics, and Poland. The Magyars precipitated the decisive break between the Byzantine and western zones of influence. They settled in the region known as Hungary today, setting themselves up as landowners, using the native Slavs to till the soil, and imposing their language. At the end of the tenth century the Magyar ruler, Stephen I (*997–1038), decided to accept Christianity and used German knights and monks to help him consolidate his power and convert his people. According to legend, the crown placed on Stephen's head in 1001 was sent to him by the pope. To this day it remains the most hallowed symbol of Hungarian nationhood.

By the time St. Stephen had gained his crown, the Czechs and Poles were also well on the way toward accepting Latin Christianity. The Czechs, who lived in the region of Bohemia, converted under the rule of Václav (*920–929), who gained recognition in Germany as the duke of Bohemia. Yet he and his successors did not become kings, remaining politically within the German sphere. Václav's murder by his younger brother made him a martyr and the patron saint of Bohemia, a symbol around which later movements for independence rallied.

The Poles gained a greater measure of independence than the Czechs, but they still faced severe German pressure, especially after 955. In 966, Mieszko I (c. 922–992), the leader of the Slavic tribe known as the Polanians, accepted baptism in order to forestall the attack the Germans were already mounting against pagan Slavic peoples along the Baltic coast and east of the Elbe River. Busily engaged in bringing the other Slavic tribes of Poland under his control, Mieszko adroitly shifted his alliances with various German princes as suited his needs. In 991, he placed his realm under the protection of the pope at Rome, establishing a tradition of Polish loyalty to the see of St. Peter.

Mieszko's son Bolesław the Brave (*992–1025) greatly extended Poland's boundaries, at one time or another holding sway from the Bohemian border to Kiev. In 1000 he, like Stephen the next year, gained a royal crown with papal blessing, a symbol of his independence from the German emperor. These symbols of rulership, consecrated by Christian priests and accorded a prestige almost akin to saints' relics, were among the most vital institutions of kingly rule in central Europe. Profits from slave raids provided the initial economic basis for much of the power of central European rulers. But as organized states emerged in Europe to ward them off, such forays became more difficult. Landownership and the revenues from agriculture displaced the slave trade as the chief source of profit; but this change encouraged a proliferation of regional centers of power that challenged monarchical rule. From the eleventh century onward, all the medieval Slavic states contended constantly with problems of internal division.

The Empire of Otto III

Monastic Piety and the Secular Clergy

The breakup of the Carolingian empire meant that local kings and magnates came to dominate local churches, a relationship between religious and political power that later generations would deem scandalous. Yet before about 1000, western Europeans believed that all power—worldly and spiritual—derived from God. In the age of Charlemagne, observers of political power like Alcuin argued that God had given the king his realm precisely so that through him, "God's holy Church might be ruled, exalted, and preserved for the Christian people." When Charlemagne's kingdom split up—some territories controlled by kings;

others by dukes, counts, castellans, local lords, and bishops—these rulers began to control local churches as well. Most contemporaries saw nothing wrong with this development; the political order still seemed God given.

The focal point of regional piety, however, was more often the local monastery than the local church. People in the neighborhood, both men and women, supported these monasteries by giving them land. The little monastery of Prataglia was founded in 1001 in Tuscany, Italy, by the local bishop of Arezzo, who endowed it with bits and pieces from the larger estates belonging to his cathedral. Soon other landowners in the vicinity, many of them peasants with only small holdings to their name, gave small plots and sold other land to the monastery. As Prataglia gained prestige, it attracted more and larger gifts and purchased less. But even at the height of its celebrity, Prataglia's landholdings did not lie much more than twenty-five kilometers away from the monastery and were concentrated particularly in one river valley. Prataglia was a purely local monastery.

Some monasteries, such as Cluny in France, achieved more than regional fame. Cluny was founded in 910 by a wealthy and powerful magnate, William the Pious, duke of Aquitaine, and his wife, Ingelberga. They gave the monastery to Saints Peter and Paul at Rome, renouncing their own rights over it, to protect it from potential oppressors and to guarantee the monks the independence they needed to follow the Rule of St. Benedict and spend their lives in prayer. During the tenth and eleventh centuries, donations of land poured into Cluny on an unprecedented scale. In a period of local loyalties, Cluny became an exception, a truly international institution whose monks were called upon to reform monasteries in Italy, many parts of France, Germany, the small Christian kingdoms of Spain, and England. Despite their regional loyalties and interests, eleventh-century Europeans maintained an ideal of a united Christendom that transcended boundaries and linked all Christians together into a single community.

At the beginning of the eleventh century, the secular clergy (that is, the bishops, archbishops, and priests, as distinct from the "regular clergy," the monks) were typically allied with the local nobility and, in Germany, Italy, and England, with kings who made high churchmen their agents. In Germany bishops administered lands, enforced the ban, collected tithes, and supported knights on behalf of the monarchy. Rich families enhanced their repute, power, and chances for salvation by placing their sons in bishoprics, in the process giving gifts to whoever controlled the episcopal office. Episcopal duties were relatively worldly, and in daily life the secular clergy were almost indistinguishable from the laity. Wearing the finest clothes, riding on horses, surrounded by an entourage of armed men, bishops were great lords. Parish priests also blended with their lay peers, in this case members of the lower classes. Typically married and fathers of children, parish priests were special in that they alone could perform the sacraments, most important the saying of Mass. Yet in an age when most people did not regularly take Communion, the importance of this distinction was minimal. Reacting to the worldliness of the secular church in their day, a small group of influential churchmen claimed that the priesthood should be a clearly separate order within the church and called for radical reform.

Church Reform, Papal Control, and East-West Schism

A small group of clerics and monks spearheaded the movement for church reform. Buttressing their arguments for change with their interpretation of canon law (the laws decreed over the centuries at church councils and by bishops and popes), they concentrated on two breaches of those laws: nicolaitism (clerical marriage) and simony (buying church offices). Their larger goal was expressed by their motto: free the church. They intended to free priests from the coils of mundane cares by requiring celibacy; and they meant to free church offices from the domination of the laity by ending the payments that made episcopacies lucrative sources of revenue for aristocratic families. Most of the men who promoted these ideas lived in the Rhineland (the region along the northern half of the Rhine River) or Italy, the most commercialized regions of Europe. Their familiarity with the impersonal practices of a profit economy led the reformers to interpret as crass purchases the gifts that

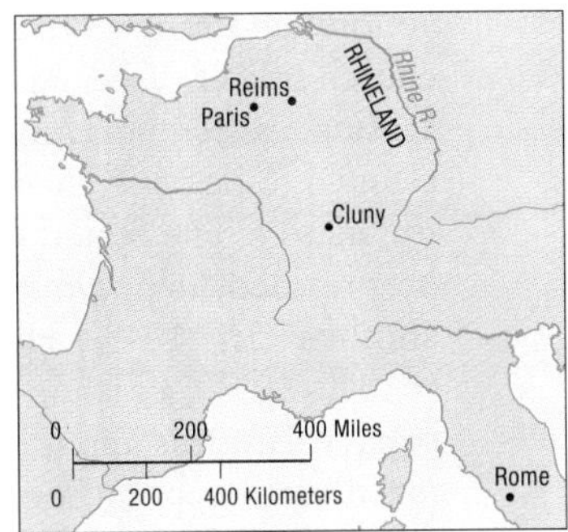

Beginnings of Church Reform

Remaking Three Societies

Byzantium	Islamic World	The West
843 Icons restored; end of iconoclasm **802–811** Reign of Emperor Nicephorus I; reconquest of Peloponnesus; attacks on Bulgaria begin **863** Cyril and Methodius sent to convert Old Moravia **c. 870–c. 1025** Macedonian renaissance **c. 899** Magyars arrive in Pannonia **913–959** Reign of Emperor Constantine VII Porphyrogenitos **976–1025** Reign of Emperor Basil II Bulgaroctonos; annexation of Bulgaria **c. 980–1015** Reign of Vladimir, prince of Russia; Russians convert to Christianity	**756–929** Emirate of Cordoba **786–809** Caliphate of Harun al-Rashid **825** Al-Khwarizmi's book on algebra published **929** Caliphate of Cordoba begins under Abd al-Rahman II **969–1171** Fatimid Dynasty in Egypt **1037** Death of Ibn Sina (Avicenna), important figure in the Islamic renaissance	**768–814** Reign of Charlemagne (sole ruler 771–814; crowned emperor in 800) **843** Treaty of Verdun; division of Carolingian empire **871–899** Reign of King Alfred the Great in England **936–973** Otto I, king in Germany and (from 962) emperor **955** Battle of Lechfeld; end of Magyar invasions **966** Mieszko I of Poland converts to Christianity **987–996** Reign of Hugh Capet; end of Carolingian rule in France **1001** Coronation of King Stephen of Hungary **1017–1035** Reign of Cnut, king of England **1049–1054** Papacy of Leo IX **1054** Schism between Roman Catholic and Greek Orthodox churches

churchmen gave in return for their offices—a practice not only acceptable but necessary in a gift economy.

In Germany Emperor Henry III (*1039– 1056) supported the reformers. Taking seriously his position as the anointed of God, Henry felt responsible for the well-being of the church. He denounced simony and refused to accept money in return for church offices. When in 1046 three men, each representing a different faction of the Roman aristocracy, claimed to be pope, Henry traveled to Italy to settle the matter. The Synod of Sutri (1046), over which he presided, deposed all three popes and elected another. In 1049, Henry appointed Leo IX (*1049–1054), a bishop from the Rhineland, to the papacy. But this appointment marked an unanticipated turning point for the emperor when Leo set out to reform the church under papal control. The Catholic church changed irrevocably during his tenure.

Leo knew canon law. He insisted, for example, that he be elected by the clergy and people of Rome before assuming the papal office. During his five years as pope, he traveled to Germany and France and held church councils. Before this time, popes had made the arduous journey across the Alps from Italy to the rest of Europe only rarely. They were, after all, mainly the bishops of Rome. But under Leo, the pope's role expanded. He sponsored the creation of a canon lawbook—the "Collection in 74 Titles"—which emphasized the pope's power. To the papal court Leo brought the most zealous reformers of his day: Humbert of Silva Candida, Peter Damian, and Hildebrand (later Gregory VII). These men played vital parts in the next episodes of the reform.

When Humbert went to Constantinople in 1054 on a diplomatic mission, he argued against the patriarch of Constantinople on behalf of the new, lofty claims of the pope. Furious at the contemptuous way he was treated, Humbert ended his mission by excommunicating the patriarch. In retaliation the emperor and his bishops excommunicated Humbert and his party, threatening them with eternal damnation. Clashes between the two churches had occurred before and had been patched up, but this one, called the Great Schism, proved insurmountable.*

In the West, Leo's claims to new power over the church hierarchy were complacently ignored at first. The Council of Reims (in France), which he called in 1049, for example, was attended by only a few bishops and boycotted by the king of France. Nevertheless, Leo made it into a forum for exercising his authority. Placing the relics of St. Remegius (the patron saint of Reims) on the altar of the church, he demanded that the attending bishops and abbots say whether or not they had purchased their offices. A few confessed guilt; some did not respond; others gave excuses. The new and extraordinary development was that all felt accountable to the pope and accepted his verdicts. One bishop was stripped of his episcopal office; another was summoned to Rome to explain himself. The power of St. Peter had come to match the force of a king's, but with a scope that encompassed the western half of Europe.

*Despite occasional thaws and liftings of the sentences, the excommunications largely remained in effect until 1965, when Pope Paul VI and the Greek Orthodox patriarch, Anthenagoras I, publicly deplored them.

Conclusion

In the early ninth century the three heirs of the Roman Empire all appeared to be organized like their "parent": centralized, monarchical, imperial. Byzantine emperors writing their learned books, Abbasid caliphs holding court in their resplendent palace at Baghdad, and Carolingian emperors issuing their directives for reform to the *missi dominici* all mimicked the Roman emperors. Yet they confronted tensions and regional pressures that tended to decentralize political power. Byzantium felt this fragmentation least, yet even there a new elite, the *strategoi*, led to decentralization and the emperor's loss of control over the countryside. In the Islamic world economic crisis, religious tension, and the ambitions of powerful dynasts decisively weakened the caliphate and opened the way to separate successor states. In the West powerful independent landowners strove with greater or lesser success (depending on the region) to establish themselves as effective rulers, and the states that would become those of modern Europe began to form.

In western Europe local conditions determined political and economic organizations. In the tenth and eleventh centuries, for example, French society was transformed by the development of territorial lordships, patrilineal families, and feudal ties. These factors figured less prominently in Germany, where a central monarchy remained, buttressed by churchmen, ministerials, and victories to the east.

The tendency toward local rule affected the church as well: monks were supported largely by local patrons, and bishoprics were filled by the sons of neighboring aristocrats, causing outraged reformers to call for drastic changes in the church. In the next century their movement would redefine the relationship between the laity and the clergy.

Suggestions for Further Reading

Source Materials

Einhard and Notker the Stammerer. *Two Lives of Charlemagne*. Translated by Lewis Thorpe. 1969. One of many translations of Einhard's important biography of Charlemagne, here paired with another biography dating from the late ninth century.

Nelson, Janet, trans. *The Annals of St.-Bertin*. 1991. Covering the period 830–882, a chronicle of the problems and resources of ninth-century kings.

Psellus, Michael. *Fourteen Byzantine Rulers: The Chronographia*. Translated by E. R. A. Sewter. 1966. A work of history written in the eleventh century by a member of the Byzantine scholarly elite.

Whitelock, Dorothy, ed. *English Historical Documents*. Vol. 1, *c. 500–1042*. 2d ed. 1979. Contains the essential primary source materials for Anglo-Saxon England.

Interpretive Studies

Ashtor, E. *A Social and Economic History of the Near East in the Middle Ages*. 1976. Stresses change in the Islamic world from the point of view of the lower classes.

Bachrach, Bernard S. *Fulk Nerra, the Neo-Roman Consul, 987–1040: A Political Biography of the Angevin Count*. 1993. The thoughts and activities of a count who created a major principality for himself and his successors.

Bloch, Marc. *Feudal Society*. Translated by L. A. Manyon. 1961. The classic synthesis of social, cultural, and economic history.

Boussard, Jacques. *The Civilisation of Charlemagne*. Translated by Frances Partridge. 1968. Surveys the Carolingian period topically, with useful maps and illustrations.

Davies, Norman. *God's Playground: A History of Poland*. Vol. 1, *The Origins to 1745*. 1982. Emphasizes the way in which Poland's history paralleled that of other European states.

Duby, Georges. *The Chivalrous Society*. Translated by Cynthia Postan. 1977. Fifteen essays by a master of social history.

———. *The Early Growth of the European Economy. Warriors and Peasants from the Seventh to the Twelfth Century*. Translated by Howard B. Clark. 1974. Explores the relationship between economy, society, and mentality.

———. *Rural Economy and Country Life in the Medieval West*. Translated by Cynthia Postan. 1968. A thorough survey that also includes primary sources, covering the subject from c. 800 to c. 1400.

Fell, Christine E., Cecily Clark, and Elizabeth Williams. *Women in Anglo-Saxon England, and the Impact of 1066*. 1984. Covers such topics as daily life, sex and marriage, family and kinship.

Fichtenau, Heinrich. *Living in the Tenth Century*. Translated by Patrick J. Geary. 1991. A discussion of important and ordinarily neglected topics, such as ideas about order and disorder, table manners, and gestures.

Frantzen, Allen J. *King Alfred*. 1986. A thoughtful analysis of Alfred's writings by a literary scholar.

Ganshof, F. L. *Feudalism*. Rev. ed. Translated by Philip Grierson. 1964. A concise discussion of the institution and its evolution.

Glick, Thomas. *Islamic and Christian Spain in the Early Middle Ages: Comparative Perspectives on Social and Cultural Formation*. 1979. Views the history of Spain as a totality rather than as the story of separate Christian and Islamic spheres.

Goitein, S. D. *A Mediterranean Society. The Jewish Communities of the Arab World as Portrayed in the Documents of the Cairo Geniza*. 4 vols. 1967–1983. Uses the *geniza* documents to explore the economy (vol. 1), the community (vol. 2), the family (vol. 3), and daily life (vol. 4) of the medieval Mediterranean.

Head, Constance. *Imperial Byzantine Portraits: A Verbal and Graphic Gallery*. 1982. Presents short biographies of each emperor along with contemporary portraits, in this way linking political authority with iconography.

Head, Thomas, and Richard Landes, eds. *The Peace of God: Social Violence and Religious Response in France around the Year 1000*. 1992. A series of essays on an important medieval social movement to contain and channel violence.

Jenkins, Romilly. *Byzantium: The Imperial Centuries. a.d. 610–1071*. 1966. A general survey.

Jones, Gwyn. *A History of the Vikings*. Rev. ed. 1984. A detailed and well-written account of the Vikings at home and abroad.

Kennedy, Hugh. *The Prophet and the Age of the Caliphates: The Islamic Near East from the Sixth to the Eleventh Century*. 1986. A solid overview of the period, concentrating on political history.

Lewis, Archibald R., and Timothy J. Runyan. *European Naval and Maritime History, 300–1500*. 1985. A revealing look at the medieval period through the prism of its naval history.

Leyser, Karl J. *Rule and Conflict in an Early Medieval Society: Ottonian Saxony*. 1979. An anthropologically informed look at one tenth-century society.

Little, Lester K. *Benedictine Maledictions: Liturgical Cursing in Romanesque France*. 1993. Discusses ritual cursing in monastic communities as a way for monks to counter their enemies.

Manteuffel, Tadeusz. *The Formation of the Polish State. The Period of Ducal Rule, 963–1194*. Translated by Andrew Gorski. 1982. A political history from the Polish point of view.

Marenbon, John. *From the Circle of Alcuin to the School of Auxerre: Logic, Theology, and Philosophy in the Early Middle Ages*. 1981. Demonstrates the continuity between Carolingian and later medieval philosophical inquiry.

McKitterick, Rosamond. *The Carolingians and the Written Word*. 1989. Discusses literacy in the Carolingian empire.

———. *The Frankish Kingdoms Under the Carolingians, 751–987*. 1983. A detailed and learned overview of the period.

Nelson, Janet. *Charles the Bald*. 1987. Shows how Charlemagne's grandson was a strong and canny ruler in a difficult period.

Ostrogorsky, George. *History of the Byzantine State*. Rev. ed. 1969. Remains the basic one-volume account of the Byzantine Empire.

Reuter, Timothy. *Germany in the Early Middle Ages, c. 800–1056*. 1991. An astute and up-to-date survey of the period.

Riché, Pierre. *Daily Life in the World of Charlemagne*. Translated by JoAnn McNamara. 1978. Takes up topics usually neglected: diet, language, travel, birth control.

Rosenwein, Barbara H. *To Be the Neighbor of Saint Peter: The Social Meaning of Cluny's Property, 909–1049*. 1989. Discusses the relationships between the monastery and its donors.

Runciman, Steven. *Byzantine Style and Civilization*. 1971. A survey of Byzantine art.

Searle, Eleanor. *Predatory Kinship and the Creation of Norman Power, 840–1066*. 1988. A fresh interpretation of the development of Normandy as a Viking creation.

Treadgold, Warren. *The Byzantine Revival, 780–842*. 1988. An integrated account of the economic, military, political, and cultural revival of the period.

Waddy, Charis. *Women in Muslim History*. 1980. A general history, covering the time of Muhammad to modern times, that looks at the changing role of women in the Islamic world.

White, Lynn, Jr. *Medieval Technology and Social Change*. 1962. Three classic essays on the relationship between medieval technology and society.

Wilson, David. *The Vikings and Their Origins. Scandinavia in the First Millennium*. 1970. Discusses the Vikings from an archaeological perspective, with many fine illustrations.

Wilson, N. G. *Scholars of Byzantium*. 1983. The history of Byzantine scholarship from the late Roman period to the fourteenth century.

CHAPTER 10

Vitality and Reform, 1054–1144

Around 1115, Guibert, the abbot of a monastery at Nogent (in France), wrote his memoirs. A remarkably intelligent and opinionated man, Guibert used his autobiography as a pulpit from which he could criticize and praise the people, movements, and ideas of his time. One man he esteemed highly was Bruno of Cologne (c. 1030–1101) who was "learned in the liberal arts and the director of higher studies" at the prominent cathedral school of Reims. Highly respected by both his many students and his peers, Bruno might have been expected to rise to the position of bishop or archbishop over a major see, the pinnacle of a career to many churchmen. But Bruno repudiated the city and his leading position there, leaving Reims because its new archbishop, Manasses, had purchased his office, or as Guibert put it, had "thrust himself by simony into the rule of that city." Guibert reported that Manasses was so worldly that he once reportedly said, "The archbishopric of Reims would be a good thing if one did not have to sing Mass for it."

In 1084, rejecting both the worldly goals of the secular clergy and the communal goals of Benedictine monks, Bruno set up a hermitage at Chartreuse, high in the Alps, on the top of "a high and dreadful cliff," in Guibert's words. The monks who gathered there lived in isolation and poverty. "They do not take gold, silver, or ornaments for their church from anyone," Guibert marveled. Yet "although they subject themselves to complete poverty, they are accumulating a very rich library." Thus began La Chartreuse, the chief house of the Carthusian order, an order still in existence. The Carthusian monks lived as hermits, eschewed

Church over State
Gratian wrote a concordance of canon laws illustrated here by a late twelfth-century artist. Its design emphasized the primacy of the Church over the State: the churchman, a saint, is on top; the king, below him, holds a sword as the symbol of his office and a scroll telling him his duties.

material wealth, and emphasized learning. In some ways their style of life was a reaction against the monumental changes rumbling through their age: their heremetic solitude ran counter to the burgeoning cities, and their austerity contrasted sharply with the opulence and power of princely courts. On the other hand, their reverence for the written word reflected the growing interest in scholarship and learning. The growth of cities and the concurrent desire of their citizens to exert more political power; church reform, including experimental forms of religious life; the revival of monarchies; and the new popularity of learning were issues that Carthusian monks and everyone else grappled with during this period.

Between 1054 and 1144, western European communities were transformed; many villages and fortifications turned into cities where traders, merchants, and artisans conducted business. Although most people still lived in less populated, rural areas, their lives were touched in many ways by a developing profit economy. Economic concerns also continued to drive changes within the church, where by the second half of the eleventh century the leadership in church reform came from the papacy. One extremely influential pope, Gregory VII, gave his name to a phase of this movement, the Gregorian Reform, a series of fundamental changes in the church that were often passionately supported by common people, both clerical and lay. In a short time the powerful forces unleashed by this reform led to the First Crusade and an important European presence in the Levant that lasted until 1144.

Redefining the role of the clergy and elaborating new political ideas, popes, kings, and princes came to exercise power in a society with a commercial economy. At the same time, city-dwellers began to demand their own governments. Monks and clerics reformulated the nature of their own communities and, like Bruno of Cologne, sought intense spiritual lives. All of these developments inspired (and in turn were inspired by) new ideas, forms of scholarship, and methods of inquiry. The rapid pace of religious, political, and economic change was matched by new developments in thought and learning.

Important Dates

1066 Norman conquest of England; Battle of Hastings

1077 Canossa: Henry IV does penance before Gregory VII

1086 Domesday Book commissioned by William I of England

c. 1090–1153 Life of St. Bernard

1095 Preaching of the First Crusade at Clermont

1097 Commune of Milan established

1122 Concordat of Worms: end of the Investiture Conflict

c. 1122 Abelard writes *Sic et Non*

1130 Norman Kingdom of Sicily established

1140 Gratian's *Decretum* published

1144 Consecration of Suger's new choir at St. Denis; beginning of Gothic architecture

The Commercial Revolution

As the population of Europe continued to expand in the eleventh century, cities, long-distance trade networks, and local markets meshed to create a profit-based economy. With improvements in agriculture and more land in cultivation, the great estates of the eleventh century produced surpluses that helped feed the new urban population and at the same time enrich the great lords, both in the cities and in the countryside. The system of territorial lordships created a class of rich and powerful men and women eager to use markets to sell their surpluses and spend their money on luxuries to enhance their style of life and their prestige. Many members of the old elite became rich from commerce, while a new urban elite arose, enriched from the same source. Wealth was power: it allowed city dwellers to become employers, princes to hire officials to do their bidding, and courtly aristocrats to become patrons.

Commerce was not new to the history of the West, of course, but the commercial economy of

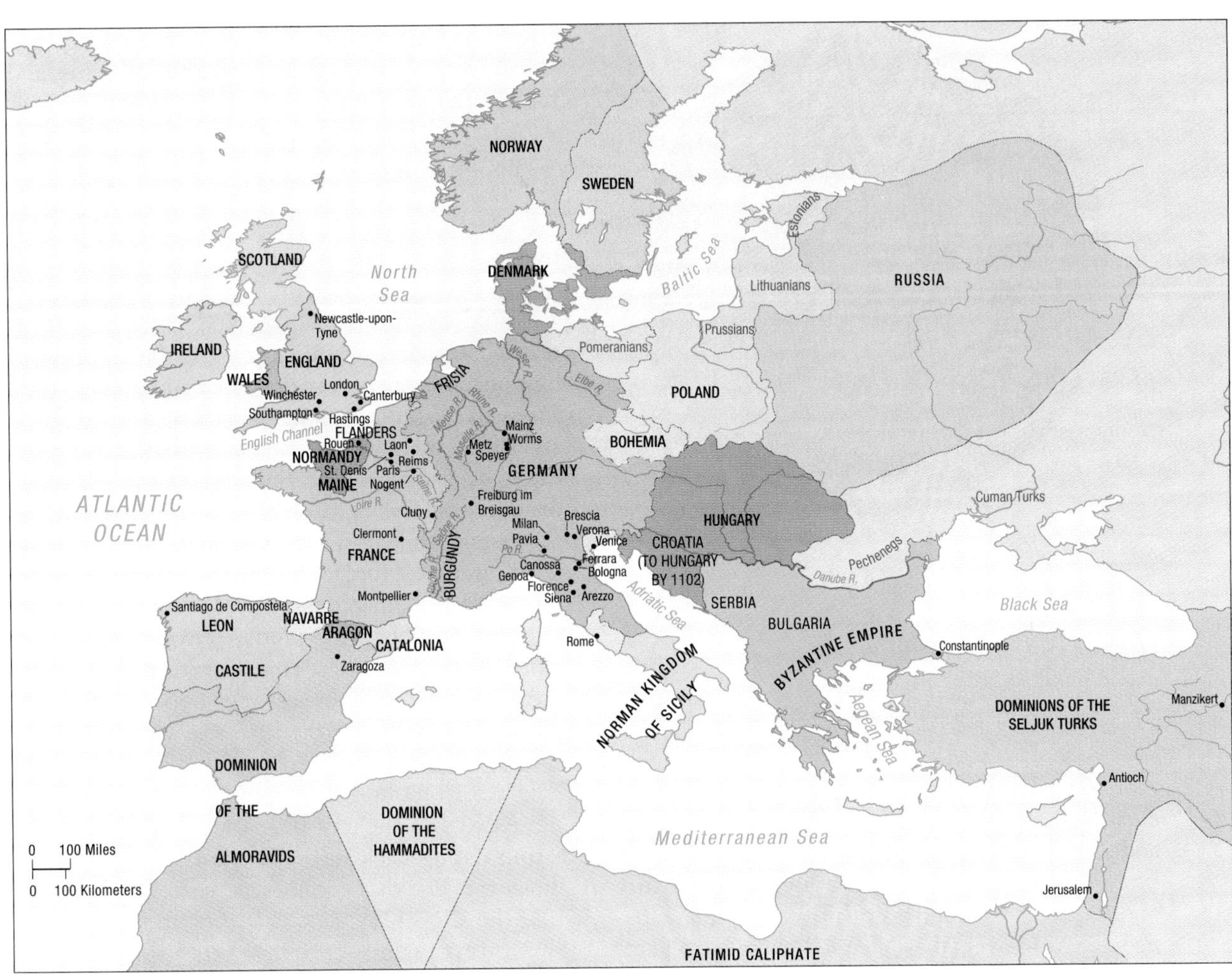

Europe and the Mediterranean, c. 1097

the Middle Ages produced the institutions that would be the direct ancestors of western businesses: corporations, banks, accounting systems, and above all, urban centers that thrived on economic vitality. Whereas ancient cities had primarily religious, social, and political functions, medieval cities were above all centers of production and economic activities.

Commercial Centers

Commercial centers developed around castles, monasteries, and within the walls of ancient towns. At Bruges (today in Belgium), for example, the castle became the magnet around which a city formed. As a medieval chronicler observed:

> *To satisfy the needs of the people in the castle at Bruges, first merchants with luxury articles began to surge around the gate; then the wine-sellers came; finally the innkeepers arrived to feed and lodge the people who had business with the prince. . . . So many houses were built that soon a great city was created.*

Thus the needs and desires of territorial lords and their families, vassals, and servants for food and luxuries drew people from the surrounding countryside and sometimes from far away. Lords had

Self-image of a City
*This coin, minted by Archbishop Anno of Cologne (*1056–1075), depicts the "image" of Cologne (Germany), a symbol of the city including towers, walls, and a grand edifice.*

reorganized their lands for greater productivity, encouraged their peasants to cultivate new land, and converted services and dues to money payments. Now, with ready cash, they happily paid for luxury goods offered by enterprising merchants and craftspeople. Moreover, they charged these merchants tolls and sales taxes, in this way profiting even more from trade. Local peasants and servants, who benefited from commerce, devoted some of their own time to reap profits as traders or craftsmen. Former servants of the bishop of Mâcon, for example, set up a bakery near the bridge of the city and sold bread to travelers. They soon grew rich.

Castles were not the only nuclei of revitalized trade. Some commercial centers clustered around Benedictine monasteries, which by the eleventh century had become large communities of several hundred monks with many needs to supply. Still other markets formed just outside the walls of older cities; these gradually merged into new and enlarged urban communities as town walls were built around them to protect their inhabitants. Sometimes peasants had surpluses and sold them at an informal market, set up in the middle of the countryside. If the surpluses continued from year to year, the market might eventually gain permanent structures. To the north, in places like Frisia, the Vikings had already established centers of wealth and trade, and these settlements became permanent, thriving towns. Along the Rhine and in other river valleys, cities sprang up to service the merchants who traversed the route between Italy and the north.

Merchants were a varied lot. Some were local traders, like the Cluniac monk who supervised a manor twenty miles to the south of his monastery and sold its surplus horses and grain at a local market. Others—mainly Jews and Italians—were long-distance traders, in great demand because they supplied the fine wines and fabrics beloved by lords and ladies, their families, and their vassals. Jews had often been involved at least part time in long-distance trade as vintners; and as lords reorganized the countryside, driving out Jewish landowners, most Jews were forced to turn to commercial activities full time. Other long-distance traders came from Italy, where urban mercantile activities had never quite ceased, and where contact with Byzantium (a great commercial center) and opportunities for plunder and trade on the high seas and in Muslim and Byzantine ports provided the background to Italy's early commercial growth.

At Reims, the city Bruno left, the middle of a forum dating back to the Roman Empire became the new home of a commercial center. As early as 1067 the king of France was writing about the many fairs in his realm—great markets held at regular intervals—that attracted large crowds. Around the marketplace at Reims grew a network of streets whose names revealed their essentially commercial functions: Street of the Butchers; Street of the Wool Market; Street of the Wheat Market.

The look and feel of such developing cities varied enormously. Nearly all included at least a marketplace, a castle, and several churches. And most had to adapt to increasingly crowded conditions. At the end of the eleventh century in Winchester, England, city plots were still large enough to accommodate houses parallel to the street; but the swelling population soon necessitated destroying these houses and building instead long, narrow, hall-like tenement houses, constructed at right angles to the thoroughfare. These were built on a frame made from strips of wood filled with wattle and daub—twigs woven together and covered with clay. If they were like the stone houses built in the late twelfth century (about which we know a good deal) they

Building and Construction
In this early twelfth-century fresco on a wall of the Romanesque church St.-Savin-sur-Gartempe in France, workers are depicted building the Tower of Babel. The commercial revolution was accompanied by a great building boom in the cities of western Europe.

had two stories: a shop or warehouse on the lower floor and living quarters above. Behind was the kitchen and perhaps also enclosures for livestock, as archaeologists have found at Southampton. In the early twelfth century even city-dwellers clung to rural pursuits, living largely off the food they raised themselves.

The construction of wattle and daub houses, churches, castles, and markets was part of a building boom that began in the tenth century and continued at an accelerated pace through the thirteenth. Specialized buildings for trade and city government were put up—charitable houses for the sick and indigent, community houses, and warehouses. In addition to individual buildings the new construction involved erecting masses of walls. Medieval cities were ringed by walls. By 1100 Speyer had three: one around its cathedral, the next just beyond the parish church of St. Moritz, the third still farther out to protect the marketplace. Within the walls lay a network of streets, often narrow, dirty, dark, and winding, made of packed clay or gravel. In English towns the main street broadened as it approached a rectangular or V-shaped marketplace. Bridges spanned the rivers; on the Meuse, for example, six new bridges were built during the eleventh century. Before the eleventh century, Europeans had depended on boats and waterways for bulky long-distance transport; now carts could haul items overland because new roads through the countryside linked the urban markets.

Although commercial centers developed throughout western Europe, they grew fastest and became most dense in regions along key waterways: the Mediterranean coasts of Italy, France, and Spain; Northern Italy along the Po River; the river system of the Rhône-Saône-Meuse; the Rhineland; the English Channel; the shores of the Baltic Sea. During the eleventh century these waterways became part of a single interdependent economy.

Tools of the Trade

The development of commercial centers betokened a new attitude toward money. Although the gift economy did not disappear, a market economy arose alongside it. The new mode of commerce marked a change in the social relations involved in economic transactions. In the gift economy, exchanges of coins, gold, and silver were components of ongoing relationships. Kings offered treasures to their followers, peasants gave dues to their lords, and pious donors presented land to the saintly patrons of churches, all in the expectation of long-term relationships. In the market economy, which thrived on the profit motive, transactions had no personal component: the obligations of the seller to the buyer and vice versa ended once a purchase was made. The value of a coin in the gift economy was determined by the friendships it made or the obligations it incurred. In the money economy, value was carefully calculated, and profit was determined by monetary gain.

As significant for the commercial revolution as this new attitude toward money was the creation of new kinds of business partnerships. Although they took many forms, all new business agreements had the common purpose of bringing people together to pool their resources and finance larger enterprises. The *commenda*, for example, an Italian invention, was a partnership established for commerce by sea. In one common arrangement, one or more investors furnished the money, and the other partners under took the risks of the actual voyage. If a trip proved successful, the investors received three-quarters of the profit and the travelers the rest. But if the voyage failed, the investors lost their outlay, and the travelers expended their time and labor to no profit. This sort of agreement had many variations. In 1073, for example, Giovanni Lissado put up 100 Venetian pounds and Sevasto Orefice put up twice as much to buy shares in a commercial voyage to Thebes. Giovanni himself was to go on the journey. He drew up a contract promising to "put to work this entire [capital] and to strive the best way I can" and if successful to divide the profits equally with Sevasto. But "if all these goods are lost because of the sea or of [hostile] people" then Sevasto would have to accept the loss of his capital. The impermanence of such partnerships (they lasted for only one voyage) meant that capital could be shifted easily from one venture to another and could therefore be used to support a variety of enterprises.

Land trade often involved a more enduring partnership. In Italy this took the form of a *compagnia*, based on the consorterial family (which pooled its resources and shared its profits among male members) and formed when family property was invested in trade. Unlike the *commenda*, in which the partners could lose no more than they had put into the enterprise, the *compagnia* left its members with joint and unlimited liability for all losses and debts. This provision enhanced family solidarity, because each member was responsible for the debts of all the others; but it also risked bankrupting entire households.

Besides partnerships, the chief tools of the commercial revolution were contracts for sales, exchanges, and loans. In a society with widely varying coinage standards, bills of exchange were crucial to international trade because they established equivalencies among different coinage systems while avoiding the need to ship actual coins from one place to another. Moreover, the terms of these bills could be used to mask loans. The church prohibited usury (profiting from loans) but loans were essential for business ventures. In the Middle Ages, as now, interest payments were the chief inducement for an investor to supply money. To circumvent the church's ban on usury, interest was often disguised as a penalty for "late payment" under the rules of the contract. This new willingness to finance business enterprises with loans signaled a changed attitude toward credit: risk was acceptable if it brought profit. Italian merchants and bankers were the pioneers in experimenting with credit institutions. Italian city governments also later invented bonds—credit investments issued to finance projects on the basis of promised returns from future revenues. Modern governments still finance public enterprises this way, though few realize we are using a medieval invention.

New forms of production matched these new methods of finance. Light industry spread in the eleventh century. Water mills, for example, not only ground grain but also powered other machines, such as flails to clean and thicken cloth and presses to extract oil. New technology to exploit deep mines provided Europeans with hitherto untapped sources of metals. Forging techniques improved, and iron was shaped into weapons as well as the tools and ploughs, that helped intensify agricultural productivity. Precious metals were fashioned into ornaments or coins, which fueled commercial activity. Such production relied on the expertise of artisans who could dye the woolens, work the metals, and mint the coins.

In part to regulate and protect these emerging industries, artisans formed guilds: local social, religious, and economic associations whose members plied the same trade. The shoemakers' guild at Ferrara began as a prayer confraternity, an association whose members gathered and prayed for one another. If a member or his wife died, the others would bear the body to the church, bury it with honors, and offer money for masses to be said for the salvation of the dead person's soul. In time this guild's membership came to be limited to shoemakers. Although mothers, wives, daughters, and female apprentices often knew how to make shoes, weave cloth, or sell goods, women did not ordinarily join guilds. Largely social and convivial fraternities, guilds undertook to regulate their members' hours, materials, and prices and to set quality standards. Although not eliminating all competition among craftsmen in the same field, the guild prevented any one artisan from gaining unfair advantages over another. Most important, the guild guaranteed each member a place in the market by controlling the production of shoes, fabrics, candles, and other items in each city.

Clearly the legitimacy and enforceability of the regulations of guilds and other trade and crafts organizations depended upon recognition by the political powers that ruled each city. Guild rules could not supersede city and church laws. But in most cities guilds and the city rulers had comfortable relationships based on mutual benefit. For example, when in 1106, twenty-three fishermen at Worms wanted exclusive rights to the wholesale fish market there, they petitioned the local bishop to give them the privilege and impose penalties on anyone who violated it. In return, they promised to give him two salmon every year and the local count one salmon a year.

Self-Government for the Cities

Townspeople seemed odd to tradition-bound commentators, accustomed to old categories of society that recognized only three classes: those who prayed (the monks and clerics), those who fought (the knights, castellans, and lords), and those who worked (the peasants). Tradesmen, artisans, ship captains, innkeepers, and money changers fit none of these categories. Townspeople themselves shared the sense that they were outsiders, and this bond often gave them a sense of solidarity with one another. But practical reasons also contributed to their feeling of common purpose: they lived in close quarters with one another; and they shared a mutual interest in sound coinage, laws that would facilitate commerce, freedom from servile dues and services, and independence to buy and sell as the market dictated. Already in the early twelfth century the king of England granted to the citizens of Newcastle-upon-Tyne the privilege that any unfree peasant who lived there unclaimed by his lord for a year and a day would be thereafter a free person. The guilds were one way townspeople expressed their mutual concerns and harnessed their collective energies. Movements for self-government were another. The general desire for personal liberty and economic freedom led many townspeople to collective action. They petitioned the political powers who ruled them—bishops, kings, counts, castellans—to allow them their own officials and law courts. Often they formed communes, sworn associations of townspeople that generally cut across the boundaries of rich and poor, merchants and craftspeople, clergy and laity.

Sometimes communes gained their independence peacefully. William Clito, who claimed the county of Flanders (today in Belgium), willingly granted the citizens of St. Omer the rights they asked for in 1127 in return for their support of his claims: he recognized them as legally free, gave them the right to mint coins, allowed them their own laws and courts, and lifted certain tolls and taxes. Although all the citizens of St. Omer benefited from these privileges, the merchant guild there profited the most, as it alone gained freedom from all tolls in the entire county of Flanders.

Those in power did not always respond favorably to townspeoples' demands for self-government, and violence sometimes ensued. Guibert of Nogent described a revolt at Laon (in northern France), where the community had chafed under the rule of the bishop. Even Guibert, who opposed communal revolt, pointed out that "the public authority" at Laon—the bishop and the nobles who followed him—"was involved in rapine and murder." Unable to gain redress peacefully, on the day before Good Friday, 1112, "a great crowd of burghers attacked the episcopal palace, armed with rapiers, double-edged swords, bows and axes, and carrying clubs and lances," killing the bishop and his men. Although the king of France, Louis VI, squelched the revolt, he finally recognized the commune of Laon in 1128.

Such collective movements for urban self-government were not confined to France, but also emerged in Italy and Germany. Except in Italy, the newly independent cities usually took their place within the framework of larger kingdoms or principalities. They sometimes retained their independence by playing off overlapping authorities in their region. In other instances lords realized they could profit economically from these self-governing cities. The town of Freiburg im Breisgau in Germany was created by a prince who wanted the benefits of a nearby market. He invited people to come to his town and live by their own laws, and he ensured their prosperity by guaranteeing safe passage for merchants going through his territory. Such resourceful lords gained from the taxes they levied on their towns more than enough to make up for what they lost in the direct exercise of power.

Unlike the towns of northern Europe, Italian cities were centers of regional political power even before the commercial revolution. Castellans constructed their fortifications and bishops ruled the countryside from such cities. The commercial revolution swelled the Italian cities with tradesmen, whose interest in self-government was often fueled by religious as well as economic concerns. At Milan in the second half of the eleventh century, popular support for ecclesiastical reform fed local discontent with the archbishop's power there. In 1097, after many clashes, the townspeople succeeded in transferring political power over Milan from the archbishop and his clergy to a government of consuls. These consuls were the leading men of the city, soldiers (*milites*) who, though neither merchants nor artisans, nevertheless claimed to speak for all the townsmen. Subsequent archbishops of Milan generally came from the same military class; they dominated the church while the consuls took charge of the laws and revenues. The title *consul* that these new governors took recalled the government of the ancient Roman Republic, affirming their status as representatives of the people. The consuls' power, like the archbishop's before them, extended beyond the town walls into the *contado*, the outlying countryside.

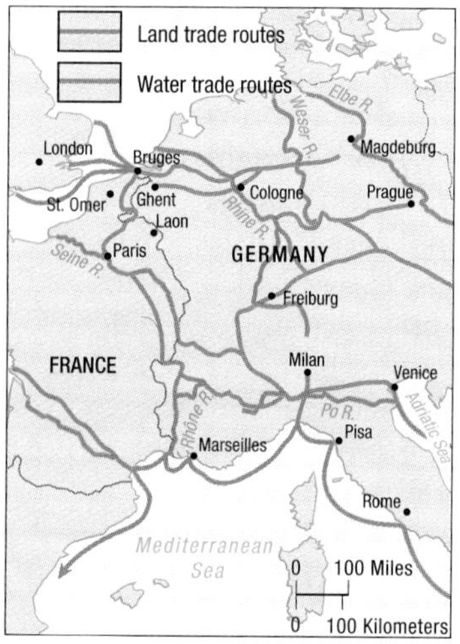

Urban Revival

Milan's experience was more representative of northern Italian cities than the experience of Venice, which did not struggle for self-government because it was already virtually independent. Nominally under the control of Byzantium until the eleventh century, it was in fact ruled by a *doge*. The doge relied on the support of Venice's great aristocratic families, whose power and wealth came from commerce in the Adriatic Sea. These aristocratic Venetian men, whose ships linked the Muslim world with Byzantium and the West, continued to dominate the city, both politically and economically, until the middle of the twelfth century, when newly successful families took on a consultative role as members of a Council of the Wise. The citizens of Venice had no interest in dominating their *contado*; they had all of the Adriatic to ply.

Papal Reform and Ensuing Struggles

The link between the development of the commune at Milan and the movement for religious reform there illustrates the interrelationship of the commercial revolution and ecclesiastical reform. Reformers who abhorred simony joined with members of the new commercial classes to replace churchmen whose worldliness distracted them from their religious mission. But economic and religious issues only partially defined the forces for change: the reform movement encompassed a new theory about how power ought to be exercised. After Leo IX (*1049–1054) had asserted his authority over local bishops in all parts of Europe, his successors immersed the papacy even more in issues outside Italy. Popes sought to extend their control and to mold the church and the world to fit an ideal vision in which their spiritual authority took precedence over secular power, so that kings were subordinate to popes. In the process of implementing this, as they supported some rulers and clashed with others, the popes too became monarchs with armies, officials, ambassadors (called legates), and elaborate revenue-raising systems.

The Papacy as a European Power

The papacy intervened in the politics of many regions of Europe. For example, in southern Italy the popes first fought against and then made peace with the Normans, the descendants of the Vikings who had settled in Normandy (in northwestern France) a century before. In the early eleventh century, Norman adventurers had come to southern Italy, hiring themselves out as warriors and fighting for the Byzantines or the Muslims, depending on who paid them best. Around the middle of the century, the Normans began to carve out territories for themselves in southern Italy. Leo IX led an army against them in 1053, delaying their settlement; but by 1059 they were there to stay. Pope Nicholas II (∗1058–1061) decided to make the best of the situation: he gave the Normans, as a fief, the "toe," "heel," and "ankle" of Italy—Calabria, Apulia, and Capua, respectively—as well as Sicily, where the Normans had begun a slow conquest that eventually led to the creation of a new Kingdom of Sicily in 1130. Most of these territories had been part of the Byzantine Empire, though Sicily had been taken by the Muslims in the ninth century. The pope's "gift" therefore was not really the territories, which were not his to give, but instead the promise of St. Peter's support, something the Normans needed in order to legitimize their power. From this investment the popes gained new and powerful vassals—a Norman army.

The Rise of the Papacy

The popes also interceded in northern Italy. In Milan they allied themselves with some members of the emerging commune, the Patarines. This group, composed of clerics and laypeople, the well-to-do and the poor, was united by the conviction that a powerful and wealthy clergy was immoral and intolerable. Like Bruno of Cologne two decades later, they considered gold and silver morally compromising. The Patarines demanded of their clergy the poverty and chastity they believed the Apostles had practiced. They dreamed of a church pure in all its members: monks, clerics, and laity. This vision fueled their opposition to the archbishop and contributed to the successful political revolt of 1097. To a papacy determined to establish the superiority of spiritual power, the Patarines were sometimes useful because they openly—and sometimes violently—opposed the churchmen the emperor had appointed. Pope Alexander II (∗1061–1073) demonstrated his solidarity with the Patarines by allowing one of their leaders to fight under his flag, the so-called banner of St. Peter.

Seizing another opportunity to assert a papal role in secular affairs, Alexander II chose sides in the question of succession to the English throne in 1066, when William, duke of Normandy, challenged the other claimant, Harold, earl of Wessex. William sought papal approval for his expedition to cross the English Channel and capture the throne. By giving William the banner of St. Peter, Alexander both legitimized the duke's claims and made the papacy a participant in the Norman conquest. "Wherever he could throughout all the world, Alexander corrected evil without compromise," wrote a contemporary, "and William gladly received from him the gift of another banner as a pledge of the support of St. Peter."

Similarly, the pope participated in wars in Spain, where he supported Christians against the dominant Muslims. With al-Andalus (Islamic Spain) extending over most of the Iberian Peninsula, independent Christian communities remained only in the far north. Political fragmentation after 1031, however, turned al-Andalus into a mosaic of small, weak lordships, or *taifas*, making the Muslims fair game for the Christians. At first the Christian kings mainly demanded tribute from the Muslims, but slowly the idea of the *reconquista*, the Christian "reconquest" of Spain, took shape. In 1064 an army composed of men from northern Spain, France, and Normandy attacked and temporarily seized the fortress of Barbastro (at Zaragoza), deep in Muslim territory. The churchmen and princes of Spain proclaimed the Peace of God just before the battle, linking the idea of Christian solidarity with hostility against non-Christians. Just before this attack on Barbastro (or possibly in connection with an expedition about ten years later), Alexander II granted an indulgence to the Christians on their way to battle: "By the authority of the holy apostles, Peter and Paul, we relieve them of penance and grant them remission [forgiveness] of sins." For Christians the

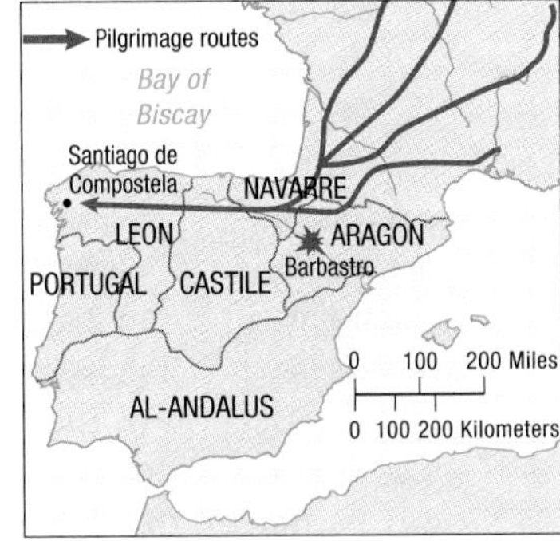

Spain in the Eleventh Century

campaign of Barbastro was a holy war, and they battled zealously. The conquerors killed the Muslim defenders, raped the women, sold the children into slavery, and loaded up on plunder. Christian victories like these forced the Islamic leaders of the *taifas* to call for help from the Almoravids in North Africa. In 1086 the Almoravids entered al-Andalus and drove back the Christians, but they then turned upon their hosts and took control of the *taifas*.

Although suffering military reverses at the hands of the Muslims after 1086, the Spanish Christians had great success in attracting western Europeans to their shrines. Pilgrims made their way across France and northern Spain to Santiago de Compostela, where St. James was said to be buried. The faithful believed that his relics worked miracles, especially for warriors. Although few women were reportedly helped by his cures, many stories were circulated of soldiers freed from their captors and of warriors victorious in battle through his intercession. St. James became the patron saint of victory against the Muslims in Spain, linking pilgrimage with military success. The popes became part of St. James's holy circle by giving special privileges to his see, eventually elevating it to an archbishopric.

Gregory VII Versus Henry IV: The Investiture Conflict

The papacy had its greatest political impact in Germany and Italy, where the emperor had checked the growth of local territorial lords by using bishops and archbishops as his trusted agents. In the hands of an anointed and pious king like Henry III (∗1039–1056), nothing seemed more natural than the union of political and religious authority. Yet contrary forces began to grow inadvertently when Leo IX, the ally of Henry III, began to use his office to enhance papal power.

In 1056, when he was just five years old, Henry IV (∗1056–1106) ascended to the German throne. Obviously, he was too young to be a strong ally of a reforming papacy or an obstacle to a pope seeking greater independence. Thus it was no accident that Nicholas II promulgated the Papal Election Decree in 1059, when Henry was only eight. The decree put the election of the pope into the hands of the College of Cardinals, which was a select group of clergy, and left the emperor's role in papal elections extremely ambiguous. The decree said simply that "in the papal election . . . due honor and reverence shall be shown our beloved son, Henry, king and emperor elect." The situation had changed radically since the days of Henry III, when Leo IX had been handpicked by the emperor.

Henry IV reached legal adulthood in 1066 and soon had to deal with Gregory VII, who became pope in 1073. Gregory (∗1073–1085) was (and remains) a controversial figure. Describing himself, he declared, "I have labored with all my power that Holy Church, the bride of god, our Lady Mother, might come again to her own splendor and might remain free, pure, and Catholic." But Henry viewed Gregory as an ambitious and evil man, who "seduced the world far and wide and stained the Church with the blood of her sons." With both king and pope competing for loyalty from the same

Emperor Henry IV
This "portrait" of Henry was made in the early twelfth century. He holds the orb and scepter of his imperial rule.

people and control over the same officials, the stage was set for a confrontation.

The clash between Henry IV and Gregory VII (and their successors) is called the Investiture Conflict. It began in 1075, when Gregory prohibited lay investiture. Specifically, investiture was the ritual by which a priest or bishop received his church and the land that went with it; more generally, it was the act that created a churchman and put him into office. Gregory's ban on lay investiture was intended as much more than a ceremonial change. He meant to revamp the very structure of the church. Gregory believed only a churchman could choose another churchman, and only a churchman could invest another. But more important, he did not consider rulers churchmen in his scheme; Gregory asserted that every temporal (that is, worldly) ruler was a layman and *only* a layman, despite the religious and spiritual roles associated with anointed kings that had developed over many centuries in the West.

The ensuing struggle was about whether the king or the pope would head the church and indeed all Christian society. The first confrontation came over the archbishopric of Milan. After Gregory forbade lay investiture, Henry decided to ignore the candidate for archbishop who had been selected and consecrated (by laying on of hands and anointment) by the Patarines but not invested by the pope. Instead Henry sent his delegates to invest a different man. Fast and furious denunciations and counterdenunciations by pope and emperor followed. In 1076, Henry called a council of German bishops who demanded that Gregory, that "false monk," resign. In reply Gregory called a synod that both excommunicated and suspended Henry from office:

> *I deprive King Henry, son of the emperor Henry, who has rebelled against [God's] Church with unheard-of audacity, of the government over the whole kingdom of Germany and Italy, and I release all Christian men from the allegiance which they have sworn or may swear to him, and I forbid anyone to serve him as king.*

The last part of this decree gave it a secular punch because it authorized anyone in Henry's kingdom to rebel against him. Henry's enemies, mostly German princes (that is, German aristocrats), now threatened to elect another king. They were motivated partly by religious sentiments, as many had established links with the papacy through their support of reformed monasteries, and partly by political opportunism, as they had chafed under the strong German king, who had tried to keep their power in check. Some bishops, such as Hermann of Metz, also joined forces with Gregory's reform party, a great blow to royal power because Henry desperately needed the troops supplied by his churchmen.

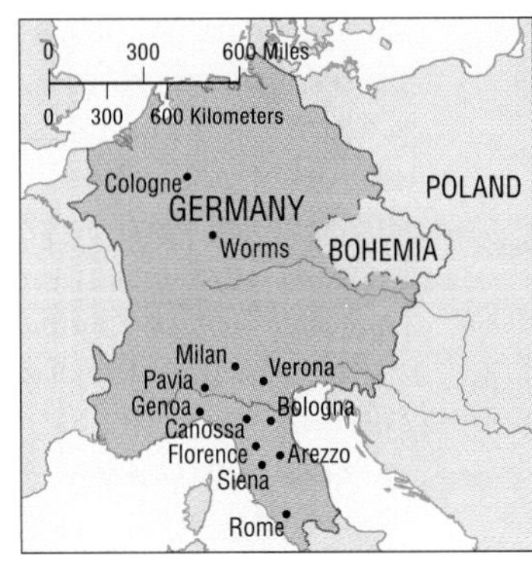

The Investiture Conflict

Attacked from all sides, Henry traveled to Gregory, who in turn was journeying northward to visit the rebellious princes. In early 1077 king and pope met at Canossa, high in central Italy's snowy Apennine Mountains. Gregory was inside a fortress there; Henry stood outside as a penitent. This posture was an astute move by Henry because no priest could refuse absolution to a penitent; Gregory had to receive Henry back into the church. But Gregory now had the advantage of the king's humiliation before the majesty of the pope. Gregory's description of Henry suggests that the pope believed himself to have triumphed:

> *There, on three successive days, standing before the castle gate, laying aside all royal insignia, barefooted and in coarse attire, he did not cease, with many tears, to beseech the apostolic help and comfort.*

Although Henry was technically back in the fold, nothing of substance had been resolved and war began. The princes elected an antiking, and Henry and his supporters elected an antipope. From 1077 until 1122 Germany was ravaged by civil war.

The Investiture Conflict was finally resolved long after Henry IV and Gregory VII had died. In 1122 the Concordat of Worms ended the fighting with a compromise that relied on a conceptual distinction between two parts of investiture—the spiritual (in which a man received the symbols of his clerical office) and the secular (in which he received the symbols of the material goods that would allow him to function). Under the terms of the concordat, the ring and staff, the symbols of pastoral office, would be given by a churchman in the first part of the ceremony. The emperor or his representative would touch the bishop with a scepter, a symbolic gesture that stood for the land and other possessions that went with his office, in the second part of the ceremony. Elections of bishops in Germany would take place "in the presence" of the emperor—that is, under his influence. In Italy the pope would have a comparable role.

Thus in the end secular rulers continued to have a part in choosing and investing churchmen, but few people any longer claimed the king was the "head of the church." Just as the new investiture ceremony broke the ritual into spiritual and secular parts, so too it implied a new notion of kingship that separated it from priesthood. The Investiture Conflict did not produce the modern distinction between church and state—that would develop only very slowly—but it set the wheels in motion.

Winners of the Investiture Conflict: German Princes and Italian Communes

The Investiture Conflict and the civil war it generated shattered the delicate balance among political and ecclesiastical powers in Germany and Italy. The German princes consolidated their lands and their positions at the expense of royal power, and the Italian communes flexed their political muscles and defied the authority of the emperor.

The disintegration of strong central authority allowed regional powers to assert themselves, much as the fragmentation of the Carolingian empire had done in France two centuries before. In Germany many nobles, including bishops, built castles and began to impose the powers of the ban over the residents of the countryside. Free peasants became serfs bound to local lords. Finding mounted warriors far superior to foot soldiers, the princes soon surrounded themselves with knights. Some of these new warriors were free men now bound to the princes as vassals; others advanced from the ranks of the ministerials, losing their servile status. In some parts of Germany the twelfth century marked the beginning of the fusing of the ranks of free knights and ministerials, and the servile origins of the ministerials were forgotten. The ministerials of the archbishop of Cologne, for example, pledged their fealty to him as their lord and received fiefs in return. Expected to go off to battle and other expeditions with him, they profited from his largess on these occasions. When they accompanied the archbishop to Rome, he gave them provisions for themselves and their servants:

> *The archbishop shall give each one of them ten marks and forty yards of cloth which is called "scarlet," and to every two knights [ministerials] he shall give a packhorse and a saddle with all that belongs to it, and two bags with a cover for them . . . and four horseshoes and twenty-four nails. After they reach the Alps the archbishop shall give each knight a mark a month for his expenses.*

These ministerials had achieved the status of the lower nobility. However, in Germany knighthood never achieved as high a status as it did in France. German members of the upper nobility scorned the titles of knight or vassal and never referred to themselves in those terms. Their conviction that vassalage was demeaning added to the German princes' resistance to becoming vassals of the king. Yet after 1122 the German king considered their homage and fealty to him a necessity. The king's power had been based on his land, his episcopacy, his ministerials, and his troops of free men. With these resources diminished, he needed to control the princes in a new way. The bonds of vassalage, the castles that dotted the countryside, the new monasteries that were founded in Germany, and the ministerial troops commanded by bishops enhanced the powers of the princes but (too often) not of the king. If he could make the princes his vassals, he could use their troops and demand their loyalty. Throughout the twelfth century the German king struggled to become the feudal lord of the princes of Germany. In the end he succeeded, but at a very high price. The princes became virtual monarchs within their own principalities, whereas the emperor, though retaining his title, became a figurehead.

As overlord of northern Italy the emperor also lost power to the communes and other movements for local self-government, which developed in the late eleventh and early twelfth century. People in cities like Pavia, Genoa, Brescia, Bologna, Siena, Arezzo, and Florence followed the lead of communes like Milan, forming town councils and governing themselves. Although many of these governments began, as in Milan, with uprisings against the city's bishop, most bishops soon learned to adapt to the new conditions. Before 1122 the bishops of Verona had been imperial appointees, foreigners who came from Germany and often the imperial court. After the Investiture Conflict, local leading families supplied the candidates from which Verona's bishops were chosen. These local men involved themselves vigorously in local affairs. For example, Bishop Tebaldus of Verona (*1135–1157) asserted his rights over the parish churches in his diocese, energetically pursued litigation on behalf of his own church's patrimony, and rebuilt his cathedral on a grand scale. His activities showed the new way in which local religious and political life would mesh in the urban centers of Italy.

The rise of the Italian communes in a time of war between the emperor and the pope left an indelible mark on these new political entities. Every commune, in Italy and elsewhere, had rival factions: conflicts between poor and rich or between competing aristocratic families raged from time to time. But in Italy a third conflict, between the supporters of the emperor and those of the pope, caused friction throughout the twelfth century. The ongoing hostilities of popes and emperors mirrored fierce communal struggles in which factions, motivated in part by local grievances, claimed to fight on behalf of the papal or imperial cause.

Religious Sanctions for Marriage

The Gregorian reform affected not only politics but also married life. When in 1125 a German bishop undertook (with the connivance of the king of Poland) a mission to convert the pagan Pomeranians (who lived along the Baltic Sea coast, now mostly in Poland), he did not simply require them to believe in Christ and be baptized. He demanded, above all, that they observe the church's laws concerning marriage, by now well established: "He forbade them to marry their godmothers or their own cousins up to the sixth and seventh generation and told them that each man should be content with only one wife."

Today we take it for granted that religious authorities exercise control over marriages and require monogamy, but in the Middle Ages the effective involvement of the church in these matters came only after the Gregorian reform. Only in the twelfth century did people regularly come to be married by a priest in church, and only then did churchmen assume jurisdiction over marital disputes, not simply in cases involving royalty but also in those of lesser aristocrats. The clergy's prohibition of marriage partners as distant as seventh cousins (marriage between such cousins was considered incest) had the potential to control dynastic alliances. Because many noble families kept their inheritance intact through a single male heir, those heirs' marriages took on great significance. The church's incest prohibitions gave the clergy a measure of power over all European states. For example, when the king of England, Henry I (*1100–1135), wanted to marry one of his daughters to William of Warenne, early of Surrey (his good friend, advisor, and important political ally), he asked Anselm, the archbishop of Canterbury, for his advice. Anselm warned against the union on the grounds that William and his prospective bride shared two ancestors several generations back. The match was broken off.

Intense ecclesiastical interest in marriage accompanied the church's increased accentuation of the sacraments and the special nature of the priest, whose chief role was to perform them. Christians believed the sacraments were the regular means by which God's heavenly grace infused mundane existence. Sacraments marked the path of life from birth to death, the route of the sinner to salvation. The priest's control over these vehicles of grace exalted his position and set him apart from everyone else. Gregory VII claimed the sacrament of the Mass was "the greatest thing in the Christian religion." No layman could perform anything equal to it. This new emphasis on the sacraments, which were now more clearly and carefully defined, along with the desire to set priests clearly apart from the laity, led to vigorous enforcement of an old element of church discipline: the celibacy of priests.

The demand for a celibate clergy had far-reaching significance for the history of the church. It distanced western clerics even further from their eastern Orthodox counterparts (who did not practice celibacy), exacerbating the schism of 1054. It also broke with traditional local practices, as clerical marriage was in some places the norm. In Normandy even the highest clergymen had wives: in the eleventh century one archbishop of Rouen was married and had three sons; a bishop of Sées was the father of an archbishop. Gregorian reformers exhorted every cleric in higher orders, from the humble parish priest to the exalted bishop, not to marry or to abandon his wife. Naturally many churchmen resisted. The historian Orderic Vitalis (1075–c.1142) reported that John, the archbishop of Rouen,

> *fulfilled his duties as metropolitan with courage and thoroughness, continually striving to separate immoral priests from their mistresses [wives]: on one occasion when he forbade them to keep concubines he was stoned out of the synod.*

Undaunted, the reformers persisted, and in 1123 the pope proclaimed all clerical marriages invalid. No wonder a poem of the twelfth century had a lady repulse a cleric's officer of love with the reply: "I refuse to commit adultery; I want to get married." Clearly clerics were no longer suitable candidates for matrimony.

The same reformers who preached against clerical marriage, however, attributed new sanctity to lay marriages. A twelfth-century thinker like Hugh of St. Victor dwelled on the sacramental meaning of marriage:

> *Can you find anything else in marriage except conjugal society which makes it sacred and by which you can assert that it is holy? . . . See now the nature of the contract by which they bind themselves in consented marriage. Henceforth and forever, each shall be to the other as a same self in all sincere love, all careful solicitude, every kindness of affection, in constant compassion, unflagging consolation, and faithful devotedness.*

Hugh saw marriage as a matter of love. The topic of love—married and unmarried, human and divine—dominated twelfth-century thought.

Important Popes

1058–1061 Nicholas II. In 1059 he proclaimed the Papal Election Decree and gave southern Italy to the Normans.

1073–1085 Gregory VII. In 1075 he forbade lay investiture; in 1076 he excommunicated Henry IV; in 1077 he was briefly reconciled with Henry at Canossa.

1088–1099 Urban II. In 1095 he preached the First Crusade (1096–1099) at the Council of Clermont.

The "Papal Monarchy"

The newly reformed and strengthened papacy enhanced its position by consolidating and imposing canon (church) law. The prohibition against clerical marriage, for example, was a law derived from decrees promulgated by meetings of churchmen at church councils and synods since the fourth century. Although canon law originated at such meetings, not until the Gregorian reform were these decrees—until now scattered here and there—compiled in a great push for systematization. This movement to organize canon law was part of a wider legal development: reformers began to study church canons in the same formal and orderly manner that legal scholars were beginning to use for Roman and other secular laws. A landmark in canon law jurisprudence was the *Concordance of Discordant Canons*, also known as the *Decretum*, compiled in about 1140 by Gratian, a monk who taught law at Bologna in northern Italy. Gratian gathered thousands of passages from the decrees of popes and councils with the intention of showing their harmony. To make conflicting canons conform to one another, he adopted the principle that papal pronouncements superseded the laws of church councils and all secular laws.

At the time Gratian was writing, the papal *curia*, or government, resembled a court of law with its own collection agency. The papacy had developed a bureaucracy to hear cases and rule on petitions. Disputed episcopal elections, for example, flooded into Rome in the wake of the Investiture Conflict. Hearing cases cost money: lawyers, judges, and courtroom clerks had to be paid. Churchmen not involved in litigation went to Rome for other sorts of benefits: to petition for privileges for their monasteries or to be consecrated by the pope, vicar of St. Peter. These services were also expensive, requiring hearing officers, notaries, and collectors. The lands owned by the papacy were not sufficient to support the growing administrative apparatus these services required, and therefore the petitioners and litigants themselves had to pay, a practice they resented. A satire written about 1100, in the style of the Gospels, made bitter fun of papal greed:

> *There came to the court a certain wealthy clerk, fat and thick, and gross, who in the*

sedition had committed murder. He first gave to the dispenser, second to the treasurer, third to the cardinals. But they thought among themselves that they should receive more. The Lord Pope, hearing that his cardinals had received many gifts, was sick, nigh unto death. But the rich man sent to him a couch of gold and silver and immediately he was made whole. Then the Lord Pope called his cardinals and ministers to him and said to them: "Brethren, look, lest anyone deceive you with vain words. For I have given you an example: as I have grasped, so you grasp also."

The First Crusade

Like other medieval rulers, the pope supported and proclaimed wars. The Crusades were a series of wars authorized by the papacy in which armies of European Christians set forth to battle non-Christians, especially Muslims in the Holy Land. In 1095 on the last day of a church council devoted to the Peace and Truce of God, Pope Urban II preached the First Crusade. Urban's sermon, occurring at a time of affirmed peace among Christians and solidarity against all violators of the Truce of God, galvanized a popular response similar to the militant fervor before the battle of Barbastro, but on a scale unprecedented in the medieval world. Armies of crusaders trekked from all parts of Europe to the Holy Land, their leaders eventually setting up fragile states in what is today the Middle East. Crusades continued throughout the following centuries to bolster or try to reconquer the lands wrested from the Muslims. Although the Crusades ultimately failed in the sense that the crusaders did not succeed in permanently retaining the Holy Land for Christendom, they were a pivotal episode in Western civilization. They marked the first stage of European overseas expansion, of what later would become imperialism.

The events that led to the First Crusade began in Asia Minor. The Muslim world had splintered into numerous small states in the tenth century; by the 1050s the fierce, nomadic, and Sunni Muslim Seljuk Turks had captured Baghdad, subjugated the caliphate, and begun to threaten Byzantium. The difficulties Emperor Romanus IV had in pulling together an army to attack the Turks in 1071 revealed how weak his position had become. Unable to muster Byzantine troops—the *strategoi* were busy defending their own districts, and provincial nobles were wary of sending support to the emperor—Romanus had to rely on a mercenary army made up of Normans, Franks, Slavs, and even Turks. This motley force met the Seljuks under Sultan Alp Arslan at Manzikert in what is today eastern Turkey. The battle was a disaster for Romanus: the Seljuks routed his army and captured him. Manzikert marked the end of Byzantine domination in the region.

The Turks, gradually settling in Asia Minor, extended their control across the empire and beyond, all the way to Jerusalem, which had been under Muslim control since the seventh century. In 1095 the Byzantine emperor Alexius I appealed to Pope Urban II (*1088–1099) for help, hoping to get new mercenary troops for a fresh offensive.

Urban II chose to interpret the request differently. At the Council of Clermont (in France) in 1095, after finishing the usual business of proclaiming the Truce of God and condemning simoniac clergy, Urban moved outside the church and addressed an already excited throng:

Oh, race of Franks, race from across the mountains, race beloved and chosen by God. . . . Let hatred depart from among you, let your quarrels end, let wars cease, and let all dissensions and controversies slumber. Enter upon the road to the Holy Sepulcher; wrest that land from the wicked race, and subject it to yourselves.

The crowd reportedly responded spontaneously in one voice: "God wills it." Historians remain divided over Urban's motives for his massive call to arms. Certainly he hoped to return the Holy Land to Christian control. He was also anxious to fulfill the goals of the Truce of God by turning the entire "race of Franks" into a peace militia dedicated to holy purposes, an army of God. Just as the Truce of God mobilized whole communities to fight against anyone who broke it, so the First Crusade impelled armed groups sworn to free the Holy Land of its enemies to form. Finally, Urban's call placed the papacy in a new position of leadership, one that complemented in a military arena the position the popes had gained in the church hierarchy.

The early Crusades involved many people. Both men and women, rich and poor, young and old participated. They abandoned their homes and braved the rough journey to the Holy Land to fight

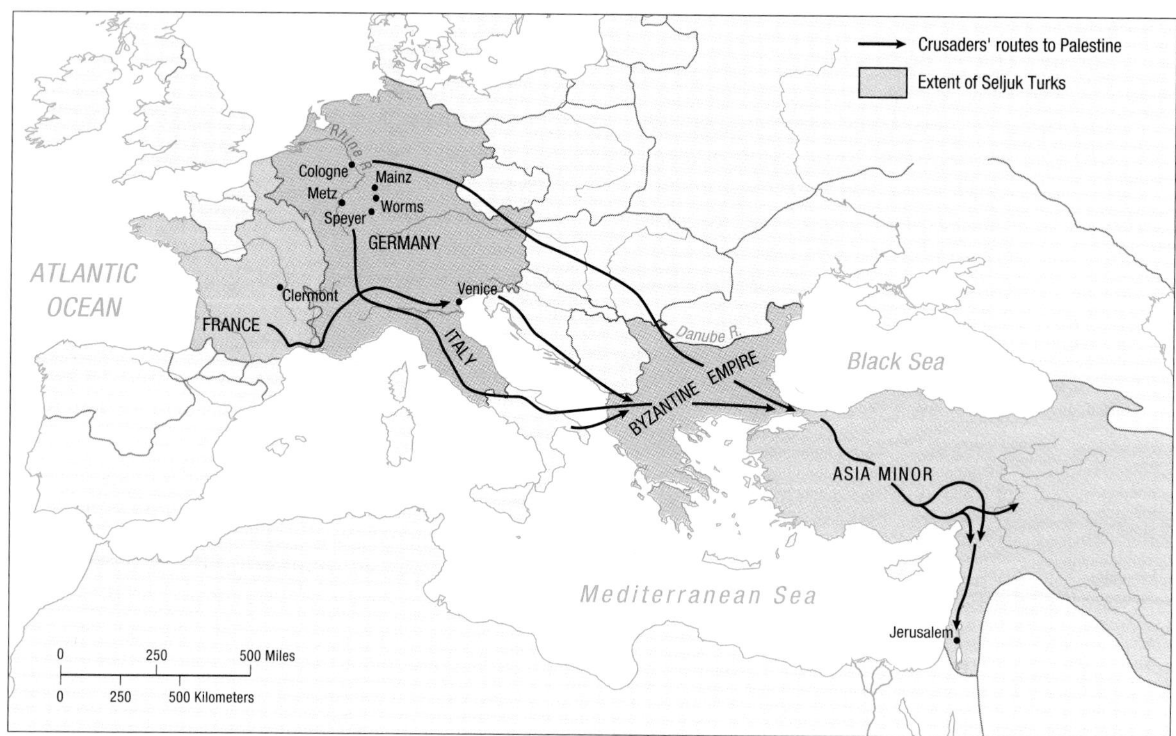

The First Crusade

for their God. They also went—especially younger sons of aristocrats, who could not expect an inheritance in Europe because of the practice of primogeniture—because they wanted land. Some knights took the cross because in addition to their pious duty they were obligated to follow their lord. Others hoped for plunder. Some crusaders were accompanied by their wives, who went partly to be with their husbands and partly to express their own militant piety. Other women went as servants; a few may have been fighters. Children and old men and women, not able to fight, sewed the hides used on siege engines—giant machines used to hurl stones at enemy fortifications. As more Crusades were undertaken during the twelfth century, the transport and supply of these armies became a lucrative business for the commercial classes of maritime Italian cities such as Venice.

The armies of the First Crusade were not organized as one military force but rather as separate militias, each commanded by a different individual. Fulcher of Chartres, an eyewitness, reported:

> *So with such a great band proceeding from western parts, gradually from day to day on the way there grew armies of innumerable people coming together from everywhere. Thus a countless multitude speaking many languages and coming from many regions was to be seen. However, all were not assembled into one army until we arrived at the city of Nicaea.*

Fulcher was speaking of the armies led by nobles and authorized by the pope. One band, not authorized by the pope, consisted of commoners. This Peasant's Crusade, which started out before the others under the leadership of an eloquent but militarily unprepared preacher, Peter the Hermit, was butchered as soon as it reached Asia Minor.

In some crusaders' minds the "wicked races" were much closer to home: some armies stopped along their way to the Holy Land to kill Jews. By this time most Jews lived in cities, many in the flourishing commercial region of the Rhineland. Under Henry IV the Jews in Speyer and elsewhere in the empire had gained a place within the government system by receiving protection from the local bishop (an imperial appointee) in return for paying a tax. Within these cities the Jews lived in their own neighborhoods—Bishop Rüdiger even built walls around the one at Speyer—and their tightly knit communities focused around the synagogue, which was a school and community center as well as a place of worship. Nevertheless, Jews also participated in the life of the larger Christian community. Archbishop Anno of Cologne dealt with Jewish moneylenders, and other Jews in Cologne were allowed to trade their wares at the fairs there. Although officials pronounced against the Jews from time to time and Jews were occasionally expelled from cities like Mainz, they were not persecuted systematically until the First Crusade. Then, as Guibert of Nogent put it, the crusaders considered it ridiculous to attack Muslims when other infidels lived in their own backyard: "That's doing our work backward." A number of Crusade leaders threatened Jews with forced conversion or death but relented when the Jews paid them money. Others, however, attacked. Jews sometimes found refuge with bishops or in the houses of Christian friends, but in many cities—Metz, Speyer, Worms, Mainz, and Cologne—they were massacred. Laden with booty from the Jewish quarters, the crusaders continued on their way to Jerusalem.

The main objective of the First Crusade—to wrest the Holy Land from the Muslims and subject it to Christian rule—was accomplished largely because of Muslim disunity. After nearly a year of ineffectual attacks, the crusaders took Antioch on June 3, 1098, killing every Turk in the city; on July 15, 1099, they seized Jerusalem. The leaders of the First Crusade set up four states—called *Outremer*, the lands "beyond the sea"—on the coastal fringe of the Muslim west. They held on to them until 1144.

The Revival of Monarchies

The establishment of states was characteristic of twelfth-century political life. Everywhere, princes and kings consolidated their rule. They found new and old ideologies to justify their hegemony; they hired officials to work for them; and they found vassals and churchmen to support them. Money gave them increased effectiveness, and the new commercial economy supplied them with increased revenues.

Louis the Fat: A Model King of France

During the Investiture Conflict the papacy had been preoccupied with the emperor, who controlled many church officials and whose title implied authority over Rome. Although the emperor's dominion was weakened after 1122, the French king, whose role had been slight in the tenth and eleventh centuries, escaped the conflict untouched. In the twelfth century he used the many institutions of French society to bolster his rule: money, money makers, vassals, castles, churchmen, lawyers, intellectuals, and artists.

Louis VI, known as Louis the Fat (*1108–1137) because by the end of his life he had become so heavy that he had to be hoisted onto his horse by a crane, was a tireless defender of royal prerogatives. We know a good deal about him and his reputation because a contemporary, Suger (1081–1152) the abbot of St. Denis, wrote Louis's biography. Suger and Louis had attended school together as boys and remained close associates until Louis's death. In fact, Suger tutored Louis's son, Louis VII (*1137–1180), and acted as regent of France when Louis VII left to lead the Second Crusade in 1147.

Suger was a chronicler and propagandist for Louis the Fat. In the area around Paris, the Ile-de-France, Louis set himself the task of consolidating territory and subduing opponents. In Suger's view these were righteous undertakings. He thought of the king as the head of a political hierarchy in which Louis had rights over the French nobles because they were his vassals or because they broke the peace. Sugar also believed Louis had a religious role: to protect the church and the poor. He viewed Louis as another Charlemagne, a ruler for all society, not merely an overlord of the nobility. Louis waged war to keep God's peace. Of course, the Gregorian reform had made its mark: Suger did not claim Louis was the head of the church, but he emphasized the royal dignity and its importance to the papacy. When Pope Paschal II arrived in France

> *for the love of God [Louis and his father] humbled their royal majesty before his feet, in the way that kings bow down with lowered diadem before the tomb of the fisherman Peter. The lord pope lifted them up and made them sit before him like devout sons of the apostles. In the manner of a wise man acting wisely, he*

conferred with them privately on the present condition of the church. Softening them with compliments, he petitioned them to bring aid to the blessed Peter and to himself, his vicar, and to lend support to the church.

Here the pope was shown needing the king's advice. Meanwhile, Suger stressed Louis's independent religious role:

Accompanied by the clergy, to whom he was always humbly attached, he turned off the road toward the well-fortified castle of Crécy. Helped by his powerful band of armed men, or rather by the hand of God, he abruptly seized the castle and captured its very strong tower as if it were simply the hut of a peasant. Having startled those criminals, he piously slaughtered the impious.

Stained Glass: Illuminating the Spirit
In this detail from a stained-glass window made for Suger's chapel of the Virgin Mary at St. Denis, Suger himself appears as the small, bowing figure. In Suger's view, the windows of the choir, glowing in rich and splendid colors, led viewers to spiritual illumination.

When Louis VI died in 1137, Suger's notion of the might and right of the king of France reflected reality in an extremely small area. The king controlled only the territory around Paris and extending southward toward the Loire valley; here he was recognized as the lord of other territorial lords. Elsewhere he was, at best, the nominal lord of powerful vassals. Nevertheless, Louis laid the groundwork for the gradual extension of royal power in France. As a lord the king could call upon his vassals to aid him in time of war (though the great ones sometimes disregarded his wishes and chose not to help). From the ban and his rights as a landlord, the king obtained many dues and taxes. He also drew revenues from Paris, a thriving city not only of commerce but also of scholarship. Officials, called provosts, enforced royal laws and collected taxes. The offices were auctioned off to the highest bidder, so in effect the provosts acted as tax-farmers for the king. With money and land, Louis could dispense the favors and give the gifts that added to his prestige and his power. Louis VI and Suger together created the territorial core and the royal ideal of the future French monarchy.

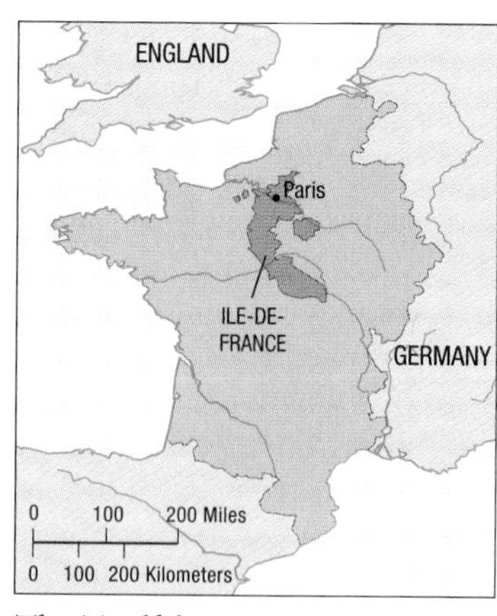

The Twelfth-Century French Monarchy

Norman England

Unlike the kings of France, who consolidated their hold gradually, the twelfth-century kings of England ruled the whole kingdom by right of conquest. When Edward the Confessor died childless in 1066, three main contenders desired the English throne: Harold, earl of Wessex, an Englishman close to the king but not of royal blood; Harald Hardrada, the king of Norway, who had unsuccessfully attempted to conquer the Danes and now turned hopefully to England; and William (1027–1087), the duke of Normandy, who claimed that Edward had promised him the throne fifteen years earlier. On his deathbed, Edward had named

Earl Harold to succeed him, and the *witan*, a royal advisory committee that had the right to choose the king, had confirmed the nomination.

When he learned that Harold had been anointed and crowned, William prepared for battle. Appealing to the pope, he received the banner of St. Peter, and with this symbol of God's approval William launched the invasion of England, filling his ships with warriors recruited from many parts of France. As a Norman writer put it:

> *He retained them all, giving them much and promising more. Many came by agreement made by them beforehand; many bargained for lands, if they should win England; some required pay, allowances and gifts.*

About a week before William's invasion force landed, Harold defeated Harald Hardrada. When he heard of William's arrival, Harold wheeled his forces south, marching them 250 miles and picking up new soldiers along the way to meet the Normans. The two armies clashed at Hastings on October 14, 1066, in one of history's rare decisive battles. Both armies had about seven or eight thousand men, Harold's in defensive position on a slope, William's attacking from below. All the men were crammed into a very small space as they began the fight. Most of the English were on foot, armed with battle-axes and stones tied to sticks, which could be thrown with great force. William's army consisted of perhaps three thousand mounted knights, a thousand archers, and the rest infantry. At first William's knights broke ranks, frightened by the fiercely thrown battle-axes of the English; but then some of the English also broke rank as they pursued the knights. William removed his helmet so his men would know him, rallying them to surround and cut down the English who had broken away. Similar skirmishes lasted the entire afternoon, and gradually Harold's troops were worn down, particularly by William's archers, whose arrows flew a hundred yards, much farther than an English battle-ax could be thrown. By dusk, King Harold was dead and his army utterly defeated. No other army gathered to oppose the successful claimant.

Some people in England supported William willingly; in fact, the first to come forward was a most illustrious woman, Queen Edith, Harold's sister and the widow of Edward the Confessor. Those English who backed William considered his victory a verdict from God, and they hoped to be granted a place in the new order themselves. But William and his men wanted to replace, not assimilate, the Anglo-Saxons. In the course of William's reign, families from the Continent almost totally supplanted the English aristocracy. And although the English peasantry remained—now with new lords—they were severely shaken. A twelfth-century historian "recorded" William's deathbed confession:

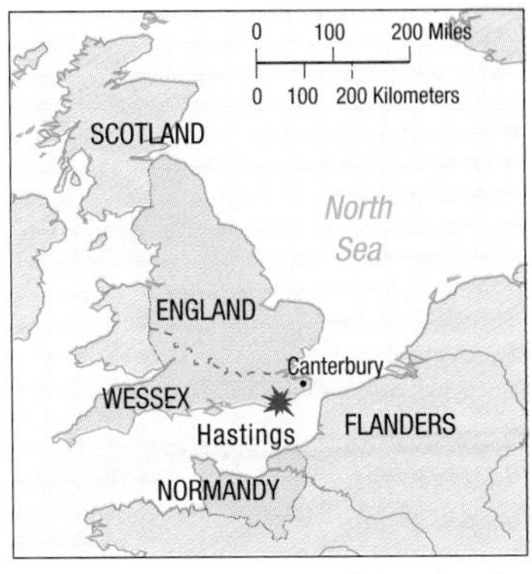

Norman Conquest of England

> *I have persecuted [England's] native inhabitants beyond all reason. Whether gentle or simple, I have cruelly oppressed them; many I unjustly disinherited; innumerable multitudes, especially in the county of York, perished through me by famine or the sword.*

Modern historians estimate that one out of five people in England died as a result of the Norman conquest.

Although the Normans destroyed a generation of English men and women, they did preserve and extend many Anglo-Saxon institutions. For example, the Norman kings used the writ to communicate orders, and they retained the old administrative divisions of shires (counties) and hundreds. But William and his successors also drew from continental institutions. Norman England became a graded political hierarchy, culminating with the king and buttressed by his castles. The land was treated as the monarch's booty; William kept about 20 percent of it for himself and divided the rest, distributing it in large but scattered fiefs to a relatively small number of his greatest vassals (his barons) and family members, lay and ecclesiastical, as well as to some lesser men, such as personal servants and soldiers. In turn these men maintained their own vassals; they owed the king military service (and the service of a fixed number of their vassals) along with certain dues and rights, such as reliefs (money paid upon

William the Conqueror
The battle of Hastings and the events leading up to it were chronicled in an extraordinary embroidery measuring about 230 feet long and 20 inches high called the Bayeaux Tapestry. The portion shown here depicts Duke Harold swearing an oath to William the Conqueror, seated on a throne.

inheriting a fief) and aids (payments made on important occasions).

These revenues and rights came from the nobles, but the king of England commanded the peasantry as well. Twenty years after his conquest, William ordered a survey and census of England, the so-called Domesday Book. It was the most extensive inventory of land, agricultural produce, taxes, and population that had ever been compiled anywhere in Europe. William

> *sent his men over all England into every shire and had them find out how many hundred hides [a measure of land] there were in the shire, or what land and cattle the king himself had in the country, or what dues he ought to receive every year from the shire. . . . So very narrowly did he have the survey to be made that there was not a single hide or yard of land, nor indeed . . . an ox or a cow or a pig left out.*

Local surveys were carried out by consulting Anglo-Saxon tax lists and by taking testimony from local jurors, men sworn to answer a series of formal questions truthfully. From these inquests scribes wrote voluminous reports filled with facts and statements from villagers, sheriffs, priests, and barons. These reports were then summarized in the Domesday Book, a concise record of England's resources that supplied the king and his officials with information such as how much and what sort of land England had, who held it, and what revenues —including the lucrative Danegeld, which was now in effect a royal tax—could be expected from it.

The Norman kings retained the Anglo-Saxon legal system, based on the shire and hundred courts. Although great lords in England set up law courts (just as on the Continent), the peculiarly English system of royal district courts continued to flourish. A sheriff appointed by the king to police the shire and muster military levies also acted as judge. If he took advantage of his position, a strong king like William could call him to account: "Summon my sheriffs by my order," began a writ from William to his magnates,

> *and tell them that they must return to my bishoprics and abbacies all the demesne, and all the demesne-land which . . . they have consented to hold or which they have seized by violence.*

William and his successors intended to control conflicts. If the disagreement involved their barons, they expected the litigants to come to "their own" court, the court of the king. "But if the dispute is between the vassals of two different lords let the plea be held in the shire court." The "men of the shire" had attended the meetings of these courts during the Anglo-Saxon period, and the practice continued under the Normans. These courts had been the sites of the regional inquests for the Domesday Book. Hence the courts had a popular as well as a royal component. Eventually the county courts would encroach on the courts of the great lords and extend the king's law across all of England to create English "common law."

The Norman conquest tied England to the languages, politics, institutions, and culture of the Continent. Modern English is an amalgam of Anglo-Saxon and Norman French, the language the Normans spoke. English commerce was linked to the wool industry in Flanders. The continental

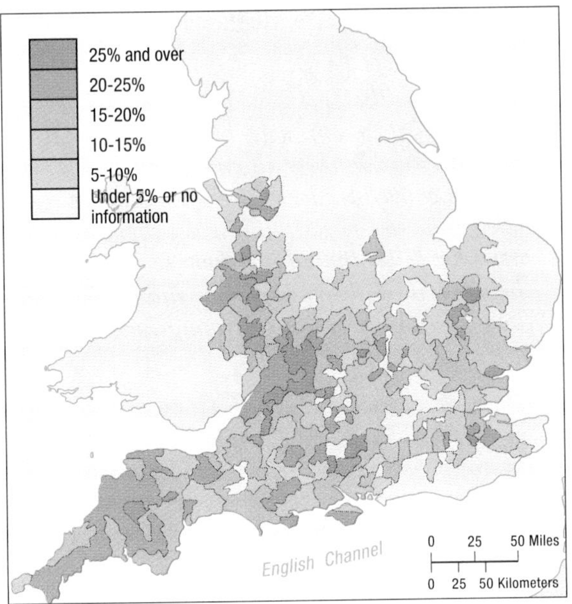

Distribution of Slaves in England in 1086 as Reported in Domesday
The Domesday Survey has been used by historians to understand issues such as the distribution of slaves in eleventh-century England. Domesday is only a partial guide to the full reality, however, because its coverage of the English shires was somewhat uneven.

movement for church reform had its counterpart in England, with a controversy similar to the Investiture Conflict: in 1097 and again from 1103 to 1107, the archbishop of Canterbury, St. Anselm (1033–1109) and the sons of William clashed over the king's prerogatives over churchmen and church offices, the same issues that had engaged Henry IV and the pope. The English compromise of 1107 anticipated the provisions of the Concordat of Worms of 1122 by rescinding the king's right to bestow the staff and ring but leaving him the right to receive the homage of churchmen before their consecration. The English Channel served as a bridge rather than a barrier to the interchange of culture. St. Anselm, the most brilliant intellect of his day, for example, was born in Italy and became abbot of the Norman monastery of Bec before his appointment as archbishop in England. Finally, the barons of England retained their estates in Normandy and elsewhere, and the kings of England often spent more time on the Continent than they did on the island. The story of England after 1066 is, in miniature, the story of Europe.

A Byzantine Revival

At the very end of the eleventh century the Byzantine Empire began to recover from the disastrous battle at Manzikert. In 1081, ten years after that debacle, the energetic soldier Alexius Comnenus seized the throne. He faced considerable unrest in Constantinople, whose populace suffered from a combination of high taxes and rising living costs; and on every side the empire was under attack—from Normans in southern Italy, Seljuk Turks in Asia Minor, and new groups in the Balkans. But Alexius I (✶1081–1118) managed to turn actual and potential enemies against one another, staving off immediate defeat. For example, he called upon the Cuman Turks to help him beat back the Pecheneg Turks, who in 1091 marched toward Constantinople. The battle was a great success for Alexius; the Pechenegs were annihilated. (Although the Cumans assisted the Byzantines in this instance, in the 1120s they attacked the empire in turn.) Similarly, Alexius asked Urban II to supply him with some western troops to fight his enemies. When he learned that crusaders rather than mercenaries were on the way, he closed the gates of Constantinople to the troops, who were eager to plunder, and negotiated their transport to Asia Minor. He also extracted an oath from their leaders (which was later broken, however) that formerly Byzantine cities captured by the crusaders be returned to him. His daughter, Anna Comnena (1083–c. 1148), later wrote an account of the Crusades from the Byzantine perspective in a book about her father, the *Alexiad*: to her the crusaders were barbarians and her father the consummate statesman and diplomat:

> *[A large contingent of crusaders arrived], a numberless heterogeneous host gathered together from almost all the Keltic lands [lands of the Franks] with their leaders (kings and dukes and counts and even bishops). The emperor sent envoys to greet them as a mark of friendship and forwarded politic letters. It was typical of Alexius: he had an uncanny prevision and knew how to seize a point of vantage before his rivals. Officers appointed for this particular task were ordered to provide*

> *victuals on the journey—the pilgrims must have no excuse for complaint for any reason whatever. Meanwhile they were eagerly pressing on to the capital. . . . With the idea of enforcing the same oath that Godfrey [a Crusade leader who had arrived earlier] had taken, Alexius . . . refuted their objections with no difficulty at all and harried them in a hundred ways until they were driven to take the oath.*

To wage all the wars he had to fight, Alexius relied less on the peasant-farmers and the *theme* system than on mercenaries and great magnates armed and mounted like western knights and accompanied by their own troops. In return for their services he gave these nobles *pronoia*, lifetime possession of large imperial estates and their dependent peasants. The *theme* system, under which peasant-soldiers in earlier centuries had been settled on imperial lands, gradually disappeared. Alexius conciliated the great families by giving the provincial nobility *pronoia* and satisfied the urban elite by granting them new offices. Although the emperor sometimes used church property to generate revenue, he normally got on well with the patriarch and Byzantine clergy, for emperor and church depended on one another to suppress heresy and foster orthodoxy. Anna Comnena wrote that her father imprisoned some heretics and then worked together with the church to convert them:

> *He sent for [the heretics] every day and personally taught them, with frequent exhortations, to abandon their abominable cult. Certain church leaders were told to make daily visits to the rest, to instruct them in the orthodox faith and advise them to give up their heretical ideas. And some did change for the better and were freed from prison, but others died in their heresy.*

The emperors of the Comnenian dynasty (1081–1185) thus bought a measure of increased imperial power, but at the price of important concessions to the nobility. The distribution of *pronoia* made the Byzantine Empire resemble a kingdom like England, where the great barons received fiefs in return for military service. However, at first the *pronoia* could not be inherited, nor could their holders subdivide them to give to their own warriors. In this way the emperor retained more direct authority over every level of the Byzantine populace than did the rulers of Europe.

Alexius's son, John II (✷1118–1143), regained Byzantine control of much of Asia Minor, decimated the tribes that had invaded the Balkans, firmly reestablished Byzantine dominion over the Slavic groups of Serbia and Bulgaria, and held off Hungarian incursions from the north. When John died in a hunting accident in 1143, Byzantium again occupied a formidable position in Europe and Asia Minor.

Despite Byzantium's unsettled political affairs, Constantinople in the eleventh and early twelfth centuries remained a rich, sophisticated, and highly cultured city. Sculptors strove to depict ideals of human beauty and elegance; mosaicists recognized body weight and physical presence over pattern and design. Churches built during the period were decorated with a scheme of mosaics meant to show the hierarchy of the cosmos and the calendar of the church. Significant innovations occurred in the realm of scholarship and literature. The neo-Platonic tradition of late antiquity had always permeated all aspects of Byzantine religious and philosophical thought, but now scholars renewed their interest in the wellsprings of classical Greek philosophy, particularly Plato and Aristotle. Some

Byzantine Revival Under the Comnenians

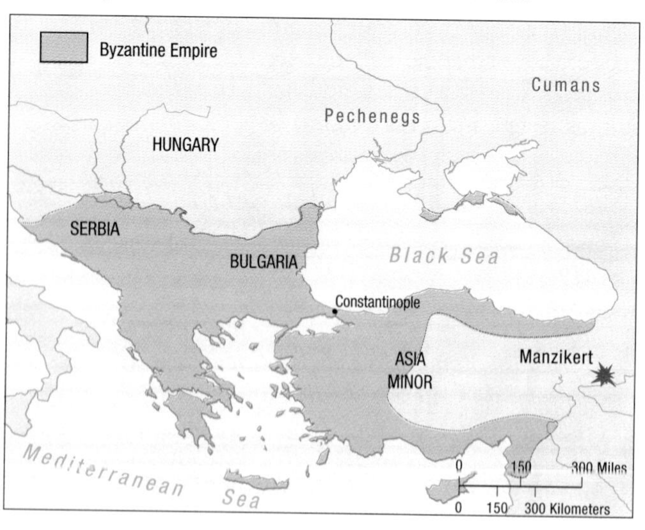

scholars sought so enthusiastically to reconcile ancient Greek philosophy with Christianity that they found themselves accused of abandoning essential Christian beliefs. The rediscovery of ancient culture inspired Byzantine writers to reintroduce old forms into the grammar, vocabulary, and rhetorical style of Greek literature. Anna Comnena wrote her *Alexiad* in this newly learned Greek:

> *I, Anna, daughter of the Emperor Alexius and the Empress Irene, born and bred in the Purple, not without some acquaintance with literature—having devoted the most earnest study to the Greek language, in fact, and being not unpracticed in rhetoric and having read thoroughly the treatises of Aristotle and the dialogues of Plato. . . . I, having realized the effects wrought by time, desire now by means of my writings to give an account of my father's deeds.*

The revival of ancient Greek writings, especially Plato's, in eleventh- and twelfth-century Byzantium had profound consequences for both eastern and western European civilization in centuries to come as these ideas slowly penetrated European culture.

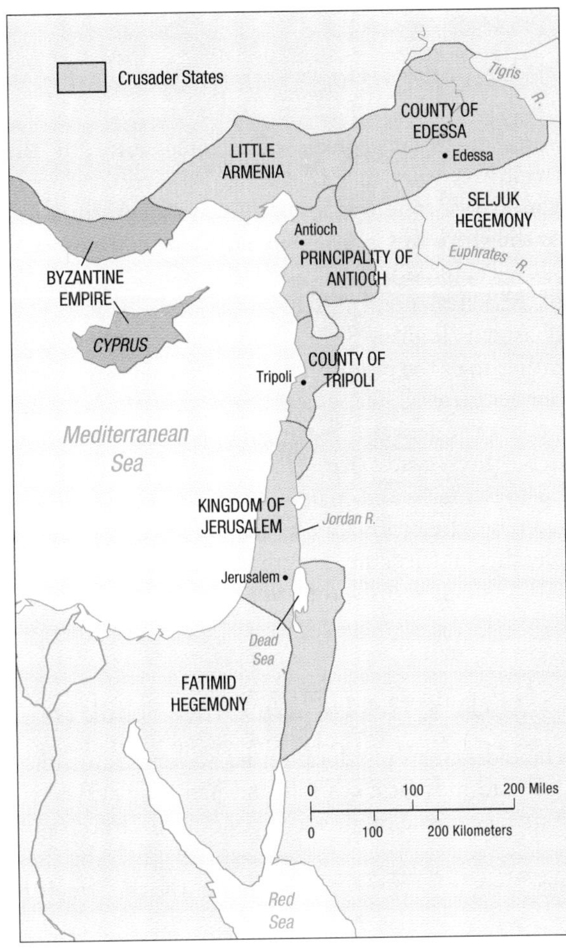

Outremer: The Crusader States

A West European Outpost: Outremer

Like Norman England, the states of Outremer were created by conquest. The crusaders carved out four tiny regions around Edessa, Antioch, Jerusalem, and (after a major battle in 1109) Tripoli. Like England, these states were feudal lordships, with a ruler at the apex of a triangular scheme of vassals. The ruler granted fiefs to his own vassals, and some of these men in turn gave portions of their holdings as fiefs to some of their own vassals. Many other vassals simply lived in the households of their lords.

Thus foreign knights, who imposed their rule on indigenous populations with vastly different customs and religions, ruled Outremer. Although European peasants clearly differed from knights and nobles by occupation, dress, and style of life, they often lived near the upper class on the same estates, and they shared the same religion. In Outremer, by contrast, the Europeans lived in towns and had little in common with the Muslims, Jews, and even native Arab-speaking Christians who tilled the soil.

The ruling classes of the Latin (or western) states of Outremer held on to their positions precariously. They were constantly on the alert against wars with their Muslim neighbors and occasionally with the Byzantines and with one another. When a new Seljuk chieftain, Zengi, succeeded in uniting Muslim forces behind him, the Latin rulers could not hold out against him. Edessa fell in 1144, and the slow but steady shrinking of Outremer began. Despite numerous new crusades, most Europeans were simply not willing to commit the vast resources and personnel that would have been necessary to maintain outposts in the Levant. Outremer fell to the Muslims permanently in 1291.

New Forms of Western Scholarship

Some historians speak of a renaissance of the twelfth century, but this revival of scholarship in western Europe was in many ways a continuation of the work of Carolingian and Ottonian scholars. Now centered in the cities and pursued by crowds of avid students, twelfth-century scholarship emphasized logical, legal, and theoretical studies rather than the predominantly literary ones of earlier centuries. The focus of study shifted partly because of practical career demands and opportunities—the need for lawyers, doctors, and businessmen—and partly because of intangible factors—the rationality of the profit economy, the pleasure of thrusting arguments home with words rather than swords, and the excitement of urban diversity.

Abelard, Heloise, and Other Scholars

The old system of education had centered in cathedral and monastic schools and had long served to train clerics and monks to carry out the church services. Around the beginning of the twelfth century, however, hundreds and eventually thousands of students sought teachers at the cathedral schools in urban centers like Reims, Paris, Bologna, and Montpellier. One contemporary described a typical student in this way:

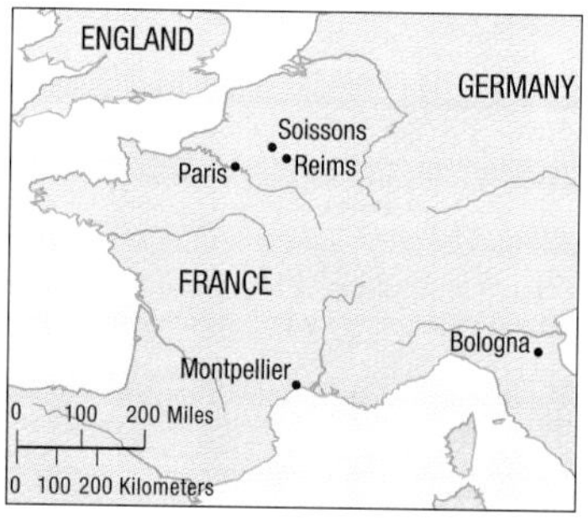

The Intellectual Revival

> *Instilled with an insatiable thirst for learning, whenever [the young monk Gilbert of Liège] heard of somebody excelling in the arts, he rushed immediately to that place and drank whatever delightful potion he could draw from the master there. . . . Later, after having filled himself with the sweet honey of knowledge like a bee flying across bloomy fields he returned to the sanctuary of his monastery.*

For Gilbert and other students a good lecture had the excitement of theater. Teachers at cathedral schools found themselves forced to find larger halls to accommodate the crush of students. Other teachers simply declared themselves "masters" and set up shop by renting a room. If they could prove their mettle in the classroom, they had no trouble finding paying students.

Many young men in the early twelfth century were "wandering scholars" like Gilbert of Liège. As far as we know, these scholars were all male; and because schools had hitherto been the training ground for clergymen, all were considered clerics, whether or not they had been ordained. Wandering became a way of life as the consolidation of castellanies, counties, and kingdoms made violence against travelers less frequent. Urban centers soon responded to the needs of transients with markets, taverns, and lodgings. Using Latin, Europe's common language, students could drift from, say, Italy to Germany, England, and France, wherever a noted master had settled. Along with crusaders, pilgrims, and merchants, students made the roads of Europe very crowded indeed.

We know a good deal about one of these early students, who later became a master: Peter Abelard (1079–1142). Born into a family of the petty nobility, destined for a career as a warrior and lord, Abelard instead became a pioneering thinker. He wrote a virtual autobiography in his *Historia calamitatum* (*Story of My Calamities*). There Abelard described his shift from the life of the warrior to the no less glorious life of the scholar:

> *I was so carried away by my love of learning, that I renounced the glory of a soldier's life, made over my inheritance and rights of the eldest son to my brothers, and withdrew from the court of Mars [war] in order to kneel at the feet of Minerva [learning].*

Arriving eventually at Paris, Abelard studied with William of Champeaux and then challenged his teacher's scholarship. Later Abelard began to lecture and to gather students of his own.

His fame as a teacher was such that a cleric named Fulbert gave Abelard room and board and engaged him as tutor for Heloise (c. 1100–c. 1163/1164), Fulbert's niece. Heloise was one of the few learned women of the period to leave any traces.

Brought up under Fulbert's guardianship, she had been sent as a young girl to a convent school, where she received a thorough grounding in literary skills. Her uncle had hoped to continue her education at home. Abelard, however, became her lover as well as her tutor. "Our desires left no stage of love-making untried," wrote Abelard in his *Historia*. At first their love affair was kept secret. But Heloise became pregnant, and Abelard insisted they marry. They did so clandestinely to prevent damaging Abelard's career, for the new emphasis on clerical celibacy meant that Abelard's professional success and prestige would have been compromised if news of his marriage were made public. Thus after they were married, Heloise and Abelard rarely saw one another. Fulbert, suspecting foul play with regard to his niece, decided to punish Abelard. He paid a servant to castrate Abelard, and soon after, both husband and wife entered separate monasteries.

For Heloise, separation from Abelard was a lasting blow. Although she became a successful abbess, carefully tending to the physical and spiritual needs of her nuns, she continued to call on Abelard for "renewal of strength." In a series of letters addressed to him, she poured out her feelings as "his handmaid, or rather his daughter, wife, or rather sister":

> *You know, beloved, as the whole world knows, how much I have lost in you, how at one wretched stroke of fortune that supreme act of flagrant treachery robbed me of my very self in robbing me of you. . . . You alone have the power to make me sad, to bring me happiness or comfort.*

For Abelard, however, the loss of Heloise and even his castration were not the worst disasters of his life: the cruelest blow came later, and it was directed at his intellect. Having applied "human and logical reasons" (as he put it) to the Trinity, he saw his book on the subject condemned at the Council of Soissons in 1121 and was forced to throw it into the flames. Bitterly weeping at the injustice, Abelard lamented, "this open violence had come upon me only because of the purity of my intentions and love of our Faith which had compelled me to write."

Abelard had written the treatise on the Trinity for his students, maintaining that "words were useless if the intelligence could not follow them, [and] that nothing could be believed unless it was first understood." The demand that logic—not just reason, but the application of technical rules—illuminate a matter of faith was something relatively new. It typifies the shift in the emphasis of intellectual life from literary studies to logic and to the second part of the "liberal arts," the *quadrivium*.

The Liberal Arts and Other Subjects

In the Middle Ages, as in ancient Rome, students still had to learn grammar, the first step of the seven liberal arts. Grammar was part of the *trivium*, which consisted of three areas of study—grammar, rhetoric, and logic (or dialectic)—that were considered the foundation of education. Logic, involving the technical analysis of texts as well as the application and manipulation of mental constructs, was a transitional subject leading to the second, higher part of the liberal arts, the *quadrivium*. This comprised four areas of study in what we might call theoretical math and science: arithmetic, geometry, music (theory rather than practice), and astronomy. Above all, logic delighted Abelard, who originally came to Paris to hear William of Champeaux (c. 1070–c. 1120) speak about the existence of universals, ideas such as "man," "truth," and "goodness." But Abelard soon engaged in hot debate with William. Logic excited enormous interest at the time because people wanted to be sure that what they were trying to prove with words was in fact true. They saw logic as the tool that could reveal and clarify each issue.

At the heart of the debate over universals was the nature of the individual. The *nominalist* position held that each individual was unique. For example, Tom and Harry (and Carol, for that matter) may be called "man" (a word that includes both males and females), but that label (to the nominalist) is merely a convenience, a manner of speaking. In reality (in the nominalist view) Tom and Harry and Carol are so unlike that each can be truly comprehended only as separate and irreducible entities. Only very few people in Abelard's time argued this position, in part because it led to clearly heretical results: applied to the Trinity, it shattered the unity of the Father, Son, and Holy Ghost, leaving the idea of the Trinity an empty name. (The word *name* in Latin is *nomen*, from which *nominalist* was derived.)

The *realist* position, argued by William of Champeaux, was more acceptable in the twelfth century. Realists argued that the "real," the essential, aspect of the individual was the universal qualities of its group. Thus Tom and Harry and Carol were certainly different, but their differences were inessential "accidents." In truth (argued the realists) all three people must be properly comprehended as "man." This view also raised theological problems—if taken to an extreme, the Trinity would melt into one. And it certainly did not satisfy a man like Abelard, who was adamant about his own individuality.

Abelard created his own position, called modified realism, by focusing on the observer, who sees "real" individuals and who abstracts "real" universals from them. The key for Abelard was the nature of the knower: the concept of "man" was formed by the knower observing the similarities between Tom, Harry, and Carol and deriving a universal concept that allowed him (or her) to view individuals properly in its light. Abelard's treatise on ethics was entitled *Know Thyself*, after the motto of the Delphic oracle and Socrates' philosophy of virtue through self-knowledge. Interested above all in the knower, Abelard went on to discuss interior motivation:

> *When the same thing is done by the same man at different times, by the diversity of his intention . . . his action is now said to be good, now bad.*

This is why Abelard so mourned the burning of his book on the Trinity, for in his view it had sprung from the purest intentions and was burned out of the basest motives.

Later in the twelfth century, scholars discovered that Aristotle had once elaborated a view parallel to Abelard's, but until the middle of the twelfth century very little of Aristotle's work was available in Europe because it had not been translated from Greek into Latin. Most of the Church Fathers had considered Aristotle's philosophy irrelevant and had not incorporated it into the Christian worldview. The only works of Aristotle available in Latin were his basic treatises on logic, which Abelard relied upon when launching his own system. However nearly the full corpus of Aristotle's philosophy had been translated into Arabic by the eleventh and twelfth centuries. Ibn Sina (Avicenna), the great Muslim scientist and doctor, also commented on Aristotle, showing how Aristotle's philosophy fit into neo-Platonism. By the mid-twelfth century, Christian and Jewish European scholars were translating Aristotle's works, along with Muslim scholars' commentaries on them, from Arabic into Latin (and Hebrew). (Later scholars translated Aristotle from the original Greek.) In a sense, early twelfth-century scholars like Abelard, with their pioneering efforts in logic, opened the way for Christian Europe to welcome Aristotle. By the thirteenth century, Aristotle had become the primary philosopher for *scholastics* (the scholars of the European medieval universities).

Around 1122–1123, shortly after writing his book on the Trinity, Abelard prepared an unusual textbook, the *Sic et Non* (*Yes and No*). It covered 156 questions, among them issues such as: "That God is one and the contrary"; "That all are permitted to marry and the contrary"; "That it is permitted to kill men and the contrary." Arrayed on both sides of each question were the words of authorities: the Bible, the church fathers, the letters of popes. Abelard argued that his method "excites young readers to the maximum of effort in inquiring into the truth." In fact, in Abelard's view the inquiring student followed the model of Christ himself, who as a boy sat among the rabbis, questioning them. The juxtaposition of authoritative sentences was nothing new; what was new was calling attention to their contradictions. The formula of *Sic et Non* was characteristic of the work of scholars in the urban schools, though those who came after Abelard were careful to reconcile the contradictions. Gratian used a similar method in his study of canon law, juxtaposing variant canons and then suggesting how to resolve their contradictions. The same development was occurring even before the time of Abelard and Gratian in the area of secular—particularly Roman—law.

Roman law had been passed down, at least in manuscripts in northern Italy, but regional laws and customs were the principal basis of legal practice until the eleventh century, which saw a renewed interest in codes of law. At Pavia in the mid-eleventh century, law teachers might be found surrounded by clutches of students, much as the masters at Paris attracted followings several decades later. Here the laws, mainly Lombard laws but also Roman laws, were subject to systematic exposition and to disputes over interpretations.

By the end of the eleventh century, Italian jurists were applying these analytical methods to Roman law alone. Justinian's law books attracted readers in the West, and within a few decades each study became institutionalized. At Bologna, Irnerius (died c. 1129) was the guiding light of a law school where students studied Lombard, Roman, or canon law. Men skilled in canon law served popes and bishops; and popes, kings, princes, and communes all found that Roman law, which claimed the emperor as its fount, justified their claims to power.

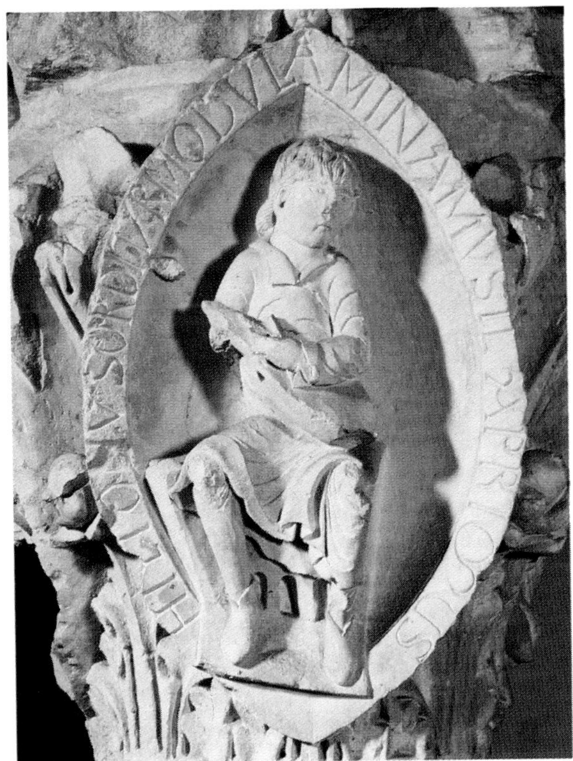

Gregorian Chant
This side of a capital atop a column in the choir at Cluny shows a musician personifying the first tone of the Gregorian chant. Notice how the shape of the sculpture echoes the shape of the architectural element—the capital—that it decorates. This subordination to architectural form was characteristic of Romanesque sculpture.

Religious Life in the Age of Reform and Commerce

Monks continued to repudiate the world in this age of reform, but as the nature of the world changed, so did the character of their repudiation. By the end of the eleventh century, the so-called black monks, the "old-fashioned" Benedictine monks and nuns, spent nearly the entire day in a gigantic and splendidly outfitted church singing an expanded and complex liturgy. Rejecting the extravagance of this life, the so-called white monks and the nuns who followed them promoted a life of pared-down liturgy within the plainest of churches. Numerous forms of monastic life flourished. Many of these new religious foundations enjoyed enormous popularity and attracted the most able men and women of the period.

Black Monks and Artistic Splendor

The monks and nuns who dyed their habits black and followed the Rule of St. Benedict reached the height of their popularity in the eleventh century. Monasteries often housed hundreds of monks; convents for nuns were usually less populated. Cluny was one of the largest monasteries, with some four hundred brothers in the mid-eleventh century.

The chief occupation of the monks, as befitted (in their view) citizens of the *City of God*, was prayer. The black monks and nuns devoted themselves to singing the Psalms and other prayers specified in the Rule of St. Benedict, adding to them still more Psalms. The rule called for chanting the entire psalter—150 psalms—over the course of a week, but some monks, like those at Cluny, chanted that number in a day.

Their devotions were neither private nor silent. Black monks had to know not only the words but also the music that went with the divine office; they had to be musicians. The music of the Benedictine monastery was plainchant (also known as Gregorian chant), which consisted of melodies, each sung in unison, without accompaniment. Although chant was rhythmically free, lacking a regular beat, its melodies ranged from extremely simple to highly

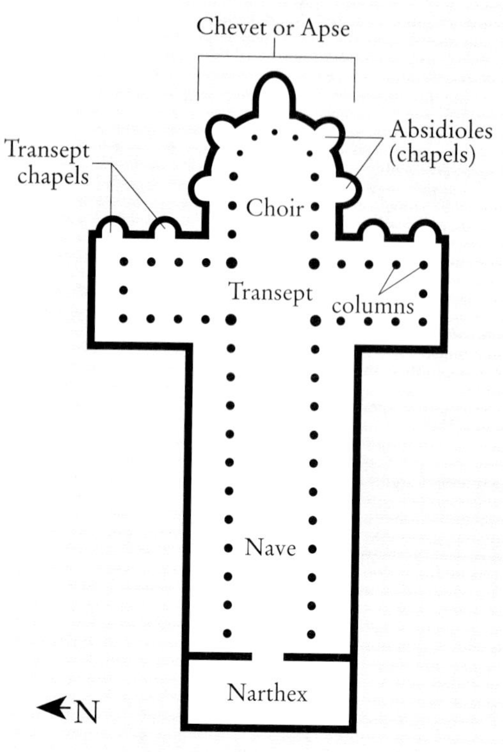

Schematic Romanesque Church

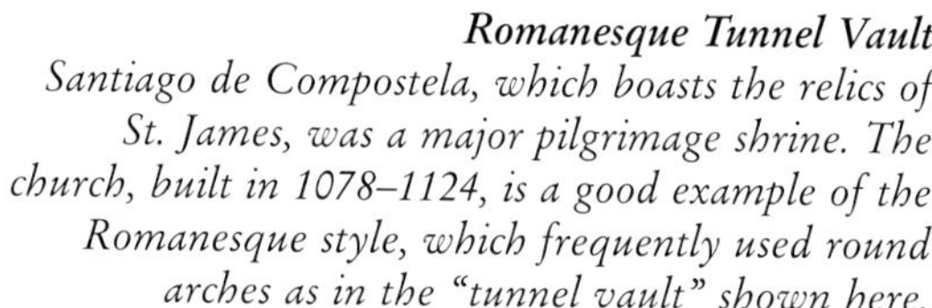

Romanesque Tunnel Vault
Santiago de Compostela, which boasts the relics of St. James, was a major pilgrimage shrine. The church, built in 1078–1124, is a good example of the Romanesque style, which frequently used round arches as in the "tunnel vault" shown here.

ornate and embellished. By the twelfth century a large repertoire of melodies had grown up, at first through oral composition and transmission, then in written notation, which first appeared in manuscripts of the ninth century.

The melodies preserved by this early notation probably originated in Rome and had been introduced into northern Europe at the behest of Charlemagne, who wanted to unify the liturgical practices of his empire. Musical notation was developed to help monks remember unfamiliar melodies and to ensure that they were sung in approximately the same way in all parts of the Carolingian realm. The melodies were further mastered and organized at this time by fitting them into the Byzantine system of eight modes, or scales. This music survived the dissolution of the Carolingian empire and remained the core music of the Catholic Church into the twentieth century.

At Cluny, where singing the liturgy occupied nearly the entire day and part of the night, the importance of music was made visible—the modes were personified and depicted in sculpture on some of the columns circling the choir of the church. The church of Cluny, rebuilt around 1100, was enormous. Constructed of stone, it must have reverberated with the voices of the hundreds of monks who sang in it.

Cluny was part of the building boom that saw the construction or repair of town walls, dwellings, mills, castles, monasteries, and churches. The style of many of these buildings, like the church of

These three images come from the Romanesque church of St. Lazarus at Autun, France. They were sculpted c. 1120–1135 by the master craftsman Gislebertus, one of a handful of medieval artists we know by name, or by one of the stone carvers under his tutelage.

(left) ***The Fall of Simon Magus***
The legend of Simon's plunge and the devil who waits for him (on the right) was already popular in the early Christian period.

(below left) ***Suicide of Judas***
Devils leer on each side in this depiction of the suicide of Judas.

(above) ***Eve***
Eve is shown as beautiful but serpentine.

Cluny, was Romanesque. Although they varied greatly, most Romanesque churches had massive stone and masonry walls decorated on the interior with paintings in bright colors. The various parts of the church—the chapels in the *chevet* (the east end), for example—were handled as discrete units, retaining the forms of cubes, cones, and cylinders. Inventive sculptural reliefs, both inside and outside the church, enlivened these pristine geometrical forms. Emotional and sometimes frenzied, Romanesque sculpture depicted themes ranging from the horrors of the Last Judgment to the beauty of Eve.

In such a setting, gilded reliquaries and altars made of silver, precious gems, and pearls were the fitting accoutrements of worship. Prayer, liturgy, and music in this way complemented the gift economy: richly clad in vestments of the finest materials, intoning the liturgy in the most splendid of churches, monks and priests offered up the gift of prayer to God; in return they begged for the gift of salvation of their souls and the souls of all the faithful.

New Monastic Orders of Poverty

Not all agreed that such opulence pleased or praised God. At the end of the eleventh century the new commercial economy and the profit motive that fueled it led many to reject wealth and to embrace poverty as a key element of religious life. The Carthusian order, founded by Bruno of Cologne, was one such group. Each monk took a vow of silence and lived as a hermit in his own small hut. Monks occasionally joined others for prayer in a common prayer room, or oratory. When not engaged in prayer or meditation, the Carthusians copied manuscripts. They considered this task part of their religious vocation, a way to preach God's word with their hands rather than their mouths. The Carthusian order grew slowly. Each monastery was limited to only twelve monks, the number of the Apostles.

The Cistercians, on the other hand, expanded rapidly. Rejecting even the conceit of blackening their cowls, they left their habits the original color of wool (hence their nickname, the white monks). The Cistercian order began as a single monastery, Cîteaux (in Latin, *Cistercium*), founded in 1098. It grew to include more than three hundred monasteries spread throughout Europe by the middle of the twelfth century. Despite the Cistercian order's official repudiation of female Cistercian houses, many nunneries followed its lead and adopted its customs. Women were as anxious as men to live the life of simplicity and poverty that they believed the Apostles had enjoyed and endured.

The guiding spirit and preeminent Cistercian abbot was St. Bernard (c. 1090–1153), who arrived at Cîteaux in 1112 along with about thirty friends and relatives. But even before Bernard's arrival, the program of the new order had been set. A chronicle of the order reports that

> *They rejected anything opposed to the [Benedictine]* Rule: *frocks, fur tunics, linsey-woolsey shirts and cowls, straw for beds and various dishes of food in the refectory, as well as lard and all other things which ran counter to the letter of the* Rule.

Although they held up the Rule of St. Benedict as the foundation of their customs, the Cistercians elaborated a style of life all their own. Largely supported, as the black monks were, by land donations from pious nobles and knights, the Cistercians created a class of lay monks called *conversi* to till the soil and reap the harvest. Drawn from the peasantry, the *conversi* were clearly a second-class group living separately from the monks. Although they could enter the monastic church, they were confined to the back. The *conversi* and the "real" monks hardly ever saw one another.

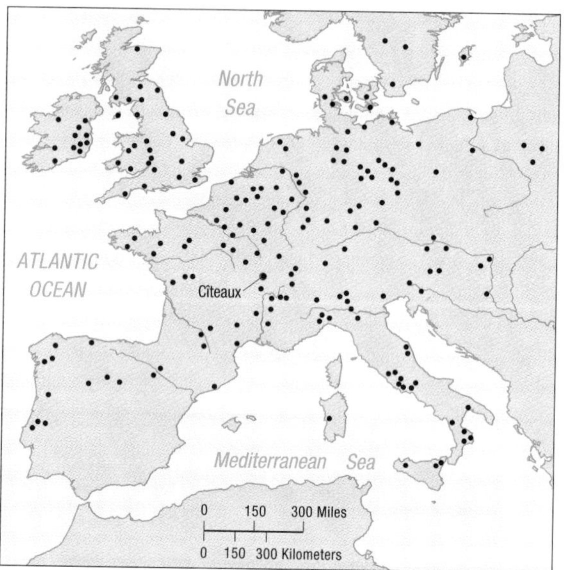

The Spread of Cistercian Monasticism in the Twelfth Century

Cistercian churches, though built of stone, were initially unlike the great Romanesque churches of the black monks. They were remarkably standardized; the church and the rest of the buildings of any Cistercian monastery were almost exactly like those of any other. The churches were small, made of smoothly hewn, undecorated stone. Wall paintings and sculpture were prohibited. St. Bernard wrote a scathing attack on Romanesque sculpture in which he acknowledged, in spite of himself, its exceptional allure:

> *What is the point of ridiculous monstrosities in the cloister where there are brethren reading—I mean those extraordinary deformed beauties and beautiful deformities? What are those lascivious apes doing, those fierce lions, monstrous centaurs, half-men and spotted leopards? . . . It is more diverting to decipher marble than the text before you, and to spend the whole day in gazing at such singularities in preference to meditating upon God's laws.*

The Cistercians had no such diversions, but the simplicity of their buildings and of their clothing also had its beauty. Illuminated by the pure white light that came through clear glass windows, Cistercian houses were luminous, cool, and serene.

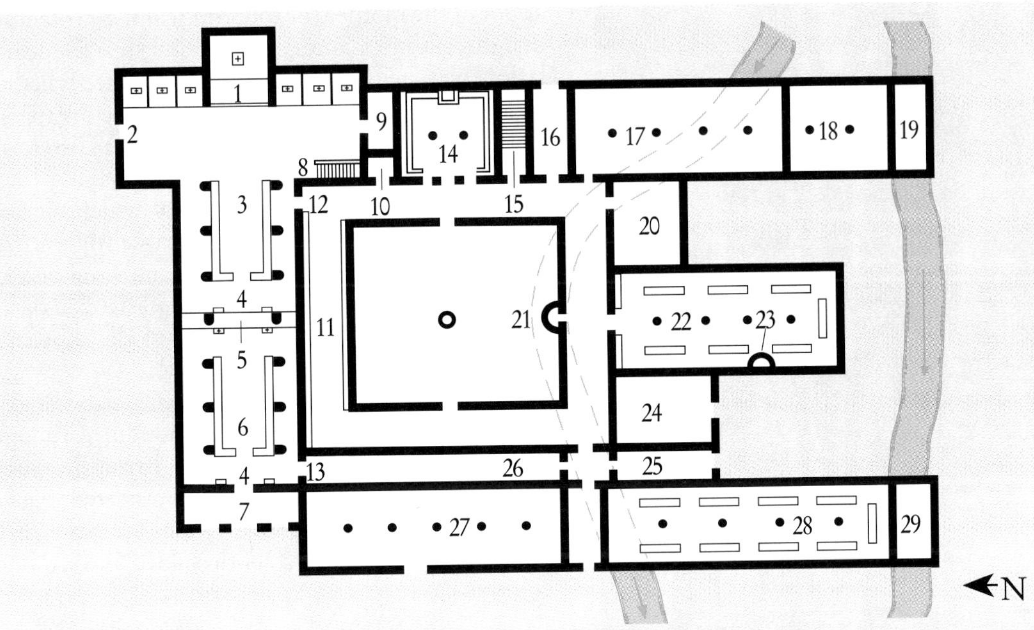

1 Sanctuary
2 Lych gate, the door through which bodies were carried from the funeral service to the graveyard
3 Monks' choir
4 Benches for the sick
5 Rood screen, separating the monks' choir from that of the conversi
6 Choir of the conversi, or lay brothers
7 Narthex
8 Night stairs from the church to the dormitory
9 Sacristy
10 'Armarium', where books were kept
11 Benches for reading, and for the 'maundy' ceremony of foot-washing
12 Monks' entry
13 Lay brothers' entry
14 Chapter house
15 Stairs from the cloister to the dormitory, which extended over the whole range 14–19
16 Parlor
17 Monks' common room
18 Room for novices
19 Latrine (used from the upper storey)
20 Calefactorium, or warming room
21 Fountain, for washing
22 Refectory (Dining room)
23 Pulpit, for reading during the meal
24 Kitchen
25 Cellarer's parlor
26 'Lane' or 'alley' of the lay brothers
27 Cellar, or storeroom
28 Lay brothers' refectory. The dormitory of the conversi, or lay brothers, extended over the whole range 27–28
29 Latrines for the lay brothers

Schematic Cistercian Monastery
All Cistercian monasteries were built on a similar plan, illustrated here. The church was integrated with the other monastic buildings, half of which were used by the monks and half by the "lay brothers." Because of their emphasis on purity, the monks built their monastery near a stream.

True to this emphasis on purity, the communal liturgy of the Cistercians was simplified and shorn of the many additions that had been tacked on in the houses of black monks. Only the *opus Dei* (the liturgy) as prescribed in the Rule of St. Benedict—plus one daily mass—was allowed. Even the music for the chant was changed; the Cistercians rigorously suppressed the B flat, even though doing so made the melody discordant, because of their insistence on strict simplicity.

Cistercian Architecture
The whiteness and simplicity of Cistercian churches may be seen in this view of the south transept of the church at Pontigny, France.

With their time partly freed from the choir, the white monks dedicated themselves to private prayer and contemplation and to monastic administration. In some ways these activities were antithetical—one internal and the other external. The Cistercian *Charter of Charity*, in effect a constitution of the order, provided for a closely monitored network of houses, and each year the Cistercian abbots met to hammer out legislation for all the monasteries. The abbot of the mother (or founding) house visited the daughter houses annually to make sure the legislation was being followed. Each house, whether mother or daughter, had large and highly organized farms and grazing lands called granges. Cistercian monks spent much of their time managing their estates and flocks of sheep, both of which yielded handsome profits by the end of the twelfth century. Clearly part of the agricultural and commercial revolutions of the Middle Ages, the Cistercian order made managerial expertise a part of the monastic life.

At the same time, the Cistercians elaborated a spirituality of intense personal emotion. Although St. Bernard and Abelard clashed—Bernard argued that Abelard was "presumptuously prepared to give a reason for everything, even of those things which are above reason"—they both valued inward and emotional awareness. As Bernard said,

> *often enough when we approach the altar to pray our hearts are dry and lukewarm. But if we persevere, there comes an unexpected infusion of grace, our breast expands as it were, and our interior is filled with an overflowing love; and if somebody should press upon it then, this milk of sweet fecundity would gush forth in streaming richness.*

The Cistercians emphasized not only human emotion but also Christ's and Mary's humanity. While pilgrims continued to stream to the tombs and reliquaries of saints, the Cistercians dedicated all their churches to the Virgin Mary, for whom they had no relics, because for them she signified the model of a loving mother. Indeed the Cistercians regularly used maternal imagery (as Bernard's description invoking the metaphor of a flowing breast illustrates) to describe the nurturing care provided to humankind by Jesus himself. The Cistercian God was approachable, human, protective, and even mothering.

Similar views of God were held by many who were not members of the Cistercian orders; their spirituality signaled wider changes. For example, around 1099, St. Anselm wrote a theological treatise entitled *Why God Became Man* in which he argued that since Man had sinned, Man had to redeem himself. St. Anselm's work represented a new theological emphasis on the redemptive power of human charity, including that of Jesus as a human being. The crusaders had trodden the very place of Christ's crucifixion, making his humanity both more real and more problematic to people who walked in the holy "place of God's humiliation and our redemption," as one chronicler put it. Yet this new stress on the loving bonds that tied Christians together also led to the persecution of others, like Jews and Muslims, who lived outside the Christian community.

St. Denis and the Beginning of Gothic

About ten years after Bernard had written about approaching the altar "dry and lukewarm," Suger, the abbot of St. Denis and biographer of Louis the Fat, wrote about the new altar at St. Denis that he had encased in gold and studded with precious gems:

> *When—out of my delight in the beauty of the house of God—the loveliness of the many-colored gems has called me away from external cares, and worthy meditation has induced me to reflect on the diversity of the sacred virtues . . . then it seems to me . . . that I can be transported from this inferior [world on earth] to that higher world [in Heaven].*

For Suger, color and light had a mystical effect, transporting the worshipper from the "slime of earth" to the "purity of Heaven," an idea Suger had read in the writings of a neo-Platonist Syrian theologian who lived about 500. Suger and most of his contemporaries mistakenly believed this theologian to be Dionysius the Areopagite, a disciple of St. Paul, whom they further misidentified as St. Denis (Dionysius in Latin), Apostle to the Gauls. Since Suger's monastery was dedicated to St. Denis, he and his monks read the Syrian thinker's mystical theology of light with the reverence due a patron saint. In this theology, God was the Father of lights, and the emanations of his light flowed through a hierarchy of beings, from angels down to the vilest matter. For Suger, precisely because people were trapped in material and mortal bodies, they could rise to God through their senses:

> *Every creature, visible or invisible, is a light brought into being by the Father of the lights. . . . This stone or that piece of wood is a light to me. . . . For I perceive that it is good and beautiful. . . . As I perceive such and similar things in this stone they become lights to me, that is to say, they enlighten me.*

When Suger embarked on a program to rebuild St. Denis, in about 1135, he turned this theology of light into an architectural style, later called Gothic. The term *Gothic* was not Suger's. It was coined centuries later by people who criticized medieval architecture as ungainly and barbaric, like the Visigoths who had sacked Rome. Although distinctions between Romanesque and Gothic are artificial since both evolved alongside one another and often shared many elements, certain characteristic features of each style can be isolated. Gothic churches were, by Romanesque standards, compact in length and unified in structure, without clear geometrical building blocks. For example, the chapels of Suger's rebuilt chevet, completed in 1144, were not separated from one another like cylinders but rather flowed together. The walls, so important in the Romanesque church, were largely replaced by stained glass in the Gothic. As the sun shone into the church, the glass glowed. As Suger put it in a poem, "And bright is the noble edifice which is pervaded by the new light." By "new light" Suger meant not just the sun but also the "clarity" of the Father of lights, God himself, who "brightens" the minds of men. Being in the church was a glance at heaven.

The Capetian monarchs associated themselves with St. Denis as they sought to extend their power. Already in 1124, for example, before riding out to a particularly important battle, Louis VI went to the church of St. Denis to obtain its banner and proclaimed the saint "the special patron and, after God, special protector of the realm." At the same time, Louis confirmed the church's right to hold a lucrative fair. About fifteen years later, when Suger rebuilt the portals (doorway areas) at the west end of St. Denis, he had them decorated with the figures of Old Testament kings, queens, and patriarchs. Their presence signified the interdependence between the monarchy and the church. Gothic architecture was the creation of a fruitful melding of royal and ecclesiastical interests and ideals in the north of France.

Conclusion

The commercial revolution and the building boom it spurred profoundly changed the look of Europe. Thriving cities of merchants and artisans brought trade, new wealth, and new institutions to the West. Mutual and fraternal organizations like the commune, the *compagnia*, and the guilds expressed and reinforced the solidarity and economic interest of city-dwellers. But many rural people were wary of urban life and its cash economy; church reformers warned against the buying and selling of church offices; and monastic reformers sought to escape money by stressing austerity and poverty.

Political consolidation accompanied economic growth, as kings and popes exerted their authority and tested its limits. The Gregorian reform pitted the emperor against the pope and in the end two separate political hierarchies emerged, the secular and the ecclesiastical. The two might cooperate, as Suger and Louis VI showed in their mutual respect, admiration, and dependence; but they might also clash, as Anselm did with the sons of William the Conqueror. Secular and religious leaders developed new and largely separate systems of administration, reflecting in political life the new distinctions, such as clerical celibacy and allegiance to the pope, that differentiated clergy and laity. Although in some ways growing apart, the two groups never worked so closely as in the Crusades, military pilgrimages inspired by the pope and led by lay lords.

The commercial economy, political stability, and ecclesiastical needs fostered the growth of schools and the achievements of new scholarship. Young men like Abelard, who a generation before would have become knights, now sought learning to enhance their careers and bring personal fulfillment. Women like Heloise could gain an excellent basic education in a convent and then go on to higher studies, as she did, with a tutor. Logic fascinated students because it seemed to clarify what was real about themselves, the world, and God. Churchmen like St. Bernard, who felt that faith could not be analyzed, rejected scholarship based on logic.

While black monks added to their hours of worship, built lavish churches, and devoted themselves to the music of the plainchant, a reformer like St. Bernard insisted on an intense, interior spiritual life in a monastery austerely and directly based on the Rule of St. Benedict. Other reformers, like Bruno of Cologne, sought the high mountaintop for its isolation and hardship. These reformers repudiated urban society, yet unintentionally reflected it: the Cistercians were as interested as any student in their interior state of mind and as anxious as any tradesman in the success of their granges, and the Carthusians were dedicated to their books.

The early twelfth century saw a period of renaissance and reform in the church, monarchies, and scholarship. The later twelfth century would be an age when people experimented with and rebelled against various forms of authority.

Suggestions for Further Reading

Source Materials

Benton, John F., ed. *Self and Society in Medieval France: The Memoirs of Abbot Guibert of Nogent (1064?–c. 1125)*. 1970. An autobiography by an outspoken and opinionated critic of his age.

Peters, Edward, ed. *The First Crusade. The Chronicle of Fulcher of Chartres and Other Source Materials*. 1971. Various sources brought together to chronicle the First Crusade.

Radice, Betty, trans. *The Letters of Abelard and Heloise*. 1974. Includes Abelard's famous *Historia calamitatum*, which is essentially his autobiography, along with other letters.

Suger. *The Deeds of Louis the Fat*. Translated by Richard C. Cusimano and John Moorhead. 1992. A biography of Louis written by his friend, Abbot Suger of St. Denis.

Tierney, Brian, ed. *The Crisis of Church and State, 1050–1300*. 1964. A collection of documents illustrating papal and royal clashes, with useful introductions by the editor.

Interpretive Studies

Barraclough, Geoffrey. *The Origins of Modern Germany*. 1963. Although written at the end of World War II, remains a useful and passionate account of medieval German political history.

Benson, Robert L., and Giles Constable, eds. with the assistance of Carol Lanham. *Renaissance and Renewal in the Twelfth Century*. 1982. Contains articles by experts on key aspects of the intellectual and religious life of the twelfth century.

Berman, Constance Hoffman. *Medieval Agriculture, the Southern French Countryside and the Early Cistercians. A Study of Forty-Three Monasteries*. 1986. Details the nature of Cistercian economic activities.

Bouchard, Constance B. *Holy Entrepreneurs: Cistercians, Knights, and Economic Exchange in Twelfth-Century Burgundy*. 1991. An important book on Cistercian economic activities.

———. *Sword, Miter, and Cloister: Nobility and the Church in Burgundy, 980–1198*. 1987. Shows the role of nobles in the movement for church and monastic reform.

Braunfels, Wolfgang. *Monasteries of Western Europe. The Architecture of the Orders*. 1972. An excellent survey of monastic architecture.

Bynum, Caroline Walker. *Jesus as Mother: Studies in the Spirituality of the High Middle Ages*. 1982. Discusses the imagery of twelfth- and thirteenth-century religious writing.

Cattin, Giulio. *Music of the Middle Ages*. 2 vols. Translated by Steven Botterill. 1984. An excellent survey that includes some primary source readings.

Chibnall, Marjorie. *Anglo-Norman England 1066–1166*. 1986. A discussion of the impact of the Norman conquest that stresses the way both Anglo-Saxon and Norman institutions were adapted and shaped after 1066.

Dillard, Heath. *Daughters of the Reconquest: Women in Castilian Town Society, 1100–1300*. 1984. Examines the roles of women in Christian Spain.

Douglas, David C. *William the Conqueror: The Norman Impact Upon England*. 1967. A very readable account of political events by an eminent scholar.

Duby, Georges. *Medieval Marriage: Two Models from Twelfth-Century France*. Translated by Elborg Forster. 1978. Studies clerical and lay notions of marriage.

Dunbabin, Jean. *France in the Making, 843–1180*. 1985. Explores the ways in which a sense of community emerged in France.

Erdmann, Carl. *The Origin of the Idea of Crusade*. Translated by Marshall W. Baldwin and Walter Goffart. 1977. A translation from German of one of the most important studies of the crusading idea.

Finucane, Ronald C. *Soldiers of the Faith: Crusaders and Moslems at War*. 1983. Views the Crusades as an interaction between Muslims and Christians.

Fletcher, R. A. *St. James' Catapult: The Life and Times of Diego Gelmírez of Santiago de Compostela*. 1984. Biography of Diego Gelmírez, a bishop of the pilgrimage center of Santiago de Compostela, illuminating the politics, religion, and mentality of the eleventh century.

Fuhrmann, Horst. *Germany in the High Middle Ages c. 1050–1200*. Translated by Timothy Reuter. 1986. An excellent survey that emphasizes social as well as political issues.

Geary, Patrick J. *"Furta Sacra": Thefts of Relics in the Central Middle Ages*. 1978. Discusses a little-known aspect of medieval economic and religious life—the "pious theft" of relics.

Green, Judith A. *The Government of England Under Henry I*. 1986. Examines the extraordinary growth of institutions of government during the early twelfth century.

Hallam, Elizabeth M. *Capetian France, 987–1328*. 1980. A good survey, with many helpful maps and tables.

———. *Domesday Book Through Nine Centuries*. 1986. A beautifully illustrated and comprehensive account of the origins and uses of the Domesday Book.

Haskins, Charles Homer. *The Renaissance of the Twelfth Century*. 1927. A classic exposition of the intellectual developments of the twelfth century.

Hyde, J. K. *Society and Politics in Medieval Italy: The Evolution of Civil Life, 1000–1350*. 1973. Surveys the emergence and history of the Italian communes.

Kapelle, William E. *The Norman Conquest of the North. The Region and Its Transformation, 1000–1135*. 1979. A new perspective on the Norman Conquest of England, stressing northern England's continuity with its Anglo-Saxon past and its staunch opposition to Norman encroachments.

Lewis, Andrew W. *Royal Succession in Capetian France*. 1981. Explores the royal notion of kin within the context of the French nobility's dynastic sensibilities.

Little, Lester K. *Religious Poverty and the Profit Economy in Medieval Europe*. 1978. Discusses the relationship between the commercial economy and new religious sensibilities in the twelfth and thirteenth centuries.

Lopez, Robert S. *The Commercial Revolution of the Middle Ages, 950–1350*. 1976. A survey of the medieval commercial economy by a first-rate historian.

Murray, Alexander. *Reason and Society in the Middle*

Ages. 1978. A fresh view of the renaissance of the twelfth century.

Newman, Charlotte A. *The Anglo-Norman Nobility in the Reign of Henry I: The Second Generation.* 1988. Looks at noble families in the generation following the Norman conquest, emphasizing the position of women, children, and bastards in noble society.

Nichols, John A., and Lillian Thomas Shank, eds. *Distant Echoes: Medieval Religious Women.* Vol. I. 1984. A collection of essays on women's monastic experience, concentrating on the tenth through the thirteenth centuries.

O'Callaghan, Joseph F. *A History of Medieval Spain.* 1975. A useful survey of medieval Spanish history that covers both Islamic and Christian societies.

Riley-Smith, Jonathan. *The First Crusade and the Idea of Crusading.* 1986. Traces the ways in which the idea of the First Crusade preached by Urban II was reinterpreted by the crusaders themselves and by writers of the next generation.

Spiegel, Gabrielle M. "The Cult of Saint Denis and Capetian Kingship." *Journal of Medieval History* 1 (1975): 43–69. Shows the relationship between the French monarchy and the monastery of St. Denis.

Tabacco, Giovanni. *The Struggle for Power in Medieval Italy.* 1989. A history of Italy focusing on its changing power structures.

Treadgold, Warren, ed. *Renaissances Before the Renaissance. Cultural Revivals of Late Antiquity and the Middle Ages.* 1984. Articles by experts on such cultural revivals as the Macedonian (at Byzantium), Carolingian, and twelfth-century renaissances.

CHAPTER

11

An Age of Confidence, 1144–1215

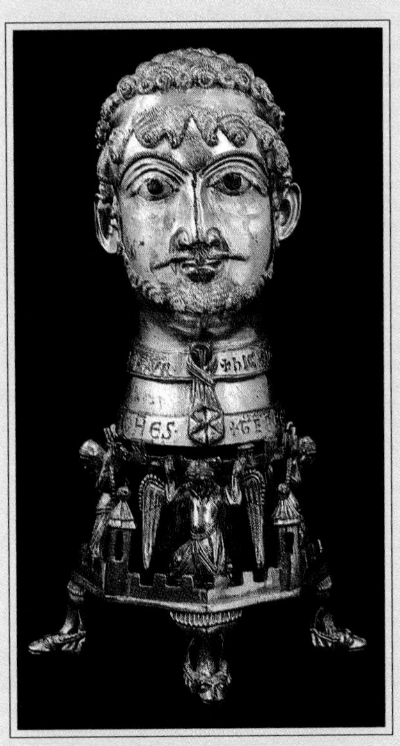

Frederick Barbarossa
This twelfth-century bronze head of Frederick Barbarossa is not so much a portrait as the embodiment of the "firmness" that so impressed contemporaries.

In 1155, King Frederick Barbarossa of Germany (*1152–1190) met representatives of the fledgling Roman commune on his way to Rome, where he intended to be crowned emperor. Recalling the glory of the Roman Empire, these ambassadors of the "senate and people of Rome" claimed that they alone could make Frederick emperor. To deliver the imperial title, they demanded five thousand pounds of gold "as expense money." Frederick, "inflamed with righteous anger," according to his uncle and biographer, Otto of Freising, interrupted them. Rome was not theirs to give, he retorted. The spotlight of history that Rome had once basked in had shifted onto him: "Do you wish to know the ancient glory of your Rome? The worth of senatorial dignity? The impregnable disposition of the army camp? . . . Behold our state. All these things are to be found with us. All these have descended to us, together with the empire."

Frederick's self-assertion and confidence characterized an age in which participants in emerging institutions of government, commerce, and religion commanded enhanced authority. He shared with the ambassadors of the Roman commune, with whom he was for the moment at odds, a newly precise and proud notion of his rights and goals. Kings, princes, popes, city-dwellers, and even heretics in the second half of the twelfth century were acutely conscious of themselves as individuals and as members of like-minded groups with identifiable objectives and plans to promote and perpetuate their aims. For example, by about 1200 many schools, which in the early twelfth century had crystallized around charismatic teachers like Peter Abelard, became permanent institutions called universities. Staffs of literate government officials now preserved both official documents and important papers; lords reckoned their profits with the help of accountants; craft guilds and religious associations defined and regulated their membership.

The new institutions of the late twelfth century reflected the post-Gregorian division between religious and secular authority. Asserting a new, confident secularism, Frederick called his empire "holy" (*sacrum,* sacred). In his view, the newly named Holy Roman Empire, although a secular state, was nevertheless so precious, worthwhile, and God-given that it, like the church, was sacred. Rather than place king above priest or priest above king, Frederick asserted a new autonomy for secular power and authority.

Important Dates

1135–1154 Reign of King Stephen and civil war in England

1147–1149 Second Crusade

1152–1190 Reign of Emperor Frederick Barbarossa

1166 Assize of Clarendon; extension of common law in England

1176 Battle of Legnano; Frederick Barbarossa defeated in northern Italy

1180–1223 Philip II Augustus rules as king of France

1182–1226 Life of St. Francis

1198–1216 Papacy of Innocent III

c. 1200 Incorporation of University of Paris

Governments as Institutions

By the end of the twelfth century, Europeans for the first time began to speak of their rulers not as kings of a people (for example, king of the Franks) but as kings of territories (for example, king of France). This new designation reflected an important change in medieval rulership. However strong rulers had been, their political power had been personal (depending on ties of kinship, friendship, and vassalage) rather than territorial (touching all who lived within the borders of their state). Because new patrilineal families now provided clearly defined lines of inheritance and because a renewed interest in Roman legal concepts supplied models for strong, central rule, the process of state building began to encompass clearly delineated regions, most strikingly in western Europe but in central and eastern Europe as well.

Western European rulers now began to employ professional administrators, sometimes, as in England, through a system so institutionalized that government did not require the king's presence to function. In other regions, such as Germany, bureaucratic administration did not develop very far. In eastern Europe it hardly began at all.

Consolidated and Fragmented Realms in Eastern Europe and Byzantium

Although local rulers in central and eastern Europe controlled certain regions for a time, few of them consolidated their hold for long periods. An exception was Leopold VI, duke of Austria (∗1194–1230), who owned most of the land in his duchy, promoted trade and the growth of towns like Vienna, and patronized poets who sang of aristocratic virtues. Because most of the noble families who might have challenged him had either died out or been eliminated by his predecessors, his power was nearly unopposed.

A more characteristic pattern, especially in eastern Europe, alternated building and fragmenting states. Just before Leopold began to rule Austria, for example, his neighbor to the east, King Béla III of Hungary (∗1172–1196), was emulating rulers in the West. With his marriage to a French princess and employment of at least one scholar from Paris, he allowed French cultural influences to flourish. In his palace, built in Romanesque style, he enjoyed an annual income from his estates, tolls, dues, and taxes equal to that of the richest western monarchs. But the wars between Béla's sons in the decades that followed his death splintered the monarchical holdings, and in a sequence familiar earlier in western Europe, aristocratic supporters divided royal wealth.

Russia underwent a similar process. Although twelfth-century Kiev was politically fragmented, autocratic princes to the north constructed Suzdal', the nucleus of the later Muscovite state. The borders of Suzdal' were definite; well-to-do towns like Moscow prospered; monasteries and churches dotted its countryside; the other princes of Russia recognized its ruler as the "grand prince." Yet in 1212 this nascent state began to crumble as the sons of the grand prince fought one another for territory, much as Béla's sons had done in Hungary.

Twelfth-Century Russia

Although the Byzantine Empire was already a consolidated, bureaucratic state, after the death of John II (✶1118–1143) it gradually ruptured. Thus while the West developed administrative institutions, the Comnenian emperors who ruled during the twelfth century downgraded the old civil servants, elevated their relatives to high offices, and favored the military elite. Byzantine rule grew more personal and western rule became more bureaucratic, the two gradually becoming more like one another.

The Rise and Fall of the German Monarchy

In electing Frederick I Barbarossa king, the princes of Germany acted with rare unanimity. For decades they had enjoyed their independence, building castles on their properties and establishing control over whole territories. Ensuring that the emperors who succeeded Henry V (1081–1125) would be weak, the princes supported only rulers who agreed to give them new lands and powers. The ruler's success depended on balancing the many conflicting interests of his own royal and imperial offices, his family, and the German princes. He also had to contend with the increasing influence of the papacy and the Italian communes, which forged alliances with one another and with the German princes, preventing the consolidation of power under a strong German ruler during the first half of the twelfth century.

The tensions between the imperial and prince-papal positions had led to civil wars in Germany before Frederick's accession. The sides were represented by two families: the Staufer, often called the Hohenstaufen in German or Ghibellines in Italian,* fought for the imperial party; their opponents, the prince-papal party, were the Welfs,† or Guelphs in Italian. (The enmity between these families became so legendary that their names remained attached to the two sides, imperial and papal, even after the families themselves had receded in importance.) Warfare between these groups raged almost continually during the first half of the twelfth century. In Franconia, for example, in one typical year the Staufer dukes first fought King Lothar III at Nuremberg, then wheeled around to face down the Welf duke of Bavaria. Exhausted from constant battles, by 1152 all parties longed for peace, and in Frederick they seemed to have a candidate who could end the strife: his mother was a Welf, his father a Staufer. Otto of Freising, whose contemporary accounts of the king's career provide most of our information about the period, saw in Frederick the image of Christ as the "cornerstone" that joined two houses and reconciled enemies.

Frederick's appearance impressed his contemporaries—the name *Barbarossa* refers to his red-blond hair and beard. But even more, Otto explained, he inspired those around him by his "firmness." He affirmed royal rights, even when he handed out duchies and allowed others to name bishops, because in return for these political powers Frederick required the princes to concede that they held their rights and territories from him as their feudal lord. By making them his vassals, although with near royal rights within their principalities, Frederick defined the princes' relationship to the German king: they were powerful yet personally subordinate to him. In this way Frederick hoped to save the

*These names derived from their properties: *Hohenstaufen* came from the castle and estates at Staufen, and *Ghibellines* came from the Italian name for their nearby estates at Waiblingen.

†*Welf* means "whelp" or "cub."

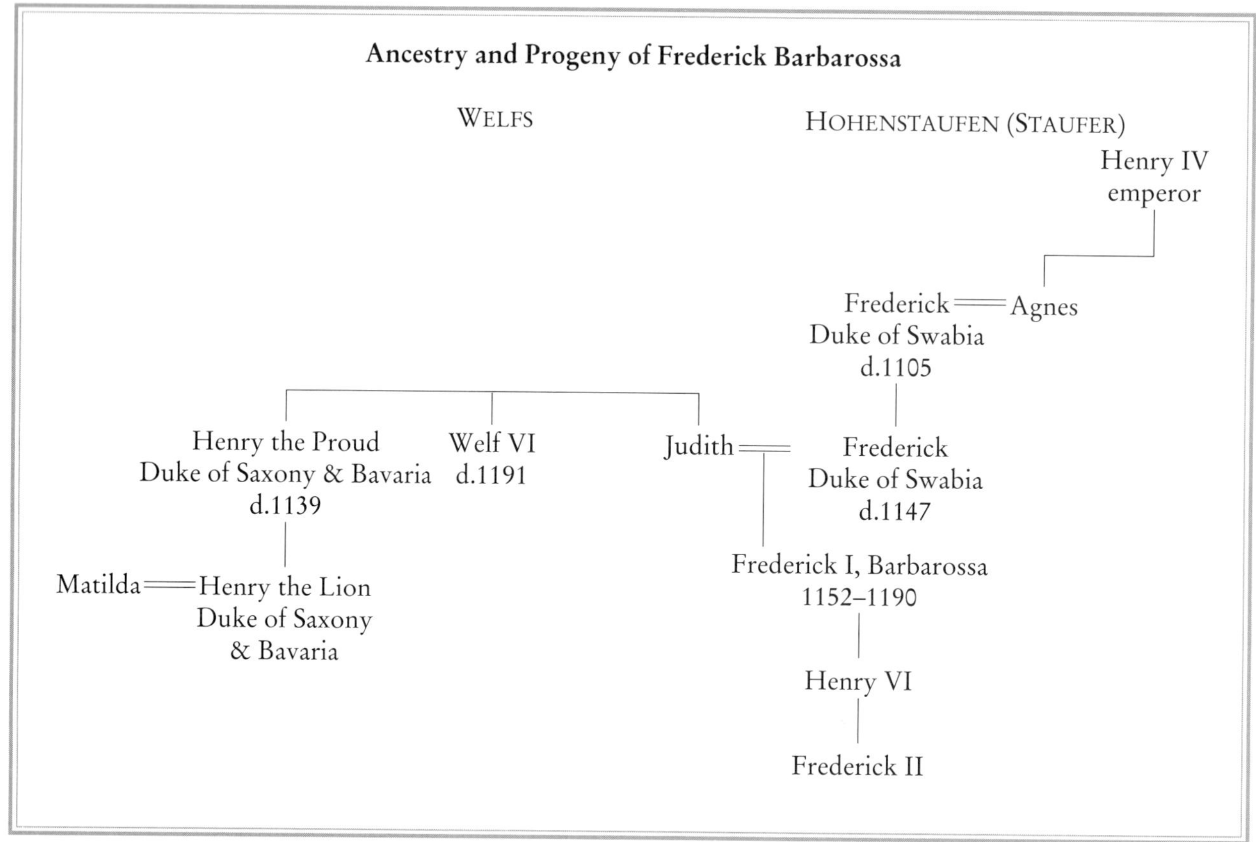

monarchy and to coordinate royal and princely rule, thus ending Germany's chronic civil wars.

Frederick also declared royal prerogatives outside Germany, as his comments to the "ambassadors" of Rome illustrated; but his words antagonized Pope Hadrian IV (*1154–1159), who thought the papacy, not Frederick, represented the glory of Rome. Frederick further angered the pope when he married Beatrice, heiress to vast estates in Burgundy and Provence. Her inheritance enabled Frederick to establish a powerful political and territorial base centering in what is now Switzerland. From there he moved into Italy, threatening the pope's sphere of influence.

Since the Investiture Conflict, the emperor had ruled Italy in name only. The communes of the northern cities guarded their liberties jealously. The pope claimed jurisdiction over Rome and, since the time of Charlemagne, the right to anoint the emperor. In Frederick's day a fresco on one wall of the Lateran palace (the pope's residence) went further: it showed the German king Lothar III receiving the imperial crown from the pope as if the empire were a papal fief, as the papacy would have liked the world to believe. Soon after Frederick's imperial coronation, Hadrian's envoys arrived at a meeting called by the emperor at Besançon in 1157 with a letter detailing the dignities, honors, and other *beneficia* the pope had showered on Frederick. The word *beneficia* incensed the assembled company of Frederick's supporters because it meant not only "benefits" but also "fiefs," as if Frederick were the pope's vassal. The incident opened old wounds from the Gregorian period, revealing the gulf between papal and imperial conceptions of worldly authority.

Although papal claims meant that conquering Italy would be especially problematic, northern

Central Europe in the Age of Frederick Barbarossa, 1152–1190

The Self-Image of the Papacy
In this sixteenth-century sketch of a lost twelfth-century fresco on a wall of the Lateran palace, Lothar III (on the far right) receives the imperial crown from the pope. A verse below the painting reads: "After he becomes the vassal of the pope, he receives the crown from the pope," implying that the empire was a papal fief.

Italy enticed Frederick. Control there would make his base in Swabia (in southwest Germany) a central rather than a peripheral part of his empire, and the flourishing commercial cities of Italy would make him rich. Taxes on agricultural production there alone would yield 30,000 silver talents annually, an incredible sum, equal to the annual income of the richest ruler of the day, the king of England.

Alternately negotiating with and fighting against the great Lombard cities, especially Milan, Frederick achieved military control in Italy in 1158. No longer able to use Italian bishops as royal governors as German kings had done earlier—the Investiture Conflict had effectively ended that practice—Frederick insisted that the communes be governed by podestas, magistrates from outside the commune appointed (or at least authorized) by the king, who would collect revenues on his behalf. The heavy hand of these officials, many of them ministerials from Germany, created enormous resentment. Markward von Brumbach, for example, podesta at Milan, immediately ordered an inventory of all taxes due the emperor, and he levied new and demeaning labor duties, even demanding the citizens to carry the wood and stones of their plundered city to Pavia, twenty-five miles away, for use in constructing new houses there. By 1167 most of the cities of northern Italy had joined with Pope Alexander III (*1159–1181) to form the Lombard League against Frederick. With his defeat at the Battle of Legnano in 1176, Frederick sued for peace. The battle marked the triumph of the city over the crown in Italy, which would not have a centralized government until the nineteenth century; its political history would instead be that of its various regions and their dominant cities.

Thus the development of government institutions in the later twelfth century did not always benefit kings. Despite Frederick I Barbarossa's creative use of the podestas and of the feudal institutions of vassalage and fief, the truly lasting governments of Italy and Germany were the communes, the principalities, and the papal states. A German monarch would have one more chance to rule effectively in Italy and Germany, when Frederick's grandson, Frederick II, would become king; but the opportunity would be lost.

Henry the Lion: A New Style of Princely Rulership

During Frederick I Barbarossa's reign many princes of Germany enjoyed near royal status, acting as independent rulers of their principalities, though acknowledging Frederick as their feudal lord. One of the most powerful was a Welf who took the family name as his symbol and called himself Henry the Lion. Married to Matilda, daughter of the English King Henry II and Queen Eleanor of Aquitaine, Henry was duke of Saxony and Bavaria, a territory stretching across Germany from north to south. A self-confident and aggressive ruler, Henry not only dominated his territory by investing bishops, collecting dues from his demesnes, and exercising judicial rights and duties but also actively extended his rule, especially in Slavic regions, pushing northeast past the Elbe River to reestablish episcopal sees and to build the commercial emporium of Lübeck.

Lord of many vassals, commander of a large army composed chiefly of ministerials and some Slavic reinforcements, Henry, like Frederick, realized that government institutions could enforce his authority and help him maintain control of his territories. Ministerials acted not only as his soldiers but as his officials as well; they collected his taxes and his share of profits from tolls, mints (like kings, Henry took a percentage of the silver to be minted into coins), and markets. Because they were unfree, Henry could shuffle them about or remove them at will. At court his steward, treasurer, and stable marshal were all ministerials. Other officials were notaries, normally clerics, who wrote and preserved some of his legal acts. Thus Henry the Lion created a small staff to carry on the day-to-day administration of his principality without him. Here, as elsewhere, administration no longer depended entirely on the personal involvement of the ruler.

Monument of Henry the Lion
Henry the Lion had this monumental lion cast from iron in 1166. It had a double meaning, signifying both his family name and his power.

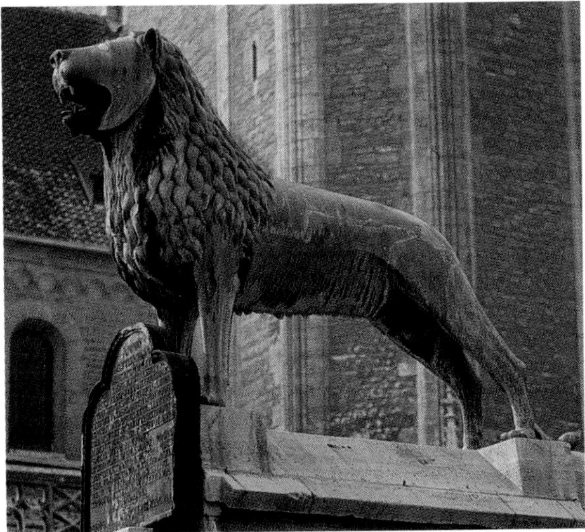

Yet like kings, princes could fall. Henry's growing power so threatened other princes, and even Frederick, that in 1179, Frederick called Henry to the king's court for violating the peace. When Henry chose not to appear, Frederick exercised his authority as Henry's feudal lord and charged him with violating his duty as a vassal. Because Henry refused the summons to court and avoided serving his lord in Italy, Frederick condemned him, confiscated his holdings, and drove him out of Germany in 1180. Although he wished to retain Henry's duchy for himself, Frederick had to divide and distribute it to supporters whose aid he needed to enforce his decrees against Henry.

Late twelfth-century kings and emperors often found themselves engaged in this balancing act of ruling yet placating their powerful lords. The process almost always involved a gamble. Successfully challenging one recalcitrant prince-vassal meant negotiating costly deals with the others, since their support was vital. Rulers like Frederick often lost as much as they gained in such actions, usually defeating the targeted truant but ending up with little to show for it after paying off all the favors required to win. Not until the early thirteenth century would a ruler emerge with enough power, skill, and sheer luck to control what he confiscated: about a quarter-century later, King Philip II (Augustus) of France denounced King John of England and duke of Normandy and expropriated the duchy of Normandy. This effort consolidated rather than sapped Philip's power.

England: Unity Through Law

By the mid-twelfth century the English kings had established the most well-developed system of administration and record keeping in Europe.

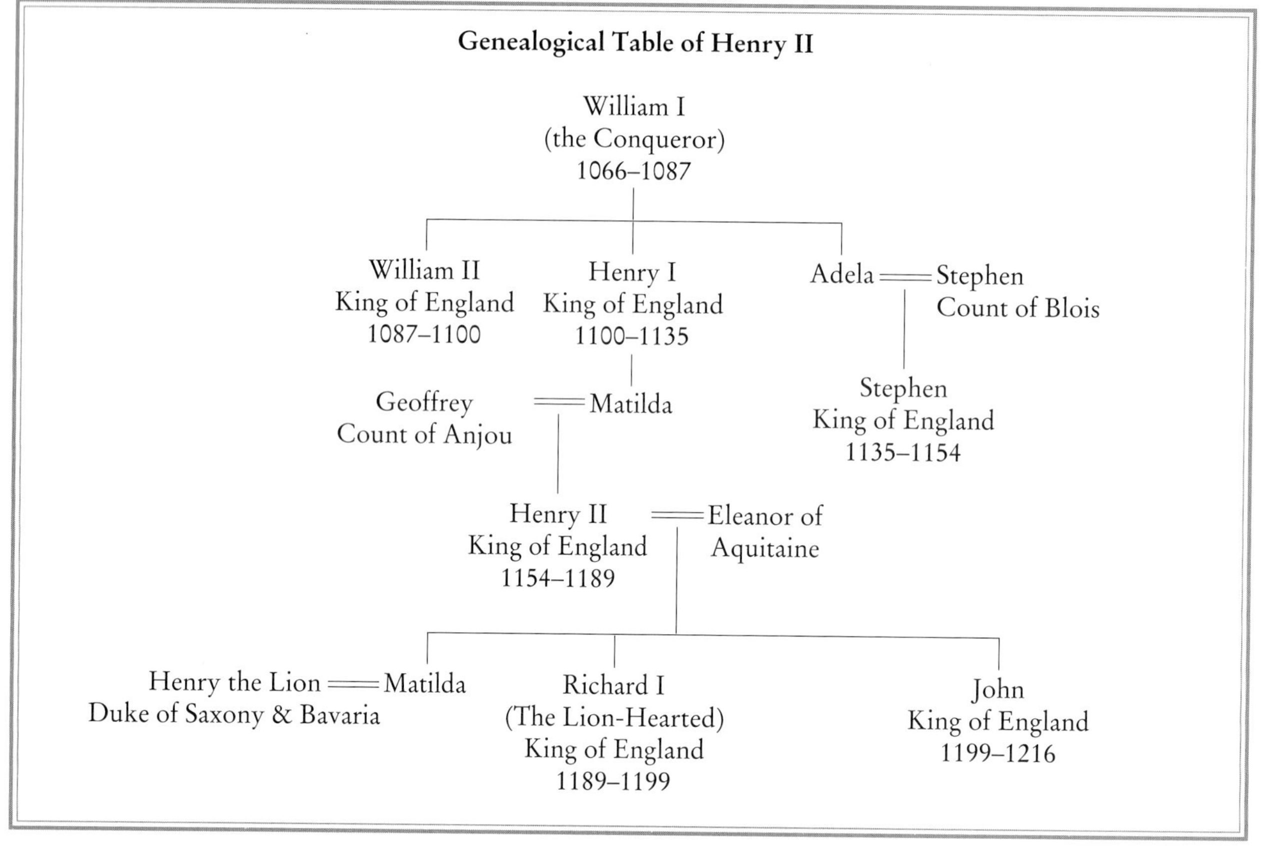

Genealogical Table of Henry II

English institutions reflected both the Anglo-Saxon tradition of conveying the king's orders via writs and the Norman tradition of retaining the ruler's control over his officials, over taxes (paid in cash), and over court cases involving all capital crimes. In addition, the very circumstances of the English king favored the growth of an administrative staff: his frequent travels to and from the Continent meant that officials needed to work in his absence, and his enormous wealth meant that he could afford them. King Henry II (✱1154–1189) was the driving force in extending and strengthening the institutions of English government.

Henry II became king in the wake of a civil war that threatened the new Norman dynasty in England. Henry I (✱1100–1135) had died without a male heir and had unsuccessfully called the great barons to swear that his daughter Matilda would rule after him. The Norman barons could not imagine a woman ruling them, and they feared her husband, Geoffrey of Anjou, their perennial enemy. The man who succeeded to the throne, Stephen of Blois, was the son of Henry's sister, Adela. With Matilda's son, the future Henry II, only two years old, the struggle for the control of England during Stephen's reign (✱1135–1154) became part of a larger territorial contest between the house of Anjou and the house of Blois. Continual civil war in England, as in Germany, benefited the lay magnates and high churchmen, who gained new privileges and powers as the monarch's authority waned. Newly built private castles, already familiar on the Continent, now appeared in England. But Stephen's coalition of barons, high clergymen, and townsmen eventually fell apart, causing him to agree to the accession of Matilda's son, Henry of Anjou. Thus Henry II became the first Angevin king of England.* His marriage to Eleanor of

*Henry's father was Geoffrey of Anjou, nicknamed Plantagenet from the *genêt*, a shrub he liked. Historians sometimes use the sobriquet to refer to the entire dynasty, so Henry II was the first *Plantagenet* as well as the first *Angevin* king of England.

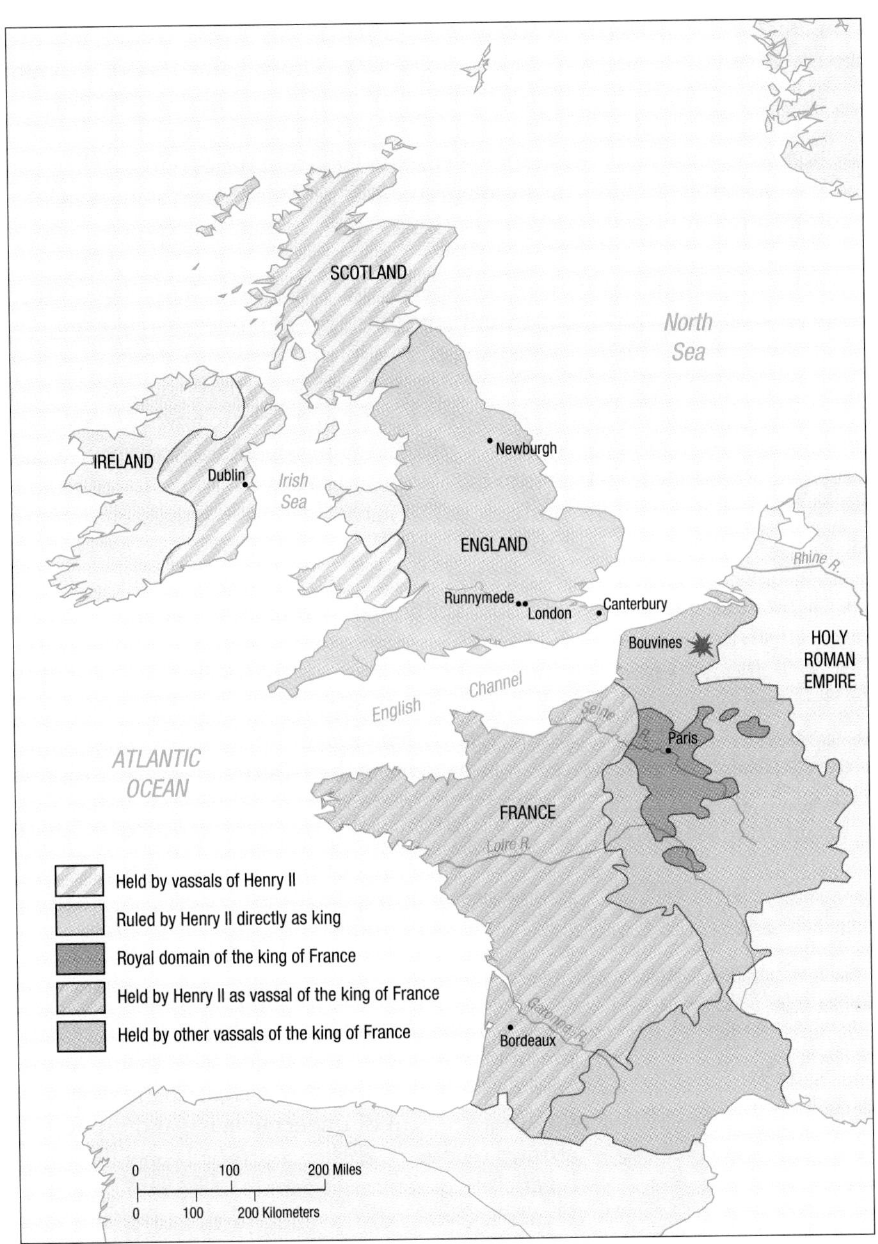

The Monarchy of Henry II: England and France

Aquitaine brought the enormous inheritance of the duchy of Aquitaine to the English crown. Although he remained the vassal of the king of France for his continental lands, Henry in effect ruled a territory that stretched from England to southern France.

Henry valued Eleanor because she was duchess of Aquitaine and because she bore him sons to maintain his dynasty. Before her marriage to Henry in 1152, Eleanor had been married to King Louis VII of France; he had the marriage annulled because she had borne him only daughters. Nevertheless, as queen of France, Eleanor had enjoyed an important position: she disputed with St. Bernard, the most renowned churchman of the day; she accompanied her husband on the Second Crusade, bringing more troops than he did; and she determined to separate from her husband even before he considered leaving her. But she lost much of her power under her

English husband, for Henry dominated her just as he would dominate his barons. Turning to her offspring in 1173, Eleanor, disguised as a man, tried to join her eldest son, Henry the Younger, in a plot against his father. But the rebellion was put down, and she spent most of the years thereafter, until King Henry's death in 1189, confined under guard at Winchester Castle.

When Henry II became king of England, he immediately sought to reassert royal authority over the barons newly ensconced in their castles. He razed new strongholds and regained crown lands. Then he proceeded to extend monarchical power, imposing royal justice by developing a system of royal courts. "Throughout the realm," wrote a contemporary admirer, "he appointed judges and legal officials to curb the audacity of wicked men and dispense justice to litigants according to the merits of their case." Henry's courts augmented the role of the crown in both criminal and civil cases by claiming jurisdiction over certain heinous crimes such as murder and offering the option of royal justice for others. At the Assize of Clarendon in 1166, for example, Henry ordered local free men across the entire kingdom to meet under oath, constituting themselves into a grand jury to declare who in their district was suspected of murder, robbery, and theft. Those named were brought before Henry's justices for judgment; even if cleared of the particular crime they were accused of, they were expelled from the country if they had notorious reputations. This new system of justice made the king's power felt everywhere, and it increased his income with confiscated lands and fines collected from criminals. Henry later added arson and rape to the list of crimes that, like murder, were deemed to violate "the king's peace."

Castle of Henry II
Henry II rebuilt or took over many castles in order to counter the power of English barons who held private castles. This castle in Suffolk is the only one that Henry built from scratch.

Henry's stiffest opposition to the extension of royal courts came from the church, where a separate system of trial and punishment had long been available to the clergy and to others who enjoyed church protection. Jealous of their prerogatives, churchmen refused to submit to the jurisdiction of Henry's courts, and the ensuing contest between Henry II and his appointed archbishop, Thomas Becket (1118–1170), became the greatest battle between the church and the state in the twelfth century. The conflict over jurisdiction simmered for six years, until Henry's henchmen murdered Thomas, unintentionally turning him into a martyr. Although Henry's role in the murder remained ambiguous, he had to do penance for the deed largely because of public outcry. In the end both church and royal courts expanded to address the concerns of a society becoming increasingly litigious.

For civil cases, Henry regularly used *justices in eyre* (*eyre* from the Latin *iter*, or "journey"), who made circuits throughout the kingdom to hear cases in which free men and women who owned property disputed such issues as rights to inheritance, dowries, the land of underage heirs, and properties claimed by others. Earlier courts had generally relied on duels between the litigants to determine verdicts. Henry's system of traveling justice offered a new option, an inquest under royal supervision. It also gave the king a new source of revenue. For example, a widow named Mabel might dispute the possession of a parcel of land at Stoke with a man named Ralph. By purchasing a royal writ she could set the wheels of the king's new justice in motion. The writ would order the sheriff to summon a jury of twelve free men from Stoke to declare in front of the justices whether Ralph or Mabel had the better right to possess the land. The power of the king would then back the verdict. Thus English kings used the law to enhance their power and income.

The Martyrdom of Thomas Becket
After years of quarreling with Becket, Henry uttered the words that sent some of his men to Becket's cathedral to kill him. In this miniature, Henry's knights murder Becket before the altar. Becket's martyrdom gave the clerical cause a strength it had lacked in his lifetime.

A contemporary legal treatise known as *Glanvill*, after its presumed author, applauded the new system for its efficiency, speed, and conclusiveness: "This legal institution emanates from perfect equity. For justice, which after many and long delays is scarcely ever demonstrated by the duel, is advantageously and speedily attained through this institution." *Glanvill* might have added that the king also speedily gained a large treasury; the Exchequer, as the financial bureau of England came to be called, recorded all the fines paid for judgments and the sums collected for writs. The amounts, entered on parchment sewn together and stored in rolls, became the Receipt Rolls and Pipe Rolls, the first of many such records of the English monarchy and an indication that writing had become a mechanism for institutionalizing royal power in England.

The English monarchy was rich; it received revenues from its courts, income from its demesne lands in England and on the Continent, taxes from its cities, and customary feudal dues (aids) from its barons and knights for such occasions as the knighting of the king's eldest son and the marriage of the king's eldest daughter. Dependent on the increasingly commercial society of the late twelfth century, the English kings encouraged their knights and barons not to serve them personally in battle but instead to pay the king a tax called *scutage* in lieu of service. The monarchs preferred to hire mercenaries both as troops to fight external enemies and as police to enforce the king's will at home.

In 1214, however, the English army was defeated on the Continent. In 1204 the king of France, Philip II (*1180–1223), had confiscated the northern French territories of King John (*1199–1216), the son and heir of Henry II. Between 1204 and 1214, John added to the crown revenues and forged an army to fight Philip. To finance his plans, he repeatedly forced his vassals to pay ever-increasing scutages and extorted money in the form of new feudal aids. He compelled the widows of his vassals to marry men of his choosing or pay him a hefty fee if they refused. In 1214 the defeat of his forces at the Battle of Bouvines caused discontented English barons to rebel openly against the king. At Runnymede in June 1215, John agreed to the charter of baronial liberties that has come to be called the Magna Carta, or "Great Charter."

The Magna Carta was essentially a conservative document defining the "customary" obligations and rights of the nobility and forbidding the king to break from these customs without consulting his barons. For example, one provision specified that:

> *No scutage or aid shall be imposed in our kingdom unless by common counsel of our kingdom [i.e., in consultation with the barons], except for ransoming our person, for making our eldest son a knight, and for once marrying our eldest daughter [all of these being customary]; and for these only a reasonable aid shall be levied . . .*

The Magna Carta also maintained that all free men in the land had certain customs and rights in common, and that the king must uphold these customs and rights:

> *No free man shall be arrested or imprisoned or disseised [dispossessed] or outlawed or exiled or in any way victimized, neither will we attack him or send anyone to attack him, except by the lawful judgment of his peers or by the law of the land.*

In this way, the Magna Carta documented the subordination of the king to custom; it implied that the king was not above the law. The growing royal power of the king was matched by the self-confidence of the English barons, certain of their rights and eager to articulate them.

France: From Acorn to Oak

Whereas the power of the English throne led to a baronial movement to curb it, the weakness of the French monarchy ironically led to its expansion. Unencumbered by Italian territorial claims like those of Frederick I and enriched by revenues from new communes like Laon, by the mid-twelfth century the king of France had carved out a compact kingdom in the middle of equally compact principalities. When Philip II, who eventually bested the English King John, became king, the Ile-de-France was sandwiched between territory controlled by the counts of Flanders, Champagne, and Anjou. By far the most powerful ruler on the Continent, King Henry II of England was both the count of Anjou and the duke of Normandy; he also held the duchy of Aquitaine through his wife and exercised hegemony over Poitou and Brittany.

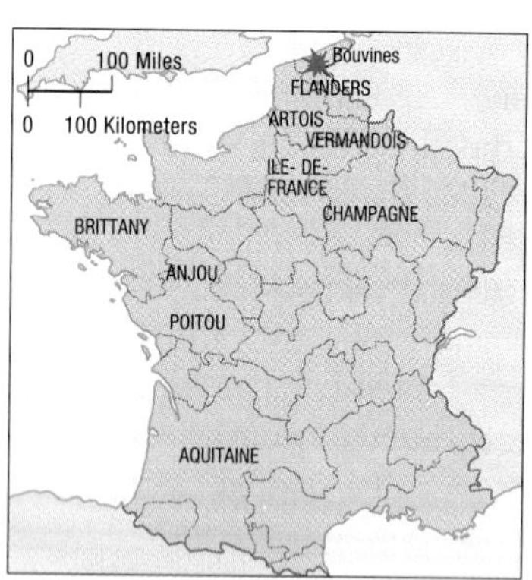

The Consolidation of France

Henry and the counts of Flanders and Champagne vied to control the newly crowned, fourteen-year-old king of France. Philip, however, quickly learned to play them off against one another, in particular by setting the sons of Henry II against their father. For example, Philip helped Henry the Younger rebel against his father in 1183 by sending the young man a contingent of mercenary troops. Despite his apparent political competence, contemporaries were astounded when Philip successfully gained territory: he wrested Vermandois and Artois from Flanders in the 1190s and Normandy, Anjou, Maine, Touraine, and Poitou from King John of England in 1204. A contemporary chronicler dubbed him Philip Augustus, the augmenter.

Modern historians are less impressed with Philip's conquests than with his ability to keep and administer his new territories.* Philip instituted a new kind of French administration run, as in England, by officials who kept accounts and files of outgoing and incoming documents. Before Philip's day the decrees of the French king, like those of Frederick I and Henry the Lion, had been written down and saved by the recipient—if they were recorded at all. For example, when a monastery wanted a confirmation of its privileges from the king, its own scribes wrote the document for its archives to preserve it against possible future challenges. Those documents the king did keep generally followed him in his travels like personal possessions; but most royal arrangements were committed to memory rather than written down. In 1194, Philip Augustus lost his meager cache of documents, along with much treasure, when he had to leave his baggage train behind in a battle with the king of England. After 1194, written decrees replaced this essentially oral tradition.

Whereas German rulers employed ministerials to do the daily work of government, Philip, like the English king, relied largely on members of the lesser nobility—knights and clerics, many of whom were "masters" educated in the city schools of France. They served as officers of his court; as *prévôts*, who oversaw the king's demesne and collected his taxes; and as *baillis* (or *sénéchaux* in the south), who not only supervised the *prévôts* but also functioned as regional judges, presiding over courts (called *assizes*, from the Old French word for "seatings") that met monthly, making the king's power felt locally as never before.

Nevertheless, before 1204 the French king's territory was minuscule compared to the vast regions

*Philip was particularly successful in imposing royal control in Normandy; later French kings gave most of the other territories to collateral members of the royal family.

Ribbed Gothic Vault
This Gothic cathedral at Mantes (France) was begun during the lifetime of Philip Augustus. During the century following 1140, architectural features such as the pointed arch and the ribbed vault were adopted in much of northern France, and their aesthetic and structural possibilities were explored.

held by the English king. Although it seems logical to us today that the French king would inevitably rule all of France, twelfth-century observers would not have been surprised if France had become the cornerstone of the English king's power, with England functioning merely as his "offshore outpost." True, some pivotal forces led to the extension of the French king's power and the territorial integrity of France. The Second Crusade brought together many French lords as vassals of the king and united them against a common foe. The language they spoke was becoming increasingly uniform and "French." Nevertheless, royal personalities and strategies that worked accidentally rather than by plan largely determined that Philip would conquer Normandy and thereby gain a commanding position in France. In 1204, having declared his vassal, the duke of Normandy (who was, of course, also the English king, John), disobedient for not coming to court when summoned, Philip confiscated most of John's continental territories. He confirmed this triumph decisively at the Battle of Bouvines ten years later, in which, mainly by luck, Philip's armies routed the major opponents and took others prisoner. With the English threat safely across the channel, the French monarch could boast being the richest and most powerful ruler in France. Unlike Frederick I Barbarossa, who was compelled to divide the territory he had seized from Henry the Lion among the German princes, Philip had sufficient support and resources to keep tight hold on Normandy. He received homage and fealty from most of the Norman aristocracy; his *baillis* carefully carried out their work there in accordance with Norman customs. For ordinary Normans the change from duke to king brought few changes.

The Growth of a Vernacular High Culture

In consolidating their power, kings, barons, and princes supported new kinds of literature and music. The second half of the twelfth century saw a flood of literature often meant to be read aloud or sung, sometimes with accompanying musical instruments, to a large audience of clerics, knights, castellans, and counts, and their mothers, wives, daughters, and sons. Although not overtly political, these new works, written in the vernacular (that is, the spoken language rather than Latin), celebrated and extolled the lives of the nobility. They provided a common experience in a common language under the aegis of the court. Whether in the cities of Italy or the more isolated courts of northern Europe, patrons and patronesses, enriched by their seigneuries and by the commercial growth of the twelfth century, now spent their profits on the arts.

Vernacular literature thrived at the court of Henry the Lion and Matilda, whose wealth and power allowed them to support writers and artists, some of whom reworked French and English narra-

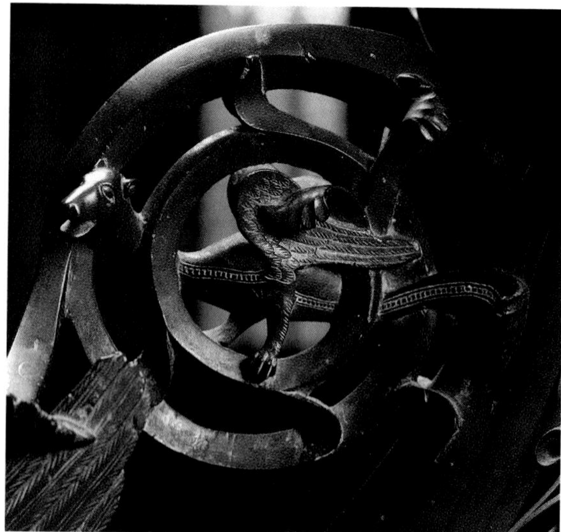

Princely Patronage of Churches
Henry the Lion and his wife Matilda commissioned many church ornaments. This detail from an iron candlestick that they commissioned depicts a winged dragon.

tive poetry into German. Poetry in the language of everyday life appealed to a wide audience, revealing the new self-confidence of German culture in the age of Frederick. Henry even had his clerics compile a brief encyclopedia of knowledge about the world and God, the *Lucidarius*, one of the earliest prose pieces in Germany. Henry and Matilda also contributed handsomely to building new churches in cities such as Lübeck and Brunswick, commissioned illuminated manuscripts, and ordered the production of fine gold reliquaries and church furnishings. Their patronage not only helped develop the German language but also heightened their prestige as aristocrats.

Poets of Love and Play: The Troubadours

Already at the beginning of the twelfth century the grandfather of Eleanor of Aquitaine, Duke William of Poitiers (1071–1127), had written lyric poems in Occitan, the vernacular of southern France. Perhaps influenced by love poetry in Arabic and Hebrew from al-Andalus, his own poetry in turn provided a model for poetic forms that gained popularity through repeated performances. The final four-line stanza of one such poem demonstrates the composer's skill with words:

Per aquesta fri e tremble,	*For this one I shiver and tremble,*
quar de tan bon' amor l'am;	*I love her with such a good love;*
qu'anc no cug qu'en nasques semble	*I do not think the like of her was ever born*
en semblan de gran linh n'Adam.	*in the long line of Lord Adam*

The rhyme scheme of this poem appears to be simple—*tremble* goes with *semble*, *l'am* with *n'Adam*—but the entire poem has five earlier verses, all six lines long and all containing the *-am*, *-am* rhyme in the fourth and sixth lines, while every other line within each verse rhymes as well.

Troubadours, lyric poets who wrote in Occitan, varied their rhymes and meters endlessly to dazzle their audience with brilliant originality. Most of their rhymes and meters resemble Latin religious poetry of the same time, indicating that the vernacular and Latin religious cultures shared the same milieu. Such similarity is also evident in the troubadour's choice of subjects. The most common topic, love, echoed the twelfth-century emphasis on the emotional relationship between God and humankind. The Cistercians expressed this new emotional connection when they dedicated their churches to the Virgin Mary, thinking of her role less as Queen of Heaven and more as mother, with the monks "curled up against her breast." The troubadours also sang about feelings while inventing new variations of nuance and imagery. When William of Poitiers sang of his "good love" for a woman unlike any other born in the line of Adam, the words could be interpreted in two ways. They reminded listeners of the Virgin, a woman unlike any other, but they also referred to William's

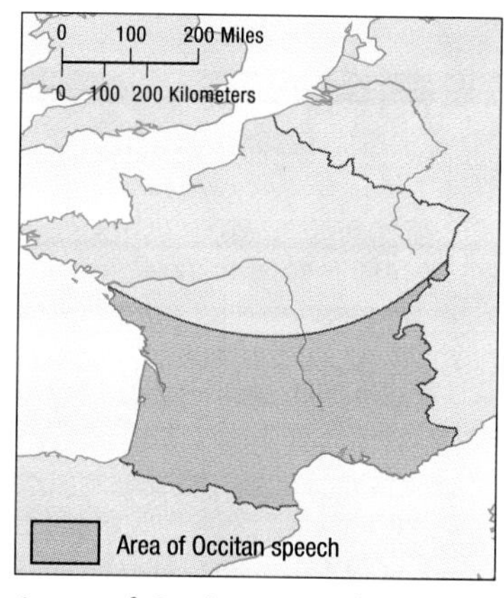

Areas of Occitan Speech

lover, recalled in another part of the poem, where he had complained

If I do not get help soon
and my lady does not give me love,
by Saint Gregory's holy head I'll die
if she doesn't kiss me in a chamber or under
a tree.

His lady's character is ambiguous here: she is like Mary, but she is also his mistress.

Later troubadours, both male and female, expressed prevalent views of love much as popular singers do today. The Contessa de Dia (c. 1060–1140; probably the wife of the lord of Die, in France) wrote about her unrequited love for a man:

Of things I'd rather keep in silence I must
sing:
so bitter do I feel toward him
whom I love more than anything.
With him my mercy and fine manners
*[*cortesia*] are in vain,*
my beauty, virtue and intelligence.
For I've been tricked and cheated
as if I were completely loathesome.

The idea of *cortesia* is key to troubadour verse: it refers to courtesy, the refinement of people living at court, and the struggle to achieve an ideal of beauty, virtue, and intelligence. The Contessa's fine manners proved that her love was courteous. Historians and literary critics sometimes use the term *courtly love* to refer to one particular mix of eroticism, ritual, and rules in the new courtly ideal: the poet expresses overwhelming love for a beautiful married noblewoman far above him in status and therefore unattainable. The theme of courtly love created a fantasy world in which women controlled the happiness and even the lives of men and were valued for their youth, beauty, and status, not their reproductive capabilities. Little wonder that Eleanor of Aquitaine and other aristocratic women paid and protected troubadours to sustain these illusions. Yet powerful men at princely courts enjoyed troubadour music as well; it did not threaten the reality of power relations between men and women or change the view that aristocratic women were valuable mainly as heiresses and mothers of sons.

Music was part of the charm of troubadour poetry, which was always sung, typically by a *jongleur* (musician). Unfortunately, we have no record of troubadour music before the thirteenth century, and even then for only a fraction of the poems. By this time music was written on four- and five-line staves, so we can at least determine relative pitches, and modern musicians can sing some troubadour songs with the hope of sounding reasonably like the original. This is the earliest popular music that can be re-created authentically. For example, the beginning of a song by the troubadour Bernart de Ventadorn, transcribed in the modern G-clef and key of C, goes as shown below. Each syllable normally corresponds to one note, except for the notes tied together with a slur, which were sung more quickly so as not to drag out the syllable's length too much.

From southern France the lyric love song spread to Italy, northern France, England, and Germany—regions in which Occitan was a foreign language and instruments probably accompanied performances that would otherwise bore audiences who did not understand the words. Similar poetry appeared in other vernacular languages: the minnesingers (literally "love singers") sang in

Troubadour Song
The songs of Raimon de Miraval, like those of other troubadours, were not written down until the thirteenth century. Here the song that begins A penas *is set to music with a five-line staff.*

German; the trouvères sang in the Old French of northern France. One trouvère was the English King Richard I (*Coeur de Lion*, or "the Lion-Hearted"), son of Henry II and Eleanor of Aquitaine. Taken prisoner in 1192 by Duke Leopold VI of Austria, Richard wrote a poem expressing his longing not for a lady but for the good companions of war, the knightly "youths" he had joined in battle:

They know well, the men of Anjou and Touraine,
those bachelors, now so magnificent and safe,
that I am arrested, far from them, in another's hands.
They used to love me much, now they love me not at all.
There's no lordly fighting now on the barren plains,
because I am a prisoner.

The Literature of Epic and Romance

The yearning for the battlefield was not as common a topic in lyric poetry as love, but long narrative poems about heroic deeds (chansons de geste) appeared frequently in vernacular writing, after a long oral tradition, at about the same time as William of Poitiers began to write about his shivering and trembling love. Like the songs of the troubadours, these poems implied a code of behavior for aristocrats, this time on the battlefield. By the end of the twelfth century, warriors wanted a guide for conduct and a common class identity. Nobles and knights had begun merging into one class because they felt threatened from below by newly rich merchants and from above by newly powerful kings. Their ascendancy on the battlefield, where they were used to unhorsing one another with lances and long swords and taking prisoners rather than killing their opponents, was also beginning to wane in the face of mercenary infantrymen who wielded long hooks and knives that ripped easily through chain mail. A knightly ethos and sense of group solidarity emerged in the face of these social, political, and military changes.

Thus the protagonists of heroic poems yearned not for love but for battle, as in Raoul de Cambrai:

The armies are in sight of one another. They go forward cautiously and reconnoitre as they go. The cowards tremble as they march, but the brave hearts rejoice for the battle.

Examining the moral issues that made war both tragic and inevitable, the poet plays on the often contradictory values of his society, in *Raoul* a vassal's right to a fief versus a son's right to his father's land. *Raoul* tells of an emperor who made the grievous error of granting Raoul a fief claimed by the sons of the vassal who first held it. Complicating matters further is Raoul's squire and friend, Bernier, a member of the family against whom Raoul must fight to win his fief. Thus filial duties clash with principles of friendship and vassalage. Raoul attacks the land that he claims, killing Bernier's mother in the process and forcing Bernier to replace his oath of vassalage with one of vengeance: "Noble vassals," he cries to his men, "can you give me good advice? My lord Raoul hates me, for he has burnt my mother in the chapel yonder. God grant I may live long enough to avenge her." The poet matches delight in the sheer physicality of battle with the agony of loss:

Young Bernier was resolute and bold. He pulled forth his sharp sword and struck the son of Guerri such a blow on his pointed helmet that the flowers and stones were scattered, the headpiece of his hauberk was pierced and he was cloven to the teeth. . . . Guerri rode away, for he hardly knew what he was doing. As he rode back over the upland his grief for his sons [he lost his other son in the same battle] became even greater, and it was a pitiful sight to see him tearing his hair with his hands.

Whereas these vernacular narrative poems, later called epics, focused on war, other poems, later called romances, explored the relationships between men and women. These romances reached their zenith of popularity during the late twelfth and early thirteenth centuries. The legend of King Arthur inspired a romance by Chrétien de Troyes (c. 1150–1190) in which a heroic knight, Lancelot, in love with the wife of his lord, comes across a comb bearing some strands of Queen Guinevere's radiant hair:

Never will the eye of man see anything receive such honour as when [Lancelot] begins to adore these tresses. A hundred thousand times he raises them to his eyes and mouth, to his forehead and face. . . . He would not exchange them for a cartload of emeralds and carbuncles, nor does he think that any sore or illness can afflict him now; he holds in contempt essence of pearl, treacle, and the cure for pleurisy; even for St. Martin and St. James he has no need.

At one level this is a commentary on the meaning of relics. Chrétien evokes the familiar imagery of relics as items of devotion. Making Guinevere's hair an object of adoration not only conveys the depth of Lancelot's feeling but also pokes a bit of fun at him. Like the troubadours, the romantic poets delighted in the interplay between religious and amorous feelings. Just as the ideal monk merges his will in God's will, Chrétien's Lancelot's loses his will to the queen. For example, when she sees Lancelot—the greatest knight in Christendom—fighting in a tournament, she tests him by sending him a message to do his "worst":

When he heard this, he replied: "Very willingly," like one who is altogether hers. Then he rides at another knight as hard as his horse can carry him, and misses his thrust which should have struck him. From that time till evening he continued to do as badly as possible in accordance with the Queen's desire.

The Romance of King Arthur
The story of King Arthur gained currency in the twelfth century, inspiring numerous romances and artistic representations.

Such an odd, funny, and pitiful moment, when the greatest of all knights subjects his pride to the whim of a lady, presents one aspect of a new kind of hero, a chivalric knight. The word *chivalry* comes from the French word *cheval*, meaning "horse"; the chivalric hero is a warrior constrained by a code of refinement, fair play, and devotion to an ideal.

New Lay and Religious Associations

Codes of behavior, not only for knights but for all groups, became increasingly important as society grew more complex. Commercial growth in the twelfth century gradually created a new social hierarchy. In the cities and in other areas touched by the commercial revolution, new groups, new identities, and new values both challenged and transformed the knightly ethos. Whereas in the early twelfth century, communes provided their leading citizens with self-government, the second half of the century saw new forms of association delineate commercial society more precisely. As towns grew and their social structures became more varied, guilds, universities, and religious movements offered men and women new affiliations and allegiances.

The new money economy now extended to the countryside, blurring the distinction between rural districts and towns in many parts of northern Europe as it had already done in the tenth-century Italy. In the late twelfth century new lay and religious associations arose principally in regions with the greatest commercial development: northern Italy, the Rhineland, and southern France. We can trace these groups best in the cities, where the documents are more plentiful, but they had their counterparts in the countryside as well.

The Penetration of the Commercial Revolution

By the middle of the twelfth century the commercial revolution had altered rural as well as urban life. On the great estates of the rich, farms were now organized to make money rather than merely sustain the estates' inhabitants. Great lords hired trained, literate agents to administer their estates, calculate profits and losses, and make marketing decisions. Aristocrats needed money not only because they relished luxuries but also because their honor and authority continued to depend on their personal generosity, patronage, and displays of wealth. In the late twelfth century, when some townsmen could boast fortunes that rivaled the riches of the landed aristocracy, the economic pressures on the nobles increased as their extravagance exceeded their incomes. Most went into debt.

The lord's need for money changed peasant life, so that peasants too became integrated into the developing commercial economy. As the population increased, the demand for food required more farmland. By the middle of the twelfth century the isolated and sporadic attempts to cultivate new land had become a regular and coordinated activity. Great lords offered special privileges to peasants who would do the backbreaking work of plowing marginal land. In 1154 the bishop of Neissen (eastern Germany) announced that

> *I have brought together and established in an uncultivated and almost uninhabited place energetic men coming from the province of Flanders, and . . . I have given in stable, eternal and hereditary possession to them and to all their descendants, the village called Kühren.*

Experts in drainage, these Flemish settlers had rights to the land they reclaimed and owed only light monetary obligations to the bishop, who nevertheless expected to reap a profit from their tolls and tithes. In effect the bishop and the settlers together created the new village of Kühren. Similar encouragement came from lords throughout Europe, especially in northern Italy, England, Flanders and the other Low Countries, and Germany. In Flanders the great monasteries sponsored drainage projects; and canals linking the cities to the agricultural regions let ships ply the waters to virtually every nook and cranny of the region. With its dense population, Flanders provided not only a natural meeting ground for long-distance traders from England and France but also numerous markets for local traders.

Sometimes free peasants acted on their own initiative to clear land and relieve the pressure of overpopulation, as when the small freeholders in England's Fenland region cooperated to build banks and dikes to claim the land that led out to the North Sea. Villages were founded on the drained land, and villagers shared responsibility for repairing and maintaining the dikes even as each peasant family farmed its new holding individually.

On old estates the rise in population strained to the breaking point the manse organization, in which each household was settled on the land that supported it. Twenty peasant families might live on what had been—in the tenth century—the manse of one family. Labor services and dues had to be recalculated with the manse supporting so many more people, and peasants and their lords often commuted services and dues into money rents, payable once a year. Although peasant men gained more control over their plots—they could sell them, will them to their sons, or even designate a small portion for their daughters—they had either to pay extra taxes for these privileges or, like communes, join together to buy their collective liberty for a high price, paid out over many years to their lord. Peasants, like town citizens, gained a new sense of identity and solidarity as they bargained with a lord keen to increase his income at their expense.

Peasants now owed more taxes to support the new administrative apparatuses of monarchs and princes. Kings' demands for money from their subjects filtered , either directly or indirectly, to the lowest classes. In Italy the cities themselves often imposed and enforced dues on the peasants, normally tenant farmers who leased their plots in the *contado*, the countryside surrounding each city. In the mid-twelfth century at Florence the urban officials, working closely with the bishop, dominated the roads and river valleys of the *contado*, collecting taxes from its cultivators, calling up its men to fight, and importing its food into the city. Therefore peasants' gains from rising prices, access to markets, greater productivity, and increased personal freedom were partially canceled out by their cash burdens. Peasants of the late twelfth century ate better than their forebears, but they also had more burdens.

Urban Corporations: The Craft Guilds and Universities

As the guilds in the towns and cities developed from confraternities for religious devotion, convivial feasting, charitable activities, and craft regulation, these organizations became interested in drawing up increasingly detailed statutes and rules to protect themselves and control the activities of their members. Guild regulations determined working hours, fixed wages, and set standards for materials and products.

Guilds naturally wanted to protect themselves and expand their influence, but communal governments did not always consider these goals to be in the city's best interest. Bread was too important a commodity in Italian towns, for example, for the communes to allow bakers to form a guild. And communes sometimes fixed prices to ensure that the guilds would not drive prices higher than town consumers could bear. But communes also supported guild efforts to control wages, reinforcing guild regulations with statutes of their own.

When great lords rather than communes governed a city, they too tried to control and protect the guilds. King Henry II of England, for example, eagerly gave some guilds in his Norman duchy special privileges so that they would depend on him:

> *Know that I have conceded and, by this my charter, have confirmed to my tanners of Rouen their guild, dyeing and greasing processes, and all customs and laws of their guild . . . and [I have confirmed] that no one [else] may perform their craft in Rouen.*

The tanners of Rouen sold raw materials to the shoemakers, who had their own guild. The manufacture of finished products often required the cooperation of several guilds. Producing wool cloth involved numerous guilds—shearers, weavers, fullers, dyers—generally working under the supervision of the merchant guild that imported the raw wool. Some guilds were more prestigious than others: in Florence, for example, professional guilds of notaries and judges ranked above craft guilds.

Within each guild existed another kind of hierarchy among the artisans or merchants themselves, with apprentices at the bottom, journeymen and -women in the middle, and masters at the top. Apprentices were boys and occasionally girls placed under the tutelage of a master for a number of years to learn a trade. Normally the child's parents made the formal contract; but sometimes the children themselves took the initiative, as did a young man named John at Genoa in 1180 when he apprenticed himself to a turner, an expert in the use of the lathe. John promised to serve his master faithfully for five years, do whatever was expected of him, and not run away. In turn, his master promised to give him food, clothing, shelter, and a small salary; to teach him the turner's art; and to give him a set of tools after the five years were up.

It would take many more years for a young person like John to become a master, however. First he would likely spend many years as a day laborer, a journeyman, hired by a master who needed extra help. Journeymen and -women did not live with their masters; they worked for them for a wage. This marked an important stage in the economic history of the West. For the first time, workers were neither slaves nor dependents but free and independent wage earners. Although we know more about journeymen than journeywomen, we know that at least a few day workers were female; invariably they received wages far lower than their male counterparts. Sometimes a married couple worked at the same trade and hired themselves out as a team. Often journeymen and -women had to be guild members—for their dues and so their masters could keep tabs on them.

Masters occupied the top of the guild hierarchy. Almost exclusively men, they dominated the offices and policies of the guild, hired journeymen, and recruited and educated apprentices. They drew up the guild regulations and served as chief overseers, inspectors, and treasurers. Because the number of masters was few and the turnover of official posts frequent, most masters eventually had a chance to serve as guild officers. Occasionally they were elected, but more often they were appointed from among the masters of the craft by the governor—whether a prince or a commune—of the city.

During the late twelfth century, women's labor in some trades gradually declined in importance. In Flanders, for example, as the manufacture of woolen cloth shifted from rural areas to cities, women participated less in the process. Only isolated manors still needed a *gynaeceum*, where female dependents spun, wove, and sewed garments. Instead new-style large looms in cities like Ypres and Ghent were run by men working in pairs. They produced a heavy-weight cloth superior to the fabric made on the lighter looms that women had worked. Similarly, women once ground grain tediously into flour by hand; but water mills and animal-powered mills gradually took the place of female labor, and most millers who ran the new machinery were male. Some women were certainly artisans and traders, and their names occasionally appeared in guild memberships. But they did not become guild officers, and they played no official role in town government. Their families were dominated by men. Bernarda Cordonaria (Shoemaker) was not the only woman in Toulouse at the beginning of the thirteenth century who took her last name not from her own trade but from her husband's craft.

Another nearly exclusively male group that developed by the end of the twelfth century was the university, an institution formed by students and masters from the spontaneous growth of schools around particular teachers in the early part of the century. Students and masters together formed a guild (*universitas*), and with special privileges from popes or kings, who valued the services of scholars, they formed small, virtually independent jurisdictions within the town. Historians sometimes speak of the hostility between "town" and "gown." Yet university towns often depended on scholars to patronize local restaurants, shops, and hostels.

Oxford, once a sleepy town where a group of students clustered around one or two masters, became in the twelfth century a center of royal administration, church courts, the study of canon law, and the teaching of Roman law, theology, and the liberal arts. It had about three hundred students by 1209, and masters gradually came to regulate student discipline, proficiency, and housing. Because all scholars were considered clerics, they had special privileges from civil law. When a student at Oxford was suspected of killing his mistress, however, the townspeople took his punishment into their own hands, sparking a revolt by the masters, who refused to teach and left town; some of them went to Cambridge to found a university there. The papacy defended the masters' strike, whereas King John supported the town. In 1214, when John was politically weak and forced to seek the pope's aid, he had to allow a papal legate to patch up a peace at Oxford that favored the university. According to the agreement, the townspeople had to rent lodgings and sell food to the students at reasonable prices, and they had to pay a yearly stipend for poor students. The local bishop appointed a chancellor to receive the money and to hear, every year, town representatives swear to uphold the agreement. Soon the masters themselves named the chancellor.

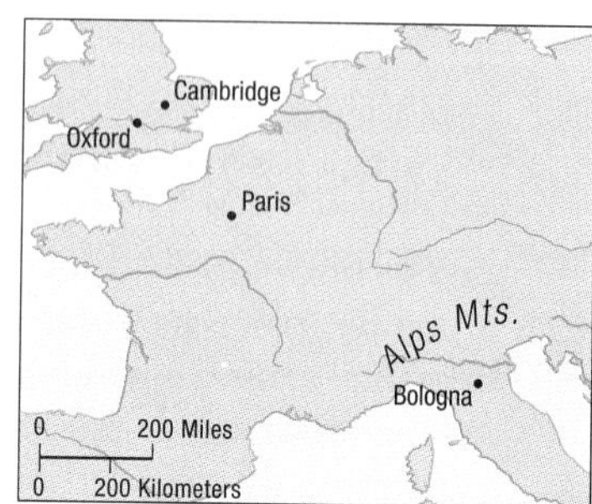

University Cities

At the University of Paris the students and masters also sought autonomy, but here the king guaranteed their rights. When in 1200 a clash between students and Parisians, led by the royal provost, left several students dead, the masters appealed to the king. Philip Augustus issued a charter that promised the students that his officials at Paris would not "lay hands on a student for any offense whatever." A few years later the masters formed a formal guild in which they swore an oath of fraternity, determined proper dress, agreed to follow a certain "order in lectures and disputations," and committed themselves to attend one another's funerals. They already had the right to determine which students were proficient enough to become masters themselves.

Bologna, long a center of legal studies, had two guilds: one of students and one of professors. Unlike young men interested in the liberal arts, Bologna's growing crowds of students were mostly men in their thirties or forties seeking career advancement through expertise in Roman and canon law. As at universities in other cities, the Bolognese students incorporated themselves by "nationality." Two "nations" coexisted at Bologna: Italian (the Cismontanes) and non-Italian (the Ultramontanes).* Each nation protected its members. The nations wrote statutes, elected rectors, and attempted to exact concessions and privileges from the citizens of Bologna and the masters of law. The students participated in the appointment of masters and the payment of their salaries, even though by 1215 the professors at Bologna had organized a guild of their own. Hostility between students and masters sometimes led to the students' boycotting classes, leaving the city, and canceling their teachers' payments. These actions brought the professors to heel. At Bologna the students dominated the university.

Religious Fervor and Dissent

Conflict over authority in the new universities was mirrored in the religious fervor that developed about 1200, when individual piety and new religious movements involved ever greater numbers of lay women and men. For women in particular, mass involvement in new sorts of piety was unprecedented, even in the monasteries of the past. Now beckoning to women of every age and every walk of life, the new piety spread beyond the convent, punctuating the routines of daily life with Scriptural reading, fasting, and charity. Some of this intense religious response developed into official, orthodox movements within the church; other religious movements so threatened established doctrine that church leaders declared them heretical.

St. Francis (c. 1182–1226) founded the most famous orthodox religious movement—the Franciscans. Francis was a child of the commercial revolution. Although expected to follow his well-to-do father in the cloth trade at Assisi, Francis began to experience doubts, dreams, and illnesses, which spurred him to religious self-examination. Eventually he renounced his family's wealth, dramatically marking the decision by casting off all his clothes and standing naked before his father, a crowd of spectators, and the bishop of Assisi. Francis then went about preaching penance to anyone who would listen. Clinging to poverty as if, in his words, "she" was his "lady," he accepted no money, walked without shoes, wore only one coarse tunic, and refused to be cloistered. Intending to follow the model of Christ, he received, as his biographers put it, a miraculous gift of grace: the stigmata, the five wounds of the crucified Christ.

By all accounts Francis was a spellbinding speaker, and he attracted many followers. Recognized as a religious order by the pope, the Brothers of St. Francis (or friars, from the Latin meaning "little brothers") spent their time preaching, ministering to lepers, and doing manual labor. Eventually they dispersed, setting up fraternal groups throughout Italy and then in France, Spain, the Holy Land, and eventually Germany and England. Unlike Bruno of Cologne and the Cistercians, who had rejected cities, the friars sought town life, sleeping in dormitories on the outskirts and becoming part of urban community life, preaching to crowds and begging for their daily bread. St. Francis converted women, too. In 1212 an eighteen-year-old noblewoman named Clare formed the nucleus of a community of pious women, the future Order of the Sisters of St. Francis. At first the women worked alongside the friars; but the church disapproved of their activities in the world, and soon Franciscan sisters were confined to cloisters under the Rule of St. Benedict.

Clare was one of many women who experimented with different styles of religious expression. Some women joined convents; others became recluses or sought membership in new lay sisterhoods. In northern Europe at the end of the twelfth century, lay women who lived together in informal pious communities were called Beguines. Without permanent vows or an established rule, the Beguines chose to be celibate (though they were free to leave the beguinage to marry) and often made their living

Cismontane means "from this side of the mountains," that is, the Alps, whereas *Ultramontane* means "from the other side of the mountains."

by weaving cloth or working with the sick and old. Although their daily occupations were ordinary, the Beguines' private, internal lives were often emotional and ecstatic, infused with the combined imagery of love and religion so pervasive in both monasteries and courts. One renowned Beguine, Mary of Oignies, who like St. Francis was said to have received the stigmata, felt herself to be a pious mother entrusted with the Christ child:

> *Sometimes it seemed to her that for three or more days she held [Christ] close to her so that He nestled between her breasts like a baby, and she hid Him there lest He be seen by others. Sometimes she kissed him as though He were a little child and sometimes she held Him on her lap as if He were a gentle lamb.*

Intensely focused on the life of Christ, men and women in the late twelfth century made his childhood, agony, death, and presence in the Eucharist the most important experiences of their own lives.

According to the established church, the Eucharist required an ordained priest to consecrate the wine and bread. In the late twelfth century, however, some reformers opened the consecration to the laity, a practice the church condemned as heretical. This was just one of a veritable explosion of heretical ideas and doctrines contradicting those officially accepted by church authorities. The idea of heresy was of course not new in the twelfth century. But the Gregorian reform had created for the first time in the West a clear church hierarchy headed by a pope who could enforce a single doctrine, discipline, and dogma. Such clearly defined orthodoxy meant that people would, for the first time in western Europe, perceive heresy as a serious problem. The growth of cities, commerce, and intellectual life fostered a new sense of community for many Europeans. But when intense religious feeling led to the fervent espousal of new religious ideas, established authorities often felt threatened and took steps to preserve their power.

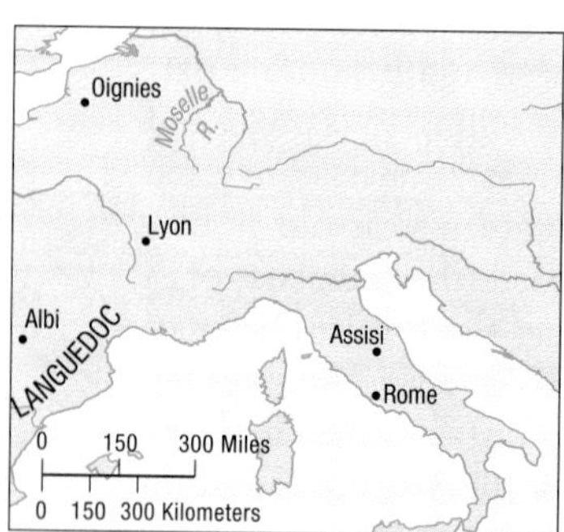

Franciscans, Heretics, and Reformers

Frederick Barbarossa's outraged reply to the representatives of the Roman commune, for example, was in part a rejection of a heretical cleric named Arnold of Brescia, leader of the commune. As Otto of Freising described him, Arnold was "a disparager of the clergy and of bishops, a persecutor of monks, a flatterer only of the laity." His heresy was both social and religious: "He used to say that neither clerics that owned property . . . nor monks with possessions could in any wise be saved. . . . Besides this, he is said to have held unreasonable views with regard to the sacrament of the altar and infant baptism." We do not know precisely what Arnold taught because we have only the reports of his orthodox critics. We do know that his radical critique of clerical riches and his questioning the meaning of the Eucharist and the efficacy of infant baptism were prevalent heretical ideas.

Among the most visible heretics were dualists, who saw the world torn between good and evil. Already important in Bulgaria and Asia Minor, dualism became a prominent ingredient in the religious life in Italy, Languedoc (a part of southern France), and the Rhineland by the end of the twelfth century. Described collectively as Cathars, or "Pure Ones," these groups believed the Devil had created the material world. Therefore they renounced the world, abjuring wealth, sex, and meat. Their repudiation of sex reflected some of the attitudes of eleventh-century church reformers (whose orthodoxy, however, was never in doubt), while their rejection of wealth echoed the same concerns that moved Bruno of Cologne to forswear city life and led St. Francis to embrace poverty. In many ways the heretics simply took these attitudes to an extreme; but unlike orthodox reformers, they also challenged the efficacy and value of the church hierarchy.

Attracting both men and women, and giving women access to the highest positions in the Cathar hierarchy, Cathars young and old, literate and unlettered saw themselves as followers of Christ's original message; as members of one condemned group protested, "the bishop who had given sentence was a heretic and not they." At Lombers in Languedoc, where they were called Albigensians,*

*The name was derived from the town of Albi, near Lombers.

they explained their ideas concerning the Eucharist with complete assurance:

> *They answered that those who received worthily were saved; and those who received unworthily, procured to themselves damnation; and they said that [the Eucharist] was consecrated by every good man, whether an ecclesiastic or a layman; and they answered nothing else, because they would not be compelled to answer concerning their faith.*

The church condemned other, nondualist, groups as heretical not on doctrinal grounds but because these groups allowed their lay members to preach, challenging the authority of the church hierarchy. In Lyon (in southeastern France) in the 1170s, for example, a rich merchant named Waldo decided to take literally the Gospel message "If you wish to be perfect, then go and sell everything you have, and give to the poor" (Matt. 19:21, Latin Vulgate Bible). The same message had inspired countless monks and would worry the church far less several decades later, when St. Francis established his new order. But when Waldo went into the street and gave away his belongings, announcing "I am really not insane, as you think," he scandalized not only the bystanders but the church as well. Refusing to retire to a monastery, Waldo and his followers, men and women called Waldensians, lived in poverty and went about preaching, quoting the Gospel in the vernacular so that everyone could understand. But the papacy rebuffed Waldo's bid to preach freely; and the Waldensians—denounced, excommunicated, and expelled from Lyon—wandered to Languedoc, Italy, northern Spain, and the Moselle valley.

European Aggression Within and Without

Classifying a particular group as a threat to society was a common method of asserting political and religious control in the second half of the twelfth century. Segregated from Christian society, vilified, and persecuted, those who were singled out, principally Jews and heretics, provided a rallying point for popes, princes, and Christian armies. Taking the offensive against those defined as different also meant launching campaigns to defeat peoples on Christendom's borders, a trend begun earlier with the First Crusade and the *reconquista* of Spain. In the early thirteenth century, war against the Muslims to the south, the unbelievers to the north, and the Byzantine Empire to the east made crusading a permanent feature of medieval life. Even the West did not escape: the crusade waged against the Albigensians starting in 1208 in southern France replaced the ruling class and eclipsed the court culture of the troubadours there.

Jews as Strangers, Heretics as Threats

Socially isolated and branded as outcasts, Jews and heretics helped define the larger society as orthodox. Like lepers, whose disease cut them off from ordinary communities, Jews were believed to threaten the health of those around them. Lepers had to wear a special costume, were forbidden to touch children, could not eat with those not afflicted, and were housed in leprosaria; Jews were similarly segregated from emerging Christian institutions, though they were not confined to hospices. Forced off their lands during the eleventh century, most ended up in the cities as craftsmen, merchants, or moneylenders, providing capital for the developing commercial society, whose Christian members

Jewish Communities

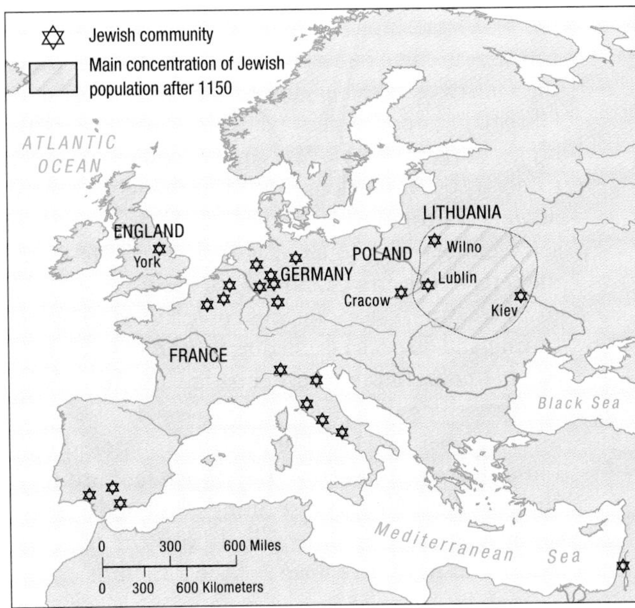

The Jew as the Other
Beginning in the second half of the twelfth century, Jews were increasingly portrayed as different from Christians, with beady eyes, hooked noses, and tall pointed hats. In this illustration clerics are borrowing money from a Jew in a conical hat.

were prohibited from charging interest as usury forbidden by Christ. The growing monopoly of the guilds forced Jews out of the crafts: in effect Jews were compelled to become "usurers" because other fields were closed to them. The slang and derogatory "to Jew," meaning "to cheat like a moneylender," was first used, in its Latin form (*judaizare*), around the mid-twelfth century by St. Bernard. Even with Christian moneylenders available, lords, especially kings, borrowed from Jews and encouraged others to do so because, along with their newly asserted powers, European rulers claimed the Jews as their serfs and Jewish property as their own. "Jews are the serfs of the crown and belong exclusively to the royal treasury," was one view proclaimed in Spain. In England a special exchequer of the Jews created in 1194 collected unpaid debts due after the death of a Jewish creditor.

Even before 1194, Henry II had imposed new and arbitrary taxes on the Jewish community. Similarly in France, persecuting Jews and confiscating their property benefited both the treasury and the authoritative image of the king. For example, early in his reign Philip Augustus's agents surprised Jews at sabbath worship in their synagogues and seized their goods, demanding that they redeem their own property for a large sum of money. Shortly thereafter, Philip declared forfeit 80 percent of all debts owed to Jews; the remaining 20 percent was to be paid directly to the king. About a year later, in 1182, Philip expelled the Jews from the Ile-de-France:

> *The king gave them leave to sell each his movable goods. . . . But their real estate, that is, houses, fields, vineyards, barns, winepresses, and such like, he reserved for himself and his successors, the kings of the French.*

When Philip allowed the Jews to return, in 1198, he intended for them to be moneylenders or money changers exclusively, whose activities would be taxed and monitored by his officials.

Limiting Jews to moneylending in an increasingly commercial economy also served the interests of lords in debt to Jewish creditors. For example, in 1190, local nobles orchestrated a brutal attack on the Jews of York (in England) to rid themselves of their debts and of the Jews to whom they owed money. Churchmen too used credit in a money economy but resented the fiscal obligations it imposed. One of the most virulent attacks against the Jews came from Peter the Venerable, a twelfth-century abbot of Cluny, who wrote an entire book about the "obstinacy" of the Jews, including a chapter on their "absurd and utterly stupid tales." But Peter's mockery was hardly disinterested; Cluny was deeply in debt—in part to the Jews in its neighborhood—when he became its abbot. The papacy, with agents and bureaucrats to support, also depended on credit granted by professional moneylenders. With their drive to create centralized territorial states and their desire to make their power known and felt, powerful rulers of Europe—churchmen and laity alike—exploited and coerced the Jews while drawing upon and encouraging a wellspring of elite and popular anti-Jewish feeling.

The sentiment against Jews grew over time. Ever since the Roman Empire had become Christian, Jews had been seen as different from Christians, and imperial law had prohibited them from, for example, owning Christian slaves or marrying Christian women. Canon laws had added to these restrictions, and in the twelfth century intellectuals elaborated objections against Jewish doctrine. These official views now merged with sensational popular stories. For example, after a little boy was murdered at Norwich, in England, Thomas of Monmouth, a local monk, charged that the child was the victim of a Jewish conspiracy. Each year, Thomas imagined, a conclave of rabbis met to decide on a place to sacrifice a Christian child. The story became commonplace, told with local variations, and typically caused the lynching of local Jews. Although Jews must have looked exactly like Christians—contemporaries complained that no one could tell the two apart—Jews now became clearly identified in sculpture and in drawings by conical hats and, increasingly, by demeaning features.

Attacks against Jews coincided with campaigns against heretics, whose beliefs spread in regions where political control was less centralized, as, for example, in southern France. By the end of the twelfth century, however, church and secular powers combined to stamp out heresies. These efforts were not always violent. Papal legates preached to heretics to convert them. The Dominican order, for example, developed after about 1205 from papal missions to Languedoc to address heretical groups. Its founder, St. Dominic (1170–1221), recognized that preachers of Christ's word who came on horseback, followed by a crowd of servants, and wearing fine clothes had no moral leverage with their audience. Therefore, like their adversaries the Cathars, the Dominicans rejected material riches and instead went about on foot, preaching and begging. Like the Franciscans, whom they resembled both organizationally and spiritually, the Dominicans were called friars.

However, the church sometimes resorted to armed force in its campaign against heretics. In 1208 the murder of a papal legate in southern France prompted Pope Innocent III (*1198–1216) to demand that northern princes take up the sword, invade Languedoc, wrest the land from the heretics, and populate it with orthodox Christians. This Albigensian Crusade marked the first time the pope offered warriors fighting an enemy in Christian Europe all the spiritual and temporal benefits of a crusade to the Holy Land: he suspended their monetary debts and promised their sins would be forgiven after forty days' service. Like all crusades, the Albigensian Crusade had political as well as religious dimensions. It pitted southern French princes, like Raymond VI, count of Toulouse (1194–1222), against northern leaders like Simon IV de Montfort l'Amaury (c. 1160–1218), a castellan from the Ile-de-France eager to demonstrate his piety and win new possessions. After twenty years of fighting, from 1209 to 1229, leadership would be taken over by the Capetian kings of France, southern resistance broken, and Languedoc brought under the control of the French crown.

More Crusades to the Holy Land

The second half of the twelfth century saw new crusades outside western Europe. When in 1144 the Muslim ruler of Syria captured the Christian city of Edessa, at the northernmost edge of Outremer, the news fired churchmen, particularly the pope and St. Bernard, to preach a new crusade, the Second Crusade (1147–1149), undertaken to resecure Edessa and to attack Damascus, a Muslim stronghold. The crusaders' crushing defeat helped create a Muslim hero, Nur al-Din, who united Syria under his command and presided over a renewal of Sunni Islam. His successor, Saladin, became all too well known to Europeans at the time of the Third Crusade.

Saladin and the Christian king of Jerusalem fought over Egypt, which Saladin ruled by 1186 together with Syria. Effectively squeezed between two Islamic pincers, Outremer lost Jerusalem to Saladin's armies in 1187. The Third Crusade (1189–1192), called to retake Jerusalem, marked a military and political watershed for Outremer. The European outpost survived, but it was reduced to a narrow strip of land. Christians could continue to enter Jerusalem as pilgrims, but Islamic hegemony over the Holy Land would remain a fact of life for centuries.

Led by the greatest rulers of Europe—Frederick I Barbarossa, Philip II Augustus, Leopold of Austria, and Richard I the Lion-Hearted—the Third Crusade refracted the political tensions among the European ruling class as the leaders quarreled among themselves. Richard, in particular, seemed to cultivate enmities: he argued with Philip about dividing the spoils of war; he fought with the king of Sicily and then patched up a peace by promising to support him against Frederick's son, Henry VI (1165–1197); he seized Cyprus from a

Battle of Hattin
In 1187 the Christian forces from Outremer were utterly defeated by Saladin's army. The Third Crusade was organized by the princes of Europe in response to calls for help from the few survivors. In this thirteenth-century depiction of the battle, the Muslims, led by Saladin, are on the left.

relative of the Byzantine emperor (thereby destroying the possibility of good relations with Constantinople); and he offended Leopold at the siege of Acre. These seemingly personal tensions reflected the hostility between the kings of England and France. Leopold, for example, was Philip's ally. Captured by Leopold and held for a huge ransom by Henry VI on his return home, Richard had good reason to write his plaintive poem bemoaning his captivity and the lost "love" of former friends.

Frederick I went overland on the Third Crusade, passing through Hungary and Bulgaria* and descending into the Byzantine Empire. "But the Greeks were worse than the Bulgarians," wrote a contemporary chronicler:

> *At the command of the Greek emperor they showed the army no kindness and even refused to sell them anything to eat.... It made Frederick angry to receive such treatment from Christians, and so he permitted his army to plunder the country.*

*Bulgaria regained its independence in 1185 after a successful rebellion against Byzantine rule.

Such hostilities made the Third Crusade a dress rehearsal for the Fourth Crusade (1202–1204), called by Pope Innocent III as part of his more general plan to define, invigorate, and impose his brand of Christianity on both believers and nonbelievers. From the first, Innocent intended to direct a new crusade that would reverse the failures of the past. The pope, in Innocent's view, was "less than God but greater than man, judge of all men and judged by none." Forces beyond Innocent's control, however, took over the Fourth Crusade, whose warriors sacked Constantinople in 1204. Prejudices, religious zeal, and self-confidence had become characteristic of western European attitudes toward the Greeks. The mutual mistrust between Byzantium and the West dated from eighth-century theological differences that stoked the flames of envy and disdain: "In every respect," wrote a Frenchman about Constantinople at the time of the Second Crusade, "she exceeds moderation; for, just as she surpasses other cities in wealth, so, too, does she surpass them in vice."

Such attitudes help explain the course of events from 1202 to 1204. The crusading army turned out to be far smaller than had been expected. Its leaders

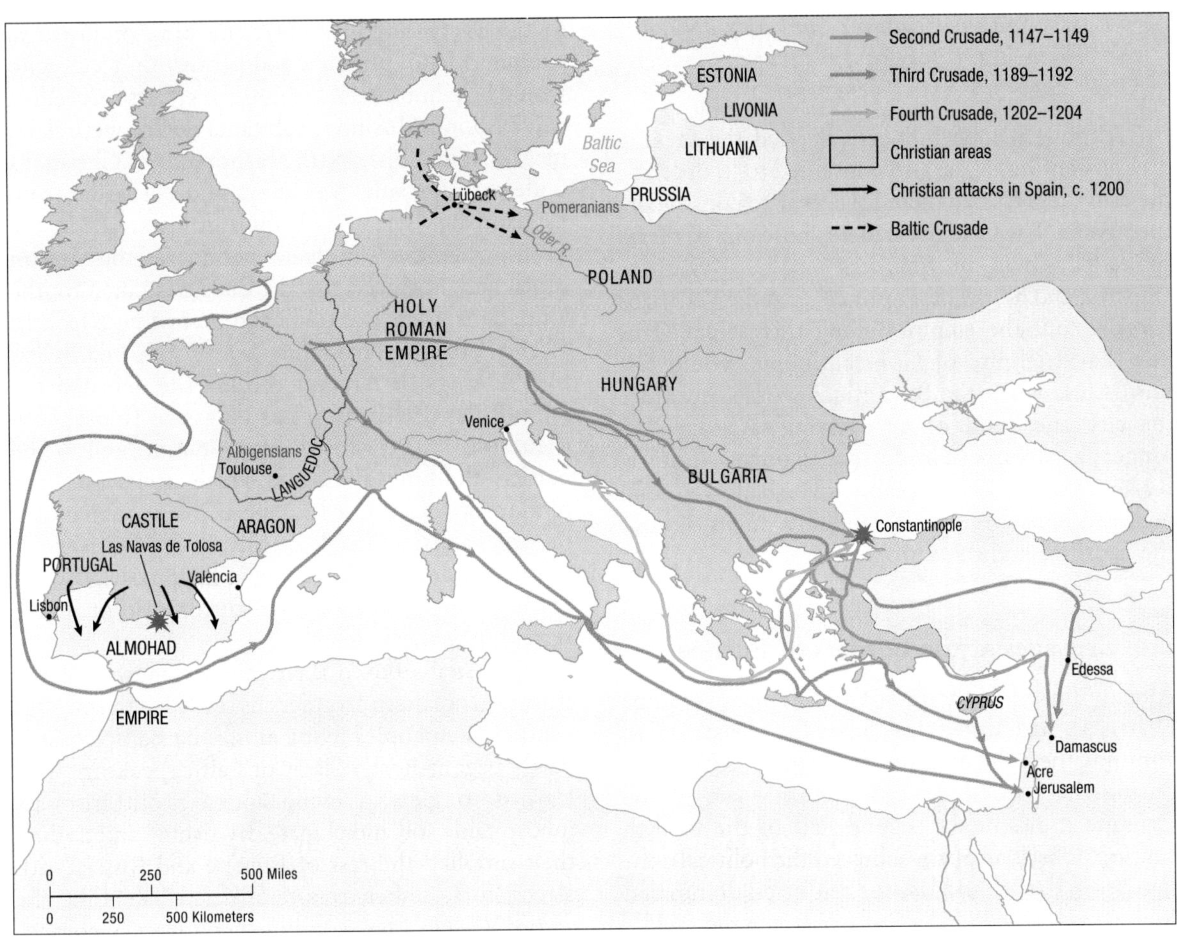

Crusades and Anti-Heretic Campaigns, 1144–1261

could not pay the Venetians, who had fitted out a large fleet of ships in anticipation of carrying multitudes of warriors across the water to Jerusalem. Seizing the opportunity to enhance its commercial hegemony, the Venetians convinced the Crusade's leaders to pay their way by attacking Zara, a Christian city but Venice's competitor in the Adriatic. The Venetians then turned their sights toward Constantinople, hoping to control it and gain a commercial monopoly there. They persuaded the crusaders to join them on behalf of a member of the ousted imperial family, Alexius, who claimed the Byzantine throne and promised the crusaders that he would reunite the eastern with the western church and fund the expedition to the Holy Land. Most of the crusaders convinced themselves that the cause was noble. "Never," wrote a contemporary, "was so great an enterprise undertaken by any people since the creation of the world." The siege took nearly a year, but on April 12, 1204, the crusaders sacked Constantinople, killing, plundering, and ransacking the city for treasure and relics. When one crusader discovered a cache of relics, a chronicler recalled, "he plunged both hands in and, girding up his loins, he filled the folds of his gown with the holy booty of the Church." But, of course, the Byzantines saw the same events as a great tragedy. The bishop of Ephesus wrote:

> *And so the streets, squares, houses of two and three stories, sacred places, nunneries, houses for nuns and monks, sacred churches, even the Great Church of God and the imperial palace, were filled with men of the enemy, all of them maddened by war and murderous in spirit. . . . [T]hey tore children from their mothers and*

mothers from their children, and they defiled the virgins in the holy chapels, fearing neither God's anger nor man's vengeance.

Although Pope Innocent decried the sacking of Constantinople, he also consented to it, ordering the crusaders to stay there for a year to consolidate their gains. The Crusade leaders chose one of themselves—Baldwin of Flanders—to be Byzantine emperor, and he, the other princes, and the Venetians parceled out the empire among themselves. This new Latin empire of Constantinople would last until 1261, when the Byzantines would recapture the city and some of its outlying territory. No longer a strong heir to the Roman Empire, Byzantium in 1204 became overshadowed and hemmed in by the stronger military might of both the Muslims and the Europeans.

Crusades at the Borders of Europe

Already linked to the First Crusade because Pope Urban II had urged the Spanish Christians to continue the fight at home, the Spanish *reconquista* during the Second Crusade became part of the Crusade itself. In the second half of the twelfth century, Christian Spain achieved the political configuration that would last for centuries, dominated to the east by the kingdom of Aragon; in the middle by Castile, whose ruler styled himself emperor; and in the southwest by Portugal, whose ruler similarly transformed his title, from prince to king. The three leaders competed for territory and power, but above all they sought an advantage against the Muslims to the south.

Muslim disunity aided the Christian conquest of Spain. The Muslims of al-Andalus were themselves beset, from the south, by a new group of Muslims from North Africa, the Almohades. Claiming religious purity, the Almohades declared their own holy war against the Andalusians. These simultaneous threats caused alliances in Spain to be based on political as well as religious considerations. The Muslim ruler of Valencia, for example, declared himself a vassal of the king of Castile and bitterly opposed the Almohades' expansion.

But the crusading ideal held no room for such subtleties. During the 1140s, armies under the command of the kings of Portugal, Castile, and Aragon scored resounding victories against Muslim cities. Enlisting the aid of crusaders on their way to the Holy Land in 1147, the king of Portugal promised land, plunder, and protection to all who would help him attack Lisbon. His efforts succeeded, and Lisbon's Muslim inhabitants fled or were slain, its Mozarabic bishop (the bishop of the Christians under Muslim rule) was killed, and a crusader from England was set up as bishop in his stead. In the 1170s, when the Almohades conquered the Muslim south and advanced toward the cities taken by the Christians, their exertions had no lasting effect. In 1212 a Christian crusading army of Spaniards led by the kings of Aragon and Castile defeated the Almohades decisively at Las Navas de Tolosa. "On their side 100,000 armed men or more fell in the battle," the king of Castile wrote afterward, "but of the army of the Lord . . . incredible though it may be, unless it be a miracle, hardly 25 or 30 Christians of our whole army fell. O what happiness! O what thanksgiving!" The decisive turning point in the *reconquista* was reached.

Christians flexed their military muscles along Europe's northern frontiers as well. By the twelfth century the peoples living along the Baltic coast—partly pagan; mostly Slavic or Baltic speaking—had learned to glean a living and a profit from its inhospitable soil and climate. By fishing and trading they supplied the rest of Europe and Russia with slaves, furs, amber, wax, and dried fish. Like the earlier Vikings, they combined commercial competition with outright raiding, so that the Danes and the Saxons (that is, the Germans in Saxony) both benefited and suffered from their presence. When St. Bernard began to preach the Second Crusade in Germany, he discovered that the Germans were indeed itching to attack the infidels—those across the Elbe! St. Bernard pressed the pope to add these northern heathens to the list of those against whom holy war should be launched and urged their conversion or extermination. Thus began the Northern Crusades, whose start paralleled the Second Crusade in 1147. These Crusades continued intermittently until the early fifteenth century.

The King of Denmark, Valdemar I (*1157–1182), and the Saxon duke Henry the Lion led the first phase of the Northern Crusades. Their initial attacks on the Slavs were uncoordinated—in some instances they even fought each other. But in key raids in the 1160s and 1170s the two leaders worked together briefly to bring much of the region west of the Oder River under their control. They took some land outright—Henry the Lion

Valdemar I, Crusader of the North
King Valdemar I of Denmark had his image cast on this penny, along with a palm leaf (a symbol of pilgrimage) and, on the reverse, a flag with a cross (a symbol of crusade).

apportioned conquered territory to his followers, for example—but more often the Slavic princes surrendered and had their territories reinstated once they became vassals of the Christian rulers. Meanwhile, churchmen arrived: the Cistercians, for example, came long before the first phase of fighting had ended, confidently building their monasteries to the very shores of the Oder River. Slavic peasants surely suffered from the conquerors' fire and pillage, but the Northern Crusades ultimately benefited all the ruling classes—Danish, German, and Slavic. The newly converted peoples paid abundant tithes to their bishops, and once converted, Slavic princes found it advantageous for both their eternal salvation and their worldly profit to join new crusades to areas still farther to the east.

Although less well known than the Crusades to the Holy Land, the Northern Crusades had far more lasting effects: they settled the Baltic region with German-speaking lords and peasants and forged a permanent relationship between the very north of Europe and its neighbors to the south and west. With the Baltic dotted with churches and monasteries and its peoples dipped into baptismal waters, the region would gradually adopt the institutions of western medieval society—cities, guilds, universities, castles, and manors. The Livs (whose region was eventually known as Livonia) were conquered by 1208, and their bishop sent knights northward to conquer the Estonians. The Prussians would be conquered with the cooperation between the Polish and German aristocracy; German peasants eventually settled Prussia. Only the Lithuanians successfully resisted western conquest, settlement, and conversion.

Religion and Politics in an Age of Ambition

1144 Fall of Edessa to the Turks; in response, the Second Crusade and the Northern Crusades launched

1152–1190 Reign of Frederick Barbarossa

- **1157** Tension with Pope Hadrian IV at the Diet of Besançon
- **1167** Italian policy provokes the formation of the Lombard League
- **1176** Lombard League defeats Frederick at the Battle of Legnano
- **1180** Engineers the fall of Henry the Lion
- **1190** Dies on the Third Crusade (1189–1192)

1154–1189 Reign of Henry II, king of England (on the Continent he was duke of Anjou, Normandy, and Maine, and his wife, Eleanor, was duchess of Aquitaine)

- **1166** Extends the scope of common law in England with the Assize of Clarendon

1180–1223 Reign of Philip II Augustus, king of France

- **1182** Expels the Jews from the royal demesne
- **1204** Conquers Normandy and other territory
- **1214** Makes good his claim on Normandy at the Battle of Bouvines

1182–1226 Life of St. Francis; the mendicant order he founded was recognized by Pope Innocent III

1199–1216 Reign of John, king of England

- **1215** Assents to the Magna Carta under great pressure from barons

1204–1205 Fourth Crusade; Constantinople sacked (1204)

1209–1229 Albigensian Crusade

1212 Battle of Las Navas de Tolosa; most of Spain in Christian hands

Conclusion

The second half of the twelfth century saw the consolidation of Europe's new political configuration, reaching the limits of a continental expansion that stretched from the Baltic to the Strait of Gibraltar. European settlements along the coast of the Levant, on the other hand, were nearly obliterated. When western Europeans sacked Constantinople, Europe and the Islamic world became the dominant political forces in the West.

Powerful territorial kings and princes now began to establish the institutions of bureaucratic authority. They hired staffs to handle their accounts, write down acts, collect taxes, issue writs, and preside over courts. Flourishing cities, a growing money economy, and trade and manufacturing provided the finances necessary to support the personnel and offices now used by medieval governments. Clerical schools and, by the end of the twelfth century, universities, became the training grounds for the new administrators.

Rulers were not alone in their quest to document, define, and institutionalize their power. The second half of the twelfth century was a great age of organization. Associations, which had earlier been fluid, now solidified into well-defined corporations—craft guilds and universities, for example—with statutes providing clearly articulated rights, obligations, and privileges to their members. Developing out of the commercial revolution, such organizations in turn made commercial activities a permanent part of medieval life.

Religious associations also formed. The Franciscans, Dominicans, Waldensians, and Albigensians—however dissimilar their beliefs—all articulated specific creeds and claimed distinctiveness. In rejecting wealth and material possessions, they revealed how deeply the commercial revolution had affected the moral life of some Europeans, who could not accept the profit motive inherent in a money economy. In emphasizing preaching they showed that a lay population, already Christian, now yearned for a more intense and personal spirituality.

New piety, new exclusivity, and new power arose in a society both more confident and less tolerant. After about 1147, crusaders fought more often and against an increasing variety of foes. With heretics setting forth their beliefs, the church, led by the papacy, now defined orthodoxy and declared dissenters its enemies. The Jews, who had once been fairly well integrated into the Christian community, were treated ambivalently, alternately used and abused. The Slavs and Balts became targets for new evangelical zeal; the Greeks became the butt of envy, hostility, and finally enmity. European Christians still considered Muslims arrogant heathens, and the deflection of the Fourth Crusade did not stem the zeal of popes to call for new crusades to the Holy Land.

Confident and aggressive, the men leading Christian Europe in the following decades of the thirteenth century would attempt to impose their rule, legislate morality, and create a unified worldview impregnable to attack. But this drive for order would be countered by unexpected varieties of thought and action, by political and social tensions, and by intensely personal religious quests.

Suggestions for Further Reading

Source Materials

Chrétien de Troyes. *Yvain: The Knight of the Lion.* Translated by Burton Raffel. 1987. One of the most famous medieval romances.

Goldin, Frederick. *Lyrics of the Troubadours and Trouvères: Original Texts, with Translations.* 1973. Contains some of the major troubadour poems, with the original and English versions on facing pages.

The Little Flowers of Saint Francis. Translated by L. Sherley-Price. 1959. Stories about the deeds of St. Francis, told by his disciples.

Otto of Freising. *The Deeds of Frederick Barbarossa.* Translated by Charles C. Mierow. 1953. The chief source for the reign of Frederick I by an important historian who was also Frederick's uncle.

Peters, Edward, ed. and trans. *Heresy and Authority in Medieval Europe*. 1980. Contains important source readings for medieval heresies and the responses to them.

The Song of Roland. Translated by Patricia Terry. 1965. The most famous Old French epic.

Interpretive Studies

Baldwin, John W. *The Government of Philip Augustus. Foundations of French Royal Power in the Middle Ages*. 1986. Details the transition to bureaucratic kingship.

Bartlett, Robert. *The Making of Europe: Conquest, Colonization, and Cultural Change, 950–1350*. 1993. Looks at both external and internal effects of European expansion and expansionism.

Boswell, John. *Christianity, Social Tolerance, and Homosexuality: Gay People in Western Europe from the Beginning of the Christian Era to the Fourteenth Century*. 1980. Studies shifting attitudes toward homosexuals, who, like lepers and Jews, were vilified in the twelfth century.

Christiansen, Eric. *The Northern Crusades: The Baltic and the Catholic Frontier, 1100–1525*. 1980. A well-written account of these less well-known crusades, which had more lasting consequences than those to the Holy Land.

Clanchy, Michael T. *From Memory to Written Record, 1066–1307*. 1979. Traces the development of an oral to a written culture in England.

Duby, Georges. *William Marshall*. 1985. Uses the life of one knight to illuminate the world of an entire class.

Fuhrmann, Horst. *Germany in the High Middle Ages, c. 1050–1200*. Translated by Timothy Reuter. 1986. Especially useful for tracing shifting notions of German kingship.

Gold, Penny Shine. *The Lady and the Virgin: Image, Attitude, and Experience in Twelfth-Century France*. 1985. Examines the image of women in art, literature, and life.

Hallam, Elizabeth M. *Capetian France, 987–1328*. 1980. A good overview of the period, with excellent bibliographies, maps, and figures.

Jordan, Karl. *Henry the Lion: A Biography*. Translated by P. S. Falla. 1986. A useful study of the great Welf prince of Germany.

Kazhdan, A. P., and Ann Wharton Epstein. *Change in Byzantine Culture in the Eleventh and Twelfth Centuries*. 1985. Considers the many ways in which Byzantine culture was transformed before the Fourth Crusade.

Kendrick, Laura. *The Game of Love: Troubadour Wordplay*. 1988. Discusses troubadour songs from the point of view of literary criticism.

Lewis, Andrew W. *Royal Succession in Capetian France: Studies on Familial Order and the State*. 1981. Studies the relationship between ideas about the family and the development of the French monarchy.

Little, Lester K. *Religious Poverty and the Profit Economy in Medieval Europe*. 1978. Places the heretics and friars in the historical context of a newly commercial society.

Moore, R. I. *The Formation of a Persecuting Society: Power and Deviance in Western Europe, 950–1250*. 1987. Explores the nature and causes of persecution of heretics, Jews, lepers, and homosexuals in the Middle Ages.

Newman, Barbara. *Sister of Wisdom: St. Hildegard's Theology of the Feminine*. 1987. An illuminating study of Hildegard of Bingen, who had a theology that relied predominantly on feminine imagery.

Nicholas, David. *Medieval Flanders*. 1992. An excellent survey of this socially turbulent and commercially flourishing region.

O'Callaghan, Joseph F. *A History of Medieval Spain*. 1975. A general survey of the period.

Page, Christopher. *Voices and Instruments of the Middle Ages: Instrumental Practice and Songs in France, 1100–1300*. 1986. Explores the relationship between songs and the use of musical instruments.

Queller, Donald E. *The Fourth Crusade: The Conquest of Constantinople, 1201–1204*. 1977. A well-written narrative of the events.

Reynolds, Susan. *Kingdoms and Communities in Western Europe, 900–1300*. 1984. Sheds light on the importance and prevalence of communities such as villages, guilds, and kingdoms.

Wakefield, Walter L. *Heresy, Crusade, and Inquisition in Southern France, 1100–1250*. 1974. An analytical narrative of events related to the Albigensian Crusade.

Warren, William L. *Henry II*. 1973. A massive and authoritative biography.

———. *King John*. 1978. A judicious assessment of the king and his times.

CHAPTER

12

The Quest for Order and Control, 1215–1320

Vault of Amiens Cathedral
The Gothic church was made of stone, but it created an illusion of lightness. The glass formed a band of light just below the vault, and the vault seemed to perch above it without weight. In fact the great thrust of the vault was carried down to earth by the piers, the walls of the aisles, and the flying buttresses.

In the summertime, King Louis IX of France (*1226–1270) would go to the woods near his castle of Vincennes on the outskirts of Paris. "Then," his biographer, Joinville, recounted, "he would sit down with his back against an oak, and make us all sit round him. Those who had any suit to present could come to speak to him without hindrance. The king would address them directly and ask, 'Is there anyone here who has a case to be settled?' Those who had one would stand up. Then he would say, 'Keep silent all of you, and you shall be heard in turn, one after the other.'" Thus the king dispensed justice.

The image of the good king, out in the warm air, lounging under a shady tree, accessible to all his people, righting wrongs, and giving wise counsel conveyed order, peace, harmony, and control. The king could not personally hear all the grievances of his people, of course; yet the fair and wise king who maintained harmonious relations in his realm was an ideal of the thirteenth century. Kings settling disputes, church councils striving to define and organize a diverse European population, scholastics working to reconcile conflicting theological ideas, poets contemplating the design of a teeming universe—all participated in the quest for order and control. Reminding his subjects of the wise King Solomon uniting his people in a godly society, Louis IX symbolized the proper relationship between ruler and subject; not long after his death, the church declared him a saint. The quest for control, however, contained a paradox: as different factions imposed the various brands of order they favored on society, clashes over power, ideology, and territory that jeopardized the very possibility of peace ensued.

The Royal Dignity
The young St. Louis sits at the top right; his mother, who acted as his regent during his minority, sits opposite him. Below is a scribe taking down dictation from a monk.

While the Fourth Lateran Council sought to define the nature of the Eucharist and control its use within the church, female mystics in the intimacy of their homes denied themselves all food except the consecrated Host, giving it a meaning in their lives never dreamt of by priests. On the international stage of high politics, Pope Innocent IV declared a crusade against the Christian emperor, Frederick II, and launched a war that ended only when the last male in the Staufer dynasty had been killed. Thus behind the supposed harmony in the thirteenth century lurked wildly diverse ideas and ideals.

Important Dates

1215 Fourth Lateran Council
1220–1250 Reign of Emperor Frederick II
1225–1274 Life of St. Thomas Aquinas
1226–1270 Reign of St. Louis (Louis IX), king of France
1258–1265 Baronial revolt against Henry III of England
1265 Parliament called by Simon de Montfort includes representatives of the commons
1285–1314 Reign of Philip the Fair of France
1294–1303 Papacy of Boniface VIII
1302 Meeting of the Estates at Paris
1309–1378 Avignon Papacy ("Babylonian Captivity")

The Church's Mission

Ever since the Gregorian reform of the eleventh century the papacy had conceived of salvation as implying a mission that included reforming the secular world. In the Gregorian period this task had focused on the king, because in Gregory's view a godless king threatened the redemption of all his subjects. Later, in the twelfth century, the church sought to purify social institutions, extending its influence over courts, government administrations, and new urban corporations. Now in the thirteenth century, churchmen elaborated coherent intellectual bases for their actions. Above all, they applied logic to theological questions, creating a rigorously argued understanding of God and an intellectual system embracing all aspects of life and the afterlife.

The Fourth Lateran Council

With his call in 1213 for a great new council to prepare for a new crusade and to reform the church, Pope Innocent III (*1198–1216) asserted the grand plan of the papacy: to order the world in the image of heaven. Claiming spiritual rather than temporal grounds for his actions, Innocent saw himself as an intermediary between earth and heaven: "[The pope is] set between God and man, lower than God but higher than man, who judges all and is judged by no one." Such a view justified political and military intervention, including the expansion of the papal states. Previously a student of theology at Paris and of law at Bologna, Innocent had learned at school the traditions that informed his view of the papacy.

The Fourth Lateran Council, over which Innocent presided in 1215, produced comprehensive legislation in just three days, mainly because the pope and his committees had prepared it beforehand. They envisioned a thorough regulation of Christian life, with canons (provisions) aimed at reforming not only the clergy but also the laity. One canon declared as dogma the meaning of the Eucharist, a matter of debate in centuries past: "[Christ's] body and blood are truly contained in the sacrament of the altar under the species of bread and wine, the bread being transubstantiated into the body and the wine into the blood by the divine power." *Transubstantiation,* a word coined by twelfth-century scholars, was a technical term to explain the belief that though the Eucharist continued to *look* like bread and wine, after consecration the wafer became the actual flesh and the wine the real blood of Christ. The Fourth Lateran Council's emphasis on transubstantiation reinforced the gulf between the clergy and the laity. Only the clergy could celebrate this mystery (that is, transform the bread and wine into Christ's body and blood), through which God's grace was transmitted to the faithful.

Some canons affected laypeople's lives even more directly, regardless of social status, by defining the relationship of the laity to the sacraments. One required Christians to attend Mass and to confess their sins to a priest at least once a year. Others codified the traditions of marriage, in which the church had involved itself more and more since the twelfth century. Now besides declaring marriage a sacrament and claiming jurisdiction over marital disputes, the Fourth Lateran Council decreed that marriage bans (announcements) had to be made publicly by local priests to ensure that people from the community could voice any objections to the marriage. For example, the intended spouses might be related within degrees prohibited by the church.

Innocent III
This fresco of Innocent III shows him as a young man of aristocratic bearing. He was indeed a member of a very powerful noble family.

Priests now became responsible for ferreting out this information and identifying any other impediments to the union. The canons further insisted that children conceived within clandestine or forbidden marriages were illegitimate; they could not inherit from their parents or become priests.

The council also made the status of Jews obvious and public: "We decree that [Jews] of either sex in every Christian province and at all times shall be distinguished from other people by the character of their dress in public." Like all the council's legislation, this decree took effect only when secular authorities enforced it. But sooner or later Jews almost everywhere had to wear a badge as a sign of their second-class status.

The council's longest decree blasted heretics: "Those condemned as heretics shall be handed over to the secular authorities for punishment." If the secular authority did not "purge his land of heretical filth," he was to be excommunicated, his vassals released from their oaths of fealty, and his land taken over by orthodox Christians. Such actions rarely occurred in practice; but they reveal the council's intense hostility against "any whose life and habits differ from the normal way of living of Christians."

Scholasticism

Just as the members of the Fourth Lateran Council considered all aspects of worldly life crucial to salvation, so contemporary thinkers linked human and divine activities. Called scholastics, these men taught in the universities, modeling their thought on Aristotle's comprehensive and logical philosophical scheme, which embraced physical, moral, psychological, and aesthetic phenomena. The scholastics believed the whole world, created by God, revealed the divine plan. They built on the methods of twelfth-century scholars—on Peter Abelard's *Sic et Non,* for example, and on Muslim commentators of Aristotle such as Ibn Rushd (1126–1193), a Cordoban legal scholar and physician known in the Latin West as Averoës. The scholastics pondered questions about human morality as well as issues more narrowly theological; they sought nothing less than to reconcile reason and revelation, earth and heaven.

Some scholastics considered scientific questions, observing the natural world to develop their ideas. Albertus Magnus (c. 1200–1280), for example, was a major theologian, but he also contributed to the fields of biology, botany, astronomy, and physics. His treatise *On Animals* shows he was a perceptive naturalist: "The swan," he noted, "belongs to the class of geese and, like a goose, has a serrated beak whose dentate edge resembles the saw-toothed blade of a sickle; it uses this beak to strain the mud in search of food and then chews what it finds with the serrated edges." In physics he discussed the commentaries of Averoës and Avicenna on Aristotle's view of motion. He advocated considering motion as inhering in the moving object itself rather than dependent upon an outside mover. Later scholastics separated the idea of motion (for example, of a ball rolling across a field) from other sorts of fluctuations (for example, of a knife rusting). These distinctions helped scientists in the sixteenth and seventeenth centuries arrive at the modern notion of inertia.

One of Albertus's students was St. Thomas Aquinas (c. 1225–1274), perhaps the most famous scholastic. Huge of build, renowned for his composure in debate, Thomas came from a noble Neapolitan family that had hoped to see him become a powerful bishop rather than a poor university professor. When he was about eighteen years old he thwarted his family's wishes and joined the Dominicans. Soon he was studying at Cologne with Albertus. At thirty-two he became a master at the University of Paris, traveling often to Rome and Naples.

Thomas, like other scholastics, considered Aristotle "the Philosopher," the authoritative voice of human reason, which he sought to pair with divine revelation in a universal and harmonious scheme. In 1273 he published his monumental *Summa Theologiae,* which covered all important human and divine topics. After dividing each topic into questions and building upon methods such as Abelard's to discuss each one thoroughly and systematically, Thomas concluded each question with a decisive position and a refutation of opposing views.

For example, Thomas analyzed each sin individually; for the sin of cheating, he isolated four questions, called articles. The first article asked, "Is it lawful to sell a thing for more than its worth?" Following the article, Thomas introduced the point with which he disagreed, the objection, by citing an authority—in this case civil law:

> Objection I: *It seems that it is lawful to sell a thing for more than its worth. For in human transactions, civil laws determine what is just. According to these laws it is just for buyer and seller to deceive one another. Therefore it is lawful to sell a thing for more than its worth.*

For this particular article, Thomas had two further objections, one a quote taken out of context from St. Augustine and the other a point by Aristotle.

After the objections came the "On the contrary" section, the position with which Thomas agreed, the *non* to the *sic* posed by the objections:

> On the contrary, *It is written [Matt. 7:12]: "Do unto others what you would have them do unto you." Now no man wants to buy something for more than its worth. Therefore no one should sell a thing to anyone else for more than its worth.*

Thomas then began an extended discussion of the question, prefaced by the words *I answer that.* Unlike Abelard, whose method left differences unresolved, Thomas wanted to reconcile the two points of view, and so he pointed out that price and worth depended on the particular circumstances of the buyer and seller and concluded that charging more than a seller had originally paid could be legitimate at times.

For townspeople engaged in commerce and worried about Biblical prohibitions on money-making, Thomas's ideas about cheating addressed burning questions. Hoping to go to heaven as well as reap the profits of their business ventures, laypeople listened eagerly to preachers who delivered their sermons in the vernacular but who based their ideas on the Latin *summae* (treatises) of St. Thomas and other scholastics. Thomas's conclusions aided townspeople in justifying their worldly activities.

Thomas's article ended with a "Reply" to each of the objections:

> Reply Objection I: *As stated above, human law is given to the people, many of whom lack virtue; it is not given to the virtuous alone. Therefore human law cannot forbid all that is contrary to virtue.*

Thus Thomas did not declare civil law, the authority of the first objection, invalid but rather incorporated it into a moral universe in which it had clear limitations. He rated human law low in the hierarchy of divine and human inventions. Such ranking characterized the way in which Thomas and other scholastics attuned ideas and institutions. They did not deny differences and contradictions; rather they defined and distinguished among them, constructing a conceptual hierarchy.

In his own day, St. Thomas was a controversial figure, and his ideas, emphasizing reason, were by no means universally accepted. Yet even Thomas departed from Aristotle, who had explained the universe through human reason alone. In Thomas's view, God, nature, and reason were in harmony, so that Aristotle's arguments could be used to explore both the human and the divine order, but with some exceptions. "Certain things that are true about God wholly surpass the capability of human reason, for instance that God is three and one," Thomas wrote. But he thought these exceptions rarely occurred.

Other scholastics emphasized God's role in human knowledge. St. Bonaventure (1221–1274), for example, argued that we know something truly because our minds are illuminated by divine light, a light that can come only from God because He alone is unchangeable, eternal, and creative. Bonaventure used St. Augustine, rather than Aristotle, as his key authority and based his philosophical position on Augustine's neo-Platonism.

The synthetic work of the mid-thirteenth-century scholastics continued for another generation. Yet at the beginning of the fourteenth century, cracks began to appear. In the *summae* of John Duns Scotus (c. 1266–1308), for example, the world and God were less compatible. For John, as for Bonaventure, human reason could know truth only through the "special illumination of the uncreated light," that is, by divine illumination. But for Scotus this illumination came not as a matter of course but only when God chose to intervene. People experienced God as willful rather than reasonable. John thus separated the divine and secular realms; reason could not soar to God.

Religious Institutions and Town Life

Many scholastics were friars. Albertus Magnus and Thomas Aquinas, for example, belonged to the Dominican order; St. Bonaventure was a Franciscan. Both orders insisted on travel, preaching, and poverty, vocations that pulled the friars into cities and towns, where laypeople eagerly listened to their words and supported them with food and shelter. Although St. Francis had wanted his followers to sleep wherever they found themselves, most Franciscans and Dominicans lived in convents just outside cities by the second quarter of the thirteenth century. As their numbers grew, nearly every moderately sized city had such houses outside its walls—414 Dominican houses for men by 1277 and more than 1,400 Franciscan houses by the early fourteenth century. About a fifth of these Franciscan convents housed nuns, who, entirely unlike their male counterparts, lived in strict seclusion. Yet they too ministered to the world by taking in the sick. The mendicant orders further tied their members to the lay community through tertiaries, a Third Order of affiliated men and women who adopted many Franciscan practices—prayer and works of charity, for example—while continuing to live in the world, raise families, and tend to the normal tasks of daily life, whatever their occupation. Even St. Louis, king of France, was a tertiary.

Thirteenth-century scholastics taught at universities. At the University of Paris, for example, Thomas Aquinas debated with other masters, lectured to students, and wrote his great *summae* linking the doctrinal concerns of the friars, the economic concerns of the townspeople, and the scholarly concerns of the university. In turn, his students preached the results of Thomas's scholarship to the lay community: as one scholastic explained, "First the bow is bent in study, then the arrow is released in preaching."

The thirteenth century was a great age of preaching, as large numbers of learned friars and other scholars took to the road to speak to throngs of townsfolk. For example, when Berthold, a Franciscan who traveled the length and breadth of Germany giving sermons, came to a town, a high tower was set up for him outside the city walls. A pennant advertised his presence and let people know which way the wind would blow his voice. St. Anthony of Padua preached in Italian to huge audiences lined up hours in advance to be sure they would have a place to hear him.

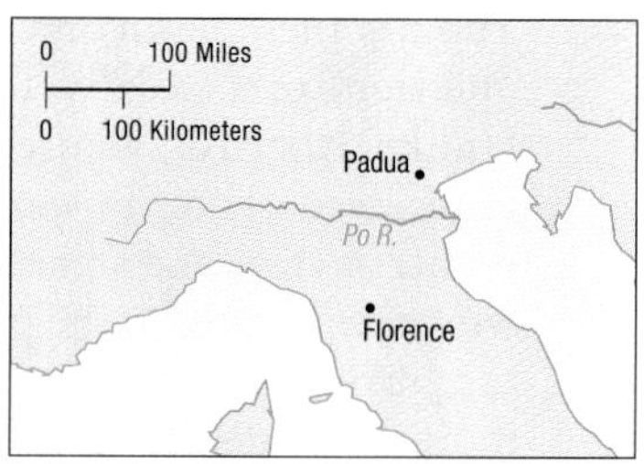

Florence and Padua

Friars and Usurers
Friars ministered to city dwellers and commented on their activities. In this illumination from c. 1250, a Franciscan and Dominican refuse offerings from two usurers, whose profession they are thus shown to condemn.

New Syntheses in Writing and Music

Thirteenth-century literary writers, like preachers, often expressed complicated ideas and feelings in the vernacular. Like the scholastics, Dante Alighieri (1265–1321) harmonized disparate traditions, but in his case these included the scholastic vision of the universe, romantic poetry, and monastic spirituality. He combined these in the dramatic and expressive Italian poem *Commedia,* later known as the *Divine Comedy.*

The *Divine Comedy* is the story of Dante's (and allegorically of all people's) journey through Hell, Purgatory, and Paradise. Dante describes his passage from Hell to Paradise so precisely that the reader can map and time his movements. Influenced by the scientific work of scholastics like Albertus Magnus, Dante's trip explores matter and motion at the same time it details Dante's approach to God.

Three major characters guide Dante: first Virgil, second a young woman named Beatrice, and finally St. Bernard. Dante regarded Virgil, who leads him through Hell and most of Purgatory, as the supreme pagan poet, representing the best of the classical literary tradition, much as Aristotle embodied philosophy for the scholastics. Beatrice (a character based on Beatrice Portinari, a woman Dante had loved and idealized) guided him through the last part of Purgatory and most of Paradise. Dante had met the real Beatrice in their native Florence, where she had died in her twenties; in his poem she symbolized the connection between human and divine love and the temporal and spiritual world. At the very end of the trip through Paradise, St. Bernard, the Cistercian abbot, leads Dante to God. Bernard's devotion to the Virgin

The Last Judgment
In Italy the artistic style of the mid-thirteenth century borrowed much from Byzantine models. This mosaic of the damned at the Last Judgment decorates the vault of the baptistery at Florence.

Mary and in turn her solicitude for Bernard epitomized for Dante the highest form of love. Such love merited the poet the most precious gift—the vision of God:

> *What I then saw is more than tongue can say.*
> *Our human speech is dark before the vision.*
> *The ravished memory swoons and falls away.*

Reflecting his own social and political concerns, Dante delighted in putting his enemies into Hell and his protectors into Paradise. Exiled from Florence by an opposing political faction, the bitter Dante prophesied:

> *Their bestiality will be made known*
> *by what they do; while your fame shines the brighter*
> *for having become a party of your own.*

Here the "you" refers to Dante, who thought of himself as a one-man party for unity and peace.

Like Dante, other writers of the period tried to harmonize the Aristotelian universe with the mysteries of faith. But they did not always follow the scholastic model in doing so. The anonymous author of the *Quest of the Holy Grail* (c. 1225), for example, used an Arthurian romance (a tale involving the knights of King Arthur's Round Table), onto which he grafted theological and ecclesiastical teachings. His Lancelot is a sinner, spiritually blinded by his adultery with Guinevere. Galahad—whose virginity symbolizes both spiritual purity and chivalric gallantry—is the hero of the tale; he alone experiences the bliss of seeing fully the splendor of the grail:

> *a man [Josephus] came down from heaven garbed in a bishop's robes, and with a crozier in his hand and mitre on his head; four angels bore him on a glorious throne, which they set down next to the table supporting the Holy Grail . . . [On the table was a Holy Vessel. Josephus] took from the Vessel a host made in the likeness of bread. As he raised it aloft there descended from above a figure like to a child, whose countenance glowed and blazed as bright as fire; and he entered into the bread, which quite distinctly took on human form.*

Familiar characters were thus used to teach a lesson about the Eucharist, human morality, and the well-ordered universe.

Musicians, like poets, developed new forms that bridged sacred and secular subjects in the thirteenth and early fourteenth centuries. This connection appears in the most distinctive musical form of the thirteenth century, the *motet* (from the French *mot,* meaning "word"). The motet is an example of polyphony, music that consists of two or more melodies performed simultaneously. Before about 1215 almost all polyphony was sacred; purely secular polyphony was not common before the fourteenth century. The motet, a unique combination of the sacred and the secular, evidently originated in Paris, the center of scholastic culture as well.

The typical thirteenth-century motet has three melody lines (or "voices"). The lowest, usually from a liturgical chant melody, typically has no words and may have been played on an instrument rather than sung. The remaining melodies have different texts, either Latin or French (or one of each), which are sung simultaneously. Latin texts were usually sacred, whereas French ones were secular, dealing with themes such as love and springtime. In one example the top voice chirps in quick rhythm about a lady's charms ("Fair maiden, lovely and comely; pretty maiden, courteous and pleasing, delicious one . . . "); the middle voice slowly and lugubriously laments the "malady" of love; and the lowest voice sings a liturgical melody. The motet thus wove the sacred (the chant melody in the lowest voice) and the secular (the French texts in the upper voices) into a sophisticated tapestry of music. Johannes de Grocheo, writing in Paris around 1300, pronounced the motet far too subtle for ignorant people to appreciate. Like the scholastic *summae,* the motets were written by and for a clerical elite. Yet they also touched the lives of ordinary people. At least one motet included the calls of street vendors, and others reflected student life in the Paris cafes.

Complementing the motet's complexity was the development of a new notation for rhythm. By the eleventh century, musical notation could indicate pitch but had no way to denote the duration of the notes. Music theorists of the thirteenth century, however, developed increasingly precise methods to indicate rhythm. Franco of Cologne, for example, in his *Art of Measurable Song,* used different shapes to mark the number of beats each note should be held. His system became the basis of modern musical notation. Because each note could be allotted whatever duration the composer specified, notation with fixed beats allowed written music to express new and complicated rhythms. Thus music also reflected both the melding of the secular and the sacred and the possibilities of greater order and control.

The Order of High Gothic Art and Architecture

The drive for order and harmony also inspired developments in Gothic architecture. Gothic was largely an urban style popular across France, England, Spain, Germany, and the Low Countries. The construction of a Gothic church created jobs and promoted commerce, as new cathedrals required a small army of quarrymen, builders, carpenters, and glass cutters. Bishops, papal legates, and clerics planned and helped pay for these grand cathedrals, but townspeople generously financed and filled them. At Chartres (in France), for example, guilds raised money to pay for stained-glass windows, which depicted their patron saint; the shoemakers built their window to the Virgin Mary. The towns- people had good reason to support the church. Not only was the cathedral at Chartres a major shrine of the Virgin—it housed her blouse—but it was

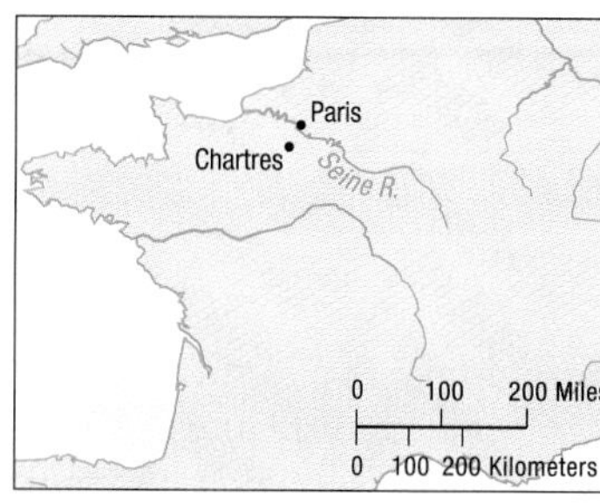

Chartres and Paris

Chartres Cathedral
The exterior of a Gothic church had an opaque and bristling look due to the patina of its stained glass and to its flying buttresses. Here Chartres cathedral towers above the other buildings. Little wonder that civic pride as well as religious piety focused on cathedrals.

Chartres's Portal Program
At Chartres three flanking portals were used to present a complex and unified message in stone sculpture, as in this south portal complex. The left portal depicts the Martyrs, the right the Confessors, and the center the Last Judgment.

Christ Showing His Wounds
On the tympanum of the central door of the south portal, a wounded Christ sits between two intercessors, revealing both his human suffering and his divine power in one image.

also the town's center of commercial activity. In its crypt, wine merchants plied their trade, while just outside vendors sold every sort of goods. During great fairs honoring important holy days in Mary's life, pilgrims thronged the streets, the poor buying small lead figures of the Virgin, the rich purchasing wearable replicas of her blouse.

Workers began rebuilding the cathedral at Chartres after a fire in 1194 had burned all but the west facade. Learned masters, architects, and sculptors together created, in stone and glass, an image of heaven that made the cathedral a physical parallel to the scholastic *summae.* Just as St. Thomas Aquinas had presented the design of his arguments with utter clarity, so the Gothic church revealed its structure without disguise; and just as Thomas had bridged the earthly and celestial realms, so the cathedral elicited a response beyond reason, evoking a sense of awe.

Even today the church's exterior bristles with flying buttresses; these along with thick interior piers (pillars) and side aisles support the thrust of the vault, relieving the walls of the roof's heavy downward weight. Windows of stunning stained glass are set in the walls. The ribs of the vault start from the top of each regularly spaced pier, tying the building together formally, much like the repetition of the articles and objections in a Thomistic argument. Yet like the scholastic tension between reason and faith, the strain between what is visible and rational and what defies reason is evident at Chartres cathedral. One knows the vault is heavy and pushes down on the piers, yet one "sees" the ribbed arches springing upward from the piers and the vault floating above on a band of light.

Gothic sculpture also reflected the triumphs and limits of knowledge, with each sculptural element part of a larger whole. On the south portal of Chartres cathedral, for example, stone figures and scenes surround three doors. The central pillar depicts Christ the teacher flanked by his Apostles. Over the central door, on the tympanum (the semicircular area above the doorway), two scenes illustrate the relationship between this world and the next. Below, Christ appears as judge in the Last Judgment while gleeful devils on his left "welcome" souls to hell; above this scene, Christ as the Son of Man shows his wounds. Christ the teacher thus establishes the church that leads to salvation because of his suffering on the cross. The two side portals address the same themes: the left tympanum shows the martyrdom of St. Stephen, who followed Christ in suffering; the right portrays several scenes of the good works necessary for redemption. Like Dante's *Divine Comedy,* these images represent a pilgrimage from this world to eternal life, with each element leading toward heaven. Working within a tradition of Gothic style, yet also experimenting with new combinations, the builders of Chartres

Orvieto Cathedral
In Italy Gothic elements were used only selectively. The cathedral of Orvieto shown here was begun c. 1290. Its builders chose to use round arches and abundant wall space decorated with patterns of light and dark.

Baptistery Pulpit by Nicola Pisano
The Italian sculptor Nicola Pisano drew upon many traditions, including those of the classical world. Here the panel of the Magi adoring the Christ child is part of a complex program of sculpture on a pulpit at Pisa.

cathedral used elements from earlier Gothic churches, such as the cathedral at Laon, where one tympanum had also placed the Last Judgment below the sculpture of Christ as Son of Man. At Chartres, however, the scene became part of a coherent scheme that could be read across three doors.

The Gothic style varied by region, no more so than in Italy, where local traditions prevailed. The outer walls of the cathedral at Orvieto, for example, alternate bricks of light and dark color, providing texture instead of glass and light; and the vault over the large nave is round rather than pointed, recalling the Roman aqueducts that could still be seen in Italy when the builders were designing the cathedral. With no flying buttresses and relatively few portals surrounded by sculpture, Italian churches conveyed a spirit of austerity and spareness, even though they incorporated other characteristically "Gothic" features. San Andrea, in Vercelli, for example, had pointed arches and a rose window in the apse. The importance of walls and the interplay between light- and dark-colored elements in the interior made Italian churches very different from French Gothic cathedrals.

The Italian sculptor Nicola Pisano (c. 1220–1278?) fused Gothic sculptural forms with classical Roman styles. Nicola's baptistery pulpit at Pisa shows drapery much like that in contemporary French figural sculpture, and the themes depicted (scenes from Christ's life) stretch across several panels, as at Chartres cathedral; but the heads of the figures are clearly based on ancient reliefs. Nicola's work thus synthesized several traditions.

By the early fourteenth century the expansive sculptures so prominent in architecture were reflected in painting as well. This new style is evident in the paintings of Giotto (1266–1337), a Florentine artist. For example he filled the walls of a private chapel at Padua with frescoes depicting scenes from Christ's life. In these frescoes he experimented with the illusion of depth. Giotto's figures, appearing weighty and voluminous, expressed a range of emotions as they seemed to move across interior and exterior spaces. In bringing sculptural realism to a flat surface, Giotto changed the emphasis of painting, which had been predominantly symbolic, decorative, and intellectual. His works instead stressed three-dimensionality, illusional space, and human emotion. By melding earthy sensibilities with religious themes, Giotto found yet another way to bring together the natural and divine realms.

Giotto's Pietà
The grieving Mary of Giotto's pietà is an example of the artist's ability to depict deeply personal human feeling. This scene is part of a large cycle of frescos that Giotto painted on the walls of a private chapel at Padua. Private patronage of such art went hand-in-hand with interest in celebrating individuality.

The Politics of Control

The quest for order, control, and harmony also became part of the political agendas of princes, popes, and cities. These rulers and institutions imposed—or tried to—their authority more fully and systematically through taxes, courts, and sometimes representative institutions. The roots of modern European parliaments and of the U.S. Congress can be traced to this era. In the thirteenth century both secular and church rulers endeavored to expand their spheres of power and eliminate opposition. This process forced them to increase their sources of revenues to pay for new militias and officials in an era of economic contraction.

Limits of Economic Growth

Economic expansion in the early thirteenth century had benefited from the demographic growth and land reclamation that had begun in the tenth century. But by 1300 the only land left uncleared in France and England was marginal or unworkable with the tools of the day. People produced more than ever before, but families also had more hungry mouths to feed: by the end of the thirteenth century, a single plot in England, for example, was divided into twenty tiny parcels for the progeny of the original peasant holder. In the region around Paris, one small farm had fragmented into seventy-eight pieces. The last known French *villeneuve* ("new town") was founded in 1246; after that new settlements ceased. Population growth seems to have leveled off by then, but the static supply of farmland meant that France and England from the mid-thirteenth century onward faced sudden and severe grain shortages. Climatic changes compounded the demographic situation. In 1309 an extremely wet growing season ruined the grain harvest in southern and western Germany; the towns, where food had to be imported, were especially hard hit. When heavy and persistent rains inundated Flanders in 1315, grain prices soared. A chronicler lamented,

> *The people were in such great need that it cannot be expressed. For the cries that were heard from the poor would move a stone, as they lay in the streets with woe and great complaint, swollen with hunger and remaining dead of poverty, so that many were thrown by set numbers, sixty and even more, into a pit.*

Warfare also took its toll on economic life. In attempts to consolidate their rule, princes hired mercenary troops but paid them such poor wages that they plundered the countryside even when they were not fighting. Warring armies had always disrupted farms, ruining the fields as they passed; but in the thirteenth century, burning became a battle tactic, used both to devastate the enemy's territory and to teach a lesson. Here too the cities felt the repercussions. A city's own army could defend its walls against roving troops, but it could not stop the flow of refugees who streamed in seeking safety. Lille's population, for example, nearly doubled as a result of the wars between Flanders and France during the first two decades of the thirteenth century. Meanwhile, like other Flemish cities, Lille had to impose new taxes on its population to pay for its huge war debts.

Pressed by war debts, the need for food, and the desire for gain, landlords and town officials alike strove to get more money. Everywhere, customary and other dues were deemed inadequate. In 1315 the king of France offered liberty to all his serfs, but mainly to assess a new war tax on all free men. In other parts of France, lords imposed a *taille,* an annual money payment; many peasants went into debt to pay it. Professional moneylenders set up loan offices in the countryside; or wealthy neighbors served as unofficial creditors. Although richer peasants might prosper as creditors, the cycle of loan, debt, and payment left poorer peasants even more impoverished.

In other areas, such as Italy, England, and southern Germany, lords found it useful to give their peasants short-term leases. Bypassing the fixed and customary dues whose value decreased as prices rose, these lords simply charged a rent that changed with the market. In Bavaria, for example, the abbot of Baumburg met with his peasants each year to announce new leases and negotiate new rents. In Italy, where peasants had long labored under twenty-five-year leases, landlords and cities introduced a short-term lease. This new lease enabled one monastery in Milan to double its rental income.

To enforce their new taxes and lease arrangements, great lords, both lay and ecclesiastical, installed local agents eager to collect taxes and to draft young village men into military service. These officials lived near the villages in fortified houses and maintained a watchful eye on local conditions. They kept account books and computed their profits and costs. One calculated, for example, that

> *You can well have three acres weeded for a penny, and an acre of meadow for fourpence, and an acre of waste meadow for threepence-halfpenny. . . . And know that five men can well reap and bind two acres a day of each kind of [grain], more or less. And where each takes twopence a day then you must give five-pence an acre.*

Although the cities were affected by the crises in the countryside during the thirteenth century, they were cushioned from their most devastating effects. In many instances the cities acted as lords over local cultivators, with rights to tax and requisition food as needed. Wars brought grief to some cities, but others profited from weapons trade. The textile industry in the older cities of Flanders declined after 1270 because a political dispute cut off supplies of wool from England; but new textile centers arose to replace them. Throughout the thirteenth century the "busts" of the business cycle were followed by "booms," so that despite hints of serious decline, such as the cessation of population growth in Florence, major decreases in business activity in the urban sector would become clear only later in the fourteenth century.

The Clash of Imperial and Papal Aims

Thirteenth-century kings and princes everywhere worked to expand and consolidate their territories as well as their taxes. With the aid of salaried agents and the backing of lawyers schooled in Roman and canon law, this impulse for growth proceeded with thoroughness even when the enlarged territory ultimately split apart, as happened when Frederick II (1194–1250) attempted to unite the kingdom of Sicily with the empire of his father, Henry VI, and his grandfather, Frederick I Barbarossa. Frederick II, called in his own day the *stupor mundi,* or "won-

Europe in the Time of Frederick II, 1212–1250

der of the world," spanned two cultures, as heir to Sicily on his mother's side and to Germany through his father. In Sicily he dealt with a diverse and cosmopolitan population of Jews, Muslims, and Christians; employed Muslim servants and concubines at court; and drew upon Byzantine and Norman traditions to rule his kingdom. From Byzantium he had the model of the late Roman emperor, fount of law and head of the church; from the Normans he acquired his position as feudal monarch holding sway over his barons. The Norman conquerors of Sicily had become vassals of the pope, so the king also had (at least theoretically) both the obligation of defending the pope and the honor of representing him. In Germany, however, Frederick found a different set of traditions; there Christian princes, often churchmen with ministerial retinues, were acutely aware of their constitutive role in kingship and their government rights and privileges.

Frederick wanted to retain both his kingdoms, but the popes feared the papal states would be encircled and strangled; and the popes themselves were interested in territorial expansion. Already, Innocent III had raised money and troops to make good his claim to "all the land from Radicofani [in the north] to Ceprano [in the south], the exarchate of Ravenna, Pentapolis, the march, the duchy of Spoleto [and so on]." From these regions the pope expected dues and taxes, military service, and the profits of justice.

Almost as soon as he was crowned emperor, in 1220, Frederick's policies alienated the papacy, and he and his successors struggled against the popes, often in outright warfare, through almost

Frederick II
Emperor Frederick II was interested not only in politics but also in the natural world. On the margins of a treatise on falconry that he wrote, Frederick is depicted as both ruler and teacher.

the entire thirteenth century. Frederick had a three-pronged strategy. First, he left Germany to the princes, granting them concessions that allowed them to turn their principalities into virtually independent states in exchange for their support or neutrality. Second, Frederick revamped the government of Sicily to give him more control and yield greater profits. The *Constitutions of Melfi*, a collection of old and new laws issued by Frederick in 1231, touched upon every important aspect of his kingdom. Anxious that official documents be legible, for example, he declared that notaries must use a simple style of handwriting; concerned that Jews and Muslims were unfairly persecuted, he allowed them to initiate court cases. The *Constitutions* exhorted agents of the government to be just, specifying that no justiciar could hold court where his family held lands (and thus be disposed to rule in their favor). For Frederick, as for other kings, justice produced profits, as the royal treasury pocketed fines and many of the expenses required for litigation. Frederick's declaration of a royal monopoly on salt, iron, and other minerals and his control over grain exports from Sicily assured him even more fiscal bounty. Third, Frederick looked to Lombardy to provide the crucial foothold he needed for the survival of the Holy Roman Empire. Not surprisingly, however, some northern Italian cities revived the Lombard League, partly to support the pope and partly to oppose Frederick, whose rule threatened them with the loss of rights and taxes. Although in 1237 Frederick won a key victory against the league at Cortenuova, his very success jeopardized him: Pope Innocent IV (∗1243–1254) excommunicated him and then declared him a heretic. In 1245, at the Council of Lyon (held in France, to be far from Frederick's forces) Frederick was excommunicated and deposed; his vassals and subjects were absolved of their fealty to him; and all were forbidden to support him. By 1248, papal legates were preaching a crusade against Frederick and all his supporters.

Frederick's death from dysentery in 1250 did not end the struggle between his dynasty and the papacy. But long before the fighting ended, his territorial vision had been shattered. The German princes won their independence, so that between 1254 and 1273, a period called the Great Interregnum, Germany had virtually no king. Finally in 1273 the princes elected Rudolf (∗1273–1291), whose family, the Habsburgs, was new to imperial power. Rudolf used the imperial title to consolidate his own principality in Swabia (southwestern Germany), but he did not try to maintain traditional imperial prerogatives. Although emperors continued to be crowned for centuries thereafter, they wielded power based on their estates and principalities rather than on a tradition of imperial rights. A fragmented Germany would endure until the nineteenth century.

Sicily was also severed from imperial rule. In 1254, Pope Innocent IV asked Henry III of England to accept the crown of Sicily on behalf of the king's second son, Edmund. When Henry could not rally the support the papacy required, however, the offer was rescinded. In 1262, Pope Urban IV (∗1261–1264) called upon Charles, the count of Anjou and brother of France's king Louis IX, to lead a crusade

Sicily and Italy at the End of the Thirteenth Century

against Sicily and its ruler, Frederick's son Manfred. Promised troops, ships, and the proceeds from a crusading tax levied on French churchmen, Charles marched into Sicily in 1266, killed Manfred, and took the title of king. As a result, France was tied to southern Italy. Rebellion soon followed, however, beginning in 1282 during the so-called Sicilian Vespers, and forces loyal to Manfred's daughter called in her husband, the king of Aragon (in Spain), to take Sicily's throne and oust the Angevins. The move left two enduring claimants to Sicily's crown: the kings of Aragon and the house of Anjou. And it spawned a long war that impoverished the region.

In the struggle between pope and emperor, the pope had clearly won, at a moment that marked a high point in the political power of the medieval papacy. Innocent's attack on Frederick's orthodoxy had been so convincing that even Dante—no friend of the papacy—placed Frederick in the circle of Hell reserved for heretics. Nevertheless, others agreed with Frederick II's view that the popes' tampering with secular matters had demeaned and sullied their office: "these men who feign holiness," Frederick sneered, referring to the popes, are "drunk with the pleasures of the world." Scattered throughout Germany were groups of devout (but heretical) Christians who believed Frederick was a divine scourge sent to overpower a materialistic papacy. The papacy won the war against the Staufer, but at a cost. Even St. Louis criticized the popes for doing "new and unheard of things."

The Separation of Royal and Ecclesiastical Power

The power and prestige of the king of France increased greatly under St. Louis, who vigorously imposed his laws and justice over much of France while maintaining generally excellent relations with the pope. The influence of the *Parlement** of Paris, the royal court of justice, increased significantly during his reign. Originally a changeable and moveable body, part of the king's personal entourage when he dealt with litigation, it was now permanently housed in Paris and staffed by professional judges who heard cases and recorded their decisions. Louis also thoroughly restructured the administration of Paris by appointing a salaried official there. The interests of good government and fiscal well-being went hand-in-hand. As Joinville pointed out:

> *People came to [Louis's kingdom] for the good justice to be obtained. Population and prosperity so increased that the revenue from sales of land, death duties, commerce and other sources was double what the king received before.*

Louis's subjects began to develop a new ideal of kingship, that of a ruler who was less concerned with military matters than with staying home to administer justice and maintain civil peace. Although Louis remained in France for long periods, he left home more often than his subjects would have liked, twice leading unsuccessful crusades to the Holy Land. When Louis took his second crusading vow, Joinville complained:

> *I considered that all those who had advised the king to go on this expedition committed mortal sin. For at that time [before the king left] the state of the country was such that there was perfect peace throughout the kingdom . . . while ever since King Louis went away the state of the kingdom has done nothing but go from bad to worse.*

Because Louis had died on this crusade, Joinville's words here implicitly criticized the government of Louis' successor, Philip III (✱1270–1285). However, he was also making a point about good

*Although *Parlement* and *Parliament* are very similar words, both deriving from the French word *parler,* meaning "to speak," the institutions they named were very different. The Parlement of France was a law court, whereas the English Parliament, although beginning as a court to redress grievances, had by 1327 become above all a representative institution. The major French representative assembly, the Estates General, first convened at the beginning of the fourteenth century.

rulership, praising the steady administrator above the heroic crusader.

Accepting limits on his power in relation to the church, Louis did not demand greater jurisdiction over churchmen; but he deftly maintained the royal dignity while recognizing church authority. Joinville liked to tell of a confrontation between the king and a French bishop:

> *Your Majesty [said the bishop], the archbishops and bishops here present have charged me to tell you that the honor of Christendom is declining in your hands. It will decline still further unless you give some thought to it, because no man stands in fear of excommunication at this present time. We therefore require your Majesty to command your bailiffs and your other officers of the law to compel all persons who have been under sentence of excommunication for a year and a day to make their peace with the Church.*

Louis responded by saying that he would be happy to intervene if he were allowed to judge each case himself. The bishop refused, denying the king jurisdiction in spiritual matters. Then, concluded Joinville,

> *The King replied that he in his turn would not give them knowledge of such matters as fell within his jurisdiction, nor order his officers to compel all excommunicated persons to obtain absolution, irrespective of whether sentence of excommunication had been rightly or wrongly pronounced. "For if I did so," he added, "I should be acting contrary to God's laws and the principles of justice."*

Thus without questioning the church's power in spiritual matters such as excommunication, Louis asserted the independence of his own temporal authority.

The Birth of Representative Institutions

As thirteenth-century monarchs and princes expanded their powers, they devised formal institutions to enlist more broadly based support: all across Europe, from Spain to Poland, from England to Hungary, rulers summoned parliaments. These grew out of the ad hoc advisory sessions kings had held with their nobles and clergy, men who informally represented the two most powerful classes, or orders, of medieval society. In the thirteenth century the advisory sessions turned into solemn, formal meetings of representatives of the orders to the king's Great Council, the origin of parliamentary sessions. Although these bodies differed from place to place, the impulse behind their creation was similar. Beginning as assemblies where kings celebrated their own royal power and prestige and where the orders simply assented to royal policy, they eventually became organs through which people not ordinarily at court could articulate their wishes.

The orders, which evolved from the idealized functional categories of the tenth century (those who pray, those who fight, and those who work), consisted of the clergy, nobles, and commoners of the realm. Unlike modern "classes," which are defined largely by economic status, medieval orders cut across economic boundaries. The "order of clerics," for example, embraced the clergy from the most humble parish priest to the most exalted archbishop and pope. The "order of commoners" theoretically included both rich merchants and poor peasants. But the notion of orders was an idealized abstraction; in practice thirteenth-century kings did not so much command representatives of the orders to come to court as they simply summoned the most powerful members of their realm, whether clerics, nobles, or important townsmen, to support their policies. In thirteenth-century León (present-day Spain), for example, the king sometimes called only the clergy and nobles; sometimes, especially when he wanted the help of their militias, he sent for representatives of the towns. As townsmen gradually began to participate regularly in advisory sessions, kings came to depend upon them and their support. In turn commoners became more fully integrated into the work of royal government.

The *cortes* of Castile-León were among the earliest representative assemblies called to the king's court and the first to include townsmen. As the *reconquista* pushed southward across the Iberian Peninsula, Christian kings called for settlers to occupy new frontiers. Enriched by plunder, fledgling villages soon burgeoned into major commercial centers. Like the cities of Italy, Spanish towns dominated the countryside. Their leaders—called *caballeros villanos,* or "city horsemen," because they were rich enough to fight on horseback—monopolized the municipal offices. In 1188, when King

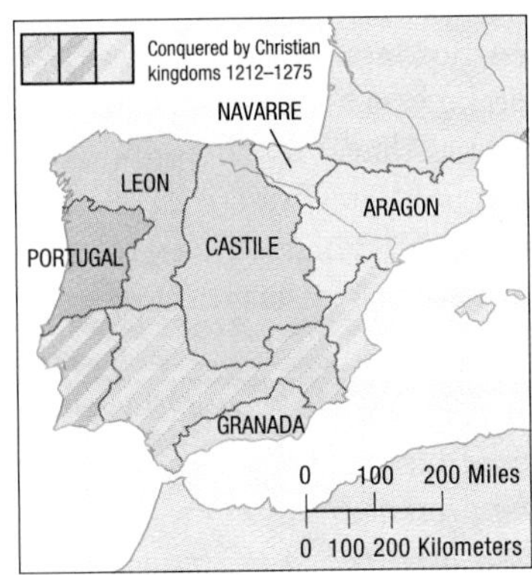

Spain in the Thirteenth Century

Alfonso IX (*1188–1230) had summoned townsmen to the *cortes,* the city caballeros served as their representatives, agreeing to Alfonso's plea for military and financial support and for help in consolidating his rule. Once convened at court (Toledo, Burgos, and Seville were favorite places) these wealthy townsmen joined bishops and noblemen in formally counseling the king and assenting to royal decisions. They played a role, for example, in recognizing Berenguela, the daughter of King Alfonso X (*1252–1284), as his heir in 1254. They were also present in 1277 when the *cortes* granted the same king a special tax to defend his king-dom, and two years later reluctantly agreed to still another levy. Thus beginning with Alfonso X, Castilian monarchs regularly called on the *cortes* to participate in major political and military issues and to assent to new taxes to finance them.

The English Parliament also developed at a time of royal strength, when the twelfth-century King Henry II had consulted prelates and barons at Great Councils. Henry II had used these parliaments as his tool, but the government of Henry III (*1216–1272) marked a change. Crowned at the age of nine, Henry III was king in name only during the first sixteen years of his reign, when England was governed by a council consisting of a few barons, professional administrators, and a papal legate. Although not quite "government by Parliament," this council set a precedent for baronial self-rule later, when Henry's popularity plummeted.

Periodically during the first half of Henry's reign the barons would make sure that he reaffirmed the provisions of the Magna Carta, which (in their view at least) gave them an important and permanent role in royal government as the king's advisors and a solid guarantee of their customary rights and privileges. As late as 1237, when Henry needed money to pay for military campaigns against Louis IX (whom he was fighting for the lands lost by John), the barons insisted that he reissue the Magna Carta in return for their agreement to pay an extraordinary feudal aid. But Henry had no intention of consistently soliciting or heeding the barons' advice, preferring instead to listen to a group of nobles from Poitiers, his half-brothers by his mother's second marriage, and favoring another faction of notables from Savoy (today in southeastern France), his wife's relatives. He further alienated the barons because all his military objectives ultimately failed. At the same time, he estranged the English clergy by allowing the pope to appoint "foreigners" (mostly Italians) to well-endowed church positions. Many nobles and commoners alike complained that Henry was acting arbitrarily and unjustly.

When in 1254, Henry agreed to accept the Sicilian crown from the pope on behalf of his son Edmund, he also promised to pay the papacy's enormous war debt, incurred in its ongoing battle against the Staufer kings. Henry tried to raise the money, but the barons thwarted his attempts. The pope, angry that payments were not forthcoming, threatened to excommunicate Henry. In 1258, matters came to a head when a parliament of great magnates, lay and clerical, met at Oxford to discuss the papal demands. The barons, enraged and determined not to be deluded again by a temporary reissue of the Magna Carta, threatened to rebel; they forced Henry to dismiss his foreign advisors; to rule with the advice of a Council of Fifteen chosen jointly by the barons and the king; and to make his chief officers, such as the treasurer and chancellor, more professional by limiting their terms and making them accountable to the council.

The new government, controlled by the barons, swiftly repudiated the Sicilian crown and the financial commitments that went with it and made peace with Louis IX. But when it appointed new judges to consider local grievances, some barons defected, for the reforms struck at their own local authority. Torn by factions, the baronial party grew weaker, whereas Henry rallied new support. The pope even absolved him from his promise at Oxford. Both sides—the baronial reformers and the monarchists—were armed and intransigent, and in 1264 civil war erupted. At the battle of Lewes in the same year, the leader of the baronial opposition, Simon de Montfort (c. 1208–1265), routed the king's forces, captured the king, and became England's de facto ruler. Because only a minority of the barons followed Simon, he sought new support by convening a parliament in 1265, to which he summoned not only the earls, barons, and churchmen who backed him but also representatives from the towns, the "commons"—and he appealed for their help. Thus for the first time the commons were given a voice in government. Even though Simon's brief rule ended that very year and Henry's son Edward I (✱1272–1307) became a rallying point for royalists, the idea of representative government in England had emerged, born out of the interplay between royal initiatives and baronial revolts.

The Collision of Pope and King

In France, too, the king sometimes called local assemblies representing the orders; but a French national representative body—the Estates General—originated in the conflict between Pope Boniface VIII and King Philip IV (Philip the Fair) (✱1285–1314). This confrontation seemed at the time simply one more episode in the ongoing struggle between medieval popes and rulers for power and authority. On both sides arguments about jurisdictions and rights echoed themes raised in the eleventh century during the Gregorian reform movement and in the twelfth and early thirteenth centuries during the clashes between popes and emperors. But western European kings now, at the end of the thirteenth century, had more power, making the standoff between Boniface and Philip a turning point that weakened the papacy and strengthened the monarchy.

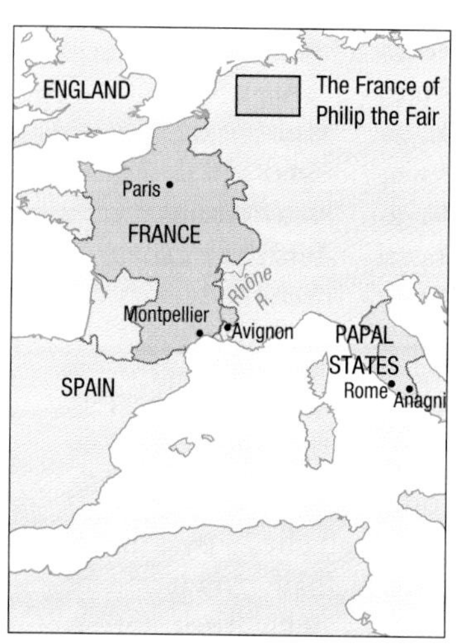

The Reign of Philip the Fair

When Boniface VIII (✱1294–1303) became pope, France's Philip the Fair and England's Edward I had just begun a war, which the kings financed by taxing their prelates along with everyone else, as if they were preparing for a crusade and could expect church support. Without even pretending any concern for clerical autonomy, Edward's men, for example, forced open church vaults to confiscate money for the royal coffers.

For the kings of both England and France the principle of national sovereignty now allowed them to claim jurisdiction over all people, even churchmen, who lived within their borders. For the pope, however, the principle at stake was his role as head of the clergy. Boniface asserted that only the pope could authorize the taxation of clerics, and in 1296 he issued the bull* *Clericis Laicos,* which conveyed in sharp language his anger over royal taxation of the clergy:

> *That laymen have been very hostile to the clergy antiquity relates; and it is clearly proved by the experiences of the present time. For not content with what is their own the laity strive for what is forbidden and loose the reins for things unlawful.*

Boniface threatened to excommunicate kings who taxed prelates without papal permission, and he called upon clerics to disobey any such royal orders.

Edward and Philip reacted swiftly to *Clericis Laicos.* Taking advantage of the important role English courts played in protecting the peace, Edward declared that all clerics who refused to pay his taxes would be considered outlaws—literally "outside the law." Clergymen who were robbed, for example, would have no recourse against their attackers; if accused of crimes, they would have no defense in court. Relying on a different strategy, Philip forbade the exportation of precious metals, money, or jewels, effectively sealing French borders. Immediately the English clergy cried out for legal protection, while the papacy itself cried out for the revenues it had long enjoyed from France. Just one year after issuing *Clericis Laicos,* Boniface backed down, conceding that kings had the right to tax their clergy in emergencies.

In 1301, Philip the Fair tested his jurisdiction in southern France by arresting Bernard Saisset, the bishop of Pamiers, on a charge of treason for slandering the king by comparing him to an owl, "the handsomest of birds which is worth absolutely nothing." Saisset's imprisonment violated the principle, maintained both by the pope and by French law, that a clergyman was not subject to lay justice. Boniface's angry reaction declared that the pope "holds the place on earth of Him who is alone lord and master," and that Philip should never imagine "that you have no superior or that you are

*An official papal document was called a bull from the *bulla,* or seal, that was used to authenticate it.

Philip the Fair and Edward I
Philip the Fair on the right and Edward I on the left confront each other in this contemporary sketch, written on a copy of the truce that the two kings declared in 1298. The impassive look on Philip's face is consistent with Bernard Saisset's wry comparison of Philip and an owl.

not subject to the head of the ecclesiastical hierarchy," suggesting that the pope was the king's superior in matters both temporal and spiritual. Philip quickly seized the opportunity to deride and humiliate Boniface, directing his agents to forge and broadly circulate a new papal letter, a parody of the original, which read, "We want you to know that you are subject to us in spiritualities and temporalities." At the same time, he convened representatives of the clergy, nobles, and townspeople to explain, justify, and propagandize his position. This new assembly, which met at Paris in 1302, was the ancestor of the Estates General,* which would meet sporadically for centuries thereafter—for the last time in 1789, at the beginning of the French Revolution. Most of those present at the assembly of 1302 supported Philip, wrote letters of protest to the cardinals, and referred to Boniface not as pope but as "he who now presides over the government of the Church."

Boniface's reply, the bull *Unam Sanctam,* intensified the situation to fever pitch with the words: "Therefore we declare, state, define and pronounce that it is altogether necessary to salvation for every human creature to be subject to the Roman Pontiff." At meetings of the king's inner circle, Philip's agents declared Boniface a false pope and accused him of sexual perversion, various crimes, and heresy: "He has a private demon whose advice he follows in all things. . . . He is a Sodomite and keeps concubines. . . . He has had many clerics killed in his presence, rejoicing in their deaths . . . ," and so on. The king sent his commissioners to the various provinces of France to convene local meetings to popularize his charges against Boniface and gain support. These meetings, which included clergy, local nobles, townspeople, and even villagers, almost unanimously denounced the pope, although a few nobles, such as the officials of Montpellier, demurred. Perhaps the most striking support came from the clergy, who were beginning to view themselves as members of a free Gallican church largely independent of the papacy. Finally in 1303, royal agents, acting under Philip's orders, invaded Boniface's palace at Anagni (southeast of Rome) to capture the pope, bring him to France, and try him. Fearing for the pope's life, however, the people of Anagni joined forces and drove the French agents out of town. Yet even after such public support for the pope, the king had won. Boniface died very shortly thereafter, and the next two popes quickly pardoned Philip and his agents for their actions.

Significantly, the second of those popes, Clement V (✱1305–1314) was a Frenchman. Though he sought a path of compromise with the cardinals faithful to the memory of Boniface VIII, civil strife prevented him from entering Italy. After moving about in France for several years, Clement finally in 1309 set up his headquarters at Avignon, a central location for Germany, France, and Italy. Here the popes remained until 1378. The period from 1309 to 1378 came to be called the Babylonian Captivity by Europeans sensitive to having the popes live far from Rome, on the Rhône River. Fourteenth-century popes continued to preside over a wealthy and busy ecclesiastical

*In France the various orders—clergy, nobles, and commoners—were called "estates."

enterprise, but the pope's prestige and authority had diminished. The delicate balance between church and state, a hallmark of the years of St. Louis, reflecting as much a search for harmony as a quest for power, broke down by the end of the thirteenth century. The quest for control led not to harmony but to confrontation and extremism. Recognizing new limits, the Avignon popes established a sober and efficient organization that took in regular revenues and gave the popes more say than ever before in the appointment of churchmen. They would, however, slowly abandon the idea of leading all of Christendom and tacitly recognize the growing power of the secular states to regulate their own internal affairs.

The Fate of the Communes

Like kings, the cities of northern and central Italy asserted their power, but on a lesser scale. Florence, for example, imposed its rule still more firmly on its *contado,* where serfdom had long ago given way to the system of short-term land leasing and sharecropping. Statutes drawn up by the Italian city governments supported the interests of landowners in the city rather than the cultivators. At Bologna, for example, the laws demanded tenant farmers plow the land fully four times before sowing seed; this measure was meant to ensure greater yield, but it greatly burdened the country folk.

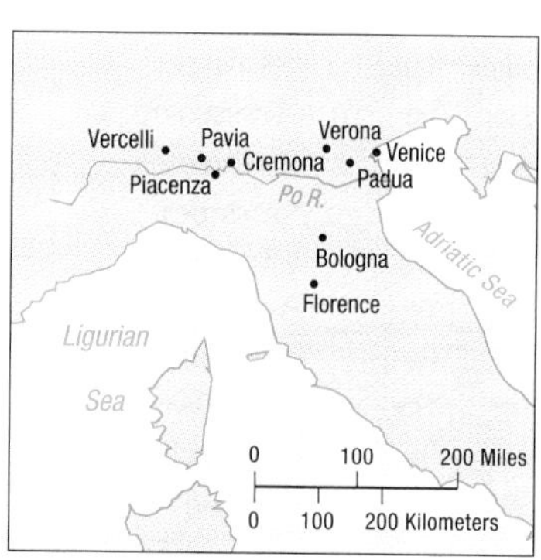

Major Cities of Northern and Central Italy

With such statutes, Italian cities regulated, ordered, and controlled the countryside. Control over the communal government meant power to tax and distribute the revenues, make appointments to both clerical and government positions, and market the food produced by the *contado.* Dominated by rival noble families, the cities were arenas of strife during the wars between the popes and the Staufer, with the Guelph nobles and their allies taking up the papal cause and the Ghibellines championing the emperor. Hiding behind these labels, however, were often self-interested communal factions who struggled to undermine one another and appropriate their opponents' power and property.

In the course of the thirteenth century still newer groups, generally from the nonnoble classes, also attempted to take over the reins of power in the commune. The *popolo,* as such groups were called, incorporated members of other city associations—craft and merchant guilds, parishes, and the commune itself. In fact, the *popolo* was itself a kind of alternative commune, a sworn association in each city, dedicated to upholding the interests of its members. Generally the wealthier craftsmen rather than the poor joined the *popolo:* at Padua, for example, the right to elect *popolo* officers was denied to "sailors, gardeners, agricultural labourers, landless men and herdsmen." Despite the exclusivity of its membership, the *popolo* welcomed the military aid of the lower classes. Armed and militant, the *popolo* demanded a share in city government, particularly to gain a voice in matters of taxation. In 1222 at Piacenza, for example, the *popolo's* members won half the government offices; a year later they and the nobles worked out a plan to share the

Siena Communal Palace
This communal palace, built at Siena between 1297 and 1310, expresses the enormous power Italian city governments wanted to hold over both the citizens within the walls and the peasants who lived in the outlying contado.

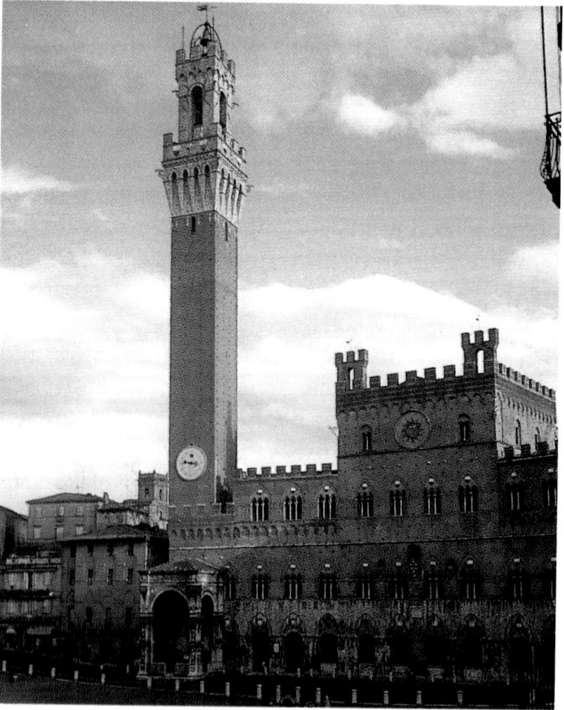

election of their city's podesta. Such power sharing often resulted from the *popolo's* struggle. In some cities nobles overcame and dissolved the *popolo;* but others virtually excluded the nobles from government. Constantly confronting one another, quarreling, feuding, and compromising, such factions as the Guelphs, Ghibellines, nobles, and *popolo* turned Italian cities into centers of civil discord.

Weakened by this constant friction, the communes were tempting prey for great regional nobles who, allying with one or another faction, tried to establish themselves as *signori* (singular, *signore,* meaning "lord") of the cities, keeping the peace at the price of repression. Ezzelino da Romano, for example, whose family commanded knightly vassals and great swaths of land in the countryside around Venice, seized control over most of the cities surrounding Verona by allying himself with Frederick II and his supporters. Here, as in other cities, the commune gave way to the *signoria* (a state ruled by a signore), with one family dominating the government. Based in one city, the signore extended his authority to neighboring cities as well. Oberto Pallavicini, with a following of German mercenaries, for example, first gained Cremona and then had himself declared "perpetual podesta" at Pavia, Vercelli, and Piacenza. The fate of Piacenza over the course of the thirteenth century was typical: first dominated by nobles, its commune eventually granted the *popolo* a voice by the first quarter of the thirteenth century; but then by the middle of the century the signore's power eclipsed both the nobles and the *popolo*.

The Mongol Invasions in a Fragmented East

Outside western Europe the fragmentation of political power left the East vulnerable to invasions from Asia in the thirteenth century. Byzantium had a tradition of central authority and administration, but military and economic factors weakened its government. With Constantinople seized by western Europeans in the Fourth Crusade, a Byzantine "government in exile" moved to parts of Greece and Asia Minor. In 1261, Michael VIII Palaeologus (*1261–1282) recaptured Constantinople and reestablished the Byzantine Empire. But Byzantium's position was precarious. It had to combat renewed invasions by western princes and protect its eastern flank, where the Ottoman Turks had seized territories. These military emergencies prevented the Byzantine emperors from restoring central government with the old *theme* system. Instead the empire's lands were divvied up among members of the imperial family and other aristocrats, and what taxes were collected more often ended up in the pockets of local magnates than the coffers of the emperor.

Nevertheless, Byzantium remained strong enough to deter an attack from the Mongols, whose invasions elsewhere across Russia, eastern Europe, and Asia constituted one of the most astonishing movements of the Middle Ages. On the northern border of China in present-day Mongolia, various tribes of mixed ethnic origins and traditions fused into an aggressive army under the leadership of Chingiz (or Genghis) Khan (c. 1162–1227) at the beginning of the thirteenth century. In part, economic necessity impelled them, because climatic changes had reduced the grasslands that sustained their animals and their nomadic way of life. But their advance out of Mongolia also represented the political strategy of Chingiz, who reckoned that military offensives would keep the tribes united under him. By 1215 the Mongols (also called the Tatars or Tartars) held Beijing and most of northern China. Some years later they moved through central Asia and skirted the Caspian Sea. In the 1230s they began concerted attacks in Europe—in Russia, Poland, and Hungary, where their formidable armies and tactics were no match for weak native princes. Only the death of their Great Khan, Chingiz's son Ögödei (1186–1241), and disputes over his succession prevented a concentrated assault on Germany. In the course of the 1250s the Mongols took Iran, Baghdad, and Damascus, stopped in their conquest of the Muslim world only by the Egyptian armies.

The Mongols' sophisticated and devastating military tactics led to their overwhelming success. Organizing their campaigns at meetings held far in advance of their planned attack, they devised two- and three-flank operations. The invasion of Hungary, for example, was two-pronged: one division of their army arrived from Russia while the other moved through Poland and Germany. Perhaps half the population of Hungary perished in the assault as the Mongols, fighting mainly on horseback, with heavy lances and powerful bows and arrows whose shots traveled far and penetrated deeply, crushed the Hungarian army of mixed infantry and cavalry.

The attack on the West began with Russia, where the Mongols had the most lasting impact. At Vladimir in Suzdal', the strongest Russian principality, they broke through the defensive walls of the cities and burned the populace huddled for protection in the cathedral. Their most important victory in Russia was the capture of Kiev in 1240. Making the mouth of the Volga River the center of their power in Russia, the Mongols dominated all of Russia's principalities for about two hundred years.

The Mongol empire in Russia, later called the Golden Horde ("golden" probably from the color of their leader's tent; "horde" from a Turkish word meaning "camp"), adopted much of the local government apparatus. The Mongols standardized the collection of taxes and the recruitment of troops by basing them on a population census, and they allowed Russian princes to continue ruling as long as they paid homage and tribute to the khan. The Mongol overlords even exempted the Russian church from their taxes. At Ryazan (southeast of Moscow), for example, the traditional princely dynasty continued to sit upon the throne, and there (in the words of a later writer), "The pious Grand Prince Ingvar . . . renewed the land of Ryazan and built churches and monasteries, he consoled newcomers and gathered together the people." Alexander Nevsky, grand prince of Novgorod (✷1252–1263), came from an old ruling family, but he personally owed his accession to the throne to Mongol support, and he continued to rely on their help as he skirmished with the Swedes, Germans, and Lithuanians who raided his principality; feuded with other claimants to his throne; and put down rebels who opposed his submission to the Mongols.

The Mongol invasions changed the political configuration of Europe and Asia. Because the Mongols were willing to deal with westerners, one consequence of their conquests was to open China to Europeans for the first time. Some missionaries, diplomats, and merchants traveled overland to China; others set sail from the Persian Gulf (where, in Iran, the Mongols had set up a khanate) and rounded India before arriving in China. Some hoped to enlist the aid of the Mongols against the Muslims; others expected to make new converts to Christianity; still others dreamed of lucrative trade routes. The most famous of these travelers was Marco Polo (1254–1324), son of a merchant family from Venice. Marco's father and uncle had already been to China and met Khubilai, the Great Khan,

The Mongol Empire After 1259

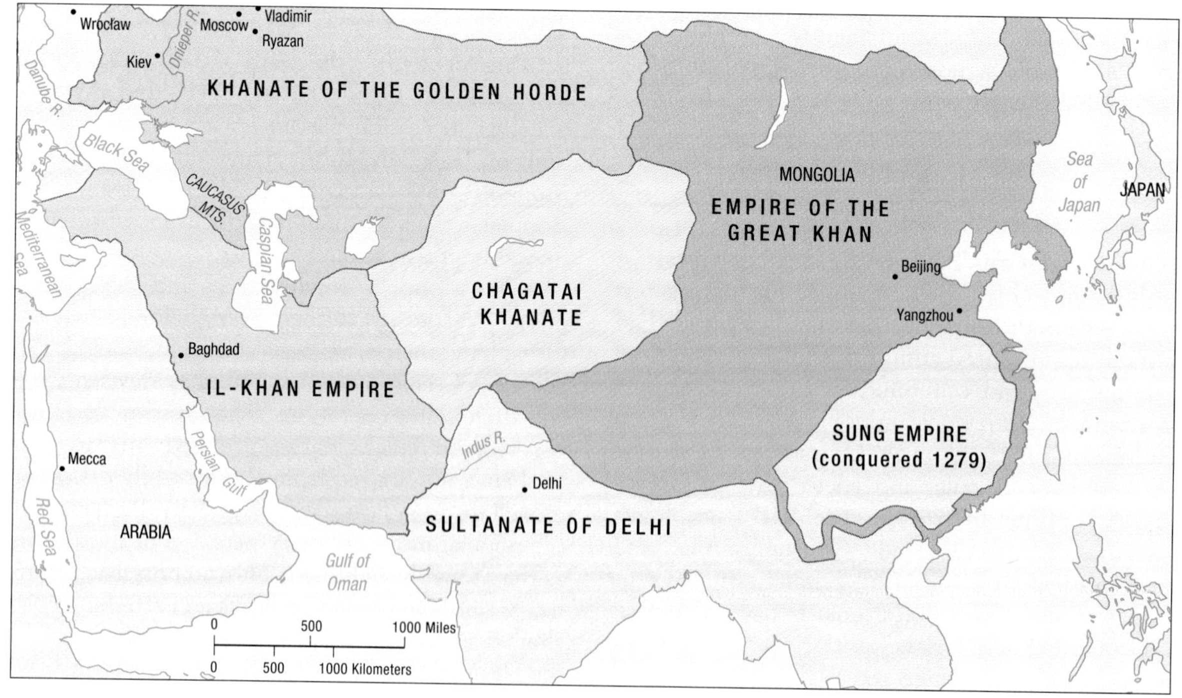

Mongols
In 1258, under the leadership of Hülegü, the Mongols captured Baghdad and brought the Abbasid Caliphate to an end. This Persian manuscript shows the Mongol army besieging a citadel.

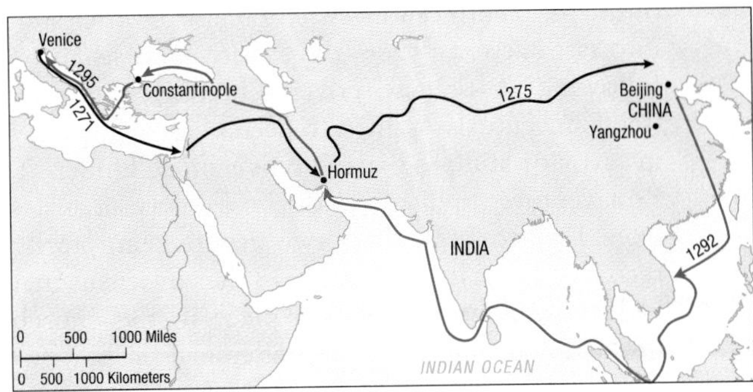

Marco Polo's Travels to and from China

who reportedly used them as envoys to ask the pope to send "men able to show by clear reasoning that the Christian religion is better than [that of the Mongols]." The delegation sent back to China, however, consisted not of missionaries but of the Polos—father, uncle, and now son—who traveled through lands where, as Marco later described, the water was "so bitter that no one could bear to drink it. Drink one drop of it and you void your bowels ten times over." After three or four years of travel, mostly on foot, the Polos' party arrived at the court of Khubilai, north of Beijing.

Marco Polo stayed in China for about seventeen years. The Mongols welcomed him: ruling as conquerors in China, they trusted foreigners more than native Chinese and willingly received Europeans. In fact, evidence suggests that an entire community of Venetian traders lived in the city of Yangzhou in the mid-thirteenth century. Both women and men dwelled in this community; Catherine Vilioni, an unmarried girl from a prosperous family of traders, died there in 1342.

Merchants paved the way for missionaries. Friars, preachers to the cities of Europe, became missionaries to new continents as well. In 1289 the pope made the Franciscan John of Monte Corvino his envoy to China. Preaching in India along the way, John arrived in China four or five years after setting out, converted one local ruler, and built a church. A few years later, now at Beijing, he boasted that he had converted six thousand people, constructed two churches, translated the New Testament and Psalms into the native language, and met with the Great Khan.

The Limits of Control

Regulation and control characterized much of the thirteenth century, from the Mongols' insistence on counting the Russian population in order to tax and recruit it, to the Fourth Lateran Council's desire to direct Christian worship and behavior, to St. Louis' attempts to legislate a moral community: "I would willingly," Louis said, "be branded with a hot iron if all filthy oaths could be abolished in my Kingdom." Uniformity and conformity were sometimes achieved; even when they were not, variations could often be tolerated. For example, in the middle of the thirteenth century the Franciscan order split into two factions. One (the Spirituals) insisted on following St. Francis' poverty literally; the other (the Conventuals) wanted to deemphasize austerity in favor of studying at the universities. Under St. Bonaventure, the general of the Franciscan order from 1257 to 1274, these two groups temporarily reconciled. Yet in 1317 and 1318 the consensus that had allowed both groups a place in the church broke down, and the pope condemned the Spirituals. Many joined illegal and unregulated fringe groups whose existence revealed a paradox: the quest for control created whole classes of people apparently out of control. Religious and political institutions found that their coercive power had limits.

The Food of Piety

The Fourth Lateran Council's promulgation of the doctrine of transubstantiation and the requirement that the laity receive Holy Communion at least once a year placed new emphasis on the holiness of the Eucharist, and the wine and wafer became objects of adoration. Now regularly denied to the laity, the cup became a privilege for priests, and the Mass became a priestly ritual of consecration rather than of communion by the congregation. Priests elevated the Host so all could see it, while bells rang and incense burned. In the *Quest of the Holy Grail,* the Eucharist was the Christ child himself. No wonder this "food" held extraordinary meaning for many. Yet the church's attempt to define and control the Eucharist produced unintended results.

From the thirteenth to the sixteenth centuries, some pious women throughout western Europe ate nothing but the Eucharist. Some women would eat spoiled foods so that their eating might become a sacrifice and a kind of martyrdom, but others refused all other foods. Angela of Foligno (1248–1309), for example, reported that the consecrated wafer swelled in her mouth and tasted sweeter than any other food. She wanted to relish it on her tongue but knew it should be swallowed right away; it went down "with that savor of unknown meat," and Angela was so moved that her hands trembled. For women like Angela, eating the Host was literally eating God, for this is how they understood the church's teaching that the consecrated wafer was actually Christ's body. In the minds of these holy women the Crucifixion thus became a kind of sacrificial feast. Angela had a vision in which the friars at Foligno suckled from the wound in Christ's side, participating fully and truly in his death. Eating Christ became a way to imitate him, and renouncing other food could become part of service to others, for many of these pious women gave the poor the food they refused to eat. These women lived in every sort of urban setting. They might be lay women—daughters, wives, and mothers living at home—or they might be Beguines or nuns living in cloistered or semi-cloistered communities. Angela of Foligno fed and ministered to the sick as a member of the tertiaries. Even if not engaged in community service, holy women felt their suffering itself was a work of charity, helping to release souls from purgatory.

Although men dominated the institutions that governed political, religious, and economic affairs, women found ways to control their own lives and to some extent the lives of those around them. Typically involved with meal preparation and feeding, these holy women found a way to use their monopoly over ordinary food to gain new kinds of social and religious power that could force the clergy to confront female piety. Insisting on distancing themselves from "normal" food, these pious women became "holy vessels" into which only the Eucharist could enter, and they often gained exceptional prestige. Some became seers and prophetesses. If a pious woman doubted the morality of her priest, for example, she might vomit out the Host, mortifying the priest publicly; or she might even bypass her priest altogether and receive the Eucharist directly from Christ in the form of a vision.

The Suppression of Heretics

Most holy women of the late Middle Ages were not considered heretics, and they did not openly defy clerical authority. Dissenters who refused to accept church doctrine, such as the Cathars of southern France, however, had been condemned as heretics at the time of the Albigensian Crusade (1209–1229). After the crusade the region came under royal control, but the continuing presence of heretics led church authorities to set up inquisitorial tribunals. An inquisition was simply an inquiry, a method long used by secular rulers to summon people together, either to discover facts or to uncover and punish crimes. The church in its zeal to end heresy and save souls used it to ferret out "heretical depravity." Calling suspects to testify in the 1230s and 1240s, inquisitors, aided by secular authorities, would round up virtually entire villages and interrogate everyone. By the mid-fourteenth century, Catharism had been eradicated.

First the inquisitors typically called the people of a district to a "preaching," where they gave a sermon and promised clemency to those who confessed their heresy promptly. Then at a general inquest they questioned each man and woman who seemed to know something about heresy: "Have you ever seen any heretics or Waldenses? Have you heard them preach? Attended any of their ceremonies? Adored heretics?" The judges assigned relatively lenient penalties to those who were not aware that they held heretical beliefs and to heretics who quickly recanted. But unrepentant heretics were burned at the stake, because the church believed such people threatened the salvation of all. Their ashes were sometimes tossed into the water so they could not serve as diabolical relics. Anyone who died while still a heretic could not be buried in consecrated ground. Raymond VII, the count of Toulouse, saw the body of his father—who died excommunicate—rot in its coffin as the pope denied all requests for its burial. Houses where heretics had resided or even simply entered were burned and the sites turned into garbage dumps. Children of heretics could not inherit any property nor become priests, even if they adopted orthodox views.

In the thirteenth century, for the first time, long-term imprisonment became a tool to repress heresy, even if the heretic had confessed: "It is our will," wrote one tribunal, "that [Raymond Maurin and Arnalda, his wife,] because they have rashly transgressed against God and holy church . . . be thrust into perpetual prison to do condign penance, and we command them to remain there in perpetuity." The inquisitors also used imprisonment to force someone to recant, to give the names of other heretics, or to admit a plot. Guillaume Agasse, for example, confessed to participating in a wicked (and imagined) meeting of leprosaria directors who planned to poison all the wells. As the quest for religious control spawned wild fantasies of conspiracy, the inquisition pinned its paranoia on real people.

The inquisition also created a new group—penitent heretics—who lived on as marginal people. Like Jews, now forced to wear yellow badges as a mark of disgrace, penitent heretics were stigmatized by huge yellow fabric crosses sewn on the front and back of their shirts. To ensure that the crosses would be visible, the penitent was forbidden to wear yellow clothing. Moreover, every Sunday and every feast day repentant heretics had to attend church twice; and during religious processions these men and women were required to join with the clergy and the faithful, carrying large branches in their hands as a sign of their penance.

The Quest for Control

c. 1162–1227 Chingiz Khan, Mongol leader, dominates northern China and Central Asia to the Caspian Sea

- **1240** Mongols capture Kiev, beginning the Golden Horde

1216–1272 Reign of Henry III, king of England

- **1258–1265** The barons, led by Simon de Montfort, revolt
- **1265** Simon convenes the first Parliament including commons

1220–1250 Reign of Emperor Frederick II, ruler of Germany and Sicily

- **1245** Deposed by the pope at Council of Lyon
- **1248** Crusade launched against him

1226–1270 Reign of St. Louis (Louis IX), king of France; increased the functions of Parlement and reformed royal administration

1273–1291 Reign of Rudolf I of Hapsburg, emperor after the Great Interregnum in Germany (1254–1273)

1285–1314 Reign of Philip the Fair (Philip IV), king of France

- **1294–1303** Embroiled in disputes with Boniface VIII
- **1302** Calls first meeting of the Estates at Paris

1309–1378 Avignon Papacy

Conclusion

In different ways the conflict between Boniface VIII and Philip the Fair of France, the mystical visions of pious women, and the creation of a class of permanent penitents all showed the limits of medieval control. Although Boniface saw himself as a supreme power to whom everyone was subject, he failed to impose his will on Philip, who was equally certain of his own exalted position. Philip, though undermining much of the papacy's power, ultimately failed to control the popes, now staying in nearby Avignon. Similarly, priests who claimed a monopoly on the mysteries of the Eucharist encountered pious women who influenced its meaning and its use. The inquisition too could not control subversive fantasies, even those of its own making, although it effectively quelled overt heresy.

The quest to dominate through new institutions was matched by new achievements in scholarship and the arts. Thirteenth-century scholastics sought philosophical control by harmonizing the thinking of the pagan Aristotle with a sophisticated Christian theology. Preachers communicated to ordinary people ideas expounded in the learned halls of the universities. Artists and architects integrated sculpture, stone, and glass to depict religious themes and fill the light-infused space of Gothic churches. Musicians wove together disparate melodic and poetic lines into motets. Writers melded heroic and romantic themes with theological truths and mystical visions.

Political leaders also aimed at order and control: to increase their revenues, expand their territories, and enhance their prestige. The kings of England and France and the governments of northern and central Italian cities partially succeeded in achieving these goals. The king of Germany failed bitterly, and Germany remained fragmented until the nineteenth century.

But the harmonies became discordant at the end of the thirteenth century. The balance between church and state achieved under St. Louis, for example, disintegrated into irreconcilable claims to power in the time of Boniface and Philip. The carefully constructed tapestry of St. Thomas' *summae*, which wove together Aristotle's secular philosophy and divine scripture, began to unravel in the teachings of John Duns Scotus. The eclectic Italian Gothic style, which gathered together indigenous as well as northern elements, gave way to a new artistic style, that of Giotto, whose work would be the foundation of Renaissance art in the fourteenth century.

Suggestions for Further Reading

Source Materials

Dante. *The Divine Comedy*. A classic with many translations. Two highly recommended versions are by Mark Musa and John Ciardi.

Joinville, Jean de, and Geoffroy de Villehardouin. *Chronicles of the Crusades*. Translated by M. R. B. Shaw. 1963. Contains Joinville's *Life of St. Louis* and an account of the Fourth Crusade.

Pegis, Anton C., ed. *Introduction to St. Thomas Aquinas*. 1945. Contains excerpts from the *Summa Theologiae* (here entitled *Summa Theologica*) and the *Summa Contra Gentiles*.

Quest of the Holy Grail. Translated by P. M. Matarasso. 1969. Written as a kind of pious answer to Arthurian romance literature. Introduces Sir Galahad to the Round Table.

Interpretive Studies

Abulafia, David. *Frederick II: A Medieval Emperor*. 1988. Stresses the continuity between Frederick's political vision and the outlooks of his forebears and contemporaries.

Bynum, Caroline Walker. *Holy Feast and Holy Fast: The Religious Significance of Food to Medieval Women*. 1987. A sensitive and insightful discussion of late medieval women mystics.

Campbell, Mary B. *The Witness and the Other World: Exotic European Travel Writing, 400–1600*. 1989.

Places the writings of Marco Polo, Columbus, and others into the wider arena of the development of travel literature.

Duby, Georges. *The Age of the Cathedrals: Art and Society, 980–1420.* 1981. An overview of the high and late Middle Ages with special emphasis on the significance of artistic expression.

Erler, Mary, and Maryanne Kowaleski. *Women and Power in the Middle Ages.* 1988. A collection of essays that explores the various ways and the different times in which women exercised power.

Fennell, John. *The Crisis of Medieval Russia, 1200–1304.* 1983. Discusses Russia under the Mongols.

Fernández-Armesto, Felipe. *Before Columbus: Exploration and Colonization from the Mediterranean to the Atlantic, 1229–1492.* 1987. Makes the important point that the exploration of the New World was not the sudden invention of Columbus but rather grew out of long-time activities along the Atlantic seaboard.

Katzenellenbogen, Adolf. *The Sculptural Programs of Chartres Cathedral.* 1959. The classic analysis of the meaning of the west, south, and north portal complexes of Chartres cathedral.

Klapisch-Zuber, Christiane, ed. *A History of Women in the West.* Vol. 2, *Silences of the Middle Ages.* 1992. A series of essays focusing on such issues as medieval medical views of women, medieval preaching directed at women, and ideal images of women.

Larner, John. *Italy in the Age of Dante and Petrarch, 1216–1380.* 1980. A thoughtful synthesis of economic, political, and social changes in a crucial period of Italian history.

McCall, Andrew. *The Medieval Underworld.* 1979. Discusses the people on the fringes of medieval society: criminals, prostitutes, and heretics.

Morgan, David. *The Mongols.* 1986. A look at the Mongols and their history in all parts of their empire.

Nicholas, David. *Medieval Flanders.* 1992. Discusses the social, economic, and political development of a key region in the Middle Ages.

O'Callaghan, Joseph F. *The Cortes of Castille-León, 1188–1350.* 1989. A study of one of the earliest representative assemblies. Also notes comparable events elsewhere in Europe.

Panofsky, Erwin. *Gothic Architecture and Scholasticism.* 1951. A brilliant discussion of the affinities between Gothic architecture and medieval *summae* as well as between Gothic architects and scholastics.

Partner, Peter. *The Lands of St. Peter: The Papal State in the Middle Ages and the Early Renaissance.* 1972. Looks at the papal monarchy from the point of view of the lands it ruled or claimed to rule directly.

Phillips, J. R. S. *The Medieval Expansion of Europe.* 1988. Emphasizes the importance of European contact with other continents and cultures before the age of Columbus.

Powers, James F. *A Society Organized for War: The Iberian Municipal Militias in the Central Middle Ages, 1000–1284.* 1988. Discusses the rise and character of "frontier towns" in the age of the *reconquista.*

Sargent, Steven D., ed. and trans. *On the Threshold of Exact Science: Selected Writings of Anneliese Maier on Late Medieval Natural Philosophy.* 1982. Translations of important articles that show the originality and integrity of medieval scientific thought.

Smart, Alastair. *The Dawn of Italian Painting, 1250–1400.* 1978. An introduction to an era of transition in Italian art, written by an art historian.

Southern, R. W. *Robert Grosseteste: The Growth of an English Mind in Medieval Europe.* 1986. Discusses an important English scholastic and political figure.

Stacey, Robert. *Politics, Policy, and Finance Under Henry III, 1216–1245.* 1987. Covers the early, often overlooked years of Henry's reign.

Strayer, Joseph R. *The Reign of Philip the Fair.* 1980. The definitive biography of this king.

Wood, Charles T. *Philip the Fair and Boniface VIII: State vs. Papacy.* 2d ed. 1971. Presents the different ways historians have viewed the personalities, issues, and events involved in the confrontation between Philip and Boniface.

CHAPTER 13

The Collapse of Medieval Order, 1320–1430

A chronicle written in the first years of the fifteenth century contains a terse entry for 1349: "In the year of Our Lord 1349," noted an anonymous cleric of Mainz (in Germany), "both the mighty and the powerless, the rich and the poor, the old and the young traveled around all lands, beating themselves cruelly with whips, doing penance with prayers and hymns, and reading fictive and false writings against the Christian faith. At that time also, the Jews were almost everywhere in the world slaughtered by Christians." The chronicler certainly exaggerates the numbers of people involved, but the events he describes accurately depict the fourteenth century. After decades of increasing control through religious and political institutions, order now gave way to chaos and violence. Groups of flagellants, who performed self-inflicted acts of violence as a form of penance, roamed the empire. Jews were persecuted on a scale not surpassed until the twentieth century. Christians massacred Jews throughout the Holy Roman Empire, southern France, Aragon, and Castile, ravaging the once-flourishing Jewish culture of the Middle Ages.

Both the flagellant movement and the antisemitic violence were manifestations of a more general crisis. In the mid-fourteenth century a series of disasters scourged a society already weakened by overpopulation, economic stagnation, social conflicts, and war. These disasters—famine, climatic changes, and disease—brought European civilization to its knees in 1348 through 1350. The plague (also called the Black Death) wiped out at least a third of Europe's population. With recurring plagues and continuous warfare through the second half of the fourteenth century, population density

The Dance of Death
Sudden death was an ever-present reality in premodern European life. One of the most widespread popular religious images was that of the Dance of Death, showing a grim skeletal figure leading young and old, rich and poor, relentlessly to the grave. In this example, a powerful clergyman vainly resists his fate.

would not reach thirteenth-century levels again until the sixteenth, and in many areas not until the eighteenth, century.

Dynastic conflicts, popular uprisings, and an external menace to the Christian nobility as the Muslim Ottoman Turks advanced steadily into southeastern Europe all undermined political authority and threatened the social order. During the later Middle Ages, the idea of universal Christendom that had sustained the Crusades receded, while loyalties to state, community, and social group deepened. The papacy, the very symbol of Christian unity and authority, remained divided by the claims of rival popes and challenged by heretical movements.

Early fifteenth century Europe stood at a turning point. Crises of confidence and control that had led to retrenchment and depressed economic growth brought about challenges to established power by the lower social classes. The cultural and religious ferment of the Late Middle Ages, however, produced an atmosphere of anxiety.

Important Dates

1315–1317 Famine in Europe
1337 Beginning of the Hundred Years' War
1346 Battle of Crécy
1348–1350 The Black Death
1349–1351 Anti-Jewish massacres in the Empire
1358 Jacquerie uprising in France
1378 Beginning of the Great Schism in the papacy
1381 English peasant uprising
1389 Ottomans defeat Serbs at Kossovo
1414–1417 Council of Constance
1415 Execution of Jan Hus; Hussite Revolution in Bohemia begins
1430 Joan of Arc saves French monarchy

Origins and Results of the Demographic Collapse

At least a generation before the Black Death, at the end of the thirteenth century, European economic growth had slowed and then stopped. By 1300 the economy could no longer support Europe's swollen population. Having cleared forests and drained swamps, the peasant masses now divided their plots into ever smaller parcels and farmed marginal lands; their income and the quality of their diet eroded. In the great urban centers, where thousands depended on steady employment and cheap bread, a bad harvest, always followed by sharply rising food prices, meant hunger and eventual famine. A cooling of the European climate contributed to the crisis in the food supply. Modern studies of tree rings indicate that fourteenth-century Europe entered a colder period, with a succession of severe winters beginning in 1315. The extreme cold upset an ecological system already overtaxed by human cultivation. Crop failures were widespread. In many cities of northwestern Europe the price of bread tripled in a month, and thousands starved to death. Some Flemish cities, for example, lost 10 percent of their population. But the Great Famine of 1315 to 1317 was only the first in a series of catastrophes the overpopulated and undernourished society of fourteenth-century Europe faced. Death, in the form of an epidemic, mowed down masses of weakened bodies in mid-century.

The Spread of the Plague

Brought to Russia and western Asia via caravans and ships from central, east, and southeast Asia, the bubonic plague spread rapidly along the trade routes that linked all parts of Europe. From its breeding ground in central Asia, the plague passed eastward into China, where it decimated the population and wiped out the remnants of the tiny Italian merchant community in Yangzhou. Bacteria-carrying fleas, living on black rats, transmitted the disease. They traveled back to Europe alongside valuable cargoes of silk, porcelain, and spices. In 1347 the Genoese colony in Caffa in the Crimea contracted the plague from the Tatars. Fleeing by ship in a desperate but futile attempt to escape the disease, the Genoese in turn communicated the plague to the seaports of the Mediterranean; by January 1348 the Black Death had infected Sicily, Sardinia, Corsica, and Marseilles. Six months later the plague had spread to Aragon, all of Italy, the Balkans, and most of France. The disease then crept

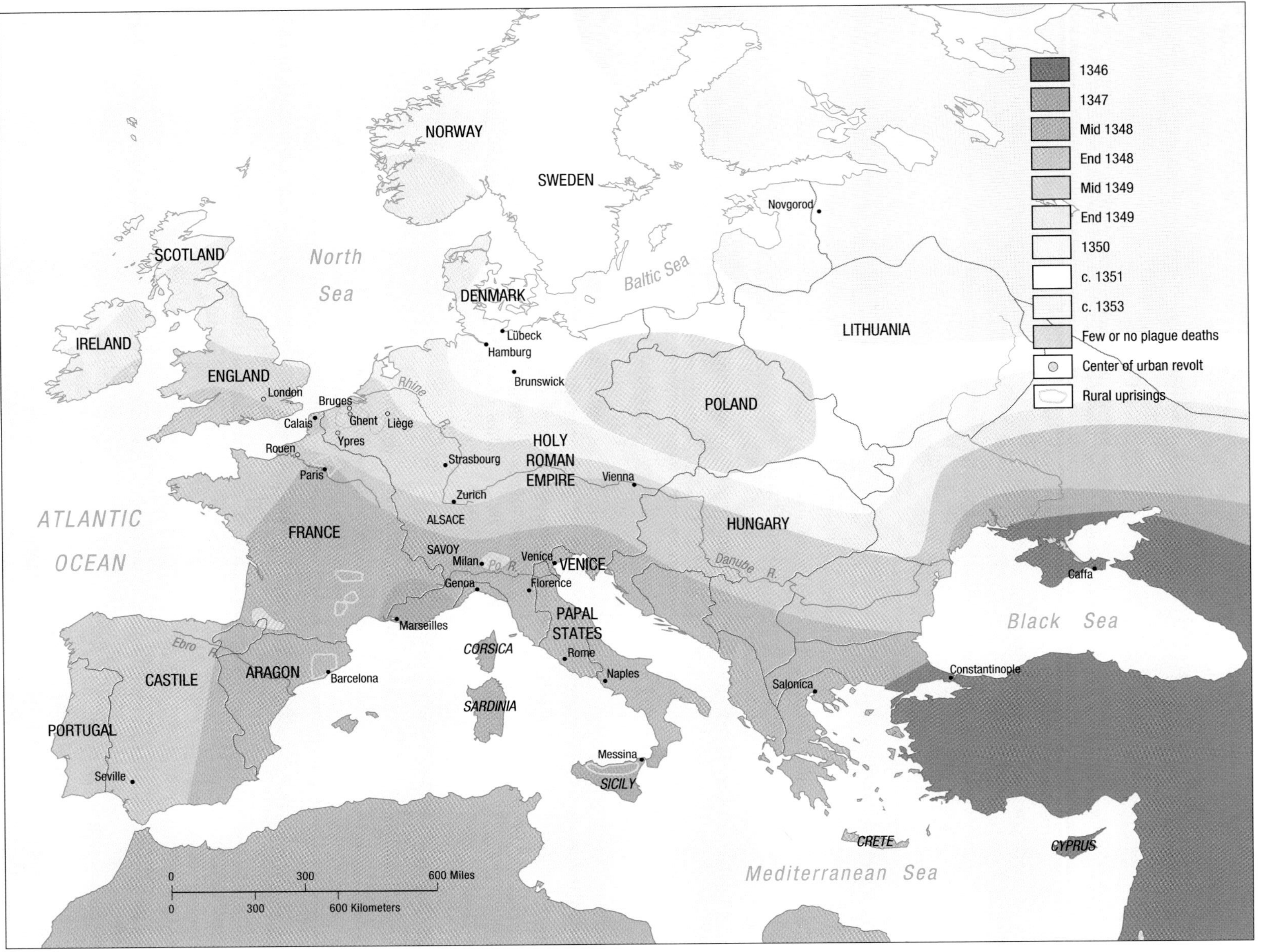

Advance of the Black Death

northward to Germany, England, and Scandinavia, reaching the Russian city of Novgorod in 1350.

Nothing like the Black Death had struck Europe since the great plague in the sixth century. The Italian writer Giovanni Boccaccio reported that the plague

> *. . . first betrayed itself by the emergence of certain tumors in the groin or the armpits, some of which grew as large as a common apple, others as an egg. . . . From the two said parts of the body this . . . began to propagate and spread itself in all directions indifferently; after which the form of the malady began to change, black spots or livid making their appearance in many cases on the arm or the thigh or elsewhere, now few and large, now minute and numerous.*

Inhabitants of cities, where crowding and filth increased the chances of contagion, died in massive numbers. Florence lost almost two-thirds of its population of ninety thousand; Siena lost half its people; Paris, the largest city of western Europe, came off relatively well, losing only a quarter of its two hundred thousand inhabitants. Most cities the plague visited on its deadly journey lost roughly half their population in less than a year. Rural areas seem to have suffered fewer mortalities, but regional differences were pronounced.

Helplessness and incomprehension worsened the terror of the plague. The Black Death was not particular: old and young, poor and rich were equally affected, although the wealthy had a better chance of not contracting the disease if they escaped to their country estates before the epidemic hit their city. Medical knowledge of the time could not explain the plague's causes. The medical faculty of the University of Paris blamed the calamity on the stars. In a report prepared for King Philip VI of France in 1348, the professors of medicine described a conjunction of Saturn, Mars, and Jupiter in the house of Aquarius in 1345, resulting in widespread death and pestilence on Earth. Various treatments were used in an attempt to combat the plague, ranging from bloodletting, a traditional cure to balance the body's four humors; to the commonsensical lying quietly in bed; to the desperate suggestion of breathing in the vapors of latrines to ward off the sickness. Many people believed air poisoning caused the disease, and when news of an outbreak reached them they reacted by walling in their neighbors. In the search for someone to blame, others accused Jews of poisoning wells and loosed the murderous rage that led to antisemitic violence.

The devastation of 1348 was only the beginning of an age of epidemics. The plague recurred and cut down Europeans repeatedly. Further outbreaks occurred in 1361, 1368–1369, 1371, 1375, 1390, and 1405; they continued, with longer dormant intervals, into the eighteenth century. Plagues and wars caused a significant long-term decrease in population. Although general figures are unavailable, detailed local studies convey the magnitude of the destruction wreaked by the Black Death and war. In eastern Normandy, for example, the population in 1368 was only 42 percent of its height in 1314, and it fell to its nadir in the fifteenth century.

Flagellants, Preachers, and Jews: Responses to the Plague

Some believed the plague was God's way of chastising a sinful world and sought to save themselves by confessing their sins. In 1349, bands of men wearing tattered clothes, marching in pairs, carrying flags, and following their own leaders appeared in southern Germany. When they reached a town or village they visited the local church and, to the great astonishment of the congregation and the alarm of the clergy, sang hymns while publicly whipping themselves, according to strict rituals, until blood flowed. The flagellants, as they soon came to be called, cried out to God for mercy and called upon the spectators to repent their sins.

From southern Germany the flagellants moved throughout the Holy Roman Empire. In groups of several dozen to many hundred, they traveled and attracted great excitement. The flagellants' flamboyant piety moved many laypeople, but most of the clergy distrusted a lay movement that seemed to challenge the official church. At its inception, the flagellant movement comprised men only from respectable social groups, such as artisans and merchants. Converts who joined the wandering bands, however, often came from the margins of society, and discipline seems to have broken down. In 1350 the church declared the flagellants heretical and suppressed them.

In some communities the religious fervor the flagellants aroused spawned violence directed at the Jews. From 1348 to 1350, antisemitic persecutions, beginning in southern France and spreading through Savoy to the Holy Roman Empire, destroyed many Jewish communities in central and western Europe. Between November 1348 and February 1351 violence against Jews erupted in at least one hundred German cities. Sometimes the clergy incited the attacks against the Jews, calling them Christ-killers, accusing them of poisoning wells and kidnapping and ritually slaughtering Christian children, and charging them with stealing and desecrating the Host (the communion wafer that Christians believed became the body of Christ during Mass). Economic resentment fueled antisemitism in some areas, as those in debt turned on creditors, often Jews, in towns throughout Europe. Perhaps most cynical were the nobility of Alsace, heavily indebted to Jewish bankers, who sanctioned the murder of Jews to avoid repaying money they had borrowed.

Many antisemitic incidents were spontaneous, with mobs plundering Jewish quarters and killing those who refused baptism. Authorities orchestrated some of the violence, however, seeking a focus for the widespread anger and fear the plague caused. Relying on contemporary chronicles, historians have long linked the arrival of the Black Death with anti-Jewish violence. More recent historical research shows that in some cities the antisemitic violence actually preceded the epidemic. This revised chronology of events demonstrates official complicity and even careful premeditation in the destruction of Jewish communities. For example, in 1349 the magistrates of Nuremberg obtained approval from Emperor Charles IV before organizing a persecution directed by the city government. Thousands of German Jews were slaughtered. Many fled to Poland, where the incidence of plague was low and where the authorities welcomed Jews as productive taxpayers. In western and central Europe, however, the persecutions of 1348 to 1350 destroyed the financial power of the Jews, who had benefited from the commercial revolution of the thirteenth century, and culminated in waves of expulsions in the fifteenth century.

Social, Economic, and Cultural Consequences of the Plague

Although the Black Death took a horrible human toll, the disaster actually profited some people. In an overpopulated society with limited resources, massive death opened the ranks for advancement. For example, after 1350, landlords had difficulty acquiring new tenant farmers without making concessions in land contracts; the vast army of priests found more benefices* to support them; and workers received much higher wages because the supply of laborers had dwindled. The Black Death and the resulting decline in urban population meant a lower demand for grain relative to the supply and thus a drop in cereal prices. Noble landlords all across Europe had to adjust to these new circumstances. Some revived seigneurial demands for labor services; others looked to their central government for legislation to regulate wages; and still others granted favorable terms to peasant proprietors, often after bloody peasant revolts. Many noblemen lost a portion of their wealth and a measure of their autonomy and political influence. Consequently, European nobles became more dependent on war and on their monarchs to supplement their incomes and enhance their power.

For the peasantry and the urban working population the higher wages generally meant an improvement in living standards. To compensate for the lower demand and price for grain, many peasants and landlords turned to stock breeding and grape and barley cultivation. As European agriculture diversified, peasants and artisans consumed more beer, wine, meat, cheese, and vegetables, a better and more varied diet than their forebears in the thirteenth century had eaten. The reduced cereal prices also stimulated sheep raising in place of farming, so that a portion of the settled population, especially in the English midlands and in Castile, became migratory.

Because of the shrinking population and thus less of a demand for food, cultivating marginal fields was no longer profitable, and in areas settled during the previous centuries of demographic and geographic expansion, many settlements were simply abandoned. In the hundred years following the Black Death, for example, some four hundred fifty large English villages and many smaller hamlets disappeared. In central Europe east of the Elbe River, where German peasants had migrated, large tracts of cultivated land reverted to forest. Estimates suggest that some 80 percent of all villages in parts of Thuringia vanished.

*A *benefice* is an ecclesiastical office that is funded by an endowment; priests collected the revenues from the endowment.

Also as a result of the plague, urban resources shifted from manufacturing for a mass market to producing for a highly lucrative, if small, luxury market. The drastic loss in urban populations had reduced the demand for such mass-manufactured goods as cloth. Fewer people now possessed proportionately greater concentrations of wealth. Per capita income increased at every social level because of inheritance. In the southern French city of Albi the proportion of citizens possessing more than 100 livres doubled between 1343 and 1357, while the number of poor people, those with less than 10 livres, declined by half.

Faced with the possibility of imminent and untimely death, the urban populace sought immediate gratification. The Florentine Matteo Villani described the newfound desire for luxury in his native city in 1351: "the common people . . . wanted the dearest and most delicate foods . . . while children and common women clad themselves in all the fair and costly garments of the illustrious who had died." Those with means increased their consumption of luxuries: silk clothing, hats, doublets (snug fitting men's jackets), and boots from Italy; expensive jewelry; and spices from Asia became fashionable in northwestern Europe. Whereas agricultural prices continued to decline, prices of manufactured goods, particularly luxury items, remained constant and even rose as demand for them outstripped supply.

The long-term consequences of this new consumption pattern spelled the end for the traditional woolen industry that had produced for a mass market. Diminishing demand for wool caused hardships for woolworkers, and social and political unrest shook many older industrial centers dependent on the cloth industry. In the Flemish clothing center of Ypres, production figures fell from a high of ninety thousand pieces of cloth in 1320 to fewer than twenty-five thousand by 1390. In Ghent, where 44 percent of all households earned their livelihood as weavers and fullers (a person who shrinks and thickens wool) and where some 60 percent of the working population depended on the textile industry, the woolen market's slump meant constant labor unrest.

Hard Times for Business

Compared to the commercial prosperity of the twelfth and thirteenth centuries, the Late Middle Ages was an age of retrenchment for those in business. During the commercial revolution, merchants had invented many techniques of the modern capitalist economy, such as banking, credit, and currencies with established rates of exchange. International bankers, all Italians, had become financiers to kings and popes. As the fourteenth-century crises afflicted the business community, a climate of pessimism and caution permeated commerce, especially during the second half of the century.

The first major crisis that undermined Italian banks was the financing of a war between France and England in which English king, Edward III, borrowed heavily from the largest Italian banking houses, the Bardi and Peruzzi of Florence. Edward was resorting to a traditional financial arrangement, dating back to the 1280s, between the English crown and Italian financiers. With many of their assets tied up in loans to the English monarchy, the Italian bankers had no choice but to extend new credits, hoping vainly to recover their initial investments. In the early 1340s, however, Edward defaulted on his loans. Adding to their problems, the Florentine bankers were forced to make war loans at home. These once-illustrious and powerful banks could not rebound from the losses they incurred because of these strains. In 1343 the banking house of the Peruzzi fell, followed by the Bardi in 1346. This international financial crisis also bankrupted the Acciaiuoli, the third-largest Florentine banking house. Other Florentine bankers, notably the Medici, founded in 1397, eventually replaced these international giants, though on a smaller scale.

This breakdown in the most advanced economic sector reflected the general recession. Merchants were less likely to take risks and more willing to invest their money in local government bonds than in venture capital. Fewer merchants traveled to Asia, partly because of the danger of being attacked by the Ottoman Turks on the overland routes that had once been protected by the Mongols. Late fourteenth-century Italian merchants no longer hazarded long overland journeys to eastern Asia, as Marco Polo and his father had done a hundred years earlier. The Medici of Florence, who would dominate Florentine politics during the Renaissance, stuck close to home, investing part of their banking profits in art and politics and relying mostly on business agents (factors) to conduct their affairs in other European cities.

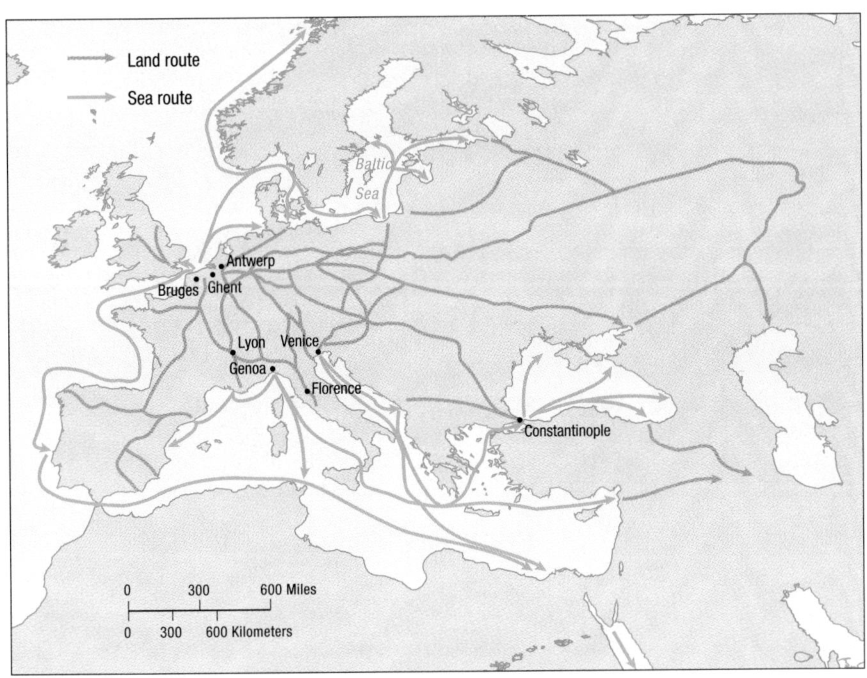

Trade in the Late Fourteenth Century

Historians have argued that this fourteenth-century economic depression diverted capital away from manufacturing and to investments in the arts and luxuries for immediate consumption. Instead of plowing their profits back into their businesses, merchants acquired land, built sumptuous townhouses, purchased luxury items, and invested in bonds. During the last decades of the fourteenth century, the maritime insurance in the great merchant republics of Venice and Genoa rose, also reflecting the pessimism of the times. The grim reality of the plague motivated many merchants to forgo long-term investments, such as in manufacturing, and instead to seek short-term profits, such as in trading luxury foods.

The most important trade axis continued to link Italy with the Low Countries. Italian cities produced silk, wool, jewelry, and other luxury goods northern Europeans desired, and they also imported spices, gold, and other coveted products from Asia and Africa. Traveling either by land through Lyons or by sea around Gibraltar, these products reached Bruges, Ghent, and Antwerp, where they were transshipped to England, northern Germany, Poland, and Scandinavia. The reverse flow carried raw materials and silver, the latter to help balance the trade between northern Europe and the Mediterranean. Diminished production and trade eventually caused turmoil in northern Europe and a crisis for financiers in the Low Countries. Bruges, the financial center for northwestern Europe, saw its power fade during the fifteenth century when a succession of its money changers went bankrupt. The Burgundian dukes eventually enacted a series of monetary laws that undermined Bruges's financial and banking community and, by extension, the city's political autonomy as well.

Challenges to Spiritual Authority

After Philip the Fair of France humiliated Pope Boniface VIII, the papacy's prestige had suffered a heavy blow when the papal seat was transferred from Rome to Avignon (bordering the French kingdom) in 1309. Until 1378 the Avignon popes were all Frenchmen. Many now called for church reform. Some clerics supported establishing a church council to limit papal power; others argued against the papacy's secular powers; some dissenters even

The Palace of the Popes at Avignon *For over a century the papacy resided not at Rome but in the small southern French city of Avignon. The massive papal palace attests to the size and complexity of the bureaucracy that grew up to serve the church's needs.*

rejected the very legitimacy of the Roman church. But the most serious challenge to the late medieval church was the coalescence of social, economic, and religious discontent expressed in new movements offering alternative visions and institutions for the faithful's spiritual guidance and salvation.

Papal Authority and Dissent

Papal government continued to grow even after Avignon became the papal residence. In the fourteenth century the papacy's institutions were more sophisticated than those of secular states. A succession of popes, all lawyers by training, concentrated on consolidating the financial and legal powers of the church, mainly through appointments and taxes. Claiming the right to assign all benefices, the popes gradually secured authority over the clergy throughout western and central Europe. Under the skillful guidance of John XXII (*1316–1334), papal rights increased incrementally without causing much protest. By the second half of the century the popes had secured the right to appoint all major benefices and many minor ones. To gain these lucrative positions, potential candidates often made gifts to the papal court to win favor. The imposition of papal taxes on all benefice holders developed from taxation to finance the Crusades. Out of these precedents the papacy instituted a regular system of papal taxation that produced the money to consolidate papal government.

Papal government, the *curia*, consisted of the pope's personal household, the Sacred College of Cardinals, and the church's financial and judicial apparatus. Combining elements of monarchy and oligarchy, the *curia* developed a bureaucracy that paralleled the organization of secular government. The pope's relatives often played a major role in his household; many popes came from extended noble lineages, and they often gave their family members preferential treatment (hence the term *nepotism*, from the Latin *nepos*, meaning "nephew"—but often a euphemism for the pope's illegitimate children—which denotes showing favoritism to one's kin). The papal household expanded rapidly in Avignon. As patrons of the arts the popes brought writers and artists into their households. Francesco Petrarch, the most famous poet of the age, worked in Avignon as a young man, before achieving his success.

After the pope, the cardinals, as a collective body, were the most elevated entity in the church.

Like great nobles in royal courts, the cardinals, many of them nobles, advised and aided the pope. They maintained their own households, employing scores of scribes, servants, and retainers. Together, the cardinals were strong enough to challenge papal authority; indeed factions of cardinals played an instrumental role in the fourteenth-century crisis of the church.

Papal bureaucracy consisted of the apostolic chamber (to manage finances), the chancery (to deal with a mountain of correspondence with all corners of Christendom), and the papal tribunal (to adjudicate ecclesiastical disputes). Most posts went to clerics with legal training, thus accentuating the juristic and administrative character of the highest spiritual authority in Christendom. During the fourteenth and fifteenth centuries, the papal army also grew, as the popes sought to restore and control the Papal States in Italy.

William of Ockham (c. 1285–1349) and Marsilius of Padua (c. 1290–1343) sharply criticized the papal monarchy, which had been developing since the twelfth century. Asserting the poverty of Christ, Ockham, an English Franciscan, denounced the papal pretension to worldly power and wealth. Rejecting further the confident synthesis of Christian doctrine and Aristotelian philosophy by Thomas Aquinas, Ockham denied that universal concepts had any reality in nature. Instead, Okham asserted, such concepts as "man" or "papal infallability" were mere representations, words in the mind. Perceiving and analyzing these ideals offered no assurance that they expressed truth. Observation and human reason were limited as means to understand the universe and to know God. Consequently, God might be capricious, contradictory, or many rather than one. Denying the possibility of an evil or erratic God, Ockham emphasized the covenant between God and his faithful. God promises to act consistently—for example, to reward virtue and punish vice. Ockham stressed simplicity in his explanations of universal concepts. His insistence that shorter explanations were superior to wordy ones became known as "Ockham's razor." Yet Ockham's so-called nominalism threatened the established order in which the church was the supreme theological authority. Ockham believed church power derived from the congregation of the faithful, both laity and clergy, not from the pope or the church council. Imprisoned by Pope John XXII for heresy, Ockham escaped in 1328 and found refuge with Emperor Louis of Bavaria.

Another antipapal refugee at the imperial court was Marsilius of Padua, a citizen of an Italian commune, a physician and lawyer by training, and the rector of the University of Paris. Marsilius attacked the very basis of papal power in *The Defender of the Peace* (1324). The true church, Marsilius argued, was constituted by the people, who had the right to select the head of the church, either through the body of the faithful or through a "human legislator." Papal power, Marsilius asserted, was the result of historical usurpation, and its exercise represented tyranny. In 1327, Pope John XXII, the living target of the treatise, decreed the work heretical. *The Defender of the Peace* would become an important intellectual justification for the Protestant reformers of the sixteenth century.

The Great Schism

While papal authority resided in Avignon, many voices urged the popes to return to Rome, the see of St. Peter. For three years (1367–1370), Urban V did return to Rome, where he received the Holy Roman emperor Charles IV in 1368 and the Byzantine emperor John V Palaeologus in 1369. The Byzantine ruler had come to seek western help to fight off the Ottoman Turks. In exchange for John's agreement to submit to Rome's spiritual authority and his promise to end the schism between the Catholic and Greek Orthodox churches, Urban called for a crusade to the East. But war broke out again between England and France, and Urban needed peace in the West as a prerequisite for the crusade. To conduct his diplomacy, Urban returned to Avignon, but he died before achieving anything.

By the second half of the fourteenth century the Avignon papacy had taken on a definitive French character. All five popes elected between 1305 and 1378 were natives of southern France, as were many of the cardinals and most of the *curia*. Moreover, French parishes provided half of the papacy's income. Nonetheless, Gregory XI, elected to the pontificate in 1371, was determined to return to Rome, where he expected to exert greater moral force to organize a crusade against the Muslim Ottomans. Before he could carry out his plans, however, Florence declared war against the Papal

States in 1375, and Gregory hastened to Rome to prevent the collapse of his territorial power in Italy.

Gregory died in 1378. Sixteen cardinals—one Spanish, four Italian, and eleven French—met in Rome to elect the new pope. Although many in the *curia* were homesick for Avignon, the Roman people, determined to keep the papacy and its revenues in Rome, clamored for the election of a Roman. An unruly crowd rioted outside the conclave, drowning out the cardinals' discussions. Fearing for their lives, the cardinals hurriedly elected the archbishop of Bari, an Italian, who took the title of Urban VI. If the cardinals thought they had elected a weak man who would both do their bidding and satisfy the Romans, Urban's immediate attempt to curb the cardinals' power dispelled any such illusions. Thirteen cardinals retired to Anagni, elected Clement VII, and returned to Avignon.

Thus began the Great Schism that political divisions in Europe perpetuated. Charles V of France, who did not want the papacy to return to Rome, immediately recognized Clement, his cousin, as did the rulers of Sicily, Scotland, Castile, Aragon, Navarre, Portugal, Ireland, and Savoy. One of the enemies of Charles V, Richard II of England, professed allegiance to Urban and was followed by the rulers of Flanders, Poland, Hungary, most of Germany, and central and northern Italy. Faithful Christians were equally divided in their loyalties. Catherine of Siena (1347–1380), a famous religious woman, and Vincent Ferrer (1350–1419), a popular Dominican preacher, supported Urban and Clement, respectively. All Christians theoretically found themselves deprived of the means of salvation, as bans from Rome and Avignon each placed a part of Christian Europe under interdict forbidding the performance of sacraments. Because neither pope would step down willingly, the leading intellectuals in the church tried to end the schism.

Religious Schism

The Conciliar Movement

According to canon law, only a pope could summon a general council of the church. But given the state of confusion in Christendom, many intellectuals argued that the crisis justified calling a general council to represent the body of the faithful, over and against the head of the church. Jean Gerson, chancellor of the University of Paris, spoke for all the conciliarists when he asserted that "the pope can be removed by a general council celebrated without his consent and against his will." He justified his claim by reasoning that "normally a council is not legally . . . celebrated without papal calling. . . . But, as in grammar and in morals, general rules have exceptions. . . . Because of these exceptions a superior law has been ordained to interpret the law."

The first attempt to resolve the question of church authority came in 1409, at the Council of Pisa, attended by cardinals who had defected from the two popes. The council asserted its supremacy by declaring both popes deposed and electing a new pontiff. When the popes at Rome and Avignon refused to yield, Christian Europe found itself in the embarrassing position of choosing among three popes. Pressure to hold another council then came from central Europe, where a new heretical movement, ultimately known as Hussitism, undermined orthodoxy from Bohemia to central Germany. Threatened politically by challenges to church authority, Emperor Sigismund pressed the Pisan pope John XXIII to convene a church council at Constance in 1414.

The cardinals, bishops, and theologians assembled in Constance felt compelled to combat heresy, heal the schism, and reform the church. They ordered Jan Hus, the Prague professor and inspiration behind the Bohemian movement, burned at the stake in spite of an imperial safe conduct he had been promised, but this act failed to suppress dissent. They deposed John XXIII because of tyrannical behavior, condemning him as an antipope. The Roman pope, Gregory, accepted the council's authority and resigned in 1415. At its closing in 1417 the council also deposed Benedict XIII, the "Spanish mule," who refused to abdicate the Avignon papacy and lived out his life in a fortress in Spain, still regarding himself as pope and surrounded by his own *curia*. The rest of Christendom, however, hailed Martin V as the new pope. The council had taken a stand against heresy and had achieved unity under one pope.

Church reform, however, would have to wait. The council could not agree on a system under which the pope would share power with a church council, and the Council of Constance was too large and cumbersome to facilitate reform, even though delegates from various states convened and voted together. The delegates did declare the supremacy of general councils and attempted to ensure continuity in conciliar government by directing the church to call new councils periodically. But the powerful prelates who dominated the three years of meetings at Constance were unwilling to limit their own privileges or to accept the laity as equals in matters of salvation.

Critics of Papal Power

1320 Dissidents from the Franciscan Order, known in Italy as the Fraticelli, attack papal wealth

1324 Marsilius of Padua, a legal scholar, denies the legitimacy of papal supremacy in *Defender of the Peace*

1328 Pope John XXII imprisons the English Franciscan and philosopher William of Ockham for criticizing papal power

1378 John Wycliffe advances the view that the true church is a community of believers rather than a clerical hierarchy in *On the Church*

1414 Wycliffe's followers, called Lollards, rebel in England

1415 The Council of Constance condemns two Prague professors, Jan Hus and Jerome of Prague, for criticizing papal and clerical privileges

1436 Radical followers of Hus, known as Taborites, suffer defeat in their attempt to create a Christian community in Bohemia free from papal authority

Dissenters and Heretics

Religious conflict in the later Middle Ages took a variety of forms. The dissatisfaction manifested as squabbling within the papacy, but perhaps more significantly as opposition to the papacy and religious expression outside the official church and even political dissent and social unrest.

After the great struggle in 1317 and 1318 between the papacy and the Franciscan Spirituals, who advocated apostolic poverty and rejected the wealth of the church, their remnants sought protection in central and southern Italy, where they came to be called the Fraticelli. Many civic and village authorities tolerated the Fraticelli because the lower classes sympathized with them, admiring their vows of evangelical poverty, and because they opposed the pope, whom they identified as the Antichrist, echoing the views of many poorer Italians. The cloth workers residing in the poorer districts of Florence supported them. During the crisis of the 1370s the Fraticelli were among the voices preaching antipapal rhetoric. Because the Italian city-states curbed the Inquisition's power, few Fraticelli were tried for heresy. The movement's gradual decline after 1400 removed the threat of their contributing to any further social unrest.

Unlike the Fraticelli, the Free Spirits did not oppose the pope, yet the church still labeled them heretics.The Free Spirits practiced an extreme form of mysticism. They asserted that humans and God were of the same essence and that individual believers could attain salvation, even sanctity, without the church and its sacraments. In the fourteenth century the Free Spirits found supporters among the Beguines, pious lay women who lived together, and the Beghards, men who did not belong to a particular religious order but who led pious lives by begging for their sustenance. Living in community houses (beguinages), the Beguines imitated the convent lives of nuns but did not submit to clerical control. First prevalent in northern Europe, beguinages sprang up rapidly in the Low Countries and the Rhineland, regions of heavy urbanization. This essentially urban development represented the desire by large segments of society to achieve salvation through piety and good works, as many began to feel that the clergy did not adequately address their spiritual needs.

For the church the discovery of Free Spirits among the Beghards and Beguines raised the larger question of ecclesiastical control, for this development threatened to eliminate the boundary between the laity and the clergy. In the 1360s, Emperor

Charles IV and Pope Urban V extended the Inquisition to Germany in a move to crush this heresy. In the cities of the Rhineland, fifteen mass trials took place between 1320 and 1430, most around the turn of the century. Through condemnations and the subjection of beguinages under the mendicant orders, the church contained potential dissent. Throughout the fifteenth century the number of beguinages continued to drop.

Intellectual dissent, social unrest, and nationalist sentiment combined to create a powerful anticlerical movement in England that became known as Lollardy. John Wycliffe (c. 1330–1384), who inspired the movement, was an Oxford professor. Initially employed as a royal apologist in the struggle between state and church, Wycliffe gradually developed ideas that challenged the very foundations of the Roman church. His treatise *On the Church,* composed in 1378, advanced the view that the true church was a community of believers rather than a clerical hierarchy. In other writings, Wycliffe repudiated monasticism, excommunication, the Mass, and the priesthood, substituting reliance on Bible reading and individual conscience in place of the official church as the path to salvation. Responsibility for church reform, Wycliffe believed, rested with the king, whose authority exceeded that of the pope.

Not only did Wycliffe gather around him like-minded intellectuals at Oxford, but he also influenced and reflected a widespread anticlericalism in late medieval England. Wycliffe actively promoted the use of English in religious writing. He and his disciples attempted to translate the Bible into English and to popularize its reading throughout all ranks of society, although he died before completing the project. His supporters included members of the gentry, but most were artisans and other humbler urban people who had some literacy. The church hierarchy called them Lollards (from *lollar,* meaning "idler"). Religious dissent was key in motivating the 1381 peasant uprising, and the radical preacher John Ball was only one of many common priests who supported the revolt. Real income for parish priests had fallen steadily after the Black Death. The sympathy of these impoverished clergy lay with the common folk against the great bishops, abbots, and lords of the realm.

Wycliffe had powerful protectors, foremost among them John of Gaunt, duke of Lancaster and brother of King Edward III. After Wycliffe's death, however, the English bishops quickly suppressed intellectual dissent at Oxford. In 1401, Parliament passed a statute to prosecute heretics. The only Lollard revolt occurred when John Oldcastle, a knight inspired by Wycliffe's ideas, plotted an assault on London. It was suppressed in 1414. But in spite of persistent persecutions, Lollardy survived underground during the fifteenth century and resurfaced during the Reformation.

The Hussite Revolution

In Bohemia religious dissent became a vehicle for social and political revolutions and the most fundamental manifestation of the crisis of the Later Middle Ages. In the Hussite revolt, nationalist, religious, and social dissenters challenged the very legitimacy of the Christian order in Europe.

Under Emperor Charles IV the pace of economic development and social change in the Holy Roman Empire quickened. Prague, the capital, became one of Europe's great cities: the new silver mine at Kutná Hora boosted its economic growth, and the first university in the empire was founded there in 1348. Many German merchants and artisans migrated to Bohemian cities, and many Czech peasants, uprooted from the land, flocked to the cities in search of employment. The hard times of the later fourteenth century turned this diverse society into a potentially explosive mass when heightened expectations of commercial and intellectual growth collided with the grim realities of plague and economic problems. Tax protests, urban riots, and ethnic conflicts signaled growing unrest, but it was religious discontent that became the focus for popular revolt.

Critics of the clergy, often clergy themselves, decried the moral conduct of priests and prelates who held multiple benefices, led dissolute lives, and ignored their pastoral duties. Living in a state of mortal sin, many argued, how could the clergy legitimately perform the sacraments? Advocating greater lay participation in the Mass and in the reading of Scripture, religious dissenters drew some of their ideas from the writings of Wycliffe, whose work was introduced following the marriage of the Bohemian princess Anna to Richard II of England in 1383. Among those influenced by Wycliffe's ideas were Jan Hus and his follower, Jerome of Prague, both Prague professors, ethnic Czechs, and leaders of a reform party in Bohemia. Although

Jan Hus at the Stake
Wearing the humiliating garb traditional on such occasions (including a cap with dancing devils), Hus is about to be burned. News of his execution touched off a religious and nationalist uprising in Bohemia. To this day Jan Hus is revered by the Czech people as a national hero.

the reform party attracted adherents from all social groups among Czech speakers, the German minority, who dominated the university and urban elites in Prague, opposed it because of ethnic rivalry. The Bohemian nobility protected Hus; the common clergy were rebelling against the bishops; and the artisans and workers in Prague were ready to back the reform party by force. Their disparate social interests all focused on one symbolic but passionately felt demand: communion in both bread and wine (*utraque* in Latin, meaning "both") at Mass. In traditional Roman liturgy the chalice was reserved for the clergy; the Utraquists, as their opponents called them, also wanted to drink from the chalice, showing a measure of equality between laity and clergy.

Despite a guarantee of safety from Emperor Sigismund of the Holy Roman Empire, Hus was burned at the stake while attending the Council of Constance. Jerome of Prague also died at the stake. Hus's death caused a national uproar, and the reform movement, focusing thus far on religious issues, burst forth as the Hussite revolution with two main streams: the radical Taborites and the more moderate Prague Hussites. In Prague the moderate faction triumphed over the radicals. With the nobility and the merchant community as its backbone, the Prague Hussites became the party of tradition and order. They wanted to reform the church but not to subvert the secular social hierarchy. Many nobles supported the Hussite cause as an excuse to seize church properties and had no intention of yielding to the radicals' egalitarian demands. Prepared for a dialogue with Sigismund and the papacy, the Prague Hussites instead faced an escalating conflict between the Taborites and the emperor in the provinces.

Sigismund's initial repression in the provinces was brutal, and many dissenters were massacred. To organize their defense, Hussites gathered at a mountain in southern Bohemia, which they called Mt. Tabor after the mountain in the New Testament where the transfiguration of Christ took place. These Taborites began to restructure their community according to the Bible. Like the first Christian church, they initially practiced communal ownership of goods and thought of themselves as the only true Christians awaiting the return of Christ and the end of the world. As their influence spread the Taborites compromised with the surrounding social order, collecting tithes from peasants and retaining magistrates in towns under their control. The leaders among the Taborites were radical priests, who ministered to the godly community in Czech, exercised moral and judicial leadership, and even led the people into battle. One famous Taborite was the general Procop the Shaven (so named because he was clean shaven even though most Taborite priests usually wore beards.).

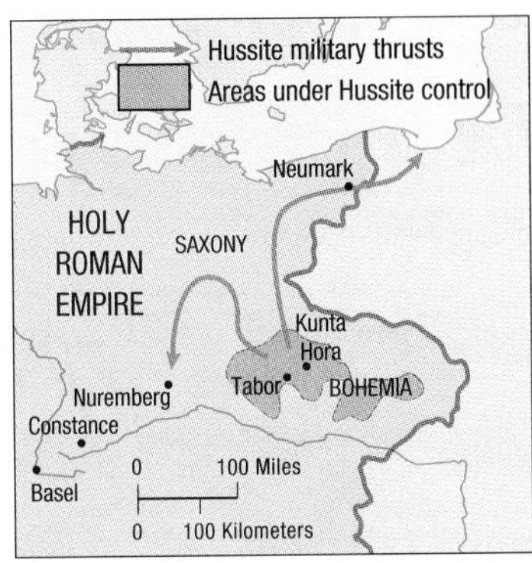

The Hussite Revolution

Modeling themselves after the Israelites of the Old Testament and the first Christians of the New Testament, the Taborites impressed even their enemies. Aeneas Sylvius Piccolomini, the future Pope Pius II (✱1458–1464), observed that "among the Taborites you will hardly find a woman who cannot demonstrate familiarity with the Old and New Testaments." The Taborite army, drawn from many social classes and led by priests, repelled five attacks by the "crusader" armies from neighboring

Germany, triumphing over their enemies using a mixture of religious fervor and military technology, such as a wagon train to protect the infantry from cavalry charges. They would not be defeated until 1436, and then only by the combined forces of the Hussites and royalists, who were eager for a compromise with Rome. By suppressing the more radical revolution of the Taborites, the Bohemians in turn retained the right to receive communion in both bread and wine until the sixteenth century.

Disintegration of the Political Order

The crises of the fourteenth century affected political allegiances as well as social and religious tensions. Just as many people no longer blindly accepted the church's dictates, so did citizens refuse to trust the politicians in power to serve the ordinary person's best interests. The ideology of Christian solidarity, always stronger in theory than in practice, dissolved in the face of national rivalries, urban and rural revolts, and the military resurgence of the Muslims. The conflict between the English and the French that came to be called the Hundred Years' War destroyed the lives of countless thousands of noncombatants as well as soldiers. Commoners—town residents and peasants—challenged the political status quo, wanting a share of the power their rulers wielded over them or at least a say in how they were governed. The Ottoman Turks battled Christian Europe in a bloody jihad (Holy War), reclaiming the land westerners had conquered in the Crusades in West Asia (now the Middle East). The political crises of the Late Middle Ages shaped the pattern of conflicts for the next two hundred years.

From Knights to Mercenaries

Although the nobility continued to dominate European society in the Late Middle Ages, their social and political roles gradually but fundamentally transformed. Even though the nobility encompassed a wide range of people, from great magnates whose power and wealth rivaled kings to humble knights who lived much like peasants, two developments in the later Middle Ages affected all of them: the agrarian crisis and the changing nature of warfare.

The nobles had traditionally been defined as the warrior class and supported by the profits from the land they owned. In the wake of the Black Death, their income from their land dwindled as food prices declined. Forced to seek additional revenues, knights turned enthusiastically to war. The extended Anglo-French conflict of this time largely reflected an English nobility addicted to the glory and profit of war. Noblemen from many nations served willingly in foreign campaigns, forming units at their own expense, motivated solely by material gain. The English knight John Hawkwood put it best: "Do you not know that I live by war and peace would be my undoing?" Captain of an army that sold its services to various Italian states vying for power, Hawkwood represented the new soldier: the mercenary who lived a life of violence and whose loyalty was given to the side that paid the most. Led by noble captains, these mercenary bands terrorized France for most of the Hundred Years' War, which devastated France from 1337 to 1453. During interludes of peace, they earned money fighting in Castile.

As if to compensate for the cynical reality of mercenary warfare, the European nobility emphasized the traditional knightly ethos in an effort to rationalize their authority by appealing to moral and aesthetic values. Arthurian romances became a vogue, not only in reading but also in life. Edward III of England, for example, created the Order of the Garter in 1344 to revive the ideal of chivalry. During truces, English and French knights jousted, glorifying mock combat according to the rules of chivalry. According to the chronicler Jean Froissart, English and French knights scorned their German counterparts for failing to follow the rules of war and observe the rituals that masked the exercise of violence and power.

Yet chivalric combat waged by knights on horseback was quickly yielding to new military realities. By the last decades of the fourteenth century, cannons were common in European warfare. New military technologies—firearms, siege equipment, and fortifications, for example—undermined the nobility's preeminence as a fighting force. A full war chest, which meant a well-equipped fighting force, counted more than valor and often determined the outcome of battles. The nobles were forced to become entrepreneurs to maintain their social eminence, be it as military captains or

A joust
Evolving out of the practice bouts that knights used to keep in fighting trim, by the late Middle Ages the joust had become a stylized show mounted before courtiers and townspeople on special occasions. Many knights were virtual professional athletes, working a regular circuit of jousts at which they competed for rich purses.

estate managers. Many turned to state service to reinforce their social stations. By appointing nobles to the royal household, as military commanders and councilors, kings and princes could further consolidate the power of emerging states.

The Hundred Years' War

The Hundred Years' War had no single political or diplomatic cause, although warring monarchs claiming preeminence for their dynasties provided a justification. A protracted struggle in western Europe that involved the nobility of almost every nation, the war was sparked by conflicting French and English interests in Aquitaine in southwestern France. As part of the French royal policy of centralizing jurisdiction, in 1337, Philip VI of France confiscated Aquitaine, which had been held by the English monarchs as a fief of the French crown. To recover his lands, Edward III of England, the only surviving male heir of Philip the Fair, laid claim to the French throne.

Elaborate chivalric behavior, savage brutality, and unabashed profiteering permeated the Hundred Years' War. One episode at the battle of Crécy (1346), recounted by the chronicler Froissart, illustrates both the grandeur and the futility of chivalric combat. John of Luxembourg, the king of Bohemia, took the French side, and although he was old and blind he insisted that his vassals guide him into battle "so that he could strike one blow with his sword"; he and his attendants were all killed, falling side by side on the battlefield. Warfare in this era involved defined rules whose application depended on social status. English and French knights took one another prisoner and showed all the formal courtesy required by chivalry—but they slaughtered captured common soldiers like cattle. Overall the pattern of war was not pitched battles but a series of raids in which English fighters plundered cities and villages, causing terrible destruction. English knights financed their own campaigns, and war was expected to turn a profit, either in captured booty or in ransom paid to free noble prisoners of war. As the conflict dragged on, English and Gascon (Gascony, a province in southwestern France controlled by the English crown) warriors formed their own armies that plundered and terrorized the countryside or sold their services to some faction of the French nobility.

Historians divide the Hundred Years' War into three periods: the first marked by English triumphs, the second in which France slowly gained the upper hand, and the third ending in the English expulsion from France.

In the first period, from 1338 to 1360, the English won several famous victories such as Crécy, in which the vastly outnumbered English knights and longbowmen routed the French cavalry. In another victory at Poitiers (1356), Edward the Black Prince (heir to the English throne, named for his black armor) defeated a superior French army and captured the French king John and a host of important noblemen, whom they ransomed for hefty sums. Divided and demoralized, the French signed the peace treaty of Brétigny in 1360, ceding vast territories in the southwest to England.

The second phase of the war lasted from 1361 to 1413. Taking advantage of the Black Prince's death and Edward III's failing health, the French, commanded by Bertrand du Guesclin, the constable of France, chipped away at the English conquests. In Charles V (∗1364–1380) and his brother, Philip the Bold (the duke of Burgundy, ∗1364–1404), the French finally found energetic leaders who could

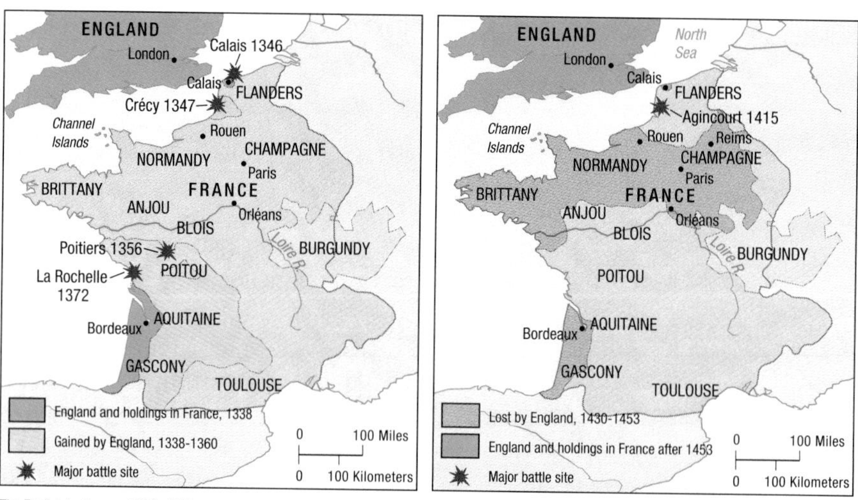

The Hundred Years' War

The English in France, 1338–1360

The English in France, 1413–1453

resist the English. In 1372, aided by a Castilian fleet, a French force took La Rochelle, long an English stronghold in Gascony. In 1386, in the aftermath of a peasant revolt in England, the French even assembled a fleet to conquer England. Although unsuccessful in landing an army, the French raided English ports into the early fifteenth century.

At the turn of the century a new set of players entered the political stage. In 1399 the English noble Henry Bolingbroke forced Richard II (grandson of Edward III) to abdicate. The coup made Bolingbroke Henry IV of England (∗1399–1413), whose story was later made famous (and much distorted) by Shakespeare's plays. Factional strife poisoned French political unity. The struggle for power began in 1392 after Charles VI (∗1380–1422), called the Mad King of France, suffered his first bout of insanity. Two factions then began to coalesce—one around John of Burgundy (the son of Philip the Bold) and the other around the duke of Orléans. In 1407, Burgundian agents assassinated the duke, whose followers, called the Armagnacs, sought vengeance and plunged France into civil war. When both parties appealed for English support in 1413, the young King Henry V (∗1413–1422), who had just succeeded his father Henry IV, launched a full-scale invasion of France.

The third phase of the war (1413–1453) began when Henry V crushed the French at Agincourt (1415). Unlike the earlier battles of Crécy and Poitiers, however, this isolated victory achieved little in the long run. Three parties now struggled for domination. Henry occupied Normandy and claimed the French throne; the dauphin (heir apparent to the French throne), son of Charles VI and later Charles VII of France (∗1422–1461), ruled central France with the support of the Armagnacs; and the duke of Burgundy held a vast territory in the northeast that included the Low Countries. Burgundy was thus able to broker war or peace by shifting support first to the English and then to the French. English power reached its height under Henry VI (∗1422–1461) during the 1420s, when combined English and Burgundian rule extended over all of France north of the Loire. But the English could not establish firm control. In Normandy a savage guerrilla war harassed the English army. Driven from their villages by pillaging and murdering soldiers, the Norman peasants retreated into forests, formed armed bands, and attacked the English. The miseries of war inspired prophecies of miraculous salvation; among the predictions was the belief that a virgin would deliver France from the English invaders.

At the court of the dauphin, in 1429, a sixteen-year-old peasant girl presented herself and her vision to save France. Born in a village in Lorraine, Joan of Arc, *la Pucelle* (The Maid), as she always referred to herself, grew up in a war-ravaged country longing for divine deliverance. The young maid, guided by an inner voice, presented herself as God's messenger to the local noble, who was sufficiently

Joan of Arc at Orléans
Joan of Arc's career as a charismatic military leader was an extraordinary occurrence in fifteenth-century France. In this manuscript illumination Joan, in full armor, directs French soldiers as they besiege the English at Orléans. The victory she gained here stunned the French people.

impressed to equip Joan with horse, armor, and a retinue and to send her to the dauphin's court. (According to her later testimony, Joan ran away from home when her father threatened to drown her because she refused an arranged marriage.) Her hair cut short, dressed in armor and holding a sword, Joan of Arc's extraordinary appearance inspired the French to trust in divine providence and turn the tide. In 1430 she accompanied the French army that raised the siege of Orléans, was wounded, and showed great courage in battle. Upon her urging, the dauphin traveled deep into hostile Burgundian territory to be anointed King Charles VII of France at Reims cathedral, thus strengthening his legitimacy by the traditional ritual of coronation.

Yet as captain of her own company of troops, Joan's fortunes declined after Reims. She promised to capture Paris and attacked the city on the Feast of the Virgin Mary, thus violating one of the holiest religious feast days. After the Anglo-Burgundian defenders drove her back, the French began to lose faith in The Maid. When the Burgundians captured her in 1431 during a minor skirmish, Charles and his forces did little to save her. Still, Joan was a powerful heroic and divine symbol, and the English were determined to undermine her legitimacy. In a trial conducted by French theologians in Anglo-Burgundian service, Joan was accused of false prophecy, suspected of witchcraft because she wore male clothes and led armies, and tricked into recanting her prophetic mission. Almost immediately, however, she retracted her confessions, returned the female attire given her after an English soldier had raped her in prison, and reaffirmed her divine mission. The English then burned her at the stake as a relapsed heretic.

After Joan's death the English position crumbled when their alliance with the Burgundians fell apart in 1435. The duke of Burgundy recognized Charles VII as king of France, and Charles entered Paris in 1437. Skirmish by skirmish, the English were driven off French soil, retaining only the port of Calais when hostilities ceased in 1453. Two years later the French church rescinded the 1431 verdict that had condemned Joan of Arc as a heretic.

Popular Uprisings

English and French knights triumphed at the expense of the common people. French peasants and townsfolk were taxed, robbed, raped, and murdered by marauding bands. Their English counterparts had to pay ever higher taxes to support their kings'

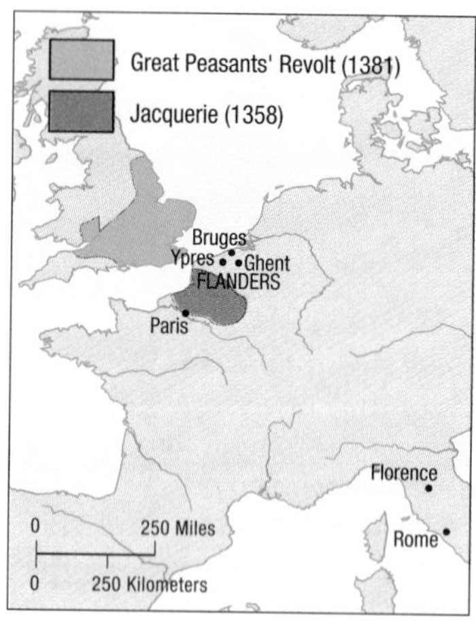

Popular Uprisings of the Late 1300s

wars. Popular uprisings, fueled by widespread resentment, now contributed to the general disintegration of political and social order. In 1358 a short but savage rebellion erupted in the area around Paris, shocking the nobility. And in 1381 a more widespread and broadly based revolt broke out in England. Although both rebellions were suppressed, rural and urban uprisings continued through the later Middle Ages, indicating the deep social conflicts that would reshape society.

Historians have traditionally described the 1358 Jacquerie, named after the jacket (*jacque*) worn by serfs, as a "peasant fury," implying that it represented simply a spontaneous outburst of aimless violence. More recent research, however, reveals the complex social origins of the movement. The revolt broke out after the capture of King John at the battle of Poitiers, when the Estates of France met to discuss monarchical reform and national defense. Unhappy with the heavy war taxes and the incompetence of the warrior nobility, the townspeople sought greater political influence under Étienne Marcel, the provost of the merchants of Paris. Through its merchants' and artisans' guilds, the Parisian commune (the citizens and government of Paris) now assumed a new political importance. In the absence of royal authority the common people vied with the nobles for control of government, and a clash between peasants and nobles near Paris lead to a massive uprising.

Long prey to arrogant and powerful noble lords, and lacking the protection of city walls, rural artisans, wealthy peasants, minor royal functionaries, and even a few rural priests joined the rebellion of townspeople, who began to destroy manor houses and castles near Paris, massacring entire noble families in a savage class war. Contemporaries were astonished at the intensity and violence of the Jacquerie. The chronicler Froissart, sympathetic to the nobility, reflected the views of the ruling class in describing the rebels as "small, dark, and very poorly armed." As for the violence, Froissart continues, "They thought that by such means they could destroy all the nobles and gentry in the world. . . ." Noble repression was even more savage, as thousands of rebels died in battles and were executed. In Paris the rebel leader Marcel was killed in factional strife, but urban rebellions continued into the fifteenth century.

In 1381 in England rural and urban discontent intensified as landlords, peasants, and workers pursued increasingly opposing interests. For the landowning class, composed of both ecclesiastical and secular lords, the Black Death and recurring plagues meant a steady erosion of income, as noble lords, forced to pay higher wages because of the labor shortage, also paid higher prices for goods. Most resorted to seigneurial rights and coercion to make up for the loss of income, either by restraining the free movement of labor or by levying fines on free tenants and serfs alike. For the lowest echelons in rural society, the serfs and agricultural workers, these new restrictions on their recently improved economic opportunities only deepened resentment. For the peasant elite, the free proprietors who man-

The English Peasant Uprising, 1381
In this manuscript illumination, depicting a much more orderly scene than must have been the reality, a host of rebellious peasants led by John Ball (on horseback) confronts troops gathered under the royal banners of England and St. George. Such confrontations, all too frequent in late-medieval and early modern Europe, always ended with the same result, as well-armed soldiers mowed down desperate village folk.

aged to acquire more land and increase their income, the new economic conditions gave them more confidence in challenging the lord's power. The renewed exercise of seigneurial authority combined with a novel sense of peasant power created the conditions for a general rural uprising.

The trigger for the English peasant revolt was the imposition of a poll tax passed by Parliament in 1377 to raise money for the war against France. Unlike traditional subsidies to the king, the poll tax was levied on everyone. In May 1381 a revolt broke out to protest these taxes to finance a war that benefited only the king and the nobility. Rebels in Essex and Kent joined bands in London who confronted the king. The famous couplet of the radical preacher John Ball, who was executed after the revolt, expressed the rebels' egalitarian, antinoble sentiment:

When Adam delved [dug] and Eve span
Who was then a gentleman?

Forced to confront the rebels, the young king Richard II agreed to abolish serfdom and impose a ceiling on land rent, concessions immediately rescinded after the rebels' defeat. The revolt spread to many parts of England before it was suppressed. Although a current of discontent survived in the religious dissent and egalitarian views of the Lollards, market forces quickly began to dominate the manorial economy, and villeinage effectively disappeared as landlords came to accept the forces of supply and demand. Free labor, land rents, and a market for goods would eventually be accepted ways of life in fifteenth-century England.

Urban Life and Insurrections

The German saying "City air makes you free" referred to serfs who fled bondage and gained their freedom after residing for a year and a day in towns that had their own charters of rights. For some, medieval cities were places of heady excitement and possibilities in the Later Middle Ages. But as the great social melting pots of the fourteenth century, cities experienced much turmoil, as war, plague, and related economic crises led to challenges to political authority. Ghent, Rome, and Florence reveal the different patterns of social conflicts.

In the middle of Flanders, the most densely populated and urbanized region of Europe, stood the great industrial city of Ghent. In 1350, after the plague, the population was sixty thousand, smaller only than Paris and London in Europe north of the Alps. For over a century, Flanders had been Europe's industrial and financial heartland, importing raw wool from England, manufacturing fine cloth in the Flemish cities, and exporting woolen goods to all parts of Europe. Bankers, money changers, and merchants from all nations congregated in Bruges, second in size and importance only to Ghent.

Because the region depended on trade for food and goods, Flanders was especially sensitive to the larger political and economic changes. Between 1323 and 1328, unrest spread from rural Flanders to Bruges and Ypres, as citizens refused to pay the tithe to the church and taxes to the count of Flanders. Later the Hundred Years' War undermined the woolen industry as Edward III of England declared a trade embargo, thus halting shipments of raw materials to Flemish industries. Although Flanders was a French fief, weavers and other artisans opposed their count's pro-French policy. From 1338 to 1345, under the leadership of Jacques van Arteveld, the burghers (citizens) of Ghent rebelled against their prince. In the revolutionary years of 1377 through 1383, the townspeople of Ghent sought an alliance with the commune of Paris, fielded an army to battle the count, and held out into the fifteenth century despite their disastrous defeat by the French army at Roosebeke in 1382. Thus the urban insurrections in Flanders became part of the economic and political struggles of the Hundred Years' War. The English Channel became a pirate's lair, as English and French sailors plundered merchant ships and raided coastal ports.

In Italy revolts in Rome and Florence resulted in part from the long absence of the popes during the Avignon papacy. Factional violence between powerful noble clans in Rome fueled popular hatred of local magnates and provided the background for the dramatic episode of the Roman commune. The Florentine chronicler Giovanni Villani narrates that "on May 20, 1347 . . . a certain Cola di Rienzo had just returned to Rome from a mission on behalf of the Roman people to the court of the Pope, to beg him to come and live, with his court, in the see of St. Peter, as he should do." Although unsuccessful in his mission to Avignon, Rienzo so impressed the Romans with his speech that they proclaimed him "tribune of the people," a title harking back to the plebians' representatives in the ancient

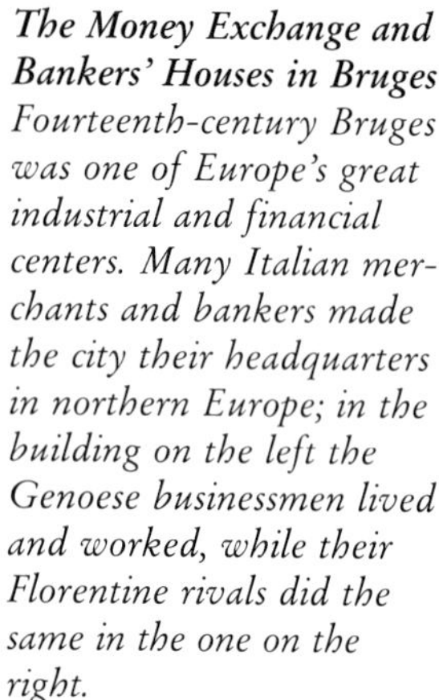
The Money Exchange and Bankers' Houses in Bruges *Fourteenth-century Bruges was one of Europe's great industrial and financial centers. Many Italian merchants and bankers made the city their headquarters in northern Europe; in the building on the left the Genoese businessmen lived and worked, while their Florentine rivals did the same in the one on the right.*

Roman Republic. "Certain of the Orsini and the Colonna," continues Villani, "as well as other nobles, fled from the city to their lands and castles to escape the fury of the tribune and the people."

Son of an innkeeper and orphaned early in life, Rienzo (1313–1354) became a notary. Inspired by his reading of ancient Roman history, Rienzo and his followers took advantage of the nobles' flight and tried to remake their city in the image of classical Roman republicanism. In their efforts to achieve social equality they pursued an antinoble campaign. Rienzo also invented elaborate civic rituals to honor the commune, thereby elevating the body of citizens, with himself as their leader, to equal status with the emperor and the pope. Noble plottings and Rienzo's own extravagant schemes eventually caused his downfall, and although he briefly returned to power in 1354, he was soon assassinated. The Roman commune, however, represented more than a passing episode; its historical models and inspirations were the ancient Roman Republic and contemporary Franciscan ideas of divine justice and social equality. These twin themes of classical antiquity and religious devotion would represent European ideals during the next two centuries.

Economic and political dissatisfaction also spurred revolt in Florence, the center of banking and the woolen industry in southern Europe and one of the largest European cities in the fourteenth century. There the large population of woolworkers depended on the wool merchants, who controlled both the supply of raw material and the marketing of finished cloth. Unlike artisans in other trades, woolworkers were prohibited from forming their own guild and thus constituted a politically unrepresented wage-earning working class. As the wool industry declined in the wake of the plague and falling demand, unemployment became an explosive social problem. During the summer of 1378, the lower classes, many of them woolworkers, rose against the regime, demanding a more egalitarian social order. The immediate cause of the uprising was the war against the papacy, called the War of the Eight Saints (1375–1378) after the eight magistrates who directed Florentine foreign policy, and popular dissatisfaction with their performance galvanized broad opposition to the government. A coalition of artisans and merchants, supported by woolworkers, demanded more equitable power sharing with the bankers and wealthy merchants who controlled city government. By midsummer, crowds thronged the streets; citizens paralyzed the government; and woolworkers set fire to the palaces of the rich and demanded the right to form their own guild. The insurrection was subsequently called the Ciompi rebellion, meaning the uprising by the "little people." Alarmed by the radical turn of events, the guild artisans turned against their worker allies and defeated them in fierce street battles. The revolt ended with a restoration of the patrician regime, although Ciompi exiles continued to plot worker revolts into the 1380s.

The Ciompi rebellion, like the uprisings in Rome and Flanders, signaled a pattern of change in late medieval Europe. Although they represented a continuation of the communal uprisings of the eleventh and twelfth centuries, which helped establish town governments in some parts of Europe, the primary causes were the disruptions of the Black Death and the subsequent economic depression. Seeking to establish a more egalitarian regime, the Ciompi espoused some of the antipapal notions of the Fraticelli. But as significant as their motivations was their failure. Urban revolts did not redraw the political map of Europe, nor did they significantly alter the distribution of power. Instead they were subsumed by larger political transformations from which the territorial states would emerge as the major political forces.

Fragmentation and Power Amid Changing Forces

During the fourteenth century, central Europe established institutional forms that lasted, with minor variations, until the Holy Roman Empire dissolved in the early nineteenth century. The four most significant developments were the shift of political focus from the South and West to the East, the changing balance of power between the emperor and the princes, the development of cities, and the rise of self-governing communes in the Alps.

Three of the five German kings in this period belonged to the House of Luxembourg: Charles IV (*1347–1378), Wenceslas (*1378–1400), and Sigismund (*1410–1437). Having obtained Bohemia by marriage, the Luxembourg dynasty based its power in the East, and Prague became the imperial capital. This change accelerated social and religious ferment within Bohemia, leading to the Hussite revolution in the early fifteenth century. From the standpoint of the Holy Roman Empire, the Luxembourgs' basing themselves in Bohemia initiated a shift of power within the empire, away from the Rhineland and Swabia toward east central Europe. This trend would be consolidated when an unbroken series of Austrian Habsburgs were elected emperor after 1440. Except for a continuous involvement with northern Italy, theoretically a part of the Holy Roman Empire, German institutions became more closely allied with eastern rather than western Europe. For example, the Holy Roman Empire's first university, named the Charles University after its royal founder, Charles IV, was at Prague. Bohemians and Hungarians also began to exert more influence in imperial politics.

Another development that separated Germany from western Europe was the fragmentation of political authority at a time when French, English, and Castilian monarchs were consolidating their power. For Charles IV, even his coronation as emperor in 1355 did not translate into more power at home. The Bohemian nobility still refused to recognize his supreme authority, and the German princes secured from him a constitutional guarantee for their own sovereignty. In 1356, Charles had to agree to the Golden Bull, which required the German king to be chosen by seven electors: the archbishops of Mainz, Cologne, and Trier; and four princes, including the king of Bohemia, the elector of Saxony, the count of the Palatinate, and the margrave of Brandenburg. The imperial electoral college also guaranteed the existence of numerous local and regional power centers, a distinctive feature in German history into the modern age.

Although no single German city rivaled Paris, London, Florence, or Ghent in population, urban communes made Germany the economic equal of northern Italy and the Low Countries. But powerful princes prevented the urban communes from evolving into city republics like those in Italy. In 1388, for example, the count of Württemberg defeated the Swabian League of cities, formed in 1376. Nevertheless, the cities were at the forefront of economic growth. In the great imperial cities of southern Germany, subject only to the emperor and represented at the Imperial Diet (a periodic meeting of the leading princes, nobles, and city representatives of the Holy Roman Empire), the leading patrician mercantile families had a voice in imperial politics. Nuremberg and Augsburg became centers of the north-south trade, linking Poland, Bohemia, and the German lands with the Mediterranean. During the fifteenth century, German

Central and Eastern Europe in the Thirteenth and Fourteenth Centuries

burghers would overtake their Italian counterparts in finance and the production of handicraft. In northern Germany the Hanseatic League, under the leadership of Lübeck, united the many towns trading between the Baltic and the North Sea. At its zenith in the fifteenth century, the Hanseatic fleet controlled the Baltic, and the league was a power to be reckoned with by kings and princes.

Another sign of political fragmentation was the growth of self-governing peasant and town communes in the high Alpine valleys that became the Swiss Confederation. In 1291 the peasants of Uri, Schwyz, and Unterwalden had sworn a perpetual alliance against their Habsburg overlord. After defeating a Habsburg army in 1315, these free peasants took the name of "Confederates" and developed a new alliance that would become Switzerland. By 1353, Luzerne, Zurich, Glarus, Zug, and Bern had joined the confederation. Its recognition in 1415 by Emperor Sigismund established the new entity as a polity, unique in its rejection of noble lordship. The Swiss Confederation grew into the sixteenth century, defeating armies sent by different princes to undermine its liberties.

Two large monarchies took shape in northeastern Europe. In the early twelfth century, Poland had splintered into petty duchies, and the Mongol invasion of the 1240s caused frightful devastation. But recovery was under way by 1300, and unlike almost every other part of Europe, Poland experienced an era of demographic and economic expansion in the fourteenth century. Both Jewish and German settlers, for example, helped build thriving towns like Cracow. Monarchical consolidation followed. King Casimir III (*1333–1370) won recognition in most of the country's regions for his royal authority, embodied in comprehensive law codes. A problem that persisted throughout his reign, however, was conflict with the neighboring princes of Lithuania—Europe's last pagan rulers, who for centuries fiercely resisted Christianization by the German crusading order, the Teutonic Knights, based in Prussia and Livonia (modern Latvia). After the Mongols overran Russia, Lithuania extended its rule southward, offering west Russian princes protection against Mongol and Muscovite rule. By the late fourteenth century a vast Lithuanian principality had arisen, embracing modern Lithuania, Belarus, and Ukraine. Casimir III's death in 1370 without a son and the failure of a new dynasty to take hold opened the way for the joining of Poland and Lithuania. In 1386 the Lithuanian prince Jogailo accepted Roman Catholic baptism, married the young queen of Poland, and later assumed the Polish crown. Under the Jagiellonian dynasty, Poland and Lithuania kept separate legal systems. Catholicism and Polish culture prevailed among the principality's upper class, although most native Lithuanian village folk remained pagan for several centuries. With only a few interruptions, the Polish-Lithuanian federation would last for five centuries. In 1410 it won a resounding victory over the Teutonic Knights, and by 1454 it regained from the crusaders direct access to the Baltic Sea at Danzig (today Gdansk).

Between Islam and Christianity

Two regions at opposite ends of the Mediterranean—Spain and Byzantium—were unusual in medieval Europe for their religious and ethnic diversity. As a result of the Spanish Reconquista of the twelfth and thirteenth centuries, the Iberian Christian kingdoms contained large religious and ethnic minorities. In Castile, where historians estimate the population before the plague at between 4 million and 5 million, some three hundred thousand inhabitants were Muslims and Jews. In Aragon, of the 1 million people in 1359, perhaps 3 percent to 4 percent belonged to these two religious minorities. In the Iberian peninsula the Christian kingdoms continued to consolidate their gains against Muslim Granada through internal colonization, bringing sizable minority populations into newly Christian regions. At the same time, the orthodox Byzantine Empire, hardly recovered from the Fourth Crusade, fought for its survival against the Ottoman Turks. In the Balkans and Anatolia, the Ottomans created a multiethnic state, but one different from the model of the Hispanic kingdoms.

In the mid-fourteenth century, the Iberian peninsula encompassed six areas: Portugal, Castile, Navarre, Aragon, and Catalonia—all Christian—and Muslim Granada. Among these territories, Castile and Aragon were the most important, both politically and economically. For example, the monarchy of Aragon, which included the prosperous seaport of Barcelona, enhanced its commercial domination of the western Mediterranean by expanding into Sicily and Sardinia. The Muslim population concentrated in the south: from the Algarve in Portugal, eastward across Andalusia and Murcia, to Valencia. As Christian conquerors and settlers advanced, most Muslims (called Moors) were driven out of the cities or if allowed to stay were confined to specific quarters. Initially, Muslims could own property, practice their religion, and elect their own judges, but conditions worsened for them in the fifteenth century as fears of rebellions and religious prejudices intensified among Christians. Many Muslims were captured by Christian armies and became slaves who worked in Christian households or on the large estates, the *latifundia*, granted by the Castilian kings to the crusading orders, the church, and powerful noble families. Slavery existed on a fairly large scale at both ends of the Mediterranean, where Christian and Muslim civilizations confronted one another: in Iberia, North Africa, Asia Minor, and the Balkans.

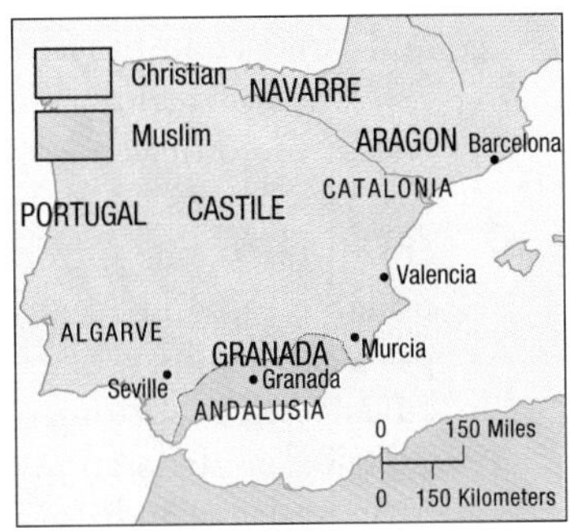

Christian Expansion in Iberia

Unlike the Muslims, Jews congregated exclusively in cities, where they practiced many urban professions. Prior to 1391 they encountered few social obstacles to advancement. Jewish physicians and tax collectors made up part of the administration of Castile, but the Christian populace resented their social prominence and wealth. Moreover, the religious fervor and sense of crisis in the later fourteenth century intensified the ever-present intolerance toward Jews. In June 1391, incited by the sermons of the priest Fernando Martínez, a mob attacked the Jewish community in Seville, plundering, burning, and killing all who refused baptism. The antisemitic violence spread to other cities in Andalusia, Castile, Valencia, Aragon, and Catalonia. Sometimes the authorities tried to protect the Jews, who were legally the king's property. In Barcelona the city government tried to suppress the mob until the riot became a popular revolt that threatened the rich and the clergy. About half of the two hundred thousand Castilian Jews converted to Christianity to save themselves; another twenty-five thousand were murdered or fled to Portugal and Granada. The survivors were to face even more discrimination and violence in the fifteenth century.

The fourteenth century also saw a great power rise at the other end of the Mediterranean. Under Osman I (1280–1324) and his son Orhan Gazi (1324–1359), the Ottoman dynasty became a formidable force in Anatolia and the Balkans, where political disunity opened the door for Ottoman advances. The Ottomans were one of several Turkish tribal confederations in central Asia. As converts to Sunni Islam and as warriors, the Ottoman cavalry raided Byzantine territory. In 1326, Orhan captured Bursa on the Marmara Sea, across from Constantinople, and two years later defeated a Byzantine army led by Emperor Andronicus III (✶1328–1341). In 1341 both contenders for the Byzantine imperial throne hoped to defeat the other with Ottoman aid; as payment they invited the swift Turkish cavalry to plunder Byzantine territory, thus opening Europe to Ottoman conquest.

Ottoman Expansion in the Balkans

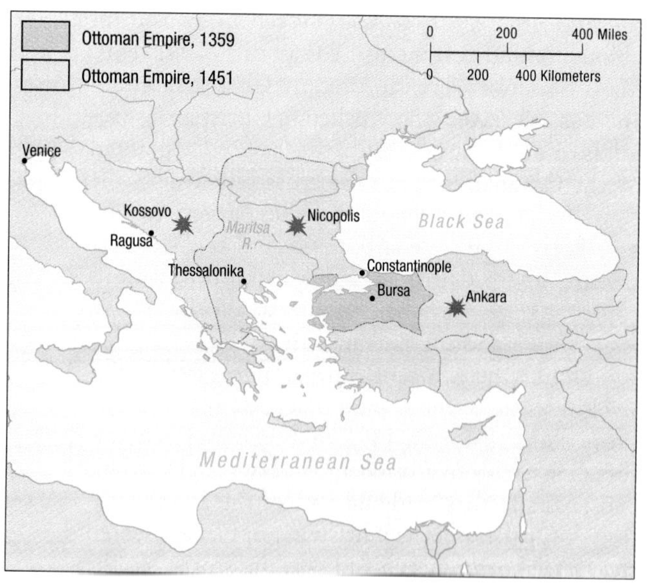

Under Murat I (✶1360–1389), the Ottomans reduced the Byzantine Empire to the city of Constantinople and the status of a vassal state. In 1364, Murat defeated a joint Hungarian-Serbian army at the Maritsa River, alerting Europe for the first time to the threat of an Islamic invasion. In 1366, Pope Urban V called for a crusade, but the Christian kingdoms in the West were already warring. In the Balkans the Ottomans skillfully exploited the political fragmentation to maintain their influence. Fortunately for the Ottomans, Serbian, Albanian, Wallachian, Bulgarian, and Byzantine interests rarely coincided. Moreover, Venice, Genoa, and Ragusa (today Dubrovnik in Croatia) each pursued separate commercial interests. The Latin principalities in Greece established after the Fourth Crusade were also disunified. Thus an Ottoman army allied with the Bulgarians and even some Serbian princes won the battle of Kossovo (1389), destroying the last organized Christian resistance south of the Danube. The Ottomans secured control of southeastern Europe after 1396, when they crushed a crusading army summoned by Pope Boniface IX and consisting of knights from many countries at Nicopolis.

It would be misleading to interpret the Ottoman invasion only as a continuation of the struggle between Christendom and Islam. The battle for territory transcended the boundaries of faith. Christian princes as vassals and Christian slave soldiers, the *Yeni Çeri,* or Janissaries (meaning the New Force, the Ottoman infantry), fought for the sultan against other Turkish princes in Anatolia. The Janissaries, Christian children the sultan raised as Muslims, constituted the fundamental support of the Ottomans. They formed a service class, the *devshirme,* which was both dependent on and loyal to the ruler.

At the sultan's court, Christian women were prominent in the harem; thus many Ottoman princes had Greek or Serbian mothers. In addition to the Janissaries, Christian princes and converts to Islam served in the emerging Ottoman administration. In areas conquered by the Ottomans, existing religious and social structures remained intact when local people accepted Ottoman suzerainty (overlordship) and paid taxes. Only in areas of persistent resistance did the Ottomans drive out or massacre the inhabitants, settling Turkish tribes in their place. A distinctive pattern of Balkan history was thus established at the beginning of the Ottoman conquest: the extreme diversity of ethnic and religious communities woven together in the fabric of an efficient central state.

By the mid-fourteenth century the territory of the Byzantine Empire consisted of only Constantinople, Thessalonika, and a narrow strip of land in modern-day Greece. Byzantium never recovered from the Fourth Crusade. During the fourteenth century, three civil wars (1321–1328, 1341–1347, 1376–1379) between rivals to the throne, the Black Death, and numerous Ottoman incursions devastated the land and the population. Constantinople was saved in 1402 from a five-year siege by the Ottomans when Mongol invaders crushed another Ottoman army near Ankara in Asia Minor. Although the empire's fortunes declined, Byzantium experienced a religious and cultural ferment, as the elites compensated for their loss of power in a search for past glory and asserted their cultural superiority as Greeks over the militarily stronger but to them culturally inferior Ottomans and Latins. The majority asserted the superiority of the Greek orthodox faith and opposed the reunion of the Roman and Greek churches, a political price for western European military aid. Still others adhered to tradition, attacking any departures from ancient literary models and Byzantine institutions. A handful, such as the scholar George Gemistos (1353–1452), abandoned Christianity and embraced Platonic philosophy. Gemistos even changed his name (meaning "full" in Greek) to Plethon, its classical equivalent, which sounds like the name of Plato (Platon in Greek). Only a minority, such as Demetrius Kydones (c. 1376), an imperial minister, urged people to learn from the strengths of the Latin West. The scholar Manuel Chrysoloras became professor of Greek in Florence in 1397, thus establishing the study of ancient Greece in western Europe.

Toward the Renaissance: The Social Order and Cultural Change

An abundance of written and visual records documenting the lives of all social groups has survived from the fourteenth century. Much of our knowledge of the period comes from the vernacular literature that transcended traditional linguistic and thematic boundaries. Sources ranging from chronicles of dynastic conflicts and noble chivalry to police records of criminality paint a vivid picture of late medieval society, showing the changed relations between town and country, noble and commoner, and men and women. These sources reveal the impact the crisis had on their lives, as Europeans struggled to adjust to uncertainties and changes related to the plague, war, and religious dissent. New material wealth allowed some to enjoy more prosperous lives, but the disruptions and dislocations caused by various crises forced many on the margins of society—the poor, beggars, and prostitutes—into a violent underworld of criminality.

As the Byzantines recovered their appreciation of Greek antiquity, so did Italians revive ancient Roman culture. This cultural movement focused initially on imitating classical Latin rhetoric, but it later extended to the other disciplines of the humanities, such as the study of history, and finally blossomed into a broad cultural movement. This movement, which inspired brilliant achievements in the visual arts and vernacular literature, came to be called the Renaissance (meaning "rebirth").

The Household

Family life and the household economy formed the fabric of late medieval society. In contrast to the nobility and great merchants, whose power rested on their lineages, most Europeans lived in a more confined social world, surrounded by kin and neighbors. The focus of their lives was the house, where parents and children, and occasionally a grandparent or other relative, lived together. This pattern generally characterized both urban and rural society. In some peasant societies, such as in

Languedoc (southern France), brothers and their families shared the same roof; but the nuclear family was by far the dominant social model.

Compared to the nobility, residing in castles, artisans and peasants lived modestly. For those of medium wealth the family dwelling usually consisted of a two- to three-story building in the city and a single farmhouse in the countryside. For these social groups the household usually served as both work and private space; shopkeepers and craftspeople used their ground floors as workshops and storefronts, reserving the upper stories for family life. By our standards late medieval urban life was intolerably crowded, with little privacy. Neighbors could easily spy on each other from adjoining windows or even come to blows, as did two Florentine neighbors who argued over the installation of a second-story latrine that emptied out on a neighbor's property. In rural areas the family house served a variety of productive purposes, not least to shelter the farm animals during the winter.

In a society with an unequal distribution of power between women and men, the worlds of commerce and agriculture were those in which women came closest to partnership with their husbands. As a consequence of the plague and labor shortages, women found themselves in relatively favorable working positions. In cities all over Europe, women worked in retail trade. They sold dairy products, foods, meat, cloth, salt, flour, and fish; brewed beer; spun and wove cloth; and often acted as their husband's informal business partner. Although excluded from many handicrafts and professions and barred from all but a few guilds, fourteenth-century women played a crucial role in the urban economy, especially when widowed. Experienced in their late husband's business, owners of valuable assets, they represented attractive marriage candidates for ambitious men. Daughters of guild artisans similarly influenced their husband's economic advancement. The degree to which women participated in public life, however, varied with class and region. Women in Mediterranean Europe, especially in upper-class families, lived more circumscribed lives than their counterparts in northern Europe. The former, for example, could not dispose of personal property without the consent of males, be they fathers, husbands, or grown sons, whereas the latter regularly represented themselves in legal transactions and testified in court. Partnership in marriage characterized the peasant household. True, men and women performed different tasks, such as plowing and spinning, but many chores required cooperation. During harvests, all hands were mobilized. The men usually reaped with sickles, while the women gleaned the fields. Viticulture (cultivating grapes for wine making) called for full cooperation between the sexes: both men and women worked equally in picking grapes and trampling them to make wine. Because the

June
Real farmwork in fourteenth-century France was never as genteel as in this miniature painting, part of a series illustrating the months of the year in a beautiful devotional book created for the duke of Berry. Nevertheless, the scene does faithfully represent the haying and suggests the gendered division of village labor, as the men swing their scythes and the women wield rakes.

February
As in all the miniatures in the duke of Berry's prayerbook, this cozy scene shows how the late-medieval nobility liked to imagine their peasants and livestock lived—both securely housed in warm and separate shelters, while the customary work of rural society goes on peacefully.

household constituted the basic unit of agricultural production, most partners remarried quickly after a spouse died. The incidence of households headed by a single person, usually a poor widow, was much lower in villages than in cities. Studies of court records for fourteenth-century English villages show relatively few reports of domestic violence, perhaps reflecting the economic dependency between the sexes. Violence against women was more visible in urban societies where many women worked as servants and prostitutes.

The improved material life of the middle classes was represented in many visual images of the Late Middle Ages. Italian and Flemish paintings of the late fourteenth and early fifteenth centuries depicted the new comforts of urban life such as fireplaces and private latrines. Painters developed an interest in material objects: beds, chests, rooms, curtains, and buildings provided the ubiquitous background of Italian paintings of the period. In rural areas the new prosperity could be seen in more elaborate farmhouses with greater differentiation between private and work space for the peasant elite. An illustration in *The Book of Hours* (1416), commissioned by the duke of Berry, brother of the French king, depicts a romanticized view of country life that might have characterized the peasant elite. Surrounded by a low fence, the compound includes the family house, a granary, and a shed. Animals and humans no longer intermingled, as they had in the thirteenth century and still did in poorer peasant households. The picture shows peasants warming themselves and drying their laundry in front of the fire, while the sheep are safe and warm in the shed.

The Underclasses

If family life and the household economy formed the fabric of late medieval society, the world of poverty and criminality represented its torn fringes. Indeed the boundary between poor and criminal was very thin. Fourteenth-century society resembled a pyramid, with a broad base of underclasses—poor peasants and laborers in the countryside, workers and servants in the cities. Still one level lower were the marginal elements of society, straddling the line between legality and criminality.

Women featured prominently in the underclasses, reflecting the unequal distribution of power between the sexes. In Mediterranean Europe some 90 percent of slaves were women in domestic servitude. Their actual numbers were small—several hundred in fourteenth-century Florence, for example—because only rich households could afford slaves. They came from Muslim or Greek Orthodox countries and usually served in upper-class households in the great commercial city republics of Venice, Florence, and Ragusa. Urban domestic service was also the major employment for girls from the countryside, who worked to save money

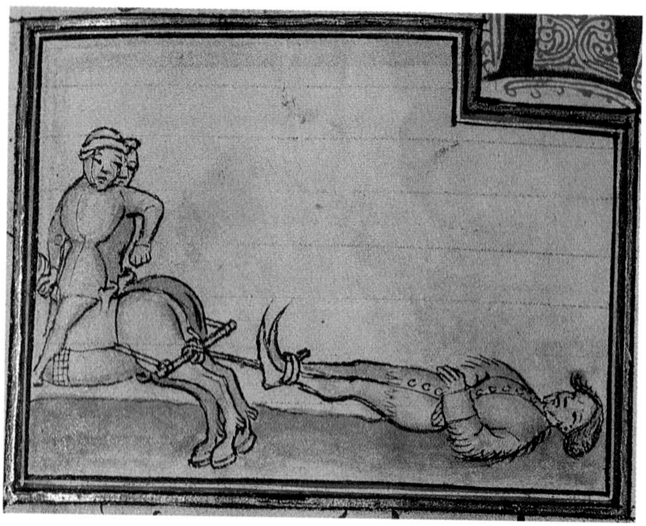

A Baron Tortured
This illumination, from a French chronicle, shows the torture meted out to a Gascon baron, Jordan de Lille, to punish his rebelliousness. Such degrading penalties (normal for ordinary transgressors) were occasionally inflicted on nobles to emphasize the gravity of their offenses.

for their dowries. In addition to the usual household chores, women also worked as wet nurses.

Given their exclusion from many professions and their powerlessness, many poor women found prostitution the only available means of living. Male violence forced many women into prostitution: rape stripped away their social respectability and any prospects for marriage. Condemned by the church, prostitutes were tolerated throughout the Middle Ages, but in the fourteenth and fifteenth centuries, the government intensified its attempts to control sexuality by institutionalizing prostitution. Restricted to particular quarters in cities, supervised by officials, sometimes under direct government management, prostitutes found themselves confined to brothels, increasingly controlled by males. In legalizing and controlling prostitution, officials aimed to maintain the public order. In Florence such state sponsorship provided a means to check homosexuality and concubinage. Female sexuality directed by the state in this way also helped define and limit the role of women in society at large. Although their legal status improved in the Late Middle Ages, prostitutes had only partial legal rights, similar to those of Jews, and were constantly subject to violence.

Men populated the violent criminal underworld. Organized gangs prowled the larger cities. In Paris, a city teeming with thieves, thugs, beggars, prostitutes, and vagabonds, the Hundred Years' War led to a sharp rise in crime. In 1389, for example, police officials tracked down a criminal ring, arresting many for highway robbery and murder. Gang members were mostly artisans who vacillated between work and crime. Sometimes disguised as clerics, they robbed, murdered, and extorted from prostitutes. Often they served as soldiers. War was no longer an occupation reserved for knights but had become a vocation that absorbed young men from poor backgrounds. Initiated into a life of plunder and killing, discharged soldiers adjusted poorly to civilian life; between wars, these men turned to crime.

A central feature of social marginality was mobility. Mostly young, lacking stable families, those on society's fringes wandered extensively, begging and stealing. Criminals were also found among the clergy. While some were lay men who assumed clerical disguises to escape the rigors of secular courts, others were bona fide clerics who turned to crime to make ends meet during an age of steadily declining clerical income. "Decent society" treated these marginal elements with suspicion and hatred. Townspeople and peasants distrusted travelers and vagabonds. During the later Middle Ages, attitudes against poverty hardened. New laws restricted vagabonds and begging clerics, although cities and guilds began building hospitals and almshouses to deal with these social problems.

Middle-Class Writers and the Birth of Humanism

From the epics and romances of the twelfth and thirteenth centuries, vernacular literature blossomed in the fourteenth. Poetry, stories, and chronicles composed in Italian, French, English, and other national languages helped articulate a new sense of aesthetics. No longer did Latin and the church culture dominate the intellectual life of Europe, and no longer were writers principally clerics or aristocrats.

The great writers of late medieval Europe were of bourgeois (urban middle-class) origins, from families that had done well in government or church service or in commercial enterprises. Unlike the troubadours, with their aristocratic backgrounds, the men and women who wrote vernacular literature in this age typically came from the cities, and their audience was the literate laity. Francesco Petrarch (1304–1374), "crowned" as the poet laureate of his age in Rome, was born in Arezzo, where his father, a notary, lived in political exile from Florence. His younger contemporary and friend, Giovanni Boccaccio (1313–1375), was also Florentine. Boccaccio's father worked for the Florentine banking firm of Bardi in Paris, where Boccaccio was born; for generations the family had been small landowners outside Florence. Geoffrey Chaucer (1340–1400?) was the first great vernacular poet of medieval England. His father was a wealthy wine merchant; Chaucer worked as a servant to the king and controller of customs in London. Even writers who celebrated the life of the nobility were children of commoners. Although born in Valenciennes to a family of moneylenders and merchants, Jean Froissart (1337–1410), whose chronicle vividly describes the events of the Hundred Years' War, was an ardent admirer of chivalry. Christine de Pizan (1365–1429), whose numerous works defended feminine honor against misogyny, was the daughter of a Venetian municipal counselor.

Life in all its facets found expression in the new vernacular literature, as writers told of love, greed, and salvation. In *Songs* (*Canzoniere*), Petrarch juxtaposes divine and carnal desires to create beautiful short poems, praising the beauty of his idealized love for Laura, a young Florentine woman he admired from afar, and the Virgin Mary; after Petrarch the sonnet became the standard form for love poetry. Boccaccio's *Decameron* popularized the short story, as the characters in this novella told sensual and bizarre tales in the shadow of the Black Death. These stories reflect the world of the Italian merchant, drawing on Boccaccio's own experiences in banking and commerce. Members of different social orders parade themselves in Chaucer's *Canterbury Tales,* journeying together on a pilgrimage. In colorful verse written in Middle English, Chaucer makes his world come alive. He describes a merchant on horseback: "A marchant was ther with a forked berd/ In mottelee, and hye on horse he sat/ up-on his heed a Flaundrish bever hat/ his botes clasped faire and fetisly. . . . For sothe he was a worthy man with-alle/ but sooth to seyn, I noot how men him calle." Chaucer also vividly portrayed other social classes—yeomen, London guildsmen, and minor officials. Whereas Chaucer created his characters from a middle-class urban society, Froissart, in *Chronicles,* idealized the world of knightly exploits and the castle, a world of glory and riches, where people are only vaguely aware of the misery of the poor.

Noble patronage was crucial to the growth of vernacular literature, a fact reflected in the careers of the most famous writers. Perhaps closest to the model of an independent man of letters, Petrarch nonetheless relied on powerful patrons at various times: his early career began at the papal court in Avignon, where his father worked as a notary; during the 1350s, he enjoyed the protection and patronage of the Visconti duke of Milan. For Boccaccio, who started out in the Neapolitan world of

Christine de Pizan Presents Her Book to Queen Isabella *Illustrations depicting an author ceremoniously kneeling to present a book to a patron were commonplace in the Late Middle Ages and Renaissance. Notice that this stylized scene depicts the exclusively female sphere of the queen of France and her ladies-in-waiting.*

commerce, the court of King Robert of Naples initiated him into the world of letters. Chaucer served in administrative posts and on many diplomatic missions, during which he met Petrarch and Boccaccio. Noble patronage shaped the literary creations of Froissart and Christine de Pizan. Froissart owed his early career to Count John of Hainault and later enjoyed the favors of the English and French royal houses, respectively, a shift discernible in the changed sympathies of his chronicle of the Hundred Years' War. Christine grew up in the French royal household, where her father served as court astrologer. Commissioned to write the official biography of King Charles V, Christine would have been unable to produce most of her writings without the patronage of women in the royal household. She presented her most famous work, *The Book of the City of Ladies* (1405), a defense of women's reputation and virtue, to Isabella of Bavaria, the queen of France and wife of Charles VI. Christine's last composition was a poem praising Joan of Arc, restorer of French royal fortunes, and like Christine herself, a distinguished woman in a world otherwise dominated by men.

Vernacular literature blossomed not at the expense of Latin but alongside a classical revival. In spite of the renown of their Italian writings, Petrarch and Boccaccio, for example, took great pride in their Latin works. Latin represented the language of salvation and was also the international language of learning. The Vulgate Bible was the only sanctioned version, although the Lollard Bible, intended for the laity, was the first English translation of Latin Scripture. Professors taught and wrote in Latin; students spoke it as best as they could; priests celebrated Mass and dispensed sacraments in Latin; and theologians composed learned treatises in Latin. Church Latin was very different from the Latin of the ancient Romans, both in syntax and in vocabulary. In the second half of the fourteenth century, writers began to imitate the rather antiquated "classical" Latin of Roman literature. In the forefront of this literary and intellectual movement, Petrarch traveled to many monasteries in search of long-ignored Latin manuscripts. For writers like Petrarch, medieval church Latin was an artificial, awkward language, whereas classical Latin, and after its revival, Greek too, was the mother tongue of the ancients. Thus the classical writings of Greece and Rome represented true vernacular literature, only more authentic, vivid, and glorious than the poetry and prose written in Italian and other contemporary European languages. Classical allusions and literary influences abound in the works of Boccaccio, Chaucer, Christine de Pizan, and others. The new intellectual fascination with the ancient past also stimulated translations of these works into the vernacular.

Italy led this new intellectual movement that came to be called humanism. In its original sense, humanism was simply the study of the seven liberal arts that constituted the introductory curriculum at universities before students moved on to the professional fields of theology, medicine, and law. Italian lawyers and notaries had a long-standing interest in classical rhetoric because eloquence was an essential skill of their profession. Gradually the imitation of ancient Roman rhetoric led to the absorption of ancient ideas. In the writings of Roman historians such as Livy and Tacitus, fifteenth-century Italian civic elites (many of them lawyers) found echoes of their own devout patriotism. Between 1400 and 1430 in Florence, which at the time was at war with the duchy of Milan, the study of the humanities evolved into a republican ideology that historians call civic humanism. Under the leadership of three chancellors—Coluccio Salutati (1331–1406), Leonardo Bruni (1374–1444), and Poggio Bracciolini (1380–1459)—the Florentines waged a highly successful propaganda war on behalf of virtuous republican Florence against tyrannical Milan, invoking the memory of the overthrow of Etruscan tyrants by the first Romans. Thus the study of ancient civilization was not only an antiquarian quest but a call to public service and political action.

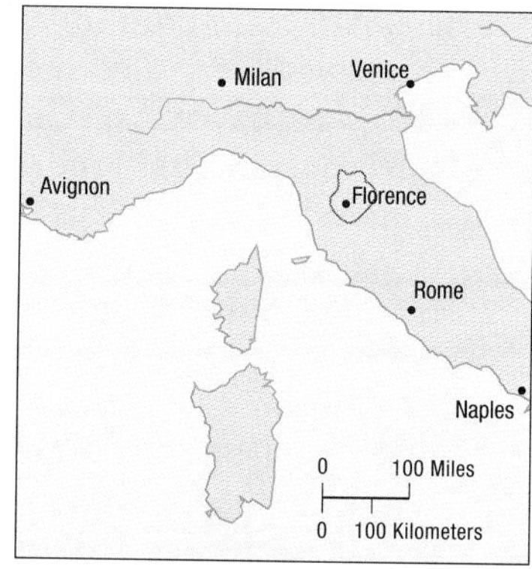

Italy at the Dawn of the Renaissance

Conclusion

The word *crisis* implies a turning point, a decisive moment, and during the hundred-plus years between 1320 and 1430, European civilization faced such a time. Departing from the path of expansion, it instead entered a period of uncertainty, disunity, and contraction. The traditional order, achieved during the optimism and growth of the High Middle Ages, was undermined in the mid-fourteenth century, most obviously by the Black Death and the Hundred Years' War, both of which decimated the population and altered agricultural production and seigneurial relations between lords and peasants. Empire and papacy, long symbols of unity, crumbled into political disintegration and spiritual malaise in the later Middle Ages.

In the eastern Mediterranean, European civilization retreated in the face of Ottoman Turk advances. Christian Europe continued to grow, however, in the Iberian Peninsula; for the next three centuries the Mediterranean would become the arena for struggles between Christian and Islamic empires. The papacy would clamor for new crusades.

Although instrumental in ending the Great Schism, the conciliar movement failed to limit supreme papal power, identified by its critics as the source of spiritual discontent. Traumatized, perhaps by the crisis of authority, the next generations of popes would concentrate on consolidating their worldly power and wealth. Successful in repressing or compromising with the Lollard, Hussite, and other heretical movements, the church would focus its attention on control and would neglect, to their future regret, the spiritual needs of a laity increasingly estranged from domination by a clerical elite.

The disintegration of universal order hastened the consolidation of some states, as countries such as England and France developed political, linguistic, and cultural boundaries that largely coincided. Other areas, such as Castile, Portugal, and the Ottoman Empire, included different linguistic and religious groups under one political authority. Still other regions, principally central Europe and Italy, remained divided into competing city-states characterized more by the sense of local differences than by their linguistic similarity.

The artistic productions of the age best reflect the new aesthetic sensibilities. Conscious of their departure from the past, writers and artists—principally in Italy—invented new forms to express their ideas. In the process, they created an elegant and sophisticated vernacular Italian literature that was much admired and imitated in other countries. Those devoted to Latin literature turned not to the language of the church but to the classical models of ancient Rome, harking back to the splendor of Roman civilization and institutions. The ancient past also inspired a creative revolution in the visual arts. In the 1420s and 1430s, a new generation in Florence discovered the beauty of the human form and classical space. They created a new style, more individualistic and innovative, that would characterize a cultural blooming in the fifteenth century.

Suggestions for Further Reading

Source Materials

Froissart, Jean. *Chronicles.* Translated by Geoffrey Brereton. 1968. A judicious selection of the highlights of Froissart's massive chronicle of the Hundred Years' War, particularly informative on the feudal nobility's ethos.

Joan of Arc: By Herself and Her Witnesses. Edited by Régine Pernoud. 1966. Contains documents on the life of Joan of Arc arranged chronologically, including important transcripts of her trial.

Pizan, Christine de. *The Book of the City of Ladies.* Translated by Earl Jeffrey Richards. 1982. Written by the celebrated author of the French court, a book defending the honor and virtues of women.

Interpretive Studies

Allmand, Christopher. *The Hundred Years' War: England and France at War, c. 1300–1450.* 1988. A readable survey of the recent literature.

Bois, Guy. *The Crisis of Feudalism: Economy and Society in Eastern Normandy, c. 1300–1550.* 1984. A stimulating, difficult book that analyzes the relationship between socioeconomic changes and warfare using a Marxist perspective.

Branca, Vittore. *Boccaccio: The Man and His Works.* 1976. A masterly synthesis by one of the leading Boccaccio scholars.

Duby, Georges. *A History of Private Life: II. Revelations of the Medieval World.* 1988. A collection of fascinating essays that portray social history; profusely illustrated.

Geremek, Bronisław. *The Margins of Society in Late Medieval Paris.* 1987. An intriguing and scholarly portrait of the Parisian underworld by a leading Polish historian and leader in the Solidarity movement.

Hanawalt, Barbara A., ed. *Women and Work in Preindustrial Europe.* 1986. Ten essays on the history of working women between the thirteenth and sixteenth centuries in western and central Europe.

Hilton, R. H., and T. H. Aston, eds. *The English Rising of 1381.* 1984. The most recent research on the English uprising, as well as on the Jacquerie and the Ciompi revolts.

Kaminsky, Howard. *A History of the Hussite Revolution.* 1967. A detailed narrative based on extensive primary research.

Leff, Gordon. *Heresy in the Later Middle Ages: The Relation of Heterodoxy to Dissent, c. 1250–1450.* 1967. Stresses the fluid landscape of theological and religious dissent; includes the Fraticelli, Free Spirits, Lollards, and Hussites.

Leuschner, Joachim. *Germany in the Late Middle Ages.* 1980. The best survey in English: balanced, readable, and particularly good on political and urban history.

Miskimin, Harry A. *The Economy of Early Renaissance Europe, 1300–1460.* 1975. A succinct and authoritative synthesis.

Mollat, Michel, and Philippe Wolff. *The Popular Revolutions of the Late Middle Ages.* 1973. A wide-ranging narrative and analysis of the many urban revolts and peasant uprisings from 1280 to 1435 by two prominent French medievalists.

Nichols, David. *The van Arteveldes of Ghent: The Varieties of Vendetta and the Hero in History.* 1988. Two generations of this leading merchant family set against the political and social background of Ghent.

Oakley, Francis. *Council Over Pope? Towards a Provisional Ecclesiology.* 1969. A succinct introduction to the history and doctrines of conciliarism and their implications for church history.

O'Callaghan, Joseph F. *A History of Medieval Spain.* 1975. A massive survey of Spanish history; a good reference book.

Ozment, Steven. *The Age of Reform, 1250–1550: An Intellectual and Religious History of Late Medieval and Reformation Europe.* 1980. A particularly lucid exposition of intellectual history of the Late Middle Ages.

Renouard, Yves. *The Avignon Papacy, 1305–1403.* 1970. A lively, comprehensive account of the Great Schism and the growth of papal government.

Rörig, Fritz. *The Medieval Town.* 1967. A succinct analysis of late medieval German cities by a leading social and economic historian.

Shaw, Stanford J. *History of the Ottoman Empire and Modern Turkey. Vol. I. Empire of the Gazia: The Rise and Decline of the Ottoman Empire, 1280–1808.* 1976. A detailed narrative, particularly good on political and institutional history.

Warner, Marina. *Joan of Arc: The Image of Female Heroism.* 1981. A careful and brilliant analysis of Joan's life and her legend after death.

Ziegler, Philip. *The Black Death.* 1970. The best synthesis of the vast literature on the plague.

CHAPTER

14

Renaissance Europe, 1430–1493

Reflecting on the history of the Italian states between 1434 and 1494, the Florentine historian Niccolò Machiavelli (1469–1527) commented on the relationship between war and peace, culture and chaos:

> *Usually provinces go most of the time, in the changes they make, from order to disorder and then pass again from disorder to order, for worldly things are not allowed by nature to stand still. . . . For virtue gives birth to quiet, quiet to leisure, leisure to disorder, disorder to ruin; and similarly, from ruin, order is born; from order, virtue; and from virtue, glory and good fortune. Whence it has been observed by the prudent that letters come after arms and that . . . captains [of war] arise before philosophers. For, as good and ordered armies give birth to victories and victories to quiet, the strength of well-armed spirits cannot be corrupted by a more honorable leisure than that of letters, nor can leisure enter into well-instituted cities with a greater and more dangerous deceit.*

Machiavelli brilliantly described the paradox of the Renaissance—a time of intense political and social conflicts, and simultaneously a period of immense cultural creativity. In painting, literature, architecture, philosophy, and history and political thought, new ideas and forms gave identity and meaning to an unstable, changeable world. For Europeans of the fifteenth century, that unstable world was defined by an incessant quest for glory on the part of ruling elites of the Renaissance states and by the disruption of that order at the turn of the century.

***Donatello,* Gattamelata**
Consciously based on Roman statues of mounted emperors, this depiction of a relatively minor professional soldier (ironically nicknamed "Honey Cat") in the Venetian service at Padua attests to the power of classical models in fifteenth-century Italian public art.

Fifteenth-Century Economy and the Renaissance State

By the fifteenth century a handful of Italian states had swallowed up the many city-republics that had dotted Italy during the Middle Ages. Locked in an intense competition between powerful republics (Florence and Venice), principalities (Naples and Milan), and the papacy, the Italian states developed an elaborate system of warfare and diplomacy that, by mid-century, served to create a balance of power. Having withstood heretical attacks and the challenge of the conciliar movement, the popes saw the consolidation of their monarchical power as a church priority, leading most of them to participate eagerly in the rivalry among the states.

Outside Italy the process of state building intensified during the fifteenth century, and rulers used diplomacy, military might, and symbols of power and authority (for example, court ceremonies, linguistic unity, and the reduction of urban autonomy) to bring autonomous regions under central control. The most instructive example in western Europe was Burgundy (part of today's France and Low Countries), whose spectacular rise and fall demonstrated the fragility of a political construction that cut across three linguistic regions and followed no natural geographic boundary. In eastern Europe thousand-year-old Byzantium fell victim to the expanding Ottoman Empire, which was to remain a European presence until the early twentieth century. Some European states also achieved permanent successes, such as the further consolidation of the monarchy and the central government in Spain, Muscovy-Russia, France, and England.

The Italian States: Republics and Principalities

With the exception of the Papal States, the Italian states of the Renaissance can be divided into two broad categories: republics that preserved the traditional institutions of the medieval commune by allowing a civic elite to control political and economic life, and principalities ruled by one dynasty. The most powerful and influential states were the republics Venice and Florence and the principalities the duchy of Milan and the kingdom of Naples. In addition to these "Big Four," a handful of smaller states, such as Siena, Ferrara, and Mantua (Siena a republic and the other two principalities), stood out as important cultural centers during the Renaissance.

The picturesque gondolas beloved by contemporary tourists symbolize Venice's long history as a powerful maritime republic. During the fifteenth and sixteenth centuries, Venice, a city built on a lagoon, ruled an extensive colonial empire that extended from the Adriatic to the Aegean Sea. Venetian merchantmen sailed the Mediterranean, the Atlantic coast, and the Black Sea; Christian pilgrims to Palestine booked passage on Venetian ships; in 1430 the Venetian navy numbered some forty-five galleys (large warships propelled by sails and oars), three hundred sailing ships, and three thousand smaller vessels, mustering a total of over thirty thousand sailors in a population of only one hundred fifty thousand. Symbolizing their intimacy with and dominion of the sea, the Venetians celebrated an annual "Wedding of the Sea" on Ascension Day. Amid throngs of spectators and foreign dignitaries, the Venetian doge (the elected duke) sailed out to the Adriatic, threw a golden ring into its waters to renew the union, and intoned, "Hear us with favor, O Lord. We worthily entreat Thee to grant that this sea be tranquil and quiet for our

Important Dates

1440s Gutenberg introduces the printing press
1453 Fall of Constantinople; end of Byzantium
1454 Treaty of Lodi; power balance in Italy
1460–85 War of the Roses; Tudor dynasty ascendant
1462–1505 Reign of Ivan III of Muscovy
1467–92 Height of Florentine Renaissance
1471–84 Reign of Pope Sixtus IV; Renaissance in Rome
1474–1516 Spain unified under Isabella of Castile and Ferdinand of Aragon
1477 Death of Charles the Bold; end of Burgundy
1478 Inquisition established in Spain
1492 Columbus's first voyage; Christians conquer Muslim Granada and expel Jews from Spain

men and all others who sail upon it." This prayer epitomized the importance of maritime power in the Venetian economy, for the city and its ruling class depended on long-distance trade for their prosperity. Control of the seas was vital, and Venetian noblemen were both sailors and warriors.

In the early fifteenth century, however, Venetians faced threats from the mainland. From 1425 to 1454, Venice fought the expanding duchy of Milan and brought its growth to a standstill, defending Venice's substantial territorial dominion on the Italian mainland. The second and greater danger came from the eastern Mediterranean, where the Ottoman Turks finally captured Byzantine Constantinople in 1453. Although a long campaign against the Turks (1463–1479) ended in defeat for Venice, this rivalry would be subsumed in a larger conflict between Christian Europe and Muslim Ottoman that would continue to the end of the seventeenth century.

By the Renaissance an oligarchy of aristocratic merchants ruled Venice and controlled all government functions. The Venetian constitution stated that only hereditary noblemen could serve in the Great Council. Their number in the fifteenth century fluctuated between two thousand and twenty-five hundred, although only between one thousand and fifteen hundred ever showed up for the Great Council meetings. Through a complicated electoral process (eleven steps were involved), the nobility elected a doge for life. Sometimes glory in war elevated a man to this highest office, as it did Pietro Mocenigo, a victorious admiral in the Turkish war. Other doges had extensive political and diplomatic experience. Limited in authority, the doge was the first among equals of the greatest Venetian nobles, who exercised power collectively via the Senate and the Council of Ten, institutions less unwieldy than the Great Council. Through military service, public office, financial sacrifices, and charity to the poor, the Venetian nobility dominated a republic remarkable for its political consensus and internal peace. Overseas trade and colonial territories benefited most social classes in Venice, who shared in the maritime profits as sailors, soldiers, and workers. A society with a strict hierarchy of classes and a tradition of conserving this social order, the Venetian Republic was widely admired for its political stability. The epithet *Serenissima Repubblica* (Most Serene Republic) pointed to the sharp contrast between Venice's stability and the political turmoil of the other Italian states.

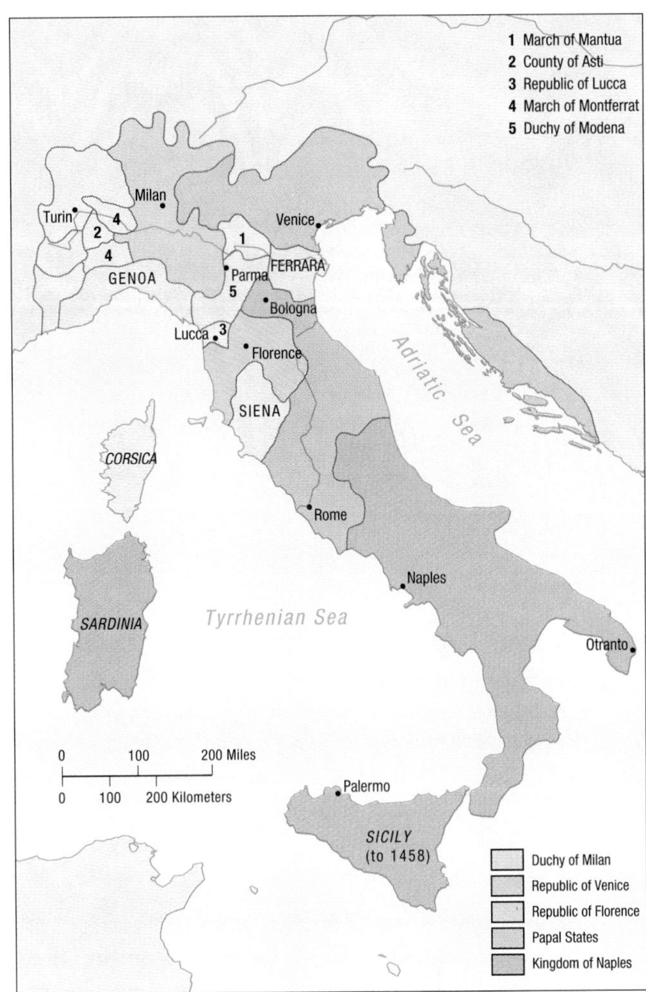

Political Map of Italy, c. 1450

Unlike serene Venice, Florence was in constant agitation: responsive to political conflicts, new ideas, and artistic styles. Like Venice, Florence described its government in the language of ancient Roman republicanism. Florentine liberty, however, rested on the subjugation of other city-republics, and Florentine armies systematically imposed their rule on the rest of Tuscany. Within Florence, despite the rhetoric of civic humanism, the social base of republican government continued to narrow in the early fifteenth century. Before 1434 a small oligarchy of four hundred thirty to five hundred seventy men ruled the quarter-million people of Florence and its

Sacred and Social Body
The Venetian state used lavish, dignified ceremony to impress citizens and visitors with its grandeur and to symbolize its divine protection. Here the great Venetian Renaissance painter Gentile Bellini depicts one such scene, a procession of the Eucharist across the Piazza San Marco uniting in common purpose the clergy and the Venetian governing elite.

subject territories. This ruling elite, too, had its own elite—an inner circle of some eighty to one hundred twenty men who consistently held the principal offices and three hundred fifty to four hundred fifty men of lesser prestige who served as the clients of the inner circle and occupied the minor offices.

Despite a system of rotation and short office terms designed to encourage political participation and prevent the entrenchment of power, the Medici family emerged victorious in 1434 in a factional struggle. Cosimo de' Medici (1388–1464), leader of the strongest faction, exiled scores of rivals and inaugurated a new era during which power increasingly became concentrated in his household. Although they maintained the traditional republican institutions and symbols, the Medici and their supporters controlled access to public office by manipulating the elaborate electoral process with screening, nominations, eligibility lists, and ad hoc committees. Pope Pius II, a native of Siena, traditionally a city in bitter rivalry with Florence, did not mince words when he described Medici power: "Cosimo, having thus disposed of his rivals, proceeded to administer the state at his pleasure and amassed wealth. . . . In Florence he built a palace fit for a king." As head of one of the largest banks of Europe, Cosimo de' Medici used his immense wealth to influence politics. Even though he did not hold any formal political office, Cosimo wielded influence in government through business associates and clients who were indebted to him for loans, political appointments, and other favors.

As the largest bank in Europe, the Medici Bank handled papal finances, and branch offices were also established in many Italian cities and the major northern European financial centers. With a total of 90,000 florins of original capital (72,000 from the Medici family), the Medici Bank (including its subsidiary wool and silk manufacturing interests) gained a profit of 290,000 florins between 1435 and 1450. (By comparison, the total public debt of the Florentine government in 1428 to 1429 amounted to 2.78 million florins.) Assiduously avoiding the trappings of princely power and scrupulously up-

Lorenzo de' Medici, "the Magnificent"
Grandson of Cosimo and ruler of Florence from 1467 to his death in 1492, Lorenzo epitomized the Renaissance prince, although he paid lip-service to republican institutions. He was equally skilled as a statesman, a patron of art and learning, a poet of haunting love- and drinking-songs, and—as his broken nose testifies—an athlete.

holding the republican facade, Cosimo de' Medici was nonetheless not above cheating the republic. In his 1459 tax return, for example, he declared only 3,000 florins for the capital of the Milanese branch of the bank; the actual investment totaled 13,500 florins. Backed by this immense private wealth, Cosimo became the arbiter of war and peace, the regulator of law, more master than citizen. Yet the prosperity and security that Florence enjoyed made him popular as well. At his death, Cosimo was lauded as the "father of his country" (*pater patriae*)—much to the irritation of his opponents.

Cosimo's death encouraged these opponents. In 1466 several patricians raised the banner of ancient republican liberty by opposing Piero de' Medici, Cosimo's son. But the opposition, lacking unity and fearful of arousing another popular revolt that might engulf the entire ruling class, was crushed by Piero. Piero's son, Lorenzo (called "the Magnificent"), who assumed power in 1467, bolstered the regime's legitimacy with his lavish patronage of the arts. In 1478 Lorenzo narrowly escaped an assassination attempt while attending Mass in the so-called Pazzi conspiracy, named after its principal instigators. Two years after Lorenzo's death in 1494, the Medici were driven from Florence. They returned in 1512, only to be driven out again in 1527. In 1530 the republic was finally defeated, and Florence became a duchy under the Medici family.

Unlike Florence, with its republican aspirations, the duchy of Milan had been ruled by one dynasty since the fourteenth century. The most powerful Italian principality, Milan was known as a military state relatively uninterested in the support of the arts but with a first-class armaments and textile industry in the capital city and rich farmlands in Lombardy. Until 1447 the duchy was ruled by the Visconti dynasty, a group of powerful lords whose plans to unify all of northern and central Italy failed due to the combined opposition of Venice, Florence, and other Italian powers. In 1447 the last Visconti duke died without a male heir, and the nobility then proclaimed Milan to be the Ambrosian republic (named after the city's patron saint, Saint Ambrose), thus bringing the Visconti rule to a close.

For three years the new republic struggled to maintain Milan's political and military strength. Cities that the Visconti family had subdued rebelled against Milan, and the two great republics of Venice and Florence plotted its downfall. Milan's ruling nobility, seeking further defense, appointed Francesco Sforza, who had married the illegitimate daughter of the last Visconti duke, to the post of general. Sforza promptly turned against his employers, claiming the duchy as his own. A bitter struggle between the nobility and the bourgeoisie in Milan further undermined the republican cause, and in 1450, Sforza entered Milan in triumph.

To consolidate his rule, Francesco constructed an imposing moated fortress in the middle of Milan, a structure that dominates the heart of the city to this day. Equipped with sixty-two drawbridges, the fortress housed twelve hundred soldiers ready to crush any civic rebellion. Military strength coupled with economic growth won over erstwhile supporters of the republic. Francesco promoted manufacturing and commerce and curbed the privileges of the nobility in an attempt to broaden his government's social base.

The Sforzas never felt completely secure in their rule. Francesco's successors used both violent as well as artistic means to establish order and legitimacy. This dichotomy was epitomized by Francesco's son, Galeazzo Maria. A cruel and brutal man, he was devoted to music, paying thirty-three singers from northern Europe extravagant stipends to satisfy his musical tastes. Yet life in this sumptuous court could turn brutal at a moment's notice. In 1475, Galeazzo casually ordered a tailor thrown into prison because he had spoiled a courtier's doublet of crimson silk. A year later, while attending Mass, the tyrant himself was assassinated by three noblemen avenging their honor.

The power of the Sforza dynasty reached its height during the 1490s. In 1493, Duke Ludovico married his niece Bianca Maria to Maximilian, the newly elected Holy Roman emperor, promising an immense dowry in exchange for the emperor's legitimation of his rule. But the newfound Milanese glory was soon swept aside by France's invasion of Italy in 1494, and the duchy itself eventually came under Spanish rule.

After a struggle for succession between Alfonso of Aragon and René d'Anjou, a cousin of the king of France, the kingdoms of Naples and Sicily came under Aragonese rule between 1435 and 1494. Unlike the northern Italian states, Naples was dominated by powerful feudal barons who retained jurisdiction and taxation over their own vast estates. Alfonso I (∗1435–1458), called "the Magnanimous" for his generous patronage of the arts, promoted the urban middle class to counter baronial rule, using as his base the city of Naples, the only large urban center in a relatively rural kingdom. Alfonso's son, Ferante I (∗1458–1494), continued his father's policies: two of his chief ministers—Francesco Coppola and Antonello Petrucci—hailed from humble backgrounds (mercantile and farming families, respectively), and Petrucci was himself a notary. With their private armies and estates intact, however, the barons constantly threatened royal power, and in 1462 many rebelled against Ferante, supporting instead the Anjou claim. More ruthless than his father, Ferante readily crushed the opposition. He kept rebellious barons in the dungeons of his Neapolitan castle and confiscated their properties. When his own ministers Coppola and Petrucci plotted against him in 1486, siding with yet another baronial rebellion, Ferante feigned reconciliation, then arrested them at a banquet and executed the two men and their families.

Embroiled in Italian politics, Alfonso and Ferante shifted their alliances among the papacy, Milan, and Florence. But the greater threat to Neapolitan security came from external forces. In 1480, Ottoman forces captured the Adriatic port of Otranto, where they massacred the entire male population. And in 1494 a French invasion ended the Aragonese dynasty in Naples, although, as in Milan, France's claim would eventually be superseded by that of Spain.

The Burgundian State

Locked in a fierce competition in the peninsula, the Italian states paid little attention to large territorial states emerging in the rest of Europe that would soon overshadow Italy with their military power and economic resources. Burgundy, whose rise during the fifteenth century was a result of military might and careful statecraft, is just such an example. The spectacular success of the Burgundian dukes—and the equally dramatic demise of Burgundian power—bears testimony to the artful creation of the Renaissance state, paving the way for the development of the European nation-state.

Part of the French royal house, the Burgundian dynasty expanded its power rapidly by acquiring territory, primarily in the Netherlands. Between 1384 and 1476 the Burgundian state filled the territorial gap between France and Germany, extending from the Swiss border in the south to Friesland, Germany, in the north. Through purchases, inheritance, and conquests, the dukes ruled over French-, Dutch-, and German-speaking subjects, creating a state that resembled a patchwork of provinces and regions, each jealously guarding its laws and traditions. The Low Countries with their flourishing cities constituted the state's economic heartland, and the region of Burgundy

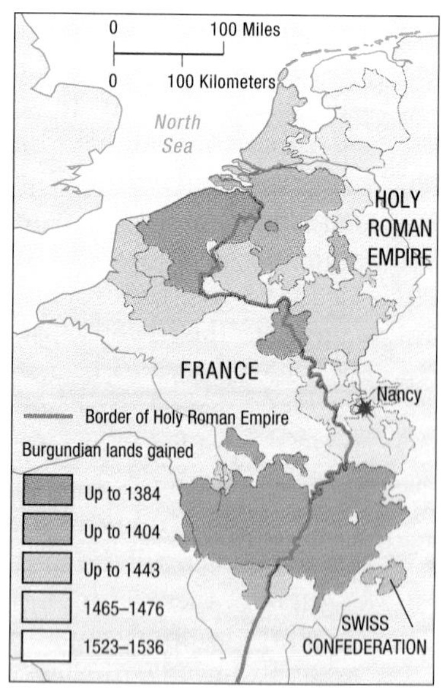

The Expansion of Burgundy

itself, which gave the state its name, offered rich farmlands and vineyards. Unlike England, whose insular character made it a natural geographical unit; or France, whose geography was forged in the national experience of repelling English invaders; or Castile, whose national identity came from centuries of warfare against Islam, Burgundy was an artificial creation whose coherence depended entirely on the skillful exercise of statecraft.

At the heart of Burgundian politics was the personal cult of its dukes. Philip the Good (*1418–1467) and his son, Charles the Bold (*1467–1477), were very different kinds of rulers, but both were devoted to enhancing the prestige of their dynasty and the security of their dominion. A bon vivant who fathered many illegitimate children, Philip was a lavish patron of the arts who commissioned numerous illuminated manuscripts, chronicles, tapestries, paintings, and music in his efforts to glorify Burgundy. Charles, on the other hand, was addicted to hunting and war and spent more time on war campaigns than at court, preferring to drill his troops rather than seduce noblewomen. Personally courageous (hence his nickname), he died in 1477 when his army was routed by the Swiss at Nancy.

The Burgundians' success depended in large part on their personal relationship with their subjects. Not only did the dukes travel constantly from one part of their dominion to another, as did the Italian rulers, they also staged elaborate ceremonies to enhance their power and promote their legitimacy. Princely entries into cities and at ducal weddings, births, and funerals became the centerpieces of a "theater" state in which the dynasty provided the only link among very diverse territories. New rituals became propaganda tools. In 1430, for example, Philip the Good created the Order of the Golden Fleece, inviting the greatest noblemen of his lands to join this latter-day Jason as his Argonauts. Philip's revival of chivalry in the ducal court transformed the semi-independent nobility into courtiers more closely tied to the prince.

In addition to sponsoring political propaganda, the Burgundian rulers created institutions to administer their geographically dispersed state by developing a financial bureaucracy and a standing army. But maintaining the army, one of the largest in Europe, left the dukes chronically short of money. They were forced to sell political offices to raise funds, which led to an inefficient and corrupt bureaucracy. The final demise of the Burgundian state had two sources: the loss of its duke, Charles the Bold, who died without a male heir; and an alliance between France and the Holy Roman Empire. When Charles fell in battle in 1477, France seized the duchy of Burgundy. The Netherlands remained loyal to Mary, Charles's daughter, and through her husband, the future Holy Roman Emperor Maximilian, some of the Burgundian lands and the dynasty's political and artistic legacy passed on to the Habsburgs.

The Marriage of Philip the Good and Isabella of Portugal in 1430
The Burgundian court embodied to the highest degree the ideals of late medieval courtly style. This painting, executed in the workshop of the Flemish master Jan van Eyck, conveys the atmosphere of chivalric fantasy in which the Burgundian court enveloped itself.

New Monarchies and Empires

Other rulers had more success than the Burgundian dukes in preserving their states. After the mutually ruinous Hundred Years' War, both France and England turned inward. The Iberian Peninsula saw the long war against the Muslims come to an end and the unification of Castile and Aragon. Central Europe's Holy Roman emperors nominally ruled over a bewildering mass of virtually independent principalities and cities. On Christian Europe's eastern fringe, Muscovy emerged as a new power when it threw off Mongol rule and started on a long path of expansion. And in the Balkans the Ottoman Turks completed their conquest of the Byzantine Empire.

Except for the Italian states, the Swiss Confederation, and some semiautonomous German urban leagues, monarchy was the prevalent form of government in the Renaissance. A mid-century period of turmoil gave way to the restructuring of central monarchical power in the last decades of the fifteenth century. Notably, the rulers Henry VII (∗1485–1509) of England, Louis XI (∗1461–1483) of France, and joint monarchs Isabella (∗1474–1504) of Castile and Ferdinand (∗1479–1516) of Aragon all developed stronger, institutionally more complex central governments in which middle-class lawyers played an increasingly prominent role.

In England civil war at home followed defeat in the Hundred Years' War. Henry VI (∗1422–1461), ascended to the throne as a child, proved in maturity to be a weak and, on occasion, mentally unstable monarch. He was unable to control the great lords of the realm, who sowed the seeds of anarchy with their numerous private feuds; between 1450 and 1455 six of the thirty-six peers in the House of Lords were imprisoned at some time for violence. Henry was held in contempt by many, particularly his cousin Richard, the duke of York (d. 1460), who resented bitterly that the House of Lancaster had usurped the throne in 1399, depriving the House of York of its legitimate claim. In 1460, York rebelled; although he was killed in battle, his son, later crowned Edward IV (∗1461–1483), defeated and deposed Henry. England's intermittent civil wars, later called the War of the Roses (after the white and red roses worn by the Yorkists and Lancastrians, respectively), continued until 1485, fueled at home by factions among nobles and regional discontent and abroad by Franco-Burgundian intervention. Edward IV crushed the Lancastrian claim in 1470 at the battle of Tewesbury, and the Yorkist succession died in 1485 when Richard III (∗1483–1485), Edward's younger brother, died at the battle of Bosworth. The ultimate victor was Henry Tudor, who married Elizabeth of York, the daughter of Edward IV, and became Henry VII (∗1485–1509). The Tudor claim benefited from Richard's notoriety: Richard was widely suspected of obtaining the throne by murdering his young nephews, two of Edward IV's sons—a sinister legend that Shakespeare gave even more fantastic proportions one century later in his famous play *Richard III*.

Unlike the Hundred Years' War, which had devastated large areas of France, the War of the Roses did relatively little damage to England's soil. Except for the campaign of 1460 to 1461, the battles were short, and, in the words of the French chronicler Philippe de Commynes (c. 1447–1511), " . . . England enjoyed this peculiar mercy above all other kingdoms, that neither the country, nor the people nor the houses, were wasted, destroyed or demolished, but the calamities and misfortunes of the war fell only upon the soldiers, and especially on the nobility." As a result, the English economy continued to grow during the fifteenth century. Its cloth industry expanded considerably, and the English now used much of the raw wool that they had been exporting to the Low Countries to manufacture goods at home. London merchants, taking a more vigorous role in trade, also assumed greater political prominence not only in the governance of London but as bankers to kings and members of Parliament; they constituted a small minority in the House of Commons, which was dominated by the country gentry. In the countryside the landed classes—the nobility, the gentry, and the yeomanry (free farmers)—benefited from rising farm and land-rent income as the population increased slowly but steadily. Some peasants lost their farms when landlords enclosed large tracts of arable land to convert into sheep pastures.

A similar postwar development took place in the Iberian monarchies. Decades of civil war over the royal successions began to wane only in 1469, when Isabella of Castile and Ferdinand of Aragon married. Retaining their separate titles, the two monarchs ruled jointly over their domains, which retained traditional laws and privileges. Their union represented the first step toward the creation of a unified Spain out of two medieval kingdoms. Isabella and Ferdinand limited the privileges of the nobility and allied themselves with the cities, relying on the *Hermandad* (civic militia) to enforce justice and on lawyers to staff the royal council. Like Henry VII of England, Isabella and Ferdinand seldom summoned the representative assemblies (respectively, Parliament and the *Cortes*) because these institutions represented the interests of the nobility, not of the people.

The united strength of Castile and Aragon brought the *reconquista* to a close with the final crusade against the Muslims. After more than a century of peace, war broke out in 1478 between Granada, the last Iberian Muslim state, and the Catholic royal forces. Weakened by internal strife, Granada finally fell in 1492. Two years later, in recognition of the crusade, Pope Alexander VI bestowed the title "Catholic monarchs" on Isabella and Ferdinand, ringing in an era in which militant Catholicism shaped Spanish national consciousness itself.

The Unification of Spain

The relative religious tolerance of the Middle Ages, in which Iberian Muslims, Jews, and Christians had lived side by side, now yielded to the demand for religious conformity. Catholicism became both a test of one's loyalty and an instrument of state authority. In 1478 royal jurisdiction introduced the Inquisition to Spain primarily as a means to control the *conversos* (Jewish converts to Christianity), whose elevated positions in the economy and the government aroused widespread resentment from the so-called Old Christians. *Conversos* often were suspected of practicing their ancestral religion in secret while pretending to adhere to their new Christian faith. Some Old Christians saw a person's refusal to eat pork, for example, as a sign of covert apostasy (betrayal of one's faith). Appointed by the monarchs, the clergy (the "inquisitors") presided over tribunals set up to investigate those suspected of religious deviancy. The accused, who were arrested on charges based on anonymous denunciations and information gathered by the inquisitors, could defend themselves but not confront their accusors. The wide spectrum of punishments ranged from monetary fines, to the *auto de fé* (a sort of public confession), to burning at the stake. After the fall of Granada many Moors were forced to convert or resettle in Castile, and in 1492 the Jewish communities had to choose between exile and conversion.

France, too, was recovering from its war years. Although France won the Hundred Years' War, it emerged in the shadow of the brilliant Burgundian court. Under Charles VII (∗1422–1461) and Louis XI (∗1461–1483), the French monarchy embarked upon a slow process of expansion and recovery. Abroad, Louis fomented rebellion in England, his traditional enemy, first by helping the Lancastrians and later by aiding Henry Tudor. At home, however, lay the more dangerous enemy, Burgundy. In 1477, with the death of Charles the Bold, Louis dealt a death blow to the duchy by seizing large tracts of Burgundian territory. France's horizons expanded even more when Louis inherited most of southern France after the royal collateral line of Anjou died out. By the end of the century, France had doubled its territory, almost assuming its modern-day boundary. To strengthen royal power at home, Louis promoted industry and commerce, imposed permanent salt and land taxes (called the *gabelle* and the *taille*) on his subjects, maintained the first standing army in western Europe, and dispensed with the Estates of France. The French kings further increased their power with important concessions from the papacy. With the 1438 Pragmatic Sanction of Bourges, Charles asserted the superiority of a general church council over the pope. Harking back to a long tradition of the High Middle Ages, the Sanction of Bourges established what would come to be known as Gallicanism (after Gaul, the ancient Roman name for France), in which the French king would effectively control ecclesiastical revenues and the appointment of French bishops.

Royal power was not absolute, however, because Louis XI failed to curb the power of the great magnate families. Unlike the English nobility, whose strength had been decimated by the War of the Roses, the French nobility remained eager for military adventure. Partly to divert the attention of the warlike nobility and also motivated by dynastic claims on Naples, the French monarchy would invade Italy in 1494, a new adventure abroad that would have disastrous consequences for French royal authority in the sixteenth century.

The rise of strong, new monarchies in western Europe contrasted sharply with the weakness of centralized state authority in central and eastern Europe, where developments in Hungary, Bohemia, and Poland resembled the Burgundian model of personal dynastic authority. Under Matthias Corvinus (✱1456–1490), the Hungarian king who briefly united the Bohemian and Hungarian crowns, an eastern European empire seemed to be emerging. A patron of the arts and a humanist, Matthias created a great library in Hungary that, unfortunately, was dispersed after his death. He repeatedly defeated the encroaching Austrian Habsburgs and even occupied Vienna in 1485. His empire did not outlast his death in 1490, however. The powerful Hungarian magnates, who enjoyed the constitutional right to elect the king, refused to acknowledge his son's claim to the throne.

Eastern Europe in the Fifteenth Century

Poland's nobility, who followed the eastern European model of succession (the nobility elected the monarch), always chose from the Jagiellonian dynasty, which by hereditary right ruled Lithuania as well. The Jagiellonians stepped into the power vacuum created by the death of Corvinus. Casimir IV, king of Poland and grand prince of Lithuania after 1444, succeeded in having his son, Władysław, elected king of Bohemia in 1471 and king of Hungary in 1490. The Jagiellonians owed their success in Bohemia and Hungary to the nobility's fear that a native prince, once enthroned, might curb their own power—power entrenched in Poland's laws and in its emerging parliament, or *Sejm*. When Casimir died in 1492, the union of these aristocratic realms dissolved amid disputes over succession. Only in 1506 would Poland and Lithuania again form a loosely united "commonwealth" under a single Jagiellonian ruler.

In the Balkans, under Sultan Mehmed II (✱1451–1481), the Ottoman Empire became a serious threat to all of Christian Europe. After he ascended the throne, Mehmed proclaimed a holy war and laid siege to Constantinople in 1453. A city of one hundred thousand, the Byzantine capital could muster only six thousand defenders (including a small contingent of Genoese) against an Ottoman force estimated at between two hundred thousand and four hundred thousand men. The city's fortifications, many of which dated from the time of Emperor Justinian, were no match for fifteenth-century canons. The defenders held out for fifty-three days: while the Christian defenders confessed their sins and prayed for divine deliverance, in desperate anticipation of the Second Coming, the Muslim besiegers pressed forward, urged on by the certainty of rich spoils and Allah's promise of a final victory over the infidel Rome. Finally the defenders were overwhelmed, and the last Byzantine emperor, Constantine Palaeologus, died in battle. Some sixty thousand residents were carried off in slavery, and the city was sacked. Mehmed entered Constantinople in triumph, rendered thanks to Allah in Church of St. Sophia, which had been turned into a mosque, and was remembered as "the Conqueror." Greek Constantinople became Turkish Istanbul, but Byzantine culture managed to survive in the Greek Orthodox church, thanks to the religious toleration in the Ottoman Empire.

Ivan III
Taking the imperial title of tsar, Ivan pushed the boundaries of Muscovy in all directions. Here he is depicted with a saintly visage in the tradition of Russian Orthodox icon painting.

North of the Black Sea and east of Poland-Lithuania, a very different polity was taking shape. In the second half of the fifteenth century the princes of Muscovy embarked on a spectacular path of success that would make their state the largest on earth. Subservient to the Mongols in the fourteenth century, the Muscovite princes began to assert their independence with the collapse of Mongol power. Ivan III (*1462–1505) was the first Muscovite prince to claim an imperial title, referring to himself as the tsar (from the name *Caesar*) of all the lands of Rus. In 1471, Ivan defeated the city-state of Novgorod, whose territories encompassed a vast region in northern Russia. Six years later he abolished the local civic government of this proud city, which had enjoyed independent trade with economically thriving cities of central Europe. To consolidate his autocratic rule and wipe out memories of past freedoms, in 1484 and 1489, Ivan forcibly relocated thousands of leading Novgorodian families to lands around Moscow. He also expanded his territory to the south and east when his forces pushed back the Mongols, now fragmented into different khanates along the Volga River.

Unlike monarchies in western and eastern Europe, whose powers were bound by corporate rights and laws, Ivan's Russian monarchy claimed absolute property rights over all lands and subjects. The expansionist Muscovite state was shaped by two traditions: religion and service. After the fall of the Byzantine Empire, the tsar was the Russian Orthodox church's only defender of the faith against Islam and Catholicism. Orthodox propaganda thus gave imperial legitimation by proclaiming Moscow the "Third Rome," (the first two being Rome and Constantinople) and praising the tsar's autocratic power as the best protector of the faith. The Mongol system of service to rulers also deeply informed Muscovite statecraft. Ivan III and his descendants considered themselves heirs to the steppe empire of the Mongols. In their conception of the state as private dominion, their emphasis on autocratic power, and the division of the populace into a landholding service elite and a vast majority of taxpaying subjects, the Muscovite princes created a state more in the political tradition of the central Asian steppes and the Ottoman Empire than of western Europe.

Renaissance Diplomacy

Many features of diplomacy among today's nation-states first appeared in fifteenth-century Europe. By mid-century, competition between states and the extension of warfare served to make diplomatic conventions into institutions in Italy and western Europe. The first diplomatic handbook, composed in 1436 by Frenchman Bernard du Rosier, later archbishop of Toulouse, declared that the business of the diplomat was "to pay honor to religion . . . and the Imperial crown, to protect the rights of kingdoms, to offer obedience . . . to confirm friendships . . . make peace . . . to arrange past disputes and remove the cause for future unpleasantness."

The emphasis on ceremonies, elegance, and eloquence (Italians referred to ambassadors as "orators") masked the complex game of diplomatic intrigue and spying. In the fifteenth century a resident ambassador was to keep a continuous stream of foreign political news flowing to the home government, not just conduct the traditional temporary diplomatic missions. In some cases the presence of semiofficial agents developed into full-fledged ambassadorships: the Venetian em-

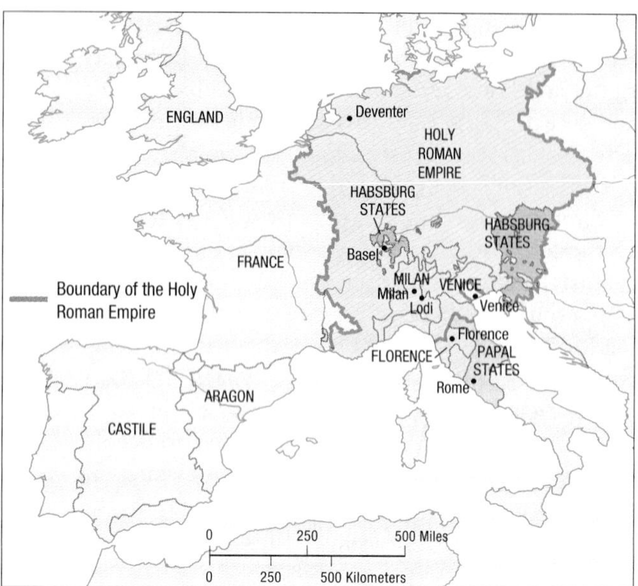

Renaissance Diplomacy and the Church

bassy to the sultan's court in Istanbul developed out of the merchant-consulate that had represented the body of all Venetian merchants, and Medici Bank branch managers eventually acted as political agents to the Florentine republic.

One mid-century episode illustrates the role of diplomatic ceremony as ritualized aggression. A Sienese ambassador at Naples, comporting himself in the grandiose style of his city, regularly appeared before King Alfonso of Naples dressed in gold brocade. The king's custom, in contrast, was to dress in black, with just a gold chain around his neck. Annoyed by the ostentation of the ambassador—who, after all, represented a minor city-state in comparison to the kingdom of Naples—Alfonso arranged to give audience in a tiny room occupied by all the ambassadors. He ordered that everyone in the crowd jostle and bump up against the Sienese ambassador. In the words of a Florentine bookseller, Vespasiano da Bisticci, who related this anecdote, " . . . when they came out of the room no-one could help laughing when they saw the brocade, because it was crimson now, with the pile all crushed and the gold fallen off it . . . it looked the ugliest rag in the world. When he saw him go out of the room with his brocade all ruined and messed up, the King could not stop laughing."

Foremost in the development of diplomacy was Milan, a state with political ambition and military might. Under the Visconti dukes, Milan sent ambassadors to Aragon, Burgundy, the Holy Roman Empire, and the Ottoman Empire. For seven years, from 1425 to 1432, an imperial diplomat resided in Milan while the Visconti's interests were likewise represented in Vienna. Under the Sforza dynasty Milanese diplomacy continued to function as a cherished form of statecraft. For generations Milanese diplomats at the French court sent home an incessant flow of information on the rivalry between France and Burgundy. Francesco Sforza, founder of the dynasty, also used his diplomatic corps to extend his political patronage. In letters of recommendation to the papacy, Francesco would comment on the political desirability of potential ecclesiastical candidates by using code words, sometimes supplemented with instructions to his ambassador to the papacy to indicate his true intent regardless of the "coded" letter of recommendation. In more sensitive diplomatic reports ciphers were routinely used in order to prevent them from being intercepted by hostile powers.

As the center of Christendom, Rome became the diplomatic hub of Europe. During the 1490s well over 243 diplomats were stationed in Rome, whereas 161 were represented at the court of Emperor Maximilian, 135 at the French court, and 100 in Milan. The papacy sent out far fewer envoys, and only at the end of the fifteenth century were papal nuncios, or envoys, permanently represented in the European states. In the 1490s there were 60 papal nuncios, whereas 138 imperial, 159 French, and 165 Milanese ambassadors appeared in European courts. The primary diplomatic effort of fifteenth-century popes—calling a crusade against the Ottomans—met with little practical success; the Christian princes were too embroiled in their own quarrels to march against Istanbul.

Italy's Renaissance diplomacy achieved its most outstanding achievement with the negotiation of a general peace treaty that settled the decades of warfare engendered by Milanese expansion and civil war. The Treaty of Lodi (1454) established a complex balance of power among the major Italian states and maintained relative stability in the peninsula for half a century. Renaissance diplomacy eventually failed, however, when more powerful northern European neighbors invaded in 1494, leading to the collapse of the whole Italian state system.

The Renaissance Church

Although the church council had restored the papacy in 1417, after the Great Schism the popes found their authority unduly restricted. In 1432, Pope Eugenius IV (*1431–1449) unsuccessfully tried to claim the sole right to convene church councils. Instead he was forced to abide by the reform decrees passed by the Council of Basel in 1433, which included restrictions on papal income and limitations on the number of cardinals. Between 1427 and 1436, papal revenues declined by almost two-thirds. In 1438, Eugenius ordered the Council of Basel to reconvene in a papal city in order to facilitate discussions that would lead to the short-lived union between the Roman and Greek Orthodox churches. Many church fathers in Basel refused to dissolve their council, and instead elected an antipope, Felix V (*1439–1449). Eventually papal authority triumphed over conciliarism, reflecting a trend that was taking place in the west European Renaissance states: the ascendancy of kingship over parliamentary government. The defection of several prominent conciliarists, such as Nicholas of Cusa (1401–1464), had turned the tide, and by 1447 most conciliarists were supporting Eugenius's successor, Nicholas V (*1447–1458), and urging the antipope Felix V to abdicate. In 1460 the humanist pope Pius II (*1458–1464) established papal supremacy in the church when he forbade appeals to councils beyond papal authority.

From the second half of the fifteenth century on, the Italian aristocracy began to dominate the papacy: Pius II came from the Piccolomini family, part of Siena's urban aristocracy; Sixtus IV (*1471–1484) hailed from the della Rovere, a noble family living near Savona in Liguria; and Innocent VIII (*1484–1492) from the Cibo family in Genoa, who had spent his youth in the Neapolitan court, where he had fathered three illegitimate children. With its character shaped by noble lineage and family loyalties, the papal court became a resource for family patronage, a trend initiated by Sixtus's appointment as cardinals of his nephews, who also became his close policy advisors. The popes' aristocratic tastes also transformed medieval Rome, with its desolate ruins and delapidated churches, into one of Europe's major cultural centers. Pius II, who had written erotic Latin poetry in his youth, sponsored a circle of humanists at court, and Sixtus established the Vatican Library, built the first bridge across the Tiber, and commissioned the Sistine Chapel, the papal chapel that, although not completed until long after his death, would glorify his name.

While the Renaissance papacy immersed itself in Italian politics and culture, a new style of religious devotion was evolving in northern Europe's heavily urbanized Low Countries and the Rhineland. Emphasizing inner spirituality and practical charity, this "modern devotion," as contemporaries called it, helped to bridge the gap between the clergy and the laity. By emphasizing inner spirituality, Christian morality, and works of charity, the modern devotion called into question the official church's emphasis on external ceremony and theological doctrine. Representative of this synthesis between official and popular religion was the Brethren of Common Life, a religious organization founded in the late fourteenth century by Gert Groote (1340–1384) in Deventer in the Netherlands that was flourishing rapidly in northern Europe.

Private Life and the State

Just as lineage and descent shaped political power in dynastic states in the fourteenth century, the state itself, through its institutions and laws, now attempted to shape families and households. Florence introduced a census, established a dowry fund and a hospital for abandoned children, and tried to regulate the sexual behavior of its citizens. Considerations of state power intruded into the most intimate personal concerns: sexual intimacy, marriage, and childbirth could not be separated from the values of the ruling classes. With a society dominated by upper-class, patriarchal households, Renaissance Italy specified rigid roles for men and women, making marriage a vehicle for consolidating a hierarchy of classes that was further reinforced by the subordination of women.

The Florentine Social Hierarchy

To deal with a mounting fiscal crisis, in 1427 the government of Florence ordered that a comprehensive tax record of households in the city and territory be compiled. Completed in 1430, this survey represented the most detailed population

Florence, c. 1490
Astride the Arno River, Florence was a typically crowded medieval Italian city. What made Florence unusual was its relatively large population, its wealth, and the splendid flowering of art and literature that this wealth supported.

census then taken in European history. From the census's mass of fiscal and demographic data, historians have been able to reconstruct a detailed picture of Florence—the most important city of the Renaissance and a city whose historical records are unparalleled in their detail.

The state of Florence, roughly the size of Massachusetts, had a population of more than two hundred sixty thousand. Tuscany, the area in which the Florentine state is located, was one of the most urbanized regions of Europe (together with Lombardy and Flanders), where 27 percent of the people lived in the largest ten cities. With thirty-eight thousand inhabitants, the capital city of Florence (as distinguished from the state of Florence) claimed 14 percent of the total population; the next largest city, Pisa, numbered only seventy-three hundred. The wealth of the city of Florence made its dominance even more striking: it possessed 67 percent of the state's declared wealth. As the center of its universe, the city's brilliance outshone that of the state's other cities and towns, and cast a long shadow over a countryside whose predominant form of agriculture was practiced by sharecroppers working for urban landlords. Florence illustrates the intensely urban character of Italian Renaissance civilization.

Straddling the Arno River, Florence was a beautiful, thriving city with a defined social hierarchy. In describing class divisions the Florentines themselves referred to the "little people" and the "fat people." Some 60 percent of all households belonged to the "little people"— workers, artisans, petty merchants—whose household possessions did not exceed 200 florins in value. In 1430 an unskilled worker could expect to make 23 florins annually, while a skilled worker earned almost double that wage. The "fat people," roughly our middle class, comprised 30 percent of the urban population. At the very bottom of the hierarchy were slaves and servants, largely women employed in domestic service. Whereas the small number of slaves were of Balkan origin, the much larger population of domestic servants came to the city from the surrounding countryside as contracted wage earners. At the top a tiny elite of patricians, bankers, and wool merchants controlled the state with their enormous wealth. In fact, the richest 1 percent of the urban households (approximately one hundred families) owned more than one-quarter of the city's wealth and one-sixth of Tuscany's total wealth. The patricians in particular owned almost all government bonds, a lucrative investment with interest rates frequently over 15 percent and guaranteed by a state they dominated.

Surprisingly, men seem to have outnumbered women in the 1427 survey. For every one hundred women there were one hundred ten men, unlike most populations, which have women as the majority. In addition to female infanticide, which was occasionally practiced, the survey itself reflected the society's bias against women: persistent underreporting of women probably explained the statistical abnormality; and married daughters, young girls, and elderly widows frequently disappeared from the memories of householders just as they often escape the attention of historians. Most people, men and women alike, lived in households with at least six inhabitants, although the greatest number of households consisted of variants on the basic conjugal family. Among the urban patriciate and the landowning peasantry, the extended family held sway. Households of more than ten members, with married brothers living under one roof, were common both in Florence and in the countryside. The number of children in a family, it seems, reflected class differences as well. Wealthier families had more children; childless couples existed almost exclusively among the poor, who were also more likely to abandon the infants they could not feed.

The Strozzi Palace, Florence
The Strozzi, a powerful and wealthy family of medieval Florence, surrendered most of its political influence to the Medici. Behind the walls of their imposing palace, the Strozzi flourished as patrons of art and learning. The interior courtyard was rebuilt in the classical style of the fifteenth century.

Family Alliances

Wealth and class also clearly determined family structure and the pattern of marriage and childbearing. In a letter to her eldest son, dated 1447, Alessandra Strozzi announced the marriage of her daughter, Caterina, to the son of Parente Parenti. She described the young groom, Marco Parenti, as "a worthy and virtuous young man, and . . . the only son, and rich, 25 years old, and keeps a silk workshop; and they have a little political standing." The dowry was set at 1,000 florins, a substantial sum—but for 400 to 500 florins more, Alessandra admitted, Caterina would have fetched a husband from a more prominent family.

The Strozzi belonged to one of Florence's most distinguished traditional families, but at the time of Caterina's betrothal the family had fallen into political disgrace. Alessandra's husband, an enemy of the Medici, was exiled in 1434; her son, Filippo, a rich merchant in Naples, lived under the same political ban. Although Caterina was clearly marrying beneath her social station, the marriage represented an alliance in which money, political status, and family standing all balanced out in the end. More an alliance between families than the consummation of love, a marriage was usually orchestrated by the male head of a household. In this case, Alessandra, as a widow, shared the matchmaking responsibility with her eldest son and other male relatives. Eighteen years later, when it came time to find a wife for Filippo, Marco Parenti, the brother-in-law, would also serve as matchmaker.

The upper-class Florentine family was patrilineal in structure; it traced descent and determined inheritance through the male line. Because the distribution of wealth depended on this patriarchal system, women occupied an ambivalent position in the household. A widow found herself torn between loyalty to her children and to her own paternal family, who pressured her to remarry and form a new family alliance. A daughter could claim inheritance only through her dowry, and she often disappeared from family records after her marriage. A wife seldom emerged from the shadow of her husband, and consequently the lives of many women have been lost to history.

In the course of a woman's life, her family often pressured her to conform to conventional expectations. At the birth of a daughter, most wealthy Florentine fathers would open an account at the Dowry Fund, a public fund established in 1425 to raise state revenues and a major investment instrument for the Florentine upper classes. In 1433 the fund paid annual interest of between 15 percent and 21 percent, and fathers could hope to raise handsome dowries by the time their daughters became marriagable in their late teens. The Dowry Fund supported the structure of the marriage market, in which the circulation of wealth and women consolidated the social coherence of the ruling classes.

Women's subordination in marriages often reflected the age differences between spouses. In Renaissance Italy most women married, before age twenty, husbands ten years older who were financially and socially established. The Italian marriage pattern contrasted sharply with the northern European model, in which partners were much closer in age. Significant age disparity also left many women widowed in their twenties and thirties, and remarriage was difficult for many. A widow's father and brothers often would want her to remarry to keep the patrimony (in the form of a dowry) circulating through a new family alliance. A widow, however, could not bring her children into her new marriage because they belonged to her first husband's family. Faced with the choice between her children and her paternal family, not to mention her own happiness, a widow could only hope to gain greater autonomy in her old age, when she could advance the fortunes of her adult sons.

The fictional Griselda from the last tale of Boccaccio's *Decameron* (1353) was the archetype of the meek and submissive wife. Completely dependent on her husband, Griselda did not even own her wedding ring and clothes. After her husband orders her to return his gifts to her after the wedding, he sends her away naked to test her loyalty. Only when Griselda proves her sexual fidelity does her husband receive her back with gifts and affection. The Griselda story, immensely popular in the Renaissance, illustrates the utter powerlessness of the married woman who had no dowry.

In northern Europe, however, women enjoyed a relatively more secure position. In England, the Low Countries, and Germany, for example, women played a significant role in the economy—not only in the peasant household, in which everyone worked, but especially in the town, serving as peddlers, weavers, seamstresses, shopkeepers, midwives, and brewers. In Cologne, for example, women could join one of several artisans' guilds, and in Munich they ranked among some of the richest brewers. Women in northern Europe shared inheritances alongside their brothers, retained control of their dowries, and had the right to represent themselves before the law. Italian men who traveled to the north marveled at the differences in gender relations, denigrating English women as violent and brazen and disapproving of the mixing of genders in German public baths.

The Regulation of Sexuality

Child care also reflected the class differences in Renaissance life. Florentine middle- and upper-class fathers arranged business contracts for most infants to go to wet nurses for breast-feeding; the baby often spent a prolonged period of time away from the family. Such elaborate child care was beyond the reach of the poor, who often abandoned their children to strangers or to public charity.

By the beginning of the fifteenth century, Florence's two hospitals were accepting large numbers of abandoned children, in addition to the sick and infirm. In 1445 the government opened a foundling hospital, the *Ospitale degl' Innocenti*, to deal with the large number of abandoned children. These unfortunate children came from two sources: poor families who were unable to feed another mouth, especially in times of famine, war, and economic depression; and women who had given birth out of wedlock. A large number of the latter were domestic slaves or servants who had been impregnated by their masters; in 1445 one-third of the first hundred foundlings at the newly opened hospital were children of the unequal liaisons between masters and

Griselda
The tale of Griselda was retold by many late medieval and Renaissance writers. In this illustration of the bestowal of a wedding ring, Griselda symbolizes the fidelity and dependence expected of a bride.

women slaves. For some women the foundling hospital provided an alternative to infanticide. Over two-thirds of abandoned infants were girls, a clear indicator of the inequality between the sexes. Although Florence's government employed wet nurses to care for the foundlings, the large number of abandoned infants overtaxed the hospital's limited resources. The hospital's death rate among infants was much higher than the already high infant mortality rate of the time.

Illegitimacy in itself did not necessarily carry a social stigma in fifteenth-century Europe. Most upper-class men acknowledged and supported their illegitimate children as a sign of virility, and illegitimate children of noble lineage often rose to social and political prominence. Any social stigma was borne primarily by the woman, whose ability to marry usually became compromised. Shame and guilt sometimes drove some poor single mothers to kill their infants, a crime for which they paid with their own lives.

In addition to prosecuting infanticide, the public regulation of sexuality focused on prostitution and homosexuality. While prescribing marital fidelity and chastity as feminine virtues, Renaissance society allowed greater freedoms when it came to male heterosexuality. As the 1415 statute that established government brothels in Florence declared, state-sponsored prostitution was intended "to eliminate a worse evil by a lesser one." Concurrent with its higher tolerance of prostitution, the Renaissance state had a low tolerance of homosexuality. In 1432, the Florentine state appointed magistrates "to discover—whether by means of secret denunciation, accusations, notifications, or any other method—those who commit the vice of sodomy, whether actively or passively. . . . " The government set fines for homosexual acts and carried out death sentences against pederasts.

Fifteenth-century European magistrates took violence against women less seriously than the sanctions against illegal male sexual behavior, as the different punishments indicate. In Renaissance Venice, for example, the typical jail sentence for rape and attempted rape was only six months. Magistrates often treated noblemen with great leniency, and handled rape cases according to class distinctions. For example, Agneta, a young girl living with a government official, was abducted and raped by two millers, who were sentenced to five years in prison; several servants who abducted and raped a slave woman were sentenced to three to four months in jail; and a nobleman who abducted and raped Anna, a slave woman, was freed. The gender and social class of both victim and rapist clearly were major factors in determining the sentence. Social inequalities placed noblemen at the top of the hierarchy and slave women at the bottom.

The Sanctification of Kinship

Throughout Europe, in keeping with the emphasis on family relationships, expressions of piety used the Holy Family as a symbol of everyday life. The Holy Family, an ordinary working family, gave the common people a religious identification: Jesus' family life became the model and reflection of their own kin. Numerous images of Jesus depicted him surrounded by his relatives—his parents, Joseph and Mary; his grandparents, Joachim and Anne; his uncles, aunts, and cousins. The world of the extended family was, of course, the reality of daily life. Popular woodcuts from Alsace showed the child Jesus riding on his hobbyhorse or helping with the wine harvest. A woodcut from the Netherlands represented the Holy Family as the ideal household; Joseph, the carpenter, a hard-working father; Mary, the loving mother; and Jesus, the sweet, well-behaved child. By adopting the Holy Family as their own, ordinary people were also sanctifying their own lives.

The cult of the Virgin Mary and her mother, St. Anne, was particularly popular. These two women symbolized maternal care and mercy in a religion anchored in the harsh judgment of sins and the horrible postmortem tortures of purgatory and hell. St. Anne became the patron saint of miners and pregnant women; a popular concoction, St. Anne's water, promised a childbirth free from fevers and pains. As the mother of God, Mary personified the ideal of maternal love. Representations of the Madonna and child were the single most frequent motif in paintings, wood sculpture, and woodcuts.

The sanctification of family and daily life presented a more accessible piety than that which the church had traditionally provided through clerical chastity, cloisters, and religious orders. The common aspects of the Holy Family now suggested that keeping the traditions of household and marriage could lead one to eternal salvation. In addition to church sacraments and doctrines, neighborly charity and love of kin assumed importance. And the virtues of charity and mercy that guided Christ's life inspired laypeople to show the same qualities in their own actions.

Widening Mental Horizons

Recovering from the devastating plagues and wars that had ravaged fourteenth-century Europe, fifteenth-century society could lend support to the arts. In addition to their traditional ecclesiastical and noble patronage, the urban elites, facing a less favorable climate for business investment due to lower rates of return and greater insecurity, sought to enhance their prestige by investing more heavily in culture. The consumers, producers, and content of these new artistic achievements offer a new view of the world and humankind's place in it.

The consumers of Renaissance art—the people who commissioned paintings, buildings, and musical and literary works—belonged in overwhelming numbers to the upper classes. The Catholic church was the single largest patron of the arts, followed by princes, bankers, rich merchants, and corporate sponsors (craft guilds and confraternities, or voluntary associations for religious laypeople). Religious themes featured prominently in the works, especially in music and the visual arts. Italy, the Low Countries, and Germany were particularly rich in artistic talent. In representing their world, Renaissance artists fulfilled both the taste of their patrons and their own artistic ideals and assumptions. Their created world of religious devotion was also one of natural beauty, human achievement, and secular glory.

Recovery of the Past

A new activism that focused on the human achievements of this world rather than on other-worldly salvation intensified Europeans' interest in Greek and Roman civilizations. The focus of this new movement, or *studia humanitatis*, which spread from Italy to northern Europe, was rhetoric; beautiful orations and writings became a mark of the elite and a claim to fame.

By the early fifteenth century the study of classical Latin (which had begun in the late fourteenth century) as well as classical and biblical Greek had become fashionable among a small intellectual elite, first in Italy and, gradually, throughout Europe. The fall of Constantinople in 1453 sent Greek scholars to Italy for refuge, giving extra impetus to the revival of Greek learning in the West. Venice and Florence assumed leadership in this new field—the former by virtue of its commercial and political ties to the eastern Mediterranean, the latter thanks to the patronage of Cosimo de' Medici, who sponsored the Byzantine refugee Gemistos Pletho, the Italian Marsilio Ficino, (1433–1499), and other Florentines, all of whom were part of the

Leonardo da Vinci,* The Last Supper *(1495–1497)
Adorning the dining hall of a Milan monastery, Leonardo's mural painting is one of the artist's masterpieces—but also a technical failure. He used a novel technique that would permit him to follow his accustomed slow, painstaking pace. Sadly, the result was rapid deterioration. But enough of the work survives to reveal the Apostles' individual features and Leonardo's dramatic psychological insights.

discussion group called the Platonic Academy. Thinkers of the second half of the fifteenth century had more curiosity about Platonic and various mystical neo-Platonic ideas—particularly alchemy, numerology, and natural magic—than about the serious study of natural phenomena and universal principles.

In Latin learning the fifteenth century continued in the tradition of Petrarch. Reacting against the painstaking logic and abstract language of scholastic philosophy, the humanists of the Renaissance advocated eloquence and style in their discourse, imitating the writings of Cicero and other great Roman authors. The Roman influence manifested itself especially in the transformation of historians' writings. Roman historians served as models for Italian humanists, who used the classical genre to explore the role of human agency in political affairs. Through their activities as educators and civil servants, professional humanists gave new vigor to the humanist curriculum of grammar, rhetoric, poetry, history, and moral philosophy. By the end of the fifteenth century European intellectuals considered a good command of classical Latin, with perhaps some knowledge of Greek, as one of the requirements of an educated man. This humanist revolution would weigh heavily in determining school curricula up to the middle of the nineteenth century and even beyond.

Most humanists did not consider the study of ancient cultures as a conflict with their Christian faith. In "returning to the sources"—a famous slogan of the time—philosophers attempted to harmonize the disciplines of Christian faith and ancient learning. The foremost Platonic scholar of the Renaissance, Ficino, a man deeply attracted to natural magic, was a priest. He argued that the immortality of the soul, a Platonic idea, was perfectly compatible with Christian doctrine, and that much of ancient wisdom actually foreshadowed later Christian teachings.

As a group the humanists were far from homogeneous, although they were overwhelmingly wellborn. Some were professional scholars, others high-ranking civil servants, still others rich patricians who had acquired a taste for learning. Many were notaries or government officials. In early fifteenth-century Florence, the humanists' active involvement in civic life shaped the general tone of their writings. Salutati, Bruni, and Poggio, who questioned the medieval ideal of contemplative learning, embodied the humanists' efforts to use ancient knowledge of humanity and nature in active participation in political and social life.

The social diversity of the humanists was matched by the wide spectrum of their political philosophy. Humanists in Florence and Venice lauded the virtues of the republican city-states of Athens and Rome; in contrast, humanists in Milan, who enjoyed the patronage of princes, applied their literary talent in praise of strong, often autocratic rulers. Whereas Florentine humanists modeled their praise of republicanism after the Romans Livy and Cicero, humanists serving the duke of Milan drew their inspiration from the writings of Suetonius's biographies of Roman emperors.

The Advent of Printing

The invention of mechanical printing aided greatly in making the Latin classics and other texts widely available. Printing with moveable type—a radical departure from the old practice of copying by hand—was invented in the 1440s by a German goldsmith in Mainz, Germany, by the name of Johannes Gutenberg (c. 1400–1470). Mass production of identical books and pamphlets made the world of print more accessible to a literate audience. Two preconditions proved essential for the advent of printing: the existence of commercial production of manuscripts and the industrial production of paper.

Paper making came to Europe from China via Arab intermediaries. By the fourteenth century paper mills were operating in Italy, producing paper that was more fragile but much cheaper than parchment or vellum—the animal skins that Europeans had hitherto used for writing. To produce paper, old rags were soaked in a chemical solution, beaten by mallets into a pulp, washed with water, treated, and dried in sheets—a method that produces good-quality paper even today. The commercial production of paper in the fourteenth and fifteenth centuries was the first stage in the rapid growth of manuscript books, leading to the invention of mechanical printing.

By the fifteenth century a brisk industry in manuscript books flourished in Europe's university towns and major cities. The production was in the hands of stationers, who organized workshops, known as *scriptoria*, for producing manuscripts, and acted as retail booksellers. The largest stationers, in Paris or Florence, were extensive operations. The Florentine Vespasiano da Bisticci, for example, created a library for Cosimo de' Medici by employing forty-five copyists to complete two hundred volumes in twenty-two months. Nonetheless, bookmaking in *scriptoria* was slow and expensive.

Printing—or "mechanically writing," as contemporaries called it—was not unknown: the Chinese had been printing by woodblocks since the tenth century, and woodcut pictures made their appearance in Europe in the early fifteenth century. The real technological breakthrough, however, came with the invention of the printing press. The process involved casting different durable metal molds to represent the alphabet. The letters, cast in relief at the end of the mold, were set to represent the text on a page. Pressed in ink against a sheet of paper, the imprint could be repeated numerous times with only a small amount of human labor. In 1467 two German printers established the first press in Rome and produced twelve thousand volumes in five years, a feat that in the past would have required one thousand scribes working full time for the same number of years.

After the 1440s printing spread rapidly from Germany to other European countries. Mainz, Cologne, Strasbourg, Nuremberg, Basel, and Augsburg had major presses; many Italian cities had established their own by 1480. In the 1490s the German city of Frankfurt-am-Main became an international meeting place for printers and booksellers. The Frankfurt Book Fair, where printers from different nations exhibited their newest titles, represented a major international cultural event and remains an unbroken tradition to this day.

The Origins and Diffusion of Printing

Early books from the presses were still rather exclusive and inaccessible, especially to a still largely illiterate population. Perhaps the most famous early book, Gutenberg's two-volume edition of the Latin Bible, was an unmistakable luxury item. Altogether 185 copies were printed—35 in vellum (requiring 5,000 calfskins) and 150 in paper (50,000 sheets in all). First priced at well over what a fifteenth-century professor could earn in a year, the Gutenberg Bible has always been one of the most expensive books in history, both for its rarity and exquisite crafting. (In 1987 Volume One of the Gutenberg Bible—a vellum copy—sold in the United States for $4.9 million.) Like many inventors throughout history, Gutenberg did not reap the material benefits of his invention, and he died impoverished.

Assessing the long-term impact of printing is more difficult than telling the story of its invention. Some historians argue that the advent of the printed word gave rise to a "communications revolution" more significant than, for example, the widespread use of the personal computer today. The multiplication of standardized texts could have altered the thinking habits of Europeans by freeing individuals from the necessity to memorize everything they had learned; it certainly made possible the relatively speedy and inexpensive dissemination of knowledge, and it facilitated intellectual exchange and created a more effective community of scholars. The creation of the book market transformed the structure of intellectual life. The audience for texts was now larger, impersonal, no longer dependent on personal patronage or church sponsorship. Printing facilitated the free expression and exchange of ideas, and its disruptive potential did not go unnoticed by political and ecclesiastical authorities. Emperors and bishops in Germany, the homeland of the printing industry, moved quickly to issue censorship regulations.

From Artisan to Artist

Like the copyists before them, the printers who ran the new presses saw themselves as artisans practicing a craft. The result might be genuinely artistic, but the producer did not think of himself as an artist, uniquely gifted. The artist, as opposed to the artisan, was a new animal to the Renaissance. In exalting the status of the artist, Leonardo da Vinci (1452–1519), painter, architect, and inventor who was himself trained in the artisan tradition, described his freedom to create, as a gentleman of leisure: "The painter sits at his ease in front of his work, dressed as he pleases, and moves his light brush with the beautiful colors . . . often accompanied by musicians or readers of various beautiful works." If this picture fits in with today's image of the creative genius, so do the stories about Renaissance painters and their eccentricities: some were violent, others absentminded; some worked as hermits, others cared little for money. Leonardo himself was described by his contemporaries as "capricious," and his work habits (or lack of them) irritated at least one employer.

The point of these stories about "genius," often told by Renaissance artists themselves, was to convince society that the artists' works were unique and their talents priceless. During the fifteenth century the artist's status in society underwent a gradual transformation. Instead of being an artisan laboring by hand to produce a given object, the artist claimed respect and recognition for his unique genius. Although artists wished to create as their genius dictated, the reality was that most relied on wealthy patrons for their support. And not all patrons of the arts allowed artists to work without restrictions. While Ludovico Sforza, the duke of Milan (*1452–1508), appreciated Leonardo's genius, a man like Borso d'Este, the duke of Ferrara (*1450–1471), paid for his art by the square foot. For every successful artist—such as the painter Andrea Mantegna (1431–1506), who was ennobled by Pope Innocent VIII—there were many others who painted marriage chests and look-alike madonnas for middle-class homes.

For painters the conditions of work fell into three categories: long-term service in princely courts, commissioned piecework, and production for the market. Mantegna, for example, worked from 1460 until his death in 1506 for the Gonzaga princes of Mantua. In return for a monthly salary and other gifts, he promised to paint panels and frescoes (paintings on a wet plaster surface). His masterpieces—fresco scenes of courtly life with vivid and accurate portraits of members of the princely family—decorated the walls of the ducal palace. In practice, however, Mantegna sometimes was treated more as a skilled worker in service to the prince than as an independent artist: he was once asked to adorn the ducal tapestry with life sketches of farm animals.

The workshop—the norm of production in Florence and in northern European cities such as Nuremberg and Antwerp—afforded the artist greater autonomy. As heads of workshops, artists

Fresco of the Camera degli Sposi
In 1474 Andrea Mantegna completed a cycle of frescos for the Gonzaga family, who ruled the duchy of Mantua in northern Italy. Mantegna's work, a masterpiece of perspective technique, creates a stunning illusion of greatly extended space.

trained apprentices and negotiated contracts with clients, with the most famous artists fetching good prices for their work. Studies of art contracts have shown that in the course of the fifteenth century artists gained greater control over their work. Early on in the century clients routinely stipulated detailed conditions to works of art. Gold paint or "ultramarine blue" were among the most expensive pigments, and consumers clearly wanted to ensure that painters did not skimp on material. Clients might also determine the arrangement of figures in a picture, leaving little more than the execution to the artist. After mid-century, however, such specific directions became less common. In 1487, for example, Filippino Lippi (1457–1504), in his contract to paint frescoes in the Strozzi chapel, specified that the work should be " . . . all from his own hand and particularly the figures." The shift underscores the increasing recognition of the unique skills of individual artists. Famous artists developed a following, and wealthy consumers came to pay a premium for work done by a master instead of apprentices.

A market system for the visual arts emerged in the Renaissance, initially in the Low Countries. Limited at first to smaller altarpieces, woodcuts, engravings, sculpture, and pottery paintings, the art market began to extend to larger panel paintings. In the fifteenth century most large-scale art was commissioned by specific patrons, but the art market, for which artists produced works without prior arrangement for sale, was to develop into the major force for artistic creativity, a force that still prevails in contemporary society. A vigorous trade in religious art sprang up in Antwerp, which was becoming the major market and financial center in Europe. Ready-made altarpieces were sold to churches and consumers from as far away as Scandinavia, and merchants could buy small portable religious statues to take along on their travels. The commercialization of art celebrated the new context of artistic creation itself: artists working in an open, competitive, urban civilization.

Representation in Perspective

An inventory of over two thousand paintings executed in Italy between 1420 and 1539 shows that about 87 percent dealt with religious subjects, more than half representations of the Virgin Mary and the rest portraits of Christ or the saints. Of those paintings with secular subjects, some two-thirds were portraits.

The predominance of religious themes in art reflected the continuing significance of church patronage and the importance of religion and the social uses of religious art in Renaissance society. The papal court in Rome was the greatest patron of the fifteenth-century arts. Beginning with Six-

Botticelli,
Adoration of the Magi
In this painting, commissioned by the Medici in the 1470s, the Holy Family appears surrounded by Florentine notables, including (many art historians believe) Cosimo de' Medici, his son, and his grandson as the Three Kings. Besides exalting the Medici, the painting also symbolizes the union between Christ and humanity.

tus IV, the Roman pontiffs embarked upon an ambitious plan that was to transform entirely the physical appearance of the Eternal City. Lay patrons commissioned religious art for two purposes: as a work of charity and piety and as a demonstration of personal power and wealth. For example, Sandro Botticelli's (1447–1510) *Adoration of the Magi* honors the Medici family of Florence along with the Holy Family: at the painting's extreme left is the young Lorenzo (later called "the Magnificent" because he patronized the arts), and touching the feet of the infant Jesus is Piero, the Medici patriarch.

Beyond the predominance of religious themes and homage to the powerful, certain stylistic innovations, through ways of depicting the world as the eye perceives it, distinguished Renaissance art from its predecessors. The Italian painters were keenly aware of their new techniques, and criticized the Byzantine and the northern Gothic stylists for their "flat" depictions of the human body and the natural world. The highest accolade for a Renaissance artist was to be described as an "imitator of nature"; nature, not design books or master painters, was the teacher of artists. Leonardo described how "painting . . . compels the mind of the painter to transform itself into the mind of nature itself and to translate between nature and art, setting out, with nature, the causes of nature's phenomena regulated by nature's laws. . . ." To imitate nature, Leonardo continued, required the technique of visual perspective, which helped to render three dimensions on a flat surface. A contemporary biography of Filippo Brunelleschi (1377–1446), the sculptor and architect, provided perhaps its earliest definition: "what the painters nowadays call perspective . . . is in practice the good and systematic diminution or enlargement, as it appears to men's eyes, of objects that are respectively remote or close at hand—of buildings, plains, mountains and landscapes of every kind. . . ."

The use of visual perspective—an illusory three-dimensional space on a two-dimensional surface and the ordered arrangement of painted objects from one single viewpoint—became one of the distinctive features of Western art. Neither Persian, Chinese, Byzantine, nor medieval Western art—all of which has been more concerned with conveying symbolism than reality—expressed this aesthetic for order through perspectival composition. Un-

***Leonardo da Vinci, Perspective Drawing** (detail)*
Leonardo was a master of the technique of having all planes recede to a vanishing point. Architectural settings lent themselves readily to perspectival draftsmanship. This drawing illustrates the means by which Renaissance artists achieved their three-dimensional effect.

derlying the idea of perspective was a new Renaissance worldview: humans asserting themselves over nature in painting and design by controlling space. The eye of the beholder became the organizing principle of the natural world in that it detected the "objective" order in nature.

Human perception now dominated artistry, a tenet illustrated so aptly by Mantegna's frescoes for the Gonzaga Palace and the paintings of Piero della Francesca (1420–1492). Completed between 1465 and 1474, Mantegna's frescoes in the palace's bridal chamber (*Camera degli sposi*), his most brilliant achievement, create an illusory extension of reality, a three-dimensional representation of life, as the actual living space in the chamber "opens out" to the painted landscape on the walls. Piero della Francesca, who apprenticed in Florence, was so fascinated by perspective that he wrote a book about it. In the fresco *The Flagellation of Christ*, della Francesca sets his detached and expressionless figures in a geometrical world of columns and tiles, framed by intersecting lines and angles. Human existence, if della Francesca's painting can be taken as a reflection of his times, was shaped by human design, in accordance with the human faculties of

***Piero della Francesca,* The Flagellation of Christ**
Active in Urbino in the mid-fifteenth century, the Tuscan artist Piero della Francesca was a master of dramatic perspective design, as exemplified in this small panel painting. His use of cool colors and his imaginative manipulation of geometrical space has spurred a favorable reevaluation of his art by twentieth-century critics.

reason and observation. Thus the artificially constructed urban society of the Renaissance was the ideal context in which to understand the ordered universe.

The Idea of Human Dignity

In practicing perspective a painter needed some knowledge of mathematics and optics, in addition to the usual mastery of color and line. Thus the Renaissance sought to unite artistic creativity and scientific knowledge. Architecture, which required an artist's eye as well as a scientist's knowledge, attracted some of the greatest minds of the age. Brunelleschi was a great Florentine architect whose designs included the dome of the city's cathedral, modeled after ancient Roman ruins; the *Ospitale degl' Innocenti* for abandoned children; and the interiors of several Florentine churches. Son of a lawyer and a goldsmith by training, Brunelleschi also invented machines to help with architectural engineering.

Another Florentine architect, Leon Battista Alberti (1404–1472), came from a wealthy merchant family. A lawyer and papal official, Alberti's theoretical interest in the arts led him to become an architect. One of his first buildings, the Rucellai Palace in Florence (1446), shows a strong classical influence and inaugurated a trend in the construction of urban palaces for the Florentine ruling elite. Although Alberti undertook architectural designs for many princes, his significance lies more in his theoretical works, which influenced his contemporaries. In a book on painting dedicated to Brunelleschi, Alberti analyzed the technique of perspective as the method of imitating nature. In *On Architecture*, modeled after the ancient Roman book by Vitruvius, Alberti argued for large-scale urban planning, with monumental buildings set on open squares, harmonious and beautiful in their proportions. His ideals were put into action by successive popes in the urban renewal of Rome, and they served to transform that unruly medieval town into a geometrically constructed monument to architectural brilliance by recalling the grandeur of its ancient origins.

Ancient history also supplied Renaissance Europe with symbolic heroes and great men. The political propaganda of the Burgundian court, for example, regularly praised the dukes as contemporary Caesars and Alexanders or compared them to the mythological hero Hercules. This marriage between classical antiquity and Renaissance propaganda graced the lesser courts of Europe, too, from Milan to Ferrara. For the most famous *condottieri* (military captains) of the time, bronze statues were cast, in the manner of those cast in ancient Rome—such as Donatello's (c. 1386–1466) *Gattamelata* (meaning "honey cat"), the nickname of a successful Venetian mercenary who actually had not won many battles. The increasing number of portraits in Renaissance painting also illustrates this new, elevated view of human existence. Initially limited to representations of pontiffs, monarchs, princes, and patricians, portraiture of the middle classes became more widespread toward the end of the fifteenth century. Painters from the Low Countries such as Jan van Eyck distinguished themselves in this genre; their portraitures achieved a sense of detail and reality unsurpassed until the advent of photography.

The ideal of a universal man, as exemplified by Alberti and other artists, was elaborated by Giovanni Pico della Mirandola (1463–1494). Born to a noble family, Pico avidly studied Latin and Greek philosophy. He befriended Ficino, Florence's leading Platonic philosopher, and enjoyed the patronage of Lorenzo de' Medici (1449–1492), who provided him with a villa after the papacy condemned some of his writings. Pico's oration, *On the Dignity of Man*, embodied the optimism of Renaissance philosophy. To express his marvel at the human species, Pico imagined God's words at his creation of Adam: "In conformity with your free judgment, in whose hands I have placed them, you are confined by no bounds, and you will fix limits of nature for yourself." Pico's construct placed humankind at the center of the universe as the measure of all things, and "the molder and maker of himself." In his efforts to reconcile Platonic and Christian philosophy, Pico stressed both the classical emphasis on human responsibility in shaping society and the religious trust in God's divine plan.

Renaissance Europe's glorification of males transformed religious culture at a fundamental level: it gave the traditional doctrine of the humanity of Christ a new emphasis, one supported both by popular preachers and in sermons at the papal court. The visual arts used representations of the Virgin and child as their central image. These paintings emphasized the human emotions of the Holy Mother and child. They expressed the humanistic beliefs of the times by depicting divinity's participation in human nature: Christ as a suckling infant, his genitals signifying both the sexuality and innocence of the divine child.

New Musical Harmonies

If Italy set the standards for the visual arts in Europe, it was more open to musical styles from the northern countries. At around 1430, simultaneous with the revival of painting in the Low Countries, a new style of music appeared that would dominate composition for the next two centuries. Instead of writing pieces with one major melodic line, composers were writing for three to four instrumental or human voices, each equally important in expressing a melodic line in harmony with the others. This new style, known as polyphonic (many sounds) music, found its greatest expression in the Burgundian Netherlands, although many musicians sought employment in Italy and in France.

The leader of this new musical movement was Guillaume Dufay (1400–1474), a native of Cambrai, whose musical training began in the cathedral choir of his hometown. His successful career took him to all the cultural centers of the Renaissance, where nobles sponsored new compositions and maintained a corps of musicians for court and religious functions. In 1438, Dufay composed festive music to celebrate the completion of the cathedral dome in Florence designed by Brunelleschi. Dufay expressed the harmonic relationship among the four voices in ratios that matched the mathematically precise dimensions of Brunelleschi's architecture. After a period of employment at the papal court, Dufay returned to his native north and composed music for the Burgundian and French courts.

Dufay's career was typical. His younger counterpart, Johannes Ockeghem (c. 1420–1495), whose influence rivaled Dufay's, worked almost exclusively at the French court. Other composers were more mobile: Josquin des Prés (1440–1521), another Netherlander, wrote music in Milan, Ferrara, Florence, Paris, and at the papal court. The new style of music was beloved by the elites: Lorenzo de' Medici sent Dufay a love poem to set to music, and the great composer maintained a lifelong relationship with the family.

Within Renaissance polyphony were three main musical genres: the canon (central texts) of the Catholic Mass; the motet, which used both sacred and secular texts; and the secular *chanson,* often using the tunes of folk dances. Composers often adapted folk melodies for sacred music, expressing religious feeling primarily through human voices, and not using instruments such as the tambourine and the lute, which were indispensible for dances. Small ensembles of wind and string instruments with contrasting sounds performed with singers in the fashionable courts of Europe. Also in use in the fifteenth century were the new keyboard instruments—the harpsichord and clavichord—which could play several harmonic lines at once.

The Renaissance and the Jews

Although a few Christian intellectuals were willing to explore Jewish learning, the larger Christian world in the fifteenth century remained intolerant of religious differences. Already devastated by the persecutions of the fourteenth century, many Jewish communities, especially those in the Holy Roman Empire and Spain, faced expulsion or exile during the Renaissance. Jews in Christian Europe were divided into two main groups—the German-speaking Ashkenazim and the Spanish-speaking Sephardim, each with its own cultural and liturgi-

Jewish Centers in Fifteenth-Century Europe

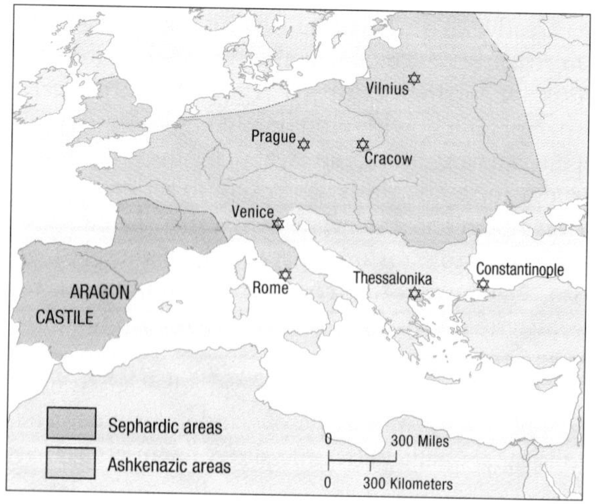

cal tradition. Additional Jewish communities, including many in Palestine and Egypt, existed under Ottoman protection. Multicultural by definition, the Jews of the Renaissance adhered to their ancestral religion and language, Hebrew, while participating in the culture of their surrounding Gentile societies, speaking Castilian, Portuguese, Italian, German, Turkish, or Arabic in daily life. In addition to the male-dominated religious culture of rabbinic learning, a secular culture flourished in the Jewish communities in which both men and women read vernacular literature (including translations from Christian authors) and took part in festivals such as carnival. Excluded from most trades by Christian authorities, Jews took on specific professions: the wealthier practiced medicine and moneylending, the middle classes peddled small wares and slaughtered animals for their communities, and the lower classes became servants in rich households or subsisted on community charity.

The single most dramatic event for the Jews of Renaissance Europe was their 1492 expulsion from Spain, the country with the largest and most vibrant Jewish communities. On the eve of the expulsion, approximately two hundred thousand Jews were living in Castile and Aragon. To that must be added roughly three hundred thousand *conversos* (Jewish converts to Christianity), many of whom maintained clandestine ties to Judaism and had relatives who had resisted the pressure to convert. Fearful that real or imagined Judaizers would corrupt the purity of Christianity, the Spanish Inquisition maintained close surveillance of the *conversos*, feeding popular resentment toward all Jews for their perceived economic privileges and religious differences. In 1492, Ferdinand and Isabella ordered all Jews in their kingdoms to convert to Christianity or leave. Well over one hundred thousand Jews chose exile. The priest Andrés Bernáldez described the expulsion with these sympathetic words: "Just as with a strong hand and outstretched arm, and much honor and riches, God through Moses had miraculously taken the other people of Israel from Egypt, so in these parts of Spain they had . . . to go out with much honor and riches, without losing any of their goods, to possess the holy promised land, which they confessed to have lost through their great and abominable sins which their ancestors had committed against God." The exiles departed for Portugal, North Africa, Italy, and the Ottoman Empire, settling in Thessalonika, Istanbul, and Palestine, thus extending the Sephardic diaspora (*diaspora* is Greek for "dispersion") to the entire Mediterranean.

On the Threshold of World History

The fifteenth century represented the first era of world history. The significance of the century lies not so much in the European "discovery" of Africa and the Americas, but in the breakdown of cultural frontiers that European colonial expansion inaugurated. Before the maritime expansion of Portugal and Spain, Europe had remained at the periphery of world history. Thirteenth-century Mongols were more interested in conquering China and Persia—lands with sophisticated cultures—than in invading Europe; Persian historians of the early fifteenth century dismissed Europeans as "barbaric Franks"; and China's Ming dynasty rulers, who sent maritime expeditions to Southeast Asia and East Africa around 1400, seemed unaware of the Europeans, even though Marco Polo and other Italian merchants had appeared at the court of the preceding Mongol Yuan dynasty. In the fifteenth century the ingenuity, endurance, and greed of the Portuguese and Castilians were motivation enough for them to seek direct and permanent contact with non-European peoples. For the first time Native American peoples were brought into a larger historical force that threatened to destroy not only their culture but their very existence. European exploitation, conquest, and racism helped to define this historical era, in which, in the transition from the medieval to the modern world, Europeans left the Baltic and the Mediterranean for wider oceans.

The Hanseatic "Lake"

Long before the voyages of exploration, European ships were roaming in waters closer to home. In the thirteenth century, on northern Europe's Baltic coast, a merchant league emerged that came to be called the Hanseatic League (*Hansa* means a band of merchants). By the fifteenth century it had expanded into an international association of merchants with extensive diplomatic and military power.

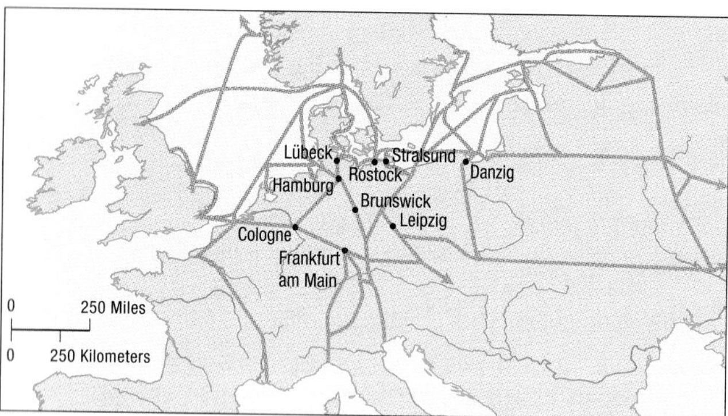

Hanseatic Towns

At the league's height, merchants from Bruges, Flanders, to Reval (today Tallin, Estonia) claimed Hanseatic privileges; about eight towns were full members and a further one hundred enjoyed associate status as Hanseatic towns. The Hanseatic League came to dominate maritime trade in the North Sea and the Baltic.

Several German-speaking seaports made up the core of the Hanseatic League. Lübeck, Hamburg, Rostock, Stralsund, and Danzig (today Gdansk, Poland)—all governed by merchant elites linked by marriage and business interests—provided most of the league's finances, personnel, and political direction. Annual Hanseatic conventions, usually held in Lübeck, decided on common policies and arbitrated disputes between members. The league set up a trade structure between eastern and western Europe: Hanseatic merchants and ships carried timber, fur, and honey from Russia, iron ore from Sweden, herring from Norway, and grain from Poland to the German, English, and Flemish cities of the West. In turn, western Europe's financial and manufacturing centers sent capital and manufactured goods back in the other direction.

By the end of the fifteenth century, however, the Hanseatic League faced serious competition. In a series of wars, the Danish monarchy tried to seize the league's Baltic trade. In the West, England and the Low Countries adopted policies that favored local merchants over the Hansa. Worst of all, intense competition among leading Hanseatic cities destroyed the league's cohesion. Antwerp, Amsterdam, and Hamburg, all league members, would replace the league as individual entrepôts (intermediary trade centers) in the next century. The decline of the Hanseatic League underlines the changing importance of trade in Europe after the Atlantic voyages: the Baltic Sea became a backwater as Europeans discovered new avenues for trade. The northern Hanseatic League remained a mere lake in comparison to the ocean of trade that was developing to the south and west.

The Changing Frontiers of Christian Europe

1433 Portuguese begin exploring West African coast

c. 1450 Portuguese establish fortified trading post in Guinea in central Africa

1453 Muslim Ottoman Turks capture Constantinople, capital of the Greek Orthodox Byzantine Empire

1478–1488 Bartholomeu Dias reaches Cape of Good Hope

1480s The Christian state of Muscovy defeats its former ruler, the Mongols

1492 Christians destroy Granada, the last Muslim state on the Iberian peninsula; Columbus's first voyage

The Divided Mediterranean

The Mediterranean Sea, which had dominated medieval maritime trade, lost its preeminence to the Atlantic Ocean in the second half of the fifteenth century. The Atlantic became Europe's door to the world, whereas the Mediterranean was divided into Christian and Muslim halves. Unlike the Arabs, who had never developed a strong navy, the Ottomans embarked upon an ambitious naval program to transform their empire into a major maritime power. The Mediterranean was to remain divided until the demise of the Turkish navy in the seventeenth century. War and piracy disrupted its flow of trade: the Venetians mobilized all their resources to fight off Turkish advances, and the Genoese largely abandoned the eastern Mediterranean, turning instead to the trade opportunities presented by the Atlantic voyages sponsored by the Castilian and Portuguese crowns.

The Mediterranean states used ships made with comparatively backward naval technology. The most common ship, the galley—a flat-bottomed vessel propelled by sails and oars—dated from the time of ancient Rome. Most galleys could not withstand open-ocean voyages, although Florentine and Genoese galleys still made long journeys to Flanders and England, hugging the coast for protection. The galley's dependence on manpower was a more serious handicap. Because prisoners of war and convicted criminals toiled as oarsmen in both Christian and Muslim ships, victory in war or the enforcement of criminal penalties were crucial to a state's ability to float large numbers of galleys. Slavery, too, a traditional Mediterranean institution, sometimes provided the necessary labor.

Although it was divided into Muslim and Christian zones, the Mediterranean still provided a significant opportunity for cultural exchange. Sugar cane came to the western Mediterranean from western Asia. From the Balearic Islands off Spain (under Aragonese rule), the crop then traveled to the Canary Islands in the Atlantic, where the native population was enslaved by Spain to work the new sugar plantations. In this way, slavery was exported from the western Mediterranean to the Atlantic, and then on to the New World.

Different ethnic groups also moved across this maritime cultural frontier. After Granada fell in 1492, many Muslims fled to North Africa and continued to raid the Spanish coast. When Castile expelled its Jews, some of them settled in North Africa, more in Italy, and many in the Ottoman Empire, Greek-speaking Thessalonika, the Jewish quarter of Istanbul, and Palestine. Conversant in two or three languages, Spanish Jews often served as intermediaries between the Christian West and Muslim East. Greeks occupied a similar position. Most Greeks in the homeland adhered to the Greek Orthodox church under Ottoman protection, but some converted to Islam and entered imperial service, making up a large part of the Ottoman navy. The Greeks on Crete, Chios, and other Aegean islands, however, lived under Italian rule, some of them converting to Roman Catholicism and entering Venetian, Genoese, and Spanish service.

New Geographical Horizons

Looking back, the sixteenth-century Spanish historian Francisco López de Gómara described Spain's maritime voyages to the East and West Indies as "the greatest event since the creation of the world, apart from the incarnation and death of him who created it." This first phase of European overseas expansion, which began in 1433 with Portugal's systematic exploration of the West African coast, culminated in 1519 to 1522 with Spain's circumnavigation of the globe.

In many ways a continuation of the struggle against Muslims in the Iberian Peninsula, Portugal's maritime voyages displayed that country's mixed motives of piety, glory, and greed. The Atlantic explorations depended for their success on several technological breakthroughs, such as the lateen sail adapted from the Arabs (it permitted a ship to tack against headwinds), new types of sailing vessels, and better charts and instruments. But the sailors themselves were barely touched by the expanding mental universe of the Renaissance; what motivated these explorers was a combination of crusading zeal and medieval adventure stories, such as the tales of Marco Polo and John Mandeville. Behind the spirit of the crusade lurked stories of vast gold mines in West Africa (the trade across the Sahara was controlled by Arabs) and the mysterious Christian kingdom established by Prester John (actually the Coptic Christian kingdom of Abyssinia, or Ethiopia, in East Africa). Moreover the Portuguese hoped to reach the spice-producing lands of South and Southeast Asia in order to circumvent the Ottoman Turks, who controlled the lands between Europe and Asia.

By 1415 the Portuguese had captured Ceuta on the Moroccan coast, thus establishing a foothold in Africa. Thereafter Portuguese voyages sailed farther and farther down the West African coast. By mid-century the Portuguese chain of forts had reached Guinea and could protect the gold and slave trades. By 1478 to 1488, Bartholomeu Dias could take advantage of the prevailing winds in the South Atlantic to reach the Cape of Good Hope. A mere ten years later (1497–1499), under the captainship of Vasco da Gama, a Portuguese fleet rounded the cape and reached Calicut, India, the center of the spice trade.

In 1455, Pope Nicholas V sanctioned Portuguese overseas expansion, commending King John II's crusading spirit and granting him and his successors the monopoly on trade with inhabitants of the newly "discovered" regions. At home the royal house of Portugal financed the fleets, with crucial roles played by Prince Peter, regent of the throne between 1440 and 1448; his more famous younger brother, Prince Henry the Navigator; and King John II. As governor of the Order of Christ, a noble crusading order, Henry financed many voyages out of the order's revenues; Peter and John used the state's income to support the enterprise. Private monies also helped, as leading Lisbon merchants participated in financing the gold and slave trades off the Guinea coast.

After the voyages of Christopher Columbus, Portugal's interests clashed with the Crown of Castile's new maritime activities. Papal diplomacy resulted eventually in the Treaty of Tordesillas (1494), by which the two royal houses divided the maritime world between them. A demarcation 370 leagues west of the Cape Verdes Islands divided the Atlantic Ocean, reserving for Portugal the African coast and the route to India and giving Castile the oceans and lands to the west.

The Voyages of Columbus

Historians agree that Christopher Columbus (1451–1506) was born of Genoese parents; beyond that, we have little accurate information about this man who conjoined the history of Europe and the Americas. As a young man, Columbus sailed and traveled in the Mediterranean, living for a time on the Greek island of Chios, then a Genoese colony. In 1476 he arrived in Portugal, apparently a survivor in a naval battle between a Franco-Portuguese and a Genoese fleet; in 1479 he married a Portuguese noblewoman. He spent the next few years mostly in Portuguese service, gaining valuable experience in regular voyages down the west coast of Africa. In 1485, after the death of his wife, Columbus settled in Spain.

Fifteenth-century Europeans already knew that Asia lay beyond the vast Atlantic Ocean, and *The Travels of Marco Polo*, written more than a century earlier, still exerted a powerful hold on European images of the East. Columbus read it many times, along with other travel books, and proposed to sail westward across the Atlantic to reach the lands of the Khan, unaware that the Mongol Empire had already collapsed in East Asia. Vastly underestimating the distances, he dreamed of finding a new route to the East's gold, spices, and lost Christians, and partook of the larger European vision that had inspired the Portuguese voyages. (His critics had a much more accurate idea of the globe's size and of the difficulty of the venture.) But after the Portuguese and French monarchs rejected his proposal, Columbus found royal patronage with the recently proclaimed Catholic monarchs Isabella of Castile and Ferdinand of Aragon.

In August 1492, equipped with a modest fleet of three ships and about ninety men, Columbus set sail for the Atlantic. The contract stipulated that Columbus would claim Castilian sovereignty over any new land and inhabitants and share any profits with the crown. Reaching what is today the Bahamas on October 12, Columbus mistook the islands to be part of the East Indies, not far from Japan and "the lands of the Great Khan." Exploring the Caribbean islands, the Castilian crew encountered communities of peaceful Indians, the Arawaks, who were awed by the Europeans' military technology, not to mention their appearance. Exchanging gifts of beads and broken glass for Arawak gold—an exchange that evoked Columbus's admiration for the trusting nature of the Indians—the crew established peaceful relationships with many communities. Yet in spite of many positive entries in the ship's log referring to Columbus's personal goodwill toward the Indians, the Europeans' objectives were clear: search for gold, subjugate the Indians, and propagate Christianity.

Leaving behind a small garrison on the West Indian island of Hispaniola, Columbus returned to Spain, parading the gold and Indians he had brought from the New World. Religion and greed were the twin motives of European contact with Native American civilization. In his log entry dated December 26, 1492, Columbus expressed his dreams for the future: by the time of his return, he hoped that the small garrison would have accumulated such quantities of gold and spices "that within three years the Sovereigns will prepare for and undertake the conquest of the Holy Land."

Excited by the prospect of easy riches, many flocked to join the second voyage. When Columbus departed Cadiz in September 1493, he commanded seventeen ships that carried between twelve hundred and fifteen hundred men, many believing all they had to do was "to load the gold into the ships." Failing to find the imaginary gold mines and spices, however, the colonial enterprise quickly switched its focus to finding contenders for the slave trade. Columbus and his crew first enslaved the Caribs, enemies of the Arawaks; in 1494, Columbus proposed a regular slave trade based in Hispaniola. They exported enslaved Indians to Spain, and slave traders sold them in Seville. Soon the Spaniards began importing sugar cane from Madeira, forcing

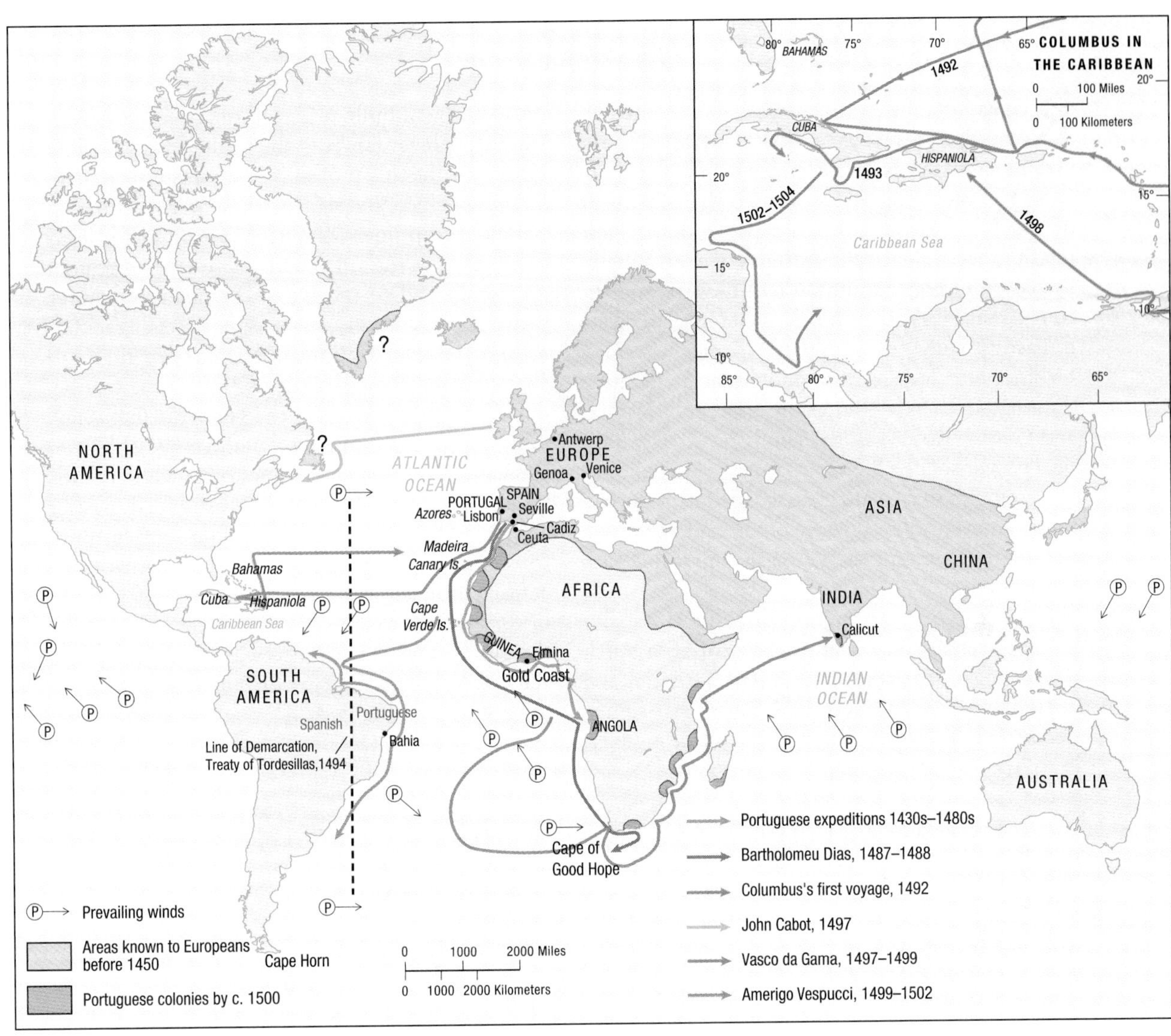

Voyages of Exploration to c. 1500

large numbers of Indians to work on plantations to produce enough sugar for export to Europe.

Columbus himself was edged out of this new enterprise. When the Spanish monarchs realized the vast potential for material gain that lay in their new dominions, they asserted direct royal authority by sending officials and priests to the Americas. Columbus's place in history embodied the fundamental transformations of his age. A Genoese in the service of Portuguese and Spanish employers, Columbus had a career that illustrated the changing balance between the Mediterranean and the Atlantic waters. As the fifteenth-century Ottomans drove Genoese merchants out of the eastern Mediterranean, they turned to the Iberian Peninsula. Columbus was one of many Genoese adventurers who served the Spanish and Portuguese crowns. The Portuguese and Spanish search for gold, spices, and slaves in the New World mirrored the well-established pattern of Portuguese colonialism in Africa, a ruthless enterprise that Europeans justified in the name of religion. The voyages of 1492–1493 would eventually draw the triangle of exchange among Europe, the Americas, and Africa, an exchange gigantic in its historical significance and brutal in its human cost.

Conclusion

Renaissance Europe's interest in ancient culture was in fact a quest for identity. Ideas, idioms, and the political and cultural forms of ancient Greece and Rome shaped the self-image of the Renaissance elites and provided a stable medium for a politically unstable world. One of the central idioms common to antiquity and the Renaissance was the power of the family: princely dynasties ruled over Milan, Naples, Ferrara, Urbino, and Monferrato, and patrician families dominated the city-states of Florence, Venice, and Genoa. Rooted in the family structure, political power shaped the very nature of households, informing marriage alliances, distributing power (most unevenly) between women and men, and regulating domestic production and biological reproduction.

An extraordinary period of cultural creativity, the Renaissance seemed to express a spirit of optimism, of unlimited human potential and achievement. Yet underneath the secular confidence stirred a great anxiety. Renaissance civilization had been built, after all, on a century of instability. Never far from the brilliance of worldly glory was the threat of sin and divine punishment. Sin, repentance, and reform: these were the themes behind the numerous sermons calling for crusades against the Ottomans. The 1490s brought an abrupt end to the Italian Peninsula's relative peace and prosperity, destroying forever the delicate balance of optimism and anxiety that had shaped Renaissance culture.

The 1490s were also the years during which Christopher Columbus set sail for the Indies in the name of the Spanish monarchs, when the interests of the Valois and Habsburg dynasties clashed, and when Italy became a battleground for soldiers of many nations. The turn of the century signaled the dawn of a new era of world history shaped by European attempts to dominate the globe. The Renaissance was to give way to a century during which Europeans would struggle for power and for faith.

Suggestions for Further Reading

Source Materials

Brucker, Gene A., ed. *The Society of Renaissance Florence: A Documentary Study.* 1971. Topically arranged documents from the archive.

Fuson, Robert H., ed. *The Log of Christopher Columbus.* 1987. An accessible, scholarly translation.

Molho, Anthony, ed. *Social and Economic Foundations of the Italian Renaissance.* 1969. Includes primary and secondary sources.

Gragg, Florence A., trans., Leona C. Gabel, ed. *Memoirs of a Renaissance Pope: The Commentaries of Pius II.* 1962. An abridged version of insights from a leading Renaissance personality.

Interpretive Studies

Baxandall, Michael. *Painting and Experience in Fifteenth Century Italy: A Primer in the Social History of Pictorial Style.* 1972. A brilliant synthesis of art history and social history.

Boxer, C. R. *Four Centuries of Portuguese Expansion, 1415–1825.* 1969. A succinct survey.

Brucker, Gene A. *Giovanni and Lusanna: Love and Marriage in Renaissance Florence.* 1986. A good story, expertly told.

Burke, Peter. *The Italian Renaissance: Culture and Society in Italy.* 1986. Strong on social and cultural history.

Dollinger, Philippe. *The German Hansa.* 1970. Definitive.

Gilmore, Myron P. *The World of Humanism, 1453–1517.* 1952. Still a classic narrative.

Herlihy, David, and Christiane Klapisch-Zuber. *Tuscans and Their Families: A Study of the Florentine Catasto of 1427.* 1978. An English abridgement of the original French work.

Klapisch-Zuber, Christiane. *Women, Family, and Ritual in Renaissance Italy.* 1985. A collection of original essays on women's history.

Martin, Henri-Jean, and Lucien Febvre. *The Coming of the Book: The Impact of Printing 1450–1800.* 1976. The best comprehensive survey.

Martines, Lauro. *Power and Imagination: City-States in Renaissance Italy.* 1979. A tour de force.

Mattingly, Garrett. *Renaissance Diplomacy.* 1954. Still unsurpassed.

Murray, Peter, and Linda Murray. *The Art of the Renaissance.* 1963. Balanced discussion of Italian and northern European achievements.

Prevenier, Walter, and Wim Blockmans. *The Burgundian Netherlands.* 1986. Richly illustrated text by the two leading scholars on the subject.

CHAPTER 15

The Struggle for Faith and Power, 1494–1560

Hille Feiken left the city of Münster, Germany, on June 16, 1534, elegantly dressed, bedecked with jewels, and determined to kill. Münster, which religious radicals had declared a holy city, lay under siege by armies loyal to its bishop, Franz von Waldeck. After reading the Book of Judith in the Apocrypha, Hille decided to deliver her city by imitating an ancient Israelite heroine named Judith. According to the Book of Ruth, Judith had approached the Assyrian general Holofernes, whose army was attacking Jerusalem. Charmed by Judith's beauty, Holofernes tried to seduce her; but after he had fallen into a drunken sleep, Judith cut off his head. Terrified, the Assyrian forces fled Jerusalem. Obsessed with this story, Hille crossed enemy lines and tried to persuade the commander of the besieging troops to take her to the bishop, promising to reveal a secret means of capturing the city without further fighting. Unfortunately, a defector recognized Hille and betrayed her. She was beheaded, in her own words, "for going out as Judith and trying to make the Bishop of Münster into a Holofernes."

Hille Feiken and the other besieged radicals in Münster were Anabaptists, part of a sect whose members believed themselves to be a community of saints amid a hopelessly sinful world. To prove their faith, adult Anabaptists received a second baptism in anticipation of the imminent Second Coming of Christ and the Last Judgment. The Anabaptists' determination to form a holy community tore at the foundations of the medieval European social and political order, and they met merciless persecution from the authorities. The Münster uprising represented an extreme (and uncharacteristically

Martin Luther

This painting by the German artist Lucas Cranach, one of the best-known likenesses of the reformer, captures Luther's firm faith in God and in his mission, an image that supporters of the Lutheran Reformation were at great pains to project.

violent) outburst of Anabaptist fervor—destined, as we shall see, to be brutally crushed.

Anabaptism was only one dimension of the Reformation, which had been set in motion by the German friar Martin Luther in 1517 and had become a sweeping movement to uproot church abuses and restore early Christian teachings. Hille Feiken's story was a sign of the times. Inspired by Luther—but often going far beyond what he would condone—ordinary men and women attempted to remake their heaven and earth. For more than two generations, such people's demands for freedom of worship and conscience occasionally were expressed in violent uprisings. Their story intertwined with bloody struggles among princes for domination in Europe, an age-old conflict now complicated by the clash of rival faiths. In the end the princes would prevail over both a divided Christendom and a restless people. Protestant or Catholic, European monarchs expanded their power at the expense of the church and disciplined their subjects in the name of piety and order.

Important Dates

1494 French invade Italy; beginning of Valois-Habsburg struggles

1517 Martin Luther criticizes sale of indulgences; beginning of Reformation

1519 Spanish conquest of Mexico

1520 Reformer Huldrych Zwingli breaks with Rome

1525 Revolution in central Europe

1529 Formation of a "Protestant" party

1529–1558 Reign of Charles V

1529–1536 Henry VIII is head of the Anglican church

1532–1536 Spanish conquest of Peru

1534–1535 Anabaptist Kingdom of Münster

1541 John Calvin established permanently in Geneva

1545–1563 Council of Trent

1546–1547 War of Schmalkaldic League

1555 Religious Peace of Augsburg

1559 Treaty of Cateau-Cambrésis

A New Heaven and a New Earth

In the last book of the Bible, Revelation (also known as the Apocalypse), the prophet St. John the Evangelist foretells the passing of the old world and the coming of a new heaven and earth presided over by Christ. At the beginning of the sixteenth century, Europeans expected the Last Judgment to arrive soon. Indeed, the times seemed desperate. The Turks were advancing on Christian Europe while Christian princes fought among themselves. Some critics of the church labeled the pope as none other than the terrifying figure of the Antichrist, whose evil reign (according to Revelation) would end with Christ's return to earth.

It was in this frightening atmosphere that Martin Luther questioned the fundamental principles behind the church's teachings and practices. From its origins as a theological dispute in 1517, Luther's reform movement sparked explosive protests. By the time of his death in 1546, half of western Europe had renounced allegiance to Rome. Denying the Roman church's claim to absolute truth, a variety of Protestant churches asserted that they embodied the "simple and pure" Christianity of earliest apostolic times. In turn, ordinary people sometimes defied the new Protestant clergy and took religious reform into their own hands.

The Crisis of Faith

It was the established church, not Christian religion, that proved deficient to believers in Europe. Numerous signs before the Reformation pointed to an intense spiritual anxiety among the laity. People went on pilgrimages; new shrines sprang up, especially ones dedicated to the Virgin Mary and Christ; prayer books printed in various vernacular languages as well as Latin sold briskly. Alongside the sacraments and rituals of the official church, laypeople practiced their own rituals for healing and salvation.

Only a thin line separated miracles, which the church could accept, and magic, which it rejected. Clerics who wanted to reform the church denounced superstitions and the insatiable popular appetite for the sacred, but others readily exploited gullible laypeople. Perhaps the most notorious scandal prior to the Reformation occurred in the Swiss city of Basel. There in 1510 several Dominicans claimed that the Virgin Mary had worked "miracles" that they themselves had concocted. For a while their plot brought in crowds of pilgrims, but when the deception was uncovered, the perpetrators were burned at the stake.

The worst excesses in popular piety conjured up the religious and racial intolerance that had plagued Christian Europe throughout the Middle Ages. In the generation before the Reformation, Jews were frequently accused of ritually slaughtering Christian children and torturing the consecrated Eucharist, or Host, the consecrated bread that Christians believed was the body of Christ. Thus in 1510 a priest in Brandenburg accused local Jews of stealing and torturing the Eucharist. When, according to legend, the consecrated bread bled, the Jews were imprisoned and killed. A shrine dedicated to the bleeding Host attracted thousands of pilgrims seeking fortune and health.

Often the church gave external behavior more weight than spiritual intentions. For example, the number of prayers recited seemed to count for more than the believer's spiritual attitude. A case in point was the sacrament of penance—the confessing of sins and receiving of forgiveness, one of the central pillars of Christian morality and of the Roman church. On the eve of the Reformation, a mass of regulations defined the gradations of human sinfulness. For example, even married couples could sin if they had intercourse on one of the church's many holy days or made love "in lust" instead of for procreation. The church similarly regulated other kinds of behavior by, for example, prohibiting the eating of meat during feast days and censoring blasphemous language.

In receiving the sacrament of penance, sinners were expected to examine their conscience and sincerely confess their sins to a priest; in practice, however, confession proved highly unsatisfactory to many Christians. First, for those with religious scruples the demands of confession intensified their anxiety about salvation. Some could not get peace of mind because they were unsure if they had remembered to confess all their sins; others trembled before God's anger and doubted his mercy. Second, some priests abused their authority by demanding sexual or monetary favors in return for penance. They seduced or blackmailed female parishioners and excommunicated debtors who failed to pay church taxes or loans from the clergy. Such reported incidents, although by no means widespread, seriously compromised the sanctity of the priestly office and sacrament. Finally, the practice of substituting monetary fines for religious tasks (such as pilgrimage or prayer) in penance suggested that the church was more interested in making money than saving souls—the charge, we shall see, that ignited Luther's reform movement.

To its critics, the Roman church was burdened by a vast, unresponsive, and sometimes corrupt clerical bureaucracy. Scandals involving church officialdom multiplied. In 1498 the archbishop of Cosenza, Bartolomeo Flores, the former private secretary to Pope Alexander VI, was sentenced to life imprisonment for having forged, with accomplices, more than three thousand papal bulls (documents that exempted holders from the church's many rules). For example, a Portuguese woman of royal blood had received permission to leave her nunnery and marry the late king's illegitimate son; a priest was allowed to marry without losing his position; and many clerics had bought the right to hold multiple benefices (ecclesiastical positions), a widespread abuse of canon law.

If papal dispensation could be bought, parishioners could also invest in the afterlife. Although a sincere confession saved a sinner from hell, he or she still faced doing penance, either in this life or the next. To alleviate suffering after death in purgatory, a pious person could go on pilgrimage, attend mass, do holy works, contribute to the church, and buy indulgences. A German prince, Frederick the Wise of Saxony (who later became Luther's protector), amassed the largest collection of relics outside of Italy. By 1518 his castle church contained 17,443 holy relics, including a piece of Moses' burning bush, parts of the holy cradle and swaddling clothes, thirty-five fragments of the true cross, and the Virgin Mary's milk. A diligent and pious person who rendered appropriate devotion to each of these relics could earn exactly 127,799 years and 116 days of remission from purgatory.

Dissatisfaction with the official church and its inflexible rules prompted several reform efforts prior to the Reformation; these were, however, limited to certain monastic houses and dioceses. More important, the church was losing touch with the religious sensibilities of the laypeople, who often resented clerical privileges. Urban merchants and artisans yearned for a religion more meaningful to their daily life and for a clergy more responsive to their needs. They wanted priests to preach edifying sermons, to administer the sacraments conscientiously, and to lead moral lives. They criticized the church's rich endowments that provided income for children of the nobility, who cared little about the salvation of townspeople. And they generously donated money to establish new preacherships for university-trained clerics, overwhelmingly from urban backgrounds and often from the same social classes as the donors. These young clerics, most of them schooled in humanism, often criticized the established church and hoped for reform.

Erasmus of Rotterdam
The great Dutch humanist was famous for his edition of the original Greek text of the New Testament, depicted here in the open book. Many contemporary portraits of Erasmus exist, attesting to his renown.

A Christian Commonwealth?

Sickened by the endless warfare among Christian princes and outraged by the abuse of power, a generation of Christian humanists dreamed of ideal societies based on peace and morality. Within their own Christian society, these intellectuals sought to realize the ethical ideals of the classical world. Scholarship and social reform became inseparable goals. Two men, the Dutch scholar Desiderius Erasmus (c. 1466–1536) and the English lawyer Thomas More (1478–1535), stood out as outstanding representatives of these "Christian humanists," who, unlike Italian humanists, placed their primary emphasis on Christian piety.

Erasmus dominated the humanist world of early sixteenth-century Europe just as Cicero had dominated the glory of ancient Roman letters. He was on intimate terms with kings and popes, and his reputation extended across Europe. Following a brief stay in a monastery as a young man, Erasmus dedicated his life to scholarship. After studying in Paris, Erasmus traveled to Venice and served as an editor with Aldus Manutius, the leading printer of Latin and Greek books.

Through his books and letters, both disseminated by Manutius's printing press, Erasmus's fame spread. In the *Adages* (1500), a collection of quotations from ancient literature offering his witty and wise commentaries on the human experience, Erasmus established a reputation as a superb humanist dedicated to educational reform. Themes explored in the *Adages* continued in the *Colloquies* (1523), a compilation of Latin dialogues intended as language-learning exercises, in which Erasmus exerted his sharp wit to criticize the morals of his time. Lamenting poor table manners, Erasmus advised his cultivated readers not to pick their noses at meals, not to share half-eaten chicken legs, and not to speak while stuffing their mouths. Turning to political matters, he mocked the corruption of the clergy and the bloody ambitions of Christian princes.

Only through education, Erasmus believed, could individuals reform themselves and society. His goal was a unified, peaceful Christendom in which charity and good works, not empty ceremonies, would mark true religion; in which learning and piety would dispel the darkness of ignorance. Many of these ideas were elaborated in *Handbook of the Militant Christian* (1503), an eloquent plea for a simple religion devoid of greed and the lust for power. In *The Praise of Folly* (1509), Erasmus satirized values held dear by his contemporaries. Ignorance, humility, and poverty represented the true Christian virtues in a world that worshiped pomposity, power, and wealth, he said. The wise appeared foolish, he concluded, for their wisdom and values were not of this world.

Inspired by the Gospel ideal of Christianity, Erasmus devoted years to preparing a new Latin edition of the New Testament from the original Greek; it was published in 1516 by the Froben Press in Basel. Moved by the pacifism of the apostolic church, Erasmus admonished the young future emperor Charles V to rule as a just Christian prince. Erasmus vented his anger by ridiculing the warrior-pope Julius II and expressed deep sorrow for the brutal warfare that had been ravaging Europe for decades.

A man of peace and moderation, Erasmus found himself challenged by angry younger men and radical ideas once the Reformation took hold. Erasmus eventually decided in favor of Christian unity over reform and schism. His dream of Christian pacifism shattered, he lived to see dissenters executed—by Catholics and Protestants alike—for speaking their conscience. Erasmus spent his last years in Freiburg and died in Basel, isolated from the Protestant community, his writings condemned in Rome and ignored by many leaders of the Catholic church, which was divided over the intellectual legacy of its famous son.

If Erasmus found himself abandoned by his times, his good friend Thomas More, to whom *The Praise of Folly* was dedicated,* met a genuinely tragic fate. Having attended Oxford and the Inns of Court, where English lawyers were trained, More had legal talents that served him well in government. Variously a member of Parliament and a royal ambassador, he proved a competent and loyal servant to Henry VIII. In 1529 this ideal servant to the king became lord chancellor, but, tired of court intrigue and in protest against Henry's divorce, More resigned his position in 1532. As we shall see, he would later pay with his life for upholding conscience over political expediency.

More's best-known work, *Utopia* (1516), which describes an imaginary land inspired by the recent voyages of discovery, was intended as a critique of his own society. A just, equitable, and hardworking community, Utopia (meaning both "no place" and "best place" in Greek) was the opposite of England. In Utopia everyone worked on the land for two years; no private property meant there was no greed; and since they were served by public schools, communal kitchens, hospitals, and nurseries, Utopians had no need for money. Ded-

***Albrecht Dürer,* The Knight, Death, and the Devil**
An illustration for Erasmus's The Handbook of the Militant Christian, *this great engraving is often interpreted as depicting a Christian clad in the armor of righteousness on a path through life beset by death and demonic temptations. It aptly symbolizes the European mentality during the Reformation.*

*The Latin title, *Encomium Moriae* ("The Praise of More"), was a pun on More's name.

icated to the pursuit of knowledge and natural religion, with equal distribution of goods and few laws, Utopia knew neither crime nor war. But unlike More's "Nowhereland," in the real world social injustice bred crime and warfare. Deprived of their livelihood, desperate men became thieves, and "thieves do make quite efficient soldiers, and soldiers make quite enterprising thieves." More believed that politics, property, and war fueled human misery, whereas for his Utopians, "fighting was a thing they absolutely loathe. They say it's a quite subhuman form of activity, although human beings are more addicted to it than any of the lower animals."

More's tolerant and rational society did have a few oddities—voluntary slavery, for instance, and strictly controlled travel. Although premarital sex brought severe punishment, prospective marriage partners could examine one another naked before making their final decisions. Men headed Utopia's households and exercised authority over women and children. And Utopians did not shy away from declaring war on their neighbors to protect their way of life. Nevertheless, this imaginary society was paradise compared to a Christian Europe battered and devastated by the French invasion of Italy in 1494.

The Struggle for Domination

A prosperous, fragmented land, Italy in 1494 to 1559 was the battlefield for the great powers of western Europe. The struggle began when Charles VIII of France (∗1483–1498) laid claim to the Neapolitan crown. Welcomed into Italy by the Milanese and Florentines, who were playing political games of their own, the French army easily conquered Naples. French successes soon gave way to defeat as the political winds shifted and the Italian states scrambled to remake alliances in order to preserve the balance of power. A second invasion, under Louis XII (∗1498–1515), only sucked France deeper into a quagmire that yielded no permanent conquests.

The first phase of the Italian Wars, as these general European conflicts came to be called, lasted until 1520. On one side stood France and its Italian allies, usually Florence and Venice; on the other were shifting anti-French alliances that included the papacy, Spain, the Holy Roman Empire, and various Italian states, each pursuing its own gain. In the battlefields of northern Italy, French cavalry and artillery challenged fierce Swiss fighters, who served as papal and imperial mercenaries. At the battle of Marignano (1515), the young French king Francis I (∗1515–1547) conquered Milan, dealing a crushing blow to the Swiss.

The French king soon encountered a formidable opponent, Charles V (∗1520–1558). Thanks to a series of dynastic unions, Charles had inherited the largest empire Europe had ever known. At the age of nineteen he became the ruler of the Low Countries, Spain and Spain's Italian and New World dominions, and the Austrian Habsburg lands. The next year, in 1520, Charles was elected Holy Roman emperor.

The church offered paltry moral guidance in this conflict among Christian princes; indeed, the Vicar of Christ, as the pope was known, was simply one more participant in the power struggle. During the fifty years before the Reformation, popes had tried to subjugate the lands over which they had long been nominal rulers. The names they chose signified the style of the vainglorious papacy:* Rodrigo Borgia took the name of the ancient Macedonian conqueror by naming himself Pope Alexander VI (∗1492–1503); his successor, Giuliano della Rovere, called himself Julius II (∗1503–1513) after another strongman from ancient history, Julius Caesar. Adopting the names of ancient conquerors reflected the papal self-image; the pope was not only the supreme spiritual head of Christendom but also a mighty prince who ruled over an extensive territory.

Alexander VI and Julius II both came from powerful noble bloodlines. The Borgias of Aragon ranked among the twenty most prestigious noble lineages in Valencia. The della Roveres, from Liguria in northern Italy, married into French royalty. Both Alexander and Julius owed their ecclesiastical careers to

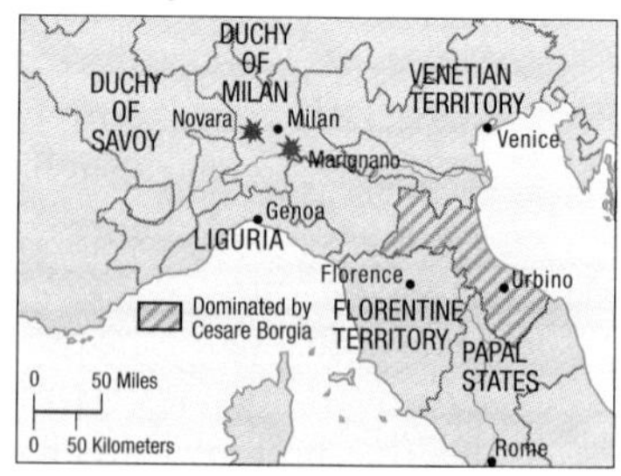

Central Italy in the Beginning of the Sixteenth Century

*For centuries each newly elected pope had followed the custom of choosing a new name. The custom continues to this day.

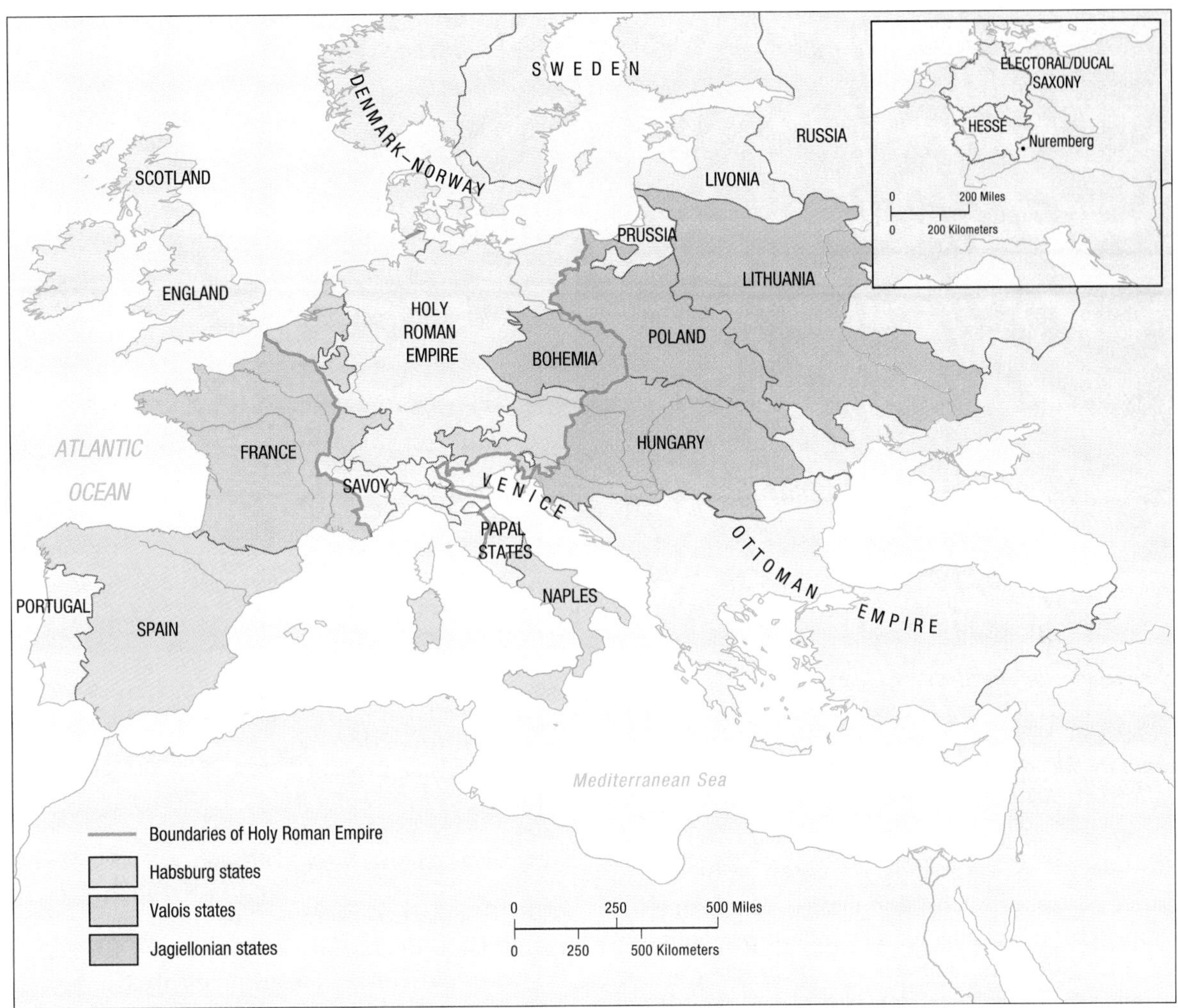

Europe, 1494–1519

family connections: their respective uncles were two popes, Calixtus III (*1455–1458) and Sixtus IV (*1471–1484). This practice of promoting nephews and sons to positions of power within the papal state led to the coining of the term *nepotism* (*nepos* in Latin means "nephew"). Family connections proved equally important in the sixteenth century, when two members of the Medici family ascended the papal throne as Leo X (*1513–1521) and Clement VII (*1523–1534).

In their private lives these princes of the church often behaved as their secular relatives did. Both before and after his election, Alexander VI fathered children—a practice generally tolerated in Rome. For Alexander, winning back the papal state was crucial for the papacy's survival. Competing as one of the Italian powers, the papacy was drawn into the dangers and allures of secular power politics. In a papal court torn by factional struggles, the appointment of nephews as cardinals was the only reliable means to preserve papal power. Cesare Borgia, Alexander's son, served as his father's trusted advisor when he was a cardinal. After the death of his brother (rumors circulated that Cesare murdered him), Cesare renounced his cardinalate to carve a principality out of the papal lands—an effort that collapsed when Julius II succeeded Alexander. But in spite of his bitter hatred for the Borgias, Julius continued their policies. Leading a papal army, Julius crushed the petty lords who

Michelangelo, The Sistine Chapel Ceiling
Depicting the Creation of the world and the Fall of Man, these magnificent frescos were painted by Michelangelo on a commission by Julius II to adorn the chapel in St. Peter's Basilica built by the pope's uncle, Sixtus IV. Recent restoration has revealed the vibrant colors of Michelangelo's original work, which had been obscured by centuries of smoke and grime.

ruled parts of the papal dominions, centralizing administration and augmenting church revenues.

To glorify his imperial image, Julius also became a great patron of the arts. His patronage led to the completion of the Sistine Chapel, begun under his uncle, Sixtus IV. The chapel's ceilings were graced by the brush of the Florentine artist Michelangelo, who also designed a grandiose but never-completed tomb for Julius based on the model of tombs for Roman emperors. Julius hoped to undertake a crusade against the Turks, a project proclaimed but unfulfilled by other popes since the mid-fifteenth century. Such a crusade, however, remained only a dream as long as Italy was threatened by foreign arms.

A Failed Reform: Savonarola, Machiavelli, and Florence

Nowhere amid this power struggle was the papacy's moral bankruptcy more apparent than in its treatment of Girolamo Savonarola (1452–1498), a Dominican friar in Florence. On November 1, 1494, Savonarola mounted the pulpit in the Florentine Cathedral before a swollen and frightened crowd of Florentines who sought solace in his terrifying words. "You know that years ago great tribulations were announced before there was any noise or smell of these wars launched by the men from over the mountains which we are now witnessing," roared the preacher. "You also know that not two full years have passed since I said to you: Behold the terrible swift sword of the Lord! Not I but God was responsible for this prediction to you, and behold, it has come and it is coming."

This "terrible swift sword" was the French army under King Charles VIII, on its way across the border to claim the Neapolitan throne. The Florentines, having just overthrown the Medici regime that had dominated their city since 1434, awaited the French king with trepidation. On November 5 they delegated Savonarola to head an embassy to Charles. During Charles's subsequent stay in Florence, Savonarola persuaded the king to depart in peace and proceed on to Naples as the instrument of God's wrath, sparing Florence.

Delivered from the French army, the Florentines hailed Savonarola as a great prophet.

For the next three and a half years, Savonarola held sway in Florence. He admonished the citizens to repent, proclaimed Florence a New Jerusalem, and denounced Alexander VI for corruption. His followers burned games, profane images, erotic books, playing cards, and all sorts of worldly "vanities." But gradually the Florentines tired of Savonarola's prophetic wrath, and when Alexander excommunicated him they turned him over to the church. On May 23, 1498, on the pope's explicit orders, Savonarola was hanged and burned for heresy.

In the crowd of spectators at Savonarola's execution was Niccolò Machiavelli (1469–1527), a Florentine civil servant. Machiavelli felt that Savonarola's rise and fall taught a valuable lesson in power. "It was the purity of his life, the doctrines he preached, and the subjects for his discourses that sufficed to make the people have faith in him," Machiavelli would write years later. But the people are fickle, he would note, and persuasion alone cannot maintain power: "Thus it comes about that all armed prophets have conquered, and unarmed ones failed." Savonarola was an example of an unarmed prophet "who failed entirely in his new rules when the multitude began to disbelieve in him, and he had no means of holding fast those who had believed or of compelling the unbelievers to believe." In short, Machiavelli would assert, the exercise of political power owed little to ethics.

Years later, after he lost office, Machiavelli set his political observations down on paper. In 1513 he dedicated a short political treatise, *The Prince*, to Giuliano de' Medici, whom papal troops had just restored to power in Florence. In this treatise (not published until 1531), Machiavelli pondered the laws of power as manifested by the political events of his day. Stripping politics of its ethical and religious veneer, Machiavelli held up Cesare Borgia, Alexander's son, as the model of a ruthless and successful prince. The aim of politics, according to Machiavelli, was to conquer fortune with human will and power.

In his admiration of power and in separating politics from morality, Machiavelli used the language of male domination to articulate power politics. Fortune, a feminine noun in Italian, is opposed by *virtù*, or manly strength (from the Latin *vir*, meaning "man"); princes must use violence to subject fortune to their will in order to prosper. Fortune, personified as feminine power, resembles the force of nature—ever-changing and fickle. A prince would soon come to grief, Machiavelli argued, if he were to depend entirely on fortune: "But I do feel this: that it is better to be rash than timid, for Fortune is a woman, and the man who wants to hold her down must beat and bully her. . . . Like a woman, too, she is always a friend of the young, because they are less timid, more brutal, and take charge of her more recklessly."

As satire and as objective political analysis, *The Prince* offered remarkable insights into the relationship between power and faith. To the strongman, or prince, Machiavelli conceded the possibility to control chaos by understanding the principles of politics. The exercise of power, according to Machiavelli, justified the use of religion as an instrument of rule, a view that scandalized his contemporaries. In spite of his perhaps despairing cynicism, Machiavelli was a republican, a patriot who wanted to restore the glory of Florence and expel the invaders from Italy. Although *The Discourses*, his extended commentary on the ancient Roman historian Livy, echoed Machiavelli's republicanism and patriotism, it was *The Prince* that made him notorious. The term *Machiavellian* quickly took on the negative meaning it still has today, and the machinations of Italian princes, these descendants of the ancient Romans, would horrify many pilgrims from the Holy Roman Empire.

The Reformation Begins

Since the mid-fifteenth century many clerics had tried to reform the church, criticizing clerical abuses and calling for moral rejuvenation, but their efforts came up against the church's inertia and resistance. Outside the clergy, many laypeople had become alienated from the church, feeling that its personnel and doctrines were indifferent to their spiritual needs. At the beginning of the sixteenth century widespread popular piety and anticlericalism existed side by side, fomenting an explosive mixture of need and resentment. A young German friar, tormented by his own religious doubts, was to become the spokesman for a generation.

THE PROGRESS OF THE REFORMATION

1517 Martin Luther publicizes the Ninety-five Theses attacking the sale of indulgences

1525 Death of Thomas Müntzer, a radical reformer who had urged revolution and extermination of the ungodly

1529 German princes who support Luther protest the condemnation of religious reform by Charles V at the Imperial Diet of Speyer, hence the sobriquet "Protestants"

1529–1536 The English Parliament establishes King Henry VIII as head of the Anglican church, severing ties to Rome

1531 Death of Huldrych Zwingli at the Battle of Kappel

1534–1535 A group of Anabaptists control the city of Münster, Germany, in a failed experiment to create a holy community

1541 John Calvin establishes himself permanently in Geneva, making that city a model of Christian reform and discipline

Martin Luther and the German Nation

Son of a miner and entrepreneur, Martin Luther (1483–1546) studied law, pursuing a career open to ambitious young men from middle-class families, which had been urged on him by his father. His true vocation, however, lay with the church. Caught in a storm on a lonely road one midsummer's night, the young student grew terrified by the thunder and lightning. Martin implored the help of St. Anne, the mother of the Virgin Mary, and promised he would enter a monastery if she protected him. Thus, to the chagrin of his father, Luther abandoned law for theology and entered the Augustinian order.

In the monastery the young Luther, finding no spiritual consolation in the sacraments of the church, experienced a religious crisis. Appalled at his own sense of sinfulness and the weakness of human nature, he lived in terror of God's justice in spite of frequent confessions and penance. A pilgrimage to Rome only deepened Luther's unease with the institutional church. Coming to his aid, a sympathetic superior sent Luther to study theology, a course of study that gradually led him to experience grace and insight into salvation. Luther recalled his monastic days in these words shortly before his death:

> *Though I lived as a monk without reproach, I felt that I was a sinner before God with an extremely disturbed conscience. I could not believe that he was placated by my satisfaction [in penance]. I did not love, yes, I hated the righteous God who punishes sinners, and secretly . . . I was angry with God. . . . Nevertheless, I beat importunately upon Paul [in Romans 1:17]. . . . At last, by the mercy of God, meditating day and night, I gave heed to the context of the words, namely, "In [the gospel] the righteousness of God is revealed, as it is written, 'He who through faith is righteous shall live.'" There I began to understand that the righteousness of God is that by which the righteous live by a gift of God, namely by faith. And this is the meaning: the righteousness of God is revealed by the gospel, namely, the passive righteousness with which merciful God justifies us by faith. . . . Here I felt that I was altogether born again and had entered paradise itself.*

Luther followed this tortuous spiritual journey while serving as a professor of theology at the University of Wittenberg, recently founded by Frederick the Wise, Elector of Saxony. But events conspired to make Luther a public figure. In 1516 the new archbishop of Mainz, Albrecht of Brandenburg, commissioned a Dominican friar to sell indulgences in his archdiocese (which included Saxony); the proceeds would help cover the cost of constructing St. Peter's Basilica in Rome and also partly defray Archbishop Albrecht's expenses in pursuing his election. Such blatant profiteering outraged many, including Luther. In 1517, Luther composed ninety-five theses—propositions for an academic debate—that questioned indulgence peddling and the purchase of church offices. Once they became

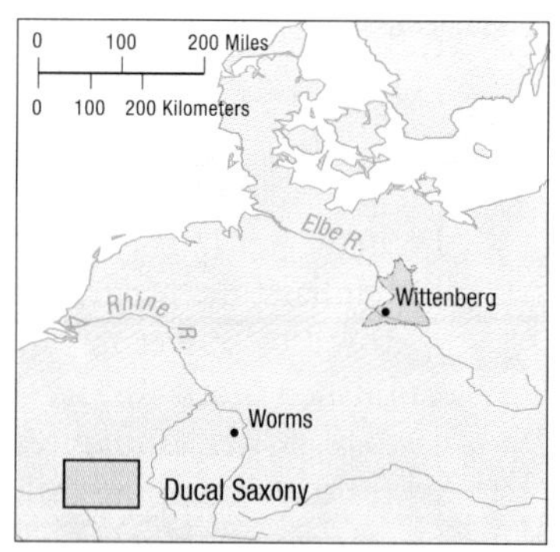

Luther's World

public, the theses unleashed a torrent of pent-up resentment and frustration in the laypeople.

What began as a theological debate in a provincial university soon engulfed the Holy Roman Empire. Two groups predominated among Luther's earliest supporters: younger humanists and those clerics who shared Luther's critical attitude toward the church establishment. It is difficult to generalize about these early clerical rebels, or "evangelicals," as they would call themselves, after the Gospels.* None of the evangelicals came from the upper echelons of the church; many were from urban middle-class backgrounds, and most were university-trained and well educated. As a group their profile differed from that of the poorly educated rural clergy, or from their noble clerical superiors, who often owed their ecclesiastical dignities to family influence rather than theological learning. The evangelicals also stood apart in that they represented those social groups most ready to challenge clerical authority—merchants, artisans, and literate urban laypeople.

Initially, Luther presented himself as the pope's "loyal opposition." In 1520 he composed three treatises. In *Freedom of a Christian*, which he wrote in Latin for the learned and addressed to Pope Leo X, Luther argued that the Roman church's numerous rules and its stress on "good works" were useless. He insisted that faith, not good works, would save sinners from damnation, and he sharply distinguished between true Gospel teachings and invented church doctrines. Basing himself on St. Paul and St. Augustine, Luther argued that by his suffering on the cross Christ had freed humanity from the guilt of sin, and that only through faith in God's justice and mercy could believers be saved. Thus the church's laws of behavior had no place in the search for salvation. Luther suggested instead "the priesthood of all believers," arguing that the Bible provided all the teachings necessary for Christian living, and that a professional caste of clerics should not hold sway over laypeople. *Freedom of a Christian* was immediately translated into German and was published widely. Its slogans "by faith alone," "by Scripture alone," and "the priesthood of all believers" came to encapsulate the reform movement.

In his second treatise, *To the Nobility of the German Nation*, which he wrote in German, Luther appealed to German nationalism. He denounced the corrupt Italians in Rome who were cheating and exploiting his compatriots and called upon the German princes to defend their nation and reform the church. This appeal to secular rulers to become church reformers had a long tradition dating back to the Investiture Conflict of the eleventh century. Luther's third major treatise, *On the Babylonian Captivity of the Church*, which he composed in Latin mainly for a clerical audience, condemned the papacy as the embodiment of the Antichrist.

From Rome's perspective, the "Luther Affair," as church officials called it, was essentially a matter of clerical discipline. Rome ordered Luther to obey his superiors and keep quiet. But the church establishment had seriously misjudged the gravity of the situation. Luther's ideas, published in numerous German and Latin editions, spread rapidly throughout the Holy Roman Empire, unleashing forces that Luther could not control. Social, nationalist, and religious protests fused into an explosive mass, one very similar to the Czech revolution that Jan Hus had inspired a century earlier. Like Hus, Luther appeared before an emperor: in 1521 he defended his faith before Charles V at the Imperial Diet of Worms, where he shocked Germans by declaring his admiration for the Czech heretic. But unlike Hus, Luther did not suffer martyrdom because he enjoyed the protection of Frederick the Wise.

During the 1520s the anti-Roman evangelicals included many German princes, city officials, professors, priests, and ordinary men and women, particularly in the cities; essentially, the early Reformation was an urban movement. As centers of publishing and commerce, German towns became natural distribution points for Lutheran propaganda. Moreover, urban people proved particularly receptive to Luther's message: many were literate and were eager to read the Scriptures, and merchants and artisans resented the clergy's tax-exempt status and the competition from monasteries and nunneries that produced their own goods. Magistrates began to curtail clerical privileges and subordinate the clergy to municipal authority. Luther's message—that clerical intercession was not necessary for a Christian's salvation—spoke to

*The word *Gospel*, meaning "good tidings," comes from the Old English translation of the Greek word *evangelion*.

the townspeople's spiritual needs and social vision. Inspired by Luther's message, many reform priests led their urban parishioners away from Roman liturgy, and from Wittenberg the reform movement quickly fanned out into a torrent of many streams.

Zwingli and the Swiss Confederation

While Luther provided the religious leadership for Protestant northern Germany, Germany's south came under the strong influence of the Reformation movement that had emerged in the poor, mountainous country of Switzerland. The Swiss Confederation (made up of thirteen cantons) had declared its independence from the Holy Roman Empire in 1291, although it would not be internationally recognized until 1648. In the late fifteenth and early sixteenth centuries, Switzerland's chief source of income was the export of soldiers: hardy Swiss peasants fought as mercenaries in papal, French, and imperial armies, earning respect as fierce pikemen. Military captains recruited and organized young men from village communes; the women stayed behind to farm and tend animals. Many young Swiss men died on the battlefields of Italy, and many others returned maimed for life. In 1520 the chief preacher of the Swiss city of Zurich, Huldrych Zwingli (1484–1531), criticized his superior, Cardinal Matthew Schinner, for sending the country's young men off to serve as cannon fodder in papal armies.

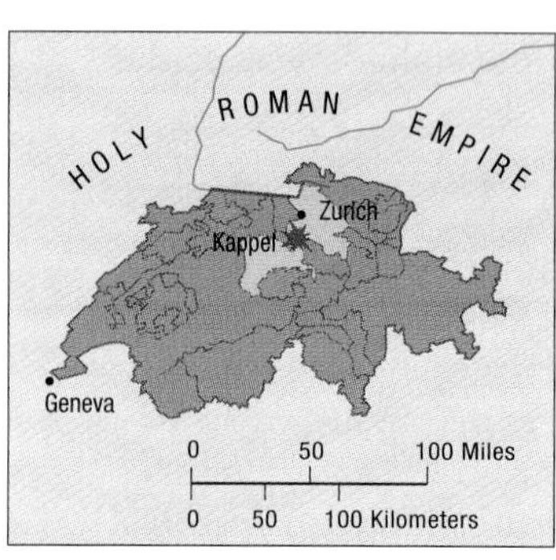

Zwingli's World

The son of a Swiss village leader, Zwingli became a reformer independently of Martin Luther. After completing his university studies, Zwingli was ordained as a priest and served as an army chaplain for several years, during which he witnessed the bloody battles of Novara and Marignano. Deeply influenced by Erasmus, whom he met in 1515, Zwingli adopted the Dutch humanist's vision of social renewal through education. In 1520, Zwingli openly declared himself a reformist and attacked the church rituals of fasting and clerical celibacy, and corruption among the ecclesiastical hierarchy.

Under Zwingli's leadership, the city and canton of Zurich served as the center for the Swiss reform movement. Guided by his vision of a theocratic (church-directed) society that would unite religion, politics, and morality, Zwingli refused to draw any distinction between the ideal citizen and the perfect Christian—an idea radically different from Luther's. While defending the reform movement in Zurich against the Catholic cantons, Zwingli also rooted out internal dissent.

Luther and Zwingli also differed in their view of the role of the Eucharist, or Holy Communion. Luther insisted that Christ was truly present in this central Christian rite, although not in the strict Catholic sense. Zwingli, influenced by Erasmus, viewed the Eucharist as simply a ceremony symbolizing Christ's union with believers.

In 1529, troubled by these differences and other disagreements, evangelical princes and magistrates assembled the major reformers at Marburg, in central Germany. After several days of intense discussions, the north German and Swiss reformers managed to resolve many doctrinal differences, but Luther and Zwingli failed to agree on the meaning of the Eucharist. Thus the German and Swiss reform movements continued on separate paths. The issue of Holy Communion would later divide Lutherans and Calvinists as well.

Although the Reformation spread from Zurich to other cities in Switzerland, five rural cantons in the heartland of the Swiss mercenary trade remained Catholic. Failing to settle their differences through political negotiations and theological debates, the Swiss plunged into civil war in 1531, with the five Catholic cantons fielding an army against Zurich. Marching as a chaplain with the citizen army from his hometown, Zwingli was killed in the battle of Kappel that same year. His enemies quartered and burned his body. The leadership of the Swiss reform movement was taken up by Zwingli's son-in-law, Heinrich Bullinger.

The Gospel of the Common People

While Zwingli was challenging the Roman church, some laypeople in Zurich secretly pursued their own path to reform. Taking their cue from the New Testament's descriptions of the first Christian community, these men and women believed that true faith was based on reason and free will. They found the baptism of infants invalid—how could a baby knowingly choose Christ?, they asked—and instead baptized one another as thinking adults. They came to be called Anabaptists—those who were rebaptized. Because the early church councils had explicitly condemned rebaptism, the Zurich Anabaptists challenged the new evangelical church, which saw itself as the source of the early Christian revival. The practice of rebaptism symbolized the Anabaptists' determination to withdraw from a social order corrupted (as they saw it) by power and evil; as pacifists who were rejecting the authority of courts and magistrates, they considered themselves a community of true Christians unblemished by sin.

Zwingli immediately attacked the Anabaptists for their refusal to bear arms and swear oaths of allegiance, sensing quite accurately that they were repudiating his theocratic order. When persuasion failed to convince the Anabaptists of their errors, Zwingli urged Zurich magistrates to carry out the death sentence against them. Thus the Reformation's first martyrs of conscience were victims of its evangelical reformers. Nevertheless, Anabaptism spread quickly from Zurich to many cities in southern Germany, despite the Holy Roman Empire's general condemnation of the movement in 1529. Vehemently antiestablishment, the Anabaptist movement, which included some ex-priests, drew its leadership primarily from the artisan class and its members from the middle and lower classes—men and women attracted by a simple message of peace and salvation.

Meanwhile, Luther found that he could no longer control the religious protests that were springing up throughout the Holy Roman Empire. Between 1520 and 1525 many city governments, often under intense popular pressure and sometimes in sympathy with the evangelicals, allowed the reform movement to sweep away church authority. Local officials appointed new clerics who were committed to reforming Christian doctrine and ritual. The turning point came in 1525, when the crisis of church authority exploded in a massive rural uprising that threatened the entire social order.

The church was the largest landowner in the Holy Roman Empire: about one-seventh of the empire's territory consisted of ecclesiastical principalities in which bishops and abbots exercised both secular and churchly power. Luther's anticlerical message struck home with peasants who were paying taxes to both their lord and the church. In the spring of 1525 many peasants in south and central Germany rose in rebellion, sometimes inspired by wandering preachers. The princes of the church, the rebels charged, were wolves in sheep's clothing, fleecing Christ's flock to satisfy their sanctimonious greed. Some urban workers and artisans joined the peasant bands, plundering monasteries, refusing to pay church taxes, and demanding village autonomy, the abolition of serfdom, and the right to appoint their own pastors. The more radical rebels called for the destruction of the entire ruling class. In Thuringia the rebels were led by an ex-priest, Thomas Müntzer, who promised to chastise the wicked and thus clear the way for the Last Judgment.

Müntzer (c. 1489–1525) was a volatile young man who led an unsettled life. Visiting Prague, he came under the influence of the Hussites (followers of Jan Hus). Unlike Luther, who had close ties to Frederick the Wise, Müntzer was a simple pastor in the small Saxon town of Allstedt. Convinced that the Last Judgment was at hand and that he himself was a latter-day prophet and an instrument of God, Müntzer tried to convince the Saxon princes to take up God's sword to destroy the ungodly. Frederick was not persuaded, and Luther took great alarm at Müntzer's radicalism. Anticipating repression, Müntzer fled Allstedt, only to return to Thuringia when the commoners rose in rebellion.

The revolution of 1525, known as the Peasants War, split the reform movement. Fearing a social revolution, princes and city authorities turned against the rebels. In Thuringia Catholic and evangelical princes joined hands to crush Müntzer and his supporters. All over the empire princes defeated peasant armies, hunted down their leaders, and uprooted all opposition. By the end of the year more than one hundred thousand had been killed and others maimed, imprisoned, or exiled. Luther had tried to mediate the conflict, chastising the princes for their brutality toward the peasants but also warning the rebels against mixing religion and social protest. Luther believed that rulers were ordained by God and thus must be obeyed even if they were tyrants. The Kingdom of God belonged not to this world but to the next, he insisted, and the body of true Christians (as opposed to the in-

The Revolution of 1525 in Germany

stitutional church, in which sinners and Christians mingled) remained known only to God. Luther considered Müntzer's mixing of religion and politics the greatest danger to the Reformation, nothing less than "the Devil's work." When the rebels ignored Luther's appeal and followed more radical preachers, Luther called on the princes to restore the divinely ordained social order. Fundamentally conservative in its political philosophy, the new evangelical church would henceforth depend for its sustenance on established political authority.

Emerging as the champions of an orderly religious reform, many German princes eventually confronted Emperor Charles V, who supported Rome. In 1529, Charles declared the Roman faith the empire's only legitimate religion. The German princes protested, proclaiming their allegiance to the reform cause, and their party came to be called the Protestants. During the 1530s religious schism assumed political forms. In 1531 Protestant princes and imperial cities formed the Schmalkaldic League, a mutual defense alliance against the Catholic emperor.

The common people, however, did not disappear from the Reformation movement. Disillusioned by the new alliance between religion and politics, some Anabaptists turned to violence. In 1534 one incendiary group, believing that the end of the world was imminent, gained control of the northwest German city of Münster. Proclaiming themselves a community of saints, this group of Anabaptists, imitating the ancient Israelites, were initially governed by twelve elders. Later, Jan of Leiden, a Dutch tailor who claimed to be the prophesied leader—a second "King David"—defeated an attack by the bishop of Münster, who had besieged the city. During this short-lived social experiment the Münster Anabaptists abolished private property in imitation of the early Christian church and dissolved traditional marriages, allowing men to have multiple wives like Old Testament patriarchs. As the siege tightened, messengers left Münster in search of relief while the leaders exhorted the faithful to remain steadfast in the hope of the Second Coming of Christ. Hille Feiken, as we have seen, tried to assassinate the bishop himself. But with food and hope exhausted, a soldier betrayed the city to the besiegers in June 1535. The leaders of the Münster Anabaptists died in battle or were horribly executed. Nevertheless, the Anabaptist movement in northwestern Europe would survive as the determined pacifist Mennonite congregation until this day, eventually spreading its membership from Russia to the United States.

A Contest for Mastery and a Continuing Reformation

In the sixteenth century new patterns of conflicts, generated by the Reformation, superimposed themselves on traditional dynastic strife. In every land rulers faced new and complex questions of power and faith: Are religious dissenters rebels by definition? Should dissenters be tolerated? Is peace preferable to religious unity? Can subjects assassinate or rebel against a ruler with different religious beliefs, and can the church sanction these acts? Who would succeed to the throne—is bloodline more important than religion? The conflicts that these questions raised would shape European history for more than a century beyond the Reformation.

The Giants Clash

While the Reformation was taking hold in Germany and common people were beginning to assert themselves, the great powers fought it out. The second phase of the Italian Wars was not confined to Italian battlefields; the Habsburg-Valois dynastic conflict escalated instead into a larger conflagration. A succession of battles, treaties, and alliances revealed the combatants' basic motives. Francis I was obsessed with conquering Milan, an ambition that a warlike French nobility, in search of booty and glory, supported. Defeated at Pavia (1525), Francis was captured, sent to Spain, and forced to sign a peace treaty. Upon his release the French king repudiated the treaty and even sought Turkish aid in defeating the Habsburg army.

All this prevented Charles V from dealing with the religious schism in his own empire. A devout monarch who dreamed of leading a crusade, Charles found himself embroiled in Italian and German politics. The Italian states were suspicious of joint imperial-Spanish domination, and German Protestant princes were hostile to an overmighty Catholic overlord such as Charles. Caught between Francis and Charles—the two most powerful Christian princes—the popes tried to promote a peace settlement, to be followed by a crusade against the Turks, while constantly shifting allegiances to prevent Italy's domination by either power. Not wanting to be left out, Henry VIII of England jumped into the fray, switching back and forth between sides to maximize his gains. The smaller Italian powers struggled for survival, acting as client states of one or the other protagonist.

In this arena of power politics, Christian and Muslim arms clashed in Hungary and the Mediterranean. The Ottoman Empire reached its apogee under Sultan Suleiman I "the Magnificent" (∗1520–1566). In 1526 a Turkish expedition destroyed the Hungarian army at Mohács. Three years later the Ottoman army unsuccessfully laid siege to Vienna. In 1535, Charles V led a campaign to capture Tunis, the lair of North African pirates under Ottoman suzerainty. Desperate to overcome superior imperialist forces, Francis I eagerly forged an alliance with the Turkish sultan. Coming to the aid of the French, the Turkish fleet be-

The Battle of Pavia (1525)
This crushing defeat of the French forces (including many Swiss mercenaries) by the Habsburg armies, shown here in a Flemish tapestry, by no means ended the bloody rivalry of Francis I and Charles V.

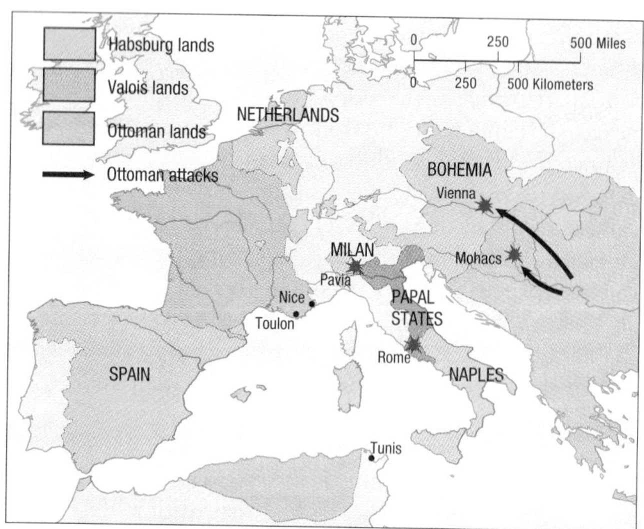

Habsburg-Valois-Ottoman Wars

sieged imperial-occupied Nice. Francis even ordered all inhabitants of nearby Toulon to vacate their town so that he could turn it into a Muslim colony for eight months, complete with a mosque and slave market.

With the deaths of Francis I and Henry VIII in 1547, the Italian Wars entered a new phase, and for the next twelve years the Habsburg-Valois struggle dominated central Europe. The new French king, Henry II (*1547–1559), the son of Francis, supported the German Protestants, while the papacy, terrorized by the imperial sacking of Rome in 1527, was torn by fear and hatred of the Catholic emperor Charles.

The sixteenth century marked the beginning of superior Western military technology. When Charles VIII of France invaded Italy in 1494, the size of his army and its artillery had awed the Italians. Over the next generations, all armies grew in size, and their firepower became ever more deadly. With new weapons and larger armies, the costs of war soared. For example, heavier artillery pieces meant that the rectangular walls of medieval cities had to be transformed into fortresses with jutting forts and gun emplacements. In 1542 to 1550—its years of conflict with Scotland and France—England spent about £450,000 per year on its armies; total royal revenues for the same period amounted to only £200,000 per year. To pay these bills, England devalued its coinage (the sixteenth-century equivalent of printing more paper money), causing prices to rise rapidly during those years.

Other European powers fell into similar predicaments. Charles V boasted the largest army in Europe—one hundred forty-eight thousand men stationed in central Europe, the Netherlands, Italy, Spain, and North Africa during 1552—but he also sank ever deeper into debt. Between 1520 and 1532, Charles borrowed 5.4 million ducats (gold coins), primarily to pay his troops; from 1552 to 1556 his war loans soared to 9.6 million ducats. Francis I, his opponent, similarly overspent. During three years of truce (1535–1537), Francis saved 1.5 million French pounds for his war chest; when war broke out again, he spent more than 4.5 million in a single season. On his death in 1547, Francis owed the bankers of Lyon almost 7 million French pounds—approximately the entire royal income for that year.

The European powers literally fought themselves into bankruptcy. In the 1520s, Francis and Charles had to pay 14 to 18 percent interest on their loans. Taxation, the sale of offices, and outright confiscations failed to bring in enough money to satisfy the war machine. Both the Habsburg and the Valois kings looked to their leading bankers to finance their costly wars. The Italian, German, and Swiss banking houses in Lyon provided a steady stream of loans to the French monarchy. The Lyon bankers financed Charles VIII's Italian campaign in 1494 and supplied Francis with annual loans after 1542. The Habsburg Spanish monarchy relied on a consortium of Genoese, Florentine, and German banks.

Foremost among the financiers of the warring princes was the Fugger bank, the largest such international enterprise in sixteenth-century Europe. Based in the south German imperial city of Augsburg, the Fugger family and their associates built an international financial empire that helped to make kings. The enterprise began with Jakob Fugger (1459–1525), nicknamed "the Rich," who became the personal banker to Charles V's grandfather, Emperor Maximilian I. Constantly short of cash, Maximilian had granted the Fugger family numerous mining and minting concessions. The Fugger empire reaped handsome profits from its Habsburg connections: in addition to collecting interest and collaterals, the Fugger banking house, with branches in the Netherlands, Italy, and Spain, transferred funds for the emperor across the scattered Habsburg domains. To pay for the service of providing and accepting bills of exchange, the Fuggers charged substantial fees. By the end of his life, Maximilian was so deeply in debt to Jakob Fugger that he had to pawn the royal jewels.

In 1519, Jakob Fugger assembled a consortium of German and Italian bankers to secure the imperial election of Maximilian's grandson, Charles of Ghent. The consortium raised a huge sum, which went toward gifts for the electors. To block Francis I, Charles's only serious rival, the bankers refused to accept Francis's bills of exchange. The French king had to pay the German electors in sacks of gold, but it was too little too late, and Charles V became emperor. For the next three decades the alliance between Europe's largest international bank and its largest empire tightened. Between 1527 and 1547 the Fugger bank's assets grew from 3 million guldens (Germany's currency) to over 7 million; roughly 55 percent of the assets were from loans to the Habsburgs, with the Spanish dynasty taking the lion's share. Nothing revealed the power of international banking more than a letter Jakob Fugger wrote to Charles V in 1523 to recoup his investment in the 1519 imperial election, asking the emperor "[to] graciously recognize my faithful, humble service, dedicated to the greater well-being of Your Imperial Majesty, and that you will order that the money which I have paid out, together with the interest upon it, shall be reckoned up and paid, without further delay."

Charles barely stayed one step ahead of his creditors, and his successors gradually lost control of the Spanish state finances. To service debts, European monarchs sought revenues in war and tax increases. But paying for troops and crushing rebellions took more money and more loans. The cycle of financial crises and warfare persisted until the late eighteenth century.

The Reformation Continues: Calvin, France, and Geneva

Under the leadership of John Calvin (1509–1564), another wave of reform pounded at the gates of Rome. Born in Picardy, in northern France, to the secretary of the bishop of Noyon, Calvin benefited from his family connections and received a scholarship to study in Paris and Orléans, where he took a law degree. A gifted intellectual who was attracted to humanism, Calvin could have enjoyed a brilliant career in government or church service. Instead, experiencing a crisis of faith, he sought eternal salvation through intense theological study.

Influenced by the leading French humanist Lefèvre d'Étaples and Bishop Briçonnet of Meaux, who sought to reform the church from within, Calvin gradually crossed the line from loyal opposition to questioning fundamental Catholic teachings. His conversion came about after a lengthy and anxious intellectual battle. Unlike Luther, who described his life in vivid detail, Calvin generally revealed nothing about personal matters.

During Calvin's youth the Reformation gained partisans in France. On Sunday, October 18, 1534, Parisians found ribald broadsheets denouncing the Catholic Mass posted on church doors. Smuggled into France from the Protestant and French-

John Calvin
This woodcut of Calvin in Geneva praises him for completing the work of Jan Hus and Martin Luther in overthrowing the Antichrist. Such linking of the reformers in a common tradition was a frequently evoked image in the visual propaganda of the Protestant Reformation.

speaking parts of Switzerland, the broadsheets unleashed a wave of repression in the capital. Rumors of a Protestant conspiracy and massacre circulated, and magistrates swiftly promoted a general persecution of reformist groups throughout France, including the hitherto unmolested religious dissidents. This so-called Affair of the Placards signaled a national crackdown on church dissenters. Hundreds of French Protestants were arrested, scores were executed, and many more, including Calvin, fled abroad.

On his way to Strasbourg, Germany, a haven for religious dissidents, Calvin stopped in Geneva—the city where he would find his life's work. This French-speaking city-republic had renounced allegiance to its bishop in anticipation of religious reform. The local reformer Guillaume Farel threatened Calvin with God's curse if he did not stay and labor in Geneva. This frightening appeal succeeded. Under Calvin and Farel the reform party became embroiled in a political struggle between two civic factions: their supporters, many of whom were French refugees, and the opposition, represented by the leading Old Genevan families, who resented the moralistic regulations of the new, foreigner-run clerical regime. A political setback in 1538 drove Calvin and Farel from Geneva, but Calvin returned in 1541 after his supporters triumphed and remained until his death in 1564.

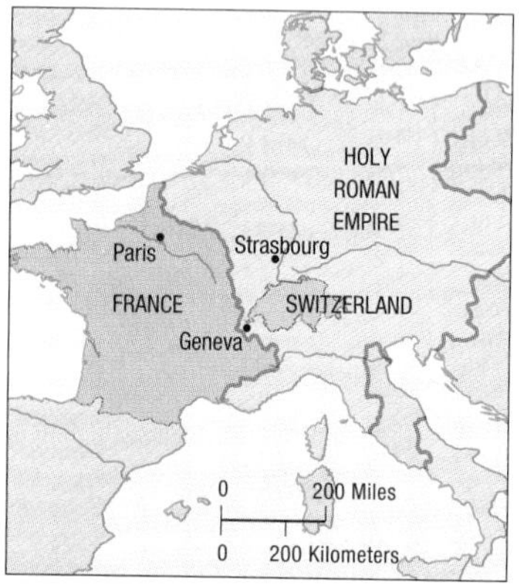

Calvin's World

Under Calvin's inspiration and moral authority, Geneva became a disciplined Christian republic, modeled after the ideas in Calvin's *The Institutes of the Christian Religion*. The first edition of this book—Calvin's masterpiece and a brilliant intellectual accomplishment—appeared in 1536, but because Calvin continued to revise his ideas, the final Latin and French editions were not published until 1559 and 1561, respectively. No reformer prior to Calvin had expounded on the doctrines, organization, history, and practices of Christianity in such a systematic, logical, and coherent manner.

Calvin followed Luther's doctrine of salvation to its ultimate logical conclusion: if God is almighty and humans cannot earn their salvation, then no Christian can be certain of salvation. Developing the doctrine of "predestination," Calvin agreed that God had ordained every man, woman, and child to salvation or damnation—even before the creation of the world. Although God's intention was hidden from human intellect, the knowledge that a small group of "elect" would be saved illuminated the purposes of history and morality.

The elect, in Calvinist theology, were known only to God; in practice, however, Calvinist congregations often functioned as moral communities whose members voluntarily subjected themselves to religious and social discipline. A fourfold office made up of pastors, elders, deacons, and teachers defined the Calvinist church. Fusing church and society, Geneva became a single moral community, a development strongly demonstrated by the insignificant rate of extramarital births in the sixteenth century. Praised by supporters as a community less troubled by crime and sin and attacked by critics as a coercive despotism, Geneva under Calvin exerted a powerful influence on the course of the Reformation. Like Zwingli, Calvin did not tolerate dissenters. While passing through Geneva the Spanish physician Michael Servetus was arrested because he had published books attacking Calvin and questioning the doctrine of the Trinity. Upon Calvin's advice, Servetus was executed by the authorities. (Calvin did not, however, approve of the method of execution: burning at the stake.) Although Calvin came under criticism for Servetus's death, Geneva became the new center of the Reformation, the place from which pastors trained for mission work and books propagating Calvinist doctrines were exported. The Calvinist movement spread to France, the Netherlands, England, Scotland, Germany, Poland, Hungary, and eventually New England, becoming the established form of the Reformation in many of these countries.

The Divided Realm

The monarchs of Europe viewed religious divisions as a dangerous challenge to the unity of their realms and the stability of their rule. If they were to tolerate religious dissent, Protestantism might become a banner of the opposition. In addition, religious differences intensified the formation of noble factions, which exploited the situation when weak monarchs or children ruled. These themes are essential to any understanding of the Reformation in France, Scotland, and England.

As we have seen, the French king Francis I tolerated Protestants up until the Affair of the Placards in 1534. However, persecutions of Huguenots—as Calvinists were called in France—were sporadic, and the Reformed church grew steadily in strength. During the 1540s and 1550s many French noble families converted to Calvinism. Under noble protection, the Reformed church was able to organize quite openly and hold synods (church meetings), especially in southern and western France. Some of the most powerful noble families, such as the Montmorency and the Bourbon, openly professed Protestantism. The French monarchy tried to maintain a balance of power between Catholic and Huguenot and between hostile noble factions. Francis and his successor, Henry II, both succeeded to a degree. But after Henry's death in a jousting accident the weakened monarchy could no longer hold together the fragile realm. After 1560 France plunged into decades of religious wars.

The English monarchy played the central role in shaping that country's religious reform. Until 1527, Henry VIII (*1509–1547) firmly opposed the Reformation, even receiving the title "Defender of the Faith" from Pope Leo X for his treatise against Luther. Under his chancellors, Cardinal Thomas Wolsey (1475–1530) and Thomas More, Henry vigorously suppressed Protestantism and executed its leaders.

The challenge to Rome in England came from two sources: the native roots of Lollardy, whose adherents could still be found among urban artisans in the early sixteenth century; and the German reformers, whose works were smuggled into the country by English merchants abroad, especially by the Company of Merchant Adventurers, which had close ties to the Hanseatic League. During the 1520s English Protestants were few in number—a few clerical dissenters (particularly at Cambridge University) and, more significantly, a small but influential noble faction at court and a mercantile elite in London.

King Henry VIII changed all that. By 1527 the king wanted to divorce his wife, Katharine of Aragon (d. 1536), the daughter of Ferdinand and Isabella of Spain. The eighteen-year marriage had produced a daughter, Princess Mary. Henry desperately needed a male heir. Moreover, he was in love with Anne Boleyn, a lady-in-waiting at court and a strong supporter of the Reformation. Henry claimed that his marriage to Katharine had never been valid because she was the widow of his older brother, Arthur. This first marriage, which apparently was never consummated, had been annulled by Pope Julius II in 1509 so that a second marriage, between Henry and Katharine, could cement the dynastic alliance between England and Spain. Now, in 1527, Henry asked the reigning pope, Clement VII, to annul his predecessor's annulment.

Around "the king's great matter" unfolded a struggle for political and religious domination. The Catholic cause lost out when Henry failed to secure a papal dispensation from Clement VII, who, in addition to the dictates of his conscience, was also a virtual pawn of Emperor Charles V, Katharine's nephew, who had occupied Rome in 1527. Disappointed, Henry turned to the Protestant faction. He dismissed Wolsey and More and chose two Protestants as his new loyal servants: Thomas Cromwell (1485–1540) as chancellor and Thomas Cranmer (1489–1556) as archbishop of Canterbury. Under their leadership the English Parliament passed a number of acts between 1529 and 1536 that severed ties between the English church and Rome, established Henry as the head of the so-called Anglican church, invalidated the claims of Katharine and Princess Mary to the throne, recognized Henry's marriage to Anne Boleyn, and allowed the English crown to confiscate the properties of the monasteries.

By 1536, Henry had grown tired of Anne Boleyn, who had given birth to the future Queen Elizabeth I but had produced no sons. The king had her beheaded on the charge of adultery, an act that he defined as treason. Thereafter Henry married four other wives. The third, Jane Seymour, bore him a son, Edward, and the fifth, Katharine Howard, he had beheaded. Thomas More went to the block in 1535 for treason—that is, for refusing to recognize Henry as "the only supreme head on earth of the Church of England"—and Thomas Cromwell suffered the same fate in 1540 when he lost favor. When Henry died in 1547, the Anglican church, nominally Protestant, still retained much traditional Catholic doctrine and ritual. But the principle of royal supremacy in religious matters would remain a lasting feature of Henry's reforms.

Under Edward VI (*1547–1553) and Mary Tudor (*1553–1558), official religious policies oscillated between Protestant reforms and Catholic restoration. In spite of regional revolts, royal power remained firm. The boy king Edward furthered the Reformation by welcoming prominent religious refugees from the continent. With Mary Tudor's accession, however, everything was reversed, and English Protestants suffered a baptism of blood. Close to three hundred Protestants perished at the stake, and more than eight hundred fled to Germany and Switzerland. Finally, after Anne Boleyn's daughter Elizabeth succeeded her half-sister to the throne in 1558, the Protestant cause again gained momentum; it eventually defined the character of the English nation.

Still another pattern of religious politics unfolded in Scotland, where powerful noble clans directly challenged royal power. Up until the 1550s Protestants had been a small minority in Scotland, who were easy to suppress if they did not enjoy the protection of sympathetic local lords. The most prominent Scottish reformer, John Knox (1514–1572), spent many of his early years in exile in England and on the Continent. But when Scotland's powerful noble clans, caught in the conflict between crown and nobility, turned to Calvinism, the Protestant cause finally triumphed.

The queen regent, Mary of Guise (d. 1560), stood at the center of Scotland's conflict. After the death of her husband, James V (d. 1542), Mary of Guise cultivated the support of her native France. Her daughter and heir to the throne, Mary Stuart, had been educated in France and was married to the dauphin Francis, son of Henry II. The queen regent also surrounded herself with French advisors and soldiers. Alienated by this pro-French policy, by 1558 to 1559 many Scottish noblemen had joined the pro-English and anti-French Protestant party. Misogyny also played a part in Protestant propaganda, skillfully exploiting the era's suspicion of female rulers and regents. In 1558, John Knox published *The First Blast of the Trumpet Against the Monstrous Regiment [Rule] of Women*, a diatribe against both Mary Tudor and Mary of Guise. Knox declared that "to promote a woman to bear rule, superiority, dominion, or empire above any realm, nation, or city is repugnant to nature, contumely to God, a thing most contrarious to his revealed will and approved ordinance and, finally, it is the subversion of good order, of all equity and justice." In 1560, the Protestant party won, and the Scottish Parliament adopted a reformed confession of faith (a document setting out doctrines).

The Catholic Renewal

Many voices for reform had echoed within the Catholic church long before Luther, but the papacy had failed to sponsor any significant change. In response to events in the empire, however, a Catholic reform movement gathered momentum in Italy during the 1530s and 1540s. Drawn from the elite, especially the Venetian upper class, the Catholic evangelicals stressed biblical ethics and moral discipline. Gian Matteo Giberti, bishop of Verona from 1524 to 1543, resigned his position in the Roman *curia* to concentrate on his pastoral duties. Another cardinal, Gasparo Contarini (1483–1542), who was descended from a Venetian noble family and had served the republic as ambassador to Charles V, was elevated to cardinal, where he labored to heal the schism within the church.

A new mood of austerity descended on Rome. In 1527, to punish Pope Clement VII for his part in the anti-imperial coalition, Charles V sent his army into Rome. His unpaid and undisciplined German troops, many of them Lutheran, pillaged and terrorized the city. The Florentine historian Francesco Guicciardini described the humiliation suffered by the great princes of the church: "[M]any prelates were captured by soldiers, especially by the German mercenaries, who because of their hatred for the Roman Church, were cruel and insolent, contemptuously leading priests throughout Rome mounted on asses and mules. . . . Many were most cruelly tormented and died during the torture. . . ." This "second invasion of barbarians" shocked the Italians, who saw it as punishment for their sins.

Under Pope Paul III (*1534–1549) and his successors, the papacy finally took the lead in church reform. The Italian nobility played a leading role, and Spaniards and Italians of all classes provided the backbone for this movement, sometimes called the Counter-Reformation. The Counter-Reformation's crowning achievements were the calling of a general church council and the founding of new religious orders.

In 1545, Pope Paul III and Charles V convened a general church counsel at Trent, a town on the border between the Holy Roman Empire and Italy. The Council of Trent, which met sporadically over the next seventeen years and finally completed its work in 1562, shaped the essential character of Catholicism, as it would remain until the 1960s. It reasserted the supremacy of clerical authority over laypeople, stipulating that bishops reside in their dioceses (instead of absenting themselves and living off church revenues) and that seminaries be established in each diocese to train priests. The council also confirmed and clarified church doctrine and sacraments. For the sacrament of the Eucharist, the counsel asserted that the bread actually *became* Christ's body—a rejection of all Protestant positions on this issue so emphatic as to preclude compromise. For the sacrament of marriage, the counsel stipulated that all unions must henceforth take place in churches and be registered by the parish clergy.

Catholic Reform

The energy of the Counter-Reformation expressed itself most vigorously in the founding of new religious orders. The most important of these, the Society of Jesus, was established by a Spanish nobleman, Ignatius of Loyola (1491–1556). Imbued with tales of chivalric romances and the national glory of the *reconquista,* Ignatius eagerly sought to prove his mettle as a soldier. In 1521, while defending the Spanish border fortress of Pamplona against a French attack, he sustained a severe leg injury. During his convalescence Ignatius read lives of the saints; once he recovered, he abandoned his quest for military glory in order to serve the church.

After diligent university studies (Latin did not come easily to a man of thirty-one) in Spain and Paris, Ignatius went on a pilgrimage to the Holy Land. Attracted by his austerity and piety, young men gravitated to this charismatic figure. Thanks to Ignatius's noble birth and Cardinal Contarini's intercession, Ignatius gained a hearing before the pope, and in 1540 the church recognized his little band, known as the Jesuits. Organized on military principles, with Ignatius as its first general, the

Ignatius Loyola
The founder of the Society of Jesus, as imagined by the early seventeenth century artist Peter Paul Rubens, is depicted exorcising a demon from a possessed woman. Such imagery was not typical of contemporary representations of the first Jesuits, though they (like virtually all Christians of the age) believed in the reality of witchcraft and the devil.

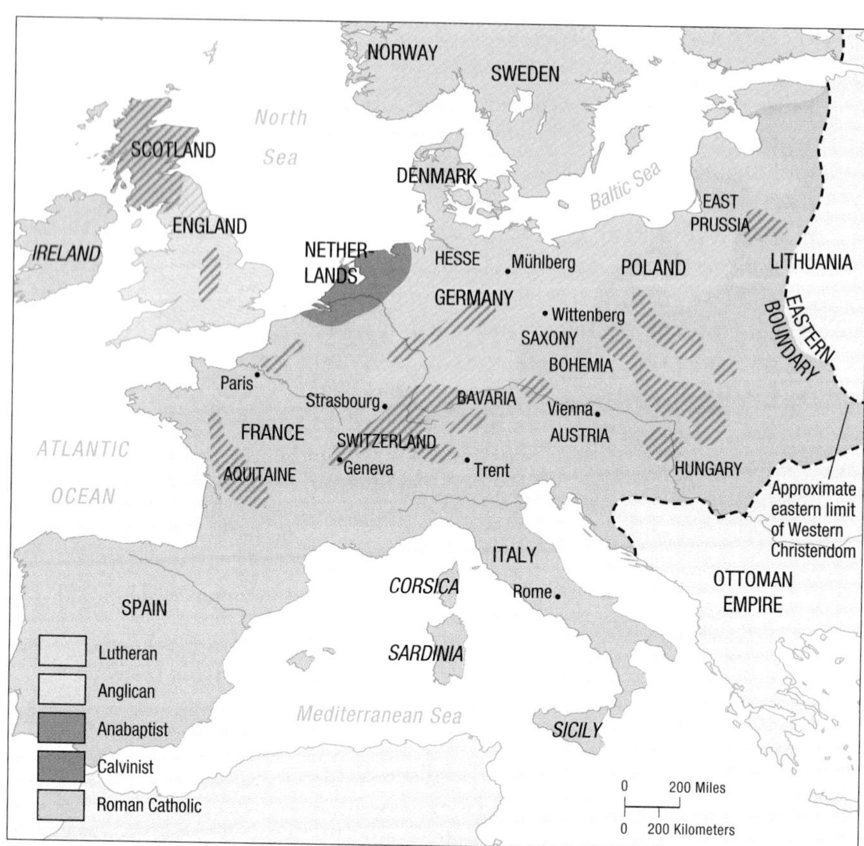

The Religious Balance in Europe, c. 1560

Jesuits became the most vigorous defenders of papal authority. Europe had one thousand Jesuits by the time of Ignatius's death in 1556. The society continued to expand, reclaiming souls who had been lost to the Reformation. Jesuit missionaries played a key role in the global Portuguese maritime empire and brought Roman Catholicism to Africans, Asians, and Native Americans.

The Religious Peace of Augsburg, 1555

While Catholic forces were gathering strength in Italy and Spain, confessional confrontation in the Holy Roman Empire led to military alliances. The Protestant Schmalkaldic League, headed by the Elector of Saxony and Philip of Hesse (the two leading Protestant princes), included most of the imperial cities, the chief source of the empire's wealth. On the other side, allied with Emperor Charles V, were the bishops and the few remaining Catholic princes. During the 1530s, Charles had to concentrate on fighting the French and the Turks. But now, having temporarily secured the western Mediterranean, he turned to central Europe to try to resolve the growing religious differences there.

In 1541, Charles convened an Imperial Diet at Regensburg, only to see negotiations between Protestant and Catholic theologians break down rapidly. The schism within the church seemed permanent. Vowing to crush the Schmalkaldic League, the emperor secured French neutrality in 1544 and papal support in 1545. Luther died in 1546. In the following year, war broke out. Using seasoned Spanish veterans and German allies, Charles occupied the German imperial cities in the south, restoring Catholic patricians and suppressing the Reformation. In 1547, he defeated the Schmalkaldic League armies at Mühlberg and captured the leading Protestant princes. Jubilant, Charles proclaimed a decree, the "Interim," which restored Catholics' right to worship in Protestant lands while permitting Lutherans to observe Holy Communion with both bread and wine. The final religious settlement would depend on the decision of the Council of Trent. Protestant resistance to the Interim was deep and widespread: many pastors went into exile, and riots broke out in many cities.

For Charles V, the reaction of his former allies proved far more alarming than Protestant resistance. His success had upset the balance of power. With Spanish troops controlling Milan and Naples and Spanish bishops vocal in the Council of Trent, Pope Julius III (*1550–1552) feared that papal authority would be subjugated by imperial might. In the Holy Roman Empire Protestant princes spoke out against "imperial tyranny," referring to Charles's imprisonment of the Elector of Saxony and Philip of Hesse. Jealously defending their traditional liberties against an overmighty emperor, the Protestant princes, led by Duke Maurice of Saxony, a Protestant and former imperial ally, raised arms against Charles. The princes declared war in 1552, chasing a surprised, armyless, and practically bankrupt emperor back to Italy.

Forced to construct an accord, Charles V agreed to the Peace of Augsburg in 1555. The settlement recognized the Evangelical (Lutheran) church in the empire, accepted the secularization of church lands but "reserved" the still-existing ecclesiastical territories (mainly the bishoprics) for Catholics, and, most important, established the principle that all princes, whether Catholic or Lutheran, enjoyed the sole right to determine the religion of their lands and subjects. Significantly, Calvinist, Anabaptist, and other dissenting groups were excluded from the settlement. The religious revolt had culminated in a princes' Reformation. As the constitutional framework for the Holy Roman Empire, the Augsburg settlement preserved a fragile peace in central Europe until 1618, but the exclusion of Calvinists would plant the seed for future conflict.

Exhausted by decades of war and disappointed by the disunity in Christian Europe, Emperor Charles V resigned his many thrones in 1555 and 1556, leaving his Netherlandish-Burgundian and Spanish dominions to his son, Philip, and his Austrian lands to his brother, Ferdinand. Retiring to a monastery in southern Spain, the most powerful of the Christian monarchs spent his last years quietly seeking salvation. His son and successor as king of Spain, Philip II (*1556–1598), found nothing but trouble. By the 1550s the Spanish monarchy could contract a loan only by paying 49 percent interest.

Charles V at Mühlberg
The great Venetian artist Titian painted a series of portraits of Charles V at stages of his career and showing various degrees of the emperor's success or failure (see also page 529). Titian here captures the emperor's sense of triumph at having finally crushed the German Protestant princes in battle in 1547. Charles's triumph was to be short-lived.

In 1557, Philip's financial crises came to a head, and he was forced to default on his loans.

Unending wars had left France even more exhausted than Spain. Henry II declared bankruptcy in 1557. In 1559 he agreed to the Treaty of Cateau-Cambrésis, in which France agreed to give up its conquests in Italy in exchange for peace and a marriage alliance with the Habsburg dynasty, leaving Spain as the western world's unchallenged leader for the rest of the century.

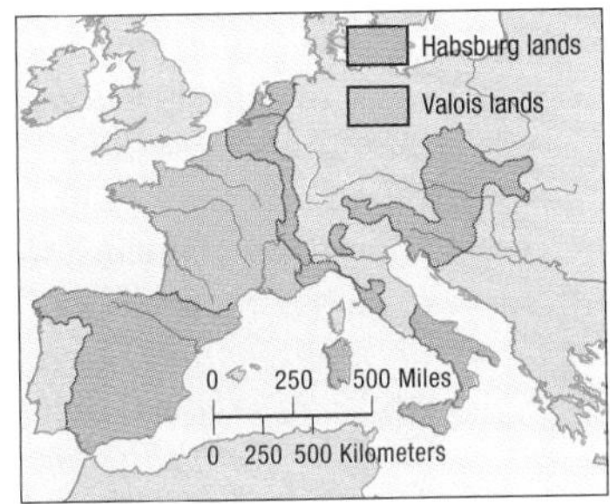

Habsburg and Valois Lands in 1559

For the Glory of God and the Prince

In northern Europe noble patrons and the royal court provided the institutional context behind the brilliant scientific, artistic, and literary achievements of the early sixteenth century, all of which adopted styles from the Italian Renaissance. While painters and poets glorified emperors and popes, the common people sought enjoyment from popular festivals such as the carnival. Highly sophisticated artists often looked to popular themes for inspiration, thus keeping the elite and popular cultures closely connected.

The Court

European princes used the institution of the royal court to bind their nobility and impress their subjects. Briefly defined, the court was the prince's household. Around the ruling family, however, a small community coalesced, made up of household servants, noble attendants, councilors, officials, artists, and soldiers. During the sixteenth century this political elite developed a sophisticated culture.

The French court of Francis I became the largest in Europe after the demise of the Burgundian dukes. In addition to the prince's household, the royal family also set up households for other members: the queen and the queen mother each had her own staff of maids and chefs, as did each of the royal children. The royal household employed officials to handle finances, guard duty, clothing, and food; in addition, physicians, librarians, musicians, dwarfs, animal trainers, and a multitude of hangers-on bloated its size. By 1535 the French court numbered 1,622 members, excluding the nonofficial courtiers.

Although Francis built many palaces (the most magnificent at Fontainbleu), the French court was often on the move. It took no fewer than eighteen thousand horses to transport the people, furniture, and documents—not to mention the dogs and falcons for the royal hunt. Hunting, in fact, was a passion for the men at court; it represented a form of mock combat, essential in the training of a military elite. Francis himself loved war games: in 1518 he staged a mock battle at court involving twelve hundred "warriors" and he himself led a party to lay siege to a model town during which several players were accidentally killed. Three years later, Francis almost lost his own life when, while

Carnival
Traditionally the day of merrymaking before the onset of the rigors of Lent (a tradition that survives in twentieth-century Mardi Gras festivities), carnival was one occasion on which the rules of social hierarchy and Christian morality were temporarily relaxed. Both Catholic and Protestant reformers considered carnival an occasion for sin and tried to rein it in.

storming a house during another mock battle, he was hit on the head by a burning log.

Italy gave Europe the ideological justification for the court culture. Two writers in particular were the most eloquent spokesmen for the culture of "courtesy": Ludovico Ariosto (1474–1533), in service at the Este court in Ferrara, and Baldassare Castiglione (1478–1529), a servant of the duke of Urbino and the pope. Considered one of the greatest Renaissance poets, Ariosto composed a long epic poem, *Orlando Furioso* ("The Mad Roland"), that represented court culture as the highest synthesis of Christian and classical values. Set against the historic struggle between Charlemagne and the Arabs, the poem tells the love story of Bradamente and Ruggiero. But before the separated lovers are reunited, the reader meets scores of characters and hundreds of adventures. The poem tells of imprisonments, betrayals, sieges, combats, jousts, and rescues, and takes the reader to caverns and far-off islands, Europe, Africa, and Asia. Modeled after Greek and Roman poetry, especially after the works of Virgil and Ovid, *Orlando Furioso* also

Francis I of France
Athlete, bon vivant, *lover, and Renaissance king, Francis I is depicted here as a self-satisfied young man in full splendor. The artist, Jean Clouet, was one of the finest French painters of the early sixteenth century, deeply influenced by the Italian style that Francis also loved.*

Fontainbleu
A French royal residence near Paris, this palatial complex represented the shifting of court life from urban centers to self-contained rural spaces, away from the turmoil and dangers of city life.

followed the tradition of the medieval chivalric romance. The tales of combat, valor, love, and magic captivated the court's noble readers, who, through this highly idealized fantasy, enjoyed a glimpse of their own world. In addition, the poem's characters represent the struggle between good and evil, and between Christianity and Islam, that was so much a part of the crusading spirit of the early sixteenth century.

Equally popular was *The Courtier* by the suave diplomat Castiglione. Like Ariosto, Castiglione tried to represent court culture as a synthesis of military virtues and literary and artistic cultivation. Speaking in eloquent dialogues, Castiglione's characters debate the qualities of an ideal courtier. The true courtier, Castiglione asserted, was a gentleman who spoke in a refined language and carried himself with nobility and dignity in the service of his prince and his lady. Clothing assumed a significant symbolism in *The Courtier*; in the words of one character, "I am not saying that clothes provide the basis for making hard and fast judgments about a man's character. . . . But I do maintain that a man's attire is also no small evidence for what kind of personality he has. . . ." The significance of outward appearance in court culture reflected the rigid distinctions between the classes and the sexes in sixteenth-century Europe. In Castiglione's words, the men at court had to display "valor," and the women "feminine sweetness."

The Sacred and Secular Patronage of Music

In musical composition, polyphony continued as the dominant style throughout the sixteenth century. But the Reformation strongly influenced musical life in other ways. In Catholic Europe the church and to a lesser extent the princely courts still employed and commissioned the leading musicians. The two leading composers of the sixteenth century, Orlando de Lassus (1532–1594) and Giovanni Pierluigi da Palestrina (1525–1594), were both in papal service as choirmasters. Lassus, a Fleming by birth, went to Munich in 1556 to enter the service of the Bavarian court, the most important German Catholic principality in the Holy Roman Empire. A prolific composer, Lassus left some three hundred ninety secular songs in Italian, French, and German, as well as approximately five hundred motets and other substantial sacred vocal works. Palestrina is remembered for his sacred music, especially for his polyphonies that accompanied the Liturgy of the Mass, in which he reaffirmed Catholic tradition by using themes from Gregorian chants.

In Protestant Europe the chorale emerged as a new musical form. In an attempt to engage the congregation in active worship, Martin Luther, an accomplished lutenist himself, composed many hymns in German. Unlike Catholic services, for which professional musicians sang in Latin, Protestant services enjoined the congregation to sing in unison. Drawing from Catholic sacred music as well as secular folk tunes, Luther and his collaborators wrote words to accompany familiar melodies. The best known of Luther's hymns, "Ein' feste Burg," became the beloved English Protestant hymn "A Mighty Fortress" and inspired many subsequent variations.

Protestants sang hymns to signify their new faith. During the Peasants War of 1525, Thomas Müntzer and the peasant rebels implored God's intercession by singing the hymn "Oh Come, Thou Holy Spirit" before they were mowed down by the knights and mercenaries in a one-sided slaughter. Eyewitnesses also reported Protestant martyrs singing hymns before their executions. In Lutheran Germany hymnals and prayer books adorned many urban households; the intimate relationship among religious devotion, bourgeois culture, and musical literacy would become a characteristic of Germany in later centuries.

The Beginning of the New Science

The first half of the sixteenth century laid the foundations for the scientific revolution that would take place one century later. The most important changes in sixteenth-century scientific thought were brought about by humanism and a new emphasis on observation. By reexamining the Greco-Roman past, the new humanist education encouraged scholars to view the traditional Greek scientific texts with a critical eye. The advent of printing, another prerequisite to the new science, meant that new scientific ideas and more accurate, stunningly illustrated texts could be circulated. The encounter with the New World—and with its fauna and flora, previously unknown to Europeans—also stimulated scientific advances. This expansion of the European global perspective seemed to inspire new questions about the cosmos, too. Amid all these changes, the university remained the most important institution for scientific work, seconded by the patronage of the church and secular rulers.

Among the many early sixteenth-century scientists whose work formed a bridge between medieval and modern science, three stood above the rest: Andreas Vesalius (1514–1564), who prepared the way for modern anatomy; Theophrastus Bombastus von Hohenheim, better known as Paracelsus (1493–1541), who laid the path for modern pharmacology and chemistry; and Nicolaus Copernicus (1473–1543), who fundamentally revised the human picture of the cosmos.

Educated in Paris and in Padua, Italy, Vesalius achieved distinction in 1543 for his *De Fabrica* ("On the Construction of the Human Body"). Until the early sixteenth century, medical knowledge in Christian Europe had been based on the writings of the second-century Greek physician Galen. Deriving his anatomical knowledge of the human body from partial dissections, Galen had made numerous inaccurate assertions about the body's composition and functioning. For more than a century before Vesalius, medical faculties in European universities revived the public dissection of cadavers. Drawing upon this accumulated knowledge, and sensing the need for accurate, graphic drawings of human anatomy such as those drafted by Leonardo da Vinci, Vesalius prepared his illustrated anatomical text as a revision of Galen's work. Reluctant at first to refute him, Vesalius eventually rejected Galen's authority in the 1555 second edition of *De Fabrica,* which was becoming the most influential anatomy textbook.

If Vesalius's original intent was merely to revise Galen, Paracelsus, a man given to forceful statements, had Galen's text burned at the University of Basel, where he was a professor of medicine. Paracelsus experimented with new drugs, performed operations (unlike most academic physicians of his day, who never went beyond medical theory), and developed a synthesis of religious, medical, and philosophical ideas. Through his deep interest in magic, alchemy, and astrology, Paracelsus became the forerunner of chemical and pharmaceutical progress. Also unorthodox in his other views, he strongly condemned the persecution of religious dissenters.

Although Paracelsus might have been sympathetic to Protestantism, science did not recognize religious boundaries. A clergyman in the Polish church, Nicolaus Copernicus never would have dreamed that his ideas would give rise to a confrontation between religion and science. A protégé of a Polish archbishop, Copernicus studied medicine and canon law first in Cracow and then in the Italian cities of Bologna, Padua, and Ferrara. He returned to Poland in 1506 and entered ecclesiastical service. Developing his ideas over two decades, in 1543 Copernicus on his death bed published *On the Revolution of the Celestial Spheres* through the efforts of a Protestant German admirer and with the cooperation of Catholic prelates, but with a preface (not by Copernicus) that presented the work only as a curious paradox and not as a hypothesis to be taken seriously.

Nevertheless, Copernicus's work threw down a revolutionary challenge to authority. Hitherto, Europeans had derived their view of the universe from the second-century Greek astronomer Ptolemy. Fully compatible with the Judeo-Christian and Greco-Roman traditions and approved by the Catholic church, Ptolemaic astronomy put the earth at the center of the cosmos. Above earth were fixed the moon, the stars, and the planets in concentric crystalline spheres; beyond these fixed spheres dwelt God and the angels. The planets revolved around earth at the command of God, the *primum mobile* ("prime mover"). According to this scheme, the planets would revolve in perfectly circular obits, a theory belied by the actual elliptical paths that could be observed and calculated. To explain these inconsistencies, Ptolemy postulated orbits within orbits, which he called epicycles. His mathematical proofs were extremely cumbersome, to say the least. Copernicus discovered that by placing the sun instead of the earth at the center of this system of spheres, he could eliminate many epicycles from the calculations. Inspired only by the elegance of his simpler mathematics but unable to resolve many difficulties in his theory, Copernicus nevertheless forthrightly questioned traditional astronomy and set the agenda for future generations of scientists. The clash between astronomy and religion would come later, when confessional struggles permeated all aspects of European life.

The Artists and the Christian Knight

In the early years of the sixteenth century, before the Reformation, the Holy Roman emperor and the pope still represented the hope of Christian regeneration. Europe stood under the threat of the Turks, the church badly needed reform, and Christendom longed for justice and peace. Through their patronage of artists, the Habsburg emperors, the French kings, and the Catholic popes created glorified self-images, representations of their era's hopes.

The use of art for political glorification was nothing new, but below the glorified surface of sixteenth-century art flowed an undercurrent of idealism. For all his political limitations, Emperor Maximilian I was a visionary who dreamed of restoring Christian chivalry and even toyed with the idea of ruling as pope and emperor. He appointed the Nuremberg artist Albrecht Dürer (1471–1528) as court painter, to represent the Habsburg vision of universal Christian emperorship. Dürer's design for Maximilian's triumphal carriage in 1518 positioned the figures of Justice, Temperance, Prudence, and Fortitude at a level above the seated emperor, with other allegorical figures—Reason, Nobility, and Power—also in attendance.

For many artists, Emperor Charles V embodied the ideal Christian knight. The Venetian painter Titian (1477–1576) captured the emperor's life on canvas four times between 1532 and 1550. His 1532 portrait depicts a grand prince in his early thirties. Two portraits from 1548 and 1550, which Titian completed after Charles's victory over the Schmalkaldic League, present a man of deep ambiguity. Titian's equestrian portrait of Charles after his victory at Mühlberg (page 523) shows a Christian knight, somber and pious. In the later painting (page 529), the seated emperor, at the height of his success, seems burdened by his office. Charles's favorite was the *Gloria*, one of the two Titians he took with him to his monastic retirement: it shows the kneeling emperor wrapped in a white death shroud joining the throng of the saved to worship the Trinity.

The Habsburg dynasty did not monopolize artistic self-glorification, however. The Florentine Michelangelo Buonarroti (1475–1564) matured his multiple talents in the service of the Medici family, although his artistry served many masters. After the overthrow of the Medici he was commissioned to sculpt an eighteen-foot statue of David, an Old Testament symbol of the restored Florentine republic. He became Pope Julius II's favorite artist, painting with furious energy the Sistine Chapel (including the ceiling) and working on a never-finished tomb and sculpture for that same warrior-pope. Later, Michelangelo was commissioned by Paul III, the first pope of the Counter-Reformation, to design palaces in Rome; in 1547, he became the chief architect of St. Peter's Basilica. Since Michelangelo's art commemorated both the famous and infamous of sixteenth-century Italy, his works

The Triumph of Maximilian I
A failure in virtually all his political schemes, the emperor Maximilian brilliantly succeeded in propagandizing his image as a triumphant Caesar. He commissioned the foremost German artist of the day, Albrecht Dürer, to execute a series of woodcuts depicting the German nobility and imperial court celebrating his grandeur in a seemingly endless procession.

The Burden of Rulership: Charles V
Not long after his victory at Mühlberg, Titian depicted Charles in a very different mood: worn down by a lifetime of striving without lasting success to unite Christendom under Habsburg rule, to purify the church, and to crush heresy and rebellion.

sometimes shared the fates of his patrons. In 1511, the people of Bologna rose in rebellion against Pope Julius II and tore down Michelangelo's fourteen-foot statue of the pope, melting it to cast a cannon. Most of Michelangelo's art has survived, however—a testimony both to his genius and to the grandiose self-image of the papacy and its remarkable self-confidence in the age of the Reformation.

New Worlds

The sixteenth century inaugurated a new era of world history. Portuguese and Spanish vessels, followed later by English, French, and Dutch ships, sailed across the Atlantic, Indian, and Pacific oceans, bringing with them people, merchandise, crops, and disease in a global exchange that would shape the modern world. In these encounters—at times peaceful but often brutal—Europeans imposed their culture on others through conquest, colonial settlement, and religious missions, all the while debating and marveling at the strange new worlds they had entered.

The Voyage to the East

Lured by the gold mines of West Africa, the Portuguese gradually extended their explorations down Africa's Atlantic coast, establishing garrisons at the Cape Verde Islands, Guinea, São Tomé, and Luanda (in present-day Angola). In 1499, Vasco da Gama reached India, and twenty-three years later Ferdinand Magellan, a Portuguese sailor in Spanish service, led the first expedition to circumnavigate the globe. By 1517 a chain of Portuguese forts dotted the Indian Ocean: at Mozambique, Hormuz (at the mouth of the Persian Gulf), Goa (in India), Colombo (in modern-day Sri Lanka), and Malacca (modern-day Malaysia). By 1557 the Portuguese had taken up residence in East Asia: in Macao on the south China coast and in Nagasaki, Japan.

Adapting to local conditions, the Portuguese employed a combination of force and diplomacy, their primary object being to control trade rather than territory. Exploiting and perpetuating tribal warfare in West Africa, the Portuguese traded in gold and "pieces," as African slaves were called, a practice condemned at home by some conscientious clergymen. A canon at Evora cathedral, Manoel Severim de Faria, observed that "one cannot yet see any good effect resulting from so much butchery; for this is not the way in which commerce can flourish and the preaching of the gospel progress. . . ." Critical voices, however, could not deny the enormous profits that the slave trade

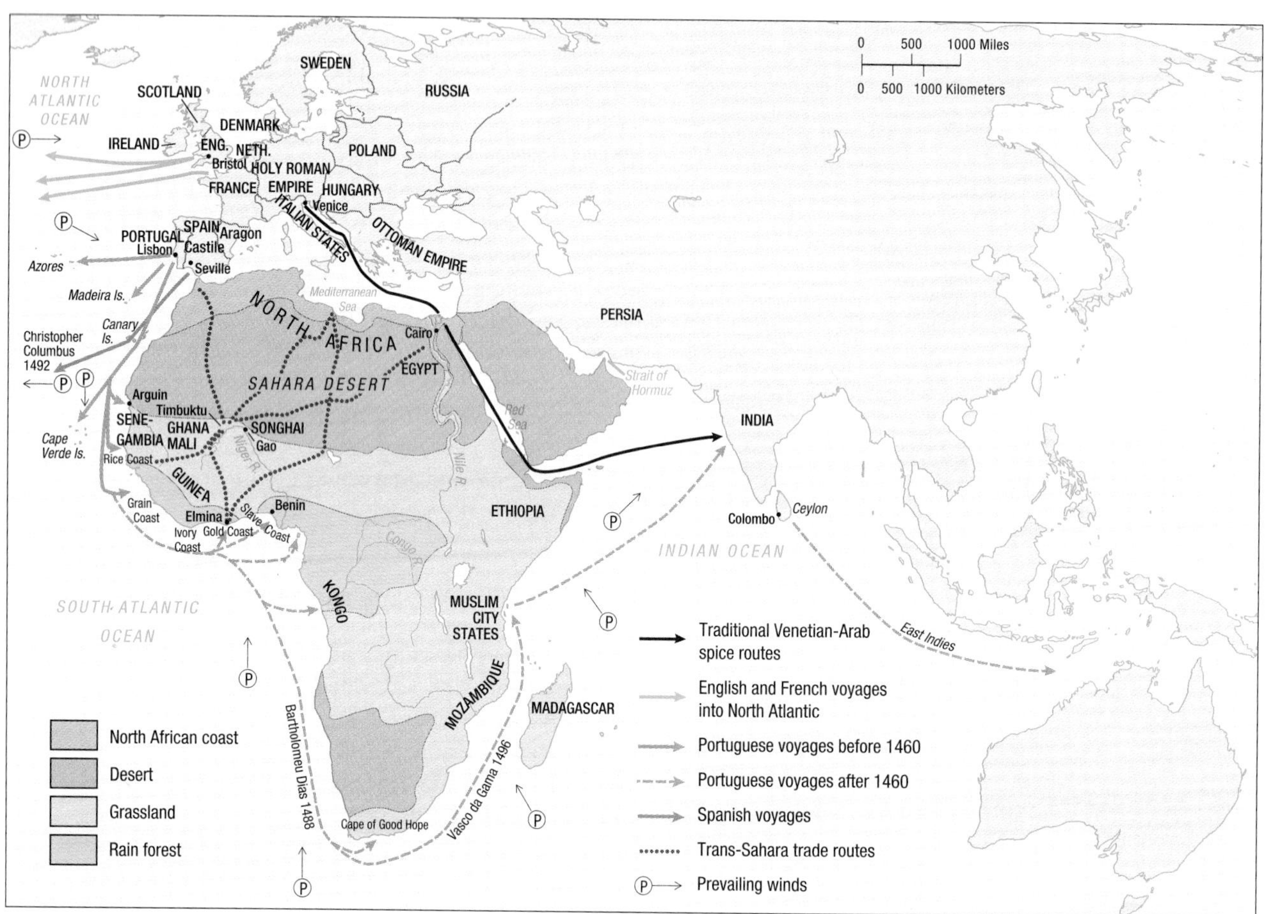

Europe, Africa, and India, c. 1500

brought to Portugal. Most slaves toiled in the sugar plantations of Brazil and the Atlantic islands; a fortunate few labored as domestic servants in Portugal, where freedmen and slaves constituted a distinct African minority in Lisbon.

America: Paradise or Hell?

On the eve of the European invasion, the native peoples of the Americas were divided into many sedentary and nomadic societies. Among the settled peoples, the largest political and social organizations centered in the Mexican and Peruvian highlands. The Aztecs and the Incas ruled over subjugated Indian populations in their respective empires. With an elaborate religious culture and a rigid social and political hierarchy, the Aztecs and Incas based their civilizations in large, urban capitals.

The Spanish explorers organized their expeditions to the mainland from a base in the Caribbean. Two prominent leaders, Hernando Cortés (1485–1547) and Francisco Pizarro (1470–1541), gathered men and arms and set off in search of gold. Catholic priests accompanied the fortune hunters to bring Christianity to allegedly uncivilized peoples and thus to justify brutal conquests. His small band swelled by peoples who had been subjugated by the Aztecs, Cortés captured the Aztec capital, Tenochtitlán, in 1519. Two years later Mexico, then named New Spain, was added to Charles V's empire. To the south, Pizarro conquered the Andean highlands, exploiting a civil war between rival Incan kings. After 1536, Lima became the administrative capital of the lands of the Spanish empire in the Andean region.

By the mid-sixteenth century the Spanish empire, built on greed and justified by its self-

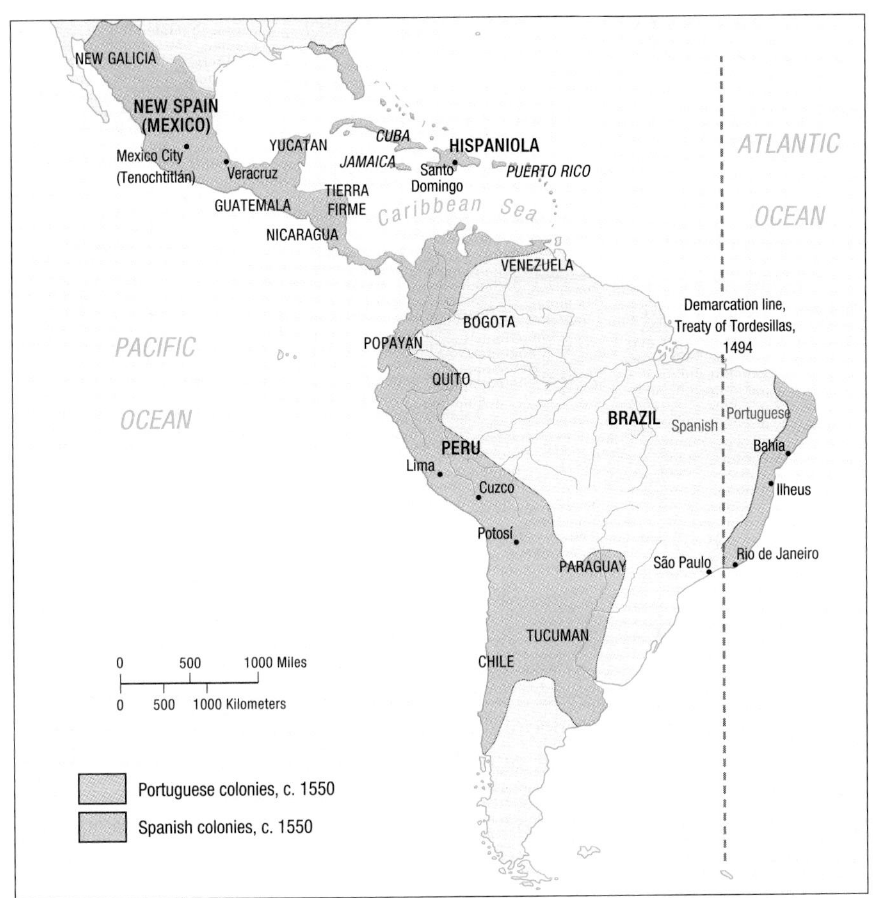

The Spanish Conquest of Mexico and Peru

proclaimed Catholic mission, stretched unbroken from Mexico to Chile. In addition to the Aztecs and Incas, the Spaniards also subdued the Mayans on the Yucatán peninsula, a people with a sophisticated knowledge of cosmology and arithmetic. The gold and silver mines in Mexico proved a treasure trove for the Spanish crown, but the real prize was the discovery of vast silver deposits in Potosí (today in Bolivia). Precious metals from Spanish America would supply the major revenues for the Spanish monarchy during the second half of the sixteenth century—in insufficient quantity to save the crown from bankruptcies, but enough to fuel seemingly endless inflation.

Not to be outdone by the Spaniards, other European powers joined the scramble for gold in the New World. In 1500 a Portuguese fleet landed at Brazil, but Portugal did not begin colonizing until 1532, when it established a permanent fort on the coast. In North America the French went in search of a "northwest passage" to China. By 1504 French fishermen had appeared in Newfoundland. Thirty years later Jacques Cartier led three voyages that explored the St. Lawrence River as far as Montreal. An early attempt in 1541 to settle Canada failed due to the harsh winter and Indian hostility. More permanent settlements in Canada and the present-day United States would have to wait until the seventeenth century.

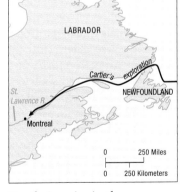

North America in the Sixteenth Century

Although the Indian populations were devastated by European diseases, the encounter in the Americas opened a new chapter in global ecological history. New World crops were introduced to the Old: maize, beans, and potatoes to enrich the European diet and tobacco to stimulate the senses. The exchange was by no means one-way. Nostalgic for home, Europeans imported familiar animals and crops: they introduced horses and sheep to the Americas and planted wheat in place of maize. Convinced of their technological and cultural superiority, European settlers attempted to remake the Americas in their own image, imposing their language and spreading their religion among the continents' first inhabitants.

"Preaching with the Sword and Rod of Iron"

Frustrated in his efforts to convert the Brazilian Indians, a Jesuit missionary wrote to his superior in Rome in 1563 that "for this kind of people it is better to be preaching with the sword and rod of iron." This attitude was common among Christian missionaries in the Americas and Africa, despite the isolated voices that condemned Europeans' abuse of native populations. The Dominican Bartolomé de Las Casas (1474–1566), an Erasmian idealist, was perhaps the most severe critic of colonial brutality in Spanish America, yet even he argued that Africans, constitutionally more suitable for labor, should be imported to the plantations in the Americas to relieve the Indians, who were being worked to death. Under the influence of Las Casas and his followers, the Spanish crown tried to curb the excesses of European settlers by placing the Indians under its protection, a policy whose success was determined by the struggle among missionaries, *conquistadores*, and royal officials for the bodies and souls of native populations.

To ensure rapid Christianization, European missionaries focused initially on winning over local elites. The recommendation of a Spanish royal official in Mexico City was typical: he wrote to the crown in 1525,

> *In order that the sons of caciques [chiefs] and native lords may be instructed in the faith, Your Majesty must command that a college be founded wherein there may be taught . . . to the end that they may be ordained priests. For he who shall become such among them, will be of greater profit in attracting others to the faith than will fifty [European] Christians.*

The Portuguese followed a similar policy in Africa and Asia. A number of young African nobles went to Portugal to be trained in theology, among them Dom Henry, a son of King Afonso I of Kongo, a Portuguese ally. In East Asia Christian missionaries under Portuguese protection again concentrated their efforts on the elites, preaching the gospel to Confucian scholar-officials in China and to the samurai (the warrior aristocracy) in Japan. Measured in numbers alone, the missionary enterprise seemed highly successful: by the second half of the sixteenth century vast multitudes of Native Americans had become nominal Christians, and thirty years after Francis Xavier's 1549 landing in Japan the Jesuits could claim over one hundred thousand Japanese converts.

After an initial period of relatively little racial discrimination, the Catholic church in the Americas and Africa adopted strict rules based on color. For example, the first Mexican Ecclesiastical Provincial Council in 1555 declared that holy orders were not to be conferred on Indians, *mestizos* (people of mixed European-Indian parentage), and mulattos (people of mixed European-African heritage); along with descendants of Moors, Jews, and persons who had been sentenced by the Spanish Inquisition, these groups were deemed "inherently unworthy of the sacerdotal office." Europeans reinforced their sense of racial superiority with their perception of the "treachery" that Native Americans and Africans exhibited whenever they resisted domination.

A different conversion tactic applied to Asia. There, European missionaries, who admired Chinese and Japanese civilization and were not backed by military power, used the sermon rather than the sword to win converts. But they too resisted ordaining indigenous priests because they implicitly connected European ethnicity with Christianity.

Discipline and Property

The emergence of a new urban, middle-class culture accompanied the sixteenth-century religious changes. More visible in Protestant Europe, marriage reforms, an emphasis on literacy, a new educational agenda, and the Protestant work ethic came together to represent a watershed in European civilization. Other changes transcended the Protestant-Catholic divide and represented the culmination of developments that stretched back to the Middle Ages: the advent of public relief for the poor, the condemnation of vagrancy, and a general disciplining of society. Many modern ideas and institutions had their origins in the sixteenth century.

The Bible

Prior to the Reformation the Latin Vulgate was the only Bible authorized by the church, although many vernacular translations circulated. The Vulgate contains errors of translation from the Greek and Hebrew, as humanists such as Erasmus pointed out. Nevertheless, textual authority was predicated upon church authority, and textual revisions touched a raw nerve in the church. The challenges to the Roman church from the Hussite and Lollard movements drew their legitimacy from the Scriptures; one of their chief aims was to translate the Bible into vernacular. Although most sixteenth-century Europeans were illiterate, the Bible assumed for them a new importance because biblical stories were transmitted by pictures and the spoken word as well as through print. As an independent source of Christian beliefs and customs, the Bible had the potential to subvert the established order.

In 1522, Martin Luther translated Erasmus's Greek New Testament into German, the first vernacular translation based on the original language of the Gospels. Illustrated with woodcuts, more than two hundred thousand copies of Luther's New Testament were printed over twelve years, an immense number for the time. In 1534, Luther completed a translation of the Old Testament. Peppered with witty phrases and colloquial expressions, Luther's Bible was a treasure chest of the German language, and it remains to this day the standard version. The popular reception of Luther's Bible was primed by a huge appetite for the story of salvation: between 1466 and 1522 more than twenty translations of the Bible had appeared in the various German dialects. Widespread among urban households, the German Bible—or, more commonly, the Gospels—occupied a central place in a family's history. Generations passed on valuable editions; pious citizens often bound the Scriptures with family papers or other reading material. To counter Protestant success, Catholic German Bibles appeared—the first was Johann Eck's 1537 translation from the Vulgate—thus authorizing and encouraging Bible reading by the Catholic laity, a sharp departure from medieval church practice.

The relationship between Scripture reading and religious reform also highlighted the history of early French and English Bibles. In the same year that Luther's German New Testament appeared in print, the French humanist Jacques Lefèvre d'Étaples (1455–1530) translated the Vulgate New Testament into French. Sponsored by Guillaume Briçonnet, the bishop from Meaux, who wanted to distribute free copies of the New Testament to the poor, the enterprise represented an early attempt to reform the French church without breaking with Rome. The Meaux reformers had been protected expressly by royal authority. With King Francis I captive in Madrid after the battle of Pavia (1525), the Parlement of Paris (the kingdom's leading law court) and the queen regent dispersed the reformers on suspicion of heresy.

Although individual books of the Bible circulated among the Lollards, a complete edition of the English Bible was not readily available in the fifteenth century. Sensing the dangerous association that could be made between the vernacular Bible and heresy, England's church hierarchy reacted swiftly. In a country with few printing presses, the first English Protestants could not publish their writings at home. Inspired by Luther's Bible during a visit to Wittenberg, the Englishman William Tyndale (1495–1536) translated the Bible into English. After he had his translation printed in Germany and the Low Countries, Tyndale smuggled copies into England with the help of the Merchant Adventurers, a sympathetic English merchant group based in Antwerp and Brussels. After Henry VIII's break with Rome and adoption of the Reformation, the new Protestant archbishop of Canterbury, Thomas Cranmer, promoted an English Bible based on Tyndale's translation.

Although the vernacular Bible occupied a central role in Protestantism, Bible reading did not become widespread until the early seventeenth century. Educational reform and the founding of new schools proceeded slowly throughout the sixteenth century, thus limiting the number of literate people. Furthermore, the complete Bible was a relatively expensive book inaccessible to poorer households. But, perhaps most important of all, the Protestant clergy, like their Catholic counterparts, grew suspicious of unsupervised Bible reading. Just as the first reformers cited Scripture against Rome, ordinary men and women drew their own lessons from the vernacular Bible, questioning and challenging the authority of the new Protestant establishment.

Indoctrinating the Young

To implant Christ's kingdom, one must change hearts and minds, argued Luther in a plea to the princes and magistrates of the Holy Roman Empire. He urged them to establish schools, supported by confiscated church property, in order to educate boys and girls in the knowledge and fear of God. The ordinance for a girls' school in Göttingen spelled out that the school's purpose was "to initiate and hold girls in propriety and the fear of God. To fear God, they must learn their catechism, beautiful psalms, sayings, and other fine Christian and holy songs and little prayers. . . ."

The Reformation replaced late medieval church schools with a state school system. Controlled by state officials who examined, appointed, and paid teachers, the new educational system aimed to train obedient, pious, and hardworking Christian citizens. Discipline, not new ideas, informed sixteenth-century pedagogy. Teachers frequently used the rod to inculcate discipline while students memorized their catechisms, prayers, and other tidbits of Christian texts. In addition to reading and writing, girls' schools included domestic skills in their curriculum.

A two-tier system existed in Protestant education. Ideally, every parish had its German school for children between six and twelve; in practice, not surprisingly, educational reform was much more successful in cities than in the countryside. To train future pastors, scholars, and officials, the Protestant church developed a secondary system of humanist schools. As the fruition of pre-Reformation ideals, these higher schools for boys, called the *gymnasia,* were intended to prepare students for university study. Greek and Latin classics constituted the core of the curriculum, to which was added religious instruction.

In Catholic Europe educational reforms at the primary level proceeded unevenly. In northern and central Italian cities, most girls and boys received some education; this strong pedagogic tradition dated back to at least the thirteenth century. Concerning other Catholic territories, such as Spain, France, and south Germany, our knowledge is fragmentary. But if Catholics lagged behind Protestants in promoting primary education, they did succeed in establishing an excellent system of secondary education through the Jesuit colleges. Established to compete as university preparatory schools with the Protestant *gymnasia*, hundreds of Jesuit colleges dotted the landscape of Spain, Portugal, France, Italy, Catholic Germany, Hungary, Bohemia, and Poland by the late sixteenth century. Among their alumni would be princes (Duke Maximilian I of Bavaria, Emperor Ferdinand II of Austria), philosophers (the seventeenth-century French philosopher René Descartes), lawyers, churchmen, and officials—the elite of Catholic Europe.

God's Poor and Vagabonds

In the early sixteenth century secular governments began to take over the institutions of public charity from the church. This broad development, which took place in both Catholic and Protestant Europe, marked two trends that had become apparent during the late Middle Ages: the rise of a work ethic simultaneously with a growing hostility toward the poor, and the massive poverty brought about by population growth.

Based on an agrarian economy that had severe technological limitations, European society again felt the pressure of population growth on its food resources. By 1490 the cycle of demographic collapse and economic depression triggered by the Black Death of 1348 had passed. Between 1490 and 1560 a new cycle of rapid economic and population growth created prosperity and stress. Yet a series of bad harvests or pillaging troops could drive thousands from the countryside. Wandering and begging in cities was by no means novel. But the reaction to poverty was new.

Sixteenth-century moralists decried the crime and sloth of vagabonds. Rejecting the notion that the poor played a central role in the Christian moral economy, and that charity and prayers united rich and poor, these moralists cautioned against charlatans and criminals who brought disease in their wake. Instead, they said, one should distinguish between the genuine poor, or "God's Poor," and vagabonds; the latter, who were able-bodied, should be forced to work. This critique of poverty implicitly repudiated monasticism; it labeled monks and friars as social parasites who lived off the labor of others.

The Reformation provided an opportunity to reform poor relief. In Nuremberg (1522) and Strasbourg (1523) magistrates centralized poor relief with church funds. Instead of using decentralized, private initiative, magistrates appointed officials to head urban agencies that would certify the "genuine poor" and distribute welfare funds to them. This initiative progressed rapidly in urban areas, where poverty was most visible, transcending religious divides. During the 1520s cities in the Low Countries and Spain passed ordinances that prohibited begging and instituted public charity. In 1526 the Spanish humanist Juan Luis Vives wrote a Latin treatise, *On the Support of the Poor*, that was soon translated into French, Italian, German, and English. National measures followed urban initiatives: in 1531, Henry VIII asked justices of the peace (unpaid local magistrates) to license the poor in England and to differentiate between those who were capable of working and those who could not; in 1540, Charles V imposed a welfare tax in Spain to augment that country's inadequate system of private charity.

More prevalent in Protestant areas, public relief for the poor became a permanent feature of government once private charity ceased to be considered a "good work" necessary to earn salvation. In fact, the number of voluntary donations took a significant drop once poor relief was introduced. The new work ethic acquired a distinctly Protestant aura in that it equated laziness with a lack of moral worth (and frequently associated laziness with Catholics) and linked hard work and prosperity with piety and divine providence. In Catholic lands, in contrast, collective charity persisted, supported as it was by a theology of good works, by societies (in Italy and Spain, for example) more sharply divided between the noble rich and the poor, and by the elites' sense of social responsibility.

"What God Joined Together"

The Protestant reformers' fundamental goal was to establish order and discipline in worship and in society—one of the aims of the Catholic Counter-Reformation as well—by decrying sexual immorality and praising the family unit. The idealized patriarchal family provided a bulwark against the forces of disorder. Protestant magistrates who established marital courts and promulgated new marriage laws also closed brothels and inflicted harsher punishments for sexual deviancy.

The new marriage laws aimed to reform the traditional sexual regime. Prior to the Reformation marriages had been private affairs between families; some couples never even registered their marriages with the church, despite the Fourth Lateran Council's clear stipulation in 1215 that marriage was a sacrament. Under canon law the Catholic church recognized any promise made between two consenting adults (age twelve for females, fourteen for males) as a marriage. In rural areas and among the urban poor, most couples simply lived together as common-law husband and wife. The problem with the old marriage laws had been their complexity and the difficulties of enforcement. Often young men readily promised marriage in a passionate moment only to renege later. The overwhelming number of cases in Catholic church courts involved young women seeking to enforce marriage promises after they had exchanged their personal honor (that is, their virginity) for the greater honor of marriage.

The Reformation proved more effective in suppressing these so-called "clandestine marriages" than the late medieval church. Protestant governments asserted greater official control over marriages, and governments in the Counter-Reformation followed suit. A marriage was legitimate only if it had been registered by an official and a pastor. In many Protestant countries, the new marriage ordinances also required parental consent, thus giving the householders immense power in regulating marriage and the transmission of family property.

Enjoined to become obedient spouses and affectionate companions in Christ, women approached this new sexual regime with ambivalence. The new marriage laws stipulated that women could seek divorce on account of desertion, impotence, and flagrant abuse, although in practice the marriage courts encouraged reconciliation. These changes from earlier marriage laws came with a price, however: a woman's role took on the more limited definition of obedient wife, helpful companion, and loving mother. Now the path to religious power was closed to women. Unlike Catherine of Siena, Teresa of Avila, or other female Catholic saints, Protestant women could not renounce family, marriage, and sexuality to attain recognition and power in the church.

In the fervor of the early Reformation years, the first generation of Protestant women attained greater equality than subsequent generations. Katherina Zell, who had married the reformer Matthew Zell, defended her equality by citing Scripture to a critic. The critic had invoked St. Paul to support his argument that women should remain silent in church; Katherina retorted, "I would remind you of the word of this same apostle that in Christ there is no male nor female." Further quoting the Book of Joel, she recited the prophecy that "[God] will pour forth [his] spirit upon all flesh and your sons and your daughters will prophesy."

Katherina was much more than the ideal pastor's wife, however. In 1525 she helped to feed and clothe the thousands of refugees who flooded Strasbourg after their defeat in the Peasants War. In 1534 she published a collection of hymns. She encouraged her husband to oppose Protestant persecution of dissenters. After Matthew's death in 1548, Katherina continued to feed the sick, the poor, and the imprisoned. Outraged by the intolerance of a new breed of Protestant clergy, she reprimanded the prominent Lutheran pastor Ludwig Rabus for his persecution of dissenters: "You behave as if you had been brought up by savages in a jungle." Comparing the Anabaptists to beasts pursued by hunters and wild animals, she praised them for bearing witness to their faith "in misery, prison, fire, and water." Rebuking Rabus, she wrote: "You young fellows tread on the graves of the first fathers of this church in Strasbourg and punish all who disagree with you, but faith cannot be forced."

A more typical role model for the average Protestant woman was Katherina von Bora (1499–1550), who married Martin Luther in 1525. Sent to a nunnery at the age of ten, Katherina, along with other nuns in her convent, responded to the reformers' calls attacking monasticism. With the help of Luther, she and other nuns escaped by hiding in empty barrels that had contained smoked herring. After their marriage, the couple lived in the former Augustinian cloister in Wittenberg, which the Elector of Saxony had given to Luther. Katie, as Luther affectionately called her, ran the establishment, feeding their children, relatives, and student boarders. Although she deferred to Luther—she addressed him as "Herr Doktor"—Katherina defended a woman's right as an equal in marriage. When Luther teased her about Old Testament examples of polygyny, Katherina retorted, "Well, if it comes to that, I'll leave you and the children and go back to the cloister." Accepting her prescribed role in a patriarchal household—one of the three estates in the new Christian society of politics, household, and church—Katherina von Bora represented the ideal Protestant woman.

Conclusion

Mocking the warlike popes, the Dutch humanist Erasmus compared his times to those of the early Christian Church. In *The Praise of Folly* he satirized Christian prelates and princes, who "continued to shed Christian blood," the same blood as that of the martyrs who had built the foundations of Christianity. Turning from the papacy to the empire, Erasmus and many intellectuals of his generation saw in Emperor Charles V the model Christian prince. As the most powerful ruler in all Europe, Charles was hailed as the harbinger of peace, the protector of justice, and the foe of the infidel Turks. For the generation that came of age before the Reformation, Christian humanism—and its imperial embodiment—represented an ideal for political and moral reform that would save Christendom from corruption and strife.

The Reformation changed this dream of peace and unity. Instead of leading a crusade against Islam—a guiding vision of his life—Charles V wore himself out in the ceaseless struggle against King Francis I of France and the German Protestants. Instead of the Christian faith of charity and learning that Erasmus had envisioned, Christianity split into a number of hostile camps that battled one another with words and swords. Instead of the intellectual unity of the generation of Erasmus, More, and Dürer, the mid-sixteenth-century cultural landscape erupted in a burst of confessional statements and left in its wake a climate of censorship, repression, and inflexibility.

Christians continued to shed Christian blood. After the brutal suppression of popular revolts in the 1520s and 1530s, religious persecution became a Christian institution: Luther called on the princes to kill rebellious peasants in 1525, Zwingli advocated the drowning of Anabaptists, and Calvin supported the death sentence for Michael Servetus. Meanwhile, in Catholic lands persecutions and executions provided Protestants with a steady stream of martyrs. The two peace settlements in the 1550s failed to provide long-term solutions: the Peace of Augsburg (1555) gradually disintegrated as the religious struggles in the empire intensified, and the Treaty of Cateau-Cambrésis (1559) was but a brief respite in a century of crisis.

Suggestions for Further Reading

Source Materials

Essential Works of Erasmus. Edited by W. T. H. Jackson. 1965.

Guicciardini, Francesco. *The History of Italy*. Translated by Sidney Alexander. 1969. The events from 1490 to 1534, written by a participant.

Hillerbrand, Hans J., ed. *The Protestant Reformation*. 1969. Strong on religious documents.

The Prince and Selected Discourses: Machiavelli. Translated by Daniel Donno. 1966.

Interpretive Studies

Bainton, Roland. *Women of the Reformation in Germany and Italy*. 1971. Fifteen portraits; lively.

Blickle, Peter. *The Revolution of 1525*. 1981. Stresses the role of the common people in the early Reformation movement.

Bouwsma, William J. *John Calvin: A Sixteenth Century Portrait*. 1988. Intellectual biography at its best.

Brady, Thomas A. *Turning Swiss: Cities and Empire, 1450–1550*. 1985. A grand synthesis of social and political history of central Europe.

Crosby, Alfred W. *The Colombian Exchange: Biological and Cultural Consequences of 1492*. 1972.

Elliott, J. H. *The Old World and the New, 1492–1650*. 1970. A thought-provoking essay.

Elton, G.R. *Reformation Europe, 1517–1559*. 1963. Clear political history is its strong point.

Evennet, Henry Outram. *The Spirit of the Counter-Reformation*. 1968. Short and stimulating.

Febvre, Lucien. *Life in Renaissance France*. 1977. An old classic, strong on cultural history.

Hsia, R. Po-chia. *The Myth of Ritual Murder: Jews and Magic in the Reformation*. 1988. Analyzes the impact of the Reformation on antisemitism.

Knecht, R.J. *Francis I*. 1982. The standard biography.

Oberman, Heiko A. *Luther: Man Between God and Devil*. 1990. A forceful biography.

Ozment, Steven E. *The Reformation in the Cities*. 1975. Successfully re-creates the religious and psychological appeal of the Reformation movement.

Parker, Geoffrey. *The Military Revolution: Military Innovation and the Rise of the West, 1500–1800*. 1988. A good synthesis.

Partridge, Loren, and Randolph Starn. *A Renaissance Likeness: Art and Culture in Raphael's Julius II*. 1980. Collaborative interpretation by a historian and an art historian.

Pitkin, Hanna F. *Fortune Is a Woman: Gender and Politics in the Thought of Niccolò Machiavelli*. 1984. Original and brilliant interpretation based on psychoanalysis, gender theories, and political history.

Prodi, Paolo. *The Papal Prince. One Body and Two Souls: The Papal Monarchy in Early Modern Europe*. 1982. An extremely informative interpretation.

Scribner, R.W. *For the Sake of Simple Folk: Popular Propaganda for the German Reformation*. 1981. Pioneering study of woodcuts and visual propaganda in the Reformation.

Strauss, Gerald. *Luther's House of Learning: Indoctrination of the Young in the German Reformation*. 1978. Stresses the failure of the Reformation to change social habits.

Trevor-Roper, Hugh. *Princes and Artists: Patronage and Ideology at Four Habsburg Courts, 1517–1633*. 1976.

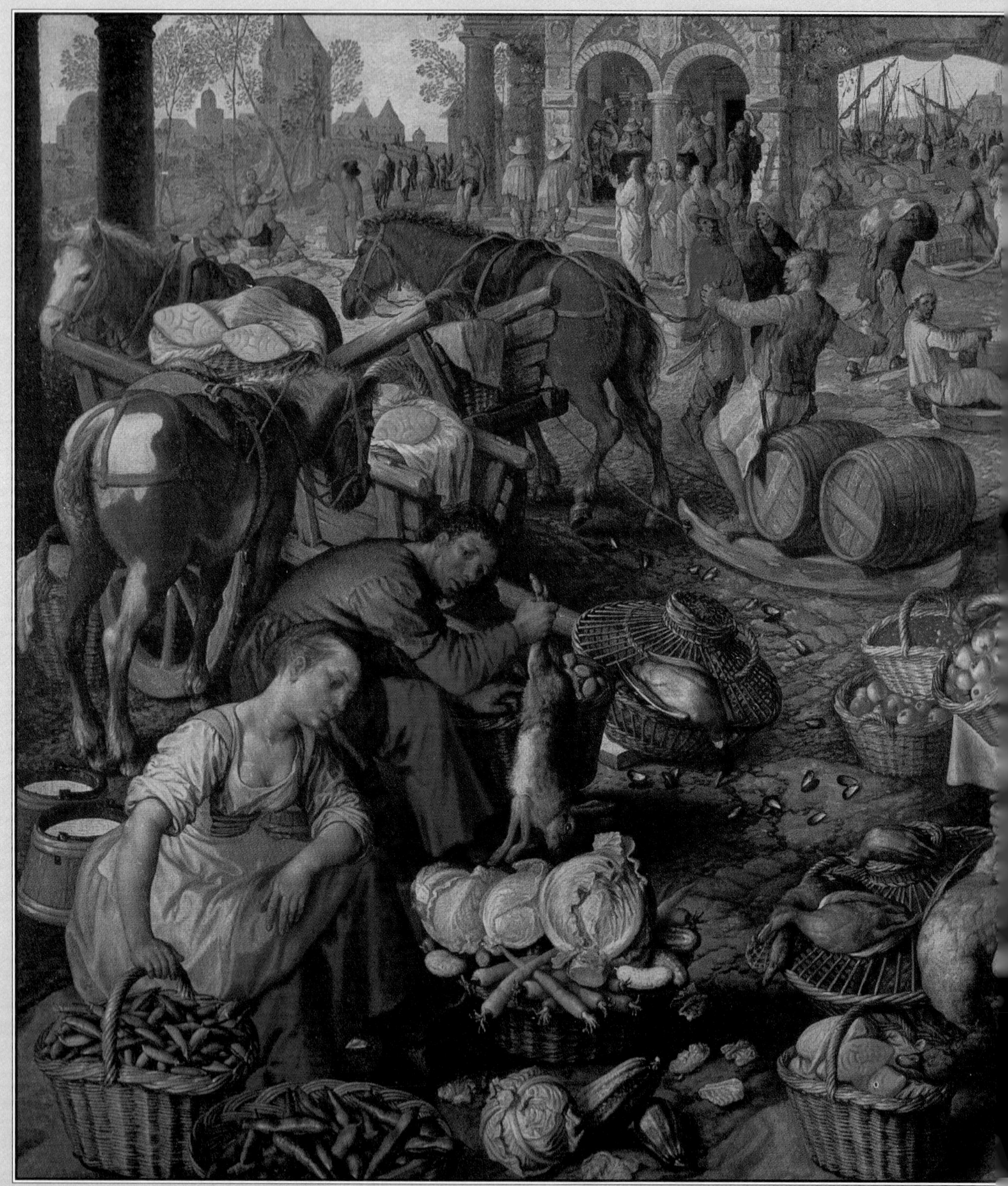

Joachim Beuckelaer, Market in the Country

PART III

The Take-off of the West, 1560–1894

After various peoples had settled the European continent and the British Isles and started forming centralized states with distinctive national identities, their dreams and ambitions ranged far beyond Europe. The voyages of "discovery" and conquest launched at the end of the 1400s gave rise to new forms of colonial rule. Settlers moved permanently from their home countries in Europe to found new colonies in the Americas—and later, in the 1800s, in Africa and Asia. Although relatively small, European countries thus assumed domination over much of the world, either directly, through colonization, or indirectly, through control of world trade.

European dynastic competition reflected these changes. Increasingly, European countries fought wars on a global scale. After

1650 the center of economic, political, and cultural power within Europe shifted from the Mediterranean to the northwestern Atlantic corner as the Dutch, English, and French wrested control of the seas from the Portuguese, Spanish, and Italians. In the next century, new forms of industrial growth radiated slowly eastward and southward from northwest Europe as new coal and iron deposits—now crucial to economic development—were discovered.

A constellation of factors catalyzed Europe's transformation from a backwater of the Roman Empire into the center of world power and wealth. The sixteenth-century religious movement known as the Reformation simultaneously shattered Catholicism's unity in western Europe and sapped the might of the one remaining imperial structure, the Holy Roman Empire. The disputes and conflicts spawned by the Reformation opened the door to new intellectual and political developments, including the idea of toleration of religious differences and of the separation of church and state. The collapse of Catholic uniformity also sparked scientific breakthroughs. Inspired by Greek ideas transmitted through Arab sources, Europeans strove not only to understand nature but to harness its energies. The scientific revolution of the 1600s provided scholars with the intellectual tools needed to understand every form of motion, from the movement of the planets in the heavens to the trajectory of cannonballs on the earth. Every great civilization had pursued scientific discoveries, but unlike others European societies relentlessly applied scientific principles to everyday life. Leading figures in the philosophic movement known as the Enlightenment held science up as the standard for *all* forms of truth, subjecting economic techniques, social relations, even religious beliefs to scientific scrutiny.

As scientific learning spread broadly through popular lectures and demonstrations, the work of academies and clubs, and university teaching, applied science reshaped the European economies and, gradually, the world landscape. The perfection of the steam engine in particular made possible not only deeper mines and the advent of factories organized around power looms but also the birth of the railroad. Travel and trade boomed, and every detail of daily life was soon affected. With the comforts and conveniences of life steadily increasing, "improvement" became a motto for the age. But industrialization had its costs. As little children toiled in dank and dangerous mines, and as working-class families crowded in sooty, polluted, urban slums, reformers and writers rallied to publicize—and to ease—their plight. And although the new technologies afforded Europeans an indisputable military edge over the rest of the world, they also fueled dangerous conflicts among the European powers at home.

The political organization of Europe also seemed to confer comparative advantages over the rest of the world. Larger than tribal organizations or city-states but smaller than the mighty empires of the ancient world, European states coalesced around national groupings. The variety of nation-states that emerged appeared best able to profit from the innovations of science, industry, and colonial exploitation. To maximize their advantages, rulers developed ever-larger bureaucracies and armies. Faced with the obvious success of such coherent nation-states as France and Great Britain, previously disunited national groups—most notably the Germans and the Italians—created their own distinctive national states. As soon as they became nations, they joined the scramble for colonial position, which in turn provoked new jealousies and rivalries. In the twentieth century, it would become apparent just how deadly national rivalries could turn.

By the late 1500s and 1600s, Europeans considered themselves "modern," that is, distinct from the peoples who lived in traditional societies. Europeans believed that as moderns, they had surpassed the achievements of the ancients. One measure of their modernity was the role of women as arbiters of manners and taste. Most European men rejected the idea of women's participation in political life, but they expected women to rule over the home and to assume responsibility for the moral improvement of society. The revolutions in science and industry confirmed and even reinforced Europeans' feelings of superiority not only to peoples of the past—especially those of the Dark, or Middle, Ages—but also to peoples living elsewhere in their world. This sense of superiority prompted them eagerly to pursue the colonization of "backward" native peoples in Asia and Africa and to condone, and even actively to support, the revived, expanding institution of human slavery.

Paradoxically, Europeans also came to associate their modernity with "freedom" and "democracy," words that gained currency in the 1700s at the very time of the greatest expansion of the slave system in the colonies. In the 1600s and 1700s, beginning in that same northwestern corner of Europe and its offshoots in the British North American colonies, people of the "middling sort"—merchants, lawyers, and landowners—agitated for an active role in politics. Rather than accept the traditional leadership of aristocratic elites, who in most countries dominated the armed forces and the state bureaucracy, they insisted on votes and offices for themselves as responsible male propertyowners. In this way began bitter struggles (which continue to this day) over the definition of democratic citizenship. The English Revolution of the 1640s and the American and French revolutions of the 1770s and 1780s demonstrated the explosive power of this issue. The French Revolutionary and Napoleonic wars revealed the advantages of mass armies commanded by men of talent who ascended the ranks, over traditional armies made up of unwilling conscripts or mercenaries and led by aristocrats with no connection to their men.

During the 1800s every European country faced the same question: whether to modernize and democratize (meaning to include all men as voters and potential officeholders) or to modernize and avoid democratization. By the end of the 1800s, much of western Europe had moved halfway toward democratization while still excluding women from politics. In eastern Europe, however, the question remained more unresolved. The twentieth century would show both the promise and perils of democracy.

CHAPTER 16

Religious Warfare and Crises of Authority, 1560–1640

One of the earliest German novels, *The Adventures of a Simpleton* by Grimmelshausen, tells an awful story from the early seventeenth-century religious wars. Looking up from playing his bagpipe, the boy Simplicius finds himself surrounded by enemy cavalrymen who drag him back to his father's farm; ransack the house; rape the maid, his mother, and his sister; force water mixed with dung down the farmhand's throat; and hold Simplicius's father's feet to the fire until he tells them where he hid his gold and jewels. The invaders then torture nearby peasants with thumbscrews, throw one alive into an oven, and strangle another with a crude noose. Simplicius hides in the woods but can still hear the cries of the suffering peasants and see his family's house burn down.

Grimmelshausen's story came out of his personal experience of the Thirty Years' War, as the wars of 1618 to 1648 came to be known. These wars grew out of an international crisis in the relationship between religious and political authority. In the wake of the Reformation, the dream of universal Christendom lay shattered. Although Catholics and Protestants continued to believe that state power and religious authority should be linked, the violence of religious conflicts began to undermine traditional connections between religion and politics. The devastations wrought by religious warfare convinced rulers and their advisers to strengthen state power. The Thirty Years' War would show that the interests of states had begun to outweigh those of religion. Bureaucracies, armies, and the powers of rulers all expanded, making wars more dangerous to and state power more intrusive in the lives of ordinary

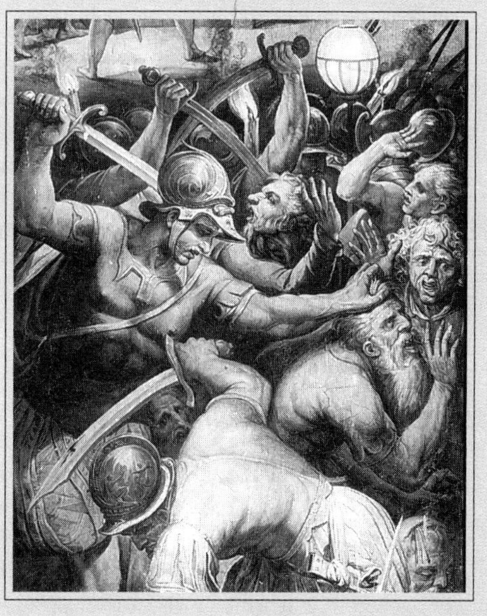

Massacre Motivated by Religion
The Italian artist Vasari painted the St. Bartholomew's Day Massacre (1572) for one of the public rooms in the pope's residence. Despite the scene's gruesomeness, both the pope and the artist intended to celebrate a Catholic victory over Protestant "heresy."

people. In a precarious world, religion gave many, whether Protestant or Catholic, the strength to accept hardship and turmoil as God's testing of their souls. In the realm of public policy, however, religious motivations eventually had to bend as state power increasingly diverged from religious sanctions.

Although particularly dramatic and deadly, the church-state crisis was only one of a series of economic, political, and cultural upheavals. In the early seventeenth century a major economic downturn resulted in food shortages, famine, and disease, creating greater burdens for states. Simultaneously, a secular (nonreligious) world view developed as the scientific revolution challenged age-old assumptions about heaven and earth. Scientists, writers, military men, and politicians all helped foster a belief in science and reason. Their emerging view of a world ruled by mechanical principles included a new vision of the social order governed by scientific laws and state powers. The scientific revolution did not prevent the persecution of witches, refute the persistent belief in magic, or alleviate the turbulence stirred by religious and dynastic conflicts. But it did set in motion forces that would ultimately help make western Europe the world's dominant power.

Important Dates

1562 French Wars of Religion begin

1566 Revolt of Calvinists in the Netherlands against Spain begins

1569 Formation of Commonwealth of Poland-Lithuania

1571 Battle of Lepanto marks victory of West over Ottomans at sea

1587 Mary Queen of Scots executed

1588 Defeat of the Spanish Armada against England

1598 French Wars of Religion end with Edict of Nantes

1618 Thirty Years' War begins

1620 Defeat of the Czechs by Imperial armies at the Battle of White Mountain

1628 Charles I grants Petition of Right in England

1629 Emperor Ferdinand issues Edict of Restitution taking back Catholic lands confiscated by Lutherans

1635 France joins the Thirty Years' War by declaring war on Spain

1648 Peace of Westphalia ends the Thirty Years' War

State Power and Religious Conflict

The Peace of Augsburg (1555) had produced relative calm in central Europe by confirming the uneasy balance between Catholic and Lutheran German princes. John Calvin and his successors, however, made Geneva the headquarters for a religious revolution that threatened to shift the balance of power between Protestants and Catholics and within Protestantism itself. Calvinists challenged Catholic dominance in France, Scotland, Poland-Lithuania, and the Spanish-ruled Netherlands. They continued to attract adherents in the German states as well, and in England they sought to influence the new Protestant monarch, Elizabeth I. In 1558 one of the Catholic bishops under Elizabeth's predecessor, Mary Tudor, warned: "The wolves be coming out of Geneva and other places of Germany and have sent their books before, full of pestilent doctrines, blasphemy and heresy to infect the people." Calvinist preachers from Geneva converted thousands and organized new communities of men and women willing to oppose even monarchs who resisted their message. Their successes upset the international equilibrium.

French Religious Wars

Calvinist inroads in France had begun in 1555, when the Genevan Company of Pastors took charge of missionary work. Supplied with false passports and often disguised as merchants, the pastors moved rapidly among clandestine congregations, mostly in towns near Paris or in the south. Some ministers were former Catholic priests; most were laymen from middle-class or noble French families. Nobles provided military protection to local congregations and helped set up a national synod to organize the secret French Calvinist—or Huguenot—church.

Conversion to Calvinism in French noble families often began with the noblewomen, some

Peter Brueghel the Elder's,* The Triumph of Death, *c. 1562
Neither riches nor power can hold back the hand of death, represented in this work by a variety of terrifying skeletal figures. The painting seems to predict the death and destruction that would soon ravage much of Europe.

of whom sought intellectual independence as well as spiritual renewal in the new faith. Charlotte de Bourbon, for example, escaped from a Catholic convent, fled to Heidelberg, and eventually married William of Orange, leader of the anti-Spanish resistance in the Netherlands. Jeanne d'Albret, wife of Antoine de Bourbon and mother of the future French king Henry IV, became a Calvinist and convinced many of her clan to convert to Calvinism, though her husband died fighting for the Catholic side. Calvinist noblewomen protected pastors, provided money and advice, and helped found schools and establish relief for the poor. Calvinism also appealed to the wives of urban craftsmen, merchants, and professionals.

Religious divisions in France often reflected political disputes among noble families. About one-third of the nobles joined the Huguenots—a much larger proportion than in the general population. The Huguenots usually followed the lead of the Bourbon family. The most uncompromisingly anti-Protestant Catholic nobles took their cues from the Guise family. The Catholic royal family was caught between these two powerful factions, each with its own military organization. The situation grew even more volatile when Henry II (*1547–1559) died unexpectedly in a tournament and his young son Francis II (*1559–1560) succumbed soon after, leaving the ten-year-old Charles IX (*1560–1574) king, with the Italian queen mother, Catherine de Medicis, as regent. France thus had no ruler who could command respect and obedience in difficult times. Catherine, a Roman Catholic, urged limited toleration for the Huguenots in an attempt to maintain political stability, but her influence was severely limited. As one ambassador commented, "It is sufficient to say that she is a woman, a foreigner, and a Florentine to boot, born of a simple house, altogether beneath the dignity of the Kingdom of France." Unwilling to obey a foreign woman of less-than-royal birth, the factions consolidated their forces, making general warfare inevitable.

For more than thirty years, French Catholics and Huguenots battled sporadically but fiercely. Both sides committed terrible atrocities. Priests and pastors were murdered, and massacres became frighteningly commonplace. Denouncing their enemies as idol worshipers, Huguenots destroyed altars and statues in Catholic churches. Catholics considered the Huguenots corrupt and polluted, deserving of the most horrible death. At Auxerre, for example, a Catholic mob slaughtered one hundred fifty Huguenots, dragged their naked bodies through the streets, and threw them into the river. Huguenots took their revenge on monasteries and abbeys, sometimes killing monks and nuns. Peasants, both Catholic and Protestant, suffered enormously from the ravages of hostile armies.

The most notorious atrocities occurred in the St. Bartholomew's Day Massacre, so-called because it began on the eve of St. Bartholomew's Day, the night of August 23, 1572. On August 22, assassins failed in their attempt to kill the Huguenot leader, Gaspard de Coligny. Panicking at the thought of Huguenot revenge and perhaps herself implicated in the botched plot, Catherine de Medicis convinced Charles IX to order the killing of the major Calvinist leaders, including Coligny. A bloodbath resulted. Catholic mobs murdered three thousand Huguenots in Paris, ten thousand in the provinces. Joyfully, the pope ordered the church bells rung throughout Catholic Europe; Spain's Philip II wrote Catherine that it was "the best and most cheerful news which at present could come to me." Protestants everywhere were horrified.

Repression did not solve the monarchy's problems, and the religious division was further complicated when a Protestant became heir to the crown. Two years after the massacre, Charles IX died, and his brother Henry III (*1574–1589) became king. Henry III, like his brother before him, failed to produce an heir; he would be the last of the Valois monarchs. Next in line for the throne was none other than the Protestant Bourbon leader, Henry of Navarre. Yet for the moment, Henry III and Catherine de Medicis perceived an even greater threat in the Guises and their newly formed Catholic League, which had requested Spanish support in rooting out Protestantism in France. Henry and Catherine felt compelled to cooperate with Henry of Navarre because the league, believing the king was not taking a strong enough stand against the Protestants, began to encourage disobedience. Henry III responded with a fatal trick. In 1588 he summoned the two Guise leaders to a meeting outside Paris and had his men kill them. A few months later a fanatical monk stabbed Henry

French Wars of Religion

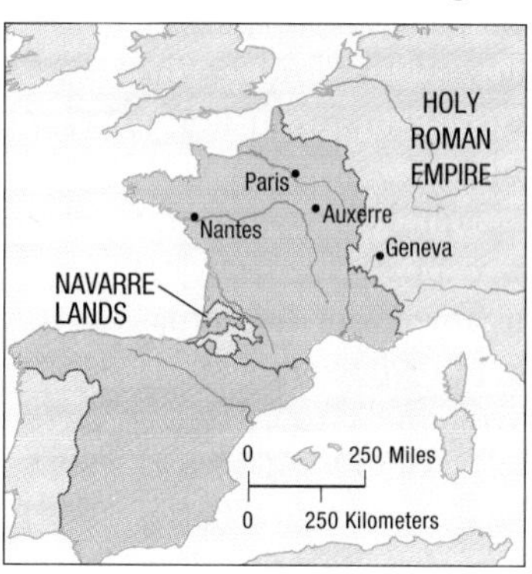

The French Wars of Religion

1555 Genevan Company of Pastors begins Calvinist missionary work in France

1559 Henry II dies in a tournament and is succeeded by his sickly son Francis II, who reigns only one year

1560 Charles IX becomes king at age ten; his mother Catherine de Medicis is regent

1562 Warfare between Catholics and Protestants begins

1572 Saint Bartholemew's Day Massacre results in killing of thousands of Protestants all over France

1574 Henry III succeeds his brother Charles X but produces no heirs to the throne

1589 Henry III assassinated by a Catholic dissatisfied with his policies

1593 Henry IV, the Protestant heir to the throne, renounces Protestantism and embraces Catholicism

1598 Henry IV grants toleration to Protestants in Edict of Nantes, ending the religious wars

III to death, and Henry of Navarre became Henry IV (*1589–1610).

The new king soon realized that to establish control over the war-weary country he had to place the interests of the French state ahead of his Protestant faith. In 1593, therefore, Henry IV publicly embraced Catholicism (for the third time!) reputedly explaining his conversion with the phrase, "Paris is worth a Mass." Within a few years he defeated the last Catholics who refused to believe him sincere and drove out the Spanish, who had intervened militarily to block his accession. In 1598 he made peace with Spain, and in the Edict of Nantes he granted the Huguenots a large measure of religious toleration. The approximately 1.25 million Calvinists became a legally protected minority within an officially Catholic kingdom of some 18 million to 20 million people. Protestants were free to worship in specified towns and were allowed their own troops, fortresses, and even courts. The religious wars in France were over.

A New Relationship Between State and Religion: The *Politiques*

The Edict of Nantes would have been inconceivable earlier, when religious minorities seemed inherently treasonous. It represented a new arrangement prompted by the very practical need to pacify a religious minority too large to ignore and impossible to eradicate. Religious divisions proved especially threatening in the late sixteenth century because religious doctrines were now used to justify political resistance. Both Luther and Calvin had worried about this issue, and they had not advocated outright rebellion. After the St. Bartholomew's Day Massacre, however, Huguenot pamphleteers developed a constitutional theory of the right of resistance. Civil society, they held, rested on an implicit contract between the ruler and his magistrates, who represented the people; if a ruler broke that contract by tyranny or idol worship (which for the Calvinists meant Catholicism), the magistrates could justly depose him or her. The Protestant William of Orange used this argument to justify the Netherlands' struggles with Catholic Spain, and after Henry IV became king, Catholic writers took the same line, arguing that a heretical monarch such as Henry IV had no right to the throne.

In response to this growing challenge to established authority, some writers and statesmen began to insist that the need for political order and social stability superseded the importance of religious conformity. Called the *politiques* because of their emphasis on political concerns, they argued that a strong state must establish its independence from religious conflicts. One *politique* writer, Michel de Montaigne (1533–1592), explained the necessity of restraint in religious matters: "We see many whom passion drives outside the bounds of reason and makes them sometimes adopt unjust, violent, and even reckless courses." Montaigne advocated skepticism toward traditional beliefs; the words "all that is certain is that nothing is certain" were painted on the beams of his study. The *politiques'* most influential political analyst was Jean Bodin (1530–1596), who wrote *The Six Books of the Republic* (1576). Examining the different forms of government, Bodin concluded that only virtually unlimited monarchical power, under which subjects have no rights of resistance, offered hope for order. Bodin's ideas laid the foundation for absolutism (the idea that the monarch should be the sole and uncontested source of power) in the seventeenth century.

Henry IV's decision to compromise on religion in order to strengthen state power gave the *politiques* great hopes for a reign of toleration and stability. But the new king needed more than a good theory. To ensure his own safety and the succession of his heirs, he had to reestablish monarchical authority. Shrewdly mixing personal charm and effective bureaucratic development, Henry created a new splendid image of monarchy and extended his government's control. Like England's Elizabeth I, he cultivated rituals that glorified the monarch as a symbol of state power. Both rulers managed to control potentially fatal religious divisions, in part by rallying their subjects and officials around their own persons. Paintings, songs, court festivities, and royal processions all celebrated the ruler as a kind of mythological figure. Henry was depicted as an expert hunter, rider, fencer, dancer, and patron of the arts and learning.

Henry also fortified the monarchy by tapping new sources of revenue and by developing a new class of officials to counterbalance the fractious nobility. In 1604 his chief minister, the duke of Sully (1560–1641), introduced a new fee known as the *paulette,* which made administrative and judicial offices much easier to inherit. For some time the French crown had earned considerable revenue by selling offices to qualified bidders. Now, in exchange

Elizabeth I of England *Portraits of the monarch, whether in full-scale paintings or miniatures given as gifts, reminded subjects of the queen's glory, power, and authority.*

for the new annual payment, officeholders could not only own their offices but also pass them on to heirs or sell them to someone else. Because these offices carried prestige and often ennobled their holders, rich middle-class merchants and lawyers with aspirations to higher social status found them attractive. By buying offices they could become part of a new social elite known as the "nobility of the robe" (named after the robes that magistrates wore, much like those judges wear today). The nobility of the robe owed its status to the king, and the monarchy acquired a growing bureaucracy, though at the cost of granting broad autonomy to new officials who could not be dismissed. New income raised by the increased sale of offices reduced the state debt and eventually allowed Sully to balance the budget. Henry left the kingdom in good enough working order to ensure his son's succession, deter the renewal of religious warfare, and build the base for a strong monarchy. His efforts did not, however, prevent his own assassination in 1610 after nineteen unsuccessful attempts.

English Protestantism

Like Henry IV of France, Elizabeth I of England (*1558–1603) aimed to reestablish a strong monarchy, and against great obstacles she achieved her goal. England remained politically stable during her reign despite persistent troubles over religion. Having succeeded her half-sister, Mary Tudor, after five years of weak government and nearly constant religious unrest, Elizabeth returned England to Protestantism. Replacing the pope as the ultimate religious authority, Elizabeth assumed control as "supreme governor" of the Church of England. She insisted on retaining some Catholic ritual and an "episcopal" system in which the monarch appointed all bishops. Issued in 1563, the Church of England's Thirty-Nine Articles of Religion incorporated these elements of Catholicism along with such Calvinist doctrines as predestination.

England's political stability depended not only on preventing civil strife but also on ensuring a Protestant succession, situations that required Elizabeth's continual maneuvering over many years. She adroitly manipulated the prejudices of the age: "I know that I have the body of a weak and feeble woman," she once told Parliament, all the while insisting on her prerogatives as ruler. In the early years of her reign, the unmarried Elizabeth considered several possible dynastic alliances. She held out the prospect of marriage as long as her Catholic cousin, Mary, Queen of Scots, stood next in line to inherit the English throne. Scottish Calvinist nobles, however, forced Mary to abdicate in 1568 in favor of her year-old son, James, who was then raised as a Protestant. By the time of Elizabeth's death in 1603, her advisers had arranged

Mary, Queen of Scots
Even in prison, Mary served as a rallying point for Catholics who resented Elizabeth's reinstatement of Anglicanism. Elizabeth ordered her execution in 1587.

for James to become king of both England and Scotland, ensuring a Protestant succession.

Elizabeth had to parry challenges not only from Catholics but also from Puritans, strict Calvinists who opposed the vestiges of Catholic ritual in the Church of England. After Elizabeth became queen many English Protestants returned from exile. They soon became highly influential in English Protestant circles, but Elizabeth resisted their demands for drastic changes in church ritual and governance. Tacitly permitting English Catholics to worship in private, she allowed Catholicism to be kept alive by aristocrats who could afford to maintain their own chapels. Of those who considered themselves Catholic in the 1550s and 1560s, only a few were prepared to resist the new religious settlement violently. When they did rise up in support of Mary, Queen of Scots, in the Northern Rebellion of 1568–1569, they were immediately defeated. The Puritans, for their part, saw no need for armed rebellion, working instead from within to influence the Church of England.

During Elizabeth's reign the Puritans established a reputation for strict moral lives and for "plainness" in religion, characteristics that would grow more important in the seventeenth century. Puritan ministers constantly preached against the Church of England's "popish attire and foolish disguising . . . tithings, holy days, and a thousand more abominations." Puritan efforts focused largely on church administration, attempting to place control in the hands of a local presbytery made up of the minister and the elders of the congregation. They had in mind something like the Presbyterian Church of Scotland, which was reorganized by the Scottish Calvinist nobility after Mary's expulsion. Elizabeth rejected any attempt to undercut bishops' authority or to substitute a presbyterian church government.

Elizabeth and her successor, James I (*1603–1625), regarded any attack on the church administration as an attack on the government as well. James echoed Elizabeth's thoughts when in response to Puritan critics of the church hierarchy he snapped, "No bishop, no king." Yet both Elizabeth and James relied on Puritan councilors and supported Puritans in high positions in the Church of England. At Puritan urging, in 1604 a new translation of the Bible—the Authorized Version, or King James Bible—was initiated; published in 1611, it encouraged laypeople to read the Scriptures. Meanwhile, the Church of England's authority reached into many aspects of life. Education was an ecclesiastical monopoly; bishops supervised the censorship of books; and local parish officials oversaw such matters as poor relief and the control of vagrants. An example of religious intervention in daily life can be seen in the Oxfordshire market town of Banbury, where in 1589, Puritan officials ordered maypoles taken down and suppressed traditional merrymaking such as morris dances and Sunday fairs. The sheriff and ultimately the highest royal officials overruled them. But even games and dances had become religious and therefore political issues, and Puritan attacks on the Church of England threatened government authority in daily life.

By the early seventeenth century the chief characteristics of Puritan teaching included a deep hatred of "popery" (the ceremonial trappings of Catholicism); a dedication to preaching, the instructional element of religion; an emphasis on keeping the Sabbath without such distractions as games and dancing; and an abhorrence of "licentious" behavior, such as theatrical productions that lacked a moral message. Puritan moral reform took place at every level, from the highest reaches of state power to the family. The family was the "Seminary of the Church and Common-wealth," and the master of the family should "make his house a little church." By stressing religious instruction within the family, Puritans inevitably focused much attention on the roles of wives and mothers. Puritan writers insisted that marriage existed for mutual spiritual comfort and companionship as well as for procreation, and mothers were expected to be counselors and religious mentors for their children. Although this emphasis on mothers' responsibilities accorded women a special importance, most Puritans continued to insist that fathers be the unquestioned heads of families. Children were supposed to stand or kneel in their parents' presence and generally to respect authority. Still, Puritan families also spawned religious and political resistance with their emphasis on Bible reading, studying catechism at home, and questioning the authority of those who did not agree with the Puritan program.

Believing themselves God's elect, English Puritans developed a fervent sense of mission about their predestined role—and England's, as an "elect nation," in international politics. In Elizabethan and particularly Puritan eyes, Catholic Spain became a diabolical force. Conversely, to pious Spanish Catholics, heretical England increasingly seemed not only a political rival but also a sinkhole of sin and error. Spanish Catholicism strove, as sternly as did Elizabethan Puritanism, to render the state a fit instrument of God's purpose. Yet the Spanish monarch, like his English and French counterparts, had to cope with a turbulent nobility and an inefficient bureaucracy at home. Against this backdrop of monarchies struggling to master chaos and earn divine favor, England and Spain headed toward a confrontation that would, before the end of the sixteenth century, engage them in hostilities on three continents.

Spanish Imperial and Religious Power

A deeply religious Catholic who was equally committed to his royal duties, Philip II (✶1556–1598) came to the Spanish throne at age twenty-eight. Spanish Catholics joined their monarch in passionately rejecting the "heresy" of Protestantism and in vigorously opposing Muslim or Jewish influence; the Spanish Inquisition, which remained in force throughout Philip's reign, enforced religious conformity. Like Elizabeth and Henry IV, Philip cultivated an image of power and authority. He built a great gray granite palace, the Escorial, but had it constructed in the mountains, half-palace, half-monastery. There he lived in a small room and dressed in somber black. Most of all, observed the Venetian ambassador, he liked "being by himself." Philip nonetheless relished the prerogatives of ruling; he personally supervised his gardens and building projects and oversaw the acquisition of paintings and books for his collections.

Philip faced enormous responsibilities because his empire was rich and far-flung. The Spanish colonies in the New World (called "the Indies") were just beginning to be settled, and their systematic exploitation commenced when silver mines opened in the 1540s. As the colonies funneled many of their profits into the Spanish economy, Spain prospered—for a while. Philip meanwhile contracted four successive marriages with the Portuguese, English, French, and Austrian royal families. His brief marriage to Mary Tudor (Mary I of England) did not produce an heir, but it and his subsequent marriage to the daughter of Henry II of France gave him reason enough for involvement in English and French affairs. In 1580, when the king of Portugal died without a direct heir, Philip took over this neighboring realm with its rich empire in Africa, India, and the Americas. The combined empires gave Spain an advantage at sea.

Religious conflict in Spain had an inevitable international dimension. Between 1568 and 1571 the Moriscos—Muslim converts to Christianity who secretly remained faithful to Islam—revolted in the south. Only distance and lack of resources prevented the Ottoman Turks from coming to their aid. As the Turks pushed into Hungary, the Spanish joined the pope and the Venetians in 1571 to defeat them in a great sea battle off the Greek coast at Lepanto. Although both sides suffered heavy losses—more than half the combatants were killed or wounded—the Christian allies drove the Turkish fleet out of the western Mediterranean. At home the Spanish forcibly resettled ninety thousand Morisco rebels in small groups in Castile.* When even this failed to squelch Muslim practices, two hundred seventy-five thousand Moriscos were expelled from Spain, most of them sent to France or North Africa.

Whereas in Spain the Inquisition successfully rooted out any sign of Protestant heresy, the Calvinists of Philip's northern possession, the Netherlands, were less easily intimidated: they

*Castile was one of the kingdoms united by the monarchy to form the Spanish state.

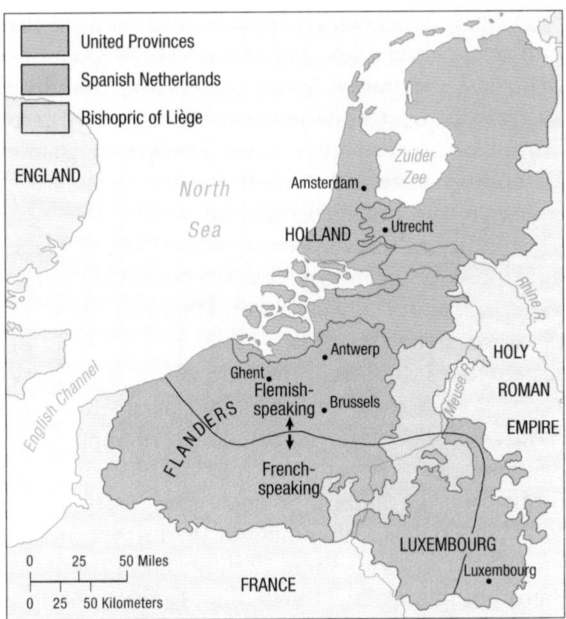

The Netherlands During the Revolt, c. 1580

were far away and accustomed to being left alone. In 1566, Calvinists attacked Catholic churches, smashing objects of devotion. To punish his unruly subjects, Philip sent an army commanded by the duke of Alba (1507–1582). Philip's emissaries executed over eleven hundred people during the next six years, alienating much of the local population. Prince William of Orange (1533–1584) emerged as the leader of the anti-Spanish resistance in the Netherlands. He encouraged exiles and pirates known as the Sea Beggars to invade the northern ports, and their success sparked urban revolts. The Spanish responded with even more force, culminating in 1576 when Philip's long-unpaid mercenary armies mutinied and sacked Antwerp, then Europe's wealthiest commercial city. In eleven days of horror known as the Spanish Fury, seven thousand people perished. Out of this bloody confrontation emerged an alliance, the Pacification of Ghent (1576), between the ten southern provinces, largely Catholic, and the seven northern provinces, which had more Protestants. Under William of Orange local forces expelled the Spaniards in 1577.

Important religious, ethnic, and linguistic differences prevented enduring unity. The southern provinces remained Catholic (although, ironically, Calvinism got its start there), in parts French-speaking, and suspicious of the increasingly strict Calvinism in the north. William himself—once a Catholic, then a Lutheran, and only belatedly a Calvinist—did not always steer a steady course. In 1579 the southern provinces broke with William and returned to the Spanish fold. In the north the United Provinces (as they were then known), deposed Philip. Despite the 1584 assassination of William of Orange, outlawed by Philip II as "an enemy of the human race," Spanish troops never regained control in the north. Spain would not formally recognize the United Provinces (called more commonly the Dutch Republic) as independent until 1648, but by the end of the sixteenth century the Dutch Republic was a self-governing state sheltering a variety of religious groups.

Oligarchy and Religious Toleration in the Dutch Republic

The princes of Orange resembled a ruling family in the Dutch Republic (sometimes incorrectly called "Holland" after the most populous of the seven provinces), but their powers were limited and largely unofficial. Europeans living under monarchy wondered how the Dutch could live without a central authority figure or even a strong central administration, but the Dutch Republic developed instead an oligarchy (government by a few members of the elite class). Urban merchant and professional families (the "regents") controlled the towns and provinces. This was no democracy: governing explicitly included "the handling and keeping quiet of the multitude." In the absence of a national bureaucracy, a single legal system, and a central court, each province governed itself and sent delegates to the one common institution, the haphazardly organized States-General, largely run by the strongest individual provinces and their ruling families.

Well situated for maritime commerce, the Dutch Republic developed a thriving economy based on shipping and shipbuilding. Whereas aristocrats elsewhere focused on their landholdings, the Dutch looked for investments in trade. Amsterdam was the main European money market for two centuries after the municipally backed Bank of Amsterdam was established in 1609. The city was also a primary commodities market and a chief supplier of arms—to allies, neutrals, and even enemies. Dutch entrepreneurs produced goods at lower prices than anyone else, and they marketed them more efficiently. Dutch traders favored free trade in Europe because they could compete at an advantage. They controlled many overseas markets thanks to their preeminence in seaborne commerce; by 1670 the Dutch commercial fleet was larger than those of England, France, Spain, Portugal, and the Austrian Empire combined. Expanding opportunities for making money attracted immigrants from all over Europe, especially from the southern Netherlands, which remained under Spanish rule.

Because commercial capitalism—making money from investments in money or trade in commodities—fostered an openness to trading with anyone anywhere, it is perhaps not surprising that Dutch society appeared generally more tolerant of religious pluralism than the other European states. One-third of the Dutch population remained Catholic, and the secular authorities interfered little with it, although they did ban public worship. Because Protestant sects could generally count on toleration from the regents, they remained peaceful. The Netherlands had a relatively large Jewish population (many Jews had settled there after being driven out of Spain and Portugal), and from 1597, Jews could worship openly in their synagogues. Its relative openness to various religions helped make the Dutch Republic one of Europe's chief intellectual and scientific centers in the seventeenth and eighteenth centuries.

Religious Conflict and the International Balance of Power

Religion had long fueled conflict between Christian powers and the Muslim warrior states, and in the late sixteenth and early seventeenth centuries the Catholic Habsburgs continued the wars against Turkish Islam in eastern Europe. Since the Reformation, however, religious division increasingly divided Europe into internally battling factions. Western European religious conflicts threatened to become international when dissidents appealed to their sympathizers abroad for help. William of Orange, for example, sought help from the German Lutherans and from Protestants in France and England; English and Irish Catholics looked to the Catholic powers for assistance. These religious struggles inevitably exacerbated long-standing dynastic competition between the chief western European powers. In eastern Europe messianic Orthodoxy pitted Muscovite Russia against religiously mixed Poland-Lithuania.

By the early seventeenth century, nonetheless, state interests began to eclipse religious concerns as states looked for new alliances. Happening neither all at once nor very smoothly, this process of change failed to prevent the outbreak of the Thirty Years' War in 1618, with the devastating effects so vividly told in Grimmelshausen's tale of Simplicius. Beginning as yet another religiously motivated conflict within the Holy Roman Empire, the wars ended in a major realignment of the European balance of power, with some Catholic and Protestant states becoming allies for the first time.

Conflict Between England and Spain

Although, as one Englishman admitted, Philip II of Spain was "the most potent Monarch of Christendome," even he could not curb the Dutch rebels or stop the English from sending their fellow Protestants military aid and political advisers. Mary, Queen of Scots, brought the conflict between Elizabeth I and Philip to a head. The French-raised and Catholic queen had been under house arrest in England since fleeing her rebellious Calvinist subjects in 1568. As the great granddaughter of Henry VII, she had valid claims to the English throne, and her very presence rallied English Catholics who resented Elizabeth's church settlement. For the nearly twenty years of her imprisonment, she joined every Catholic plot against the English queen. In 1586 still more evidence of her intrigues came to light: a letter in which she offered her succession rights to Philip II, England's archenemy. Despite her reluctance to agree to the execution of another monarch, Elizabeth had Mary beheaded in 1587. In response, Pope Sixtus V decided to subsidize a Catholic crusade under Philip's leadership against the heretical queen, "the English Jezebel."

At the end of May 1588, Philip II sent his armada of one hundred thirty ships from Lisbon toward the English Channel. The Spanish king's motives were at least as political and economic as they were religious; he now had an excuse to strike

Anglo-Spanish War, 1580s

at the country whose pirates raided his shipping and encouraged Dutch resistance, and he hoped to use his fleet to ferry thousands of troops from the Netherlands across the channel to invade England itself. After several inconclusive engagements, the English scattered the Spanish Armada close to the French coast by sending blazing fireships into their midst. A gale then forced the Spanish to flee around Scotland. When the armada limped home in September, half the ships had been lost and thousands of sailors were dead or starving. Protestants everywhere rejoiced; Elizabeth struck a medal with the words, "God blew, and they were scattered." In his play *King John* a few years later (1596), Shakespeare wrote, "This England never did, nor never shall, Lie at the proud foot of a conqueror." A Spanish monk lamented, "Almost the whole of Spain went into mourning."

When Philip II died in 1598, his great empire had begun to lose its luster. The Dutch revolt ground on, and Henry IV seemed firmly established in France. The costs of fighting the Dutch, the English, and the French mounted up, and in the 1590s pervasive crop failures and the plague made hard times even worse. In his novel *Don Quixote* (1605, 1616) the Spanish novelist and playwright Miguel de Cervantes (1547–1616) captured the sadness of Spain's loss of grandeur. Cervantes's hero, a minor nobleman, reads so many romances and books of chivalry that he loses his wits and wanders the countryside hoping to recreate the heroic deeds of times past. His "tilting at windmills" provides an apt metaphor for a declining military aristocracy and a sense of thwarted ambition.

Eastern Europe: The Clash of Faiths and Empires

After the Christian naval triumph at Lepanto in 1571, the Austrian Habsburgs continued to battle the Ottoman armies in the Danube basin. The Habsburgs worked to consolidate the resources of their Bohemian and Austrian lands, of the slender strip of western Hungary they controlled, and of the Holy Roman Empire. But they had to make numerous concessions to the nobility of these lands in order to keep raising the money to hire mercenary armies capable of fighting the Turks in the series of inconclusive engagements that dragged on until the early seventeenth century.

Religious Divisions in Europe, c. 1600

Ottoman power had reached its zenith during the reign of Suleiman the Magnificent (*1520–1566) and gradually declined thereafter. Defeat at Lepanto did not end Ottoman attacks in the western Mediterranean and did not hold off Turkish fleets, which subsequently seized Venetian-held Cyprus in 1573. Meanwhile Ottoman rule went unchallenged in the Balkans, where the Turks allowed their Christian subjects to cling to the Orthodox faith (and be taxed) rather than forcibly converting them to Islam. Orthodox Christians thus enjoyed relative toleration and were unlikely to look to the West for aid. Even less inclined to turn westward were the numerous and prosperous Sephardic Jewish communities of the Ottoman Empire, now joined by Jews expelled from Spain. Islam itself provided a powerful unifying force for the Turks and those conquered peoples or western "renegades" who embraced it, enabling the Ottoman Empire to withstand the sapping of the sultans' authority after Suleiman's death. The late sixteenth-century Ottoman monarchs became mere puppets of palace intrigues led by their elite troops, the Janissaries. However, the Habsburgs lacked the strength to drive the Ottomans back, and the Ottoman Empire still remained strong enough to avoid crumbling from within.

Whereas in the Balkans Orthodox Christians were obliged to collaborate with Ottoman power, in the Russian lands they found a champion in the Muscovite tsars. Building upon the base laid by his grandfather Ivan III, Tsar Ivan IV (*1533–1584) fought to make Muscovy the center of a mighty Russian empire. Ivan brought the entire Volga valley under Muscovite control and initiated Russian expansion eastward into Siberia. In 1558 he struck out to the west, vainly attempting to seize the decaying state of the German-crusader knights in present-day Estonia and Latvia to provide Russia direct access to the Baltic Sea. Given to unpredictable fits of rage, Ivan killed numerous *boyars* (nobles), tortured priests, sacked the city of Novgorod on hearing rumors that it was siding with Lithuania, and killed his own son with an iron rod during a quarrel. His epithet "the Terrible" reflects not only the terror he unleashed but also the awesome impression he evoked. Cunning, intelligent, morbidly suspicious, and cruel, Ivan came to embody barbarism in the eyes of westerners. An English visitor wrote that Ivan's actions had bred "a general hatred, distreccion [distraction], fear and discontentment throw his kyngdom. . . . God has a great plague in store for this people." Such warnings did not keep away the many westerners drawn to Moscow by opportunities to buy furs and sell western cloth and military hardware.

Two formidable foes blocked Ivan's way: Sweden (which then ruled Finland as well) and Poland-Lithuania. Both hoped to annex the eastern Baltic provinces, and both feared Russian expansionism. Poland and the Grand Duchy of Lithuania, united into a single commonwealth in 1569, controlled territory stretching from the Baltic Sea to deep within present-day Ukraine and Belarus. It was the largest state lying wholly within the boundaries of Europe. Poland-Lithuania, like the Dutch Republic, constituted one of the great exceptions to the general European trend toward greater monarchical authority. The Polish and Lithuanian nobles elected their king, who tried to mediate between the great magnates soon dominant in the legislature (*Sejm*) and the gentry or lesser nobility.

Russia, Poland-Lithuania, and Sweden in the Late 1500s

The Protestant Reformation made inroads in Poland-Lithuania in the sixteenth century when many nobles converted to Lutheranism or Calvinism. The Protestants soon split into antagonistic camps, however: antitrinitarians, Anabaptists, and religious pacifists all found adherents among the Poles, Lithuanians, and many Italian religious refugees in the commonwealth. Fearful of religious persecution by the Catholic majority, the nobility insisted that their kings accept the principle of religious toleration as a prerequisite for election. The nobles' successful demand for limited monarchy and religious toleration greatly impressed the beleaguered French Huguenots in the 1570s and was closely studied (and sharply criticized) by Jean Bodin in his *Six Books of the Republic.* Ultimately, the French *politiques* embraced the idea of a stronger rather than a weaker monarchy as the best guarantee of civil peace and religious liberty. In Poland-Lithuania the nobles' insistence on maintaining their "golden liberty" ensured the survival of pockets of Protestantism until the mid-seventeenth century. Protected by the kings and magnates, the numerous Jewish communities remained prosperous during the late sixteenth and early seventeenth centuries.

Ivan's successors in Russia soon faced a serious threat from Poland-Lithuania. Boris Godunov (*1598–1605) became tsar when the last of Ivan's heirs perished, but he too died before his reform plans could take shape. Before Boris's death a usurper claiming to be Ivan IV's dead son Dmitri had appeared with Polish-Lithuanian backing, and in the turmoil this "false Dmitri" won the Russian crown—only to be quickly overthrown. A terrible period of chaos known as the Time of Troubles ensued, during which the king of Poland-Lithuania tried to put his son on the Russian throne. In 1613 an army of nobles, townspeople, and peasants finally drove out the westerners and installed a nobleman who established an enduring new dynasty: Michael Romanov (*1613–1645). With the return of peace, Muscovite Russia resumed the process of state building. Reorganizing tax gathering and military recruitment and continuing to create a service nobility to whom the peasantry was increasingly subject, the first Romanovs laid the foundations of the powerful Russian empire that would emerge late in the seventeenth century under Peter the Great.

The Thirty Years' War, 1618–1648

East-West contrasts sharpened during the long series of wars fought in central Europe in the first half of the seventeenth century. The lengthy campaigns that devastated much of Europe's heartland had their origins in the ethnic and religious differences that divided the huge Holy Roman Empire. The empire embraced some eight major ethnic groups, and its people were Catholic and Protestant (Lutheran, Calvinist, and Anabaptist). Catholics held the preponderance of power because the imperial Habsburg dynasty and four of the seven electors who chose the emperor were of that faith. The balance of religious and political power never stabilized because control of some territories within the empire shifted from one religious group to another. Moreover, the Peace of Augsburg (1555) did not recognize Calvinism. Yet after 1555, Calvinism made inroads in Lutheran areas, and by 1613 two of the three Protestant imperial electors had become Calvinists. In addition, the Counter-Reformation—especially the zealous campaigns of the Jesuits—had won many Protestant cities back to Catholicism. The already fragile Augsburg settlement had no mechanism for resolving conflicts among the many minor princes and the emperor, and the disputing parties thus turned to war.

Fighting first broke out in Bohemia, whose relationship to the Holy Roman Empire resembled that of the Netherlands under Spanish rule. The Habsburgs held not only the imperial crown but also a collection of royal crowns (Bohemia was one) administered separately. When the devoutly Catholic Habsburg heir Archduke Ferdinand was crowned king of Bohemia in 1617, he began to curtail the religious freedom previously granted to Protestants. A resistance movement led by the largest ethnic group, the Czechs, quickly formed. In 1618 a group of Czech Protestant noblemen cornered two of the king's Catholic advisers and in the "defenestration of Prague" threw them out a window in the royal castle onto a dung heap far below. A Protestant assembly then formed a provisional government and appealed to other Protestants in the empire for help. A year later, when Ferdinand was elected emperor (as Ferdinand II, *1619–1637), the rebellious Bohemians deposed him and chose the young Calvinist Frederick V of the Palatinate (*1616–1623) to replace him. A quick series of clashes ended in 1620 when the imperial armies defeated the Czechs and their allies at the Battle of White Mountain, outside Prague. For the Czechs, White Mountain joined the martyrdom of Jan Hus in 1415 as symbols of the cruel squashing of their budding tradition of self-determination.

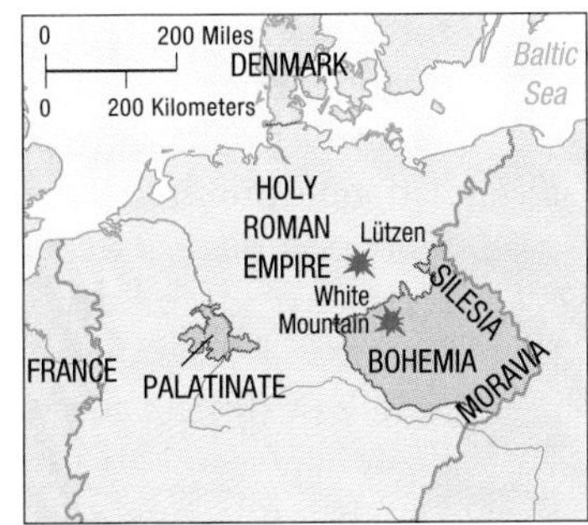

The Thirty Years' War

White Mountain did not end the war. Private mercenary armies commanded by soldiers of fortune began to form during the fighting, and the emperor had virtually no control over them. The amazing

The Thirty Years' War

1618 "Defenestration of Prague" opens the Thirty Years' War when Czech Protestants resist Austrian Catholic rule

1620 Austrians defeat Czechs and their allies at the Battle of White Mountain

1629 In the Edict of Restitution, Emperor Ferdinand II outlaws Calvinism and takes back Catholic properties previously confiscated by Lutherans

1632 Gustavus Adolphus of Sweden, a Lutheran, invades German lands with the aid of subsidies from the Catholic French government

1635 France openly joins the hostilities by declaring war on Spain and allying with the Dutch

1644 Opening of peace negotiations

1648 Peace of Westphalia ends the Thirty Years' War

career of the century's best-known soldier of fortune, Albrecht von Wallenstein (1583–1634), showed how political advantage and personal gain could confuse the expected division along religious lines. A Czech-speaking noble Bohemian Protestant by birth, Wallenstein took the Habsburg side during the Bohemian phase of the war and amassed a fortune in the process. In 1625 he offered to raise an army for Ferdinand, and within three years he had one hundred twenty-five thousand soldiers, who occupied and plundered much of northern Germany with the emperor's approval. The Lutheran king of Denmark, Christian IV (*1596–1648), invaded to protect the north German Protestants and to extend his influence. Despite Dutch and English encouragement, Christian lacked adequate military support and Wallenstein's forces soon defeated him.

Emboldened by his general's victories, Ferdinand issued the Edict of Restitution in 1629, outlawing Calvinism and reclaiming Catholic church properties confiscated by the Lutherans. With Protestant interests in jeopardy, Gustavus Adolphus (*1611–1632) of Sweden invaded Germany in 1630. Declaring his support for the Protestant cause, he clearly intended to gain control over trade in northern Europe as well (he had already ejected the Poles from present-day Latvia and Estonia in 1619). Now the primacy of political motives became obvious, for the Catholic French government, which hoped to block Spanish intervention in the war and to win influence and perhaps territory in the empire, subsidized Gustavus. The publication of the treaty between the Lutheran and Catholic powers to fight the Catholic Habsburgs showed that state interests now outweighed all other considerations. According to the treaty, France paid Sweden 1 million livres annually for five years for "the safeguarding of the Baltic and Oceanic Seas, the liberty of commerce, and the relief of the oppressed states of the Holy Roman Empire."

The Swedish king promptly defeated the imperial army and occupied the Catholic parts of southern Germany before he was killed at the battle of Lützen against Wallenstein in 1632. After eliminating Gustavus Adolphus, Wallenstein tried to parlay his military success into even greater personal influence and was rumored to be negotiating with Protestant powers. Ferdinand dismissed his general and had his henchmen assassinate him. The war dragged on. France openly joined the fray in 1635 by declaring war on Spain and soon after forged an alliance with the Calvinist Dutch in their struggle for independence. The conflict now effectively pitted France against the Spanish and Austrian Habsburgs. Not until 1644 did peace negotiations open, and only four years later, with the Peace of Westphalia, did they finally come to a close. France and Spain nonetheless continued fighting until 1659.

The Consequences of Constant Warfare

The central European wars accelerated changes in military armaments and tactics that had been evolving since the early sixteenth century. Improvements in artillery led states to build large defensive fortifications, and the increasing use of gunpowder weapons resulted in tactics that maximized opportunities to give fire. Soon the infantry, consisting of long, narrow lines of troops firing muskets joined by tightly packed formations of pike-carrying foot soldiers, overshadowed the cavalry. Everywhere, the size of armies increased dramatically. Most armies in the 1550s had fewer than fifty thousand men, but Gustavus Adolphus led one hundred thousand in 1631, and by the end of the seventeenth century, Louis XIV of France would have four hundred thousand soldiers. The cost of larger armies and new weapons such as cannon and warships strained the resources of every state.

Maintaining discipline in these huge armies required new, harsher methods. Drill, combat training, and a clear chain of command became essential. Newly introduced uniforms created—as their name suggests—a new standardization, but these outfits soon lost their distinctiveness in the conditions of early modern warfare. An Englishman who fought for the Dutch army in 1633 described how he slept on the wet ground, got his boots full of water, and "at peep of day looked like a drowned ratt."

Innovations came from many quarters. The Italians developed stronger fortifications to withstand shelling and assault. The Spanish became known for their military administration and medical facilities on the battlefield; they set up the first permanent military hospital. The Dutch introduced identical-caliber weapons and illustrated military textbooks. Gustavus Adolphus's Swedes used small, mobile units of thirty men each who could fire in lines rather than from squares.

To field larger armies, governments needed offices for supply and administration, new sources of funds, and more soldiers, often from social classes that had not usually served before. Although mercenaries still predominated in many armies, rulers began to recruit more of their own subjects. Volunteers proved easiest to find in dire economic times, when the threat of starvation induced men to accept the bonus offered for signing up. A Venetian general explained the motives for enlisting: "To escape from being craftsmen [or] working in a shop; to avoid a criminal sentence; to see new things; to pursue honour (though these are very few) . . . all in the hope of having enough to live on and a bit over for shoes, or some other trifle that will make life supportable." The men all had to be paid, however, and governments often fell short, leading to frequent mutinies, looting, and pillaging.

Not only were the larger armies more difficult to supply, but they also attracted all sorts of displaced people desperately in need of provisions. In the last year of the Thirty Years' War, for example, the Imperial-Bavarian Army had forty thousand men entitled to draw rations—and more than one hundred thousand wives, prostitutes, servants, children, maids, and camp followers who had to scrounge for their own food. The bureaucracies of early seventeenth-century Europe simply could not cope with such demands. Consequently, armies and their hangers-on had to live off the countryside. If an army could not successfully occupy a territory, then it plundered the land so its goods would not fall into enemy hands. The horrific results were scenes like that witnessed by Simplicius.

Jacob Duck, **Soldiers' Quarters,** *c. 1635*
Wherever they went, armies attracted all kinds of followers.

Some towns were battered by up to ten or eleven sieges during the Thirty Years' War, and the invaders slaughtered many urban citizens when the cities fell. But on the whole the worst suffering took place in the countryside. Peasants fled their villages, which their attackers often burned down. At times, desperate peasants revolted and looted nearby castles and monasteries. War and intermittent outbreaks of plague cost some German towns one-third of their population; in certain locales two-fifths of the rural population perished. Bohemia lost more than a third of its population. As a poet of the time asked, "But we human beings, what are we? A house of grim pain . . . A scene of rude fear and adversity."

Economic Crisis and Realignment

The Thirty Years' War was waged against a backdrop of fundamental economic change. After a century of rising prices, caused partly by huge inflows of gold and silver from the New World and partly by population growth, prices began to level off and even to drop, and in most places the rate of population growth slowed. With fewer goods being produced, international trade fell into recession. Agricultural yields also declined. Just when states attempted to field ever-expanding standing armies, peasants and townspeople alike were less able to pay the escalating taxes needed to finance the wars. Famine and disease trailed grimly behind economic crisis and war, in some areas causing large-scale uprisings and revolts, already foreshadowed in Russia's Time of Troubles. Behind the scenes of rebellion, the economic balance of power began to shift as northwestern Europe, especially England and the Dutch Republic, rose to dominate international markets.

The Causes of Economic Crisis

The seventeenth-century economic crisis came as a shock after nearly one hundred fifty years of growth. The religious and dynastic wars of the late sixteenth century occurred during a time of population increase and general inflation. Even though religious and political turbulence led to population decline in some cities, such as Antwerp, overall rates of growth remained impressive: in the sixteenth century, parts of Spain doubled in population, and England's population grew by 70 percent. The supply of precious metals swelled too: improvements in mining techniques in central Europe raised the output of silver and copper mines, and in the 1540s new silver mines were discovered in Mexico and Peru. Spanish gold imports peaked in the 1550s, silver in the 1590s. This flood of precious metals combined with population growth to fuel an astounding increase in food prices (400 percent in the sixteenth century) and a more moderate rise in the cost of manufactured goods. Real wages rose much more slowly, at about half the rate of increase in food prices. Governments always overspent revenues, and by the end of the century, most of Europe's rulers faced deep deficits.

Economic crisis did not strike everywhere at the same time, but the warning signs were unmistakable. From the Baltic to the East Indies, foreign trade slumped as war and an uncertain money supply made business riskier. After 1625, silver imports to Spain declined, partly because so many of the Indians who worked in Spanish colonial mines died from disease. Textile production fell in many countries, and in some places it nearly collapsed, largely because of decreased demand and a shrinking labor force. Even the slave trade stagnated, though its growth would resume after 1650.

Demographic slowdown also signaled economic trouble. Overall, Europe's population may have actually declined, from 85 million in 1550 to 80 million in 1650. In the Mediterranean growth had stopped in the 1570s. The most sudden reversal occurred in central Europe as a result of the Thirty Years' War: the Holy Roman Empire lost about one-fourth of its population in the 1630s and 1640s. Population continued to grow only in England and Wales, the Netherlands (both the Dutch Republic and the Spanish Netherlands), and Scandinavia.

Agricultural production reflected differences in population growth. Where population stagnated or declined, agricultural prices dropped because of less demand, and farmers who produced for the market suffered as the prices they received declined. Many reacted by converting grain-growing land to pasture or vineyards, because the prices of other foods fell less than the price of grain. Interest in agricultural innovations diminished. In some places peasants abandoned their villages and left land to waste, as had happened in the late fourteenth century. The only country that emerged unscathed from the economic crisis was the Dutch Republic, principally because it had long excelled in agricultural innovation. Inhabiting Europe's most densely populated area, the Dutch developed systems of field drainage, crop rotation, and animal husbandry that provided high yields of grain for both people and animals. Their foreign trade, textile industry, agricultural production, and population all grew. After the Dutch, the English fared best.

Historians have long disagreed about the causes of the early seventeenth-century economic downturn. Some cite the inability of agriculture to support a rising population by the end of the sixteenth century; others the extensive mid-century wars, the states' demands for more taxes, the irreg-

Louis Le Nain,
Peasant's Repast, *1642*
This painting depicts the simplicity and poverty of peasant life, but also its dignity. Notice the darkness of the men's clothing and the lack of shoes for some. Bread appears clearly as the center of the meal.

ularities in money supply due to primitive banking practices, or the waste caused by middle-class expenditures in the desire to emulate the nobility. To this list of causes, recent researchers have added climatic changes. Studies of tree rings, glacier movements, and dates of grape harvests have led experts to call the seventeenth century a "little ice age": glaciers advanced, average temperatures fell, and winters were often exceptionally severe. Cold winters and wet summers meant bad harvests, and these natural disasters ushered in a host of social disasters. When the harvest was bad, prices shot back up, and many could not afford to feed themselves.

Grain had become the essential staple of most Europeans' diets. Since the late Middle Ages, most of Europe's citizens (outside the Netherlands and England) ate little meat; only the wealthy could afford it. Most people consumed less butter, eggs, poultry, and wine and more grain products, ranging from bread to beer. The average adult European now ate more than four hundred pounds of grain per year. Peasants lived on bread, soup with a little fat or oil, peas or lentils, garden vegetables in season, and only occasionally a piece of meat or fish. In most places the poor existed on the verge of starvation; one contemporary observed that "the fourth part of the inhabitants of the parishes of England are miserable people and (harvest time excepted) without any subsistence."

Famine and Disease

The threat of food shortages haunted Europe whenever harsh weather destroyed crops, and local markets were vulnerable to problems of food distribution. Customs barriers inhibited local trade, overland transport moved at a snail's pace, bandits disrupted traffic, and the state or private contractors commandeered available food for the perpetually warring armies. Usually the adverse years differed from place to place, but from 1594 to 1597 most of Europe suffered from shortages, and the resulting famine led to revolts from Ireland to Muscovy. To head off social disorder, the English government drew up a new Poor Law in 1597 that required each community to support its poor, and many other governments also increased relief efforts.

Most people did not respond to their dismal circumstances by rebelling or mounting insurrections. They simply left their huts and hovels and took to the road in search of food and charity. Overwhelmed officials recorded pitiful tales of suffering. Women and children died while waiting in line for food at convents or churches. Husbands left their wives and families to search for better conditions in other parishes or even other countries. Those left behind might be reduced to eating chestnuts, roots, bark, and grass. In eastern France in 1637, a witness reported that "The roads were paved with people. . . . Finally it came to cannibalism." Eventually compassion gave way to fear, as these hungry vagabonds, who sometimes banded together to beg for bread, became more aggressive, occasionally threatening to burn a barn if they were not given food.

Successive bad harvests led to malnutrition, which weakened people, making them more susceptible to such epidemic diseases as the plague, typhoid fever, typhus, dysentery, smallpox, and influenza. Disease did not spare the rich, though many epidemics hit the poor hardest. The plague was feared most, because in one year it could cause the death of up to one-half of a town's or village's population and because it struck with no discernible pattern. Nearly 5 percent of France's population died in the plague of 1628 to 1632.

Patterns of Landholding and Family Life

Other effects of economic crisis were less visible than famine and disease, but no less momentous. The most important was the peasantry's changing status. Peasants had many obligations, including rent and—if the land had been subject to a lord's control in the past—various dues such as fees for inheriting or selling land and tolls for using mills, wine presses, or ovens. States collected an overwhelming array of taxes, ranging from direct taxes on land to taxes on such consumer goods as salt, an essential preservative. Protestant and Catholic churches alike exacted a 10 percent tax, or tithe, which they often collected in the field during harvest time. Millions of peasants lived on an economic margin that made these burdens nearly intolerable; any reversal of fortune could force them into the homeless world of vagrants and beggars, who (in France, for example) numbered in the hundreds of thousands.

In the seventeenth century the mass of peasants became more sharply divided into rich and poor. In England, the Dutch Republic, northern France, and northwestern Germany, the peasantry was disappearing: agricultural innovation gave some peasants the means to become farmers who rented substantial holdings, produced for the market, and in good times enjoyed relative comfort and higher status. Those who could not afford to plant new crops such as maize (American corn), buckwheat, and potatoes, or use techniques that ensured higher yields, became simple laborers, with little or no land of their own. The minimum plot of land needed to feed a family varied depending on the richness of the soil, available improvements in agriculture, and distance from markets. For example, only two acres could support a family in Flanders, as opposed to ten acres in Muscovy. One-half to four-fifths of the peasants did not have even this much land. They descended deeper into debt during difficult times and often lost their land to wealthier farmers or city officials intent on developing rural estates. In eastern Europe the situation was radically different because the noble landlords tied their peasants to the land, making them serfs.

The economic crisis directly affected family life. One-fifth to one-quarter of all children died in their first year; half, before age twenty. In 1636 an Englishman described his grief when his twenty-one-month-old son died, revealing the anguish the loss of so many babies brought: "We both found the sorrow for the loss of this child, on whom we had bestowed so much care and affection . . . far to surpass our grief for the decease of his three elder brothers, who dying almost as soon as they were born, were not so endeared to us as this [one] was." Demographic historians have shown that European families reacted almost immediately to economic crisis. During bad harvests they postponed marriages and had fewer children. When hard times passed, more of them married and they had more children.

We might assume that families would have more children to compensate for high death rates, but beginning in the early seventeenth century and continuing until the end of the eighteenth, families in all ranks of society started to limit the number of children. Because methods of contraception were not widely known, they did this by marrying later; the average age at marriage rose from the early

Philippe de Champaigne,* The Children of Habert de Montmor, *1649
Pictures of children separate from their parents became more common in the 1600s. These are the children of an ennobled judge; their clothing reflects the family's wealth. Even among the rich, three of the seven children in the family died before reaching adulthood. Here, as was the custom, the youngest boys wear clothes like those of girls.

twenties to the late twenties during the seventeenth century. The later a couple married, the fewer children they would have. The average family had about four children. Poorer families seem to have had fewer children (two or three for the poorer people in the cities) and wealthier ones more (an average of five, for example, in the English aristocracy). Peasant couples, especially in eastern and southeastern Europe, had more children than urban couples because cultivation still required intensive manual labor.

Why was postponing marriage—and smaller family size—seen as a response to economic crisis? If couples had many children, they would have to divide the family fortune to pay dowries for the girls and give the boys something to live on. With the family farm or shop already hard-pressed, families could not afford these expenses, so limits on the number of children were essential. The trend toward family limitation was more general, however, for it affected all social groups and continued even after the crisis had passed. Evidently, people came to see smaller families as a means to increase their standard of living; even English aristocrats had fewer children by the end of the century.

The consequences for individuals must have been profound. Young men and women were expected to put off marriage (*and* sexual intercourse) until their mid- to late twenties—if they were among the lucky 50 percent who lived that long and not among the 10 percent who never married. Because both the Reformation and Counter-Reformation had stressed sexual fidelity and abstinence before marriage, the number of births out of wedlock was relatively small (2–5 percent of births); premarital intercourse was generally tolerated only after a couple had announced their engagement. Although abstinence before one's late twenties must have posed many a moral dilemma, women particularly benefited directly from family limitation; fewer than 10 percent now died in childbirth, an experience all women feared because of the great risks. Even in the richest and most enlightened homes, childbirth sometimes occasioned an atmosphere of panic. To allay their fears, women sometimes depended upon magic stones and special pilgrimages and prayers. Midwives delivered most babies; physicians were scarce, and even if they did attend a birth they were generally less helpful. The English woman Alice Thornton described in her diary how her doctor bled her to prevent a miscarriage after a fall; her son died anyway in a breech birth that almost killed her too.

Women also felt the effects of economic change. As hard times limited demand in some areas and urban commerce began to move beyond the guild system into national and international trade networks in others, opportunities within guilds were restricted to men. Widows who had been able to take over their late husband's trade now found themselves excluded or limited to short tenures. Because people assumed that almost all women would marry and that women's work was secondary to men's or a form of temporary support for the family, women always earned lower wages. Many went into domestic service until they married, some for their entire lives. As town governments began to fear the effects of "masterless" people, they carefully regulated women's work as servants, requiring them to stay in their positions unless they could prove mistreatment by a master.

The Changing Economic Balance in Europe

The long-term consequences of the economic crisis varied from region to region. The economies of southern and eastern Europe declined, whereas those of the northwest emerged stronger. Northern Italian industries were eclipsed, and Spanish commerce with the New World dropped. With growing populations and geographical positions that promoted overseas trade, England and the Dutch Republic became the leading mercantile powers. Amsterdam replaced Seville, Venice, Genoa, and Antwerp as the center of European trade and commerce. The plague also had differing effects. Whereas central Europe and the Mediterranean countries took generations to recover from its ravages, northwestern Europe quickly replaced its lost population, no doubt because this area's people had suffered less from the malnutrition related to the economic crisis and from the plague itself.

East-West differences overshadowed those between northern and southern regions. Because labor shortages coincided with economic recovery, peasants in western Europe gained more independence. In most places they became free to buy and sell property and to pass it on through inheritance. All but remnants of serfdom disappeared from western Europe. By contrast, from the Elbe River east to Muscovy, nobles reinforced their dominance over peasants, thanks to cooperation from rulers and lack of resistance from villagers, whose community traditions—particularly in Poland, Bohemia, and the eastern German states—had always acknowledged nobles' rights of lordship.

The price rise of the sixteenth century prompted the eastern European nobles, especially in Polish and eastern German lands, to increase their holdings and step up their production of grain for western markets. To raise production, they demanded more rent and heavier dues from their peasants, whom the government decreed must stay in their villages. Although noble landlords lost income in the economic downturn of the first half of the seventeenth century, the peasants gained nothing. They became further indebted to their landlords; those who were still free became less so, and those who were already dependent became serfs—completely tied to the land. A city official from Pomerania might complain of "this barbaric and as it were Egyptian servitude," but townspeople had no power to fight the nobles. Most places still supported a social system ranging from freedom to serfdom, but in Muscovy the complete enserfment of the peasantry would eventually be recognized in the Code of Laws in 1649. Although enserfment produced short-term profits for landlords, in the long run it retarded economic development in eastern Europe and kept most of the population in a stranglehold of illiteracy and hardship.

The Scramble for Political Authority

As rulers expanded their bureaucracies, extended their powers of taxation, and boosted the size of their armies, they inevitably encountered resistance, especially because ordinary people, already strained economically and emotionally, found it difficult to meet government's increasing demands. The most sustained struggle for political authority took place in England between the crown and Parliament. Yet despite many setbacks, most states emerged by 1640 with more authority over their subjects' resources than ever before. The number of state-salaried employees multiplied, paperwork proliferated, and appointment to office depended more and more on university education in the law. Rulers themselves also had to change. Military prowess, once almost a prerequisite for a monarch, became less important than a knowledge of accounting and an ability to shrewdly navigate the maze of international issues. Although court pageantry still demanded constant attention, rulers had to learn to rely on bureaucrats. A few became bureaucrats themselves: Philip II, for example, insisted on seeing much of the government's incoming paperwork, and he took state papers with him wherever he went. Once when the royal family went sailing, he sat at his desk signing papers while others in the court danced.

Monarchical Authority

To make their power obvious, many rulers carefully nurtured the theatricality of court life that had developed in the fifteenth and sixteenth centuries. In addition to the pageants and plays put on for the court, even the rulers' meals became state occasions governed by precise ritual. In Spain regulations that set the wages, duties, and ceremonial functions of every official prescribed court etiquette. Hundreds, even thousands, of people made up such a court. The court of Philip IV (*1621–1665), for example, numbered seventeen hundred. In the 1630s he built a second palace outside Madrid, the Buen Retiro. There the courtiers lived amid parks and formal gardens, artificial ponds, grottoes, an iron aviary (which led some critics to call the whole thing a "chicken coop"), a wild animal cage, a courtyard for bullfights, and rooms filled with sculptures and paintings. At the Buen Retiro and elsewhere, rulers began collections that would become some of Europe's great museums.

Rising taxes and increasing demands for military supplies also reflected the growth of state power. Supporting armies and monarchical trappings required more money and more people to staff the armies, supervise tax collection, and oversee the extension of royal power. The great nobles often resisted being molded into docile officials or courtiers, so to enforce their will monarchs turned to personal favorites, often chosen from the lesser nobility, who created new client networks. For example, Axel Oxenstierna (1583–1654) directed the Swedish government during the reign of Gustavus Adolphus and also handled the transition to the regency when the king died in battle.

One of the most powerful royal favorites was Cardinal Richelieu (1585–1642), chief minister in France between 1625 and 1642. Richelieu directed the monarchy of Henry IV's son, Louis XIII (*1610–1643), and his name became synonymous with the phrase *reason of state.* The contrast between

***Jusepe Leonardo,* Palace of the Buen Retiro in 1636–1637**
This painting depicts Philip IV's imposing new palace as it appeared in the 1630s.

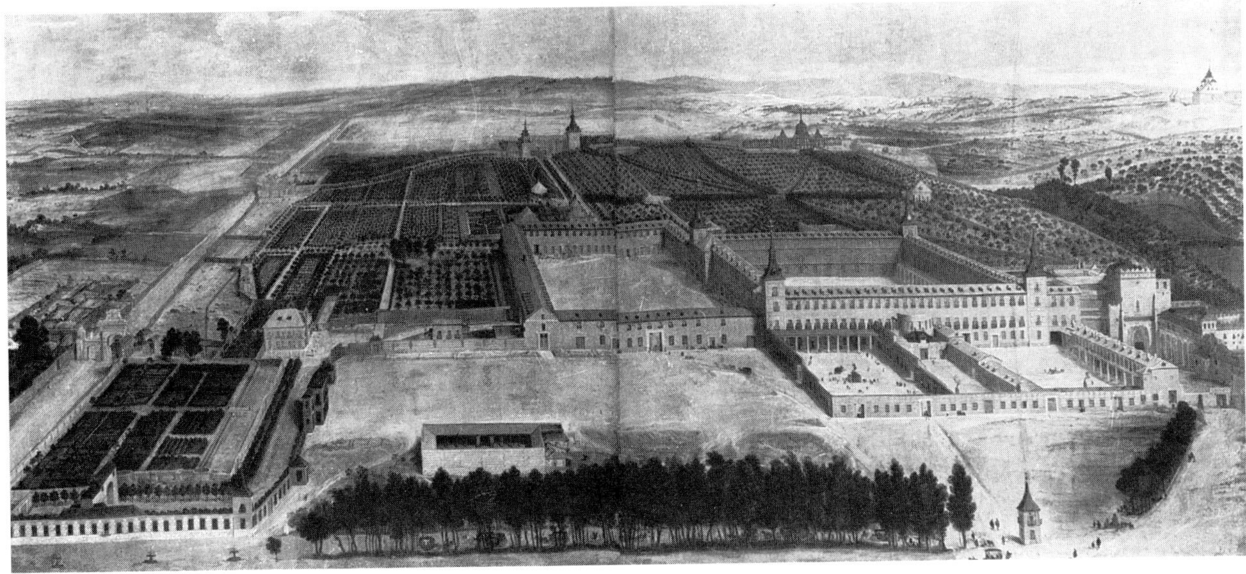

Richelieu's foreign and domestic policies indicates that by the seventeenth century even the rhetoric of religious difference did not interfere with political interests. While supporting Protestant states abroad, Richelieu silenced Protestants within France by banning their political organizations and separate law courts. He also crushed noble resistance to his rule and extended the use of intendants—delegates from the king's council dispatched to the provinces to oversee police, army, and financial affairs. This expansion of state authority allowed Richelieu to double the rate of land tax in just eight years, between 1635 and 1643.

Even before the Peace of Westphalia ended the Thirty Years' War, Spain already suffered from the effects of its participation in the conflicts, as calls for more men and taxes provoked revolts in several provinces. Philip IV faced an inescapable financial problem: while silver shipments from America declined, his armies needed ever more money to fight the Dutch and French. After a twelve-year truce between Spain and the Dutch Republic expired in 1621, the two states struggled for another twenty-seven years. At issue was not only control over the Dutch homeland but also dominance in the colonies, for the Dutch carried the war to Brazil, which newly independent Portugal recovered only in 1654. Much to Philip's chagrin, his brother-in-law, Louis XIII of France, allied himself to the Dutch Protestant rebels in 1635 and began a war with Spain that lasted until 1659. "The king of France," wrote Philip, "defying God, law, and nature, . . . has gone to war with me . . . in support of heresy."

Diego Rodríguez de Silva Velázquez,
The Count-Duke of Olivares
Velázquez painted Philip IV and many members of his court, including his chief minister Olivares, shown here as an energetic and powerful man of action, wearing the armor and sword of a military noble.

Raising money for these wars meant more taxes. Philip's mentor and chief minister, Gaspar de Guzmán, count-duke of Olivares (1587–1645), undertook a wide-ranging program to increase revenues by establishing new taxes, such as a state monopoly on salt (so effective in France), and by standardizing tax collection throughout the land. Spain was actually a union of several kingdoms, including Aragon, Valencia, and Portugal, each with their own representative institutions (*cortes*). Many provinces retained the constitutional right to approve new taxation, and they resisted the innovations. Olivares aimed to install a system in which all provinces paid relatively equal amounts so that most of the burden would not continue to fall on the central province of Castile; he described his program as "one king, one law, one coinage," a policy that actually meant an attack on the special privileges of many provinces. In almost every state of Europe, these regional privileges hindered the growth of central state power. In 1640 the northeastern province of Catalonia resisted Olivares's demands for more money and supplies for the war with France. This spark produced a revolutionary explosion throughout the Spanish monarchy.

All European states searched frantically for more revenues. In addition to raising taxes, governments frequently resorted to currency depreciations, the sale of newly created offices, forced loans, and manipulation of the embryonic stock and bond markets. When all else failed, they declared bankruptcy. The Spanish government, for example, did so three times in the first half of the seventeenth century. In these times of plague, famine, and stagnating growth, poor peasants and city workers could hardly bear new demands for money. The governments' creditors and the highest-ranking nobles also had grievances. Rebellion often resulted.

In the late sixteenth century most popular rebellions had originated in religious quarrels. Pockets of religious revolt still remained in the early seventeenth century, even outside the area of the Thirty Years' War, but in many places opposition to royal taxation set off new uprisings. From Portugal to Muscovy, peasants and city-dwellers resisted new impositions by forming makeshift armies and battling royal forces. With their colorful banners, unlikely leaders, unusual names (the *Nu-Pieds,* or "Bare-Footed," in France, for example), and crude weapons, the rebels were no match for state armies, but they did keep officials worried and troops occupied. These "days of shaking" also contributed to the massive constitutional and political revolts of the 1640s.

Constitutional Resistance in England

Although they lacked her political shrewdness, Elizabeth's Stuart successors were far from incompetent, and they faced less overwhelming problems than rulers of the continental states, partly because England stayed out of the Thirty Years' War. England's population was relatively small (one-fourth the size of France's) and homogeneous, but ethnic differences troubled relations among Scotland, Ireland, and England, all now ruled separately by the king of England. The crown had originally needed less money for armies because the surrounding seas offered these island states natural protection. Yet though the continental empires survived the seventeenth-century crisis, the Stuarts did not. The English crown was relatively poor—English per capita taxes were only a quarter of those in France—but when it needed more money, taxpayers were reluctant to pay. Subjects used Parliament, dominated by men from the gentry, or landowning, classes, to organize opposition. The very cohesion of the English state made possible the first successful national revolution, which would break out in 1640.

From the first, the Stuarts seemed destined to antagonize their parliaments. James I insisted on repeatedly making an issue of what Elizabeth had always left implicit: that he ruled by divine right and was accountable only to God. In his view, "The state of monarchy is the supremest thing on earth; for kings are not only God's lieutenants on earth, but even by God himself they are called gods." Like continental rulers, James needed more revenue; Elizabeth had left many debts, and inflation eroded the crown's income from its own properties. James tried every expedient to avoid asking Parliament for more money: he raised customs duties and sold noble titles and commercial monopolies. In the process he alienated the old nobility as well as ordinary people. Puritans found him unreceptive to their demands to reform the Church of England and criticized his court as too lavish. Many people were troubled by his obvious infatuation with George Villiers (1592–1628), the duke of Buckingham, who on the king's behalf pursued an unpopular Spanish marriage for Prince Charles and, when that failed, precipitated a disastrous and inconclusive war with Spain. None of these actions endeared the king to Parliament.

When Charles I (*1625–1649) succeeded his father, the antagonism between Parliament and king increased, even though Charles eventually stopped selling titles and cut back on court expenses. Supporting the court was still very expensive, however, because Charles not only entertained thousands of courtiers with masques (court dramas based on mythology or allegory) and plays but also continued to add to the impressive royal collection of Italian and Dutch paintings. The leaders of the House of Commons wanted to reassert Parliament's constitutional claims, and in 1628 they forced Charles to agree to a Petition of Right that outlined the rights of his subjects: the king promised not to levy taxes without parliamentary consent or to imprison critics without good cause. Later that year the duke of Buckingham was assassinated. He had used his position as a favorite of James and then of Charles to add to his relatives' fortunes, and he had encouraged the sale of offices and honors. The assassination devastated Charles. He blamed the leaders of Parliament for it and tried to halt continuing parliamentary agitation about royal policy by refusing to call Parliament between 1629 and 1640. Now the king's ministers had to find every loophole possible to raise revenues without parliamentary action. They tried to turn "ship money," a levy on seaports in times of emergency, into an annual tax collected everywhere in the country. The crown won the ensuing court case, but many subjects still refused to pay what they considered an illegal tax.

Attempting to clamp down, the king's minister Thomas Wentworth, earl of Strafford (1593–1641), and the archbishop of Canterbury, William Laud (1573–1645), initiated a policy called "thorough"—essentially a ruthless effort to use the royal and ecclesiastical courts to reestablish crown control over local affairs. As Wentworth wrote to Laud, "a little violence and extraordinary means" were needed. The religious part of the policy outraged many, especially among the Puritans, who hated Laud for emphasizing the ceremonies and liturgies of the Church of England and making it seem more like Catholicism. Charles married a French Catholic and seemed receptive to a Catholic-Anglican rapprochement. Laud used all available courts, especially the king's personally controlled High Court of Star Chamber, to persecute his Puritan critics—whipping, pillorying, branding them, sometimes even cutting off their ears or splitting their noses. But when Laud tried to apply his policies to Scotland, they backfired completely; the stubborn Presbyterian Scots rioted against the imposition of the Anglican prayer book—the Book of Common Prayer—and in 1640 they invaded northern England. To raise money to fight the war, Charles called Parliament into session. This was a fateful step.

Settlements in the New World

Across the seas in the New World colonies, Europeans experimented with new forms of political and economic authority that would eventually transform the populations and even the landscapes of the Americas. The English established precedents for North American colonization when in the 1580s they founded settlements in Ireland by driving the Irish clans from their strongholds and claiming the land for English and Scottish Protestants. When the Irish resisted with guerrilla warfare, English generals waged total war, destroying harvests and burning villages; one lined the path to his headquarters with Irish heads. Declaring the Irish "savages," the English forced them to submit. A few decades later, they would use the same tactics against the "savage" North American natives.

In settling the New World, Europeans acted on political and religious as well as economic motives. At the beginning of the seventeenth century, the English, Dutch, and French began competing with the Spanish and Portuguese in establishing both trading outposts and permanent settlements. Because Spain and Portugal (annexed to Spain between 1580 and 1640) were still the major powers in the New World, other prospective colonizers had to carve niches in seemingly less hospitable places, especially North America, considered inferior to South and Central America.

Governments chartered private joint-stock companies to enrich investors by importing fish, furs, tobacco, and precious metals, if they could be found, and to develop new markets for European products. These efforts were pure mercantilism (government-sponsored policies to increase national wealth). But in New England, religion motivated the Puritan colonists, who sought refuge from religious persecution. Some colonists justified their mission by promising to convert the native population to Christianity. As John Smith told his followers in Virginia, "The gaining provinces addeth to the King's Crown; but the reducing heathen people to civility and true religion bringeth honour to the King of Heaven." The native North Americans, however, resisted conversion to Protestantism much more resolutely than did the Indians of Mexico, Peru, and Canada to Catholicism. Protestantism did not mesh at all with native culture because it demanded a conversion experience based on a Christian notion of sin. Catholicism, in contrast, stressed rituals that were more accessible to the native populations. As a result, France and Spain were more successful in their colonial efforts to convert American natives.

In establishing permanent colonies, the Europeans created whole new communities across the Atlantic. Originally, the warm climate of Virginia made it an attractive spot, but the *Mayflower*, which had sailed for Virginia with its sectarian emigrants,* landed far to the north, near Cape Cod, Massachusetts, where in 1620 the settlers founded New Plymouth Colony. As the religious situation

*The "Pilgrim" settlers of Plymouth belonged to a tiny English sect that, unlike the Puritans, attempted to separate from the Church of England.

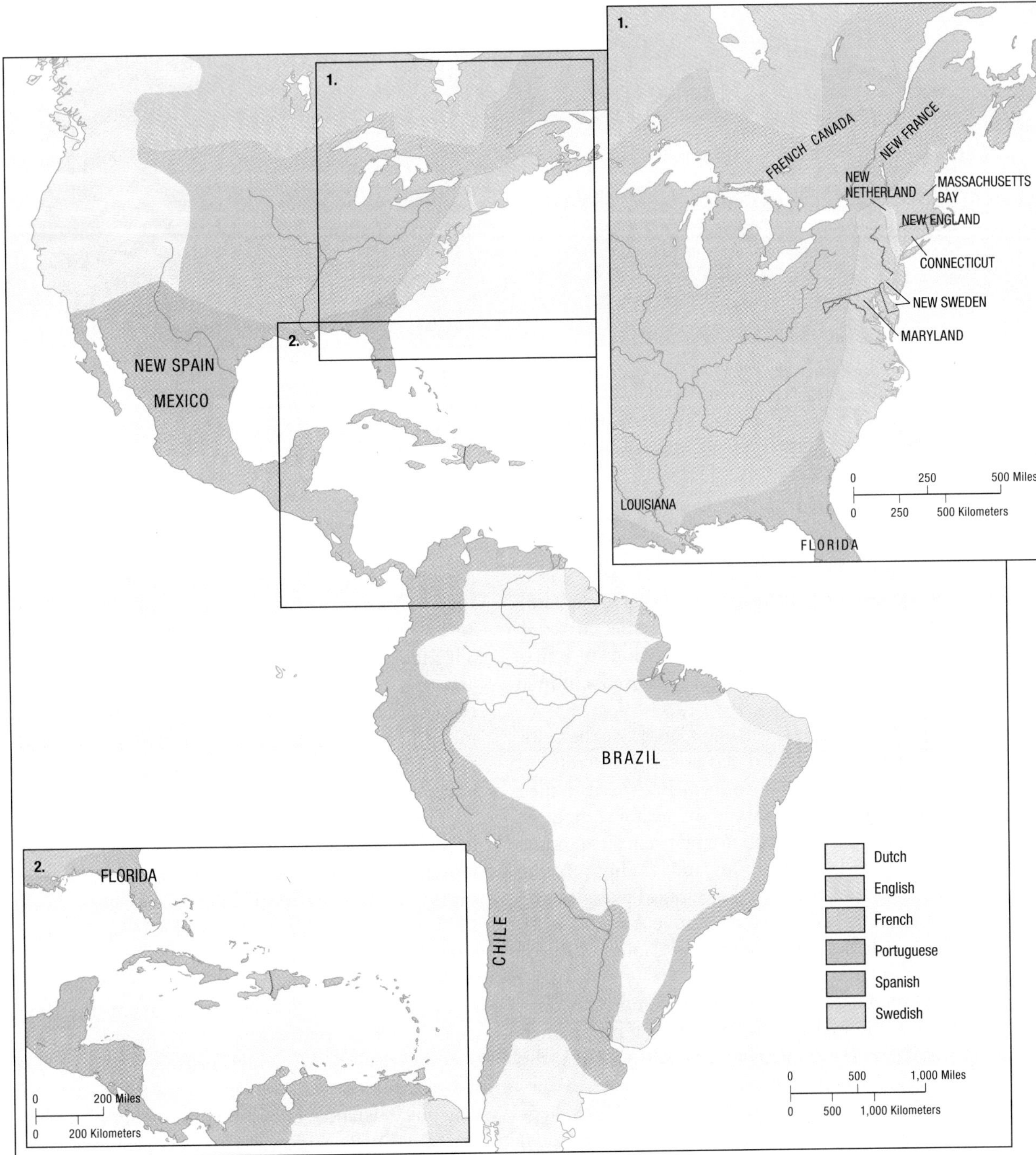

European Colonization of the Americas

for English Puritans worsened, wealthier people became willing to emigrate, and in 1629 a prominent group of Puritans incorporated themselves as the Massachusetts Bay Company. They founded a virtually self-governing colony headquarted in Boston. Migrating settlers, including dissident Puritans, soon founded new settlements in Connecticut and Rhode Island. Catholic refugees from England established a much smaller colony in Maryland, although the colony soon had a Protes-

Paolo Farinati, **America,** *1595*
Europeans found the "savages" of newly discovered lands fascinating and terrifying and often described them as cannibals. Here a half-nude Indian seems to have been successfully converted to Christianity (he holds a crucifix in one hand), but his comrades are roasting human flesh.

tant majority. By the 1640s the American colonies had more than fifty thousand people—not including the Indians, whose numbers had been decimated in epidemics and wars—and the foundations of representative government in locally chosen colonial assemblies.

The French began settling Canada at the same time, but because the French government refused to let Protestants emigrate from France, it denied itself a ready population for the establishment of permanent colonies abroad. Many French emigrants quickly turned to trapping and trading in the woods, and they were not discouraged from leaving the settlements and marrying Native Americans. In 1640, Canada had only about three thousand European inhabitants.

Mainland North America was not the only target for colonial settlement. Faced with Spanish and Portuguese dominance in South America, the French and English turned to the Caribbean islands. For a while the fierce native Caribs kept them, like the Spanish, off the most fertile islands, but in the 1620s and 1630s they finally occupied St. Kitts (English and French), Barbados (English), Martinique (French), and Guadeloupe (French). The West Indies, as they were called, proved ideal for a plantation economy of tobacco and sugar cane. At first, white indentured servants, bound to a master for a specified period, supplied the labor; black slaves were brought in during most of the seventeenth century, principally by Dutch traders. Virginia had only one hundred fifty blacks in 1640, and it is not clear whether they were slaves. The earliest black inhabitants were probably treated as indentured servants and freed, if they survived, after a number of years. A trend toward lifelong black servitude, however, was already evident.

The biggest threat to the Spanish and Portuguese came from Dutch traders and pirates. The Dutch West India Company, incorporated in 1621, captured a large strip of the Brazilian coast in the 1620s and 1630s (but lost it in the 1650s), and the company's fleets interrupted Spanish maritime trade in the Caribbean. The Dutch learned the techniques of sugar cultivation from the Portuguese, whose plantations in northern Brazil had become the world's chief source of sugar. The Dutch introduced sugar cultivation to the Caribbean islands. Dutch colonies from New Amsterdam (New York) to Curaçao provided ports for trade, and Dutch fleets carried much of the trade of the English and French colonies, too (including slaves). By the 1650s the English would become so obsessed with Dutch commercial success that they would be willing to go to war to break its hold.

All Coherence Gone: A Clash of World Views

Just as state interests became separated from religious motives and often came to supersede religious alliances, so too did a new secular and scientific attitude challenge religion and the orthodox view of a Judeo-Christian universe. During the late sixteenth and early seventeenth centuries, both art and science began to break some of their bonds with religion. The visual arts, for example, more frequently depicted secular subjects. Gradually, many came to doubt old certainties of an ordered universe, with the earth fixed between heaven and hell. The English poet John Donne (1572–1631) captured the new sense of doubts when he lamented,

> *'Tis all in pieces, all coherence gone,*
> *All just supply, and all Relation.*

Yet traditional attitudes did not wither away. Belief in magic and witches pervaded all levels of society. People of all classes accepted supernatural explanations for natural phenomena and for the ordered universe, now threatened by new scientific and political ideas.

New Relations Expressed in the Arts

Writers, artists, and composers created works that reflected new secular attitudes and contemporary uncertainties about the proper sources of authority. Some of these works appeared in the new permanent professional theater companies of the last quarter of the sixteenth century. In previous centuries, traveling companies made their living by playing at urban religious festivals and by repeating their performances in small towns and villages along the way. In London, Seville, and Madrid, the first professional acting companies performed before paying audiences in the 1570s. A huge outpouring of play writing followed. The Spanish playwright Lope de Vega (1562–1635) alone wrote more than fifteen hundred plays. Between 1580 and 1640, three hundred English playwrights produced works for a hundred different companies of actors. Theaters did a banner business despite Puritan opposition in England and Catholic clerical objections in Spain to performances lacking a clear moral lesson. Puritan denunciations of the theater's "hideous obscenities" and "detestable matchless iniquities" did not stop countless shopkeepers, apprentices, lawyers, and court nobles from crowding into open-air theaters to see everything from bawdy farces to profound tragedies.

The most enduring and influential playwright of the time was the Englishman William Shakespeare (1564–1616), son of a glovemaker, who wrote three dozen plays and acted in one of the chief troupes. Although Shakespeare's plays were not set in contemporary England, they reflected the concerns of his age: the nature of power and the crisis of authority. His greatest tragedies—*Hamlet* (1601), *King Lear* (1605), and *Macbeth* (1606)—show the uncertainty and even chaos that result when power is misappropriated or misused. In each play, family relationships are linked to questions about the legitimacy of government, just as they were for Elizabeth herself. Hamlet's mother marries the man who murdered his royal father and usurped the crown; two of Lear's daughters betray him when he tries to divide his kingdom; Macbeth's wife persuades him to murder the king and seize the throne. Some of Shakespeare's female characters, like Lady Macbeth, are as driven, ambitious, powerful, and tortured as the male protagonists; others, like Queen Gertrude in *Hamlet*, reflect the ambiguity of women in public life—they were not expected to act with authority, and their lives were subject to men's control.

Shakespeare's stories of revenge, exile, political instability, broken families, betrayal, witchcraft, madness, suicide, and murder clearly mirrored the anxieties of the period. One character in the final act describes the tragic story of Hamlet as one "Of carnal, bloody, and unnatural acts; Of accidental judgments, casual slaughters; Of deaths put on by cunning and forced cause." Like many real-life people, Shakespeare's tragic characters found little peace in the turmoil of their times.

New styles of painting reflected such concerns less directly, but they too showed the desire for changed standards. In the late sixteenth century a new artistic style known as Mannerism developed in the Italian states and soon spread across Europe. Mannerism was an almost theatrical style that

Mannerist Painting
El Greco considered The Burial of Count Orgaz *his greatest work. Painted in 1588 for a Spanish Catholic church, it commemorates a local miracle, in which St. Stephen and St. Augustine descended from heaven to lay the Count of Orgaz in his tomb.*

allowed painters to distort perspective to convey a message or emphasize a theme. The great Mannerist painter, a Greek called El Greco, was trained in Venice and Rome before he moved to Spain in the 1570s. His paintings encapsulated the Mannerist style: he crowded figures or objects into every available space, used larger-than-life or elongated figures, and created new and often bizarre visual effects. This style departed abruptly from precise Renaissance perspective. The religious intensity of El Greco's pictures shows that faith still motivated many artists, as it did much political conflict.

The most important new style in seventeenth-century high art was the baroque, which, like Mannerism, originated in the Italian states. As is the case with many such terms, *baroque* was not used as a label by people living in the seventeenth century; in the eighteenth century, art critics coined the word to mean shockingly bizarre, confused, and extravagant, and until a hundred years ago, art historians and collectors largely disdained the baroque. Stylistically, the baroque rejected Renaissance classicism: in place of the classical emphasis on line, harmonious design, unity, and clarity, the baroque featured curves, exaggerated lighting, intense emotions, release from restraint, and even a kind of artistic sensationalism.

In church architecture and painting the baroque melodramatically reaffirmed the emotional depths of the Catholic faith and glorified both church and monarchy. The Catholic church encouraged the expression of religious feeling through art because its emotional impact helped strengthen the ties between the faithful and the Counter-Reform church. As an urban and spectacular style, the baroque was well suited to public festivities and display. Along with religious festivals, civic processions, and state funerals that served the interests of the church and state, baroque portraits, such as the many portraits of Philip IV by Diego Velázquez, celebrated authority.

Closely tied to the Counter-Reformation, the baroque style spread from Rome to other Italian states and then into central Europe. The Catholic Habsburg territories, including Spain and the Spanish Netherlands, embraced the style. The Spanish built baroque churches in their American colonies as part of a massive conversion campaign. Within Europe, Protestant countries largely resisted the baroque, as we can see by comparing Dutch artists with Flemish painters from the Spanish Netherlands. The first great baroque painter was an Italian-trained Fleming, Peter Paul Rubens (1577–1640). A devout Catholic, Rubens painted vivid, exuberant pictures on religious themes, packed with figures. His was an extension of the theatrical baroque style, conveying ideas through broad gestures and dramatic poses. The great Dutch Protestant painters of the next generation, such as Rembrandt van Rijn (1606–1669), sometimes used Biblical subjects, but their pictures were more realistic and focused on everyday scenes. Many of them suggested the Protestant concern for an inner life and personal faith rather than the public expression of religiosity.

Baroque Painting
With his 2,000 paintings, Rubens defined the new baroque style, which emphasized monumentality, vastness of space, animation, almost violent movement, striking colors, luxury, and spiritual exaltation. As shown in this 1616 painting, The Fall of the Damned, *the baroque was never bland!*

As in the visual arts, differences in musical style during the late sixteenth and early seventeenth centuries reflected religious divisions. The new Protestant churches developed their own distinct music, which differentiated their worship from the Catholic Mass and also marked them as Lutheran or Calvinist. Lutheran composers developed a new form, the strophic hymn, or chorale, a religious text set to a tune that is then enriched through harmony. Calvinist congregations, in keeping with their emphasis on simplicity and austerity, avoided harmony and more often sang in unison, thereby encouraging participation.

A new secular musical form, the opera, grew up parallel to the baroque style in the visual arts. First influential in the Italian states, opera combined music, drama, dance, and scenery in a grand sensual display, often with themes chosen to please the monarchy and the aristocracy. Operas could be based on typically baroque sacred subjects or on traditional stories. Like Shakespeare, opera composers often turned to familiar stories their audiences would recognize and readily follow. One of the dominant composers of opera—and perhaps the most innovative—was Claudio Monteverdi, whose work contributed to the development of both opera and the orchestra. His first operatic production, *Orfeo* (1607), was the first to require an orchestra of about forty instruments and to include instrumental as well as vocal sections.

The Mechanical Universe

During a time of upheaval and war, a quiet revolution in scientific ideas gathered momentum among Europe's intellectual elite. It would have far-reaching implications. The revolution began with astronomy, in debates over the motion of the heavens. In 1543, Nicolaus Copernicus had argued that the earth and planets revolved around the sun and could be analyzed mathematically. Most important was the Copernican notion that the sun, not the earth, was the center of the universe, an assertion that challenged long-established ancient and religious claims.

Motion provided the key to this new science. Since Aristotle, scientists had upheld the ancient view that objects in their natural state were at rest; now it appeared that motion, not rest, was the natural order of the universe. If so, then the same principles of mechanical movement might be common not only in everyday events like the fall of an object but also to such less-evident phenomena as the movement of the planets or the collisions of the tiniest particles of matter. The idea that the whole universe operated mechanically and predictably profoundly threatened established Christian beliefs, especially because Catholic doctrine held that the heavens were perfect and unchanging while the earth was "corrupted." The new science of motion erased this distinction, making all motion the same. If all nature partook of the motion of particles, then science might explain the movement of objects and inner workings of animals and humans—perhaps even the actions of states.

Despite their implications, Copernicus's views aroused little opposition during the latter half of the sixteenth century. A notable exception was the Italian monk Giordano Bruno (1548–1600), who taught Copernican theory all over Europe and extended its logic by arguing for an infinite universe; the Inquisition arrested him and burned him at the stake. As time passed, astronomers gathering new data on celestial motion became increasingly uncertain about the virtues of the Ptolemaic theory that the sun revolved around the earth. At the beginning of the seventeenth century, the Ptolemaic system began to crumble beneath the work of the German Johannes Kepler (1571–1630) and the Italian Galileo Galilei (1564–1642). Kepler followed Copernicus in asserting that mathematics could describe the movements of the heavens, and between 1609 and 1619 he published his three laws of planetary motion. Kepler's laws provided mathematical backing for the Copernican view—the heliocentric, or sun-centered, system—and directly challenged the claim long held, even by Copernicus, that planetary motion is circular. Kepler's first law stated that the orbits of the planets are ellipses, with the sun always at one focus of the ellipse.

Galileo provided the critical evidence to support the Copernican view. This Italian scholar had already designed a military compass when he heard in 1609 that two Dutch astronomers had built a telescope. He quickly made an even better one and published his findings for all the world to read. Using the telescope, he observed the moon, Jupiter's four satellites, the phases of Venus, and sunspots; his findings led him to dismiss the Ptolemaic system. The planets and the sun were no more perfect than the earth, he realized, and other planets also had moons. Galileo described the earth as a moving part of a larger system, which the Copernican view described more accurately.

Galileo then tried to make a connection between planetary motion and motion on earth. The Aristotelian view that a body's natural state is at rest meant that it must constantly be pushed to keep moving. Galileo insisted that a body would keep moving as long as nothing stopped its motion. Galileo's new way of thinking about bodies in motion would be crucial for the later theories of Sir Isaac Newton. He imagined geometrical bodies moving in absolutely empty space. This leap required abstract reasoning beyond the observation of natural phenomena and made mathematics the vehicle for scientific explanation. As Galileo wrote:

> *Philosophy is written in this grand book, the universe, which stands continually open to our gaze. But the book cannot be understood unless one first learns to comprehend the language and read the letters in which it is composed. It is written in the language of mathematics, and its characters are triangles, circles, and other geometric figures without which it is humanly impossible to understand a single word of it; without these, one wanders about in a dark labyrinth.*

With this new mathematical language—and by implication, without the aid of the Bible or the church—people could understand God's creation.

To reach a lay audience, Galileo published his views in Italian rather than Latin. He appealed to the merchants and aristocrats of Florence by arguing that the new science was useful for everyday projects and by using comparisons to accounting and commercial exchanges. The new science, he insisted, suited "the minds of the wise" (whether lay or clerical) but not "the shallow minds of the common people." If the Bible were wrong about motion in the universe, the error was that the Scriptures used common language to appeal to the lower orders. The Catholic church responded quickly to Galileo's challenge. In 1616 the church forbade him to teach that the earth moves and in 1633 accused him of not obeying the earlier order. Forced to appear before the Inquisition, he agreed to publicly recant his assertion that the earth moved to save himself from torture and death. Afterward he lived under house arrest and could publish his work only in the Dutch Republic, which had become a haven for scientists and thinkers. Scientific research, like economic growth, would come to be centered in the northern, Protestant countries, where it was less constrained by church control.

Scientific Method

Despite the opposition of the Catholic church and of clergy of various faiths, the intellectual elite in the 1630s began to accept the Copernican view. Ancient learning, the churches and their theologians, and even cherished popular beliefs seemed to be undermined by a new standard of truth based on systematic observation, experiments, and rational deduction. Two men were chiefly responsible for spreading the prestige of the scientific method beyond the realm of science into the intellectual mainstream: the English writer and politician Sir Francis Bacon (1561–1626) and the French mathematician and philosopher René Descartes (1596–1650). Respectively, they represented the two essential halves of scientific method: inductive reasoning through observation and experimental research, and deductive reasoning from self-evident principles.

In *The Advancement of Learning* (1605), Bacon attacked reliance on ancient writers. The minds of the medieval scholars, he said, had been "shut up in the cells of a few authors (chiefly Aristotle, their dictator) as their persons were shut up in the cells of monasteries and colleges," and they could therefore produce only "cobwebs of learning" that were "of no substance or profit." Advancement would take place only through the collection, comparison, and analysis of information. Knowledge, in Bacon's view, must be empirically based (that is, gained by observation). Although not a scientist, Bacon supported the scientific method over popular beliefs, which he rejected as "fables and popular errors." Claiming that God had called the Catholic church "to account for their degenerate manners and ceremonies," Bacon looked to the English state, which he served as lord chancellor, and to the Protestant Reformation for evidence of rational principles in action.

Descartes, a French Catholic who served in the Thirty Years' War, also espoused rationality, but, unlike Bacon, he sought to test accepted doctrine with mathematical principles. Descartes agreed with Bacon's denunciation of traditional learning, but he argued for reliance on mathematics and logic (deductive method) rather than experiments (inductive method). His major contribution to mathematics was the invention of analytic geometry. Descartes aimed to establish science on philosophical foundations that would secure the authority of both church and state, yet he was so worried about the consequences of his work that he chose to move to the more hospitable atmosphere of the Dutch Republic.

In his *Discourse on Method* (1637), which became the most important piece of propaganda for the new methods of learning, Descartes argued—in French, not Latin—for a rational, deductive model of scientific knowledge, in which mathematical and mechanical principles would provide the way to understand all of nature, including the actions of people and states. Prior assumptions and ancient writings must be repudiated in favor of "the human will operating according to reason." Begin with the simple and go on to the complex, he asserted, and believe only those ideas that present themselves "clearly and distinctly." Descartes believed that rational individuals would see the necessity of strong state power and that only "meddling and restless spirits" would plot against it. Descartes insisted that human reason could not only unravel the secrets of nature but also prove the existence of God. Nevertheless, his books were banned in many places.

Ultimately, scientific method combined both experiment and deductive reason. The new understanding of motion, both in the heavens and on earth, soon had important applications in such fields as navigation, cartography, mechanics, ballistics, fortification, surveying, and even astrology. Startling discoveries took place in medicine, too, especially Englishman William Harvey's demonstration of the circulation of blood (1628). The heart, according to Harvey, was "a piece of machinery." The body too was part of the mechanical universe.

Magic and Witchcraft

Despite the new emphasis on clear reasoning, observation, and independence from past authorities, science had not yet become as separate from magic as might be expected. Many scholars studied alchemy along with physics. Elizabeth I maintained a court astrologer who was also a serious mathematician, and many writers distinguished between "natural magic," which was close to experimental science, and evil "black magic." One of the leading astronomers of the time, Tycho Brahe (1546–1601), defended his studies of alchemy and astrology as part of natural magic. For many of the greatest minds, magic and science were still closely linked.

In a world in which most people believed in astrology, magical healing, divination, prophecy, and ghosts, we should not be surprised that many of Europe's learned people also firmly believed in witchcraft. The same Jean Bodin who argued against religious fanaticism insisted on death for

David Teniers the Younger, **Witches' Sabbath,** *c. 1650*
This painting captures many of the popular views about female witches, including their alliance with the devil and with the devil's strange, monstrous troupe of followers.

witches—and even for those who did not believe in the dangers of witches. In France alone, 345 books and pamphlets on witchcraft appeared between 1550 and 1650. Witchcraft trials peaked in Europe between 1560 and 1640, the very time of the celebrated breakthroughs of the new science. Many people, including state officials, lawyers, and judges, believed that scientific reasoning confirmed the existence and danger of witches. Montaigne was one of the few notable people to speak out against executing accused witches: "It is taking one's conjectures rather seriously to roast someone alive for them," he wrote in 1580.

Belief in witches was not new in the sixteenth century. Witches had long been thought capable of almost anything: passing through walls, traveling through the air, destroying crops, and causing personal catastrophes from miscarriages to demonic possession. What was new was the official persecution of witches, justified by the notion that witches were agents of Satan whom the righteous must oppose. In a time of economic crisis, plague, warfare, and the clash of religious differences, witchcraft trials provided an outlet for social stress and anxiety, legitimated by state power. At the same time, the trials seem to have been part of the religious reform movement itself. In much of Europe the spread of the trials coincided with the arrival of reform-minded clergy, whether Protestant or Catholic.

The victims of the persecution were overwhelmingly female; 80 percent of the accused witches in about one hundred thousand trials in Europe and North America during the sixteenth and seventeenth centuries were women. About a third were sentenced to death. Before 1400 (when witchcraft trials were rare), nearly half of those accused had been men. Some historians argue that this gender difference indicates that the trials expressed a hatred of women that came to a head during conflicts over the Reformation. Official descriptions of witchcraft oozed lurid details of sexual orgies, incest, homosexuality, and cannibalism, in which women acted as the devil's sexual slaves. Catholic and Protestant reforming clergy attacked the presumably wild and undisciplined sexuality of women as the most obvious manifestation of popular unruliness, peasant superstitiousness, and heretical tendencies. Lawyers and judges followed their lead.

Although people of any social station might be accused of witchcraft, those of certain social groups repeatedly found themselves on trial. Among the most commonly accused were beggar women. The accusers were almost always better off than those they accused, and they seem to have reacted out of a sense of guilt for having been slow to respond to pleas for charity. Because elderly spinsters and widows were often poor, perceived as socially marginal, and thus thought likely to hanker after revenge on those more fortunate, they were far more likely to be accused. Another commonly accused woman was the midwife, who was a prime target for suspicion in a time when childbirth was dangerous and frightening and medical care rudimentary at best. Although sometimes venerated for their special skill, midwives also numbered among the thousands of largely powerless women persecuted for their imagined consorting with the devil.

Conclusion

The witchcraft persecutions underscore the trauma that characterized these times. The trials took place all over Europe (and later in parts of North America), but they concentrated especially in the German lands of the Holy Roman Empire, an area of great religious division and the cockpit of the Thirty Years' War. Constant religious conflicts, marauding armies, escalating demands for new taxes, economic decline, disease, and sometimes starvation shattered the lives of many ordinary Europeans. In response to the uncertainties of the age, some people blamed the poor widow or the upstart midwife for their problems; others joined desperate revolts; still others left for more fortunate spots or emigrated overseas. A few among the literate elite began to look to the new science for a sense of certainty and order in a time of turmoil.

Out of the chaos and sense of crisis emerged several new patterns that had important long-term effects. The balance of political and economic power shifted from the Mediterranean world to the north—primarily to France and the Dutch Republic. Many Europeans now wanted governments that would maintain internal peace, even if it meant losing absolute religious uniformity. The growing disengagement of political motives from religious ones did not mean that violence or conflict had ended, but it did strengthen the rulers' power. An expanded scale of warfare required more state involvement. The growth of state power directly changed the lives of ordinary people; more men went into the armies and most families paid more taxes. This extension of state power was only just beginning; it would be one of the chief factors that defined the modern world, even into the twentieth century.

Suggestions for Further Reading

Source Materials

Drake, Stillman, ed. *Discoveries and Opinions of Galileo.* 1957. Translations with excellent introductions to some of Galileo's most important works on the new science.

Kors, Alan C., and Edward Peters. *Witchcraft in Europe, 1100–1700: A Documentary History.* 1972. Original documents from all over Europe including selections from trial transcripts.

Rabb, Theodore K. *The Thirty Years' War.* 2d ed. 1972. A useful collection of differing views of historians and participants.

Interpretive Studies

Ashton, Trevor H., ed. *Crisis in Europe.* 1965. Still the best collection of essays on the interrelated aspects of the seventeenth-century crises.

Bonney, Richard. *The European Dynastic States, 1494–1660.* 1991. Provides a good overview of social and economic developments as well.

Braudel, Fernand. *The Mediterranean and the Mediterranean World in the Age of Philip the Second.* 2 vols. Translated by Siân Reynolds. 1972–1973. A very influential view of the long-term development of the Mediterranean region.

Buisseret, David. *Henry IV.* 1984. A readable biography of the French king.

Davis, Natalie Zemon. *Society and Culture in Early Modern France.* 1975. An anthropologically informed set of essays on social and cultural life that includes pathbreaking work on women's participation in French Protestantism.

De Vries, Jan. *The Economy of Europe in an Age of Crisis, 1600–1750.* 1976. An excellent and thorough overview of the economic crisis.

Elliot, J. H. *Richelieu and Olivares.* 1984. A brief, readable comparative study of two great statesmen from France and Spain.

Hall, A. Rupert. *From Galileo to Newton.* Rev. ed. 1981. A clearly written history of the major scientific breakthroughs and their significance.

Jacob, Margaret C. *The Cultural Meaning of the Scientific Revolution.* 1988. Includes excellent chapters on the social context of the scientific revolution.

Levack, Brian P. *The Witch-hunt in Early Modern Europe.* 1987. Synthesizes research on the witchcraft persecutions.

Limm, Peter. *The Thirty Years' War.* 1984. Includes documents as well as reviews of controversies about the war.

Lynch, John. *Spain Under the Habsburgs.* Vol. 1, *Empire and Absolutism: 1516–1598.* 1964. A solid, thorough account of Spain under Philip II.

Mattingly, Garrett. *The Armada.* 1959. Describes the decisive sea battle between the English and the Spanish with grace and verve.

Mitterauer, Michael, and Reinhard Sieder. *The European Family: Patriarchy to Partnership from the Middle Ages to the Present.* Translated by Karla Oosterveen and Manfred Hörzinger. 1982. A summary of modern research in family history, especially in eastern Europe.

Morse, David. *England's Time of Crisis: From Shakespeare to Milton.* 1989. A cultural history of England that links the most important writings of the time to political events.

Parker, David. *The Making of French Absolutism.* 1983. An excellent introduction to the origins of the French absolutist state; concentrates on the period from the religious wars to Louis XIV.

Parker, Geoffrey. *Europe in Crisis, 1598–1648.* 1979. The best one-volume textbook on the first half of the seventeenth century.

———. *The Military Revolution: Military Innovation and the Rise of the West, 1500–1800.* 1988. A cogent overview of the military revolution with an interesting emphasis on its effects on the colonies.

Parker, Geoffrey, and Lesley M. Smith. eds. *The General Crisis of the Seventeenth Century.* 1978. A collection of essays by specialists who critically examine the idea of a "general crisis" in the seventeenth century.

Parry, J. H. *The Age of Reconnaissance.* 1981. A useful and concise overview of the early colonies in the New World.

Redondi, Pietro. *Galileo, Heretic.* Translated by Raymond Rosenthal. 1987. A fascinating and controversial piece of detective work that uncovers the Catholic church's reasons for condemning Galileo.

Skinner, Quentin. *The Foundations of Modern Political Thought.* Vol. 2, *The Age of Reformation.* 1978. A new interpretation of the origins of constitutionalism in Reformation writings about the right of resistance.

Strong, Roy. *The Cult of Elizabeth: Elizabethan Portraiture and Pageantry.* 1977. A copiously illustrated analysis of the use of court ritual to emphasize royal power.

Thomas, Keith. *Religion and the Decline of Magic.* 1971. A fascinating and rich description of beliefs in magic and witchcraft in England.

Thornton, John. *Africa and Africans in the Making of the Atlantic World, 1400–1680.* 1992. The early history of relations between Africans and Europeans.

CREDITS

Text

p. 213, chart, "Roman Imperial Silver Coinage, 27 B.C.–A.D. 272" from *The Archeology of the Roman Empire* by Kevin Greene, published by B. T. Batsford Ltd., London and reproduced with permission.

p. 273, figures from Clive Foss, *Ephesus After Antiquity: A Late Antique Byzantine and Turkish City,* reprinted with the permission of Cambridge University Press.

p. 279, figure adapted from *The Venture of Islam* by Marshall Hodgson, 1974, p. 168. Reprinted by permission of The University of Chicago Press.

p. 286, drawing of Tours c. 600, based on Henri Galinie, "Archeologie et topographie Historique de Tours-IVeme-XIeme Siecle," *Zeitschrift Fur Archolaogie des Mittelalters,* 6 (1978); 33–56, figures 2 and 4. Reprinted by permission of Dr. Rudolf Habelt GmbH.

p. 361, map adapted from *Domesday England* by H. C. Darby, 1977, reprinted with the permission of Cambridge University Press.

p. 371, diagram of Cistercian monastery from *Monasteries of Western Europe* by Wolfgang Braunfels, p. 75, figure 61, Copyright © 1972. Reprinted by permission of Princeton University Press.

p. 390, lines from Frederick Goldin, ed. and trans. *Lyrics of the Troubadours and Trouveres, Original Texts with Translations,* Anchor Press 1973. Reprinted by permission of Doubleday, a division of Bantam, Doubleday, Dell Publishing Group, Inc.

p. 391, "Of things I'd rather keep in silence . . . ," from Meg Bogin, *The Women Troubadours,* 1976, p. 85, W. W. Norton Publishers.

pp. 391, 392, lines from Frederick Goldin, ed. and trans. *Lyrics of the Troubadours and Trouveres, Original Texts with Translations,* Anchor Press 1973. Reprinted by permission of Doubleday, a division of Bantam, Doubleday, Dell Publishing Group, Inc.

p. 392, from *Raoul de Cambrai: An Old French Feudal Epic,* trans. Jessie Crosland, Cooper Square Publishers, 1966, Rowman & Littlefield Publishers Inc.

Photograph

Prologue

p. xxxvi, Erich Lessing/Art Resource, NY; p. xxxix, M. Shostak/Anthro-Photo; pp. xli–xliv Erich Lessing/Art Resource, NY.

Part I

p. 1, Nimatallah/Art Resource, NY

Chapter 1

p. 3, The University of Pennsylvania Museum, Philadelphia, neg. # CBS 7051; p. 6, Hirmer Fotoarchiv; p. 7, The University of Pennsylvania Museum, Philadelphia, neg. # T4-28c3; p. 12 (top), Copyright British Museum; p. 12 (bottom), Lila AbuLughod/Anthro-Photo; p. 13, Giraudon/Art Resource, NY; p. 15, Courtesy, Museum of Fine Arts, Boston; p. 18, The National Trust Photographic Library/Art Resource, NY; p. 19, Erich Lessing/Art Resource, NY; p. 27, The Metropolitan Museum of Art, Rogers Fund and Contribution from Edward S. Harkness, 1929 (29.3.2); p. 28, Griffith Institute, Ashmolean Museum, Oxford.

Chapter 2

p. 37, Copyright British Museum; p. 39, British School at Athens. Photo credit: Popham/Sackett; p. 42, Courtesy of the Oriental Institute of the University of Chicago; p. 46, American School of Classical Studies at Athens: Agora Excavations; p. 47, From A. M. Snodgrass: *Archaic Greece* © 1980, J. M. Dent & Sons, Ltd., London; courtesy of the author and The Orion Publishing Group Ltd.; p. 48, Antikensammlungen und der Glyptothek in München; p. 50, Makron, Greek, Attic, Red-figure *Kylix,* (72,55) 480 B.C., wheel thrown, slip decorated earthenware. Ht. 4 11/32 in.; Diam. with handles 14 5/32 in. The Toledo Museum of Art, Toledo, Ohio; Gift of Edward Drummond Libbey; p. 54, The Metropolitan Museum of Art, Rogers Fund, 1911 (11.210.1); p. 55, George Obremski/The Image Bank; p. 58, Hirmer Fotoarchiv; p. 59, The Metropolitan Museum of Art, Purchase, Walter C. Baker Gift, 1956 (56.11.1). Rollout Photograph by Justin Kerr; p. 65, Anne van der Vaeren /The Image Bank.

Chapter 3

p. 75, Scala/Art Resource, NY; p. 82, Photo Deutsches Archäologisches Institut Athens; p. 85, American School of Classical Studies at Athens: Agora Excavations; p. 86, Alberto Incrocci/The Image Bank; p. 87, Guido Alberto Rossi/The Image Bank; p. 88, Copyright British Museum; p. 91, Copyright British Museum; p. 93, Roberto Valladares/The Image Bank; p. 96, H. L. Pierce Fund. Courtesy, Museum of Fine Arts, Boston; p. 97, The Master and Fellows of Corpus Christi College, Cambridge; p. 105, Staatliche Museen zu Berlin. Photo: Jürgen Liepe, 1990 © Bildarchiv Preussischer Kulturbesitz, Berlin.

Chapter 4

p. 111, Scala/Art Resource, NY; p. 113, Copyright British Museum; p. 114, William Francis Warden Fund. Courtesy, Museum of Fine Arts, Boston; p. 116, Copyright British Museum; p. 125, Erich Lessing/Art Resource, NY; p. 130, Scala/Art Resource, NY; p. 132, Staatliche Museen zu Berlin. © Bildarchiv Preussischer Kulturbesitz, Berlin; p. 135, Copyright British Museum; p. 137, Scala/Art Resource, NY; p. 138 (left), Scala/Art Resource, NY; p. 138 (right), The Metropolitan Museum of Art, Rogers Fund, 1909. (09.39); p. 140, Weinberg-Clark/The Image Bank.

Chapter 5

p. 147, Copyright British Museum; p. 150, Scala/Art Resource, NY; p. 151, Scala/Art Resource, NY; p. 161 (top), Scala/Art Resource, NY; p. 161 (bottom), Scala/Art Resource, NY; p. 163, Alinari/Art Resource, NY; p. 165, Sopr. Archeologica di Pompei (M. Grimoldi); p. 168, Scala/Art Resource, NY; p. 170, From Olaf Höckmann: *Antike Seefahrt,* © 1985, Beck's Archäologishce Bibliothek, Munich; p. 173, Scala/Art Resource, NY; p. 183, Copyright British Museum; p. 184, Museo Capitolino, Rome. S. Rissone (M. Grimoldi).

Chapter 6

p. 187, Scala/Art Resource, NY; p. 190, The American Numismatic Society; p. 192, Scala/Art Resource, NY; p. 194 (left), Scavi Ostia Antica (M. Grimoldi); p. 194 (right), Erich Lessing/Art Resource, NY; p. 195, Art Resource, NY; p. 204, Scala/Art Resource, NY; p. 206, Sopr. Archeologica delle Prov. di Napoli e Caserta (M. Grimoldi); p. 210, Art Resource, NY; p. 214, Lozovet/The Image Bank; p. 217, Scala/Art Resource, NY; p. 221, Scala/Art Resource, NY.

Chapter 7

p. 225, Giraudon/Art Resource, NY; p. 233, Copyright, Martha Cooper/Peter Arnold, Inc.; p. 235, Scala/Art Resource, NY; p. 242, Erich Lessing/Art Resource, NY; p. 246, William Karel/Sygma; p. 248, Archäologisches Landesmuseum, Schleswig; p. 253, Musée du Bardo, Tunisia; p. 258, Alinari/Art Resource, NY; p. 262, Scala/Art Resource, NY; p. 263 (left), Deutsches Archäologisches Institut (M. Grimoldi); p. 263 (right), Art Resource, NY.

Part II

pp. 266–267, Art Resource, NY

Chapter 8

p. 269, By permission of the British Library; p. 273, The Walker Trust, University of St. Andrews Library, Scotland; p. 277, Kurgan-Lisnet/Liaison; p. 278, Bibliothèque Nationale, Paris; p. 282, Copyright British Museum; p. 283, Clive Foss Architectural Photographs, Cambridge; p. 287, Bibliothèque Nationale, Paris; p. 288, Prähistorische Staatssammlung, Munich; p. 289, Musée Alfred Bonno, Chelles; p. 292, York Castle Museum; p. 293, By permission of the British Library; p. 296, S. Rissone (M. Grimoldi).

Chapter 9

p. 303, Hessische Landes- und Hochschul- Bibliothek, Darmstadt; p. 304, Biblioteca Nazionale Marciana di Venezia; p. 306, Victoria & Albert Museum, London/Art Resource, NY; p. 307, Bibliothèque Nationale, Paris; p. 308, Erzbischöfliches Diözesanmuseum Köln; p. 313, Pro Bibliotheca Academiae Scientiarum Hungaricae; p. 314, Reproduced by kind permission of the Trustees of the Chester Beatty Library, Dublin; p. 321, By permission of the British Library; p. 322, Giraudon/Art Resource, NY; p. 324, Werner Forman Archive/Art Resource, NY; p. 328, KL Weyarn I, Bayerisches Hauptstaatsarchiv; p. 332, Bayerische Staatsbibliothek; p. 333, Ashmolean Museum, Oxford.

Chapter 10

p. 341, Staatsbibliothek Preussischer Kulturbesitz © Bildarchiv Preussischer Kulturbesitz, Berlin; p. 344, Staatliche Museen zu Berlin © Bildarchiv Preussischer Kulturbesitz, Berlin; p. 345, Giraudon/Art Resource, NY; p. 350, The Master and Fellows of Corpus Christi College, Cambridge; p. 358, Owen Franken, Paris; p. 360, Erich Lessing/Art Resource, NY; p. 367, Erich Lessing/Art Resource, NY; p. 368 (right), Foto Marburg/Art Resource, NY; p. 369 (top left), © Caisse Nationale des Monuments Historiques et des Sites/SPADEM; p. 369 (bottom left), Giraudon/Art Resource, NY; p. 369 (right), Erich Lessing/Art Resource, NY; p. 372, © Caisse Nationale des Monuments Historiques et des Sites/SPADEM.

Chapter 11

p. 377, Deutscher Kunstverlag; p. 382, Barb. lat. 2738, fol. 104v-105r, Foto Biblioteca Vaticano; p. 383, Erich Lessing/Art Resource, NY; p. 386, Photo: Bridgeman Art Library/John Bethell; p. 387, By permission of the British Library; p. 389, © Caisse Nationale des Monuments Historiques et des Sites/SPADEM; p. 390, Photo by Jutta Brüdern, courtesy of Der Braunschweiger Dom; p. 392, Biblioteca Ambrosiana, Milano; p. 393, Alinari/Art Resource, NY; p. 400, Bayerische Staatsbibliothek; p. 402, The Master and Fellows of Corpus Christi College, Cambridge; p. 405, National Museum, Copenhagen.

Chapter 12

p. 409, Erich Lessing/Art Resource, NY; p. 410, The Pierpont Morgan Library, New York. M.240, f.8; p. 411, Scala/Art Resource, NY; p. 414, Bibliothèque Nationale, Paris; p. 415, Scala/Art Resource, NY; p. 416, Giraudon/Art Resource, NY; p. 417, Owen Franken; p. 418, Scala/Art Resource, NY; p. 419, Scala/Art Resource, NY; p. 422, Cod. Pal. lat. 1071, fol. iv, Foto Biblioteca Vaticano; p. 427, Public Record Office, London; p. 428, Monique Salaber/Liaison; p. 431, Bibliothèque Nationale, Paris/Photo: Bridgeman Art Library.

Chapter 13

pp. 437, 444, Giraudon/Art Resource, NY; p. 449, The Hulton Deutsch Collection; pp. 450, 453, Giraudon/Art Resource, NY; p. 454, Bridgeman/Art Resource, NY; p. 456, By permission of the Houghton Library, Harvard University; pp. 462, 463, Giraudon/Art Resource, NY; p. 464, Erich Lessing/Art Resource, NY; p. 465, Bridgeman/Art Resource, NY.

Chapter 14

p. 469, Cameraphoto/Art Resource, NY; p. 472, Erich Lessing/Art Resource, NY; p. 473, National Gallery of Art, Washington, DC; p. 475, Giraudon/Art Resource, NY; p. 479, Sovfoto/Eastfoto; pp. 482, 483, Scala/Art Resource, NY; p. 485, Erich Lessing/Art Resource, NY; pp. 487, 490, 491, 492, Scala/Art Resource, NY.

Chapter 15

p. 501, The Metropolitan Museum of Art, Gift of Robert Lehman, 1955. (55.220.2); p. 504, Victoria & Albert Museum

London/Art Resource, NY; p. 505, Art Resource, NY; p. 508, Scala/Art Resource, NY; p. 515, Alinari/Art Resource, NY; p. 517, Snark/Art Resource, NY; p. 521, Erich Lessing/Art Resource, NY; pp. 523, 524, Scala/Art Resource, NY; p. 525, Giraudon/Art Resource, NY; p. 528, Foto Marburg/Art Resource, NY; p. 529, Giraudon/Art Resource, NY.

Part III
pp. 538–539, Alinari/Art Resource, NY

Chapter 16
p. 543, Alinari/Art Resource, NY; p. 545, Scala/Art Resource, NY; p. 548, Private Collection; p. 549, Victoria & Albert Museum/Art Resource, NY; p. 557, North Carolina Museum of Art, Raleigh, Purchased with funds from the State of North Carolina; p. 559, Giraudon/Art Resource, NY; p. 561, Scala/Art Resource, NY; p. 563, Patrimonio Nacional, Madrid; p. 564, Scala/Art Resource, NY; p. 568, *America,* fresco, 1595, Paolo Farinati. Villa Della Torre, Mezzane di Sotto, Verona; p. 570, Giraudon/Art Resource, NY; pp. 571, 574, Erich Lessing/Art Resource, NY.

INDEX

This index includes a guide to pronouncing proper names and terms that may be unfamiliar to the English-speaking reader. The purpose of the guide is to provide an acceptable indication of pronunciation of selected foreign terms.

Accent marks indicate the syllable to be stressed.

The following symbols are used to indicate the pronunciation of certain vowels, consonants, and letter clusters.

Long vowels

a = ay	as in *date (dayt)*
e = ee	as in *even (ee vn)*
i = ī	as in *size (sīz)*
o = ō	as in *soap (sōp)*
u = oo	as in *flute (floot)*

Short vowels

a	as in *map*
ah	broad a as in *father*
e	as in *met*
uh	as in *but* or *banana*

Other sounds

oy	as in *coin*
zh	as in *vision*
ny	as in *signoria* (si • nyo • ree′ • uh)
x	a guttural sound produced at the back of the throat, as in German *Bach* or Russian *Khrushchev*

French and Polish nasal vowels are indicated by *ahn, ehn, ihn, ohn,* and *uhn.*

Page numbers in italic refer to illustrations and captions.
Page numbers followed by "n." refer to footnotes.

Normans, 325; Hundred Years' War and, 452; papacy and, 348–349; William I (the Conqueror), 349, 358–361
North Africa, Arab conquest of, 282
North America: exploration of, 531–532; settlements in, 566–568
Northern Rebellion (1568–1569), 549
Nossis of Locri, Greek poet, 137
Nouy, battle of (1044), 327
Novara, battle of (sixteenth century), 512
Novgorod: Black Death in, 440; fifteenth-century, 479
Noyon (noh • yohn'), bishop of, 517
Numerian (noo • me' • ri • an), Roman emperor (✱283–284), 227
Nu-Pieds (noo-pee' • ay), 565
Nur al-Din, 401

Occitan (ahk' • i • tan), 390
Ockeghem, Johannes (ok' • eh • gem, yo • ha' • nes) (c. 1420–1495), 494
Octavian (ahk • tay' • vee • an). *See* Augustus
Octavianus (ahk • tay • ve • ah' • noos). *See* Augustus
Octavius (ahk • tay' • vee • us), Gaius. *See* Augustus
Odoacer (o • do • ah' • ser), non–Roman general, 252
Odysseus, 48
Odyssey, The (Homer), 48, 52, 172, 262
Ögödei, Mongol ruler (1186–1241), 429
Old Testament, 217
Oleg, Dnieper valley chief, 310
Oligarchic, 57
Oligarchy (o • li • gar' • kee), 57, 60–64
Olivares, count-duke of. *See* Guzmán, Gaspar de
Olympias (o • lim' • pee • as), queen of Macedonia, 124–125, 129
Olympic Games, 48–49
On Agriculture (Cato), 172
On Animals (Albertus Magnus), 412
On Architecture (Alberti), 493
On the Babylonian Captivity of the Church (Luther), 511
On the Church (Wycliffe), 448
On the Dignity of Man (Pico della Mirandola), 493
On the Nature of Things (Lucretius), 184
On the Revolution of the Celestial Spheres (Copernicus), 527
On the Rivers of Europe (Callimachus), 136
On the Support of the Poor (Vives), 535
Oppius, Roman tribune (215 B.C.), 162
Optimates (op • tee • maht' • ays), 175
Optimius, Roman consul, 175
Order of the Garter (1344), 451
Order of the Golden Fleece (1430), 475
Orefice, Sevasto, 346
Orestes, Roman commander, 252
Orfeo (Monteverdi), 571
Orhan Gazi (or' • han gah' • zee), Ottoman ruler (1324–1359), 460
Origen (o' • ri • jen), Christian theologian (c. 185–255), 222, 243, 247
Origins, The (Cato), 172
Orlando Furioso ("The Mad Roland") (Ariosto), 525–526
Orléans (or • lay • ahn'), duke of, 452
Orsini (or • see' • nee) family, 456
Orvieto cathedral, 418, *418*
Osman I, founder of the Ottoman Empire (1280–1324), 460
Ospitale degl' Innocenti (oh • spih • tah' • leh deh • lihn • oh • chen' • tee), 484, 493
Ostracism (ahs' • tra • sizm), 82–83
Ostracon (ahs' • trak • on), 82, *82*
Ostrogoths, 252, 270, 294
Oswy, Northumbrian king, 293
Otho, Roman emperor (✱A.D. 69), 215
Otranto (oh • trahn' • to), 474
Otto I, king of Germany and emperor (✱936–973), 325, 330–331, 333
Otto II, king of Germany and emperor (✱973–983), 331
Otto III, king of Germany and emperor (✱983–1002), 331
Ottoman Empire: fifteenth-century expansion into the Adriatic port of Otranto, 474; fifteenth-century expansion into the Balkans, 478; fighting with the Habsburgs in the Danube basin, 553–554; fourteenth-century expansion in the Balkans, 460–461; Habsburg-Valois-Ottoman wars, 515–517
Ottonian kings, 331–332
Otto of Freising (frī' • zing), historian and biographer, 377, 379, 398
Outremer (oo' • tre • mer), 357, 363, 401
Ovid, Roman poet (43 B.C.–A.D. 17), 198
Oxenstierna, Axel, Swedish minister (1583–1654), 563
Oxford University, 396
Oxus River, 130, 139

Pacification of Ghent (1576), 551
Pagans, confrontation between Christians and, 232–234, 237–238
Palace of the Buen Retiro (Leonardo), *563*
Palaeologus (pay • lay • o • lo' • gus), Byzantine emperor, 478
Palatine Hill, 151
Paleolithic period: knowledge and beliefs of hunter-gatherers, xl–li; spread and organization of people in, xxxviii–xl
Palestrina, Giovanni Pierluigi da (pah • les • tree' • nah, jo • vah' • nee pyer • loo • ee' • jee dah), musician (1525–1594), 526
Pallavicini, Oberto, 429
Palmyra (pal • mī' • rah), 214, *214*
Pamplona (pahm • ploh' • nah), Spanish fortress, 521
Pan-Hellenism, 122
Pannonia, 270, 271
Papacy: Avignon popes, 428, 443; Babylonian Captivity, 427; Byzantium and political tensions, 296–297; Carolingians and, 297–298, 317–318; celibacy of priests, development of, 353–354; church reform and, 335–337; conciliar movement, 446–447; conflict between Philip IV and Pope Boniface VIII, 426–428; conflict with monarchies in the thirteenth century, 420–424; Counter-Reformation and, 520–522; *curia,* 203, 354, 444; Donation of Constantine, 318; East-West schism (Great Schism), 336–337, 337n.; as a European power, 348–350; fifteenth-century, 481; fifteenth-century art and, 490–491; First Crusade, 355–357; fourteenth-century challenges to, 443–450; German conflict with, during the twelfth century, 380, *382;* Great Schism, 337, 337n., 445–446; Gregory the Great impact on, 295–296; hierarchy and dissent issues, 444–445; Investiture Conflict, 350–353; Lateran Council, Fourth, 410–412; Lombards and, 297; name selection by, 506, 506n.; origin of, 232; "papal monarchy," 354–355, 445; papal palace at Avignon, *444;* post–Carolingian, 330; reform and ensuing struggles, 348–357; religious sanctions for marriage, 353–354; as rulers in the sixteenth century, 506–508; separation of royal and ecclesiastical power, 423–424; sixteenth-century regulations and scandals, 506–508; thirteenth century and role of, 410–414; twelfth-century heretics and, 401; War of the Eight Saints, 456–457
Papal Election Decree (1059), 350
Paper making, 488